k_{SIMPLE}	Nominal risk-free rate of interest; also referred to as i_{SIMPLE}
k_{ps}	Cost of preferred stock
k_{RF}	Rate of return on a risk-free security
k_s	(1) Cost of retained earnings
	(2) Required return on a stock
M	Maturity value of a bond
M/B	Market-to-book ratio
MCC	Marginal cost of capital
MIRR	Modified internal rate of return
N	Calculator key denoting number of periods
n	Life of a project
NPV	Net present value
NWC	Net working capital
P_o	Price of the stock today
P	Sales price per unit of product sold
P/E	Price/earnings ratio
PMT	Periodic level payment of an annuity
PV	Present value
PVA_n	Present value of an annuity for n years
PVIF	Present value interest factor for a lump sum
PVIFA	Present value interest factor for an annuity
Q	Quantity produced or sold
r	Correlation coefficient
ROA	Return on assets
ROE	Return on equity
RP	Risk premium
RP_M	Market risk premium
S	Sales in dollars
SML	Security Market Line
Σ	Summation sign (capital sigma)
σ	Standard deviation (lowercase sigma)
σ^2	Variance
t	Time period
T	Marginal income tax rate
TIE	Times interest earned
v	Variable cost as a percent of selling price
V	Variable cost per unit
V_d	Bond value
V_{ps}	Preferred stock value
VC	Total variable costs
WACC	Weighted average cost of capital
YTC	Yield to call
YTM	Yield to maturity

Essentials of Managerial Finance

Eleventh Edition

Essentials of Managerial Finance

Eleventh Edition

J. Fred Weston
Anderson Graduate School of Management
University of California, Los Angeles

Scott Besley
University of South Florida

Eugene F. Brigham
University of Florida

THE DRYDEN PRESS
Harcourt Brace College Publishers

Fort Worth   Philadelphia   San Diego   New York   Orlando   Austin   San Antonio
Toronto   Montreal   London   Sydney   Tokyo

Executive Editor: Mike Reynolds
Development Editor: Shana Lum
Project Editor: Jim Patterson
Art Director: Brian Salisbury
Production Manager: Ann Coburn
Permissions Editor: Adele Krause
Product Manager: Craig Johnson
Marketing Coordinator: Kelly Whidbee

Copyeditor: Carolyn Crabtree
Proofreader: Roberta Kirchhoff
Indexer: Sylvia Coates
Text Type: 10/12 Garamond

Cover Image: © Tommy Flynn, Photonica

Some material in this work previously appeared in ESSENTIALS OF MANAGERIAL FINANCE, Tenth Edition, copyright © 1993, 1990, 1987, 1985, 1982, 1979, 1977, 1972, 1971, 1968 by The Dryden Press. All rights reserved.

Address for orders:
The Dryden Press
6277 Sea Harbor Drive
Orlando, FL 32887-6777
1-800-782-4479, or 1-800-433-0001 (in Florida)

Address for editorial correspondence:
The Dryden Press
301 Commerce Street, Suite 3700
Fort Worth, TX 76102

ISBN: 0-03-010199-9

Library of Congress Catalog Card Number: 95-67304

Printed in the United States of America

  7 8 9 0 1 2 3 4   048   9 8 7 6 5 4 3

The Dryden Press
Harcourt Brace College Publishers

THE DRYDEN PRESS SERIES IN FINANCE

THE HB COLLEGE OUTLINE SERIES

Preface

Essentials of Managerial Finance is intended for use in the introductory finance course. The textbook begins with a discussion of basic concepts, including accounting statements, security markets, interest rates, taxes, risk analysis, time value of money, and the basics of security valuation. Subsequent chapters explain how financial managers can help maximize their firms' values by improving decisions in such areas as working capital management, capital budgeting, and choice of capital structure. This organization has three important advantages:

1. Explaining early in the book how accounting data are used, how financial markets operate, and how security prices are determined helps students understand how managerial finance can affect the value of the firm. Also, early coverage of such key concepts as risk analysis, time value, and valuation techniques permits their use and reinforcement throughout the remainder of the book.
2. Structuring the book around markets and valuation enhances continuity as this organization helps students see how the various topics relate to one another.
3. Most students—even those who do not plan to major in finance—are generally interested in stock and bond valuation, rates of return, and the like. Because people's ability to learn a subject is a function of their interest and motivation, and because *Essentials* begins by showing the relationships between security markets, stock values, and managerial finance, this organization is good from a pedagogic standpoint.

Now in its eleventh edition, *Essentials* has grown over the course of time, not only in size but also in the long list of practical and theoretical developments it covers. On the recommendation of reviewers, we turned a discerning eye to the table of contents to determine if our coverage was truly "essential" for the first undergraduate course. What we saw were a few topics that had been melded into *Essentials* that, because of level or simply the primary objectives of typical undergraduate managerial finance courses, really belonged in a more advanced book. We did not categorically omit these topics; instead, we placed some of them, such as modified internal rate of return, in appendices so as to not interrupt the flow of the chapter but to offer instructors the option of covering the topic. By improving the organization and topic coverage of *Essentials,* we feel that the eleventh edition will be a valuable tool for students learning about managerial finance for the first time.

Relationship with Our Other Books

As the body of knowledge expanded, it first became difficult, then impossible, to provide everything one needs to know about managerial finance in one textbook, especially an undergraduate book. This recognition has led us to limit the scope of this book and also to write other textbooks to deal with the materials that cannot be included in *Essentials.* Lou Gapenski and Gene Brigham have co-authored both an intermediate undergraduate textbook (*Intermediate Financial Management,* Fifth Edition) and a comprehensive textbook aimed primarily at MBAs (*Financial Management: Theory and Practice,* Seventh Edition).

The relationship between *Essentials* and these more advanced books deserves special comment. First, we recognize that the advanced books are often used by students who have used *Essentials* in the introductory undergraduate course, so we wanted to avoid excessive overlap but also to be sure to expose students to alternative points of view on controversial subjects. To avoid unnecessary overlap, both we and our reviewers were on the alert to eliminate excessive duplications. We should note, though, that our students in advanced courses invariably tell us that they find it helpful to have the more difficult materials repeated—they need the review. Students also say they like the fact that the style and notation used in our upper-level books are consistent with those in the introductory textbook, as this makes learning easier. Regarding alternative points of view, we have made every effort to take a moderate, middle-of-the-road approach, and where serious controversy exists, we have tried to present the alternative points of view. Reviewers were asked to consider this point, and their comments have helped us eliminate potential biases.

Intended Market and Use

As noted above, *Essentials* is intended for use as an introductory textbook. The key chapters can be covered in a one-term course, and, supplemented with cases and some outside readings, the book can also be used in a two-term course. If it is used in a one-term course, the instructor probably will cover only selected chapters, leaving the others for students either to examine on their own or to use as references in conjunction with work in later courses. Also, we have made every effort to write the chapters in a flexible, modular format, which helps instructors cover the material in a different sequence should they choose to do so.

Major Changes in the Eleventh Edition

The theory and practice of finance are dynamic, and as new developments occur, they should be incorporated into a textbook such as this one. Also, working with a team of reviewers, we are constantly looking for ways to improve the book in terms of clarity and student understanding. As a result, several important changes were made in this edition, the most important of which are discussed below.

Financial Forecasting and Control

Based upon the feedback from many professors, we merged Chapters 7 and 8 from the tenth edition into our "new" Chapter 4: "Financial Forecasting and Control." This improvement allowed us to have a more concise discussion, include leverage (a change we explain below), and pair this coverage more closely with financial statement analysis. This new Chapter 4 incorporates more use of ratios, better relating the significance of forecasting, planning, and control to the evaluation of financial strength of the firm.

Coverage of Leverage

As instructors, we have always had difficulty deciding when to teach leverage, and then as authors, where to put the discussion of leverage in *Essentials*. In the tenth edition, operating leverage was presented twice, with nearly identical discussions, and financial leverage presented only once in relation to capital structure. As we thought about this inconsistency, we reasoned that both operating and financial leverage essentially are measures of risk and would be best covered in the chapter that first introduces risk: Chapter 4, "Financial Forecasting and Control."

Alternative Financing Arrangements and Corporate Restructuring

In the tenth edition, *Essentials* covered hybrid financing instruments and restructuring techniques in two separate chapters. As we considered the idea of making *Essentials* truly essential, we found that most instructors did not have the time to cover these chapters fully and primarily only got through a brief overview of leasing. And while the information on mergers and acquisitions is interesting and often in the news, we believe that explaining the valuation of mergers was beyond the scope of the first undergraduate course. The result of these thoughts was Chapter 20, "Alternative Financing Arrangements and Corporate Restructuring," which covers preferred stock characteristics, leasing, options and warrants, convertibles, leveraged buyouts, and mergers and acquisitions. Our approach with this chapter was to provide a brief introduction to each of these instruments, detailing their major characteristics, advantages and disadvantages, and use in financial management.

Capital Budgeting Coverage

As mentioned previously, our mission to refocus *Essentials* as an undergraduate book resulted in several topics being moved to appendices. Part V was primarily affected by our efforts, with modified internal rate of return and other more technical topics now in appendices. Our emphasis in the core of the chapters is the basics of capital budgeting, although the appendices allow for flexibility of coverage.

Ethical Dilemmas

For the past five years or so, ethics has become an important buzzword in business education. We felt that it was crucial to introduce managerial finance students to ethical issues early and often throughout the course. For nearly half of the chapters in the eleventh edition, we have added a feature called "Ethical Dilemma." We present an ethical situation based upon a true story and ask students to make the decision. These "Ethical Dilemmas" expose students to the relationship between ethics and business, promote critical thinking and decision-making skills, and provide interesting vehicles for class discussion. In the Instructor's Manual you will find the real company (if you choose to reveal it to your students), information about the situation described, and key discussion points for the class.

A Managerial Perspective and Industry Practice

Although these boxed articles are not new to *Essentials,* we want to draw attention to them because of the fact that nearly all of them are new to this edition. "A Managerial Perspective" is an interesting and engaging lead-off for student reading and/or for a class lecture. "Industry Practice" shows the application of the concepts in real financial management decisions.

Unifying Example

To illustrate the interrelation of all managerial finance concepts, we have developed one example company, Unilate Textiles, throughout *Essentials.* This provides students with a sense of continuity across chapters and also is a fresh change for instructors who have used *Essentials* for several years.

Supplementary Materials

A number of items are available free of charge to adopting instructors:

1. **Instructor's Manual.** This comprehensive manual contains answers to all text questions and problems, a detailed set of lecture notes (including suggestions for using the transparency acetates described below), discussion guidelines for the Ethical Dilemmas, detailed solutions to integrative problems, and suggested course outlines.
2. **Transparencies.** A comprehensive set of transparency masters and acetates that includes approximately 40 color acetates.
3. **Test Bank.** The *Test Bank* contains approximately 1,000 class-tested questions and problems. We have carefully evaluated all of the questions and problems for the appropriateness. In particular, to reduce redundancy, we have weeded out the true/false questions that also appear in multiple-choice questions. There is still a generous offering of true/false questions, multiple-choice conceptual questions, multiple-choice problems (that can easily be modified to short answer problems by removing the answer choices), and financial calculator problems. The test bank is available in computerized format, featuring Dryden's computerized test bank program EXAMaster+. EXAMaster+ has many features which allow the instructor to modify test questions, select items by key words, scramble tests for multiple sections, and test completely on the computer. EXAMaster+ is available for IBM 3.5", Windows, and Macintosh systems. For instructors more comfortable with WordPerfect, we also offer the test bank in WordPerfect 5.1 format. Our endnote system makes for easy test creation, because the answers automatically follow the questions into an answer key.
4. **Lecture Presentation Software.** Instructors who have used presentation programs such as Harvard Graphics, Microsoft PowerPoint, Aldus Persuasion, and Lotus Freehand have discovered the visual power of "electronic transparencies." We have created our Lecture Presentation Software (LPS) as an alternative to acetates. The LPS is essentially a slide show that outlines the Integrative Problem solutions as well as other key information from each chapter. The

software is available for use with PowerPoint, and those instructors with access to this program can easily make alterations to fit their course.

5. **Blueprints and "Course-Pack."** The *Blueprints* supplement is provided to instructors free of charge, and it (or selected parts of it) can be copied in an off-campus copy center and sold to students for only the copying cost. We do this with the chapters we cover in our course, and we add some items such as the syllabus, several old exams, instructions on the use of financial calculators, and other course-specific materials. Other instructors have only the transparencies copied or some transparencies plus the solutions to some of the end-of-chapter problems. In any event, we encourage instructors to construct their own "course-packs," drawing from materials we have provided, to facilitate their students' learning.

6. **Video Series.** *The Dryden Press Financial Management Video Series* have six volumes of tapes to highlight key concepts, illustrate the relation of the concepts to real companies through CBS news footage, and motivate your students' understanding of finance. For information on the contents of particular volumes, please contact your Dryden sales representative.

7. **Problem Disk.** A disk containing *Lotus 1-2-3* models for the computer-related end-of-chapter problems is also available.

8. **Supplemental Problems.** Another set of additional problems, organized according to topic and level of difficulty, will be provided to instructors who request it.

A number of additional items are available for purchase by students:

1. **Study Guide.** This supplement outlines the key sections of each chapter, provides students with self-test questions, and also provides a set of problems and solutions similar to those in the text and in the *Test Bank*. Since many instructors are now using multiple-choice exams, we have increased coverage of exam-type questions and problems in the new study guide.

2. **Cases.** *Cases in Financial Management: Dryden Request* by Eugene F. Brigham and Louis C. Gapenski is well suited for use with *Essentials,* especially for two-semester sequences. The cases provide real-world applications of the methodologies and concepts developed in this book. In addition, all of the cases are available in a customized format, so your students pay only for the cases you will use.

3. **Readings Books.** One readings book, *Issues and Readings in Managerial Finance* (The Dryden Press, 1995), edited by Ramon E. Johnson, provides an excellent mix of theoretical and practical articles which can be used to supplement the textbook. Another supplemental reader is *Advances in Business Financial Management: A Collection of Readings* (The Dryden Press, 1996), edited by Philip L. Cooley, which provides a broader selection of articles from which to choose.

4. **Finance with Lotus 1-2-3: Text and Models.** In its second edition, this text by Eugene F. Brigham, Dana A. Aberwald, and Louis C. Gapenski (The Dryden Press, 1992) enables students to learn, on their own, how to use *Lotus 1-2-3* and apply it to financial decisions.

5. **Financial Analysis with Microsoft Excel** and **Financial Analysis with Lotus for Windows.** These two new books by Timothy Mayes and Todd Shank

(The Dryden Press, 1996) fully integrate the teaching of spreadsheet analysis with the basic finance concepts. These books are perfect companions to *Essentials* in courses where computer work is highly emphasized.

The Dryden Press will provide complimentary supplements or supplement packages to those adopters qualified under our adoption policy. Please contact your sales representative to learn how you may qualify. If as an adopter or potential user you receive supplements you do not need, please return them to your sales representative or send them to:

Attn: Returns Department
Troy Warehouse
465 South Lincoln Drive
Troy, MO 63379

Acknowledgments

This book reflects the efforts of a great many people over a number of years. For the Eleventh Edition, we are indebted to the following professors who provided their input on our ideas and gave us many of their own for improving the book:

William Baker, *Stockton State College*
Douglas Bible, *Louisiana State University*
Stephen Caples, *McNeese State University*
Shin-Herng Michelle Chu, *California State Polytechnic University-Pomona*
Paul F. Conway, *University of Notre Dame*
Ed Daley, *Virginia Military Institute*
V. Sivarama Krishnan, *Cameron University*
Douglas Leary, *St. John's University*
Iqbal Mansur, *Widener University*
Massoud Metghalchi, *University of Houston-Victoria*
Charlie Narron, *Mars Hill College*
Gladson Nwanna, *Morgan State University*
Phil Pennell, *Guilford College*
Glenn Petry, *Washington State University*
Ralph Pope, *California State University-Sacramento*
Murli Rajan, *University of Scranton*
Jim Reinemann, *College of Lake County*
Robert Ritzcovan, *Mercy College*
Ramesh Shah, *Widener University*
John Teall, *Pace University*
Randy Trostle, *Elizabethtown College*
Gautam Vora, *The University of New Mexico*
Sally Jo Wright, *Sangamon State University*

Next, we would like to thank the following professors, whose reviews and comments have helped prior editions and our companion books: Mike Adler, Syed Ahmad, Ed Altman, Bruce Anderson, Ron Anderson, Bob Angell, Vince Apilado, Henry Arnold, Bob Aubey, Gil Babcock, Peter Bacon, Kent Baker, Robert Balik, Tom Bankston, Les Barenbaum, Charles Barngrover, Bill Beedles, Moshe Ben-

Horim, Bill Beranek, Tom Berry, Will Bertin, Dan Best, Roger Bey, Dalton Bigbee, John Bildersee, Russ Boisjoly, Keith Boles, Geof Booth, Jerry Boswell, Kenneth Boudreaux, Helen Bowers, Oswald Bowlin, Don Boyd, G. Michael Boyd, Pat Boyer, Joe Brandt, Elizabeth Brannigan, Greg Brauer, Mary Broske, Dave Brown, Kate Brown, Bill Brueggeman, Stephen G. Buell, Ted Byrley, Bill Campsey, Bob Carlson, Severin Carlson, David Cary, Steve Celec, Don Chance, Antony Chang, Susan Chaplinsky, Jay Choi, S. K. Choudhary, Lal Chugh, Maclyn Clouse, Margaret Considine, Phil Cooley, Joe Copeland, David Cordell, Marcia Cornett, M. P. Corrigan, John Cotner, Charles Cox, David Crary, John Crockett, Jr., Roy Crum, Brent Dalrymple, Bill Damon, Joel Dauten, Steve Dawson, Sankar De, Fred Dellva, James Desreumaux, Bodie Dickerson, Bernard Dill, J. David Diltz, Gregg Dimkoff, Les Dlabay, Mark Dorfman, Gene Drzycimski, Dean Dudley, David Durst, Ed Dyl, Richard Edelman, Charles Edwards, John Ellis, Dave Ewert, John Ezzell, Michael Ferri, Jim Filkins, John Finnerty, Susan Fischer, Steven Flint, Russ Fogler, Dan French, Michael Garlington, David Garraty, Jim Garven, Adam Gehr, Jr., Jim Gentry, Philip Glasgo, Rudyard Goode, Walt Goulet, Bernie Grablowsky, Theoharry Grammatikos, Reynold Griffith, Ed Grossnickle, John Groth, Alan Grunewald, Manak Gupta, Sam Hadaway, Don Hakala, Paul Halpern, Gerald Hamsmith, William Hardin, John Harris, Paul Hastings, Bob Haugen, Steve Hawke, Del Hawley, Robert Hehre, George Hettenhouse, Hans Heymann, Kendall Hill, Roger Hill, Tom Hindelang, Linda Hittle, Ralph Hocking, J. Ronald Hoffmeister, Robert Hollinger, Jim Horrigan, John Houston, John Howe, Keith Howe, Steve Isberg, Jim Jackson, Kose John, Craig Johnson, Keith Johnson, Ramon Johnson, Ray Jones, Frank Jordan, Manual Jose, Alfred Kahl, Gus Kalogeras, Mike Keenan, Bill Kennedy, James Keys, Carol Kiefer, Joe Kiernan, Rick Kish, Don Knight, Dorothy Koehl, Jaroslaw Komarynsky, Duncan Kretovich, Harold Krogh, Charles Kroncke, Don Kummer, Joan Lamm, Larry Lang, P. Lange, Howard Lanser, John Lasik, Edward Lawrence, Martin Lawrence, Wayne Lee, Jim LePage, Jules Levine, John Lewis, Jason Lin, Chuck Linke, Bill Lloyd, Susan Long, Judy Maese, Bob Magee, Ileen Malitz, Phil Malone, Lewis Mandell, Terry Maness, Chris Manning, S. K. Mansinghka, Terry Martell, D. J. Masson, John Mathys, John McAlhany, Andy McCollough, Ambrose McCoy, Thomas McCue, Bill McDaniel, John McDowell, Charles McKinney, Robyn McLaughlin, Jamshid Mehran, Larry Merville, Rick Meyer, Jim Millar, Ed Miller, John Mitchell, Carol Moerdyk, Bob Moore, Barry Morris, Gene Morris, Fred Morrissey, Chris Muscarella, David Nachman, Tim Nantell, Don Nast, Bill Nelson, Bob Nelson, Bob Niendorf, Tom O'Brien, Dennis O'Connor, John O'Donnell, Jim Olsen, Robert Olsen, Jim Pappas, Stephen Parrish, Glenn Petry, Jim Pettijohn, Rich Pettit, Dick Pettway, Hugo Phillips, H. R. Pickett, John Pinkerton, Gerald Pogue, Eugene Poindexter, R. Potter, Franklin Potts, R. Powell, Chris Prestopino, Jerry Prock, Howard Puckett, Herbert Quigley, George Racette, Bob Radcliffe, Bill Rentz, Ken Riener, Charles Rini, John Ritchie, Pietra Rivoli, Antonio Rodriguez, James Rosenfeld, E. N. Roussakis, Dexter Rowell, Jim Sachlis, Abdul Sadik, Thomas Scampini, Kevin Scanlon, Frederick Schadler, Mary Jane Scheuer, Carl Schweser, David Scott, John Settle, Alan Severn, Sol Shalit, Frederic Shipley, Dilip Shome, Ron Shrieves, Neil Sicherman, J. B. Silvers, Clay Singleton, Joe Sinkey, Stacy Sirmans, Jaye Smith, Patricia Smith, Patrick Smith, Steve Smith, Don Sorensen, David Speairs, Ken Stanly, Ed Stendardi, Alan Stephens, Don Stevens, Jerry Stevens, Glen Strasburg, Philip Swensen, Ernest Swift, Paul Swink, Gary Tallman, Dular Talukdar, Dennis Tanner, Craig Tapley, Russ Taussig, Richard Teweles, Ted Teweles, Francis C. Thomas, Andrew Thompson, John Thompson, Dogan Tirtiroglu, Marco

Tonietti, William Tozer, George Trivoli, George Tsetsekos, Ricardo Ulivi, David Upton, Howard Van Auken, Pretorious Van den Dool, Pieter Vandenberg, Paul Vanderheiden, JoAnn Vaughan, Jim Verbrugge, Patrick Vincent, Steve Vinson, Susan Visscher, John Wachowicz, Mike Walker, Sam Weaver, Kuo-Chiang Wei, Bill Welch, Robert J. Wiley, Norm Williams, Tony Wingler, Ed Wolfe, Don Woods, Michael Yonan, Dennis Zocco, and Kent Zumwalt.

Special thanks are due to Chris Barry, Texas Christian University, who wrote many of the small business sections; to Dilip Shome, Virginia Polytechnic Institute, who helped greatly with the capital structure chapter; and to Roy Crum, University of Florida, who coauthored the multinational finance chapter. Dana Aberwald worked closely with us at every stage of the revision; her assistance was absolutely invaluable. Also, Louis Gapenski worked closely with us on the integrative problems and offered advice on many other parts of the book. In addition, Steve Bouchard and Chad Hamilton of the University of Florida worked through and/or discussed with us all or major parts of the book and supplements to help eliminate errors and confusing sections. Finally, the Dryden Press staff, including Shana Lum, Jim Patterson, Brian Salisbury, Ann Coburn, Adele Krause, Craig Johnson, and Kelly Whidbee, helped greatly with all phases of the text development and production.

Errors in the Text

At this point, most authors make a statement like this: "We appreciate all the help we received from the people listed above, but any remaining errors are, of course, our own responsibility." And generally there are more than enough remaining errors. As a part of our quest for clarity, we resolved to avoid this problem in *Essentials,* and as a result of our error-detection procedures, we are convinced that it is virtually free of mistakes.

Some of our colleagues suggested that if we are so confident about the book's accuracy, we should offer a reward to people who find errors. With that in mind, but primarily because we want to detect any remaining errors and correct them in subsequent printings, we hereby offer a reward of $10 per error to the first person who reports it to us. (Any error that has follow-through effects is counted as two errors only.) Two accounting students have set up a foolproof audit system to make sure we pay—accounting students tend to be skeptics! Please report any errors to Scott Besley at the address below.

Conclusion

Finance is, in a real sense, the cornerstone of the enterprise system—good financial management is vitally important to the economic health of business firms, and hence to the nation and the world. Because of its importance, finance should be widely and thoroughly understood, but this is easier said than done. The field is relatively complex, and it is undergoing constant change in response to shifts in economic conditions. All of this makes finance stimulating and exciting but also challenging and sometimes perplexing. We sincerely hope that *Essentials* will meet its own challenge by contributing to a better understanding of our financial system.

J. Fred Weston
Anderson Graduate School of Management
University of California, Los Angeles
Los Angeles, California 90024

Scott Besley
College of Business Administration
University of South Florida
Tampa, Florida 33620-5500

Eugene F. Brigham
College of Business
University of Florida
Gainesville, Florida 32611-7160

September 1995

Brief Contents

Contents

Essentials of Managerial Finance

Eleventh Edition

PART I

Introduction to Managerial Finance

CHAPTER 1

An Overview of Managerial Finance

For two decades, William Bennett headed Circus Circus Enterprises, which he and co-founder William Pennington built into a major gaming organization through their vision that gambling could be mass-marketed with the allure of cheap travel junkets and low-stakes games. But, on July 8, 1994, relenting to pressure from stockholders, Bennett resigned from his powerful position as chairman of the board of directors. The stockholders forced Bennett out primarily because they saw the price of Circus Circus stock drop by almost 60 percent during the previous six months, and they attributed this devaluation largely to the fact that Bennett ruled the firm much like a dictator with his own agenda. The bottom line was that stockholders believed the value of their investment suffered under Bennett's administration—in their minds, the stockholders' best interests were not being served. Maurice Saatchi, chairman and co-founder of Saatchi and Saatchi PLC, a worldwide advertising agency with such accounts as British Airways and Mars (a candy manufacturer), can empathize with Bennett because he was forced to resign in December 1994, also because stockholders did not believe he had their best interests in mind. For the same reason, in 1994, the stockholders of Circus Circus and John Labatt Ltd., a Toronto-based beer brewer, turned down proposals from top management that would have made the firms less attractive as takeover candidates, because the proposals were viewed as being beneficial to management rather than to the stockholders. In each of these instances, stockholders made it clear that they are the owners of the firms, and, as such, top management should strive to achieve the stockholders' primary goal of value maximization.

When conflicts occur between managements' goals (for example, job security, substantial compensation) and the owners' goal (increased value), management should "do what is right for the company and its owners." To reduce the chances of conflicts in goals and ensure the goals of stockholders are pursued, many firms now require their senior managers to own stock in the companies they run. Such firms as Eastman Kodak, Xerox, Union Carbide, and Hershey Foods, to name a few, have policies that force those who are in top management positions to also be owners of the firm. It is believed

Continued

that if managers also are owners, they will be more "in tune" with the other stockholders' interests and less inclined to pursue activities harmful to the stock's value. There is evidence that supports this contention—firms with executives that own substantial amounts of stock do very well.

As you read this chapter, think about some of the issues raised above: As a stockholder in a company, what goal (or set of goals) would you like to see pursued? To what extent should top managers let their personal goals influence the decisions they make concerning how the firm is run? Would you, as an outside stockholder, feel more comfortable that your interests were being represented better if the firm's top managers also owned large amounts of the firm's stock? What factors should management consider when trying to "boost" the value of the firm's stock?

"Why should I study finance?" As a student, you might be asking yourself this question right now. To answer this question, we need to ask another: What role does "finance" play in the successful operation of a firm? As we will see in this chapter and in the chapters that follow, proper financial management will help any business provide better products to its customers at lower prices, pay higher salaries to its employees, and still provide greater returns to investors who put up the funds needed to form and operate the business. Because the economy—both national and worldwide—consists of customers, employees, and investors, sound financial management contributes to the well-being of both individuals and the general population.

The purpose of this chapter is to provide an overview of managerial finance. After you finish the chapter, you should have a reasonably good idea of how finance knowledge is used in business. You should also have a better understanding of (1) some of the forces that will affect managerial finance in the future; (2) the way businesses are organized; (3) where finance fits in a firm's organizational structure relative to such areas as accounting, marketing, production, and personnel; and (4) the goals of a firm and the way financial managers can contribute to achieving these goals.

Career Opportunities in Finance

The study of finance consists of three interrelated areas: (1) *money and capital markets,* which deals with many of the topics covered in macroeconomics; (2) *investments,* which focuses on the decisions of individuals and financial and other institutions as they choose securities for their investment portfolios; and (3) *managerial finance,* or "business finance," which involves the actual management of the firm. Although our concern in this text primarily is with managerial finance, each of these areas is related, so a financial manager should have a good understanding of capital market operations and the way investors evaluate and choose securities. The career opportunities within each field are many and varied, but financial managers must have a knowledge of all three areas if they are to do their jobs well. The purpose of this section is to give you a general idea of the areas in which finance graduates can expect to work.

Money and Capital Markets

Many finance majors go to work for financial institutions, including banks, insurance companies, savings and loans, and credit unions. For success here one needs a knowledge of the factors that cause interest rates to rise and fall, the regulations to which financial institutions are subject, and the various types of financial instruments (mortgages, auto loans, certificates of deposit, and so on). One also needs a general knowledge of all aspects of business administration, because the management of a financial institution involves accounting, marketing, personnel, and computer systems, as well as managerial finance.

Investments

Finance graduates who go into investments generally work for stock brokerage firms, banks, investment companies, or insurance companies. The three main functions in the investments area are (1) sales, (2) the analysis of individual securities, and (3) determination of the optimal mix of securities for a given investor. As a finance graduate, you might get a job performing any one or some combination of these tasks.

Managerial Finance

Managerial finance is the broadest of the three areas, and the one with the greatest number of job opportunities. Managerial finance is important in all types of businesses, whether they are public or private, deal with financial services, or are manufacturers. The types of jobs one encounters in managerial finance range from decisions regarding plant expansions to choosing what types of securities to issue to finance expansion. Financial managers also have the responsibility for deciding the credit terms under which customers can buy, how much inventory the firm should carry, how much cash to keep on hand, whether to acquire other firms (merger analysis), and how much of the firm's earnings to plow back into the business versus pay out as dividends.

Regardless of which area you go into, you will need to have some knowledge of all three. For example, a banker lending to businesses cannot perform well without a good understanding of managerial finance, because he or she must be able to judge how well a business is operated. The same holds for one of Merrill Lynch's security analysts, and even stockbrokers must have an understanding of general financial principles if they are to give intelligent advice to their customers. At the same time, corporate financial managers need to know what their bankers are thinking about, and how investors are likely to judge their corporations' performances and thus determine their stock prices. So, if you decide to make finance your career, you will need to know something about all three areas.

 Self-Test Questions

What are the three main areas of finance?

If you have definite plans to go into one area, why is it necessary that you know something about the other areas?

Managerial Finance in the Twentieth Century

When managerial finance emerged as a separate field of study in the early 1900s, the emphasis was on the legal aspects of mergers, the formation of new firms, and the various types of securities that firms could issue to raise funds. This was a time when industrialization was sweeping the country; "big" was considered power, so many takeovers and mergers were used to create large corporations. During the Great Depression of the 1930s, however, an unprecedented number of business failures caused the emphasis in finance to shift to bankruptcy and reorganization, to corporate liquidity, and to regulation of security markets. During the 1940s and early 1950s, finance continued to be taught as a descriptive, institutional subject, viewed more from the standpoint of an outsider rather than from that of management. But, with the advent of the computer for general business use, the focus began to shift toward the insider's point of view and the importance of financial decision making to the firm. A movement toward theoretical analysis began during the 1960s, and the focus of managerial finance shifted to managerial decisions regarding the choice of assets and liabilities necessary to maximize the value of the firm. The focus on valuation continued through the 1980s, but the analysis was expanded to include (1) inflation and its effects on business decisions; (2) deregulation of financial institutions and the resulting trend toward large, broadly diversified financial services companies; (3) the dramatic increase in both the use of computers for analysis and the electronic transfer of information; and (4) the increased importance of global markets and business operations. In today's fast-paced, technologically driven world, the area of managerial finance continues to evolve. But, to this point, the two most important trends during the 1990s have been the continued globalization of business and a further increase in the use of electronic technology.

The Globalization of Business

Four factors have made the trend toward globalization mandatory for many businesses: (1) Improvements in transportation and communications have lowered shipping costs and made international trade more feasible. (2) The political clout of consumers who desire low-cost, high-quality products has helped lower trade barriers designed to protect inefficient, high-cost domestic manufacturers. (3) As technology has advanced, the cost of developing new products has increased, and, as development costs rise, so must unit sales if the firm is to be competitive. (4) In a world populated with multinational firms able to shift production to wherever costs are lowest, a firm whose manufacturing operations are restricted to one country cannot compete unless costs in its home country happen to be low, a condition that does not necessarily exist for many U.S. corporations. As a result of these four factors, most manufacturers must produce and sell globally to survive.

Service companies, including banks, advertising agencies, and accounting firms, also are being forced to "go global" to better serve their multinational clients. There will, of course, always be some purely domestic companies, but you should keep in mind that the most dynamic growth, and the best opportunities, often are with companies that operate worldwide.

Computer Technology

Many large companies currently have networks of personal computers linked to one another, to the firm's own mainframe computers, and to their customers' and suppliers' computers. Some companies, like General Motors, require their suppliers to be linked electronically so orders and payments can be made via the computer. As the 1990s progress, we will see continued advances in the use of electronic technology in managerial finance, and this technology will revolutionize the way financial decisions are made. One result of this "electronic revolution" that we have seen already is the increased use of quantitative analysis via computer models for financial decision making. Therefore, it is clear the next generation of financial managers will need stronger computer and quantitative skills than were required in the past.

 Self-Test Questions

How has managerial finance changed from the early 1900s to the 1990s?

How might a person become better prepared for a career in managerial finance?

Increasing Importance of Managerial Finance

The historical trends discussed in the preceding section have greatly increased the importance of managerial finance. In earlier times the marketing manager would project sales, the engineering and production staffs would determine the assets necessary to meet those demands, and the financial manager's job was simply to raise the money needed to purchase the required plant, equipment, and inventories. That situation no longer exists—decisions now are much more coordinated, and the financial manager generally has direct responsibility for the control process.

Eastern Airlines and Delta can be used to illustrate both the importance of managerial finance and the effects of financial decisions. In the 1960s, Eastern's stock sold for more than $60 per share while Delta's sold for $10. By the mid-1990s, Delta had become one of the world's strongest airlines, and its stock was selling for more than $53 per share. Eastern, on the other hand, had gone bankrupt and was no longer in existence. Although many factors combined to produce these results, financial decisions exerted a major influence. Because Eastern had traditionally used a great deal of debt while Delta had not, Eastern's costs increased significantly, and its profits were lowered, when interest rates rose during the 1980s. Rising rates had only a minor effect on Delta. Further, when fuel price increases made it imperative for the airlines to buy new, fuel-efficient planes, Delta was able to do so, but Eastern was not. Finally, when the airlines were deregulated, Delta was strong enough to expand into developing markets and to cut prices as necessary to attract business, but Eastern was not.

The Delta–Eastern story, and others like it, illustrates how important proper financial planning is to long-run corporate survival; such awareness has increased the emphasis placed on the managerial finance function. Indeed, the value of managerial finance is reflected in the fact that more chief executive officers (CEOs) in the top 1,000 U.S. companies started their careers in finance than in any other functional area.

It also is becoming increasingly important for people in marketing, accounting, production, personnel, and other areas to understand finance in order to do a good job in their own fields. People in marketing, for instance, must understand how marketing decisions affect and are affected by funds availability, by inventory levels, by excess plant capacity, and so on. Similarly, accountants must understand how accounting data are used in corporate planning and are viewed by investors.

Thus, *there are financial implications in virtually all business decisions, and nonfinancial executives simply must know enough finance to work these implications into their own specialized analyses.*[1] Because of this, every student of business, regardless of major, should be concerned with finance.

Self-Test Questions

Explain why financial planning is important to today's chief executives.

Why do marketing people need to know something about managerial finance?

The Financial Manager's Responsibilities

The financial manager's task is to make decisions concerning the acquisition and use of funds for the greatest benefit of the firm. Here are some specific activities that are involved:

1. **Forecasting and planning.** The financial manager must interact with other executives as they look ahead and lay the plans that will shape the firm's future position.

2. **Major investment and financing decisions.** A successful firm generally has rapid growth in sales, which requires investments in plant, equipment, and inventory. The financial manager must help determine the optimal sales growth rate, and he or she must help decide on the specific assets to acquire and the best way to finance those assets. For example, should the firm raise funds by borrowing (debt) or by selling stock (equity)? If the firm uses debt (borrows), should it be long-term or short-term?

3. **Coordination and control.** The financial manager must interact with other executives to ensure that the firm is operated as efficiently as possible. All business decisions have financial implications, and all managers—financial and otherwise—need to take this into account. For example, marketing decisions affect sales growth, which in turn influences investment requirements. Thus, marketing decision makers must consider how their actions affect (and are affected by) such factors as the availability of funds, inventory policies, and plant capacity utilization.

---

[1]It is interesting that the course "Managerial Finance for Nonfinancial Executives" has the highest enrollment in most executive development programs.

4. Dealing with the financial markets. The financial manager must deal with the money and capital markets. As we will see in Chapter 2, each firm affects and is affected by the general financial markets where funds are raised, where the firm's securities are traded, and where its investors are either rewarded or penalized.

In summary, financial managers make decisions regarding which assets their firms should acquire, how those assets should be financed, and how the firm should manage its existing resources. If these responsibilities are performed optimally, financial managers will help to maximize the value of their firms, thus maximizing the long-run welfare of those who buy from or work for the company.

Self-Test Question

What are four specific activities with which financial managers are involved?

Alternative Forms of Business Organization

There are three main forms of business organization: (1) proprietorships, (2) partnerships, and (3) corporations. In terms of numbers, about 80 percent of businesses are operated as proprietorships, while the remainder are divided equally between partnerships and corporations. Based on dollar value of sales, however, about 80 percent of all business is conducted by corporations, about 13 percent by proprietorships, and about 7 percent by partnerships. Because most business is conducted by corporations, we will concentrate on them in this book. However, it is important to understand the differences among the three forms.

Proprietorship

PROPRIETORSHIP
An unincorporated business owned by one individual.

A **proprietorship** is an unincorporated business owned by one individual. Starting a proprietorship is fairly easy—just begin business operations. However, in most cases, even the smallest business must be licensed by the municipality (city, county, or state) in which it operates.

The proprietorship has three important advantages: (1) It is easily and inexpensively formed, (2) it is subject to few government regulations, and (3) the business is taxed like an individual, not a corporation.

The proprietorship also has four important limitations: (1) The proprietor has unlimited personal liability for business debts, which can result in losses that exceed the money he or she has invested in the company; (2) it is difficult for a proprietorship to obtain large sums of capital, because the firm's financial strength often is based on the financial strength of the sole owner; (3) transferring ownership is somewhat difficult—disposing of the business is similar to selling a house; and (4) the life of a business organized as a proprietorship is limited to the life of the individual who created it. For these reasons, individual proprietorships are confined primarily to small business operations. However, businesses frequently are started as proprietorships and then converted to corporations when their growth causes the disadvantages of being a proprietorship to outweigh the advantages.

Partnership

PARTNERSHIP
An unincorporated business owned by two or more persons.

A **partnership** is like a proprietorship, except there are two or more owners. Partnerships can operate under different degrees of formality, ranging from informal, oral understandings to formal agreements filed with the secretary of the state in which the partnership does business. Most legal experts would recommend the partnership agreement be put in writing.

The advantages of a partnership are the same as those of a proprietorship: (1) formation is easy and relatively inexpensive, (2) a partnership is subject to few government regulations, and (3) the business is taxed like an individual, not a corporation.

The disadvantages also are similar to those associated with proprietorships: (1) unlimited liability, (2) limited life of the organization, (3) difficulty of transferring ownership, and (4) difficulty of raising large amounts of capital.

Regarding liability, the partners can potentially lose all their personal assets, even those assets not invested in the business, because under partnership law each partner is liable for the business's debts. Therefore, if any partner is unable to meet his or her *pro rata* claim in the event the partnership goes bankrupt, the remaining partners must make good on the unsatisfied claims, drawing on their personal assets if necessary. The partners of the national accounting firm Laventhol and Horwath, a huge partnership that went bankrupt at the end of 1992 as a result of suits filed by investors who relied on faulty audit statements, currently are learning all about the perils of doing business as a partnership. Thus, a Texas partner who audits a savings and loan that goes under can bring ruin to a millionaire New York partner who never went near the S&L.[2]

The first three disadvantages—unlimited liability, impermanence of the organization, and difficulty of transferring ownership—lead to the fourth, the difficulty partnerships have in attracting substantial amounts of funds. This is no particular problem for a slow-growing business, but if a business's products really catch on, and if it needs to raise large amounts of funds to capitalize on its opportunities, the difficulty in attracting funds becomes a real drawback. Thus, growth companies such as Hewlett-Packard and Apple Computer generally begin life as a proprietorship or partnership, but at some point they find it necessary to convert to a corporation.

Corporation

CORPORATION
A legal entity created by a state, separate and distinct from its owners and managers, having unlimited life, easy transferability of ownership, and limited liability.

A **corporation** is a legal entity created by a state. It is separate and distinct from its owners and managers. This separateness gives the corporation three major advantages:

1. **Unlimited life.** A corporation can continue after its original owners and managers are deceased.

---

[2]However, it is possible to limit the liabilities of some of the partners by establishing a *limited partnership,* wherein one (or more) partner is designated the *general partner* and the others *limited partners.* Limited partnerships are quite common in the area of real estate investment, but they do not work well with most types of businesses, including accounting firms, because one partner rarely is willing to assume all the business's risk. Recently, the "Big 6" accounting firms reorganized themselves as limited liability partnerships, which are partnerships in which only the assets of the partnership and the "engagement" partner (partner in charge of the situation) are at risk.

2. **Easy transferability of ownership interest.** Ownership interests can be divided into shares of stock, which in turn can be transferred far more easily than can proprietorship or partnership interests.

3. **Limited liability.** To illustrate the concept of limited liability, suppose you invested $10,000 to become a partner in a business that subsequently went bankrupt owing creditors $1 million. Because the owners are liable for the debts of a partnership, you could be assessed for a share of the company's debt, and you could be held liable for the entire $1 million if your partners could not pay their shares—this is what we mean by unlimited liability. On the other hand, if you invested $10,000 in the stock of a corporation that then went bankrupt, your potential loss on the investment would be limited to your $10,000 investment.[3]

These three factors—unlimited life, easy transferability of ownership interest, and limited liability—make it much easier for corporations than for proprietorships or partnerships to raise money in the general capital markets.

The corporate form of business offers significant advantages over proprietorships and partnerships, but it does have two primary disadvantages: (1) Corporate earnings are subject to double taxation—the earnings of the corporation are taxed, and then any earnings paid out as dividends are taxed again as income to the stockholders. (2) Setting up a corporation, and filing required state and federal reports, is more complex and time-consuming than for a proprietorship or a partnership.

Although a proprietorship or a partnership can commence operations without much paperwork, setting up a corporation requires that the incorporators hire a lawyer to prepare a charter and a set of bylaws. The *charter* includes the following information: (1) name of the proposed corporation, (2) types of activities it will pursue, (3) amount of capital stock, (4) number of directors, and (5) names and addresses of directors. The charter is filed with the secretary of the state in which the firm will be incorporated; when it is approved, the corporation officially exists.[4] Then, after the corporation is in operation, quarterly and annual financial and tax reports must be filed with state and federal authorities.

The *bylaws* are a set of rules drawn up by the founders of the corporation to aid in governing the internal management of the company. Included are such points as (1) how directors are to be elected (all elected each year, or perhaps one-third each year for three-year terms); (2) whether the existing stockholders will have the first right to buy any new shares the firm issues; and (3) procedures for changing the bylaws themselves, should conditions require it.

For the following reasons, the value of any business other than a very small one probably will be maximized if it is organized as a corporation:[5]

1. Limited liability reduces the risks borne by investors; other things held constant, *lower risk means higher value.*

---

[3]In the case of small corporations, the limited liability feature is often a fiction, since bankers and credit managers frequently require personal guarantees from the stockholders of small, weak businesses.

[4]Most major U.S. corporations are chartered in Delaware, which has, over the years, provided a favorable legal environment. It is not necessary for a firm to be headquartered, or even to conduct operations, in its state of incorporation.

[5]Each of these reasons (topics) will be discussed in more detail later in the book.

2. Corporations can attract funds more easily than can unincorporated businesses, and these funds can be invested in *growth opportunities* that help increase the firm's value.

3. Corporate ownership can be transferred more easily than ownership of either a proprietorship or a partnership. Therefore, all else equal, *investors would be willing to pay more* for a corporation than a proprietorship or partnership—this means that the corporate form of organization can enhance the value of a business.

4. Corporations are taxed differently than proprietorships and partnerships, and some of the *tax differences are beneficial* for corporations.

As we will see later in the chapter, most firms are managed with value maximization in mind, and this, in turn, has caused most large businesses to be organized as corporations.

Self-Test Questions

What are the key differences between sole proprietorships, partnerships, and corporations?

Explain why the value of any business other than a very small one probably will be maximized if it is organized as a corporation.

Finance in the Organizational Structure of the Firm

Organizational structures vary from firm to firm, but Figure 1-1 presents a fairly typical picture of the role of finance within a corporation. The chief financial officer—who has the title of vice-president: finance—reports to the president. The financial vice-president's key subordinates are the treasurer and the controller. In most firms the treasurer has direct responsibility for managing the firm's cash and marketable securities, for planning how funds are raised, for selling stocks and bonds to raise funds, and for overseeing the corporate pension fund. The treasurer also supervises the credit manager, the inventory manager, and the director of capital budgeting (who analyzes decisions related to investments in fixed assets). The controller is responsible for the activities of the accounting and tax departments.

Self-Test Question

Identify the two subordinates who report to the firm's chief financial officer, and indicate the primary responsibilities of each.

The Goals of the Corporation

Business decisions are not made in a vacuum—decision makers have some objective in mind. *Throughout this book we operate on the assumption that management's primary goal is* **stockholder wealth maximization,** which, as we will see, translates into *maximizing the value of the firm, which is measured by the*

FIGURE 1-1

Place of Finance in a Typical Business Organization

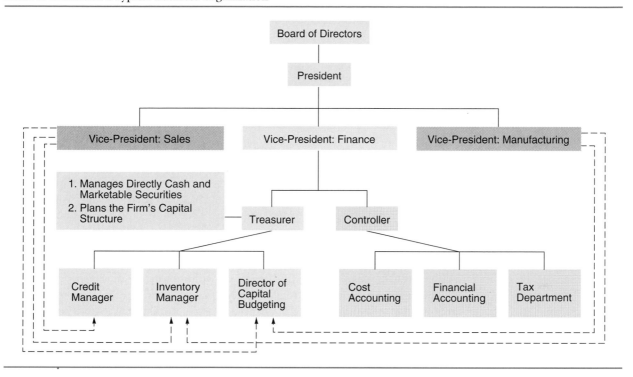

STOCKHOLDER WEALTH MAXIMIZATION
The appropriate goal for management decisions; considers the risk and timing associated with expected earnings per share in order to maximize the price of the firm's common stock.

price of the firm's common stock. Firms do, of course, have other objectives—in particular, managers, who make the actual decisions, are interested in their own personal satisfaction, in their employees' welfare, and in the good of the community and of society at large. Still, for the reasons set forth in the following sections, *stock price maximization is the most important goal of most corporations.*

Managerial Incentives to Maximize Shareholder Wealth

The stockholders own the firm and elect the management team. Management, in turn, is supposed to operate in the best interests of the stockholders. As a stockholder of a company, you probably would want the managers to make decisions that would maximize the value of the stock you own, including dividends. We know, however, that because the stock of most large firms is widely held, the managers of large corporations have a great deal of latitude in making business decisions. This being the case, might not managers pursue goals other than stock price maximization? For example, some have argued that the managers of a large, well-entrenched corporation could work just hard enough to keep stockholder returns at a "reasonable" level and then devote the remainder of their efforts and resources to public service activities, to employee benefits, to higher executive salaries, or to golf.

It is almost impossible to determine whether a particular management team is trying to maximize shareholder wealth or is merely attempting to keep stockholders satisfied while pursuing other goals. For example, how can we tell whether employee or community benefit programs are in the long-run best interests of the stockholders? Similarly, are relatively high executive salaries really necessary to attract and retain excellent managers, or just another example of managers taking advantage of stockholders?

It is impossible to give definitive answers to these questions. However, we do know that the managers of a firm operating in a competitive market will be forced to undertake actions that are reasonably consistent with shareholder wealth maximization. If they depart from this goal, they run the risk of being removed from their jobs. We will have more to say about the conflict between managers and shareholders later in the chapter.

Social Responsibility

SOCIAL RESPONSIBILITY
The concept that businesses should be actively concerned with the welfare of society at large.

NORMAL PROFITS/RATES OF RETURN
Those profits and rates of return that are close to the average for all firms and are just sufficient to attract capital.

Another issue that deserves consideration is **social responsibility:** Should businesses operate strictly in their stockholders' best interests, or are firms also responsible for the welfare of their employees, customers, and the communities in which they operate? Certainly firms have an ethical responsibility to provide a safe working environment, to avoid polluting the air or water, and to produce safe products. However, socially responsible actions have costs, and it is questionable whether businesses would incur these costs voluntarily. If some firms do act in a socially responsible manner while others do not, then the socially responsible firms will be at a disadvantage in attracting funds. To illustrate, suppose the firms in a given industry have **profits** and **rates of return on investment** that are close to **normal**—that is, close to the average for all firms and just sufficient to attract capital. If one company attempts to exercise social responsibility, it will have to raise prices to cover the added costs. If the other businesses in its industry do not follow suit, their costs and prices will be lower. The socially responsible firm will not be able to compete, and it will be forced to abandon its efforts. Thus, any voluntary socially responsible acts that raise costs will be difficult, if not impossible, in industries that are subject to keen competition.

What about oligopolistic firms with profits above normal levels—cannot such firms devote resources to social projects? Undoubtedly they can, and many large, successful firms do engage in community projects, employee benefit programs, and the like to a greater degree than would appear to be called for by pure profit or wealth maximization goals.[6] Still, publicly owned firms are constrained in such actions by financial market factors. To illustrate, suppose a saver who has funds to invest is considering two firms. One firm devotes a substantial part of its resources to social actions, while the other concentrates on profits and stock prices. Most investors are likely to shun the socially oriented firm, thus putting it at a disadvantage in the capital market. After all, why should the stockholders of one corporation subsidize society to a greater extent than those of other businesses? For this reason, even highly profitable firms (unless they are closely held rather than publicly owned) generally are constrained against taking unilateral cost-increasing social actions.

Does all this mean that firms should not exercise social responsibility? Not at all, but it does mean that most significant cost-increasing actions will have to be

---

[6]Even firms like these often find it necessary to justify such projects at stockholder meetings by stating that these programs will contribute to long-run profit maximization.

mandatory rather than voluntary, at least initially, to ensure that the burden falls uniformly on all businesses.

Stock Price Maximization and Social Welfare

If a firm attempts to maximize its stock price, is this good or bad for society? In general, it is good. Aside from such illegal actions as attempting to form monopolies, violating safety codes, and failing to meet pollution control requirements, *the same actions that maximize stock prices also benefit society.* First, note that stock price maximization requires efficient, low-cost plants that produce high-quality goods and services at the lowest possible cost. Second, stock price maximization requires the development of products that consumers want and need, so the profit motive leads to new technology, to new products, and to new jobs. Finally, stock price maximization necessitates efficient and courteous service, adequate stocks of merchandise, and well-located business establishments—these factors all are necessary to maintain a customer base that is necessary for producing sales, and thus profits. Therefore, actions that help a firm increase the price of its stock also are beneficial to society at large. This is why profit-motivated, free-enterprise economies have been so much more successful than socialistic and communistic economic systems. Because managerial finance plays a crucial role in the operation of successful firms, and because successful firms are absolutely necessary for a healthy, productive economy, it is easy to see why finance is important from a social standpoint.[7]

 Self-Test Questions

What is management's primary goal?

What would happen if one firm attempted to exercise costly social responsibility, while its competitors did not exercise social responsibility?

How does the goal of stock price maximization benefit society at large?

Managerial Actions to Maximize Shareholder Wealth

PROFIT MAXIMIZATION
The maximization of the firm's net income.
EARNINGS PER SHARE (EPS)
Net income divided by the number of shares of common stock outstanding.

To maximize the price of a firm's stock, what types of actions should its management take? First, consider the question of stock prices versus profits: Will **profit maximization** also result in stock price maximization? In answering this question, we must consider the matter of total corporate profits versus **earnings per share (EPS)**.

---

[7]People sometimes argue that firms, in their efforts to raise profits and stock prices, increase product prices and gouge the public. In a reasonably competitive economy, which we have, prices are constrained by competition and consumer resistance. If a firm raises its prices beyond reasonable levels, it will simply lose its market share. Even giant firms like General Motors lose business to the Japanese and Germans, as well as to Ford and Chrysler, if they set prices above levels necessary to cover production costs plus a "normal" profit. Of course, firms *want* to earn more, and they constantly try to cut costs, develop new products, and so on, and thereby earn above-normal profits. Note, though, that if they are indeed successful and do earn above-normal profits, those very profits will attract competition which will eventually drive prices down, so again the main long-term beneficiary is the consumer.

INDUSTRY PRACTICE

The Shareholders Meeting—Is It Just a Ritual?

Each year, nearly every American company that is publicly traded holds a shareholders meeting (1) to provide information concerning the previous year's performance, (2) to fill vacancies on the board of directors, and (3) to make decisions about major issues facing the firm.

A century ago, when a firm was held by a few shareholders who typically lived close to the main factory or headquarters, the annual meeting was used to communicate with the owners and reach a consensus concerning matters affecting the future of the firm's operations. Today, the shareholders of most large American firms are scattered around the world, making it difficult to schedule a single meeting that all shareholders can attend. Further, disclosure laws that have been enacted in the twentieth century require that publicly traded firms inform *all* shareholders of major developments via periodic financial reports, proxy statements, and other published reports, and the technology used to communicate this information has improved significantly, especially in the past two decades. So the annual meeting is no longer seen as the most important means to communicate with stockholders. Instead, the shareholders meeting has become an expensive ritual for many large corporations—for some firms the cost exceeds $1 million.

Will shareholders meetings of large corporations become a thing of the past? Perhaps. Consider the fact that most of the largest corporations in the United States are owned by institutional investors, such as mutual funds, insurance companies, and pension funds. If these investors want to know anything about the actions of a company, they simply call or fax the company's top management—they do not wait until the annual shareholders meeting to find out the answers to important questions they have today. In addition, companies now are required to provide shareholders with proxy statements that include much greater and more simplified financial information than ever before. The proxy statement, which must be mailed to shareholders prior to the shareholders meeting, includes information concerning the major issues that will be addressed at the annual meeting, and it provides a medium by which shareholders can vote

on the issues without actually attending the meeting. Most investors who own small amounts of large companies do not attend the annual meeting, so they rely on proxy voting to convey their feelings about the major issues facing the firms they own. The new disclosure rules require that proxy statements include information about executive compensation and firm performance, both in the current year and for the past five years. The financial data, including changes in the firm's stock price and the dividends paid, must be presented in graphical form along with comparative data of similar companies and some market index like the New York Stock Exchange Composite Index. The Securities and Exchange Commission (SEC) has mandated these new disclosure rules to help *all* investors become better informed about how executives are paid relative to the performance of their firms.

Modern technology and existing disclosure requirements have helped to decrease the role of the annual shareholders meeting—much of the business that used to take place at the shareholders meeting now is performed at other times, using modern communications media. So it seems the shareholders meeting as we know it today is more of a ritual than a functional activity. Consequently, in the future, we probably will see shareholders meetings change significantly, perhaps even disappear. Some suggestions are: (1) If shareholders meetings must be held, get them over with as quickly as possible. (2) Rather than hold a single, centrally located meeting, have a series of regional seminars to keep stockholders informed. (3) Eliminate shareholders meetings altogether—use proxy voting and surveys to conduct business and to determine stockholders' opinions.

It is clear that, as communication technology improves and disclosure requirements become more stringent, shareholders' relationships with companies will continue to change.

SOURCE: "Stop Us Before We Meet Again," *The Wall Street Journal,* March 18, 1994, p. A10, And "Your Money Matters: Weekend Report;Revolutionary Proxies: Read Them and Reap," *The Wall Street Journal,* January 29, 1994, p. C1.

For example, suppose Xerox had 100 million shares outstanding and earned $400 million, or $4 per share. If you owned 100 shares of the stock, your share of the total profits would be $400. Now suppose Xerox sold another 100 million shares and invested the funds received in assets that produced $100 million of income. Total income would rise to $500 million, but earnings per share would decline from $4 to $500/200 = $2.50. Now your share of the firm's earnings would be only $250, down from $400. You (and other current stockholders) would have suffered an earnings dilution, even though total corporate profits had risen. Therefore, other things held constant, *if management is interested in the well-being of its current stockholders, it should concentrate on earnings per share rather than on total corporate profits.*

Will maximization of expected earnings per share always maximize stockholder welfare, or should other factors be considered? Think about the *timing of the earnings.* Suppose Xerox had one project that would cause earnings per share to rise by $0.20 per year for 5 years, or $1 in total, while another project would have no effect on earnings for 4 years but would increase earnings by $1.25 in the fifth year. Which project is better—in other words, is $0.20 per year for 5 years better or worse than $1.25 in Year 5? The answer depends on which project adds the most to the value of the stock, which in turn depends on the time value of money to investors. Thus, timing is an important reason to concentrate on wealth as measured by the price of the stock rather than on earnings alone.

Another issue relates to *risk.* Suppose one project is expected to increase earnings per share by $1, while another is expected to raise earnings by $1.20 per share. The first project is not very risky—if it is undertaken, earnings will almost certainly rise by about $1 per share. However, the other project is quite risky, so, although our best guess is that earnings will rise by $1.20 per share, we must recognize the possibility that there might be no increase whatsoever, or even a loss. Depending on how averse stockholders are to risk, the first project might be preferable to the second.

The riskiness inherent in projected earnings per share also depends on *how the firm is financed.* As we shall see, many firms go bankrupt every year, and the greater the use of debt, the greater the threat of bankruptcy. *Consequently, although the use of debt financing might increase projected EPS, debt also increases the riskiness of projected future earnings.*

Another issue is the matter of paying dividends to stockholders versus retaining earnings and reinvesting them in the firm, thereby causing the earnings stream to grow over time. Stockholders like cash dividends, but they also like the growth in EPS that results from plowing earnings back into the business. The financial manager must decide exactly how much of the current earnings to pay out as dividends rather than to retain and reinvest—this is called the **dividend policy decision.** The optimal dividend policy is the one that maximizes the firm's stock price.

We see, then, that the firm's stock price is dependent on the following factors:

DIVIDEND POLICY DECISION
The decision as to how much of current earnings to pay out as dividends rather than to retain for reinvestment in the firm.

1. Projected earnings per share
2. Timing of the earnings stream
3. Riskiness of the projected earnings
4. Use of debt
5. Dividend policy

Every significant corporate decision should be analyzed in terms of its effect on these factors and hence on the price of the firm's stock. For example, suppose Occidental Petroleum's coal division is considering opening a new mine. If this is done, can it be expected to increase EPS? Is there a chance that costs will exceed estimates, that prices and output will fall below projections, and that EPS will be reduced because the new mine was opened? How long will it take for the new mine to show a profit? How should the capital required to open the mine be raised? If debt is used, by how much will this increase Occidental's riskiness? Should Occidental reduce its current dividends and use the cash thus saved to finance the project, or should it maintain its dividends and finance the mine with external capital? Managerial finance is designed to help answer questions like these, plus many more.

Self-Test Questions

Will profit maximization always result in stock price maximization?

Identify five factors that affect the firm's stock price, and explain the effects of each of them.

Agency Relationships

An *agency relationship* exists when one or more people (the principals) hire another person (the agent) to perform a service and then delegate decision-making authority to that agent. Important agency relationships exist (1) between stockholders and managers and (2) between stockholders and creditors (debtholders).

Stockholders versus Managers

AGENCY PROBLEM
A potential conflict of interest between (1) the principals (outside shareholders) and the agent (manager) or (2) stockholders and creditors (debtholders).

A potential **agency problem** arises whenever the manager of a firm owns less than 100 percent of the firm's common stock. If a firm is a proprietorship managed by the owner, the owner-manager will presumably operate the business in a fashion that will improve his or her own welfare, with welfare measured in the form of increased personal wealth, more leisure, or perquisites.[8] However, if the owner-manager incorporates and sells some of the firm's stock to outsiders, a potential conflict of interests immediately arises. For example, the owner-manager might now decide not to work as hard to maximize shareholder wealth because less of this wealth will go to him or her, or to take a higher salary or enjoy more perquisites because part of those costs will fall on the outside stockholders. This potential conflict between two parties, the principals (outside shareholders) and the agent (manager), is an agency problem.

In general, if a conflict of interest exists, what can be done to ensure that management treats the outside stockholders fairly? Several mechanisms are used to motivate managers to act in the shareholders' best interests. These include (1) the threat of firing, (2) the threat of takeover, and (3) managerial compensation.

---

[8]Perquisites are executive fringe benefits, such as luxurious offices, use of corporate planes and yachts, personal assistants, and general use of business assets for personal purposes.

1. **The threat of firing.** Until recently, the probability of a large firm's management being ousted by its stockholders was so remote that it posed little threat. This situation existed because ownership of most firms was so widely distributed, and management's control over the proxy (voting) mechanism was so strong, that it was almost impossible for dissident stockholders to gain enough votes to overthrow the managers. Today, however, 55 percent of the stock of an average large corporation is owned by a relatively few large institutions rather than by thousands of individual investors, and the institutional money managers have the clout to influence a firm's operations. Major corporations whose managements have been ousted include United Airlines, Disney, and IBM.

HOSTILE TAKEOVER
The acquisition of a company over the opposition of its management.

2. **The threat of takeover. Hostile takeovers** (where management does not want the firm to be taken over) are most likely to occur when a firm's stock is undervalued relative to its potential. In a hostile takeover, the managers of the acquired firm generally are fired, and any who are able to stay on lose the power they had prior to the acquisition. Thus, managers have a strong incentive to take actions that maximize stock prices. In the words of one company president, "If you want to keep control, don't let your company's stock sell at a bargain price."

POISON PILL
An action taken by management to make a firm unattractive to potential buyers and thus avoid a hostile takeover.

Actions to increase the firm's stock price and to keep it from being a bargain obviously are good from the standpoint of the stockholders, but other tactics that managers can use to ward off a hostile takeover might not be. Two examples of questionable tactics are *poison pills* and *greenmail*. A **poison pill** is an action a firm can take that practically kills it and thus makes it unattractive to potential suitors. Examples include Disney's plan to sell large blocks of its stock at low prices to "friendly" parties, Scott Industries' decision to make all of its debt immediately payable if its management changed, and Carleton Corporation's decision to give huge retirement bonuses, which represented a large part of the company's wealth, to its managers if the firm was taken over (such payments are called *golden parachutes*). **Greenmail,** which is like blackmail, occurs when (1) a potential acquirer (firm or individual) buys a block of stock in a company, (2) the target company's management becomes frightened that the acquirer will make a tender offer and gain control of the company, and (3) to head off a possible takeover, management offers to pay greenmail, buying the stock owned by the potential raider at a price above the existing market price without offering the same deal to other stockholders. A good example of greenmail was Disney's buy-back of 11.1 percent of its stock from Saul Steinberg's Reliance Group, giving Steinberg a quick $60 million profit. A group of stockholders sued, and Steinberg and the Disney directors were forced to pay $45 million to Disney stockholders.

GREENMAIL
A situation in which a firm, trying to avoid a takeover, buys back stock at a price above the existing market price from the person(s) trying to gain control of the firm.

3. **Structuring managerial incentives.** Increasingly, firms are tying managers' compensation to the company's performance, and this motivates managers to operate in a manner consistent with stock price maximization.

EXECUTIVE STOCK OPTION
A type of incentive plan that allows managers to purchase stock at some future time at a given price.

In the 1950s and 1960s, most performance-based incentive plans involved **executive stock options,** which allowed managers to purchase stock at some future time at a given price. Because the value of the options was tied directly to the price of the stock, it was assumed that granting options would provide an incentive for managers to take actions that would maximize the stock's price. This type of managerial incentive lost favor in the 1970s, however, because the general stock market declined, and stock prices did not necessarily reflect companies' earnings growth. Incentive plans should be based on those factors over which managers have control, and, because they cannot control the general stock market, stock option plans were not good incentive devices. Therefore, although 61 of the 100 largest U.S. firms used stock options as their sole incentive compensation in 1970, not even one of the largest 100 companies relied exclusively on such plans in 1995.

PERFORMANCE SHARES
A type of incentive plan in which managers are awarded shares of stock on the basis of the firm's performance over given intervals with respect to earnings per share or other measures.

An important incentive plan now is **performance shares,** which are shares of stock given to executives on the basis of performance as measured by earnings per share, return on assets, return on equity, and so on. For example, Honeywell uses growth in earnings per share as its primary performance measure. If the company achieves a targeted average growth in earnings per share, the managers will earn 100 percent of their shares. If the corporate performance is above the target, Honeywell's managers can earn even more shares. But, if growth is below the target, they get less than 100 percent of the shares.

All incentive compensation plans—executive stock options, performance shares, profit-based bonuses, and so forth—are designed to accomplish two things. First, these plans provide inducements to executives to act on those factors under their control in a manner that will contribute to stock price maximization. Second, the existence of such performance plans helps companies attract and retain top-level executives. Well-designed plans can accomplish both goals.

Stockholders versus Creditors

A second agency problem involves conflicts between stockholders and creditors (debtholders). Creditors lend funds to the firm at rates that are based on (1) the riskiness of the firm's existing assets, (2) expectations concerning the riskiness of future asset additions, (3) the firm's existing capital structure (that is, the amount of debt financing it uses), and (4) expectations concerning future capital structure changes. These are the factors that determine the riskiness of the firm's debt, so creditors base the interest rate they charge on expectations regarding these factors.

Now suppose the stockholders, acting through management, cause the firm to take on new ventures that have much greater risk than was anticipated by the creditors. This increased risk will cause the value of the outstanding debt to fall. If the risky ventures are successful, all the benefits will go to the stockholders because the creditors only get a fixed return. However, if things go sour, the bondholders will have to share the losses. What this amounts to, from the stockholders' point of view, is a game of "heads I win, tails you lose," which obviously is not a good game for the bondholders.

Similarly, if the firm increases its use of debt in an effort to boost the return to stockholders, the value of the old debt will decrease, so we have another "heads I win, tails you lose" situation. To illustrate, consider what happened to RJR Nabisco's bondholders when, in 1988, RJR's chief executive officer announced his plan to take the company private with funds the company would borrow (termed a *leveraged buyout*). Stockholders saw their shares jump in value from $56 to over $90 in just a few days, but RJR's bondholders suffered losses of approximately 20 percent. Investors immediately realized that taking RJR Nabisco private would cause the amount of its debt to rise dramatically, and thus its riskiness would soar. This, in turn, led to a huge decline in the price of RJR's outstanding bonds. Ultimately, RJR's management was not successful in its buyout attempt. But Nabisco was purchased by another company for more than $100 per share—what a gain for the stockholders!

Can and should stockholders, through their managers/agents, try to expropriate wealth from the firm's creditors? In general, the answer is no. First, because such attempts have been made in the past, creditors today protect themselves reasonably well against stockholder actions through restrictions in credit agreements. Second, if potential creditors perceive that a firm will try to take advantage of them in unethical ways, they will either refuse to deal with the firm or else require a much higher than normal rate of interest to compensate for the risks of such "sneaky" actions. Thus, firms that try to deal unfairly with creditors either lose access to the debt markets or are saddled with higher interest rates, both of which decrease the long-run value of the stock.

In view of these constraints, it follows that the goal of maximizing shareholder wealth requires fair play with creditors: Stockholder wealth depends on continued access to capital markets, and access depends on fair play and abiding by both the letter and the spirit of credit agreements. Managers, as agents of both the creditors and the stockholders, must act in a manner that is fairly balanced between the interests of these two classes of security holders. Similarly, because of other constraints and sanctions, management actions that would expropriate wealth from any of the firm's **stakeholders** (employees, customers, suppliers, and so on) will ultimately be to the detriment of shareholders. Therefore, maximizing shareholder wealth requires the fair treatment of all stakeholders.

STAKEHOLDERS
Individuals or entities that have an interest in the well-being of a firm—stockholders, creditors, employees, customers, suppliers, and so on.

Self-Test Questions

What is an agency relationship, and what two major agency relationships affect managerial finance?

Give some examples of potential agency problems between stockholders and managers.

List several factors that motivate managers to act in the shareholders' interests.

Give an example of how an agency problem might arise between stockholders and creditors.

The External Environment

Although managerial actions affect the value of a firm's stock, external factors also influence stock prices. Among these factors are legal constraints, the general level of economic activity, the tax laws, and conditions in the stock market. Figure 1-2 diagrams these general relationships. Working within the set of external constraints shown in the box at the extreme left, management makes a set of long-run strategic policy decisions that chart a course for the firm. These policy decisions, along with the general level of economic activity and the level of corporate income taxes, influence the firm's expected profitability, the timing of its

FIGURE 1-2

Summary of Major Factors Affecting Stock Prices

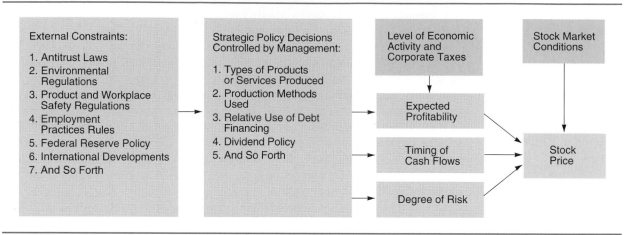

cash flows, their eventual transfer to stockholders in the form of dividends, and the degree of risk inherent in projected earnings and dividends. Profitability, timing, and risk all affect the price of the firm's stock, but so does another factor, conditions in the stock market as a whole, because all stock prices tend to move up and down together to some extent.

Self-Test Question

Identify some factors beyond a firm's control that influence its stock price.

Business Ethics

The word *ethics* is defined in Webster's dictionary as "standards of conduct or moral behavior." Business ethics can be thought of as a company's attitude and conduct toward its employees, customers, community, and stockholders. High standards of ethical behavior demand that a firm treat each party with which it deals in a fair and honest manner. A firm's commitment to business ethics can be measured by the tendency of the firm and its employees to adhere to laws and regulations relating to such factors as product safety and quality, fair employment practices, fair marketing and selling practices, the use of confidential information for personal gain, community involvement, bribery, and illegal payments to foreign governments to obtain business.

There are many instances of firms engaging in unethical behavior. For example, in recent years the employees of several prominent Wall Street investment banking houses have been sentenced to prison for illegally using insider information on proposed mergers for their own personal gain, and E. F. Hutton, a large brokerage firm, lost its independence through a forced merger after it was convicted of cheating its banks out of millions of dollars in a check kiting scheme. Drexel

Burnham Lambert, one of the largest investment banking firms, went bankrupt, and its "junk bond king," Michael Milken, who had earned $550 million in just one year, was sentenced to 10 years in prison plus charged a huge fine for securities-law violations. And, even more recently, Salomon Brothers Inc. was implicated in a Treasury-auction bidding scandal that resulted in the removal of key officers and a significant reorganization of the firm.

In spite of all this, the results of a recent study indicate that the executives of most major firms in the United States believe that their firms should, and do, try to maintain high ethical standards in all their business dealings. Further, most executives believe that there is a positive correlation between ethics and long-run profitability. For example, Chemical Bank suggested that ethical behavior has increased its profitability because such behavior (1) avoids fines and legal expenses, (2) builds public trust, (3) attracts business from customers who appreciate and support its policies, (4) attracts and keeps employees of the highest caliber, and (5) supports the economic viability of the communities in which it operates.

Most firms today have in place strong codes of ethical behavior, and they conduct training programs designed to ensure that all employees understand the correct behavior in different business situations. However, it is imperative that top management—the chairperson, president, and vice-presidents—be openly committed to ethical behavior, and that they communicate this commitment through their own personal actions as well as through company policies, directives, and punishment/reward systems.

Self-Test Questions

How would you define "business ethics"?

Is "being ethical" good for profits in the long run? In the short run?

Organization of the Book

Part I consists of two background chapters. In this chapter, we have discussed the goals of the firm and the philosophy of managerial finance. Chapter 2 describes how financial markets operate, how interest rates are determined, and how our tax system affects both stock prices and managerial decisions.

Part II deals with forecasting and control. First, Chapter 3 describes the key financial statements, shows how analysts appraise a firm's performance, and explains how the various aspects of managerial finance relate to one another. Then, in Chapter 4, we focus on projecting future financial statements under different strategic plans and operating conditions.

Part III includes topics related to the theory of valuation. First, in Chapter 5, we see how risk is measured and how it affects security prices and rates of return. Then, Chapter 6 discusses the time value of money and its effects on asset values and rates of return. Finally, Chapter 7 explains how risk and time value jointly determine stock and bond values in the marketplace.

Beginning with Part IV (Chapters 8 through 12), we examine short-term, day-to-day operating decisions. From accounting, we know that assets which are expected to be converted to cash within a year, such as inventories and accounts receivable, are called *current assets,* and that liabilities which must be paid off within a year are called *current liabilities.* The management of current assets and current liabilities is known as *working capital management.* In Chapters 8 through 12, we see how the proper amounts of cash, inventories, and accounts receivable are determined, and how these current assets should be financed.

Part V, "Strategic Long-Term Investment Decisions: Capital Budgeting," applies the concepts covered in Parts I through III to long-term, fixed asset decisions. Here we move into the execution phase of the long-range strategic planning process, considering the vital subject of *capital budgeting.* Because major capital expenditures take years to plan and implement, and decisions in this area generally are not reversible and hence affect the firm's operations for many years, their effect on the firm's value is significant.

Parts VI and VII focus on long-term financial decisions: What are the principal sources and forms of long-term capital, how much does each type of financing cost, and how does the method of financing affect the value of the firm? These sections use most of the valuation concepts developed earlier in the book, and here we analyze such key issues as the optimal debt/equity mix and dividend policy. Part VII serves to integrate the long-term strategic aspects of the book and to show how the parts fit together. Part VII also includes a chapter on "International Managerial Finance." As we have mentioned, the importance of the globalization of businesses will continue to increase significantly.

It is worth noting that some instructors may choose to cover the chapters in a sequence different from their order in the book. The chapters are modular and self-contained, so such a reordering will present no major difficulties.

ETHICAL DILEMMA   *Chances Are What They Don't Know Won't Hurt Them!*

Futuristic Electronic Technologies (FET) recently released a new advanced electronic micro system to be used by financial institutions, large corporations, and governments to process and store financial data, including taxes, automatic payroll payments, and so on. Even though the technology used in the creation of the product was developed by FET, it is expected FET's competitors will soon possess similar technology. So, in order to beat the competition to the market, FET introduced its new micro system a little earlier than originally planned. In fact, laboratory testing had not been fully completed before the product reached the market. The tests are complete now, and the final results suggest the micro system might be flawed with respect to how some data are retrieved and processed. The tests are not conclusive, though, and even if additional testing proves a flaw does exist, according to FET, it is of minuscule importance because the problem seems to occur for only one out of 100 million retrieval and processing attempts. The financial ramifications associated with the flaw are unknown at this time.

Assume you are one of FET's senior executives whose annual salary is based on the performance of the firm's common stock. You realize that if FET recalls the affected micro system the stock price will suffer; thus, your salary for the year will be less than you expected. To complicate matters, you just purchased a very expensive house based on your salary expectations for the next few years—those expectations will not come true unless the new micro system is a success for FET. As one of the senior executives, you will help determine what course of action FET will follow with respect to the micro system. What should you do? Should you encourage FET to recall the micro system until further testing is completed? Or is there another course of action you can suggest?

Goals and Resources in the Small Firm

Although small business is a vital contributor to the financial health of our economy, the businesses themselves often are fragile and susceptible to failure because of poor management, particularly financial management.

Significant differences exist between small and big businesses regarding the way they are owned, the way they are managed, and the financial and managerial resources at their disposal. These differences make it necessary to modify managerial finance principles for application in the small business area. Two especially important differences are resource shortages and goal conflicts.

RESOURCE SHORTAGES. It is not unusual for the founders of a small business to have full responsibility for all phases of the firm's operations. In fact in many cases, these individuals are reluctant to relinquish any responsibilities even when the firm grows significantly. So management in small firms often is spread very thin, with one or two key individuals taking on far more responsibility than they can handle properly. If you talk to small business operators, you often will hear, "This is my business, and I need to keep active in every aspect of the operations in order to monitor its pulse—no one can do this for me." Unfortunately, it is this attitude that keeps most small businesses small.

Not only is management often spread thin in small firms, but such firms have great difficulty acquiring the new funds needed for expansion. Until a firm achieves a fairly substantial size, say $15 million or so in sales, it cannot sell stock or bonds to the general public. Further, if the company does have a public stock offering at the first opportunity, its costs will be quite high in comparison to larger firms' costs of issuing stock. For example, it took Richard Smyth four tries and substantial expense to find a company that was willing to underwrite a $5.5 million initial public offering for Vista 2000 Inc., a small firm that develops and markets home safety devices in Roswell, Georgia. In general, small firms have very limited access to public capital markets. Access to nonpublic markets also is limited. For example, banks sometimes are reluctant to lend substantial amounts to small firms that lack a financial history, and relatives' resources only extend so far.

Small firms thus have constraints both on their managerial talent and on their ability to obtain adequate capital. It is no wonder small firms often fail, given their poor (or overworked) management and lack of capital.

GOAL CONFLICTS. Small businesses also differ from large firms with regard to corporate goals. Earlier in the chapter we pointed out that share price maximization is taken to be the goal of all firms. For a small firm, often the owner's livelihood is the business, because a substantial portion of the owner's wealth is bet on the success of the business. Generally, the small business owner is not diversified at all—every bit of wealth is invested in the business. Given this level of commitment and lack of a fall-back position, small business owners take a very different posture toward risk-taking than would a typical investor in a public company. Most public investors hold a well-diversified portfolio of assets, and their employment incomes generally come from jobs in altogether separate industries. On the other hand, both the salary and investment income of a small business owner generally are dependent on the success of one company. This makes the risk exposure of the small business owner quite high.

The owner-managers of small firms are keenly interested in the value of their firms, even if this value cannot be observed in the market. But the motives of small business owners are complex. Some owners are motivated primarily by such considerations as the desire to be their "own boss," even if this means not letting the firm grow at the fastest rate possible or be as profitable as it could be. In other words, there is value to being in control, and that value is not easily measurable. As a result, we often observe small businesses taking actions, such as refusing to bring in new stockholders even when they badly need new capital, that do not make sense when judged on the basis of value maximization but that do make sense when seen in the light of the personal objectives of the owners.

To the extent that the goals of the small firm differ from value maximization, some of the prescriptions in this text might not be entirely applicable. However, most of the tools we develop will be useful for small businesses, even though the tools might have to be modified somewhat. In any event, brief *Small Business* sections in various chapters will serve as our vehicle for discussing issues of special importance to small firms.

Summary

This chapter has provided an overview of managerial finance. The following key concepts are covered.

- Managerial finance has undergone significant changes over time, but four issues have received the most emphasis in recent years: (1) **inflation** and its effects on interest rates, (2) **deregulation** of financial institutions, (3) a dramatic increase in the **use of telecommunications** for transmitting information **and of computers** for analyzing the effects of alternative financial decisions, and (4) the increased importance of **global financial markets and business operations.**
- **Financial managers** are responsible for obtaining and using funds in a way that will **maximize the value of their firms.**
- Finance consists of three interrelated areas: (1) **money and capital markets,** (2) **investments,** and (3) **managerial finance.**
- The three main forms of business organization are the **proprietorship,** the **partnership,** and the **corporation.**
- Although each form of organization offers some advantages and disadvantages, **most business is conducted by corporations because this organizational form maximizes most firms' values.**
- The **primary goal** of management should be to **maximize stockholders' wealth,** and this means **maximizing the price of the firm's stock.** Further, actions that maximize stock prices also increase social welfare.
- An **agency problem** is a potential conflict of interests that can arise between (1) the owners of the firm and its management or (2) the stockholders and the creditors (debtholders).
- There are a number of ways to **motivate managers to act in the best interests of stockholders,** including (1) the **threat of firing,** (2) the **threat of takeovers,** and (3) properly structured **managerial incentives.**
- The **price of the firm's stock** depends on the firm's **projected earnings per share,** the **timing of its earnings,** the **riskiness of the projected earnings,** its **use of debt,** and its **dividend policy.**
- **Small businesses** are quite important in the aggregate, so we shall discuss small business issues throughout the text.

Questions

1-1   What are the three principal forms of business organization? What are the advantages and disadvantages of each?

1-2   Would the "normal" rate of return on investment be the same in all industries? Would "normal" rates of return change over time? Explain.

1-3   Would the role of the financial manager be likely to increase or decrease in importance relative to other executives if the rate of inflation increased? Explain.

1-4   Should stockholder wealth maximization be thought of as a long-term or a short-term goal—for example, if one action would probably increase the firm's stock price from a current level of $20 to $25 in 6 months and then to $30 in 5 years, but another action would probably keep the stock at $20 for several years then increase it to $40 in 5 years, which action would be better? Can you think of some specific corporate actions that might have these general tendencies?

1-5   Drawing on your background in accounting, can you think of any accounting procedure differences that might make it difficult to compare the relative performance of different firms?

1-6   Would the management of a firm in an oligopolistic or in a competitive industry be more likely to engage in what might be called "socially conscious" practices? Explain your reasoning.

1-7   What is the difference between stock price maximization and profit maximization? Under what conditions might profit maximization not lead to stock price maximization?

1-8   If you were the president of a large, publicly owned corporation, would you make decisions to maximize stockholders' welfare or your own personal interests? What are some actions stockholders could take to ensure that management's interests and those of stockholders coincided? What are some other factors that might influence management's actions?

1-9   The president of United Semiconductor Corporation made this statement in the company's annual report: "United's primary goal is to increase the value of the common stockholders' equity over time." Later on in the report, the following announcements were made:

    a.   The company contributed $1.5 million to the symphony orchestra in San Francisco, its headquarters city.

    b.   The company is spending $500 million to open a new plant in Mexico. No revenues will be produced by the plant for 4 years, so earnings will be depressed during this period versus what they would have been had the decision not been made to open the new plant.

    c.   The company is increasing its relative use of debt. Whereas assets were formerly financed with 35 percent debt and 65 percent equity, henceforth the financing mix will be 50–50.

    d.   The company uses a great deal of electricity in its manufacturing operations, and it generates most of this power itself. Plans are to utilize nuclear fuel rather than coal to produce electricity in the future.

    e.   The company has been paying out half of its earnings as dividends and retaining the other half. Henceforth, it will pay out only 30 percent as dividends.

Discuss how United's stockholders, customers, and labor force would react to each of these actions, and then how each action might affect United's stock price.

Self-Test Problem

(Solution appears in Appendix B)

ST-1   Define each of the following terms:

Key terms

    a.   proprietorship; partnership; corporation

    b.   stockholder wealth maximization

    c.   hostile takeover

    d.   social responsibility; business ethics

    e.   normal profits; normal rate of return

    f.   agency problem; agency costs

    g.   poison pill; greenmail

    h.   performance shares; executive stock option

    i.   profit maximization

    j.   earnings per share

    k.   dividend policy decision

    l.   small business versus large business

CHAPTER 2

The Financial Environment: Markets, Institutions, Interest Rates, and Taxes

In December 1991, after 17 months of recession, the Federal Reserve decided to take action to decrease interest rates in an effort to "prop up the economy" and push it toward recovery. Although interest rates had declined an average of 3 percent to 4 percent during the previous two years, the economy remained stagnant—experts predicted no growth, or even negative growth for 1992. Consequently, to stimulate an economic recovery, the Fed announced it was going to (1) cut the discount rate that it charged on loans to banks from 4.5 percent to 3.5 percent, its lowest level in 27 years, and (2) lower the federal funds rate (the interest rate charged on overnight loans between banks) from 4.5 percent to 4 percent. This announcement came as a surprise, because the rate cuts were the biggest in a decade. Previous Fed actions had been small, cautious quarter-point reductions that had been announced with minimum fanfare to keep the financial markets convinced of the Fed's commitment to fight inflation.

The financial system responded immediately to the Fed's announcement. Morgan Guaranty Trust Co. cut its prime lending rate from 7.5 percent to 6.5 percent, and other large banks followed Morgan's actions. Both short-term and long-term interest rates decreased to levels not seen in years.

The Fed continued its support for lower interest rates for the next couple of years. In fact, at the end of 1993, the yield on 30-year Treasury bonds had dipped to a record low of 5.8 percent, the yield on Treasury bills was around 3 percent, and the federal funds rate actually dropped below 3 percent. These low rates helped encourage borrowing and capital investment, which in turn helped the economy move closer to recovery. The policy makers at the Fed were happy—right? Not exactly. The Fed was worried that the record low interest rates would result in a recovery with too much growth too quickly, which would create "runaway" inflation and push us back into a recessionary economy.

Continued

In an effort to keep the economic recovery from "getting out of hand," the Fed increased interest rates six times during 1994. This action caused both short-term and long-term interest rates to increase during the year—some short-term rates increased by nearly 3 percent, and long-term rates increased by about 2.5 percent. But, just as the Fed had hoped, the increased rates slowed economic growth to about 2.5 percent, and inflation leveled off at less than 3 percent. If the economy stalls again, or if it shows signs of growing too rapidly, surely the Fed will react again by changing interest rates in the appropriate direction.

In the past few years interest rates have changed dramatically. Such changes affect both businesses and individuals. Whether business or individual, when we borrow we would like the rates to be low. During 1992 and 1993, when the rates were very low, many firms and individuals replaced higher interest loans with lower interest loans (refinanced). On the other hand, when rates are low, those who depend on the income from their investments suffer. Thus, interest rate changes affect all of us.

As you read this chapter, think about (1) all the factors the Fed must consider before attempting to change interest rates, and (2) the effects of interest rate changes on inflation, on the financial markets, and on the economy as a whole.

SOURCE: "Changing Its Course, The Fed Boldly Tries to Bolster the Economy," *The Wall Street Journal,* December 23, 1991, "The Fed Holds Steady for Now—But Beware of the Ides of November," *Business Week,* October 10, 1994, and subsequent news releases.

Financial managers must understand the environment and markets within which businesses operate. Therefore, in this chapter, we examine the markets where firms raise funds, securities are traded, and stock prices are established, as well as the institutions that operate in these markets. In the process, we will explore the principal factors that determine money costs in the economy. In addition, because taxes are critically important in financial decisions, we discuss some key features of the U.S. tax laws.

The Financial Markets

Businesses, individuals, and government units often need to raise funds. For example, suppose Carolina Power & Light (CP&L) forecasts an increase in the demand for electricity in North Carolina, and the company decides to build a new power plant. Because CP&L almost certainly will not have the $2 billion or so necessary to pay for the plant, the company will have to raise these funds in the financial markets. Or suppose Mr. Fong, the proprietor of a San Francisco hardware store, decides to expand into appliances. Where will he get the money to buy the initial inventory of TV sets, washers, and freezers? Similarly, if you want to buy a home that costs $100,000, but you have only $20,000 in savings, how can you raise the additional $80,000?

On the other hand, some individuals and firms have incomes greater than their current expenditures, so they have funds available to invest. For example, Carol

Hawk has an income of $36,000, but her expenses are only $30,000, while Microsoft recently announced its desire to invest over $1.5 billion.

People and organizations wanting to borrow money are brought together with those having surplus funds in the **financial markets.** Note that "markets" is plural—there are a great many different financial markets, each one consisting of many institutions, in a developed economy such as ours. Each market deals with a somewhat different type of instrument in terms of the instrument's maturity and the assets backing it. Also, different markets serve different types of customers, or operate in different parts of the country. Here are some of the major types of markets:

FINANCIAL MARKETS
"Mechanisms" by which borrowers and lenders get together.

1. *Physical asset markets* (also called *tangible* or *real* asset markets) are those for such products as wheat, autos, real estate, computers, and machinery. *Financial asset markets* deal with stocks, bonds, notes, mortgages, and other *claims on real assets* with respect to the distribution of future cash flows.

MONEY MARKETS
The financial markets in which funds are borrowed or loaned for short periods (generally less than one year).

2. **Money markets** are the markets for debt securities with maturities of less than one year. The New York and London money markets have long been the world's largest, but Tokyo is rising rapidly. **Capital markets** are the markets for long-term debt and corporate stocks. The New York Stock Exchange, which handles the stocks of the largest U.S. corporations, is a prime example of a capital market.

CAPITAL MARKETS
The financial markets for stocks and long-term debt (generally one year or longer).

3. *Mortgage markets* deal with loans on residential, commercial, and industrial real estate, and on farmland, while *consumer credit markets* involve loans on autos and appliances as well as loans for education, vacations, and so on.

4. *World, national, regional, and local markets* also exist. Thus, depending on an organization's size and scope of operations, it might be able to borrow all around the world, or it might be confined to a strictly local, even neighborhood, market.

PRIMARY MARKETS
Markets in which corporations raise funds by issuing new securities.

5. **Primary markets** are the markets in which corporations raise new capital. If GE were to sell a new issue of common stock to raise capital, this would be a primary market transaction. The corporation selling the newly created stock receives the proceeds from the sale in a primary market transaction. **Secondary markets** are markets in which existing, already outstanding securities are traded among investors. Thus, if Edgar Rice decided to buy 1,000 shares of IBM stock, the purchase would occur in the secondary market. The New York Stock Exchange is a secondary market, because it deals in outstanding, as opposed to newly issued, stocks and bonds. Secondary markets also exist for mortgages, various other types of loans, and other financial assets. The corporation whose securities are being traded is not involved in a secondary market transaction and, thus, does not receive any funds from such a sale.

SECONDARY MARKETS
Markets in which securities and other financial assets are traded among investors after they have been issued by corporations and public agencies, such as municipalities.

Other classifications could be made, but this breakdown is sufficient to show that there are many types of financial markets.

A healthy economy is dependent on efficient transfers of funds from people who are net savers to firms and individuals who need funds. Without efficient transfers, the economy simply could not function: Carolina Power & Light could not raise capital, so Raleigh's citizens would have no electricity; you would not be able to buy the house you want; Carol Hawk would have no place to invest her savings; and so on. Obviously, the level of employment and productivity, hence our standard of living, would be much lower. Therefore, it is absolutely essential that our financial markets function efficiently—not only quickly, but also at a low cost.[1]

Table 2-1 lists the most important instruments traded in the various financial markets. The instruments are arranged from those with the lowest maturities (money market instruments) to those with the highest maturities (capital market instruments). As we go through the book, many of these instruments will be discussed in much greater detail. For example, we will see that there actually are many varieties of corporate bonds, ranging from "plain vanilla flavored" bonds, to bonds that are convertible into common stocks, and to bonds whose interest payments vary depending on the rate of inflation. Still, the table gives an idea of the characteristics and costs of the instruments traded in the major financial markets.

Self-Test Questions

Distinguish between physical asset markets and financial asset markets.

What is the difference between spot and futures markets?

Distinguish between money and capital markets.

What is the difference between primary and secondary markets?

Why are financial markets essential for a healthy economy?

Financial Institutions

Funds are transferred between those who have funds to invest (savers) and those who need the funds (borrowers) by the three different processes diagrammed in Figure 2-1:

1. A *direct transfer* of money and securities, as shown in the top section, occurs when a business sells its stocks or bonds directly to savers (investors) without going through any type of financial institution. The business delivers its securities to savers, who in turn give the firm the money it needs.

2. As shown in the middle section, a transfer also can go through an *investment banking house* such as Morgan Stanley, which serves as a middleman and facilitates the issuance of securities. The company sells its stocks or bonds to the investment bank, which in turn sells these same securities to savers. The business's securities and the savers' money merely "pass through" the investment banking house. However, the investment bank does buy and hold the securities for a period of time, so it is taking a chance—it might not be able to resell them to savers for as much as it paid. Because new securities are involved and the corporation receives money from the sale, this is a primary market transaction. It should be noted that investment banking has nothing to

---

[1]As the countries that made up the former Soviet Union and the Eastern European nations move toward capitalism, just as much attention must be paid to the establishment of cost-efficient financial markets as to electrical power, transportation, communications, and other infrastructure systems. Economic efficiency simply is impossible without a good system for allocating capital within the economy.

TABLE 2-1

Summary of Major Market Instruments, Market Participants, and Security Characteristics

Instrument (1)	Market (2)	Major Participants (3)	Security Characteristics		
			Riskiness (4)	Maturity (5)	Interest Rate on 1/13/95[a] (6)
U.S. Treasury bills	Money	Sold to institutional investors by U.S. Treasury to finance federal expenditures	Default-free	91 days to 1 year	6.4%
Banker's acceptances	Money	Firm's promise to pay, guaranteed by bank	Low degree of risk if guaranteed by a strong bank	Up to 180 days	6.3
Commercial paper	Money	Issued by financially secure firms to large investors	Low default risk	Up to 270 days	6.2
Negotiable certificates of deposit (CDs)	Money	Issued by major money-center commercial banks to large investors	Riskier than Treasury bills	Up to 1 year	6.5
Money market mutual funds	Money	Invest in Treasury bills, CDs, and commercial paper; held by individuals and businesses	Low degree of risk	No specific maturity (instant liquidity)	5.5
Eurodollar market time deposits	Money	Issued by banks outside U.S.	Default risk is a function of issuing bank	Up to 1 year	6.3
Consumer credit loans	Money	Issued by banks/credit unions/finance companies to individuals	Risk is variable	Variable	Variable 10–15%
U.S. Treasury notes and bonds	Capital	Issued by U.S. government	No default risk, but price can decline if interest rates rise	1 to 30 years	7.8
Mortgages	Capital	Borrowings from commercial banks and S&Ls by individuals and businesses	Risk is variable	Up to 30 years	9.1
State and local government bonds	Capital	Issued by state and local governments to individuals and institutional investors	Riskier than U.S. government securities, but exempt from most taxes	Up to 30 years	6.6

[a]Interest rates are for longest maturity securities of the type and for the strongest securities of a given type. Thus, the 8.5% interest rate shown for corporate bonds reflects the rate on 30-year, Aaa bonds. Lower-rated bonds had higher interest rates.

(continued)

TABLE 2-1

continued

Instrument (1)	Market (2)	Major Participants (3)	Security Characteristics		
			Riskiness (4)	Maturity (5)	Interest Rate on 1/13/95[a] (6)
Corporate bonds	Capital	Issued by corporations to individuals and institutional investors	Riskier than U.S. government securities, but less risky than preferred and common stocks; varying degree of risk within bonds depending on strength of issuer	Up to 40 years	8.5%
Leases	Capital	Similar to debt in that firms can lease assets rather than borrow and then buy the assets	Risk similar to corporate bonds	Generally 3 to 20 years	Similar to bond yields
Preferred stocks	Capital	Issued by corporations to individuals and institutional investors	Riskier than corporate bonds, but less risky than common stock	Unlimited	3–5%
Common stocks[b]	Capital	Issued by corporations to individuals and institutional investors	Risky	Unlimited	2.5–6.0%

[a]Interest rates are for longest maturity securities of the type and for the strongest securities of a given type. Thus, the 8.5% interest rate shown for corporate bonds reflects the rate on 30-year, Aaa bonds. Lower-rated bonds had higher interest rates.

[b]Common stocks are expected to provide a "return" in the form of dividends and capital gains rather than interest. Of course, if you buy a stock, while you may *expect* to earn 10 percent on your money, the stock's price may decline and cause you to experience a 100 percent loss. The rates given for preferred and common stock represent the average returns investors would have earned during the previous year, 1994, if market indexes were purchased.

do with the traditional banking process as we know it—investment banking deals with the issuance of new securities, not deposits and loans.

3. Transfers can also be made through a *financial intermediary,* such as a bank or a mutual fund. Here the intermediary obtains funds from savers, issuing its own securities or liabilities in exchange, and then uses the money to lend out or to purchase another business's securities. For example, a saver might give dollars to a bank, receiving from it a certificate of deposit, and then the bank might lend the money to a small business in the form of a mortgage loan. Thus, intermediaries literally create new forms of capital—in this case, certificates of deposit, which are both safer and more liquid than mortgages and thus are better securities for most savers to hold. The existence of intermediaries greatly increases the efficiency of the financial markets.

FIGURE 2-1

Diagram of the Capital Formation Process

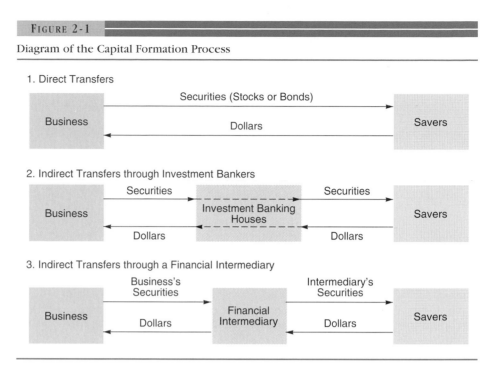

1. Direct Transfers

| Business | Securities (Stocks or Bonds) → / ← Dollars | Savers |

2. Indirect Transfers through Investment Bankers

Business — Securities → / ← Dollars — Investment Banking Houses — Securities → / ← Dollars — Savers

3. Indirect Transfers through a Financial Intermediary

Business — Business's Securities → / ← Dollars — Financial Intermediary — Intermediary's Securities → / ← Dollars — Savers

---

For simplicity, we assumed that the entity needing capital is a business, and specifically a corporation, but it is easy to visualize the demander of funds as a home purchaser, a government unit, and so on.

Direct transfers of funds from savers to businesses are possible and do occur on occasion, but it is generally more efficient for a business to enlist the services of an **investment banker.** Merrill Lynch, Morgan Stanley, and Goldman Sachs are examples of financial service corporations that offer investment banking services. Such organizations (1) help corporations design securities with the features that currently are most attractive to investors, (2) buy these securities from the corporation, and (3) then resell them to savers. Although the securities are sold twice, this process really is one primary market transaction, with the investment banker acting as a middleman as funds are transferred from savers to businesses.

The **financial intermediaries** shown in the third section of Figure 2-1 do more than simply transfer money and securities between borrowers and savers— they literally create new financial products. Because the intermediaries generally are large, they gain economies of scale in analyzing the creditworthiness of potential borrowers, in processing and collecting loans, and in pooling risks, and thus helping individual savers diversify—that is, "not put all their financial eggs in one basket." Further, a system of specialized intermediaries can enable savings to do more than just draw interest. For example, individuals can put money into banks and get both interest income and a convenient way of making payments (checking), or put money into life insurance companies and get both interest income and protection for their beneficiaries.

In the United States and other developed nations, a large set of specialized, highly efficient financial intermediaries has evolved. Competition and government policy have created a rapidly changing arena, however, such that different types

INVESTMENT BANKER
An organization that underwrites and distributes new issues of securities; helps businesses and other entities obtain needed financing.

FINANCIAL INTERMEDIARIES
Specialized financial firms that facilitate the transfer of funds from savers to borrowers.

I'd Like to Apply for a Loan; By the Way, How Much Is the Broccoli Today?

Since the deregulation of the 1980s, it has become more difficult to separate the functions of various financial institutions. Besides taking deposits and lending money, many large banking organizations now provide services traditionally associated with insurance companies and stock brokerage firms. And, likewise, mutual funds and other nonbank providers of financial services have entered the world of banking. For example, CS First Boston, Incorporated, a large securities firm, has entered into a partnership with Credit Suisse, a large Swiss bank, to provide large commercial loans in the United States. Securities firms such as First Boston and Merrill Lynch have provided small commercial loans for years, and many securities firms have actively bought and sold bank loans in the secondary market. But the First Boston–Credit Suisse partnership is the first attempt in the United States to supply large commercial loans on an ongoing basis.

To become more competitive with nonbank rivals such as securities firms, banks are moving away from traditional banking practices. More and more, banks have become aggressive competitors for customers. For example, in their effort to get close to customers, some banks have located limited branch operations in local supermarkets. In 1994, there were approximately 2,100 branches in supermarkets, up from the 1990 total of about 900. The fast-paced growth of supermarket branches is expected to continue because these operations are less expensive than free-standing branches, and because supermarket branches reach many customers that would not otherwise use the banks' services.

As the competition between nonbank firms and banks heats up, the lines differentiating financial institutions from each other will become more blurred. In fact, banks currently are hiring people with experience in the securities industry, while securities firms are hiring commercial lenders. It probably won't be long before you can get the mortgage for your house at the same place you buy IBM's common stock, which might also be the place you fill your grocery needs.

---

of institutions currently perform services formerly reserved for others. This trend, which will continue, has blurred institutional distinctions. Still, there remains a degree of institutional identity, and here are the major classes of intermediaries:

1. *Commercial banks,* the traditional "department stores of finance," serve a wide variety of customers. Historically, the commercial banks were the major institutions that handled checking accounts and through which the Federal Reserve System expanded or contracted the money supply. Today, however, several other institutions also provide checking services and significantly influence the effective money supply. Conversely, commercial banks provide an ever-widening range of services, including trust operations, stock brokerage services, and insurance.

   Note that commercial banks are quite different from investment banks. Commercial banks lend money, whereas investment banks help companies raise capital from other parties.[2]

---

[2]Prior to 1933, commercial banks offered investment banking services, but the Glass-Steagall Act, passed in that year, prohibited commercial banks from engaging in investment banking. Thus, the Morgan Bank was broken up into two separate organizations, one of which is now the Morgan Guaranty Trust Company, a commercial bank, while the other is Morgan Stanley, a major investment banking house, which is not considered a financial intermediary. Note also that Japanese and European banks can offer both commercial and investment banking services. This severely hinders U.S. banks in global competition, so recent legislative efforts have been aimed at improving the international competitiveness of U.S. banks.

2. *Savings and loan associations (S&Ls),* which have traditionally served individual savers and residential and commercial mortgage borrowers, take the funds of many small savers and then lend this money to home buyers and other types of borrowers. Because the savers obtain a degree of liquidity that would be absent if they bought the mortgages or other securities directly, perhaps the most significant economic function of the S&Ls is to "create liquidity" that otherwise would be lacking. Also, the S&Ls have more expertise in analyzing credit, setting up loans, and making collections than individual savers, so they reduce the cost and increase the availability of real estate loans. Finally, the S&Ls hold large, diversified portfolios of loans and other assets and thus spread risks in a manner that would be impossible if small savers were making mortgage loans directly. Because of these factors, savers benefit by being able to invest their savings in more liquid, better managed, and less risky accounts, whereas borrowers benefit by being able to obtain more capital, and at lower costs, than would otherwise be possible.[3]

3. *Credit unions* are cooperative associations whose members have a common bond, such as being employees of the same firm. Members' savings are loaned only to other members, generally for auto purchases, home improvements, and the like. Credit unions often are the cheapest source of funds available to individual borrowers.

4. *Pension funds* are retirement plans funded by corporations or government agencies for their workers and administered primarily by the trust departments of commercial banks or by life insurance companies. Pension funds invest primarily in bonds, stocks, mortgages, and real estate.

5. *Life insurance companies* take savings in the form of annual premiums, then invest these funds in stocks, bonds, real estate, and mortgages, and finally make payments to the beneficiaries of the insured parties. In recent years life insurance companies have also offered a variety of tax-deferred savings plans designed to provide benefits to the participants when they retire.

6. *Mutual funds* are investment companies that accept money from savers and then use these funds to buy various types of financial assets such as stocks, long-term bonds, and short-term debt instruments. These organizations pool funds and thus reduce risks through diversification. They also achieve economies of scale, which lower the costs of analyzing securities, managing portfolios, and buying and selling securities. Different funds are designed to meet the objectives of different types of savers. Hence, there are income funds for those who prefer current income, growth funds for savers who are willing to accept significant risks in the hope of higher returns, and still other funds that are used as interest-bearing checking accounts (the **money market mutual funds**). There are literally hundreds of mutual funds with dozens of different goals and purposes.

MONEY MARKET MUTUAL FUND A mutual fund that invests in short-term, low-risk securities and allows investors to write checks against their accounts.

Financial institutions historically have been heavily regulated, with the primary purpose of ensuring the safety of the institutions and thus protecting depositors. However, these regulations—which have taken the form of prohibitions on nationwide branch banking, restrictions on the types of assets the institutions can

---

[3]*Mutual savings banks,* which are similar to S&Ls, operate primarily in the northeastern states, accept savings primarily from individuals, and lend mainly on a long-term basis to home buyers and consumers.

buy, ceilings on the interest rates they can pay, and limitations on the types of services they can provide—have tended to impede the free flow of funds from surplus to deficit areas, and thus have hurt the efficiency of our financial markets. Recognizing this fact, Congress has authorized some major changes, and more will be forthcoming.

The result of the ongoing regulatory changes has been a blurring of the distinctions among the different types of institutions. Indeed, the trend in the United States today is toward huge financial service corporations, which own banks, S&Ls, investment banking houses, insurance companies, pension plan operations, and mutual funds, and which have branches across the country and even around the world. Interestingly, at one time, Sears, Roebuck, one of the largest retailing organizations in the United States, also owned a large insurance company (Allstate Insurance), a leading brokerage and investment banking firm (Dean Witter), the largest real estate brokerage firm (Coldwell Banker), a mortgage company (Sears Mortgage), a huge credit card business, and a host of other related businesses. By the end of 1994, Sears had sold the real estate organization and had spun off the mortgage company in an effort to pare down its operations. Other financial service corporations, most of which started in one area and have now diversified to cover most of the financial spectrum, include Transamerica, Merrill Lynch, American Express, Citicorp, Fidelity, and Prudential.

Self-Test Questions

Identify the three different ways capital is transferred between savers and borrowers.

What is the difference between a commercial bank and an investment bank?

Distinguish between investment banking houses and financial intermediaries.

List the major types of intermediaries and briefly describe each one's function.

What effect do you think regulatory changes and competitive pressures will have on financial institutions in the future?

The Stock Market

As noted earlier, secondary markets are those in which outstanding, previously issued securities are traded. By far the most active secondary market, and the most important one to financial managers, is the stock market. It is here that the prices of firms' stocks are established, and, because the primary goal of managerial finance is to maximize the firm's stock price, a knowledge of this market is essential for anyone involved in managing a business.

The Stock Exchanges

There are two basic types of stock markets: (1) *organized exchanges,* which include the New York Stock Exchange (NYSE), the American Stock Exchange (AMEX), and several regional exchanges, and (2) the less formal *over-the-counter market.* Because the organized exchanges have actual physical market locations and are easier to describe and understand, we will consider them first.

ORGANIZED SECURITY EXCHANGES
Formal organizations with physical locations where auction markets are conducted in designated ("listed") securities. The two major U.S. stock exchanges are the New York Stock Exchange (NYSE) and the American Stock Exchange (AMEX).

The **organized security exchanges** are tangible physical entities. Each of the larger ones occupies its own building, has specifically designated members, and has an elected governing body—its board of governors. Members are said to have "seats" on the exchange, although everybody stands up. These seats, which are bought and sold, give the holder the right to trade on the exchange. There are 1,366 seats on the New York Stock Exchange, and in December 1994, NYSE seats were selling for about $760,000, down nearly $100,000 from the previous month's price.

Most of the larger investment banking houses operate *brokerage departments,* which own seats on the exchanges and designate one or more of their officers as members. The exchanges are open on all normal working days, with the members meeting in a large room equipped with telephones and other electronic equipment that enable each member to communicate with his or her firm's offices throughout the country.

Like other markets, security exchanges facilitate communication between buyers and sellers. For example, Merrill Lynch (the largest brokerage firm) might receive an order in its Atlanta office from a customer who wants to buy 100 shares of IBM stock. Simultaneously, Dean Witter's Denver office might receive an order from a customer wishing to sell 100 shares of IBM. Each broker communicates by wire with the firm's representative on the NYSE. Other brokers throughout the country also are communicating with their own exchange members. The exchange members with *sell orders* offer the shares for sale, and they are bid for by the members with *buy orders.* Thus, the exchanges operate as *auction markets.*[4]

The Over-the-Counter Market

OVER-THE-COUNTER MARKET
A large collection of brokers and dealers, connected electronically by telephones and computers, that provides for trading in securities not listed on the organized exchanges.

If a security is not traded on an organized exchange, it is said to be traded *over the counter.* In contrast to the organized security exchanges, the **over-the-counter market** is an intangible organization that consists of a network of brokers and dealers around the country. An explanation of the term *over-the-counter* will help clarify exactly what this market is. The exchanges operate as auction

[4]The NYSE actually is a modified auction market, wherein people (through their brokers) bid for stocks. Originally—about two hundred years ago—brokers would literally shout, "I have 100 shares of Union Pacific for sale; how much am I offered?" and then sell to the highest bidder. If a broker had a buy order, he or she would shout, "I want to buy 100 shares of Union Pacific; who'll sell at the best price?" The same general situation still exists, although the exchanges now have members known as *specialists* who facilitate the trading process by keeping an inventory of shares of the stocks in which they specialize. If a buy order comes in at a time when no sell order arrives, the specialist will sell off some inventory. Similarly, if a sell order comes in, the specialist will buy and add to inventory. The specialist sets a *bid price* (the price the specialist will pay for the stock) and an *asked price* (the price at which shares will be sold out of inventory). The bid and asked prices are set at levels designed to keep the inventory in balance. If many buy orders start coming in because of favorable developments or sell orders come in because of unfavorable events, the specialist will raise or lower prices to keep supply and demand in balance. Bid prices are somewhat lower than asked prices, with the difference, or *spread,* representing the specialist's profit margin.

Special facilities are available to help institutional investors such as mutual funds or pension funds sell large blocks of stock without depressing their prices. In essence, brokerage houses which cater to institutional clients will purchase *blocks* (defined as 10,000 or more shares) and then resell the stock to other institutions or individuals. Also, when a firm has a major announcement which is likely to cause its stock price to change sharply, it will ask the exchanges to halt trading in its stock until the announcement has been made and digested by investors. Thus, when Texaco announced that it planned to acquire Getty Oil, trading was halted for one day in both Texaco and Getty stocks.

markets—buy and sell orders come in more or less simultaneously, and exchange members match these orders. If a stock is traded less frequently, perhaps because it is the stock of a new or small firm, few buy and sell orders come in, and matching them within a reasonable length of time would be difficult. To avoid this problem, some brokerage firms maintain an inventory of such stocks—they buy when individual investors want to sell and sell when investors want to buy. At one time the inventory of securities was kept in a safe, and the stocks, when bought and sold, literally were passed over the counter.

Today, the over-the-counter market is defined to include all facilities that are needed to conduct security transactions not conducted on the organized exchanges. These facilities consist of (1) the relatively few *dealers* who hold inventories of over-the-counter securities and who are said to "make a market" in these securities, (2) the thousands of *brokers* who act as *agents* in bringing these dealers together with investors, and (3) the computers, terminals, and electronic networks that provide a communications link between dealers and brokers. The dealers who make a market in a particular stock continuously quote a price at which they are willing to buy the stock (the *bid price*) and a price at which they will sell shares (the *asked price*). Each dealer's prices, which are adjusted as supply and demand conditions change, can be read off computer screens all across the country. The spread between bid and asked prices represents the dealer's markup, or profit.

Brokers and dealers who make up the over-the-counter market are members of a self-regulating body known as the *National Association of Security Dealers (NASD)*, which licenses brokers and oversees trading practices. The computerized trading network used by NASD is known as the *NASD Automated Quotation System (NASDAQ)*, and *The Wall Street Journal* and other newspapers contain information on NASDAQ transactions.

In terms of numbers of issues, the majority of stocks are traded over the counter. However, because the stocks of larger companies are listed on the exchanges, about two-thirds of the dollar volume of stock trading takes place on the exchanges.

Self-Test Questions

What are the two basic types of stock markets, and how do they differ?

Where are the greatest number of stocks traded, over-the-counter market or the stock markets?

The Cost of Money

PRODUCTION OPPORTUNITIES
The returns available within an economy from investment in productive (cash-generating) assets.

In a free economy, funds are allocated through the price system. *The interest rate is the price paid to borrow funds, whereas in the case of equity capital, investors expect to receive dividends and capital gains.* The factors that affect the supply of and demand for investment capital, and hence the cost of money, are discussed in this section.

The four most fundamental factors affecting the cost of money are (1) **production opportunities,** (2) **time preferences for consumption,** (3) **risk,** and

TIME PREFERENCES FOR CONSUMPTION
The preferences of consumers for current consumption as opposed to saving for future consumption.

RISK
In a financial market context, the chance that a financial asset will not earn the return promised.

INFLATION
The tendency of prices to increase over time.

(4) **inflation.** To see how these factors operate, visualize an isolated island community where the people survive on fish. They have a stock of fishing gear which permits them to live reasonably well, but they would like to have more fish. Now suppose Mr. Crusoe has a bright idea for a new type of fishnet that would enable him to double his daily catch. However, it would take him a year to perfect his design, build his net, and learn how to use it efficiently, and Mr. Crusoe probably would starve before he could put his new net into operation. Therefore, he might suggest to Ms. Robinson, Mr. Friday, and several others that if they would give him one fish each day for a year, he would return two fish a day during all of the next year. If someone accepted the offer, then the fish which Ms. Robinson or one of the others gave to Mr. Crusoe would constitute *savings;* these savings would be *invested* in the fishnet; and the extra fish the net produced would constitute a *return on the investment.*

Obviously, the more productive Mr. Crusoe thought the new fishnet would be, the higher his expected return on the investment would be and the more he could afford to offer potential investors for their savings. In this example we assume that Mr. Crusoe thinks he will be able to pay, and thus he has offered, a 100 percent rate of return—he has offered to give back two fish for every one he received. He might have tried to attract savings for less—for example, he might have decided to offer only 1.5 fish next year for every one he receives this year, which would represent a 50 percent rate of return to Ms. Robinson and the other potential savers.

How attractive Mr. Crusoe's offer appears to a potential saver would depend in large part on the saver's *time preference for consumption.* For example, Ms. Robinson might be thinking of retirement, and she might be willing to trade fish today for fish in the future on a one-for-one basis. On the other hand, Mr. Friday might be unwilling to "lend" a fish today for anything less than three fish next year, because he has a wife and several young children to feed with his current fish. Mr. Friday would be said to have a high time preference for consumption and Ms. Robinson a low time preference. Note also that if the entire population is living right at the subsistence level, time preferences for current consumption would necessarily be high, aggregate savings would be low, interest rates would be high, and capital formation would be difficult.

The risk inherent in the fishnet project, and thus in Mr. Crusoe's ability to repay the loan, also affects the return investors require: The higher the perceived risk, the higher the required rate of return. Also, in a more complex society there are many businesses like Mr. Crusoe's, many goods other than fish, and many savers like Ms. Robinson and Mr. Friday. Further, people use money as a medium of exchange rather than barter with fish. When money is used, rather than fish, its value in the future, which is affected by inflation, comes into play: The higher the expected rate of *inflation,* the larger the required return.

Thus, we see that the interest rate paid to savers depends in a basic way (1) on the rate of return producers expect to earn on invested capital, (2) on savers' time preferences for current versus future consumption, (3) on the riskiness of the loan, and (4) on the expected future rate of inflation. The returns borrowers expect to earn by investing the funds they borrow set an upper limit on how much they can pay for savings, while consumers' time preferences for consumption establish how much consumption they are willing to defer, hence how much they will save at different levels of interest offered by borrowers. Higher risk and higher inflation also lead to higher interest rates.

Self-Test Questions

What is the price paid to borrow money called?

What is the "price" of equity capital?

What four fundamental factors affect the cost of money?

Interest Rate Levels

Funds are allocated among borrowers by interest rates: Firms with the most profitable investment opportunities are willing and able to pay the most for capital, so they tend to attract it away from less efficient firms or from those whose products are not in demand. Of course, our economy is not completely free in the sense of being influenced only by market forces. Thus, the federal government has agencies that help designated individuals or groups obtain credit on favorable terms. Among those eligible for this kind of assistance are small businesses, certain minorities, and firms willing to build plants in areas with high unemployment. Still, most capital in the U.S. economy is allocated through the price system.

Figure 2-2 shows how supply and demand interact to determine interest rates in two capital markets. Markets A and B represent two of the many capital markets in existence. The going interest rate, which can be designated as either k or i but for purposes of the discussion here is designated as k, initially is 10 percent for the low-risk securities in Market A.[5] Borrowers whose credit is strong enough to qualify for this market can obtain funds at a cost of 10 percent, and investors who want to put their money to work without much risk can obtain a 10 percent return. Riskier borrowers must obtain higher-cost funds in Market B. Investors who are more willing to take risks invest in Market B expecting to earn a 12 percent return but also realizing that they might actually receive much less (or much more).

If the demand for funds declines, as it typically does during business recessions, the demand curves will shift to the left, as shown in Curve D_2 in Market A. The market-clearing, or equilibrium, interest rate in this example declines to 8 percent. Similarly, you should be able to visualize what would happen if the Federal Reserve tightens credit as it did throughout 1994: The supply curve, S_1, would shift to the left, and this would raise interest rates and lower the level of borrowing in the economy.

Capital markets are interdependent. For example, if Markets A and B were in equilibrium before the demand shift to D_2 in Market A, this means that investors were willing to accept the higher risk in Market B in exchange for a risk premium of 12% − 10% = 2%. After the shift to D_2, the risk premium would initially increase to 12% − 8% = 4%. This much larger premium probably would induce some of the lenders in Market A to shift to Market B; this, in turn, would cause the supply curve in Market A to shift to the left (or up) and that in Market B to shift to the right. The transfer of capital between markets would raise the interest rate in Market A and lower it in Market B, thus bringing the risk premium back closer to the original level, 2 percent. For example, in 1994, when the Federal Reserve effectively raised rates on Treasury securities, the rates on corporate bonds and mortgages followed.

---

[5]In Chapter 6, when the time value of money is discussed, the term i is used to denote interest rate, because this corresponds to the interest rate key on most financial calculators.

FIGURE 2-2

Interest Rates as a Function of Supply and Demand for Funds

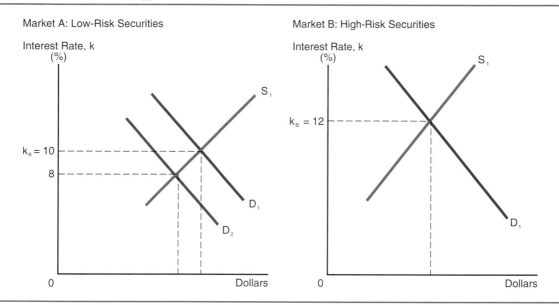

Market A: Low-Risk Securities

Interest Rate, k (%)

$k_A = 10$
8
S_1
D_1
D_2

0   Dollars

Market B: High-Risk Securities

Interest Rate, k (%)

S_1
$k_B = 12$
D_1

0   Dollars

There are many capital markets in the United States. U.S. firms also invest and raise funds throughout the world, and foreigners both borrow and lend funds in the United States. There are markets in the United States for home loans, farm loans, business loans, government loans, and so on. For each type of capital, there is a price, and these prices change over time as shifts occur in supply and demand conditions. Figure 2-3 shows how long- and short-term interest rates to business borrowers have varied since the 1950s. Notice that short-term interest rates are especially prone to rise during booms and then fall during recessions. (The shaded areas of the chart indicate recessions.) When the economy is expanding, firms need capital, and this demand for capital pushes rates up. Also, inflationary pressures are strongest during business booms, and that also exerts upward pressure on rates. Conditions are reversed during recessions, such as the one in 1991 and 1992. Slack business reduces the demand for credit, the rate of inflation falls, and the result is a drop in interest rates.

These tendencies do not hold exactly—the period after 1984 is a case in point. The price of oil fell dramatically in 1985 and 1986, reducing inflationary pressures on other prices and easing fears of serious long-term inflation. Earlier, these fears had pushed interest rates to record levels. The economy from 1984 to 1987 was fairly strong, but the declining fears about inflation more than offset the normal tendency of interest rates to rise during good economic times, and the net result was lower interest rates.[6]

---

[6]Short-term rates are responsive to current economic conditions, whereas long-term rates primarily reflect long-run expectations for inflation. As a result, short-term rates are sometimes above and sometimes below long-term rates. The relationship between long-term and short-term rates is called the *term structure of interest rates*. This topic is discussed later in the chapter.

FIGURE 2-3

Long- and Short-Term Interest Rates, 1960–1994

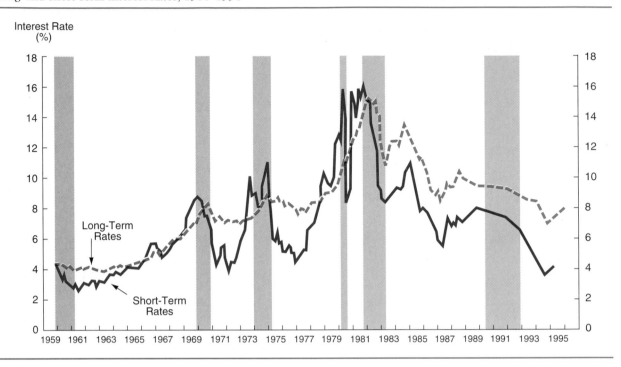

NOTES:

a. The shaded areas designate business recessions.

b. Short-term rates are measured by four- to six-month loans to very large, strong corporations, and long-term rates are measured by AAA corporate bonds.

SOURCE: *Federal Reserve Bulletin.*

The relationship between inflation and long-term interest rates is highlighted in Figure 2-4, which plots rates of inflation along with long-term interest rates. Prior to 1965, when the average rate of inflation was about 1 percent, interest rates on the least risky bonds (AAA-rated) generally ranged from 4 percent to 5 percent. As the war in Vietnam accelerated in the late 1960s, the rate of inflation increased, and interest rates began to rise. The rate of inflation dropped after 1970 and so did long-term interest rates. However, the 1973 Arab oil embargo was followed by a quadrupling of oil prices in 1974, which caused a spurt in inflation, which in turn drove interest rates to new record highs in 1974 and 1975. Inflationary pressures eased in late 1975 and 1976 but then rose again after 1976. In 1980, inflation rates hit the highest level on record, and fears of continued double-digit inflation pushed interest rates up to historic highs. From 1981 through 1986, the inflation rate dropped sharply, and in 1986 inflation was only 1.1 percent, the lowest level in 25 years. In 1993, interest rates dropped to historical lows—the Treasury bill yield actually dropped below 3 percent. Currently (1995), inflation is in the 3 percent range, Treasury bill rates are above 5.5 percent, and interest rates to strong corporations are about 8.5 percent.

FIGURE 2-4

Relationship between Annual Inflation Rates and Long-Term Interest Rates 1960–1994

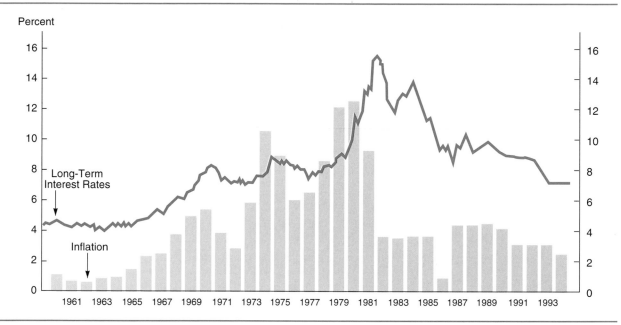

NOTES:

a. Interest rates are those on AAA long-term corporate bonds.

b. Inflation is measured as the annual rate of change in the Consumer Price Index (CPI).

SOURCE: *Federal Reserve Bulletin.*

 Self-Test Questions

How are interest rates used to allocate capital among firms?

What happens to market-clearing, or equilibrium, interest rates in a capital market when the demand for funds declines? What happens when inflation increases or decreases?

Why does the price of capital change during booms and recessions?

How does risk affect interest rates?

How does a change in rates in one financial market affect the rates in other financial markets?

The Determinants of Market Interest Rates

In general, the quoted (or nominal) interest rate on a debt security, k, is composed of a real risk-free rate of interest, k*, plus several premiums that reflect inflation, the riskiness of the security, and the security's marketability (or liquidity). This relationship can be expressed as follows:

$$2\text{-}1 \qquad \text{Quoted interest rate} = k = k^* + IP + DRP + LP + MRP$$

In Equation 2-1, the variables are defined as follows:

k = the quoted, or *nominal,* rate of interest on a given security.[7] There are many different securities, hence many different quoted interest rates.

k^* = the *real risk-free rate of interest* (k^* is pronounced "k-star")

IP = inflation premium

DRP = default risk premium

LP = liquidity, or marketability, premium

MRP = maturity risk premium

We discuss the components whose sum makes up the quoted, or nominal, rate on a given security in the following sections.

The Real Risk-Free Rate of Interest, k^*

REAL RISK-FREE RATE OF INTEREST, k^*
The rate of interest that would exist on default-free U.S. Treasury securities if no inflation were expected.

The **real risk-free rate of interest, k^*,** is defined as the interest rate that would exist on a security with a *guaranteed* payoff (termed a riskless, or risk-free security) if inflation was expected to be zero during the investment period. It can be thought of as the rate of interest that would exist on short-term U.S. Treasury securities in an inflation-free world. The real risk-free rate changes over time depending on economic conditions, especially (1) on the rate of return corporations and other borrowers are willing to pay to borrow funds, and (2) on people's time preferences for current versus future consumption. It is difficult to measure the real risk-free rate precisely, but most experts think that in the United States k^* has fluctuated in the range of 1 percent to 4 percent in recent years.

The Nominal, or Quoted, Risk-Free Rate of Interest, k_{RF}

NOMINAL (QUOTED) RISK-FREE RATE, k_{RF}
The rate of interest on a security that is free of all risk; k_{RF} is proxied by the T-bill rate or the T-bond rate. k_{RF} includes an inflation premium.

The **nominal,** or **quoted, risk-free rate, k_{RF},** is the *real risk-free rate plus a premium for expected inflation:* $k_{RF} = k^* + IP$. If we combine $k^* + IP$ and let this sum equal k_{RF}, then Equation 2-1 becomes:

$$2\text{-}2 \qquad k = k_{RF} + DRP + LP + MRP$$

To be strictly correct, the risk-free rate should mean the interest rate on a security that has absolutely no risk at all—one that has no risk of default, no maturity risk, no liquidity risk, and no risk of loss if inflation increases. No such security exists

---

[7]The term *nominal* as it is used here means the *stated* rate as opposed to the real rate, which is adjusted to remove the effects of inflation. If you bought a 30-year Treasury bond in January 1995, the quoted, or nominal, rate would be about 8 percent, but if inflation was expected to average 5 percent over the next 10 years, the real rate would be about 8% − 5% = 3%.

in the real world; hence, there is no observable truly risk-free rate. However, there is one security that is free of most risks—a U.S. Treasury bill (T-bill), a short-term security issued by the U.S. government. Treasury bonds (T-bonds), longer-term government securities, are free of default and liquidity risks, but T-bonds are exposed to some risk due to changes in the general level of interest rates.

If the term *risk-free rate* is used without either the term *real* or the term *nominal,* people generally mean the quoted (nominal) rate, and we will follow that convention in this book. Therefore, when we use the term *risk-free rate,* k_{RF}, we mean the nominal risk-free rate, which includes an inflation premium equal to the average expected inflation rate over the life of the security. In general, we use the T-bill rate to approximate the short-term risk-free rate, and the T-bond rate to approximate the long-term risk-free rate. So, whenever you see the term *risk-free rate,* assume that we are referring either to the quoted U.S. T-bill rate or to the quoted T-bond rate.

Inflation Premium (IP)

Inflation has a major impact on interest rates because it erodes the purchasing power of the dollar and lowers the real rate of return on investments. To illustrate, suppose you saved $1,000 and invested it in a certificate of deposit that matures in 1 year and will pay 5 percent interest. At the end of the year you will receive $1,050—your original $1,000 plus $50 of interest. Now suppose the inflation rate during the year is 10 percent, and it affects all items equally. If beer had cost $1 per bottle at the beginning of the year, it would cost $1.10 at the end of the year. Therefore, your $1,000 would have bought $1,000/$1 = 1,000 bottles at the beginning of the year but only $1,050/$1.10 = 955 bottles at year's end. Thus, *in real terms,* you would be worse off—you would receive $50 of interest, but it would not be sufficient to offset inflation. In this case, you would be better off buying 1,000 bottles of beer (or some other storable asset such as land, timber, apartment buildings, wheat, or gold) than investing in the certificate of deposit.

INFLATION PREMIUM (IP)
A premium for expected inflation that investors add to the real risk-free rate of return.

Investors are well aware of all this, so when they lend money, they build in an **inflation premium (IP)** equal to the *average inflation rate expected over the life of the security.* Therefore, if the real risk-free rate of interest, k^*, is 3 percent, and if inflation is expected to be 4 percent (and hence IP = 4%) during the next year, then the quoted rate of interest on 1-year T-bills would be 7 percent. In early January of 1995, the expected 1-year inflation rate was about 3 percent, and the yield on 1-year T-bills was about 6.4 percent. This implies that the real risk-free rate on short-term securities at that time was about 3.4 percent.

Default Risk Premium (DRP)

The risk that a borrower will *default* on a loan, which means not to pay the interest or the principal, also affects the market interest rate on a security: The greater the default risk, the higher the interest rate lenders charge (demand). Treasury securities have no default risk; thus, they generally carry the lowest interest rates on taxable securities in the United States. For corporate bonds, the better the bond's overall credit rating, the lower its default risk, and, consequently, the lower its interest rate.[8] Here are some representative interest rates on long-term bonds in January 1995:

	Rate	DRP
U.S. Treasury	7.8%	—
AAA	8.5	0.7%
AA	8.7	0.9
A	9.0	1.2

DEFAULT RISK PREMIUM (DRP)
The difference between the interest rate on a U.S. Treasury bond and a corporate bond of equal maturity and marketability.

The difference between the quoted interest rate on a T-bond and that on a corporate bond with similar maturity, liquidity, and other features is the **default risk premium (DRP).** Therefore, if the bonds listed above were *otherwise similar,* the default risk premium would be DRP = $k - k_{RF}$, which are the values given above. Default risk premiums vary somewhat over time, but the January 1995 figures are representative of levels in recent years.

Liquidity Premium (LP)

Liquidity generally is defined as the ability to convert an asset to cash on short notice and "reasonably" capture the amount initially invested. Assets have varying degrees of liquidity, depending on the characteristics of the market in which they are traded. For instance, there exist very active and easily accessible secondary markets for financial assets like government notes and bonds and the stocks and bonds of large corporations, but the markets for real estate are limited because they are geographically constrained. Therefore, most financial assets are considered more liquid than real assets. Of course, the most liquid asset of all is cash, and the more easily an asset can be converted to cash at a price that substantially recovers the initial amount invested, the more liquid it is considered. Consequently, short-term financial assets generally are more liquid than long-term financial assets. Because liquidity is important, investors evaluate liquidity and include **liquidity premiums (LP)** when market rates of securities are established. Although it is very difficult to accurately measure liquidity premiums, a differential of at least two and probably four or five percentage points exists between the least liquid and the most liquid financial assets of similar default risk and maturity.

LIQUIDITY PREMIUM (LP)
A premium added to the rate on a security if the security cannot be converted to cash on short notice and at close to the original cost.

Maturity Risk Premium (MRP)

U.S. Treasury securities are free of default risk in the sense that one can be virtually certain that the federal government will pay interest on its bonds and will also pay them off when they mature. Therefore, the default risk premium on Treasury securities essentially is zero. Further, active markets exist for Treasury securities, so their liquidity premiums also are close to zero. Thus, as a first approximation, the rate of interest on a Treasury bond should be the risk-free rate, k_{RF}, which is

---

[8]Bond ratings, and bonds' riskiness in general, will be discussed in detail in Chapter 19. For now, merely note that bonds rated AAA are judged to have less default risk than bonds rated AA, AA bonds are less risky than A bonds, and so on. Ratings are designated AAA or Aaa, AA or Aa, and so forth, depending on the rating agency. In this book the designations are used interchangeably.

INTEREST RATE RISK
The risk of capital losses to which investors are exposed because of changing interest rates.

MATURITY RISK PREMIUM (MRP)
A premium that reflects interest rate risk; bonds with longer maturities have greater interest rate risk.

REINVESTMENT RATE RISK
The risk that a decline in interest rates will lead to lower income when bonds mature and funds are reinvested.

equal to the real risk-free rate, k^*, plus an inflation premium, IP. However, an adjustment is needed for long-term Treasury bonds. The prices of long-term bonds decline sharply whenever interest rates rise, and because interest rates can and do occasionally rise, all long-term bonds, even Treasury bonds, have an element of risk called **interest rate risk.** As a rule, the bonds of any organization, from the U.S. government to General Motors, have more interest rate risk the longer the maturity of the bond.[9] Therefore, a **maturity risk premium (MRP),** which is higher the longer the years to maturity, must be included in the required interest rate.

The effect of maturity risk premiums is to raise interest rates on long-term bonds relative to those on short-term bonds. This premium, like the others, is extremely difficult to measure, but (1) it seems to vary over time, rising when interest rates are more volatile and uncertain, then falling when interest rates are more stable, and (2) in recent years, the maturity risk premium on 30-year T-bonds appears to have been generally in the range of one or two percentage points.[10]

We should mention that although long-term bonds are heavily exposed to interest rate risk, short-term investments are heavily exposed to **reinvestment rate risk.** When short-term investments mature and the proceeds are reinvested, or "rolled over," a decline in interest rates would necessitate reinvestment at a lower rate, and hence would lead to a decline in interest income. To illustrate, suppose you had $100,000 invested in 1-year certificates of deposit, and you lived on the income. In 1981, short-term rates were about 15 percent, so your income would have been about $15,000. However, your income would have declined to about $9,000 by 1983, and to just $6,500 by 1995. Had you invested your money in long-term T-bonds in 1981, when the long-term and short-term rates were nearly equal, your income (but not the value of the principal) would have been stable—about $15,000 per year.[11] Thus, although "investing short" preserves one's principal, the interest income provided by short-term investments varies from year to year, depending on reinvestment rates.

Self-Test Questions

Write out an equation for the nominal interest rate on any debt security.

Distinguish between the real risk-free rate of interest, k^*, and the nominal, or quoted, risk-free rate of interest, k_{RF}.

---

[9]For example, if someone had bought a 30-year Treasury bond for $1,000 in 1972, when the long-term interest rate was 7 percent, and held it until 1981, when long-term T-bond rates were about 14.5 percent, the value of the bond would have declined to about $514. That would represent a loss of almost half the money, and it demonstrates that long-term bonds, even U.S. Treasury bonds, are not riskless. However, had the investor purchased short-term T-bills in 1972 and subsequently reinvested the principal each time the bills matured, he or she would still have had about $1,000. This point will be discussed in detail in Chapter 7.

[10]The MRP has averaged 1.3 percentage points over the past 65 years. See *Stocks, Bonds, Bills, and Inflation: 1994 Yearbook* (Chicago: Ibbotson Associates, 1994).

[11]Long-term bonds also have some reinvestment rate risk. To actually earn the quoted rate on a long-term bond, the interest payments must be reinvested at the quoted rate. However, if interest rates fall, the interest payments must be reinvested at a lower rate; thus, the realized return would be less than the quoted rate.

How is inflation considered when interest rates are determined by investors in the financial markets? Explain.

Does the interest rate on a T-bond include a default risk premium? Explain.

Distinguish between liquid and illiquid assets, and identify some assets that are liquid and some that are illiquid.

Briefly explain the following statement: "Although long-term bonds are heavily exposed to interest rate risk, short-term bills are heavily exposed to reinvestment rate risk."

The Term Structure of Interest Rates

TERM STRUCTURE OF INTEREST RATES
The relationship between yields and maturities of securities.

YIELD CURVE
A graph showing the relationship between yields and maturities of securities.

"NORMAL" YIELD CURVE
An upward-sloping yield curve.

INVERTED ("ABNORMAL")
YIELD CURVE
A downward-sloping yield curve.

A study of Figure 2-3 reveals that at certain times, such as in 1995, short-term interest rates were lower than long-term rates, whereas at other times, such as in 1980 and 1981, short-term rates were higher than long-term rates. The relationship between long- and short-term rates, known as the **term structure of interest rates,** is important to corporate treasurers, who must decide whether to borrow by issuing long- or short-term debt, and to investors, who must decide whether to buy long- or short-term bonds. Thus, it is important to understand (1) how long- and short-term rates are related to each other and (2) what causes shifts in their relative positions.

To begin, we can find in a source such as *The Wall Street Journal* or the *Federal Reserve Bulletin* the interest rates on Treasury bonds of various maturities at a given date. For example, the tabular section of Figure 2-5 presents interest rates for different maturities on two different dates. The set of data, when plotted on a graph such as that in Figure 2-5, is called the **yield curve** for that date. The yield curve changes both in position and in slope over time. In March of 1980, all rates were relatively high, and short-term rates were higher than long-term rates, so the yield curve on that date was *downward sloping*. However, in January of 1995, all rates had fallen, and short-term rates were lower than long-term rates, so the yield curve at that time was *upward sloping*. Had we drawn the yield curve during January of 1982, it would have been essentially horizontal, because long-term and short-term bonds on that date had about the same rate of interest (see Figure 2-3).

Historically, in most years, long-term rates have been above short-term rates, so usually the yield curve has been upward sloping. For this reason, people often call an upward-sloping yield curve a **"normal" yield curve** and a yield curve that slopes downward an **inverted,** or **"abnormal," yield curve.** Thus, in Figure 2-5, the yield curve for March 1980 was inverted, but the one for January 1995 was normal. In the next section, we discuss three explanations for the shape of the yield curve and why an upward sloping yield curve is considered normal.

Term Structure Theories (Explanations)

Several theories have been proposed to explain the shape of the yield curve. The three major ones are (1) the expectations theory, (2) the liquidity preference theory, and (3) the market segmentation theory.

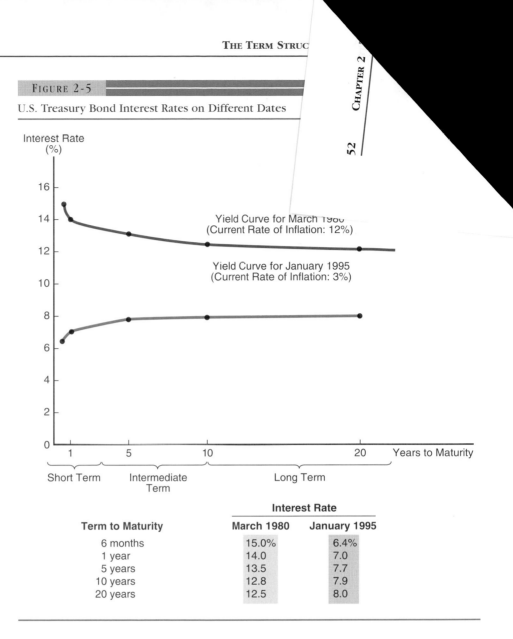

FIGURE 2-5

U.S. Treasury Bond Interest Rates on Different Dates

		Interest Rate	
Term to Maturity		March 1980	January 1995
6 months		15.0%	6.4%
1 year		14.0	7.0
5 years		13.5	7.7
10 years		12.8	7.9
20 years		12.5	8.0

EXPECTATIONS THEORY
The theory that the shape of the yield curve depends on investors' expectations about future inflation rates.

EXPECTATIONS THEORY The **expectations theory** states that the yield curve depends on *expectations* concerning future inflation rates. Specifically, k_t, the nominal interest rate on a U.S. Treasury bond that matures in t years, is found as follows under the expectations theory:

$$k_t = k^* + IP_t$$

Here k^* is the real risk-free interest rate, and IP_t is an inflation premium that is equal to the *average expected rate of inflation* over the t years until the bond matures. Under the expectations theory, the maturity risk premium (MRP) is assumed to be zero, and, for Treasury securities, the default risk premium (DRP) and liquidity premium (LP) also are zero.

To illustrate, suppose that in late December of 1995 the real risk-free rate of interest was $k^* = 3\%$ and expected inflation rates for the next 3 years were as follows:[12]

Year	Expected Annual (1-year) Inflation Rate	Expected Average Inflation Rate from 1995 to Indicated Year (IP_t)
1996	2%	2%/1 = 2%
1997	4%	(2% + 4%)/2 = 3%
1998	9%	(2% + 4% + 9%)/3 = 5%

Given these expectations, the following interest rate pattern should exist:

Bond Type	Real Risk-free Rate (k^*)		Inflation Premium: Average Expected Inflation Rate (IP_t)		Nominal Treasury Bond Rate for Each Maturity ($k_{T\text{-}bond}$)
1-year bond	3%	+	2%	=	5%
2-year bond	3%	+	3%	=	6%
3-year bond	3%	+	5%	=	8%

If the yields on these hypothetical bonds were plotted, the yield curve would be upward sloping, similar to the January 1995 yield curve in Figure 2-5. Had the pattern of expected inflation rates been reversed, with inflation expected to fall from 9 percent to 2 percent over the three-year period, the pattern of interest rates would produce an inverted yield curve like the March 1980 yield curve in Figure 2-5.

LIQUIDITY PREFERENCE THEORY
The theory that, all else equal, lenders prefer to make short-term loans rather than long-term loans; hence, they will lend short-term funds at lower rates than long-term funds.

LIQUIDITY PREFERENCE THEORY The **liquidity preference theory** states that long-term bonds normally yield more than short-term bonds for two reasons: (1) Investors generally prefer to hold short-term securities, because such securities are more liquid in the sense that they can be converted to cash with little danger of loss of principal. Investors will, therefore, generally accept lower yields on short-term securities, and this leads to relatively low short-term rates. (2) Borrowers, on the other hand, generally prefer long-term debt, because short-term debt exposes them to the risk of having to repay the debt under adverse conditions. Accordingly, borrowers want to "lock into" long-term funds, which means they are willing to pay a higher rate, other things held constant, for long-term funds than for short-term funds—this also leads to relatively low short-term rates. Thus, lender and borrower preferences both operate to cause short-term rates to be lower than long-term rates. Taken together, these two sets of preferences—and hence the liquidity preference theory—imply that under normal conditions, a positive maturity risk premium (MRP) exists, and the MRP increases with years to maturity, causing the yield curve to be upward sloping.

---

[12]Technically, we should be using geometric averages rather than arithmetic averages, but the differences are not material in this example. For a discussion of this point, see Robert C. Radcliffe, *Investment: Concepts, Analysis, and Strategy,* 4th ed. (New York: HarperCollins College Publishers, 1994), Chapter 5.

MARKET SEGMENTATION
THEORY
The theory that each
borrower and lender has a
preferred maturity and that
the slope of the yield curve
depends on the supply of
and demand for funds in
the long-term market
relative to the short-term
market.

MARKET SEGMENTATION THEORY   Briefly, the **market segmentation theory** states that each lender and each borrower has a preferred maturity. For example, a person borrowing to buy a long-term asset like a house, or an electric utility borrowing to build a power plant, would want a long-term loan. However, a retailer borrowing in September to build its inventories for Christmas would prefer a short-term loan. Similar differences exist among savers—for example, a person saving to take a vacation next summer would want to lend in the short-term market, but someone saving for retirement 20 years hence would probably buy long-term securities.

The thrust of the market segmentation theory is that the slope of the yield curve depends on supply/demand conditions in the long-term and short-term markets. Thus, according to this theory, the yield curve could at any given time be either flat, upward sloping, or downward sloping. An upward-sloping yield curve would occur when there was a large supply of short-term funds relative to demand, but a shortage of long-term funds. Similarly, a downward-sloping curve would indicate relatively strong demand for funds in the short-term market compared to that in the long-term market. A flat curve would indicate balance between the two markets.

Various tests of the theories explaining the shape of the yield curve have been conducted, and these tests indicate that all three theories have some validity. Thus, the shape of the yield curve at any given time is affected (1) by expectations about future inflation, (2) by liquidity preferences, and (3) by supply/demand conditions in long- and short-term markets. One factor might dominate at one time, another at another time, but all three affect the term structure of interest rates.

Self-Test Questions

What is a yield curve, and what information would you need to draw this curve?

Discuss each of the following theories: (1) market segmentation theory, (2) liquidity preference theory, and (3) expectations theory.

Distinguish between the shapes of a "normal" yield curve and an "abnormal" yield curve, and explain when each might exist.

Other Factors that Influence Interest Rate Levels

In addition to inflationary expectations, liquidity preferences, and the supply/demand situation, other factors also influence both the general level of interest rates and the shape of the yield curve. The four most important factors are (1) Federal Reserve policy, (2) the level of the federal budget deficit, (3) the foreign trade balance, and (4) the level of business activity.

Federal Reserve Policy

As you probably learned in your economics courses, (1) the money supply has a major effect on both the level of economic activity and the rate of inflation, and (2) in the United States, the Federal Reserve Board controls the money supply. If the Fed wants to control growth in the economy, as it did in 1994, it slows growth in the money supply. Initially, such an action causes interest rates to increase and inflation to stabilize. The reverse holds if the Fed loosens the money supply.

To illustrate, in 1994 the Fed tightened up the money supply six times to control the pace of the existing economic recovery in an effort to keep inflation in check. The Fed primarily deals in the short-term end of the market, so this tightening had the direct effect of pushing short-term interest rates up sharply. Long-term rates followed, but the very fact the Fed was taking action to keep inflationary pressures under control affected investors' expectations concerning inflation, which caused long-term rates to level off and even drop slightly in some financial markets.

During periods when the Fed actively intervenes in the markets, the yield curve will be distorted. Short-term rates will be temporarily "too low" if the Fed is easing credit, and "too high" if it is tightening credit. Long-term rates are not affected as much by Fed intervention.

Federal Deficits

If the federal government spends more than it takes in from tax revenues, it runs a deficit, and that deficit must be covered either by borrowing or by printing money. If the government borrows, this added demand for funds pushes up interest rates. If it prints money, this increases expectations for future inflation, which also drives up interest rates. Thus, the larger the federal deficit, other things held constant, the higher the level of interest rates. Whether long- or short-term rates are more affected depends on how the deficit is financed, so we cannot state, in general, how deficits will affect the slope of the yield curve.

Foreign Trade Balance

Businesses and individuals in the United States buy from and sell to people and firms in other countries. If we buy more than we sell (that is, if we import more than we export), we are said to be running a *foreign trade deficit*. When trade deficits occur, they must be financed, and the main source of financing is debt. In other words, if we import $200 billion of goods but export only $100 billion, we run a trade deficit of $100 billion, and we must borrow the $100 billion.[13] Therefore, the larger our trade deficit, the more we must borrow, and as we increase our borrowing, this drives up interest rates. Also, foreigners are willing to hold U.S. debt only if the interest rate on this debt is competitive with interest rates in other countries. Therefore, if the Federal Reserve attempts to lower interest rates in the United States, causing our rates to fall below rates abroad, then foreigners will sell U.S. bonds, those sales will depress bond prices, and the result will be higher U.S. rates. Thus, the existence of a deficit trade balance hinders the Fed's ability to combat a recession by lowering interest rates.

The United States has been running annual trade deficits since the mid-1970s, and the cumulative effect of these deficits is that the United States is by far the largest debtor nation of all time. As a result, our interest rates are very much influenced by interest rate trends in other countries around the world (higher rates

---

[13]The deficit could also be financed by selling assets, including gold, corporate stocks, entire companies, and real estate. The United States has financed its massive trade deficits by all these means in recent years, but the primary method has been by borrowing.

abroad lead to higher U.S. rates). Because of all this, U.S. corporate treasurers—and anyone else who is affected by interest rates—must keep up with developments in the world economy.

Business Activity

Figure 2-3, presented earlier, can be examined to see how business conditions influence interest rates. Here are the key points revealed by the graph:

1. Because inflation increased from 1955 to 1981, the general tendency during this period was toward higher interest rates. However, since the 1981 peak, the trend has generally been downward.
2. Until 1966, short-term rates were almost always below long-term rates. Thus, in those years the yield curve was almost always "normal" in the sense that it was upward sloping.
3. The shaded areas in the graph represent recessions, during which both the demand for money and the rate of inflation tend to fall, and, at the same time, the Federal Reserve tends to increase the money supply in an effort to stimulate the economy. As a result, there is a tendency for interest rates to decline during recessions. Currently, in early 1995, the economy is in the midst of a recovery. The Fed's actions to raise interest rates are efforts to control the economy so it does not grow too quickly.
4. During recessions, short-term rates decline more sharply than long-term rates. This occurs because (1) the Fed operates mainly in the short-term sector, so its intervention has the strongest effect here, and (2) long-term rates reflect the average expected inflation rate over the next 20 to 30 years, and this expectation generally does not change much, even when the current rate of inflation is low because of a recession.

Self-Test Questions

Other than inflationary expectations, liquidity preferences, and normal supply/demand fluctuations, name four additional factors which influence interest rates, and explain their effects.

How does the Fed stimulate the economy? How does the Fed affect interest rates?

Interest Rate Levels and Stock Prices

Interest rates have two effects on corporate profits. First, because interest is a cost, the higher the rate of interest, the lower a firm's profits, other things held constant. Second, interest rates affect the level of economic activity, and economic activity affects corporate profits. Interest rates obviously affect stock prices because of their effects on profits, but, perhaps even more important, they have an effect due to competition in the marketplace between stocks and bonds. If interest rates rise sharply, investors can get higher returns in the bond market, which induces them to sell stocks and to transfer funds from the stock market to the bond market. A massive sale of stocks in response to rising interest rates obviously would depress stock prices. Of course, the reverse occurs if interest rates decline. Indeed, the bull market of December 1991, when the Dow Jones Industrial Index rose 10 percent in less than a month, was caused almost entirely by the sharp drop in long-term interest rates. On the other hand, the poor performance exhibited by the market in 1994—common stocks declined on average by more than 3 percent—resulted from sharp increases in interest rates.

Self-Test Question

In what two ways do changes in interest rates affect stock prices?

Interest Rates and Business Decisions

The yield curve for January 1995, shown earlier in Figure 2-5, indicates that short-term rates were lower than long-term rates at that time. Suppose it is January 1995, and you own a company that has decided to (1) build a new plant that has a 20-year life and will cost $10 million, and (2) raise the funds to build the plant by selling an issue of debt (or borrowing) rather than by issuing stock. If you borrow on a short-term basis—say for one year—the rate on the loan might be 6.5 percent, so the interest cost for the year would be $650,000; whereas, if you use long-term (20-year) financing, the rate might be 8.5 percent, and the interest cost for the year would be $850,000. Therefore, at first glance, it would seem that you should use short-term debt to finance the new plant.

However, this could prove to be a horrible mistake. If you use short-term debt, you will have to renew your loan every year, and the rate charged on each new loan will reflect the then-current short-term rate. Interest rates could return to their March 1980 levels, so by 1996 you could be paying 14 percent, or $1.4 million interest per year. These high interest payments would cut into, and perhaps eliminate, your profits. Your reduced profitability could easily increase your firm's risk to the point where its bond rating would be lowered, causing lenders to increase the risk premium built into the interest rates they charge, which in turn would force you to pay even higher rates. These very high interest rates would further reduce your profitability, worrying lenders even more, and making them reluctant to renew your loan. If your lenders refused to renew the loan and demanded payment, as they have every right to do, you might have trouble raising the cash. If you had to make price cuts to convert physical assets to cash, you might incur heavy operating losses, or, ultimately, even bankruptcy.

On the other hand, if you use long-term financing, your interest costs would remain constant at $850,000 per year, so an increase in interest rates in the economy would not hurt you. You might even be able to buy up some of your bankrupt competitors at bargain prices—bankruptcies increase dramatically when interest rates rise, primarily because many firms do use short-term debt.

Does all this suggest that firms should always avoid short-term debt? Not necessarily. If inflation falls in the next few years, so will interest rates. If you had borrowed on a long-term basis for 8.5 percent in January 1995, your company would be at a major disadvantage if competitors who used short-term debt in 1995 could borrow at a cost of only 5 percent or 6 percent in subsequent years. On the other hand, large federal deficits might drive inflation and interest rates up to new record levels. In that case, you would wish you had borrowed on a long-term basis in 1995.

Financing decisions would be easy if we could develop accurate forecasts of future interest rates. Unfortunately, predicting future interest rates with consistent accuracy is somewhere between difficult and impossible—people who make a living by selling interest rate forecasts say it is difficult, but many others say it is impossible.

Even if it is difficult to predict future interest rate *levels,* it is easy to predict that interest rates will *fluctuate*—they always have, and they always will. This being the case, sound financial policy calls for using a mix of long- and short-term debt as well as equity in such a manner that the firm can survive in most interest rate environments. Further, the optimal financial policy depends in an important way on the nature of the firm's assets—the easier it is to sell off assets and thus to pay off debts, the more feasible it is to use large amounts of short-term debt. This makes it more feasible to finance current assets than fixed assets with short-term debt. We will return to this issue later in the book, when we discuss working capital policy.

 Self-Test Questions

If short-term interest rates are lower than long-term rates, why might a firm still choose to finance with long-term debt?

Explain the following statement: "The optimal financial policy depends in an important way on the nature of the firm's assets."

The Federal Income Tax System

The value of any financial asset, including stocks, bonds, and mortgages, as well as the values of most real assets such as manufacturing plants or even entire firms, depends on the stream of cash flows produced by the asset. For the most part, cash flows from an asset consist of usable income plus depreciation, and usable income means income after taxes.

Our tax laws can be changed by Congress, and in recent years changes have occurred almost every year. Indeed, a major change has occurred, on average, every 3 to 4 years since 1913, when our federal income tax system began. Further, certain parts of our tax system are tied to the rate of inflation, so changes occur automatically each year, depending on the rate of inflation during the previous year. Therefore, although this section will give you a background on the basic nature of our tax system, you should consult current rate schedules and other data published by the Internal Revenue Service (and available in U.S. post offices) to determine your personal or business taxes.

The Federal Tax Code is separated into two sections: (1) tax laws that are applicable to individuals, and (2) tax laws that are applicable to corporations. Certainly, the tax code for individuals applies to persons such as individuals and families, while the corporate tax code applies to businesses that are organized as corporations. For businesses that are not corporations, the corporate tax code is not applicable; so, proprietorships and partnerships are taxed according to the individual tax code. The income from partnerships and proprietorships is reported by the individual owners as personal income. Generally, then, the tax rates for corporations and the tax rates for proprietorships and partnerships differ.

At the end of 1994, federal income tax rates for individuals went up to almost 40 percent, and, when state and city income taxes were included, the marginal tax rate on an individual's income could have exceeded 45 percent. Corporate profits were subject to federal income tax rates of up to 39 percent, in addition to state income taxes. Because of the magnitude of the tax bite, taxes play an important role in many financial decisions.

Congress and the administration continuously debate the merits of different changes in the tax laws. Some people want to raise taxes to reduce our huge deficits and to help rebuild our inner cities. But others think reducing taxes will help stimulate the economy and reduce deficits by producing greater revenues for the government. It is clear the tax laws will change in coming years—they always do. At some point, depreciation schedules might be liberalized, and capital gains might be taxed at a lower rate. Even in the unlikely event that Congress does not change the tax laws, changes still will occur because certain aspects of the tax calculation are tied to the rate of inflation. Thus, by the time you read this section, tax rates and other factors might be different from those we provide. Still, this section should give you an understanding of the basics of our tax system.

Taxes are so complicated that university law schools offer master's degrees in taxation to practicing lawyers, many of whom also have the CPA certification. In a field complicated enough to warrant such detailed study, we can cover only the highlights. This really is enough, though, because business managers and investors should, and do, rely on tax specialists rather than trust their own limited knowledge. Still, it is important to know the basic elements of the tax system to understand the impact taxes have on cash flows.

Individual Income Taxes

PROGRESSIVE TAX
A tax that requires a higher percentage payment on higher incomes. The personal income tax in the United States is progressive.

Individuals pay taxes on wages and salaries, on investment income (dividends, interest, and profits from the sale of securities), and on the profits of *proprietorships and partnerships*. Our tax rates are **progressive**—that is, the higher one's income, the larger the percentage paid in taxes. The individual tax rates for 1994 are provided in the appendix, Table 2A-1. In this section, we discuss some of the general topics applicable to those who are affected by the individual tax code section.

TAXABLE INCOME
Gross income minus exemptions and allowable deductions as set forth in the Tax Code.

1. **Taxable income** is defined as gross income less a set of exemptions and deductions that are spelled out in the instructions to the tax forms individuals must file. When filing a tax return in 1995 for the tax year 1994, each taxpayer will receive an exemption of $2,450 for each dependent, including the taxpayer, which reduces taxable income. However, this exemption is indexed to rise with inflation, and the exemption is phased out for high-income taxpayers. Also, certain expenses, such as mortgage interest paid, state and local income taxes paid, and charitable contributions, can be deducted and thus be used to reduce taxable income; but again, high-income taxpayers lose some of this benefit.

MARGINAL TAX RATE
The tax applicable to the last unit of income.

2. The **marginal tax rate** is defined as the tax on the last unit of income. The marginal tax rate is represented by the tax bracket you are in. For example, if you are single and your taxable income is $50,000, then your marginal tax rate is 28 percent. As Table 2A-1 shows, marginal rates begin at 15 percent, rise to 28 percent, then to 31 percent, and so on.

AVERAGE TAX RATE
Taxes paid divided by
taxable income.

3. One can calculate **average tax rates** from the data in Table 2A-1. The average tax rate equals the percent of taxable income that is paid in taxes. For example, if Jill Smith, a single individual, had taxable income of $35,000, her tax bill would be $3,412.50 + ($35,000 − $22,750)(0.28) = $3,412.50 + $3,430.00 = $6,842.50. Her average tax rate would be $6,842.50/$35,000 = 19.55% versus a marginal rate of 28 percent. If Jill received a raise of $1,000, bringing her income to $36,000, she would have to pay $280 of it as taxes, so her after-tax raise would be $720. In addition, her social security taxes would increase.

TAXES ON DIVIDEND AND INTEREST INCOME Dividend and interest income received by individuals from corporate securities is added to other income and thus is taxed at the rates shown in Table 2A-1. Because corporations pay dividends out of earnings that already have been taxed, there is *double taxation* of corporate income.

It should be noted that under U.S. tax laws, interest on most state and local government bonds, called *municipals* or *"munis,"* is not subject to federal income taxes. Thus, investors get to keep all the interest received from most municipal bonds but only a fraction of the interest received from bonds issued by corporations or by the U.S. government. This means that a lower-yielding muni can provide the same after-tax return as a higher-yielding taxable corporate bond. For example, a taxpayer in the 31 percent marginal tax bracket who could buy a muni that yielded 10 percent would have to receive a before-tax yield of 14.5 percent on a corporate or U.S. Treasury bond to have the same after-tax income:

$$\frac{\text{Equivalent pretax yield}}{\text{on a taxable investment}} = \frac{\text{Yield on tax-free investment}}{1 - \text{Marginal tax rate}}$$

$$= \frac{10\%}{1 - 0.31} = 14.5\%$$

If we know the yield on the taxable bond (investment), we can use the following equation to find the equivalent yield on a muni (tax-free investment):

$$\frac{\text{Yield on}}{\text{tax-free investment}} = \left(\frac{\text{Pretax yield on}}{\text{taxable investment}}\right) \times (1 - \text{Marginal tax rate})$$

$$= 14.5\% \times (1 - 0.31) = 14.5\% (0.69) = 10.0\%$$

The exemption from federal taxes stems from the separation of federal and state powers, and its primary effect is to help state and local governments borrow at lower rates than otherwise would be available to them.

INTEREST PAID BY INDIVIDUALS For the most part, the interest paid by individuals on loans is *not* tax deductible. The principal exception is the interest paid on mortgage financing used to purchase a house for personal residence, which is tax deductible. The effect of tax deductible interest payments is to lower the actual cost of the mortgage to the taxpayer. For example, if Staci Jones has an 8 percent mortgage on her house and she has a marginal tax rate equal to 36 percent, the after-tax cost of her mortgage is:

$$\text{After-tax rate} = 8\% \ (1 - 0.36) = 5.12\%.$$

CAPITAL GAIN OR LOSS
The profit (loss) from the sale of a capital asset for more (less) than its purchase price.

CAPITAL GAINS VERSUS ORDINARY INCOME Assets such as stocks, bonds, and real estate are defined as *capital assets.* If you buy a capital asset and later sell it for more than your purchase price, the profit is called a **capital gain;** if you suffer a loss, it is called a **capital loss.** An asset sold within one year of the time it was purchased produces a *short-term gain or loss,* whereas one held for more than one year produces a *long-term gain or loss.* Thus, if you buy 100 shares of Disney stock for $40 per share and sell it for $50 per share, you will have a capital gain of 100 × $10, or $1,000. However, if you sell the stock for $30 per share, you will have a $1,000 capital loss. If you sell the stock for exactly $40 per share, you will have neither a gain nor a loss; you simply get back the $4,000 you originally invested, and no tax is due.

From 1921 through 1986, long-term capital gains were taxed at substantially lower rates than ordinary income. For example, in 1986 long-term capital gains were taxed at only 40 percent of the tax rate on ordinary income. The tax law changes that took effect in 1987 eliminated this differential, and from 1987 through 1990 all capital gains income (both long-term and short-term) was taxed as if it were ordinary income. However, beginning in 1991, the maximum tax rate on long-term capital gains was capped at 28 percent.

There has been a great deal of controversy over the proper tax rate for capital gains. It has been argued that lower tax rates on capital gains (1) stimulate the flow of venture capital to new, start-up businesses, which generally provide capital gains as opposed to dividend income, and (2) cause companies to retain and reinvest a high percentage of their earnings in order to provide their stockholders with lightly taxed capital gains as opposed to highly taxed dividend income. Thus, it has been argued that elimination of the favorable rates on capital gains has retarded investment and economic growth. The proponents of preferential capital gains tax rates lost the argument in 1986, but in 1990 they did succeed in getting the rate capped at 28 percent versus the top marginal rate of about 40 percent. You should not be surprised if the capital gains differential is changed again.

BUSINESS VERSUS PERSONAL EXPENSES *Individuals* pay taxes on the income generated by proprietorships and partnerships they own—the income *"passes through"* to the owners of these types of businesses. Therefore, we need to differentiate business expenses, which are tax deductible, from personal expenses, which are not tax deductible. Generally speaking, an allowable business expense is a cost incurred to generate business revenues. On the other hand, if the expense is incurred for personal benefit (use), it is considered a personal expense. For instance, Loretta Kay owns a house in which she lived until last month, at which time she moved and rented the house to a group of college students. Three months ago, the plumbing burst in the kitchen, and Loretta had to call the plumber for repairs. The repairs cost $1,000. Is this a tax deductible expense? No, because the house was Loretta's personal residence at the time. Last night, Loretta had to call the plumber again to fix pipes that had burst in the house she now has rented to the students—the repairs cost $1,200. Is this a tax deductible expense? Yes, the expense was incurred for business purposes because the house now is rental property, which is considered a business operation.

Corporate Income Taxes

The corporate tax structure is shown in the appendix, Table 2-2A. The structure is similar to the individual rates. However, there are some areas where the corporate tax code and the individual tax code differ significantly. We discuss some of the differences in this section.

INTEREST AND DIVIDEND INCOME RECEIVED BY A CORPORATION   Interest income received by a corporation is taxed as ordinary income at regular corporate tax rates. However, 70 percent of the dividends received by one corporation from another corporation is excluded from taxable income, while the remaining 30 percent is taxed at the ordinary tax rate.[14] Thus, a corporation earning over $12 million with a 35 percent marginal tax rate would pay only $(0.30)(0.35) = 0.105 = 10.5\%$ of its dividend income as taxes, so its effective tax rate on intercorporate dividends would be 10.5 percent. If this firm received $10,000 in dividends from another corporation, its after-tax dividend income would be $8,950:

$$\text{After-tax income} = \text{Before-tax income} - \text{Taxes}$$
$$= \$10,000 - \$10,000\,[(0.30)(0.35)]$$
$$- \$10,000(1 - 0.105) = \$10,000\,(.895) = \$8,950$$

If the corporation pays its own after-tax income out to its stockholders as dividends, the income ultimately is subjected to triple taxation: (1) the original corporation is taxed first, (2) then the second corporation is taxed on the dividends it receives, and (3) the individuals who receive the final dividends are taxed again. This is the reason for the 70 percent exclusion on intercorporate dividends.

INTEREST AND DIVIDENDS PAID BY A CORPORATION   A firm's operations can be financed with either debt or equity capital. If the firm uses debt, it must pay interest on this debt (to banks and to bondholders), whereas if it uses equity, it will pay dividends to the equity investors (stockholders). The interest paid by a corporation is deducted from its operating income to obtain its taxable income, but the dividends paid are not deductible. Therefore, a firm needs $1 of pretax income to pay $1 of interest, but if it is in the 35 percent tax bracket, it needs $1.54 of pretax income to pay $1 of dividends:

$$\frac{\text{Pretax income needed}}{\text{to pay \$1 of dividends}} = \frac{\$1}{1 - \text{Tax rate}} = \frac{\$1}{1 - 0.35} = \$1.54$$

---

[14]The size of the dividend exclusion actually depends on the degree of ownership. Corporations that own less than 20 percent of the stock of the dividend-paying company can exclude 70 percent of the dividends received; firms that own over 20 percent but less than 80 percent can exclude 80 percent of the dividends; and firms that own over 80 percent can exclude the entire dividend payment. Because most companies own less than 20 percent of other companies, we will assume a 70 percent dividend exclusion.

Of course, it generally is not possible to finance exclusively with debt capital, and the risk of doing so would offset the benefits of the higher expected income. Still, *the fact that interest is a deductible expense has a profound effect on the way businesses are financed—our tax system favors debt financing over equity financing.* This point is discussed in more detail in Chapters 15 and 16.

CORPORATE CAPITAL GAINS Before 1987, corporate long-term capital gains were taxed at lower rates than ordinary income, as was true for individuals. Under current law, however, corporations' capital gains are taxed at the same rates as their operating incomes.

CORPORATE LOSS CARRY-BACK AND CARRY-FORWARD Ordinary corporate operating losses can be carried back (**carry-back**) to each of the preceding 3 years and carried forward (**carry-forward**) for the next 15 years to offset taxable income in those years. For example, an operating loss reported in 1996 could be carried back and used to reduce taxable income in 1993, 1994, and 1995, and carried forward, if necessary, and used in 1997, 1998, and so on, to the year 2011 to offset future taxable income. The loss is applied first to the earliest year, then to the next earliest year, and so on, until losses have been used up or the 15-year carry-forward limit has been reached.

> **TAX LOSS CARRY-BACK AND CARRY-FORWARD**
> Losses that can be carried backward or forward in time to offset taxable income in a given year.

To illustrate, partial income statements for Apex Corporation are given in Table 2-2. In 1993, 1994, and 1995, Apex produced positive taxable income amounts, and it paid the appropriate taxes each of these years, which totaled $224 million. However, in 1996, Apex experienced a taxable loss equal to $700 million. The carry-back feature allows Apex to write off this taxable loss against positive taxable income beginning in 1993. Note that the loss is large enough that the *adjusted* taxable incomes for 1993–1995 equal zero. This permits Apex to recover the amount of taxes paid in those years. Thus, Apex would amend the tax forms filed in 1993–1995, and it would receive a tax refund equal to $224 million. After adjusting the previous three years' tax forms, Apex still would have $60 million of unrecovered loss from 1996 to carry forward through the year 2010, if necessary. The purpose of permitting firms to treat losses like this is to avoid penalizing corporations whose incomes fluctuate substantially from year to year.

ACCUMULATED EARNINGS TAX Corporations could refrain from paying dividends to permit their stockholders to avoid personal income taxes on dividends. To prevent this, the Tax Code contains an **improper accumulation** provision which states that earnings accumulated by a corporation are subject to penalty rates *if the purpose of the accumulation is to enable stockholders to avoid personal income taxes.* A cumulative total of $250,000 (the balance sheet item "retained earnings") is by law exempted from the accumulated earnings tax for most corporations. This is a benefit primarily to small corporations.

> **IMPROPER ACCUMULATION**
> Retention of earnings by a business for the purpose of enabling stockholders to avoid personal income taxes.

The improper accumulation penalty applies only if the retained earnings in excess of $250,000 are shown to be *unnecessary to meet the reasonable needs of the business.* A great many companies do indeed have legitimate reasons for retaining more than $250,000 of earnings. For example, earnings might be retained and used to pay off debt, to finance growth, or to provide the corporation with a cushion against possible cash drains caused by losses. How much a firm should properly accumulate for uncertain contingencies is a matter of judgment.

TABLE 2-2

Apex Corporation: Partial Income Statements for 1993–1996 (millions of dollars)

Original Statement	1993	1994	1995	1996
Taxable income	$200	$260	$180	$(700)
Taxes (35%)	(70)	(91)	(63)	245
Net income	$130	$169	$117	$(455)

Adjusted Statement	1993	1994	1995	Total Effect of Carry-back
Original taxable income	$200	$260	$180	
Carry-back credit	(200)	(260)	(180)	$640
Adjusted taxable income	0	0	0	
Taxes (35%)	0	0	0	
Adjusted net income	$ 0	$ 0	$ 0	
Taxes originally paid	70	91	63	$224

Tax refund = $224

Loss available to carry forward in 1997–2011 = $700 − $640 = $60

CONSOLIDATED CORPORATE TAX RETURNS If a corporation owns 80 percent or more of another corporation's stock, it can aggregate income and file one consolidated tax return; thus, the losses of one company can be used to offset the profits of another. (Similarly, one division's losses can be used to offset another division's profits.) No business ever wants to incur losses (you can go broke losing $1 to save 34¢ in taxes), but tax offsets do make it more feasible for large, multidivisional corporations to undertake risky new ventures or ventures that will suffer losses during a developmental period and profits thereafter.

Taxation of Small Businesses: S Corporations

S CORPORATION
A small corporation which, under Subchapter S of the Internal Revenue Code, elects to be taxed as a proprietorship or a partnership yet retains limited liability and other benefits of the corporate form of organization.

The Internal Revenue Code provides that small businesses (less than 35 stockholders) which meet certain restrictions as spelled out in the code can be set up as corporations and thus receive the benefits of the corporate form of organization—especially limited liability—yet still be taxed as proprietorships or partnerships rather than as corporations. These corporations are called **S corporations.** For a corporation that elects S corporation status for tax purposes, all the income of the business is reported as personal income by the owners, and it is taxed at the rates that apply to individuals. This would be preferred by owners of small corporations in which all or most of the income earned each year is distributed as dividends because the income would be taxed only once at the individual level.

Self-Test Questions

Explain what is meant by the statement: "Our tax rates are progressive."

Are tax rates progressive for all income ranges?

Explain the difference between marginal tax rates and average tax rates.

What are capital gains and losses, and how are they differentiated from ordinary income?

How does the federal income tax system tax corporate dividends received by a corporation and those received by an individual? Why is this distinction made?

Briefly explain how tax loss carry-back and carry-forward procedures work.

Depreciation

Depreciation plays an important role in income tax calculations. Congress specifies, in the Tax Code, the life over which assets can be depreciated for tax purposes and the methods of depreciation that can be used. Because these factors have a major influence on the amount of depreciation a firm can take in a given year, and thus on the firm's taxable income, depreciation has an important effect on taxes paid and cash flows from operations. We will discuss how depreciation is calculated, and how it affects income and cash flows, when we discuss the subject of capital budgeting in Chapters 13 and 14.

Summary

In this chapter we discussed the nature of financial markets, the types of institutions that operate in these markets, how interest rates are determined, some of the ways in which interest rates affect business decisions, and the Federal income tax system. The following key concepts were covered.

- There are many different types of **financial markets.** Each market serves a different region or deals with a different type of security.
- Transfers of capital between borrowers and savers take place (1) by **direct transfers** of money and securities; (2) by transfers through **investment bankers,** who act as middlemen; and (3) by transfers through **financial intermediaries,** which create new securities.
- The **stock market** is an especially important market because this is where stock prices (which are used to "grade" managers' performances) are established.
- There are two basic types of stock markets—the **organized exchanges** and the **over-the-counter market.**
- Capital is allocated through the price system—a price must be paid to "rent" money. Lenders charge **interest** on funds they lend, while equity investors receive **dividends** and **capital gains** in return for letting firms use their money.
- Four fundamental factors affect the cost of money: (1) **production opportunities,** (2) **time preferences for consumption,** (3) **risk,** and (4) **inflation.**
- The **risk-free rate of interest, k_{RF},** is defined as the real risk-free rate, k^*, plus an inflation premium (IP): $k_{RF} = k^* + IP$.
- The **nominal (or quoted) interest rate** on a debt security, k, is composed of the real risk-free rate, k^*, plus premiums that reflect inflation (IP), default risk (DRP), liquidity (LP), and maturity risk (MRP):

$$k = k^* + IP + DRP + LP + MRP.$$

- If the **real risk-free rate of interest and the various premiums were constant over time,** interest rates in the economy would be stable. However, both the real rate and the premiums—especially the premium for expected inflation—**do change over time, causing market interest rates to change.** Also, Federal Reserve intervention to increase or decrease the money supply, as well as international currency flows, lead to fluctuations in interest rates.
- The relationship between the yields on securities and the securities' maturities is known as the **term structure of interest rates,** and the **yield curve** is a graph of this relationship.
- The yield curve is normally **upward sloping**—this is called a **normal yield curve**—but the curve can **slope downward** (an **inverted yield curve**) if the demand for short-term funds is relatively strong or if the rate of inflation is expected to decline.
- **Interest rate levels have a profound effect on stock prices.** Higher interest rates (1) slow down the economy, (2) increase interest expenses and thus lower corporate profits, and (3) cause investors to sell stocks and transfer funds to the bond market. Each of these factors tends to depress stock prices.
- The value of any asset depends on the stream of **after-tax cash flows** it produces. Tax rates and other aspects of our tax system are changed by Congress every year or so.
- In the United States, income tax rates are **progressive**—the higher one's income, the larger the percentage paid in taxes, up to a point.
- Assets such as stocks, bonds, and real estate are defined as **capital assets.** If a capital asset is sold for more than the purchase price, the profit is called a **capital gain.** If the capital asset is sold for a loss, it is called a **capital loss.**
- **Interest income** received by a corporation is taxed as ordinary income; however, **70 percent of the dividends received by one corporation from another is excluded from taxable income.**
- Because **interest paid by a corporation is a deductible expense** while dividends are not, our tax system favors debt financing over equity financing.
- Ordinary corporate operating losses can be **carried back** to each of the preceding 3 years and **carried forward** for the next 15 years to offset taxable income in those years.
- **S corporations** are small businesses that have the limited-liability benefits of the corporate form of organization yet obtain the benefits of being taxed as a partnership or a proprietorship.

Questions

2-1 What are financial intermediaries, and what economic functions do they perform?

2-2 Suppose interest rates on residential mortgages of equal risk were 8 percent in California and 10 percent in New York. Could this differential persist? What forces might tend to equalize rates? Would differentials in borrowing costs for businesses of equal risk located in California and New York be more or less likely to exist than differentials in residential mortgage rates? Would differentials in the cost of money for New York and California firms be more likely to exist if the firms being compared were very large or if they were very small?

2-3 What would happen to the standard of living in the United States if people lost faith in the safety of our financial institutions? Why?

2-4   How does a cost-efficient capital market help to reduce the prices of goods and services?

2-5   Which fluctuate more, long-term or short-term interest rates? Why?

2-6   Suppose you believe that the economy is just entering a recession. Your firm must raise capital immediately, and debt will be used. Should you borrow on a long-term or a short-term basis? Why?

2-7   Suppose a new process was developed which could be used to make oil out of seawater. The equipment required is quite expensive but it would, in time, lead to very low prices for gasoline, electricity, and other types of energy. What effect would this have on interest rates?

2-8   Suppose a new and much more liberal Congress and administration were elected, and their first order of business was to take away the independence of the Federal Reserve System and to force the Fed to greatly expand the money supply. What effect would this have
   a. On the level and slope of the yield curve immediately after the announcement?
   b. On the level and slope of the yield curve that would exist two or three years in the future?

2-9   It is a fact that the federal government (1) encouraged the development of the savings and loan industry; (2) virtually forced the industry to make long-term, fixed-interest-rate mortgages; and (3) forced the savings and loans to obtain most of their capital as deposits that were withdrawable on demand.
   a. Would the savings and loans be better off in a world with a "normal" or an inverted yield curve?
   b. Would the savings and loan industry be better off if the individual institutions sold their mortgages to federal agencies and then collected servicing fees or if the institutions held the mortgages that they originated?

2-10   Suppose interest rates on Treasury bonds rose from 7 percent to 14 percent as a result of higher interest rates in Europe. What effect would this have on the price of an average company's common stock?

2-11   Suppose you owned 100 shares of General Motors stock, and the company earned $6 per share during the last reporting period. Suppose further that GM could either pay all its earnings out as dividends (in which case you would receive $600) or retain the earnings in the business, buy more assets, and cause the price of the stock to go up by $6 per share (in which case the value of your stock would rise by $600).
   a. How would the tax laws influence what you, as a typical stockholder, would want the company to do?
   b. Would your choice be influenced by how much other income you had? Why might the desires of a 35-year-old doctor differ with respect to corporate dividend policy from those of a pension fund manager or a retiree living on a small income?
   c. How might the corporation's decision with regard to the dividends it pays influence the price of its stock?

2-12   What does *double taxation of corporate income* mean?

2-13   If you were starting a business, what tax considerations might cause you to prefer to set it up as a proprietorship or a partnership rather than as a corporation? Would you consider the average or the marginal tax rate more relevant?

2-14   Explain how the federal income tax structure affects the choice of financing (use of debt versus equity) of U.S. business firms.

Self-Test Problems

(Solutions Appear in Appendix B)

Key Terms

ST-1 Define each of the following terms:
 a. money market; capital market
 b. primary market; secondary market
 c. investment banker; financial service corporation
 d. financial intermediary
 e. mutual fund; money market fund
 f. organized security exchanges; over-the-counter market
 g. production opportunities; time preferences for consumption
 h. real risk-free rate of interest, k*; nominal risk-free rate of interest, k_{RF}
 i. inflation premium (IP)
 j. default risk premium (DRP)
 k. liquidity; liquidity premium (LP)
 l. interest rate risk; maturity risk premium (MRP)
 m. reinvestment rate risk
 n. term structure of interest rates; yield curve
 o. "normal" yield curve; inverted ("abnormal") yield curve
 p. market segmentation theory; liquidity preference theory; expectations theory
 q. progressive tax
 r. marginal and average tax rates
 s. capital gain or loss
 t. tax loss carry-back and carry-forward
 u. S corporation

Inflation rates

ST-2 Assume that it is now January 1, 1996. The rate of inflation is expected to be 6 percent throughout 1996. However, increased government deficits and renewed vigor in the economy are then expected to push inflation rates higher. Investors expect the inflation rate to be 7 percent in 1997, 8 percent in 1998, and 9 percent in 1999. The real risk-free rate, k*, currently is 3 percent. Assume that no maturity risk premiums are required on bonds with 5 years or less to maturity. The current interest rate on 5-year T-bonds is 11 percent.
 a. What is the average expected inflation rate over the next 4 years?
 b. What should be the prevailing interest rate on 4-year T-bonds?
 c. What is the implied expected inflation rate in 2000, or Year 5, given that bonds which mature in that year yield 11 percent?

Form of business and taxes

ST-3 John Thompson is planning to start a new business, JT Enterprises, and he must decide whether to incorporate or do business as a sole proprietorship. Under either form, Thompson will initially own 100 percent of the firm, and tax considerations are important to him. He plans to finance the firm's expected growth by drawing a salary just sufficient for his family living expenses, which he estimates will be about $40,000, and by retaining all other income in the business. Assume that as a married man with one child, Thompson has income tax exemptions of 3 × $2,450 = $7,350 and he estimates that his itemized deductions for each of the three years will be $9,000. He expects JT Enterprises to grow and to earn income of $60,000 in 1996, $90,000 in 1997, and $110,000 in 1998. Which form of business organization will allow Thompson to pay the lowest taxes (and retain the most income) during the period from 1996 to 1998? Assume that the tax rates given in the appendix are applicable for all future years. (Social security taxes would also have to be paid, but ignore them.)

Problems

Note: By the time this book is published, Congress may have changed rates and/or other provisions of current tax law—as noted in the chapter, such changes occur fairly often. Work all problems on the assumption that the information in the chapter is still current.

Yield curves   **2-1**   Suppose you and most other investors expect the rate of inflation to be 7 percent next year, to fall to 5 percent during the following year, and then to remain at a rate of 3 percent thereafter. Assume that the real risk-free rate, k*, is 2 percent and that maturity risk premiums on Treasury securities rise from zero on very short-term bonds (those that mature in a few days) by 0.2 percentage points for each year to maturity, up to a limit of 1.0 percentage point on 5-year or longer-term T-bonds.

    a. Calculate the interest rate on 1-, 2-, 3-, 4-, 5-, 10-, and 20-year Treasury securities, and plot the yield curve.

    b. Now suppose Exxon, a AAA-rated company, had bonds with the same maturities as the Treasury bonds. As an approximation, plot an Exxon yield curve on the same graph with the Treasury bond yield curve. (Hint: Think about the default risk premium on Exxon's long-term versus its short-term bonds.)

    c. Now plot the approximate yield curve of Long Island Lighting Company, a risky nuclear utility.

Yield curve   **2-2**   The following yields on U.S. Treasury securities were taken from The *Wall Street Journal* of January 18, 1995:

Term	Rate
6 months	6.5%
1 year	7.0
2 years	7.4
3 years	7.6
4 years	7.7
5 years	7.7
10 years	7.9
20 years	7.9
30 years	8.0

Plot a yield curve based on these data. Discuss how each term structure theory can explain the shape of the yield curve you plot.

Inflation and interest rates   **2-3**   It is January 1, 1995. Inflation currently is about 3 percent; throughout 1994, the Fed took action to maintain inflation at this level. However, the economy is in a recovery, and reports indicate that inflation is expected to increase during the next 5 years. Assume that *at the beginning* of 1995, the rate of inflation *expected* for 1995 is 5 percent; for 1996, it is *expected* to be 6 percent; for 1997, it is *expected* to be 8 percent; and, for 1998 and every year thereafter, it is *expected* to settle at 4 percent.

    a. What was the average expected inflation rate over the 5-year period 1995–1999? (Use the arithmetic average.)

    b. What average nominal interest rate, over the 5-year period, would be expected to produce a 2 percent real risk-free rate of return on 5-year Treasury securities?

    c. Assuming a real risk-free rate of 2 percent and a maturity risk premium which starts at 0.1 percent and increases by 0.1 percent *each year,* estimate the interest rate in January 1995 on bonds that mature in 1, 2, 5, 10, and 20 years, and draw a yield curve based on these data.

    d. Describe the general economic conditions that could be expected to produce an upward-sloping yield curve.

e. If the consensus among investors in early 1995 had been that the expected rate of inflation for every future year was 6 percent (that is, $I_t = I_{t+1} = 6\%$ for $t = 1$ to ∞), what do you think the yield curve would have looked like? Consider all the factors that are likely to affect the curve. Does your answer here make you question the yield curve you drew in part c?

Loss carry-back, carry-forward   **2-4**   The Angell Company has made $150,000 before taxes during each of the past 15 years, and it expects to make $150,000 a year before taxes in the future. However, in 1995 the firm incurred a loss of $650,000. The firm will claim a tax credit at the time it files its 1995 income tax return, and it will receive a check from the U.S. Treasury. Show how it calculates this credit, and then indicate the firm's tax liability for each of the next 5 years. Assume a 30 percent tax rate on all income to ease the calculations.

Loss carry-back, carry-forward   **2-5**   The projected taxable income of the Glasgo Corporation, formed in 1996, is indicated in the table below. (Losses are shown in parentheses.) What is the corporate tax liability for each year? Use tax rates as shown in the appendix.

Year	Taxable Income
1996	$ (95,000)
1997	70,000
1998	55,000
1999	80,000
2000	(150,000)

Form of organization   **2-6**   Kate Brown has operated her small repair shop as a sole proprietorship for several years, but projected changes in her business's income have led her to consider incorporating.

Brown is married and has two children. Her family's only income, an annual salary of $45,000, is from operating the business. (The business actually earns more than $45,000, but Kate reinvests the additional earnings in the business.) She itemizes deductions, and she is able to deduct $6,000. These deductions, combined with her four personal exemptions for $4 \times \$2,450 = \$9,800$, give her a taxable income of $45,000 − $6,000 − $9,800. (Assume the personal exemption remains at $2,450.) Of course, her actual taxable income, if she does not incorporate, would be higher by the amount of reinvested income. Brown estimates that her business earnings before salary and taxes for the period 1996 to 1998 will be:

Year	Earnings before Salary and Taxes
1996	$65,000
1997	85,000
1998	95,000

a. What would her total taxes (corporate plus personal) be in each year under
  (1) A non-S corporate form of organization? (1996 tax = $7,380)
  (2) A proprietorship? (1996 tax = $8,836)
b. Should Brown incorporate? Discuss.

Personal taxes   **2-7**   Margaret Considine has this situation for the year 1995: salary of $60,000; dividend income of $10,000; interest on IBM bonds of $5,000; interest on state of Florida municipal bonds of $10,000; proceeds of $22,000 from the sale of IBM stock purchased in 1984 at a cost of $9,000; and proceeds of $22,000 from the November 1995 sale of IBM stock purchased in October 1995 at a cost of $21,000. Margaret gets one exemption ($2,450), and she has allowable itemized deductions of $5,000;

Forecasting, Planning, and Control

CHAPTER 3

Analysis of Financial Statements

A MANAGERIAL PERSPECTIVE

U.S. firms must make "full and fair" disclosure of their operations by publishing various financial statements and other reports required by the Securities and Exchange Commission, the Financial Accounting Standards Board, and the American Institute of Certified Public Accountants. Unfortunately, these groups often do not consult with each other concerning the disclosure requirements. As a result, the average size of the annual reports sent to stockholders continues to increase each year. In fact, according to Ernst & Young, a large national accounting firm, from 1972 to 1992, the average size of an annual report of a large, national company has increased from 35 to 65 pages, the number of pages of footnotes to the financial statements has increased from 4 to 17, and the amount of space management uses for its discussions has grown from 3 to 12 pages—if this growth continues, in the year 2012 annual reports will be at least 120 pages in length.

In most cases, annual reports are used to convey more than financial results; some firms use the annual report as an opportunity to showcase top management and sell the future of the company, without regard to the financial information. So, often, work on the report begins as much as six months before its publication, and most firms hire professional designers and writers to ensure that the final product looks sharp and reads well. Some firms pride themselves in the unique packaging designs used. For example, since 1977, McCormick & Company has used one of the spices and seasonings it produces to scent the paper on which its annual report is printed—the scent for 1993 was Chinese Five Spice. Also in 1993, Eskimo Pie Corporation fashioned its annual report to resemble an ice cream bar, complete with a stick.

In most instances, the puffery contained in annual reports detracts from the primary purpose to provide objective financial information about the firm. For that reason, Wall Street analysts and other sophisticated investors prefer more straightforward financial disclosure documents, such as 10-Ks, which contain more detailed and unadorned information and which must by law be filed with the Securities and Exchange Commission.

Continued

Of course, there are companies that use the annual report as originally intended—to communicate the financial position of the firm. One such firm is General Motors, whose 1992 "lean and mean" annual report was a drastic departure from previous publications. In fact, instead of a color photograph of a car, the cover of the report contained a statement from GM's CEO concerning the dramatic changes that had been implemented. Similarly, when constructing the annual report for Berkshire Hathaway, legendary chairman Warren Buffett says, "I assume I have a very intelligent partner who has been away for a year and needs to be filled in on all that's happened." Consequently, in his letters he often admits mistakes and emphasizes the negative. Buffett also uses his letters to educate his shareholders and to help them interpret the data presented in the rest of the report. Berkshire Hathaway's annual reports contain no photographs, colored ink, bar charts, or graphs, freeing readers to focus on the company's financial statements and Buffett's interpretation of them. Some CEOs might contend that such a barebones approach is too dull for the average stockholder and, further, that some readers may actually be intimidated by the information overload.

More and more, firms are recognizing that the "slick" annual report has (1) lost its credibility with serious seekers of financial information, and (2) become increasingly more expensive to produce. In 1993, Johnson & Johnson saved more than $400,000 by decreasing the size of its annual report by 18 pages and mailing it using third class postage; Pfizer's report was trimmed by 10 pages; and U.S. Surgical decided to eliminate its annual report by including the required information with the annual proxy statements sent to shareholders.

As you read this chapter, think about the kinds of information corporations provide their stockholders. Do the basic financial statements provide adequate data for investment decisions? What other information might be helpful? Also, consider the pros and cons of Chairman Buffett's decision to include frank, and frequently self-critical, letters in his company's annual reports. Would you suggest that other companies follow suit?

Financial statement analysis involves a comparison of a firm's performance with that of other firms in the same line of business, which often is identified by the firm's industry classification. Generally speaking, the analysis is used to determine the firm's financial position in order to identify its current strengths and weaknesses and to suggest actions that might enable the firm to take advantage of its strengths and correct its weaknesses.

Financial statement analysis is important not only for the firm's managers but also for the firm's investors and creditors. Internally, financial managers use the information provided by financial analysis to help make financing and investment decisions to maximize the firm's value. Externally, stockholders and creditors use financial statement analysis to evaluate the attractiveness of the firm as an investment by examining its ability to meet its current and expected financial obligations.

In this chapter, we discuss how to evaluate a firm's current position. Then, in the remaining chapters, we will examine the types of actions that a firm can take to improve its financial position and thus to increase the price of its stock.

For the most part, this chapter should be a review of what you learned in accounting. However, accounting focuses on how financial statements are made, whereas our focus is on how they are used by management to improve the firm's performance and by investors (either stockholders or creditors) to examine the firm's financial position when evaluating its attractiveness as an investment.

Financial Statements and Reports

ANNUAL REPORT
A report issued annually by a corporation to its stockholders. It contains basic financial statements as well as management's opinion of the past year's operations and the firm's prospects.

Of the various reports corporations issue to their stockholders, the **annual report** probably is the most important. Two types of information are given in this report. First, a verbal section, often presented as a letter from the chairman, describes the firm's operating results during the past year and then discusses new developments that will affect future operations. Second, the annual report presents four basic financial statements—the *income statement,* the *balance sheet,* the *statement of retained earnings,* and the *statement of cash flows.* Together, these statements give an accounting picture of the firm's operations and financial position. Detailed data are provided for the two most recent years, along with historical summaries of key operating statistics for the past five or ten years.[1]

The quantitative and verbal information contained in the annual report are equally important. The financial statements report what actually has happened to the firm's financial position and to its earnings and dividends over the past few years, whereas the verbal statements attempt to explain why things turned out the way they did. For example, Table 3-1 shows that Unilate Textiles' earnings decreased by $1 million in 1995 to $62 million versus $63 million in 1994. In the annual report, management reported that the 1.6 percent earnings drop resulted from losses associated with a poor cotton crop and from increased costs due to a 3-month strike and a retooling of the factory. However, management then went on to paint a more optimistic picture for the future, stating that full operations had been resumed, that several unprofitable businesses had been eliminated, and that 1996 profits were expected to increase. Of course, an increase in profitability might not occur, and analysts should compare management's past statements with subsequent results to determine if management's optimism is justified. In any event, *the information contained in an annual report is used by investors to form expectations about future earnings and dividends.* Therefore, the annual report obviously is of great interest to investors.

For illustrative purposes, we will use data taken from Unilate Textiles, a manufacturer and distributor of a wide variety of textiles and clothing items. Formed in

---

[1]Firms also provide quarterly reports, but these are much less comprehensive than the annual reports. In addition, larger firms file even more detailed statements, giving breakdowns for each major division or subsidiary, with the Securities and Exchange Commission (SEC). These reports, called *10-K reports,* are made available to stockholders upon request to a company's corporate secretary. Finally, many larger firms also publish *statistical supplements,* which give financial statement data and key ratios going back 10 to 20 years.

1980 with the merger of three family-owned firms in North Carolina, Unilate has grown steadily and has earned a reputation for being one of the best firms in its industry.

The Income Statement

INCOME STATEMENT
A statement summarizing the firm's revenues and expenses over an accounting period, generally a quarter or a year.

The **income statement,** often referred to as the profit and loss statement, presents the results of business operations during a specified period of time, such as a quarter or a year. The statement summarizes the revenues generated and the expenses incurred by the firm during the accounting period. Table 3-1 gives the 1994 and 1995 income statements for Unilate Textiles. Net sales are shown at the top of each statement, after which various costs, including income taxes, are subtracted to obtain the net income available to common stockholders. A report on earnings and dividends per share is given at the bottom of the statement. In managerial finance, earnings per share (EPS) is called "the bottom line," denoting that, of all the items on the income statement, EPS is the most important. Unilate earned $2.48 per share in 1995, down from $2.52 in 1994, but it still raised the per share dividend from $1.08 to $1.17.

It is important to remember that not all the amounts shown on the income statement represent cash flows. Recall from what you learned in accounting that, for most corporations, the income statement is generated using the accrual method of accounting. This means revenues are recognized when they are

---

TABLE 3-1

Unilate Textiles: Comparative Income Statements for Years Ending December 31
(millions of dollars, except per share data)

	1995	1994
Net sales	$ 1,500	$ 1,435
Cost of goods sold	(1,220)[a]	(1,175)
Gross profit	$ 280	$ 260
Fixed operating expenses except depreciation	(90)	(85)
Depreciation	(50)	(40)
Earnings before interest and taxes (EBIT)	$ 140	$ 135
Interest	(36)	(30)
Earnings before taxes (EBT)	$ 104	$ 105
Taxes (40%)	(42)	(42)
Net income	$ 62	$ 63
Preferred dividends	(0)	(0)
Earnings available to common shareholders	$ 62	$ 63
Common dividends	(29)	(27)
Addition to retained earnings	$ 33	$ 36
Per-share data:		
Common stock price	$23.00	$24.00
Earnings per share (EPS)[b]	$ 2.48	$ 2.52
Dividends per share (DPS)[b]	$ 1.17	$ 1.08

[a]Here, and throughout the text, parentheses are used to denote negative numbers, and all numbers are rounded.

[b]Unilate has 25,000,000 shares of common stock outstanding.

earned, not when the cash is received, and expenses are realized when they are incurred, not when the cash is paid. This point will be addressed further later in the chapter.

The Balance Sheet

BALANCE SHEET
A statement of the firm's financial position at a specific point in time.

The **balance sheet** shows the financial position of a firm at a specific point in time. This financial statement indicates the investments made by the firm in the form of assets and the means by which the assets were financed—whether the funds were raised by borrowing (liabilities) or by selling ownership shares (equity). Unilate's year-end 1994 and 1995 balance sheets are given in Table 3-2. The top portion (normally referred to as the left-hand side) of the balance sheet shows that on December 31, 1995, Unilate's assets totaled $850 million, while the bottom portion (normally referred to as the right-hand side) shows the liabilities and equity, or the claims against these assets. The assets are listed in order of their "liquidity," or the length of time it typically takes to convert them to cash. The claims are listed in the order in which they must be paid: Accounts payable generally must be paid within 30–60 days, accruals are payable within 60–90 days, and so on, down to the stockholders' equity accounts, which represent ownership and need never be "paid off."

TABLE 3-2				

Unilate Textiles: December 31 Comparative Balance Sheets (millions of dollars)

		1995		1994
Assets				
Cash and marketable securities		$ 20		$ 40
Accounts receivable		180		160
Inventories		270		200
Total Current Assets		470		400
Gross plant and equipment	680		600	
Less: Accumulated depreciation	300		250	
Net plant and equipment		380		350
Total Assets		$850		$750
Liabilities and Equity				
Accounts payable		$ 30		$ 15
Accruals		60		55
Notes payable		40		35
Total Current Liabilities		130		105
Long-term bonds		297		255
Total Liabilities		427		360
Preferred stock		0		0
Common stock (25,000,000)		130		130
Retained earnings		293		260
Owners' equity		423		390
Total Liabilities and Equity		$850		$750

Some additional points about the balance sheet are worth noting:

1. **Cash versus other assets.** Although the assets are all stated in terms of dollars, only cash represents actual money. Receivables are bills others owe Unilate; inventories show the dollars the company has invested in raw materials, work-in-process, and finished goods available for sale; and net fixed assets reflect the amount of money Unilate paid for its plant and equipment when it acquired those assets less the amount that has been written off (depreciated) since the acquisition of those assets. Unilate can write checks at present for a total of $20 million (versus current liabilities of $130 million due within a year). The noncash assets should produce cash over time, but they do not represent cash in hand, and the amount of cash they would bring if they were sold today could be higher or lower than the values at which they are carried on the books (their book values).

2. **Liabilities versus stockholders' equity.** The claims against assets are of two types—liabilities (or money the company owes) and the stockholders' ownership position.[2] The balance sheet must *balance,* so the **common stockholders' equity, or net worth,** is a residual that represents the amount stockholders would receive if all the firm's assets could be sold at their book values and all the liabilities could be paid at their book values. Unilate's 1995 net worth is:

$$\text{Assets} \quad - \quad \text{Liabilities} \quad = \quad \text{Stockholders' equity}$$

$$\$850 \text{ million} \quad - \quad \$427 \text{ million} \quad = \quad \$423 \text{ million}$$

Suppose assets decline in value—for example, suppose some of the accounts receivable are written off as bad debts. If liabilities remain constant, the value of the stockholders' equity must decline. Therefore, the risk of asset value fluctuations is borne by the stockholders. Note, however, that if asset values rise (perhaps because of inflation), these benefits will accrue exclusively to the stockholders. The change in the firm's net worth is reflected by changes in the retained earnings account; if bad debts are written off on the asset (left-hand) side of the balance sheet, the retained earnings balance is reduced on the liabilities and equity (right-hand) side.

3. **Preferred versus common stock.** Chapter 20 includes a detailed discussion of preferred stock and its use as a source of financing. As we will see, preferred stock is a hybrid, or a cross between common stock and debt. In the event of bankruptcy, the payoff to preferred stock ranks below debt but above common stock. Common stockholders, who are the "true" owners of the firm, often view preferred stock as another form of debt because, like debt, the payment to preferred stockholders (dividend) is fixed, so preferred stockholders do not benefit if the company's earnings grow. Also, most financial analysts combine

COMMON STOCKHOLDERS' EQUITY (NET WORTH)
The capital supplied by common stockholders— capital stock, paid-in capital, retained earnings, and, occasionally, certain reserves.

---

[2]One could divide liabilities into (1) debts owed to someone and (2) other items, such as deferred taxes, reserves, and so on. Because we do not make this distinction, the terms *debt* and *liabilities* are used synonymously. It should be noted that firms occasionally set up reserves for certain contingencies, such as the potential costs involved in a lawsuit currently in the courts. These reserves represent an accounting transfer from retained earnings to the reserve account. If the company wins the suit, retained earnings will be credited, and the reserve will be eliminated. If it loses, a loss will be recorded, cash will be reduced, and the reserve will be eliminated.

preferred stock with debt when evaluating the financial position of a firm, because, even though it is not a liability, the preferred dividend is considered a fixed obligation of the firm. Therefore, when the term "equity" is used in finance, we generally mean "common equity." Like most firms, Unilate Textiles does not use preferred stock financing.

4. **Breakdown of the common equity account.** A detailed discussion of the common equity accounts is given in Chapter 18. At this point, it is important to note that often the common equity section is divided into three accounts—common stock, paid-in capital, and retained earnings. The **retained earnings** account is built up over time as the firm "saves," or reinvests, a part of its earnings rather than paying everything out as dividends. The other two common equity accounts arise from the issuance of stock to raise capital.

   RETAINED EARNINGS
   That portion of the firm's earnings that has been saved rather than paid out as dividends.

   The breakdown of the common equity accounts shows whether the company actually earned the funds reported in its equity accounts or whether the funds came mainly from selling stock. This information is important both to creditors and to stockholders. For instance, a potential creditor would be interested in the amount of money the owners put up, while stockholders would want to know the form in which the money was put up. In the remainder of this chapter, we generally aggregate the three common equity accounts and call this sum common equity or net worth.

5. **Accounting alternatives.** Not every firm uses the same method to determine the account balances shown on the balance sheet. For instance, Unilate uses the FIFO (first-in, first-out) method to determine the inventory value shown on its balance sheet. It could have used the LIFO (last-in, first-out) method. During a period of rising prices, compared to LIFO, FIFO will produce a higher balance sheet inventory value but a lower cost of goods sold, thus a higher net income.

   In some cases, a company uses one accounting method to construct financial statements provided to stockholders and another accounting method for tax purposes, internal reports, and so on. For example, a company will use the most accelerated method permissible to calculate depreciation for tax purposes, because accelerated methods lower the taxable income. At the same time, the company might use straight line depreciation for constructing financial statements reported to stockholders, because a higher net income results. There is nothing illegal or unethical with this practice, but, when evaluating firms, users of financial statements must be aware that more than one accounting alternative is available for constructing financial statements.

6. **The time dimension.** The balance sheet can be thought of as a snapshot of the firm's financial position *at a point in time*—for example, on December 31, 1994. Thus, on December 31, 1994, Unilate had $40 million of cash and marketable securities, but this account had been reduced to $20 million by the end of 1995. The income statement, on the other hand, reports on operations *over a period of time*—for example, during the calendar year 1995. Unilate's 1995 sales amounted to $1.5 billion, and its net income available to common stockholders was $62 million. The balance sheet changes every day as inventories are increased or decreased, as fixed assets are added or retired, as bank loans are increased or decreased, and so on. Companies whose businesses are seasonal have especially large changes in their balance sheets during the year. For example, most retailers have large inventories just before Christmas but low inventories and high accounts receivable just after Christmas. Therefore,

firms' balance sheets will change over the year, depending on the date on which the statement is constructed. Unilate has observed balance sheet changes during the year that are similar to those experienced by retailers.

Statement of Retained Earnings

Changes in the common equity accounts between balance sheet dates are reported in the **statement of retained earnings.** Unilate's statement is shown in Table 3-3. The company earned $62 million during 1995, it paid out $29 million in common dividends, and it retained $33 million for reinvestment in the business. Thus, the balance sheet item "retained earnings" increased from $260 million at the end of 1994 to $293 million reported at the end of 1995. Note that the balance sheet account "retained earnings" represents a claim *against assets,* not assets per se. Further, firms retain earnings primarily to expand the business, and this means investing in plant and equipment, in inventories, and so on, *not* necessarily in a bank account. Changes in retained earnings represent the recognition that income generated by the firm during the accounting period has been reinvested in assets rather than paid out as dividends to stockholders. In other words, changes in retained earnings result because common stockholders allow the firm to reinvest in itself funds that otherwise could be distributed as dividends. Thus, *retained earnings as reported on the balance sheet do not represent cash and are not "available" for the payment of dividends or anything else.*[3]

Accounting Income versus Cash Flow

When you studied the construction of income statements in accounting, the emphasis probably was on determining the net income of the firm. In finance, however, we focus on *cash flows.* The value of an asset (or a whole firm) is determined by the cash flows it generates. The firm's net income is important, but cash flows are even more important, because cash is needed to continue normal business operations such as the payment of financial obligations, the purchase of assets, and the payment of dividends.

As we discussed in Chapter 1, the goal of the firm should be to maximize the price of its stock. Because the value of any asset, including a share of stock, depends on the cash flows produced by the asset, managers should strive to maximize cash flows available to investors over the long run. A business's **cash flows** include the cash receipts and the cash disbursements. The income statement contains revenues and expenses, some of which are cash items and some of which are noncash items. Generally the largest noncash item included on the income statement is depreciation, which is an operating cost. We need to understand the role of depreciation for the recognition of income, as well as the impact depreciation has on cash flows.

---

[3]The amount reported in the retained earnings account is *not* an indication of the amount of cash the firm has. Cash (as of the balance sheet date) is found in the cash account—an asset account. A positive number in the retained earnings account indicates only that in the past, according to generally accepted accounting principles, the firm has earned an income, but its dividends have been less than its reported income. Even though a company reports record earnings and shows an increase in the retained earnings account, it still may be short of cash.

The same situation holds for individuals. You might own a new BMW (no loan), lots of clothes, and an expensive stereo, and, hence, have a high net worth, but if you had only 23 cents in your pocket plus $5 in your checking account, you would still be short of cash.

TABLE 3-3

Unilate Textiles: Statement of Retained Earnings for the Year Ending December 31, 1995 (millions of dollars)

Balance of retained earnings, December 31, 1994	$260
Add: 1995 net income	62
Less: 1995 dividends to stockholders	(29)
Balance of retained earnings, December 31, 1995	$293

Depreciation results because we want to match revenues and expenses, not because we want to match cash inflows and cash outflows, to compute the income earned by the firm during a specific accounting period. When a firm purchases a long-term asset, it is intended to be used to produce revenues for multiple years in the future. The cash payment for the asset occurs on the date of purchase. But, because the productive capacity of the asset is not used up in the year of purchase, its full cost is not recognized as an expense in that year. Rather, the value of the asset is expensed away over its lifetime, because, as it is used to generate revenues, the value of the asset declines. Depreciation is the means by which the reduction in the asset's value, which is an operating cost, is matched with the revenues the asset helps to produce. For example, if a machine with a life of 5 years and a zero expected salvage value was purchased in 1994 for $100,000, the total $100,000 cost is not expensed in 1994; instead, it is charged against production over the machine's 5-year depreciable life. The annual depreciation charge is deducted from sales revenues, along with other operating costs such as labor and raw materials, to determine income. However, because funds were expended back in 1994, the depreciation charged against income in 1995 through 1999 is not a cash outlay, as are labor or raw materials charges. The bottom line is that *depreciation is a noncash charge used to compute net income, so, if net income is used to obtain an estimate of the net cash flow from operations, the amount of depreciation must be added back to the income figure.*

To see how depreciation affects cash flows, consider the following simplified income statement (Column 1) and cash flow statement (Column 2). Here we assume that all sales revenues were received in cash during the year and that all costs except depreciation were paid in cash during the year. Cash flows are seen to equal net income plus depreciation:

	Income Statement (1)		Cash Flows (2)	
Sales revenues		$750		$750
Cost, except depreciation	(525)		(525)	
Depreciation (DEP)	(75)		—	
Total operating costs		(600)		(525) (Cash costs)
Earnings before taxes		$150		$225 (Pre-tax cash flow)
Taxes (40%)		(60)		(60) (From Column 1)
Net income (NI)		$ 90		
Add back depreciation		75		
Net cash flow = NI + DEP		$165		$165

INDUSTRY PRACTICE

The Accuracy of Financial Statements

It is not unusual for companies to restate their financial statements because small accounting irregularities are discovered after the statements are published. In most cases, the irregularities are immaterial, and would be considered "honest mistakes." Sometimes, however, firms use accounting methods that are considered inappropriate in order to inflate operating results.

In 1994, both California Micro Devices Corporation, producer of thin-film electronic chips, and PerSeptive Biosystems, maker of biotechnology equipment, restated their financial statements to correct accounting errors. California Micro Devices extended its quarterly accounting periods beyond the ending dates to inflate the results reported for each period. This practice, in combination with other actions, produced a year-end earnings figure that was inflated by more than $20 million—the reported net income was $5 million, when it really should have been a net loss of between $15 million and $20 million. Similarly, PerSeptive Biosystems inflated its sales by using very liberal sales terms, by allowing contingent purchases, and by recording instruments loaned to customers as sales. Prior to the restatement, PerSeptive reported a net loss of $5.6 million; after the restatement, the loss was $34 million.

The stocks of both companies suffered significant losses when the accounting irregularities were disclosed. At the beginning of 1995, the stock of California Micro Devices was selling for $3.875, significantly less than the record price of $23.625 reached in July, not long after the inflated financial statements were released. PerSeptive's stock price declined 36 percent to $4.50 when it was announced the financial statements were being restated; in total, mounting accounting problems caused the stock's value to decrease from its high of $32.25 during the previous year.

In addition to significant stock decreases, California Micro Devices and PerSeptive Biosystems probably will be sued by investors, creditors, or any other parties that might have been hurt financially because they relied on the information provided in the inflated financial statements.

SOURCES: "California Micro Finds Irregularities Inflating Earnings," *The Wall Street Journal,* January 10, 1995, p. B7; and "PerSeptive Restates Its Results for Much of Past 2 Fiscal Years," *The Wall Street Journal,* December 28, 1994, p. B5.

As we will see in Chapter 7, a stock's value is based on the cash flows that investors expect it to provide in the future. Although any individual investor could sell the stock and receive cash for it, the *cash flow* provided by the stock itself is the expected future dividend stream, and that expected dividend stream provides the fundamental basis for the stock's value.

ACCOUNTING PROFIT
A firm's net income as reported on its income statement.

Because dividends are paid in cash, a company's ability to pay dividends depends on its cash flows. Cash flows generally are related to **accounting profit,** which is simply net income reported on the income statement. Although companies with relatively high accounting profits generally have relatively high cash flows, the relationship is not precise. Therefore, investors are concerned with cash flow projections as well as profit projections.

Firms can be thought of as having two separate but related bases of value: *existing assets,* which provide profits and cash flows, and *growth opportunities,* which represent opportunities to make new investments that will increase future profits and cash flows. The ability to take advantage of growth opportunities often depends on the availability of the cash needed to buy new assets, and the cash flows from existing assets are often the primary source of the funds used to make profitable new investments. This is another reason why both investors and managers are concerned with cash flows as well as profits.

OPERATING CASH FLOWS
Those cash flows that arise
from normal operations;
the difference between
cash collections and
cash expenses.

For our purposes, it is useful to divide cash flows into two classes: (1) *operating cash flows* and (2) *other cash flows.* **Operating cash flows** are those that arise from normal operations, and they are, in essence, the difference between cash collections and cash expenses, including taxes paid. Other cash flows arise from borrowing, from the sale of fixed assets, or from the repurchase of common stock. Our focus here is on operating cash flows.

Operating cash flows can differ from accounting profits (or net income) for two primary reasons:

1. All the taxes reported on the income statement might not have to be paid during the current year, or, under certain circumstances, the actual cash payments for taxes might exceed the tax figure deducted from sales to calculate net income. The reasons for these tax cash flow differentials are discussed in detail in accounting courses.

2. Sales might be on credit, hence not represent cash, and some of the expenses (or costs) deducted from sales to determine profits might not be cash costs. Most important, depreciation is not a cash cost.

Thus, operating cash flows could be larger or smaller than accounting profits during any given year. The effect of the major noncash expense, depreciation, was discussed above, and we will consider the cash flow implications of credit sales as opposed to sales for cash in a later chapter.

The Cash Flow Cycle

As a company like Unilate goes about its business, it sells products. Sales lead (1) to a reduction of inventories, (2) to an increase in cash or accounts receivable, and (3) if the sales price exceeds the cost of the item sold, to a profit. So, when Unilate sells its products, both the income statement and the balance sheet are affected. It is critical that you understand (1) businesses deal with physical units like autos, computers, or aluminum, (2) physical transactions are translated into dollar terms through the accounting system, and (3) the purpose of financial analysis is to examine the accounting numbers in order to determine how efficiently the firm produces and sells physical goods and services and to evaluate the financial position of the firm.

Several factors make financial analysis difficult. One of them is the variations that exist in accounting methods among firms. As was discussed previously, different methods of inventory valuation and depreciation can lead to differences in reported profits for otherwise identical firms, and a good financial analyst must be able to adjust for these differences if he or she is to make valid comparisons among companies. Another factor involves timing—an action is taken at one point in time, but its full effects cannot be accurately measured until some later period.

CASH FLOW CYCLE
The way in which actual
net cash, as opposed to
accounting net income,
flows into or out of the
firm during some
specified period.

To understand how timing influences the financial statements, we must understand the **cash flow cycle** as set forth in Figure 3-1. In the figure, rectangles represent balance sheet accounts—assets and claims against assets—whereas circles represent income items and cash flow activities that affect balance sheet accounts. Each rectangle can be thought of as a reservoir, and there is a certain amount of the asset or liability in the reservoir (account) on each balance sheet date. Various transactions cause changes in the accounts, just as adding or subtracting water

Figure 3-1

Cash and Materials Flows within the Firm (millions of dollars)

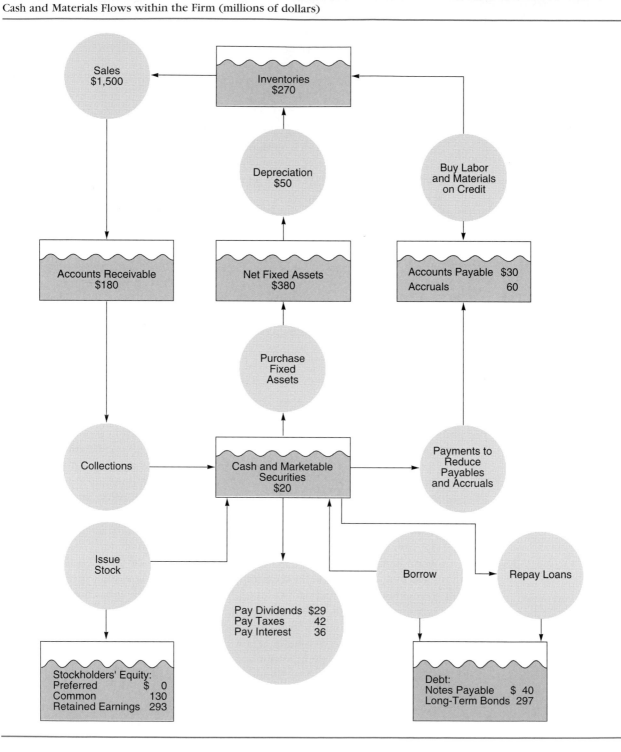

changes the level in a reservoir. The direction of the change in each reservoir is indicated by the direction of the arrow(s) connected to that reservoir. For example, because collecting an account receivable reduces the receivables reservoir but increases the cash reservoir, an arrow goes *from* the accounts receivable reservoir *to* the collections circle, then *from* the collections circle *to* the cash and marketable securities reservoir.

The cash account is the focal point of the figure. Certain events, such as collecting accounts receivable or borrowing money from the bank, will cause the cash account to increase, while the payment of taxes, interest, dividends, and accounts payable will cause it to decline. Similar comments could be made about all the balance sheet accounts—their balances rise, fall, or remain constant depending on events that occur during the period under study, which for Unilate is January 1, 1995, through December 31, 1995.

Projected increases in sales might require the firm to raise cash by borrowing from its bank or by selling new stock. For example, if Unilate anticipates an increase in sales, it will (1) expend cash to buy or build fixed assets; (2) step up purchases of raw materials, thereby increasing both raw materials inventories and accounts payable; (3) increase production, which will lead to an increase in both accrued wages and work-in-process; and (4) eventually build up its finished goods inventory. Some cash will have been expended and hence removed from the cash account, and the firm will have obligated itself to expend still more cash within a few weeks to pay off its accounts payable and its accrued wages. These cash-using events will have occurred *before* any new cash has been generated from sales. Even when the expected sales do occur, there still will be a lag in the generation of cash until receivables are collected—because Unilate grants credit for 30 days, it will have to wait 30 days after a sale is made before cash comes in. Depending on how much cash the firm had at the beginning of the build-up, on the length of its production-sales-collection cycle, and on how long it can delay payment of its own payables and accrued wages, Unilate might have to obtain substantial amounts of additional cash by selling stock or bonds, or by borrowing from the bank.

If the firm is profitable, its sales revenues will exceed its costs, and its cash inflows eventually will exceed its cash outlays. However, even a profitable business can experience a cash shortage if it is growing rapidly. It might have to pay for plant, materials, and labor before cash from the expanded sales starts flowing in. For this reason, rapidly growing firms generally require large bank loans or capital from other sources.

An unprofitable firm, such as Eastern Airlines before its bankruptcy, will have larger cash outlays than inflows. This, in turn, will lower the cash account and also cause a slowdown in the payment of accrued wages and accounts payable, and it might also lead to heavy borrowings. Accordingly, liabilities rise to excessive levels in unprofitable firms. Similarly, an overly ambitious expansion plan will result in excessive inventories and fixed assets, while too lenient a credit/collection policy will result in high accounts receivable, which eventually will result in bad debts and reduced profits.

If a firm runs out of cash and cannot obtain enough to meet its obligations, then it cannot operate, and it will have to declare bankruptcy. In fact, Eastern Airlines and thousands of other companies have been forced to do just that. Therefore, an accurate cash flow forecast is a critical element in managerial finance.[4] Financial analysts are well aware of all this, and they use the analytical techniques discussed in the remainder of this chapter to help discover cash flow problems before they become serious.

Statement of Cash Flows

The graphic cash flow analysis set forth in Figure 3-1 is converted into numerical form and reported in annual reports as the **statement of cash flows.** This statement is designed to show how the firm's operations have affected its cash position by examining the investment (uses of cash) and financing decisions (sources of cash) of the firm. The information contained in the statement of cash flows can help answer such questions as: Is the firm generating the cash needed to purchase additional fixed assets for growth? Is growth so rapid that external financing is required both to maintain operations and for investment in new fixed assets? Does the firm have excess cash flows that can be used to repay debt or to invest in new products? This information is useful both for financial managers and investors, so the statement of cash flows is an important part of the annual report.

Constructing a statement of cash flows is relatively easy. First, to some extent, the cash flow effects of a firm's operations are shown in its income statement. For example, Unilate reported its 1995 net income as $62 million, which we know includes a $50 million depreciation expense that is a noncash operating cost. So, if the $50 million depreciation expense is added back to the $62 million net income, we have an *estimate* of cash flows from normal operations equal to $112 million. But, for most firms, some of the reported revenues have not been collected and some of the reported expenses have not been paid at the time the income statement is constructed. In order to adjust the *estimate* of cash flows obtained from the income statement and to account for cash flows not reflected in the income statement, we need to examine the impact of changes in the balance sheet accounts during the year in question, which is fiscal year 1995 for Unilate. Looking at the changes in the balance sheet accounts from the beginning to the end of the year, we want to identify which items provided cash (source) and which items used cash (use) during the year. To determine whether a change in a balance sheet account was a source or a use of cash, we can use the following simple rules:

Sources of Cash:	Uses of Cash:
↑ **in a liability or equity account:** borrowing funds or selling stock provides the firms with cash	↓ **in a liability or equity account:** paying off a loan or buying back stock uses cash
↓ **in an asset account:** selling inventory or collecting receivables provides cash	↑ **in an asset account:** buying fixed assets or buying more inventory uses cash

Using these rules, we can identify which changes in Unilate's balance sheet accounts provided cash and which changes used cash during 1995. Table 3-4 shows the results of this identification. In addition, the table includes the cash flow information contained in Unilate's 1995 income statement.

---

[4]The mechanics of a cash forecast are explained in Chapter 9 along with a more detailed discussion of cash management.

TABLE 3-4

Unilate Textiles: Cash Sources and Uses during 1995 (millions of dollars)

			Change	
	12/31/95	12/31/94	Sources	Uses
Balance Sheet Changes:				
Cash and marketable securities	$ 20	$ 40	$ 20	
Accounts receivable	180	160		$ 20
Inventory	270	200		70
Gross plant and equipment	680	600		80
Accounts payable	30	15	15	
Accruals	60	55	5	
Notes payable	40	35	5	
Long-term bonds	297	255	42	
Common stock (25,000,000)	130	130		
Income Statement Information:				
Net income	$ 62			
Add: Depreciation	50			
Gross cash flow from operations	$112		112	
Dividend payment	29			29
Totals			$199	$199

The information contained in Table 3-4 can be used to construct the statement of cash flows shown in Table 3-5.[5] Each balance sheet change in Table 3-4 is classified as resulting from (1) operations, (2) long-term investments, or (3) financing activities. Operating cash flows are those associated with the production and sale of goods and services. The amount of net income plus depreciation is the primary operating cash flow, but changes in accounts payable, accounts receivable, inventories, and accruals are also classified as operating cash flows, because these accounts are directly affected by the firm's day-to-day operations. Investment cash flows arise from the purchase or sale of plant, property, and equipment. Financing cash inflows result from issuing debt or common stock, while financing outflows occur when the firm pays dividends or repays debt. The cash inflows and outflows from these three activities are summed to determine their impact on the firm's cash position during the year, which is measured by the change in the cash and marketable securities accounts.

The top part of Table 3-5 shows cash flows generated by and used in operations—for Unilate, operations provided net cash flows of $42 million. The operating cash flows are generated principally from the day-to-day operations of the firm, and this amount can be determined by adjusting the net income figure to account for noncash items. The day-to-day operations of Unilate in 1995 provided

[5]There are two different formats for presenting the cash flow statement. The method we present here is called the *indirect method.* Cash flows from operations are calculated by starting with net income, adding back expenses not paid out of cash, and subtracting revenues that do not provide cash. Using the *direct method,* operating cash flows are found by summing all revenues that provide cash and then subtracting all expenses that are paid in cash. Both formats produce the same result, and both are accepted by the Financial Accounting Standards Board.

TABLE 3-5

Unilate Textiles: Statement of Cash Flows for the Period Ending December 31, 1995 (millions of dollars)

Cash Flows from Operating Activities:		
Net income	$ 62	
Additions to net income		
Depreciation[a]	50	
Increase in accounts payable	15	
Increase in accruals	5	
Subtractions from net income		
Increase in accounts receivable	(20)	
Increase in inventory	(70)	
Net cash flow from operations		$ 42
Cash Flows from Long-Term Investing Activities:		
Acquisition of fixed assets		$(80)
Cash Flows from Financing Activities:		
Increase in notes payable	$ 5	
Increase in bonds	42	
Dividend payment	(29)	
Net cash flow from financing		$ 18
Net change in cash		$(20)
Cash at the beginning of the year		40
Cash at the end of the year		$ 20

[a]Depreciation is a noncash expense that was deducted when calculating net income. It must be added back to show the correct cash flow from operations.

$112 million of funds; however, the increases in inventories and investment in receivables during the year accounted for a combined use of funds equal to about 80 percent of this amount. The second section shows long-term investing activities. Unilate purchased fixed assets totaling $80 million; this was its only investment activity during 1995. Unilate's financing activities, shown in the lower section of Table 3-5, included borrowing from banks (notes payable), selling new bonds, and paying dividends to its common stockholders. Unilate raised $47 million by borrowing, but it paid $29 million in dividends, so its net inflow of funds from financing activities during 1995 was $18 million.

When all these sources and uses of cash are totaled, we see that Unilate had a $20 million cash shortfall during 1995. It met that shortfall by drawing down its cash and marketable securities holdings by $20 million, as shown in Table 3-2, the firm's balance sheet, and Table 3-4.

Unilate's statement of cash flows should be of some concern to the financial manager and to outside analysts. The company generated $42 million cash from operations, it spent an additional $80 million on new fixed assets, and it paid out another $29 million in dividends. It covered these cash outlays by borrowing heavily, by selling off marketable securities, and by drawing down its bank account. Obviously, this situation cannot continue year after year, so something will have to be done. We will consider some of the actions the financial manager might recommend, but first we must examine the financial statements in more depth.

 ### Self-Test Questions

Identify the two types of information given in the annual report.

Describe these four basic financial statements: (1) the income statement, (2) the balance sheet, (3) the statement of retained earnings, and (4) the statement of cash flows.

Explain the following statement: "Retained earnings as reported on the balance sheet do not represent cash and are not 'available' for the payment of dividends or anything else."

Differentiate between operating cash flows and other cash flows.

List two reasons why operating cash flows can differ from net income.

In accounting, the emphasis is on the determination of net income. What is emphasized in finance, and why is that emphasis important?

Assuming that depreciation is the only noncash cost, how can someone calculate a business's cash flow?

Describe the general rules for identifying whether changes in balance sheet accounts represent sources or uses of cash.

Ratio Analysis

Financial statements provide information about a firm's position at a point in time as well as its operations over some past period. However, the real value of financial statements lies in the fact that they can be used to help predict the firm's financial position in the future, and to determine expected earnings and dividends. From an investor's standpoint, *predicting the future is what financial statement analysis is all about,* while from management's standpoint, *financial statement analysis is useful both as a way to anticipate future conditions and, more important, as a starting point for planning actions that will influence the future course of events.*

An analysis of the firm's ratios generally is the first step in a financial analysis. The ratios are designed to show relationships between financial statement accounts *within* firms and *between* firms. Translating accounting numbers into relative values, or ratios, allows us to compare the financial position of one firm to another, even if their sizes are significantly different. For example, Firm A might have debt of $5,248,760 and interest charges of $419,900, while Firm B might have debt of $52,647,980 and interest charges of $3,948,600. Which company is stronger? The true burden of these debts, and the companies' ability to repay them, can be ascertained (1) by comparing each firm's debt to its assets and (2) by comparing the interest it must pay to the income it has available for payment of interest. Such comparisons are made by ratio analysis.

In the paragraphs that follow, we will calculate the 1995 financial ratios for Unilate Textiles and then evaluate those ratios in relation to the industry averages.[6] Note that all dollar amounts in the ratio calculations are in millions, except where per share values are used.

Liquidity Ratios

LIQUID ASSET
An asset that can be easily converted into cash without significant loss of its original value.

LIQUIDITY RATIOS
Ratios that show the relationship of a firm's cash and other current assets to its current liabilities.

CURRENT RATIO
This ratio is calculated by dividing current assets by current liabilities. It indicates the extent to which current liabilities are covered by assets expected to be converted to cash in the near future.

A **liquid asset** is one that can be easily converted to cash without significant loss of its original value. Converting assets, especially current assets such as inventory and receivables, to cash is the primary means by which a firm obtains the funds needed to pay its current bills. Therefore, a firm's "liquid position" deals with the question of how well the firm is able to meet its current obligations. Short-term, or current, assets are more easily converted to cash (more liquid) than long-term assets. So, in general, one firm would be considered more liquid than another firm if it has a greater proportion of its total assets in the form of current assets.

Unilate has debts totaling $130 million that must be paid off within the coming year. Will it have trouble satisfying those obligations? A full liquidity analysis requires the use of cash budgets (described in Chapter 9), but by relating the amount of cash and other current assets to the firm's current obligations, ratio analysis provides a quick, easy-to-use measure of liquidity. Two commonly used **liquidity ratios** are discussed in this section.

CURRENT RATIO   The **current ratio** is calculated by dividing current assets by current liabilities:

$$\text{Current ratio} = \frac{\text{Current assets}}{\text{Current liabilities}}$$

$$= \frac{\$470}{\$130} = 3.6 \text{ times}$$

Industry average $= 4.1$ times

Current assets normally include cash, marketable securities, accounts receivable, and inventories. Current liabilities consist of accounts payable, short-term notes payable, current maturities of long-term debt, accrued income taxes, and other accrued expenses (principally wages).

If a company is getting into financial difficulty, it begins paying its bills (accounts payable) more slowly, borrowing more from its bank, and so on. If current liabilities are rising faster than current assets, the current ratio will fall, and this could spell trouble. Because the current ratio provides the best single indicator of the extent to which the claims of short-term creditors are covered by assets that

---

[6]In addition to the ratios discussed in this section, financial analysts also employ a tool known as common size balance sheets and income statements. To form a *common size* balance sheet, one simply divides each asset and liability item by total assets and then expresses the result as a percentage. The resultant percentage statement can be compared with statements of larger or smaller firms, or with those of the same firm over time. To form a common size income statement, one simply divides each income statement item by sales.

are expected to be converted to cash fairly quickly, it is the most commonly used measure of short-term solvency. Care must be taken when examining the current ratio, just as it should be when examining any ratio individually. For example, just because a firm has a low current ratio, even one below 1.0, this does not mean the current obligations cannot be met.

Unilate's current ratio of 3.6 is below the average for its industry, 4.1, so its liquidity position is somewhat weak. Still, because current assets are scheduled to be converted to cash in the near future, it is highly probable that they could be liquidated at close to their stated value. With a current ratio of 3.6, Unilate could liquidate current assets at only 28 percent of book value and still pay off current creditors in full.[7]

Although industry average figures are discussed later in some detail, it should be noted at this point that an industry average is not a magic number that all firms should strive to maintain—in fact, some very well managed firms will be above the average while other good firms will be below it. However, if a firm's ratios are far removed from the average for its industry, an analyst should be concerned about why this variance occurs. Thus, a significant deviation from the industry average should signal the analyst (or management) to *check further*, even if the deviation is considered to be in the "good" direction. For example, we know that Unilate's liquidity position currently is below average. But what would you conclude if Unilate's current ratio actually was nearly twice that of the industry, perhaps 8.0×? Is this good? Maybe not. Because current assets, which are considered liquid, generally generate lower rates of return than long-term assets, it might be argued that firms with too much liquidity are not investing wisely.

QUICK (ACID TEST) RATIO
This ratio is calculated by deducting inventories from current assets and dividing the remainder by current liabilities. The quick ratio is a variation of the current ratio.

QUICK, OR ACID TEST, RATIO   The **quick,** or **acid test, ratio** is calculated by deducting inventories from current assets and then dividing the remainder by current liabilities:

$$\text{Quick, or acid test, ratio} = \frac{\text{Current assets} - \text{Inventories}}{\text{Current liabilities}}$$

$$= \frac{\$470 - \$270}{\$130} = \frac{\$200}{\$130} = 1.5 \text{ times}$$

Industry average = 2.1 times

Inventories typically are the least liquid of a firm's current assets, hence they are the assets on which losses are most likely to occur in the event of liquidation. Therefore, a measure of the firm's ability to pay off short-term obligations without relying on the sale of inventories is important.

The industry average quick ratio is 2.1, so Unilate's ratio value of 1.5 is low in comparison with the ratios of other firms in its industry. Still, if the accounts

[7]1/3.6 = 0.278, or 28 percent. Note that 0.278 ($470) = $130, which is the amount of current liabilities.

receivable can be collected, the company can pay off its current liabilities even without having to liquidate its inventory.

Our evaluation of the liquidity ratios suggests that Unilate's liquidity position currently is poor. To get a better idea of why Unilate is in this situation, we must examine its asset management ratios.

Asset Management Ratios

ASSET MANAGEMENT RATIOS
A set of ratios that measures how effectively a firm is managing its assets.

The second group of ratios, the **asset management ratios,** measures how effectively the firm is managing its assets. These ratios are designed to answer this question: Does the total amount of each type of asset as reported on the balance sheet seem reasonable, too high, or too low in view of current and projected sales levels? Firms invest in assets to generate revenues both in the current period and in future periods. To purchase their assets, Unilate and other companies must borrow or obtain funds from other sources. If they have too many assets, their interest expenses will be too high, hence their profits will be depressed. On the other hand, because production is affected by the capacity of assets, if assets are too low, profitable sales might be lost because the firm is unable to manufacture enough products.

INVENTORY TURNOVER RATIO
The ratio calculated by dividing cost of goods sold by inventories.

INVENTORY TURNOVER   The **inventory turnover ratio** is defined as cost of goods sold divided by inventories:[8]

$$\text{Inventory turnover ratio} = \frac{\text{Cost of goods sold}}{\text{Inventories}}$$

$$= \frac{\$1,220}{\$270} = 4.5 \text{ times}$$

Industry average = 7.4 times

As a rough approximation, each item of Unilate's inventory is sold out and re-stocked, or "turned over," 4.5 times per year.[9]

Unilate's turnover of 4.5 times is much lower than the industry average of 7.4 times. This suggests that Unilate is holding excessive stocks of inventory; excess

---

[8]Some compilers of financial ratio statistics, such as Dun & Bradstreet, use the ratio of sales to inventories carried at cost to represent inventory turnover. If this form of the inventory turnover ratio is used, we must recognize that the true turnover will be overstated, because sales are stated at market prices while inventories are carried at cost.

[9]"Turnover" is a term that originated many years ago with the old Yankee peddler, who would load up his wagon with goods, then go off on his route to peddle his wares. The merchandise was his "working capital," because it was what he actually sold, or "turned over," to produce his profits, whereas his "turnover" was the number of trips he took each year. Annual sales divided by inventory equaled turnover, or trips per year. If he made 10 trips per year, stocked 100 pans, and made a gross profit of $5 per pan, his annual gross profit would be (100) ($5) (10) = $5,000. If he went faster and made 20 trips per year, his gross profit would double, other things held constant.

stocks are, of course, unproductive and represent an investment with a low or zero rate of return. Unilate's low inventory turnover ratio makes us question the current ratio. With such a low turnover, we must wonder whether the firm is holding damaged or obsolete goods (for example, textile types and patterns from previous years) not actually worth their stated value.

Care must be used when calculating and using the inventory turnover ratio, because purchases of inventory, thus the cost of goods sold figure, occur over the entire year, whereas the inventory figure is for one point in time. For this reason, it is better to use an average inventory measure.[10] If the firm's business is highly seasonal, or if there has been a strong upward or downward sales trend during the year, it is essential to make such an adjustment. To maintain comparability with industry averages, however, we did not use the average inventory figure.

DAYS SALES OUTSTANDING (DSO)
The ratio calculated by dividing accounts receivable by average sales per day; indicates the average length of time it takes the firm to collect for credit sales.

DAYS SALES OUTSTANDING   **Days sales outstanding (DSO),** also called the "average collection period" (ACP), is used to evaluate the firm's ability to collect its credit sales in a timely manner. It is calculated by dividing average daily sales into accounts receivable to find the number of days' sales that are tied up in receivables. Thus, the DSO represents the average length of time that the firm must wait after making a sale before receiving cash, which is the average collection period. Unilate has about 43 days' sales outstanding, well above the 32-day industry average.[11]

$$\text{DSO} = \frac{\text{Days sales}}{\text{outstanding}} = \frac{\text{Receivables}}{\text{Average sales per day}} = \frac{\text{Receivables}}{\left[\dfrac{\text{Annual sales}}{360}\right]}$$

$$= \frac{\$180}{\left[\dfrac{\$1,500}{360}\right]} = \frac{\$180}{\$4.167} = 43.2 \text{ days}$$

$$\text{Industry average} = 32.1 \text{ days}$$

---

[10]Preferably, the average inventory value should be calculated by summing the monthly figures during the year and dividing by 12. If monthly data are not available, one can add the beginning and ending figures and divide by 2; this will adjust for growth but not for seasonal effects. Using the approach, Unilate's average inventory for 1995 would be $235 = ($200 + $270)/2, and its inventory turnover would be 5.2 = $1,220/$235, which still is well below the industry average given above.

[11]To compute DSO using this equation, we have to assume all the firm's sales are credit. We usually compute DSO in this manner, because information on credit sales generally is unavailable, so total sales must be used. Because all firms do not have the same percentage of credit sales, there is a chance that the days sales outstanding will be somewhat in error. Also, note that by convention the financial community generally uses 360 rather than 365 as the number of days in the year for purposes such as this. Finally, it would be better to use average receivables, either an average of the monthly figures or (beginning receivables + ending receivables)/2 = ($160 + $180)/2 = $170 in the formula. Had the annual average receivables been used, Unilate's DSO would have been $170/$4.17 = 40.8 days. The 40.8-day figure is the more accurate one, but because the industry average was based on year-end receivables, we used 43.2 days for our comparison. The DSO is discussed further in Chapter 10.

The DSO also can be evaluated by comparison with the terms on which the firm sells its goods. For example, Unilate's sales terms call for payment within 30 days, so the fact that 43 days' sales, not 30 days', are outstanding indicates that customers, on the average, are not paying their bills on time. If the trend in DSO over the past few years has been rising, but the credit policy has not been changed, this would be even stronger evidence that steps should be taken to improve the time it takes to collect accounts receivable. This seems to be the case for Unilate, because its 1994 DSO was about 40 days.

FIXED ASSETS TURNOVER RATIO
The ratio of sales to net fixed assets.

FIXED ASSETS TURNOVER   The **fixed assets turnover ratio** measures how effectively the firm uses its plant and equipment to help generate sales. It is the ratio of sales to net fixed assets:

$$\text{Fixed assets turnover ratio} = \frac{\text{Sales}}{\text{Net fixed assets}}$$

$$= \frac{\$1,500}{\$380} = 3.9 \text{ times}$$

Industry average $= 4.0$ times

Unilate's ratio of 3.9 times is almost equal to the industry average, indicating that the firm is using its fixed assets about as intensively (efficiently) as are the other firms in the industry. Unilate seems to have neither too much nor too few fixed assets in relation to other firms.

Care should be taken when using the fixed assets turnover ratio to compare different firms. Recall from accounting that all of the balance sheet accounts are stated in terms of historical costs. Inflation has caused the value of many assets that were purchased in the past to be seriously understated. Therefore, if we were comparing an old firm that had acquired many of its fixed assets years ago at low prices with a new company that had acquired its fixed assets only recently, we probably would find that the old firm had a higher fixed assets turnover. However, this would be more reflective of the inability of accountants to deal with inflation than of any inefficiency on the part of the new firm. The accounting profession is trying to devise ways to make financial statements better reflect current values rather than historical values. If balance sheets were actually stated on a current value basis, this would eliminate the problem of comparisons, but at the moment the problem still exists. Because financial analysts typically do not have the data necessary to make adjustments, they must simply recognize that a problem exists and deal with it judgmentally. In Unilate's case, the issue is not a serious one because all firms in the industry have been expanding at about the same rate; thus, the balance sheets of the comparison firms are indeed comparable.[12]

---

[12]See FASB #33, *Financial Reporting and Changing Prices* (September 1979), for a discussion of the effects of inflation on financial statements and what the accounting profession is trying to do to provide better and more useful balance sheets and income statements.

TOTAL ASSETS TURNOVER RATIO
The ratio calculated by dividing sales by total assets.

TOTAL ASSETS TURNOVER   The final asset management ratio, the **total assets turnover ratio,** measures the turnover of all of the firm's assets. It is calculated by dividing sales by total assets:

$$\text{Total assets turnover ratio} = \frac{\text{Sales}}{\text{Total assets}}$$

$$= \frac{\$1,500}{\$850} = 1.8 \text{ times}$$

Industry average $= 2.1$ times

Unilate's ratio is somewhat below the industry average, indicating that the company is not generating a sufficient volume of business given its investment in total assets. To become more efficient, sales should be increased, some assets should be disposed of, or a combination of these steps should be taken.

Our examination of Unilate's asset management ratios shows that its fixed assets turnover ratio is very close to the industry average, but its total assets turnover is below average. The fixed assets turnover ratio excludes current assets, while the total assets turnover ratio does not. Therefore, comparison of these ratios confirms our conclusion from the analysis of the liquidity ratios—Unilate seems to have a liquidity problem. The fact that the inventory turnover ratio and the average collection period are below average suggests, at least in part, the poor liquidity might be attributable to problems with inventory and receivables management. Slow sales and slow collections of credit sales suggest Unilate might rely more heavily on external funds, such as loans, than the industry to pay current obligations. Examining the debt management ratios will help us determine if this actually is the case.

Debt Management Ratios

FINANCIAL LEVERAGE
The use of debt financing.

The extent to which a firm uses debt financing, or **financial leverage,** has three important implications: (1) By raising funds through debt, stockholder ownership is not diluted. (2) Creditors look to the equity, or owner-supplied funds, to provide a margin of safety; if the stockholders have provided only a small proportion of the total financing, the risks of the enterprise are borne mainly by its creditors. (3) If the firm earns more on investments financed with borrowed funds than it pays in interest, the return on the owners' capital is magnified, or "leveraged."

Financial leverage (borrowing) affects the expected rate of return realized by stockholders for two reasons: (1) the interest on debt is tax deductible while dividends are not, so paying interest lowers the firm's tax bill, all else equal; and (2) usually the rate a firm earns from its investments in assets is different from the rate at which it borrows. If the firm has healthy operations, it generally invests the funds it raises at a rate of return that is greater than the interest rate on its debt. In combination with the tax advantage debt has compared to stock, the higher investment rate of return produces a magnified positive return to the stockholders. Under these conditions, leverage works to the advantage of the firm and its stockholders. Unfortunately, financial leverage is a two-edged sword. When the firm experiences poor business conditions, typically sales are lower and costs are higher than expected, but the cost of borrowing still must be paid. The *costs* (interest payments) associated with borrowing are contractual and do not vary with sales, and they must be paid to keep the firm from potential bankruptcy. Therefore, the required interest payments might be a very significant burden for a firm that has liquidity problems. In fact, if the interest payments are high enough, a firm with a positive operating income actually could end up with a negative return to stockholders. Under these conditions, leverage works to the detriment of the firm and its stockholders.

A detailed discussion of financial leverage is given in the next chapter. For the purposes of ratio analysis, we need to understand that firms with relatively high debt ratios have higher expected returns when the business is normal or good, but they are exposed to risk of loss when the business is poor. Thus, firms with low debt ratios are less risky, but they also forgo the opportunity to leverage up their return on equity. The prospects of high returns are desirable, but investors are averse to risk. Therefore, decisions about the use of debt require firms to balance higher expected returns against increased risk. Determining the optimal amount of debt for a given firm is a complicated process, and we defer a discussion of this topic until Chapter 16. For now we will simply look at two procedures analysts use to examine the firm's debt in a financial statement analysis: (1) They check balance sheet ratios to determine the extent to which borrowed funds have been used to finance assets, and (2) they review income statement ratios to determine how well operating profits can cover fixed charges such as interest. These two sets of ratios are complementary, so analysts use both types.

DEBT RATIO

The ratio of total debt to total assets. It is a measure of the percentage of funds provided by creditors.

DEBT RATIO   The **debt ratio,** which is the ratio of total debt to total assets, measures the percentage of the firm's assets financed by creditors (borrowing):

$$\text{Debt ratio} = \frac{\text{Total debt}}{\text{Total assets}}$$

$$= \frac{\$130 + \$297}{\$850} = \frac{\$427}{\$850} = 0.502 = 50.2\%$$

Industry average = 45.0%

Total debt includes both current liabilities and long-term debt. Creditors prefer low debt ratios, because the lower the ratio, the greater the cushion against creditors' losses in the event of liquidation. The owners, on the other hand, can benefit from leverage because it magnifies earnings, thus the return to stockholders. But too much debt often leads to financial difficulty, which eventually might cause bankruptcy.

Unilate's debt ratio is 50.2 percent; this means that its creditors have supplied about half the firm's total financing. Because the average debt ratio for this industry is 45 percent, Unilate might find it difficult to borrow additional funds without first raising more equity capital through a stock issue. Creditors might be reluctant

TIMES-INTEREST-EARNED (TIE) RATIO
The TIE ratio is computed by dividing earnings before interest and taxes (EBIT) by interest charges; measures the ability of the firm to meet its annual interest payments.

to lend the firm more money, and management would be subjecting the firm to a greater chance of bankruptcy if it sought to increase the debt ratio much further by borrowing additional funds.[13]

TIMES INTEREST EARNED   The **times-interest-earned (TIE) ratio** is determined by dividing earnings before interest and taxes (EBIT in Table 3-1) by the interest charges:

$$\text{Times-interest-earned (TIE) ratio} = \frac{\text{EBIT}}{\text{Interest charges}}$$

$$= \frac{\$140}{\$36} = 3.9 \text{ times}$$

Industry average = 6.5 times

The TIE ratio measures the extent to which operating income can decline before the firm is unable to meet its annual interest costs. Failure to meet this obligation can bring legal action by the firm's creditors, possibly resulting in bankruptcy. Note that earnings before interest and taxes, rather than net income, is used in the numerator. Because interest is paid with pre-tax dollars, the firm's ability to pay current interest is not affected by taxes.

Unilate's interest is covered 3.9 times. Because the industry average is 6.5 times, compared to firms in the same business, Unilate is covering its interest charges by a low margin of safety. Thus, the TIE ratio reinforces our conclusion based on the debt ratio that Unilate would face difficulties if it attempted to borrow additional funds.

FIXED CHARGE COVERAGE RATIO
This ratio expands the TIE ratio to include the firm's annual long-term lease payments and sinking fund payments.

FIXED CHARGE COVERAGE   The **fixed charge coverage ratio** is similar to the times-interest-earned ratio, but it is more inclusive because it recognizes that many firms lease assets and also must make sinking fund payments. Leasing has become widespread in certain industries in recent years, making this ratio preferable to the times-interest-earned ratio for many purposes. Unilate's annual long-term lease payments are $10 million, and it must make an annual $8 million sinking fund payment to help retire its debt. Because sinking fund payments must be paid with after-tax dollars, whereas interest and lease payments are paid with pre-tax dollars, the sinking fund payment must be divided by (1 − Tax rate) to find the before-tax income required to pay taxes and still have enough left to make the sinking fund payment.[14]

---

[13]The ratio of debt to equity also is used in financial analysis. The debt to assets (D/A) and debt to equity (D/E) ratios are simply transformations of each other, because total debt plus total equity must equal total assets:

$$D/E = \frac{D/A}{1 - D/A}, \text{ and } D/A = \frac{D/E}{1 + D/E}$$

[14]Note that $8/ (1 − 0.4) = $13.33. Therefore, if the company had pre-tax income of $13.33, it could pay taxes at a 40 percent rate and have exactly $8 left with which to make the sinking fund payment. Thus, to pay an $8 sinking fund requirement, Unilate needs $13.33 of pre-tax income. Dividing by (1 − T) is called "grossing up" an after-tax value to find the corresponding pre-tax value.

Fixed charges include interest, annual long-term lease obligations, and sinking fund payments, and the fixed charge coverage ratio is defined as follows:

$$\text{Fixed charge coverage ratio} = \frac{\text{EBIT} + \text{Lease payments}}{\text{Interest charges} + \text{Lease payments} + \left[\dfrac{\text{Sinking fund payments}}{(1 - \text{Tax rate})}\right]}$$

$$= \frac{\$140 + \$10}{\$36 + \$10 + \dfrac{\$8}{(1 - 0.4)}} = 2.5 \text{ times}$$

Industry average = 5.8 times

In the numerator of the fixed charge coverage ratio, the lease payments are added to EBIT because we want to determine the firm's ability to cover its fixed charges from the income generated before any fixed charges are deducted. The EBIT figure represents the firm's operating income, net of lease payments, so the lease payments must be added back.

Unilate's fixed charges are covered only 2.5 times, as opposed to an industry average of 5.8 times. Again, this indicates that the firm is weaker than average, and this points out the difficulties Unilate probably would encounter if it attempted to increase its debt.

Our examination of Unilate's debt management ratios indicates that the company has a debt ratio *above* the industry average, and it has coverage ratios significantly *below* the industry average. This suggests that Unilate is in a relatively dangerous position with respect to leverage (debt). In fact, Unilate might have great difficulty borrowing additional funds until its debt position improves. If Unilate cannot pay its current obligations as a result, it might be forced into bankruptcy. To see how Unilate's debt position has affected its profits, we next examine the profitability ratios.

PROFITABILITY RATIOS
A group of ratios showing the effect of liquidity, asset management, and debt management on operating results.

Profitability Ratios

Profitability is the net result of a number of policies and decisions. The ratios examined thus far provide some information about the way the firm is operating, but the **profitability ratios** show the combined effects of liquidity, asset management, and debt management on operating results.

NET PROFIT MARGIN ON SALES
This ratio measures net income per dollar of sales; it is calculated by dividing net income by sales.

NET PROFIT MARGIN ON SALES   The **net profit margin on sales,** calculated by dividing net income by sales, gives the profit per dollar of sales:

$$\text{Profit margin on sales} = \frac{\text{Net Income}}{\text{Sales}}$$

$$= \frac{\$62}{\$1,500} = 0.041 = 4.1\%$$

Industry average $= 4.7\%$

Unilate's profit margin is below the industry average of 4.7 percent, indicating that its costs are too high relative to sales revenues. Remember, according to the debt ratio, Unilate has a greater proportion of debt than the industry average; and the times interest earned ratio shows that Unilate's interest payments on its debt are not covered as well as the rest of the industry. This is one reason Unilate's profit margin is low. To see this, we can compute the ratio of EBIT (operating income) to sales, which is called the *operating profit margin.* Unilate's operating profit margin of 9.3 percent is exactly the same as the industry, so the cause of the low net profit margin is the relatively high interest attributable to the firm's above-average use of debt.

RETURN ON TOTAL ASSETS (ROA)
The ratio of net income to total assets; provides an idea of the overall return on investment earned by the firm.

RETURN ON TOTAL ASSETS   The ratio of net income to total assets measures the **return on total assets (ROA)** after interest and taxes:

$$\text{Return on total assets (ROA)} = \frac{\text{Net income}}{\text{Total assets}}$$

$$= \frac{\$62}{\$850} = 0.073 = 7.3\%$$

Industry average $= 10.1\%$

RETURN ON COMMON EQUITY (ROE)
The ratio of net income to common equity; measures the rate of return on common stockholders' investment.

Unilate's 7.3 percent return is well below the 10.1 percent average for the industry. This low return results from the company's above-average use of debt.

RETURN ON COMMON EQUITY   The ratio of net income to common equity measures the **return on common equity (ROE),** or the *rate of return on stockholders' investment:*[15]

$$\text{Return on common equity (ROE)} = \frac{\text{Net income available to common stockholders}}{\text{Common equity}}$$

$$= \frac{\$62}{\$423} = 0.147 = 14.7\%$$

Industry average $= 18.3\%$

---

[15]Net income to common stockholders is computed by subtracting preferred dividends from net income. Because Unilate has no preferred stock, the net income available to common stockholders is the same as the net income.

Unilate's 14.7 percent return is below the 18.3 percent industry average. This result is due to the company's greater use of debt (leverage), a point that is analyzed further later in this chapter and the next chapter.

Our examination of Unilate's profitability ratios shows that its operating results have suffered due to its poor liquidity position, its poor asset management, and its above-average debt. In the final group of ratios, we will examine Unilate's market value ratios to get an indication of how investors feel about the company's current position.

Market Value Ratios

MARKET VALUE RATIOS
A set of ratios that relate the firm's stock price to its earnings and book value per share.

The **market value ratios** represent a group of ratios that relate the firm's stock price to its earnings and book value per share. These ratios give management an indication of what investors think of the company's past performance and future prospects. If the firm's liquidity, asset management, debt management, and profitability ratios are all good, then its market value ratios will be high, and its stock price will probably be as high as can be expected. Of course, the opposite also is true.

PRICE/EARNINGS (P/E) RATIO
The ratio of the price per share to earnings per share; shows the dollar amount investors will pay for $1 of current earnings.

PRICE/EARNINGS RATIO   The **price/earnings (P/E) ratio** shows how much investors are willing to pay per dollar of reported profits. To compute the P/E ratio, we need to know the firm's earnings per share (EPS):

$$\text{Earnings per share} = \frac{\text{Net income available to common stockholders}}{\text{Number of common shares outstanding}}$$

$$= \frac{\$62}{25} = \$2.48$$

Unilate's stock sells for $23, so with an EPS of $2.48, its P/E ratio is 9.3:

$$\text{Price/earnings (PE) ratio} = \frac{\text{Market price per share}}{\text{Earnings per share}}$$

$$= \frac{\$23.00}{\$2.48} = \ 9.3 \text{ times}$$

Industry average = 11.0 times

As we will see in Chapter 7, other things held constant, P/E ratios are higher for firms with high growth prospects, but they are lower for riskier firms. Because

Unilate's P/E ratio is below those of other textile manufacturers, this suggests that the company is regarded as being somewhat riskier than most, as having poorer growth prospects, or both. From our analysis of its debt management ratios, we know Unilate has above-average risk associated with leverage, but we do not know if its growth prospects are poor.

MARKET/BOOK (M/B) RATIO
The ratio of a stock's market price to its book value.

MARKET/BOOK RATIO   The ratio of a stock's market price to its book value gives another indication of how investors regard the company. Companies with relatively high rates of return on equity generally sell at higher multiples of book value than those with low returns. First, we find Unilate's book value per share:

$$\text{Book value per share} = \frac{\text{Common equity}}{\text{Number of common shares outstanding}}$$

$$= \frac{\$423}{25} = \$16.92$$

Now we divide the market value per share by the book value per share to get a market/book (M/B) ratio of 1.4 times for Unilate:

$$\text{Market/book ratio} = \frac{\text{Market price per share}}{\text{Book value per share}}$$

$$= \frac{\$23.00}{\$16.92} = 1.4$$

Industry average $= 2.0$

Investors are willing to pay less for Unilate's book value than for that of an average textile manufacturer. This should not be surprising, because, as we discovered previously, Unilate has generated below-average returns with respect to both total assets and common equity. Generally, the stocks of firms that earn high rates of return on their assets sell for prices well in excess of their book values. For very successful firms, the market/book ratio can be as much as 10 to 15 times.

Our examination of Unilate's market value ratios indicates that investors are not excited about the future prospects of its common stock as an investment. Perhaps the investors believe Unilate is headed toward financial difficulty, or even bankruptcy, if actions are not taken to correct its liquidity and asset management problems and to improve its leverage position. A method used to get an indication of the direction a firm is headed is to evaluate the trends of the ratios over the past few years to answer the question: Is the firm's position improving or deteriorating?

Trend Analysis

TREND ANALYSIS
An analysis of a firm's
financial ratios over time;
used to determine the
improvement or
deterioration in its
financial situation.

The analysis of its ratios indicates that Unilate's current financial position is poor when compared to the industry norm. But this analysis does not tell us whether Unilate's financial position is better or worse than previous years. To determine in which direction the firm is headed, it is important to analyze trends in ratios. By examining the paths taken in the past, **trend analysis** provides information about whether the firm's financial position is more likely to improve or deteriorate in the future. A simple approach to trend analysis is to construct graphs containing both the firm's ratios and the industry averages for the past five years. Using this approach, we can examine both the direction of the movement in, and the relationships between, the firm's ratios and the industry averages. Figure 3-2 shows that Unilate's return on equity has declined since 1991, even though the industry average has been relatively stable. Other ratios could be analyzed similarly. If we were to compare Unilate's ratios from 1995 with those from 1994, we would discover Unilate's financial position has deteriorated, not strengthened—this is not a good trend.

Summary of Ratio Analysis: The Du Pont Chart

DU PONT CHART
A chart designed to show
the relationships among
return on investment,
asset turnover, the profit
margin, and leverage.

Table 3-6 summarizes Unilate's ratios, and Figure 3-3, called a **Du Pont chart** because that company's managers developed the general approach, shows the relationships between return on investment (assets), asset turnover, the profit margin, and leverage. The left-hand side of the chart develops the profit margin on sales. The various expense items are listed and then summed to obtain Unilate's total costs, which are subtracted from sales to obtain the company's net income. When we divide net income by sales, we find that 4.1 percent of each sales dollar is left over for stockholders. If the profit margin is low or trending down, one can examine the individual expense items to identify and then correct problems.

The right-hand side of Figure 3-3 lists the various categories of assets, totals them, and then divides sales by total assets to find the number of times Unilate "turns its assets over" each year. The company's total assets turnover ratio is 1.8 times.

DU PONT EQUATION
A formula that gives the
rate of return on assets by
multiplying the profit
margin by the total
assets turnover.

The profit margin times the total assets turnover is called the **Du Pont equation,** and it gives the rate of return on assets (ROA):

$$\boxed{\begin{array}{c} \textbf{3-1} \\ \text{ROA} = \text{Net profit margin} \times \text{Total assets turnover} \\ = \dfrac{\text{Net income}}{\text{Sales}} \times \dfrac{\text{Sales}}{\text{Total assets}} \end{array}}$$

$$= \frac{\$62}{\$1,500} \times \frac{\$1,500}{\$850} = 4.1\% \times 1.8 = 7.3\%$$

Unilate made 4.1 percent, or 4.1 cents, on each dollar of sales, and assets were "turned over" 1.8 times during the year, so the company earned a return of 7.3 percent on its assets.

FIGURE 3-2

Rate of Return on Common Equity

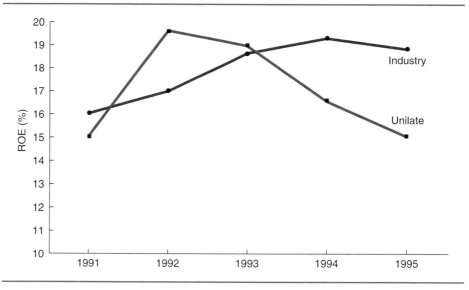

Unilate's management can use the Du Pont system to analyze ways of improving the firm's performance. Focusing on the left, or "profit margin," side of its Du Pont chart, Unilate's marketing people can study the effects of raising sales prices (or lowering them to increase volume), of moving into new products or markets with higher margins, and so on. The company's cost accountants can study various expense items and, working with engineers, purchasing agents, and other operating personnel, seek ways of holding down costs. On the "turnover" side, Unilate's financial analysts, working with both production and marketing people, can investigate ways of minimizing the investment in various types of assets.

As a result of such an analysis, Sarah Allen, Unilate's president, recently announced a series of moves designed to cut operating costs by more than 20 percent per year. Allen also announced that the company intends to concentrate its capital in markets where profit margins are reasonably high, and that if competition increases in certain of its product markets (such as the low-price end of the textiles market), Unilate will withdraw from those markets. Unilate is seeking a high return on equity, and Allen recognizes that if competition drives profit margins too low in a particular market, it then becomes impossible to earn high returns on the capital invested to serve that market. Therefore, if it is to achieve a high ROE, Unilate might have to develop new products and shift capital into new areas. The company's future depends on this type of analysis, and if it succeeds in the future, then the Du Pont system will have helped it achieve that success.

Self-Test Questions

Identify two ratios that are used to analyze a firm's liquidity position, and write out their equations.

TABLE 3-6

Unilate Textiles: Summary of Financial Ratios (millions of dollars, except per share dollars)

Ratio	Formula for Calculation	Calculation		Ratio	Industry Average	Comment
Liquidity						
Current	$\dfrac{\text{Current assets}}{\text{Current liabilities}}$	$\dfrac{\$470}{\$130}$	=	3.6×	4.1×	Low
Quick, or acid test	$\dfrac{\text{Current assets} - \text{Inventories}}{\text{Current liabilities}}$	$\dfrac{\$200}{\$130}$	=	1.5×	2.1×	Low
Asset Management						
Inventory turnover	$\dfrac{\text{Cost of goods sold}}{\text{Inventories}}$	$\dfrac{\$1,220}{\$270}$	=	4.5×	7.4×	Low
Days sales outstanding (DSO)	$\dfrac{\text{Receivables}}{\left[\dfrac{\text{Annual sales}}{360}\right]}$	$\dfrac{\$180}{\$4.167}$	=	43.2 days	32.1 days	Poor
Fixed assets turnover	$\dfrac{\text{Sales}}{\text{Net fixed assets}}$	$\dfrac{\$1,500}{\$380}$	=	3.9×	4.0×	OK
Total assets turnover	$\dfrac{\text{Sales}}{\text{Total assets}}$	$\dfrac{\$1,500}{\$850}$	=	1.8×	2.1×	Low
Debt Management						
Debt ratio	$\dfrac{\text{Total debt}}{\text{Total assets}}$	$\dfrac{\$427}{\$850}$	=	50.2%	45.0%	Poor
Times interest earned (TIE)	$\dfrac{\text{EBIT}}{\text{Interest charges}}$	$\dfrac{\$140}{\$36}$	=	3.9×	6.5×	Low
Fixed charge coverage	$\dfrac{\text{EBIT} + \text{Lease payments}}{\underset{\text{charges}}{\text{Interest}} + \underset{\text{payments}}{\text{Lease}} + \left[\dfrac{\text{Sinking fund pmt}}{(1 - \text{Tax rate})}\right]}$	$\dfrac{\$150}{\$59.33}$	=	2.5×	5.8×	Low
Profitability						
Profit margin on sales	$\dfrac{\text{Net income}}{\text{Sales}}$	$\dfrac{\$62}{\$1,500}$	=	4.1%	4.7%	Poor
Return on total assets (ROA)	$\dfrac{\text{Net income}}{\text{Total assets}}$	$\dfrac{\$62}{\$850}$	=	7.3%	10.1%	Poor
Return on common equity (ROE)	$\dfrac{\text{Net income available to common stockholders}}{\text{Common equity}}$	$\dfrac{\$62}{\$423}$	=	14.7%	18.3%	Poor
Market Value						
Price/Earnings (P/E)	$\dfrac{\text{Market price per share}}{\text{Earnings per share}}$	$\dfrac{\$23.00}{\$2.48}$	=	9.3×	11.0×	Low
Market/Book	$\dfrac{\text{Market price per share}}{\text{Book value per share}}$	$\dfrac{\$23.00}{\$16.92}$	=	1.4×	2.0×	Low

FIGURE 3-3

Du Pont Chart Applied to Unilate Textiles (millions of dollars)

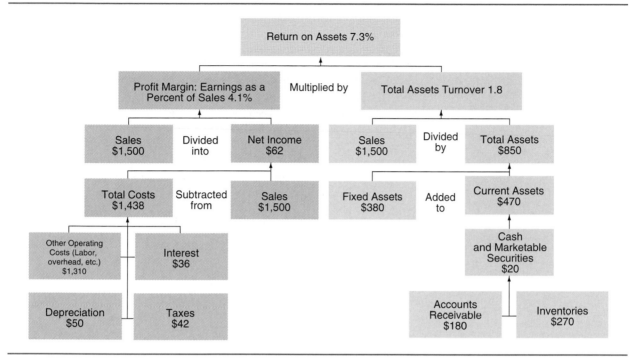

Identify four ratios that are used to measure how effectively a firm is managing its assets, and write out their equations.

Identify three ratios that are used to measure the extent to which a firm uses debt financing, and write out their equations.

Identify three ratios that show the combined effects of liquidity, asset management, and debt management on profitability, and write out their equations.

Identify two ratios that relate a firm's stock price to its earnings and book value per share, and write out their equations.

Explain how the Du Pont equation and chart combine several ratios to reveal the basic determinants of ROA.

Comparative Ratios

COMPARATIVE RATIO ANALYSIS
An analysis based on a comparison of a firm's ratios with those of other firms in the same industry.

The preceding analysis of Unilate Textiles involved a **comparative ratio analysis** because the ratios calculated for Unilate were compared with those of other firms in the same industry. Comparative ratios for a large number of industries are available from a number of sources, including Dun & Bradstreet (D&B), Robert Morris Associates, and the U.S. Commerce Department. Trade associations and individual firms' credit departments also compile industry average financial ratios. Finally, financial statement data for thousands of publicly owned corporations are available on magnetic tapes and diskettes, and because brokerage houses, banks, and other financial institutions have access to these data, security analysts can and do generate comparative ratios tailored to their specific needs. Table 3-7 provides a sample of the ratios provided by the *Almanac of Business and Industrial Financial Ratios.*

Each of the data-supplying organizations uses a somewhat different set of ratios designed for its own purposes. For example, D&B deals mainly with small firms, many of which are proprietorships, and it sells its services primarily to banks and other lenders. Therefore, D&B is concerned largely with the creditor's viewpoint, and its ratios emphasize current assets and liabilities, not market value ratios. Therefore, when you select a comparative data source, you should be sure that your emphasis is similar to that of the agency whose ratios you plan to use. Additionally, there are often definitional differences in the ratios presented by different sources, so before using a source, be sure to verify the exact definitions of the ratios to insure consistency with your past work.

Self-Test Questions

Differentiate between trend analysis and comparative ratio analysis.

Why is it necessary to conduct both trend and comparative ratio analyses?

Uses and Limitations of Ratio Analysis

As noted earlier, ratio analysis is used by three main groups: (1) *managers,* who employ ratios to help analyze, control, and thus improve the firm's operations; (2) *credit analysts,* such as bank loan officers or bond rating analysts, who analyze ratios to help ascertain a company's ability to pay its debts; and (3) *security analysts,* including both stock analysts, who are interested in a company's efficiency and growth prospects, and bond analysts, who are concerned with a company's ability to pay interest on its bonds as well as with the liquidating value of the assets in the event the company fails. In later chapters we will look more closely at the basic factors which underlie each ratio, and at that point you will get a better idea about how to interpret and use ratios.

We should also note that, although ratio analysis can provide useful information concerning a company's operations and financial condition, it does have inherent problems and limitations that necessitate care and judgment. Some potential problems are listed below:

1. Many large firms operate a number of different divisions in quite different industries, and in such cases it is difficult to develop a meaningful set of industry averages for comparative purposes. This tends to make ratio analysis more useful for small, narrowly focused firms than for large, multidivisional ones.
2. Most firms want to be better than average, so merely attaining average performance is not necessarily good. As a target for high-level performance, it is best to focus on the industry leaders' ratios.
3. Inflation has badly distorted firms' balance sheets—recorded values are historical and are often substantially different from "true" values. Further, because

TABLE 3-7

Ratios for Selected Industries

SIC Code, Line of Business, Number of Firms	Current Ratio ✕	Quick Ratio ✕	Debt Ratio %	Days Sales Outstanding Days	Inventory Turnover ✕	Total Asset Turnover ✕	Before-Tax Profit Margin %	Return on Assets %	Return on Equity %
2050 Bakery Products (1455)	1.5	0.9	53.5	116.1	1.9	1.9	3.9	12.5	15.8
2735 Book Publishing (8173)	1.1	0.7	71.5	105.9	3.6	0.7	3.6	8.1	9.0
2830 Drugs (874)	1.2	0.7	50.5	92.3	3.9	0.7	14.2	16.7	19.9
3430 Plumbing & Heating (1152)	2.7	1.4	44.5	76.6	3.5	1.0	4.6	10.0	8.2
5030 Lumber & Construction (11,613)	1.6	0.9	70.4	40.0	8.6	3.0	0.5	6.7	4.9
5700 Home Furnishings (19,578)	2.2	1.0	55.9	39.1	3.7	2.2	3.0	10.7	15.0

SOURCE: *1994 Almanac of Business and Industrial Financial Ratios*

SIC codes are "Standard Industrial Classification" codes used by the U.S. Government to classify companies.

inflation affects both depreciation charges and inventory costs, profits also are affected. Thus, a ratio analysis for one firm over time, or a comparative analysis of firms of different ages, must be interpreted with judgment.

4. Seasonal factors also can distort a ratio analysis. For example, the inventory turnover ratio for a textile firm will be radically different if the balance sheet figure used for inventory is the one just before versus the one just after the close of the fall fashion season. This problem can be minimized by using monthly averages for inventory (and receivables) when calculating ratios such as turnover.

"WINDOW DRESSING" TECHNIQUES
Techniques used by firms to make their financial statements look better than they actually are.

5. Firms can employ **"window dressing" techniques** to make their financial statements look stronger. To illustrate, a Chicago builder borrowed on a two-year basis on December 28, 1995, held the proceeds of the loan as *cash* for a few days, and then paid off the loan ahead of time on January 2, 1996. This improved his current and quick ratios, and made his year-end 1995 balance sheet look good. However, the improvement was strictly window dressing; a week later the balance sheet was back at the old level.

6. Different accounting practices can distort comparisons. As noted earlier, inventory valuation and depreciation methods can affect financial statements and thus distort comparisons among firms. Also, if one firm leases a substantial amount of its productive equipment, then its assets may appear low relative to sales, because leased assets often do not appear on the balance sheet. At the same time, the lease liability may not be shown as a debt. Therefore, leasing can artificially improve both the turnover and the debt ratios. However, the accounting profession has taken steps to reduce this problem, as we discuss in Chapter 20.

7. It is difficult to generalize about whether a particular ratio is "good" or "bad." For example, a high current ratio might indicate a strong liquidity position, which is good, or excessive cash, which is bad (because excess cash in the bank is a nonearning asset). Similarly, a high fixed assets turnover ratio may denote either a firm that uses its assets efficiently or one that is undercapitalized and cannot afford to buy enough assets.

8. A firm might have some ratios that look "good" and others that look "bad," making it difficult to tell whether the company is, on balance, strong or weak. However, statistical procedures can be used to analyze the net effects of a set of ratios. Many banks and other lending organizations use statistical procedures to analyze firms' financial ratios, and, on the basis of their analyses, classify companies according to their probability of getting into financial trouble.[16]

Ratio analysis is useful, but analysts should be aware of these problems and make adjustments as necessary. Ratio analysis conducted in a mechanical, unthinking manner is dangerous, but, used intelligently and with good judgment, it can provide useful insights into a firm's operations. Probably the most important and most

---

[16]The technique used is discriminant analysis. For a discussion, see Edward I. Altman, "Financial Ratios, Discriminant Analysis, and the Prediction of Corporate Bankruptcy," *Journal of Finance,* September 1968, 589–609, or Eugene F. Brigham and Louis C. Gapenski, *Intermediate Financial Management,* 5th ed. (Fort Worth, Tex.: The Dryden Press, 1996), Chapter 18.

difficult input to successful ratio analysis is the judgment used when interpreting the results to reach an overall conclusion about the firm's financial position. Your judgment in interpreting a set of ratios is necessarily weak at this point, but it will improve as you go through the remainder of the book.

Self-Test Questions

Name three types of users of ratio analysis. What type of ratios does each group emphasize?

List several potential problems with ratio analysis.

ETHICAL DILEMMA

Hocus-Pocus—Look, An Increase in Sales!

Dynamic Energy Wares (DEW) manufactures and distributes products that are used to save energy and to help reduce and reverse the harmful environmental effects of atmospheric pollutants. DEW relies on a relatively complex distribution system to get the products to its customers—large companies, which account for nearly 30 percent of total sales, purchase directly from DEW, while smaller companies and retailers that sell to individuals are required to purchase from one of the 50 independent distributors that are contractually obligated to *exclusively* sell DEW's products.

DEW's accountants have just finished the financial statements for the third quarter of the fiscal year, which ended three weeks ago. The results are terrible—profits are down 30 percent from this time last year when a downturn in sales began. Profits are depressed primarily because DEW continues to lose market share to a competitor that started business nearly two years ago.

Senior management has decided it needs to take action that will boost sales in the fourth quarter so that year-end profits are "more acceptable." So, starting immediately, DEW will (1) eliminate all direct sales, which means large companies now must purchase from DEW's distributors like the smaller companies and retailers, (2) require distributors to maintain certain minimum inventory levels, which are much higher than previous levels, and (3) form a task force to study and propose ways the firm can recapture lost market share.

The financial manager, who is your boss, has asked you to attend a hastily called meeting of DEW's distributors to announce the implementation of the changes in operations. At the meeting, the distributors will be informed that they must increase inventory to the required minimum level before the end of DEW's current fiscal year or face losing the distributorship. According to your boss, the reason for this requirement is to ensure distributors can meet the increased demand they will gain because the large companies no longer will be allowed to purchase directly from DEW. But, the sales forecast you have been working on for the past couple of months indicates distributors' sales are expected to decline by almost 10 percent during the next year, thus the added inventories might be extremely burdensome to the distributors. When you approached your boss about this, she said, "Tell the distributors not to worry! We won't require payment for six months, and any of the additional inventory that remains unsold after nine months can be returned. But, they *must* take delivery of the inventory within the next two months."

It appears the actions implemented by DEW will produce favorable year-end sales results for the current fiscal year. Do you agree with the decisions made by DEW's senior management? Will you be comfortable announcing the decisions to DEW's distributors? How would you respond to a distributor who says "DEW doesn't care about us, the company just wants to look good, no matter who gets hurt—that's unethical?" What are you going to say to your boss? Are you going to the distributors' meeting?

SMALL BUSINESS

Financial Analysis in the Small Firm

Financial ratio analysis is especially useful for small businesses, and readily available sources provide comparative data by size of firm. For example, Robert Morris Associates provides comparative ratios for a number of small-firm classes, including the size range of zero to $250,000 in annual sales. Nevertheless, analyzing a small firm's statements presents some unique problems. We examine here some of those problems from the standpoint of a bank loan officer, one of the most frequent users of ratio analysis.

When examining a small-business credit prospect, a banker essentially is making a prediction about the ability of the company to repay its debt. In making this prediction, the banker is particularly concerned about indicators of liquidity and about continuing prospects for profitability, especially with respect to the firm's ability to generate cash flows. Bankers like to do business with a new customer if it appears that loans can be paid off on a timely basis and that the company will remain in business and therefore be a customer of the bank for some years to come. Thus, both short-run and long-run viability are of interest to the banker. At the same time, the banker's perceptions about the business are important to the owner-manager, because the bank probably will be the firm's primary source of funds.

The first problem the banker is likely to encounter is that, unlike the bank's bigger customers, the small firm might not have audited financial statements. Further, the statements that are available might have been produced on an irregular basis (for example, in some months or quarters but not in others). If the firm is young, it might have historical financial statements for only one year, or perhaps none at all. Also, the financial statements might not have been produced by a reputable accounting firm but by the owner's brother-in-law.

The quality of its financial data could therefore be a problem for a small business that is attempting to establish a banking relationship. In addition, for a given set of financial ratios, a small firm might be riskier than a larger one. Small firms often produce a single product or rely heavily on a single customer, or both. For example, several years ago a company called Yard Man Inc. manufactured and sold lawn equipment. Most of Yard Man's sales were to Sears, so most of its revenues and profits were due to its Sears account. When Sears decided to drop Yard Man as a supplier, the company was left without its most important customer. Yard Man is no longer in business. Because large firms typically have a broad customer base, they are not as exposed to a loss of a large portion of their business. Similarly, Coleco manufactured and sold the extremely popular Cabbage Patch dolls. The phenomenal popularity of the dolls was a great boon for Coleco, but when the public lost interest in the Cabbage Patch fad, the company was forced into bankruptcy.

The extension of credit to a small company, and especially to a small owner-managed company, often involves yet another risk that is less of a problem for larger firms—namely, dependence on the leadership of a single key individual whose unexpected death could cause the company to fail. For such a firm, it is important to have a plan of management succession clearly specified so creditors are assured the business will continue without interruption if some sort of disaster befalls the "key" manager. In addition, the firm could carry "key person insurance," payable to the bank or other creditors for the purposes of retiring the loan in the event of the key person's death.

In summary, to determine the financial strength of a small firm, the financial analyst must "look beyond the ratios" and analyze the viability of the firm's products, customers, management, and market. Ratio analysis is only the first step in a sound evaluation of the firm's ability to repay its debt and meet its other financial obligations.

Summary

The primary purposes of this chapter were (1) to describe the basic financial statements and (2) to discuss techniques used by investors and managers to analyze the statements. The following key concepts are covered.

- The four basic statements contained in the annual report are the **balance sheet,** the **income statement,** the **statement of retained earnings,** and the

statement of cash flows. Investors use the information provided in these statements to form expectations about the future levels of earnings and dividends, and about the firm's riskiness.

- **Operating cash flows** differ from reported **accounting income.** Investors should be more interested in a firm's projected cash flows than in reported earnings, because it is cash, not paper profits, that is paid out as dividends and plowed back into the business to produce growth.

- **Financial statement analysis** generally begins with the calculation of a set of **financial ratios** designed to reveal the relative strengths and weaknesses of a company as compared to other companies in the same industry, and to show whether the firm's position has been improving or deteriorating over time.

- **Liquidity ratios** show the relationship of a firm's current assets to its current liabilities, and thus indicate the firm's ability to meet its current obligations.

- **Asset management ratios** measure how effectively a firm is managing its assets.

- **Debt management ratios** reveal (1) the extent to which the firm is financed with debt and (2) its likelihood of defaulting on its debt obligations.

- **Profitability ratios** show the combined effects of liquidity, asset management, and debt management policies on operating results.

- **Market value ratios** relate the firm's stock price to its earnings and book value per share, providing an indication of how investors regard the firm's future prospects.

- **Trend analysis** is important, because it reveals whether the firm's ratios are improving or deteriorating over time.

- The **Du Pont chart** is designed to show how the profit margin on sales, the assets turnover ratio, and the use of debt interact to determine the rate of return on investment.

- In analyzing a small firm's financial position, ratio analysis is a useful starting point. However, the analyst must also (1) examine the quality of the financial data, (2) ensure that the firm is sufficiently diversified to withstand shifts in customers' buying habits, and (3) ensure that the firm has a plan for the succession of its management.

Ratio analysis has limitations, but used with care and judgment, it can be very helpful. The interpretation of the computed ratio values is the most important ingredient for reaching a conclusion regarding both the existing and the prospective financial position of a firm.

Questions

3-1   What four statements are contained in most annual reports?

3-2   If a "typical" firm reports $20 million of retained earnings on its balance sheet, could its directors declare a $20 million cash dividend without any qualms whatsoever? Explain why or why not.

3-3   Describe the changes in balance sheet accounts that would constitute sources of funds. What changes would be considered uses of funds?

3-4   Financial ratio analysis is conducted by four groups of analysts: managers, equity investors, long-term creditors, and short-term creditors. What is the primary emphasis of each of these groups in evaluating ratios?

3-5 What are some cares that must be taken when using ratio analysis? What is the most important aspect of ratio analysis?

3-6 Profit margins and turnover ratios vary from one industry to another. What differences would you expect to find between a grocery chain like Safeway and a steel company? Think particularly about the turnover ratios and the profit margin, and think about the Du Pont equation.

3-7 How does inflation distort ratio analysis comparisons, both for one company over time (trend analysis) and when different companies are compared? Are only balance sheet items or both balance sheet and income statement items affected?

3-8 If a firm's ROE is low and management wants to improve it, explain how using more debt might help. Could using too much debt be a detriment?

3-9 How might (a) seasonal factors and (b) different growth rates distort a comparative ratio analysis? Give some examples. How might these problems be alleviated?

3-10 Below are the balance sheets for Batelan Corporation for the fiscal years 1994 and 1995. In the column to the right of the balance sheet amounts, indicate whether the change in the account balance represents a source or a use of cash for the firm. Place a (+) in the space provided to indicate a source of funds, a (−) to indicate a use of funds, and a (0) if it cannot be determined whether the change was a source or a use of cash.

	1995	1994	Source (+) or Use (−)?
Cash	$ 400	$ 500	_____
Accounts receivable	250	300	_____
Inventory	450	400	_____
Current assets	1,100	1,200	
Net property and equipment	1,000	950	_____
Total assets	$2,100	$2,150	
Accounts payable	$ 200	$ 400	_____
Accruals	300	250	_____
Notes payable	400	200	_____
Current liabilities	900	850	
Long-term debt	800	900	_____
Total liabilities	1,700	1,750	
Common stock	250	300	_____
Retained earnings	150	100	_____
Total equity	400	400	
Total liabilities and equity	$2,100	$2,150	

From these balance sheets, can you tell whether Batelan generated a positive or negative net income during 1995? Can you tell if dividends were paid? Explain.

3-11 Indicate the effects of the transactions listed in the following table on total current assets, current ratio, and net income. Use (+) to indicate an increase, (−) to indicate a decrease, and (0) to indicate either no effect or an indeterminate effect. Be prepared to state any necessary assumptions, and assume an initial current ratio of more than 1.0. (Note: A good accounting background is necessary to answer some of these questions; if yours is not strong, just answer the questions you can handle.)

	Total Current Assets	Current Ratio	Effect on Net Income
a. Cash is acquired through issuance of additional common stock.	———	———	———
b. Merchandise is sold for cash.	———	———	———
c. Federal income tax due for the previous year is paid.	———	———	———
d. A fixed asset is sold for less than book value.	———	———	———
e. A fixed asset is sold for more than book value.	———	———	———
f. Merchandise is sold on credit.	———	———	———
g. Payment is made to trade creditors for previous purchases.	———	———	———
h. A cash dividend is declared and paid.	———	———	———
i. Cash is obtained through short-term bank loans.	———	———	———
j. Short-term notes receivable are sold at a discount.	———	———	———
k. Marketable securities are sold below cost.	———	———	———
l. Advances are made to employees.	———	———	———
m. Current operating expenses are paid.	———	———	———
n. Short-term promissory notes are issued to trade creditors in exchange for past due accounts payable.	———	———	———
o. Ten-year notes are issued to pay accounts payable.	———	———	———
p. A fully depreciated asset is retired.	———	———	———
q. Accounts receivable are collected.	———	———	———
r. Equipment is purchased with short-term notes.	———	———	———
s. Merchandise is purchased on credit.	———	———	———
t. The estimated taxes payable are increased.	———	———	———

Self-Test Problems

(Solutions Appear in Appendix B)

ST-1 Define each of the following terms:

Key terms

   a. annual report; income statement; balance sheet
   b. equity, or net worth; paid-in capital; retained earnings
   c. cash flow cycle
   d. statement of retained earnings; statement of cash flows
   e. depreciation; inventory valuation methods
   f. liquidity ratios: current ratio; quick, or acid test, ratio
   g. asset management ratios: inventory turnover ratio; days sales outstanding (DSO); fixed assets turnover ratio; total assets turnover ratio
   h. financial leverage: debt ratio; times-interest-earned (TIE) ratio; fixed charge coverage ratio
   i. profitability ratios: profit margin on sales; return on total assets (ROA); return on common equity (ROE)
   j. market value ratios: price/earnings (P/E) ratio; market/book (M/B) ratio; book value per share

k. trend analysis; comparative ratio analysis
l. Du Pont chart; Du Pont equation
m. "Window dressing"; seasonal effects on ratios

Debt ratio ST-2 K. Billingsworth & Co. had earnings per share of $4 last year, and it paid a $2 dividend. Total retained earnings increased by $12 million during the year, while book value per share at year-end was $40. Billingsworth has no preferred stock, and no new common stock was issued during the year. If Billingsworth's year-end debt (which equals its total liabilities) was $120 million, what was the company's year-end debt/assets ratio?

Ratio analysis ST-3 The following data apply to A.L. Kaiser & Company (millions of dollars):

Cash and marketable securities	$100.00
Fixed assets	$283.50
Sales	$1,000.00
Net income	$50.00
Quick ratio	2.0×
Current ratio	3.0×
DSO	40.0 days
ROE	12.0%

Kaiser has no preferred stock—only common equity, current liabilities, and long-term debt.

a. Find Kaiser's (1) accounts receivable (A/R), (2) current liabilities, (3) current assets, (4) total assets, (5) ROA, (6) common equity, and (7) long-term debt.

b. In part a, you should have found Kaiser's accounts receivable (A/R) = $111.1 million. If Kaiser could reduce its DSO from 40 days to 30 days while holding other things constant, how much cash would it generate? If this cash were used to buy back common stock (at book value) and thus reduce the amount of common equity, how would this affect (1) the ROE, (2) the ROA, and (3) the debt ratio?

Problems

Ratio analysis 3-1 Data for Unilate Textiles' 1994 financial statements are given in Table 3-1 and Table 3-2 in the chapter.

a. Compute the 1994 values of the ratios indicated below:

	1994 Values	
Ratio	**Unilate**	**Industry**
Current ratio	_____	3.9×
Days sales outstanding	_____	33.5 days
Inventory turnover	_____	7.2×
Fixed asset turnover	_____	4.1×
Debt ratio	_____	45.0%
Net profit margin	_____	4.6%
Return on assets	_____	9.9%

b. Briefly comment on Unilate's 1994 financial position. Can you see any obvious strengths or weaknesses?

c. Compare Unilate's 1994 ratios with its 1995 ratios, which are presented in Table 3-6 in the chapter. Comment on whether you believe Unilate's financial position improved or deteriorated during 1995.

d. What other information would be useful for projecting whether Unilate's financial position is expected to get better or worse in the future?

Ratio analysis   3-2   Data for Campsey Computer Company and its industry averages follow.

a. Calculate the indicated ratios for Campsey.

b. Construct the Du Pont equation for both Campsey and the industry.

c. Outline Campsey's strengths and weaknesses as revealed by your analysis.

d. Suppose Campsey had doubled its sales as well as its inventories, accounts receivable, and common equity during 1995. How would that information affect the validity of your ratio analysis? (Hint: Think about averages and the effects of rapid growth on ratios if averages are not used. No calculations are needed.)

Campsey Computer Company: Balance Sheet as of December 31, 1995

Cash	$ 77,500	Accounts payable	$129,000
Receivables	336,000	Notes payable	84,000
Inventories	241,500	Other current liabilities	117,000
Total current assets	$655,000	Total current liabilities	$330,000
Net fixed assets	292,500	Long-term debt	256,500
		Common equity	361,000
Total assets	$947,500	Total liabilities and equity	$947,500

Campsey Computer Company: Income Statement for Year Ended December 31, 1995

Sales	$ 1,607,500
Cost of goods sold	(1,353,000)
Gross profit	254,500
Fixed operating expenses except depreciation	(143,000)
Depreciation	(41,500)
Earnings before interest and taxes	70,000
Interest	(24,500)
Earnings before taxes	45,500
Taxes (40%)	(18,200)
Net income	$ 27,300

Ratio	Campsey	Industry Average
Current ratio	_____	2.0 ×
Days sales outstanding	_____	35 days
Inventory turnover	_____	5.6 ×
Total assets turnover	_____	3.0 ×
Profit margin on sales	_____	1.2 %
Return on assets	_____	3.6 %
Return on equity	_____	9.0 %
Debt ratio	_____	60.0 %

Balance sheet analysis   **3-3**   Complete the balance sheet and sales information in the table that follows for Isberg Industries using the following financial data:
Debt ratio: 50%
Quick ratio: 0.80×
Total assets turnover: 1.5×
Days sales outstanding: 36 days
Gross profit margin on sales: (Sales − Cost of goods sold)/Sales = 25%
Inventory turnover ratio: 5×

Balance Sheet

Cash	_____	Accounts payable	_____
Accounts receivable	_____	Long-term debt	60,000
Inventories	_____	Common stock	_____
Fixed assets	_____	Retained earnings	97,500
Total assets	$300,000	Total liabilities and equity	
Sales	_____	Cost of goods sold	_____

Du Pont analysis   **3-4**   The Finnerty Furniture Company, a manufacturer and wholesaler of high-quality home furnishings, has experienced low profitability in recent years. As a result, the board of directors has replaced the president of the firm with a new president, Elizabeth Brannigan, who has asked you to make an analysis of the firm's financial position using the Du Pont chart. The most recent industry average ratios, and Finnerty's financial statements, are as follows:

Industry Average Ratios

Current ratio	2×	Fixed assets turnover	6×
Debt ratio	30%	Total assets turnover	3×
Times-interest-earned	7×	Profit margin on sales	3%
Inventory turnover	8.5×	Return on total assets	9%
Days sales outstanding	24 days	Return on common equity	12.9%

Finnerty Furniture Company: Balance Sheet as of December 31, 1995 (millions of dollars)

Cash	$ 45	Accounts payable	$ 45
Marketable securities	33	Notes payable	45
Net receivables	66	Other current liabilities	21
Inventories	159	Total current liabilities	$111
Total current assets	$303	Long-term debt	24
		Total liabilities	$135
Gross fixed assets	225		
Less depreciation	78	Common stock	114
Net fixed assets	$147	Retained earnings	201
		Total stockholders' equity	$315
Total assets	$450	Total liabilities and equity	$450

Finnerty Furniture Company: Income Statement for Year Ended December 31, 1995 (millions of dollars)

Net sales	$795.0
Cost of goods sold	(660.0)
Gross profit	$135.0
Selling expenses	(73.5)
Depreciation expense	(12.0)
Earnings before interest and taxes	$ 49.5
Interest expense	(4.5)
Earnings before taxes (EBT)	45.0
Taxes (40%)	(18.0)
Net income	$ 27.0

   a. Calculate those ratios that you think would be useful in this analysis.
   b. Construct a Du Pont equation for Finnerty, and compare the company's ratios to the industry average ratios.
   c. Do the balance sheet accounts or the income statement figures seem to be primarily responsible for the low profits?
   d. Which specific accounts seem to be most out of line in relation to other firms in the industry?
   e. If Finnerty had a pronounced seasonal sales pattern, or if it grew rapidly during the year, how might that affect the validity of your ratio analysis? How might you correct for such potential problems?

Ratio analysis   **3-5**   The Cary Corporation's forecasted 1996 financial statements follow, along with some industry average ratios.
   a. Calculate Cary's 1996 forecasted ratios, compare them with the industry average data, and comment briefly on Cary's projected strengths and weaknesses.
   b. What do you think would happen to Cary's ratios if the company initiated cost-cutting measures that allowed it to hold lower levels of inventory and substantially decreased the cost of goods sold? No calculations are necessary. Think about which ratios would be affected by changes in these two accounts.

Cary Corporation: Forecasted Balance Sheet as of December 31, 1996

Cash	$ 72,000
Accounts receivable	439,000
Inventories	894,000
Total current assets	$1,405,000
Land and building	238,000
Machinery	132,000
Other fixed assets	61,000
Total assets	$1,836,000
Accounts and notes payable	$ 432,000
Accruals	170,000
Total current liabilities	$ 602,000
Long-term debt	404,290
Common stock	575,000
Retained earnings	254,710
Total liabilities and equity	$1,836,000

Cary Corporation Forecasted Income Statement for 1996

Sales	$4,290,000
Cost of goods sold	(3,580,000)
Gross operating profit	$ 710,000
General administrative and selling expenses	(236,320)
Depreciation	(159,000)
Miscellaneous	(134,000)
Earnings before taxes (EBT)	$ 180,680
Taxes (40%)	(72,272)
Net income	$ 108,408
Number of shares outstanding	23,000

Per-Share Data

EPS	$4.71
Cash dividends	$0.95
P/E ratio	5×
Market price (average)	$23.57

Industry Financial Ratios (1996)[a]

Quick ratio	1.0×
Current ratio	2.7×
Inventory turnover[b]	5.8×
Days sales outstanding	32 days
Fixed assets turnover[b]	13.0×
Total assets turnover[b]	2.6×
Return on assets	9.1%
Return on equity	18.2%
Debt ratio	50.0%
Profit margin on sales	3.5%
P/E ratio	6.0×

[a]Industry average ratios have been constant for the past four years.
[b]Based on year-end balance sheet figures.

Exam-Type Problems

The problems included in this section are set up in such a way that they could be used as multiple-choice exam problems.

Ratio calculation **3-6** Assume you are given the following relationships for The Zumwalt Corporation:

Sales/total assets	1.5×
Return on assets (ROA)	3%
Return on equity (ROE)	5%

Calculate Zumwalt's profit margin and debt ratio.

Liquidity ratios **3-7** The Hindelang Company has $1,312,500 in current assets and $525,000 in current liabilities. Its initial inventory level is $375,000, and it will raise funds as additional notes payable and use them to increase inventory. How much can Hindelang's short-term debt (notes payable) increase without pushing its current ratio below 2.0? What will be the firm's quick ratio after Hindelang has raised the maximum amount of short-term funds?

Ratio calculations   **3-8**   The W.F. Bailey Company had a quick ratio of 1.4, a current ratio of 3.0, an inventory turnover of 5 times, total current assets of $810,000, and cash and marketable securities of $120,000 in 1995. If the cost of goods sold equaled 86 percent of sales, what were Bailey's annual sales and its DSO for 1995?

Times-interest-earned ratio   **3-9**   Wolken Corporation has $500,000 of debt outstanding, and it pays an interest rate of 10 percent annually. Wolken's annual sales are $2 million; its average tax rate is 20 percent; and its net profit margin on sales is 5 percent. If the company does not maintain a TIE ratio of at least 5 times, its bank will refuse to renew the loan, and bankruptcy will result. What is Wolken's TIE ratio?

Return on equity   **3-10**   Coastal Packaging's ROE last year was only 3 percent, but its management has developed a new operating plan designed to improve things. The new plan calls for a total debt ratio of 60 percent, which will result in interest charges of $300 per year. Management projects an EBIT of $1,000 on sales of $10,000, and it expects to have a total assets turnover ratio of 2.0. Under these conditions, the average tax rate will be 30 percent. If the changes are made, what return on equity will Coastal earn? What is the ROA?

Return on equity   **3-11**   Earth's Best Company has sales of $200,000, a net income of $15,000, and the following balance sheet:

Cash	$ 10,000	Accounts payable	$ 30,000
Receivables	50,000	Other current liabilities	20,000
Inventories	150,000	Long-term debt	50,000
Net fixed assets	90,000	Common equity	200,000
Total assets	$300,000	Total liabilities and equity	$300,000

a. The company's new owner thinks that inventories are excessive and can be lowered to the point where the current ratio is equal to the industry average, 2.5×, without affecting either sales or net income. If inventories are sold off and not replaced so as to reduce the current ratio to 2.5×, if the funds generated are used to reduce common equity (stock can be repurchased at book value), and if no other changes occur, by how much will the ROE change?

b. Now suppose we wanted to take this problem and modify it for use on an exam, that is, to create a new problem which you have not seen to test your knowledge of this type of problem. How would your answer change if (1) We doubled all the dollar amounts? (2) We stated that the target current ratio was 3.0×? (3) We said that the company had 10,000 shares of stock outstanding, and we asked how much the change in part a would increase EPS? (4) What would your answer to (3) be if we changed the original problem to state that the stock was selling for twice book value, so common equity would not be reduced on a dollar-for-dollar basis?

c. Now explain how we could have set the problem up to have you focus on changing accounts receivable, or fixed assets, or using the funds generated to retire debt (we would give you the interest rate on outstanding debt), or how the original problem could have stated that the company needed *more* inventories and it would finance them with new common equity or with new debt.

Statement of cash flows   **3-12**   The consolidated balance sheets for the Lloyd Lumber Company at the beginning and end of 1995 follow. The company bought $50 million worth of fixed assets. The charge for depreciation in 1995 was $10 million. Net income was $33 million, and the company paid out $5 million in dividends.

a. Fill in the amount of the source or use in the appropriate column.

Lloyd Lumber Company: Balance Sheets at Beginning and End of 1995 (millions of dollars)

	Jan. 1	Dec. 31	Change Source	Use
Cash	$ 7	$ 15	_____	_____
Marketable securities	0	11	_____	_____
Net receivables	30	22	_____	_____
Inventories	53	75	_____	_____
Total current assets	$ 90	$123		
Gross fixed assets	75	125	_____	_____
Less accumulated depreciation	25	35	_____	_____
Net fixed assets	$ 50	$ 90		
Total assets	$140	$213		
Accounts payable	$ 18	$ 15	_____	_____
Notes payable	3	15	_____	_____
Other current liabilities	15	7	_____	_____
Long-term debt	8	24	_____	_____
Common stock	29	57	_____	_____
Retained earnings	67	95	_____	_____
Total liabilities and equity	$140	$213		

NOTE: Total sources must equal total uses.

    b. Prepare a statement of cash flows.
    c. Briefly summarize your findings.

Income and cash flow analysis   **3-13** The Montejo Corporation expects 1996 sales to be $12 million. Operating costs other than depreciation are expected to be 75 percent of sales, and depreciation is expected to be $1.5 million in 1996. All sales revenues will be collected in cash, and cost other than depreciation must be paid during the year. Montejo's interest expense is expected to be $1 million, and it is taxed at a 40 percent rate.

    a. Set up an income statement and a cash flow statement (use two columns on one page) for Montejo. What is the expected cash flow from operations?

    b. Suppose Congress changed the tax laws so that Montejo's depreciation expenses doubled in 1996, but no other changes occurred. What would happen to the net income and cash flow from operations expected in 1996?

    c. Now suppose Congress, rather than increasing Montejo's 1996 depreciation, reduced it by 50 percent. How would the income and cash flows be affected?

    d. If this company belonged to you, would you prefer Congress increase or decrease the depreciation expense allowed your company? Explain why.

Integrative Problem

Financial statement analysis   **3-14** Donna Jamison was recently hired as a financial analyst by Computron Industries, a manufacturer of electronic components. Her first task was to conduct a financial analysis of the firm covering the last two years. To begin, she gathered the following financial statements and other data.

Balance Sheets	1995	1994
Assets		
Cash	$ 52,000	$ 57,600
Accounts receivable	402,000	351,200
Inventories	836,000	715,200
Total current assets	$1,290,000	$1,124,000
Gross fixed assets	$ 527,000	$ 491,000
Less accumulated depreciation	166,200	146,200
Net fixed assets	$ 360,800	$ 344,800
Total assets	$1,650,800	$1,468,800
Liabilities and Equity		
Accounts payable	$ 175,200	$ 145,600
Notes payable	225,000	200,000
Accruals	140,000	136,000
Total current liabilities	$ 540,200	$ 481,600
Long-term debt	$ 424,612	$ 323,432
Common stock (100,000 shares)	$ 460,000	$ 460,000
Retained earnings	225,988	203,768
Total equity	$ 685,988	$ 663,768
Total liabilities and equity	$1,650,800	$1,468,800

Income Statements

	1995	1994
Sales	$3,850,000	$3,432,000
Cost of goods sold	(3,250,000)	(2,864,000)
Other expenses	(430,300)	(340,000)
Depreciation	(20,000)	(18,900)
Total operating costs	$3,700,300	$3,222,900
EBIT	$ 149,700	$ 209,100
Interest expense	(76,000)	(62,500)
EBT	$ 73,700	$ 146,600
Taxes (40%)	(29,480)	(58,640)
Net income	$ 44,220	$ 87,960
EPS	$0.442	$0.880

Statement of Cash Flows (1995):

Operating Activities:

Net income	$ 44,220
Other additions (Sources of cash):	
Depreciation	20,000
Increase in accounts payable	29,600
Increase in accruals	4,000
Subtractions (Uses of cash):	
Increases in accounts receivable	(50,800)
Increase in inventories	(120,800)
Net cash flow from operations	($ 73,780)

Statement of Cash Flows (1995): *(continued)*

Long-Term Investing Activities:

Investment in fixed assets		($ 36,000)

Financing Activities:

Increase in notes payable		$ 25,000
Increase in long-term debt		101,180
Payment of cash dividends		(22,000)
Net cash flow from financing		104,180
Net reduction in cash account		($ 5,600)
Cash at beginning of year		57,600
Cash at end of year		$ 52,000

Other Data

December 31 stock price	$ 6.00	$ 8.50
Number of shares	100,000	100,000
Dividends per share	$ 0.22	$ 0.22
Lease payments	$ 40,000	$ 40,000

Industry average data for 1995:

Ratio	Industry Average
Current	2.7×
Quick	1.0×
Inventory turnover	6.0×
Days sales outstanding (DSO)	32.0 days
Fixed assets turnover	10.7×
Total assets turnover	2.6×
Debt ratio	50.0%
TIE	2.5×
Fixed charge coverage	2.1×
Profit margin	3.5%
ROA	9.1%
ROE	18.2%
Price/earnings	14.2×
Market/book	1.4×

Assume that you are Donna Jamison's assistant, and that she has asked you to help her prepare a report which evaluates the company's financial condition. Then answer the following questions.

a. What can you conclude about the company's financial condition from its statement of cash flows?

b. What is the purpose of financial ratio analysis, and what are the five major categories of ratios?

c. What are Computron's current and quick ratios? What do they tell you about the company's liquidity position?

d. What are Computron's inventory turnover, days sales outstanding, fixed assets turnover, and total assets turnover ratios? How does the firm's utilization of assets stack up against that of the industry?

e. What are the firm's debt, times-interest-earned, and fixed charge coverage ratios? How does Computron compare to the industry with respect to financial leverage? What conclusions can you draw from these ratios?

f. Calculate and discuss the firm's profitability ratios—that is, its profit margin, return on assets (ROA), and return on equity (ROE).

g. Calculate Computron's market value ratios—that is, its price/earnings ratio and its market/book ratio. What do these ratios tell you about investors' opinions of the company?

h. Use the Du Pont equation to provide a summary and overview of Computron's financial condition. What are the firm's major strengths and weaknesses?

i. Use the following simplified 1995 balance sheet to show, in general terms, how an improvement in one of the ratios, say the DSO, would affect the stock price. For example, if the company could improve its collection procedures and thereby lower the DSO from 37.6 days to 27.6 days, how would that change "ripple through" the financial statements (shown in thousands below) and influence the stock price?

Accounts receivable	$ 402	Debt	$ 965
Other current assets	888		
Net fixed assets	361	Equity	686
Total assets	$1,651	Total liabilities and equity	$1,651

j. Although financial statement analysis can provide useful information about a company's operations and its financial condition, this type of analysis does have some potential problems and limitations, and it must be used with care and judgment. What are some problems and limitations?

Computer-Related Problem

Work the problem in this section only if you are using the computer problem diskette.

Ratio analysis **3-15** Use the computerized model in the File C3 to solve this problem.

a. Refer to Problem 3-5. Suppose Cary Corporation is considering installing a new computer system which would provide tighter control of inventories, accounts receivable, and accounts payable. If the new system is installed, the following data are projected (rather than the data given in Problem 3-5) for the indicated balance sheet and income statement accounts:

Accounts receivable	$ 395,000
Inventories	700,000
Other fixed assets	150,000
Accounts and notes payable	275,000
Accruals	120,000
Cost of goods sold	3,450,000
Administrative and selling expenses	248,775
P/E ratio	6×

How do these changes affect the projected ratios and the comparison with the industry averages? (Note that any changes to the income statement will change the amount of retained earnings; therefore, the model is set up to calculate 1996 retained earnings as 1995 retained earnings plus net income minus dividends paid. The model also adjusts the cash balance so that the balance sheet balances.)

b. If the new computer were even more efficient than Cary's management had estimated and thus caused the cost of goods sold to decrease by $125,000 from the projections in part a, what effect would that have on the company's financial position?

c. If the new computer were less efficient than Cary's management had estimated and caused the cost of goods sold to increase by $125,000 from the projections in part a, what effect would that have on the company's financial position?

d. Change, one by one, the other items in part a to see how each change affects the ratio analysis. Then think about, and write a paragraph describing, how computer models like this one can be used to help make better decisions about the purchase of such things as a new computer system.

CHAPTER 4

Financial Planning and Control

In November 1994, Sony Corporation, the Japanese consumer electronics firm, wrote off more than $3.2 billion in assets, causing the book value of its assets to immediately decrease by about 30 percent and the market value of its stock to decrease by 13 percent within a one-week period. The write-off was directly attributed to Sony Pictures, the motion picture business that had been formed five years earlier with the $5 billion purchase of Columbia Pictures and Tri-Star Pictures from Coca-Cola Company. According to most analysts, the success of Sony's 1988 purchase of CBS Records, one of the world's largest record companies, teased the company into expanding its entertainment operations to the "Hollywood scene." Unfortunately, Sony did not follow the old adage: "look before you leap"—company executives seemingly did not have a formal financial plan or control mechanism for the movie business. Michael Schulhof, chairman of Sony Corporation of America, was put in charge of Sony Pictures, even though he was unknown in the motion picture industry. He hired two movie producers, neither of whom had previous experience running a movie studio, to head the production facilities. During the past five years, more than $1 billion has been spent on refurbishing studio lots and on executive perquisites such as fresh flowers, antiques, private chefs, and lavish parties. But, Sony Pictures' movie-production companies, Columbia and Tri-Star, were unable to consistently produce hit movies; in fact, most of the pictures were expensive flops, including "Last Action Hero," "I'll Do Anything," and "Mary Shelley's Frankenstein." Was Sony Pictures just unlucky? Not according to Chuck Goto, an analyst with Smith Barney, who notes that "[i]f you look at it very objectively, it's clear the company mismanaged shareholders' money" by not planning adequately. It seems the only plan Sony had was to pour money into movies, and this strategy was destined to fail because there was not adequate forecasting and control to head off any problems that arose. Sony probably will have more write-offs in the future resulting from its motion picture business—the total losses might never be known completely. But, one thing is clear, many of the problems at Sony Pictures could have been

Continued

avoided or reduced significantly if Sony Corporation had a financial plan in place before it entered the movie industry. Most analysts agree that the value of Sony Pictures at the end of 1994 was about one half of its 1989 value. At the end of 1994, Sony began "biting the bullet," hoping that its motion picture business would survive the financial frivolity exhibited in the previous five years. Sony began to evaluate the effects on forecasted earnings and stock prices of cutting certain costs, writing off additional assets, and controlling the finances associated with the motion picture businesses—a plan was devised to attempt a salvage of Sony Pictures, which provided encouragement to Sony Corporation's investors and potential investors.

SOURCES: "Last Action: Sony Finally Admits Billion-Dollar Mistake: Its Messed-Up Studio; Columbia was Mismanaged from the Very Start; Public Sale May be Next in a League of Their Own," *The Wall Street Journal*, November 18, 1994, and "Despite Recent Drop, Sony's Stock Receives Some Favorable Reviews," *The Wall Street Journal*, November 25, 1994.

In the last chapter, we focused on how to use financial statement analysis to evaluate the existing financial position of the firm. In this chapter, we will see how a financial manager can use some of the information obtained through financial statement analysis for financial planning and control of the firm's future operations.

Well-run companies generally base their operating plans on a set of forecasted financial statements. The **financial planning** process begins with a sales forecast for the next few years. Then the assets required to meet the sales targets are determined, and a decision is made concerning how to finance the required assets. At that point, income statements and balance sheets can be projected, and earnings and dividends per share, as well as the key ratios, can be forecasted.

Once the "base case" forecasted statements and ratios have been prepared, top managers want to know (1) how realistic the results are, (2) how to attain the results, and (3) what impact changes in operations will have on the forecasts. At this stage, which is the **financial control** phase, the firm is concerned with implementing the financial plans, or forecasts, and dealing with the feedback and adjustment process that is necessary to ensure the goals of the firm are pursued appropriately.

The first part of the chapter is devoted to financial planning using projected financial statements, or forecasts, and the second part of the chapter focuses on financial control using budgeting and the analysis of leverage to determine how changes in operations affect financial forecasts.

FINANCIAL PLANNING
The projection of sales, income, and assets based on alternative production and marketing strategies, as well as the determination of the resources needed to achieve these projections.

FINANCIAL CONTROL
The phase in which financial plans are implemented; control deals with the feedback and adjustment process required to ensure adherence to plans and modification of plans because of unforeseen changes.

Sales Forecasts

Forecasting is an essential part of the planning process, and a **sales forecast** is the most important ingredient of financial forecasting. The sales forecast generally starts with a review of sales during the past five to ten years, which can be expressed in a graph such as that in Figure 4-1. The first part of the graph shows five years of historical sales for Unilate Textiles, the textile and clothing manufacturer we analyzed in the last chapter. The graph could have contained ten years of sales data, but Unilate typically focuses on sales figures for the latest five years

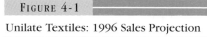

FIGURE 4-1

Unilate Textiles: 1996 Sales Projection

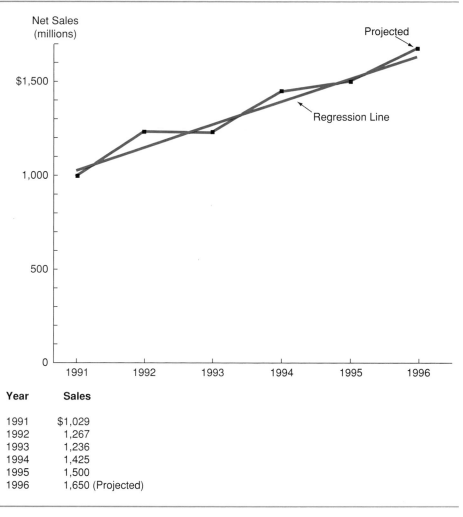

Year	Sales
1991	$1,029
1992	1,267
1993	1,236
1994	1,425
1995	1,500
1996	1,650 (Projected)

SALES FORECAST
A forecast of a firm's unit and dollar sales for some future period; generally based on recent sales trends plus forecasts of the economic prospects for the nation, region, industry, and so forth.

because the firm's studies have shown that future growth is more closely related to the recent than to the distant past.

Unilate had its ups and downs during the period from 1991 to 1995. In 1993, poor cotton production in the United States and diseased sheep in Australia resulted in low textile production, which caused 1993 sales to fall below the 1992 level. Then a significant increase in both the supply of cotton and the supply of wool in 1994 pushed sales up by 15 percent. Based on a regression analysis, Unilate's forecasters determined that the average annual growth rate in sales over the past 5 years was about 9.5 percent. To determine the forecasted sales growth for 1996, some of the factors that Unilate considered included projections of expected economic activity, competitive conditions, and product development and distribution both in the markets in which Unilate currently operates and in the markets it plans to enter in the future. Often, firms develop mathematical models such as regression equations to take into consideration such factors when forecasting future sales. Based on its historical sales trend, plans for new product and market introductions, and Unilate's forecast for the economy, the firm's planning committee has projected a 10 percent growth rate for sales during 1996. So, 1996 sales are expected to be $1,650 million, which is 10 percent higher than 1995 sales of $1,500 million.

If the sales forecast is inaccurate, the consequences possibly can be serious. First, if the market expands significantly *more* than Unilate has geared up for, the company probably will not be able to meet demand. Customers will buy competitors' products, and Unilate will lose market share, which will be hard to regain. On the other hand, if the projections are overly optimistic, Unilate could end up with too much plant, equipment, and inventory. This would mean low turnover ratios, high costs for depreciation and storage, and, possibly, write-offs of obsolete or unusable inventory. All of this would result in a low rate of return on equity, which in turn would depress the company's stock price. If Unilate had financed an unnecessary expansion with debt, its problems would, of course, be compounded. Remember from our analysis of its 1995 financial statements in the last chapter that Unilate's current financial position is somewhat weak. Thus, an accurate sales forecast is critical to the well-being of the firm.[1]

Self-Test Questions

How do past trends affect a sales forecast?

List some factors that should be considered when developing a sales forecast.

Briefly explain why an accurate sales forecast is critical to profitability.

Projected (Pro Forma) Financial Statements

Any forecast of financial requirements involves (1) determining how much money the firm will need during a given period, (2) determining how much money the firm will generate internally during the same period, and (3) subtracting the funds generated from the funds required to determine the external financing requirements. One method used to estimate external requirements is the *projected,* or *pro forma, balance sheet method.*

ADDITIONAL FUNDS NEEDED (AFN)
Funds that a firm must raise externally through borrowing or by selling new stock.

The projected balance sheet method is straightforward—simply project the asset requirements for the coming period, then project the liabilities and equity that will be generated under normal operations, and subtract the projected liabilities and equity from the required assets to estimate the **additional funds needed (AFN)** to support the level of forecasted operations. The steps in the procedure are explained below.

Step 1. Forecast the 1996 Income Statement

PROJECTED BALANCE SHEET METHOD
A method of forecasting financing requirements based on forecasted financial statements.

The **projected balance sheet method** begins with a forecast of sales. Next, the income statement for the coming year is forecasted in order to obtain an initial estimate of the amount of retained earnings the company will generate during the

---

[1]A sales forecast actually is the *expected value of a probability distribution* with many possible levels of sales. Because any sales forecast is subject to a greater or lesser degree of uncertainty, for financial planning we are often just as interested in the degree of uncertainty inherent in the sales forecast (σ sales) as we are in the expected value of sales. The concepts of probability distribution measures as they apply to corporate finance are discussed in the next chapter.

year. This requires assumptions about the operating cost ratio, the tax rate, interest charges, and the dividends paid. In the simplest case, the assumption is made that costs will increase at the same rate as sales; in more complicated situations, cost changes are forecasted separately. Still, the objective of this part of the analysis is to determine how much income the company will earn and then retain for reinvestment in the business during the forecasted year.

Table 4-1 shows Unilate's actual 1995 income statement and the initial forecast of the 1996 income statement if the conditions just mentioned exist. To create the 1996 income forecast, we assume that sales and variable operating costs will be 10 percent greater in 1996 than in 1995. In addition, it is assumed that Unilate currently operates at full capacity, so it will need to expand its plant capacity in 1996 to handle the additional operations. Therefore, in Table 4-1, the 1996 forecasts of sales, *all* operating costs, and depreciation are 10 percent greater than their 1995 levels. The result is that earnings before interest and taxes (EBIT) is forecasted to be $154 million in 1996.

To complete the initial forecast of 1996 income, we assume no change in the financing of the firm because, at this point, it is not known if additional financing is needed. But it is apparent that the 1996 interest expense will change if the amount of debt (borrowing) the firm needs to support the forecasted increase in operations changes. To forecast the 1996 dividends, we simply assume the dividend payout will be similar to what it was in 1995, about 45–50 percent of earnings per share. So the dividend per share for 1996 is forecasted to be $1.31. If the

---

TABLE 4-1

Unilate Textiles: Actual 1995 and Projected 1996 Income Statements (millions of dollars, except per share data)

	1995 Results[a]	Forecast Basis[b]	1996 Initial Forecast
Net sales	$1,500	× 1.10	$1,650
Cost of goods sold	(1,220)	× 1.10	(1,342)
Gross profit	$ 280		$ 308
Fixed operating costs except depreciation	(90)	× 1.10	(99)
Depreciation	(50)	× 1.10	(55)
Earnings before interest and taxes (EBIT)	$ 140		154
Less interest	(36)		(36)[c]
Earnings before taxes (EBT)	$ 104		$ 118
Taxes (40%)	(42)		(47)
Net Income	$ 62		$ 71
Common dividends	(29)		(33)[d]
Addition to retained earnings	$ 33		$ 38
Dividends per share	$1.17		$1.31
Number of common shares (millions)	25		25

[a]The dollar values in this financial statement, as well as the others in this section, are rounded (except per share data); so there might be rounding effects with some of the results.

[b]× 1.10 indicates "times 1 + g"; used for items that grow proportionally with sales.

[c]Indicates a 1995 figure carried over for the preliminary forecast.

[d]Indicates a projected figure. See text for explanation.

issuing long-term bonds, by selling new common stock, or by some combination of these.

The initial forecast of Unilate's financial statements has shown us that (1) higher sales must be supported by higher asset levels, (2) some of the asset increases can be financed by spontaneous increases in accounts payable and accruals and by retained earnings, and (3) any shortfall must be financed from external sources, either by borrowing or by selling new stock.

Step 3. Raising the Additional Funds Needed

Like other corporations, Unilate can raise the additional funds needed to support the forecasted increase in operations either by borrowing or by selling more stock (equity). Unilate can borrow by going to its bank for a loan or by selling a corporate bond to investors; either action will increase the firm's debt. Unilate's financial manager will base the decision of exactly how to raise the $38 million additional funds needed on several factors, including its ability to handle additional debt, conditions in the financial markets, and restrictions imposed by existing debt agreements. The decisions concerning how to best finance the firm will be discussed later in Part VI of the text. At this point, it is important to understand that, regardless of how Unilate raises the $38 million AFN, the initial forecasts of both the income statement and the balance sheet will be affected. If Unilate takes on new debt, its interest expenses will rise; and, if additional shares of common stock are sold, *total* dividend payments will increase if the *same dividend per share* is paid to common stockholders. Each of these changes, which we term *financing feedbacks,* will affect the amount of additional retained earnings originally forecasted, which in turn will affect the amount of additional funds needed.

Remember from our ratio analysis in the last chapter that we concluded Unilate has a below-average debt position. Consequently, Unilate has decided any additional funds needed to support future operations will be raised primarily by issuing new common stock. Following this financing policy should help improve Unilate's debt position as well as its overall profitability.

Step 4. Financing Feedbacks

FINANCING FEEDBACKS
The effects on the income statement and balance sheet of actions taken to finance forecasted increases in assets.

As mentioned in the previous section, one complexity that arises in financial forecasting relates to **financing feedbacks.** The external funds raised to pay for new assets create additional expenses that must be reflected in the income statement, and that lowers the initially forecasted addition to retained earnings, which means more external funds are needed. In other words, if Unilate raised the $38 million AFN by issuing new debt and new common stock, it would find both the interest expense and the total dividend payments would be higher than the amounts contained in the forecasted income statement shown in Table 4-1. Consequently, after adjusting for the higher interest and dividend payments, the addition to retained earnings would be lower than the initial forecast of $38 million. Because the retained earnings will be lower than projected, a financing shortfall will exist even after the original AFN of $38 million is considered. So, in reality, Unilate must raise more than $38 million to account for the fact that any additional external financing needed to support the expected increase in operations will reduce the forecasted addition to retained earnings, which contributes to the amount of internal financing expected to be generated from the increase in operations. To determine the amount of external financing actually needed, we have to adjust the initial forecasts of both the income statement (Step 1) and the balance sheet (Step 2) to reflect the impact of raising the additional external financing. This process has to be repeated until AFN = 0 in Table 4-2, which means Step 1 and Step 2 might have to be repeated several times to fully account for the financing feedbacks.

Table 4-3 contains the adjusted 1996 preliminary forecasts for the income statement and the balance sheet of Unilate Textiles after all the financing effects are considered. To generate the adjusted forecasts, it is assumed that of the total external funds needed, 65 percent will be raised by selling new common stock at $23 per share, 15 percent will be borrowed from the bank at an interest rate of 7 percent, and 20 percent will be raised by selling long-term bonds with a coupon interest of 10 percent. Under these conditions, it can be seen from Table 4-3 that Unilate actually needs $40 million to support the forecasted increase in operations, not the $38 million contained in the initial forecast. The additional $2 million is needed because the added amounts of debt and common stock will cause interest and dividend payments to increase, which will decrease the contribution to retained earnings by $2 million.[2]

Analysis of the Forecast

The 1996 forecast as developed above represents a preliminary forecast because we have completed only the first stage of the total forecasting process. Next, the projected statements must be analyzed to determine whether the forecast meets the firm's financial targets. If the statements do not meet the targets, then elements of the forecast must be changed.

Table 4-4 shows Unilate's 1995 ratios as they were reported in Table 3-6 of Chapter 3, plus the projected 1996 ratios based on the preliminary forecast and the industry average ratios. As we noted in Chapter 3, the firm's financial condition at the close of 1995 was weak, with many ratios being well below the industry averages. The preliminary forecast for 1996 (after financing feedbacks are considered), which assumes that Unilate's past practices will continue into the future, shows an improved debt position. But the overall financial position still is somewhat weak, and this condition will persist unless management takes some actions to improve things.

Unilate's management actually plans to take steps to improve its financial condition. The plans are to (1) close down certain operations, (2) modify the credit policy to reduce the collection period for receivables, and (3) better manage inventory so that products are turned over more often.[3] These proposed operational changes will affect both the income statement and the balance sheet, so the preliminary forecast will have to be revised again to reflect the impact of such changes. When this process is complete, management will have its final forecast. To keep things simple, we do not show the final forecast here; instead, for the remaining discussions, we assume the preliminary forecast is not substantially different and use it as the final forecast for Unilate's 1996 operations.

As we have shown, forecasting is an iterative process, both in the way the financial statements are generated and in the way the financial plan is developed.

---

[2]Appendix 4A gives a more detailed description of the iterations required to generate the final forecasts.

[3]We will discuss receivables and inventory management in detail in Part IV.

TABLE 4-3

Unilate Textiles: 1996 Adjusted Forecast of Financial Statements (millions of dollars)

INCOME STATEMENT

	Initial Forecast	Adjusted Forecast	Financing Adjustment
Net sales	$1,650	$1,650	
Cost of goods sold	(1,342)	(1,342)	
Gross profit	$ 308	$ 308	
Fixed operating costs except depreciation	(99)	(99)	
Depreciation	(55)	(55)	
Earnings before interest and taxes (EBIT)	$ 154	$ 154	
Less interest	(36)	(37)	(1)
Earnings before taxes (EBT)	$ 118	$ 117	
Taxes (40%)	(47)	(47)	0
Net income	$ 71	$ 70	
Common dividends	(33)	(34)	(1)
Addition to retained earnings	$ 38	$ 36	(2)
Dividends per share	$1.31	$1.31	
Number of common shares (millions)	25	26	

BALANCE SHEET

	Initial Forecast	Adjusted Forecast	Financing Adjustment
Cash	$ 22	$ 22	
Accounts receivable	198	198	
Inventories	297	297	
Total current assets	$517	$517	
Net plant and equipment	418	418	
Total assets	$935	$935	
Accounts payable	$ 33	$ 33	
Accruals	66	66	
Notes payable	40	46	$ 6
Total current liabilities	$139	$145	
Long-term bonds	297	305	$ 8
Total liabilities	$436	$450	
Common stock	130	156	$26
Retained earnings	331	329	$ (2)
Total owners' equity	$461	$485	
Total liabilities and equity	$897	$935	
Additional Funds Needed (AFN)	$ 38	$ 0	$38

NOTE: All values, except dividends per share, are rounded to the nearest million (dollars or shares).

	1995	Adjusted Preliminary 1996	Industry Average
TABLE 4-4			
Unilate Textiles: Key Ratios			
Current ratio	3.6	3.6	4.1
Inventory turnover	4.5	4.5	7.4
Days sales outstanding	43.2	43.2	32.1
Total assets turnover	1.8	1.8	2.1
Debt ratio	50.2%	48.1%	45.0%
Times interest earned	3.9	4.1	6.5
Profit margin	4.1%	4.3%	4.7%
Return on assets	7.3%	7.5%	10.1%
Return on equity	14.7%	14.5%	18.3%

For planning purposes, the financial staff develops a preliminary forecast based on a continuation of past policies and trends. This provides the executives with a starting point, or "straw man" forecast. Next, the model is modified to see what effects alternative operating plans would have on the firm's earnings and financial condition. This results in a revised forecast.

Self-Test Questions

What is the AFN, and how is the projected balance sheet method used to estimate it?

What is a financing feedback, and how do financing feedbacks affect the estimate of AFN?

Why is it necessary for the forecasting process to be iterative?

Other Considerations in Forecasting

We have presented a very simple method for constructing pro forma financial statements under rather restrictive conditions. In this section, we describe some other conditions that should be considered when creating forecasts.

Excess Capacity

The construction of the 1996 forecasts for Unilate were based on the assumption that the firm's 1995 operations were at full capacity, so any increase in sales would require additional assets, especially plant and equipment. If Unilate did *not* operate at full capacity in 1995, then plant and equipment would have to be increased only if the additional sales (operations) forecasted in 1996 exceeded the unused capacity of the existing assets. For example, if Unilate actually utilized only 80 percent of its fixed assets' capacity to produce 1995 sales of $1,500 million, then

$$\$1,500 \text{ million} = 0.80 \times (\text{Plant capacity})$$

$$\text{Plant capacity} = \frac{\$1,500 \text{ million}}{0.80} = \$1,875 \text{ million}$$

In this case, then, Unilate could increase sales to $1,875 million, or by 25 percent of 1995 sales, before full capacity is reached and plant and equipment would have to be increased. In general, we can compute the sales capacity of the firm if it is known what percent of assets are utilized to produce a particular level of sales:

$$\text{Full capacity sales} = \frac{\text{Sales level}}{\begin{array}{c}\text{Percent of capacity used}\\\text{to generate sales level}\end{array}}$$

If Unilate does not have to increase plant and equipment, fixed assets would remain at the 1995 level of $380 million, so the amount of AFN would be $38 million less than the initial forecast reported in Table 4-1. Coincidentally, this amount equals the AFN shown in Table 4-2, so, with no increase in plant and equipment, spontaneous financing and the addition to retained earnings will sufficiently finance Unilate's 10 percent increase in operations—no external funds are needed in this case.

In addition to the excess capacity of fixed assets, the firm could have excesses in other assets that can be used for increases in operations. For instance, in the last chapter, we concluded that perhaps Unilate's inventory level at the end of 1995 was greater than it should have been. If true, some increase in 1996 forecasted sales can be absorbed by the above-normal inventory, and production would not have to be increased until inventory levels are reduced to normal—this requires no additional financing.

In general, excess capacity means less external financing is required to support increases in operations than would be needed if the firm previously operated at full capacity.

Economies of Scale

There are economies of scale in the use of many types of assets, and when economies occur, a firm's variable cost of goods sold ratio is likely to change as the size of the firm changes (either increases or decreases) substantially. Currently, Unilate's variable cost ratio is 81.3 percent of sales; but the ratio might decrease to 80 percent of sales if operations increase significantly. If everything else is the same, changes in the variable cost ratio affect the addition to retained earnings, which in turn affects the amount of AFN.

Lumpy Assets

In many industries, technological considerations dictate that if a firm is to be competitive, it must add fixed assets in large, discrete units; such assets often are re-

LUMPY ASSETS
Assets that cannot be acquired in small increments; instead, they must be obtained in large, discrete amounts.

ferred to as **lumpy assets.** For example, in the paper industry, there are strong economies of scale in basic paper mill equipment, so when a paper company expands capacity, it must do so in large, lumpy increments. Lumpy assets primarily affect the fixed asset turnover of a firm and, consequently, the financial requirements associated with expanding. For instance, if, instead of $38 million, Unilate needed an additional $50 million in fixed assets to increase operations 10 percent, the AFN would be much greater. With *lumpy assets,* it is possible that a small

---

What is a "Good" Sales Forecast?

Managers know that sales forecasts are essential for effective planning and future survival of their businesses. In this chapter, we describe only one rather simple forecasting technique—pro forma forecasting. There are numerous forecasting techniques that can be used to predict sales; some of the procedures are quantitative and very sophisticated, while others are rather subjective in nature. Many of the quantitative methods are inexpensive to apply, and they provide more accurate forecasts than the judgmental, "seat-of-the-pants" forecasting approaches. Given the current understanding of the quantitative models, many of which are covered in the curricula offered by business schools, and the proliferation of computer technology in business, you would expect most managers to use the more sophisticated sales forecasting methods. But, a recent survey of 500 companies in the United States indicates that managers primarily rely on judgmental methods, including the manager's opinion, to formulate sales forecasts, not the more sophisticated, quantitative techniques. The managers surveyed indicated they possessed the knowledge and technology to apply the quantitative forecasting methods, but most preferred to trust their own, or their colleagues' experiences when forecasting sales. Even those managers who use quantitative methods stated that they generally subjectively adjust the forecasts resulting from these models to incorporate

qualitative factors, including knowledge of the operating environment, the product quality, and previous experience with the models. In fact, the results of the survey suggest that the primary reasons managers do not use sophisticated forecasting models is because they believe the data needed to use such models appropriately either are not relevant or are not available. Consequently, for the most part, managers believe their judgments provide sales forecasts that are as "good" as sophisticated models. "Good" might not relate to forecast accuracy, though, because about 85 percent of the survey's respondents indicated that they would prefer to either underestimate or overestimate when forecasting sales. More than 70 percent said they "underforecast" sales because when the forecast is exceeded, an explanation is not needed and a reward might even be considered; but, when actual sales turn out to be less than forecasted, job security becomes tenuous. Interestingly, the respondents who said they "overforecast" indicated that the primary reason was because they could get more staff to support the higher amount of sales. So, to many managers, forecasting sales is more of an art than a science.

SOURCE: Nada R. Sanders and Karl B. Manrodt, "Forecasting Practices in US Corporations: Survey Results," *Interfaces,* March–April 1994.

---

projected increase in sales would require a significant increase in plant and equipment, which would require a very large financial commitment.

Self-Test Question

Discuss three factors that might cause "spontaneous" assets and liabilities to change at a different rate than sales.

Financial Control—Budgeting and Leverage

In the preceding sections, we focused on financial forecasting, emphasizing how growth in sales requires additional investment in assets, which in turn generally requires the firm to raise new funds externally. In this section, we consider the planning and control systems used by financial managers when implementing the forecasts. First, we look at the relationship between sales volume and profitability under different operating conditions. These relationships provide information that is used by managers to plan for changes in the firm's level of operations, financing needs, and profitability. Later, we examine the control phase of the planning and control process, because a good control system is essential both to ensure that plans are executed properly and to facilitate a timely modification of plans if the assumptions upon which the initial plans were based turn out to be different than expected.

The planning process can be enhanced by examining the effects of changing operations on the firm's profitability, both from the standpoint of profits from operations and from the standpoint of profitability after financing effects are considered.

When Jack Smith became CEO at General Motors in 1992, he and his management team examined the operations that existed at GM at that time. They found the company's performance to be dismal, especially in North America, which produced a $10.7 billion loss in earnings before interest and taxes. Part of the solution to GM's problems was to reduce operating and financing costs in order to create more efficient operations—the hope was to break even, or to bring operating income up to zero, by 1993. That goal was accomplished, and in 1995 net income was expected to be nearly $1 billion. To achieve this turnaround, Smith and his staff at GM had to evaluate the impact on sales and net income of reducing costs through layoffs, savings in materials purchases, lowering debt, and so on. In the remainder of this chapter, we look at some of the areas Smith might have evaluated to provide information about the effects of changing GM's operations.

Operating Breakeven Analysis

OPERATING BREAKEVEN ANALYSIS
An analytical technique for studying the relationship between sales revenues, operating costs, and profits.

The relationship between sales volume and operating profitability is explored in cost-volume-profit planning, or operating breakeven analysis. **Operating breakeven analysis** is a method of determining the point at which sales will just cover operating costs; that is, the point at which the firm's production and sales operations will break even. But it also shows the magnitude of the firm's operating profits or losses if sales exceed or fall below that point. Breakeven analysis is important in the planning and control process because the cost-volume-profit relationship can be influenced greatly by the proportion of the firm's investment in assets which are fixed. A sufficient volume of sales must be anticipated and achieved if fixed and variable costs are to be covered, or else the firm will incur losses from operations. In other words, if a firm is to avoid accounting losses, its sales must cover all costs—those that vary directly with production and those that do not change as production levels change. Costs that vary directly with the level of production generally include the labor and materials needed to produce and sell the product, while the fixed operating costs generally include such costs as depreciation, rent, and insurance expenses that are incurred regardless of the firm's production level.

Operating breakeven analysis deals only with the upper portion of the income statement—the portion from sales to net operating income (NOI), or earnings before interest and taxes (EBIT). This portion generally is referred to as the *operating section,* because it contains only the revenues and expenses associated with the normal production and sales operations of the firm. Table 4-5 gives the operating section of Unilate's forecasted 1996 income statement, which was shown in Table 4-3. For the discussion that follows, we have assumed that all Unilate's prod-

TABLE 4-5

Unilate Textiles: 1996 Forecasted Operating Income (millions of dollars)

Sales (S)	$1,650
Variable cost of goods sold (VC)	(1,342)
Gross profit (GP)	308
Fixed operating costs (F)	(154)
Net operating income (NOI)	$ 154

NOTES:
Sales in units = 110 million units
Selling price per unit = $15.00
Variable costs per unit = $1,342/110 = $12.20
Fixed operating costs, which include $55 million depreciation and $99 million in other fixed costs
such as rent, insurance, and general office expenses

ucts sell for $15 each and the variable cost of goods sold per unit is $12.20, which is 81.3 percent of the selling price.

Breakeven Graph

Table 4-5 shows the net operating income (also referred to as the earnings before interest and taxes, or EBIT) for Unilate if 110 million products are produced and sold during the year. But what if Unilate doesn't sell 110 million products? Certainly, the firm's net operating income will be something other than $154 million. Figure 4-2 shows the total revenues and total operating costs for Unilate at various levels of sales, beginning with zero. According to the information given in Table 4-5, Unilate has fixed costs, which include depreciation, rent, insurance, and so on, equal to $154 million. This amount must be paid even if the firm produces and sells nothing, so the $154 million fixed cost is represented by a horizontal line. If Unilate produces and sells nothing, its sales revenues will be zero; but, *for each unit sold,* the firm's sales will increase by $15. Therefore, the total revenue line starts at the origin of the X and Y axes, and it has a slope equal to $15 to account for the dollar increase in sales for each additional unit sold. On the other hand, the line representing the total operating costs intersects the Y axis at $154 million, which represents the fixed costs incurred even when no products are sold, and it has a slope equal to $12.20, which is the cost directly associated with the production of each additional unit sold. The point at which the total revenue line intersects the total cost line is the **operating breakeven point,** because this is where the revenues generated from sales just cover the *total operating costs* of the firm. Notice that prior to the breakeven point, the total cost line is above the total revenue line, which shows Unilate will suffer operating losses because the total costs cannot be covered by the sales revenues. And, after the breakeven point, the total revenue line is above the total cost line because revenues are more than sufficient to cover total operating costs, so Unilate will realize operating profits.[4]

OPERATING BREAKEVEN POINT Represents the level of production and sales where operating income is zero; it is the point where revenues from sales just equal total operating costs.

[4]In Figure 4-2, we assume the operating costs can be divided into two distinct groups—fixed costs and variable costs. It should be noted that there are costs which are considered semi-variable (or semi-fixed). These costs are fixed for a certain range of operations, but change if operations are either higher or lower. For the analysis which follows, we have assumed there are no semi-variable costs, so that the operating costs can be separated into either a fixed component or a variable component.

FIGURE 4-2

Unilate Textiles: Operating Breakeven Chart

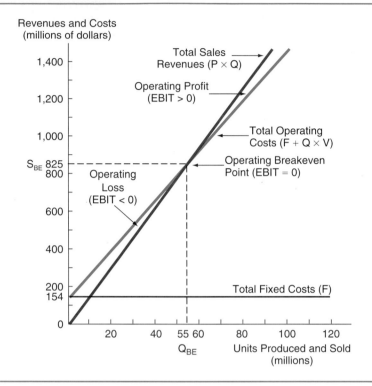

NOTES:

S_{BE} = operating breakeven in dollars

Q = sales in units; Q_{BE} = operating breakeven in units

F = fixed costs = $154 million

V = variable costs per unit = $12.20

P = price per unit = $15.00

Breakeven Computation

Figure 4-2 shows that Unilate must sell 55 million units to be at the operating breakeven point. If Unilate sells 55 million products, it will generate $825 million in sales revenues, which will be just enough to cover the $825 million total operating costs—$154 million fixed costs and $671 million variable costs (55 million units at $12.20 per unit). If we do not have a graph like Figure 4-2, how can the operating breakeven point be computed? Actually, it is rather simple. Remember, the operating breakeven point is where the revenues generated from sales just cover the total operating costs, which include both the costs directly attributable to producing each unit and the fixed operating costs that remain constant no matter the production level. As long as the selling price of each unit (the slope of the total revenue line) is greater than the variable operating cost of each unit (the slope of the total operating cost line), each unit sold will generate revenues that contribute to covering the fixed operating costs. For Unilate, this contribution (termed the *contribution margin*) is $2.80, which is the difference between the $15 selling price and the $12.20 variable cost of each unit. To compute the operating breakeven point for Unilate then, we have to determine how many units need to be sold to cover the fixed operating cost of $154 million if each unit has a contribution margin equal to $2.80. Just divide the $154 million fixed cost by the $2.80 contribution margin and you will discover the breakeven point is 55 million units, which equates to $825 million in sales revenues.

More formally, the operating breakeven point can be found by setting the total revenues equal to the total operating costs so that net operating income (NOI) is zero. In equation form, NOI = 0 if

$$\text{Sales revenues} = \begin{array}{c}\text{Total}\\\text{operating}\\\text{costs}\end{array} = \begin{array}{c}\text{Total}\\\text{variable}\\\text{costs}\end{array} + \begin{array}{c}\text{Total}\\\text{fixed}\\\text{costs}\end{array}$$

$$(P \times Q) = \text{TOC} = (V \times Q) + F$$

where P is the sales price per unit, Q is the number of units produced and sold, V is the variable operating cost per unit, and F is the total fixed operating costs. Solving for the quantity that needs to be sold, Q, produces a formula that can be used to find the number of units that need to be sold to achieve operating breakeven.

4-1

$$Q_{BE} = \frac{F}{P - V} = \frac{F}{\text{Contribution margin}}$$

Thus, the operating breakeven point for Unilate is:

$$Q_{BE} = \frac{\$154 \text{ million}}{\$15.00 - \$12.20} = \frac{\$154 \text{ million}}{\$2.80} = 55 \text{ million units}$$

In the remainder of the chapter, we omit the word "million" in the computations, and include it only in the final answer.

From Equation 4-1, we can see that the operating breakeven point is lower (higher) if the numerator is lower (higher) or if the denominator is higher (lower). Therefore, all else equal, one firm will have a lower operating breakeven point than another firm if its fixed costs are lower, if the selling price of its product is higher, if its variable operating cost per unit is lower, or if some combination of these exists. For instance, if Unilate could increase the sales price per unit from $15.00 to $16.05 without affecting either its fixed operating costs ($154 million) or its variable operating cost per unit ($12.20), then its operating breakeven point would fall to 40 million units.

The operating breakeven point also can be stated in terms of the total sales revenues needed to cover total operating costs. At this point, we just need to multiply the sales price per unit by the value computed by solving Equation 4-1, which yields $825 million for Unilate. Or, we can restate the contribution margin as a percent of the sales price per unit (this is called the *gross profit margin*), and then apply Equation 4-1. In other words,

4-2

$$S_{BE} = \frac{F}{1 - \frac{V}{P}} = \frac{F}{\text{Gross profit margin}}$$

Solving Equation 4-2 for Unilate, the operating breakeven point based on dollar sales is:

$$S_{BE} = \frac{\$154}{1 - \frac{\$12.20}{\$15.00}} = \frac{\$154}{1 - 0.8133} = \frac{\$154}{0.1867} = \$825 \text{ million}$$

Equation 4-2 shows that 18.67¢ of every $1 in sales revenues goes to cover the fixed operating costs, so $825 million worth of the product must be sold to break even.

Breakeven analysis based on dollar sales rather than on units of output is useful in determining the breakeven volume for a firm that sells many products at varying prices. This analysis requires only that total sales, total fixed costs, and total variable costs at a given level be known.

Cash Operating Breakeven Point

CASH OPERATING BREAKEVEN POINT (Q_{CBE})
The breakeven point when noncash items are subtracted from the fixed operating costs.

Firms that have fixed costs which include a large amount of noncash expenses often find it useful to compute the **cash operating breakeven point.** The purpose of computing the cash operating breakeven point is to determine the level of sales necessary to cover *cash* operating costs. To compute the cash operating breakeven point, the conventional computation given by Equation 4-1 needs to be adjusted so that the fixed costs amount includes only cash outlays:

4-3

$$Q_{CBE} = \frac{F - \text{Noncash outlays}}{P - V}$$

If Unilate's only noncash operating expense is depreciation, which is forecasted to be $55 million in 1996, then its cash operating breakeven point would be:

$$Q_{CBE} = \frac{\$154 - \$55}{\$15.00 - \$12.20} = \frac{\$99}{\$2.80} \approx 35 \text{ million units}$$

The cash operating breakeven point for Unilate is much less than the conventional operating breakeven point because noncash operating expenses (depreciation) are more than one-third of the total operating expenses. Comparison of the conventional operating breakeven point and the cash operating breakeven point can provide useful information about the firm's flow of funds from operations. For a full representation of cash flows we need to construct a cash budget. We discuss cash budgets and cash management in Chapter 9.

Using Operating Breakeven Analysis

Operating breakeven analysis can shed light on three important types of business decisions: (1) When making new product decisions, breakeven analysis can help determine how large the sales of a new product must be for the firm to achieve profitability. (2) Breakeven analysis can be used to study the effects of a general expansion in the level of the firm's operations; an expansion would cause the levels of both fixed and variable costs to rise, but it also would increase expected sales. (3) When considering modernization and automation projects, where the fixed investment in equipment is increased in order to lower variable costs, particularly the cost of labor, breakeven analysis can help management analyze the consequences of purchasing these projects.

However, care must be taken when using operating breakeven analysis. To apply breakeven analysis as we have discussed it here requires that the sales price *per unit,* the variable cost *per unit,* and the *total* fixed operating costs do not change with the level of the firm's production and sales. Within a narrow range of production and sales, this assumption probably is not a major issue. But what if the firm expects either to produce a much greater (or fewer) number of products than normal, or to expand its plant and equipment significantly? Will the numbers change? Most likely the answer is yes. Therefore, use of a single breakeven chart like the one presented in Figure 4-2 is impractical—such a chart provides useful information, but the fact that it cannot deal with changes in the price of the product, with changing variable cost rates, and with changes in fixed cost levels suggests the need for a more flexible type of analysis. Today, such analysis is provided by computer simulation. Functions such as those expressed in Equations 4-1 and 4-2 (or more complicated versions of them) can be put into a spreadsheet such as *Lotus 1-2-3* or similarly modeled with other computer software, and then variables such as sales price (P), the variable cost rate (V), and the level of fixed costs (F) can be changed. The model can instantaneously produce new versions of Figure 4-2, or a whole set of such graphs, to show what the operating breakeven point would be under different production setups and price-cost situations.

 ### *Self-Test Questions*

Is interest paid considered in operating breakeven analysis? Why or why not?

Give the equations used to calculate the operating breakeven point in units and in dollar sales.

Why might a firm compute its cash operating breakeven point rather than its conventional operating breakeven point?

Give some examples of business decisions for which operating breakeven analysis might be useful.

Identify some limitations to the use of a single operating breakeven chart.

Operating Leverage

OPERATING LEVERAGE
The existence of fixed operating costs, such that a change in sales will produce a larger change in operating income (EBIT).

If a high percentage of a firm's total operating costs are fixed, the firm is said to have a high degree of **operating leverage.** In physics, leverage implies the use of a lever to raise a heavy object with a small amount of force. In politics, people who have leverage can accomplish a great deal with their smallest word or action. *In business terminology, a high degree of operating leverage, other things held constant, means that a relatively small change in sales will result in a large change in operating income.*

Operating leverage arises because the firm has fixed operating costs that must be covered no matter the level of production. The impact of the leverage, however, depends on the actual operating level of the firm. For example, Unilate has $154 million in fixed operating costs, which are covered rather easily because the firm currently sells 110 million products, twice its operating breakeven point of 55 million units. But what would happen to the operating income if Unilate sold more or less than forecasted? To answer this question we need to determine the *degree of operating leverage (DOL)* associated with Unilate's 1996 forecasted operations.

DEGREE OF OPERATING LEVERAGE (DOL)
The percentage change in NOI (or EBIT) associated with a given percentage change in sales.

Operating leverage can be defined more precisely in terms of the way a given change in sales volume affects operating income (NOI). To measure the effect of a change in sales volume on NOI, we calculate the **degree of operating leverage (DOL),** defined as the percentage change in NOI (or EBIT) associated with a given percentage change in sales:[5]

$$4\text{-}4 \qquad DOL = \frac{\text{Percentage change in NOI}}{\text{Percentage change in sales}} = \frac{\dfrac{\Delta NOI}{NOI}}{\dfrac{\Delta Sales}{Sales}} = \frac{\dfrac{\Delta EBIT}{EBIT}}{\dfrac{\Delta Sales}{Sales}} = \frac{\dfrac{\Delta EBIT}{EBIT}}{\dfrac{\Delta Q}{Q}}$$

In effect, the DOL is an index number that measures the effect of a change in sales on operating income or EBIT.

Table 4-5 shows the NOI for Unilate is $154 million at production and sales equal to 110 million units. If the number of units produced and sold increases to 121 million, the operating income (in millions of dollars) would be:

$$NOI = 121(\$15.00 - \$12.20) - \$154 = \$185$$

So, the degree of operating leverage associated with this change is 2.0:

$$DOL = \frac{\dfrac{\$185 - \$154}{\$154}}{\dfrac{\$15(121 - 110)}{\$15(110)}} = \frac{\dfrac{\$31}{\$154}}{\dfrac{11}{110}} = \frac{20.0\%}{10.0\%} = 2.0$$

---

[5]Remember the net operating income (NOI) is the same as the earnings before interest and taxes (EBIT).

TABLE 4-6

Unilate Textiles: Operating Income at Sales Levels of 110 Million Units and 121 Million Units (millions of dollars)

	1996 Forecasted Operations	Sales Increase	Unit Change	Percent Change
Sales in units (millions)	110	121	11	+10%
Sales revenues	$1,650	$1,815	$165	+10%
Variable cost of goods sold	(1,342)	(1,476)	(134)	+10%
Gross profit	308	339	31	+10%
Fixed operating costs	(154)	(154)	(0)	0%
Net operating income (EBIT)	$ 154	$ 185	$ 31	+20%

To interpret the meaning of the value of the degree of operating leverage, remember we computed the percent change in operating income and then divided the result by the percent change in sales. Taken literally, then, Unilate's DOL of 2.0 indicates that the percent change in operating income will be 2.0 times the percent change in sales from the current 110 million units ($1,650 million). So, if the number of units sold increases from 110 million to 121 million, or by 10 percent, Unilate's operating income should increase by 2.0 times 10 percent, or by 20.0 percent; at 121 million units, operating income should be 20.0 percent greater than the $154 million generated at 110 million units of sales; the new operating income should be $185 million = 1.20 × $154 million. Table 4-6 shows a comparison of the operating incomes generated at the two different sales levels.

The results contained in Table 4-6 show that Unilate's *gross profit* would increase by $31 million, or by 10 percent, if sales increase 10 percent. The fixed operating costs remain constant at $154 million, so EBIT also increases by $31 million, and the total impact of a 10 percent increase in sales is a 20 percent increase in operating income. If the fixed operating costs were to increase in proportion to the increase in sales—that is, 10 percent—then the net operating income also would increase by 10 percent because all revenues and costs would have changed by the same proportion. But, in reality, fixed operating costs will not change (a 0 percent increase); thus, a 10 percent increase in Unilate's forecasted 1996 sales will result in an *additional* 10 percent increase in operating income. The total increase is 20 percent, which results because operating leverage exists.

Equation 4-4 can be simplified so the degree of operating leverage at a particular level of operations can be calculated as follows:[6]

---

[6]Equation 4-5 can be derived by restating Equation 4-4 in terms of the variables we have defined previously, and then simplifying the result. Starting with Equation 4-4, we have

$$\text{DOL} = \frac{\text{Percentage change in NOI}}{\text{Percentage change in sales}} = \frac{\dfrac{\Delta \text{NOI}}{\text{NOI}}}{\dfrac{\Delta \text{Sales}}{\text{Sales}}} = \frac{\dfrac{\Delta \text{EBIT}}{\text{EBIT}}}{\dfrac{\Delta Q}{Q}} \qquad 4\text{-}4$$

(continued)

Breakeven Graph

FINANCIAL BREAKEVEN POINT
The point at which EPS equals zero.

Figure 4-4 shows the earnings per share (EPS) for Unilate at various levels of EBIT. The point at which EPS equals zero is referred to as the **financial breakeven point.** As the graph indicates, the financial breakeven point for Unilate is where EBIT equals $37 million. At this EBIT level, the income generated from operations is just sufficient to cover the financing costs, including income taxes—thus EPS equals zero. To see if this is true, we can compute the EPS when EBIT is $37 million:

Earnings before interest and taxes (EBIT)	$37
Interest	(37)
Earnings before taxes (EBT)	0
Taxes (40%)	(0)
Net income	0
Earnings available to common stockholders (EAC)	$ 0

EPS = $0/26 = $0

Breakeven Computation

The results obtained from Figure 4-4 can be translated algebraically to produce a relatively simple equation that can be used to compute the financial breakeven point of any firm. First, remember the financial breakeven point is defined as the level of EBIT that generates EPS equal to zero. Therefore, at the financial breakeven point,

$$\text{4-6} \quad \text{EPS} = \frac{\text{Earnings available to common stockholders}}{\text{Number of common shares outstanding}} = 0$$

$$= \frac{(\text{EBIT} - \text{D})(1 - \text{T}) - \text{D}_{ps}}{\text{Shrs}_{\text{C}}} = 0$$

TABLE 4-8

Unilate Textiles: 1996 Forecasted Earnings Per Share (millions of dollars)

Earnings before interest and taxes (EBIT)	$154
Interest	(37)
Earnings before taxes (EBT)	117
Taxes (40%)	(47)
Net income	70
Preferred dividends	(0)
Earnings available to common stockholders	$ 70

NOTES:
Shrs$_{\text{C}}$ = number of common shares = 26 million
EPS = earnings per share = $70/26 = $2.69

where EBIT is the earnings before interest and taxes, I represents the interest payments on debt, T is the marginal tax rate, D_{ps} is the amount of dividends paid to preferred stockholders, and $Shrs_C$ is the number of common shares outstanding. Notice that EPS equals zero if the numerator in Equation 4-6, which is the earnings available to common stockholders, equals zero; so the financial breakeven point also can be stated as follows:

$$(EBIT - I)(1 - T) - D_{ps} = 0$$

Rearranging this equation to solve for EBIT gives the solution for the level of EBIT needed to produce EPS equal to zero. Therefore, the computation for a firm's financial breakeven point is

4-7

$$EBIT_{financial\ BEP} = I + \frac{D_{ps}}{(1 - T)}$$

Using Equation 4-7, the financial breakeven point for Unilate Textiles in 1996 is:

$$EBIT_{financial\ BEP} = \$37 + \frac{\$0}{1 - .4} = \$37$$

which is the same result shown in Figure 4-4.

FIGURE 4-4

Unilate Textiles: Financial Breakeven Chart

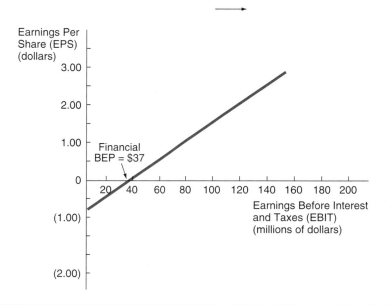

NOTES:

EPS = EAC/Shrs$_C$

EAC = Earnings available for common stockholders

Shrs$_C$ = Number of common shares outstanding

According to Equation 4-7, the amount of preferred stock dividends must be stated on a before-tax basis to determine the financial breakeven point. If a firm has no preferred stock, though, the firm only needs to cover its interest payments, so the financial breakeven point simply equals the interest expense. This is the case for Unilate, because it has no preferred stock. Because most corporations in the United States do not have preferred stock outstanding, we will not include preferred dividends in the discussions that follow. The use of preferred stock as a source of funds will be discussed in Chapter 20.

Using Financial Breakeven Analysis

Financial breakeven analysis can be used to help determine the impact of the firm's financing mix on the earnings available to common stockholders.[8] When the firm uses financing alternatives that require fixed financing costs such as interest, financial leverage exists. Financial leverage affects the financing section of the income statement like operating leverage affects the operating section. This point is discussed in the next section.

Self-Test Questions

Define the financial breakeven point. How does the financial breakeven point differ from the operating breakeven point?

Why is it important to carry out financial breakeven analysis?

Financial Leverage

FINANCIAL LEVERAGE
The existence of fixed financial costs such as interest; when a change in EBIT results in a larger change in EPS.

While operating leverage considers how changing sales volume affects operating income, **financial leverage** considers the impact a change in operating income has on earnings per share, or earnings available to common stockholders. So, operating leverage affects the operating section of the income statement, whereas financial leverage affects the financing section of the income statement. *Financial leverage takes over where operating leverage leaves off, further magnifying the effects on earnings per share of changes in the level of sales.* For this reason, operating leverage sometimes is referred to as *first-stage leverage* and financial leverage as *second-stage leverage.*

DEGREE OF FINANCIAL LEVERAGE (DFL)
The percent change in EPS that results from a given percent change in EBIT.

Like operating leverage, financial leverage arises because fixed costs exist; in this case, the fixed costs are associated with how the firm is financed. The **degree of financial leverage (DFL)** is defined as the percent change in earnings per share (EPS) that results from a given percent change in earnings before interest and taxes (EBIT), and it is computed as follows:

---

[8]The effect of financing the firm with various proportions of debt and equity will be discussed in greater detail in Chapter 16.

TABLE 4-9

Unilate Textiles: Earnings Per Share at Sales Levels of 110 Million Units and 121 Million Units (millions of dollars, except per share data)

	1996 Forecasted Operations	Sales Increase	Dollar Change	Percent Change[a]
Sales in units (millions)	110	121		
Earnings before interest and taxes (EBIT)	$154	$185	$31	+20%
Interest (I)	(37)	(37)	(0)	+ 0%
Earnings before taxes (EBT)	117	148	31	+26%
Taxes (40%)	(47)	(59)	(12)	+26%
Net income	$ 70	$ 89	$19	+26%
Earnings per share (26 million shares)	$2.69	$3.40	$0.71	+26%

[a]The dollar values are rounded to the nearest million—to compute the percent change column, non-rounded numbers were used.

4-8

$$DFL = \frac{\text{Percent change in EPS}}{\text{Percent change in EBIT}} = \frac{\dfrac{\Delta EPS}{EPS}}{\dfrac{\Delta EBIT}{EBIT}}$$

Table 4-9 shows the results of increasing Unilate's EBIT 20 percent. The increase in EPS is 26 percent, which is 1.3 times the change in EBIT; so, the DFL for Unilate equals 1.3.

The degree of financial leverage at a particular level of EBIT can be computed easily by using the following equation:[9]

4-9

$$DFL = \frac{EBIT}{EBIT - I} = \frac{EBIT}{EBIT - [\text{Financial BEP}]}$$

---

[9]Equation 4-9 can be derived easily by expanding Equation 4-8, rearranging the terms, and then simplifying the results. If we use EPS and EBIT to indicate the 1996 forecasted EPS and EBIT, respectively, and EPS* and EBIT* to indicate the EPS and EBIT that would exist after a change in sales volume, then

$$DFL = \frac{\dfrac{\Delta EPS}{EPS}}{\dfrac{\Delta EBIT}{EBIT}} = \frac{\dfrac{EPS^* - EPS}{EPS}}{\dfrac{EBIT^* - EBIT}{EBIT}}$$

For Unilate, the computation for 1996 forecasted earnings per share is

(continued)

Using Equation 4-9, the DFL for Unilate Textiles at EBIT equal to $154 million (sales of 110 million units) is

$$DFL_{110} = \frac{\$154}{\$154 - \$37} = \frac{\$154}{\$117} = 1.3$$

The interpretation of the DFL value is the same as for the degree of operating leverage, except the starting point for evaluating financial leverage is the earnings before interest and taxes (EBIT) and the ending point is earnings per share (EPS). So, because the DFL for Unilate is 1.3, the company can expect a 1.3 percent change in EPS for every 1 percent change in EBIT; a 20 percent increase in EBIT results in a 26 percent (20 percent × 1.3) increase in earnings available to common stockholders, thus the same percent increase in EPS (the number of common shares outstanding do not change). Unfortunately, the opposite also is true—if Unilate's 1996 EBIT is 20 percent below expectations, its EPS will be 26 percent below the forecast of $2.69, or $1.99.

The value of the degree of financial leverage found using Equation 4-9 pertains to one specific initial EBIT level. If the level of sales changes, and thus the EBIT changes, so does the value computed for DFL. For example, at sales equal to 80 million units, Unilate's EBIT would be $70 million = [80 ($15.00 − $12.20)] − $154, and the DFL value would be

$$DFL_{80} = \frac{\$70}{\$70 - \$37} = \frac{\$70}{\$33} = 2.1$$

Compared to sales equal to 110 million units, at sales equal to 80 million units Unilate would have greater difficulty covering the fixed financing costs, so its DFL

(continued)

$$EPS = \frac{(EBIT - I)(1 - T)}{Shrs_C}$$

where $Shrs_C$ is the number of common shares outstanding. The percent change in EPS can be written and simplified as follows:

$$\Delta EPS = \frac{\dfrac{(EBIT^* - I)(1 - T)}{Shrs_C} - \dfrac{(EBIT - I)(1 - T)}{Shrs_C}}{\dfrac{(EBIT - I)(1 - T)}{Shrs_C}} = \frac{(EBIT^* - I)(1 - T) - (EBIT - I)(1 - T)}{(EBIT - I)(1 - T)}$$

$$= \frac{EBIT^* - EBIT}{(EBIT - I)}$$

Substituting this relationship into the computation of DFL, we have

$$DFL = \frac{\dfrac{(EBIT^* - EBIT)}{EBIT - I}}{\dfrac{(EBIT^* - EBIT)}{EBIT}} = \frac{(EBIT^* - EBIT)}{(EBIT - I)} \times \frac{EBIT}{(EBIT^* - EBIT)}$$

$$= \frac{EBIT}{EBIT - I} = \frac{EBIT}{EBIT - [Financial\ BEP]}$$

4-9

If a firm has preferred stock, the relationship given in Equation 4-7 can be substituted in the above equation for the financial breakeven point.

is much greater. At EBIT equal to $70 million (80 million units of sales), Unilate is close to its financial breakeven point (EBIT equal to $37 million), and its degree of financial leverage is high. So, the more difficulty a firm has covering its fixed financing costs with operating income, the greater its degree of financial leverage. In general, then, the *higher* the DFL for a particular firm, the *closer* the firm is to its financial breakeven point, and the *more sensitive* its earnings per share is to a change in operating income. *Greater sensitivity implies greater risk; thus, it can be stated that firms with higher DFLs generally are considered to have greater financial risk than firms with lower DFLs.*

Self-Test Questions

What does the term "high degree of financial leverage" imply, and what are some implications of having a high degree of financial leverage?

Give the general equation used to calculate the degree of financial leverage. Compare the equation for DFL to the equation for times interest earned given in Chapter 3.

Combining Operating and Financial Leverage (DTL)

Our analysis of operating leverage and financial leverage has shown that (1) the greater the degree of operating leverage (or fixed operating costs for a particular level of operations), the more sensitive EBIT will be to changes in sales volume, and (2) the greater the degree of financial leverage (or fixed financial costs for a particular level of operations), the more sensitive EPS will be to changes in EBIT. Therefore, if a firm has a considerable amount of both operating and financial leverage, then even small changes in sales will lead to wide fluctuations in EPS. Look at the impact leverage has on Unilate's 1996 forecasted operations. We found that if the sales volume increases by 10 percent, Unilate's EBIT would increase by 20 percent; and, if EBIT increases by 20 percent, its EPS would increase by 26 percent. So, in combination, a 10 percent increase in sales volume would result in a 26 percent increase in EPS. This shows the impact of total leverage, which is the combination of both operating leverage and financial leverage, with respect to Unilate's current forecasted operations.

DEGREE OF TOTAL LEVERAGE (DTL)
The percent change in EPS resulting from a change in sales.

The **degree of total leverage (DTL)** is defined as the percent change in EPS resulting from a change in sales volume. This relationship can be written

$$4\text{-}10 \qquad \begin{array}{c} \text{Degree of} \\ \text{total leverage} \end{array} = \text{DTL} = \frac{\dfrac{\Delta \text{EPS}}{\text{EPS}}}{\dfrac{\Delta \text{Sales}}{\text{Sales}}} = \frac{\dfrac{\Delta \text{EBIT}}{\text{EBIT}}}{\dfrac{\Delta \text{Sales}}{\text{Sales}}} \times \frac{\dfrac{\Delta \text{EPS}}{\text{EPS}}}{\dfrac{\Delta \text{EBIT}}{\text{EBIT}}} = \text{DOL} \times \text{DFL}$$

Combining the equations for DOL (Equations 4-5 and 4-5a) and for DFL (Equation 4-9), Equation 4-10 can be restated as follows:

$$4\text{-}11 \quad \text{DTL} = \frac{\text{Gross Profit}}{\text{EBIT}} \times \frac{\text{EBIT}}{\text{EBIT} - [\text{Financial BEP}]} = \frac{\text{Gross Profit}}{\text{EBIT} - [\text{Financial BEP}]}$$

$$= \frac{S - VC}{\text{EBIT} - I} = \frac{Q(P - V)}{[Q(P - V) - F] - I}$$

Using Equation 4-11, at 110 million units of sales the degree of total leverage for Unilate would be

$$\text{DTL}_{110} = \frac{110(\$15.00 - \$12.20)}{110(\$15.00 - \$12.20) - \$154 - \$37}$$

$$= \frac{\$308}{\$154 - \$37} = \frac{\$308}{\$117}$$

$$= 2.6$$

According to Equation 4-10, we could have arrived at the same result for DTL by multiplying the degree of operating leverage by the degree of financial leverage, so the DTL for Unilate would be 2.0 x 1.3 = 2.6. This value indicates that for every one percent change in sales volume, Unilate's EPS will change by 2.6 percent; a 10 percent increase in sales will result in a 26 percent increase in EPS. This is exactly the impact expected.

The value of DTL can be used to compute the new earnings per share (EPS*) after a change in sales volume. We already know that Unilate's EPS will change by 2.6 percent for every one percent change in sales. So EPS* resulting from a 10 percent increase in sales can be computed as follows:

$$\text{EPS*} = \text{EPS}[1 + (.10)(2.6)] = \$2.69 \text{ x } (1 + .26) \approx \$3.40$$

which is the same result given in Table 4-9 (rounding effects exist).

The degree of combined (total) leverage concept is useful primarily for the insights it provides regarding the joint effects of operating and financial leverage on earnings per share. The concept can be used to show management, for example, that a decision to automate a plant and to finance the new equipment with debt would result in a situation where a 10 percent decline in sales would result in a nearly 50 percent decline in earnings, whereas with a different operating and financial package, a 10 percent sales decline would cause earnings to decline by only 15 percent. Having the alternatives stated in this manner gives decision makers a better idea of the ramifications of alternative actions with respect to the firm's level of operations and how those operations are financed.

Self-Test Questions

What information is provided by the degree of total (combined) leverage?

What does the term "high degree of total leverage" imply?

Using Leverage and Forecasting for Control

From the discussions in the previous sections, it should be clear what the impact on income would be if the 1996 sales forecast for Unilate Textiles is different than expected. If sales are greater than expected, both operating and financial leverage will magnify the "bottom line" impact on EPS (DTL = 2.6). But the opposite also holds. Consequently, if Unilate does not meet its forecasted sales level, leverage will result in a magnified loss in income compared to what is expected. This will occur because production facilities might have been expanded too greatly, inventories might be built up too quickly, and so on; the end result might be that the firm suffers a significant income loss. This loss will result in a lower than expected addition to retained earnings, which means the plans for additional external funds needed to support the firm's operations will be inadequate. Likewise, if the sales forecast is too low, then, if the firm is at full capacity, it will not be able to meet the additional demand, and sales opportunities will be lost—perhaps forever. In the previous sections, we showed only how changes in operations (1996 forecasts) affect the income generated by the firm; we did not continue the process to show the impact on the balance sheet and the financing needs of the firm. To determine the impact on the financial statements, the financial manager needs to repeat the steps discussed in the first part of this chapter. It is at this stage the financial manager needs to evaluate and act on the feedback received from the forecasting and budgeting processes. In effect, then, the forecasting (planning) and control of the firm is an ongoing activity, a vital function to the long-run survival of any firm.

The forecasting and control functions described in this chapter are important for several reasons. First, if the projected operating results are unsatisfactory, management can "go back to the drawing board," reformulate its plans, and develop more reasonable targets for the coming year. Second, it is possible that the funds required to meet the sales forecast simply cannot be obtained; if so, it obviously is better to know this in advance and to scale back the projected level of operations than to suddenly run out of cash and have operations grind to a halt. Third, even if the required funds can be raised, it is desirable to plan for their acquisition well in advance. Finally, any deviation from the projections needs to be dealt with to improve future forecasts and the predictability of the firm's operations to ensure the goals of the firm are being pursued appropriately.

Self-Test Question

Why is it important that the forecasting and control of the firm be an ongoing activity?

ETHICAL DILEMMA   *Competition-Based Planning—Promotion or Payoff?*

A few months ago, Kim Darby, financial manager of Republic Communications Corporation (RCC), contacted you about a job opening in the financial planning division of the company. RCC is a well-established firm that has offered long-distance phone service in the United States for more than three decades. But recent deregulation in the telecommunications industry has RCC concerned,

SMALL BUSINESS

Planning Is Everything

Skypix, an aerial photography business, started like many small businesses—as a hobby. Harlan Accola and his brother Conrad began selling aerial pictures of farms and other property when they were in high school to "make a few bucks" and pay some bills. When their sideline caught on in 1980, the brothers went into business in earnest. Because business was booming, they figured their hobby filled a niche that could be very successful. Harlan Accola hired bookkeepers and accountants to construct the financial statements requested by banks when the company needed to borrow funds. But, he didn't think those financial statements were very important to Skypix— they were just something the banks required to ensure the loans were OK. Harlan admits he would take the statement prepared by his CPA, look at the "bottom line" to make sure the firm was profitable, and then throw it into a desk drawer. The company's financial plan was very simple—make sure cash was available to pay the bills due next week.

As long as sales could be made, Harlan thought Skypix would survive because profits would be generated. Unfortunately, by 1986, the Accolas discovered that profits didn't always translate into the cash needed to pay the bills. Skypix was significantly past due on many of its bills, and the bank demanded payment on a $240,000 loan that had provided much of its operating cash flow; even worse, it owed the Internal Revenue Service overdue taxes. How did Skypix and the Accolas end up in this mess? Like many small businesses Skypix operated without a formal financial plan.

Times have changed for the Accolas. In 1986, the brothers realized that a lack of planning could cause their business to be completely destroyed. So they reorganized the company to ensure the bank and all other creditors would be paid, and they renamed the company American Images to signal a new beginning. With the new beginning came the commitment to develop a planning process for the business to follow when generating sales and cash flow forecasts. In 1993, the Accolas hired Dennis Kearns, a controller with many years of experience in accounting and financial planning, to help build a formal procedure for financial planning that better utilized the company's computer system. In addition, Harlan Accola decided to implement some of the ideas he had read about including employees in the planning process, so he invited each of the department heads to participate in the formulation of the company's financial goals. Before participating in the planning session, though, the department heads were instructed to discuss the departmental forecasts with the employees to ensure the forecasts were realistic and to ensure each employee understood his or her responsibility with respect to attaining the company's overall forecast.

The formal planning process seems to be working well for American Images. In 1994, the company had revenues of nearly $5 million, and the future prospects (plans) appear good. Harlan Accola attributes the turnaround to the improvement in the financial planning process. In the future, his plans are to better educate managers about the use of financial statements, especially the income statement, so they can better understand how their departments fit into the overall goals of American Images. The Accolas certainly would agree that "planning is everything"— financial planning is important to the success of any business, but it is especially critical to the survival of small, upstart companies like American Images.

SOURCE: Jay Finegan, "Everything According to Plan," *Inc.*, March 1995.

because competition has increased significantly—today there are many more firms offering long-distance services than five years ago. In fact, RCC has seen its profits decline along with market share since deregulation began. Kim Darby indicated that RCC wants to reverse this trend by improving the company's planning function so that long-distance rates can be set to better attract and keep customers in the future. According to her, that is the reason she contacted you.

When she first called, Kim told you RCC would like to hire you because you are one of the "up-and-comers" in the telecommunications industry. You have worked at National Telecommunications, Inc. (NTI), one of RCC's fiercest competitors, since you graduated from college four years ago, helping to develop their rate-setting program, which many consider the best in the industry.

Taking the position at RCC would be comparable to a promotion with a $30,000 salary increase and provide greater chances for advancement than your current position at NTI. So, after interviewing with RCC and talking to friends and family, a couple of days ago you informally accepted the job at RCC—you have not yet notified NTI of your decision.

Earlier today, Kim called to see if you could start your new position in a couple of weeks. RCC would like you to start work as soon as possible because it wants to begin a redesign of its rate-setting plan in an effort to regain market share. During the conversaton, Kim mentioned that it would be helpful if you could bring the rate-setting program and some rate-setting information with you to your new job—it will help RCC rewrite its rate-setting program. In an attempt to allay any reservations you might have, Kim told you that NTI sells its software to other companies and any rate setting information is available to the public through states' public service commissions, so everything you bring really is well known in the industry and should be considered in the public domain. And, according to Kim, RCC is not going to copy the rate-setting program—her attitude is "what is wrong with taking a look at it as long as we don't copy the program?" If you provide RCC with NTI's rate-setting program, you know it will help the company to plan better, and better planning will lead to increased market share and higher stock prices. An improved rate-setting plan might net RCC as much as $200 million each year, and RCC has a very generous bonus system to reward employees that help the company improve its market position. If you do not provide the software, you might start your new job "off on the wrong foot." What should you do?

Summary

The first part of this chapter described in broad outline how firms project their financial statements and determine their external funding requirements. The second part of the chapter included a discussion of how we can evaluate the effects of changes in forecasts on the income of the firm. The key concepts covered are listed below.

- **Financial planning** involves making projections of sales, income, and assets based on alternative production and marketing strategies and then deciding how to meet the forecasted financial requirements.
- **Financial control** deals with the feedback and adjustment process that is required (1) to ensure that plans are followed or (2) to modify existing plans in response to changes in the operating environment.
- The **projected, or pro forma, balance sheet method** is used to forecast financial requirements.
- A firm can determine the amount of **additional funds needed (AFN)** by estimating the amount of new assets necessary to support the forecasted level of sales and then subtracting from that amount the spontaneous funds that will be generated from operations. The firm can then plan to raise the AFN through bank borrowing, by issuing securities, or both.
- **Operating breakeven analysis** is a method of determining the point at which sales will just cover costs, and it shows the magnitude of the firm's operating profits or losses if sales exceed or fall below that point.
- The **operating breakeven point** is the sales volume at which total operating costs equal total revenues and operating income (EBIT) equals zero. The equation used to compute the operating breakeven point is

$$Q_{BE} = \frac{F}{P - V} = \frac{F}{\text{contribution margin}}$$

Self-Test Problems

(Solutions Appear in Appendix B)

Key terms

ST-1 Define each of the following terms:
  a. sales forecast
  b. projected balance sheet method
  c. spontaneously generated funds
  d. dividend payout ratio
  e. pro forma financial statement
  f. additional funds needed (AFN)
  g. financing feedback
  h. financial planning; financial control
  i. operating breakeven analysis; operating breakeven point, Q_{BE}; cash operating breakeven point, Q_{CBE}
  j. financial breakeven analysis; financial breakeven point (EPS level)
  k. operating leverage; degree of operating leverage (DOL)
  l. financial leverage; degree of financial leverage (DFL)
  m. combined (total) leverage; degree of total leverage (DTL)

Operating leverage and breakeven analysis

ST-2 Olinde Electronics Inc. produces stereo components that sell for P = $100. Olinde's fixed costs are $200,000; 5,000 components are produced and sold each year; EBIT is currently $50,000; and Olinde's assets (all equity financed) are $500,000. Olinde estimates that it can change its production process, adding $400,000 to investment and $50,000 to fixed operating costs. This change will (1) reduce variable costs per unit by $10 and (2) increase output by 2,000 units, but (3) the sales price on all units will have to be lowered to $95 to permit sales of the additional output. Olinde has tax loss carry-forwards that cause its tax rate to be zero. Olinde uses no debt, and its average cost of funds is 10 percent.
  a. Should Olinde make the change?
  b. Would Olinde's degree of operating leverage increase or decrease if it made the change? What about its operating breakeven point?
  c. Suppose Olinde was unable to raise additional equity financing and had to borrow the $400,000 to make the investment at an interest rate of 8 percent. Use the Du Pont equation to find the expected ROA of the investment. Should Olinde make the change if debt financing must be used?
  d. What would Olinde's degree of financial leverage be if the $400,000 was borrowed at the 8 percent interest rate? What would its financial breakeven point be?

Problems

Pro forma statements and ratios

4-1 Magee Computers makes bulk purchases of small computers, stocks them in conveniently located warehouses, and ships them to its chain of retail stores. Magee's balance sheet as of December 31, 1995, is shown here (millions of dollars):

Cash	$ 3.5		Accounts payable	$ 9.0
Receivables	26.0		Notes payable	18.0
Inventories	58.0		Accruals	8.5
Current assets	$ 87.5		Current liabilities	$ 35.5
Net fixed assets	35.0		Long-term bonds	6.0
			Common stock	15.0
			Retained earnings	66.0
Total assets	$122.5		Total liabilities and equity	$122.5

Sales for 1995 were $350 million, while net income for the year was $10.5 million. Magee paid dividends of $4.2 million to common stockholders. Sales are projected to increase by $70 million, or 20 percent, during 1996. The firm is operating at full capacity. Assume that all ratios remain constant.

a. Construct Magee's pro forma balance sheet for December 31, 1996. Assume that all external capital requirements are met by bank loans and are reflected in notes payable. Do not consider any financing feedback effects.

b. Now calculate the following ratios, based on your projected December 31, 1996, balance sheet. Magee's 1995 ratios and industry average ratios are shown here for comparison:

	Magee Computers 12/31/96	Magee Computers 12/31/95	Industry Average 12/31/95
Current ratio	_____	2.5×	3.0×
Debt/total assets	_____	33.9%	30.0%
Return on equity	_____	13.0%	12.0%

c. Now assume that Magee grows by the same $70 million but that the growth is spread over 5 years—that is, that sales grow by $14 million each year. Do not consider any financing feedback effects.

(1) Construct a pro forma balance sheet as of December 31, 2000, using notes payable as the balancing item.

(2) Calculate the current ratio, total debt/total assets ratio, and rate of return on equity as of December 31, 2000. [Hint: Be sure to use total sales, which amount to $1,960 million, to calculate retained earnings but 2000 profits to calculate the rate of return on equity—that is, return on equity = (2000 profits)/(12/31/00 equity).]

d. Do the plans outlined in parts a and/or c seem feasible to you? That is, do you think Magee could borrow the required capital, and would the company be raising the odds on its bankruptcy to an excessive level in the event of some temporary misfortune?

Additional funds needed **4-2** Noso Textile's 1995 financial statements are shown below.

Noso Textile:
Balance Sheet as of December 31, 1995
(thousands of dollars)

Cash	$ 1,080	Accounts payable	$ 4,320
Receivables	6,480	Accruals	2,880
Inventories	9,000	Notes payable	2,100
Current assets	$16,560	Current liabilities	$ 9,300
Net fixed assets	12,600	Long-term bonds	3,500
		Common stock	3,500
		Retained earnings	12,860
Total assets	$29,160	Total liabilities and equity	$29,160

Noso Textile:
Income Statement for December 31, 1995
(thousands of dollars)

Sales	$36,000
Operating costs	(32,440)
Earnings before interest and taxes	$ 3,560
Interest	(560)
Earnings before taxes	$ 3,000
Taxes (40%)	(1,200)
Net income	$ 1,800
Dividends (45%)	$ 810
Addition to retained earnings	$ 990

a. Suppose 1996 sales are projected to increase by 15 percent over 1995 sales. Determine the additional funds needed. Assume that the company was operating at full capacity in 1995, that it cannot sell any of its fixed assets, and that any required financing will be borrowed as notes payable. Also, assume that assets, spontaneous liabilities, and operating costs are expected to increase by the same percentage as sales. Use the projected balance sheet method to develop a pro forma balance sheet and income statement for December 31, 1996. (Do not incorporate any financing feedback effects. Use the pro forma income statement to determine the addition to retained earnings.)

b. Use the financial statements developed in part a to incorporate the financing feedback as a result of the addition to notes payable. (That is, do the next financial statement iteration.) For the purpose of this part, assume that the notes payable interest rate is 10 percent. What is the AFN for this iteration?

Degree of leverage   **4-3**   Van Auken Lumber's 1995 income statement is shown below.

Van Auken Lumber:
Income Statement for December 31, 1995
(thousands of dollars)

Sales	$36,000
Cost of goods sold	(25,200)
Gross profit	$10,800
Fixed operating costs	(6,480)
Earnings before interest and taxes	$ 4,320
Interest	(2,880)
Earnings before taxes	$ 1,440
Taxes (40%)	(576)
Net income	$ 864
Dividends (50%)	$ 432

a. Compute the degree of operating leverage (DOL), degree of financial leverage (DFL), and degree of total leverage (DTL) for Van Auken Lumber.

b. Interpret the meaning of each of the numerical values you computed in part a.

c. Briefly discuss some ways Van Auken can reduce its degree of total leverage.

External financing
requirements

4-4 The 1995 balance sheet and income statement for the Woods Company are shown below.

Woods Company:
Balance Sheet as of December 31, 1995
(thousands of dollars)

Cash	$ 80	Accounts payable	$ 160
Accounts receivable	240	Accruals	40
Inventories	720	Notes payable	252
Current assets	$1,040	Current liabilities	$ 452
Fixed assets	3,200	Long-term debt	1,244
		Common stock	1,605
		Retained earnings	939
Total assets	$4,240	Total liabilities and equity	$4,240

Woods Company:
Income Statement for the Year Ending
December 31, 1995
(thousands of dollars)

Sales	$8,000
Operating costs	(7,450)
Earnings before interest and taxes	$ 550
Interest	(150)
Earnings before taxes	$ 400
Taxes (40%)	(160)
Net income	$ 240

Per share data

Common stock price	$16.96
Earnings per share (EPS)	$1.60
Dividends per share (DPS)	$1.04

a. The firm operated at full capacity in 1995. It expects sales to increase by 20 percent during 1996 and expects 1996 dividends per share to increase to $1.10. Use the projected balance sheet method to determine how much outside financing is required, developing the firm's pro forma balance sheet and income statement, and use AFN as the balancing item.

b. If the firm must maintain a current ratio of 2.3 and a debt ratio of 40 percent, how much financing, after the first pass, will be obtained using notes payable, long-term debt, and common stock?

c. Make the second pass financial statements incorporating financing feedbacks, using the ratios in part b. Assume that the interest rate on debt averages 10 percent.

Operating breakeven analysis

4-5 The Weaver Watch Company manufactures a line of ladies' watches that is sold through discount houses. Each watch is sold for $25; the fixed costs are $140,000 for 30,000 watches or less; variable costs are $15 per watch.

a. What is the firm's gain or loss at sales of 8,000 watches? Of 18,000 watches?

b. What is the operating breakeven point? Illustrate by means of a chart.

c. What is Weaver's degree of operating leverage at sales of 8,000 units? Of 18,000 units? (Hint: Use Equation 4-5 to solve this problem.)

d. What happens to the operating breakeven point if the selling price rises to $31? What is the significance of the change to the financial manager?

e. What happens to the operating breakeven point if the selling price rises to $31 but variable costs rise to $23 a unit?

Operating breakeven analysis   **4-6**   The following relationships exist for Dellva Industries, a manufacturer of electronic components. Each unit of output is sold for $45; the fixed costs are $175,000, of which $110,000 are annual depreciation charges; variable costs are $20 per unit.

a. What is the firm's gain or loss at sales of 5,000 units? Of 12,000 units?

b. What is the operating income breakeven point?

c. What is the cash breakeven point?

d. Assume Dellva is operating at a level of 4,000 units. Are creditors likely to seek the liquidation of the company if it is slow in paying its bills?

Financial leverage   **4-7**   Gordon's Plants has the following partial income statement for 1995:

Earnings before interest and taxes	$4,500
Interest	(2,000)
Earnings before taxes	$2,500
Taxes (40%)	(1,000)
Net income	$1,500
Number of common shares	1,000

a. If Gordon's has no preferred stock, what is its financial breakeven point? Show the amount you come up with actually is the financial breakeven by recreating the portion of the income statement shown above for that amount.

b. What is the degree of financial leverage for Gordon's at EBIT equal to $4,500? What does this value mean?

c. If Gordon's actually has preferred stock that requires payment of dividends equal to $600, what would be the financial breakeven point? Show the amount you compute is the financial breakeven by recreating the portion of the income statement shown above for that amount.

Exam-Type Problems

The problems in this section are set up in such a way that they could be used as multiple-choice exam problems.

Operating leverage   **4-8**   The Niendorf Corporation produces teakettles, which it sells for $15 each. Fixed costs are $700,000 for up to 400,000 units of output. Variable costs are $10 per kettle.

a. What is the firm's gain or loss at sales of 125,000 units? Of 175,000 units?

b. What is the breakeven point? Illustrate by means of a chart.

c. What is Niendorf's degree of operating leverage at sales of 125,000 units? Of 150,000 units? Of 175,000 units? (Hint: You may use either Equation 4-5 or 4-5a to solve this problem.)

Long-term financing needed   **4-9**   At year-end 1995, total assets for Shome Inc. were $1.2 million and accounts payable were $375,000. Sales, which in 1995 were $2.5 million, are expected to increase by 25 percent in 1996. Total assets and accounts payable are proportional to sales and that relationship will be maintained. Shome typically uses no current liabilities other than accounts payable. Common stock amounted to $425,000 in

1995, and retained earnings were $295,000. Shome plans to sell new common stock in the amount of $75,000. The firm's profit margin on sales is 6 percent; 40 percent of earnings will be paid out as dividends.

    a. What was Shome's total debt in 1995?

    b. How much new, long-term debt financing will be needed in 1996? (Hint: AFN − New stock = New long-term debt.) Do not consider any financing feedback effects.

Degree of operating leverage   **4-10**   *a.* Given the following graphs, calculate the total fixed costs, variable costs per unit, and sales price for Firm A. Firm B's fixed costs are $120,000, its variable costs per unit are $4, and its sales price is $8 per unit.

    b. Which firm has the higher degree of operating leverage? Explain.

    c. At what sales level, in units, do both firms earn the same profit?

Breakeven Charts for Problem 4-10

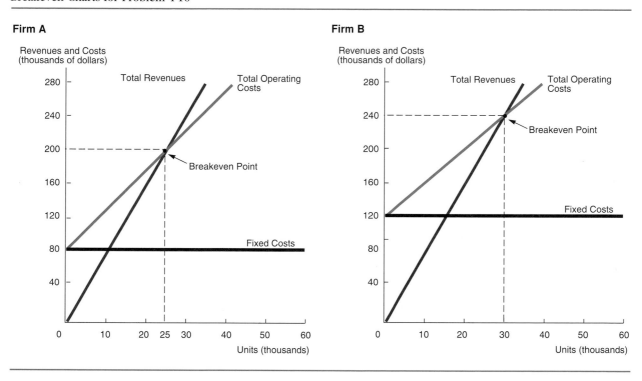

Additional funds needed   **4-11**   The McGill Company's sales are forecasted to increase from $1,000 in 1995 to $2,000 in 1996. Here is the December 31, 1995, balance sheet:

Cash	$ 100	Accounts payable	$ 50
Accounts receivable	200	Notes payable	150
Inventories	200	Accruals	50
Current assets	$ 500	Current liabilities	$ 250
Net fixed assets	500	Long-term debt	400
		Common stock	100
		Retained earnings	250
Total assets	$1,000	Total liabilities and equity	$1,000

McGill's fixed assets were used to only 50 percent of capacity during 1995, but its current assets were at their proper levels. All assets except fixed assets increase at the same rate as sales, and fixed assets would also increase at the same rate if the current excess capacity did not exist. McGill's after-tax profit margin is forecasted to be 5 percent, and its payout ratio will be 60 percent. What is McGill's additional funds needed (AFN) for the coming year? Ignore financing feedback effects.

Breakeven analysis and leverage

4-12 Straight Arrow Company manufactures golf balls. The following income statement information is relevant for Straight Arrow in 1996:

Selling price per sleeve of balls (P)	$5.00
Variable cost of goods sold (% of price, P)	75%
Fixed operating costs	$50,000
Interest expense	$10,000
Preferred dividends	$0.00
Marginal tax rate	40%
Number of common shares	20,000

a. What level of sales does Straight Arrow need to achieve in 1996 to breakeven with respect to *operating income*?

b. At its operating breakeven, what will be the EPS for Straight Arrow?

c. How many sleeves of golf balls (units) does Straight Arrow need to sell in 1996 to attain the financial breakeven point? (Hint: An easy way to look at this problem is to consider how many sleeves of balls (units) *beyond those needed for operating breakeven* Straight Arrow needs to sell to cover its fixed financial charges. Note that Straight Arrow has no preferred stock.)

d. If Straight Arrow expects its sales to be $300,000 in 1996, what is its degree of operating leverage, its degree of financial leverage, and its degree of total (combined) leverage? Based on the degree of total leverage, compute the earnings per share you would expect in 1996 if sales actually turn out to be $270,000.

Integrative Problem

Forecasting, breakeven, and leverage

4-13 Sue Wilson is the new financial manager of Northwest Chemicals (NWC), an Oregon producer of specialized chemicals sold to farmers for use in fruit orchards. She is responsible for constructing financial forecasts and for evaluating the financial feasibility of new products.

PART I. FINANCIAL FORECASTING

Sue must prepare a financial forecast for 1996 for Northwest. NWC's 1995 sales were $2 billion, and the marketing department is forecasting a 25 percent increase for 1996. Sue thinks the company was operating at full capacity in 1995, but she is not sure about this. The 1995 financial statements, plus some other data, are given in Table IP4-1.

Assume that you were recently hired as Sue's assistant, and your first major task is to help her develop the forecast. She asked you to begin by answering the following questions.

a. Assume that NWC was operating at full capacity in 1995 with respect to all assets. Estimate the 1996 financial requirements using the projected financial statement approach, making an initial forecast plus one additional pass to determine the effects of financing feedbacks. Assume that (1) each type of asset as well as payables, accruals, and fixed and variable costs grow at the same rate as sales; (2) the payout ratio is held constant at 30 percent; (3) external funds

TABLE IP4-1

Financial Statements and Other Data on NWC (millions of dollars)

A. 1995 Balance Sheet

Cash and securities	$ 20	Accounts payable and accruals	$ 100
Accounts receivable	240	Notes payable	100
Inventories	240	Total current liabilities	$ 200
Total current assets	$ 500	Long-term debt	100
		Common stock	500
Net fixed assets	500	Retained earnings	200
Total assets	$1,000	Total liabilities and equity	$1,000

B. 1995 Income Statement

Sales	$2,000.00
Less: Variable costs	(1,200.00)
Fixed costs	(700.00)
Earnings before interest and taxes	$ 100.00
Interest	(16.00)
Earnings before taxes	$ 84.00
Taxes (40%)	(33.60)
Net income	$ 50.40
Dividends (30%)	(15.12)
Addition to retained earnings	$ 35.28

C. Key Ratios

	NWC	Industry	Comment
Profit margin	2.52	4.00	
Return on equity	7.20	15.60	
Days sales outstanding (360 days)	43.20 days	32.00 days	
Inventory turnover	5.00×	8.00×	
Fixed assets turnover	4.00×	5.00×	
Total assets turnover	2.00×	2.50×	
Total debt ratio	30.00%	36.00%	
Times interest earned	6.25×	9.40×	
Current ratio	2.50	3.00	
Payout ratio	30.00%	30.00%	

needed are financed 50 percent by notes payable and 50 percent by long-term debt (no new common stock will be issued); and (4) all debt carries an interest rate of 8 percent.

b. Calculate NWC's forecasted ratios, and compare them with the company's 1995 ratios and with the industry averages. How does NWC compare with the average firm in its industry, and is the company expected to improve during the coming year?

c. Suppose you now learn that NWC's 1995 receivables and inventories were in line with required levels, given the firm's credit and inventory policies, but that excess capacity existed with regard to fixed assets. Specifically, fixed assets were operated at only 75 percent of capacity

(1) What level of sales could have existed in 1995 with the available fixed assets? What would the fixed assets/sales ratio have been if NWC had been operating at full capacity?

(2) How would the existence of excess capacity in fixed assets affect the additional funds needed during 1996?

d. Without actually working out the numbers, how would you expect the ratios to change in the situation where excess capacity in fixed assets exists? Explain your reasoning.

e. Based on comparisons between NWC's days sales outstanding (DSO) and inventory turnover ratios with the industry average figures, does it appear that NWC is operating efficiently with respect to its inventories and accounts receivable? If the company were able to bring these ratios into line with the industry averages, what effect would this have on its AFN and its financial ratios? (Note: Inventories and receivables will be discussed in detail in later chapters.)

f. How would the following affect the AFN: (1) the dividend payout ratio changes, (2) the profit margin changes, (3) plant capacity changes, and (4) NWC begins buying from its suppliers on terms that permit it to pay after 60 days rather than after 30 days. (Consider each item separately and hold all other things constant.)

PART II. BREAKEVEN ANALYSIS AND LEVERAGE
One of NWC's employees recently proposed that NWC should expand its operations and sell its chemicals in retail establishments such as Home Depot, Builder's Square, Scotty's, and so on. To determine the feasibility of the idea, Sue needs to perform a breakeven analysis. The fixed costs associated with producing and selling the chemicals to retail stores would be $60 million, the selling price per unit is expected to be $10, and the variable cost ratio would be the same as it is currently.

a. What is the operating breakeven point both in dollars and in number of units for the employee's proposal?

b. Draw the operating breakeven chart for the proposal. Should the employee's proposal be adopted if NWC can produce and sell 20 million units of the chemical?

c. If NWC can produce and sell 20 million units of its product to retail stores, what would be its degree of operating leverage? What would be NWC's percent increase in operating profits if sales actually were 10 percent higher than expected?

d. Assume NWC has excess capacity, so it does not need to raise any additional external funds to implement the proposal. What would be its degree of financial leverage and its degree of total leverage? If the actual sales turned out to be 10 percent greater than expected, as a percent, how much greater would the earnings per share be?

e. Explain how breakeven analysis and leverage analysis can be used for planning the implementation of this proposal.

Computer-Related Problem

Work the problem in this section only if you are using the computer problem diskette.

Forecasting   4-14   Use the model in File C4 to solve this problem. Stendardi Industries' 1995 financial statements are shown in the following table.

Stendardi Industries:
Balance Sheet as of December 31, 1995
(millions of dollars)

Cash	$ 4.0	Accounts payable	$ 8.0
Receivables	12.0	Notes payable	5.0
Inventories	16.0	Current liabilities	$13.0
Current assets	$32.0	Long-term debt	12.0
Net fixed assets	40.0	Common stock	20.0
		Retained earnings	27.0
Total assets	$72.0	Total liabilities and equity	$72.0

Stendardi Industries:
Income Statement for December 31, 1995
(millions of dollars)

Sales	$80.0
Operating costs	(71.3)
Earnings before interest and taxes	$ 8.7
Interest	(2.0)
Earnings before taxes	$ 6.7
Taxes (40%)	(2.7)
Net income	$ 4.0
Dividends (40%)	$1.60
Addition to retained earnings	$2.40

Assume that the firm has no excess capacity in fixed assets, that the average interest rate for debt is 12 percent, and that the projected annual sales growth rate for the next 5 years is 15 percent.

a. Stendardi plans to finance its additional funds needed with 50 percent short-term debt and 50 percent long-term debt. Using the projected balance sheet method, prepare the pro forma financial statements for 1996 through 2000, and then determine (1) additional funds needed, (2) the current ratio, (3) the debt ratio, and (4) the return on equity.

b. Sales growth could be 5 percentage points above or below the projected 15 percent. Determine the effect of such variances on AFN and the key ratios.

c. Perform an analysis to determine the sensitivity of AFN and the key ratios for 2000 to changes in the dividend payout ratio as specified in the following, assuming sales grow at a constant 15 percent. What happens to AFN if the dividend payout ratio (1) is raised from 40 to 70 percent or (2) is lowered from 40 to 20 percent?

APPENDIX 4A Projected Financial Statements—Including Financing Feedbacks

In the chapter, we discussed the procedure used to construct pro forma financial statements. The first step is to estimate the level of operations and then project the impact such operations will have on the financial statements of the firm. We found that when a firm needs additional external financing, its existing interest and dividend payments will change—thus, the values initially projected for the financial statements will be affected.

TABLE 4A-1

Unilate Textiles: 1996 Forecast of Financial Statements (millions of dollars)

INCOME STATEMENT

	Initial Pass	Feed-back	Second Pass	Final Pass
Earnings before interest and taxes (EBIT)	$154.0		$154.0	$154.0
Less interest	(36.0)	+1.2	(37.2)	(37.2)
Earnings before taxes (EBT)	$118.0		$116.8	$116.8
Taxes (40%)	(47.2)	−0.5	(46.7)	(46.7)
Net income	$ 70.8		$ 70.1	$ 70.1
Common dividends	(32.8)	+1.4	(34.2)	(34.2)
Addition to retained earnings	$ 38.0	−2.1	$ 35.9	$ 35.9
Dividends per share	$1.31		$1.31	$1.31
Number of common shares (millions)	25.00		26.07	26.13

BALANCE SHEET

	Initial Pass	Feed-back	Second Pass	Final Pass
Cash	$ 22.0		$ 22.0	$ 22.0
Accounts receivable	198.0		198.0	198.0
Inventories	297.0		297.0	297.0
Total current assets	$517.0		$517.0	$517.0
Net plant and equipment	418.0		418.0	418.0
Total Assets	$935.0		$935.0	$935.0
Accounts payable	$ 33.0		$ 33.0	$ 33.0
Accruals	66.0		66.0	66.0
Notes payable	40.0	+5.7	45.7	+0.3 → 46.0
Total current liabilities	$139.0		$144.7	$145.0
Long-term bonds	297.0	+7.5	304.5	+0.5 → 305.0
Total liabilities	$436.0		$449.2	$450.0
Common stock	130.0	+24.5	154.5	+1.5 → 156.0
Retained earnings	331.3		329.2	329.0
Total owners' equity	$461.3		$483.7	$485.0
Total Liabilities and Equity	$897.3	+37.7	$932.9	+2.3 → $935.0
Additional funds needed (AFN)	$ 37.7		$ 2.1	$ 0.0

Therefore, to recognize these *financing feedbacks,* the construction of projected financial statements needs to be an iterative process. In this appendix, we give an indication of the iterative process for constructing the pro forma statements for Unilate. Table 4A-1 contains the initial projected statements shown in Tables 4-1 and 4-2 of the chapter, then some of the subsequent passes used to adjust the forecasted statements are given. According to the discussion in the chapter, the forecasted statements first are constructed assuming only retained earnings and spontaneous financing are available to support the forecasted operations. This first pass is necessary to provide an indication of the additional external funds needed—Unilate needs almost $38 million. But if Unilate raises this additional amount by borrowing from the bank and by issuing new bonds and new common stock, then its interest and dividend payments will increase. This can be seen by examining the income statement constructed in the second pass to show the effects of raising the $37.7 million additional funds needed. Because Unilate would have additional debt, it would have to pay $1.2 million more interest; and, because it has more shares of common stock outstanding, it would have to pay $1.4 million more dividends. Consequently, as the second pass balance sheet shows, if Unilate raises only the $37.7 million AFN (additional funds needed) initially computed, it would still find a need for funds—the AFN would be $2.1 million—because the addition to retained earnings would be lower than originally expected. As it turns out, Unilate actually would need to raise $40 million to support the forecasted 1996 operations.

PART III

Essential Concepts in Managerial Finance

Risk and Rates of Return

1994 was a year most investors wish they could erase. The performances of the major stock markets could only be classified as abysmal—stocks traded on the New York Stock Exchange (NYSE), on the American Stock Exchange (AMEX), and over the counter (OTC) on average, decreased by more than 3 percent. USAir stock, which trades on the NYSE, lost nearly two thirds of its value because the company had difficulty handling its high operating costs and the costs of air mishaps in the highly competitive airline industry; the stock of Greyhound Lines, a bus transportation company traded on the AMEX, decreased by more than 85 percent because many travelers took advantage of low air fares; and, stockholders of Media Vision Technology, a manufacturer of personal computer add-ons that is traded over the counter, saw their stock fall from $43.75 to $0.09, a loss of nearly 100 percent, because the firm went into bankruptcy. Even as these stocks experienced debilitating losses, other stocks provided very handsome, if not unbelievable, gains. United Inns, a hotel company traded on the NYSE, more than tripled its stock price in 1994; EXX, the toy manufacturer that holds the rights to the Mighty Morphin Power Ranger toys, saw the value of its stock increase by nearly 1,300 percent, from $1.63 to $22.25 on the AMEX; and, the stock of MicroTouch Systems, which is an OTC company that manufactures screens for computers, jumped from $6.88 to $37.63, an increase of almost 450 percent. As these examples show, investors that "put all their eggs in one basket," faced considerable risk in the stock markets—they could have either won or lost significant sums. Unfortunately, even those investors that diversified by holding mutual funds experienced a loss in value from 1½ percent to 4½ percent. To be sure, 1994 was a year of great uncertainty for the stock markets—the risk of investing in stocks frightened away many "average" investors.

Should investors panic? The answer is a resounding NO! In fact, many investment strategists would suggest that the 1994 results generated in the stock markets opened up great opportunities for future investment, because many stocks were artificially depressed at the beginning of 1995. In any

Continued

event, most strategists would tell investors not to overreact—investors often make a very serious mistake by leaving the market after bad years. Instead, investors should stay in the market, but diversify according to their own risk preferences.

As times change, strategies and portfolio mixes need to be changed to meet new conditions, but it is important for you to understand the basic concepts of risk and return and how diversification works. You will discover that investors can create portfolios of securities to reduce risk without reducing the average return on their investments. After reading this chapter, you should have a better understanding of how risk affects investment returns and how to evaluate risk when selecting investments such as those described above.

In this chapter we take an in-depth look at how investment risk should be measured and how it affects security prices and rates of return. Recall that in Chapter 2, when we examined the determinants of interest rates, we defined the real risk-free rate, k^*, to be the rate of interest on a risk-free security in the absence of inflation. The actual interest rate on a particular debt security was shown to be equal to the real risk-free rate plus several premiums that reflect both inflation and the riskiness of the security in question. In this chapter we define more precisely what the term *risk* means as it relates to securities, we examine procedures managers use for measuring risk, and we discuss the relationship between risk and return. Then, in Chapters 6 and 7, we extend these relationships to show how they interact to determine security prices in the financial markets. Business executives should understand these concepts and use them as they plan the actions that will shape their firms' futures.

We will demonstrate in this chapter that each investment—each stock, bond, or physical asset—has two types of risk: (1) diversifiable risk and (2) nondiversifiable risk. The sum of these two components is the investment's total risk. Diversifiable risk should not be important to rational, informed investors, because they can eliminate its effects by diversifying it away. The really significant risk is nondiversifiable risk—this risk is bad in the sense that it cannot be eliminated, and if you invest in anything other than riskless assets such as short-term Treasury bills, you will be exposed to it. In the balance of the chapter we will explain these risk concepts and show you how risk enters into the decision process.

Defining and Measuring Risk

Risk is defined in *Webster's Dictionary* as "a hazard; a peril; exposure to loss or injury." Thus, for most, risk refers to the chance that some unfavorable event will occur. If you engage in skydiving, you are taking a chance with your life—skydiving is risky. If you bet on the horses, you are risking your money. If you invest in speculative stocks (or, really, *any* stock), you are taking a risk in the hope of making an appreciable return.

Most people view risk in the manner we just described—a chance of loss. In reality, *risk* occurs when we cannot be certain about the outcome of a particular activity or event, so we are not sure what will occur in the future. Consequently, *risk* results from the fact that an action such as investing can produce more than one outcome in the future. To illustrate the riskiness of financial assets, suppose you have a large amount of money to invest for one year. You could buy a Treasury security that has an expected return equal to 8 percent. The rate of return expected from this investment can be determined quite precisely, because the chances of the government defaulting on Treasury securities is negligible; the outcome essentially is guaranteed, which means this is a risk-free investment. On the other hand, you could buy the common stock of a newly formed company that has developed technology to extract petroleum from the mountains in South America without defacing the landscape and without harming the ecology. The technology has yet to be proven economically feasible, so it is not known what returns the common stockholders will receive in the future. Experts who have analyzed the common stock of the company have determined that the *expected*, or average long-run, return for such an investment is 30 percent; each year, the investment could yield a positive return as high as 900 percent, but there also is the possibility the company will not survive, in which case the entire investment will be lost, so the return will be −100 percent. The return investors receive each year cannot be determined precisely because more than one outcome is possible—this is a risky investment. Because there is a significant danger of actually earning considerably less than the expected return, investors probably would consider the stock to be quite risky. But there also is a very good chance the actual return will be greater than expected, which, of course, is an outcome we gladly accept. So, when we think of investment risk, along with the chance of actually receiving less than expected, we should consider the chance of actually receiving more than expected. If we consider investment risk from this perspective, then we can define **risk** as the chance of receiving an actual return other than expected, which simply means there is *variability in the returns* or outcomes from the investment. Therefore, investment risk can be measured by the variability of the investment's returns.

Investment risk, then, is related to the possibility of actually earning a return other than expected—the greater the variability of the possible outcomes, the riskier the investment. However, we can define risk more precisely, and it is useful to do so.

RISK
The chance that an outcome other than expected will occur.

Probability Distributions

PROBABILITY DISTRIBUTION
A listing of all possible outcomes, or events, with a probability (chance of occurrence) assigned to each outcome.

An event's *probability* is defined as the chance that the event will occur. For example, a weather forecaster might state, "There is a 40 percent chance of rain today and a 60 percent chance that it will not rain." If all possible events, or outcomes, are listed, and if a probability is assigned to each event, the listing is called a **probability distribution.** For our weather forecast, we could set up the following probability distribution:

Outcome (1)	Probability (2)	
Rain	0.40 =	40%
No rain	0.60 =	60
	1.00	100%

The possible outcomes are listed in Column 1, while the probabilities of these outcomes, expressed both as decimals and as percentages, are given in Column 2. Notice that the probabilities must sum to 1.0, or 100 percent.

Probabilities can also be assigned to the possible outcomes (or returns) from an investment. If you buy a bond, you expect to receive interest on the bond, and those interest payments will provide you with a rate of return on your investment. The possible outcomes from this investment are (1) that the issuer will make the interest payments or (2) that the issuer will fail to make the interest payments. The higher the probability of default on the interest payments, the riskier the bond; and the higher the risk, the higher the rate of return you would require to invest in the bond. If instead of buying a bond you invest in a stock, you will again expect to earn a return on your money. A stock's return will come from dividends plus capital gains. Again, the riskier the stock—which means the greater the variability of the possible payoffs—the higher the stock's expected return must be to induce you to invest in it.

With this in mind, consider the possible rates of return (dividend yield plus capital gain or loss) that you might earn next year on a $10,000 investment in the stock of either Martin Products Inc. or U.S. Electric. Martin manufactures and distributes computer terminals and equipment for the rapidly growing data transmission industry. Because its sales are cyclical, its profits rise and fall with the business cycle. Further, its market is extremely competitive, and some new company could develop better products that could literally bankrupt Martin. U.S. Electric, on the other hand, supplies electricity which is an essential service, and because it has city franchises that protect it from competition, its sales and profits are relatively stable and predictable.

The rate-of-return probability distributions for the two companies are shown in Table 5-1. Here we see that there is a 20 percent chance of a boom, in which case both companies will have high earnings, pay high dividends, and enjoy capital gains; there is a 50 percent probability of a normal economy and moderate returns; and there is a 30 percent probability of a recession, which will mean low

TABLE 5-1

Probability Distributions for Martin Products and U.S. Electric

State of the Economy	Probability of This State Occurring	Rate of Return on Stock if This State Occurs	
		Martin Products	**U.S. Electric**
Boom	0.2	110%	20%
Normal	0.5	22	16
Recession	0.3	−60	10
	1.0		

TABLE 5-2

Calculation of Expected Rates of Return: Martin Products and U.S. Electric

State of the Economy (1)	Probability of This State Occurring (2)	Martin Products		U.S. Electric	
		Return if This State Occurs (3)	Product: (2) × (3) = (4)	Return if This State Occurs (5)	Product: (2) × (5) = (6)
Boom	0.2	110%	22%	20%	4%
Normal	0.5	22	11	16	8
Recession	0.3	−60	−18	10	3
	1.0		$\hat{k} = 15\%$		$\hat{k} = 15\%$

earnings and dividends as well as the possibility of capital losses. Notice, however, that Martin Products' rate of return could vary far more widely than that of U.S. Electric. There is a fairly high probability that the value of Martin's stock will vary substantially, resulting in a loss of 60 percent or a gain of 110 percent, while there is no chance of a loss for U.S. Electric and its maximum gain is 20 percent.[1]

Self-Test Questions

What does "investment risk" mean?

Set up illustrative probability distributions for (1) a bond investment and (2) a stock investment.

Expected Rate of Return

EXPECTED RATE OF RETURN, $\hat{k}$
The rate of return expected to be realized from an investment; the mean value of the probability distribution of possible results.

Table 5-1 provides the probability distributions showing the possible outcomes for investing in Martin Products and U.S. Electric. We can see that the most likely outcome is for the economy to be normal, in which case Martin will return 22 percent and U.S. Electric will return 16 percent. But other outcomes also are possible, so we need to summarize the information contained in the probability distributions into a single measure that considers all these possible outcomes—that measure is the expected value, or expected rate of return, for the investments.

Simply stated, the **expected value (return)** is the *weighted average* of the outcomes, where the weights we use are the probabilities. Table 5-2 shows how the expected rates of return for Martin Products and U.S. Electric are computed— we multiply each possible outcome by the probability it will occur and then

---

[1]It is, of course, completely unrealistic to think that any stock has no chance of a loss. Only in hypothetical examples could this occur. To illustrate, the price of Columbia Gas's stock dropped from $34.50 to $20.00 in just three hours on June 19, 1991. All investors were reminded that any stock is exposed to some risk of loss, and those investors who bought Columbia Gas learned this lesson the hard way.

sum the results. We designate the expected rate of return, $\hat{k}$, which is termed "k-hat."[2]

The expected rate of return can be calculated using the following equation:[3]

$$\text{5-1} \quad \text{Expected rate of return} = \hat{k} = Pr_1k_1 + Pr_2k_2 + \ldots + Pr_nk_n$$

$$= \sum_{i=1}^{n} Pr_ik_i$$

Here k_i is the ith possible outcome, Pr_i is the probability the ith outcome will occur, and n is the number of possible outcomes. Thus, $\hat{k}$ is a weighted average of the possible outcomes (the k_i values), with each outcome's weight being its probability of occurrence. Using the data for Martin Products, we obtain its expected rate of return as follows:

$$\hat{k} = Pr_1(k_1) + Pr_2(k_2) + Pr_3(k_3)$$

$$= 0.2(110\%) + 0.5(22\%) + 0.3(-60\%)$$

$$= 15\%$$

Notice the expected rate of return does not equal any of the possible payoffs for Martin Products given in Table 5-2. Stated simply, the expected rate of return represents the average payoff investors will receive from Martin Products if the probability distribution given in Table 5-2 does not change over a long period. If the probability distribution for Martin Products is correct, then 20 percent of the time the future economic condition will be termed a boom, so investors will earn a 110 percent rate of return; 50 percent of the time the economy should be normal and the investment payoff will be 22 percent; and 30 percent of the time the economy should be recessionary and the payoff will be a loss equal to 60 percent. On average, then, Martin Products' investors will earn 15 percent.

We can graph the rates of return to obtain a picture of the variability of possible outcomes; this is shown in the Figure 5-1 bar charts. The height of each bar signifies the probability that a given outcome will occur. The range of probable returns for Martin Products is from +110 to −60 percent, with an expected return of 15 percent. The expected return for U.S. Electric also is 15 percent, but its range is much narrower.

---

[2]In Chapter 7, we will use k_d to signify the return on a debt instrument and k_s to signify the return on a stock. In this section, however, we discuss only returns on stocks; thus, the subscript s is unnecessary, and we use the term $\hat{k}$ rather than $\hat{k}_s$.

[3]The second form of the equation is simply a shorthand expression in which sigma (Σ) means "sum up," or add the values of n factors. If i = 1, then $Pr_ik_i = Pr_1k_1$; if i = 2, then $Pr_ik_i = Pr_2k_2$; and so on until i = n, the last possible outcome. The symbol $\sum_{i=1}^{n}$ simply says, "Go through the following process: First, let i = 1 and find the first product; then let i = 2 and find the second product; then continue until each individual product up to i = n has been found, and then add these individual products to find the expected rate of return."

FIGURE 5-1

Probability Distributions of Martin Products' and U.S. Electric's Rates of Return

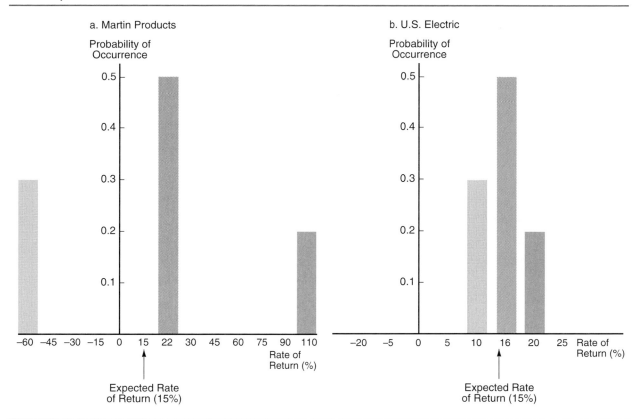

Continuous versus Discrete Probability Distributions

DISCRETE PROBABILITY DISTRIBUTION
The number of possible outcomes is limited, or finite.

Thus far we have assumed that only three states of the economy can exist: recession, normal, and boom. So the probability distributions given in Table 5-1 are called **discrete** because there is a finite, or limited, number of outcomes. Actually, of course, the state of the economy could range from a deep depression to a fantastic boom, and there are an unlimited number of possibilities in between. Suppose we had the time and patience to assign a probability to each possible state of the economy (with the sum of the probabilities still equaling 1.0), and to assign a rate of return to each stock for each state of the economy. We would have a table similar to Table 5-1, except that it would have many more entries in each column. This table could be used to calculate expected rates of return as shown previously, and the probabilities and outcomes might be approximated by continuous curves such as those presented in Figure 5-2. Here we have changed the assumptions so that there is essentially a zero probability that Martin Products' return will be less than −60 percent or more than 110 percent, or that U.S. Electric's return will be less than 10 percent or more than 20 percent, but virtually any return within these limits is possible. These probability distributions are **continuous** because, in each case, the number of outcomes possible is unlimited—U.S. Electric's return could be 10.01 percent, 10.001 percent, and so on.

CONTINUOUS PROBABILITY DISTRIBUTION
The number of possible outcomes is unlimited, or infinite.

FIGURE 5-2

Continuous Probability Distributions of Martin Products' and U.S. Electric's Rates of Return

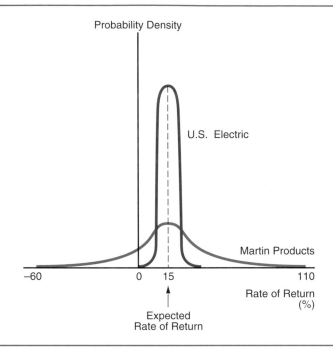

NOTE: The assumptions regarding the probabilities of various outcomes have been changed from those in Figure 5-1. There the probability of obtaining exactly 16 percent return for U.S. Electric was 50 percent; here it is *much smaller*, because there are many possible outcomes instead of just three. With continuous distributions, it is more appropriate to ask what the probability is of obtaining at least some specified rate of return than to ask what the probability is of obtaining exactly that rate. This topic is covered in detail in statistics courses.

The *tighter the probability distribution*, the *less variability* there is and the more likely it is that the actual outcome will be close to the expected value; consequently, the less likely it is that the actual return will be much different from the expected return. Thus, *the tighter the probability distribution, the lower the risk assigned to a stock.* Because U.S. Electric has a relatively tight probability distribution, its *actual* return is likely to be closer to its 15 percent expected return than is that of Martin Products.

Measuring Risk: The Standard Deviation

Because we have defined risk as the variability of returns, we can measure risk by examining the tightness of the probability distribution associated with the possible outcomes. In general, the width of a probability distribution indicates the amount of scatter, or variability, of the possible outcomes. Therefore, *the tighter the probability distribution of expected returns, the less its variability—thus the smaller the risk associated with the investment.* According to this definition, U.S. Electric is much less risky than Martin Products, because the actual payoffs that are possible are closer to the expected return for U.S. Electric than for Martin Products.

To be most useful, any measure of risk should have a definite value—we need a measure of the tightness of the probability distribution. The measure we probably use most often is the **standard deviation,** the symbol for which is **σ** (pronounced "sigma"). The smaller the standard deviation, the tighter the probability distribution, and, accordingly, the lower the riskiness of the investment. To calculate the standard deviation, we proceed as shown in Table 5-3, taking the following steps:

STANDARD DEVIATION, σ
A measure of the tightness, or variability, of a set of outcomes.

1. We calculate the expected rate of return:

5-1
$$\text{Expected rate of return} = \hat{k} = \sum_{i=1}^{n} Pr_i k_i$$

For Martin, we previously found $\hat{k} = 15\%$.

2. First, we subtract the expected rate of return ($\hat{k}$) from each possible outcome (k_i) to obtain a set of deviations from ($\hat{k}$):

$$\text{Deviation}_i = k_i - \hat{k}$$

VARIANCE, σ²
The standard deviation squared.

3. Next, we square each deviation, multiply the result by the probability of occurrence for its related outcome, and then sum these products to obtain the **variance** of the probability distribution:

5-2
$$\text{Variance} = \sigma^2 = \sum_{i=1}^{n} (k_i - \hat{k})^2 Pr_i$$

4. Finally, we take the square root of the variance to obtain the standard deviation:

TABLE 5-3

Calculating Martin Products' Standard Deviation

Payoff k_i (1)		Expected Return $\hat{k}$ (2)		$k_i - \hat{k}$ (3)	$(k_i - \hat{k})^2$ (4)	Probability (5)	$(k_i - \hat{k})^2 Pr_i$ (4) × (5) = (6)
110%	−	15%	=	95	9,025	0.2	(9,025)(0.2) = 1,805.0
22	−	15	=	7	49	0.5	(49)(0.5) = 24.5
(60)	−	15	=	−75	5,625	0.3	(5,625)(0.3) = 1,687.5
						Variance = σ^2 =	3,517.0
						Standard deviation = $\sigma_M = \sqrt{\sigma_M^2} = \sqrt{3,517}$ =	59.3%

$$\text{Standard deviation} = \sigma = \sqrt{\sigma^2} = \sqrt{\sum_{i=1}^{n} (k_i - \hat{k})^2 Pr_i}$$

Thus, the standard deviation is a weighted average deviation from the expected value, and it gives an idea of how far above or below the expected value the actual value is likely to be. Martin's standard deviation is seen in Table 5-3 to be $\sigma_M = 59.3\%$, and, using these same procedures, we find U.S. Electric's standard deviation to be 3.6 percent. The larger standard deviation of Martin Products indicates a greater variation of returns, thus a greater chance that the expected return will not be realized; therefore, Martin Products would be considered a riskier investment than U.S. Electric, using this measure of risk.[4]

COEFFICIENT OF VARIATION (CV)
Standardized measure of the risk per unit of return; calculated as the standard deviation divided by the expected return.

Another useful measure to evaluate risky investments is the **coefficient of variation (CV),** which is the standard deviation divided by the expected return:

$$\text{Coefficient of variation} = CV = \frac{\text{Risk}}{\text{Return}} = \frac{\sigma}{\hat{k}}$$

The coefficient of variation shows the risk per unit of return, and it provides a more meaningful basis for comparison when the expected returns on two alternatives are not the same. Because U.S. Electric and Martin Products *have the same*

---

[4]In the example, we described the procedure for finding the mean and standard deviation when the data are in the form of a known probability distribution. If only sample returns data over some *past period* are available, the standard deviation of returns can be estimated using this formula:

$$\text{Estimated } \sigma = S = \sqrt{\frac{\sum_{t=1}^{n} (\bar{k}_t - \bar{k}_{Avg})^2}{n - 1}} \tag{5-3a}$$

Here $\bar{k}_t$ ("k bar t") denotes the past realized rate of return in Period t, and $\bar{k}_{Avg}$ is the average annual return earned during the last n years. Here is an example:

Year	$\bar{k}_t$
1993	15%
1994	−5
1995	20

$$\bar{k}_{Avg} = \frac{15 + (-5) + 20}{3} = 10\%$$

$$\text{Estimated } \sigma = S = \sqrt{\frac{(15 - 10)^2 + (-5 - 10)^2 + (20 - 10)^2}{3 - 1}}$$

$$= \sqrt{\frac{350}{2}} = 13.2\%$$

The historical σ often is used as an estimate of the future σ. Much less often, and generally incorrectly, $\bar{k}_{Avg}$ for some past period is used as an estimate of $\hat{k}$, the *expected* future return. Because past variability is likely to be repeated, σ might be a good estimate of future risk, but it is much less reasonable to expect that the past *level* of return (which could have been as high as +100% or as low as −50%) is the best expectation of what investors think will happen in the future.

expected return, it is not necessary to compute the coefficient of variation to compare the two investments. In this case, most people would prefer to invest in U.S. Electric, because it offers the same expected return with lower risk. The firm with the higher standard deviation, Martin, must have the higher coefficient of variation because the means for the two stocks are equal, but the numerator in Equation 5-4 will be greater for Martin. In fact, the coefficient of variation for Martin is 59.3%/15% = 3.95 and that for U.S. Electric is 3.6%/15% = 0.24. Thus, Martin is more than 16 times riskier than U.S. Electric on the basis of this criterion.

The coefficient of variation is more useful when we consider investments which have different expected rates of return *and* different levels of risk. For example, Biobotics Corporation is a biological research and development firm which, according to stock analysts, offers investors an expected rate of return equal to 35 percent with a standard deviation of 7.5 percent. Biobotics offers a higher expected return than U.S. Electric, but it also is riskier. So, with respect to both risk and return, which is a better investment? If we calculate the coefficient of variation for Biobotics, we find it equals 7.5%/35% = 0.21, which is slightly less than U.S. Electric's coefficient of variation of 0.24. Consequently, Biobotics actually has less risk per unit of return than U.S. Electric, even though its standard deviation is higher. In this case, the additional return offered by the Biobotics investment is more than sufficient to compensate for the additional risk.

The probability distributions for U.S. Electric and Biobotics are graphed in Figure 5-3. U.S. Electric has the smaller standard deviation, hence the more peaked probability distribution. But it is clear from the graph that the chances of a really high return are greater for Biobotics than for U.S. Electric, because Biobotics' expected return is so high. *Because the coefficient of variation captures the effects of both risk and return, it is a better measure for evaluating risk in situations*

FIGURE 5-3

Comparison of Probability Distributions and Rates of Return for U.S. Electric and Biobotics Corporation

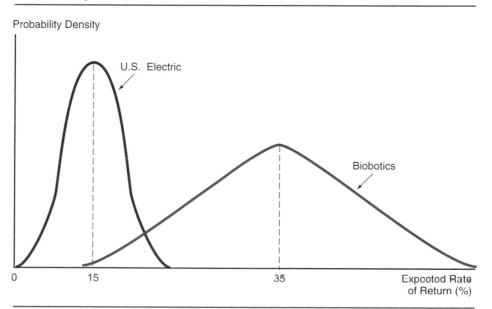

Probability Density

U.S. Electric

Biobotics

0   15   35   Expected Rate
                                                        of Return (%)

where investments differ with respect to both their amounts of total risk and their expected returns.

Risk Aversion and Required Returns

Suppose you have worked hard and saved $1 million, which you now plan to invest. You can buy a 10 percent U.S. Treasury note, and at the end of 1 year you will have a sure $1.1 million, which is your original investment plus $100,000 in interest. Alternatively, you can buy stock in R&D Enterprises. If R&D's research programs are successful, your stock will increase in value to $2.2 million; however, if the research is a failure, the value of your stock will go to zero, and you will be penniless. You regard R&D's chances of success or failure as being 50-50, so the expected value of the stock investment is $1,100,000 = 0.5($0) + 0.5($2,200,000). Subtracting the $1 million cost of the stock leaves an expected profit of $100,000, or an expected (but risky) 10 percent rate of return:

$$\begin{aligned} \text{Expected rate} \atop \text{of return} &= \frac{\text{Expected ending value} - \text{Beginning value}}{\text{Beginning value}} \\[2ex] &= \frac{\$1,100,000 - \$1,000,000}{\$1,000,000} \\[2ex] &= \frac{\$100,000}{\$1,000,000} = 0.10 = 10\% \end{aligned}$$

Thus, you have a choice between a sure $100,000 profit (representing a 10 percent rate of return) on the Treasury note and a risky expected $100,000 profit (also representing a 10 percent expected rate of return) on the R&D Enterprises stock. Which one would you choose? If you choose the less risky investment, you are *risk averse.* Most investors are indeed risk averse, and certainly the average investor is risk averse, at least with regard to his or her "serious money." Because this is a well-documented fact, we shall assume **risk aversion** throughout the remainder of the book.

RISK AVERSION
Risk-averse investors require higher rates of return to invest in higher-risk securities.

What are the implications of risk aversion for security prices and rates of return? The answer is that, other things held constant, the higher a security's risk, the higher the return investors demand, thus the less they are willing to pay for the investment. To see how risk aversion affects security prices, we can analyze the situation with U.S. Electric and Martin Products stocks. Suppose each stock sold for $100 per share and each had an expected rate of return of 15 percent. Investors are averse to risk, so there would be a general preference for U.S. Electric because there is less variability in its payoffs (less uncertainty). People with money to invest would bid for U.S. Electric rather than Martin stock, and Martin's stockholders would start selling their stock and using the money to buy U.S. Electric stock. Buying pressure would drive up the price of U.S. Electric's stock, and selling pressure would simultaneously cause Martin's price to decline.

RISK PREMIUM, RP
The portion of the expected return that can be attributed to the additional risk of an investment; it is the difference between the expected rate of return on a given risky asset and that on a less risky asset.

These price changes, in turn, would cause changes in the expected rates of return on the two securities. Suppose, for example, that the price of U.S. Electric stock was bid up from $100 to $150, whereas the price of Martin's stock declined from $100 to $75. This would cause U.S. Electric's expected return to fall to 10 percent, while Martin's expected return would rise to 20 percent. The difference in returns, 20% − 10% = 10%, is a **risk premium, RP,** which represents the compensation investors require for assuming the *additional* risk of Martin stock.

This example demonstrates a very important principle: *In a market dominated by risk-averse investors, riskier securities **must** have higher expected returns, as estimated by the average investor, than less risky securities, because if this situation does not hold, investors will buy and sell investments and prices will continue to change until the higher risk investments have higher expected returns than the lower risk investments.* We will consider the question of how much higher the returns on risky securities must be later in the chapter, after we see how diversification affects the way risk should be measured. Then, in Chapter 7, we will see how risk-adjusted rates of return affect the price investors are willing to pay for a security.

Self-Test Questions

Which of the two stocks graphed in Figure 5-2 is less risky? Why?

How is the standard deviation associated with an investment calculated?

Why is the standard deviation used as a measure of risk?

Which is a better measure of risk: (1) standard deviation or (2) coefficient of variation? Explain.

What is meant by the following statement: "Most investors are risk averse"?

How does risk aversion affect relative rates of return?

Portfolio Risk and the Capital Asset Pricing Model

CAPITAL ASSET PRICING MODEL (CAPM)
A model based on the proposition that any stock's required rate of return is equal to the risk-free rate of return plus a risk premium, where risk reflects diversification.

In the preceding section we considered the riskiness of investments held in isolation. We used the standard deviation to measure the risk of an investment because it provides an indication of the total variability of the investment's possible payoffs.[5] Now we analyze the riskiness of investments held in portfolios. As we shall see, holding a stock as part of a portfolio generally is less risky than holding the same stock all by itself. This fact has been incorporated into a procedure called the **Capital Asset Pricing Model (CAPM),** used to analyze the relationship between risk and rates of return. The CAPM is an extremely important analytical tool in both managerial finance and investment analysis. In fact, the 1990 Nobel Prize was awarded to the developers of the CAPM, Professors Harry Markowitz and William F. Sharpe, in part because of their work in this area. In the following sections we discuss the elements of the CAPM.[6]

Portfolio Risk and Return

Most financial assets are not held in isolation; rather, they are held as parts of portfolios. Banks, pension funds, insurance companies, mutual funds, and other financial institutions are required by law to hold diversified portfolios. Even individual investors—at least those whose security holdings constitute a significant

---

[5]A *portfolio* is a collection of investment securities. If you owned some General Motors stock, some Exxon stock, and some IBM stock, you would be holding a three-stock portfolio. For the reasons set forth in this section, the majority of all stocks are held as parts of portfolios.

[6]The CAPM is a relatively complex subject, and we present only its basic elements in this text. For a more detailed discussion, see any standard investments textbook.

part of their total wealth—generally hold stock portfolios, not the stock of only one firm. This being the case, from an investor's standpoint the fact that a particular stock goes up or down is not very important; what is important is the return on his or her portfolio, and the portfolio's risk. Logically, then, the risk and return characteristics of an investment should *not* be evaluated in isolation; rather, the risk and return of an individual security should be analyzed in terms of how that security affects the risk and return of the portfolio in which it is held.

To illustrate, Payco American is a collection agency company that operates several offices nationwide. The company is not well known, its stock is not very liquid, its earnings have fluctuated quite a bit in the past, and it doesn't even pay a dividend. All this suggests that Payco is risky and that its required rate of return, k, should be relatively high. However, Payco's k always has been quite low in relation to those of most other companies. This indicates that investors regard Payco as low-risk in spite of its uncertain profits and its nonexistent dividend stream. The reason for this somewhat counterintuitive fact has to do with diversification and its effect on risk. Payco's stock price rises during recessions, whereas other stocks tend to decline when the economy slumps. Therefore, holding Payco in a portfolio of "normal" stocks tends to stabilize returns on the entire portfolio.

EXPECTED RETURN ON A PORTFOLIO, $\hat{k}_P$
The weighted average expected return on the stocks held in the portfolio.

PORTFOLIO RETURNS   The **expected return on a portfolio, $\hat{k}_P$,** simply is the weighted average of the expected returns on the individual stocks in the portfolio, with the weights being the fraction of the total portfolio invested in each stock:

5-5

$$\hat{k}_P = w_1\hat{k}_1 + w_2\hat{k}_2 + \ldots + w_n\hat{k}_n$$

$$= \sum_{j=1}^{N} w_j\hat{k}_j$$

Here the $\hat{k}_j$'s are the expected returns on the individual stocks, the w_j's are the weights, and there are N stocks in the portfolio. Note that w_1 (1) is the proportion of the portfolio's dollar value invested in Stock 1 (that is, the value of the investment in Stock 1 divided by the total value of the portfolio) and (2) the w_j's must sum to 1.0.

In January 1996, a security analyst estimated that the following returns could be expected on four large companies:

	Expected Return, $\hat{k}$
Lotus Development	14%
General Electric	13%
Arctic Oil	20%
Citicorp	18%

If we formed a $100,000 portfolio, investing $25,000 in each stock, the expected portfolio return would be 16.25%:

$$\hat{k}_P = w_1\hat{k}_1 + w_2\hat{k}_2 + w_3\hat{k}_3 + w_4\hat{k}_4$$

$$= 0.25(14\%) + 0.25(13\%) + 0.25(20\%) + 0.25(18\%)$$

$$= 16.25\%.$$

REALIZED RATE OF RETURN, k̄
The return that is actually earned. The actual return (k̄) usually is different from the expected return (k̂).

Of course, after the fact and a year later, the actual **realized rates of return, k̄,** on the individual stocks—the $\bar{k}_j$, or "k-bar," values—will almost certainly be different from their expected values, so $\bar{k}_P$ will be somewhat different from $\hat{k}_P = 16.25\%$. For example, Lotus stock might double in price and provide a return of +100%, whereas Citicorp stock might have a terrible year, fall sharply, and have a return of −75%. Note, though, that those two events would be somewhat offsetting, so the portfolio's return might still be close to its expected return, even though the individual stocks' actual returns were far from their expected returns.

PORTFOLIO RISK As we just saw, the expected return of a portfolio is simply a weighted average of the expected returns of the individual stocks in the portfolio. However, unlike returns, the riskiness of a portfolio, σ_P, generally is *not* a weighted average of the standard deviations of the individual securities in the portfolio; the portfolio's risk usually is *smaller* than the weighted average of the stocks' σs. In fact, at least theoretically, it is possible to combine two stocks which by themselves are quite risky as measured by their standard deviations and to form a portfolio which is completely riskless, with $\sigma_P = 0$.

To illustrate the effect of combining securities, consider the situation in Figure 5-4. The bottom section gives data on rates of return for Stocks W and M individually, and also for a portfolio invested 50 percent in each stock. The three top graphs show the actual historical returns for each investment from 1991 to 1995, and the lower graphs show the probability distributions of returns, assuming that the future is expected to be like the past. The two stocks would be quite risky if they were held in isolation, but when they are combined to form Portfolio WM, they are not risky at all. (Note: These stocks are called W and M because their returns graphs in Figure 5-4 resemble a W and an M.)

The reason Stocks W and M can be combined to form a riskless portfolio is that their returns move opposite to each other—when W's returns fall, those of M rise, and vice versa. The relationship between two variables is called *correlation,* and the **correlation coefficient, r,** measures the degree of the relationship between the variables.[7] In statistical terms, we say that the returns on Stocks W and M are perfectly negatively correlated, with $r = -1.0$.

CORRELATION COEFFICIENT, r
A measure of the degree of relationship between two variables.

The opposite of perfect negative correlation, with $r = -1.0$, is perfect positive correlation, with $r = +1.0$. Returns on two perfectly positively correlated stocks would move up and down together, and a portfolio consisting of two such stocks would be exactly as risky as the individual stocks. This point is illustrated in Figure 5-5, where we see that the portfolio's standard deviation is equal to that of the individual stocks. Thus, diversification does nothing to reduce risk if the portfolio consists of perfectly positively correlated stocks.

Figures 5-4 and 5-5 demonstrate that when stocks are perfectly negatively correlated ($r = -1.0$), all risk can be diversified away, but when stocks are perfectly

[7]The *correlation coefficient,* r, can range from +1.0, denoting that the two variables move in the same direction with exactly the same degree of synchronization every time movement occurs, to −1.0, denoting that the variables always move with the same degree of synchronization, but in opposite directions. A correlation coefficient of zero suggests that the two variables are not related to each other—that is, changes in one variable are *independent* of changes in the other.

FIGURE 5-4

Rate of Return Distributions for Two Perfectly Negatively Correlated Stocks (r = −1.0) and for Portfolio WM

a. Rates of Return

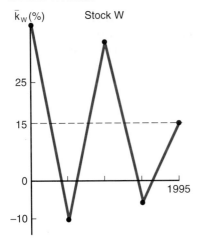

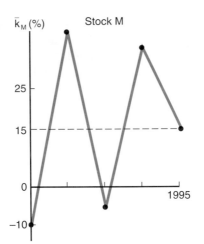

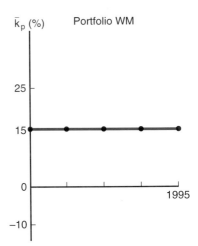

b. Probability Distributions of Returns

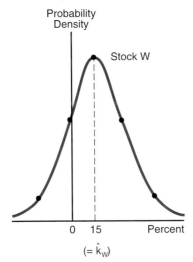

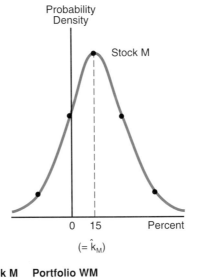

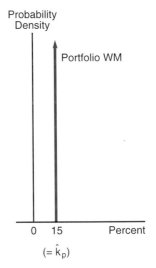

Year	Stock W (k_W)	Stock M (k_M)	Portfolio WM (k_p)
1991	40%	(10%)	15%
1992	(10)	40	15
1993	35	(5)	15
1994	(5)	35	15
1995	15	15	15
Average return	15%	15%	15%
Standard deviation	22.6%	22.6%	0.0%

FIGURE 5-5

Rate of Return Distributions for Two Perfectly Positively Correlated Stocks (r = +1.0) and for Portfolio MM′

a. Rates of Return

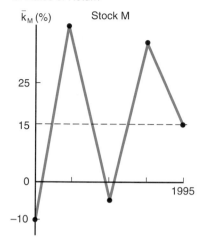

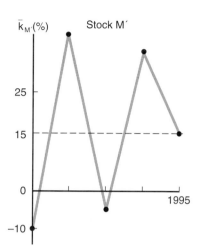

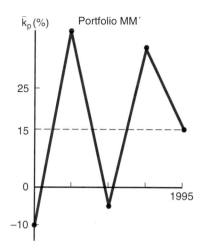

b. Probability Distributions of Returns

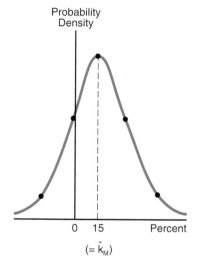

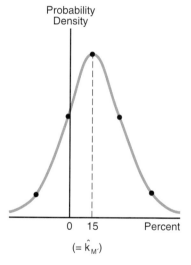

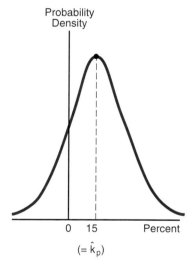

Year	Stock M (k_M)	Stock M' (k_M')	Portfolio MM' (k_p)
1991	(10%)	(10%)	(10%)
1992	40	40	40
1993	(5)	(5)	(5)
1994	35	35	35
1995	15	15	15
Average return	15%	15%	15%
Standard deviation	22.6%	22.6%	22.6%

positively correlated (r = +1.0), diversification is ineffective. In reality, most stocks are positively correlated, but not perfectly so. On average, the correlation coefficient for the returns on two randomly selected stocks would be about +0.6, and for most pairs of stocks, r would lie in the range of +0.5 to +0.7. *Under such conditions, combining stocks into portfolios reduces risk but does not eliminate it completely.* Figure 5-6 illustrates this point with two stocks whose correlation coefficient is r = +0.67. The portfolio, which consists of 50 percent of each stock, has an average return of 15.0 percent, which is exactly the same as the average return for each of the two stocks, but its standard deviation is 20.6 percent, which is less than the standard deviation of either stock. Thus, the portfolio's risk is *not* an average of the risks of its individual stocks—diversification has reduced, but not eliminated, risk.

From these two-stock portfolio examples, we have seen that in one extreme case (r = −1.0), risk can be completely eliminated, while in the other extreme case (r = +1.0), diversification does no good. In between these extremes, combining two stocks into a portfolio reduces, but does not eliminate, the riskiness inherent in the individual stocks.

What would happen if we included more than two stocks in the portfolio? *As a rule, the riskiness of a portfolio is reduced as the number of stocks in the portfolio increases.* If we added enough stocks, could we completely eliminate risk? In general, the answer is no, but the extent to which adding stocks to a portfolio reduces its risk depends on the *degree of correlation* among the stocks: *The smaller the positive correlation coefficient, the lower the risk in a large portfolio.* If we could find a set of stocks whose correlations were negative, all risk could be eliminated. *In the typical case, where the correlations among the individual stocks are positive but less than +1.0, some, but not all, risk can be eliminated.*

To test your understanding, would you expect to find higher correlations between the returns on two companies in the same or in different industries? For example, would the correlation of returns on Ford's and General Motors' stocks be higher, or would the correlation coefficient be higher between either Ford or GM and IBM, and how would those correlations affect the risk of portfolios containing them?

Answer: Ford's and GM's returns have a correlation coefficient of about 0.9 with one another because both are affected by auto sales, but only about 0.6 with those of IBM.

Implications: A two-stock portfolio consisting of Ford and GM would be riskier than a two-stock portfolio consisting of Ford or GM plus IBM. Thus, to minimize risk, portfolios should be diversified *across* industries.

Firm-Specific Risk versus Market Risk

As noted earlier, it is very difficult, if not impossible, to find stocks whose expected returns are not positively correlated—most stocks tend to do well when the national economy is strong and do poorly when it is weak.[8] Thus, even very

---

[8]It is not too hard to find a few stocks that happened to rise because of a particular set of circumstances in the past while most other stocks were declining; it is much harder to find stocks that could logically be *expected* to go up in the future when other stocks are falling. Payco American, the collection agency discussed earlier, is one of those rare exceptions.

FIGURE 5-6

Rate of Return Distributions for Two Partially Correlated Stocks (r = +0.67) and for Portfolio WY

a. Rates of Return

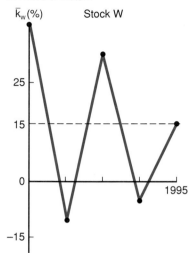

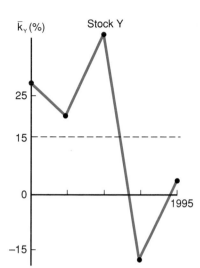

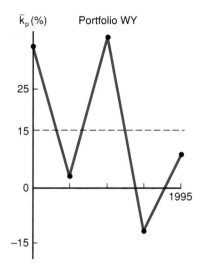

b. Probability Distribution of Returns

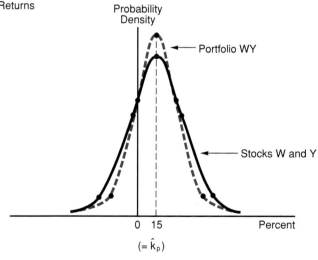

Year	Stock W ($\bar{k}_W$)	Stock Y ($\bar{k}_Y$)	Portfolio WY ($\bar{k}_p$)
1991	40%	28%	34%
1992	(10)	20	5
1993	35	41	38
1994	(5)	(17)	(11)
1995	15	3	9
Average return	15%	15%	15%
Standard deviation	22.6%	22.6%	20.6%

large portfolios end up with a substantial amount of risk, but the risk generally is less than if all the money was invested in only one stock.

To see more precisely how portfolio size affects portfolio risk, consider Figure 5-7, which shows how portfolio risk is affected by forming larger and larger portfolios of randomly selected stocks listed on the New York Stock Exchange (NYSE). Standard deviations are plotted for an average one-stock portfolio, for a two-stock portfolio, and so on, up to a portfolio consisting of all 1,500-plus common stocks that were listed on the NYSE at the time the data were graphed. The graph illustrates that, in general, the riskiness of a portfolio consisting of average NYSE stocks tends to decline and to approach some minimum limit as the size of the portfolio increases. According to data accumulated in recent years, σ_1, the standard deviation of a one-stock portfolio (or an average stock), is approximately 28 percent. A portfolio consisting of all the stocks in the market, which is called the *market portfolio,* would have a standard deviation, σ_M, of about 15.1 percent, which is shown as the horizontal dashed line in Figure 5-7.

Thus, almost half of the riskiness inherent in an average individual stock can be eliminated if the stock is held in a reasonably well diversified portfolio, which is one containing 40 or more stocks. Some risk always remains, however, so it is virtually impossible to diversify away the effects of broad stock market movements that affect almost all stocks.

FIGURE 5-7

Effects of Portfolio Size on Portfolio Risk for Average Stocks

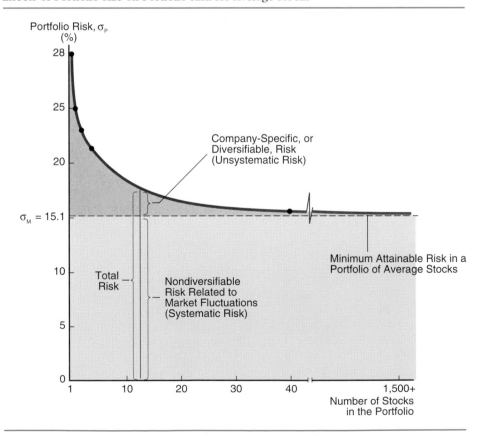

That part of the risk of a stock which can be eliminated is called *diversifiable,* or *firm-specific,* or *unsystematic, risk;* that part which cannot be eliminated is called *nondiversifiable,* or *market,* or *systematic, risk.* The name is not especially important, but the fact that a large part of the riskiness of any individual stock can be eliminated is vitally important.

FIRM-SPECIFIC RISK
That part of a security's risk associated with random outcomes generated by events, or behaviors, specific to the firm; it *can* be eliminated by proper diversification.

Firm-specific risk is caused by such things as lawsuits, strikes, successful and unsuccessful marketing programs, the winning and losing of major contracts, and other events that are unique to a particular firm. Because the actual outcomes of these events essentially are random, their effects on a portfolio can be eliminated by diversification—bad events in one firm will be offset by good events in another. **Market risk,** on the other hand, stems from factors that systematically affect most firms, such as war, inflation, recessions, and high interest rates. Because most stocks tend to be affected similarly (negatively) by these *market* conditions, systematic risk cannot be eliminated by diversification.

MARKET RISK
That part of a security's risk that *cannot* be eliminated by diversification, because it is associated with economic, or market, factors that systematically affect most firms.

We know that investors demand a premium for bearing risk; that is, the higher the riskiness of a security, the higher the expected return required to induce investors to buy (or to hold) it. However, if investors are primarily concerned with *portfolio risk* rather than the risk of the individual securities in the portfolio, how should the riskiness of an individual stock be measured? The answer, as provided by the Capital Asset Pricing Model (CAPM), is this: *The relevant riskiness of an individual stock is its contribution to the riskiness of a well-diversified portfolio.* In other words, the riskiness of General Electric's stock to a doctor who has a portfolio of 40 stocks or to a trust officer managing a 150-stock portfolio is the contribution that the GE stock makes to the portfolio's riskiness. The stock might be quite risky if held by itself, but if most of its risk can be eliminated by diversification, then its **relevant risk,** which is its *contribution to the portfolio's risk,* might be small.

RELEVANT RISK
The risk of a security that cannot be diversified away, or its market risk. This reflects a security's contribution to the risk of a portfolio.

A simple example will help make this point clear. Suppose you are offered the chance to flip a coin once; if a head comes up, you win $20,000, but if it comes up tails, you lose $16,000. This is a good bet—the expected return is 0.5($20,000) + 0.5(−$16,000) = $2,000. However, it is a highly risky proposition, because you have a 50 percent chance of losing $16,000. Thus, you might well refuse to make the bet. Alternatively, suppose you were offered the chance to flip a coin 100 times, and you would win $200 for each head but lose $160 for each tail. It is possible that you would flip all heads and win $20,000, and it is also possible that you would flip all tails and lose $16,000, but the chances are very high that you would actually flip about 50 heads and about 50 tails, winning a net of about $2,000. Although each individual flip is a risky bet, collectively you have a low-risk proposition, because most of the risk has been diversified away. This is the idea behind holding portfolios of stocks rather than just one stock, except that with stocks all the risk cannot be eliminated by diversification—those risks related to broad, systematic changes in the stock market will remain.

Are all stocks equally risky in the sense that adding them to a well-diversified portfolio would have the same effect on the portfolio's riskiness? The answer is no. Different stocks will affect the portfolio differently, so different securities have different degrees of relevant risk. How can the relevant risk of an individual stock be measured? As we have seen, all risk except that related to broad market movements can, and presumably will, be diversified away. After all, why accept risk that can easily be eliminated? *The risk that remains after diversifying is market risk, or risk that is inherent in the market, and it can be measured by evaluating the degree to which a given stock tends to move up and down with the market.* In the next section, we develop a measure of a stock's market risk, and then, in a later section, we introduce an equation for determining the required rate of return on a stock, given its market risk.

The Concept of Beta

Remember the relevant risk associated with an individual stock is based on its systematic risk, which depends on how sensitive the firm's operations are to economic events such as interest rate changes and inflationary pressures. Because the general movements in the financial markets reflect movements in the economy, the market risk of a stock can be measured by observing its tendency to move with the market, or with an average stock that has the same characteristics as the market. The measure of a stock's sensitivity to market fluctuations is called its **beta coefficient,** and it generally is designated with a Greek β. Beta is a key element of the CAPM.

An *average-risk stock* is defined as one that tends to move up and down in step with the general market as measured by some index, such as the Dow Jones Industrial Index, the S&P 500 Index, or the New York Stock Exchange Composite Index. Such a stock will, *by definition,* have a beta, β, of 1.0, which indicates that, in general, if the market moves up by 10 percent, the stock also will move up by 10 percent, while if the market falls by 10 percent, the stock likewise will fall by 10 percent. A portfolio of such β = 1.0 stocks will move up and down with the broad market averages, and it will be just as risky as the averages. If β = 0.5, the stock is only half as volatile as the market—it will rise and fall only half as much—and a portfolio of such stocks will be half as risky as a portfolio of β = 1.0 stocks. On the other hand, if β = 2.0, the stock is twice as volatile as an average stock, so a portfolio of such stocks will be twice as risky as an average portfolio. The value of such a portfolio could double—or halve—in a short time, and if you held such a portfolio, you could quickly become a millionaire—or a pauper.

Figure 5-8 graphs the relative volatility of three stocks. The data below the graph assume that in 1993 the "market," defined as a portfolio consisting of all stocks, had a total return (dividend yield plus capital gains yield) of k_M = 10%, and Stocks H, A, and L (for High, Average, and Low risk) also had returns of 10 percent. In 1994 the market went up sharply, and the return on the market portfolio was k_M = 20%. Returns on the three stocks also went up: H soared to 30 percent; A went up to 20 percent, the same as the market; and L only went up to 15 percent. Now suppose that the market dropped in 1995, and the market return was k_M = −10%. The three stocks' returns also fell, H plunging to −30 percent, A falling to −10 percent, and L going down only to k_L = 0%. Thus, the three stocks all moved in the same direction as the market, but H was by far the most volatile; A was just as volatile as the market; and L was less volatile than the market.

Beta measures a stock's volatility relative to an average stock (or the market), which has β = 1.0, and a stock's beta can be calculated by plotting a line like those in Figure 5-8. The slopes of the lines show how each stock moves in response to a movement in the general market—indeed, *the slope coefficient of such a "regression line" is defined as a beta coefficient.* (Procedures for actually calculating betas are described in Appendix 5A.) Betas for literally thousands of companies are calculated and published by Merrill Lynch, *Value Line,* and numerous other organizations. The beta coefficients of some well-known companies are

FIGURE 5-8

Relative Volatility of Stocks H, A, and L

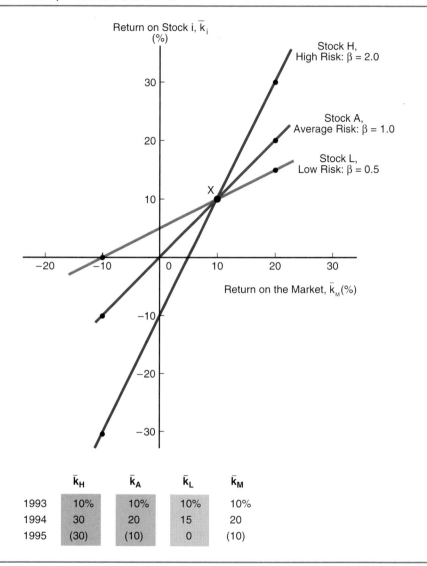

	$\bar{k}_H$	$\bar{k}_A$	$\bar{k}_L$	$\bar{k}_M$
1993	10%	10%	10%	10%
1994	30	20	15	20
1995	(30)	(10)	0	(10)

NOTE: These three stocks plot exactly on their regression lines. This indicates that they are exposed only to market risk. Mutual funds which concentrate on stocks with a specific degree of market risk would have patterns similar to those shown in the graph.

shown in Table 5-4. Most stocks have betas in the range of 0.50 to 1.50, and the average for all stocks is 1.0 by definition.[9]

If a higher-than-average-beta stock (one whose beta is greater than 1.0) is added to an average-beta (β = 1.0) portfolio, then the beta, and consequently the riskiness, of the portfolio will increase. Conversely, if a lower-than-average-beta stock

---

[9]In theory, betas can be negative—if a stock's returns tend to rise when those of other stocks decline, and vice versa, then the regression line in a graph such as Figure 5-8 will have a downward slope, and the beta will be negative. Note though, that *Value Line* follows 1,700 stocks, and none have negative betas. Payco American, the collection agency company, might have a negative beta, but it is too small to be followed by *Value Line* and most other services that calculate and report betas.

TABLE 5-4

Illustrative List of Beta Coefficients

Stock	Beta
Apple Computer	1.30
General Motors	1.15
Johnson & Johnson	1.15
General Electric	1.10
Anheuser Busch	1.10
Hershey Foods	1.00
Heinz	0.95
IBM	0.95
Pacific Gas & Electric	0.75
Energen Corp.[a]	0.60

SOURCE: *Value Line*, January 20, 1995.

[a]Energen is a gas distribution company. It has a monopoly in much of Alabama, and its rates are adjusted every 3 months to keep its profits relatively constant.

(one whose beta is less than 1.0) is added to an average-risk portfolio, the portfolio's beta and risk will decline. *Thus, because a stock's beta measures its contribution to the riskiness of a portfolio, theoretically beta is the correct measure of the stock's riskiness.*

The preceding analysis of risk in a portfolio setting is part of the Capital Asset Pricing Model (CAPM), and we can summarize our discussion to this point as follows:

1. A stock's risk consists of two components—*market risk* and *firm-specific risk.*
2. *Firm-specific risk* can be eliminated through diversification, and most investors do indeed diversify, either by holding large portfolios or by purchasing shares in a mutual fund. We are left, then, with *market risk,* which is caused by general movements in the stock market and which reflects the fact that most stocks are systematically affected by certain overall economic events like war, recessions, and inflation. Market risk is the only relevant risk to a rational, diversified investor, because he or she should already have eliminated firm-specific risk.
3. Investors must be compensated for bearing risk—*the greater the riskiness of a stock, the higher its required return.* However, compensation is required only for risk that cannot be eliminated by diversification. If risk premiums existed on stocks with high diversifiable risk, well-diversified investors would start buying these securities and bidding up their prices, and their final (equilibrium) expected returns would reflect only nondiversifiable market risk.

An example might help clarify this point. Suppose half of Stock A's risk is market risk (it occurs because Stock A moves up and down with the market). The other half of A's risk is diversifiable. You hold only Stock A, so you are exposed to all its risk. As compensation for bearing so much risk, *you want* a risk premium of 8 percent above the 6 percent T-bond rate. Thus, the return you demand from this investment is 14% = 6% + 8%. But suppose other investors, including your professor, are well diversified; they also hold Stock A, but they have eliminated its diversifiable risk and thus are exposed to only half as much risk as you. Therefore, their risk premium will be only half as large as yours, and they will *require* a return of only 10% = 6% + 4% to invest in the stock.

If the stock actually yielded more than 10 percent in the market, others, including your professor, would buy it. If it yielded the 14 percent you demand, you would be willing to buy the stock, but the well-diversified investors would compete with you to acquire it, thus bid its price up and its yield down, and this would keep you from getting the stock at the return you need to compensate you for taking on its *total risk.* In the end, you would have to accept a 10 percent return or else keep your money in the bank. Thus, risk premiums in a market populated with *rational* investors will reflect only market risk.

4. The market risk of a stock is measured by its *beta coefficient,* which is an index of the stock's relative volatility. Some benchmark values for beta are:
   $\beta = 0.5$: Stock is only half as volatile, or risky, as the average stock.
   $\beta = 1.0$: Stock is of average risk.
   $\beta = 2.0$: Stock is twice as risky as the average stock.
5. *Because a stock's beta coefficient determines how the stock affects the riskiness of a diversified portfolio, beta is the most relevant measure of a stock's risk.*

Portfolio Beta Coefficients

A portfolio consisting of low-beta securities will itself have a low beta, because the beta of any set of securities is a weighted average of the individual securities' betas:

5-6

$$\beta_P = w_1\beta_1 + w_2\beta_2 + \ldots + w_N\beta_N$$

$$= \sum_{j=1}^{N} w_j\beta_j$$

Here β_P is the beta of the portfolio, and it reflects how volatile the portfolio is in relation to the market; w_j is the fraction of the portfolio invested in the jth stock; and β_j is the beta coefficient of the jth stock. For example, if an investor holds a $105,000 portfolio consisting of $35,000 invested in each of 3 stocks, and each of the stocks has a beta of 0.7, then the portfolio's beta will be $\beta_{P1} = 0.7$:

$$\beta_{P1} = 0.33(0.7) + 0.33(0.7) + 0.33(0.7) = 0.7$$

Such a portfolio will be less risky than the market: it should experience relatively narrow price swings and have relatively small rate-of-return fluctuations. In terms of Figure 5-8, the slope of its regression line would be 0.7, which is less than that for a portfolio of average stocks.

Now suppose one of the existing stocks is sold and replaced by a stock with $\beta_j = 2.5$. This action will increase the riskiness of the portfolio from $\beta_{P1} = 0.7$ to $\beta_{P2} = 1.3$:

$$\beta_{P2} = 0.33(0.7) + 0.33(0.7) + 0.33(2.5) = 1.3$$

Had a stock with $\beta_j = 0.2$ been added, the portfolio beta would have declined from 0.7 to 0.53. Adding a low-beta stock, therefore, would reduce the riskiness of the portfolio.

Self-Test Questions

Explain the following statement: "A stock held as part of a portfolio generally is less risky than the same stock held in isolation."

What is meant by perfect positive correlation, by perfect negative correlation, and by zero correlation?

In general, can the riskiness of a portfolio be reduced to zero by increasing the number of stocks in the portfolio? Explain.

What is meant by diversifiable risk and nondiversifiable risk?

What is an average-risk stock?

Why is beta the theoretically correct measure of a stock's riskiness?

If you plotted the returns on a particular stock versus those on the Dow Jones Industrial Index over the past 5 years, what would the slope of the line you obtained indicate about the stock's risk?

The Relationship between Risk and Rates of Return

In the preceding section we saw that, under the CAPM theory, beta is the appropriate measure of a stock's relevant risk. Now we must specify the relationship between risk and return: For a given level of beta, what rate of return will investors require on a stock in order to compensate them for assuming the risk? To begin, let us define the following terms:

$\hat{k}_j$ = *expected* rate of return on the jth stock.

k_j = *required* rate of return on the jth stock. Note that if $\hat{k}_j$ is less than k_j, you would not purchase this stock, or you would sell it if you owned it. If $\hat{k}_j$ is greater than k_j, you would want to buy the stock, and you would be indifferent if $\hat{k}_j = k_j$.

k_{RF} = risk-free rate of return. In this context, k_{RF} is generally measured by the return on U.S. Treasury Securities.

β_j = beta coefficient of the jth stock. The beta of an average stock is $\beta_A = 1.0$.

k_M = required rate of return on a portfolio consisting of all stocks, which is the market portfolio. k_M also is the required rate of return on an average ($\beta_A = 1.0$) stock.

$RP_M = (k_M - k_{RF})$ = market risk premium. This is the additional return over the risk-free rate required to compensate an average investor for assuming an average amount of risk. Average risk means $\beta_A = 1.0$.

$RP_j = (k_M - k_{RF})\beta_j$ = risk premium on the jth stock. The stock's risk premium is less than, equal to, or greater than the premium on an average stock, depending on whether its beta is less than, equal to, or greater than 1.0. If $\beta_j = \beta_A = 1.0$, then $RP_j = RP_M$.

MARKET RISK PREMIUM, RP$_M$
The additional return over the risk-free rate needed to compensate investors for assuming an average amount of risk.

The **market risk premium, RP$_M$,** depends on the degree of aversion that investors on average have to risk.[10] Let us assume that at the current time, Treasury bonds yield $k_{RF} = 9\%$ and an average share of stock has a required return of $k_M = 13\%$. Therefore, the market risk premium is 4 percent:

$$RP_M = k_M - k_{RF} = 13\% - 9\% = 4\%$$

It follows that if one stock were twice as risky as another, its risk premium would be twice as high, and, conversely, if its risk were only half as much, its risk premium would be half as large. Further, we can measure a stock's relative riskiness by its beta coefficient. Therefore, if we know the market risk premium, RP$_M$, and the stock's risk as measured by its beta coefficient, β_j, we can find its risk premium as the product $RP_M \times \beta_j$. For example, if $\beta_j = 0.5$ and $RP_M = 4\%$, then RP_j is 2 percent:

5-7

$$\text{Risk premium for Stock j} = RP_j = RP_M \times \beta_j$$

$$= 4\% \times 0.5$$
$$= 2.0\%$$

As the discussion in Chapter 2 implies, the required return for any investment can be expressed in general terms as:

$$\text{Required return} = \text{Risk-free return} + \text{Premium for risk}$$
$$k_j \qquad = \qquad k_{RF} \qquad + \qquad RP_j$$

According to the discussion presented above, then, the required return for Stock j can be written as

5-8

$$\text{SML: } k_j = k_{RF} + (RP_M)\beta_j$$
$$= k_{RF} + (k_M - k_{RF})\beta_j$$

---

[10]This concept, as well as other aspects of CAPM, is discussed in more detail in Chapter 3 of Eugene F. Brigham and Louis C. Gapenski, *Intermediate Financial Management,* Fifth Edition (Fort Worth, Tex.: The Dryden Press, 1996). It should be noted that the risk premium of an average stock, $k_M - k_{RF}$, cannot be measured with great precision because it is impossible to obtain precise values for the expected *future* return on the market, k_M. However, empirical studies suggest that where long-term U.S. Treasury bonds are used to measure k_{RF} and where k_M is an estimate of the expected return on the S&P 400 Industrial Stocks, the market risk premium varies somewhat from year to year, and it has generally ranged from 4 to 8 percent during the past 20 years.

Chapter 3 of *Intermediate Financial Management* also discusses the assumptions embodied in the CAPM framework. Some of the assumptions of the CAPM theory are unrealistic and, because of this, the theory does not hold exactly.

$$= 9\% + (13\% - 9\%)(0.5)$$

$$= 9\% + 4\%(0.5)$$

$$= 11\%$$

SECURITY MARKET LINE (SML)

The line that shows the relationship between risk as measured by beta and the required rate of return for individual securities. SML = Equation 5-8.

Equation 5-8 is the equation for CAPM equilibrium pricing, and it generally is called the **Security Market Line (SML).**

If some other stock were riskier than Stock j and had $\beta_{j2} = 2.0$, then its required rate of return would be 17 percent:

$$k_{j2} = 9\% + (4\%)2.0 = 17\%$$

An average stock, with $\beta_A = 1.0$, would have a required return of 13 percent, the same as the market return:

$$k_A = 9\% + (4\%)1.0 = 13\% = k_M$$

As noted above, Equation 5-8 is called the Security Market Line (SML) equation, and it is often expressed in graph form, as in Figure 5-9, which shows the SML when $k_{RF} = 9\%$ and $k_M = 13\%$. Note the following points:

FIGURE 5-9

The Security Market Line (SML)

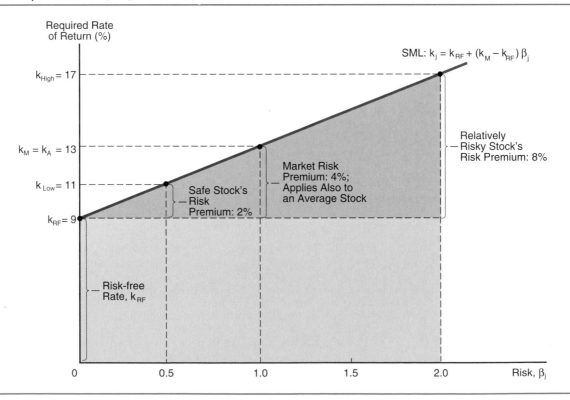

1. *Required rates of return* are shown on the vertical axis, while risk as measured by beta is shown on the horizontal axis. This graph is quite different from the one shown in Figure 5-8, where the returns on individual stocks were plotted on the vertical axis and returns on the market index were shown on the horizontal axis. The slopes of the three lines in Figure 5-8 represented the three stocks' betas, and these three betas are now plotted as points on the horizontal axis in Figure 5-9.

2. Riskless securities have $\beta_j = 0$; therefore, k_{RF} appears as the vertical axis intercept in Figure 5-9.

3. The slope of the SML reflects the degree of risk aversion in the economy; the greater the average investor's aversion to risk, (1) the steeper the slope of the line, (2) the greater the risk premium for any stock, and (3) the higher the required rate of return on stocks.[11] These points are discussed further in a later section.

4. The values we worked out for stocks with $\beta_j = 0.5$, $\beta_j = 1.0$, and $\beta_j = 2.0$ agree with the values shown on the graph for k_{Low}, k_A, and k_{High}.

Both the Security Market Line and a company's position on it change over time due to changes in interest rates, investors' risk aversion, and individual companies' betas. Such changes are discussed in the following sections.

The Impact of Inflation

As we learned in Chapter 2, interest amounts to "rent" on borrowed money, or the price of money; thus, k_{RF} is the price of money to a riskless borrower. We also learned that the risk-free rate as measured by the rate on U.S. Treasury securities is called the *nominal,* or *quoted,* rate, and it consists of two elements: (1) a *real inflation-free rate of return, k*,* and (2) an *inflation premium, IP,* equal to the anticipated rate of inflation.[12] Thus, $k_{RF} = k^* + IP$.

If the expected rate of inflation increases 2 percent, this would cause k_{RF} to increase 2 percent. Such a change is shown in Figure 5-10. Notice that under the CAPM, the increase in k_{RF} also causes an *equal* increase in the rate of return on all risky assets because the inflation premium is built into the required rate of return of both riskless and risky assets.[13] For example, the risk-free return

---

[11]Students sometimes confuse beta with the slope of the SML. This is a mistake. The slope of any line is equal to the "rise" divided by the "run," or $(Y_1 - Y_0)/(X_1 - X_0)$. Consider Figure 5-9. If we let $Y = k$ and $X = \beta$, and we go from the origin to $\beta = 1.0$, we see that the slope is $(k_M - k_{RF})/(\beta_M - \beta_{RF}) = (13 - 9/(1 - 0) = 4$. Thus, the slope of the SML is equal to $(k_M - k_{RF})$, the market risk premium. In Figure 5-9, $k_j = 9\% + (4\%)\beta_j$, so a doubling of beta (for example, from 1.0 to 2.0) would produce a 4 percentage point increase in k_j.

[12]Long-term Treasury bonds also contain a maturity risk premium, MRP. Here we include the MRP in k^* to simplify the discussion.

[13]Recall that the inflation premium for any asset is equal to the average expected rate of inflation over the life of the asset. Thus, in this analysis we must assume either that all securities plotted on the SML graph have the same life or else that the expected rate of future inflation is constant.

It also should be noted that k_{RF} in a CAPM analysis can be proxied by either a long-term rate (the T-bond rate) or a short-term rate (the T-bill rate). Traditionally, the T-bill rate was used, but in recent years there has been a movement toward use of the T-bond rate because there is a closer relationship between T-bond yields and stocks than between T-bill yields and stocks. See *Stocks, Bonds, Bills, and Inflation: 1994 Yearbook* (Chicago: Ibbotson Associates, 1994), for a discussion.

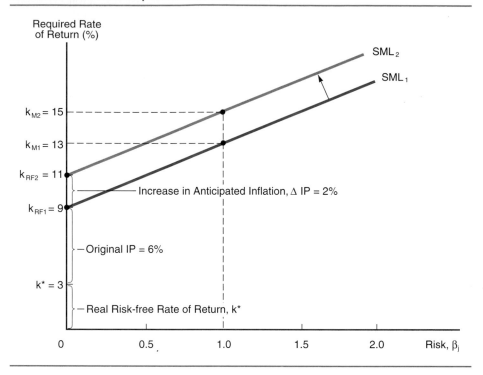

FIGURE 5-10

Shift in the SML Caused by an Increase in Inflation

increases from 9 percent to 11 percent, and the rate of return on an average stock, k_M, increases from 13 percent to 15 percent—all securities' returns increase by two percentage points.

Changes in Risk Aversion

The slope of the Security Market Line reflects the extent to which investors are averse to risk—the steeper the slope of the line, the greater the average investor's risk aversion. If investors are *indifferent* to risk, and if k_{RF} is 9 percent, then risky assets would also provide an expected return of 9 percent: If there is no risk aversion, there would be no risk premium, so the SML would be horizontal. As risk aversion increases, so does the risk premium and, thus, the slope of the SML.

Figure 5-11 illustrates an increase in risk aversion. If the market risk premium rises from 4 percent to 6 percent, k_M rises from $k_{M1} = 13\%$ to $k_{M2} = 15\%$. The returns on other *risky* assets also rise, with the effect of this shift in risk aversion being more pronounced on riskier securities. For example, the required return on a stock with $\beta_j = 0.5$ increases by only one percentage point, from 11 percent to 12 percent, whereas that on a stock with $\beta_j = 1.5$ increases by three percentage points, from 15 percent to 18 percent.

FIGURE 5-11

Shift in the SML Caused by Increased Risk Aversion

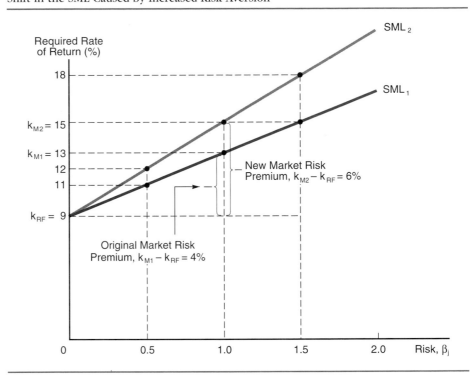

Changes in a Stock's Beta Coefficient

As we shall see later in the book, a firm can affect its beta risk through changes in the composition of its assets as well as through its use of debt financing. A company's beta can also change as a result of external factors, such as increased competition in its industry, or the expiration of basic patents. When such changes occur, the required rate of return also changes and this will affect the price of the firm's stock. For example, consider Unilate Textiles, with a beta equal to 1.0. Now suppose some action occurred that caused Unilate's beta to increase from 1.0 to 1.5. If the conditions depicted in Figure 5-9 held, Unilate's required rate of return would increase from

$$k_1 = k_{RF} + (k_M - k_{RF})\beta_j$$

$$= 9\% + (13\% - 9\%)1.0$$

$$= 13\%$$

to

$$k_2 = 9\% + (13\% - 9\%)1.5$$

$$= 15\%$$

Any change that affects the required rate of return on a security, such as a change in its beta coefficient or in expected inflation, will have an impact on the price of the security. We will examine in detail the relationship between a security's required rate of return and its stock price in Chapter 7.

Self-Test Questions

Differentiate between the expected rate of return ($\hat{k}$) and the required rate of return (k) on a stock. Which would have to be larger to get you to buy the stock?

What are the differences between the relative volatility graph (Figure 5-8), where "betas are made," and the SML graph (Figure 5-9), where "betas are used"? Consider both how the graphs are constructed and the purpose for which they were developed.

What happens to the SML graph when inflation (1) increases or (2) decreases?

What happens to the SML graph when risk aversion (1) increases or (2) decreases? What would the SML look like if investors were indifferent to risk—that is, had zero risk aversion?

How can a firm influence its market, or beta, risk?

Physical Assets versus Securities

In a book on managerial finance for business firms, why do we spend so much time on the riskiness of stocks? Why not begin by looking at the riskiness of such business assets as plant and equipment? The reason is that, *for a management whose goal is stock price maximization, the overriding consideration is the riskiness of the firm's stock, and the relevant risk of any physical asset must be measured in terms of its effect on the stock's risk.* For example, suppose Goodyear Tire Company is considering a major investment in a new product, recapped tires. Sales of recaps and hence earnings on the new operation are highly uncertain, so it would appear that the new venture is quite risky. However, suppose returns on the recap business are negatively correlated with Goodyear's regular operations—when times are good and people have plenty of money, they buy new tires, but when times are bad, they tend to buy more recaps. Therefore, returns would be high on regular operations and low on the recap division during good times, but the opposite situation would occur during recessions. The result might be a pattern like that shown in Figure 5-4 earlier in the chapter for Stocks W and M. Thus, what appears to be a risky investment when viewed on a stand-alone basis might not be very risky when viewed within the context of the company as a whole.

This analysis can be extended to the corporation's owners—the stockholders. Because the stock of Goodyear is owned by diversified stockholders, the real issue each time the company makes a major asset investment is this: How does this investment affect the risk of our stockholders? Again, the stand-alone risk of an individual project might look quite high, but viewed in the context of the project's effect on stockholders' risk, it might not be very large. We will address this subject again in Chapter 14, where we will examine the effects of capital budgeting projects on companies' beta coefficients and thus on their risk to stockholders.

Self-Test Questions

Explain the following statement: "The stand-alone risk of an individual project may look quite high, but viewed in the context of a project's effect on stockholders' risk, the project's risk might not be very large."

How would the correlation between returns on the project and other assets' returns affect the preceding statement?

A Word of Caution

A word of caution about betas and the Capital Asset Pricing Model (CAPM) is in order. Although these concepts are logical, the entire theory is based on *ex ante,* or expected, conditions, yet we have available only *ex post,* or past, data. Thus, the betas we calculate show how volatile a stock has been in the *past,* but conditions can change, and the stock's *future volatility,* which is the item of real concern to investors, might be quite different from its past volatility. Although the CAPM represents a significant step forward in security pricing theory, it does have some potentially serious deficiencies when applied in practice, so estimates of k_j found through use of the SML might be subject to considerable error—many investors and analysts use the CAPM and the concept of β to provide "ball park" figures for further analysis.

ETHICAL DILEMMA

RIP—Retire in Peace

Retirement Investment Products (RIP) offers a full complement of retirement planning services and a diverse line of retirement investments that have varying degrees of risk. With the investment products available at RIP, investors could form retirement funds with any level of risk preferred, from risk-free to extremely risky. RIP's reputation in the investment community is impeccable, because the service agents who advise clients are required to fully inform their clients of the risk possibilities that exist for any investment position, whether it is recommended by an agent or requested by a client. Since 1950, RIP has built its investment portfolio of retirement funds to $60 billion, which makes it one of the largest providers of retirement funds in the United States.

You work for RIP as an investment analyst. One of your responsibilities is to help form recommendations for the retirement fund managers to evaluate when making investment decisions. Recently, Howard, a close friend from your college days who now works for SunCoast Investments, a large brokerage firm, called to tell you about a new investment that is expected to earn very high returns during the next few years. The investment is called a "Piggy-back Asset Investment Device," or PAID for short. Howard told you that he really does not know what this acronym means or how the investment is constructed, but all the reports he has read indicate PAIDs should be a hot investment in the future, therefore the returns should be very handsome for those who get in now. The one piece of information he did provide you was that a PAID is a rather complex investment that consists of a combination of securities whose values are based on numerous debt instruments issued by government agencies, including the Federal National Mortgage Association, the Federal Home Loan Bank, and so on. Howard made it clear that he would like you to consider recommending to RIP that PAIDs be purchased through SunCoast Investments. The commissions from such a deal would bail him and his family out of a financial crisis that resulted because they had bad luck with their investments in the 1994 financial markets. Howard has indicated that somehow he would reward you if RIP invests in PAIDs through SunCoast, because, in his words: "You would literally be saving my life." You told Howard you would think about it, and call him back.

Further investigation into PAIDs has yielded little additional information than what previously was provided by Howard. The new investment is intriguing because its expected return is extremely high compared to similar investments. So, earlier this morning, you called Howard to quiz him a little more about the return expectations and to try to get an idea concerning the riskiness of PAIDs. But Howard was unable to adequately explain the risk associated with the investment, though he reminded you that the debt of U.S. Government agencies is involved. As he says, "how much risk is there with government agencies?"

The PAIDs are very enticing because RIP can attract more clients if it can increase the return offered on its investments. If you recommend the new investment and the higher returns pan out, you will earn a very sizable commission. In addition, you will be helping Howard out of his financial situation, because his commissions will be substantial if the PAIDs are purchased through SunCoast Investments. Should you recommend the PAIDs as an investment?

Summary

The primary goals of this chapter were (1) to show how risk is measured in financial analysis and (2) to explain how risk affects rates of return. The key concepts covered are listed below.

- **Risk** can be defined as the chance that some event other than expected will occur.
- Most rational investors hold **portfolios of stocks,** and they are more concerned with the risks of their portfolios than with the risks of individual stocks.
- The **expected return** on an investment is the mean value of its probability distribution of possible returns.
- The **higher the probability** that the actual return will be *significantly different* from the expected return, the **greater the risk** associated with owning an asset.
- The average investor is **risk averse,** which means that he or she must be compensated for holding risky securities; therefore, riskier securities must have higher expected returns than less risky securities.
- A stock's risk consists of (1) **company-specific risk,** which can be eliminated by diversification, plus (2) **market,** or **beta, risk,** which cannot be eliminated by diversification.
- The **relevant risk** of an individual security is its contribution to the riskiness of a well-diversified portfolio, which is the security's **market risk.** Because market risk cannot be eliminated by diversification, investors must be compensated for it.
- A stock's **beta coefficient, β,** is a measure of the stock's market risk. Beta measures the extent to which the stock's returns move with the market.
- A **high-beta stock** is more volatile than an average stock, while a **low-beta stock** is less volatile than an average stock. An **average stock** has β = 1.0.
- The **beta of a portfolio** is a **weighted average** of the betas of the individual securities in the portfolio.
- The **Security Market Line (SML)** equation shows the relationship between a security's risk and its required rate of return. The return required for any secur-

ity j is equal to the **risk-free rate** plus the **market risk premium** times the **security's beta:** $k_j = k_{RF} + (k_M - k_{RF})\beta_j$.

- Even though the expected rate of return on a stock generally is equal to its required return, a number of things can happen to cause the required rate of return to change: (1) the **risk-free rate can change** because of changes in anticipated inflation, (2) a **stock's beta can change,** or (3) **investors' aversion to risk can change.**

In the next two chapters, we will see how a security's rate of return affects its value. Then, in the remainder of the book, we will examine the ways in which a firm's management can influence a stock's riskiness and hence its price.

Questions

5-1   The probability distribution of a less risky expected return is more peaked than that of a riskier return. What shape would the probability distribution have for (a) completely certain returns and (b) completely uncertain returns?

5-2   Security A has an expected return of 7 percent, a standard deviation of expected returns of 35 percent, a correlation coefficient with the market of −0.3, and a beta coefficient of −0.5. Security B has an expected return of 12 percent, a standard deviation of returns of 10 percent, a correlation with the market of 0.7, and a beta coefficient of 1.0. Which security is riskier? Why?

5-3   Suppose you owned a portfolio consisting of $250,000 worth of long-term U.S. government bonds.
   a. Would your portfolio be riskless?
   b. Now suppose you hold a portfolio consisting of $250,000 worth of 30-day Treasury bills. Every 30 days your bills mature and you reinvest the principal ($250,000) in a new batch of bills. Assume that you live on the investment income from your portfolio and that you want to maintain a constant standard of living. Is your portfolio *truly* riskless?
   c. Can you think of any asset that would be completely riskless? Could someone develop such an asset? Explain.

5-4   A life insurance policy is a financial asset. The premiums paid represent the investment's cost.
   a. How would you calculate the expected return on a life insurance policy?
   b. Suppose the owner of a life insurance policy has no other financial assets—the person's only other asset is "human capital," or lifetime earnings capacity. What is the correlation coefficient between returns on the insurance policy and returns on the policyholder's human capital?
   c. Life insurance companies have to pay administrative costs and sales representatives' commissions; hence, the expected rate of return on insurance premiums is generally low, or even negative. Use the portfolio concept to explain why people buy life insurance in spite of negative expected returns.

5-5   If investors' aversion to risk increased, would the risk premium on a high-beta stock increase more or less than that on a low-beta stock? Explain.

Self-Test Problems

(Solutions Appear in Appendix B)

ST-1   Define the following terms, using graphs or equations to illustrate your answers wherever feasible:

Key terms

    a. risk; probability distribution
    b. expected rate of return, $\hat{k}$
    c. continuous probability distribution
    d. standard deviation, σ; variance, σ^2; coefficient of variation, CV
    e. risk aversion; realized rate of return, $\bar{k}$
    f. risk premium for Stock j, RP_j; market risk premium, RP_M
    g. Capital Asset Pricing Model (CAPM)
    h. expected return on a portfolio, $\hat{k}_p$
    i. correlation coefficient, r
    j. market risk; company-specific risk; relevant risk
    k. beta coefficient, β; average stock's beta, β_A
    l. Security Market Line (SML); SML equation
    m. slope of SML as a measure of risk aversion

Realized rates of return   **ST-2**   Stocks A and B have the following historical returns:

Year	Stock A's Returns, k_A	Stock B's Returns, k_B
1991	(10.00)%	(3.00)%
1992	18.50	21.29
1993	38.67	44.25
1994	14.33	3.67
1995	33.00	28.30

    a. Calculate the average rate of return for each stock during the period 1991 through 1995. Assume that someone held a portfolio consisting of 50 percent of Stock A and 50 percent of Stock B. What would have been the realized rate of return on the portfolio in each year from 1991 through 1995? What would have been the average return on the portfolio during this period?
    b. Now calculate the standard deviation of returns for each stock and for the portfolio. Use Equation 5-3a in Footnote 4.
    c. Looking at the annual returns data on the two stocks, would you guess that the correlation coefficient between returns on the two stocks is closer to 0.9 or to -0.9?
    d. If you added more stocks at random to the portfolio, which of the following is the most accurate statement of what would happen to σ_p?
        (1) σ_p would remain constant.
        (2) σ_p would decline to somewhere in the vicinity of 15 percent.
        (3) σ_p would decline to zero if enough stocks were included.

Problems

Expected returns   **5-1**   Suppose you won the Florida lottery and were offered (1) $0.5 million or (2) a gamble in which you would get $1 million if a head were flipped but zero if a tail came up.
    a. What is the expected value of the gamble?
    b. Would you take the sure $0.5 million or the gamble?
    c. If you choose the sure $0.5 million, are you a risk averter or a risk seeker?
    d. Suppose you actually take the sure $0.5 million. You can invest it in either a U.S. Treasury bond that will return $537,500 at the end of a year or a common stock that has a 50-50 chance of being either worthless or worth $1,150,000 at the end of the year.
        (1) What is the expected dollar profit on the stock investment? (The expected profit on the T-bond investment is $37,500.)

(2) What is the expected rate of return on the stock investment? (The expected rate of return on the T-bond investment is 7.5 percent.)

(3) Would you invest in the bond or the stock?

(4) Exactly how large would the expected profit (or the expected rate of return) have to be on the stock investment to make you invest in the stock, given the 7.5 percent return on the bond?

(5) How might your decision be affected if, rather than buying one stock for $0.5 million, you could construct a portfolio consisting of 100 stocks with $5,000 invested in each? Each of these stocks has the same return characteristics as the one stock—that is, a 50-50 chance of being worth either zero or $11,500 at year-end. Would the correlation between returns on these stocks matter?

Security Market Line   **5-2**   The McAlhany Investment Fund has total capital of $500 million invested in five stocks:

Stock	Investment	Stock's Beta Coefficient
A	$160 million	0.5
B	120 million	2.0
C	80 million	4.0
D	80 million	1.0
E	60 million	3.0

The current risk-free rate is 8 percent, whereas market returns have the following estimated probability distribution for the next period:

Probability	Market Return
0.1	10%
0.2	12
0.4	13
0.2	16
0.1	17

a. Compute the expected return for the market.

b. Compute the beta coefficient for the investment fund. (Remember, this is a portfolio.)

c. What is the estimated equation for the Security Market Line (SML)?

d. Compute the fund's required rate of return for the next period.

e. Suppose John McAlhany, the president, receives a proposal for a new stock. The investment needed to take a position in the stock is $50 million, it will have an expected return of 18 percent, and its estimated beta coefficient is 2.0. Should the new stock be purchased? At what expected rate of return should McAlhany be indifferent to purchasing the stock?

Realized rates of return   **5-3**   Stocks A and B have the following historical returns:

Year	Stock A's Returns, k_A	Stock B's Returns, k_B
1991	(18.00)%	(14.50)%
1992	33.00	21.80
1993	15.00	30.50
1994	(0.50)	(7.60)
1995	27.00	26.30

a. Calculate the average rate of return for each stock during the period 1991 through 1995.

b. Assume that someone held a portfolio consisting of 50 percent of Stock A and 50 percent of Stock B. What would have been the realized rate of return on the portfolio in each year from 1991 through 1995? What would have been the average return on the portfolio during this period?

c. Calculate the standard deviation of returns for each stock and for the portfolio. (Use Equation 5-3a in Footnote 4.)

d. Calculate the coefficient of variation for each stock and for the portfolio.

e. If you are a risk-averse investor, would you prefer to hold Stock A, Stock B, or the portfolio? Why?

Exam-Type Problems

The problems included in this section are set up in such a way that they could be used as multiple-choice exam problems.

Expected returns   **5-4**   The market and Stock J have the following probability distributions:

Probability	k_M	k_J
0.3	15%	20%
0.4	9	5
0.3	18	12

a. Calculate the expected rates of return for the market and Stock J.

b. Calculate the standard deviations for the market and Stock J.

c. Calculate the coefficients of variation for the market and Stock J.

Expected returns   **5-5**   Stocks X and Y have the following probability distributions of expected future returns:

Probability	X	Y
0.1	(10)%	(35)%
0.2	2	0
0.4	12	20
0.2	20	25
0.1	38	45

a. Calculate the expected rate of return, $\hat{k}$, for Stock Y ($\hat{k}_X = 12\%$).

b. Calculate the standard deviation of expected returns for Stock X ($\sigma_Y = 20.35\%$). Now calculate the coefficient of variation for Stock Y. Is it possible that most investors might regard Stock Y as being less risky than Stock X? Explain.

Required rate of return   **5-6**   Suppose $k_{RF} = 8\%$, $k_M = 11\%$, and $k_B = 14\%$.

a. Calculate Stock B's beta.

b. If Stock B's beta were 1.5, what would be B's new required rate of return?

Required rate of return   **5-7**   Suppose $k_{RF} = 9\%$, $k_M = 14\%$, and $\beta_j = 1.3$.

a. What is k_j, the required rate of return on Stock j?

b. Now suppose k_{RF} (1) increases to 10 percent or (2) decreases to 8 percent. The slope of the SML remains constant. How would this affect k_M and k_j?

c. Now assume k_{RF} remains at 9 percent but k_M (1) increases to 16 percent or (2) falls to 13 percent. The slope of the SML does not remain constant. How would these changes affect k_j?

Portfolio beta   **5-8**   Suppose you hold a diversified portfolio consisting of a $7,500 investment in each of 20 different common stocks. The portfolio beta is equal to 1.12. Now suppose you have decided to sell one of the stocks in your portfolio with a beta equal to 1.0 for $7,500 and to use these proceeds to buy another stock for your portfolio. Assume the new stock's beta is equal to 1.75. Calculate your portfolio's new beta.

Portfolio required return   **5-9**   Suppose you are the money manager of a $4 million investment fund. The fund consists of 4 stocks with the following investments and betas:

Stock	Investment	Beta
A	$ 400,000	1.50
B	600,000	(0.50)
C	1,000,000	1.25
D	2,000,000	0.75

If the market required rate of return is 14 percent and the risk-free rate is 6 percent, what is the fund's required rate of return?

Required rate of return   **5-10**   Stock R has a beta of 1.5, Stock S has a beta of 0.75, the expected rate of return on an average stock is 15 percent, and the risk-free rate of return is 9 percent. By how much does the required return on the riskier stock exceed the required return on the less risky stock?

Integrative Problem

Risk and return   **5-11**   Assume that you recently graduated with a major in finance, and you just landed a job in the trust department of a large regional bank. Your first assignment is to invest $100,000 from an estate for which the bank is trustee. Because the estate is expected to be distributed to the heirs in about one year, you have been instructed to plan for a one-year holding period. Further, your boss has restricted you to the following investment alternatives, shown with their probabilities and associated outcomes. (Disregard for now the items at the bottom of the data; you will fill in the blanks later.)

		Returns on Alternative Investments					
		Estimated Rate of Return					
State of the Economy	Probability	T-Bills	High Tech	Collections	U.S. Rubber	Market Portfolio	2-Stock Portfolio
Recession	0.1	8.0%	(22.0%)	28.0%	10.0%	(13.0%)	
Below Average	0.2	8.0	(2.0)	14.7	(10.0)	1.0	
Average	0.4	8.0	20.0	0.0	7.0	15.0	
Above average	0.2	8.0	35.0	(10.0)	45.0	29.0	
Boom	0.1	8.0	50.0	(20.0)	30.0	43.0	
$\hat{k}$							
σ							
CV							
β							

The bank's economic forecasting staff has developed probability estimates for the state of the economy, and the trust department has a sophisticated computer program which was used to estimate the rate of return on each alternative under each state of the economy. High Tech Inc. is an electronics firm; Collections Inc.

collects past-due debts; and U.S. Rubber manufactures tires and various other rubber and plastics products. The bank also maintains an "index fund" which owns a market-weighted fraction of all publicly traded stocks; you can invest in that fund and thus obtain average stock market results. Given the situation as described, answer the following questions.

a. (1) Why is the T-bill's return independent of the state of the economy? Do T-bills promise a completely risk-free return? (2) Why are High Tech's returns expected to move with the economy whereas Collections' are expected to move counter to the economy?

b. Calculate the expected rate of return on each alternative and fill in the row for $\hat{k}$ in the table above.

c. You should recognize that basing a decision solely on expected returns is only appropriate for risk-neutral individuals. Since the beneficiaries of the trust, like virtually everyone, are risk averse, the riskiness of each alternative is an important aspect of the decision. One possible measure of risk is the standard deviation of returns. (1) Calculate this value for each alternative, and fill in the row for σ in the table above. (2) What type of risk is measured by the standard deviation? (3) Draw a graph which shows *roughly* the shape of the probability distributions for High Tech, U.S. Rubber, and T-bills.

d. Suppose you suddenly remembered that the coefficient of variation (CV) is generally regarded as being a better measure of total risk than the standard deviation when the alternatives being considered have widely differing expected returns. Calculate the CVs for the different securities, and fill in the row for CV in the table above. Does the CV produce the same risk rankings as the standard deviation?

e. Suppose you created a two-stock portfolio by investing $50,000 in High Tech and $50,000 in Collections. (1) Calculate the expected return ($\hat{k}_p$), the standard deviation (σ_p), and the coefficient of variation (CV_p) for this portfolio and fill in the appropriate rows in the table above. (2) How does the riskiness of this 2-stock portfolio compare to the riskiness of the individual stocks if they were held in isolation?

f. Suppose an investor starts with a portfolio consisting of one random selected stock. What would happen (1) to the riskiness and (2) to the expected return of the portfolio as more and more randomly selected stocks were added to the portfolio? What is the implication for investors? Draw two graphs to illustrate your answer.

g. (1) Should portfolio effects impact the way investors think about the riskiness of individual stocks? (2) If you chose to hold a one-stock portfolio and consequently were exposed to more risk than diversified investors, could you expect to be compensated for all of your risk; that is, could you earn a risk premium on that part of your risk that you could have eliminated by diversifying?

h. The expected rates of return and the beta coefficients of the alternatives as supplied by the bank's computer program are as follows:

Security	Return ($\hat{k}$)	Risk (Beta)
High Tech	17.4%	1.29
Market	15.0	1.00
U.S. Rubber	13.8	0.68
T-bills	8.0	0.00
Collections	1.7	(0.86)

(1) What is a beta coefficient, and how are betas used in risk analysis? (2) Do the expected returns appear to be related to each alternative's market risk?

(3) Is it possible to choose among the alternatives on the basis of the information developed thus far? Use the data given at the start of the problem to construct a graph that shows how the T-bills', High Tech's, and Collections' beta coefficients are calculated. Then discuss what betas measure and how they are used in risk analysis.

i. (1) Write out the Security Market Line (SML) equation, use it to calculate the required rate of return on each alternative, and then graph the relationship between the expected and required rates of return. (2) How do the expected rates of return compare with the required rates of return? (3) Does the fact that Collections has a negative beta make any sense? What is the implication of the negative beta? (4) What would be the market risk and the required return of a 50-50 portfolio of High Tech and Collections? Of High Tech and U.S. Rubber?

j. (1) Suppose investors raised their inflation expectations by 3 percentage points over current estimates as reflected in the 8 percent T-bill rate. What effect would higher inflation have on the SML and on the returns required on high- and low-risk securities? (2) Suppose instead that investors' risk aversion increased enough to cause the market risk premium to increase by 3 percentage points. (Inflation remains constant.) What effect would this have on the SML and on returns of high- and low-risk securities?

Computer-Related Problem

Work the problem in this section only if you are using the computer problem diskette.

Realized rates of return   **5-12**   Using the computerized model in File C5, rework Problem 5-3, assuming that a third stock, Stock C, is available for inclusion in the portfolio. Stock C has the following historical returns:

Year	Stock C's Return, k_C
1991	32.00%
1992	(11.75)
1993	10.75
1994	32.25
1995	(6.75)

a. Calculate (or read from the computer screen) the average return, standard deviation, and coefficient of variation for Stock C.

b. Assume that the portfolio now consists of 33.33 percent of Stock A, 33.33 percent of Stock B, and 33.33 percent of Stock C. How does this affect the portfolio return, standard deviation, and coefficient of variation versus when 50 percent was invested in A and in B?

c. Make some other changes in the portfolio, making sure that the percentages sum to 100 percent. For example, enter 25 percent for Stock A, 25 percent for Stock B, and 50 percent for Stock C. (Note that the program will not allow you to enter a zero for the percentage in Stock C.) Notice that $\hat{k}_p$ remains constant and that σ_p changes. Why do these results occur?

d. In Problem 5-3, the standard deviation of the portfolio decreased only slightly, because Stocks A and B were highly positively correlated with one another. In this problem, the addition of Stock C causes the standard deviation of the portfolio to decline dramatically, even though $\sigma_C = \sigma_A = \sigma_B$. What does this indicate about the correlation between Stock C and Stocks A and B?

e. Would you prefer to hold the portfolio described in Problem 5-3 consisting only of Stocks A and B or a portfolio that also included Stock C? If others react similarly, how might this affect the stocks' prices and rates of return?

APPENDIX 5A	# Calculating Beta Coefficients

The CAPM is an *ex ante* model, which means that all the variables represent before-the-fact, *expected* values. In particular, the beta coefficient used in the SML equation should reflect the expected volatility of a given stock's return versus the return on the market during some *future* period. However, people generally calculate betas using data from some *past* period and then assume that the stock's relative volatility will be the same in the future as it was in the past.

To illustrate how betas are calculated, consider Figure 5A-1. The data at the bottom of the figure show the historical realized returns for Stock J and for the market over the past five years. The data points have been plotted on the scatter diagram, and a regression line has been drawn. If all the data points had fallen on a straight line, as they did in Figure 5-8 in the chapter, it would be easy to draw an accurate line. If they do not, as in Figure 5A-1, then you must fit the line either "by eye" as an approximation or with a calculator or a computer.

Recall what the term *regression line,* or *regression equation,* means: The equation $Y = \alpha + \beta X + \epsilon$ is the standard form of a simple linear regression. It states that the dependent variable, Y, is equal to a constant, α (the Y intercept), plus β times X, where β is the slope coefficient and X is the independent variable, plus an error term, ϵ. Thus, the rate of return on the stock during a given time period (Y) depends on what happens to the general stock market, which is measured by $X = \bar{k}_M$.

Once the data have been plotted and the regression line has been drawn on graph paper, we can estimate its intercept and slope, the α and β values in $Y = \alpha + \beta X$. The intercept, α, simply is the point where the line cuts the vertical axis. The slope coefficient, β, can be estimated by the "rise over run" method. This involves calculating the amount by which $\bar{k}_j$ increases for a given increase in $\bar{k}_M$. For example, we observe in Figure 5A-1 that $\bar{k}_j$ increases from -8.9 to $+7.1$ percent (the rise) when $\bar{k}_M$ increases from 0 to 10.0 percent (the run). Thus β, the beta coefficient, can be measured as follows:

$$\text{beta} = \beta = \frac{\text{Rise}}{\text{Run}} = \frac{\Delta Y}{\Delta X} = \frac{7.1 - (-8.9)}{10.0 - 0.0} = \frac{16.0}{10.0} = 1.6$$

Note that rise over run is a ratio that is using any two arbitrarily selected points on the line.

The regression line equation enables us to predict a rate of return for Stock J, given a value of $\bar{k}_M$. For example, if $\bar{k}_M = 15\%$, we would predict $\bar{k}_j = -8.9\% + 1.6(15\%) = 15.1\%$. However, the actual return probably would differ from the predicted return. This deviation is the error term, ϵ_j, for the year, and it varies randomly from year to year depending on company-specific factors. Note, though, that the higher the correlation coefficient, the closer the points lie to the regression line, and the smaller the errors.

If you have taken a statistics course that covered regression analysis, you are aware that five observations are not sufficient to attain valid results. In actual practice, monthly rather than annual returns are generally used for $\bar{k}_j$ and $\bar{k}_M$, and five years of data are often employed; thus, there would be $5 \times 12 = 60$ data points on the scatter diagram. Also, in practice one would use the *least squares method* for finding the regression coefficients α and β; this procedure minimizes the squared values of the error terms. It is discussed in statistics courses.

The least squares value of beta can be obtained quite easily with a financial calculator. The procedures that follow explain how to find the values of beta and the slope using a Hewlett-Packard 10B. We show the steps for a HP-10B because it is one of the popular, inexpensive calculators. The procedures for other calculators are nearly identical. But, if you do not have a HP-10B, consult the manual for your calculator to ensure you are following the proper procedures.

FIGURE 5A-1

Calculating Beta Coefficients

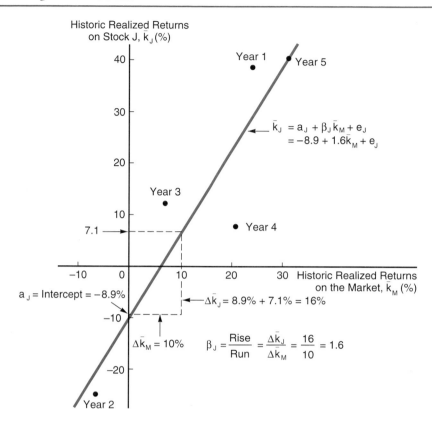

Year	Market ($\bar{k}_M$)	Stock J ($\bar{k}_J$)
1	23.8%	38.6%
2	(7.2)	(24.7)
3	6.6	12.3
4	20.5	8.2
5	30.6	40.1
Average $\bar{k}$	14.9%	14.9%
$\sigma_{\bar{k}}$	15.1%	26.5%

Hewlett-Packard 10B[1]

1. Press ▒ Clear all to clear your memory registers.
2. Enter the first X value ($\bar{k}_M = 23.8$ in our example), press INPUT , and then enter the first Y value ($\bar{k}_j = 38.6$) and press Σ+ . Be *sure* to enter the X variable first.

---

[1]The Hewlett-Packard 17B calculator is even easier to use. If you have one, see Chapter 9 of the *Owner's Manual.*

3. Repeat Step 2 until all values have been entered.
4. To display the vertical axis intercept, press 0 ▮▮ $\hat{y}, m$. Then -8.9219 should appear.
5. To display the beta coefficient, b, press ▮▮ SWAP . Then 1.6031 should appear.
6. To obtain the correlation coefficient, press ▮▮ $\hat{x}, r$ and then ▮▮ SWAP to get r = 0.9134.

Putting it all together, you should have this regression line.

$$\bar{k}_j = -8.92 + 1.60\bar{k}_M.$$

$$r = 0.9134.$$

Problems

Beta coefficients and rates of return

5A-1 You are given the following set of data:

	Historical Rates of Return ($\bar{k}$)	
Year	Stock Y($\bar{k}_Y$)	NYSE ($\bar{k}_M$)
1	3.0%	4.0%
2	18.2	14.3
3	9.1	19.0
4	(6.0)	(14.7)
5	(15.3)	(26.5)
6	33.1	37.2
7	6.1	23.8
8	3.2	(7.2)
9	14.8	6.6
10	24.1	20.5
11	18.0	30.6
Mean	9.8%	9.8%
$\sigma_{\bar{k}}$	13.8	19.6

a. Construct a scatter diagram graph (*on graph paper*) showing the relationship between returns on Stock Y and the market as in Figure 5A-1; then draw a free-hand approximation of the regression line. What is the approximate value of the beta coefficient? (If you have a calculator with statistical functions, use it to calculate beta.)

b. Give a verbal interpretation of what the regression line and the beta coefficient show about Stock Y's volatility and relative riskiness as compared with other stocks.

c. Suppose the scatter of points had been more spread out but the regression line was exactly where your present graph shows it. How would this affect (1) the firm's risk if the stock were held in a one-asset portfolio and (2) the actual risk premium on the stock if the CAPM held exactly? How would the degree of scatter (or the correlation coefficient) affect your confidence that the calculated beta will hold true in the years ahead?

d. Suppose the regression line had been downward sloping and the beta coefficient had been negative. What would this imply about (1) Stock Y's negative riskiness and (2) its probable risk premium?

e. Construct an illustrative probability distribution graph of returns (see Figure 5-6) for portfolios consisting of (1) only Stock Y, (2) 1 percent each of 100 stocks with beta coefficients similar to that of Stock Y, and (3) all stocks (that is, the distribution of returns on the market). Use as the expected rate of return the arithmetic mean as given previously for both Stock Y and the market and assume that the distributions are normal. Are the expected returns "reasonable"—that is, is it reasonable that $\hat{k}_Y = \hat{k}_M = 9.8\%$?

f. Now suppose that in the next year, Year 12, the market return was 27 percent, but Firm Y increased its use of debt, which raised its perceived risk to investors. Do you think that the return on Stock Y in Year 12 could be approximated by this historical characteristic line?

$$\hat{k}_Y = 3.8\% + 0.62(\hat{k}_M) = 3.8\% + 0.62(27\%) = 20.5\%$$

g. Now suppose $\bar{k}_Y$ in Year 12, after the debt ratio was increased, had actually been 0 percent. What would the new beta be, based on the most recent 11 years of data (that is, Years 2 through 12)? Does this beta seem reasonable—that is, is the change in beta consistent with the other facts given in the problem?

Security Market Line   **5A-2**   You are given the following historical data on market returns, $\bar{k}_M$, and the returns on Stocks A and B, $\bar{k}_A$ and $\bar{k}_B$.

Year	$\bar{k}_M$	$\bar{k}_A$	$\bar{k}_B$
1	29.00%	29.00%	20.00%
2	15.20	15.20	13.10
3	(10.00)	(10.00)	0.50
4	3.30	3.30	7.15
5	23.00	23.00	17.00
6	31.70	31.70	21.35

k_{RF}, the risk-free rate, is 9 percent. Your probability distribution for k_M for next year is as follows:

Probability	k_M
0.1	(14%)
0.2	0
0.4	15
0.2	25
0.1	44

a. Determine graphically the beta coefficients for Stocks A and B.

b. Graph the Security Market Line and give its equation.

c. Calculate the required rates of return on Stocks A and B.

d. Suppose a new stock, C, with $\hat{k}_C = 18$ percent and $\beta_C = 2.0$ becomes available. Is this stock in equilibrium; that is, does the required rate of return on Stock C equal its expected return? Explain. If the stock is not in equilibrium, explain how equilibrium will be restored.

CHAPTER 6

The Time Value of Money

Even as a student, you should be thinking about retirement. Don't laugh—most experts would agree that you should have some financial plan for achieving your retirement goals when you start your professional career, or very soon afterwards, or you will find those goals will be difficult, if not impossible, to attain. Chances are that unless you create a savings plan for retirement as soon as you start your career, either you will have to work longer than you had planned to attain the desired retirement lifestyle or you will have to live below the standard of living you planned for your retirement. According to the experts, saving for retirement cannot begin too soon. Unfortunately, most Americans are professional procrastinators when it comes to saving and investing for retirement—the savings rate in the United States is only 4 percent, the lowest of any industrialized nation. One reason many people give for their lack of savings is that they expect to receive Social Security when they retire. But, don't bet on it! The ratio of workers paying into Social Security to retirees receiving benefits, which was 17 to 1 in 1950 and was down to 3.2 to 1 in 1995, will decline to less than 2 to 1 after the Year 2000. Although Congress has taken some action, unless the funds going into Social Security are increased significantly relative to the benefits expected to be paid out in the future, it is estimated the government retirement system will be running a deficit by the year 2020. The reasons Social Security system's future is in doubt are (1) the life expectancy of Americans has increased by more than 15 years since the inception of Social Security in 1935, and (2) 77 million "baby boomers" born between 1946 and 1964 will add a tremendous burden to the system beginning around 2010.

What does the retirement plight of the baby boomers (and their children) have to do with the time value of money? Actually, a great deal. A study conducted by *Money* magazine and Oppenheimer Management Corporation in 1994 indicated that Americans do little more than talk about retirement plans until late in their professional careers, in many cases too late for their retirement goals to be achievable. To be able to retire comfortably,

Continued

10 percent to 20 percent of your income should be set aside each year. For example, it is estimated that a 35-year-old who is earning $50,000 would need at least $1 million to retire at the current standard of living in 30 years. To achieve this goal, the individual would have to save about $10,500 each year at a 7 percent return, which represents more than a 20 percent annual savings. The saving would have been about one half this amount (just over $5,000) if the individual had begun saving for retirement at age 25.

The techniques and procedures covered in this chapter are exactly the ones used by experts to forecast the boomers' retirements needs, their probable wealth at retirement, and the resulting shortfall. If you study this chapter carefully, perhaps you can avoid the trap into which many people seem to be falling.

SOURCE: Penelope Wang, "How to Retire with Twice as Much Money," *Money*, October 1994.

In Chapter 1 we saw that the primary goal of managerial finance is to maximize the value of the firm's stock. We also saw that stock values depend in part on the timing of the cash flows investors expect to receive from an investment—a dollar expected soon is worth more than a dollar expected in the distant future. Therefore, it is essential that financial managers have a clear understanding of the time value of money and its impact on the value of the firm. These concepts are discussed in this chapter, where we show how the timing of cash flows affects asset values and rates of return.

The principles of time value analysis as developed here have many applications, ranging from setting up schedules for paying off loans to decisions about whether to acquire new equipment. In fact, *of all the techniques used in finance, none is more important than the concept of time value of money, or discounted cash flow (DCF) analysis.* Because this concept is used throughout the remainder of the book, it is vital that you understand time value before you move on to other topics.

Cash Flow Time Lines

CASH FLOW TIME LINE
An important tool used in time value of money analysis; it is a graphical representation that is used to show the timing of cash flows.

One of the most important tools in time value of money analysis is the **cash flow time line,** which is used to help us visualize when the cash flows associated with a particular situation occur. Constructing a cash flow time line will help you to solve problems related to the time value of money, because illustrating what happens in a particular situation generally makes it easier to set up the problem for solution. To illustrate the time line concept, consider the following diagram:

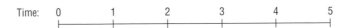

Time 0 is today; Time 1 is one period from today, or the end of Period 1; Time 2 is two periods from today, or the end of Period 2; and so on. Thus, the values on top of the tick marks represent end-of-period values. Often the periods are years, but other time intervals such as semiannual periods, quarters, months, or even days also are used. If each period on the cash flow time line represents a year, the interval from the tick mark corresponding to 0 to the tick mark corresponding to 1 would be Year 1, the interval from the tick mark corresponding to 1 to the tick mark corresponding to 2 would be Year 2, and so on. Note that each tick mark corresponds to the end of one period as well as the beginning of the next period. In other words, the tick mark at Time 1 represents the *end* of Year 1; it also represents the *beginning* of Year 2 because Year 1 has just passed.[1]

Cash flows are placed directly below the tick marks, and interest rates are shown directly above the cash flow time line. Unknown cash flows, which you are trying to find in the analysis, are indicated by question marks. For example, consider the following time line:

Time:	0	5%	1		2		3
Cash Flows:	−100						?

OUTFLOW
A payment, or disbursement, of cash for expenses, investments and so on.

Here the interest rate for each of the three periods is 5 percent; a single amount (or lump sum) cash **outflow** is made at Time 0; and the Time 3 value is an unknown **inflow.** Because the initial $100 is an outflow (an investment), it has a minus sign. Because the Period 3 amount is an inflow, it does not have a minus sign. Note that no cash flows occur at Times 1 and 2. Note also that we do not show dollar signs on time lines; this reduces clutter.

INFLOW
A receipt of cash from an investment, an employer, or other sources.

Now consider the following situation, where a $100 cash outflow is made today, and we will receive an unknown amount at the end of Time 2:

Time:	0	5%	1	10%	2
Cash Flows:	−100				?

Here the interest rate is 5 percent during the first period, but it rises to 10 percent during the second period. If the interest rate is constant in all periods, we show it only in the first period, but if it changes, we show all the relevant rates on the cash flow time line.

The cash flow time line is an essential tool for better understanding time value of money concepts—even experts use cash flow time lines to analyze complex problems. We will be using cash flow time lines throughout the book, and you should get into the habit of using them when you work problems.

Self-Test Question

Draw a 3-year cash flow time line that illustrates the following situation: (1) An outflow of $10,000 occurs at Time 0. (2) Inflows of $5,000 occur at the end of Years 1, 2, and 3. (3) The interest rate during the 3 years is 10 percent.

---

[1]For our discussions, the difference between the end of one period and the beginning of the next period is the same as one day ending and the next day beginning   it occurs in less than one second

Future Value

COMPOUNDING
The process of determining the value of a cash flow or series of cash flows some time in the future when compound interest is applied.

A dollar in hand today is worth more than a dollar to be received in the future because, if you had it now, you could invest it, earn interest, and end up with more than one dollar in the future. The process of going from today's values, which are termed present values (PV), to future values (FV) is called **compounding.** To illustrate, suppose you deposited $100 in a bank account that paid 5 percent interest each year. How much would you have at the end of one year? To begin, we define the following terms:

PV = present value, or beginning amount, in your account. Here PV = $100.

i = interest rate the bank pays on the account per year. The interest earned is based on the balance at the beginning of each year, and we assume that it is paid at the end of the year. Here i = 5%, or, expressed as a decimal, i = 0.05. Throughout this chapter, we designate the interest rate as i because that symbol is used on most financial calculators. Note, though, that in later chapters we use the symbol k to denote interest rates because k is used more often in the financial literature.

INT = dollars of interest you earn during the year = (Beginning amount) × i. Here INT = $100(0.05) = $5.

FV_n = value of your account at the end of n years in the future. Whereas PV is the value now, or the present value, FV_n is the value n years into the future, after the interest earned has been added to the account.

n = number of periods interest is earned. Here n = 1.

In our example, n = 1, so FV_n can be calculated as follows:

$$FV_n = FV_1 = PV + INT$$
$$= PV + PV(i)$$
$$= PV(1 + i)$$

$$= \$100(1 + 0.05) = \$100(1.05) = \$105.$$

FUTURE VALUE (FV)
The amount to which a cash flow or series of cash flows will grow over a given period of time when compounded at a given interest rate.

Thus, the **future value (FV)** at the end of one year, FV_1, equals the present value multiplied by 1.0 plus the interest rate. So you will have $105 in one year if you invest $100 today and 5 percent interest is paid at the end of the year.

What would you end up with if you left your $100 in the account for 5 years? Here is a cash flow time line set up to show the amount at the end of each year:

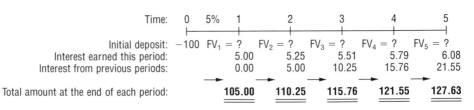

Time:	0	5%	1	2	3	4	5
Initial deposit:	−100		FV_1 = ?	FV_2 = ?	FV_3 = ?	FV_4 = ?	FV_5 = ?
Interest earned this period:			5.00	5.25	5.51	5.79	6.08
Interest from previous periods:			0.00	5.00	10.25	15.76	21.55
Total amount at the end of each period:			**105.00**	**110.25**	**115.76**	**121.55**	**127.63**

Note the following points: (1) You start by depositing $100 in the account—this is shown as an outflow at time period 0, t = 0. (2) You earn $100(0.05) = $5 of interest during the first year, so the amount at the end of Year 1 (or t = 1) is $100 + $5 = $105. (3) You start the second year with $105, so, in the second year, you earn 5 percent interest both on the $100 you invested originally and on the $5 paid to you as interest in the first year; $5.25 interest is earned in the second year, so at the end of the second year you have $110.25. Your interest during Year 2, $5.25, is higher than the first year's interest of $5, because you earned $5(0.05) = $0.25 interest on the first year's interest. (4) This process continues, and because the beginning balance is higher in each succeeding year, the annual amount of interest earned increases. (5) The total interest earned, $27.63, is reflected in the final balance at t = 5, $127.63. As you can see, the total interest earned is greater than $5 per year, which is 5 percent of the original $100 investment, because each year the interest paid was left in the account to earn additional interest the next year. The total *additional* interest earned would be $2.63—this results because interest is earned on interest already paid, which means **compounded interest** is received.

COMPOUNDED INTEREST
Interest earned on interest.

Note that the value at the end of Year 2, $110.25, is equal to

$$FV_2 = FV_1(1 + i)$$

$$= [PV(1 + i)](1 + i)$$

$$= PV(1 + i)^2$$

$$= \$100(1.05)^2 = \$110.25$$

Continuing, the balance at the end of Year 3 is

$$FV_3 = FV_2(1 + i)$$

$$= PV(1 + i)^3$$

$$= \$100(1.05)^3 = \$115.76$$

and

$$FV_5 = \$100(1.05)^5 = \$127.63$$

In general, the future value of an initial sum at the end of n years can be found by applying Equation 6-1:

6-1

$$FV_n = PV(1 + i)^n$$

Equation 6-1 and most other time value of money problems can be solved in three ways: numerically with a regular calculator, with interest tables, or with a financial calculator.

Numerical Solution

According to Equation 6-1, in order to compute the future value, FV, of an amount invested today, PV, we need to determine by what multiple the amount invested will increase in the future. As you can see, the multiple by which any amount will increase is based on the total dollar interest earned, which depends on both the interest rate and the length of time interest is earned. This multiple, termed the **Future Value Interest Factor for i and n (FVIF$_{i,n}$)**, is defined as $(1 + i)^n$.

FUTURE VALUE INTEREST FACTOR FOR i AND n (FVIF$_{i,n}$) The future value of $1 left on deposit for n periods at a rate of i percent per period—the multiple by which an initial investment grows because of the interest earned.

The value for FVIF$_{i,n}$ can be computed using a regular calculator either by (1) multiplying $(1 + i)$ by itself $n - 1$ times, or (2) using the exponential function to raise $(1 + i)$ to the nth power. For our example, you can enter $1 + i = 1.05$ into your calculator, and then multiply 1.05 by itself four times; or, if your calculator has an exponential function key, which generally is labeled y^x, you can enter 1.05 into your calculator, press the y^x function key, enter 5, and then press the = (equal) key. In either case, your answer would be 1.276282, which you would multiply by $100 to get the final answer, $127.6282, which would be rounded to $127.63.

In certain time value of money problems, it is difficult to arrive at a solution using a regular calculator. We will tell you this when we have such a problem, and in these cases we will not show a numerical solution. Also, at times we show the numerical solution just below the cash flow time line, as a part of the diagram, rather than in a separate section.

Interest Tables (Tabular Solution)

As we showed in the previous section, computing the values for FVIF$_{i,n}$ is not a very difficult task if you have a calculator handy. Table 6-1 is illustrative of the future value interest factors for i values from 4% to 6% and n values from 1 to 6 periods, while Table A-3 in Appendix A at the back of the book contains FVIF$_{i,n}$ values for a wide range of i and n values.

Because $(1 + i)^n = $ FVIF$_{i,n}$, Equation 6-1 can be rewritten as follows:

6-1a

$$FV_n = PV(1 + i)^n = PV(FVIF_{i,n})$$

To illustrate, the FVIF for our 5-year, 5 percent interest problem can be found in Table 6-1 by looking down the first column to Period 5, and then looking across that row to the 5 percent column, where we see that FVIF$_{5\%,5}$ = 1.2763. Then, the value of $100 after 5 years is found as follows:

$$FV_n = PV(FVIF_{i,n})$$

$$= \$100(FVIF_{5\%,5})$$

$$= \$100(1.2763)$$

$$= \$127.63$$

TABLE 6-1			

Future Value Interest Factors: $FVIF_{i,n} = (1 + i)^n$

Period (n)	4%	5%	6%
1	1.0400	1.0500	1.0600
2	1.0816	1.1025	1.1236
3	1.1249	1.1576	1.1910
4	1.1699	1.2155	1.2625
5	1.2167	**1.2763**	1.3382
6	1.2653	1.3401	1.4185

Financial Calculator Solution

Equation 6-1 and a number of other equations have been programmed directly into financial calculators, and such a calculator can be used to find future values. Note that calculators have five keys that correspond to the five most commonly used time value of money variables:

N I PV PMT FV

Here

   N = the number of periods; some calculators use n rather than N.

   I = interest rate per period; again, some calculators use i or INT rather than I.

   PV = present value.

   PMT = annuity payment. This key is used only if the cash flows involve a series of equal, or constant, payments (an annuity). If there are no periodic payments in the particular problem, then PMT = 0. We will use this key later in the chapter.

   FV = future value.

On some financial calculators, these keys actually are buttons on the face of the calculator, while on others they are shown on a screen after going into the time value of money (TVM) menu.

   In this chapter, we will deal with equations that involve only four of the variables at any one time—three of the variables will be known, and the calculator will then solve for the fourth (unknown) variable. In the next chapter, when we deal with bonds, we will use all five variables in the bond valuation equation.[2]

   To find the future value of $100 after 5 years at 5 percent interest using a financial calculator, note again that we are dealing with Equation 6-1:

$$FV_n = PV(1 + i)^n \qquad \textbf{(6-1)}$$

---

[2]The equation programmed into the calculator actually has five variables, one for each key. In this chapter, the value of one of the variables always is zero. It is a good idea to get into the habit of inputting a zero for the unused variable (whose value automatically is set equal to zero when you clear the calculator's memory); if you forget to clear your calculator, this procedure will help you avoid trouble.

The equation has four variables, FV_n, PV, i, and n. If we know any three, we can solve for the fourth. In our example, we can enter PV = −100, I = 5, PMT = 0, and N = 5. Then, when we press the FV key, we will get the answer, FV = 127.6282 (rounded to four decimal places). Note that on some calculators you are required to press a "Compute" (sometimes labeled CPT or COMP) key before pressing the FV key.

Many financial calculators require that all cash flows be designated as either inflows or outflows, because the computations are based on the fact that we generally pay (cash outflows) to receive benefits (cash inflows). For these calculators, you must enter cash outflows as negative numbers. In our illustration, you deposit, or put in, the initial amount (which is an outflow to you) and you take out, or receive, the ending amount (which is an inflow to you). If your calculator requires that you input outflows as negative numbers, the PV would be entered as −100. If you forget the negative sign and enter 100, then the calculator would assume you received $100 in the current period and that you must pay it back with interest in the future, so the FV would appear as −127.63, a cash outflow. Sometimes the convention of changing signs can be confusing, but, if you think about what you are doing, you should not have a problem with whether the calculator gives you a positive or a negative answer.

We also should note that financial calculators permit you to specify the number of decimal places that are displayed. For most calculators, at least twelve significant digits are used in the actual calculations. But, for the purposes of reporting the results of the computations, generally we use two places for answers when working with dollars or percentages and four places when working with decimals. *The nature of the problem dictates how many decimal places should be displayed*—to be safe, you might want to set your calculator so the floating decimal format is used, and round the final results yourself.

Technology has progressed to the point where it is far more efficient to solve most time value of money problems with a financial calculator. *However, you must understand the concepts behind the calculations and know how to set up cash flow time lines in order to work complex problems.* This is true for stock and bond valuation, capital budgeting, lease analysis, and many other important types of problems, such as retirement planning, mortgage payments, and other situations that affect you personally.

Problem Format

To help you understand the various types of time value problems, we generally will use a standard format in the book. First, we state the problem in words. Next, we diagram the problem using a cash flow time line. Then, beneath the time line, we show the equation that must be solved. Finally, we present three alternative procedures for solving the equation to obtain the answer: (1) use a regular calculator to obtain a numerical solution, (2) use the tables, or (3) use a financial calculator.

To illustrate the format, we use the 5-year, 5 percent example:

CASH FLOW TIME LINE:

EQUATION:

$$FV_n = PV(1 + i)^n = \$100(1.05)^5$$

1. NUMERICAL SOLUTION:

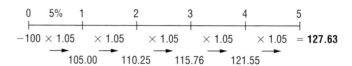

| 0 | 5% | 1 | 2 | 3 | 4 | 5 |

$-100 \times 1.05 \quad \times 1.05 \quad \times 1.05 \quad \times 1.05 \quad \times 1.05 \quad =$ **127.63**

105.00   110.25   115.76   121.55

Using a regular calculator, raise 1.05 to the 5th power and multiply by $100 to get $FV_5 = \$127.63$.

2. TABULAR SOLUTION:

Look up $FVIF_{5\%,5}$ in Table 6-1 or Table A-3 at the end of the book and then multiply by $100:

$$FV_5 = \$100(FVIF_{5\%,5}) = \$100(1.2763) = \$127.63$$

3. FINANCIAL CALCULATOR SOLUTION:

Inputs: 5   5   −100   0   ?

              N   **I**   **PV**   **PMT**   **FV**

Output: = 127.63

Note that the calculator diagram tells you to input N = 5, PV = −100, I = 5, and PMT = 0, and then to press the FV key to get the answer, 127.63. Also, note that in this particular problem, the PMT key does not really come into play, as no constant series of payments is involved.[3] Finally, you should recognize that small rounding differences often occur among the various solution methods because tables use fewer significant digits (4) than do calculators (12–14), and also because rounding sometimes is done at intermediate steps in long problems.

Graphic View of the Compounding Process: Growth

Figure 6-1 shows how $1 (or any other sum) grows over time at various interest rates. The data used to plot the curves could be obtained from Table A-3, or it could be generated with a calculator. The higher the rate of interest, the faster the rate of growth. *The interest rate is, in fact, a growth rate:* If a sum is deposited and earns 5 percent interest, then the funds on deposit will grow at a rate of 5 percent per period. Note also that time value concepts can be applied to anything that is growing—sales, population, earnings per share, or whatever.

Self-Test Questions

Explain what is meant by the following statement: "A dollar in hand today is worth more than a dollar to be received next year."

---

[3]We input PMT = 0, but if you cleared the calculator before you started, that already would have been done.

FIGURE 6-1

Relationships among Future Value, Growth, Interest Rates, and Time

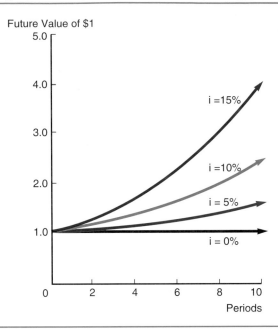

What is compounding? What is "interest on interest"?

Explain the following equation: $FV_1 = PV + INT$.

Set up a cash flow time line that shows the following situation: (1) Your initial deposit is $100. (2) The account pays 5 percent interest annually. (3) You want to know how much money you will have at the end of 3 years.

What equation could you use to solve the preceding problem?

What are the five TVM (time value of money) input keys on a financial calculator?

Present Value

OPPORTUNITY COST RATE
The rate of return on the best available alternative investment of equal risk.

Suppose you have some extra cash, and you have a chance to buy a low-risk security which will pay $127.63 at the end of 5 years. Your local bank currently is offering 5 percent interest on 5-year certificates of deposit, and you regard the security as being very safe. The 5 percent rate is defined as being your **opportunity cost rate,** or the rate of return you could earn on alternative investments of *similar risk.* How much should you pay for the security?

From the future value example presented in the previous section, we saw that an initial amount of $100 invested at 5 percent per year would be worth $127.63 at the end of 5 years. As we will see in a moment, you should be indifferent to the choice between $100 today and $127.63 at the end of 5 years, and the $100

PRESENT VALUE (PV)
The value today of a future cash flow or series of cash flows.

is defined as the **present value, or PV,** of $127.63 due in 5 years when the opportunity cost rate is 5 percent. If the price of the security is anything less than $100, you should definitely buy it because it would cost you exactly $100 to produce the $127.63 in 5 years if you earned a 5 percent return. Therefore, if you could find another investment with the same risk that would produce the same future amount ($127.63) but at a cost less than $100 (say $95.00), then you could earn a return higher than 5 percent by purchasing that investment. Similarly, if the price of the security is greater than $100, you should not buy it because it would cost you only $100 to produce the same future amount at the given rate of return. If the price is exactly $100, then you could either buy it or turn it down, because $100 is the security's fair value if it has a 5 percent expected return.

In general, *the present value of a cash flow due n years in the future is the amount which, if it were on hand today, would grow to equal the future amount.* Because $100 would grow to $127.63 in 5 years at a 5 percent interest rate, $100 is the present value of $127.63 due 5 years in the future when the opportunity cost rate is 5 percent.

DISCOUNTING
The process of finding the present value of a cash flow or a series of cash flows; the reverse of compounding.

Finding present values is called **discounting,** and it simply is the reverse of compounding—if you know the PV, you can compound to find the FV, while if you know the FV, you can discount to find the PV. When discounting, you would follow these steps:

CASH FLOW TIME LINE:

```
0    5%    1         2         3         4         5
├─────────┼─────────┼─────────┼─────────┼─────────┤
PV = ?                                          127.63
```

EQUATION:

To develop the present value, or discounting, equation, we begin with Equation 6-1:

$$FV_n = PV(1 + i)^n = PV(FVIF_{i,n})$$ **(6-1)**

and then solve for PV to yield:

6-2
$$PV = \frac{FV_n}{(1 + i)^n} = FV_n\left[\frac{1}{(1 + i)}\right]^n = FV_n(PVIF_{i,n})$$

The last form of Equation 6-2 recognizes that the interest factor $PVIF_{i,n}$ is equal to

6-2a
$$PVIF_{i,n} = \left[\frac{1}{1 + i}\right]^n$$

The term given in Equation 6-2a is called the **Present Value Interest Factor for i and n (PVIF$_{i,n}$)**.

PRESENT VALUE INTEREST FACTOR FOR i AND n (PVIF$_{i,n}$)
The present value of $1 due n periods in the future discounted at i percent per period.

1. NUMERICAL SOLUTION:

| 0 | 5% | 1 | | 2 | | 3 | | 4 | | 5 |

$-100 = \div 1.05 \qquad \div 1.05 \qquad \div 1.05 \qquad \div 1.05 \longleftarrow 127.63 \div 1.05$

105.00   110.25   115.76   121.55

Using a regular calculator, raise 1.05 to the 5th power and divide $127.63 by the result, or divide $127.63 by 1.05 five times:

$$PV = \frac{\$127.63}{(1.05)^5}$$

$$= \frac{\$127.63}{1.2763} = \$127.63(0.7835)$$

$$= \$100$$

2. TABULAR SOLUTION:

Table A-1 in Appendix A contains present value interest factors for selected values of i and n, PVIF$_{i,n}$. The value of PVIF$_{i,n}$ for i = 5% and n = 5 periods is 0.7835, so the present value of $127.63 to be received after 5 years when the opportunity cost rate is 5 percent equals:

$$PV = \$127.63(PVIF_{5\%,5}) = \$127.63(0.7835) = \$100$$

3. FINANCIAL CALCULATOR SOLUTION:

Inputs: 5   5   ?   0   127.63

| N | I | PV | PMT | FV |

Output: = −100

Enter N = 5, I = 5, PMT = 0, and FV = 127.63, and then press PV to get PV = −100.

Graphic View of the Discounting Process

Figure 6-2 shows how the present value of $1 (or any other sum) to be received in the future diminishes as the years to receipt increases. Again, the data used to plot the curves could be obtained either with a calculator or from Table A-1, and the graph shows that (1) the present value of a sum to be received at some future date decreases and approaches zero as the payment date is extended farther into the future and (2) the rate of decrease is greater the higher the interest (discount) rate. At relatively high interest rates, funds due in the future are worth very little today, and even at a relatively low discount rate, the present value of a sum due in the very distant future is quite small. For example, at a 19 percent discount rate, $1 million due in 100 years is worth only about 3¢ today. (However, 3¢ would grow to $1 million in 100 years at 19 percent.)

FIGURE 6-2

Relationships among Present Value, Interest Rates, and Time

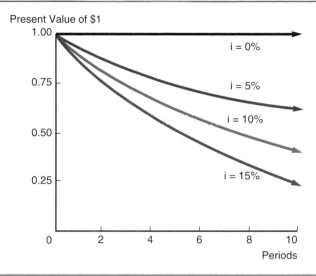

Present Value of $1

Self-Test Questions

What is meant by the term "opportunity cost rate"?

What is discounting? How is it related to compounding?

How does the present value of an amount to be received in the future change as the time is extended and as the interest rate increases?

Solving for Time and Interest Rates

At this point, you should realize that the compounding and discounting processes are reciprocals, or inverses, of one another and that we have been dealing with one equation in two different forms:

FV Form:

6-1

$$FV_n = PV(1 + i)^n = PV(FVIF_{i,n})$$

PV Form:

6-2

$$PV = \frac{FV_n}{(1 + i)^n} = FV_n\left[\frac{1}{1 + i}\right]^n = FV_n(PVIF_{i,n})$$

There are four variables in these equations—PV, FV, i, and n—and if you know the values of any three, you (or your financial calculator) can find the value of the fourth. To this point, we have known the interest rate (i) and the number of years

(n) plus either the PV or the FV. In many situations, though, you will need to solve for either i or n, as we discuss below.

Solving for i

Suppose you can buy a security at a price of $78.35 that will pay you $100 after 5 years. Here we know PV, FV, and n, but we do not know i, the interest rate you will earn on your investment. Problems such as this are solved as follows:

CASH FLOW TIME LINE:

EQUATION:

$$FV_n = PV(1 + i)^n \tag{6-1}$$

$$\$100 = \$78.35(1 + i)^5. \quad \text{Solve for } i.$$

1. NUMERICAL SOLUTION:

One method of finding the value of i is to go through a trial-and-error process in which you insert different values of i into Equation 6-1 until you find a value which "works" in the sense that the right-hand side of the equation equals $100. The solution value is i = 0.05, or 5 percent. The trial-and-error procedure is extremely tedious and inefficient for most time value problems, so it is rarely used in the "real world." Alternatively, in this case, you could solve this problem by using relatively simple algebra to find i directly:

$$FV_n = PV(1 + i)^n = PV(FVIF_{i,n})$$

$$\$100 = \$78.35(1 + i)^5$$

$$(1 + i)^5 = \frac{\$100}{\$78.35} = 1.2763 = FVIF_{i,5}$$

$$(1 + i) = (1.2763)^{\frac{1}{5}} = 1.05$$

$$i = 1.05 - 1 = 0.05$$

2. TABULAR SOLUTION:

As the computations given above show, $FVIF_{i,5} = 1.2763$. Using Table A-3, look across the Period 5 row until you find FVIF = 1.2763. This value is in the 5% column, so the interest rate at which $78.35 grows to $100 over 5 years is 5 percent.[4] This procedure can be used only if the interest rate is in the table; there-

---

[4]The solution could also be set up in present value format:

$$PV = FV_n(PVIF_{i,n})$$

$$\$78.35 = \$100(PVIF_{i,5})$$

$$PVIF_{i,5} = \$78.35/\$100 = 0.7835$$

This value corresponds to i = 5 percent in Table A-1.

fore, it will not work for fractional interest rates or where n is not a whole number. Approximation procedures can be used, but they can be laborious and inexact.

3. FINANCIAL CALCULATOR SOLUTION:

Inputs: 5   ?   −78.35   0   100

| N | I | PV | PMT | FV |

Output: = 5.0

Enter N = 5, PV = −78.35, PMT = 0, and FV = 100, and then press I to get I = 5. This procedure can be used for any interest rate or any value of n, including fractional values.

Solving for n

Suppose you know that the security will provide a return of 10 percent per year, that it will cost $68.30, and that you will receive $100 at maturity, but you do not know when the security matures. Thus, you know PV, FV, and i, but you do not know n, the number of periods. Here is the situation:

CASH FLOW TIME LINE:

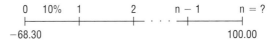

0   10%   1   2   n − 1   n = ?

−68.30   100.00

EQUATION:

$$FV_n = PV(1 + i)^n$$ **(6-1)**

$100 = $68.30(1.10)^n$. Solve for n.

1. NUMERICAL SOLUTION:

Again, you could go through a trial-and-error process wherein you substituted different values for n into the equation. You would find (eventually) that n = 4 "works," so 4 is the number of years it takes for $68.30 to grow to $100 if the interest rate is 10 percent.[5]

2. TABULAR SOLUTION:

$$FV_n = PV(1 + i)^n = PV(FVIF_{i,n})$$

$$\$100 = \$68.30(FVIF_{10\%,n})$$

$$FVIF_{10\%,n} = \frac{\$100}{\$68.30} = 1.4641$$

---

[5]The value of n also can be solved algebraically as follows:

$$\$100 = \$68.30(1.10)^n$$

$$(1.10)^n = \frac{\$100}{\$68.30} = 1.4641$$

$$\ln[(1.10)^n] = n[\ln(1.10)] = \ln(1.4641)$$

$$n = \frac{\ln(1.4641)}{\ln(1.10)} = \frac{0.3812}{0.0953} = 4.00$$

Now look down the 10% column in Table A-3 until you find FVIF = 1.4641. This value is in Row 4, which indicates that it takes 4 years for $68.30 to grow to $100 at a 10 percent interest rate.[6]

3. FINANCIAL CALCULATOR SOLUTION:

Inputs:	?	10	−68.30	0	100
	N	**I**	**PV**	**PMT**	**FV**
Output:	= 4.0				

Enter I = 10, PV = −68.30, PMT = 0, and FV = 100, and then press N to get N = 4.

Self-Test Questions

Assuming that you are given PV, FV, and the interest rate, i, write out an equation that can be used to determine the time period, n.

Assuming that you are given PV, FV, and the time period, n, write out an equation that can be used to determine the interest rate, i.

Explain how a financial calculator can be used to solve for (1) i and (2) n.

Future Value of an Annuity

ANNUITY
A series of payments of an equal amount at fixed intervals for a specified number of periods.

ORDINARY (DEFERRED) ANNUITY
An annuity whose payments occur at the end of each period.

ANNUITY DUE
An annuity whose payments occur at the beginning of each period.

FVA$_n$
The future value of an annuity over n periods.

An **annuity** is a series of equal payments made at fixed intervals for a specified number of periods. For example, $100 at the end of each of the next three years is a 3-year annuity. The payments are given the symbol PMT, and they can occur at either the beginning or the end of each period. If the payments occur at the *end* of each period, as they typically do, the annuity is called an **ordinary,** or **deferred,** annuity. If payments are made at the *beginning* of each period, the annuity is an **annuity due.** Because ordinary annuities are more common in finance, when the term *annuity* is used in this book, you should assume that the payments occur at the end of each period unless otherwise noted.

Ordinary Annuities

An ordinary, or deferred, annuity consists of a series of equal payments made at the *end* of each period. If you deposit $100 at the end of each year for 3 years in a savings account that pays 5 percent interest per year, how much will you have at the end of 3 years? To answer this question, we must find the future value of the annuity, **FVA$_n$**. Each payment is compounded out to the end of Period n, and the sum of the compounded payments is the future value of the annuity, FVA$_n$.

---

[6]The problem could also be solved as follows:

$$PV = FV_n(PVIF_{i,n})$$

$$\$68.30 = \$100(PVIF_{10\%,n})$$

$$PVIF_{10\%,n} = \$68.30/\$100 = 0.6830$$

This value corresponds to n = 4 years in Table A-1.

CASH FLOW TIME LINE:

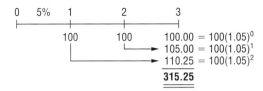

0	5%	1	2	3
		100	100	$100.00 = 100(1.05)^0$
				$105.00 = 100(1.05)^1$
				$110.25 = 100(1.05)^2$
				315.25

Here we show the regular cash flow time line as the top portion of the diagram, but we also show how each cash flow is processed to produce the value FVA_n in the lower portion of the diagram.

EQUATION:

The cash flow time line shows that we can compute the future value of the annuity simply by determining the future values of the individual payments and summing the results. Thus, the equation for the future value of an ordinary annuity can be written:

> **6-3**
> $$FVA_n = PMT(1 + i)^0 + PMT(1 + i)^1 + PMT(1 + i)^2$$
> $$+ \ldots + PMT(1 + i)^{n-1}$$
> $$= PMT \sum_{t=1}^{n} (1 + i)^{n-t} = PMT \sum_{t=0}^{n-1} (1 + i)^t$$

Notice that the first line of Equation 6-3 presents the annuity payments in reverse order of payment, and the superscript in each term indicates the number of periods of interest each payment receives. In other words, because the first annuity payment was made at the end of Period 1, interest would be earned in Period 2 through Period n only; thus, compounding would be for $n - 1$ periods rather than n periods, compounding for the second annuity payment would be for Period 3 through Period n, or $n - 2$ periods, and so on. The last annuity payment is made at the same time the computation is made, so there is no time for interest to be earned; thus, the superscript 0 represents the fact that no interest is earned. Simplifying the first line produces the last line of Equation 6-3. Using Equation 6-3, the solution for the 3-period $100 annuity would be:

$$FVA_3 = \$100(1.05)^0 + \$100(1.05)^1 + \$100(1.05)^2$$

$$= \$100 \left[\sum_{t=0}^{2} (1.05)^t \right]$$

1. NUMERICAL SOLUTION:

The lower section of the time line shows the numerical solution. The future value of each cash flow is found, and those FVs are summed to find the FV of the annuity. This is a tedious process for long annuities.

We can simplify the numerical solution somewhat by simplifying Equation 6-3:[7]

---

[7]The simplification shown in Equation 6-3a is found by applying the algebra of geometric progressions. This equation is useful in situations where the required values of i and n are not in the tables or when a financial calculator is not available.

$$6\text{-}3a \quad FVA_n = PMT\left[\sum_{t=1}^{n} (1 + i)^{n-t}\right] = PMT\left[\frac{(1 + i)^n - 1}{i}\right]$$

Using Equation 6-3a, the future value of $100 deposited at the end of each year for 3 years in a savings account that earns 5 percent interest per year is:

$$FVA_3 = \$100\left[\frac{(1.05)^3 - 1}{0.05}\right]$$

$$= \$100(3.1525)$$

$$= \$315.25$$

2. TABULAR SOLUTION:

The summation term in Equation 6-3 is called the **Future Value Interest Factor for an Annuity of n payments at i interest (FVIFA$_{i,n}$):**

$$6\text{-}3b \quad FVIFA_{i,n} = \sum_{t=1}^{n} (1 + i)^{n-t} = \frac{(1 + i)^n - 1}{i}$$

FUTURE VALUE INTEREST FACTOR FOR AN ANNUITY (FVIFA$_{i,n}$) The future value interest factor for an annuity of n periods compounded at i percent.

FVIFAs have been calculated for various combinations of i and n; Table A-4 in Appendix A contains a set of FVIFA factors. To find the answer to the 3-year, $100 annuity problem, first refer to Table A-4 and look down the 5% column to the third period; the FVIFA is 3.1525. Thus, the future value of the $100 annuity is $315.25:

$$FVA_n = PMT(FVIFA_{i,n})$$

$$FVA_3 = \$100(FVIFA_{5\%,3})$$

$$= \$100(3.1525)$$

$$= \$315.25$$

3. FINANCIAL CALCULATOR SOLUTION:

Inputs:	3	5	0	−100	?
	N	I	PV	PMT	FV
Output:					= 315.25

Note that in annuity problems, the PMT key is used in conjunction with the N and I keys, plus either the PV or the FV key, depending on whether you are trying to find the PV or the FV of the annuity. In our example, you want the FV, so press the FV key to get the answer, 315.25. Because there is no initial payment, we input PV = 0.

Annuities Due

Had the three $100 payments in the previous example been made at the *beginning* of each year, the annuity would have been an *annuity due*. On the cash flow time line, each payment would be shifted to the left one year; therefore, each payment would be *compounded for one extra year (period),* which means each payment would earn interest for an additional year.

CASH FLOW TIME LINE:

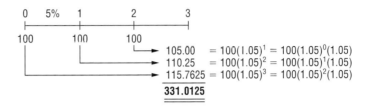

Again, the regular cash flow time line is shown at the top of the diagram, and the future value of each annuity payment at the end of year 3 is shown in the year-3 column, with the actual computations shown to the right.

1. NUMERICAL SOLUTION:

We can find the FV of each cash flow and then sum the results to find the FV of the annuity due. This procedure is shown in the lower section of the cash flow time line. Notice from the diagram that the difference between an ordinary annuity and an annuity due is that *each of the payments of the annuity due earns interest for one additional year.* So the numerical solution for an annuity due also can be found by adjusting Equations 6-3 and 6-3a to account for the fact that each payment is able to earn an additional year's interest when compared to an ordinary annuity. The solution for $FVA_{n,DUE}$ is

6-3c
$$FVA_{n,DUE} = PMT\left[\sum_{t=1}^{n}(1+i)^t\right] = PMT\left[\left\{\sum_{t=1}^{n}(1+i)^{n-t}\right\}\times(1+i)\right]$$
$$= PMT\left[\frac{(1+i)^n - 1}{i}\times(1+i)\right]$$

The future value of the three $100 deposits made at the beginning of each year into a savings account that earns 5 percent annually is:

$$FVA_{3,DUE} = \$100\left[\left\{\frac{(1.05)^3 - 1}{0.05}\right\}\times(1.05)\right]$$
$$= \$100[(3.1525)\times 1.05]$$
$$= \$331.0125$$

FVIFA$_{i,n}$(DUE)
The future value interest factor for an annuity due for n payments at i interest—FVIFA$_{i,n}$(DUE) = FVIFA$_{i,n}$ × (1 + i).

2. TABULAR SOLUTION:

As we have shown, for an annuity due, each payment is compounded for one additional period, so the future value interest factor for an *annuity due,* **FVIFA$_{i,n}$(DUE),** is equal to the FVIFA$_{i,n}$ for an ordinary annuity compounded for one additional period. In other words,

$$\text{FVIFA}_{i,n}(\text{DUE}) = \left[\frac{(1 + i)^n - 1}{i} \times (1 + i) \right]$$
$$= [(\text{FVIFA}_{i,n})(1 + i)]$$

Here is the tabular solution for FVA$_n$,DUE:

$$\text{FVA}_{n,\text{DUE}} = \text{PMT}[\text{FVIFA}_{i,n}(\text{DUE})] = \text{PMT}[(\text{FVIFA}_{i,n})(1 + i)]$$

$$\text{FVA}_{3,\text{DUE}} = \$100[(3.1525)(1.05)] = \$331.0125$$

The payments occur earlier, so more interest is earned. Therefore, the future value of the annuity due is larger—$331.01 versus $315.25 for the ordinary annuity.

3. FINANCIAL CALCULATOR SOLUTION:

Most financial calculators have a switch, or key, marked DUE or BEG that allows you to switch from end-of-period payments (ordinary annuity) to beginning-of-period payments (annuity due). When the beginning mode is activated, the display normally will show the word BEGIN, or the letters BGN. Thus, to deal with annuities due, switch your calculator to BEGIN and proceed as before:

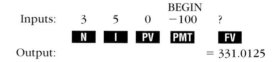

```
                                    BEGIN
Inputs:     3      5      0     -100      ?
          ┌───┐ ┌───┐ ┌────┐ ┌─────┐ ┌────┐
          │ N │ │ I │ │ PV │ │ PMT │ │ FV │
          └───┘ └───┘ └────┘ └─────┘ └────┘
Output:                              = 331.0125
```

Enter N = 3, I = 5, PV = 0, PMT = −100, and then press FV to get the answer, 331.01. Because most problems specify end-of-period cash flows, you should always switch your calculator back to END mode after you work an annuity due problem.

Self-Test Questions

What is the difference between an ordinary annuity and an annuity due?

How do you modify the FVIFA$_{i,n}$ for determining the value of an ordinary annuity in order to determine the value of an annuity due?

Which annuity has the greater future value: an ordinary annuity or an annuity due? Why?

Explain how financial calculators can be used to solve future value of annuity problems.

Present Value of an Annuity

Suppose you were offered the following alternatives: (1) a 3-year annuity with payments of $100 at the end of each year or (2) a lump sum payment today. You have no need for the money during the next three years, so if you accept the annuity, you would simply deposit the payments in a savings account that pays 5 percent interest per year. Similarly, the lump sum payment would be deposited into the same account. How large must the lump sum payment today be to make it equivalent to the annuity? Here is the setup:

CASH FLOW TIME LINE:

$$\frac{100}{(1.05)^1} = 95.238$$

$$\frac{100}{(1.05)^2} = 90.703$$

$$\frac{100}{(1.05)^3} = 86.384$$

272.325

The regular cash flow time line is shown at the top of the diagram, and the numerical solution values are on the left. The PV of the annuity, PVA_n, is $272.325.

EQUATION:

As you can see from the cash flow time line, the present value of an annuity can be determined by computing the PV of the individual payments and summing the results. The general equation used to find the PV of an ordinary annuity is shown below:

6-4

$$PVA_n = PMT\left(\frac{1}{1+i}\right)^1 + PMT\left(\frac{1}{1+i}\right)^2 + \ldots + PMT\left(\frac{1}{1+i}\right)^n$$

$$= PMT\left[\sum_{t=1}^{n}\left(\frac{1}{1+i}\right)^t\right]$$

1. NUMERICAL SOLUTION:

One method of determining the present value of the annuity is to compute the present value of each cash flow and then sum the result. This procedure is shown in the lower section of the cash flow time line diagram, where we see that the PV of the annuity is $272.325. This approach can be tedious if there is a large number of annuity payments.

The numerical solution is easier if we simplify Equation 6-4:[8]

6-4a

$$PVA_n = PMT\left[\sum_{t=1}^{n}\left(\frac{1}{1+i}\right)^t\right] = PMT\left[\frac{1 - \frac{1}{(1+i)^n}}{i}\right]$$

Using Equation 6-4a, the PV of the 3-year annuity with end-of-year payments of $100 is:

$$PVA_n = \$100\left[\frac{1 - \frac{1}{(1.05)^3}}{0.05}\right]$$

$$= \$100(2.72325)$$

$$= \$272.325$$

2. Tabular Solution:

The summation term in Equation 6-4 is called the **Present Value Interest Factor for an Annuity of n payments at i interest (PVIFA$_{i,n}$):**

$$PVIFA_{i,n} = \sum_{t=1}^{n}\left(\frac{1}{1+i}\right)^t = \frac{1 - \frac{1}{(1+i)^n}}{i}$$

Present Value Interest Factor for an Annuity (PVIFA$_{i,n}$)
The present value interest factor for an annuity of n periods discounted at i percent.

The values for PVIFA at different values of i and n are shown in Table A-2 at the back of the book.

To find the answer to the 3-year, $100 annuity problem, simply refer to Table A-2 and look down the 5% column to the third period. The PVIFA is 2.7232, so the present value of the $100 annuity is $272.32:

$$PVA_n = PMT(PVIFA_{i,n})$$

$$PVA_3 = \$100(PVIFA_{5\%,3}) = \$100(2.7232) = \$272.32$$

3. Financial Calculator Solution:

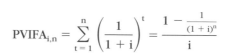

Inputs: 3   5   ?   -100   0
         N **I** **PV** **PMT** **FV**

Output: = 272.325

---

[8]The simplification shown in Equation 6-4a is found by applying the algebra of geometric progressions. This equation is useful in situations where the required values of i and n are not in the tables or when a financial calculator is not available.

Enter N = 3, I = 5, PMT = −100, and FV = 0, and then press the PV key to find PV = 272.325.

One especially important application of the annuity concept relates to loans with constant payments, such as mortgages and auto loans. With such loans, called *amortized loans, the amount borrowed is the present value of an ordinary annuity,* and the payments constitute the annuity stream. We will examine constant payment loans in more depth in a later section of this chapter.

Annuities Due

Had the three $100 payments in our earlier example been made at the *beginning* of each year, the annuity would have been an *annuity due.* On the cash flow time line, each payment would be shifted to the left one year, so each payment would be *discounted for one less year.* Here is the cash flow time line setup:

CASH FLOW TIME LINE:

$$
\begin{array}{c}
\begin{array}{ccccccc}
& & 0 & 5\% & 1 & 2 & 3 \\
& & \vdash & & \vdash & \vdash & \dashv
\end{array}
\end{array}
$$

$$\frac{100}{(1.05)^1} \times (1.05) = \frac{100}{(1.05)^0} = 100.000 \qquad 100 \qquad 100$$

$$\frac{100}{(1.05)^2} \times (1.05) = \frac{100}{(1.05)^1} = \ 95.238 \ \longleftarrow$$

$$\frac{100}{(1.05)^3} \times (1.05) = \frac{100}{(1.05)^2} = \ 90.703 \ \longleftarrow$$

$$PVA_{3,DUE} = \mathbf{285.941}$$

1. NUMERICAL SOLUTION:

Again, we can find the PV of each cash flow and then sum these PVs to find the PV of the annuity due. This procedure is illustrated in the lower section of the cash flow time line diagram. Because the cash flows occur sooner, the PV of the annuity due exceeds that of the ordinary annuity—$285.94 versus $272.32.

The cash flow time line shows that the difference between the PV of an annuity due and the PV of an ordinary annuity is that *each of the payments of the annuity due is discounted one less year.* So the numerical solution for an annuity due also can be found by adjusting Equations 6-4 and 6-4a to account for the fact each annuity payment will have the *opportunity* to earn an additional year's (period's) interest when compared to an ordinary annuity:

6-4b
$$PVA_{n,DUE} = PMT\left[\sum_{t=0}^{n-1}\left(\frac{1}{1+i}\right)^t\right] = PMT\left[\sum_{t=1}^{n}\left(\frac{1}{1+i}\right)^t \times (1+i)\right]$$

$$= PMT\left[\frac{1 - \frac{1}{(1+i)^n}}{i} \times (1+i)\right]$$

Therefore, if the three $100 payments were made at the beginning of the year, the PV of the annuity would be:

$$PV_{3,DUE} = \$100\left[\frac{1 - \frac{1}{(1.05)^3}}{0.05} \times (1.05)\right]$$

$$= \$100[(2.72325)(1.05)]$$

$$= \$100(2.85941)$$

$$= \$285.941$$

2. TABULAR SOLUTION:

We can use the PVIFAs given in Table A-2, which are computed for ordinary annuities, if we adjust these values to account for the fact that the payments associated with an annuity due occur one period earlier than the payments associated with an ordinary annuity. As the cash flow time line and the numerical solution indicate, the adjustment is rather simple—just multiply the PVIFA for an ordinary annuity by $(1 + i)$. So, the present value interest factor for an annuity due, $PVIFA_{i,n}(DUE)$, is:

$PVIFA_{i,n}(DUE)$
The present value interest factor for an annuity due for n payments at i interest—$PVIFA_{i,n}(DUE) = PVIFA_{i,n} \times (1 + i)$.

$$PVIFA_{i,n}(DUE) = \left[\frac{1 - \frac{1}{(1 + i)^n}}{i} \times (1 + i)\right]$$

$$= [(PVIFA_{i,n})(1 + i)]$$

The tabular solution for $PVA_{n,DUE}$ is

$$PVA_{n,DUE} = PMT[PVIFA_{i,n}(DUE)] = PMT[(PVIFA_{i,n})(1 + i)]$$

$$PVA_{3,DUE} = \$100[(2.7232)(1.05)]$$

$$= \$100(2.85941) = \$285.94$$

3. FINANCIAL CALCULATOR SOLUTION:

				BEGIN	
Inputs:	3	5	?	−100	0
	N	**I**	**PV**	**PMT**	**FV**
Output:			= 285.94		

Switch to the beginning-of-period mode, and then enter N = 3, I = 5, PMT = −100, and FV = 0, and then press PV to get the answer, 285.94. *Again, because most problems deal with end-of-period cash flows, don't forget to switch your calculator back to the END mode.*

Self-Test Questions

Which annuity has the greater present value: an ordinary annuity or an annuity due? Why?

Explain how financial calculators can be used to find present values of annuities.

Solving for Interest Rates with Annuities

Suppose you pay $1,155.72 for an investment that promises to pay you $250 per year for the next 6 years. If the payments are made at the end of each year, what interest rate (rate of return) will you earn on this investment? We can solve this problem as follows:

CASH FLOW TIME LINE:

0 i = ? 1	2	3	4	5	6
−1,155.72 250	250	250	250	250	250

EQUATION:

$$PVA_n = PMT(PVIFA_{i,n})$$ **(6-4)**

$$\$1{,}155.72 = \$250(PVIFA_{i\ =\ ?,6})$$

1. NUMERICAL SOLUTION:

To solve this problem numerically, you would have to use a trial-and-error process in which you plug different values for i into either Equation 6-4 or Equation 6-4a until you find the value for i where the present value of the six-year, $250 annuity is equal to $1,155.72. The solution is i = 0.08, or 8%.

2. TABULAR SOLUTION:

If we solve the equation given above for the PVIFA, we find

$$PVIFA_{i\ =\ ?,6} = \frac{\$1{,}155.72}{\$250} = 4.6229$$

Using Table A-2, look across the Period 6 row until you find PVIFA = 4.6229. This value is in the 8% column, so the interest rate at which a six-year, $250 annuity has a present value equal to $1,155.72 is 8 percent. This method cannot be used if the interest rate is not in the table; instead, you would have to use your financial calculator to solve the problem.

3. FINANCIAL CALCULATOR SOLUTION:

	Inputs:	6	?	−1,155.72	250	0
		N	**I**	**PV**	**PMT**	**FV**
	Output:		= 8.0			

Enter N = 6, PV = −1,155.72, PMT = 250, and FV = 0, and then press I to get the answer, 8.0%.

In the problem we just solved, the information that was given included the amount of the annuity payment, the *present value* of the annuity, and the number of years the annuity payment is received. If the *future value* of the annuity was given instead of the present value, to find i, we would follow the same procedures outlined above, but Equation 6-3 would be used because it applies to future values. For example, let's assume a financial institution has an investment that requires you to make annual payments equal to $250 starting at the end of this year, and in 6 years the financial institution will pay you $1,833.98. In this case, we know the amount of the annuity—$250—the length of the annuity—6 years—and the future value of the annuity—$1,833.98. What is the interest rate that you would earn on this investment? The procedure to solve this problem is the same as outlined above, except you use the FVA$_n$ equation (Equation 6-3) instead of the PVA$_n$ for the numerical and tabular solutions, and the FV key ($1,833.98) instead of the PV key for the financial calculator solution. Try it—you should get i = 0.08 = 8%.

Perpetuities

PERPETUITY
A stream of equal payments expected to continue forever.

Most annuities call for payments to be made over some finite period of time—for example, $100 per year for 3 years. However, some annuities go on indefinitely, or perpetually, and these annuities are called **perpetuities.** The present value of a perpetuity is found by applying Equation 6-5.[9]

6-5
$$PV_{PERPETUITY} = \frac{\text{Payment}}{\text{Interest rate}} = \frac{PMT}{i}$$

Perpetuities can be illustrated by some British securities issued after the Napoleonic Wars. In 1815, the British government sold a huge bond issue and used the proceeds to pay off many smaller issues that had been floated in prior years to pay for the wars. Because the purpose of the bonds was to consolidate past debts, the bonds were called **consols.** Suppose each consol promised to pay $100 per year in perpetuity. (Actually, interest was stated in pounds.) What would each bond be worth if the opportunity cost rate, or discount rate, was 5 percent? The answer is $2,000:

CONSOL
A perpetual bond issued by the British government to consolidate past debts; in general, any perpetual bond.

$$PV_{PERPETUITY} = \frac{\$100}{0.05} = \$2,000$$

Suppose the interest rate rose to 10 percent; what would happen to the consol's value? The value would drop to $1,000:

$$PV_{PERPETUITY} = \frac{\$100}{0.10} = \$1,000$$

We see that the value of a perpetuity changes dramatically when interest rates change. Perpetuities are discussed further in Chapter 7, where procedures for finding the value of various types of securities are discussed.

---

[9]The derivation of Equation 6-5 is given in Appendix 4A of Eugene F. Brigham and Louis C. Gapenski, *Intermediate Financial Management,* 5th ed. (Fort Worth, Tex.: The Dryden Press, 1996).

Self-Test Questions

What happens to the value of a perpetuity when interest rates increase?

What happens when interest rates decrease? Why do these changes occur?

Uneven Cash Flow Streams

UNEVEN CASH FLOW STREAM
A series of cash flows in which the amount varies from one period to the next.

PAYMENT (PMT)
This term designates constant cash flows.

CASH FLOW (CF)
This term designates cash flows in general, including uneven cash flows.

The definition of an annuity includes the words *constant amount*—in other words, annuities involve payments that are equal in every period. Although many financial decisions do involve constant payments, some important decisions involve uneven, or nonconstant, cash flows: For example, common stocks typically pay an increasing stream of dividends over time, and fixed asset investments such as new equipment normally do not generate constant cash flows. Consequently, it is necessary to extend our time value discussion to include **uneven cash flow streams.**

Throughout the book, we will follow convention and reserve the term **payment (PMT)** for annuity situations where the cash flows are constant, and we will use the term **cash flow (CF)** to denote cash flows in general, which includes uneven cash flows. Financial calculators are set up to follow this convention, so if you are using one and dealing with uneven cash flows, you will need to use the cash flow register.

Present Value of an Uneven Cash Flow Stream

The PV of an uneven cash flow stream is found as the sum of the PVs of the individual cash flows of the stream. For example, suppose we must find the PV of the following cash flow stream, discounted at 6 percent:

0	6%	1	2	3	4	5
PV = ?		100	200	200	200	1,000

The PV is found by applying this general present value equation:

6-6

$$PV = CF_1\left(\frac{1}{1+i}\right)^1 + CF_2\left(\frac{1}{1+i}\right)^2 + \ldots + CF_n\left(\frac{1}{1+i}\right)^n$$

$$= \sum_{t=1}^{n} CF_t\left(\frac{1}{1+i}\right)^t = \sum_{t=1}^{n} CF_t(PVIF_{i,t})$$

We can find the PV of each individual cash flow using the numerical, tabular, or financial calculator methods, and then sum these values to find the present value of the stream. Here is what the process would look like:

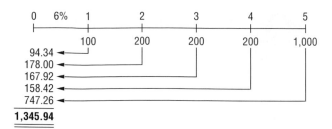

All we did was to apply Equation 6-6, show the individual PVs in the left column of the diagram, and then sum these individual PVs to find the PV of the entire stream.

The present value of any cash flow stream can always be found by summing the present values of the individual cash flows as shown above. However, cash flow regularities within the stream might allow us to use shortcuts. For example, notice that cash flows 2 through 4 represent an annuity. We can use this fact to solve the problem in a slightly different manner:

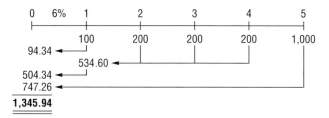

The Year 2–4 cash flows represent an ordinary annuity, so we find its PV at Year 1 (one period before the first payment). This PV ($534.60) must then be discounted back one more period to get its Year 0 value.

Problems involving uneven cash flows can be solved in one step with most financial calculators. First, you input the individual cash flows, in chronological order, into the cash flow register. Cash flows usually are designated CF_0, CF_1, CF_2, CF_3, and so on. Next, you enter the interest rate. At this point, you have substituted in all the known values of Equation 6-6, so you only need to press the NPV key to find the present value of the stream. The calculator has been programmed to find the PV of each cash flow and then to sum these values to find the PV of the entire stream. To input the cash flows for this problem, enter 0 (because CF_0 = 0), 100, 200, 200, 200, and 1000 in that order into the cash flow register, enter I = 6, and then press NPV to obtain the answer, $1,345.94.

Two points should be noted. First, when dealing with the cash flow register, the calculator uses the term NPV rather than PV. The N stands for *net*, so NPV is the abbreviation for Net Present Value, which simply is the net present value of a series of positive and negative cash flows, including CF_0. Our example has no negative cash flows, but if it did, we simply would input them with negative signs. Also, because we wanted to compute the PV, CF_0 = 0.

The second point to note is that annuities can be entered into the cash flow register more efficiently by using the N_j key. (On some calculators, you are prompted to enter the number of times the cash flow occurs, and on still other calculators the procedures for inputting data, as we discuss next, might be different. You should consult your calculator manual to determine the appropriate steps for your specific calculator.) In this illustration, you would enter CF_0 = 0,

$CF_1 = 100$, $CF_2 = 200$, $N_j = 3$ (which tells the calculator that the 200 occurs 3 times), and $CF_5 = 1000$. Then enter $I = 6$ and press the NPV key, and 1,345.94 will appear in the display. Also, note that amounts entered into the cash flow register remain in the register until they are cleared. Thus, if you had previously worked a problem with eight cash flows and then moved to a problem with only four cash flows, the calculator would assume that the last four cash flows from the first problem belonged to the second problem. Therefore, *you must be sure to clear the cash flow register before starting a new problem.*

Future Value of an Uneven Cash Flow Stream

TERMINAL VALUE
The future value of a cash flow stream.

The future value of an uneven cash flow stream (sometimes called the **terminal value**) is found by compounding each payment to the end of the stream and then summing the future values:

$$\boxed{\begin{array}{l} \textbf{6-7} \\[4pt] FV_n = CF_1(1 + i)^{n-1} + CF_2(1 + i)^{n-2} + \ldots + CF_n(1 + i)^0 \\[10pt] \qquad = \sum_{t=1}^{n} CF_t(1 + i)^{n-t} = \sum_{t=1}^{n} CF_t(FVIF_{i,n-t}) \end{array}}$$

The future value of our illustrative uneven cash flow stream is $1,801.17:

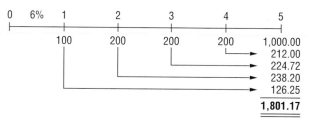

Some financial calculators have a net future value (NFV) key which, after the cash flows and interest rate have been entered into the calculator, can be used to obtain the future value of an uneven cash flow stream. In any event, it is easy enough to compound the individual cash flows to the terminal year and then to sum them to find the FV of the stream. Also, we generally are more interested in the present value of an asset's cash flow stream than in the future value because the present value represents today's value, which we can compare to the price of the asset.

Solving for i with Uneven Cash Flow Streams

It is relatively easy to solve for i *numerically or with the tables* when the cash flows are lump sums or annuities. However, it is extremely difficult to solve for i if the cash flows are uneven, as you will have to go through tedious trial-and-error calculations. With a financial calculator, though, it is easy to find the value of i. Simply input the CF values into the cash flow register and then press the IRR key. IRR stands for *internal rate of return,* which is the return on an investment. We will defer further discussion of this calculation for now and take it up later in our discussion of capital budgeting methods in Chapter 13.

Self-Test Questions

Give two examples of financial decisions that would typically involve uneven flows of cash.

What is meant by the term "terminal value"?

Semiannual and Other Compounding Periods

ANNUAL COMPOUNDING
The arithmetic process of determining the final value of a cash flow or series of cash flows when interest is added once a year.

SEMIANNUAL COMPOUNDING
The arithmetic process of determining the final value of a cash flow or series of cash flows when interest is added twice a year.

In all of our examples thus far, we have assumed that interest is compounded once a year, or annually. This is called **annual compounding.** Suppose, however, that you put $100 into a bank which states that it pays a 6 percent annual interest rate but that interest is added each six months. This is called **semiannual compounding.** How much would you accumulate at the end of one year, two years, or some other period under semiannual compounding?

To illustrate semiannual compounding, assume that $100 is placed into an account at an interest rate of 6 percent and left there for 3 years. First, consider again what happens under *annual compounding:*

1. CASH FLOW TIME LINE, EQUATION, AND NUMERICAL SOLUTION:

$$FV_n = PV(1 + i)^n = \$100(1.06)^3$$
$$= \$119.10$$

2. TABULAR SOLUTION:

$$FV_3 = \$100(FVIF_{6\%,3}) = \$100(1.1910) = \$119.10$$

3. FINANCIAL CALCULATOR SOLUTION:

Inputs:	3	6	−100	0	?
	N	**I**	**PV**	**PMT**	**FV**
Output:					= 119.10

Now consider what happens under semiannual compounding. Here we have n = 2 × 3 = 6 semiannual periods, and you will earn i = 6% ÷ 2 = 3% every six months. Note that on all types of contracts, interest always is quoted as an annual rate, and if compounding occurs more frequently than once a year, that fact is stated, along with the rate. In our example, the quoted rate is "6 percent, compounded semiannually." Here is how we find the FV after 3 years at 6 percent with semiannual compounding:

1. EQUATION AND NUMERICAL SOLUTION:

$$FV_n = PV(1 + i)^n = \$100(1.03)^6$$

$$= \$100(1.1941) = \$119.41$$

Here i = rate per period = (annual rate) ÷ (compounding periods per year) = 6% ÷ 2 = 3%, and n = the total number of periods = (years) × (compounding periods per year) = 3 × 2 = 6.

2. TABULAR SOLUTION:

$$FV_6 = \$100(FVIF_{3\%,6}) = \$100(1.1941) = \$119.41$$

Look up FVIF for 3%, 6 periods in Table A-3 and complete the arithmetic.

3. FINANCIAL CALCULATOR SOLUTION:

Inputs: 6   3   −100   0   ?

| N | I | PV | PMT | FV |

Output: = 119.41

Enter N = (years) × (periods per year) = 3 × 2 = 6, I = (annual rate) ÷ (periods per year) = 6 ÷ 2 = 3, PV = −100, and PMT = 0, and then press FV to find the answer—$119.41 versus $119.10 under annual compounding. The FV is larger with semiannual compounding because interest on interest is being earned more frequently.

Throughout the world economy, different compounding periods are used for different types of investments. For example, bank accounts generally compute interest on a daily basis; most bonds pay interest semiannually; and stocks generally pay dividends quarterly.[10] If we are to properly compare securities with different compounding periods, we need to put them on a common basis. This requires us to distinguish between the **simple, or quoted, interest rate** and the **effective annual rate.**

The simple, or quoted, interest rate in our example is 6 percent. *The effective annual rate (EAR) is defined as that rate which would produce the same ending (future) value if annual compounding had been used.* In our example, the effective annual rate is the rate that would produce an FV of $119.41 at the end of Year 3.

We can determine the effective annual rate, given the simple rate and the number of compounding periods per year, by solving this equation:

SIMPLE (QUOTED)
INTEREST RATE
The contracted, or quoted, interest rate which is used to compute the interest paid per period.

EFFECTIVE ANNUAL
RATE (EAR)
The annual rate of interest actually being earned, as opposed to the quoted rate, considering the compounding of interest.

6-8

$$\text{Effective annual rate} = EAR = \left(1 + \frac{i_{SIMPLE}}{m}\right)^m - 1.0$$

---

[10]Some banks and savings and loans even pay interest compounded continuously. Continuous compounding is discussed in Appendix 6A.

Here i_{SIMPLE} is the simple, or quoted, interest rate, and m is the number of compounding periods per year. For example, to find the effective annual rate if the simple rate is 6 percent and semiannual compounding is used, we have[11]

$$\text{Effective annual rate} = \text{EAR} = \left(1 + \frac{0.06}{2}\right)^2 - 1.0 = (1.03)^2 - 1.0$$

$$= 1.0609 - 1.0 = 0.0609 = 6.09\%$$

Semiannual compounding (or any nonannual compounding) can be handled in two ways: (1) State everything on a periodic basis rather than on an annual basis. For example, use n = 6 periods rather than n = 3 years, and use i = 3% per period rather than i = 6% per year. (2) Alternatively, find the effective annual rate by applying Equation 6-8, and then use this rate as an annual rate over the given number of years. In our example, use i = 6.09% and n = 3 years. Here are the time lines for the two alternative procedures:

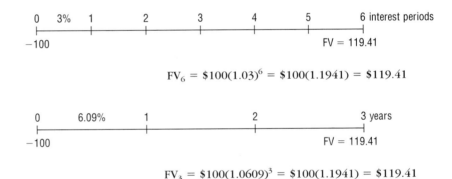

$$FV_6 = \$100(1.03)^6 = \$100(1.1941) = \$119.41$$

$$FV_3 = \$100(1.0609)^3 = \$100(1.1941) = \$119.41$$

We see that both procedures produce the same result, $119.41. Of course, once you start dealing with noninteger interest rates such as 6.09 percent, the use of a calculator or the numerical solution is essential.

The points made about semiannual compounding can be generalized as follows. When compounding occurs more frequently than once a year, we can use a modified version of Equation 6-1 to find the future value of any lump sum:

$$\text{Annual compounding: } FV_n = PV(1 + i)^n \qquad \textbf{(6-1)}$$

6-9

$$\text{More frequent compounding: } FV_n = PV\left(1 + \frac{i_{SIMPLE}}{m}\right)^{m \times n}$$

---

[11]Most financial calculators are programmed to find the EAR or, given the EAR, to find the nominal rate. This is called *interest rate conversion,* and you simply enter the nominal rate and the number of compounding periods per year and then press the EFF% key to find the EAR.

Here i_{SIMPLE} is the simple, or quoted, rate, m is the number of times compounding occurs per year, and n is the number of years. For example, when banks pay daily interest, the value of m is set at 365 and Equation 6-9 is applied.[12]

ANNUAL PERCENTAGE RATE (APR)
The periodic rate × the number of periods per year.

To illustrate further the effects of compounding more frequently than once a year, consider the interest rate charged on credit cards. Many banks charge 1.5 percent per month, and, in their advertising, they state that the **Annual Percentage Rate (APR)** is 18.0 percent. However, the true rate is the effective annual rate of 19.6 percent:[13]

$$\text{Effective annual rate} = \text{EAR} = \left(1 + \frac{0.18}{12}\right)^{12} - 1$$

$$= (1.015)^{12} - 1$$

$$= 0.196 = 19.6\%$$

Semiannual and other compounding periods can also be used for discounting, and for both lump sums and annuities. First, consider the case where we want to find the PV of an ordinary annuity of $100 per year for 3 years when the interest rate is 8 percent, compounded annually:

CASH FLOW TIME LINE:

$$
\begin{array}{ccccccc}
0 & 8\% & 1 & & 2 & & 3 \\
\vdash & & + & & + & & \dashv \\
PV = ? & & -100 & & -100 & & -100
\end{array}
$$

1. NUMERICAL SOLUTION:

Find the PV of each cash flow and sum them. Alternatively, compute the PV directly as follows:

$$PVA_3 = \$100\left[\frac{1 - \frac{1}{(1.08)^3}}{0.08}\right] = \$100(2.5771) = \$257.71$$

---

[12]To illustrate, the future value of $1 invested at 10 percent for 1 year under daily compounding is $1.1052:

$$FV_n = \$1\left(1 + \frac{0.10}{365}\right)^{365} = \$1(1.105156) = \$1.1052$$

[13]The *annual percentage rate (APR)* is the rate often used in bank loan advertisements because it meets the minimum requirements contained in "truth in lending" laws. Typically, the APR is defined as (periodic rate) × (number of periods in one year). For example, the APR on a credit card with interest charges of 1.5 percent per month is 1.5%(12) = 18.0%. The APR understates the effective annual rate because compounding is not taken into consideration. So, banks tend to use the APR when advertising what they charge on loans, but they use the effective annual rate when advertising rates on savings accounts and certificates of deposit because they want to make their deposit rates look high.

2. TABULAR SOLUTION:

$$PVA_3 = PMT(PVIFA_{8\%,3})$$

$$= \$100(2.5771) = \$257.71$$

3. FINANCIAL CALCULATOR SOLUTION:

Inputs: 3   8   ?   −100   0

| N | I | PV | PMT | FV |

Output: = 257.71

Now let's change the situation. For example, suppose the annuity calls for payments of $50 each 6 months rather than for $100 per year, and the rate is 8 percent, compounded semiannually. Here is the time line:

CASH FLOW TIME LINE:

		1		2		3 years
0	4% 1	2	3	4	5	6 6-month periods

PV = ?   −50   −50   −50   −50   −50   −50

1. NUMERICAL SOLUTION:

Find the PV of each cash flow by discounting at 4 percent. Treat each tick mark on the time line as a period, so there would be 6 periods. The PV of the annuity is $262.11 versus $257.71 under annual compounding. Solving directly, the computation is:

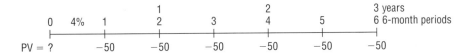

$$PVA_6 = \$50\left[\frac{1 - \frac{1}{(1.04)^6}}{0.04}\right] = \$50(5.2421) = \$262.11$$

2. TABULAR SOLUTION:

$$PVA_6 = PMT(PVIFA_{4\%,6})$$

$$= \$50(5.2421) = \$262.11$$

3. FINANCIAL CALCULATOR SOLUTION:

Inputs: 6   4   ?   −50   0

| N | I | PV | PMT | FV |

Output: = 262.11

The semiannual payments come in sooner, so they can be invested sooner, which means the $50 semiannual annuity is more valuable than the $100 annual annuity.

Self-Test Questions

What changes must you make in your calculations to determine the future value of an amount that is being compounded at 8 percent semiannually versus one being compounded annually at 8 percent?

Why is semiannual compounding better than annual compounding from a saver's standpoint?

What is meant by the terms "annual percentage rate," "effective annual rate," and "simple interest rate"?

Fractional Time Periods

In all the examples used thus far in the chapter, we have assumed that payments occur at either the beginning or the end of periods but not at some date within a period. However, we often encounter situations that require compounding or discounting over fractional periods. For example, suppose you deposited $100 in a bank that pays 10 percent interest, compounded annually. If you leave your money in the bank for 9 months, or 0.75 of the year, how much would you have in your account? Problems such as this can be handled easily, but the tables generally cannot be used.

CASH FLOW TIME LINE AND EQUATION:

```
0    10%   0.25      0.50       0.75      1.00
├─────────┼──────────┼──────────┼──────────┤
-100                            FV = ?
```

$$FV_n = PV(1 + i)^n \qquad (6\text{-}1)$$

1. NUMERICAL SOLUTION:

$$FV_{0.75} = \$100(1.10)^{0.75} = \$100(1.0741) = \$107.41$$

2. FINANCIAL CALCULATOR SOLUTION:[14]

Inputs:	0.75	10	−100	0	?
	N	**I**	**PV**	**PMT**	**FV**
Output:					= 107.41

Present values, annuities, and problems where you must find interest rates or numbers of periods can all be handled with ease. Note, though, that financial calculators are essential for many fractional year problems—the tables are useless.

Self-Test Question

Why are the tables useless for fractional time periods?

Amortized Loans

One of the most important applications of compound interest involves loans that are paid off in installments over time. Included are automobile loans, home mortgage loans, student loans, and most business debt other than very short-term loans

---

[14]Some older calculators will produce an answer of FV = 107.50. This result occurs because these calculators solve for fractional time periods using a straight-line interpolation procedure.

and long-term bonds. If a loan is to be repaid in equal periodic amounts (monthly, quarterly, or annually), it is said to be an **amortized loan.**[15]

AMORTIZED LOAN
A loan that is repaid in equal payments over its life.

To illustrate, suppose a firm borrows $1,000, and the loan is to be repaid in 3 equal payments at the end of each of the next 3 years. The lender is to receive 6 percent interest on the loan balance that is outstanding at the beginning of each year. The first task is to determine the amount the firm must repay each year, or the annual payment. To find this amount, recognize that the $1,000 represents the present value of an annuity of PMT dollars per year for 3 years, discounted at 6 percent:

CASH FLOW TIME LINE AND EQUATION:

$$\begin{array}{c c c c c}
0 \quad 6\% & 1 & 2 & 3 \\
\vdash\!\!\!\!\!-\!\!\!\!\!-\!\!\!\!\!-\!\!\!\!\!-\!\!\!\!\!-\!\!\!\!\!-\!\!\!\!\!-\!\!\!\!\!-\!\!\!\!\!-\!\!\!\!\!-\!\!\!\!\!-\!\!\!\!\!+\!\!\!\!\!-\!\!\!\!\!-\!\!\!\!\!-\!\!\!\!\!-\!\!\!\!\!-\!\!\!\!\!+\!\!\!\!\!-\!\!\!\!\!-\!\!\!\!\!-\!\!\!\!\!-\!\!\!\!\!-\!\!\!\!\!+ \\
1,000 & PMT & PMT & PMT
\end{array}$$

$$PVA_n = \frac{PMT}{(1+i)^1} + \frac{PMT}{(1+i)^2} + \frac{PMT}{(1+i)^3} = \sum_{t=1}^{3} \frac{PMT}{(1+i)^t}$$

$$\$1,000 = \sum_{t=1}^{3} \frac{PMT}{(1.06)^t}$$

Here we know everything except PMT, so we can solve the equation for PMT.

1. NUMERICAL SOLUTION:

You could follow the trial-and-error procedure, inserting values for PMT in the equation until you find a value that "works" and causes the right side of the equation to equal $1,000. This would be a tedious process, but eventually you would find PMT = $374.11. Or you could solve for PMT as follows:

$$\$1,000 = \sum_{t=1}^{3} \frac{PMT}{(1.06)^t} = PMT\left[\sum_{t=1}^{3} \frac{1}{(1.06)^t}\right] = PMT\left[\frac{1 - \frac{1}{(1.06)^3}}{0.06}\right]$$

$$\$1,000 = PMT(2.673012)$$

$$PMT = \frac{\$1,000}{2.673012} = \$374.11$$

2. TABULAR SOLUTION:

Substitute in known values and look up PVIFA for 6%, 3 periods in Table A-2:

$$PVA_3 = PMT(PVIFA_{6\%,3})$$

$$\$1,000 = PMT(2.6730)$$

$$PMT = \frac{\$1,000}{2.6730} = \$374.11$$

---

[15]The word *amortized* comes from the Latin *mors,* meaning "death," so an amortized loan is one that is "killed off" over time.

	Beginning Amount	Payment	Interest[a]	Repayment of Principal[b]	Remaining Balance
Year	(1)	(2)	(3)	(2) − (3) = (4)	(1) − (4) = (5)
1	$1,000.00	$374.11	$60.00	$314.11	$685.89
2	685.89	374.11	41.15	332.96	352.93
3	352.93	374.11	21.18	352.93	0.00

TABLE 6-2

Loan Amortization Schedule, 6 Percent Interest Rate

[a]Interest is calculated by multiplying the loan balance at the beginning of the year by the interest rate. Therefore, interest in Year 1 is $1,000(0.06) = $60.00; in Year 2, it is $685.89(0.06) = $41.15; and in Year 3, it is $352.93(0.06) = $21.18.

[b]Repayment of principal is equal to the payment of $374.11 minus the interest charge for each year.

3. FINANCIAL CALCULATOR SOLUTION:

Inputs: 3   6   1000   ?   0

N   I   PV   PMT   FV

Output: = −374.11

Enter N = 3, I = 6, PV = 1000 (the firm receives the cash), and FV = 0, and then press the PMT key to find PMT = −374.11.

Therefore, the firm must pay the lender $374.11 at the end of each of the next 3 years, and the percentage cost to the borrower, which also is the rate of return to the lender, will be 6 percent.

Each payment consists partly of interest and partly of repayment of principal. This breakdown is given in the **amortization schedule** shown in Table 6-2. The interest component is largest in the first year, and it declines as the outstanding balance of the loan decreases. For tax purposes, a business borrower reports the interest component shown in Column 3 as a deductible cost each year, while the lender reports this same amount as taxable income.

Financial calculators are programmed to calculate amortization tables—you simply enter the input data, and then press one key to get each entry in Table 6-2. If you have a financial calculator, it is worthwhile to read the appropriate section of the manual and learn how to use its amortization feature.

AMORTIZATION SCHEDULE
A schedule showing precisely how a loan will be repaid. It gives the required payment on each payment date and a breakdown of the payment, showing how much is interest and how much is repayment of principal.

Self-Test Questions

To construct an amortization schedule, how do you determine the amount of the periodic payments?

How do you determine the amount of each payment that goes to interest and to principal?

Comparison of Different Types of Interest Rates

Up to this point, we have discussed three different types of interest rates. If you will be working with relatively difficult time value problems, then it is useful to compare the three types and to know when each should be used, as we discuss below.

1. **Simple, or quoted, rate.** This is the rate that is quoted by borrowers and lenders. Practitioners in the stock, bond, mortgage, commercial loan, consumer loan, banking, and other markets express all financial contracts in terms of simple rates. So, if you talk with a banker, broker, mortgage lender, auto finance company, or student loan officer about rates, the simple rate is the one he or she normally will quote you. However, to be meaningful, the simple rate quotation also must include the number of compounding periods per year. For example, a bank might offer 8.5 percent, compounded quarterly, on CDs, or a mutual fund might offer 8 percent, compounded daily, on its money market account.

Simple rates can be compared with one another, but *only if the instruments being compared use the same number of compounding periods per year.* Thus, to compare an 8.5 percent, annual payment CD with an 8 percent, daily payment money market fund, we would need to put both instruments on an effective annual rate (EAR) basis as discussed later in this section.

Note also that the simple rate never is shown on a time line, and it is never used as an input in a financial calculator unless compounding occurs only once a year (in which case i_{SIMPLE} = periodic rate = EAR). If more frequent compounding occurs, you must use either the periodic rate or the effective annual rate as discussed below.[16]

2. **Periodic rate, i_{PER}.** This is the rate charged by a lender or paid by a borrower *each interest period.* It can be a rate per year, per 6-month period, per quarter, per month, per day, or per any other time interval (usually one year or less). For example, a bank might charge 1 percent per month on its credit card loans, or a finance company might charge 3 percent per quarter on consumer loans. We find the periodic rate as follows:

6-10

$$\text{Periodic rate} = i_{PER} = \frac{i_{SIMPLE}}{m}$$

which implies that

6-11

$$i_{SIMPLE} = (\text{Periodic rate}) \times (m) = \text{APR}$$

Here i_{SIMPLE} is the simple annual rate and m is the number of compounding periods per year. APR, which is the annual percentage rate, represents the periodic rate stated on an annual basis without considering interest compounding; it is i_{SIMPLE}. *The APR never is used in actual calculations; it is simply reported to borrowers.*

If there is one payment per year, or if interest is added only once a year, then m = 1 and the periodic rate is equal to the simple rate. But, *in all cases*

---

[16]Some calculators have a switch that permits you to specify the number of payments per year. We find it less confusing to set this switch to 1 and leave it there. We prefer to work with "periods" when more than 1 payment occurs each year because this maintains a consistency between number of periods and the periodic interest rate.

where interest is added or payments are made more frequently than annually, the periodic rate is less than the simple rate.

The periodic rate is used for calculations in problems where these two conditions hold: (1) payments occur on a regular basis more frequently than once a year, and (2) a payment is made on each compounding (or discounting) date. Thus, if you were dealing with an auto loan that required monthly payments, with a semiannual payment bond, or with an education loan that called for quarterly payments, then on your cash flow time line and in your calculations you would use the Periodic rate = $i_{SIMPLE} \div m$. The periodic rate would not be used to find the PV of an annuity calling for annual payments but where discounting occurred quarterly, because in that case the payments and discounting periods per year do not coincide.

Note that in each of the preceding examples the interest compounding period is the same as the payment period. *The periodic rate can be used directly in calculations, but only if the number of payments per year is consistent with the number of interest compounding periods.*

To illustrate use of the periodic rate, suppose you make eight quarterly payments of $100 into an account that pays 12 percent, compounded quarterly. How much would you have after two years?

CASH FLOW TIME LINE:

0	3%	1	2	3	1 4	5	6	7	2 Years 8 Quarters
		-100	-100	-100	-100	-100	-100	-100	-100 FV = ?

$$FVA_n = \sum_{t=1}^{n} PMT(1 + i)^{n-1} = \sum_{t=1}^{8} \$100(1.03)^{8-t}$$

1. NUMERICAL SOLUTION:

Compound each $100 payment at $12 \div 4 = 3$ percent for the appropriate number of periods, and then sum these individual FVs to find the FV of the payment stream, $889.23. Or compute FVA_n directly as follows:

$$FVA_8 = \$100\left[\frac{(1.03)^8 - 1}{0.03}\right] = \$100(8.8923) = \$889.23$$

2. TABULAR SOLUTION:

Look up FVIFA for 3%, 8 periods, in Table A-4, and complete the arithmetic:

$$FVA_8 = PMT(FVIFA_{3\%,8}) = \$100(8.8923) = \$889.23$$

3. FINANCIAL CALCULATOR SOLUTION:

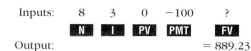

Inputs:	8	3	0	-100	?
	N	I	PV	PMT	FV
Output:					= 889.23

Input N = 2 × 4 = 8, I = 12 ÷ 4 = 3, PV = 0, and PMT = -100, and then press the FV key to get FV = 889.23.

3. **Effective annual rate (EAR).** This is the rate with which, under annual compounding (m = 1), we would obtain the same result as if we had used a given periodic rate with m compounding periods per year. The EAR is found as follows:

6-8

$$EAR = \left(1 + \frac{i_{SIMPLE}}{m}\right)^m - 1.0$$

In the EAR equation, $i_{SIMPLE} \div m$ is the periodic, i_{PER}, rate and m is the number of periods per year. For example, suppose you could borrow using either a credit card that charges 1 percent per month or a bank loan with a 12 percent quoted simple interest rate compounded quarterly. Which should you choose? To answer this question, the cost (rate) of each alternative must be expressed as an EAR:

$$\text{Credit card loan: } EAR = (1 + 0.01)^{12} - 1.0 = (1.01)^{12} - 1.0$$

$$= 1.126825 - 1.0 = 0.126825 = 12.6825\%$$

$$\text{Bank loan: } EAR = (1 + 0.03)^4 - 1.0 = (1.03)^4 - 1.0$$

$$= 1.125509 - 1.0 = 0.125509 = 12.5509\%$$

Thus, the credit card loan costs a little more than the bank loan. This result should have been intuitive to you—both loans have the same 12 percent simple rate, yet you would have to make monthly payments on the credit card versus quarterly payments under the bank loan.

Self-Test Questions

Define the simple (or quoted) rate, the periodic rate, and the effective annual rate.

How are the simple rate, the periodic rate, and the effective annual rate related? Can you think of a situation where all three of these rates will be the same?

Summary

Financial decisions often involve situations in which someone pays money at one point in time and receives money at some later time. Dollars that are paid or received at two different points in time are different, and this difference is recognized and accounted for by time value of money (TVM) analysis. We summarize below the types of TVM analysis and the key concepts covered in this chapter, using the data shown in Figure 6-3 to illustrate the various points. Refer to the figure constantly, and try to find in it an example of the points covered as you go through this summary.

- **Compounding** is the process of determining the **future value (FV)** of a cash flow or a series of cash flows. The compounded amount, or future value, is equal to the beginning amount plus the interest earned.
- Future value: $FV_n = PV(1 + i)^n = PV(FVIF_{i,n})$. (single payment)

FIGURE 6-3

Illustration for Chapter Summary (i = 4%)

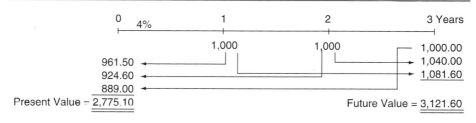

Example: $924.56 compounded for 2 years at 4 percent:

$$FV_2 = \$924.56(1.04)^2 = \$1,000$$

- **Discounting** is the process of finding the **present value (PV)** of a future cash flow or a series of cash flows; discounting is the reciprocal (inverse) of compounding.
- Present value: $PV = \dfrac{FV_n}{(1 + i)^n} = FV_n\left(\dfrac{1}{1 + i}\right)^n = PVIF_{i,n}$ (single payment)

Example: $1,000 discounted back for 2 years at 4 percent:

$$PV = \frac{\$1,000}{(1.04)^2} = \$1,000\left(\frac{1}{1.04}\right)^2 = \$1,000(0.9246) = \$924.60$$

- An **annuity** is defined as a series of equal periodic payments (PMT) for a specified number of periods.
- Future value: $FVA_n = PMT(1 + i)^0 + PMT(1 + i)^1 + PMT(1 + i)^2 + \ldots + PMT(1 + i)^{n-1}$ (annuity)

$$= PMT \sum_{t=1}^{n} (1 + i)^{n-t} = PMT\left[\frac{(1 + i)^n - 1}{i}\right] = PMT(FVIFA_{i,n})$$

Example: FVA of 3 payments of $1,000 when i = 4%:

$$FVA_3 = \$1,000(3.1216) = \$3,121.60$$

- Present value: $PVA_n = \dfrac{PMT}{(1 + i)^1} + \dfrac{PMT}{(1 + i)^2} + \ldots + \dfrac{PMT}{(1 + i)^n}$ (annuity)

$$= PMT \sum_{t=1}^{n} \left[\frac{1}{1 + i}\right]^t = PMT\left[\frac{1 - \frac{1}{(1 + i)^n}}{i}\right] = PMT(PVIFA_{i,n})$$

Example: PVA of 3 payments of $1,000 when i = 4%:

$$PVA_3 = \$1,000(2.7751) = \$2,775.10$$

- An annuity whose payments occur at the end of each period is called an **ordinary annuity.** The preceding formulas are for ordinary annuities.
- If each payment occurs at the beginning of the period rather than at the end, then we have an **annuity due.** In Figure 6-3, the payments would be shown at Years 0, 1, and 2 rather than at Years 1, 2, and 3. The PV of each payment would be larger, because each payment would be discounted back one year less; hence, the PV of the annuity also would be larger.

  Similarly, the FV of the annuity due also would be larger because each payment would be compounded for an extra year. The following formulas can be used to convert the PV and FV of an ordinary annuity to an annuity due:

$$PVA_{n,DUE} = PMT[(PVIFA_{i,n}) \times (1 + i)] = PMT[PVIFA_{i,n}(DUE)]$$

Example: PVA of 3 beginning-of-year payments of $1,000 when i = 4%:

$$PVA_{3,DUE} = \$1,000[(2.7751)(1.04)] = \$2,886.10$$

$$FVA_{n,DUE} = PMT[(FVIFA_{i,n}) \times (1 + i)] = PMT[FVIFA_{i,n}(DUE)]$$

Example: FVA of 3 beginning-of-year payments of $1,000 when i = 4%:

$$FVA_{3,DUE} = \$1,000[(3.1216)(1.04)] = \$3,246.46$$

- If the cash flow time line in Figure 6-3 were extended out forever so that the $1,000 payments went on forever, we would have a **perpetuity** whose value could be found as follows:

$$\text{Value of a perpetuity} = PVA_{PERPETUITY} = \frac{PMT}{i} = \frac{\$1,000}{0.04} = \$25,000$$

- If the cash flows in Figure 6-3 were unequal, we could not use the annuity formulas. To find the PV or FV of an **uneven series,** find the PV or FV of each individual cash flow and then sum them. However, if some of the cash flows constitute an annuity, then the annuity formula can be used to calculate the present value of that part of the cash flow stream.
- **Financial calculators** have built-in programs that perform all the operations discussed in this chapter. It would be useful for you to buy such a calculator and learn how to use it. Even if you do, though, it is essential that you understand the logical processes involved.
- Thus far in the summary we have assumed that payments are made, and interest is earned, at the end of each year, or annually. However, many contracts call for more frequent payments; for example, mortgage and auto loans call for monthly payments, and most bonds pay interest semiannually. Similarly, most banks compute interest daily. When compounding occurs more frequently than once a year, this fact must be recognized. We can use the Figure 6-3 example to illustrate the procedures. First, the following formula is used to find an **effective annual rate (EAR):**

$$\text{Effective annual rate} = EAR = \left(1 + \frac{i_{SIMPLE}}{m}\right)^m - 1.0$$

For semiannual compounding, the effective annual rate is 4.04 percent:

$$\left(1 + \frac{0.04}{2}\right)^2 - 1.0 = (1.02)^2 - 1.0 = 1.0404 - 1.0 = 0.0404 = 4.04\%$$

This rate could then be used (with a calculator but not with the tables) to find the PV or FV of each payment in Figure 6-3.

If the $1,000 per-year payments were actually payable as $500 each 6 months, you would simply redraw Figure 6-3 to show 6 payments of $500 each, but you would also need to use a periodic interest rate of 4%/2 = 2% for determining the PV or FV of the payments.

- The general equation for finding the future value for any number of compounding periods per year is:

$$FV_n = PV\left(1 + \frac{i_{SIMPLE}}{m}\right)^{n \times m}$$

where

i_{SIMPLE} = quoted interest rate

   m = number of compounding periods per year

   n = number of years

- An **amortized loan** is one that is paid off in equal payments over a specified period. An **amortization schedule** shows how much of each payment constitutes interest, how much is used to reduce the principal, and the remaining balance of the loan at each point in time.

The concepts covered in this chapter will be used throughout the remainder of the book. For example, in Chapter 7 we will apply present value concepts to the process of valuing stocks and bonds, and we will see that the market prices of securities are established by determining the present values of the cash flows they are expected to provide. In later chapters, the same basic concepts are applied to corporate decisions involving both expenditures on capital assets and determining the types of capital that should be used to pay for assets.

Questions

6-1   What is an *opportunity cost rate?* How is this rate used in time value analysis, and where is it shown on a cash flow time line? Is the opportunity rate a single number which is used in all situations?

6-2   An *annuity* is defined as a series of payments of a fixed amount for a specific number of periods. Thus, $100 a year for 10 years is an annuity, but $100 in Year 1, $200 in Year 2, and $400 in Years 3 through 10 does *not* constitute an annuity. However, the second series *contains* an annuity. Is this statement true or false?

6-3   If a firm's earnings per share grew from $1 to $2 over a 10-year period, the total *growth* would be 100 percent, but the *annual growth rate* would be *less than* 10 percent. True or false? Explain. Under what conditions would the annual growth rate *actually* be 10 percent per year?

6-4   Would you rather have a savings account that pays 5 percent interest compounded semiannually or one that pays 5 percent interest compounded daily? Explain.

6-5   To find the present value of an uneven series of cash flows, you must find the PVs of the individual cash flows and then sum them. Annuity procedures can never be of use, even if some of the cash flows constitute an annuity (for example, $100 each for Years 3, 4, 5, and 6), because the entire series is not an annuity. Is this statement true or false? Explain.

6-6   The present value of a perpetuity is equal to the payment of the annuity, PMT, divided by the interest rate, i: $PV_{PERPETUITY} = PMT/i$. What is the *sum,* or *future value,* of a perpetuity of PMT dollars per year? (Hint: The answer is infinity, but explain why.)

Self-Test Problems

(Solutions Appear in Appendix B)

Key terms   **ST-1**   Define each of the following terms:
       a.   PV; i; INT; FV_n; n; PVA_n; FVA_n; PMT; m; i_{SIMPLE}
       b. $FVIF_{i,n}$; $PVIF_{i,n}$; $FVIFA_{i,n}$; $PVIFA_{i,n}$; $FVIFA_{i,n}$(DUE); $PVIFA_{i,n}$(DUE)
       c.   opportunity cost rate
       d.   annuity; lump sum payment; cash flow; uneven cash flow stream
       e.   ordinary (deferred) annuity; annuity due
       f.   perpetuity; consol
       g.   outflow; inflow; cash flow time line
       h.   compounding; discounting
       i.   annual, semiannual, quarterly, monthly, and daily compounding
       j.   effective annual rate (EAR); simple (quoted) interest rate; APR; periodic rate
       k.   amortization schedule; principal component versus interest component of a payment; amortized loan
       l.   terminal value

Future value   **ST-2**   Assume that it is now January 1, 1996. On January 1, 1997, you will deposit $1,000 into a savings account that pays 8 percent.
       a.   If the bank compounds interest annually, how much will you have in your account on January 1, 2000?
       b.   What would your January 1, 2000, balance be if the bank used quarterly compounding rather than annual compounding?
       c.   Suppose you deposited the $1,000 in 4 payments of $250 each on January 1 of 1997, 1998, 1999, and 2000. How much would you have in your account on January 1, 2000, based on 8 percent annual compounding?
       d.   Suppose you deposited 4 equal payments in your account on January 1 of 1997, 1998, 1999, and 2000. Assuming an 8 percent interest rate, how large would each of your payments have to be for you to obtain the same ending balance as you calculated in Part a?

Time value of money   **ST-3**   Assume that it is now January 1, 1996, and you will need $1,000 on January 1, 2000. Your bank compounds interest at an 8 percent annual rate.
       a.   How much must you deposit on January 1, 1997, to have a balance of $1,000 on January 1, 2000?
       b.   If you want to make equal payments on each January 1 from 1997 through 2000 to accumulate the $1,000, how large must each of the 4 payments be?
       c.   If your father offered either to make the payments calculated in Part b ($221.92) or to give you a lump sum of $750 on January 1, 1997, which would you choose?

d. If you have only $750 on January 1, 1997, what interest rate, compounded annually, would you have to earn to have the necessary $1,000 on January 1, 2000?

e. Suppose you can deposit only $186.29 each January 1 from 1997 through 2000, but you still need $1,000 on January 1, 2000. What interest rate, with annual compounding, must you seek out to achieve your goal?

f. To help you reach your $1,000 goal, your mother offers to give you $400 on January 1, 1997. You will get a part-time job and make 6 additional payments of equal amounts each 6 months thereafter. If all this money is deposited in a bank that pays 8 percent, compounded semiannually, how large must each of the 6 payments be?

g. What is the effective annual rate being paid by the bank in Part f?

h. *Reinvestment rate risk* was defined in Chapter 2 as being the risk that maturing securities (and coupon payments on bonds) will have to be reinvested at a lower rate of interest than they were previously earning. Is there a reinvestment rate risk involved in the preceding analysis? If so, how might this risk be eliminated?

Effective annual rates   **ST-4**   Bank A pays 8 percent interest, compounded quarterly, on its money market account. The managers of Bank B want its money market account to equal Bank A's effective annual rate, but interest is to be compounded on a monthly basis. What simple, or quoted, rate must Bank B set?

Problems

Present and future values for different periods   **6-1**   Find the following values, *using the numerical solution approach,* and then work the problems using a financial calculator or the tables to check your answers. Disregard rounding errors. (Hint: If you are using a financial calculator, you can enter the known values and then press the appropriate key to find the unknown variable. Then, without clearing the TVM register, you can "override" the variable that changes by simply entering a new value for it and then pressing the key for the unknown variable to obtain the second answer. This procedure can be used in Parts b and d, and in many other situations, to see how changes in input variables affect the output variable.)

a. An initial $500 compounded for 1 year at 6 percent.

b. An initial $500 compounded for 2 years at 6 percent.

c. The present value of $500 due in 1 year at a discount rate of 6 percent.

d. The present value of $500 due in 2 years at a discount rate of 6 percent.

Present and future values for different interest rates   **6-2**   Use the tables or a financial calculator to find the following values. See the hint for Problem 6-1.

a. An initial $500 compounded for 10 years at 6 percent.

b. An initial $500 compounded for 10 years at 12 percent.

c. The present value of $500 due in 10 years at a 6 percent discount rate.

d. The present value of $1,552.90 due in 10 years at (i) a 12 percent discount rate, and (ii) a 6 percent rate. Give a verbal definition of the term *present value,* and illustrate it using a cash flow time line with data from this problem. As part of your answer, explain why present values are dependent upon interest rates.

Time for a lump sum to double   **6-3**   To the closest year, how long will it take $200 to double if it is deposited and earns the following rates? [Notes: (1) See the hint for Problem 6-1. (2) This problem cannot be solved exactly with some financial calculators. For example, if you enter PV = −200, FV = 400, and I = 7 in an HP-12C and then press the N key, you will get 11 years for Part a. The correct answer is 10.2448 years, which rounds to 10, but the calculator rounds up. However, the HP-10B and HP-17B give the correct answer. You should look up FVIF = 400/200 = 2 in the tables for Parts a, b, and c, but figure out Part d.]

a. 7 percent

b. 10 percent

c. 18 percent

d. 100 percent

Future value of an annuity   **6-4**   Find the *future value* of the following annuities. The first payment in these annuities is made at the *end* of Year 1; that is, they are *ordinary annuities*. (Note: See the hint to Problem 6-1. Also, note that you can leave values in the TVM register, switch to BEG, press FV, and find the FV of the *annuity due*.)

a. $400 per year for 10 years at 10 percent.

b. $200 per year for 5 years at 5 percent.

c. $400 per year for 5 years at 0 percent.

d. Now rework Parts a, b, and c assuming that payments are made at the beginning of each year; that is, they are *annuities due*.

Present value of an annuity   **6-5**   Find the present value of the following ordinary annuities (see note to Problem 6-4):

a. $400 per year for 10 years at 10 percent.

b. $200 per year for 5 years at 5 percent.

c. $400 per year for 5 years at 0 percent.

d. Now rework Parts a, b, and c assuming that payments are made at the beginning of each year; that is, they are *annuities due*.

Uneven cash flow stream   **6-6**   Find the present values of the following cash flow streams under the following conditions:

Year	Cash Stream A	Cash Stream B
1	$100	$300
2	400	400
3	400	400
4	400	400
5	300	100

a. The appropriate interest rate is 8 percent. (Hint: It is fairly easy to work this problem dealing with the individual cash flows. However, if you have a financial calculator, read the section of the manual which describes how to enter cash flows such as the ones in this problem. This will take a little time, but the investment will pay huge dividends throughout the course. Note that, if you do the work with the cash flow register, you must enter $CF_0 = 0$.)

b. What is the value of each cash flow stream at a 0 percent interest rate?

Effective rate of interest   **6-7**   Find the interest rates, or rates of return, on each of the following:

a. You *borrow* $700 and promise to pay back $749 at the end of 1 year.

b. You *lend* $700 and receive a promise to be paid $749 at the end of 1 year.

c. You borrow $85,000 and promise to pay back $201,229 at the end of 10 years.

d. You borrow $9,000 and promise to make payments of $2,684.80 per year for 5 years.

Future value of various   **6-8**   Find the amount to which $500 will grow under each of the following conditions:
compounding periods

a. 12 percent compounded annually for 5 years.

b. 12 percent compounded semiannually for 5 years.

c. 12 percent compounded quarterly for 5 years.

d. 12 percent compounded monthly for 5 years.

Present value of various compounding periods

6-9 Find the present value of $500 due in the future under each of the following conditions:

   a. 12 percent simple rate, compounded annually, discounted back 5 years.

   b. 12 percent simple rate, semiannual compounding, discounted back 5 years.

   c. 12 percent simple rate, quarterly compounding, discounted back 5 years.

   d. 12 percent simple rate, monthly compounding, discounted back 1 year.

Future value of an annuity for various compounding periods

6-10 Find the future values of the following ordinary annuities:

   a. FV of $400 each 6 months for 5 years at a simple rate of 12 percent, compounded semiannually.

   b. FV of $200 each 3 months for 5 years at a simple rate of 12 percent, compounded quarterly.

   c. The annuities described in Parts a and b have the same amount of money paid into them during the 5-year period and both earn interest at the same simple rate, yet the annuity in Part b earns $101.60 more than the one in Part a over the 5 years. Why does this occur?

Effective versus nominal interest rates

6-11 The First City Bank pays 7 percent interest, compounded annually, on time deposits. The Second City Bank pays 6.5 percent interest, compounded quarterly.

   a. Based on effective interest rates, in which bank would you prefer to deposit your money?

   b. Could your choice of banks be influenced by the fact that you might want to withdraw your funds during the year as opposed to at the end of the year? In answering this question, assume that funds must be left on deposit during the entire compounding period in order for you to receive any interest.

Amortization schedule

6-12 Lorkay Seidens, Inc. just borrowed $25,000. The loan is to be repaid in equal installments at the end of each of the next 5 years, and the interest rate is 10 percent.

   a. Set up an amortization schedule for the loan.

   b. How large must each annual payment be if the loan is for $50,000? Assume that the interest rate remains at 10 percent and that the loan is paid off over 5 years.

   c. How large must each payment be if the loan is for $50,000, the interest rate is 10 percent, and the loan is paid off in equal installments at the end of each of the next 10 years? This loan is for the same amount as the loan in Part b, but the payments are spread out over twice as many periods. Why are these payments not half as large as the payments on the loan in Part b?

Effective rates of return

6-13 Assume that AT&T's pension fund managers are considering two alternative securities as investments: (1) Security Z (for zero intermediate year cash flows), which costs $422.41 today, pays nothing during its 10-year life, and then pays $1,000 after 10 years or (2) Security B, which has a cost today of $500 and pays $74.50 at the end of each of the next 10 years.

   a. What is the rate of return on each security?

   b. Assume that the interest rate AT&T's pension fund managers can earn on the fund's money falls to 6 percent immediately after the securities are purchased and is expected to remain at that level for the next 10 years. What would the price of each security change to, what would be the fund's profit on each security, and what would be the percentage profit (profit divided by cost) for each security?

   c. Assuming that the cash flows for each security had to be reinvested at the new 6 percent market interest rate, (1) what would be the value attributable to each security at the end of 10 years and (2) what "actual, after-the-fact" rate of return would the fund have earned on each security? (Hint: The "actual" rate of return is found as the interest rate which causes the PV of the compounded Year 10 amount to equal the original cost of the security.)

d. Now assume all the facts as given in Parts b and c except assume that the interest rate rose to 12 percent rather than fell to 6 percent. What would happen to the profit figures as developed in Part b and to the "actual" rates of return as determined in Part c? Explain your results.

Required annuity payments   **6-14**   A father is planning a savings program to put his daughter through college. His daughter now is 13 years old. She plans to enroll at the university in 5 years, and it should take her 4 years to complete her education. Currently, the cost per year (for everything—food, clothing, tuition, books, transportation, and so forth) is $12,500, but a 5 percent inflation rate in these costs is forecasted. The daughter recently received $7,500 from her grandfather's estate; this money, which is invested in a bank account paying 8 percent interest compounded annually, will be used to help meet the costs of the daughter's education. The rest of the costs will be met by money the father will deposit in the savings account. He will make 6 equal deposits to the account in each year from now until his daughter starts college. These deposits will begin today and also will earn 8 percent interest.

a. What will be the present value of the cost of four years of education *at the time the daughter becomes 18?* [Hint: Calculate the future value of the cost (at 5%) for each year of her education, then discount three of these costs back (at 8%) to the year in which she turns 18, then sum the four costs.]

b. What will be the value of the $7,500 which the daughter received from her grandfather's estate *when she starts college at age 18?* (Hint: Compound for 5 years at 8%.)

c. If the father is planning to make the first of 6 deposits today, how large must each deposit be for him to be able to put his daughter through college?

Future value of a   **6-15**   As soon as she graduated from college, Kay began planning for her retirement. Her
retirement fund   plans were to deposit $500 semiannually into an IRA (a retirement fund), beginning six months after graduation and continuing until the day she retired, which she expected to be thirty (30) years later. Today is the day Kay retires (happy retirement). She just made the last $500 deposit into her retirement fund, and now she wants to know how much she has accumulated for her retirement. The fund earned 10 percent compounded semiannually since it was established.

a. Compute the balance of the retirement fund assuming all the payments were made on time.

b. Although Kay was able to make all the $500 deposits she planned, ten (10) years ago she had to withdraw $10,000 from the fund to pay some medical bills incurred by her mother. Compute the balance in the retirement fund based on this information.

Exam-Type Problems

The problems in this section are set up in such a way that they could be used as multiple-choice exam problems.

Present value comparisons   **6-16**   Which amount is worth more at 14 percent: $1,000 in hand today or $2,000 due in 6 years?

Growth rates   **6-17**   Martell Corporation's 1995 sales were $12 million. Sales were $6 million 5 years earlier (in 1990).

a. To the nearest percentage point, at what rate have sales been growing?

b. Suppose someone calculated the sales growth for Martell Corporation in Part a as follows: "Sales doubled in 5 years. This represents a growth of 100 percent in 5 years, so, dividing 100 percent by 5, we find the growth rate to be 20 percent per year." Explain what is wrong with this calculation.

Effective rate of return **6-18** Krystal Magee invested $150,000 eighteen (18) months ago. Currently, the investment is worth $168,925. Krystal knows the investment has paid interest *every three (3) months (that is, quarterly)*, but she doesn't know what the yield on her investment is. Help Krystal. Compute both the annual percentage rate (APR) *and* the effective annual rate of interest.

Effective rate of interest **6-19** Your broker offers to sell you a note for $13,250 that will pay $2,345.05 per year for 10 years. If you buy the note, what rate of interest (to the closest percent) will you be earning?

Effective rate of interest **6-20** A mortgage company offers to lend you $85,000; the loan calls for payments of $8,273.59 per year for 30 years. What interest rate is the mortgage company charging you?

Required lump sum payment **6-21** To complete your last year in business school and then go through law school, you will need $10,000 per year for 4 years, starting next year (that is, you will need to withdraw the first $10,000 one year from today). Your rich uncle offers to put you through school, and he will deposit in a bank paying 7 percent interest a sum of money that is sufficient to provide the four payments of $10,000 each. His deposit will be made today.
   a. How large must the deposit be?
   b. How much will be in the account immediately after you make the first withdrawal? After the last withdrawal?

Repaying a loan **6-22** Sue wants to buy a car that costs $12,000. She has arranged to borrow the total purchase price of the car from her credit union at a simple interest rate equal to 12 percent. The loan requires quarterly payments for a period of three (3) years. If the first payment is due three months (one quarter) after purchasing the car, what will be the amount of Sue's quarterly payments on the loan?

Repaying a loan **6-23** While Steve Bouchard was a student at the University of Florida, he borrowed $12,000 in student loans at an annual interest rate of 9 percent. If Steve repays $1,500 per year, how long, to the nearest year, will it take him to repay the loan?

Reaching a financial goal **6-24** You need to accumulate $10,000. To do so, you plan to make deposits of $1,750 per year, with the first payment being made a year from today, in a bank account which pays 6 percent annual interest. Your last deposit will be more than $1,750 if more is needed to round out to $10,000. How many years will it take you to reach your $10,000 goal, and how large will the last deposit be?

Present value of a perpetuity **6-25** What is the present value of a perpetuity of $100 per year if the appropriate discount rate is 7 percent? If interest rates in general were to double and the appropriate discount rate rose to 14 percent, what would happen to the present value of the perpetuity?

Loan amortization **6-26** Assume that your aunt sold her house on December 31 and that she took a mortgage in the amount of $10,000 as part of the payment. The mortgage has a quoted (or simple) interest rate of 10 percent, but it calls for payments every 6 months, beginning on June 30, and the mortgage is to be amortized over 10 years. Now, one year later, your aunt must file a Form 1099 with the IRS and with the person who bought the house, informing them of the interest that was included in the two payments made during the year. (This interest will be income to your aunt and a deduction to the buyer of the house.) To the closest dollar, what is the total amount of interest that was paid during the first year?

Automobile loan comparison **6-27** Sarah is on her way to the local Chevrolet dealership to buy a Cavalier. The list, or "sticker," price of the car is $13,000. Sarah has $3,000 in her checking account that she can use as a downpayment toward the purchase of a new car. Sarah has carefully evaluated her finances, and she has determined she can afford payments which *total* $2,400 per year on a loan to purchase the car. Sarah can borrow the money to purchase the car either through the dealer's "special financing package," which is advertised as 4.0% financing, or from a local bank, which has automobile loans at 12% interest. Each loan would be outstanding for a period of five (5) years, and the payments would be made quarterly (every three months). Sarah knows the dealer's special financing package requires that she will have to pay the sticker price for the car. But, if she uses the bank financing, she thinks she can negotiate with the dealer for a better price. Assume Sarah wants to pay $600 per payment, regardless of which loan she chooses, and the remainder of the purchase price will be a down payment that can be satisfied with any of the $3,000 in Sarah's checking account. Ignoring charges for taxes, tag, and title transfer, how much of a reduction in the sticker price must Sarah negotiate in order to make the bank financing more attractive than the dealer's special financing package?

Annuity withdrawals—an ordinary annuity versus an annuity due

6-28   Jason worked various jobs during his teenage years to save money for college. Now it is his twentieth birthday, and he is about to begin his college studies at the University of South Florida. A few months ago, Jason received a scholarship that will cover all his college tuition for a period not to exceed five (5) years. The money he has saved will be used for living expenses while he is in college; in fact, Jason expects to use all his savings while attending USF. The jobs he worked as a teenager allowed him to save a total of $10,000, which currently is invested at 12% in a financial asset that pays interest monthly. Because Jason will be a full-time student, he expects to graduate four (4) years from today, on his twenty-fourth birthday.

  a. How much can Jason withdraw every month while he is in college if the first withdrawal occurs today?

  b. How much can Jason withdraw every month while he is in college if he waits until the end of this month to make the first withdrawal?

Simple rate of return

6-29   Sue Sharpe, manager of Oaks Mall Jewelry, wants to sell on credit, giving customers 3 months in which to pay. However, Sue will have to borrow from her bank to carry the accounts payable. The bank will charge a simple 15 percent, but with monthly compounding. Sue wants to quote a simple rate to her customers (all of whom are expected to pay on time) which will exactly cover her financing costs. What simple annual rate should she quote to her credit customers?

Required annuity payments

6-30   Janet just graduated from a women's college in Mississippi with a degree in business administration, and she is about to start a new job with a large financial services firm based in Tampa, Florida. From reading various business publications while she was in college, Janet has concluded it probably is a good idea to begin planning for her retirement now. Even though she is only 25 years old and just beginning her career, Janet is concerned that Social Security will not be able to meet her needs when she retires. Fortunately for Janet, the company that has hired her has created a good retirement/investment plan that permits her to make contributions every year. So, Janet is now evaluating the amount she needs to contribute to satisfy her financial requirements at retirement. She has decided that she would like to take a trip as soon as her retirement begins (a reward to herself for many years of excellent work). The estimated cost of the trip, including all expenses such as meals and souvenirs, will be $120,000, and it will last for one year (no other funds will be needed during the first year of retirement). After she returns from her trip, Janet plans to settle down to enjoy her retirement. She estimates she will need $70,000 each year to be able to live comfortably and enjoy her "twilight years." The retirement/investment plan available to employees where Janet is going to work pays 7 percent interest compounded annually, and it is expected this rate will continue as long as the company offers the opportunity to contribute to the fund. When she retires, Janet will have to move her retirement "nest egg" to another investment so she can withdraw money when she needs it.

Her plans are to move the money to a fund that allows withdrawals at the beginning of each year; the fund is expected to pay 5 percent interest compounded annually. Janet expects to retire in forty (40) years, and, after looking at the actuarial tables, she has decided she will live another twenty (20) years after she returns from her "retirement trip" around the world. If Janet's expectations are correct, how much must she contribute to the retirement fund to satisfy her retirement plans if she makes her first contribution to the fund one year from today and the last contribution on the day she retires?

Integrative Problem

Time value of money analysis   **6-31**   Assume that you are nearing graduation and that you have applied for a job with a local bank. As part of the bank's evaluation process, you have been asked to take an examination that covers several financial analysis techniques. The first section of the test addresses time value of money analysis. See how you would do by answering the following questions.

a. Draw cash flow time lines for (1) a $100 lump sum cash flow at the end of Year 2, (2) an ordinary annuity of $100 per year for 3 years, and (3) an uneven cash flow stream of −$50, $100, $75, and $50 at the end of Years 0 through 3.

b. (1) What is the future value of an initial $100 after 3 years if it is invested in an account paying 10 percent annual interest?
(2) What is the present value of $100 to be received in 3 years if the appropriate interest rate is 10 percent?

c. We sometimes need to find how long it will take a sum of money (or anything else) to grow to some specified amount. For example, if a company's sales are growing at a rate of 20 percent per year, approximately how long will it take sales to triple?

d. What is the difference between an ordinary annuity and an annuity due? What type of annuity is shown below? How would you change it to the other type of annuity?

e. (1) What is the future value of a 3-year ordinary annuity of $100 if the appropriate interest rate is 10 percent?
(2) What is the present value of the annuity?
(3) What would the future and present values be if the annuity were an annuity due?

f. What is the present value of the following uneven cash flow stream? The appropriate interest rate is 10 percent, compounded annually.

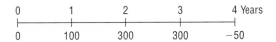

g. What annual interest rate will cause $100 to grow to $125.97 in 3 years?

h. (1) Will the future value be larger or smaller if we compound an initial amount more often than annually, for example, every 6 months, or *semiannually,* holding the stated interest rate constant? Why?
(2) Define (a) the stated, or quoted, or simple, rate, (b) the periodic rate, and (c) the effective annual rate (EAR).
(3) What is the effective annual rate for a simple rate of 10 percent, compounded semiannually? Compounded quarterly? Compounded daily?

(4) What is the future value of $100 after 3 years under 10 percent semiannual compounding? Quarterly compounding?

i. Will the effective annual rate ever be equal to the simple (quoted) rate?

j. (1) What is the value at the end of Year 3 of the following cash flow stream if the quoted interest rate is 10 percent, compounded semiannually?

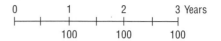

(2) What is the PV of the same stream?

(3) Is the stream an annuity?

(4) An important rule is that you should *never* show a simple rate on a time line or use it in calculations unless what condition holds? (Hint: Think of annual compounding, when $i_{SIMPLE} = EAR = i_{PER}$.) What would be wrong with your answer to questions j(1) and j(2) if you used the simple rate 10% rather than the periodic rate $i_{SIMPLE} \div 2 = 10\% \div 2 = 5\%$?

k. (1) Construct an amortization schedule for a $1,000, 10 percent annual rate loan with 3 equal installments.

(2) What is the annual interest expense for the borrower, and the annual interest income for the lender, during Year 2?

(Parts l through o require a financial calculator.)

l. Suppose on January 1, 1996, you deposit $100 in an account that pays a simple, or quoted, interest rate of 11.33463 percent, with interest added (compounded) daily. How much will you have in your account on October 1, or after 9 months?

m. Now suppose you leave your money in the bank for 21 months. Thus, on January 1, 1996, you deposit $100 in an account that pays a 12 percent effective annual interest rate. How much will be in your account on October 1, 1997?

n. Suppose someone offered to sell you a note calling for the payment of $1,000 15 months from today. The person offers to sell the note to you for $850. You have $850 in a bank time deposit that pays a 6.76649 percent simple rate with daily compounding, which is a 7 percent effective annual interest rate, and you plan to leave the money in the bank unless you buy the note. The note is not risky—you are sure it will be paid on schedule. Should you buy the note? Check the decision in three ways: (1) by comparing your future value if you buy the note versus leaving your money in the bank, (2) by comparing the PV of the note with your current bank account, and (3) by comparing the EAR on the note versus that of the bank account.

o. Suppose the note discussed in Part n had a cost of $850, but called for 5 quarterly payments of $190 each, with the first payment due in 3 months rather than $1,000 at the end of 15 months. Would it be a good investment for you?

Computer-Related Problem

Work the problem in this section only if you are using the computer problem diskette.

Amortization schedule   **6-32** Use the computerized model in File C6 to solve this problem.

a. Set up an amortization schedule for a $30,000 loan to be repaid in equal installments at the end of each of the next 20 years at an interest rate of 10 percent. What is the annual payment?

b. Set up an amortization schedule for a $60,000 loan to be repaid in 20 equal annual installments at an interest rate of 10 percent. What is the annual payment?

c. Set up an amortization schedule for a $60,000 loan to be repaid in 20 equal annual installments at an interest rate of 20 percent. What is the annual payment?

APPENDIX 6A   Continuous Compounding and Discounting

In Chapter 6, we dealt only with situations where interest is added at discrete intervals—annually, semiannually, monthly, and so forth. In some instances, though, it is possible to have instantaneous, or continuous, growth. In this appendix, we discuss present value and future value calculations when the interest rate is compounded continuously.

Continuous Compounding

CONTINUOUS COMPOUNDING
A situation in which interest is added continuously rather than at discrete points in time.

The relationship between discrete and **continuous compounding** is illustrated in Figure 6A-1. Panel a shows the annual compounding case, where interest is added once a year; Panel b shows the situation when compounding occurs twice a year; and Panel c shows interest being earned continuously. As the graphs show, the more frequent the compounding period, the larger the final compounded amount because interest is earned on interest more often.

Equation 6-9 in the chapter can be applied to any number of compounding periods per year:

$$\text{More frequent compounding} = FV_n = PV(1 + \tfrac{i_{\text{SIMPLE}}}{m})^{m \times n} \qquad \textbf{(6-9)}$$

To illustrate, let PV = $100, i = 10%, and n = 5. At various compounding periods per year, we obtain the following future values at the end of 5 years:

$$\text{Annual: } FV_5 = \$100(1 + \tfrac{0.10}{1})^{1 \times 5} = \$100(1.10)^5 \qquad = \$161.05$$

$$\text{Semiannual: } FV_5 = \$100(1 + \tfrac{0.10}{2})^{2 \times 5} = \$100(1.05)^{10} \qquad = \$162.89$$

$$\text{Monthly: } FV_5 = \$100(1 + \tfrac{0.10}{12})^{12 \times 5} = \$100(1.0083)^{60} \qquad = \$164.53$$

$$\text{Daily: } FV_5 = \$100(1 + \tfrac{0.10}{365})^{365 \times 5} = \$100(1.00027)^{1.825} = \$164.86$$

FIGURE 6A-1

Annual, Semiannual, and Continuous Compounding: Future Value with i = 25%

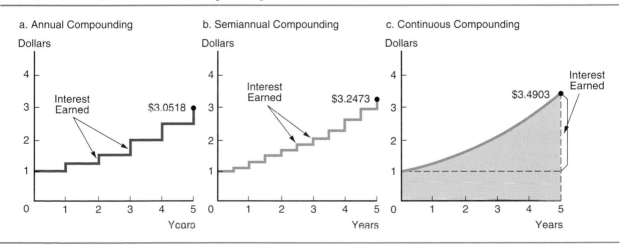

a. Annual Compounding
Dollars
Interest Earned $3.0518

b. Semiannual Compounding
Dollars
Interest Earned $3.2473

c. Continuous Compounding
Dollars
$3.4903   Interest Earned

We could keep going, compounding every hour, every minute, every second, and so on. At the limit, we could compound every instant, or continuously. The equation for continuous compounding is

6A-1

$$FV_n = PV(e^{i \times n})$$

Here e is the value 2.71828 . . . .[1] If $100 is invested for 5 years at 10 percent compounded continuously, then FV_5 is calculated as follows:

$$\text{Continuous: } FV_5 = \$100[e^{0.10(5)}] = \$100(2.71828 \ldots)^{0.5}$$

$$= \$164.872$$

Continuous Discounting

Equation 6A-1 can be transformed into Equation 6A-2 and used to determine present values under continuous discounting:

6A-2

$$PV = \frac{FV_n}{e^{i \times n}} = FV_n(e^{-i \times n})$$

Thus, if $1,649 is due in 10 years, and if the appropriate continuous discount rate, i, is 5 percent, then the present value of this future payment is

$$PV = \frac{\$1,649}{(2.7183 \ldots)^{0.5}} = \frac{\$1,649}{1.649} = \$1,000$$

---

[1]Calculators with exponential functions can be used to evaluate Equation 6A-1.

Bond and Stock Valuation

A MANAGERIAL PERSPECTIVE

On January 3, 1994, Treasury notes were selling at prices that promised investors an average return of about 5.5 percent if they were held until the year 2001. Therefore, a seven-year Treasury note with a face, or par, value equal to $10,000 that paid $275 in interest every six months had a market value equal to $10,000 on January 3, 1994. By January 3, 1995, the value of the same Treasury note was approximately $8,910. So, if you had purchased the note one year earlier, at least on paper, you would have incurred a capital loss equal to $1,090 during 1994. How could the market value of the Treasury note lose so much value in one year? The primary reason the value of this investment, as well as other debt instruments, decreased so significantly was because the Federal Reserve purposely increased interest rates six times during 1994. So at the beginning of 1995, the average return on a Treasury note with a 2001 maturity was 7.81 percent. In a single year, the return demanded by investors in Treasury notes increased about 2.3 percent, and this caused the values of these financial instruments to decrease greatly. Investors who bought the 7-year Treasury notes on January 3, 1994 experienced a loss in value equal to $1,090, but they received interest payments of $550 ($275 each six months); so those investors who sold their Treasury notes on January 3, 1995 lost 5.4 percent ($540) on their original $10,000 investment.

Could investors have fared better in the stock market or in other types of investments? Probably not. On average, the values of stocks decreased by more than 3 percent in 1994; even after considering dividends paid by the companies, the average return earned by investors was poor by any comparison. For the most part, investors were not happy with the performance of their investments in 1994, because values declined in most cases. As we write this text in 1995, it appears the stock market has reversed—the Dow Jones Industrial Average pushed above the 4500 level for the first time in history in June 1995. In addition, interest rates appear to have stablilized, so investors have greater confidence the values of their investments will not decrease significantly during the next year.

Continued

As you read this chapter, think about why the value of the Treasury notes decreased so significantly from January 1994 to January 1995 when interest rates increased 2.3 percent. What happens to the value of financial assets when the returns demanded by investors change? Are bonds and stocks affected the same? Answering these questions will help you to get a basic understanding of how stocks and bonds are valued in the financial markets. Such an understanding will help you make investments decisions, including those that are critical when establishing a retirement plan.

In Chapter 1 we noted that the goal of managerial finance is to maximize the value of firms. Then, in Chapter 5, we saw how investors determine the rates of return they require on securities, and in Chapter 6 we examined time value of money (TVM) analysis. These TVM concepts are used by managers and investors to establish the worth of any asset whose value is derived from future cash flows; such assets include real estate, factories, machinery, oil wells, coal mines, farmland, stocks, and bonds. Now, in this chapter, we use time value of money techniques to explain how investors establish the values of stocks and bonds. The material covered in the chapter obviously is important to investors, and it is equally important to financial managers. Indeed, because all important corporate decisions should be analyzed in terms of how they will affect the price of the firm's stock, it is essential that managers know how stock prices are determined.

Basic Valuation

After learning about the time value of money, you should realize that the *value* of anything, whether it is a financial asset like a stock or a bond or it is a real asset like a building or a piece of machinery, *is based on the present value of the cash flows the asset is expected to produce in the future.* On a cash flow time line, value can be depicted as follows:

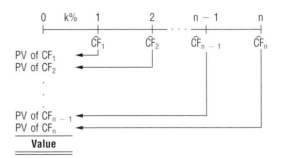

Therefore, the value of any asset can be expressed in general form as:

$$7\text{-}1 \quad \begin{matrix} \text{Asset} \\ \text{value} \end{matrix} = V = \frac{\hat{CF}_1}{(1 + k)^1} + \frac{\hat{CF}_2}{(1 + k)^2} + \cdots + \frac{\hat{CF}_n}{(1 + k)^n} = \sum_{t=1}^{n} \frac{\hat{CF}_t}{(1 + k)^t}$$

Here

$\widehat{CF}_t$ = the cash flow expected to be generated by the asset in period t

k = the return investors consider appropriate for holding such an asset. This return usually is termed the *required return,* and, as we saw in Chapter 5, it is based on both economic conditions and the riskiness of the asset.

According to Equation 7-1, the value of an asset is affected by the cash flows it is expected to generate, $\widehat{CF}$, and the return required by investors, k. As you can see, *the higher the expected cash flows, the greater the asset's value; also, the lower the required return, the greater the asset's value.* In the remainder of this chapter, we discuss how this general valuation concept can be applied to determine the value of a bond (debt) and a stock (equity).

Bond Valuation

Corporations raise capital in two forms—debt and equity. Our first task in this chapter is to examine the valuation process for bonds, the principal type of long-term debt.

BOND
A long-term debt instrument.

A **bond** is a long-term promissory note issued by a business or governmental unit. For example, suppose on January 2, 1996, Unilate Textiles borrowed $25 million by selling 25,000 individual bonds for $1,000 each. Unilate received the $25 million, and it promised to pay the bondholders annual interest and to repay the $25 million on a specified date. The lenders were willing to give Unilate $25 million, so the value of the bond issue was $25 million. But how did the investors decide that the issue was worth $25 million? As a first step in explaining how the values of this and other bonds are determined, we need to define some terms:

PAR VALUE
The face value of a stock or bond.

1. **Par value.** The **par value** is the stated face value of the bond; it usually is set at $1,000, although multiples of $1,000 (for example, $5,000) often are used. The par value generally represents the amount of money the firm borrows and promises to repay at some future date.

COUPON PAYMENT
The specified number of dollars of interest paid each period, generally each six months, on a bond.

COUPON INTEREST RATE
The stated annual rate of interest on a bond.

2. **Coupon interest rate.** The bond requires the issuer to pay a specified number of dollars of interest each year (or, more typically, each six months). When this **coupon payment,** as it is called, is divided by the par value, the result is the **coupon interest rate.** For example, Unilate's bonds have a $1,000 par value, and they pay $150 in interest each year. The bond's coupon interest is $150, so its coupon interest rate is $150 \div $1,000 = 15 percent. The $150 is the yearly "rent" on the $1,000 loan. This payment, which is fixed at the time the bond is issued, remains in force, by contract, during the life of the bond.[1]

---

[1]The term *coupon payment* comes from the fact that some time ago, most bonds literally had a number of small ($\frac{1}{2}$-by-2-inch) dated coupons attached to them, and on the interest payment date, the owner would clip off the coupon for that date and either cash it at his or her bank or mail it to the company's paying agent, who then mailed back a check for the interest. A 30-year, semiannual bond would start with 60 coupons, whereas a 5-year annual payment bond would start with only 5 coupons. Today most bonds are registered—no physical coupons are involved, and interest checks are mailed automatically to the registered owners of the bonds. Even so, people continue to use the terms *coupon* and *coupon interest rate* when discussing registered bonds.

MATURITY DATE

A specified date on which the par value of a bond must be repaid.

ORIGINAL MATURITY

The number of years to maturity at the time a bond is issued.

CALL PROVISION

A provision in a bond contract that gives the issuer the right to "recall" the bond and pay it off under specified terms prior to the stated maturity date.

3. **Maturity date.** Bonds generally have a specified **maturity date** on which the par value must be repaid. Unilate's bonds, which were issued on January 2, 1996, will mature on January 1, 2011; thus, they had a 15-year maturity at the time they were issued. Most bonds have **original maturities** (the maturity at the time the bond is issued) of from 10 to 40 years, but any maturity is legally permissible. Of course, the effective maturity of a bond declines each year after it has been issued. Thus, Unilate's bonds had a 15-year original maturity, but in 1997 they will have a 14-year maturity, and so on.

4. **Call provisions.** Often, bonds have a provision whereby the issuer can pay them off prior to maturity by "calling them in" from the investors. This feature is known as a **call provision.** If a bond is callable, and if interest rates in the economy decline, then the company can sell a new issue of low-interest-rate bonds and use the proceeds to retire the old, high-interest-rate issue, just as a homeowner can refinance a home mortgage.

5. **New issues versus outstanding bonds.** As we shall see, a bond's market price is determined primarily by the cash flows it generates, or the interest it pays, which depends on the coupon interest rate—the higher the coupon, other things held constant, the higher the market price of the bond. At the time a bond is issued, the coupon generally is set at a level that will cause the market price of the bond to equal its par value. If a lower coupon were set, investors simply would not be willing to pay $1,000 for the bond, while if a higher coupon were set, investors would clamor for the bond and bid its price up above $1,000. Investment bankers can judge quite precisely the coupon rate that will cause a bond to sell at its $1,000 par value.

A bond that has just been issued is known as a *new issue. (The Wall Street Journal* classifies a bond as a new issue for about one month after it has first been issued.) Once the bond has been in the market for a while, it is classified as an *outstanding bond,* also called a *seasoned issue.* Newly issued bonds generally sell very close to par, but the prices of outstanding bonds vary widely from par. Coupon interest payments are constant, so when economic conditions change, a bond with a $150 coupon that sold at par when it was issued will sell for more or less than $1,000 thereafter.

The Basic Bond Valuation Model[2]

Equation 7-1 shows that the value of a financial asset is based on the cash flows expected to be generated by the asset in the future. In the case of a bond, the cash flows consist of interest payments during the life of the bond plus a return of the principal amount borrowed, generally the par value, when the bond matures. In a cash flow time line format, here is the situation:

---

[2]In finance, the term *model* refers to an equation or set of equations designed to show how one or more variables affect some other variable. Thus, a bond valuation model shows the mathematical relationship between a bond's price and the set of variables that determine the price.

Here

kd = the appropriate interest rate on the bond (kd = 15% for Unilate's bond). We used the term i or I to designate the interest rate in Chapter 6 because those terms are used on financial calculators, but k, with the subscript d to designate the rate on a debt security, is normally used in finance.[3]

N = the number of years before the bond matures (N = 15 for Unilate's bond). Note that N declines each year after the bond has been issued, so a bond that had a maturity of 15 years when it was issued (original maturity = 15) will have N = 14 after one year, N = 13 after two years, and so on. Note also that at this point we assume that the bond pays interest once a year, or annually, so N is measured in years. Later on, we will deal with semiannual payment bonds, which pay interest each six months.[4]

INT = dollars of interest paid each year = Coupon rate × Par value = INT = 0.15($1,000) = $150. In calculator terminology, INT = PMT = 150.

M = the par, or face, value of the bond (M = $1,000). This amount must be paid off at maturity.

We can now redraw the cash flow time line to show the numerical values for all variables except the bond's current value:

```
     0    15%    1          2          14         15
     ├──────────┼──────────┼── ··· ──┼──────────┤
   Value        150        150        150        150
                                                1,000
                                                ─────
                                                1,150
```

Now the following general equation can be solved to find the value of any bond:

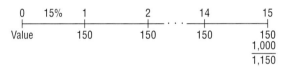

$$7\text{-}2 \qquad \begin{aligned} \frac{\text{Bond}}{\text{value}} = V_d &= \frac{\text{INT}}{(1 + k_d)^1} + \frac{\text{INT}}{(1 + k_d)^2} + \cdots + \frac{\text{INT}}{(1 + k_d)^N} + \frac{M}{(1 + k_d)^N} \\ &= \sum_{t=1}^{N} \frac{\text{INT}}{(1 + k_d)^t} + \frac{M}{(1 + k_d)^N} \end{aligned}$$

Notice the interest payments represent an annuity, and repayment of the par value at maturity represents a single, or lump sum, payment. Thus, Equation 7-2 can be rewritten for use with the tables:

---

[3]The appropriate interest rate on debt securities was discussed in Chapter 2. The bond's riskiness, liquidity, and years to maturity, as well as supply and demand conditions in the capital markets, all influence the interest rate on bonds.

[4]We should note that some bonds that have been issued either pay no interest during their lives (*zero coupon bonds*) or else pay very low coupon rates. Such bonds are sold at a discount below par, and hence they are called *original issue discount bonds*. The "interest" earned on a zero coupon bond comes at the end when the company pays off at par ($1,000) a bond which was purchased for, say, $321.97. The discount of $1,000 − $321.97 = $678.03 substitutes for interest.

7-2a

$$V_d = INT(PVIFA_{k_d, N}) + M(PVIF_{k_d, N})$$

Inserting values for our particular bond, we have

$$V_d = \sum_{t=1}^{15} \frac{\$150}{(1.15)^t} + \frac{\$1,000}{(1.15)^{15}}$$

$$= \$150(PVIFA_{15\%, 15}) + \$1,000(PVIF_{15\%, 15})$$

The value of the bond can be computed by using the three procedures discussed in Chapter 6: (1) numerically, (2) using the tables, and (3) with a financial calculator.

NUMERICAL SOLUTION:

Simply discount each cash flow back to the present and sum these PVs to find the value of the bond; see Figure 7-1 for an example. This procedure is not very efficient, especially if the bond has many years to maturity. So, alternatively, we can use the equations presented in Chapter 6 to find the solution:

$$V_d = \$150 \left[\frac{1 - \frac{1}{(1.15)^{15}}}{0.15} \right] + \$1,000 \left(\frac{1}{1.15} \right)^{15}$$

$$= \$150(5.8474) + \$1,000(0.12289)$$

$$= \$877.11 + \$122.89 = \$1,000$$

FIGURE 7-1

Time Line for Unilate Textiles' Bonds, 15% Interest Rate

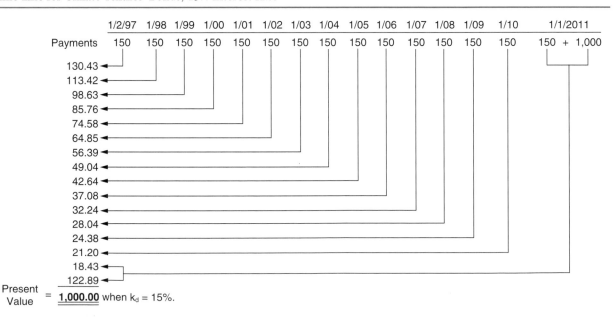

TABULAR SOLUTION:

Look up the appropriate PVIF and PVIFA values in Tables A-1 and A-2 at the end of the book, insert them into the equation, and complete the arithmetic:

$$V_d = \$150(5.8474) + \$1,000(0.1229)$$

$$- \$877.11 + \$122.90 = \$1,000.01 \approx \$1,000$$

There is a one-cent rounding error, which results from the fact that the tables only go to four decimal places.

FINANCIAL CALCULATOR SOLUTION:

In Chapter 6 we worked problems where only four of the five time value of money (TVM) keys were used, but all five keys are used with bond problems. Here is the setup:

Inputs:	15	15	?	150	1000
	N	**I**	**PV**	**PMT**	**FV**
Output:			= −1,000		

Input N = 15, k_d = I = 15, INT = PMT = 150, M = FV = 1000, and then press the PV key to find the value of the bond, $1,000. Because the PV is an outflow to the investor, it is shown with a negative sign.

Changes in Bond Values over Time

If k_d remained constant at 15 percent, what would be the value of the bond one year after it was issued? We can find this value using Equation 7-2 and the tables, but now the term to maturity is only 14 years, so N = 14. We see that V_d remains constant at $1,000:

$$V_d = \$150(5.7245) + \$1,000(0.1413) = \$999.98 \approx \$1,000.$$

With a financial calculator, just override N = 15 with N = 14, press the PV key, and you will get the same answer. The value of the bond will remain at $1,000 as long as the appropriate interest rate, k_d, remains constant at 15 percent, and k_d equals the coupon interest rate. In other words, *if the market rate associated with a bond, k_d, equals the coupon rate of interest, the bond will sell at its par value.*[5]

---

[5]The bond prices quoted by brokers are calculated as described. However, if you bought a bond between interest payment dates, you would have to pay the basic price plus accrued interest. Thus, if you purchased a Unilate bond 6 months after it was issued, your broker would send you an invoice stating that you must pay $1,000 as the basic price of the bond plus $75 interest, representing one-half the annual interest of $150. The seller of the bond would receive $1,075. If you bought the bond the day before its interest payment date, you would pay $1,000 + (364/365)($150) = $1,149.59. Of course, you would receive an interest payment of $150 at the end of the next day.

Throughout the chapter we assume that the bond is being evaluated immediately after an interest payment date. The more expensive financial calculators have a built-in calendar that permits the calculation of exact values between interest payment dates.

Now suppose interest rates in the economy fell after the Unilate bonds were issued, and, as a result, k_d fell *below the coupon rate,* decreasing from 15 to 10 percent. *Both the coupon interest payments and the maturity value remain constant,* but now the PVIF and PVIFA values used in Equation 7-2 would have to be based on a k_d equal to 10 percent. The value of the bond at the end of the first year (so N = 14) would be $1,368.31:

$$V_d = \$150(\text{PVIFA}_{10\%,14}) + \$1,000(\text{PVIF}_{10\%,14})$$

$$= \$150(7.3667) + \$1,000(0.2633)$$

$$= \$1,105.01 + \$263.30 = \$1,368.31$$

Thus, if k_d fell *below* the coupon rate, the bond would sell above par, or at a *premium.* With a financial calculator, just change k_d = I from 15 to 10, and then press the PV key to get the answer, $1,368.33. (The calculator solution and the tabular solution differ due to rounding.)

The arithmetic of the bond value increase should be clear, but what is the logic behind it? The fact that k_d has fallen to 10 percent means that if you had $1,000 to invest, you could buy new bonds like Unilate's (every day some 10 to 12 companies sell new bonds), except that these new bonds would pay $100 of interest each year rather than $150. Naturally, you would prefer $150 to $100, so you would be willing to pay more than $1,000 for Unilate's bonds to obtain its higher coupons. All investors would recognize this, and, as a result, the Unilate bonds would be bid up in price to $1,368.31, at which point they would provide the same rate of return to a potential investor as the new bonds—10 percent.

Assuming that interest rates remain constant at 10 percent for the next 14 years, what would happen to the value of Unilate's bond? It would fall gradually from $1,368.31 at present to $1,000 at maturity, when Unilate will redeem each bond for $1,000. This point can be illustrated by calculating the value of the bond 1 year later, when it has 13 years remaining to maturity. With a financial calculator, merely input the values for N, I, PMT, and FV, now using N = 13, and press the PV key to find the value of the bond, $1,355.17. Using the tables, we have

$$V_d = \$150(\text{PVIFA}_{10\%,13}) + \$1,000(\text{PVIF}_{10\%,13})$$

$$= \$150(7.1034) + \$1,000(0.2897) = \$1,355.21 \text{ (rounding difference)}$$

Thus, the value of the bond will have fallen from $1,368.31 to $1,355.21, or by $13.10. If you were to calculate the value of the bond at other future dates, the price would continue to fall as the maturity date is approached.

Notice that if you purchased the bond at a price of $1,368.31 and then sold it 1 year later with k_d still at 10 percent, you would have a capital loss of $13.10, or a total return of $150.00 − $13.10 = $136.90. Your percentage rate of return would consist of an *interest yield* (also called a *current yield*) plus a *capital gains yield,* calculated as follows:

$$\text{Interest, or current, yield} = \quad \$150/\$1,368.31 = \quad 0.1096 = \quad 10.96\%$$

$$\text{Capital gains yield} = -\$13.10/\$1,368.31 = -0.0096 = \underline{-0.96\%}$$

$$\text{Total rate of return, or yield} = \$136.90/\$1,368.31 = \quad 0.1001 \approx \underline{\underline{10.00\%}}$$

Had interest rates risen from 15 to 20 percent during the first year after issue rather than fallen, the value of the bond would have declined to $769.49:

$$V_d = \$150(\text{PVIFA}_{20\%,14}) + \$1,000(\text{PVIF}_{20\%,14})$$

$$= \$150(4.6106) + \$1,000(0.0779)$$

$$= \$691.59 + \$77.90 = \$769.49$$

In this case, the bond would sell at a *discount* of $230.51 below its par value:

$$\text{Discount} = \text{Price} - \text{Par value} = \$769.49 - \$1,000.00$$

$$= -\$230.51$$

CURRENT YIELD
The annual interest payment on a bond divided by its current market value.

The total expected future yield on the bond would again consist of a **current yield** and a capital gains yield, but now the capital gains yield would be positive. The total yield would be 20 percent. To see this, calculate the price of the bond with 13 years left to maturity, assuming that interest rates remain at 20 percent. With a calculator, enter N = 13, I = 20, PMT = 150, and FV = 1000, and then press PV to obtain the bond's value, $773.37. Using the tables, proceed as follows:

$$V_d = \$150\,(\text{PVIFA}_{20\%,13}) + \$1,000(\text{PVIF}_{20\%,13})$$

$$= \$150(4.5327) + \$1,000(0.0935)$$

$$= \$679.91 + \$93.50 = \$773.41 \text{ (rounding)}$$

Notice that the capital gain for the year is the difference between the bond's value in Year 13 and the bond's value in Year 14, or $773.41 - $769.49 = $3.92. The interest yield, capital gains yield, and total yield are calculated as follows:

$$
\begin{aligned}
\text{Interest, or current, yield} &= \ \ \$150/\$769.49 = 0.1949 = 19.49\% \\
\text{Capital gains yield} &= \ \ \$3.92/\$769.49 = 0.0051 = \ \ \underline{0.51\%} \\
\text{Total rate of return, or yield} &= \$153.92/\$769.49 = 0.2000 = \underline{\underline{20.00\%}}
\end{aligned}
$$

Figure 7-2 graphs the value of the bond over time, assuming that interest rates in the economy (1) remain constant at 15 percent, (2) fall to 10 percent and then remain constant at that level, or (3) rise to 20 percent and remain constant at that level. Of course, if interest rates do not remain constant, then the price of the bond will fluctuate. However, *regardless of what future interest rates do, the bond's price will approach $1,000 as it nears the maturity date* (barring bankruptcy, in which case the bond's value might drop to zero).

Figure 7-2 illustrates the following key points:

1. Whenever the going rate of interest, k_d, is equal to the coupon rate, a bond will sell at its par value. Normally, the coupon rate is set equal to the going interest rate when a bond is issued, so it sells at par initially.

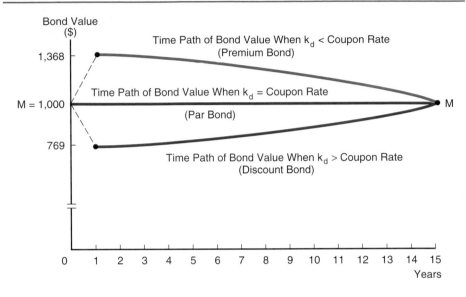

FIGURE 7-2

Time Path of the Value of a 15% Coupon, $1,000 Par Value Bond When Interest Rates Are 10%, 15%, and 20%

Year	$k_d = 10\%$	$k_d = 15\%$	$k_d = 20\%$
0	—	$1,000	—
1	$1,368.31	1,000	$ 769.49
.	.	.	.
.	.	.	.
.	.	.	.
15	1,000.00	1,000	1,000.00

NOTE: The curves for 10% and 20% have a slight bow.

DISCOUNT BOND
A bond that sells below its par value; occurs whenever the going rate of interest rises above the coupon rate.

PREMIUM BOND
A bond that sells above its par value; occurs whenever the going rate of interest falls below the coupon rate.

2. Interest rates do change over time, but the coupon rate remains fixed after the bond has been issued. Whenever the going rate of interest is *greater* than the coupon rate, a bond's price will fall *below* its par value. Such a bond sells at a discount from its face value, so it is called a **discount bond.**

3. Whenever the going rate of interest is *less* than the coupon rate, a bond's price will rise *above* its par value. Such a bond sells at a premium compared to this face value, so it is called a **premium bond.**

4. Thus, an *increase* in interest rates will cause the price of an outstanding bond to *fall,* whereas a *decrease* in rates will cause it to *rise.*

5. The market value of a bond always will approach its par value as its maturity date approaches, provided the firm does not go bankrupt.

These points are very important, because they show that bondholders can suffer capital losses or make capital gains, depending on whether interest rates rise or fall after the bond is purchased. And, as we saw in Chapter 2, interest rates do indeed change over time.

Finding the Interest Rate on a Bond: Yield to Maturity

YIELD TO MATURITY (YTM)
The average rate of return earned on a bond if it is held to maturity.

Suppose you were offered a 14-year, 15 percent coupon, $1,000 par value bond at a price of $1,368.31. What rate of interest would you earn on your investment if you bought the bond and held it to maturity? This rate is called the bond's **yield to maturity (YTM),** and it is the interest rate discussed by bond traders when they talk about rates of return. To find the yield to maturity, you could solve Equation 7-2 or 7-2a for k_d:

$$V_d = \$1,368.31 = \frac{\$150}{(1 + k_d)^1} + \cdots + \frac{\$150}{(1 + k_d)^{14}} + \frac{\$1,000}{(1 + k_d)^{14}}$$

$$= \$150(\text{PVIFA}_{k_d,14}) + \$1,000(\text{PVIF}_{k_d,14})$$

If you have a financial calculator, you would enter N = 14, PMT = 150, FV = 1000, and PV = −1368.31, and then press the I key. The calculator will blink for a few seconds, and then the answer, 10 percent, will appear.

If you do not have a financial calculator, you can substitute values for PVIFA and PVIF until you find a pair that "works" so that the present value of the interest payments combined with the present value of the repayment of the face value at maturity equals the current price of the bond. But what would be a good interest rate to use as a starting point? First, you know that the bond is selling at a premium over its par value ($1,368.31 versus $1,000), so the bond's yield to maturity must be below its 15 percent coupon rate. Therefore, you might start by trying rates below 15 percent. It could take you a while to "zero in" on the appropriate rate. It probably would be better to get an estimate of the rate by computing the *approximate* yield to maturity, which can be found with the following equation:[6]

7-3

$$\frac{\text{Approximate}}{\text{yield to maturity}} = \frac{\overset{\text{Annual}}{\text{interest}} + \overset{\text{Accrued}}{\text{capital gains}}}{\text{Average value of bond}}$$

$$= \frac{\text{INT} + \left(\dfrac{M - V_d}{N}\right)}{\left[\dfrac{2(V_d) + M}{3}\right]}$$

Equation 7-3 is based on computations of approximate yields in the past and it does not consider the time value of money, so it should be used only to approximate a bond's yield to maturity. For the bond we are examining, the approximate yield to maturity is

---

[6]The form of Equation 7-3, which gives a "good" approximation for a bond's yield to maturity, is based on the work of Gabriel A. Hawawini and Ashok Vora, "Yield Approximations: A Historical Perspective," *Journal of Finance* (March 1982): 145–156.

$$\text{Yield to maturity} = k_d \approx \frac{\$150 + \left(\frac{\$1,000 - \$1,368.31}{14}\right)}{\left[\frac{2(\$1,368.31) + \$1,000}{3}\right]}$$

$$\approx \frac{\$150 + (-\$26.31)}{\$1,245.54} = .0993 \approx 10\%$$

Inserting interest factors for 10 percent, you obtain

$$V_d = \$150(7.3667) + \$1,000(0.2633)$$

$$= \$1,105.01 + \$263.30 = \$1,368.31$$

This calculated value is equal to the market price of the bond, so 10 percent is the bond's actual yield to maturity: $k_d = \text{YTM} = 10.0\%$.[7]

The yield to maturity is identical to the total annual rate of return discussed in the preceding section. The YTM for a bond that sells at par consists entirely of an interest yield, but if the bond sells at a price other than its par value, the YTM consists of the interest yield plus a positive or negative capital gains yield. Note also that a bond's yield to maturity changes whenever interest rates in the economy change, and this is almost daily. One who purchases a bond and holds it until it matures will receive the YTM that existed on the purchase date, but the bond's calculated YTM will change frequently between the purchase date and the maturity date.[8]

Bond Values with Semiannual Compounding

Although some bonds pay interest annually, most actually pay interest semiannually. To evaluate semiannual payment bonds, we must modify the valuation equa-

---

[7]A few years ago, bond traders all had specialized tables called *bond tables* that gave yields on bonds of different maturities selling at different premiums and discounts. Because calculators are so much more efficient (and accurate), bond tables are rarely used any more.

[8]Bonds that contain call provisions (callable bonds) often are called by the firm prior to maturity. In cases where a bond issue is called, investors do not have the opportunity to earn the yield to maturity (YTM) because the bond issue is retired before the maturity date arrives. Thus, for callable bonds, we often compute the *yield to call*, rather than the yield to maturity. The computation for the yield to call is the same as for the yield to maturity, except the *call price* of the bond is substituted for the maturity (par) value, and the number of years until the bond can be called is substituted for the years to maturity. So to calculate the yield to call we modify Equation 7-2, and solve the following equation for k_d:

$$\text{Price of bond} = \sum_{t=1}^{N_C} \frac{\text{INT}}{(1 + k_d)^t} + \frac{\text{Call price}}{(1 + k_d)^{N_C}}$$

Here N_C is the number of years until the company can call the bond; Call price is the price the company must pay in order to call the bond (it often is set equal to the par value plus one year's interest); and k_d is the yield to call (YTC). To solve for the YTC, proceed just like the solution for the yield to maturity (YTM) of a bond. For example, suppose Unilate's 15 percent coupon bonds, which have a current price of $1,368.31, are callable in 9 years at $1,150. The set up for computing the YTC is:

$$\$1,368.31 = \frac{\$150}{(1 + k_d)^1} + \frac{\$150}{(1 + k_d)^2} + \cdots + \frac{\$150}{(1 + k_d)^9} + \frac{\$1,150}{(1 + k_d)^9}$$

Using your calculator, you would find the solution for the yield to call is 9.78 percent.

tion the same as we did in Chapter 6 to take into consideration interest compounding can occur more than once a year. So, Equations 7-2 and 7-2a become

$$V_d = \sum_{t=1}^{2N} \frac{\frac{INT}{2}}{\left(1 + \frac{k_d}{2}\right)} + \frac{M}{\left(1 + \frac{k_d}{2}\right)}$$

$$= \frac{INT}{2}\left(PVIFA_{\frac{k_d}{2}, 2N}\right) + M\left(PVIF_{\frac{k_d}{2}, 2N}\right)$$

To illustrate, assume now that Unilate Textiles' bonds pay $75 interest each 6 months rather than $150 at the end of each year. Thus, each interest payment is only half as large, but there are twice as many of them. When the going (simple) rate of interest is 10 percent with semiannual compounding, the value of this 15-year bond is found as follows:[9]

$$V_d = \$75 \, (PVIFA_{5\%,30}) + \$1,000(PVIF_{5\%,30})$$

$$= \$75(15.3725) + \$1,000(0.2314)$$

$$= \$1,152.94 + \$231.40 = \$1,384.34$$

With a financial calculator, enter N = 30, k = I = 5, PMT = 75, FV = 1000, and then press the PV key to obtain the bond's value, $1,384.31 (rounding difference). The value with semiannual interest payments is slightly larger than $1,380.32, the value when interest is paid annually. This higher value occurs because interest payments are received, and therefore can be reinvested, somewhat faster under semiannual compounding.

Students sometimes want to discount the *maturity (par) value* at 10 percent over 15 years rather than at 5 percent over 30 six-month periods. This is incorrect. Logically, all cash flows in a given contract must be discounted at the same periodic rate, the 5 percent semiannual rate in this instance, because this is the opportunity rate for the investor. For consistency, bond traders must use the same discount rate for all cash flows, including the cash flow at maturity, and they do.

Interest Rate Risk on a Bond

As we saw in Chapter 2, interest rates go up and down over time. Further, changes in interest rates affect the bondholders in two ways: (1) An increase in interest rates leads to a decline in the values of outstanding bonds. Because interest rates

---

[9]We also are assuming a change in the effective annual interest rate, from 10 percent to

$$EAR = (1.05)^2 - 1 = 1.1025 - 1.0 = 0.1025 = 10.25\%$$

Most bonds pay interest semiannually, and the rates quoted are on a semiannual basis. Therefore, effective annual rates for most bonds are somewhat higher than the quoted rates, which, in effect, represent the APRs for the bonds.

INTEREST RATE PRICE RISK
The risk of changes in bond prices to which investors are exposed due to changing interest rates.

INTEREST RATE REINVESTMENT RATE RISK
The risk that income from a bond portfolio will vary because cash flows have to be reinvested at current market rates.

can rise, bondholders face the risk of losses in the values of their portfolios. This risk is called **interest rate price risk.** (2) Many bondholders (including such institutional bondholders as pension funds and life insurance companies) buy bonds to build funds for some future use. These bondholders reinvest the cash flows (interest payments plus repayment of principal when the bonds mature or are called). If interest rates decline, the bondholders will earn a lower rate of return on reinvested cash flows, and this will reduce the future value of their portfolios relative to the values they would have had if interest rates had not fallen. This is called **interest rate reinvestment rate risk.**

We see, then, that any given change in interest rates has two separate effects on bondholders—it changes the current values of their portfolios (price risk), and it also changes the rates of return at which the cash flows from their portfolios can be reinvested (reinvestment rate risk). Note that these two risks tend to offset one another. For example, an increase in interest rates will lower the current value of a bond portfolio, but because the future cash flows produced by the portfolio will then be reinvested at a higher rate of return, the future value of the portfolio will be increased. In this section we will look at just how these two effects operate to affect bondholders' positions.[10]

Suppose you bought some 15 percent Unilate bonds at a price of $1,000, and interest rates subsequently rose to 20 percent by the end of the first year. As we saw before, the price of the bonds would fall to $769.49, so you would have a loss of $230.51 per bond.[11] Interest rates can and do rise, and rising rates cause a loss of value for bondholders. Thus, people or firms who invest in bonds are exposed to risk from changing interest rates, which is called *interest rate price risk.*

One's exposure to interest rate price risk is higher on bonds with long maturities than on those maturing in the near future. This point can be demonstrated by showing how the value of a 1-year bond with a 15 percent coupon fluctuates with changes in k_d and then comparing these changes with those on a 14-year bond as calculated previously. The values for a 1-year bond and a 14-year bond at several different market interest rates, k_d, are shown in Figure 7-3. The values for the bonds were computed assuming the coupon interest payments for the bonds occur annually. Notice how much more sensitive the price of the long-term bond is to changes in interest rates. At a 15 percent interest rate, both the long- and the short-term bonds are valued at $1,000. When rates rise to 20 percent, the long-term bond falls to $769.47, but the short-term bond falls only to $958.33.

For bonds with similar coupons, this differential sensitivity to changes in interest rates always holds true—the longer the maturity of the bond, the greater its price changes in response to a given change in interest rates. Thus, even if the risk of default on two bonds is exactly the same, the one with the

---

[10]Actually, we will stop far short of a full examination of the effects of interest rate changes on bondholders' positions, as such an examination would go well beyond the scope of the text. We can note, though, that a concept called "duration" has been developed to help fixed income investors deal with changing interest rates, and, with a properly structured portfolio (one that has the proper duration), most of the risks of changing interest rates can be eliminated because price risk and reinvestment rate risk can be made to exactly offset one another.

[11]You would have an *accounting* (and tax) loss only if you sold the bond; if you held it to maturity, you would not have such a loss. However, even if you did not sell, you would still have suffered a *real economic loss in an opportunity cost sense* because you would have lost the opportunity to invest at 20 percent and would be stuck with a 15 percent bond in a 20 percent market. Thus, in an economic sense "paper losses" are just as bad as realized accounting losses.

FIGURE 7-3

FIGURE 7-3

Value of Long- and Short-Term 15% Annual Coupon Rate Bonds at Different Market Interest Rates

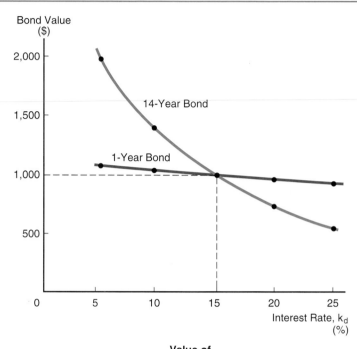

Current Market Interest Rate, k_d	Value of 1-Year Bond	Value of 14-Year Bond
5%	$1,095.24	$1,989.86
10	1,045.45	1,368.33
15	1,000.00	1,000.00
20	958.33	769.47
25	920.00	617.59

NOTE: Bond values were calculated using a financial calculator.

longer maturity typically is exposed to more price risk from a change in interest rates.[12]

The logical explanation for this difference in interest rate price risk is simple. Suppose you bought a 14-year bond that yielded 15 percent, or $150 a year. Now suppose interest rates on comparable-risk bonds rose to 20 percent. You would be stuck with only $150 of interest for the next 14 years. On the other hand, had you bought a 1-year bond, you would have had a low return for only 1 year. At the end of the year, you would get your $1,000 back, and you could then reinvest

[12]If a 10-year bond were plotted in Figure 7-3, its curve would lie between those of the 14-year bond and the 1-year bond. The curve of a 1-month bond would be almost horizontal, indicating that its price would change very little in response to an interest rate change, but a perpetuity would have a very steep slope.

it and receive 20 percent, or $200 per year, for the next 13 years. Thus, interest rate price risk reflects the length of time one is committed to a given investment.

Although a 1-year bond has less interest rate price risk than a 14-year bond, the 1-year bond exposes the buyer to more interest rate reinvestment rate risk. Suppose you bought a 1-year bond that yielded 15 percent, and then interest rates on comparable-risk bonds fell to 10 percent. After 1 year, when you got your $1,000 back, you would be able to invest it at only 10 percent, so you would lose $150 − $100 = $50 in annual interest. Had you bought the 14-year bond, you would have continued to receive $150 in annual interest payments even if rates fell. If you reinvested those coupon payments, you would have to accept a lower rate of return, but you would still be much better off than if you had been holding the 1-year bond.

Bond Prices in Recent Years

We know from Chapter 2 that interest rates fluctuate, and we have just seen that the prices of outstanding bonds rise and fall inversely with changes in interest rates. Figure 7-4 shows what has happened to the price of a typical bond, Florida Power & Light's 7⅜ percent, 30-year bond that matures in 2002. The bond prices given on the graph are the prices for the last trading day of each year; for example, on December 30, 1994, the bond sold for $945. Some of the yields associated with the bond also are reported on the graph to give you an indication of the changes in interest rates that caused the bond price changes from 1978–1994.

When FPL first issued this bond in 1972, it was worth $1,000, but in 1981 when corporate bond rates hovered around 16 percent, it sold for only $488, a significant discount from its par value. As interest rates decreased from the extraordinarily high levels of the early 1980s, the price of FPL's bond rose, and in 1993 it was selling at a premium for $1,021. By the end of 1994 (beginning of 1995), the bond again was selling for a discount, at $945. As the graph shows, if the interest rates stay at the 1994 level of 8.4 percent for the remaining 8 years of the bond's life (1995-2002), the price of the bond will gradually increase to its maturity value of $1,000 just before it matures in 2002.

Self-Test Questions

In what two primary forms do corporations raise capital?

What is meant by the terms "new issue" and "seasoned issue"?

Explain, verbally, the following equation:

$$V_d = \sum_{t=1}^{N} \frac{INT}{(1 + k_d)^t} + \frac{M}{(1 + k_d)^N}$$

Explain what happens to the price of a bond if (1) interest rates rise above the bond's coupon rate or (2) interest rates fall below the bond's coupon rate.

Write out a formula that can be used to calculate the discount or premium on a bond, and explain it.

Differentiate between interest rate price risk and reinvestment rate risk.

FIGURE 7-4

Florida Power & Light 7⅜%, 30-Year Bond: Market Value (Yield to Maturity) from 1978–1994

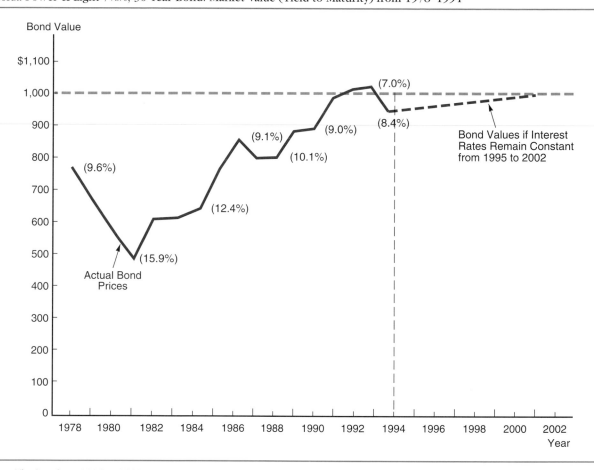

NOTE: The line from 1995 to 2002 appears linear, but it actually has a slight curve.

How is the bond valuation formula shown above changed to deal with bonds that have semiannual coupons rather than annual coupons?

Preferred Stock Valuation

Preferred stock is a hybrid—it is similar to bonds in some respects and to common stock in other respects. Preferred dividends are similar to interest payments on bonds in that they are fixed in amount and generally must be paid before common stock dividends can be paid. However, like common dividends, preferred dividends can be omitted without bankrupting the firm, and many preferred issues have no specific maturity date.

Most preferred stocks entitle their owners to regular, fixed dividend payments. If the payments last forever, the issue is a *perpetuity* whose value, V_{ps}, is found as follows:

7-4

$$V_{ps} = \frac{D_{ps}}{k_{ps}}$$

V_{ps} is the value of the preferred stock, D_{ps} is the preferred dividend, and k_{ps} is the required rate of return associated with the preferred stock. Unilate Textiles currently has no preferred stock, but it is considering raising funds with a preferred stock issue that will pay a dividend of $10 per year. If the required rate of return on this preferred stock is 10 percent, its value should be $100, found by solving Equation 7-4 as follows:

$$V_{ps} = \frac{\$10.00}{0.10} = \$100.00$$

If we know the current price of a preferred stock and its dividend, we can solve for the current rate being earned, as follows:

7-4a

$$k_{ps} = \frac{D_{ps}}{V_{ps}}$$

k_{ps} is similar to the yield to maturity of a bond, but the maturity date is infinity, ∞.

Self-Test Question

In what way is preferred stock similar to bonds, and in what respect is it similar to common stock?

Common Stock Valuation

Common stock represents an ownership interest in a corporation, but to the typical investor, a share of common stock is simply a piece of paper characterized by two features:

1. It entitles its owner to dividends, but only if the company has earnings out of which dividends can be paid and only if management chooses to pay dividends rather than to retain and reinvest all the earnings. Whereas a bond contains a *promise* to pay interest, common stock provides no such promise to pay dividends—if you own a stock, you might *expect* a dividend, but your expectations might not in fact be met. To illustrate, Long Island Lighting Company (LILCO) had paid dividends on its common stock for more than 50 years, and people expected these dividends to continue. However, when the company encountered severe problems a few years ago, it stopped paying dividends. Note, though, that LILCO continued to pay interest on its bonds; if it had not, then it would have been declared bankrupt, and the bondholders could have taken over the company.

2. Stock can be sold at some future date, hopefully at a price greater than the purchase price. If the stock actually is sold at a price above its purchase price, the investor will receive a *capital gain.* Generally, at the time people buy common stocks, they do expect to receive capital gains; otherwise, they would not buy the stocks. However, after the fact, one can end up with capital losses rather than capital gains. LILCO's stock price dropped from $17.50 to $3.75 in one year, so the *expected* capital gains on that stock turned out to be *actual* capital losses in that year.

Definitions of Terms Used in the Stock Valuation Models

Common stocks provide an expected future cash flow stream, and a stock's value is found in the same manner as the values of other financial assets—namely, as the present value of the expected future cash flow stream. The expected cash flows consist of two elements: (1) the dividends expected in each year and (2) the price investors expect to receive when they sell the stock. The expected final stock price includes the return of the original investment plus a capital gain.

We saw in Chapter 1 that managers seek to maximize the values of their firms' stocks. A manager's actions affect both the stream of cash flows to investors and the riskiness of that stream. Therefore, the manager needs to know how alternative actions are likely to affect stock prices, so at this point we develop some models to help show how the value of a share of stock is determined. We begin by defining the following terms:

D_t = dividend the stockholder expects to receive at the end of Year t. D_0 is the most recent dividend, which already has been paid; D_1 is the next dividend expected to be paid, and it will be paid at the end of this year; D_2 is the dividend expected at the end of 2 years; and so forth. D_1 represents the first cash flow a new purchaser of the stock will receive. Note that D_0, the dividend which has just been paid, is known with certainty. However, all future dividends are expected values, so the estimate of D_t might differ among investors.[13]

MARKET PRICE, P_0
The price at which a stock sells in the market.
INTRINSIC VALUE, $\hat{P}_0$
The value of an asset that in the mind of a particular investor is justified by the facts; $\hat{P}_0$ may be different from the asset's current market price.

P_0 = actual **market price** of the stock today.

$\hat{P}_t$ = *expected* price of the stock at the end of each Year t (pronounced "P hat t"). $\hat{P}_0$ is the **intrinsic**, or *theoretical,* **value** of the stock today as seen by the particular investor doing the analysis; $\hat{P}_1$ is the price expected at the end of 1 year; and so on. Note that $\hat{P}_0$ is the intrinsic value of the stock today based on a particular investor's estimate of the stock's expected dividend stream and the riskiness of that stream. Hence, whereas P_0 is fixed and is identical for all investors because it represents the price at which the stock currently can be purchased, $\hat{P}_0$ could differ among investors depending on what they feel the firm actually is worth. The caret, or "hat," is used to indicate that $\hat{P}_t$ is an

---

[13]Stocks generally pay dividends quarterly, so theoretically we should evaluate them on a quarterly basis. However, in stock valuation, most analysts work on an annual basis because the data generally are not precise enough to warrant refinement to a quarterly model. For additional information on the quarterly model, see Charles M. Linke and J. Kenton Zumwalt, "Estimation Biases in Discounted Cash Flow Analysis of Equity Capital Cost in Rate Regulation," *Financial Management* (Autumn 1984): 15–21.

estimated value. $\hat{P}_0$, the individual investor's estimate of the intrinsic value today, could be above or below P_0, the current stock price, but an investor would buy the stock only if his or her estimate of $\hat{P}_0$ were equal to or greater than P_0.

Because there are many investors in the market, there can be many values for $\hat{P}_0$. However, we can think of a group of "average," or "marginal," investors whose actions actually determine the market price. For these marginal investors, P_0 must equal $\hat{P}_0$; otherwise, a disequilibrium would exist, and buying and selling in the market would change P_0 until $P_0 = \hat{P}_0$ for an average investor.

GROWTH RATE, g

The expected rate of change in dividends per share.

g = expected **growth rate** in dividends as predicted by a marginal investor. (If we assume that dividends are expected to grow at a constant rate, g also is equal to the expected rate of growth in the stock's price.) Different investors might use different g's to evaluate a firm's stock, but the market price, P_0, is set on the basis of the g estimated by marginal, or average, investors.

REQUIRED RATE OF RETURN, k_s

The minimum rate of return on a common stock that stockholders consider acceptable.

k_s = minimum acceptable, or **required, rate of return** on the stock, considering both its riskiness and the returns available on other investments. Again, this term generally relates to marginal investors. The determinants of k_s were discussed in detail in Chapter 5.

DIVIDEND YIELD

The expected dividend divided by the current price of a share of stock.

$D_1 \div P_0$ = expected **dividend yield** on the stock during the coming year. If the stock is expected to pay a dividend of $1 during the next 12 months, and if its current price is $10, then the expected dividend yield is $1 \div $10 = 0.10 = 10\%$.

CAPITAL GAINS YIELD

The change in price (capital gain) during a given year divided by the price at the beginning of the year.

$\dfrac{\hat{P}_1 - P_0}{P_0}$ = expected **capital gains yield** on the stock during the coming year. If the stock sells for $10 today, and if it is expected to rise to $10.50 at the end of 1 year, then the expected capital gain is $\hat{P}_1 - P_0 = $10.50 - $10.00 = 0.50, and the expected capital gains yield is $0.50 \div $10 = 0.05 = 5\%$.

EXPECTED RATE OF RETURN, $\hat{k}_s$

The rate of return on a common stock that an individual stockholder expects to receive; equal to the expected dividend yield plus the expected capital gains yield.

$\hat{k}_s$ = **expected rate of return** that an investor who buys the stock actually expects to receive. $\hat{k}_s$ (pronounced "k hat s") could be above or below k_s, but one would buy the stock only if $\hat{k}_s$ were equal to or greater than k_s. $\hat{k}_s$ = expected dividend yield plus expected capital gains yield; in other words,

$$\hat{k}_s = \frac{D_1}{P_0} + \frac{\hat{P}_1 - P_0}{P_0}.$$

In our example, the expected total return = $\hat{k}_s$ = 10\% + 5\% = 15\%.

ACTUAL (REALIZED) RATE OF RETURN, $\bar{k}_s$

The rate of return on a common stock actually received by stockholders. $\bar{k}_s$ may be greater than or less than $\hat{k}_s$ and/or k_s.

$\bar{k}_s$ = **actual,** or **realized,** *after the fact* **rate of return,** pronounced "k bar s." You might expect to obtain a return of $\hat{k}_s$ = 14 percent if you buy IBM stock today, but if the market goes down, you may end up next year with an actual realized return that is much lower, perhaps even negative.

Expected Dividends as the Basis for Stock Values

Remember that according to Equation 7-1 the value of any asset is the present value of the cash flows expected to be generated by the asset in the future. In our

INDUSTRY PRACTICE

Great Expectations! But, What About the Results?

Do investors value stocks based on the cash flows they expect to receive from owning stocks? To answer this question, consider what happens to stocks' values when companies report earnings that are less than expected—stock values generally fall. Although earnings are not fully representative of the cash flows generated by firms, because dividends are paid from earnings, investors rely on earnings forecasts to form their expectations of future dividend payments. Sports & Recreation, Inc., a Tampa-based sporting goods retailer, recently discovered how earnings expectations, earnings results and stock value are related. On March 13, 1995, Sports & Recreation announced that its 1994 fourth quarter earnings were $6.7 million, or 33¢ per share, a 20 percent increase from the $5.58 million (31¢ per share) reported in the same quarter of 1993; quarterly sales of more than $129 million were up 46 percent from the previous year. Other firms could only dream of achieving the same success. Unfortunately, Sports & Recreation, which first sold stock publicly in 1992, saw the price of its stock drop by nearly 42 percent, from $18.50 to a new 52-week low of $10.75, the day after its fourth quarter earnings announcement was made. The primary reason for the $7.75 decrease in value was because investors had expected earnings per share to be 43¢ (totalling about $7.75 million), not 33¢, so the amount reported for fourth quarter earnings was more than 23 percent below estimates. Based on the lower-than-expected earnings, and the fact that Sport & Recreation had inventory levels that were considered too high as well as a weak cash flow position, investors modified their expectations concerning the potential

cash flows the company could generate in the future; and, the stock's value was adjusted accordingly.

The stock of Wellcome PLC, a British pharmaceutical manufacturer dropped by more than 2 percent on the day it was announced that an advisory committee of the Food and Drug Administration (FDA) declined to recommend approval for Wellcome's request to distribute a nonprescription version of its best selling drug Zovirax in the United States. Although the recommendation did not represent the final decision of the FDA, the stock price decrease indicated that investors adjusted their expectations to reflect the possibility that Wellcome would not be able to market the nonprescription Zovirax, a herpes medication, in the United States—the ability to distribute the drug in a new market surely would have resulted in increased future earnings, thus increased future dividends.

These examples are just two of many illustrating changes in value that occur because reported results differed from expectations, which caused investors to modify their estimates of future cash flows. We should note that reported results can differ from expectations in a positive as well as a negative direction. For example, in March 1995, Oracle Corporation, a California computer software company, reported that its 1994 earnings had increased 50 percent compared to 1993—this higher-than-expected growth caused the company's stock to increase by about 5 percent in one day. In any event, as we discuss in this chapter, valuation should be based on the present value of the future cash flows generated by an asset; so when cash flow expectations change, so does value.

discussion of bonds, we found that the value of a bond is the present value of the interest payments over the life of the bond plus the present value of the bond's maturity (or par) value. Stock prices are likewise determined as the present value of a stream of cash flows, and the basic stock valuation equation is similar to the bond valuation equation (Equation 7-2). What are the cash flows that corporations provide to their stockholders? First, think of yourself as an investor who buys a stock with the intention of holding it (in your family) forever. In this case, all that you (and your heirs) will receive is a stream of dividends, and the value of the stock today is calculated as the present value of an infinite stream of dividends:

7-5

$$\text{Value of stock} = \hat{P}_0 = \text{PV of expected future dividends}$$

$$= \frac{D_1}{(1 + k_s)^1} + \frac{D_2}{(1 + k_s)^2} + \cdots + \frac{D_\infty}{(1 + k_s)^\infty}$$

$$= \sum_{t=1}^{\infty} \frac{D_t}{(1 + k_s)^t}$$

What about the more typical case, where you expect to hold the stock for a specific (finite) period and then sell it—what will be the value of $\hat{P}_0$ in this case? Unless the company is likely to be liquidated and thus to disappear, *the value of the stock still is determined by Equation 7-5.* To see this, recognize that for any individual investor, the expected cash flows consist of expected dividends plus the expected sale price of the stock. However, the sale price the current investor receives will depend on the dividends the future investor expects. Therefore, for all present and future investors in total, expected cash flows must be based on all of the expected future dividends. To put it another way, unless a firm is liquidated or sold to another concern, the cash flows it provides to its stockholders will consist only of a stream of dividends; therefore, the value of a share of its stock must be established as the present value of that expected dividend stream that will be paid throughout the life of the company.

The general validity of Equation 7-5 also can be confirmed by asking the following question: Suppose I buy a stock and expect to hold it for 1 year. I will receive dividends during the year plus the value $\hat{P}_1$ when I sell the stock at the end of the year. But what will determine the value of $\hat{P}_1$? The answer is that it will be determined as the present value of the dividends during Year 2 plus the stock price at the end of that year, which in turn will be determined as the present value of another set of future dividends and an even more distant stock price. This process can be continued forever, and the ultimate result is Equation 7-5.[14]

Equation 7-5 is a generalized stock valuation model in the sense that the time pattern of D_t can be anything: D_t can be rising, falling, or constant, or it can even be fluctuating randomly, and Equation 7-5 still will hold. Often, however, the projected stream of dividends follows a systematic pattern, in which case we can develop a simplified (that is, easier to evaluate) version of the stock valuation model expressed in Equation 7-5. In the following sections we consider the cases of zero growth, constant growth, and nonconstant growth.

---

[14]We should note that investors periodically lose sight of the long-run nature of stocks as investments and forget that in order to sell a stock at a profit, one must find a buyer who will pay the higher price. If you analyzed a stock's value in accordance with Equation 7-5, concluded that the stock's market price exceeded a reasonable value, and then bought the stock anyway, then you would be following the "bigger fool" theory of investment—you think that you might be a fool to buy the stock at its excessive price, but you also think that when you get ready to sell it, you can find someone who is an even bigger fool. The bigger fool theory was widely followed in the summer of 1987, just before the stock market lost over one-third of its value in the October 1987 crash.

Stock Values with Zero Growth

ZERO GROWTH STOCK
A common stock whose future dividends are not expected to grow at all; that is, $g = 0$, and $D_1 = D_2 = \ldots = D_\infty$.

Suppose dividends are not expected to grow at all; instead they are expected to stay the same every year. Here we have a **zero growth stock,** for which the dividends expected in future years are equal to some constant amount—the current dividend. That is, $D_1 = D_2 = \ldots = D_\infty = D_0$. Therefore, we can drop the subscripts on D and rewrite Equation 7-5 as follows:

7-5a
$$\hat{P}_0 = \frac{D}{(1 + k_s)^1} + \frac{D}{(1 + k_s)^2} + \cdots + \frac{D}{(1 + k_s)^\infty}$$

As we noted in Chapter 5 in connection with the British consol bond and also in our discussion of preferred stocks, a security that is expected to pay a constant amount each year forever is called a perpetuity. *Therefore, a zero growth stock is a perpetuity.*

As we saw in Chapter 6, the value of any perpetuity is simply the payment divided by the discount rate, so the value of a zero growth stock reduces to this formula:

7-6
$$\text{Value of zero growth stock} = \hat{P}_0 = \frac{D}{k_s}$$

So, if we have a stock that is expected to always pay a dividend equal to $1.17, and the required rate of return associated with such an investment is 13.6%, the stock's value should be:[15]

$$\hat{P}_0 = \frac{\$1.17}{0.136} = \$8.60$$

Generally, we can find the price of a stock and the most recent dividend paid to the stockholders by looking in a financial newspaper such as *The Wall Street Journal.* Therefore, if we have a stock with constant dividends, we can solve for the expected rate of return by rearranging Equation 7-6 to produce:

7-6a
$$\hat{k}_s = \frac{D}{P_0}$$

---

[15]If you think that having a stock pay dividends forever is unrealistic, then think of it as lasting only for 50 years. Here you would have an annuity of $1.17 per year for 50 years. The PV of a 50-year annuity of $1.17 with an opportunity rate of interest equal to 13.6% would be $1.17(7.34042) = $8.59, which would differ by only a penny from that of the perpetuity. Thus, the dividends from Years 51 to infinity contribute almost nothing to the value of the stock.

Because we are dealing with an *expected rate of return,* we put a "hat" on the k value. Thus, if we bought a stock at a price of $8.60 and expected to receive a constant dividend of $1.17, our expected rate of return would be:

$$\hat{k}_s = \frac{\$1.17}{\$8.60} = 0.136 = 13.6\%$$

Normal, or Constant, Growth

NORMAL (CONSTANT) GROWTH
Growth which is expected to continue into the foreseeable future at about the same rate as that of the economy as a whole; g = a constant.

In general, investors expect the earnings and dividends of most companies to increase each year. Even though expected growth rates vary from company to company, it is not uncommon for investors to expect dividend growth to continue in the foreseeable future at about the same rate as that of the nominal gross national product (real GNP plus inflation). On this basis, we might expect the dividend of an average, or "normal," company to grow at a rate of 6 to 8 percent a year. Thus, if a **normal,** or **constant, growth** company's last dividend, which has already been paid, was D_0, its dividend in any future Year t can be forecasted as $D_t = D_0(1 + g)^t$, where g is the constant expected rate of growth. For example, if Unilate Textiles just paid a dividend of $1.17 (that is, $D_0 = \$1.17$), and if investors expect an 8.1 percent growth rate, then the estimated dividend 1 year hence would be $D_1 = \$1.17(1.081) = \$1.265$; D_2 would be $1.367; and the estimated dividend 5 years hence would be

$$D_t = D_0(1 + g)^t = \$1.17(1.081)^5 = \$1.727$$

Using this method for estimating future dividends, we can determine the current expected stock value, $\hat{P}_0$, using Equation 7-5 as set forth previously—in other words, we can find the expected future cash flow stream (the dividends), then calculate the present value of each dividend payment, and finally sum these present values to find the value of the stock. Thus, the intrinsic value of the stock is equal to the present value of its expected future dividends.

If g is constant, Equation 7-5 can be rewritten as follows:[16]

7-7

$$\hat{P}_0 = \frac{D_0(1 + g)^1}{(1 + k_s)^1} + \frac{D_0(1 + g)^2}{(1 + k_s)^2} + \cdots + \frac{D_0(1 + g)^\infty}{(1 + k_s)^\infty}$$

$$= \frac{D_0(1 + g)}{k_s - g} = \frac{D_1}{k_s - g}$$

Inserting values into the last version of Equation 7-7, we find the value of Unilate's stock is approximately $23.00:

$$\hat{P}_0 = \frac{\$1.17(1.081)}{0.136 - 0.081} = \frac{\$1.265}{0.055} = \$23$$

---

[16]The last term in Equation 7-7 is derived in Appendix 4A of Eugene F. Brigham and Louis C. Gapenski, *Intermediate Financial Management,* 5th ed. (Fort Worth, Tex.: The Dryden Press, 1996). In essence, the full-blown version of Equation 7-7 is the sum of a geometric progression, and the last term is the solution value of the progression.

CONSTANT GROWTH MODEL
Also called the Gordon Model, it is used to find the value of a stock that is expected to experience constant growth.

The **constant growth model** as set forth in the last term of Equation 7-7 is often called the Gordon Model, after Myron J. Gordon, who did much to develop and popularize it.

Note that Equation 7-7 is sufficiently general to encompass the zero growth case described earlier: If growth is zero, $g = 0$, which simply is a special case of constant growth, and Equation 7-7 is equal to Equation 7-6. Note also that a necessary condition for the derivation of the simplified form of Equation 7-7 is that k_s be greater than g. If the equation is used in situations where k_s is not greater than g, the results will be meaningless.

The concept underlying the valuation process for a constant growth stock is graphed in Figure 7-5. Dividends are growing at the rate $g = 8.1\%$, but because $k_s > g$, the present value of each future dividend is declining. For example, the dividend in Year 1 is $D_1 = D_0(1 + g)^1 = \$1.17(1.081) = \$1.265$. However, the present value of this dividend, discounted at 13.6 percent, is $PV(D_1) = \$1.265/(1.136)^1 = \$1.113$. The dividend expected in Year 2 grows to $\$1.265(1.081) = \$1.367$, but the present value of this dividend falls to \$1.06. Continuing, $D_3 = \$1.478$ and $PV(D_3) = \$1.008$, and so on. Thus, the expected dividends are growing, but the present value of each successive dividend is declining, because the dividend growth rate (8.1%) is less than the rate used for discounting the dividends to the present (13.6%).

FIGURE 7-5

Present Values of Dividends of a Constant Growth Stock: $D_0 = 1.17$, $g = 8.1\%$, $k_s = 13.6\%$

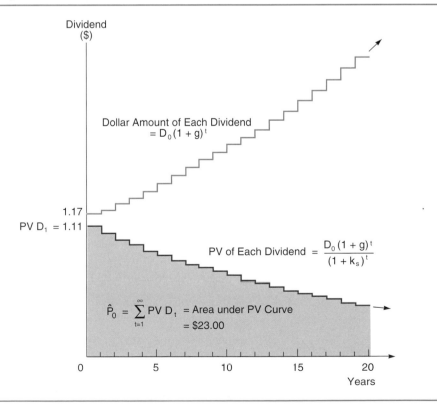

If we summed the present values of each future dividend, this summation would be the value of the stock, $\hat{P}_0$. When g is a constant, this summation is equal to $D_1/(k_s - g)$, as shown in Equation 7-7. Therefore, if we extended the lower step function curve in Figure 7-5 on out to infinity and added up the present values of each future dividend, the summation would be identical to the value given by Equation 7-7, $23.

Growth in dividends occurs primarily as a result of growth in *earnings per share (EPS)*. Earnings growth, in turn, results from a number of factors, including (1) inflation, (2) the amount of earnings the company retains and reinvests, and (3) the rate of return the company earns on its equity (ROE). Regarding inflation, if output (in units) is stable and if both sales prices and input costs rise at the inflation rate, then EPS also will grow at the inflation rate. EPS also will grow as a result of the reinvestment, or plowback, of earnings. If the firm's earnings are not all paid out as dividends (that is, if some fraction of earnings is retained), the dollars of investment behind each share will rise over time, which should lead to growth in future earnings and dividends.

Expected Rate of Return on a Constant Growth Stock

We can solve Equation 7-7 for k_s, again using the hat to denote that we are dealing with an expected rate of return:[17]

7-8

$$\begin{array}{ccccc} \text{Expected rate} \\ \text{of return} \end{array} = \begin{array}{c} \text{Expected} \\ \text{dividend yield} \end{array} + \begin{array}{c} \text{Expected growth} \\ \text{rate, or capital} \\ \text{gains yield} \end{array}$$

$$\hat{k}_s = \frac{D_1}{P_0} + g$$

Thus, if you buy a stock for a price $P_0 = \$23$, and if you expect the stock to pay a dividend $D_1 = \$1.265$ one year from now and to grow at a constant rate $g = 8.1\%$ in the future, then your expected rate of return will be 13.6 percent:

$$\hat{k}_s = \frac{\$1.265}{\$23} + 0.081 = 0.055 + 0.081 = 0.136 = 13.6\%$$

In this form, we see that $\hat{k}_s$ is the *expected total return* and that it consists of an *expected dividend yield,* $D_1/P_0 = 5.5\%$, plus an *expected growth rate or capital gains yield,* $g = 8.1\%$.

Suppose this analysis had been conducted on January 1, 1996, so $P_0 = \$23$ is the January 1, 1996 stock price and $D_1 = \$1.265$ is the dividend expected at the end of 1996. What is the expected stock price at the end of 1996 (or the begin-

---

[17]The k_s value of Equation 7-7 is a *required* rate of return, but when we transform to obtain Equation 7-8, we are finding an *expected* rate of return. Obviously, the transformation requires that $k_s = \hat{k}_s$. This equality holds if the stock market is in equilibrium, a condition that will be discussed later in the chapter.

ning of 1997)? We would again apply Equation 7-7, but this time we would use the expected 1997 dividend, $D_2 = D_1(1 + g) = \$1.265(1.081) = \$1.3672$:

$$\hat{P}_{1/1/97} = \frac{D_{1997}}{k_s - g} = \frac{\$1.3672}{0.136 - 0.081} = \$24.86$$

Now notice that $24.86 is 8.1 percent greater than P_0, the $23 price on January 1, 1996:

$$\$23(1.081) = \$24.86.$$

Thus, we would expect to have a capital gain of $24.86 − $23 = $1.86 during the year, which is a capital gains yield of 8.1 percent:

$$\text{Capital gains yield} = \frac{\text{Capital gain}}{\text{Beginning price}} = \frac{\text{Ending price} - \text{Beginning price}}{\text{Beginning price}}$$

$$= \frac{\$24.86 - \$23.00}{\$23.00} = \frac{\$1.86}{\$23.00} = 0.081 = 8.1\%$$

We could extend the analysis on out, and in each future year the expected capital gains yield would equal g = 8.1 percent, the expected dividend growth rate.

Continuing, the dividend yield in 1997 could be estimated as follows:

$$\text{Dividend yield}_{1997} = \frac{D_{1997}}{P_{1/1/97}} = \frac{\$1.3672}{\$24.86} = 0.055 = 5.5\%$$

The dividend yield for 1998 could also be calculated, and again it would be 5.5 percent. Thus, for a constant growth stock, the following conditions must hold:

1. The dividend is expected to grow forever at a constant rate, g.
2. The stock price is expected to grow at this same rate.
3. The expected dividend yield is a constant.
4. The expected capital gains yield also is a constant, and it is equal to g.
5. The expected total rate of return, $\hat{k}_s$, is equal to the expected dividend yield plus the expected growth rate: $\hat{k}_s$ = dividend yield + g.

The term *expected* should be clarified—it means expected in a probabilistic sense, as the statistically expected outcome. Thus, if we say the growth rate is expected to remain constant at 8.1 percent, we mean that the best prediction for the growth rate in any future year is 8.1 percent, not that we literally expect the growth rate to be exactly equal to 8.1 percent in each future year. In this sense, the constant growth assumption is a reasonable one for many large, mature companies.

Nonconstant Growth

Firms typically go through *life cycles*. During the early part of their lives, their growth is much faster than that of the economy as a whole; then they match the economy's growth; and finally their growth is slower than that of the economy.[18] Automobile manufacturers in the 1920s and computer software firms such as Microsoft in the 1990s are examples of firms in the early part of the cycle. Other firms, such as those in the tobacco industry or coal industry, are in the waning stages of their life cycles, so their growth is not keeping pace with the general economic growth (in some cases growth is negative). Firms whose growth is not about the same as the economy's growth are called **nonconstant growth** firms. Figure 7-6 illustrates nonconstant growth and also compares it with normal growth and zero growth.[19]

NONCONSTANT GROWTH
The part of the life cycle of a firm in which its growth either is much faster or is much slower than that of the economy as a whole.

In the figure, the dividends of the supernormal growth (growth much greater than the economy) firm are expected to grow at a 30 percent rate for 3 years, after which the growth rate is expected to fall to 8.1 percent, the assumed average for the economy. The value of this firm, like any other, is the present value of its expected future dividends as determined by Equation 7-5. In the case in which D_t is growing at a constant rate, we simplified Equation 7-5 to $\hat{P}_0 = D_1/(k_s - g)$. In the supernormal case, however, the expected growth rate is not a constant—it declines at the end of the period of supernormal growth. To find the value of such a stock, or of any nonconstant growth stock when the growth rate will eventually stabilize, we proceed in three steps:

1. Compute the value of the dividends that experience nonconstant growth, and then find the PV of these dividends.
2. *Find the price of the stock* at the end of the nonconstant growth period, *at which point it has become a constant growth stock,* and discount this price back to the present.
3. Add these two components to find the intrinsic value of the stock, $\hat{P}_0$.

Figure 7-7 can be used to illustrate the process for valuing nonconstant growth stocks, assuming the following five facts exist:

k_s = stockholders' required rate of return = 13.6%. This rate is used to discount the cash flows.

N = years of supernormal growth = 3.

g_s = rate of growth in both earnings and dividends during the supernormal growth period = 30%. (Note: The growth rate during the supernormal growth period could vary from year to year. Also, there could be several

---

[18]The concept of life cycles could be broadened to *product cycle,* which would include both small, start-up companies and large companies like IBM, which periodically introduce new products that give sales and earnings a boost. We should also mention *business cycles,* which alternately depress and boost sales and profits. The growth rate just after a major new product has been introduced, or just after a firm emerges from the depths of a recession, is likely to be much higher than the "expected long-run average growth rate," which is the proper value to use for evaluating the project.

[19]A negative growth rate indicates a declining company. A mining company whose profits are falling because of a declining ore body is an example. Someone buying such a company would expect its earnings, and consequently its dividends and stock price, to decline each year, and this would lead to capital losses rather than capital gains. Obviously, a declining company's stock price will be relatively low, and its dividend yield must be high enough to offset the expected capital loss and still produce a competitive total return. Students sometimes argue that they would not be willing to buy a stock whose price was expected to decline. However, if the annual dividends are large enough to *more than offset* the falling stock price, the stock still could provide a good return.

FIGURE 7-6

Illustrative Dividend Growth Rates

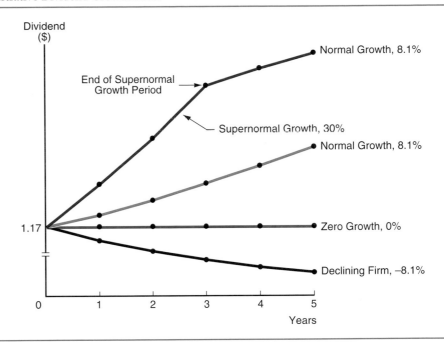

different supernormal growth periods—for example, 30% for 3 years, then 20% for 3 years, and then a constant rate.) This rate is shown directly on the time line.

g_n = rate of normal, constant growth after the supernormal period = 8.1%. This rate also is shown on the cash flow time line, after Year 3.

D_0 = last, or most current, dividend paid by the company = \$1.17.

The valuation process as diagrammed in Figure 7-7 is explained in the steps set forth below the time line. The value of the supernormal growth stock is calculated to be \$39.09.

Self-Test Questions

Explain the following statement: "Whereas a bond contains a promise to pay interest, common stock provides an expectation but no promise of dividends."

What are the two elements of a stock's expected returns?

Write out and explain the valuation model for a zero growth stock.

Write out and explain the valuation model for a constant growth stock.

How does one calculate the capital gains yield and the dividend yield of a stock?

Explain how one would find the value of a stock with nonconstant growth.

FIGURE 7-7

Process for Finding the Value of a Nonconstant Growth Stock

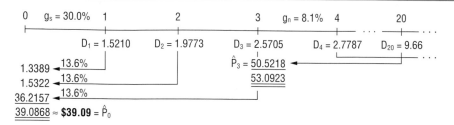

Step 1. Calculate the dividends for each year during the nonconstant growth period—$D_t = D_0(1 + g_s)^t$:

$$D_1 = \$1.17(1.30)^1 = \$1.5210$$
$$D_2 = \$1.17(1.30)^2 = \$1.9773$$
$$D_3 = \$1.17(1.30)^3 = \$2.5705$$

Show these values on the cash flow time line as cash flows for Years 1 through 3.

Step 2. The price of the stock is the PV of dividends from Year 1 to infinity. So, in theory, we could continue projecting each future dividend beyond Year 3, when normal growth of 8.1% occurs. In other words, use $g_n = 8.1\%$ to compute D_4, D_5, and so on with D_3 as the base dividend for normal growth:

$$D_4 = \$2.5705(1.081)^1 = \$2.7787$$
$$D_5 = \$2.5705(1.081)^2 = \$3.0038$$
$$\vdots$$
$$D_{20} = \$2.5705(1.081)^{17} = \$9.6617$$

We can continue this process, and then find the PV of this stream of dividends. However, we know that after D_3 has been paid in Year 3, the stock becomes a constant growth stock, so we can apply the constant growth formula at that point and find $\hat{P}_3$, which is the PV of the dividends from Year 4 through infinity as evaluated in Year 3. After the Year 3 dividend has been paid, all of the future dividends will grow at a constant rate equal to 8.1%, so

$$\hat{P}_3 = \frac{D_4}{k_s - g_n} = \frac{\$2.7787}{0.136 - 0.081} = \$50.5218$$

We show this $50.5218 on the cash flow time line as a second cash flow at Year 3. The $50.5218 is a Year 3 cash flow in the sense that the owner of the stock could sell it for $50.5218 at the end of Year 3, and also in the sense that $50.5218 is the present value equivalent of the dividend cash flows from Year 4 to infinity. Therefore, the *total cash flow* we recognize in Year 3 is the sum of $D_3 + P_3 = \$2.5705 + \$50.5218 = \$53.0923$.

Step 3. Now that the cash flows have been placed on the cash flow time line, we need to discount each cash flow at the required rate of return, $k_s = 13.6\%$. Because 13.6% is not shown in the tables, you must either compute the PVs directly or use the cash flow registers on your calculator. You can compute the PVs directly by dividing each cash flow by $(1.136)^t$. If you use the cash flow registers on your calculator, input $CF_0 = 0$, $CF_1 = 1.5210$, $CF_2 = 1.9773$, $CF_3 = 53.0923$, $I = 13.6$. The result is shown to the left below the cash flow time line.

Stock Market Equilibrium

Recall from Chapter 5 that the required return on Stock X, k_X, can be found using the Security Market Line (SML) equation as it was developed in our discussion of the Capital Asset Pricing Model (CAPM):

$$k_X = k_{RF} + (k_M - k_{RF}) \beta_X.$$

If the risk-free rate of return is 8 percent, if the market risk premium is 4 percent, and if Stock X has a beta of 2, then the marginal investor will require a return of 16 percent on Stock X, calculated as follows:

$$k_X = 8\% + (4\%) \, 2.0 = 16\%.$$

This 16 percent required return is shown as a point on the SML in Figure 7-8.

The average investor will want to buy Stock X if the expected rate of return is more than 16 percent; will want to sell it if the expected rate of return is less than 16 percent; and will be indifferent, hence will hold but not buy or sell, if the expected rate of return is exactly 16 percent. Now suppose the investor's portfolio contains Stock X, and he or she analyzes the stock's prospects and concludes that its earnings, dividends, and price can be expected to grow at a constant rate of 5 percent per year. The last dividend was $D_0 = \$2.8571$, so the next expected dividend is

$$D_1 = \$2.8571(1.05) = \$3.$$

Our average investor observes that the present price of the stock, P_0, is $30. Should he or she purchase more of Stock X, sell the present holdings, or maintain the present position?

The investor can calculate Stock X's *expected rate of return* as follows:

$$\hat{k}_x = \frac{D_1}{P_0} + g = \frac{\$3}{\$30} + 0.05 = 0.15 = 15\%.$$

This value is plotted on Figure 7-8 as Point X, which is below the SML. Because the expected rate of return is less than the required return, this average investor would want to sell the stock, as would other holders. However, few people would want to buy at the $30 price, so the present owners would be unable to find buyers unless they cut the price of the stock. Thus, the price would decline, and this decline would continue until the stock's price reached $27.27, at which point the market for this security would be in **equilibrium,** because the expected rate of return, 16 percent, would be equal to the required rate of return:

EQUILIBRIUM
The condition under which the expected return on a security is just equal to its required return, $\hat{k} = k$, and the price is stable.

$$\hat{k}_x = \frac{\$3}{\$27.27} + 0.05 = 0.11 + 0.05 = 0.16 = 16\% = k_x.$$

Had the stock initially sold for less than $27.27, say at $25, events would have been reversed. Investors would have wanted to buy the stock because its expected rate of return would have exceeded its required rate of return, and buy orders would have driven the stock's price up to $27.27.

FIGURE 7-8

Expected and Required Returns on Stock X

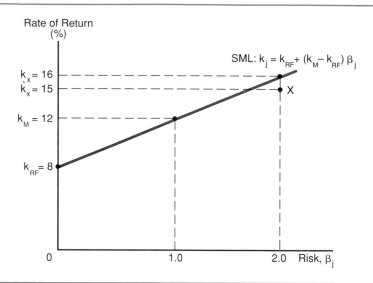

To summarize, in equilibrium these two conditions must hold:

1. The expected rate of return as seen by the average investor must equal the required rate of return: $\hat{k}_j = k_j$.
2. The actual market price of the stock must equal its intrinsic value as estimated by the average investor: $P_0 = \hat{P}_0$.

Of course, some individual investors might believe that $\hat{k}_j > k_j$ and $\hat{P}_0 > P_0$, and hence they would invest most of their funds in the stock, while other investors might have an opposite view and would sell all their shares. However, it is the average investor who establishes the actual market price, and for this investor, $\hat{k}_j = k_j$ and $P_0 = \hat{P}_0$. If these conditions do not hold, trading will occur until they do hold.

Changes in Equilibrium Stock Prices

Stock market prices are not constant—they undergo violent changes at times. For example, on October 19, 1987, the Dow Jones average dropped 508 points, and the average stock lost about 23 percent of its value in just one day. Some stocks lost over half of their value that day. To see how such changes can occur, let us assume that Stock X is in equilibrium, selling at a price of $27.27 per share. If all expectations were met exactly, during the next year the price would gradually rise to $28.63, or by 5 percent. However, many different events could occur to cause a change in the equilibrium price of the stock. To illustrate, consider again the set of inputs used to develop Stock X's price of $27.27, along with a new set of assumed input variables:

	Variable Value	
	Original	New
Risk-free rate, k_{RF}	8%	7%
Market risk premium, $k_M - k_{RF}$	4%	3%
Stock X's beta coefficient, β_X	2.0	1.0
Stock X's expected growth rate, g_X	5%	6%
Current dividend, D_0	$2.8571	$2.8571
Price of Stock X	$27.27	?

Now give yourself a test: How would the change in each variable, by itself, affect the price, and what is your guess as to the new stock price?

Every change, taken alone, would lead to an increase in the price. The first three variables influence k_x, which declines from 16 to 10 percent:

$$\text{Original } k_x = 8\% + 4\%(2.0) = 16\%.$$

$$\text{New } k_x = 7\% + 3\%(1.0) = 10\%.$$

Using these values, together with the new g value, we find that $\hat{P}_0$ rises from $27.27 to $75.71.[20]

$$\text{Original } \hat{P}_0 = \frac{\$2.8571(1.05)}{0.16 - 0.05} = \frac{\$3}{0.11} = \$27.27.$$

$$\text{New } \hat{P}_0 = \frac{\$2.8571(1.06)}{0.10 - 0.06} = \frac{\$3.0285}{0.04} = \$75.71.$$

At the new price, the expected and required rates of return will equal:[21]

$$\hat{k}_x = \frac{\$3.0285}{\$75.71} + 0.06 = 0.10 = 10\% = k_x.$$

Evidence suggests that stocks, especially those of large NYSE companies, adjust rapidly to disequilibrium situations. Consequently, equilibrium ordinarily exists for any given stock, and, in general, required and expected returns are equal. Stock prices certainly change, sometimes violently and rapidly, but this simply reflects

---

[20]A price change of this magnitude is by no means rare. The prices of *many* stocks double or halve during a year. For example, during 1994, the stock of TSX Corporation increased nearly 700 percent, from $2\frac{2}{8}$ to $18\frac{7}{8}$—the stock actually reached a high price of $24 during the year. On the other hand, Gitano's stock fell from $2.60 to $0.13, which represented a 95 percent loss for shareholders in 1994.

[21]It should be obvious by now that *actual realized* rates of return are not necessarily equal to expected and required returns. Thus, an investor might have *expected* to receive a return of 15 percent if he or she had bought TSX or Gitano stock in 1994, but, after the fact, the realized return on TSX was far above 15 percent, whereas that on Gitano was far below.

changing conditions and expectations. There are, of course, times when a stock continues to react for several months to a favorable or unfavorable development, but this does not signify a long adjustment period; rather, it simply illustrates that as more new pieces of information about the situation become available, the market adjusts to them. The ability of the market to adjust to new information is discussed in the next section.

The Efficient Markets Hypothesis

EFFICIENT MARKETS HYPOTHESIS (EMH)
The hypothesis that securities are typically in equilibrium—that they are fairly priced in the sense that the price reflects all publicly available information on each security.

A body of theory called the **Efficient Markets Hypothesis (EMH)** holds that (1) stocks are always in equilibrium and (2) it is impossible for an investor to *consistently* "beat the market" on a risk-adjusted basis. Essentially, those who believe in the EMH note that there are 100,000 or so full-time, highly trained, professional analysts and traders operating in the market, while there are fewer than 3,000 major stocks.[22] Therefore, if each analyst followed 30 stocks (which is about right, as analysts tend to specialize in the stocks in a specific industry), there would be 1,000 analysts following each stock. Further, these analysts work for organizations such as Citibank, Merrill Lynch, Paine Webber, and the like, which have billions of dollars available with which to take advantage of bargains. As a result of SEC disclosure requirements and electronic information networks, as new information about a stock becomes available, these 1,000 analysts all receive and evaluate it at approximately the same time. Therefore, the price of the stock adjusts almost immediately to reflect any new developments.

Financial theorists generally define three forms, or levels, of market efficiency:

1. The *weak form* of the EMH states that all information contained in past price movements is fully reflected in current market prices. Therefore, information about recent, or past, trends in stock prices is of no use in selecting mispriced stocks—the fact that a stock has risen for the past three days, for example, gives us no useful clues as to what it will do today or tomorrow. People who believe that weak-form efficiency exists also believe that "tape watchers" and "chartists" are wasting their time.[23]
2. The *semistrong form* of the EMH states that current market prices reflect all *publicly available* information. If this is true, no abnormal returns can be earned by analyzing stocks.[24] Thus, if semistrong-form efficiency exists, it does no good to pore over annual reports or other published data because market

---

[22]There actually are many more than 3,000 stocks traded in the United States, but many of them are stocks of small firms which are traded infrequently. The 3,000 *major* stocks include those listed on both the New York Stock Exchange and the American Stock Exchange, and other relatively large firms that institutional investors like pension funds and investment companies consider appropriate for their portfolios.

[23]Tape watchers are people who watch the NYSE tape, while chartists plot past patterns of stock price movements. Both are called "technicians," and both believe that they can see if something is happening to the stock that will cause its price to move up or down in the near future.

[24]An abnormal return is one that exceeds the return justified by the riskiness of the investment—that is, a return that plots above the SML in a graph like Figure 7-8.

prices will have adjusted to any good or bad news contained in such reports as soon as they came out. However, insiders (say, the presidents of companies), even under semistrong-form efficiency, can still make abnormal returns on their own companies' stocks.

3. The *strong form* of the EMH states that current market prices reflect all pertinent information, whether publicly available or privately held. If this form holds, even insiders would find it impossible to earn abnormal returns in the stock market.[25]

Many empirical studies have been conducted to test the three forms of market efficiency. Most of these studies suggest that the stock market is indeed highly efficient in the weak form and reasonably efficient in the semistrong form, at least for the larger and more widely followed stocks. However, the strong-form EMH does not hold, so abnormal profits can be made by those who possess inside information.

What bearing does the EMH have on financial decisions? Because stock prices do seem to reflect public information, most stocks appear to be fairly valued. This does not mean that new developments could not cause a stock's price to soar or to plummet, but it does mean that stocks, in general, are fairly priced, and the prices probably are in equilibrium—it is safe to assume $\hat{k} = k$ and $\hat{P}_0 = P_0$. However, there are certainly cases in which corporate insiders have information not known to outsiders.

Actual Stock Prices and Returns

Our discussion thus far has focused on expected stock prices and expected rates of return. Anyone who has ever invested in the stock market knows that there can be, and generally are, large differences between expected and realized prices and returns.

Figure 7-9 shows how the price of an average share of stock has varied in recent years, and Figure 7-10 shows how total realized returns have varied. The market trend has been strongly up, but it has gone up in some years and down in others, and the stocks of individual companies have likewise gone up and down. We know from theory that expected returns as estimated by an average investor always are positive, but in some years, as Figure 7-10 shows, negative returns have been realized. Of course, even in bad years some individual companies do well, so the "name of the game" in security analysis is to pick the winners. Financial managers attempt to take actions that will put their companies into the winners' column, but they don't always succeed. In subsequent chapters, we will examine the actions that managers can take to increase the odds of their firms doing relatively well in the marketplace.

---

[25]Several cases of illegal insider trading have made the news headlines recently. These cases involved employees of several major investment banking houses and even an employee of the SEC. In one famous case, Ivan Boesky admitted to making $50 million by purchasing the stock of firms he knew were about to merge. He went to jail, and he had to pay a large fine, but he helped disprove the strong-form EMH.

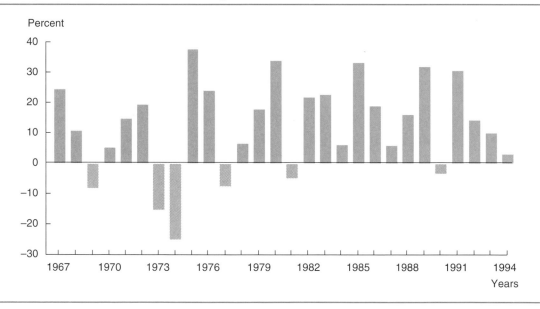

FIGURE 7-9

S&P 500 Index, 1967–1994

FIGURE 7-10

S&P 500 Index, Total Returns: Dividend Yield + Capital Gain or Loss, 1967–1994

Self-Test Questions

When a stock is in equilibrium, what two conditions must hold?

What is the major conclusion of the Efficient Markets Hypothesis (EMH)?

What is the difference between the three forms of the EMH: (1) weak form, (2) semistrong form, and (3) strong form?

If a stock is not in equilibrium, explain how financial markets adjust to bring it into equilibrium.

SMALL BUSINESS

Valuation of Small Firms

In this chapter we presented several equations for valuing a firm's common stock. These equations had one common element: They all assumed that the firm is currently paying a dividend. However, many small firms, even highly profitable ones whose stock is traded in the market, have never paid a dividend. How does one value the stock of such firms? If a firm is expected to begin paying dividends in the future, we can modify the equations presented in the chapter and use them to determine the value of the stock.

A new business often expects to have very low sales during its first few years of operation as it develops its product. Then, if the product catches on, sales will grow rapidly for several years. For example, Compaq Computer Company had only three employees when it was incorporated in 1982. Its first year was devoted to product development, and 1982 sales were zero. In 1983, however, Compaq began marketing its personal computer, and its sales hit $111 million, a record first-year volume for any new firm, and by 1986 Compaq was included in *Fortune*'s 500 largest U.S. industrial firms. Obviously, Compaq has been more successful than most new businesses, but it is common for small firms to have growth rates of 100 percent, 500 percent, or even 1,000 percent during their first few years of operation.

Sales growth brings with it the need for additional assets—Compaq could not have increased its sales as it did without also increasing its assets, and asset growth requires an increase in liability and/or equity accounts. Small firms can generally obtain some bank credit, but they must maintain a reasonable balance between debt and equity. Thus, additional bank borrowings require increases in equity, and getting the equity capital needed to support growth can be difficult for small

firms. They have limited access to the capital markets, and, even when they can sell common stock, the owners of small firms are reluctant to do so for fear of losing voting control. Therefore, the best source of equity for most small businesses is retained earnings, and for this reason most small firms pay no dividends during their rapid growth years. Eventually, though, successful small firms do pay dividends, and those dividends generally grow rapidly at first but slow down to a sustainable constant rate once the firm reaches maturity.

Finding the value of the stock of a small firm is the same as was described earlier in the chapter in the section about nonconstant growth companies, except, for most small firms, there might be numerous years in which no dividend payments are expected. If a small firm currently pays no dividend but is expected to pay dividends in the future, the value of its stock can be found as follows:

1. Estimate when dividends will be paid, the amount of the first dividend, the growth rate during the supernormal growth period, the length of the supernormal period, the long-run (constant) growth rate, and the rate of return required by investors.
2. Use the constant growth model to determine the price of the stock after the firm reaches a stable growth situation.
3. Set out on a time line the cash flows (dividends during the supernormal growth period and the stock price once the constant growth state is reached) and then find the present value of these cash flows. *That present value represents the value of the stock today.*

Summary

Corporate decisions should be analyzed in terms of how alternative courses of action are likely to affect the value of a firm. However, it is necessary to know how bond and stock prices are established before attempting to measure how a given decision will affect a specific firm's value. Accordingly, this chapter showed how bond and stock values are determined as well as how investors estimate the rates of return they expect to earn. The key concepts covered in the chapter are summarized below.

- The **value** of any asset can be found by computing the **present value of the cash flows** the asset is expected to generate during its life.

- A **bond** is a long-term promissory note issued by a business or governmental unit. The firm receives the selling price of the bond in exchange for promising to make interest payments and to repay the principal on a specified future date.
- The **value of a bond** is found as the present value of an **annuity** (the interest payments) plus the present value of a lump sum (the **principal**). The bond is evaluated at the appropriate periodic interest rate over the number of periods for which interest payments are made.
- The equation used to find the value of a bond is:

$$V_d = \sum_{t=1}^{N \times m} \frac{INT}{\left(1 + \frac{k_d}{m}\right)^t} + \frac{M}{\left(1 + \frac{k_d}{m}\right)^{N \times m}}$$

$$= INT\left(PVIFA_{\frac{k_d}{m}, N \times m}\right) + M\left(PVIF_{\frac{k_d}{m}, N \times m}\right)$$

where m equals the number of times interest is paid during the year.
- The return earned on a bond held to maturity is termed the bond's **yield to maturity (YTM).**
- The longer the maturity of a bond, the more its price will change in response to a given change in interest rates; this is called **interest rate price risk.** Bonds with short maturities, however, expose the investor to high **interest rate reinvestment rate risk,** which is the risk that income will differ from what is expected because cash flows received from bonds will have to be reinvested at different interest rates.
- Most **preferred stocks are perpetuities,** and the value of a share of perpetual preferred stock is found as the dividend divided by the required rate of return: $V_{ps} = D_{ps}/k_{ps}$.
- The **value of a share of stock** is calculated as the **present value of the stream of dividends** it is expected to provide in the future.
- The equation used to find the **value of a constant,** or **normal, growth stock** is: $\hat{P}_0 = D_1/(k_s - g)$.
- The **expected total rate of return** from a stock consists of an **expected dividend yield** plus an **expected capital gains yield.** For a constant growth firm, both the expected dividend yield and the expected capital gains yield are constant.
- The equation for $\hat{k}_s$, **the expected rate of return on a constant growth stock,** can be expressed as follows: $\hat{k}_s = D_1/P_0 + g$.
- A **zero growth stock** is one whose future dividends are not expected to grow at all, while a **nonconstant growth stock** is one whose earnings and dividends are expected to grow at a rate different from the economy as a whole over some specified time period.
- To find the **present value of a nonconstant growth stock,** (1) find the dividends expected during the nonconstant growth period, (2) find the price of the stock at the end of the nonconstant growth period, (3) discount the dividends and the projected price back to the present, and (4) sum these PVs to find the current value of the stock, $\hat{P}_0$.
- The **Efficient Markets Hypothesis (EMH)** holds that (1) stocks always are in equilibrium and (2) it is impossible for an investor to consistently "beat the market." Therefore, according to the EMH, stocks always are fairly valued ($\hat{P}_0 = P_0$),

the required return on a stock is equal to its expected return $(k = \hat{k})$, and all stocks' expected returns plot on the SML.

- Finally, in this chapter we saw that differences can and do exist between expected and actual returns in the stock and bond markets—only for short-term, risk-free assets are expected and actual (or realized) returns equal.

Questions

7-1   Describe how you should determine the value of an asset, whether it is a real asset or a financial asset.

7-2   Two investors are evaluating IBM's stock for possible purchase. They agree on the expected value of D_1 and also on the expected future dividend growth rate. Further, they agree on the riskiness of the stock. However, one investor normally holds stocks for 2 years, while the other normally holds stocks for 10 years. On the basis of the type of analysis done in this chapter, they should both be willing to pay the same price for IBM's stock. True or false? Explain.

7-3   A bond that pays interest forever and has no maturity date is a perpetual bond. In what respect is a perpetual bond similar to a no-growth common stock, and to a share of preferred stock?

7-4   "The values of outstanding bonds change whenever the going rate of interest changes. In general, short-term interest rates are more volatile than long-term interest rates. Therefore, short-term bond prices are more sensitive to interest rate changes than are long-term bond prices." Is this statement true or false? Explain.

7-5   The rate of return you would get if you bought a bond and held it to its maturity date is called the bond's yield to maturity. If interest rates in the economy rise after a bond has been issued, what will happen to the bond's price and to its YTM? Does the length of time to maturity affect the extent to which a given change in interest rates will affect the bond's price?

7-6   If you buy a callable bond and interest rates decline, will the value of your bond rise by as much as it would have risen if the bond had not been callable? Explain.

7-7   If you bought a share of common stock, you would typically expect to receive dividends plus capital gains. Would you expect the distribution between dividend yield and capital gains to be influenced by the firm's decision to pay more dividends rather than to retain and reinvest more of its earnings?

Self-Test Problems

(Solutions Appear in Appendix B)

Key terms   **ST-1**   Define each of the following terms:
    a. bond
    b. par value; maturity date; call provision
    c. coupon payment; coupon interest rate
    d. premium bond; discount bond
    e. current yield (on a bond); yield to maturity (YTM)
    f. interest rate price risk; interest rate reinvestment rate risk
    g. intrinsic value $(\hat{P}_0)$; market price (P_0)
    h. required rate of return, k_s; expected rate of return, $\hat{k}_s$; actual, or realized, rate of return, $\bar{k}_s$
    i. capital gains yield; dividend yield; expected total return
    j. zero growth stock

k. normal, or constant, growth; nonconstant growth

l. equilibrium

m. Efficient Markets Hypothesis (EMH); three forms of EMH

Stock growth rates and valuation

ST-2   You are considering buying the stocks of two companies that operate in the same industry; they have very similar characteristics except for their dividend payout policies. Both companies are expected to earn $6 per share this year. However, Company D (for "dividend") is expected to pay out all its earnings as dividends, while Company G (for "growth") is expected to pay out only one-third of its earnings, or $2 per share. D's stock price is $40. G and D are equally risky. Which of the following is most likely to be true?

a. Company G will have a faster growth rate than Company D. Therefore, G's stock price should be greater than $40.

b. Although G's growth rate should exceed D's, D's current dividend exceeds that of G, and this should cause D's price to exceed G's.

c. An investor in Stock D will get his or her money back faster because D pays out more of its earnings as dividends. Thus, in a sense, D is like a short-term bond, and G is like a long-term bond. Therefore, if economic shifts cause k_d and k_s to increase and if the expected streams of dividends from D and G remain constant, Stocks D and G will both decline, but D's price should decline farther.

d. D's expected and required rate of return is $\hat{k}_s = k_s = 15\%$. G's expected return will be higher because of its higher expected growth rate.

e. On the basis of the available information, the best estimate of G's growth rate is 10 percent.

Bond valuation

ST-3   The Pennington Corporation issued a new series of bonds on January 1, 1973. The bonds were sold at par ($1,000), have a 12 percent coupon, and mature in 30 years, on December 31, 2002. Coupon payments are made semiannually (on June 30 and December 31).

a. What was the YTM of Pennington's bonds on January 1, 1973?

b. What was the price of the bond on January 1, 1978, 5 years later, assuming that the level of interest rates had fallen to 10 percent?

c. Find the current yield and capital gains yield on the bond on January 1, 1978, given the price as determined in Part b.

d. On July 1, 1996, Pennington's bonds sold for $916.42. What was the YTM at that date?

e. What were the current yield and capital gains yield on July 1, 1996?

Constant growth stock valuation

ST-4   Ewald Company's current stock price is $36, and its last dividend was $2.40. In view of Ewald's strong financial position and its consequent low risk, its required rate of return is only 12 percent. If dividends are expected to grow at a constant rate, g, in the future, and if k_s is expected to remain at 12 percent, what is Ewald's expected stock price 5 years from now?

Nonconstant growth stock valuation

ST-5   Snyder Computer Chips Inc. is experiencing a period of rapid growth. Earnings and dividends are expected to grow at a rate of 15 percent during the next 2 years, at 13 percent in the third year, and at a constant rate of 6 percent thereafter. Snyder's *last* dividend was $1.15, and the required rate of return on the stock is 12 percent.

a. Calculate the value of the stock today.

b. Calculate $\hat{P}_1$ and $\hat{P}_2$.

c. Calculate the dividend yield and capital gains yield for Years 1, 2, and 3.

Problems

Bond valuation

7-1   Suppose Ford Motor Company sold an issue of bonds with a 10-year maturity, a $1,000 par value, a 10 percent coupon rate, and semiannual interest payments.

a. Two years after the bonds were issued, the going rate of interest on bonds such as these fell to 6 percent. At what price would the bonds sell?

b. Suppose that, 2 years after the initial offering, the going interest rate had risen to 12 percent. At what price would the bonds sell?

c. Suppose that the conditions in Part a existed—that is, interest rates fell to 6 percent 2 years after the issue date. Suppose further that the interest rate remained at 6 percent for the next 8 years. Describe what would happen to the price of the Ford Motor Company bonds over time.

Perpetual bond valuation   **7-2**   The bonds of the Lange Corporation are perpetuities with a 10 percent coupon. Bonds of this type currently yield 8 percent, and their par value is $1,000.

a. What is the price of the Lange bonds?

b. Suppose interest rate levels rise to the point where such bonds now yield 12 percent. What would be the price of the Lange bonds?

c. At what price would the Lange bonds sell if the yield on these bonds were 10 percent?

d. How would your answers to Parts a, b, and c change if the bonds were not perpetuities but had a maturity of 20 years?

Constant growth   **7-3**   Your broker offers to sell you some shares of Wingler & Co. common stock that
stock valuation   paid a dividend of $2 *yesterday.* You expect the dividend to grow at the rate of 5 percent per year for the next 3 years, and if you buy the stock you plan to hold it for 3 years and then sell it.

a. Find the expected dividend for each of the next 3 years; that is, calculate D_1, D_2, and D_3. Note that $D_0 = \$2$.

b. Given that the appropriate discount rate is 12 percent and that the first of these dividend payments will occur 1 year from now, find the present value of the dividend stream; that is, calculate the PV of D_1, D_2, and D_3, and then sum these PVs.

c. You expect the price of the stock 3 years from now to be $34.73; that is, you expect $\hat{P}_3$ to equal $34.73. Discounted at a 12 percent rate, what is the present value of this expected future stock price? In other words, calculate the PV of $34.73.

d. If you plan to buy the stock, hold it for 3 years, and then sell it for $34.73, what is the most you should pay for it?

e. Use Equation 7-7 to calculate the present value of this stock. Assume that $g = 5\%$, and it is constant.

f. Is the value of this stock dependent upon how long you plan to hold it? In other words, if your planned holding period were 2 years or 5 years rather than 3 years, would this affect the value of the stock today, $\hat{P}_0$?

Return on common stock   **7-4**   You buy a share of Damanpour Corporation stock for $21.40. You expect it to pay dividends of $1.07, $1.1449, and $1.2250 in Years 1, 2, and 3, respectively, and you expect to sell it at a price of $26.22 at the end of 3 years.

a. Calculate the growth rate in dividends.

b. Calculate the expected dividend yield.

c. Assuming that the calculated growth rate is expected to continue, you can add the dividend yield to the expected growth rate to get the expected total rate of return. What is this stock's expected total rate of return?

Constant growth   **7-5**   Investors require a 15 percent rate of return on Goulet Company's stock ($k_s = 15\%$).
stock valuation

a. What will be Goulet's stock value if the previous dividend was $D_0 = \$2$ and if investors expect dividends to grow at a constant compound annual rate of (1) −5 percent, (2) 0 percent, (3) 5 percent, and (4) 10 percent?

b. Using data from Part a, what is the Gordon (constant growth) model value for Goulet's stock if the required rate of return is 15 percent and the expected growth rate is (1) 15 percent or (2) 20 percent? Are these reasonable results? Explain.

c. Is it reasonable to expect that a constant growth stock would have $g > k_s$?

Nonconstant growth
stock valuation

7-6 Bayboro Sails is expected to pay dividends of \$2.50, \$3.00, and \$4.00 in the next three years—D_1, D_2, and D_3, respectively. After three years, the dividend is expected to grow at a constant rate equal to 4 percent per year indefinitely. Stockholders require a return of 14% to invest in the common stock of Bayboro Sails.

a. Compute the present value of the dividends Bayboro is expected to pay over the next three years.

b. For what price should investors expect to be able to sell the common stock of Bayboro at the end of three years? (Hint: The dividend will grow at a constant 4 percent in Year 4, Year 5, and every year thereafter, so Equation 7-7 can be used to find $\hat{P}_3$—the appropriate dividend to use in the numerator is D_4.)

c. Compute the value of Bayboro's common stock today, $\hat{P}_0$.

Bond valuation

7-7 In January of 1994, the yield on AAA-rated corporate bonds averaged about 5.0 percent; by the end of the year the yield on these same bonds was about 8.0 percent because the Federal Reserve increased interest rates six times during the year. Assume IBM issued a 10-year, 5.0 percent coupon bond on January 1, 1994. On the same date, GM issued a 20-year, 5.0 percent coupon bond. Both bonds pay interest *annually*. Also assume that the market rate on similar risk bonds was 5.0 percent at the time the bonds were issued.

a. Compute the market value of each bond at the time of issue.

b. Compute the market value of each bond one year after issue if the market yield for similar risk bonds was 8.0 percent on January 1, 1995.

c. Compute the 1994 capital gains yield for each bond.

d. Compute the current yield for each bond in 1994.

e. Compute the total return each bond would have generated for investors in 1994.

f. If you invested in bonds at the beginning of 1994, would you have been better off to have held long-term or short-term bonds? Explain why.

g. Assume interest rates stabilize at the January 1995 rate of 8.0 percent, and they stay at this level indefinitely. What would be the price of each bond on January 1, 2000, after six years have passed? Describe what should happen to the prices of these bonds as they approach their maturities.

Nonconstant growth
stock valuation

7-8 It is now January 1, 1996. Swink Electric Inc. has just developed a solar panel capable of generating 200 percent more electricity than any solar panel currently on the market. As a result, Swink is expected to experience a 15 percent annual growth rate for the next 5 years. By the end of 5 years, other firms will have developed comparable technology, and Swink's growth rate will slow to 5 percent per year indefinitely. Stockholders require a return of 12 percent on Swink's stock. The most recent annual dividend (D_0), which was paid yesterday, was \$1.75 per share.

a. Calculate Swink's expected dividends for 1996, 1997, 1998, 1999, and 2000.

b. Calculate the value of the stock today, $\hat{P}_0$. Proceed by finding the present value of the dividends expected at the end of 1996, 1997, 1998, 1999, and 2000 plus the present value of the stock price which should exist at the end of 2000. The year-end 2000 stock price can be found by using the constant growth equation (Equation 7-7). Notice that to find the December 31, 2000, price, you use the dividend expected in 2001, which is 5 percent greater than the 2000 dividend.

c. Calculate the expected dividend yield, D_1/P_0, the capital gains yield expected in 1996, and the expected total return (dividend yield plus capital gains yield) for 1996. (Assume that $\hat{P}_0 = P_0$, and recognize that the capital gains yield is equal to the total return minus the dividend yield.) Also calculate these same three yields for 2000.

d. How might an investor's tax situation affect his or her decision to purchase stocks of companies in the early stages of their lives, when they are growing rapidly, versus stocks of older, more mature firms? When does Swink's stock become "mature" in this example?

e. Suppose your boss tells you she believes that Swink's annual growth rate will be only 12 percent during the next 5 years and that the firm's normal growth rate will be only 4 percent. Without doing any calculations, what general effect would these growth-rate changes have on the price of Swink's stock?

f. Suppose your boss also tells you that she regards Swink as being quite risky and that she believes the required rate of return should be 14 percent, not 12 percent. Again without doing any calculations, how would the higher required rate of return affect the price of the stock, its capital gains yield, and its dividend yield?

Supernormal growth stock valuation   **7-9**   Tanner Technologies Corporation (TTC) has been growing at a rate of 20 percent per year in recent years. This same growth rate is expected to last for another 2 years.

a. If $D_0 = \$1.60$, $k = 10\%$, and $g_n = 6\%$, what is TTC's stock worth today? What are its expected dividend yield and capital gains yield at this time?

b. Now assume that TTC's period of supernormal growth is to last another 5 years rather than 2 years. How would this affect its price, dividend yield, and capital gains yield? Answer in words only.

c. What will be TTC's dividend yield and capital gains yield once its period of supernormal growth ends? (Hint: These values will be the same regardless of whether you examine the case of 2 or 5 years of supernormal growth; the calculations are very easy.)

d. Of what interest to investors is the changing relationship between dividend yield and capital gains yield over time?

Equilibrium stock price   **7-10**   The risk-free rate of return, k_{RF}, is 11 percent; the required rate of return on the market, k_M, is 14 percent; and Altman Company's stock has a beta coefficient (β) of 1.5.

a. Based on the Capital Asset Pricing Model (CAPM), what should be the required return for Altman Company's stock?

b. If the dividend expected during the coming year, D_1, is $2.25, and if $g =$ a constant 5%, at what price should Altman's stock sell?

c. Now suppose the Federal Reserve Board increases the money supply, causing the risk-free rate to drop to 9 percent and k_M to fall to 12 percent. What would this do to the price of the stock?

d. In addition to the change in Part c, suppose investors' risk aversion declines; this fact, combined with the decline in k_{RF}, causes k_M to fall to 11 percent. At what price would Altman's stock sell?

e. Now suppose Altman has a change in management. The new group institutes policies that increase the expected constant growth rate to 6 percent. Also, the new management stabilizes sales and profits and thus causes the beta coefficient to decline from 1.5 to 1.3. Assume that k_{RF} and k_M are equal to the values in Part d. After all these changes, what is Altman's new equilibrium price? (Note: D_1 goes to $2.27.)

Beta coefficients   **7-11**   Suppose Sartoris Chemical Company's management conducts a study and concludes that if Sartoris expanded its consumer products division (which is less risky than its primary business, industrial chemicals), the firm's beta would decline from 1.2 to 0.9. However, consumer products have a somewhat lower profit margin, and this would cause Sartoris's constant growth rate in earnings and dividends to fall from 7 percent to 5 percent.

a. Should management make the change? Assume the following: $k_M = 12\%$; $k_{RF} = 9\%$; $D_0 = \$2$.

b. Assume all the facts as given above except the change in the beta coefficient. How low would the beta have to fall to cause the expansion to be a good one? (Hint: Set $\hat{P}_0$ under the new policy equal to $\hat{P}_0$ under the old one, and find the new beta that will produce this equality.)

Exam-Type Problems

The problems included in this section are set up in such a way that they could be used as multiple-choice exam problems.

Bond valuation   **7-12**   The Desreumaux Company has two bond issues outstanding. Both bonds pay $100 annual interest plus $1,000 at maturity. Bond L has a maturity of 15 years and Bond S a maturity of 1 year.

a. What will be the value of each of these bonds when the going rate of interest is (1) 5 percent, (2) 8 percent, and (3) 12 percent? Assume that there is only one more interest payment to be made on Bond S.

b. Why does the longer-term (15-year) bond fluctuate more when interest rates change than does the shorter-term bond (1-year)?

Yield to maturity   **7-13**   It is now January 1, 1996, and you are considering the purchase of an outstanding Puckett Corporation bond that was issued on January 1, 1994. The Puckett bond has a 9.5 percent annual coupon and a 30-year original maturity (it matures on December 31, 2024). Interest rates have declined since the bond was issued, and the bond now is selling at 116.575 percent of par, or $1,165.75. You want to determine the yield to maturity for this bond.

a. Use Equation 7-3 to approximate the yield to maturity for the Puckett bond in 1996.

b. What is the actual yield to maturity in 1996 for the Puckett bond?

Yield to maturity   **7-14**   The Severn Company's bonds have 4 years remaining to maturity. Interest is paid annually; the bonds have a $1,000 par value; and the coupon interest rate is 9 percent.

a. Compute the *approximate* yield to maturity for the bonds if the current market price is either (1) $829 or (2) $1,104.

b. Would you pay $829 for one of these bonds if you thought that the appropriate rate of interest was 12 percent—that is, if $k_d = 12\%$? Explain your answer.

Rate of return for a perpetual bond   **7-15**   What will be the rate of return on a perpetual bond with a $1,000 par value, an 8 percent coupon rate, and a current market price of (a) $600, (b) $800, (c) $1,000, and (d) $1,500? Assume interest is paid annually.

Declining growth stock valuation   **7-16**   McCue Mining Company's ore reserves are being depleted, so its sales are falling. Also, its pit is getting deeper each year, so its costs are rising. As a result, the company's earnings and dividends are declining at the constant rate of 5 percent per year. If $D_0 = \$5$ and $k_s = 15\%$, what is the value of McCue Mining's stock?

Equilibrium rates of return   **7-17**   The beta coefficient for Stock C is $\beta_C = 0.4$, whereas that for Stock D is $\beta_D = -0.5$. (Stock D's beta is negative, indicating that its rate of return rises whenever returns on most other stocks fall. There are very few negative beta stocks, although collection agency stocks are sometimes cited as an example.)

a. If the risk-free rate is 9 percent and the expected rate of return on an average stock is 13 percent, what are the required rates of return on Stocks C and D?

b. For Stock C, suppose the current price, P_0, is $25; the next expected dividend, D_1, is $1.50; and the stock's expected constant growth rate is 4 percent. Is the stock in equilibrium? Explain, and describe what will happen if the stock is not in equilibrium.

Supernormal growth stock valuation **7-18** Assume that the average firm in your company's industry is expected to grow at a constant rate of 6 percent, and its dividend yield is 7 percent. Your company is about as risky as the average firm in the industry, but it has just successfully completed some R&D work which leads you to expect that its earnings and dividends will grow at a rate of 50 percent $[D_1 = D_0 (1 + g) = D_0(1.50)]$ this year and 25 percent the following year, after which growth should match the 6 percent industry average rate. The last dividend paid (D_0) was $1. What is the value per share of your firm's stock?

Effective annual rate **7-19** Assume that as investment manager of Florida Electric Company's pension plan (which is exempt from income taxes), you must choose between IBM bonds and AT&T preferred stock. The bonds have a $1,000 par value, they mature in 20 years, they pay $40 each 6 months, and they sell at a price of $897.40 per bond. The preferred stock is a perpetuity; it pays a dividend of $2 each quarter, and it sells for $95 per share. What is the effective annual rate of return (EAR) on the *higher* yielding security?

Simple interest rate **7-20** Tapley Corporation has a 14 percent coupon rate, semiannual payment, and $1,000 par value bonds that mature in 30 years. The bonds sell at a price of $1,353.54, and the yield curve is flat. Assuming that interest rates in the economy are expected to remain at their current level, what is the best estimate of Tapley's simple interest rate on *new* bonds?

Nonconstant growth stock valuation **7-21** Microtech Corporation is expanding rapidly, and it currently needs to retain all of its earnings, hence it does not pay any dividends. However, investors expect Microtech to begin paying dividends, with the first dividend of $1.00 coming 3 years from today. The dividend should grow rapidly—at a rate of 50 percent per year—during Years 4 and 5. After Year 5, the company should grow at a constant rate of 8 percent per year. If the required return on the stock is 15 percent, what is the value of the stock today?

Integrative Problem

Bond/stock valuation **7-22** Robert Balik and Carol Kiefer are senior vice presidents of the Mutual of Chicago Insurance Company. They are co-directors of the company's pension fund management division, with Balik having responsibility for fixed income securities (primarily bonds) and Kiefer being responsible for equity investments. A major new client, the California League of Cities, has requested that Mutual of Chicago present an investment seminar to the mayors of the represented cities, and Balik and Kiefer, who will make the actual presentation, have asked you to help them by answering the following questions.

Section I: Bond valuation   *a.* What are the key features of a bond?

   b. How is the value of any asset whose value is based on expected future cash flows determined?

   c. How is the value of a bond determined? What is the value of a 1-year, $1,000 par value bond with a 10 percent annual coupon if its required rate of return is 10 percent? What is the value of a similar 10-year bond?

   d. (1) What would be the value of the bond described in Part c if, just after it had been issued, the expected inflation rate rose by 3 percentage points, causing investors to require a 13 percent return? Would we now have a discount or a premium bond? (Hint: $PVIF_{13\%,1} = 0.8850$; $PVIF_{13\%,10} = 0.2946$; $PVIFA_{13\%,10} = 5.4262$.)

       (2) What would happen to the bond's value if inflation fell, and k_d declined to 7 percent? Would we now have a premium or a discount bond?

(3) What would happen to the value of the 10-year bond over time if the required rate of return remained at 13 percent or remained at 7 percent?

e. (1) What is the yield to maturity on a 10-year, 9 percent annual coupon, $1,000 par value bond that sells for $887.00? That sells for $1,134.20? What does the fact that a bond sells at a discount or at a premium tell you about the relationship between k_d and the bond's coupon rate?

(2) What is the current yield, the capital gains yield, and the total return in each case?

f. What is interest rate price risk? Which bond in Part c has more interest rate price risk, the 1-year bond or the 10-year bond?

g. What is interest rate reinvestment rate risk? Which bond in Part c has more interest rate reinvestment rate risk, assuming a 10-year investment horizon?

h. Redo Parts c and d, assuming the bonds have semiannual rather than annual coupons. (Hint: $PVIF_{6.5\%,2} = 0.8817$; $PVIFA_{6.5\%,2} = 1.8206$; $PVIF_{6.5\%,20} = 0.2838$; $PVIFA_{6.5\%,20} = 11.0185$; $PVIF_{3.5\%,2} = 0.9335$; $PVIFA_{3.5\%,2} = 1.8997$; $PVIF_{3.5\%,20} = 0.5026$; $PVIFA_{3.5\%,20} = 14.2124$.)

i. Suppose you could buy, for $1,000, either a 10 percent, 10-year, annual payment bond or a 10 percent, 10-year, semiannual payment bond. They are equally risky. Which would you prefer? If $1,000 is the proper price for the semiannual bond, what is the proper price for the annual payment bond?

j. What is the value of a perpetual bond with an annual coupon of $100 if its required rate of return is 10 percent? 13 percent? 7 percent? Assess the following statement: "Because perpetual bonds match an infinite investment horizon, they have little interest rate price risk."

Section II: Stock valuation

To illustrate the common stock valuation process, Balik and Kiefer have asked you to analyze the Bon Temps Company, an employment agency that supplies word processor operators and computer programmers to businesses with temporarily heavy work loads. You are to answer the following questions.

a. (1) Write out a formula that can be used to value any stock, regardless of its dividend pattern.

(2) What is a constant growth stock? How are constant growth stocks valued?

(3) What happens if the growth is constant, and $g > k_s$? Will many stocks have $g > k_s$?

b. Assume that Bon Temps has a beta coefficient of 1.2, that the risk-free rate (the yield on T-bonds) is 10 percent, and that the required rate of return on the market is 15 percent. What is the required rate of return on the firm's stock?

c. Assume that Bon Temps is a constant growth company whose last dividend (D_0, which was paid yesterday) was $2.00 and whose dividend is expected to grow indefinitely at a 6 percent rate.

(1) What is the firm's expected dividend stream over the next 3 years?

(2) What is the firm's current stock price?

(3) What is the stock's expected value one year from now?

(4) What are the expected dividend yield, the capital gains yield, and the total return during the first year?

d. Now assume that the stock is currently selling at $21.20. What is the expected rate of return on the stock?

e. What would the stock price be if its dividends were expected to have zero growth?

f. Now assume that Bon Temps is expected to experience supernormal growth of 30 percent for the next 3 years, then return to its long-run constant growth rate of 6 percent. What is the stock's value under these conditions? What is its expected dividend yield and capital gains yield in Year 1? In Year 4?

g. Suppose Bon Temps is expected to experience zero growth during the first 3 years and then to resume its steady-state growth of 6 percent in the fourth year.

What is the stock's value now? What is its expected dividend yield and its capital gains yield in Year 1? In Year 4?

b. Finally, assume that Bon Temps's earnings and dividends are expected to decline by a constant 6 percent per year—that is, g = −6%. Why would anyone be willing to buy such a stock, and at what price should it sell? What would be the dividend yield and capital gains yield in each year?

i. What does *market equilibrium* mean?

j. If equilibrium does not exist, how will it be established?

k. What is the Efficient Markets Hypothesis, and what are its three forms?

Computer-Related Problem

Work the problem in this section only if you are using the computer problem diskette.

Nonconstant growth stock valuation

7-23 Use the model on the computer problem diskette in the File C7 to solve this problem.

a. Refer to Problem 7-8. Rework Part e, using the computerized model to determine what Swink's expected dividends and stock price would be under the conditions given.

b. Suppose your boss tells you that she regards Swink as being quite risky and that she believes the required rate of return should be higher than the 12 percent originally specified. Rework the problem under the conditions given in Part e, except change the required rate of return to (1) 13 percent, (2) 15 percent, and (3) 20 percent to determine the effects of the higher required rate of return on Swink's stock price.

PART IV

Working Capital Management

CHAPTER 8

Working Capital Policy

In December 1993, Trans World Airlines (TWA) was labeled the best domestic airline for long flights and the second best for short flights by American business travelers. TWA received this accolade just one month after emerging from bankruptcy court. The future seemed rosy—employees had agreed to salary concessions in exchange for an equity position in the company, the airline had restructured its liabilities and lowered its cost structure, and the employees, with their new ownership position, appeared to possess a new-found motivation and concern for company success. Unfortunately, the nation's seventh largest airline discovered that its "new lease on life" was not a long-term contract. By the summer of 1994, TWA was struggling to find ways to cover a $135 million shortfall expected for the year. Many analysts believed the company was headed toward a second, and perhaps final, bankruptcy, primarily because it was in an extremely precarious position with respect to liquidity. The company's cash reserves were not sufficient to carry TWA through the lean sales that were expected during the coming months, and analysts were very pessimistic that needed funds could be raised with a stock or bond issue or by selling off assets. Investors also recognized TWA's liquidity problems—the company's stock fell about 50 percent in less than four months. It was obvious that TWA needed to improve its liquidity position to ensure future survival. The answer for TWA has been to reduce costs by laying off employees and by eliminating some of its flights. Although these solutions might provide short-term liquidity, the lost revenues and the customer ill will that is created might prove to be the ultimate downfall of the once-glamorous airline.

Firms strive to maintain a balance between current assets and current liabilities and between sales and each category of current assets in an effort to provide sufficient liquidity to survive, to live to maximize value in the future. As long as a good balance is maintained, current liabilities can be paid on time, suppliers will continue to provide needed inventories, and companies will be able to meet sales demands. However, if the financial situation gets out of balance, liquidity problems surface and often multiply

Continued

331

into more serious problems, perhaps even bankruptcy. For example, Merry-Go-Round Enterprises, a clothing retailer, filed for bankruptcy in January 1994 because it was having problems paying its creditors and, because of its poor financial condition, suppliers were reluctant to ship inventory needed to generate sales. As you read this chapter, consider how important liquidity, thus proper management of working capital, is to the survival of a firm. Also, consider the fact that many start-up firms never make it past the first few months of business primarily because such firms do not have formal working capital policies in place.

Generally we divide financial management decisions into the management of assets (investments) and liabilities (sources of financing) in (1) the *long term* and (2) the *short term.* In this section, we discuss *short-term financial management,* also termed **working capital management,** which typically is viewed as the management of the current assets and current liabilities of a firm. As you read this section, you will realize that a firm's value cannot be maximized in the long run unless it survives the short run. Firms fail most often because they are unable to meet their working capital needs; consequently, *sound working capital management is a requisite for firm survival.*

WORKING CAPITAL MANAGEMENT
The management of short-term assets (investments) and liabilities (financing sources).

About 60 percent of a financial manager's time is devoted to working capital management, and many of you who get jobs in finance-related fields will find your first assignment on the job will involve working capital. For these reasons, working capital policy and management is an essential topic of study. In this chapter, we provide an overview of working capital policy, and the remaining chapters in this section contain discussions of how specific working capital areas should be managed.

Working Capital Terminology

It is useful to begin the discussion of working capital policy by reviewing some basic definitions and concepts:

WORKING CAPITAL
A firm's investment in short-term assets—cash, marketable securities, inventory, and accounts receivable.

NET WORKING CAPITAL
Current assets minus current liabilities—the amount of current assets financed by long-term liabilities.

1. The term **working capital,** sometimes called *gross working capital,* generally refers to current assets.
2. **Net working capital** is defined as current assets minus current liabilities.
3. The *current ratio,* which was discussed in Chapter 3, is calculated by dividing current assets by current liabilities, and it is intended to measure a firm's liquidity. However, a high current ratio does not insure that a firm will have the cash required to meet its needs. If inventories cannot be sold, or if receivables cannot be collected in a timely manner, then the apparent safety reflected in a high current ratio could be illusory.
4. The best and most comprehensive picture of a firm's liquidity position is obtained by examining its *cash budget.* The cash budget, which forecasts cash inflows and outflows, focuses on what really counts—the firm's ability to generate sufficient cash inflows to meet its required cash outflows. Cash budgeting will be discussed in the next chapter.

WORKING CAPITAL POLICY
Decisions regarding (1) the target levels for each current asset account, and (2) how current assets will be financed.

5. Working capital policy refers to the firm's basic policies regarding (1) target levels for each category of current assets and (2) how current assets will be financed.

The term *working capital* originated with the old Yankee peddler, who would load up his wagon with goods and then go off on his route to peddle his wares. The merchandise was called working capital because it was what he actually sold, or "turned over," to produce his profits. The wagon and horse were his fixed assets. He generally owned the horse and wagon, so they were financed with "equity" capital, but he borrowed the funds to buy the merchandise. These borrowings were called *working capital* loans, and they had to be repaid after each trip to demonstrate to the bank that the credit was sound. If the peddler was able to repay the loan, then the bank would make another loan, and banks that followed this procedure were said to be employing sound banking practices.

We must distinguish between those current liabilities that are specifically used to finance current assets and those current liabilities that represent (1) current maturities of long-term debt; (2) financing associated with a construction program which, after the project is completed, will be funded with the proceeds of a long-term security issue; or (3) the use of short-term debt to finance fixed assets.

Table 8-1 contains balance sheets for Unilate Textiles constructed at three different dates. According to the definitions given, Unilate's December 31, 1995, working capital (current assets) was $470 million, and its net working capital was $470 − $130 = $340 million. Also, Unilate's year-end 1995 current ratio was 3.62.

What if the total current liabilities of $130 million at the end of 1995 included the current portion of long-term debt, say $10 million? This account is unaffected by changes in working capital policy because it is a function of past long-term debt financing decisions. Thus, even though we define long-term debt coming due in the next accounting period as a current liability, it is not a working capital decision variable in the current period. Similarly, if Unilate were building a new factory and initially financed the construction with a short-term loan which would be replaced later with mortgage bonds, the construction loan would not be considered part of working capital management. Although such accounts are not part of Unilate's working capital decision process, they cannot be ignored because they are *due* in the current period, and they must be taken into account when Unilate's managers construct the cash budget and assess the firm's ability to meet its current obligations (its liquidity position).

Self-Test Questions

Why is it important to properly manage short-term assets and liabilities?

Where did the term *working capital* originate?

The Requirement for External Working Capital Financing

Unilate's operations and the sale of textile products are very seasonal, typically peaking in September and October. Thus, at the end of September Unilate's inventories are significantly higher than they are at the end of the calendar year. Unilate offers significant sales incentives to wholesalers during August and September in *product sales.* At this point, GCP would have (1) paid *all* of the $3,375,000 wages owed its employees, so the balance of accrued wages would equal zero; (2) paid $325,000 to its suppliers, so the balance of accounts payable would decrease by $325,000; (3) received $700,000 payment from its customers, so the balance of accounts receivable would decrease by $700,000; and (4) borrowed $3,000,000 from a local bank to pay employees, so the balance of notes payable would increase by $3,000,000. At this point, the balance sheet would be:

Cash	$ 0	Accounts payable	$ 4,550,000
Accounts receivable	9,800,000	Accrued wages	0
Inventory	0	Notes payable	3,000,000
Current assets	9,800,000	Current liabilities	7,550,000
		Common equity	300,000
Fixed assets	300,000	Retained earnings	2,250,000
Total assets	$10,100,000	Total liabilities and equity	$10,100,000

But, on day 16, GCP also must conduct its normal daily business—raw materials must be purchased, and finished goods must be manufactured and sold. Because no additional cash flows will occur on this day, the purchase of raw materials will increase accounts payable by $325,000 = 50,000 × $6.50, the use of employees to manufacture finished goods will increase accrued wages by $225,000 = 50,000 × $4.50, and credit sales will increase accounts receivable by $700,000. Consequently, at the *end of day 16,* the balance sheet will be:

Cash	$ 0	Accounts payable	$ 4,875,000
Accounts receivable	10,500,000	Accrued wages	225,000
Inventory	0	Notes payable	3,000,000
Current assets	10,500,000	Current liabilities	8,100,000
		Common equity	300,000
Fixed assets	300,000	Retained earnings	2,400,000
Total assets	$10,800,000	Total liabilities and equity	$10,800,000

At this point, the accounts payable and accounts receivable balances reflect fifteen days worth of credit activities associated with the production and sales operations that took place from day 2 through day 16. On the other hand, because, at the beginning of the day, the employees were paid the wages due them for the first 15 days of business, accrued wages include only the amount owed to employees for their work to produce inventory on day 16. And, because there have not been any cash disbursements to stockholders, the balance in retained earnings represents the profits from the products sold for all 16 days GCP has been in business— $2,400,000 = $150,000 × 16 days.

At the beginning of day 17, GCP will pay for the materials it purchased on day 2. It also will receive payment for the products that were sold on day 2. This process will continue as long as the purchasing and payment patterns of both GCP and its customers do not change. So, GCP will pay out $325,000 every day to pay for materials purchased 15 days earlier (a decrease in payables), but the payables balance will remain the same from this point on because GCP also will purchase on credit raw materials valuing $325,000 (an increase in payables) every day to produce the product needed for that day's sales. Therefore, the accounts payable balance will remain constant at $4,875,000. Similarly, the balance in accounts receivable will remain at $10,500,000, because every day GCP will receive cash payments from customers totaling $700,000 (a decrease in receivables) at the same time $700,000 worth of products are sold for credit (an increase in receivables).

At this point, consider the cash flow position of GCP. From day 16 on, every day, GCP will receive cash payments from its customers which total $700,000, and it will make cash payments to its suppliers which total $325,000. But the employees are paid every 15 days, not every day. Therefore, GCP can accumulate $375,000 = $700,000 − $325,000 in cash each day until employees' salaries need to be paid again. The next time employees' salaries are paid is on day 31, so the cash account balance will increase by $375,000 for 15 days. Therefore, at the beginning of day 31, after all cash flows except accrued wages are recognized, GCP will have a cash balance equal to $5,625,000 = $375,000 × 15 days. Accrued wages will equal $3,375,000 = $225,000 × 15 days, so, after paying its employees, GCP still will have a cash balance equal to $2,250,000. This amount represents the *total cash profit* GCP has generated from the past 15 days of business. This amount can be used to pay off a portion of the bank loan, or it could be used to expand operations. In any event, once the balances in receivables and payables have stabilized because the daily adjustments to those accounts are offsetting, GCP actually realizes a *cash* profit of $150,000 per day.

As we can see from the above illustration, in general, once GCP's operations have stabilized so that the credit sales and credit purchasing patterns and the collection and payment activities stay the same day after day, the balances of accounts receivable and accounts payable will remain constant—the daily increase associated with each account will be offset by the daily decrease associated with the account. For example, every day, accounts receivable will increase by $700,000 as a result of that day's sales, but accounts receivable will decrease by the same amount because credit sales from 15 days previously are collected. Therefore, once the firm's operations have stabilized and cash collections from credit sales and cash payments for credit purchases have begun, the balance in accounts receivable and accounts payable can be computed using the following equation:

8-1	
	$$\frac{\text{Account}}{\text{balance}} = \frac{\text{Amount of}}{\text{daily activity}} \times \frac{\text{Average life}}{\text{of the account}}$$

So, for accounts receivable, the balance would be the daily credit sales times the length of time each account remains outstanding—$700,000 × 15 days = $10,500,000.

The preceding scenario will occur only if GCP's expectations, including forecasted sales, come true. What happens if GCP's forecasts are too optimistic? If GCP finds it cannot sell 50,000 units each day, its cash collections will decrease, its inventory probably will build up, and perhaps notes payable also will increase. If this pattern continues, GCP eventually might find itself in financial difficulty.

Although the illustration we used in this section is oversimplified, it should give you an indication of the interrelationships between the working capital accounts.

and so forth. Actually, of course, two factors prevent this exact maturity matching: (1) there is uncertainty about the lives of assets, and (2) some common equity must be used, and common equity has no maturity. To illustrate the uncertainty factor, Unilate might finance inventories with a 30-day loan, expecting to sell the inventories and use the cash generated to retire the loan. But if sales were slow, the cash would not be forthcoming, and the use of short-term credit could end up causing a problem (for example, look at the cash conversion cycle computed for Unilate in the previous section). Still, if Unilate makes an attempt to match asset and liability maturities, we would define this as a *moderate current asset financing policy.*

AGGRESSIVE APPROACH
A policy with which all the fixed assets of a firm are financed with long-term capital, but *some* of the firm's permanent current assets are financed with short-term, nonspontaneous sources of funds.

AGGRESSIVE APPROACH   Panel b of Figure 8-3 illustrates the situation for a relatively aggressive firm that finances all its fixed assets with long-term capital but part of its permanent current assets with short-term, nonspontaneous credit. A look back at Table 8-1 will show that Unilate actually follows this strategy. Unilate has nearly $504 million in permanent current assets (almost $914 million in permanent assets less $410 million fixed assets) projected for September 1996, so its temporary current assets must be about $690 − $504 = $186 million. However, the firm is projected to have $129 million in notes payable as well as temporary financing equal to about $100 million from peak levels of accounts payable and accruals (payables are projected to be $60 million higher than at the end of 1995, and accruals are projected to be $40 million higher). Thus, Unilate's level of temporary financing, which is nearly $229 million, exceeds its level of temporary current assets, so some part of its permanent assets are financed with temporary capital.

Returning to Figure 8-3, note that we used the term *relatively* in the title for Panel b, because there can be different *degrees* of aggressiveness. For example, the dashed line in Panel b could have been drawn *below* the line designating fixed assets, indicating that all of the permanent current assets and part of the fixed assets were financed with short-term credit; this would be a highly aggressive, extremely risky position, because the firm would be very much subject to dangers from rising interest rates as well as to loan renewal problems. However, short-term debt often is cheaper than long-term debt, and some firms are willing to sacrifice safety for the chance of higher profits.

CONSERVATIVE APPROACH
A policy in which all of the fixed assets, all of the permanent current assets, and some of the temporary current assets of a firm are financed with long-term capital.

CONSERVATIVE APPROACH   As shown in Panel c of Figure 8-3, the dashed line could also be drawn *above* the line designating permanent current assets, indicating that permanent capital is being used to finance all permanent asset requirements and also to meet some or all of the seasonal demands. In the situation depicted in our graph, the firm uses a small amount of short-term, nonspontaneous credit to meet its peak requirements, but it also meets a part of its seasonal needs by "storing liquidity" in the form of marketable securities during the off-season. The humps above the dashed line represent short-term financing; the troughs below the dashed line represent short-term security holdings. Panel c represents a very safe, conservative current asset financing policy, and generally is not as profitable as the other two approaches.

Self-Test Questions

What two key issues does working capital policy involve?

What is meant by the term *current asset financing policy*?

What are three alternative current asset financing policies? Is one best?

What distinguishes "permanent current assets" from "temporary current assets"?

Which of the three alternative current asset financing policies uses the most short-term debt?

Advantages and Disadvantages of Short-Term Financing

The three possible financing policies described above were distinguished by the relative amounts of short-term debt used under each policy. The aggressive policy calls for the greatest use of short-term debt, while the conservative policy requires the least; maturity matching falls in between. Although using short-term credit generally is riskier than using long-term credit, short-term credit does have some significant advantages. The pros and cons of short-term financing are considered in this section.

Speed

A short-term loan can be obtained much faster than long-term credit. Lenders will insist on a more thorough financial examination before extending long-term credit, and the loan agreement will have to be spelled out in considerable detail because a lot can happen during the life of a 10- or 20-year loan. Therefore, if funds are needed in a hurry, the firm should look to short-term sources.

Flexibility

If the needs for funds are seasonal or cyclical, a firm might not want to commit itself to long-term debt for three reasons. First, the costs associated with issuing long-term debt are significantly greater than the costs of getting short-term credit. Second, some long-term debts carry expensive penalties for prepayments (paying prior to maturity). Accordingly, if a firm thinks its need for funds will diminish in the near future, it should choose short-term debt for the flexibility it provides. And, third, long-term loan agreements always contain provisions, or covenants, which constrain the firm's future actions. Short-term credit agreements generally are much less onerous in this regard.

Cost of Long-Term versus Short-Term Debt

The yield curve normally is upward sloping, indicating that interest rates generally are lower on short-term than on long-term debt. Thus, under normal conditions, interest costs at the time the funds are obtained will be lower if the firm borrows on a short-term rather than on a long-term basis.

SMALL BUSINESS

Growth and Working Capital Needs

Working capital is the requirement that entrepreneurs most often underestimate when seeking funds to finance a new business. The entrepreneur generally plans for research and development and for the plant and equipment required for production. Working capital, however, frequently comes as a surprise to the entrepreneur, who probably expects to develop a product the market will immediately accept and for which the market will pay a substantial premium. This premium will, he or she assumes, lead to high profit margins, which will then "finance" all of the firm's other needs. As naive as this point of view seems, it nevertheless is common among founders of new businesses.

Rick was one of the founders of a new micro-computer software company that began seeking venture capital to support its products in early 1995. When speaking with a venture capitalist, who was concerned about the low level of funding being sought, Rick explained that the company's products had such a high profit margin that the company essentially would be self-financing. Rick claimed there would be no need for financing once the marketing was under way, because the profits would generate more than enough cash to pay for new product development.

Sally, a venture capitalist approached by Rick, was disconcerted by Rick's reasoning. She explained to Rick that the selling price of his product would not be received fully by his company because distributors and wholesalers were involved. She also pointed out that most of the sales would be on credit, so the revenues received by his company initially would be added to accounts receivable—not received as cash—and probably not collected, on average, for about 45 to 60 days. Meanwhile, Rick would have to write checks to pay for overhead, for high research and development expenses, for a marketing staff, for advertising, and so on. So instead of cash flowing in, the firm would be, on balance, paying cash out for the first few years of its life.

Rapid growth consumes cash; it does not generate cash. Rapid growth might generate profits, but profits do not pay the bills—cash does. Consider what a firm must do to sustain a high growth rate. If it is a manufacturer, the components of its assets include raw materials inventory, work-in-process inventory, finished goods inventory, and accounts receivable, as well as fixed assets. With the exception of fixed assets, these items all are components of gross working capital. When the firm produces a product, it makes an investment in each of these working capital items before any cash is received from collection of receivables, assuming all sales are credit sales.

Consider a small firm that finances its activities solely through the funds it generates. If the firm has a cash conversion cycle of 180 days cash is "turned over" only twice per year. If the company earns, say, 3 percent on its sales dollar, it has about 3 percent more money available after each cash cycle than before it. With two cycles per year, about 6 percent more is available for investment at the end of the year than at the beginning. Thus, annual growth of approximately 6 percent can be supported internally; so if the company is growing at a rate of 20 percent per year, it must either obtain funds externally or face enormous pressures.

Generally, a firm can fund more rapid growth internally either by raising the profit margin or by shortening the cash conversion cycle (increasing the number of cycles per year). To raise the profit margin, the company must raise prices, cut costs, or both. Raising prices might reduce growth (because customers will be less eager to buy at higher prices), but it might also help bring growth and financial resources more into balance. Shortening the cash conversion cycle requires reducing inventory, collecting receivables more efficiently, or paying suppliers more slowly. For example, if the cash turnover changes to four times per year from two, internally fundable growth doubles (12 percent rather than 6 percent). Improving the cash conversion cycle and thus increasing the rate at which the firm can support growth internally reduces the firm's needs for outside funds to a more manageable level.

For the small business with serious constraints on obtaining outside funds, these discretionary policies can help bring the firm's rate of growth into balance with its ability to finance that growth. Furthermore, such control on the part of management might impress bankers and others who have funds, and this might help the firm get the outside financing it would have preferred to have had all along.[1]

---

[1]Limits on growth and the concept of "sustainable growth" are explored in Chapter 6 of Robert C. Higgins, *Analysis for Financial Management*, 2nd edition (Homewood, Ill.: Irwin) 1989.

Risk of Long-Term versus Short-Term Debt

Even though short-term debt often is less expensive than long-term debt, short-term credit subjects the firm to more risk than does long-term financing. This occurs for two reasons: (1) If a firm borrows on a long-term basis, its interest costs will be relatively stable, perhaps even fixed, over time, but if it uses short-term credit, its interest expense will fluctuate widely, at times reaching quite high levels. For example, the rate banks charge large corporations for short-term debt more than tripled over a two-year period in the early 1980s, rising from 6.25 percent to 21 percent. Many firms that had borrowed heavily on a short-term basis simply could not meet their rising interest costs, and as a result bankruptcies hit record levels during that period. Similarly, in 1994, because the Federal Reserve increased rates six times during the year, short-term rates increased by more than 3 percent. (2) If a firm borrows heavily on a short-term basis, it could find itself unable to repay this debt, and it might be in such a weak financial position that the lender will not extend the loan; this too could force the firm into bankruptcy. Braniff Airlines failed during a credit crunch in the 1980s for this very reason.

Self-Test Questions

What are some advantages of short-term debt over long-term debt as a source of capital?

What are some disadvantages of short-term debt?

Summary

This chapter examined the relationship between working capital accounts, working capital policy, and alternative ways of financing current assets. The key concepts covered are listed below.

- **Working capital** refers to current assets, and **net working capital** is defined as current assets minus current liabilities. **Working capital policy** refers to decisions relating to the level of current assets and the way they are financed.
- Decisions affecting one working capital account will have an impact on other working capital accounts.
- Once the firm's operations have stabilized so that the cash inflows and the outflows into working capital accounts are the same, the account balance can be computed using the following equation:

$$\frac{\text{Account}}{\text{balance}} = \frac{\text{Amount of}}{\text{daily activity}} \times \frac{\text{Average life}}{\text{of the account}}$$

- The **inventory conversion period** is the average length of time required to convert raw materials into finished goods and then to sell them.
- The **receivables collection period** is the average length of time required to convert the firm's receivables into cash, and it is equal to the days sales outstanding.
- The **payables deferral period** is the average length of time between the purchase of raw materials and labor and paying for them.

- The **cash conversion cycle** is the length of time between paying for purchases and receiving cash from the sale of finished goods. The cash conversion cycle can be calculated as follows:

$$
\begin{array}{cccc}
\text{Cash} & \text{Inventory} & \text{Receivables} & \text{Payables} \\
\text{conversion} = \text{conversion} + & \text{collection} - & \text{deferral} \\
\text{cycle} & \text{period} & \text{period} & \text{period}
\end{array}
$$

- Under a **relaxed current asset investment policy,** a firm holds relatively large amounts of each type of current asset. Under a **restricted current asset investment policy,** the firm holds minimal amounts of these items.
- **Permanent current assets** are those current assets that the firm holds even during slack times, whereas **temporary current assets** are the additional current assets that are needed during seasonal or cyclical peaks. The methods used to finance permanent and temporary current assets constitute the firm's current asset financing policy.
- A **moderate approach** to current asset financing involves matching, to the extent possible, the maturities of assets and liabilities, so that temporary current assets are financed with short-term, nonspontaneous debt and permanent current assets and fixed assets are financed with long-term debt or equity plus spontaneous debt. Under an **aggressive approach,** some permanent current assets and perhaps even some fixed assets are financed with short-term debt. A **conservative approach** would be to use long-term capital to finance all permanent assets and some of the temporary current assets.
- The advantages of short-term credit are (1) the **speed** with which short-term loans can be arranged, (2) increased **flexibility,** and (3) the fact that short-term **interest rates** generally are **lower** than long-term rates. The principal disadvantage of short-term credit is the **extra risk** that the borrower must bear because (1) the lender can demand payment on short notice and (2) the cost of the loan will increase if interest rates rise.

Questions

8-1   How does the seasonal nature of a firm's sales influence its decision regarding the amount of short-term credit to use in its financial structure?

8-2   Assuming the firm's sales volume remained constant, would you expect it to have a higher cash balance during a tight-money period or during an easy-money period? Why?

8-3   Describe the relationships between accounts payable, inventories, accounts receivable, and the cash account by tracing the impact on these accounts of a product manufactured and sold by a company. Start with the purchase of raw materials, and conclude with the collection for the sale of the product.

8-4   Describe the cash conversion cycle. How can a financial manager use knowledge of the cash conversion cycle to better manage the working capital of a firm?

8-5   What are the advantages of matching the maturities of assets and liabilities? What are the disadvantages?

8-6   From the standpoint of the borrower, is long-term or short-term credit riskier? Explain. Would it ever make sense to borrow on a short-term basis if short-term rates were above long-term rates?

8-7 If long-term credit exposes a borrower to less risk, why would people or firms ever borrow on a short-term basis?

Self-Test Problems

(Solutions Appear in Appendix B)

Key terms **ST-1** Define each of the following terms:
    a. working capital; net working capital; working capital policy
    b. permanent current assets; temporary current assets
    c. cash conversion cycle; inventory conversion period; receivables collection period; payables deferral period
    d. relaxed current asset investment policy; restricted current asset investment policy; moderate current asset investment policy
    e. moderate, or maturity matching, current asset financing policy; aggressive current asset financing policy; conservative current asset financing policy

Current asset financing **ST-2** Vanderheiden Press Inc. and the Herrenhouse Publishing Company had the following balance sheets as of December 31, 1995 (thousands of dollars):

	Vanderheiden Press	Herrenhouse Publishing
Current assets	$100,000	$ 80,000
Fixed assets (net)	100,000	120,000
Total assets	$200,000	$200,000
Current liabilities	$ 20,000	$ 80,000
Long-term debt	80,000	20,000
Common stock	50,000	50,000
Retained earnings	50,000	50,000
Total liabilities and equity	$200,000	$200,000

Earnings before interest and taxes (EBIT) for both firms are $30 million, and the marginal tax rate is 40 percent.
    a. What is the return on equity for each firm if the interest rate on current liabilities is 10 percent and the rate on long-term debt is 13 percent?
    b. Assume that the short-term rate rises to 20 percent. While the rate on new long-term debt rises to 16 percent, the rate on existing long-term debt remains unchanged. What would be the return on equity for Vanderheiden Press and Herrenhouse Publishing under these conditions?
    c. Which company is in a riskier position? Why?

Working capital policy **ST-3** The Calgary Company is attempting to establish a current assets policy. Fixed assets are $600,000, and the firm plans to maintain a 50 percent debt ratio. The interest rate is 10 percent on all debt. The three alternative current asset policies under consideration are to carry current assets that total 40, 50, and 60 percent of projected sales. The company expects to earn 15 percent before interest and taxes on sales of $3 million. Calgary's marginal tax rate is 40 percent. What is the expected return on equity under each alternative?

Problems

Working capital accounts relationships **8-1** Go back to the GCP illustration at the beginning of the chapter. Assume the collection and payment patterns of both GCP and its customers do not change.

a. Construct the balance sheet for GCP at the close of business on day 31. Remember, the employees' salaries will have been paid at the *beginning* of the day for the *previous* 15 days they have worked, so accrued wages will include only one day of salaries (day 31).

b. How long will it take GCP to pay off the bank loan it took out on day 16 if the *daily cash profits* are used to repay the loan? (Ignore any interest costs.)

Cash conversion cycle **8-2** Look back in the chapter to Table 8-1, which showed the balance sheets for Unilate Textiles on three different dates. Unilate's sales fluctuate during the year due to the seasonal nature of its business; however, we can calculate its sales on an average day as total sales divided by 360, recognizing that daily sales will be much higher than this value during its peak selling season and much lower during its slack time. Unilate's projected sales for 1996 are $1,650 million, so daily sales are expected to average $4.583 million. The projected cost of goods sold for 1996 is $1,342 million, so daily credit costs associated with production are expected to average $3.728 million. Assume all sales and all purchases are made on credit.

a. Calculate Unilate's inventory conversion period as of September 30, 1996, and December 31, 1996. (Hint: The inventory conversion period is equal to the average number of days a product remains in inventory, and it is calculated as inventory divided by average cost of goods sold per day.)

b. Calculate Unilate's receivables collection period as of September 30, 1996, and December 31, 1996.

c. Calculate the payables deferral period as of September 30, 1996, and December 31, 1996. (Hint: The payables deferral period is equal to accounts payable divided by average daily purchases, which is the average CGS per day.)

d. Using the values calculated in Parts a through c, calculate the length of Unilate's cash conversion cycle on the two balance sheet dates.

e. In Part d, you should have found that the cash conversion cycle was longer on September 30 than on December 31. Why did these results occur?

f. Can you think of any reason why the cash conversion cycle of a firm with seasonal sales might be different during the slack selling season than during the peak selling season?

Working capital investment **8-3** Verbrugge Corporation is a leading U.S. producer of automobile batteries. Verbrugge turns out 1,500 batteries a day at a cost of $6 per battery for materials and labor. It takes the firm 22 days to convert raw materials into a battery. Verbrugge allows its customers 40 days in which to pay for the batteries, and the firm generally pays its suppliers in 30 days.

a. What is the length of Verbrugge's cash conversion cycle?

b. If Verbrugge always produces and sells 1,500 batteries a day, what amount of working capital must it finance?

c. By what amount could Verbrugge reduce its working capital financing needs if it was able to stretch its payables deferral period to 35 days?

d. Verbrugge's management is trying to analyze the effect of a proposed new production process on the working capital investment. The new production process would allow Verbrugge to decrease its inventory conversion period to 20 days and to increase its daily production to 1,800 batteries. However, the new process would cause the cost of materials and labor to increase to $7. Assuming the change does not affect the receivables collection period (40 days) or the payables deferral period (30 days), what will be the length of the cash conversion cycle and the working capital financing requirement if the new production process is implemented?

Working capital policy **8-4** The Hawley Corporation is attempting to determine the optimal level of current assets for the coming year. Management expects sales to increase to approximately $2 million as a result of an asset expansion presently being undertaken. Fixed assets total $1 million, and the firm finances 60 percent of its total assets with debt and the rest with equity (common stock). Hawley's interest cost currently is 8 percent on both short-term and longer-term debt (which the firm uses in its permanent structure). Three alternatives regarding the projected current asset level are available to the firm: (1) a tight policy requiring current assets of only 45 percent of projected sales, (2) a moderate policy of 50 percent of sales in current assets, and (3) a relaxed policy requiring current assets of 60 percent of sales. The firm expects to generate earnings before interest and taxes (EBIT) at a rate of 12 percent on total sales.

a. What is the expected return on equity under each current asset level? (Assume a 40 percent marginal tax rate.)

b. In this problem we have assumed that the level of expected sales is independent of current asset policy. Is this a valid assumption?

c. How would the overall riskiness of the firm vary under each policy?

Exam-Type Problems

The problems included in this section are set up in such a way that they could be used as multiple-choice exam problems.

Cash conversion cycle   **8-5**   The Saliford Corporation has an inventory conversion period of 60 days, a receivables collection period of 36 days, and a payables deferral period of 24 days.

a. What is the length of the firm's cash conversion cycle?

b. If Saliford's annual sales are $3,960,000 and all sales are on credit, what is the average balance in accounts receivable?

c. How many times per year does Saliford turn over its inventory?

d. What would happen to Saliford's cash conversion cycle if, on average, inventories could be turned over 8 times a year?

Cash conversion cycle and asset turnover   **8-6**   The Flamingo Corporation is trying to determine the effect of its inventory turnover ratio and days sales outstanding (DSO) on its cash flow cycle. Flamingo's 1995 sales (all on credit) were $180,000, and it earned a net profit of 5 percent, or $9,000. The cost of goods sold equals 85 percent of sales. Inventory was turned over 8 times during the year, and the DSO, or average collection period, was 36 days. The firm had fixed assets totaling $40,000. Flamingo's payables deferral period is 30 days.

a. Calculate Flamingo's cash conversion cycle.

b. Assuming Flamingo holds negligible amounts of cash and marketable securities, calculate its total assets turnover and ROA.

c. Suppose Flamingo's managers believe that the inventory turnover can be raised to 10 times. What would Flamingo's cash conversion cycle, total assets turnover, and ROA have been if the inventory turnover had been 10 for 1995?

Integrative Problem

Working capital policy and working capital financing   **8-7**   Daniel Barnes, financial manager of New York Fuels (NYF), a heating oil distributor, is concerned about the company's working capital policy, and he is considering three alternative policies: (1) a restrictive ("lean and mean" or "tight") policy, which calls for reducing receivables by $100,000 and inventories by $200,000; (2) a relaxed ("loose" or "fat cat") policy, which calls for increasing receivables by $100,000 and inventories by $200,000; and (3) a moderate policy, which would mean leaving receivables and inventories at their current levels. NYF's 1995 financial statements and key ratios, plus some industry average data, are given in Table IP8-1.

The cost of long-term debt is 12 percent versus only 8 percent for short-term notes payable. Variable costs as a percentage of sales (74 percent) would not be affected by the firm's working capital policy, but fixed costs would be affected due

TABLE IP8-1

Financial Statements and Other Data on NYF (thousands of dollars)

A. 1995 Balance Sheet

Cash and securities	$ 100	Accounts payable and accruals	$ 300
Accounts receivable	600	Notes payable (8%)	500
Inventories	1,000	Total current liabilities	$ 800
Total current assets	$1,700	Long-term debt (12%)	600
Net fixed assets	800	Common equity	1,100
Total assets	$2,500	Total liabilities and equity	$2,500

B. 1995 Income Statement

Sales	$ 5,000.00
Less: Variable costs	(3,700.00)
Fixed costs	(1,000.00)
EBIT	$ 300.00
Interest	(112.00)
Earnings before taxes	$ 188.00
Taxes (40%)	(75.20)
Net income	$ 112.80
Dividends (30% payout)	$ 33.84
Addition to retained earnings	$ 78.96

C. Key Ratios

	NYF	Industry
Profit margin	2.3%	3.0%
Return on equity	10.3%	15.0%
Days sales outstanding	43.2	30.0
Accounts receivable turnover	8.3×	12.0×
Inventory turnover	3.7	5.4
Fixed assets turnover	6.3	6.0
Total assets turnover	2.0	2.5
Debt/assets	56.0%	50.0%
Times interest earned	2.7×	4.8×
Current ratio	2.1	2.3
Quick ratio	0.9	1.3

to the storage, handling, and insurance costs associated with inventory. Here are the assumed fixed costs under the three policies:

Policy	Fixed Costs
Restrictive	$ 950,000
Moderate	1,000,000
Relaxed	1,100,000

Sales also would be affected by the policy chosen: Carrying larger inventories and using easier credit terms would stimulate sales, so sales would be highest under the relaxed policy and lowest under the restrictive policy. Also, these effects would vary depending on the strength of the economy. Here are the relationships Barnes assumes would have held in 1995:

State of the Economy	Sales (millions of dollars)		
	Restrictive	Moderate	Relaxed
Weak	$4.3	$4.5	$5.0
Average	4.7	5.0	5.5
Strong	5.3	5.5	6.0

Barnes considers the 1995 economy to be average.

You have been asked to answer the following questions to help determine NYF's optimal working capital policy.

a. How does NYF's current working capital policy as reflected in its financial statements compare with an average firm's policy? Do the differences suggest that NYF's policy is better or worse than that of the average firm in its industry?

b. Based on the 1995 ratios and financial statements, what were the company's inventory conversion period, its receivables collection period, and, assuming a 29-day payables deferral period, its cash conversion cycle? How could the cash conversion cycle concept be used to help improve the firm's working capital management?

c. Barnes has asked you to recast the 1995 financial statements, and calculate some key ratios, assuming an average economy and a restrictive (tight) working capital policy, and to check some calculations he has made. Construct these statements, and then calculate the new current ratio and ROE. Assume that common stock is used to make the balance sheet balance, but do not get into financing feedbacks. (Hint: You need to change sales, fixed costs, receivables, inventories, and common equity, plus items affected by those changes, and then calculate new ratios.)

d. Barnes himself has actually analyzed the situation for each of the policies under each economic scenario; the ROEs he has calculated are shown in Table IP8-2. What are the implications of these data for the working capital policy decision?

e. The working capital policy discussion thus far has focused entirely on current assets, and not at all on the current asset financing policy. How would you bring financing policy into the analysis?

Computer-Related Problem

Work the problem in this section only if you are using the computer problem diskette.

Working capital financing   **8-8**   Use File C8 on the computer problem diskette to solve this problem. Three companies—Aggressive, Moderate, and Conservative—have different working capital management policies as implied by their names. For example, Aggressive employs only minimal current assets, and it finances almost entirely with current liabilities plus equity. This restricted approach has a dual effect. It keeps total assets low, which tends to increase return on assets; but because of stock-outs and credit

TABLE IP8-2

ROEs under the Alternative Policies

State of the Economy	Working Capital Policy		
	Tight	Moderate	Easy
Weak	4.2%	3.2%	3.8%
Average	12.0	10.3	9.3
Strong	23.7	17.3	14.9
Average	13.3%	10.3%	9.3%

rejections, total sales are reduced, and because inventory is ordered more frequently and in smaller quantities, variable costs are increased. Condensed balance sheets for the three companies follow:

	Aggressive	Moderate	Conservative
Current assets	$225,000	$300,000	$450,000
Fixed assets	300,000	300,000	300,000
Total assets	$525,000	$600,000	$750,000
Current liabilities (cost = 12%)	$300,000	$150,000	$ 75,000
Long-term debt (cost = 10%)	0	150,000	300,000
Total debt	$300,000	$300,000	$375,000
Equity	225,000	300,000	375,000
Total liabilities and equity	$525,000	$600,000	$750,000
Current ratio	0.75:1	2:1	6:1

The cost of goods sold functions for the three firms are as follows:

Cost of goods sold = Fixed costs + Variable costs

Aggressive: Cost of goods sold	=	$300,000	+	0.70(sales)
Moderate: Cost of goods sold	=	$405,000	+	0.65(sales)
Conservative: Cost of goods sold	=	$577,500	+	0.60(sales)

Because of the working capital differences, sales for the three firms under different economic conditions are expected to vary as follows:

	Aggressive	Moderate	Conservative
Strong economy	$1,800,000	$1,875,000	$1,950,000
Average economy	1,350,000	1,500,000	1,725,000
Weak economy	1,050,000	1,200,000	1,575,000

a. Construct income statements for each company for strong, average, and weak economies using the following format:

> Sales
> Less: cost of goods sold
> Earnings before interest and taxes (EBIT)
> Less: interest expense
> Earnings before taxes (EBT)
> Less: taxes (at 40%)
> Net income (NI)

b. Compare the return on equity for the companies. Which company is best in a strong economy? In an average economy? In a weak economy?

c. Suppose that, with sales at the average-economy level, short-term interest rates rose to 20 percent. How would this affect the three firms?

d. Suppose that because of production slowdowns caused by inventory shortages, the aggressive company's variable cost ratio rose to 80 percent. What would happen to its ROE? Assume a short-term interest rate of 12 percent.

e. What considerations for the management of working capital are indicated by this problem?

CHAPTER 9

Managing Cash and Marketable Securities

A MANAGERIAL PERSPECTIVE

Cash is the oil that lubricates the wheels of business. Without adequate oil, machines grind to a halt, and a business with inadequate cash will do likewise. However, carrying cash is expensive—because cash is a nonearning asset, a firm that holds cash beyond its minimum requirements lowers its earnings potential.

Cash management is a very professional, highly refined activity. The following excerpt from a United California Bank (UCB) advertisement illustrates what is involved:

> Using any lockbox will accelerate cash flow. But a UCB Lock Box System does it with maximum efficiency. One difference is our unique city-wide zip code system for California lockbox customers. It speeds the receipt of your lockbox mail by several hours.
>
> Another difference: We work around the clock, seven days a week. So you can be sure your funds will be deposited, regardless of absenteeism or seasonal work loads.
>
> A third difference: We're the only West Coast bank using helicopters to speed collections of checks, thus reducing float.
>
> Also, using our computerized optimization models, we can determine how many lockboxes you should use, where they should be located, and how much money you'll save with them.
>
> Finally, you need not keep idle cash balances to guard against a failure to receive expected payments or to be ready for unexpected outflows. We can arrange a line of credit for you, let you know by 11 A.M. how much (if any) you need to borrow to cover the checks that have cleared, and have the money in your account by 4 P.M. Or, if your account has net inflows on a given day, we will use these funds to reduce your loan balance or to purchase securities, as you direct. With this service, you'll never have funds sitting idle.
>
> The cost is surprisingly low. Call us, and let us show you how UCB can make your cash work harder.

For some companies, these ideas make good sense. However, firms sometimes go too far with their cash management systems. For example, the general practice in the securities brokerage business (until Merrill Lynch lost a

Continued

major suit and agreed to stop doing it) was to write checks to customers located east of the Mississippi on a West Coast bank and checks to customers located west of the river on an East Coast bank. This slowed down payments on checks, deprived customers of the use of their money, and gave the brokerage firms the use of billions of dollars of their customers' money for extended periods of time. According to the SEC, this practice, although it increased brokerage firms' profits by millions of dollars each year, was "inconsistent with a broker-dealer's obligation to deal fairly with its customers."

As you read this chapter, consider just how important the various cash management techniques discussed really are. The lessons to be learned from this chapter apply to the cash holdings of individuals as well as businesses. Maybe you will be able to take some of the ideas discussed in this chapter and improve the handling of your own cash balances.

Throughout the text, we have emphasized that the primary goal of the financial manager should be to maximize the value of the firm. The discussions in Part III of the text showed that value is based on cash flows. Thus, managing cash flows is an extremely important task for a financial manager. Part of this task is determining how much cash a firm should have on hand at any time to ensure normal business operations continue uninterrupted. The solution seems simple—keep as much cash as possible. But cash is a nonproductive asset because, by itself, cash generates no return at all. So, if a firm holds more cash than it needs, shareholders' returns will not be maximized. Ideally, then, a firm would like to have *all* its cash invested in productive assets that are expected to generate positive returns. But this is not possible for most firms, because cash needs (demands) do not always coincide with cash receipts (supplies). Therefore, the ideal cash balance is somewhere between the extremes of holding as much cash as possible and holding no cash at all.

In this chapter, we discuss some of the factors that affect the amounts of cash firms hold, and we describe some of the cash management techniques currently used by businesses. In addition, we discuss the most commonly held types of marketable securities. Marketable securities are included with the discussion of cash management because these investments typically are used as a "temporary, very short-term residence" for idle cash balances that are not needed in the immediate time period. It will become apparent that marketable securities often are referred to as **"near cash" assets** because they serve many of the purposes of cash, but they offer a positive return while cash and corporate checking deposits do not.

"NEAR-CASH" ASSETS
Assets, such as marketable securities, which essentially serve the same purposes as cash; such assets are extremely liquid.

Cash Management

Even though cash is a "nonearning, or idle, asset," it is needed to pay for labor and raw materials, buy fixed assets, pay taxes, service debt, pay dividends, and so on. When possible, cash should be "put to work" by investing it in assets that have positive expected returns. Thus, the goal of the cash manager is to minimize the amount of cash the firm must hold for use in conducting its normal business activities, yet, at the same time, to have sufficient cash to (1) pay suppliers, (2) maintain its credit rating, and (3) meet unexpected cash needs. We begin our analysis with a discussion of the reasons for holding cash. For the purposes of our discussion, the term *cash* refers to the funds a firm holds that can be used for immediate cash disbursement needs—this includes the amount a firm holds in its checking accounts as well as the amount of actual currency and coin it holds.

Rationale for Holding Cash

Firms hold cash for two primary reasons:

TRANSACTIONS BALANCE
A cash balance necessary for day-to-day operations; the balance associated with routine payments and collections.

COMPENSATING BALANCE
A checking account balance that a firm must maintain to compensate a bank for services it provides.

PRECAUTIONARY BALANCES
A cash balance held in reserve for unforeseen fluctuations in cash flows.

SPECULATIVE BALANCE
A cash balance that is held to enable the firm to take advantage of any bargain purchases that might arise.

1. *Transactions.* Cash balances are necessary in business operations. Payments must be made in cash, and receipts are deposited in the cash account. Cash balances associated with routine payments and collections are known as **transactions balances.**
2. *Compensation to banks for providing loans and services.* A bank makes money by lending out funds that have been deposited with it, so the larger its deposits, the better the bank's profit position. In addition, if a bank is providing services to a customer, it might require the customer to leave a minimum balance on deposit to help offset the costs of providing the services. This type of balance, defined as a **compensating balance,** is discussed in detail later in this chapter.

Two other reasons for holding cash have been noted in the finance and economics literature: for *precaution* and for *speculation*. Cash inflows and outflows are somewhat unpredictable, with the degree of predictability varying among firms and industries. Therefore, firms need to hold some cash in reserve for random, unforeseen fluctuations in cash flows. These "safety stocks" are called **precautionary balances**—the less predictable the firm's cash flows, the larger such balances should be. However, if the firm has easy access to borrowed funds—that is, if it can borrow on short notice—its need for precautionary balances is reduced. Also, as we note later in this chapter, firms that would otherwise need large precautionary balances tend to hold highly liquid marketable securities, or *near cash,* rather than cash *per se.*

Sometimes cash balances are held to enable the firm to take advantage of bargain purchases that might arise. These funds are called **speculative balances.** However, as with precautionary balances, firms today are more likely to rely on reserve borrowing capacity and/or marketable securities portfolios than on cash *per se* for speculative purposes.

Although the cash accounts of most firms can be thought of as consisting of transactions, compensating, precautionary, and speculative balances, we cannot calculate the amount needed for each purpose, sum them, and produce a total desired cash balance, because the same money often serves more than one purpose. For instance, precautionary and speculative balances also can be used to satisfy compensating balance requirements. Firms do, however, consider all four factors when establishing their target cash positions.

Advantages of Holding Adequate Cash and Near-Cash Assets

In addition to the four motives just discussed, sound working capital management requires that an ample supply of cash be maintained for several specific reasons:

CASH DISCOUNT
A price reduction that suppliers offer customers for early payment of bills.

1. It is essential that the firm have sufficient cash and near-cash assets to take advantage of **cash discounts.** Suppliers frequently offer customers discounts for early payment of bills. As we will see in Chapter 12, the cost of not taking discounts generally is very high, so firms should have enough cash and near-cash assets to permit payment of bills in time to take discounts if such payment behavior is considered appropriate.

2. Adequate holdings of cash and near-cash assets can help the firm maintain its credit rating by keeping its current and acid test ratios in line with those of other firms in its industry. A strong credit rating enables the firm both to purchase goods from suppliers on favorable terms and to maintain an ample line of credit with its bank.

3. Cash and near-cash assets are useful for taking advantage of favorable business opportunities, such as special offers from suppliers or the chance to acquire another firm.

4. The firm should have sufficient cash and near-cash assets to meet such emergencies as strikes, fires, or competitors' marketing campaigns and to weather seasonal and cyclical downturns.

Self-Test Questions

Why is cash management important?

What are the two primary motives for holding cash?

What are the two secondary motives for holding cash as noted in the finance and economics literature?

The Cash Budget

Perhaps the most critical ingredient to proper cash management is the ability to estimate the cash flows of the firm so the firm can make plans to borrow when cash is deficient or to invest when cash is in excess of what is needed. Without a doubt, financial managers will agree that the most important tool for managing cash is the cash budget (forecast). The cash budget helps management plan investment and borrowing strategies, and it also is used to provide feedback and control to improve the efficiency of cash management in the future.

The firm estimates its general needs for cash as a part of its overall budgeting, or forecasting, process. First, it forecasts its operating activities such as expenses and revenues for the period in question. Then, the financing and investment activities necessary to attain that level of operations must be forecasted. Such forecasts entail the construction of *pro forma* financial statements, which we discussed in Chapter 4. The information provided from the *pro forma* balance sheet and income statement is combined with projections about the delay in collecting accounts receivable, the delay in paying suppliers and employees, tax payment dates, dividend and interest payment dates, and so on. All of this information is summarized in the **cash budget,** which shows the firm's projected cash inflows and outflows over some specified period. Generally, firms use a monthly cash budget forecasted over the next year plus a more detailed daily or weekly cash budget for the coming month. The monthly cash budgets are used for planning purposes and the daily or weekly budgets for actual cash control.

The cash budget provides much more detailed information concerning a firm's future cash flows than do the forecasted financial statements. Remember when we developed Unilate Textiles' 1996 forecasted financial statements in Chapter 4, net sales were projected to be $1,650 million. According to the forecasted financial statements, the net cash flow (in millions of dollars) generated from operations in 1996 are expected to be:

Net income	$70
Add: Noncash expenses (depreciation)	55
Gross cash flow from operations	$125
Adjustments to gross cash flow:	
Increase in accounts receivable	(18)
Increase in inventories	(27)
Increase in accounts payable	3
Increase in accruals	6
Total adjustments to gross cash flow	$ (36)
Net cash flow from operations	$ 89

So, in 1996, it is expected Unilate will generate $89 million cash inflow through normal production and sales operations. Much of this $89 million will be used to satisfy the financing and investment activities of the firm. Even after these activities are considered, Unilate's cash account is projected to increase by $2 million in 1996. Does this mean that Unilate will not have to worry about cash shortages during 1996? To answer this question, we must construct Unilate's cash budget for 1996.

To simplify the construction of Unilate's cash budget, we will consider only the last half of 1996 (July through December). Further, we will not list every cash flow that is expected to occur, but instead focus on the operating flows. Remember that Unilate's sales peak is in September. All sales are made on terms that allow a 2 percent cash discount for payments made within 10 days, and, if the discount is not taken, the full amount is due in 30 days. However, like most companies, Unilate finds that some of its customers delay payment for more than 90 days. Experience has shown that payment on 20 percent of Unilate's dollar sales is made within 10 days of the sale—these are the discount sales. On 70 percent of sales, payment is made during the month immediately following the sale, and payment is made on 10 percent of sales two months or more after the initial sales. To simplify the cash budget, though, we will assume the last 10 percent of sales is collected in the second month following the sale.

The costs to Unilate of cotton, wool, and other cloth-related materials average 60 percent of the sales prices of the finished products. These purchases generally are made one month before the firm expects to sell the finished products. In 1996, Unilate's suppliers have agreed to allow payment for materials to be delayed for 30 days after the purchase. Accordingly, if July sales are forecasted at $150 million, then purchases during June will amount to $90 million, and this amount actually will be paid in July.

Other cash expenses such as wages and rent also are built into the cash budget, and Unilate must make estimated tax payments of $16 million on September 15 and $10 million on December 15, while a $20 million payment for a new plant must be made in October. Assuming that Unilate's **target, or minimum, cash balance** is $5 million and that it projects $8 million to be on hand on July 1, 1996, what will the firm's monthly cash surpluses or shortfalls be for the period from July to December?

Unilate's 1996 cash budget for July through December is presented in Table 9-1. The approach used to construct this cash budget generally is termed the **disbursements and receipts method** (also referred to as **scheduling**) because the cash disbursements and cash receipts are estimated to determine the net cash flow expected to be generated each month. The format used in Table 9-1 is quite simple—it is much like balancing a checkbook; the cash receipts are lumped into one category and the cash disbursements are lumped into another category to determine the net effect monthly cash flows have on the cash position of the firm. More detailed formats can be used, depending on how the firm prefers to present the cash budget information.

The first line of Table 9-1 gives the sales forecast for the period from May through December. These estimates are necessary to determine collections for July through December. Similarly, the second line of the table gives the credit purchases expected each month based on the sales forecasts so the monthly payments for credit purchases can be determined.

The cash receipts category shows cash collections based on credit sales originating in three months (the current month and the previous two months). Take a look at the collections expected in July. Remember that Unilate expects 20 percent of the dollar sales to be collected in the month of the sales and, thus, to be affected by the 2 percent cash discount offered; 70 percent of the dollar sales will be collected one month after the sales; and the remaining 10 percent of the dollar sales will be collected two months after the sales (it is assumed there are no bad debts). So, in July, $29.4 million $= 0.20 \times (1 - 0.02) \times \$150$ million collections will result from sales in July; $87.5 million $= 0.70 \times \$125$ million will be collected from sales that occurred in June; and $10.0 million $= 0.10 \times \$100$ million will be collected from sales that occurred in May. Thus, the total collections received in July represent 20 percent of July sales (minus the discount) plus 70 percent of June sales plus 10 percent of May sales, or $126.9 million total.

The cash disbursements category shows payments for raw materials, wages, rent, and so on. Raw materials are purchased on credit one month before the finished goods are expected to be sold, but payments for the materials are not made until one month later (that is, the month of the expected sales). The cost of the raw materials is expected to be 60 percent of sales. July sales are forecasted at $150 million, so Unilate will purchase $90 million of materials in June and pay for these purchases in July. Similarly, Unilate will purchase $120 million of materials in July to meet August's forecasted sales of $200 million. Additional monthly cash disbursements include employees' salaries (which equal 21.33 percent of monthly sales), rent (which remains constant), and other operating expenses (which vary with respect to production levels). Cash disbursements that are not expected to occur monthly include taxes (September and December) and payment for the construction of additional facilities (October).

TABLE 9-1

Unilate Textiles: 1996 Cash Budget (millions of dollars)

	May	June	July	Aug	Sept	Oct	Nov	Dec
Credit Sales	$100.0	$125.0	$150.0	$200.0	$250.0	$180.0	$130.0	$100.0
Credit Purchases								
= 60% of next month's sales		90.0	120.0	150.0	108.0	78.0	60.0	
Cash Receipts:								
Collections from this month's sales								
= (0.2) (0.98) (current sales)			29.4	39.2	49.0	35.3	25.5	19.6
Collections from previous month's sales								
= (0.7) (previous month's sales)			87.5	105.0	140.0	175.0	126.0	91.0
Collections from sales two months previously								
= (0.1) (sales 2 months ago)			10.0	12.5	15.0	20.0	25.0	18.0
Total Cash Receipts			$126.9	$156.7	$204.0	$230.3	$176.5	$128.6
Cash Disbursements:								
Payments for credit purchases (1-month lag)			$ 90.0	$120.0	$150.0	$108.0	$ 78.0	$ 60.0
Wages and salaries (21.33% of monthly sales)			32.0	42.7	53.3	38.4	27.7	21.3
Rent			9.0	9.0	9.0	9.0	9.0	9.0
Other expenses			7.0	8.0	11.0	10.0	5.0	4.0
Taxes					16.0			10.0
Payment for plant construction						20.0		
Total Cash Disbursements			$138.0	$179.7	$239.3	$185.4	$119.7	$104.3
Net Cash Flow (Receipts − Disbursements)			$ (11.1)	$ (23.0)	$ (35.3)	$ 44.9	$ 56.8	$ 24.3
Beginning Cash Balance			$ 8.0	$ (3.1)	$ (26.1)	$ (61.4)	$ (16.5)	$ 40.3
Ending Cash Balance			(3.1)	(26.1)	(61.4)	(16.5)	40.3	64.6
Target (Minimum) Cash Balance			5.0	5.0	5.0	5.0	5.0	5.0
Surplus (Shortfall) Cash			$ (8.1)	$ (31.1)	$ (66.4)	$ (21.5)	$ 35.3	$ 59.6

The net cash flow line shows whether Unilate's operations are expected to generate positive or negative net cash flows each month. But this is only the beginning of the story. We need to examine the firm's cash position based on the cash balance existing at the beginning of the month and based on the *target (minimum) cash balance* desired by Unilate. The "bottom line" shows whether Unilate can expect a monthly cash surplus that can be invested temporarily in marketable securities or a monthly cash shortfall that must be financed with external sources of funds.

At the beginning of July, Unilate will have cash equal to $8 million. During July, Unilate is expected to generate a negative $11.1 million net cash flow; thus, July cash disbursements are expected to exceed cash receipts by $11.1 million. Because Unilate has only $8 million cash to begin July, ignoring any financing requirements, the cash balance at the end of July is expected to be a negative $3.1 million; effectively, if the firm doesn't find additional funding, its checking account will be overdrawn by $3.1 million. To make matters worse, Unilate has a target cash balance equal to $5 million, so, without any additional financing, its cash balance at the end of July is expected to be $8.1 million short of its target.

Unilate must make arrangements to borrow $8.1 million in July to bring the cash account balance up to the target balance of $5 million. Assuming that this amount is indeed borrowed, loans outstanding will total $8.1 million at the end of July. (We assume that Unilate did not have any loans outstanding on July 1 because its beginning cash balance exceeded the target balance.)

The cash surplus or required loan balance (shortfall) is given on the bottom line of the cash budget. A positive value indicates a cash surplus, whereas a negative value (in parentheses) indicates a loan requirement. Note that the bottom line surplus cash or loan requirement shown is a *cumulative amount*. Thus, Unilate must borrow $8.1 million in July; it has a cash shortfall during August of $23 million as reported on the Net Cash Flow line, so its total loan requirement at the end of August is $8.1 million + $23.0 million = $31.1 million, as reported on the bottom line for August. Unilate's arrangement with the bank permits it to increase its outstanding loans on a daily basis, up to a prearranged maximum, just as you could increase the amount you owe on a credit card. Unilate will use any surplus funds it generates to pay off its loans, and, because the loan can be paid down at any time, on a daily basis, the firm never will have both a cash surplus and an outstanding loan balance. If Unilate actually does have a cash surplus bottom line, these funds will be invested in short-term, temporary investments.

This same procedure is used in the following months. Sales will peak in September, accompanied by increased payments for purchases, wages, and other items. Receipts from sales also will go up, but the firm still will be left with a $35.3 million net cash outflow during the month. The total loan requirement at the end of September will hit a peak of $66.4 million, the cumulative cash plus the target cash balance.[1] This amount also is equal to the $31.1 million needed at the end of August plus the $35.3 million cash deficit for September.

Sales, purchases, and payments for past purchases will fall sharply in October, but collections will be the highest of any month because they will reflect the high September sales. As a result, Unilate will enjoy a healthy $44.9 million net cash gain during October. This net gain can be used to pay off borrowings, so loans outstanding will decline by $44.9 million, to $21.5 million.

Unilate will have an even larger cash surplus in November, which will permit it to pay off all its loans. In fact, the company is expected to have $35.3 million in surplus cash by the month's end, and another cash surplus in December will swell the excess cash to $59.6 million. With such a large amount of unneeded funds, Unilate's treasurer certainly will want to invest in interest-bearing securities or put the funds to use in some other way. Various types of investments into which Unilate might put its excess funds are discussed later in the chapter.

Before concluding our discussion of the cash budget, we should make some additional points:

1. For simplicity, our illustrative budget for Unilate omitted many important cash flows that are anticipated for 1996, such as dividends, proceeds from stock and

---

[1]This figure is calculated easily as follows:

$$\text{CASH}_{\text{Sept}} = \frac{\text{Beginning cash}}{\text{balance in July}} + (\text{Net CF})_{\text{July}} + (\text{Net CF})_{\text{Aug}} + (\text{Net CF})_{\text{Sept}} - \frac{\text{Target cash}}{\text{balance}}$$

$$= \$8 - \$11.1 - \$23.0 - \$35.3 - \$5.0 = \$(66.4)$$

bond sales, and additional fixed asset additions. Some of these are projected to occur in the first half of the year, but those that are projected for the July–December period could easily be added to the example. The final cash budget should contain all projected cash inflows and outflows.

2. Our cash budget example does not reflect interest on loans or income from investing surplus cash. This refinement could easily be added.

3. If cash inflows and outflows are not uniform during the month, we could seriously understate the firm's peak financing requirements. The data in Table 9-1 show the situation expected on the last day of each month, but on any given day during the month it could be quite different. For example, if all payments had to be made on the fifth of each month, but collections came in uniformly throughout the month, the firm would need to borrow much larger amounts than those shown in Table 9-1. In this case, we would have to prepare a cash budget identifying requirements on a daily basis.

4. Because depreciation is a noncash charge, it does not appear on the cash budget other than through its effect on taxable income, hence on taxes paid.

5. Because the cash budget represents a forecast, all the values in the table are *expected* values. If actual sales, purchases, and so on are different from the forecasted levels, then the projected cash deficits and surpluses also will differ. Thus, Unilate might end up needing to borrow larger amounts than are indicated, so it should arrange a line of credit in excess of that amount. For example, if monthly sales turn out to be only 90 percent of their forecasted levels, Unilate will need total financing equal to nearly $30 million in October, a 39 percent increase from the amount reported in the expected cash budget in Table 9-1.

6. Computerized spreadsheet programs such as *Lotus 1-2-3* are particularly well suited for constructing and analyzing cash budgets, especially with respect to the sensitivity of cash flows to changes in sales levels, collection periods, and the like. We could change any assumption, say the projected monthly sales or the time that customers pay, and the cash budget would automatically and instantly be recalculated. This would show us exactly how the firm's borrowing requirements would change if various other things changed. Also, with a computer model, it is easy to add features like interest paid on loans, interest earned on marketable securities, and so on. We have written such a model for the computer-related problem at the end of the chapter.

7. Finally, we should note that the target cash balance probably will be adjusted over time, rising and falling with seasonal patterns and with long-term changes in the scale of the firm's operations. Thus, Unilate probably will plan to maintain larger cash balances during August and September than at other times, and, as the company grows, so will its required cash balance. Also, the firm might even set the target cash balance at zero—this could be done if it carried a portfolio of marketable securities that could be sold to replenish the cash account, or if it had an arrangement with its bank that permitted the firm to borrow any funds needed on a daily basis. In that event, the target cash balance simply would be equal to zero. Note, though, that most firms would find it difficult to operate with a zero-balance bank account, just as you would, and the costs of such an operation would in most instances offset the costs associated with maintaining a positive cash balance. Therefore, most firms do set a positive target cash balance. Factors that influence the target cash balance are discussed later in the chapter.

Self-Test Questions

What is the purpose of a cash budget?

Suppose a firm's cash flows do not occur uniformly throughout the month. What impact might this have on the accuracy of the forecasted borrowing requirements?

How is uncertainty handled in a cash budget?

Is depreciation reflected in a cash budget? Explain.

Cash Management Techniques

Cash management entails more than forecasting the cash flows each month. Firms realize that proper management and control of cash flows can help make operations more efficient. Cash management has changed significantly over the past 20 years as a result of two factors. First, for much of that time, interest rates have been high relative to previous periods, which has increased the opportunity cost of holding cash and encouraged financial managers to search for more efficient ways of managing cash. Second, new technologies, particularly computerized electronic funds transfer mechanisms, have made improved cash management possible.

Most cash management activities are performed jointly by the firm and its primary bank, but the financial manager is responsible for the effectiveness of the cash management program. Effective cash management encompasses proper management of both the cash inflows and the cash outflows of a firm. More specifically, managing cash inflows and cash outflows entails (1) synchronizing cash flows, (2) using float, (3) accelerating collections, (4) getting available funds to where they are needed, and (5) controlling disbursements. Most business is conducted by large firms, many of which operate regionally, nationally, or even worldwide. They collect cash from many sources and make payments from a number of different cities. For example, companies like IBM, General Motors, and Hewlett-Packard have manufacturing plants all around the world, even more sales offices, and bank accounts in virtually every city where they do business. Their collection points typically are spread out, following sales patterns. Some disbursements are made from local offices, but most disbursements are made in the areas where manufacturing occurs or else from the home office (dividend and interest payments, taxes, debt repayments, and the like). Thus, a major corporation might have hundreds or even thousands of bank accounts, and because there is no reason to think that inflows and outflows will balance in each account, a system must be in place to transfer funds from where they currently are to where they are needed, to arrange loans to cover net corporate shortfalls, and to invest net corporate surpluses without delay. We discuss the most commonly used techniques for accomplishing these tasks in the following sections.

Cash Flow Synchronization

If you as an individual were to receive income once a year, you probably would put it in the bank, draw down your account periodically, and have an average balance during the year equal to about half your annual income. If you received income monthly instead of once a year, you would operate similarly, but now your average balance would be much smaller. If you could arrange to receive income daily and to pay rent, tuition, and other charges on a daily basis, and if you were quite confident of your forecasted inflows and outflows, then you could hold a very small average cash balance.

Exactly the same situation holds for business firms—by improving their forecasts and by arranging things so that cash receipts coincide with required cash outflows, firms can reduce their transactions balances to a minimum. Recognizing this point, utility companies, oil companies, credit card companies, and so on arrange to bill customers, and to pay their own bills, on regular "billing cycles" throughout the month. This improves the **synchronization of cash flows,** which in turn enables a firm to reduce its cash balances, decrease its bank loans, lower interest expenses, and boost profits.

SYNCHRONIZED CASH FLOWS
A situation in which cash inflows coincide with cash outflows, thereby permitting a firm to hold low transactions balances.

Check-Clearing Process

When a customer writes and mails a check, this does *not* mean that the funds are immediately available to the receiving firm. Most of us have been told by someone that "the check is in the mail," and we also have deposited a check in our account and then been told that we cannot write our own checks against this deposit until the **check-clearing** process has been completed. Our bank must first make sure that the check we deposited is good and then receive funds itself from the customer's bank before it will give us cash.

CHECK CLEARING
The process of converting a check that has been written and mailed into cash in the payee's (receiver's) account.

As shown on the left side of Figure 9-1, quite a bit of time could be required for a firm to process incoming checks and obtain the use of the money. A check must first be delivered through the mail and then be cleared through the banking system before the money can be put to use. Checks received from customers in distant cities are especially subject to delays because of mail time and also because more parties are involved. For example, assume that you receive a check and deposit it in your bank. Your bank must send the check to the bank on which it was drawn. Only when this latter bank transfers funds to your bank are the funds available for you to use. If a check is deposited in the same bank on which it was drawn, that bank merely transfers funds by bookkeeping entries from one of its depositors to another. But most deposited checks are drawn from outside banks, so the verification, or clearing process, generally is handled by a check-clearing system, termed a *clearinghouse,* set up by the Federal Reserve or a network of banks in a particular region. The length of time required for checks to clear is a function of the distance between the payer's (check writer's) bank and the payee's (depositor's) bank. In the case of private clearinghouses, the required time can range from one to three days. The maximum time required for checks to clear through the Federal Reserve System is two days, but mail delays can slow down things on each end of the Fed's involvement in the process.

Using Float

Float is defined as the difference between the balance shown in a firm's (or individual's) checkbook and the balance on the bank's records. Suppose a firm writes, on average, checks in the amount of $5,000 each day, and it takes six days for these checks to clear and to be deducted from the firm's bank account. This will cause the firm's own checkbook to show a balance $30,000 smaller than the

FIGURE 9-1

Diagram of the Check-Clearing Process

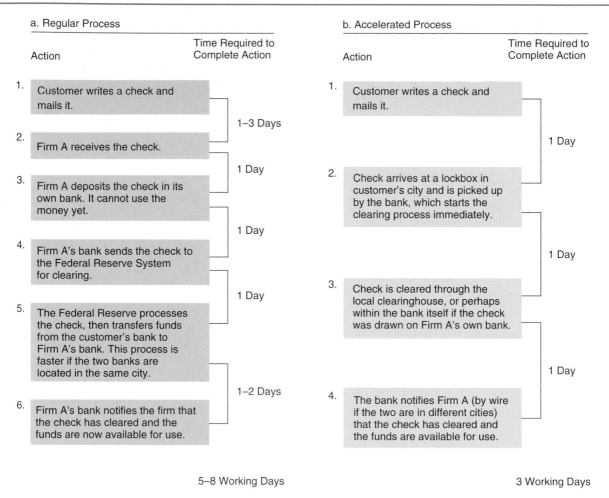

a. Regular Process

Action	Time Required to Complete Action
1. Customer writes a check and mails it.	
	1–3 Days
2. Firm A receives the check.	
	1 Day
3. Firm A deposits the check in its own bank. It cannot use the money yet.	
	1 Day
4. Firm A's bank sends the check to the Federal Reserve System for clearing.	
	1 Day
5. The Federal Reserve processes the check, then transfers funds from the customer's bank to Firm A's bank. This process is faster if the two banks are located in the same city.	
	1–2 Days
6. Firm A's bank notifies the firm that the check has cleared and the funds are now available for use.	

5–8 Working Days

b. Accelerated Process

Action	Time Required to Complete Action
1. Customer writes a check and mails it.	
	1 Day
2. Check arrives at a lockbox in customer's city and is picked up by the bank, which starts the clearing process immediately.	
	1 Day
3. Check is cleared through the local clearinghouse, or perhaps within the bank itself if the check was drawn on Firm A's own bank.	
	1 Day
4. The bank notifies Firm A (by wire if the two are in different cities) that the check has cleared and the funds are available for use.	

3 Working Days

DISBURSEMENT FLOAT
The value of the checks that have been written and *disbursed* but have not yet fully cleared through the banking system and thus have not been deducted from the account on which they were written.

COLLECTIONS FLOAT
The amount of checks that have been *received* and deposited but have not yet been credited to the account in which they were deposited.

balance on the bank's records; this difference is called **disbursement float.** Now suppose the firm also receives checks in the amount of $5,000 daily, but it loses four days while they are being deposited and cleared. This will result in $20,000 of **collections float.** In total, the firm's **net float**—the difference between $30,000 positive disbursement float and the $20,000 negative collections float—will be $10,000, which means the balance the bank shows in the firm's checking account is $10,000 greater than the balance the firm shows in its own checkbook.

If the firm's own collection and clearing process is more efficient than that of the recipients of its checks—which is generally true of larger, more efficient firms—then the firm actually could show a *negative* balance on its own books (referred to as a *red book balance*), but have a *positive* balance on the records of its bank. Some firms indicate that they *never* have positive book cash balances. One large manufacturer of construction equipment stated that, although its account, according to its bank's records, shows an average cash balance of about $20 million, its *book* cash balance is *minus* $20 million—it has $40 million of net

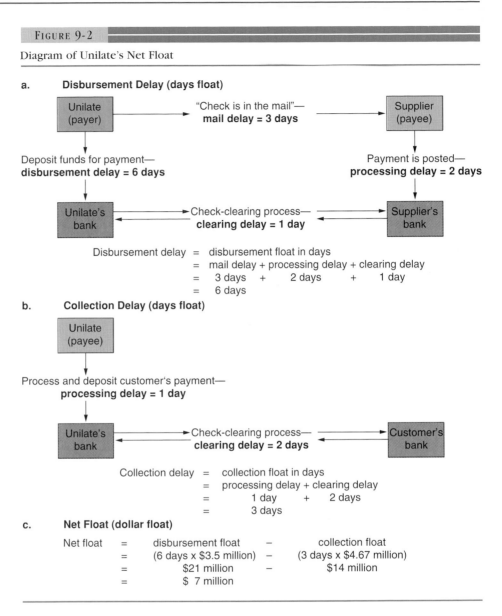

FIGURE 9-2

Diagram of Unilate's Net Float

a.   Disbursement Delay (days float)

Disbursement delay = disbursement float in days
                    = mail delay + processing delay + clearing delay
                    =   3 days   +   2 days   +   1 day
                    =   6 days

b.   Collection Delay (days float)

Collection delay = collection float in days
                  = processing delay + clearing delay
                  =   1 day   +   2 days
                  =   3 days

c.   Net Float (dollar float)

Net float = disbursement float   –   collection float
           = (6 days x $3.5 million) –   (3 days x $4.67 million)
           = $21 million   – $14 million
           = $ 7 million

NET FLOAT
The difference between disbursement float and collections float; the difference between the balance shown in the checkbook and the balance shown on the bank's books.

float. Obviously the firm must be able to forecast its disbursements and collections accurately in order to make such heavy use of float.

Delays that cause float arise because it takes time for checks (1) to travel through the mail (*mail delay*), (2) to be processed by the receiving firm (*processing delay*), and (3) to clear through the banking system (*clearing, or availability, delay*). Basically, the size of a firm's net float is a function of its ability to speed up collections on checks received and to slow down collections on checks written. Efficient firms go to great lengths to speed up the processing of incoming checks, thus putting the funds to work faster, and they try to delay their own payments as long as possible. For example, consider the net float that exists for Unilate Textiles, illustrated in Figure 9-2. When Unilate sends a check to pay its suppliers, on average it takes six days before Unilate's bank account is reduced by the amount of the check—it takes three days for the check written by Unilate to reach its supplier; it takes the supplier another two days to post the payment to accounts receivable and to prepare the check for deposit; then it takes one day for the check to clear through the banking system once it has been deposited by the supplier. So, Unilate has six days to make sure the balance in its checking account is sufficient to cover the check sent to the supplier. If Unilate's disbursements average $3.5 million a day, its *disbursement float* is $21 million = $3.5 million × 6 days. On the other hand, when Unilate receives payment from a customer, it takes an average of three days before the payment is available for use by Unilate—it takes Unilate one day to process and deposit the payment made by its customer; then it takes two days for the customer's check to clear. If Unilate's collections average $4.67 million a day, then its *collection float* is $14 million = $4.67 million × 3 days. In total, Unilate's *net float* is $7 million = $21 million − $14 million, so the balance Unilate shows in its checkbook is $7 million less than the balance shown by the bank. If Unilate can either slow down the collection on checks it has written or speed up the collection on checks it has received, net float can be increased.

Acceleration of Receipts

A firm cannot use customers' payments until they are received *and* converted into a spendable form, such as cash or an increase in a checking account balance. The sooner customers' payments can be put to use, the greater the return the firm can generate. Thus, it would benefit the firm to accelerate the collection of customers' payments and conversion of those payments into cash.

Financial managers continuously look for ways to collect receivables more quickly. If the delays caused by either the postal system, the processing of payments by the firm, or the clearing of checks through the banking system can be reduced, then receipts can be converted into a usable form sooner. Although some of these delays cannot be controlled directly by the firm, there exist several techniques both to speed collections and to get funds where they are needed sooner. In this section, we discuss lockbox plans, preauthorized debits, and concentration banking.

LOCKBOX PLAN
A procedure used to reduce float by having payments sent to post office boxes located near the customers.

LOCKBOXES A **lockbox plan** is one of the oldest and most widely used cash management tools. The term *lockbox* refers to a post office box to which customers' payments are sent, rather than to the firm's corporate headquarters. The firm arranges for a local bank to collect the checks from the post office box (perhaps several times a day) and to deposit them immediately into the company's checking account at the bank. The bank usually provides the firm with a daily record of the receipts collected, often via electronic systems that permit continuous updating of the firm's receivables accounts.

Lockboxes are geographically located in areas where a large number of customers exist. For example, a national firm headquartered in New York City might have its West Coast customers send their payments to a post office box in San Francisco, its customers in the Southwest send their checks to Dallas, and so on, rather than having all checks sent to New York City. Such arrangements reduce the delays associated with collections—the time customers' payments are in the mail (mail delay) is less because the lockbox (collection point) is located nearer the customers than the corporate headquarters; processing delay is almost completely eliminated because the collecting firm does not handle the payments; and the checks generally clear faster because the local bank is in the same Federal Reserve district as the customers' banks.

Lockbox services often can increase the availability of funds by two to five days over the "regular" system. If a firm that has credit sales equal to $5 million per day and an opportunity cost equal to 8 percent can speed up its collections by three days using a lockbox plan, its *annual* savings would be:

> **9-1**
>
> $$\frac{\text{Annual}}{\text{savings}} = \frac{\text{Credit sales}}{\text{per day}} \times \frac{\text{Decrease in}}{\text{collection delays}} \times \frac{\text{Opportunity}}{\text{cost}}$$

$$= \quad \$5 \text{ million} \times \quad 3 \text{ days} \quad \times \quad 0.08$$

$$= \quad \$1.2 \text{ million.}$$

Therefore, this firm would be willing to pay a *maximum* of $1.2 million a year for a lockbox plan to accelerate the collection of its customers' payments.

PREAUTHORIZED DEBITS   If a firm receives regular, repetitive payments from its customers, it might want to establish a **preauthorized debit system** (sometimes called preauthorized payments). With this collection/payment system, the collecting firm and its customer (paying firm) enter into an agreement whereby the paying firm's bank periodically (perhaps the first of every month) transfers funds from the paying firm's account to the collecting firm's account, even if that account is located at another bank. The paying firm's bank knows the amount to transfer because the collecting firm provides notification through its bank. These transactions also are called *checkless* or *paperless* transactions because they are accomplished without using traditional paper checks. However, a record of payment does appear on both parties' bank statements. Preauthorized debiting accelerates the transfer of funds because mail and check-clearing delays are totally eliminated, and processing delays are almost totally eliminated. Although preauthorized debits are efficient, and they appear to be the trend of the future, the pace of acceptance by payers has been much slower than originally predicted. Of course, a payer who agrees to a preauthorized debit system loses the disbursement float that is inherent in the paper-based system.

CONCENTRATION BANKING   Lockbox systems and preauthorized debits, although efficient in speeding up collections, might result in the firm's cash being spread around among many banks. **Concentration banking** is a cash management arrangement used to mobilize funds from decentralized receiving locations, whether they be lockboxes or decentralized company locations, into one or more central cash pools. The cash manager then uses these pools for short-term investing or reallocation among the firm's banks.

In a typical concentration banking arrangement, the firm's collection, or regional, banks record deposits received each day. Then, based on disbursement needs of the firm, the corporate cash manager transfers the funds from these collection points to a central bank account to achieve *cash concentration*. By pooling its cash, the firm is able to take maximum advantage of economies of scale in cash management and investment—often commissions are less per dollar on large

PREAUTHORIZED DEBIT SYSTEM
A system that allows a customer's bank to periodically transfer funds from its account to a selling firm's bank account for the payment of bills.

CONCENTRATION BANKING
A technique used to move funds from many bank accounts to a more central cash pool in order to more effectively manage cash.

investments, and there are instances where investments of larger dollar amounts earn higher returns than smaller investments (for example, super certificate of deposits).

Figure 9-3 illustrates a concentration banking arrangement that might be typical of a firm that has a lockbox collection plan. Notice the deposits in the regional banks are periodically transferred to the central, or **concentration bank,** where centralized cash management decisions are made.

One of the keys to concentration banking is the ability to quickly transfer funds from collecting banks to concentration banks. One commonly used transfer tool is the **depository transfer check (DTC).** A DTC is a nonnegotiable, unsigned document, which can be either paper or electronic, that is used just like any other check to transfer funds from one bank to another. The sole purpose of DTCs is to transfer funds between banks.

Paper DTCs are very cheap—the typical cost is less than $1—but it could take one or two days for the transferred funds to be available to the firm, because paper DTCs generally are transported via the mail. On the other hand, electronic depository transfer checks (EDTCs) are transported via computers, usually with the aid of electronic communications networks called **automated clearinghouses (ACH).** The ACH system consists of a coordinated network of ACH operators, financial institutions, and corporations that have the capabilities of transferring and processing data via computer affiliations. ACH systems guarantee one-day clearing regardless of the location of the bank on which the check was written. The ACH network sorts all transactions daily, the entries then are forwarded for processing the following day, and the processing accomplishes the actual transfer. The ACH system is relatively inexpensive if the firm has a large number of recurring transactions to process. For example, many states and large corporations use ACH transactions to automatically deposit the paychecks of their employees, and the United States government uses the ACH system for its routine payments such as Social Security. General Motors is one of the large corporations that have implemented an ACH system for the payment of their suppliers. GM's electronic system utilizes multiple banks across the nation, and it not only speeds up the payment process but also decreases uncertainty about the timing of the payment. This system benefits both GM and its suppliers because it reduces the required level of transactions and precautionary cash balances for each firm. GM's suppliers especially like the electronic system because overdue bills from GM have been reduced considerably, and suppliers take this into account when they bid for GM's business.

In addition to the automated clearinghouses, a wire transfer system, such as the *FedWire,* can be used to transfer funds. A **wire transfer** occurs when banks send messages concerning funds transfers across phone lines. The availability of funds is immediate. Because wire transfers are rather expensive (usually about $8 to $10 per transfer), they typically are used to move large sums that occur infrequently and sporadically.

Disbursement Control

Efficient cash management requires that both inflows and outflows be managed effectively. Accelerating collections represents one side of cash management, and controlling funds outflows represents the other side. In this section, we discuss three methods commonly used to control the disbursements of a firm.

CONCENTRATION BANK
A larger bank to which a firm channels funds from its local collection banks which operate lockboxes.

DEPOSITORY TRANSFER CHECK (DTC)
A nonnegotiable, unsigned instrument used for the sole purpose of transferring funds from one bank to another.

AUTOMATED CLEARINGHOUSE (ACH)
An electronic communications network that provides a means of sending data concerning funds transfers from one bank to another.

WIRE TRANSFER
A method of transferring funds between banks by sending information over telephone lines (wires); availability is immediate.

FIGURE 9-3

Concentration Banking Arrangement

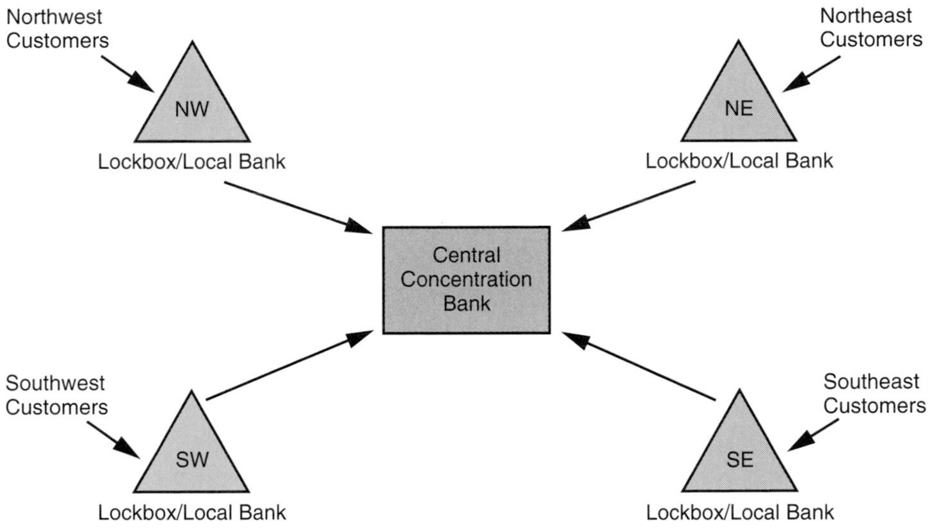

PAYABLES CENTRALIZATION   No single action controls cash outflows more effectively than the centralized processing of payables. This permits the financial manager to evaluate the payments coming due for the entire firm and to schedule the availability of funds to meet these needs on a companywide basis. Centralizing disbursements also permits more efficient monitoring of payables and float balances. Of course, there also are disadvantages to a centralized disbursement system—regional offices might not be able to make prompt payment for services rendered, which can create ill will and raise the company's operating costs. More than one firm has saved a few pennies by using a cheaper check-disbursing system but lost far more as a result of higher operating costs caused by ill will. As firms become more electronically proficient, the centralization of disbursements can be coordinated more effectively and such situations should be reduced substantially.

ZERO-BALANCE ACCOUNT (ZBA)
A special checking account used for disbursements that has a balance equal to zero when there is no disbursement activity.

ZERO-BALANCE ACCOUNTS   A **zero-balance account (ZBA)** is a special disbursement account that has a balance equal to zero when there is no disbursement activity. Typically, a firm establishes several ZBAs in a concentration bank and funds them from a master account. As checks are presented to a ZBA for payment, funds automatically are transferred from the master account. The use of zero-balance accounts is a popular method to simplify the control of disbursements and cash balances, thus reducing the amount of idle (non-interest-bearing) cash.

CONTROLLED DISBURSEMENT ACCOUNT (CDA)
A checking account in which funds are not deposited until checks are presented for payment, usually on a daily basis.

CONTROLLED DISBURSEMENT ACCOUNTS   Whereas zero-balance accounts typically are established at concentration banks, *controlled disbursement accounts (CDA)* can be set up at any bank. In fact, controlled disbursement accounts initially were used only in relatively remote banks, hence this technique originally was called *remote disbursement.* The basic technique is simple: **Controlled disbursement accounts (CDA)** are not funded until the day's checks are presented against the account. The firm relies on the bank that maintains the CDA to provide information in the morning (before 11 A.M., New York time) concerning the total amount of the checks that will be presented for payment that day. This early notification gives financial managers sufficient time to (1) wire funds to the controlled disbursement account to cover the checks presented for payment or (2) invest excess cash at midday, when money market trading is at a peak. CDAs are used by more than three-fourths of U.S. firms that have annual sales greater than $100 million.

Self-Test Questions

What is float? How do firms use float to increase cash management efficiency?

What are some methods firms can use to accelerate receipts?

What are some techniques for controlling disbursements?

Compensating Banks for Services

In addition to lending firms money, banks provide a great many services—they clear checks, operate lockbox plans, supply credit information, and the like. Because these services cost the bank money, the bank must be compensated for rendering them.

Compensating Balances

Most of the income earned by banks is derived from the interest received by lending funds obtained from deposits. So, if a firm maintains a deposit account with an average balance of $100,000, and if the bank can lend some of these funds at a net return of $8,000, the account is, in a sense, worth $8,000 to the bank. In this case, it is to the bank's advantage to provide services worth up to $8,000 to attract and hold the account.

Banks first determine the costs of the services rendered to their larger customers, and then they estimate the average account balances necessary to provide enough income to compensate for these costs. Firms can make direct fee payments for these services, but they often find it more convenient to maintain compensating balances rather than to pay monthly cash service charges to the bank. In some cases, firms maintain *minimum* checking account balances for safety/liquidity purposes; these otherwise idle balances can be used to meet compensating balance requirements.[2]

Compensating balances also are required by some banks under loan agreements. During periods when the supply of credit is restricted and interest rates are high, banks frequently require that borrowers maintain accounts that average a specified percentage of the loan amount as a condition for granting a loan; 10 percent is a typical figure. If the required balance is larger than the firm would otherwise maintain, the effective cost of the loan is increased; the excess balance

---

[2]Compensating balance arrangements apply to individuals as well as to business firms. Thus, you might get "free" checking services if you maintain a minimum balance of $500, but you are charged 25 cents per check if your balance falls below that amount during the month.

INDUSTRY PRACTICE

Banks Aren't Just Lenders Anymore—Ask A Cash Manager

Banks offer more than lending services to businesses—much more. In fact, some large banks generate as much as 50 percent or more of their profits from non-lending services. For example, at BankAmerica, corporate banking provides about 50 percent of overall income, up from 25 percent five years ago; at Continental Bank, nearly two thirds of the revenues are derived from non-lending sources; and, Chemical Bank generates more than 45 percent of its profits from services other than lending.

Competition for corporate customers is fierce, because the profits that can be made from non-lending services are very attractive. Major banks attract companies by offering a variety of electronic-based services that help to improve the efficiency of cash management. Some of the services offered include check-clearing functions, investment advisement, and cash management, including electronic lockbox systems and sweep accounts. Companies can improve the efficiency of their cash management by utilizing the services available through their banking relationships. For instance, Hewlett-Packard (HP) Company, a manufacturer of computers and business equipment, found BankAmerica could provide a national cash management system that was superior to what the company used previously. Before its relationship with BankAmerica, HP used a decentralized cash collection system, with employees scattered throughout the United States. Now, HP relies on the computer-based technology available at the

bank to coordinate its cash collections from a single location, with far fewer employees. BankAmerica offered HP a cash management package that previously the company either took care of itself or relied on more than one bank to provide. BankAmerica offered quicker check clearing, thus reduced collection float, through its national check-clearing network—more than 10 percent of all the checks written in the U.S. are cleared through one of the BankAmerica's check processing centers. Another service offered to large corporations by BankAmerica and such other banks as NationsBank and Citicorp, includes sweep accounts, which provide automatic investment of excess funds in short-term securities—excess funds are swept automatically into highly liquid investment accounts, where positive returns can be earned.

Some large banks, like BankAmerica, offer as many as 70 different services and products in an effort to attract corporate customers. Many banks believe that once they electronically link a company to computer-based services, a long-term relationship is established. Indeed, if a company relies on its bank for a national network of cash management experts, it might be difficult to "mechanically" unplug such services.

Certainly firms have become more aware of the non-lending services offered by banks, especially with respect to cash management. It no longer is considered fashionable to control cash movement from within the firm if such outside sources as banks can provide the expertise more economically.

COMPENSATING BALANCE (CB)
A deposit by a firm in a non-interest bearing account used to compensate the bank for services provided, including check clearing, lockbox arrangements, and loan servicing.

presumably "compensates" the bank for making a loan at a rate below what it could earn on the funds if they were invested elsewhere.[3]

Compensating balances (CB) can be established (1) as an *absolute minimum*—say, $100,000—below which the actual balance must never fall or (2) as a *minimum average balance*—perhaps $100,000—over some period, generally a month. The absolute minimum is a much more restrictive requirement, because the total amount of cash held during the month will be $100,000 plus the amount of the firm's transactions balances. The $100,000 in this case is "dead money" from the firm's standpoint. With a minimum average balance, however, the account could fall to zero on one day provided it was $200,000 on some other day, with the average working out to $100,000. Thus, the $100,000 in this case would be available for transactions. For business accounts, average balances are common, whereas absolute minimums are rare. But absolute balance requirements are less rare during times of extremely tight money.

---

[3]The effect of compensating balances on interest rates will be discussed in Chapter 12.

Overdraft Systems

OVERDRAFT SYSTEM
A system whereby depositors can write checks in excess of their balances, with banks automatically extending loans to cover the shortages.

One of the services provided by banks is an **overdraft system.** In such a system, if a depositor firm writes checks in excess of its actual balance, its bank automatically extends a loan to cover the shortage. The maximum amount of such loans must, of course, be established beforehand. Although statistics are not available on the usage of overdrafts in the United States, a number of firms have worked out informal, and in some cases formal, overdraft arrangements. Also, both banks and credit card companies regularly establish cash reserve systems for individuals. In general, the use of overdrafts has been increasing in recent years, and, if this trend continues, it will lead to a reduction of cash balances.

Self-Test Questions

What are compensating balances, and why are they used?

Differentiate between an absolute minimum and a minimum average compensating balance.

What are overdraft systems, and how do they work?

The Costs versus the Benefits of Cash Management

Although a number of techniques have been discussed to reduce cash balance requirements, implementing these procedures is not a costless operation. How far should a firm go in making its cash operations more efficient? As a rule, the firm should incur these expenses as long as the marginal returns exceed the marginal costs.

For example, suppose that by establishing a lockbox system a firm can reduce its investment in cash by $1 million without increasing the risk of running short of cash. Further, suppose the firm borrows at a cost of 12 percent. The lockbox system will release $1 million, which can be used to reduce bank loans and thus save $120,000 per year. If the costs of setting up and operating the lockbox system are less than $120,000, the move is a good one, but if the costs exceed $120,000, the improvement in efficiency is not worth the cost. It is clear that larger firms, with larger cash balances, can better afford to hire the personnel necessary to maintain tight control over their cash positions. Cash management is one element of business operations in which economies of scale are present.

Very clearly, the value of careful cash management depends upon the costs of funds invested in cash, which in turn depend upon the existing interest rates. In recent years, with interest rates fluctuating from relatively high levels to rather low levels, firms have been devoting a great deal of care to cash management.[4] As we write this early in 1995, the country is in a period of economic recovery, and even though interest rates are considered to be at moderate levels, the importance of cash management has become even more critical due to the need to boost profits.

---

[4]Banks also have placed considerable emphasis on developing and marketing cash management services. Because of economies of scale, banks can generally provide these services to smaller companies at lower costs than the companies could achieve themselves.

Self-Test Question

How much should a firm spend to implement methods to more effectively manage cash?

Marketable Securities

MARKETABLE SECURITIES
Securities that can be sold on short notice without loss of principal or original investment.

Realistically, the management of cash and the management of marketable securities cannot be separated—management of one implies management of the other, because the amount of marketable securities held by a firm depends on its short-term cash needs. In the first part of the chapter, we focused on cash management. Now we turn to **marketable securities,** or "near-cash" assets.

Rationale for Holding Marketable Securities

Marketable securities typically provide much lower yields than operating assets. For example, IBM holds a multibillion-dollar portfolio of marketable securities that yields about 6 percent to 7 percent, while its operating assets provide a return of about 14 percent. Why would a company such as IBM have such large holdings of low-yielding assets? There are two basic reasons for these holdings: (1) they serve as a substitute for cash balances, and (2) they are used as a temporary investment. These points are considered next.

MARKETABLE SECURITIES AS A SUBSTITUTE FOR CASH   Some firms hold portfolios of marketable securities in lieu of larger cash balances, liquidating part of the portfolio to increase the cash account when cash is needed. Most financial managers view the marketable securities account as a place to "temporarily put cash balances to work" earning a positive return during periods when these cash balances are not needed for liability payments or for longer-term investments. In such situations, the marketable securities could be used as a substitute for transactions balances, for precautionary balances, for speculative balances, or for all three. In most cases, the securities are held primarily for precautionary purposes—most firms prefer to rely on bank credit to make temporary transactions or to meet speculative needs, but they still might hold some liquid assets to guard against a possible shortage of bank credit.

A few years ago, IBM had substantially more marketable securities than it does today. Those large liquid balances had been built up primarily as a reserve for possible damage payments resulting from pending antitrust suits. When it became clear that IBM would win most of the suits, its liquidity needs declined, and the company spent some of the funds on other assets, including repurchases of its own stock. This is a good example of a firm's building up its precautionary balances to handle possible emergencies.

MARKETABLE SECURITIES HELD AS A TEMPORARY INVESTMENT   Temporary investments in marketable securities generally occur in one of the following two situations:

1. **To finance seasonal or cyclical operations.** If the firm has a conservative financing policy as we defined it back in Panel c of Figure 8-3, then its long-term capital will exceed its permanent assets, and marketable securities will be held when inventories and receivables are low. On the other hand, with a highly aggressive policy the firm will never carry any securities, and it will borrow heavily to meet peak needs. With a moderate policy, where maturities are matched, permanent assets will be matched with long-term financing, most seasonal increases in inventories and receivables will be met by short-term loans, but the firm also will carry marketable securities for short periods at certain times.

2. **To meet known financial requirements.** Marketable securities frequently are built up immediately preceding quarterly corporate tax payment dates. Further, if a major plant construction program is planned for the near future, if an acquisition is planned, or if a bond issue is about to mature, a firm might build up its marketable securities portfolio to provide the required funds.

For example, Commonwealth Edison, the electric utility serving Chicago, has a permanent, ongoing construction program, generating a continuous need for new capital. Because there are substantial fixed costs involved in stock or bond flotations, these securities are issued infrequently and in large amounts. During the 1970s, Commonwealth Edison followed the practice of selling bonds and stock *before* the capital was needed, investing the proceeds in marketable securities, and then liquidating the securities to finance plant construction. Plan A in Figure 9-4 illustrates this procedure. During the 1980s, however, Edison encountered financial stress. It was forced to use up its liquid assets and to switch to its present policy of financing plant construction with short-term bank loans and then selling long-term securities to retire the bank loans when they had built up to some target level. This policy is illustrated by Plan B of Figure 9-4.

Plan A is the more conservative, less risky policy. First, the company is minimizing its liquidity problems because it has no short-term debt hanging over its head. Second, it is sure of having the funds available to meet construction payments as they come due. On the other hand, the return earned on market-

---

FIGURE 9-4

Alternative Methods of Financing a Continuous Construction Program

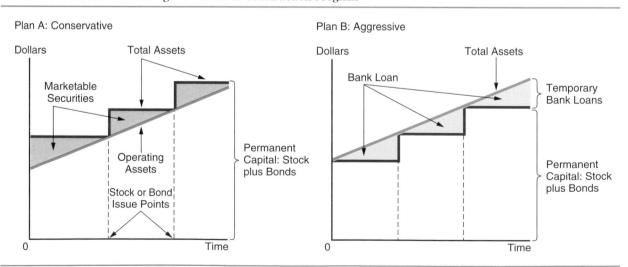

able securities generally is less than the rate at which funds can be borrowed, so following the less risky strategy has a cost.

Factors Influencing the Choice of Marketable Securities

A wide variety of securities is available to firms that choose to hold marketable securities. In this section we first consider the characteristics of marketable securities compared to other investments, and then we look at some specific instruments which are suitable investments for temporary excess cash.

MATURITY   Firms hold marketable securities in order to *temporarily* invest cash that otherwise would be idle in the short run. Cash invested in marketable securities is not needed for immediate disbursement, but it is expected to be needed in the near term, perhaps in a few days, weeks, or months. If the cash budget indicates the funds are not needed in the foreseeable future, they should be invested in longer-term investments that generally earn higher returns.

RISK   Recall that in Chapter 2 we developed this equation for determining the nominal interest rate:

$$k_{Nom} = k^* + IP + DRP + LP + MRP.$$

Here k^* is the real risk-free rate, IP is a premium for expected inflation, DRP is the default risk premium, LP is the liquidity (or marketability) risk premium, and MRP is the maturity (or interest rate) risk premium. Also, remember from Chapter 2 that the risk-free rate, k_{RF}, is equal to $k^* + IP$, and a U.S. Treasury bill comes closest to the risk-free rate. For other instruments considered appropriate as marketable securities, the default and liquidity risks are small, and the interest-rate risk is negligible. These risks are small because marketable securities mature in the short term, and the short run is less uncertain than the long run. So, default risk in the short run is lower than in the long run, and liquidity is higher for short-term investments than for long-term investments. Also, recall from Chapter 7, long-term investments, such as bonds, are much more sensitive to changes in interest rates than are prices of short-term investments. In general, then, the total risk associated with a portfolio of marketable securities, which consists of short-term investments, is less than the total risk associated with a portfolio of long-term investments. Consequently, the risk premiums included in the preceding equation generally will be lower for marketable securities than for long-term investments, hence k_{Nom} also will be less.

LIQUIDITY   We generally judge an asset's *marketability* by how quickly and easily it can be bought and sold in the financial markets. If an asset can be sold easily on short notice for close to its original purchase price, it is said to be a **liquid asset.** Because marketable securities are held as a *substitute* for cash and as a *temporary* investment, such instruments should be very liquid.

LIQUID ASSET
An asset that can be easily and quickly converted into cash at a price close to its original purchase value.

RETURN (YIELD)   As we know from earlier discussions, the higher a security's risk, the higher its required return. Thus corporate treasurers, like other investors, must make a tradeoff between risk and return when choosing marketable securities. And, because the marketable securities portfolio generally is composed of

different from the balances on the company's books. Besides, in the past, Christy has followed a very conservative approach to forecasting the daily excesses, and more often than not the amounts she transferred out of the accounts were much less than they could have been.

A recent economic downturn and a loss of business to competitors have contributed to poor earnings results for ExPers. So, after reviewing Christy's conservative forecasting record, the company's top management has directed her to transfer funds more liberally. In memo to Christy, the CEO stated:

> "We must do a better job of using float to our advantage—let's get more aggressive. First, we want you to overestimate daily deposits and to underestimate daily clearings of checks when you determine the amounts that should be transferred into interest-bearing securities each day. Specifically, increase your deposit estimates by at least 10 percent of what you normally would use, and decrease clearings by at least 15 percent of your normal estimate. Second, delay payments to our clients by two days, and use accounts at the most distant, smallest banks in our banking network. If we have to, it is easier to conceal our actions from these banks. Banks take advantage of float with our money, so let's turn the tables and take advantage of float with their money. These steps will help us recover some of the profits we have lost in recent times due to increased competition.

Christy has put you in charge of the estimates for the daily transfers of funds. According to your preliminary, and very rough estimates, if the CEO's directive is followed "to the letter," ExPers will be chronically overdrawn at its local banks. You have informed Christy of your findings, and, in essence, she said it doesn't matter, that the cash management area must do what the CEO requests. She pointed out that the overdrawn accounts could be disguised by continuously transferring funds from one bank to another before the checks have a chance to fully clear through the banking system, thus positive bank balances can be maintained in accounts that actually don't have any "real" funds. According to her, as the CEO mentioned, banks effectively do the same thing—so it can't be illegal. What should you do? What would you do if you were Christy?

Summary

In this chapter, we discussed cash and marketable securities. First, we examined some cash management techniques, and then we discussed marketable securities. The following key concepts are covered.

- The **primary goal of cash management** is to reduce the amount of cash held to the minimum necessary to conduct business.
- The **transactions balance** is the cash necessary to conduct day-to-day business, whereas the **precautionary balance** is a cash reserve held to meet random, unforeseen needs. A **compensating balance** is a minimum checking account balance that a bank requires as compensation either for services provided or as part of a loan agreement. Firms also hold **speculative balances,** which allow them to take advantage of bargain purchases. Note, though, that borrowing capacity and marketable security holdings reduce the need for both precautionary and speculative balances.
- **Effective cash management** encompasses the proper management of cash inflows and outflows, which entails (1) synchronizing cash flows, (2) using float, (3) accelerating collections, (4) determining where and when funds will be needed and insuring that they are available at the right place at the right time, and (5) controlling disbursements.
- **Disbursement float** is the amount of funds associated with checks written by a firm that are still in process and hence have not yet been deducted by the bank from the firm's account.

SMALL BUSINESS

Building a Banking Relationship to Maintain Liquidity

Building a good banking relationship is important for a small business for two reasons. The most obvious reason is that the firm may need money for working capital, expansion, equipment, and so on. A less obvious reason is that the banker may be a valuable source of financial advice for an inexperienced small-business owner. Once the bank has loaned the business money, it is in the best interest of both the bank and the business for the firm to survive. Thus, a good banker will take a genuine interest in the firm.

The banker will be concerned about and be watchful for the one thing the entrepreneur most wants to avoid—the failure of the business. To that end, the banker will follow the firm's financial progress very closely, and that watchful eye can be of great benefit to the entrepreneur.

FINDING THE RIGHT BANKER Often the small business owner does not know how to go about finding the right banker. Looking for funds, he or she might go to the nearest bank and ask for money to finance an idea or proposal. If the bank is largely a retail bank with little expertise in commercial accounts, the firm could find that it has made a terrible mistake. Businesses should shop for their banks, just like they shop for products.

The right banker should satisfy at least three conditions: (1) The banker should understand the entrepreneur's business. (2) The banker should be interested in the business and commit to follow it closely. (3) The banker should be experienced and understand the pitfalls that wipe out small firms. In addition, the bank itself should be adequately capitalized and able to offer funds at the level the business needs, and it should provide other services (such as cash management) that businesses need. Also, the banker and entrepreneur must have rapport—miscommunication could cause serious financial stress for a small business, because the banking relationship represents the small firm's liquidity lifeline.

TIPS FROM A SENIOR LOAN OFFICER The senior loan officer of a large commercial bank provides a good perspective concerning establishing a banking relationship with a small business. He summarized the points he teaches new officers to consider when reviewing a proposal to grant credit. These points can be used by the bank to improve the liquidity and the potential for survival of a small business.

First, he tells officers simply to ask, "Why do you need the money?" He wants to know not only how the funds will be used, but also why the company cannot generate funds itself. This is not to imply that the bank is taking the arrogant view that "We only lend money to people who don't need it." Rather, the loan officer needs to be sure that the entrepreneur understands the business well enough to know the answers.

Next, loan officers should carefully investigate how the loan will be repaid. If the funds will come from operating cash flows, how realistic are the cash budgets provided by the company? If it is a seasonal working capital loan, what is the company's track record for managing inventories and receivables, especially in the off season when liquidity is the key to survival? If the business is not seasonal, does the firm maintain sufficient liquidity to meet payments on debt incurred from operations?

Loan officers should realize that some working capital in a growing business essentially is permanent. Therefore, the next concern is whether management truly is in control of the business and whether the financing can be supported by assets.

The final question the loan officer asks, which is the most important of all, is: "What are your biggest problems?" A loan officer should explain that he or she isn't looking for firms that have no problems, because every firm has problems. What the banker really is trying to find out is whether the entrepreneur is perceptive and in control of the business, is frank and candid, and willing to talk honestly about the business's problems. A good small-business owner-manager will perceive problems. If the entrepreneur isn't aware of them, they can lead to business failure. If they are recognized, the problems perhaps can be solved.

CONCLUSION For a small business, a good banking relationship should be viewed as a partnership to survival and future growth potential; it can mean the difference between liquidity and illiquidity, success and failure. Establishing such a relationship is vitally important. Both sides are better off if the relationship is an open one, where the banker and the business owner understand each other and communicate honestly when dealing with the various problems of the small, but growing, firm.

- **Collections float** is the amount of funds associated with checks written to a firm that have not been cleared and hence are not yet available for use.
- **Net float** is the difference between disbursement float and collections float, and it also is equal to the difference between the balance in a firm's checkbook and the balance on the bank's records. The larger the net float, the smaller the cash balances the firm must maintain, so net float is good.
- Two techniques that can be used to speed up collections are (1) **lockboxes** and (2) **preauthorized debits.** Also, a **concentration banking system** consolidates cash into a centralized pool that can be managed more efficiently than a large number of individual accounts.
- Three techniques for controlling disbursements are (1) **payables centralization**, (2) **zero-balance accounts**, and (3) **controlled disbursement accounts.**
- The implementation of a sophisticated cash management system is costly, so all cash management actions must be evaluated to ensure that **benefits exceed costs.**
- Firms can reduce their cash balances by holding **marketable securities,** which can be sold easily on short notice at close to their quoted market values. Marketable securities serve both as a substitute for cash and as a temporary investment for funds that will be needed in the near future. Safety is the primary consideration when selecting marketable securities.

Questions

9-1 What are the two principal reasons for holding cash? Can a firm estimate its target cash balance by summing the cash held to satisfy each of the two reasons?

9-2 Explain how each of the following factors probably would affect a firm's target cash balance if all other factors were held constant.
- *a.* The firm institutes a new billing procedure that better synchronizes its cash inflows and outflows.
- *b.* The firm develops a new sales forecasting technique that improves its forecasts.
- *c.* The firm reduces its portfolio of U.S. Treasury bills.
- *d.* The firm arranges to use an overdraft system for its checking account.
- *e.* The firm borrows a large amount of money from its bank and also begins to write far more checks than it did in the past.
- *f.* Interest rates on Treasury bills rise from 5 percent to 10 percent.

9-3 What is a cash budget? For what purposes should cash budgets be created?

9-4 Why is a cash budget important even when there is plenty of cash in the bank?

9-5 Discuss why it is important for a financial manager to understand the concept of float in order to effectively manage the firm's cash.

9-6 Why would a lockbox plan make more sense for a firm that makes sales all over the United States than for a firm with the same volume of business but concentrated where the corporate headquarters are located?

9-7 What is a concentration banking system? What are the advantages and disadvantages of using concentration banking?

9-8 In general, does a firm wish to speed up or slow down collections of payments made by its customers? Why? How does the same firm wish to manage its disbursements? Why?

9-9   Would a corporate treasurer be more tempted to invest the firm's cash in long-term as opposed to short-term securities when the yield curve was upward sloping or downward sloping?

9-10   What does the term *liquidity* mean? Which would be more important to a firm that held a portfolio of marketable securities as precautionary balances against the possibility of losing a major lawsuit—liquidity or rate of return? Explain.

9-11   Firm A's management is very conservative whereas Firm B's is more aggressive. Is it true that, other things the same, Firm B would probably have larger holdings of marketable securities? Explain.

9-12   When selecting securities for portfolio investments, corporate treasurers must make a tradeoff between risk and returns. Is it true that most treasurers are willing to assume a fairly high exposure to risk to gain higher expected returns?

Self-Test Problems

(Solutions appear in Appendix B)

Key terms   **ST-1**   Define each of the following terms:
   a. transactions balance; compensating balance; precautionary balance; speculative balance
   b. cash discounts
   c. synchronized cash flows
   d. check clearing; net float; disbursement float; collections float
   e. mail delay; processing delay; clearing (availability) delay
   f. lockbox plan; preauthorized debit
   g. depository transfer check (DTC); electronic depository transfer; concentration bank
   h. overdraft system; zero-balance accounts; controlled disbursement accounts
   i. marketable securities

Float   **ST-2**   The Upton Company is setting up a new checking account with Howe National Bank. Upton plans to issue checks in the amount of $1 million each day and to deduct them from its own records at the close of business on the day they are written. On average, the bank will receive and clear the checks at 5 P.M. the third day after they are written; for example, a check written on Monday will be cleared on Thursday afternoon. The firm's agreement with the bank requires it to maintain a $500,000 average compensating balance; this is $250,000 greater than the cash balance the firm would otherwise have on deposit. It makes a $500,000 deposit at the time it opens the account.
   a. Assuming that the firm makes deposits at 4 P.M. each day (and the bank includes them in that day's transactions), how much must the firm deposit daily in order to maintain a sufficient balance once it reaches a steady state? (To do this, set up a table that shows the daily balance recorded on the company's books and the daily balance at the bank until a steady state is reached.) Indicate the required deposit on Day 1, Day 2, Day 3, if any, and each day thereafter, assuming that the company will write checks for $1 million on Day 1 and each day thereafter.
   b. How many days of float does Upton have?
   c. What ending daily balance should the firm try to maintain (1) on the bank's records and (2) on its own records?

Comparison of   **ST-3**   Kroncke Inc. has grown from a small Boston firm with customers concentrated in
transfer methods   New England to a large, national firm serving customers throughout the United States. It has, however, kept its central billing system in Boston. On average, 5 days

elapse from the time customers mail payments until Kroncke is able to receive, process, and deposit them. To shorten the collection period, Kroncke is considering the installation of a lockbox system consisting of 30 local depository banks, or lockbox operators, and 8 regional concentration banks. The fixed costs of operating the system are estimated to be $14,000 per month. Under this system, customers' checks would be received by the lockbox operator 1 day after they are mailed, and daily collections should average $30,000 at each location. The collections would be transferred daily to the regional concentration banks. One transfer mechanism involves having the local depository banks use "mail depository transfer checks," or DTCs, to move the funds to the concentration banks; the alternative would be to use electronic (wire) transfers. A DTC would cost only 75 cents, but it would take 2 days before funds were in the concentration bank and thus available to Kroncke. Therefore, float time under the DTC system would be 1 day for mail plus 2 days for transfers, or 3 days total, down from 5 days. A wire transfer would cost $11, but funds would be available immediately, so float time would be only 1 day. If Kroncke's opportunity cost is 11 percent, should it initiate the lockbox system? If so, which transfer method should be used? (Assume that there are $52 \times 5 = 260$ working days in a year.)

Problems

Disbursement float

9-1 The Garvin Company is setting up a new checking account with Barngrover National Bank. Garvin plans to issue checks in the amount of $1.6 million each day and to deduct them from its own records at the close of business on the day they are written. On average, the bank will receive and clear (that is, deduct from the firm's bank balance) the checks at 5 P.M. the fourth day after they are written; for example, a check written on Monday will be cleared on Friday afternoon. The firm's agreement with the bank requires it to maintain a $1.2 million average compensating balance; this is $400,000 greater than the cash balance the firm would otherwise have on deposit. It makes a $1.2 million deposit at the time it opens the account.

a. Assuming that the firm makes deposits at 4 P.M. each day (and the bank includes them in that day's transactions), how much must it deposit daily in order to maintain a sufficient balance once it reaches a steady state? (To do this, set up a table that shows the daily balance recorded on the company's books and the daily balance at the bank until a steady state is reached.) Indicate the required deposit on Day 1, Day 2, Day 3, Day 4, if any, and each day thereafter, assuming that the company will write checks for $1.6 million on Day 1 and each day thereafter.

b. How many days of float does Garvin carry?

c. What ending daily balance should the firm try to maintain (1) on the bank's records and (2) on its own records?

d. Explain how net float can help increase the value of the firm's common stock.

Cash budgeting

9-2 Patricia Smith recently leased space in the Southside Mall and opened a new business, Smith's Coin Shop. Business has been good, but Smith has frequently run out of cash. This has necessitated late payment on certain orders, which in turn is beginning to cause a problem with suppliers. Smith plans to borrow from the bank to have cash ready as needed, but first she needs a forecast of just how much she must borrow. Accordingly, she has asked you to prepare a cash budget for the critical period around Christmas, when needs will be especially high.

Sales are made on a cash basis only. Smith's purchases must be paid for during the following month. Smith pays herself a salary of $4,800 per month, and the rent is $2,000 per month. In addition, she must make a tax payment of $12,000 in December. The current cash on hand (on December 1) is $400, but Smith has agreed to maintain an average bank balance of $6,000—this is her target cash balance. (Disregard till cash, which is insignificant because Smith keeps only a small amount on hand in order to lessen the chances of robbery.)

The estimated sales and purchases for December, January, and February are shown below. Purchases during November amounted to $140,000.

	Sales	Purchases
December	$160,000	$40,000
January	40,000	40,000
February	60,000	40,000

a. Prepare a cash budget for December, January, and February.

b. Suppose Smith were to start selling on a credit basis on December 1, giving customers 30 days to pay. All customers accept these terms, and all other facts in the problem are unchanged. What would the company's loan requirements be at the end of December in this case? (Hint: The calculations required to answer this question are minimal.)

Cash budgeting   **9-3**   Carol Moerdyk, owner of Carol's Fashion Designs Inc., is planning to request a line of credit from her bank. She has estimated the following sales forecasts for the firm for parts of 1996 and 1997:

May	1996	$180,000
June		180,000
July		360,000
August		540,000
September		720,000
October		360,000
November		360,000
December		90,000
January	1997	180,000

Collection estimates obtained from the credit and collection department are as follows: collections within the month of sale, 10 percent; collections the month following the sale, 75 percent; collections the second month following the sale, 15 percent. Payments for labor and raw materials are typically made during the month following the one in which these costs have been incurred. Total labor and raw materials costs are estimated for each month as follows:

May	1996	$ 90,000
June		90,000
July		126,000
August		882,000
September		306,000
October		234,000
November		162,000
December		90,000

General and administrative salaries will amount to approximately $27,000 a month; lease payments under long-term lease contracts will be $9,000 a month; depreciation charges will be $36,000 a month; miscellaneous expenses will be $2,700 a month; income tax payments of $63,000 will be due in both September and December; and a progress payment of $180,000 on a new design studio must be paid in October.

Cash on hand on July 1 will amount to $132,000, and a minimum cash balance of $90,000 will be maintained throughout the cash budget period.

a. Prepare a monthly cash budget for the last six months of 1996.

b. Prepare an estimate of the required financing (or excess funds)—that is, the amount of money Carol will need to borrow (or will have available to invest)—for each month during that period.

c. Assume that receipts from sales come in uniformly during the month (that is, cash receipts come in at the rate of 1/30 each day), but all outflows are paid on the fifth of the month. Will this have an effect on the cash budget—in other words, would the cash budget you have prepared be valid under these assumptions? If not, what can be done to make a valid estimate of peak financing requirements? No calculations are required, although calculations can be used to illustrate the effects.

d. Carol produces on a seasonal basis, just ahead of sales. Without making any calculations, discuss how the company's current ratio and debt ratio would vary during the year assuming all financial requirements were met by short-term bank loans. Could changes in these ratios affect the firm's ability to obtain bank credit?

Lockbox system   **9-4**   Durst Corporation began operations 5 years ago as a small firm serving customers in the Denver area. However, its reputation and market area grew quickly, so that today Durst has customers throughout the entire United States. Despite its broad customer base, Durst has maintained its headquarters in Denver and keeps its central billing system there. Durst's management is considering an alternative collection procedure to reduce its mail time and processing float. On average, it takes 5 days from the time customers mail payments until Durst is able to receive, process, and deposit them. Durst would like to set up a lockbox collection system, which it estimates would reduce the time lag from customer mailing to deposit by 3 days—bringing it down to 2 days. Durst receives an average of $1,400,000 in payments per day.

a. How many days of collection float now exist (Durst's customers' disbursement float) and what would it be under the lockbox system? What reduction in cash balances could Durst achieve by initiating the lockbox system?

b. If Durst has an opportunity cost of 10 percent, how much is the lockbox system worth on an annual basis?

c. What is the maximum monthly charge Durst should pay for the lockbox system?

Comparison of funds transfer instruments   **9-5**   The San Francisco field office of the Metallux Corporation has sold a quantity of silver ingots for $22,500. Metallux wants to transfer this amount to its concentration bank in New York as economically as possible. Two means of transfer are being considered: (1) a mail depository transfer check (DTC), which costs $0.75 and takes three days, or (2) a wire transfer, which costs $8.00 and for which funds are immediately available in New York.

a. Metallux earns 12 percent annual interest on funds in its concentration bank. Which transfer method should Metallux use to minimize the total cost of the transfer?

b. At what dollar transfer amount would Metallux be indifferent to the two transfer procedures? (Hint: Set the cost of the two methods equal.)

c. What other factors might influence the decision?

Exam-Type Problems

The problems included in this section are set up in such a way that they could be used as multiple-choice exam problems.

Computation of float   **9-6**   Clearwater Glass Company has examined its cash management policy and found that, on average, 5 days are needed for checks the company writes to reach its bank and thus be deducted from its checking account balance (that is, disbursement delay, or float, is 5 days). On the other hand, an average of 4 days pass from the time Clearwater Glass receives payments from its customers until the funds are available for use at the bank (i.e., collection delay, or float, is 4 days). On an average day, Clearwater Glass writes checks that total $70,000, and it receives checks from customers that total $80,000.

    a. Compute the disbursement float, collection float, and net float in dollars.

    b. If Clearwater Glass has an opportunity cost equal to 10 percent, how much would it be willing to spend each year to reduce collection delay (float) by two days?

Lockbox system   **9-7**   Koehl and Daughters Inc. operates a mail-order firm doing business on the West Coast. Koehl receives an average of $325,000 in payments per day. On average it takes 4 days from the time customers mail checks until Koehl receives and processes them. Koehl is considering the use of a lockbox system to reduce collection and processing float. The system will cost $6,500 per month and will consist of 10 local depository banks and a concentration bank located in San Francisco. Under this system, customers' checks should be received at the lockbox locations 1 day after they are mailed, and daily totals will be transferred to San Francisco using wire transfers costing $9.75 each. Assume that Koehl has an opportunity cost of 10 percent and that there are $52 \times 5 = 260$ working days, hence 260 transfers from each lockbox location, in a year.

    a. What is the total annual cost of operating the lockbox system?

    b. What is the annual benefit of the lockbox system to Koehl?

    c. Should Koehl initiate the system?

Integrative Problem

Cash management and cash budgeting   **9-8**   Ray Smith, a retired librarian, recently opened a sportsman's shop called Ray's Camping & Fishing Gear, Unlimited. Ray decided at age 62 that he wasn't quite ready to stay at home, living the life of leisure. It had always been his dream to open an outdoor sportsman's shop, so his friends convinced him to go ahead. Because Ray's educational background was in literature and not in business, he hired you, a finance expert, to help him with the store's cash management. Ray is very eager to learn, so he asked you to develop a set of questions to help him understand cash management. Now answer the following questions:

    a. What is the goal of cash management?

    b. For what two primary reasons do firms hold cash?

    c. What is meant by the terms *precautionary* and *speculative* balances?

    d. What are some specific advantages for a firm holding adequate cash balances?

    e. How can a firm synchronize its cash flows, and what good would this do?

    f. You have been going through the store's checkbook and bank balances. In the process, you discovered that Ray, on average, writes checks in the amount of $1,200 each day and that it takes about 5 days for these checks to clear. Also, the firm receives checks in the amount of $1,200 daily, but loses 4 days while they are being deposited and cleared. What is the firm's disbursement float, collections float, and net float?

    g. How can a firm speed up collections and slow down disbursements?

    h. Identify two funds transfer "tools" and explain how they work. Would they be appropriate for Ray's business?

    i. Define compensating balances, overdraft systems, zero-balance accounts, and controlled disbursement accounts, and explain how each is used.

    j. Why would a firm hold marketable securities?

k. What factors should a firm consider in building its marketable securities portfolio? What are some securities that should and should not be held?

l. Your evaluation of Ray's business shows that currently its total cash and checking account balances equal $18,000, and nothing is invested in marketable securities. Ray wonders whether the company needs that much cash, given the fact cash earns no interest. He wants you to prepare a cash budget for the company for the next six months. Ray has provided you with the following figures for sales that actually occurred in the last two months of 1995 and for forecasted sales for the first eight months of 1996:

November	1995	$25,000	April	$100,000
December		22,000	May	80,000
January	1996	12,000	June	40,000
February		12,000	July	20,000
March		70,000	August	25,000

As you can see, Ray's business is very seasonal. The credit terms Ray offers allow customers to take a 2 percent discount if they pay within 10 days of the purchase date; otherwise, the full invoice amount is due within 30 days. Ray's records indicate that 40 percent of the customers have taken the discount and thus paid in the month of the sale, 50 percent have paid the following month, and 10 percent have paid during the second month after the sale. These percentages are expected to continue. Also, Ray purchases goods for resale two months prior to when they should be sold and pays for them the month after receipt, and the cost of the purchases amounts to 75 percent of sales. Thus, the $70,000 worth of goods to be sold in March will be purchased in January at a cost of $70,000 (0.75) = $52,500, and this amount will be paid in February.

   Wages, rent, administrative, and selling expenses are projected to total $8,200 per month, and depreciation expenses are expected to be $2,500 per month. Quarterly income tax payments of $8,000 must be made in March and June, and $15,000 will be needed in April to pay for the spring advertising campaign. Currently, on January 1, 1996, Ray has a total of $18,000 of cash.

(1) Prepare a cash budget for the first six months of 1996. Assume that $18,000 of cash will be on hand on January 1 and that Ray wants to begin each subsequent month with $6,000 of cash on hand (Ray's minimum desired cash balance for emergencies). What is the maximum cash surplus Ray's company will enjoy during the period studied? The maximum cash shortfall?

(2) We have assumed that all sales are collected and thus that Ray's company experiences no bad debts. Is this realistic? If not, how would bad debts be dealt with in a cash budgeting sense? For purposes of this question, assume that 3 percent of sales end up as bad debts. (Hint: Bad debts will affect collections but not purchases.)

(3) The cash budget is a *forecast,* so many of the flows are expected values rather than amounts known with certainty. If actual sales, hence collections and production, were different from the forecasted levels, then the forecasted surpluses and deficits would also be incorrect. In words, how would you expect the funds needed or surplus cash position to be affected if sales were to rise or fall 15 percent above or below the levels originally forecasted? How would the company's ability to react in a timely manner to falling sales affect the outcome? How could scenario analysis be used to help forecast the net cash inflows and required beginning-of-month cash balances? Assume zero bad debt losses.

Computer-Related Problem

Work the problem in this section only if you are using the computer problem diskette.

Cash budget

9-9 Use the model in File C9 to solve this problem.

a. Refer to Problem 9-3. Suppose that, by offering a 2 percent cash discount for paying within the month of sale, the credit manager of Carol's Fashion Designs Inc. has revised the collection percentages to 50 percent, 35 percent, and 15 percent, respectively. How will this affect the loan requirements?

b. Return the payment percentages to their base case values: 10 percent, 75 percent, and 15 percent, respectively, and the discount to zero percent. Now suppose sales fall to only 70 percent of the forecasted level. Production is maintained, so cash outflows are unchanged. How does this affect Carol's financial requirements?

c. Return sales to the forecasted level (100%), and suppose collections slow down to 3 percent, 10 percent, and 87 percent for the three months, respectively. How does this affect financial requirements? If Carol went to a cash-only sales policy, how would that affect requirements, other things held constant?

| APPENDIX 9A | ## The Baumol Model for Balancing Cash and Marketable Securities |

In this chapter, we have discussed how lockboxes, synchronized inflows and outflows, and float can reduce the required cash balance. Now we consider a formal model that can be used for establishing the target cash balance.

William Baumol first noted that cash balances are in many respects similar to inventories, and that the EOQ inventory model, which will be developed in Chapter 11, can be used to establish a target cash balance.[1] Baumol's model assumes that the firm uses cash at a steady, predictable rate—say, $1 million per week—and that the firm's cash inflows from operations also occur at a steady, predictable rate—say, $900,000 per week. Therefore, the firm's net cash outflows, or net need for cash, also occur at a steady rate—in this case, $100,000 per week.[2] Under these steady-state assumptions, the firm's cash position will resemble the situation shown in Figure 9A-1.

If our illustrative firm started at Time 0 with a cash balance of CASH = $300,000, and if its outflows exceeded its inflows by $100,000 per week, then its cash balance would drop to zero at the end of Week 3, and its average cash balance would be CASH/2 = $300,000/2 = $150,000. Therefore, at the end of Week 3 the firm would have to replenish its cash balance, either by selling marketable securities, if it had any, or by borrowing.

If CASH were set at a higher level, say, $600,000, then the cash supply would last longer (6 weeks), and the firm would have to sell securities (or borrow) less frequently, but its average cash balance would rise from $150,000 to $300,000. Brokerage or some other type of transactions cost must be incurred to sell securities (or to borrow), so holding larger cash balances will lower the transactions costs associated with obtaining cash. On

---

[1]William J. Baumol, "The Transactions Demand for Cash: An Inventory Theoretic Approach," *Quarterly Journal of Economics*, November 1952, 545-556.

[2]Our hypothetical firm is experiencing a $100,000 weekly cash shortfall, but this does not necessarily imply that it is headed for bankruptcy. The firm could, for example, be highly profitable and enjoying high earnings but be expanding so rapidly that it is experiencing chronic cash shortages that must be made up by borrowing or by selling common stock. Or the firm could be in the construction business and therefore receive major cash inflows at wide intervals but have net cash outflows of $100,000 per week between major inflows.

FIGURE 9A-1

Cash Balances under the Baumol Model's Assumptions

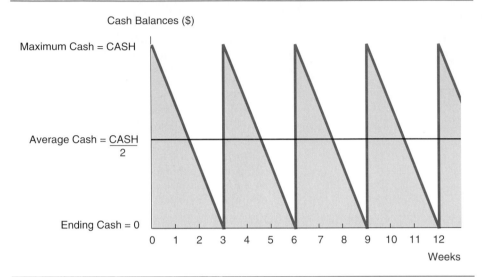

FIGURE 9A-2

Determination of the Target Cash Balance

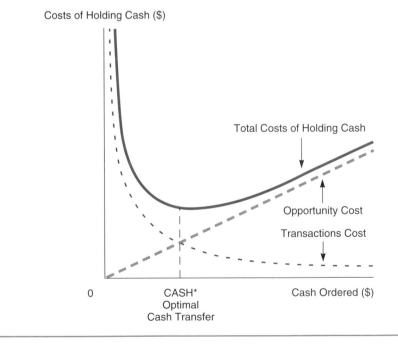

the other hand, cash provides no income, so the larger the average cash balance, the higher the opportunity cost, which is the return that could have been earned on securities or other assets held in lieu of cash. Thus, we have the situation that is graphed in Figure 9A-2. The optimal cash balance is found by using the following variables and equations:

CASH = amount of cash raised by selling marketable securities or by borrowing. CASH/2 = average cash balance.

CASH* = optimal amount of cash to be raised by selling marketable securities or by borrowing. CASH*/2 = optimal average cash balance.

O = fixed costs of making a securities trade or of obtaining a loan.

T = total amount of net new cash needed for transactions during the entire period (usually a year).

k = opportunity cost of holding cash, set equal to the rate of return forgone on marketable securities or the cost of borrowing to hold cash.

The total costs of cash balances consist of holding (or opportunity) costs plus transactions costs:[3]

9A-1

$$\frac{\text{Total}}{\text{costs}} = \quad \text{Holding costs} \quad + \quad \text{Transactions costs}$$

$$= \left(\begin{array}{c}\text{Average cash} \\ \text{balance}\end{array}\right) \times \left(\begin{array}{c}\text{Opportunity} \\ \text{cost}\end{array}\right) + \left(\begin{array}{c}\text{Number of} \\ \text{transactions}\end{array}\right) \times \left(\begin{array}{c}\text{Cost per} \\ \text{transaction}\end{array}\right)$$

$$= \frac{\text{CASH}}{2} \times (k) \quad + \quad \frac{T}{\text{CASH}} \times (O)$$

The minimum total costs are achieved when CASH is set equal to CASH*, the optimal cash transfer. CASH* is found as follows: [4]

9A-2

$$\text{CASH}^* = \sqrt{\frac{2(O)(T)}{k}}$$

Equation 9A-2 is the **Baumol model** for determining optimal cash balances. To illustrate its use, suppose O = $150; T = 52 weeks × $100,000/week = $5,200,000; and k = 15% = 0.15. Then

$$\text{CASH}^* = \sqrt{\frac{2(\$150)\,(\$5,200,000)}{0.15}} = \$101,980$$

Therefore, the firm should sell securities in the amount of $101,980 when its cash balance approaches zero, thus building its cash balance back up to $101,980. If we divide T by CASH*, we have the number of transactions per year: $5,200,000/$101,980 = 50.99 ≈ 51, or about once a week. The firm's average cash balance is $101,980/2 = $50,990 ≈ $51,000.

Notice that the optimal cash balance increases less than proportionately with increases in the amount of cash needed for transactions. For example, if the firm's size and consequently its net new cash needs doubled from $5,200,000 to $10,400,000 per year, average

---

[3]Total costs can be expressed on either a before-tax or an after-tax basis. Both methods lead to the same conclusions regarding target cash balances and comparative costs. For simplicity, we present the model here on a before-tax basis.

[4]Equation 9A-1 is differentiated with respect to CASH. The derivative is set equal to zero, and we then solve for CASH = CASH* to derive Equation 9A-2. This model, applied to inventories and called the EOQ model, is discussed further in Chapter 11.

cash balances would increase by only 41 percent, from $51,000 to $72,000. This suggests that there are economies of scale in holding cash balances, and this in turn gives larger firms an edge over smaller ones.[5]

Of course, the firm probably would want to hold a safety stock of cash designed to reduce the probability of a cash shortage to some specified level. However, if the firm is able to sell securities or to borrow on short notice—and most larger firms can do so simply by making a telephone call—the safety stock of cash can be quite low.

The Baumol model obviously is simplistic in many respects. Most important, it assumes relatively stable, predictable cash inflows and outflows, and it does not take into account any seasonal or cyclical trends. Other models have been developed to deal both with uncertainty in the cash flows and with trends. Any of these models, including the Baumol model, can provide a useful starting point for establishing a target cash balance, but all have limitations and must be applied with judgment.

Self-Test Questions

What is the purpose of the Baumol model?

Write out the equation for the model and then list its key assumptions.

Problem

Optimal funds transfer

9A-1   Bildersee Industries projects that cash outlays of $4.5 million will occur uniformly throughout the year. Bildersee plans to meet its cash requirements by periodically selling marketable securities from its portfolio. The firm's marketable securities are invested to earn 12 percent, and the cost per transaction of converting securities to cash is $27.

    a. Use the Baumol model to determine the optimal transaction size for transfers from marketable securities to cash.

    b. What will be Bildersee's average cash balance?

    c. How many transfers per year will be required?

    d. What will be Bildersee's total annual cost of maintaining cash balances? What would the total cost be if the company maintained an average cash balance of $50,000 or of $0 (it deposits funds daily to meet cash requirements)?

---

[5]This edge may, of course, be more than offset by other factors—after all, cash management is only one aspect of running a business.

CHAPTER 10

Credit Management

American Express Company has long been associated with the American Express charge card, which permits customers to purchase goods and services and pay the full amount at some later date. The charge card is not intended to be used to provide extended credit to its users—there is no provision for delaying payment beyond the payment date, or receiving credit at a specified rate of interest. So, American Express decided to tap the credit card market with the introduction of the Optima Card in 1987. Essentially the Optima Card offered the same benefits as bank credit cards like Visa and MasterCard—customers could use the card to charge purchases, and then either pay the full amount due within the designated billing period or delay payment and receive credit at the interest rate specified in the credit agreement. Given the success of the American Express charge card—in 1983, American Express commanded almost one third of the market for national charge and credit card purchases—it seemed the Optima Card credit card was destined for success. But, in reality, the Optima Card never made it; in fact, most analysts would rate the credit card as an expensive dud for the American Express Company.

Why did the Optima Card fail? Most of the signs point to the fact that American Express did not formulate a good credit policy before it introduced the new credit card. According to the experts, the credit standards originally used by American Express were relatively weak, so the company was allowing customers with rather poor credit to have the Optima Card. To compound matters, in 1989, the company relaxed its credit standards in an attempt to attract more customers; the strategy worked—more customers used the Optima Card. Unfortunately, the bad debts associated with these customers increased significantly, but the increase was not recognized until two years later, apparently because American Express had not implemented sufficient methods for monitoring its credit accounts (accounts receivable). Ultimately, the company was forced to write off significant amounts of bad debts and to reconsider its ability to compete in the credit card industry.

Continued

Managing a credit department requires fast, accurate, up-to-date information, and to help get such information, the National Association of Credit Management (a group with 43,000 member firms) persuaded TRW to develop a computer-based telecommunications network for the collection, storage, retrieval, and distribution of credit information. The TRW system contains credit data on more than 120 million individuals, and it electronically transmits credit reports that are available within seconds to its thousands of subscribers. When you apply for a credit card or a bank loan, to determine your credit history, the lender usually requests your credit report from an agency such as TRW.[3] Dun & Bradstreet has a similar electronic system that covers businesses, plus another service that provides more detailed reports through the U.S. mail.

A typical business credit report would include the following information:

1. A summary balance sheet and income statement.
2. A number of key ratios, with trend information.
3. Information obtained from the firm's suppliers telling whether it has been paying promptly or slowly and whether it has failed to make any payments recently.
4. A verbal description of the physical condition of the firm's operations.
5. A verbal description of the backgrounds of the firm's owners, including any previous bankruptcies, lawsuits, divorce settlement problems, and the like.
6. A summary rating, ranging from A for the best credit risks down to F for those that are deemed likely to default.

Although a great deal of credit information is available, it still must be processed in a judgmental manner. Computerized information systems can assist in making better credit decisions, but, in the final analysis, most credit decisions are really exercises in informed judgment.

Using Standards to Grant Credit

Although most credit decisions are subjective, many firms now use a sophisticated statistical method called *multiple discriminant analysis (MDA)* to assess credit quality. MDA is similar to multiple regression analysis where the evaluation is focused on determining which characteristics best describe a customer's ability and willingness to pay off the debt if credit is granted. These models are set up to "score" the quality of credit based on factors considered important for differentiating between potentially good and potentially bad credit customers, so these evaluation processes generally are termed **credit-scoring systems.** For example, when a firm such as Sears, Roebuck & Co. evaluates consumers' credit quality, the factors considered important for credit scoring probably would include: (1) whether the credit applicant owns his or her own home; (2) the length of time the applicant has worked at his or her current job; (3) the applicant's out-

CREDIT-SCORING SYSTEMS
Techniques used to "score" the creditworthiness of credit customers.

---

[3]We cannot cover all the details of individual credit reports here. You should be aware that you probably currently have a credit information portfolio that is maintained by a credit-reporting agency, which provides your credit and payment history to firms and banks when you apply for credit. You do have the right to know, and you probably should request, the information contained in your credit report. For more information concerning your rights and the contents of credit reports for individuals, see a *personal finance* textbook or a textbook that deals exclusively with consumer credit.

standing debt in relation to his or her annual income; and (4) the applicant's credit history with respect to the terms of credit previously granted, including whether payments were made on time. When a customer applies for a Sears credit card, each of these factors is "scored" and the sum of the scores is compared to a "standardized" value to determine if the customer will be granted credit.

One major advantage of a credit-scoring system is that a customer's credit quality is expressed in a single numerical value rather than as a subjective assessment of various factors. This is a tremendous advantage for a large firm that must evaluate many customers in many different locations using many different credit employees, because, without an automated procedure, the firm would have a hard time applying equal standards to all credit applicants. Therefore, most credit card companies, department stores, oil companies, and the like use credit-scoring systems to determine who is granted credit, and the limit allowed for credit purchases.

To illustrate the use of credit-scoring for making a decision about whether to grant a customer credit, suppose Benchwood Confectioner has historical data on all of its previous credit sales. Evaluation of the data shows that 75 percent of the customers paid on time, while the remaining 25 percent either paid late or, in some cases, went bankrupt and did not pay at all. Further, the firm has historical data on each customer's quick ratio, times-interest-earned ratio, debt ratio, years in existence, and so on. Using statistical techniques to examine this information, Benchwood's credit manager has determined that the financial measures that best indicate whether a credit customer will pay on time or will become a bad debt are the values associated with the customer's times-interest-earned ratio (TIE), quick ratio, debt ratio, and the number of years the customer has been in business.

Using discriminant analysis (MDA), the credit manager has produced the following equation to evaluate the creditworthiness of credit customers in the future:

$$\text{Credit score} = [3.0 \times (\text{TIE})] + \left[5.2 \times \left(\frac{\text{Quick}}{\text{ratio}}\right)\right] - \left[18.0 \times \left(\frac{\text{Debt}}{\text{ratio}}\right)\right] + \left[2.5 \times \left(\frac{\text{Years in}}{\text{business}}\right)\right]$$

In addition, the credit manager has determined that a score less than 30 suggests the customer is a poor credit risk, 30–45 indicates an average credit risk, and a score above 45 signifies a good credit risk.

Now consider a firm with the following characteristics that applies for credit purchases:

TIE = 4.2   Quick ratio = 3.0

Debt ratio = 0.30   Years in business = 10

According to the equation developed by Benchwood's credit manager, this customer's credit score would be $47.8 = 3.0(4.2) + 5.2(3.0) - 18.0(0.30) + 2.5(10)$. Therefore, the firm would be considered a good credit risk, and consequently it would be offered favorable credit terms.

Often, evaluating credit risks for businesses is not as easy as suggested by this example. In fact, because firms use different accounting practices for valuation to construct financial statements (e.g., FIFO versus LIFO for inventory valuation), generally it is extremely difficult to use accounting data to generate one single credit-scoring equation that can be applied universally.[4] For that reason, in commercial credit analysis, credit-scoring models generally are used at the initial stage of the investigation to screen out the extremely bad credit risks. The firms that survive the initial screening then are evaluated further to determine their strengths and weaknesses with respect to the general areas considered important to determining creditworthiness (the Cs of credit).

Self-Test Questions

Identify and briefly explain the five Cs of credit.

What are some sources of credit information?

What is a credit-scoring system?

Terms of Credit

TERMS OF CREDIT
The payment conditions offered to credit customers; the terms include the length of the credit period and any cash discounts offered.

The **terms of credit** refer to the conditions of the credit sale, especially with regard to the payment arrangements. Firms need to determine when the credit period begins, how long the customer has to pay for credit purchases before the account is considered delinquent, and whether a cash discount will be offered. An examination of the credit terms offered by firms in the United States would show great variety across industries—credit terms range from cash before delivery (CBD) and cash on delivery (COD) to allowing credit purchases with cash discounts offered for early payment. Due to the competitive nature of trade credit, however, most financial managers follow the norm of the industry in which they operate when setting credit terms for their firms.

Credit Period

CREDIT PERIOD
The length of time for which credit is granted; after that time, the credit account is considered delinquent.

The **credit period** is the length of time an account receivable can remain outstanding before it is considered delinquent; it is the time the seller permits the buyer to make payment of the full invoice amount. Generally, the credit period starts on the date reported on the invoice, but, depending on the industry standards, the payment period might start when the goods are shipped, when the goods are received by the buyer, at the beginning of the month, at the end of the month, in the middle of the month, or some other time specified by the terms of credit.

---

[4]Consumer credit evaluation is not as complicated as commercial credit evaluation, because the quantitative measures used to evaluate consumer credit contain greater consistency than those used for commercial credit. For example, we, as individuals, report our income and financing on a cash basis rather than an accrual basis. So, an individual who reports an annual disposable income of $30,000 generally has the ability to spend $30,000 in cash during the year. On the other hand, we know there are instances where firms have reported positive net incomes, but their net cash flows during the same period were negative. In a sense, as we noted in Chapter 3, firms can employ "window dressing" techniques to make their financial statements look better than they actually are. Thus, experienced credit analysts do not rely solely on the information contained in financial statements to make decisions concerning creditworthiness.

Cash Discounts

CASH DISCOUNT
A reduction in the invoice price of goods offered by the seller to encourage early payment.

It is a common practice for firms to offer cash discounts to induce purchasing firms to pay for their credit purchases before the final day of the credit period. The use of **cash discounts** for early payment is analyzed by balancing the costs and benefits of different cash discounts. For example, a firm might decide to change its credit terms from "net 30," which means that customers must pay the full invoice price within 30 days, to "2/10, net 30," which means that it will allow a 2 percent discount from the full invoice price if payment is received within 10 days, while the full invoice price must otherwise be paid within 30 days. This change should produce two benefits: (1) It should attract new customers who consider the discount to be a type of price reduction, and (2) the discount should cause a reduction in the days sales outstanding because some established customers will pay more promptly in order to take advantage of the discount. Offsetting these benefits is the dollar cost of the discounts taken. The optimal discount is established at the point where the marginal costs and benefits are exactly offsetting. The methodology for analyzing changes in the discount is developed later in the chapter.

SEASONAL DATING
Credit terms used to induce customers to buy "out of season" by not requiring payment for the purchases until the customer's selling season, no matter when the goods were shipped.

If sales are seasonal, a firm might use **seasonal dating** to establish the credit period. For example, Slimware Inc., a swimsuit manufacturer, sells on terms of 2/10, net 30, May 1 dating. This means that the effective invoice date is May 1, even if the sale was made back in January. The discount can be taken up to May 10; otherwise, the full amount must be paid on May 30. Slimware produces throughout the year, but retail sales of bathing suits are concentrated in the spring and early summer, and by offering seasonal dating, the company induces some of its customers to stock up early, saving Slimware storage costs and also "nailing down sales."

Self-Test Questions

What does the phrase *terms of credit* mean?

How can cash discounts be used to influence sales volume and the DSO?

What is seasonal dating?

Credit Collection Policy

COLLECTION POLICY
The procedures followed by a firm to collect its accounts receivables.

Collection policy refers to the procedures the firm follows to collect its credit accounts. The firm needs to determine when, and how, notification of the credit sale will be conveyed to the buyer. The quicker a customer receives an invoice, the sooner the bill *can* be paid. In a world where speed and accuracy are becoming significant factors in business, more firms have turned to electronic technology to "send" invoices to customers.

One of the most important collection policy decisions is how the past-due accounts should be handled. For example, a letter might be sent to customers when a bill is 10 days past due; a more severe letter, followed by a telephone call, might be used if payment is not received within 30 days; and the account might be turned over to a collection agency after 90 days.

INDUSTRY PRACTICE

Recessions Breed Aggressive Receivables Behavior

During a recession, or any economic downturn, generally interest rates are high, and credit is tight. Short-term credit is no exception. But, when the availability of formal short-term financing sources declines, firms increasingly turn to more informal and spontaneous sources like the trade credit provided by product suppliers. Often, it is easier for firms to rely more heavily on their suppliers for credit than to seek alternative short-term funds, such as bank loans, when the credit markets are tight. Indeed, suppliers find that customers tend to take longer to pay during economic downturns than when the economy is considered healthy; thus, both the amount and the age of receivables increase.

Do suppliers change the way they view the credit function during economic downturns? According to the credit managers of some leading companies in the United States, during economic downturns, firms often tighten their credit policies, increasing credit standards and more aggressively collecting delinquent accounts, in an effort to guard against the tendency for their customers to pay slower and for the amount of customer defaults to increase. For example, Gary Grissom, director of credit for U.S. operations for S. C. Johnson and Son, Inc., believes it is more important to identify poor credit risks during economic downturns than good economic times because the negative effects associated with delinquent payers and defaulted accounts often are more severe for suppliers during an unfavorable economy. When a company's collections slow down (its DSO increases) because its customers delay their payments, generally the company's ability to pay bills is impaired and its own payments slow down. So, if a company does not implement a more cautious credit policy when the economy slows down, it might find itself amid its own financial troubles resulting from the credit payment behavior of its customers.

Companies have used a variety of methods to help their credit departments cope with the economic downturns. For example, during the recession we experienced at the beginning of the 1990s, Pillsbury Company, based in Minneapolis, emphasized the analysis of cash flows rather than income to reduce bad debts associated with credit granting, and it more aggressively collected accounts to ensure prompt payment. In another instance, a company in the Northeast changed its standards so drastically that the rate of credit approvals dropped from 90 percent to 30 percent. For the most part, firms believe that their credit departments have to work harder and be more aggressive with the implementation of their credit policies during an economic downturn—credit policies must be tightened through stricter credit standards and terms and more aggressive collection efforts at a time when customers stretch payments longer and default more often. However, there are firms that believe such situations provide them with opportunities to increase market share if they "go against the grain." For example, Albany Ladder Company in Albany, New York, does not change its credit policy when the economy worsens. The company believes an economic downturn actually provides an opportunity for astute credit managers to improve profits. First, when sales slow down, there is more time to concentrate on collections, so a higher percentage of accounts receivable can be collected compared to when the economy and the company's business is booming. Second, firms that tighten their credit policies drive away some customers; so firms that are willing to grant more credit can attract these customers, many of which are profitable, perhaps permanently.

No matter the approach taken, credit managers seem to become more aware of their customers during economic downturns. Most would agree that the company's credit policy needs to be tightened to avoid financially stressful situations caused by increased defaults and by a general lengthening of credit payment periods. But, where some firms believe economic downturns create credit problems, other firms find new business opportunities. During recessions, should firms more aggressively collect accounts or more aggressively pursue credit customers abandoned by other firms' credit policy changes?

SOURCE: Richard H. Gamble, "Cracking the Whip: Credit Tightens Its Grip to Withstand Recession," *Corporate Cashflow* (May 1991) pp. 35–40.

Profit Potential

Thus far, we have emphasized the costs of granting credit. However, if it is possible to sell on credit and also to assess a carrying charge on the receivables that are outstanding, then credit sales can actually be *more profitable* than cash sales.

This is especially true for consumer durables (autos, appliances, clothing, and so on), but it is also true for certain types of industrial equipment. Thus, GM's General Motors Acceptance Corporation (GMAC) unit, which finances automobiles, is highly profitable, as is Sears's credit subsidiary.[7] Some encyclopedia companies even are reported to lose money on cash sales but to more than make up these losses from the carrying charges on their credit sales; obviously, such companies would rather sell on credit than for cash!

The carrying charges on outstanding credit generally are about 18 percent on a simple interest rate basis: 1.5 percent per month, so $i_{SIMPLE} = APR = 1.5\% \times 12 = 18\%$. This is equivalent to an effective annual rate of $EAR = (1.015)^{12} - 1.0 = 19.6\%$. Except in the type of situation that occurred in the early 1980s, when short-term interest rates rose to unprecedented levels, having receivables outstanding that earn over 18 percent is highly profitable.

Legal Considerations

It is illegal, under the Robinson-Patman Act, for a firm to charge prices that discriminate between customers unless these differential prices are cost-justified. The same holds true for credit—it is illegal to offer more favorable credit terms to one customer or class of customers than to another unless the differences are cost-justified.

Credit Instruments

OPEN ACCOUNT
A credit arrangement whereby an invoice is signed by the buyer when the goods are received, after which both the buyer and the seller record the credit purchase on their respective books.

PROMISSORY NOTE
A legal document that specifies the amount, interest rate, repayment schedule, and other terms and conditions of a loan; a legal IOU.

COMMERICAL DRAFT
An instrument drawn up by, and made out to, the seller that must be signed by the customer before taking possession of the goods.

SIGHT DRAFT
An instrument that calls for payment upon acceptance of the goods by the buyer.

TIME DRAFT (TRADE ACCEPTANCE)
A draft that is payable at some future date.

Most credit is offered on **open account,** which means that the only formal evidence of credit is an invoice which accompanies the shipment and which the buyer signs to indicate that goods have been received. Then the buyer and the seller each record the purchase on their books of account. Under certain circumstances, the selling firm might require the buyer to sign a **promissory note** evidencing the credit obligation. Promissory notes are useful (1) if the order is very large; (2) if the seller anticipates the possibility of having trouble collecting, because a note is a stronger legal claim than a simple signed invoice; or (3) if the buyer wants a longer-than-usual time in which to pay for the order, because in that case interest should be charged, and interest charges can be built into a promissory note.

Another instrument used in trade credit, especially in international trade, is the **commercial draft.** Here the seller draws up a draft—which is a combination check and promissory note—calling for the buyer to pay a specific amount to the seller by a specified date. This draft is then sent to the buyer's bank, along with the shipping invoices necessary to take possession of the goods. The bank forwards the draft to the buyer, who signs it and returns it to the bank. The bank then delivers the shipping documents to its customer, who at this point can claim the goods. If the draft is a **sight draft,** then upon delivery of the shipping documents and acceptance of the draft by the buyer, the bank actually withdraws money from the buyer's account and forwards it to the selling firm. If the draft is a **time draft,** payable on a specific future date, then the bank returns it to the selling firm. In this case, the draft is called a **trade acceptance,** and it amounts to

---

[7]Companies that do a large volume of sales financing typically set up subsidiary companies called *captive finance companies* to do the actual financing. Thus, General Motors, Chrysler, and Ford all have captive finance companies, as do Sears, Montgomery Ward, and General Electric.

a promissory note that the seller can hold for future payment or use as collateral for a loan. The bank, in such a situation, has served as an intermediary, making sure that the buyer does not receive title to the goods until the note (or draft) has been executed for the benefit of the seller.

A seller who lacks confidence in the ability or willingness of the buyer to pay off a time draft might refuse to ship without a guarantee of payment by the buyer's bank. Presumably, the bank knows its customer, and, for a fee, the bank will guarantee payment of the draft. In this instance, the draft is called a **banker's acceptance.** Such instruments are widely used, especially in foreign trade. They have a low degree of risk if guaranteed by a strong bank, and there is a ready market for acceptances, making it easy for the seller of the goods to sell the instrument to raise immediate cash. (Banker's acceptances are sold at a discount below face value, and then paid off at face value when they mature, so the discount amounts to interest on the acceptance. The effective interest rate on a strong banker's acceptance is a little above the Treasury bill rate of interest.)

Another type of credit instrument is the **conditional sales contract,** under which the seller retains legal ownership of the goods until the buyer has completed payment. Conditional sales contracts are used primarily for such items as machinery, dental equipment, and the like, which are often purchased on an installment basis over a period of two or three years. The significant advantage of a conditional sales contract is that it is easier for the seller to repossess the equipment in the event of default than it would be if title had been assigned to the buyer. This feature makes possible some credit sales that otherwise would not be feasible. Conditional sales contracts generally have a market interest rate built into their payment schedules.

BANKER'S ACCEPTANCE
A time draft that obligates a buyer to make a future payment, but the payment has been guaranteed by the bank.

CONDITIONAL SALES CONTRACT
A method of financing in which the seller retains title to the goods until the buyer has completed payment.

Self-Test Questions

How do profit potential and legal considerations affect a firm's credit policy?

Describe some instruments used to document trade credit transactions, and indicate when each type of instrument is likely to be used.

Analyzing Proposed Changes in Credit Policy

If the firm's credit policy is *eased* by such actions as lengthening the credit period, relaxing credit standards, following a less stringent collection policy, or offering cash discounts, then sales should increase: *Easing the credit policy stimulates sales.* Of course, if the credit policy is eased and sales increase, then costs also will increase because more labor, materials, and so on will be required to produce the additional goods. Additionally, receivables outstanding will increase, which will increase carrying costs, and bad debt and/or discount expenses also might increase. Thus, the key question when deciding on a proposed credit policy change is this: Will the firm realize a net benefit? If the added benefits expected from a credit policy change do not exceed the added costs, then the policy change should *not* be made. Easing the credit policy will stimulate sales, but, if the additional costs incurred more than offset the additional benefits derived from the additional sales, the change should not be made. On the other hand, tightening the credit policy generally will cause a contraction in sales, but the cost savings might exceed the lost revenues, in which case the policy change should be made.

We saw earlier that the 1995 DSO for Unilate Textiles was 43.2 days, which was 13.2 days greater than the credit terms it offers and 11.1 days greater than the industry average. This is not expected to differ in 1996, so Unilate wants to determine if its credit policy should be changed to reduce the average collection period. Unilate might accomplish this task by (1) making it more difficult to become a credit customer (tightening the credit standards), (2) increasing the pressure used to collect delinquent accounts, or (3) changing the credit terms to encourage customers to pay sooner. If Unilate either tightens its credit standards or puts more pressure on its customers to pay sooner, the effect probably will be a decrease in gross credit sales. On the other hand, if Unilate's credit terms are changed to offer a higher cash discount to encourage earlier payment, then gross credit sales could possibly increase.

Unilate's financial manager has proposed that the company improve its average collection period by changing both the existing collection policy and the standards applied when credit is granted. The first part of the proposal is that Unilate's collection department bill its customers sooner, and more pressure will be exerted to collect delinquent accounts sooner. It is apparent that this *tougher* collection policy will require Unilate to spend more on its collection efforts—the financial manager estimates the increase in collection costs will be $600,000 annually. The second part of the proposal calls for the credit manager to tighten existing credit standards slightly—the credit department will more closely examine the financial position of its credit customers, and suspend the credit of customers who are considered "habitually delinquent." The hope is that the tighter credit standards in combination with more careful evaluation of customers' financial position will reduce the number of customers that are "habitually delinquent" for very long periods (for instance, past due for 90 days or more). Even though Unilate has an extremely loyal customer base, it is expected that some sales will be lost to competitors if the proposed credit policy changes are implemented. The financial manager estimates the loss in credit sales resulting from this credit policy change will total $2 million annually, which is a loss of less than ⅛ percent of 1996 forecasted net sales. Because these credit policy changes will have little, if any, effect on the "good" credit customers, the financial manager does not expect there to be a change in the number of customers taking advantage of the cash discount. However, in addition to the estimated loss in sales, tightening the credit standards will increase the costs of evaluating the creditworthiness of customers because more intensive examination of each customer's financial position will be required—it is estimated the cost of evaluating receivables will increase by $400,000 annually. If the proposed credit policy changes are approved, the financial manager believes the average collection period, or DSO, for receivables can be reduced from 43.2 days to 35.6 days—this is more in line with the credit terms offered by Unilate (2/10 net 30), and it is closer to the industry average of 32.1 days. Also, if the average collection period is reduced, the amount "carried" in accounts receivable is reduced, which means less funds are "tied up" in receivables. Table 10-2 provides information about Unilate's existing credit policy and the financial manager's proposed modifications to the credit policy.

Should Unilate adopt the financial manager's proposal? To answer this question, we need to compute the marginal costs and benefits associated with changing the existing credit policy to determine if the proposal is more advantageous than the

TABLE 10-2

Unilate Textiles: Existing and Proposed Credit Policies
Expected for 1996 (millions of dollars)

	Existing Policy	Proposed Policy
Credit terms	2/10 net 30	2/10 net 30
Gross credit sales	$1,656.6	$1,654.6
Net credit sales (S)	$1,650.0	$1,648.0
Variable cost ratio (on gross sales)	81%	81%
Bad debts	$ 0	$ 0
Credit evaluation and collection costs	$16	$17
Days sales outstanding (DSO)	43.2 days	35.6 days

current policy. As Table 10-2 shows, annual sales are expected to decrease by $2 million and annual credit evaluation *and* collection costs are expected to increase by $0.6 million + $0.4 million = $1 million—together this represents a $3 million decrease in earnings before taxes. According to this information, the proposed changes do not seem to be desirable. But consider the other side of the coin—reduced sales mean reduced production costs, and it is expected that the average collection period will decline if the proposal is implemented. If sales decrease by $2 million, then the variable cost of goods sold should decrease by $2 million times the variable cost ratio, or $1.62 million = $2 million × (0.81).[8] Also, the decrease in both credit sales and average collection period, or DSO, means less funds will be "tied up" in receivables, thus the opportunity, or carrying cost, of receivables also will be less.

To compute the carrying cost, we need to determine how much Unilate has invested in receivables and the "cost" of this investment. The amount invested in receivables can be computed by determining the amount Unilate paid for the products that were sold on credit, but for which cash payment has not been received:

10-3

$$\text{Receivables investment} = \frac{\text{Average accounts}}{\text{receivable balance}} \times \frac{\text{Variable}}{\text{cost ratio}}$$

$$= \left[(\text{DSO}) \times \left(\frac{\text{Sales}}{\text{per day}} \right) \right] \times \frac{\text{Variable}}{\text{cost ratio}}$$

$$= \left[(\text{DSO}) \times \left(\frac{S}{360} \right) \right] \times v$$

Only variable costs enter this calculation because this represents the funds the firm has *tied up* in receivables, and it is this amount that must be financed—the

---

[8]In earlier chapters, we indicated Unilate's variable cost ratio is 0.8133. This is the variable cost ratio based on *net* sales, which are gross sales less the cash discounts taken; in 1996, gross sales are expected to be $1,656.6, with net sales equal to $1,650. Based on gross sales, Unilate's variable cost ratio is 0.81.

variable costs represent the firm's investment in the cost of goods sold. For Unilate, the receivables investments associated with the existing and the proposed credit policies are:

$$\text{Receivables investment}_{\text{Current}} = \left[(43.2 \text{ days}) \times \left(\frac{\$1{,}656.6 \text{ million}}{360} \right) \right] \times (0.81)$$

$$= \$198 \text{ million} \times 0.81$$

$$= \$161.0 \text{ million}$$

$$\text{Receivables investment}_{\text{Proposal}} = \left[(35.6 \text{ days}) \times \left(\frac{\$1{,}654.6 \text{ million}}{360} \right) \right] \times (0.81)$$

$$= \$163 \text{ million} \times 0.81$$

$$= \$132.5 \text{ million}$$

Once the investment in receivables is computed, the receivables carrying (opportunity) cost can be computed by determining how much return these funds would have earned if they could be invested elsewhere:

10-4

$$\frac{\text{Receivables}}{\text{carrying cost}} = \frac{\text{Receivables}}{\text{investment}} \times \frac{\text{Opportunity}}{\text{cost of funds}}$$

$$= \left\{ \left[(\text{DSO}) \times \left(\frac{S}{360} \right) \right] \times v \right\} \times k_{AR}$$

where k_{AR} represents the opportunity cost associated with the funds *tied up* in accounts receivable. Therefore, if Unilate's opportunity cost for funds invested in receivables is 8 percent, the cost of carrying receivables with the existing policy and with the proposal would be:

$$\text{Receivables carrying cost}_{\text{Current}} = \$161.0 \text{ million} \times 0.08 = \$12.9 \text{ million}$$

$$\text{Receivables carrying cost}_{\text{Proposal}} = \$132.5 \text{ million} \times 0.08 = \$10.6 \text{ million}$$

If the proposed credit policy changes are adopted, the required investment in receivables will decrease from $161.0 million to $132.5 million, which will decrease the opportunity cost of carrying receivables from $12.9 million to $10.6 million, a savings of $2.3 million.

Our analysis shows that if the financial manager's proposed credit policy changes are accepted, Unilate's taxable income will decrease by $3 million because sales will decrease by $2 million and credit evaluation and collection costs will increase by $1 million. At the same time, the lower sales will be accompanied by a $1.6 million decrease in the total variable cost of goods sold (0.81 × $2 million sales decrease), and a reduced accounts receivable investment will save the firm $2.3 million in receivables carrying costs—the total savings is $3.9 million. Because the amount of the total savings exceeds the amount of the total costs, the proposed credit policy changes should be adopted.

Table 10-3 summarizes the results of the analysis we just described, and it illustrates the general idea behind credit policy analysis. The results are presented on an after-tax basis, assuming Unilate's marginal tax rate is 40 percent.

TABLE 10-3

Unilate Textiles: Analysis of Changing Credit Policy (millions of dollars)

	Projected 1996 Revenues/Costs under *Current* Credit Policy	Projected 1996 Revenues/Costs under *Proposed* Credit Policy	Income Effect of Credit Policy Change
Gross sales	$ 1,656.6	$ 1,654.6	$(2.0)
Less: Cash discounts[a]	(6.6)	(6.6)	0.0
Net sales	1,650.0	1,648.0	(2.0)
Variable cost of goods sold	(1,342.0)	(1,340.4)	1.6
Bad debts	(0.0)	(0.0)	0.0
Credit evaluation and collection costs	(16.0)	(17.0)	(1.0)
Receivables carrying cost	(12.9)	(10.6)	2.3
Revenues net of variable production costs and credit costs	$ 279.1	$ 280.0	$ 0.9
Tax impact (40%)[b]	(111.6)	(112.0)	(0.4)
After-tax revenues	$ 167.5	$ 168.0	$ 0.5

[a]Unilate offers credit terms of 2/10 net 30—20 percent of its customers take advantage of the cash discount, so the total cash discount is $6.6 million = (0.20) (0.02) ($1,656.6 million). This value will be the same with both credit policies.

[b]For this example, it is not necessary to include the tax impact, because the marginal tax rate will not change under the proposed credit policy changes. Therefore, if the proposal is acceptable before taxes, it also is acceptable after taxes. This might not be the case if the marginal tax rate that applies to the proposal differs from the existing rate.

The combined effect of all the changes in credit policy is a projected $0.5 million annual increase in after-tax revenues, which suggests the credit policy changes would be beneficial for Unilate. There might, of course, be corresponding changes on the projected balance sheet—the lower sales might necessitate somewhat less cash and inventories. These changes, as well as any other changes, also would have to be considered in the analysis. For simplicity, we assume the only changes relevant to the decision to change the credit policy are those discussed above, and contained in Table 10-3.

The $0.5 million expected increase in after-tax revenues is, of course, an estimate, and the actual effects of the change could be quite different. In the first place, there is uncertainty—perhaps quite a lot—about the projected $2 million decrease in sales. Conceivably, if Unilate's competitors responded to the credit policy changes, the impact on sales might differ significantly. Similar uncertainties must be attached to the number of customers who would take discounts, to production costs at various sales levels, to the costs of carrying receivables, and to bad debt losses.

The analysis in Table 10-3 provides Unilate's managers with a vehicle for considering the impact of credit policy changes on the firm's income statement and balance sheet variables. However, a great deal of judgment must be applied to the decision because customers' responses to credit policy changes are very difficult to estimate. Nevertheless, this type of numerical analysis can provide a good starting point for credit policy decisions.[9]

Self-Test Questions

Describe the procedure used to evaluate a change in credit policy.

Should credit policy decisions be made more on the basis of numerical analyses or judgmental factors?

Summary

This chapter discussed receivables management. The key concepts covered are listed below.

- When a firm sells goods to a customer on credit, an **account receivable** is created.
- A firm's **credit policy** consists of four elements: (1) credit standards, (2) credit terms, (3) collection policy, and (4) monitoring receivables.
- The five Cs of credit, which are used to evaluate the credit-worthiness of customers, are **character, capacity, capital, collateral,** and **conditions.**
- Firms can use an **aging schedule** and the **days sales outstanding (DSO)** to help keep track of their receivables position and to help avoid an increase in bad debts.
- Two major sources of external credit information are **credit associations,** which are local groups that meet frequently and correspond with one another to exchange information on credit customers, and **credit reporting agencies,** which collect credit information and sell it for a fee.
- Additional factors that influence a firm's overall credit policy are (1) **profit potential** and (2) **legal considerations.**
- The basic objective of the credit manager is to increase profitable sales by extending credit to worthy customers and therefore adding value to the firm.
- If a firm **tightens its credit policy,** its sales should decrease. Actions which tighten the credit policy include shortening the credit period and tightening credit standards and collection policy. Some of these actions will increase revenues and costs, while others will decrease revenues and costs. A firm should change its credit policy only if the costs of doing so will be more than offset by the benefits.

---

[9]The approach we have taken to analyze the viability of the proposed change in credit policy normally is called the "heuristic approach." It generally is used to provide an approximation for the dollar benefit (cost) of changing credit policies. Present value techniques should be used whenever possible, because they give more precise results. But, it has been shown that the same decision will be made using either the heuristic approach or a present value approach. For an example, see J. Fred Weston and Pham D. Tuan, "Comment on Analysis of Credit Policy Changes," *Financial Management* (Winter 1980). We used the heuristic approach here to avoid the complication of when to assume the various cash flows occur—in reality, the cash flows associated with receivables occur at various times during the collection period.

Questions

10-1 Is it true that when one firm sells to another on credit, the seller records the transaction as an account receivable while the buyer records it as an account payable and that, disregarding discounts, the receivable typically exceeds the payable by the amount of profit on the sale?

10-2 What are the four elements of a firm's credit policy? To what extent can firms set their own credit policies as opposed to having to accept policies that are dictated by "the competition"?

10-3 Suppose that a firm makes a purchase and receives the shipment on February 1. The terms of trade as stated on the invoice read "2/10, net 40, May 1 dating." What is the latest date on which payment can be made and the discount still be taken? What is the date on which payment must be made if the discount is not taken?

10-4 *a.* What is the days sales outstanding (DSO) for a firm whose sales are $2,880,000 per year and whose accounts receivable are $312,000? (Use 360 days per year.)
   b. Is it true that if this firm sells on terms of 3/10, net 40, its customers probably all pay on time?

10-5 What are aging schedules, and how can they be used to help the credit manager more effectively manage accounts receivable?

10-6 Firm A had no credit losses last year, but 1 percent of Firm B's accounts receivable proved to be uncollectible and resulted in losses. Should Firm B fire its credit manager and hire A's?

10-7 Indicate by a $(+)$, $(-)$, or (0) whether each of the following events would probably cause accounts receivable (A/R), sales, and profits to increase, decrease, or be affected in an indeterminant manner:

	A/R	Sales	Profits
The firm tightens its credit standards.	_____	_____	_____
The terms of trade are changed from 2/10, net 30 to 3/10, net 30.	_____	_____	_____
The terms are changed from 2/10, net 30 to 3/10, net 40.	_____	_____	_____
The credit manager gets tough with past-due accounts.	_____	_____	_____

Self-Test Problems

(Solutions Appear in Appendix B)

Key terms **ST-1** Define each of the following terms:
   a. account receivable; days sales outstanding (DSO)
   b. aging schedule
   c. credit policy; credit period; credit standards; five Cs of credit; collection policy; credit terms
   d. cash discounts
   e. seasonal dating
   f. open account; promissory note; commercial draft; sight draft; time draft, or trade acceptance; banker's acceptance; conditional sales contract

Change in credit policy **ST-2** The Boca Grande Company expects to have sales of $10 million this year under its current operating policies. Its variable costs as a percentage of sales are 80 percent, and its required rate of return is 16 percent. Currently, Boca Grande's credit policy is net 25 (no discount for early payment). However, its DSO is 30 days, and its bad debt loss percentage is 2 percent. Boca Grande spends $50,000 per year to collect bad debts, and its marginal tax rate is 40 percent.

The credit manager is considering two alternative proposals for changing Boca Grande's credit policy. Find the expected change in net income, taking into consideration anticipated changes in carrying costs for accounts receivable, the probable bad debt losses, and the discounts likely to be taken, for each proposal. Should a change in credit policy be made?

Proposal 1: Lengthen the credit period from net 25 to net 30. Collection expenditures will remain constant. Under this proposal, sales are expected to increase by $1 million annually, and the bad debt loss percentage on *new* sales is expected to rise to 4 percent (the loss percentage on old sales should not change). In addition, the DSO is expected to increase from 30 days to 45 days on all sales.

Proposal 2: Shorten the credit period from net 25 to net 20. Again, collection expenses will remain constant. The anticipated effects of this change are a decrease in sales of $1 million per year, a decline in the DSO from 30 days to 22 days, and a decline in the bad debt loss percentage to 1 percent on all sales.

Problems

Easing credit terms   **10-1**   Bey Technologies is considering changing its credit terms from 2/15, net 30 to 3/10, net 30 in order to speed collections. At present, 40 percent of Bey's non-default customers take the 2 percent discount. Under the new terms, discount customers are expected to rise to 50 percent of the non-default customers. Regardless of the credit terms, half of the customers who do not take the discount are expected to pay on time, whereas the remainder will pay 10 days late. The change does not involve a relaxation of credit standards; therefore, bad debt losses are not expected to rise above their present 2 percent level. However, the more generous cash discount terms are expected to increase sales from $2 million to $2.6 million per year. Bey's variable cost ratio is 75 percent, the interest rate on funds invested in accounts receivable is 9 percent, and the firm's marginal tax rate is 40 percent.

a. What is the days sales outstanding before and after the change?
b. Calculate the discount costs before and after the change.
c. Calculate the dollar cost of carrying receivables before and after the change.
d. Calculate the bad debt losses before and after the change.
e. What is the incremental profit from the change in credit terms? Should Bey change its credit terms?

Credit analysis   **10-2**   Flint Distributors makes all sales on a credit basis, selling on terms of 2/10, net 30. Once a year it evaluates the creditworthiness of all its customers. The evaluation procedure ranks customers from 1 to 5, with 1 indicating the "best" customers. Results of the ranking are as follows:

Customer Category	Percentage of Bad Debts	Days Sales Outstanding	Credit Decision	Added Sales if Credit Extended to Category
1	None	10	Unlimited credit	None
2	1	12	Unlimited credit	None
3	3	20	Limited credit	$375,000
4	9	60	Limited credit	$190,000
5	16	90	Limited credit	$220,000

The variable cost ratio is 70 percent, and Flint's marginal tax rate is 40 percent. The cost of capital invested in receivables is 12 percent. What would be the effect on the profitability of extending unlimited credit to each of Categories 3, 4, and 5? (Hint: Determine the effect on the income statement of changing each policy separately. In other words, find the change in sales, change in production costs, change in receivables and cost of carrying receivables, change in bad debt costs, and so forth, down to the change in net profits. Assume that none of the customers in these three categories will take the discount.)

Relaxing collection efforts   **10-3**   The Pettit Corporation has annual credit sales of $2 million. Current expenses for the collection department are $30,000, bad debt losses are 2 percent, and the days sales outstanding is 30 days. Pettit is considering easing its collection efforts so that collection expenses will be reduced to $22,000 per year. The change is expected to increase bad debt losses to 3 percent and to increase the days sales outstanding to 45 days. In addition, sales are expected to increase to $2.2 million per year.

Should Pettit relax collection efforts if the opportunity cost of funds is 12 percent, the variable cost ratio is 75 percent, and its marginal tax rate is 40 percent?

Exam-Type Problems

The problems included in this section are set up in such a way that they could be used as multiple-choice exam problems.

Receivables investment   **10-4**   Morrissey Industries sells on terms of 3/10, net 30. Total sales for the year are $900,000. Forty percent of the customers pay on the tenth day and take discounts; the other 60 percent pay, on average, 40 days after their purchases.
  a. What is the days sales outstanding?
  b. What is the average amount of receivables?
  c. What would happen to average receivables if Morrissey toughened its collection policy with the result that all nondiscount customers paid on the thirtieth day?

Tightening credit terms   **10-5**   Helen Bowers, the new credit manager of the Muscarella Corporation, was alarmed to find that Muscarella sells on credit terms of net 50 days while industrywide credit terms have recently been lowered to net 30 days. On annual credit sales of $3 million, Muscarella currently averages 60 days' sales in accounts receivable. Bowers estimates that tightening the credit terms to 30 days would reduce annual sales to $2.6 million, but accounts receivable would drop to 35 days of sales, and the savings on investment in them should more than overcome any loss in profit.

Muscarella's variable cost ratio is 70 percent, and its marginal tax rate is 40 percent. If the interest rate on funds invested in receivables is 11 percent, should the change in credit terms be made?

Cost of carrying receivables   **10-6**   The McCollough Company has a variable operating cost ratio of 70 percent, its cost of capital is 10 percent, and current sales are $10,000. All of its sales are on credit, and it currently sells on terms of net 30. Its accounts receivable balance is $1,500. McCollough is considering a new credit policy with terms of net 45. Under the new policy, sales will increase to $12,000, and accounts receivables will rise to $2,500. If McCollough changes its credit policy to net 45, by how much will its cost of carrying receivables increase? Assume a 360-day year.

Integrative Problem

Credit policy   **10-7**   Dan Edwards, Financial Vice-President of Shield Chemicals Corporation, recently received a report from the company's marketing department recommending that Shield's credit policy be eased. Specifically, the report recommended that the credit terms be changed from 2/10, net 30 to 3/20, net 45 and that both the credit standards and the collection policy be relaxed. According to the report, such a change would cause sales to increase from $18 million to $22 million.

Currently, 63 percent of Shield's *paying* customers pay on Day 10 and take the discount, 34 percent pay on Day 30, and the remaining 3 percent pay (on average) on Day 60. Only 2 percent of sales currently end up as bad debt losses. If the new credit policy is adopted, Edwards thinks that 70 percent of *paying* customers would take the discount, 11 percent would pay on Day 45, and 19 percent would pay late, on Day 90. However, because of the relaxed credit standards, bad debt losses would rise from 2 percent to 4 percent.

Variable operating costs currently are 75 percent of sales, the cost of funds used to carry receivables is 10 percent, and Shield's marginal tax rate is 40 percent. None of these factors would change as a result of a credit policy change.

To help decide whether to adopt the new policy, Edwards has asked you to answer the following questions:

a. What four variables make up a firm's credit policy? In what direction would each be changed if the credit policy were to be *tightened?* How would each variable tend to affect sales, the level of receivables, and bad debt losses?

b. What are the 5 Cs of credit, which credit policy variables do they affect, and how are they used in credit management?

c. How are the days sales outstanding (DSO) and the average collection period (ACP) related to one another? What would the DSO be if the current credit policy is maintained? If the proposed policy is adopted?

d. What is the dollar amount of bad debt losses under the current and the proposed credit policies?

e. What is the dollar amount of discounts granted under the current and the proposed credit policies?

f. What is the dollar cost of carrying receivables under the current and the proposed credit policies?

g. What is the expected incremental profit associated with the proposed change in credit policy? Based on the analysis thus far, should the change be made?

h. If the proposed changes were made, how sure would Edwards be that the changes would actually produce the expected results? What variables in this analysis are especially uncertain? Can you think of anything that the company might do to get more accurate, less uncertain estimates of the effects of the proposed changes?

i. Suppose the company makes the proposed change, but its competitors react by making changes in their own credit terms, with the net result being that gross sales remain at the $18 million level. What would be the impact on the company's after-tax profits?

j. (1) What does the term *monitoring accounts receivable* mean?
   (2) Why would a firm want to monitor its receivables?
   (3) How might the DSO and the aging schedule be used in this process?
   (4) How would seasonal fluctuations affect the validity of the DSO and the aging schedule for monitoring purposes?

Computer-Related Problem

Work the problem in this section only if you are using the computer problem diskette.

Tightening credit terms   **10-8**   Use the model in File C10 to work this problem.

a. Refer to Problem 10-5. When Bowers analyzed her proposed credit policy changes, she found that they would reduce Muscarella's profits and, therefore, should not be enacted. Bowers has reevaluated her sales estimates since all other firms in the industry have recently tightened their credit policies. She now estimates that sales would decline to only $2,800,000 if she tightened the credit policy to net 30 days. Would the credit policy change be profitable under these circumstances?

b. On the other hand, Bowers believes that she could tighten the credit policy to net 45 days and pick up some sales from her competitors. She estimates that sales would increase to $3.3 million and that the days sales outstanding would fall to 50 days under this policy. What would be Muscarella's profits if Bowers enacted this change?

c. Bowers also believes that, if she leaves the credit policy as it is, sales will increase to $3.4 million, and the days sales outstanding will remain at 60 days. Should Bowers leave the credit policy alone or tighten it as described in either Part a or Part b? Which credit policy produces the largest profits for Muscarella Corporation?

CHAPTER 11

Inventory Management

Companies are very much concerned with their inventory policies. The cost of money used to buy and carry inventories is about 15 percent for many firms, and storage, insurance, pilferage, and obsolescence amount to another 10 to 15 percent. Thus, holding $100 of inventory for a year has a cost in the range of $25 to $30. With these high costs, holding excessive inventories literally can ruin a company. On the other hand, inventory shortages can lead to lost sales, to production interruptions, and to customer ill will; so shortages can be just as harmful as excesses.

Today many firms use computerized inventory control models to match stocks on hand with forecasted sales levels, and they coordinate closely with suppliers to reduce average inventory levels. For example, Huffy Corporation, the largest U.S. bicycle manufacturer, was able to reduce its inventory significantly by using a better inventory control process. Huffy has saved millions of dollars in interest and storage costs by keeping a pared-down inventory, with no adverse effect on sales. Similarly, in the second quarter of 1994, Gap Incorporated, a San Francisco clothing retailer, saw its income rise by 55 percent even though sales were up only 12 percent. Gap attributes its success to the fact that tighter inventory controls were implemented to reduce inventory, and the improvement in inventory management resulted in fewer markdowns and write-offs of hard-to-sell clothing lines. Similar inventory management helped Nordstrom Incorporated, a Seattle-based apparel retailer, to report earnings much greater than expected during the same time period.

Such policies of minimizing inventory amounts are not without dangers—if sales surge, inventories might not be sufficient to meet demand, causing the companies to lose sales to competitors who continue to carry higher inventories. Note, though, that if sales fall, low-inventory firms will be in better positions than firms that are overstocked, and if consumers' tastes change, companies like Huffy and Gap will be able to adapt more easily than competitors, who will be stuck with obsolete or undesirable products.

Continued

Our goal in this chapter is to examine the factors that companies like Huffy, Gap, and Nordstrom consider when they establish their inventory policies. Should every firm pare down its holding of inventory like these companies have, or are there instances where large amounts of inventory are preferable?

If the delivery of raw materials and the production of inventory could be perfectly coordinated with the arrival of demand (customers), then a firm probably would not need to carry any inventory. Firms generally find it necessary to hold some inventory because it is not known with perfect certainty when customers will arrive, when orders will be delayed, or when production problems will arise. While products are in inventory, however, they do not generate a return, and they must be financed by the company. Thus, excessive inventories are costly to the firm; but insufficient inventories also are costly because customers might purchase from competitors if products are not available when demanded (this is called a *stockout*), and future business could be lost. Thus, firms need to determine the appropriate level of inventory to hold.

In general, inventories are essential for sales, and sales are necessary for generating profits. The actual control of inventory items usually is not under the direct control of the financial manager. Rather, in manufacturing companies, production people typically have control over inventories, whereas in retail concerns this control is exercised by merchandising people. However, the financial manager still is vitally concerned with inventory levels, for he or she has responsibility for tracking factors that affect the overall profitability of the firm. And, because inventories generally amount to about 12 percent of assets for manufacturing firms and about 30 percent of assets for wholesalers and retailers, poor inventory control could cause significant harm to the firm's profitability position. You know from your study of the Du Pont equation that ineffective inventory management can result in excessive inventories, which in turn can lead to a low rate of return on invested capital. Unilate Textiles is a prime example—a low inventory turnover in 1995 resulted in a low return on equity.

Inventory management also has an effect on the cash conversion cycle, which was discussed in Chapter 8. Remember that one of the components of the cash conversion cycle is the inventory conversion period, the average length of time required to convert raw materials into finished goods and then to sell these goods. Naturally, the larger the amount of inventories held, the longer the inventory conversion period, hence the longer the cash conversion cycle. In 1995, Unilate's inventory conversion period was nearly 80 days, which accounted for more than 70 percent of its 114-day cash conversion cycle. It is apparent Unilate could improve its cash conversion period through more effective inventory management. In this chapter we discuss in general terms the basics of inventory management.

Inventories

Inventories, which can be classified as (1) *raw materials*, (2) *work-in-process*, and (3) *finished goods*, are an essential part of virtually all business operations. As is the case with accounts receivable, inventory levels depend heavily upon sales.

However, whereas receivables build up *after* sales have been made, inventories must be acquired *ahead* of sales. This is a critical difference, and the necessity of forecasting sales before establishing target inventory levels makes inventory management a difficult task. Also, because errors in the establishment of inventory levels quickly lead either to lost sales or to excessive costs of maintaining inventory, inventory management is as important as it is difficult.

Inventory management techniques are covered in depth in production management courses, but because financial managers have a responsibility both for raising the capital needed to carry inventory and for the overall profitability of the firm, we need to cover the basics of inventory management here. Two examples will make clear the importance of inventory management.

First, consider the actions of Universal Food Products, which is a large regional food processing company. Just prior to the beginning of its seasonal demand, in preparation for the increased demand it expects, Universal will begin to increase the level of inventory it holds for processing. Suppose the sales forecasts provided by Universal's management prove to be overly optimistic, so the level of sales falls well short of what was expected. Some of Universal's products are perishable—the value of these items will have to be written off against retained earnings. Those products that have longer shelf lives will be stored at a cost to Universal. Products that cannot be sold cannot generate cash inflows. But cash is needed to pay suppliers, employees, storage costs, and so on. If Universal cannot find external financing such as bank loans, it could find itself in serious financial difficulty.

Now consider a different type of situation, that of Housepro Corporation, an established appliance manufacturer. Suppose Housepro anticipates that the economy is about to get much stronger and that the demand for appliances will rise sharply. If it is to share in the expected boom, Housepro will have to increase production. This means it will have to increase inventory, and, because the inventory buildup must precede sales, additional financing will be required—some liability account, perhaps notes payable, would have to be increased to support the additional inventory.

These simple examples show that proper inventory management requires close coordination among the sales, purchasing, production, and finance departments. The sales/marketing department generally is the first to spot changes in demand. These changes must be worked into the company's purchasing and manufacturing schedules, and the financial manager must arrange any financing that will be needed to support the inventory buildup. Lack of coordination among departments, poor sales forecasts, or both, can lead to disaster.

Types of Inventory

Firms would prefer to hold little or no inventory; if it could be arranged, firms would like to time the production of their products to coincide perfectly with the arrival of demand. For example, a manufacturer would consider it ideal if a customer arrived to purchase its product just as the product came off the assembly line. If the manufacturer could time its production so that the completion of the product for sale *always* occurred at the same time a customer arrived, then it would never have to hold any finished products in inventory. This is a tough task to accomplish, because the only way a firm can ensure its production of products coincides perfectly with customers' demand is if the demand is *known with certainty.* We can safely state that no firm knows its demand with perfect certainty.

But what if a firm could forecast its demand with perfect certainty? Does that mean the firm would not have to hold any inventory? Probably not, because, generally, the production, or manufacturing, process takes *some* amount of time. The time required in production, and thus the amount of transformation the material goes through before a salable item is produced, varies according to the value added to the original materials purchased. Therefore, almost every firm finds it necessary to hold inventory in one form or another. In this section we describe the three primary types of inventory.

Raw Materials

RAW MATERIALS
The inventories purchased from suppliers which ultimately will be transformed into finished goods.

Raw materials include the inventory purchased from suppliers; it is the material a firm purchases to transform into a finished product for sale. As long as the firm has an inventory of raw materials, delays in ordering and delivery from suppliers do not affect the production process. If a firm does not have raw materials, the first stages of production would have to be stopped until such materials are received. Later in the chapter, we discuss methods currently used to reduce the amount of raw materials inventory a firm has to carry.

Work-in-Process

WORK-IN-PROCESS
Inventory in various stages of completion; some work-in-process is at the very beginning of the production process while some is at the end of the process.

Work-in-process refers to inventory units that are at various stages of completion; some of the inventory in work-in-process will be at the beginning stages of completion and some will be nearly completed. If a firm has work-in-process at every stage of the production process, then it will not have to completely shut down production if a problem arises at one of the previous production stages. For example, as long as GM has an inventory of automobiles that have passed through the first stage of production, it does not have to shut down the entire assembly line for maintenance of the machinery used in the first stage of production.

Finished Goods

FINISHED GOODS
Inventories that have completed the production process and are ready for sale.

The **finished goods** inventory represents products that are ready for sale. For these items, the production process is complete. Firms carry finished goods to ensure that orders can be filled when they are received. If a firm did not have a finished goods inventory, it would have to wait for the completion of the production process before inventory could be sold—thus demand could not be satisfied when it arrived. When demand arrives and there is no inventory to satisfy that demand, a *stockout* exists, and the firm might lose the demand to competitors, perhaps permanently.

Self-Test Questions

What are the three primary types of inventory?

What is the purpose of holding each of the three types of inventory?

Managing Inventory

Inventory management focuses on four basic questions: (1) How many units should be ordered (or produced) at a given time? (2) At what point should inventory be ordered (or produced)? (3) What inventory items warrant special attention? (4) Can changes in the costs of inventory items be hedged? The remainder of the chapter provides answers to these four questions.

Inventory Costs

The goal of inventory management is to provide the inventories required to sustain operations at the lowest possible cost. The first step in inventory management is to identify all the costs involved in purchasing and maintaining inventory. Table 11-1 gives a listing of the typical costs associated with inventory. We have broken down costs into three categories: those associated with carrying inventory, those associated with ordering and receiving inventory, and those associated with running short of inventory (stockouts).

STOCKOUT
Occurs when a firm runs out of inventory *and* customers arrive to purchase the product.

Although it could well be the most important element, at this point we will disregard the third category of costs—the costs of running short, which could result in stockouts. **Stockouts** occur when (1) a firm runs out of inventory and (2) customers arrive to purchase the product. The costs of stockouts are dealt with by adding safety stocks, as we will discuss later. Similarly, we will discuss

---

TABLE 11-1

Costs Associated with Inventory

	Approximate Annual Cost as a Percentage of Inventory Value
I. Carrying Costs	
Cost of capital tied up	12.0%
Storage and handling costs	0.5
Insurance	0.5
Property taxes	1.0
Depreciation and obsolescence	12.0
Total	26.0%
II. Ordering, Shipping, and Receiving Costs	
Ordering and production setup costs	Varies
Shipping and handling costs	2.5%
III. Costs of Running Short	
Loss of sales	Varies
Loss of customer goodwill	Varies
Disruption of production schedules	Varies

NOTE: These costs vary from firm to firm, from item to item, and also over time. The figures shown are U.S. Department of Commerce estimates for an average manufacturing firm. Where costs vary so widely that no meaningful numbers can be assigned, the term *Varies* is reported.

quantity discounts in a later section. The costs that remain for consideration at this stage, then, are carrying costs and ordering, shipping, and receiving costs.

Carrying Costs

CARRYING COSTS
The costs associated with having inventory, which include storage costs, insurance, cost of tying up funds, depreciation costs, and so on; these costs generally increase in proportion to the average amount of inventory held.

Total **carrying costs** generally increase in direct proportion to the average amount of inventory carried. Inventory carried, in turn, depends on the frequency with which orders are placed. To illustrate, if a firm sells T units per year, and if it places equal-sized orders N times per year, then Q = T/N units will be purchased with each order. If the inventory is used evenly over the year, and if no safety stocks are carried, then the average inventory, A, will be

11-1

$$\text{Average inventory} = A = \frac{\text{Units per order}}{2} = \frac{\left(\frac{T}{N}\right)}{2} = \frac{Q}{2}$$

For example, if T = 120,000 units a year and N = 4, then the firm will order Q = 30,000 units at a time, and its average inventory will be 15,000 units:

$$A = \frac{\left(\frac{120,000}{4}\right)}{2} = \frac{30,000}{2} = 15,000 \text{ units}$$

Just after a shipment arrives, the inventory will be 30,000 units; just before the next shipment arrives, it will be zero; on average, 15,000 units will be carried.

Now assume the firm purchases its inventory at a price PP = $2.50 per unit. The average inventory value is, thus, PP × A = $2.50(15,000) = $37,500. If it costs the firm an average of 10 percent to finance inventory, it will incur $3,750 in financing charges to carry the inventory for one year. Further, assume that each year the firm incurs $2,200 of storage costs (space, utilities, security, taxes, and so forth), that its inventory insurance costs are $550, and that it must mark down inventory by $1,000 because of depreciation and obsolescence. The firm's total cost of carrying the $37,500 average inventory is thus $3,750 + $2,200 + $550 + $1,000 = $7,500, and the annual percentage cost of carrying the inventory is $7,500/$37,500 = 0.20 = 20%.

Defining the annual percentage carrying cost as C, we can, in general, find the annual total carrying cost, TCC, as the percentage carrying cost, C, times the price per unit, PP, times the average inventory in units, A:

11-2

$$\text{Total carrying cost} = TCC = C \times PP \times A = C \times PP \times \left(\frac{Q}{2}\right)$$

In our example,

$$TCC = (0.20)(\$2.50)(15,000) = \$7,500$$

Ordering Costs

Although we assume that carrying costs are entirely variable and increase in direct proportion to the average size of inventory, **ordering costs** usually are fixed. For example, the costs of placing and receiving an order—generating interoffice memos, using fax transmissions or long-distance telephone calls, and taking delivery—essentially are fixed regardless of the size of an order, so this part of inventory cost simply is the fixed cost of placing and receiving orders times the number of orders placed per year.[1] We define the fixed costs associated with ordering inventories as O, and if we place N orders per year, the total ordering cost is given by Equation 11-3:

11-3

$$\text{Total ordering costs} = \text{TOC} = O \times N = O \times \left(\frac{T}{Q}\right)$$

Here TOC = total ordering cost, O = fixed costs per order, N = number of orders placed per year, and Q is the inventory quantity for each order.

To illustrate the use of Equation 11-3, if O = \$100, T = 120,000 units, and Q = 30,000 units, then TOC, the total annual ordering cost, is \$400:

$$\text{TOC} = \$100 \left(\frac{120,000}{30,000}\right) = \$100 \,(4) = \$400$$

Total Inventory Costs

Total carrying cost, TCC, as defined in Equation 11-2, and total ordering cost, TOC, as defined in Equation 11-3, can be combined to find total inventory costs, TIC, as follows:

11-4

$$\text{Total inventory costs} = \text{TIC} = \quad \text{TCC} \quad + \text{TOC}$$

$$= (C \times PP \times A) + (O \times N)$$

$$= (C \times PP)\left(\frac{Q}{2}\right) + O\left(\frac{T}{Q}\right)$$

---

[1]Note that, in reality, both carrying and ordering costs can have variable and fixed cost elements, at least over certain ranges of average inventory. For example, security and utilities charges probably are fixed in the short run over a wide range of inventory levels. Similarly, labor costs in receiving inventory could be tied to the quantity received, hence could be variable. To simplify matters, we treat all carrying costs as variable and all ordering costs as fixed. However, if these assumptions do not fit the situation at hand, the cost definitions can be changed. For example, one could add another term for shipping costs if there are economies of scale in shipping such that the cost of shipping a unit is smaller if shipments are larger. However, in most situations, shipping costs are not sensitive to order size, so total shipping costs are simply cost per unit times the units ordered (and sold) during the year. Under this condition, shipping costs are not influenced by inventory policy, and hence may be disregarded for purposes of determining the optimal inventory level and the optimal order size.

Here we see that total carrying cost equals average inventory in units, Q/2, multiplied by unit purchase price, PP, times the percentage annual carrying cost, C. Total ordering cost equals the number of orders placed per year, T/Q, multiplied by the fixed cost of placing and receiving an order, O. We will use this equation in the next section to develop the optimal inventory ordering quantity.

Self-Test Questions

What is a stockout?

What are the three categories of inventory costs?

What are some specific inventory carrying costs?

What are some inventory ordering costs?

Explain in words what Equation 11-4 computes.

The Economic Ordering Quantity (EOQ) Model

Inventories obviously are necessary, but it is equally obvious that a firm's profitability will suffer if it has too much or too little inventory. How can we determine the optimal inventory level? One commonly used approach is based on the economic ordering quantity (EOQ) model, which is described next.

Derivation of the EOQ Model

Figure 11-1 illustrates the basic premise on which the EOQ model is built—namely, that some costs rise with larger inventories while other costs decline, and there is an optimal order size (and associated average inventory) which minimizes the total costs of inventories. First, as noted earlier, the average investment in inventory depends on how frequently orders are placed and the size of each order—if we order every day, average inventory will be much smaller than if we order once a year. Further, as Figure 11-1 shows, the firm's carrying costs rise with larger orders: Larger orders mean larger average inventory, so warehousing costs, interest on funds tied up in inventory, insurance, and obsolescence costs all will increase. However, ordering costs decline with larger orders of inventories: The cost of placing orders and order handling costs will decline if we order infrequently and consequently hold larger quantities.

If the carrying and ordering cost curves in Figure 11-1 are summed, the result represents total inventory costs, TIC. The point where the TIC is minimized represents the **economic (optimum) ordering quantity (EOQ),** and this, in turn, determines the optimal average inventory level.

The EOQ is found by differentiating Equation 11-4 with respect to ordering quantity, Q, and setting the derivative equal to zero. The result is:

ECONOMIC ORDERING QUANTITY (EOQ)
The optimal quantity that should be ordered; it is this quantity that will minimize the *total inventory costs.*

11-5

$$\text{Economic ordering quantity} = \text{EOQ} = \sqrt{\frac{2(O)(T)}{(C)(PP)}}$$

FIGURE 11-1

Determination of the Optimal Order Quantity

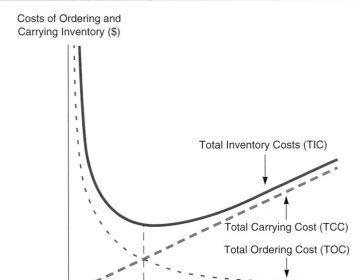

Here

EOQ = economic ordering quantity, or the optimum quantity to be ordered each
    time an order is placed

    O = fixed costs of placing and receiving an order

    T = annual sales in units

    C = annual carrying costs expressed as a percentage of average inventory
    value

    PP = purchase price the firm must pay per unit of inventory (raw materials)

EOQ MODEL
A formula for determining
the order quantity that
will minimize total
inventory costs:

$$EOQ = \sqrt{\frac{2(O)(T)}{(C)(PP)}}$$

Equation 11-5 is the **EOQ model.**[2] The primary assumptions of the model, which
will be relaxed shortly, include the following: (1) sales can be forecasted perfectly,
(2) sales are evenly distributed throughout the year, and (3) orders are received
when expected.

EOQ Model Illustration

To illustrate the EOQ model, consider the following data, supplied by Cotton Tops
Inc., a distributor of custom-designed T-shirts that supplies concessionaires at
Daisy World:

[2]The EOQ model can also be written as

$$EOQ = \sqrt{\frac{2(O)(T)}{(C)^*}},$$

where C^* is the annual carrying cost per unit expressed in dollars.

T = annual sales = 78,000 shirts per year

C = percentage carrying cost = 25 percent of inventory value

PP = purchase price per shirt = $3.84 per shirt. (The shirts sell for $9, but this is irrelevant for our purposes here.)

O = fixed cost per order = $260

Substituting these data into Equation 11-5, we find an EOQ of 6,500 units:

$$EOQ = \sqrt{\frac{2(\$260)(78,000)}{(0.25)(\$3.84)}}$$

$$= \sqrt{42,250,000} = 6,500 \text{ units}$$

With an EOQ of 6,500 shirts and annual usage of 78,000 shirts, Cotton Tops will place 78,000/6,500 = 12 orders per year. Notice that average inventory holdings depend directly on the EOQ: This relationship is illustrated graphically in Figure 11-2, where we see that average inventory = EOQ/2. Immediately after an order is received, 6,500 shirts are in stock. The usage rate, or sales rate, is 1,500 shirts per week (78,000/52 weeks), so inventories are drawn down by this amount each week. Thus, the actual number of units held in inventory will vary from 6,500 shirts just after an order is received to zero just before a new order arrives. With a 6,500 beginning balance, a zero ending balance, and a uniform sales rate, inventory will average one-half the EOQ, or 3,250 shirts, during the year. At a cost of $3.84 per shirt, the average investment in inventory will be (3,250)($3.84) = $12,480. If inventories are financed by bank loans, the loan will vary from a high of $24,960 to a low of $0, but the average amount outstanding over the course of a year will be $12,480.

FIGURE 11-2

Inventory Position without Safety Stock

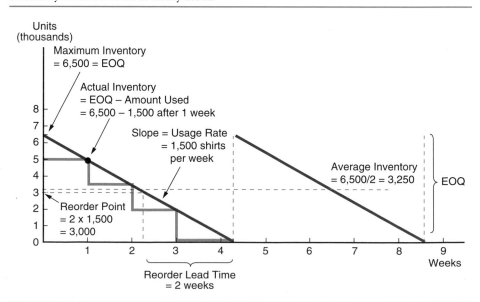

Notice that the EOQ, hence average inventory holdings, rises with the square root of sales increases. Therefore, a given increase in sales will result in a less-than-proportionate increase in inventory, so the inventory/sales ratio will tend to decline as a firm grows. For example, Cotton Tops' EOQ is 6,500 shirts at an annual sales level of 78,000, and the average inventory is 3,250 shirts, or $12,480. However, if sales were to increase by 100 percent, to 156,000 shirts per year, the EOQ would rise to about 9,192 shirts, or by only 41 percent, and the average inventory would rise by this same percentage. This suggests that there are economies of scale in holding inventories.[3]

Finally, look at Cotton Tops' total inventory costs for the year, assuming that the EOQ is ordered each time. Using Equation 11-4, we find total inventory costs of $6,240:

$$
\begin{aligned}
\text{TIC} &= \qquad \text{TCC} \qquad + \qquad \text{TOC} \\
&= \quad (\text{C} \times \text{PP})\left(\frac{Q}{2}\right) \quad + \quad \text{O}\left(\frac{T}{Q}\right) \\
&= 0.25(\$3.84)\left(\frac{6,500}{2}\right) + (\$260)\left(\frac{78,000}{6,500}\right) \\
&= \qquad \$3,120 \qquad + \qquad \$3,120 \qquad = \$6,240
\end{aligned}
$$

Note these two points: (1) The $6,240 total inventory cost represents the total of carrying costs and ordering costs, but this amount does *not* include the 78,000($3.84) = $299,520 annual cost of purchasing the inventory itself. (2) As we see both in Figure 11-1 and in the numbers just above, at the EOQ, total carrying cost (TCC) equals total ordering cost (TOC). This property is not unique to our Cotton Tops illustration; it always holds.

Table 11-2 contains the total inventory costs that Cotton Tops would incur at various order quantities, including the EOQ level. Notice that as the amount ordered increases, the total carrying costs increase but the total ordering costs decrease, and vice versa. If Cotton Tops orders less than the EOQ amount, then the higher ordering costs more than offset the lower carrying costs; if an amount greater than the EOQ is ordered, the higher carrying costs more than offset the lower ordering costs.

Setting the Reorder Point

REORDER POINT
The level of inventory at which an order should be placed.

The EOQ model assumes immediate delivery of the inventory when it is ordered. But what if a 2-week lead time is required for production and shipping? What is Cotton Tops' **reorder point,** or the inventory level at which an order should be placed? The firm sells 78,000/52 = 1,500 shirts per week. Thus, if a 2-week lag occurs between the order and the delivery, Cotton Tops must place the order when there are 3,000 shirts on hand:

---

[3]Note, however, that these scale economies relate to each particular item, not to the entire firm. Thus, a large distributor with $500 million of sales might have a higher inventory/sales ratio than a much smaller distributor if the small firm has only a few high-sales-volume items while the large firm distributes a great many low-volume items.

Table 11-2

Cotton Tops, Inc.: Total Inventory Costs for Various Order Quantities

	Quantity	Number of Orders	Total Ordering Costs	Total Carrying Costs	Total Inventory Costs
	2,000	39	$10,140	$ 960	$11,100
	3,000	26	6,760	1,440	8,200
	5,200	15	3,900	2,496	6,396
	6,000	13	3,380	2,880	6,260
EOQ	**6,500**	**12**	**3,120**	**3,120**	**6,240**
	7,800	10	2,600	3,744	6,344
	9,750	8	2,080	4,680	6,760
	19,500	4	1,040	9,360	10,400
	78,000	1	260	37,440	37,700

T = annual sales = 78,000 shirts

C = carrying cost = 25 percent

PP = purchase price = $3.84/shirt

O = ordering cost = $260/order

11-6

$$\text{Reorder point} = (\text{Lead time in weeks}) \times (\text{Weekly usage})$$

$$= 2 \times 1,500 = 3,000$$

At the end of the 2-week production and shipping period, the inventory balance will be down to zero—but just at that time, the order of new shirts will arrive.

Goods in Transit

Goods in Transit
Goods which have been ordered but have not yet been received.

If a new order must be placed before the previous order is received, a **goods-in-transit inventory** will build up. Goods in transit are goods that have been ordered but have not been received. A goods-in-transit inventory will exist if the normal delivery lead time is longer than the time between orders. This complicates matters somewhat, but the simplest solution to the problem is to deduct goods in transit when calculating the reorder point. In other words, the reorder point is calculated as follows:

11-7

$$\frac{\text{Reorder}}{\text{point}} = \left(\frac{\text{Lead time}}{\text{in weeks}} \times \frac{\text{Weekly}}{\text{usage}} \right) - \frac{\text{Goods in}}{\text{transit}}$$

Goods in transit is not an issue for Cotton Tops because the firm orders 78,000/6,500 = 12 times a year, or once a month, and the delivery lead time is 2 weeks. However, suppose that Cotton Tops ordered 1,500 shirts every 2 weeks and the delivery lead time was 3 weeks. Then, whenever an order was placed, another order of 3,000 shirts (1,500 shirts × 2 weeks) would be in transit. Therefore, Cotton Tops' reorder point would be:

$$\text{Reorder point} = (3 \times 1,500) - 3,000 = 4,500 - 3,000 = 1,500$$

In one week, Cotton Tops will receive the 3,000 shirts that are in transit (those ordered 2 weeks ago); during the week, the firm will sell 1,500 shirts, so its inventory level will be zero when the goods in transit are received.

Self-Test Questions

What is the purpose of the EOQ model?

What is the relationship between total carrying cost and total ordering cost at the EOQ?

What assumptions are inherent in the EOQ model as presented here?

EOQ Model Extensions

The basic EOQ model was derived under several restrictive assumptions. In this section, we relax some of those assumptions and, in the process, extend the model to make it more useful.

The Concept of Safety Stocks

SAFETY STOCKS
Additional inventory carried to guard against changes in sales rates or production/shipping delays.

If Cotton Tops knew for certain that both the sales rate and the order lead time would never vary, it could operate exactly as shown in Figure 11-2. However, because sales do change, and because production and shipping delays do occur, the firm must carry additional inventory, or **safety stocks.**

The concept of a safety stock is illustrated in Figure 11-3. First, note that the slope of the sales line measures the expected rate of sales. The company *expects* to sell 1,500 shirts per week, but let us assume that the maximum likely sales rate is 2,500 units each week, 1,000 more than normal. Further, assume that Cotton Tops sets the safety stock at 2,000 shirts (two weeks of *above-normal* sales), so it initially orders 8,500 shirts—the EOQ of 6,500 plus the 2,000-unit safety stock. Subsequently, it reorders the EOQ of 6,500 shirts whenever the inventory level falls to 5,000—the safety stock of 2,000 shirts plus the 3,000 shirts expected to be used while awaiting delivery of the order.

Notice that, because it has inventory equal to 5,000 units, the company could sell a maximum of 2,500 units a week during the 2-week delivery period. This maximum rate of sales is shown by the steeper dashed line in Figure 11-3. The condition that makes possible this higher maximum sales rate is the safety stock of 2,000 shirts.

The safety stock also is useful to guard against delays in receiving orders. The expected delivery time is 2 weeks, but with a 2,000-unit safety stock, the company could maintain sales at the expected rate of 1,500 units per week for an additional 1.3 weeks if production or shipping delays held up an order.

However, carrying a safety stock has a cost. The average inventory is now EOQ/2 plus the safety stock, or $6,500/2 + 2,000 = 3,250 + 2,000 = 5,250$ shirts,

Figure 11-3

Inventory Position with Safety Stock Included

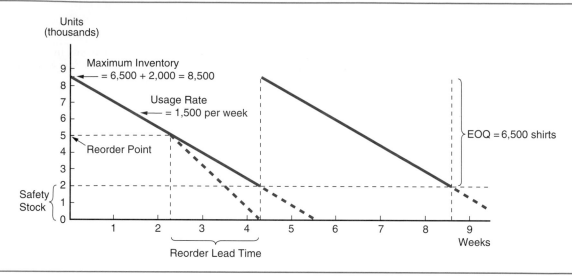

and the average inventory value is now (5,250)($3.84) = $20,160. This increase in average inventory causes an *increase* in annual inventory carrying costs equal to (Safety stock)(PP)(C) = 2,000($3.84)(0.25) = $1,920.

The optimal safety stock varies from situation to situation, but, in general, it *increases* (1) with the uncertainty of demand forecasts, (2) with the costs (in terms of lost sales and lost goodwill) that result from inventory shortages (stock-outs), and (3) with the probability that delays will occur in receiving shipments. The optimum safety stock *decreases* as the cost of carrying this additional inventory increases.

Quantity Discounts

In the form presented in Equation 11-5, the EOQ model presumes the purchase price of inventory does not change, regardless of the quantity ordered. For Cotton Tops, this means the purchase price for each shirt is $3.84, regardless of whether the shirts are ordered one at a time (Q = 1) or all at once (Q = 78,000). But what if the T-shirt manufacturer offered Cotton Tops a *quantity discount* of 1 percent on large orders? If the quantity discount applied to orders of 5,000 or more, then Cotton Tops would continue to place the EOQ order of 6,500 shirts and take the quantity discount. However, if the quantity discount required orders of 13,000 or more, then Cotton Tops' inventory manager would have to compare the savings in purchase price that would result if its ordering quantity were increased to 13,000 units versus the increase in total inventory costs caused by the departure from the 6,500-unit EOQ.

As Table 11-2 indicates, the total inventory cost at the EOQ amount is approximately $6,240. If Cotton Tops orders 13,000 shirts to take advantage of the discount, the purchase price per shirt would equal 0.99($3.84) = $3.80, so the total inventory cost would be:

$$\text{TIC} = 0.25 \times \$3.80 \times \left(\frac{13,000}{2} \right) + \$260 \times \left(\frac{78,000}{13,000} \right)$$

$$= 6,175 \qquad\qquad + \$1,560 \qquad = \$7,735$$

If Cotton Tops orders 13,000 shirts at a time, the total inventory cost increases by $1,495. But the preceding computation does not consider the cost of goods sold savings Cotton Tops will realize by taking the discount. For the entire year, Cotton Tops will save 1 percent of the initial purchase price of $3.84, so the total reduction in purchase price will be $[0.01(\$3.84)] \times 78,000 = \$2,995.20$. The net benefit from ordering 13,000 shirts to take advantage of the quantity discount will be $2,995.20 - $1,495.00 = $1,500.20, so Cotton Tops should take advantage of the quantity discount. As you can see, quantity discounts could affect significantly the optimal order quantity.

Inflation

Moderate inflation—say, 3 percent per year—can largely be ignored for purposes of inventory management, but higher rates of inflation must be explicitly considered. If the rate of inflation in the types of goods the firm stocks tends to be relatively constant, it can be dealt with quite easily—simply deduct the expected annual rate of inflation from the carrying cost percentage, C, in Equation 11-5, and use this modified version of the EOQ model to establish the working stock. The reason for making this deduction is that inflation causes the value of the inventory to rise, thus offsetting somewhat the effects of depreciation and other carrying costs factors. Because C now will be smaller, the calculated EOQ, and the average inventory, will increase. However, the higher the rate of inflation, the higher are interest rates, and this factor will cause C to increase, thus lowering the EOQ and average inventory.

On balance, there is no evidence that inflation either raises or lowers the optimal inventory of firms in the aggregate. Inflation still should be explicitly considered, however, because it will raise the individual firm's optimal holdings if the rate of inflation for its own inventories is above average (and is greater than the effects of inflation on interest rates) and vice versa.

Seasonal Demand

For most firms, it is unrealistic to assume that the demand for an inventory item is uniform throughout the year. What happens when there is seasonal demand, as would hold true for an ice cream company? Here the standard annual EOQ model obviously is not appropriate. However, the model does provide a point of departure for setting inventory parameters, which are then modified to fit the particular seasonal pattern. The procedure here is to divide the year into the seasons in which annualized sales are relatively constant, say the summer, the spring and fall, and the winter. Then the EOQ model can be applied separately to each period. During the transitions between seasons, inventory would be either run down or else built up with special seasonal orders.

Self-Test Questions

Why are inventory safety stocks required?

How would you decide whether to accept a quantity discount offer from a supplier?

What is goods-in-transit inventory?

How does goods-in-transit inventory affect the inventory reorder point?

What impact does inflation have on the EOQ?

How can the EOQ model be used when a company faces seasonal demand fluctuations?

Inventory Control Systems

RED-LINE METHOD
An inventory control procedure whereby a *red line* is drawn around the inside of an inventory-stocked bin to indicate the reorder point level.

TWO-BIN METHOD
An inventory control procedure in which an order is placed when one of two inventory-stocked bins is empty.

The EOQ model, together with safety stock analysis, can be used to establish the proper inventory level, but inventory management also involves the establishment of an *inventory control system.* Inventory control systems run the gamut from very simple to extremely complex, depending on the size of the firm and the nature of its inventories. For example, one simple control procedure is the **red-line method**—inventory items are stocked in a bin, a red line is drawn around the inside of the bin at the level of the reorder point, and the inventory clerk places an order when the red line shows. The **two-bin method** has inventory items stocked in two bins. When the working bin is empty, an order is placed and inventory is drawn from the second bin. These procedures work well for small parts, such as bolts in a manufacturing process, or for many items in retail businesses.

Computerized Systems

COMPUTERIZED INVENTORY CONTROL SYSTEM
A system of inventory control in which a computer is used to determine reorder points and to adjust inventory balances.

Larger companies employ **computerized inventory control systems.** The computer starts with an inventory count in memory. As withdrawals are made, they are recorded by the computer, and the inventory balance is revised. When the reorder point is reached, the computer automatically places an order, and when the order is received, the recorded balance is increased. Retailers such as Wal-Mart have carried this system quite far—each item has a bar code, and, as an item is checked out, the code is read, a signal is sent to the computer, and the inventory balance is adjusted at the same time the price is fed into the cash register tape. When the balance drops to the reorder point, an order is placed, in Wal-Mart's case directly from its computers to those of its suppliers.

A good inventory control system is dynamic, not static. A company such as IBM or General Motors (GM) stocks hundreds of thousands of different items. The sales (or use) of these various items can rise or fall quite separately from rising or falling overall corporate sales. As the usage rate for an individual item begins to rise or fall, the inventory manager must adjust its balance to avoid running short or ending up with obsolete items. If the change in the usage rate appears to be permanent, then the EOQ should be recomputed, the safety stock level should be reconsidered, and the computer model used in the control process should be reprogrammed.

JIT Is Not JIJ (Just in Japan) Anymore

Just-in-time (JIT) inventory management systems were introduced more than 30 years ago by Toyota Motor Corporation. The objective of JIT is to eliminate waste by timing the delivery of products from a supplier to a purchaser at the instant they are needed. To implement a JIT inventory system, a purchasing firm must find a supplier (or network of suppliers) that can provide quality products on short notice and with the assurance the products will be delivered on time. Thus, coordination is critical for JIT systems to be beneficial to both the supplier and the purchaser.

In recent times, as the economy has improved, nearly 80 percent of firms have indicated that they will not increase inventory levels like they usually do during improving economic conditions. Many inventory managers attribute this strategy to the influence of JIT inventory management systems. With much improved electronics, better synchronization between suppliers and purchasers, and a greater awareness of the impact of inventory carrying (holding) costs, many firms have recognized that improved inventory policies can result in greater profits—some form of JIT might be the answer.

A recent survey of manufacturers in the United States indicates that more than three quarters either use or intend to use JIT systems for inventory management.[1] Of those companies that already have implemented JIT, most have reduced the number of suppliers they now utilize; in fact, more than 10 percent of the companies decreased their suppliers by more than 50 percent as a result of JIT systems. More

reductions are expected as companies more fully integrate JIT. Nearly all of the companies that use JIT indicated that product price no longer is the primary consideration for selecting suppliers; rather, with JIT, the most important factor is the supplier's ability to reliably deliver products that conform to quality specifications. In addition, JIT firms are concerned with the flexibility of a supplier with respect to response to orders. To achieve the reliability and flexibility demanded by JIT users, suppliers and purchasers essentially must enter into a buyer-seller relationship that is highly coordinated and synchronized. With today's modern technology, this coordination can be attained relatively easily by electronically connecting suppliers and purchasers so that inventory levels can be monitored, inventory patterns can be analyzed, and suppliers can better plan shipments to purchasers. Unfortunately, even though they are well aware of the benefits, most companies are hesitant to allow suppliers access to their inventory records—less than half of JIT companies allow suppliers to access inventory information, and, surprisingly, only about one half of the companies use electronic ordering systems.

JIT systems have improved communications between purchasers and suppliers, and even boosted employee morale. As production managers have discovered, the implementation of JIT systems is a major commitment that requires both purchasers and suppliers to formally construct strategic plans, both in the short run and the long run. Thus, it is believed JIT inventory management will help improve productivity and product quality in the United States. To be successful, though, a JIT inventory management system should be a win-win situation—both the supplier and the purchaser must see the benefits of the system.

[1]Thomas J. Billesbach, Alan Harrison, and Simon Croom-Morgan, "Supplier Performance Measures and Practices in JIT Companies in the U.S. and the U.K.," *International Journal of Purchasing and Materials Management* (Fall 1991), 24–28.

Just-in-Time Systems

JUST-IN-TIME (JIT) SYSTEM
A system of inventory control in which a manufacturer coordinates production with suppliers so that raw materials of components arrive just as they are needed in the production process.

A relatively new approach to inventory control called the **just-in-time (JIT) system** has been developed by Japanese firms and has gained significant popularity throughout the world. Toyota provides a good example of the just-in-time system. Most of Toyota's factories, along with its suppliers, dot the countryside around Toyota City. Delivery of components is tied to the speed of the assembly line, and parts generally are delivered no more than a few hours before they are used. The just-in-time system reduces the need for Toyota and other manufacturers to carry large inventories, but it requires a great deal of coordination between the manufacturer and its suppliers, both in the timing of deliveries and the quality of the parts.

Not surprisingly, U.S. automobile manufacturers were among the first domestic firms to move toward just-in-time systems. Ford has been restructuring its production system with a goal of increasing its inventory turnover from 20 times a year to 30 or 40 times. Of course, just-in-time systems place considerable pressure on suppliers. GM formerly kept a 10-day supply of seats and other parts made by Lear Siegler; now GM sends in orders at four- to eight-hour intervals and expects immediate shipment. A Lear Siegler spokesman stated, "We can't afford to keep things sitting around either," so Lear Siegler has had to be tougher on its own suppliers.

Just-in-time systems also are being adopted by smaller firms. In fact, some production experts say that small companies are better positioned than large ones to use just-in-time methods because it is easier to redefine job functions and to educate people in small firms. One small-firm example is Fireplace Manufacturers Inc., a manufacturer of prefabricated fireplaces. The company recently had cash flow problems at a time when it carried $1.1 million in inventories to support annual sales of about $8 million. The company used just-in-time methods to trim its raw material and work-in-process inventories to $750,000, freeing up $350,000 of cash, even as sales doubled.

It has been argued that just-in-time inventory controls do not really increase overall economic efficiency because they merely shift costs of purchases to other firms farther up the supply chain. However, this view probably is incorrect—the close coordination required between the parties has led to an overall reduction of inventories throughout the production-distribution system, and hence to a general improvement in economic efficiency. This point is made by such companies as Wal-Mart and Toyota, and it is borne out by economic statistics, which indicate that inventories as a percentage of sales have been declining since the use of just-in-time procedures began.

Out-Sourcing

OUT-SOURCING
The practice of purchasing components rather than making them in-house.

Another important development related to inventories is **out-sourcing**, which is the practice of purchasing components rather than making them in-house. Thus, if GM arranged to buy radiators, axles, and other parts from suppliers rather than making them itself, it would be increasing its use of out-sourcing. Out-sourcing often is combined with just-in-time systems to reduce inventory levels. However, perhaps the major reason for out-sourcing has nothing to do with inventory policy—a bureaucratic, unionized company like GM can often buy parts from a smaller, nonunionized supplier at a lower cost than if it made them itself.

The Relationship between Production Scheduling and Inventory Levels

A final point relating to inventory levels is *the relationship between production scheduling and inventory levels*. A firm like a greeting card manufacturer has highly seasonal sales. Such a firm could produce on a steady, year-round basis, or it could let production rise and fall with sales. If it established a level production schedule, its inventories would rise sharply during periods when sales were low and then would decline during peak sales periods, but the average inventory held would be substantially higher than if production rose and fell with sales.

Our discussions of just-in-time systems, out-sourcing, and production scheduling all point out the necessity of coordinating inventory policy with manufacturing/procurement policies. Companies try to minimize *total production and distribution costs,* and inventory costs are just one part of total costs. Still, they are an important cost, and financial managers should be aware of the determinants of inventory costs and how they can be minimized.

Self-Test Questions

Describe some inventory control systems used in practice.

What are just-in-time systems? What are their advantages?

What types of operations can benefit most from just-in-time systems?

What is out-sourcing?

Describe the dependency between production scheduling and inventory levels.

Monitoring Inventory Levels

ABC System
A system used to categorize inventory to ensure that the usage rates, stock levels, delivery times, and so on of the most important inventory items are reviewed most often.

The EOQ model can give some insights into the optimal ordering quantity and average inventories for a firm's major items, but usage rates change over time, and a good inventory management system must respond promptly to such changes. One system that is used to monitor inventory EOQs and levels is the **ABC system.** Under this system, the firm analyzes each inventory item on the basis of its cost, frequency of usage, seriousness of a stock-out, reorder lead time, and other criteria. Items that are expensive, are used frequently, have serious consequences if stock-outs occur, and have long reorder lead times are put into the A category; less important items are placed in the B category; and the least important items are designated as C items. Management reviews the A items' usage rates, stock positions, and delivery times frequently—say, monthly—and adjusts the EOQ and reorder points as necessary. Category B items are reviewed and adjusted less frequently—say, every quarter—and C items are reviewed even less often, perhaps annually. Thus, inventory management resources are focused on where they will do the most good.

Major inventory changes also should be evaluated using the firm's forecasting model and cash budget. For example, increases in inventory, if not accompanied by increases in sales, would tend to decrease profitability and increase the need for additional funding. Further, cash outlays for the additional inventory would increase cash outflows as reported on the firm's cash budget. Efficient inventory management will result in relatively low levels of inventories, in low write-offs of obsolete or deteriorated inventories, and in few work stoppages or lost sales due to inventory shortages. All this, in turn, will contribute to a high total assets turnover, a high profit margin, a high return on equity, and a high stock price.

Self-Test Question

Explain the key features of the ABC system of inventory management.

ETHICAL DILEMMA

Money Back Guarantee, No Questions Asked

TradeSmart, Inc. operates 1,200 discount electronics stores throughout the United States. Trade-Smart has been quite successful in a highly competitive industry primarily because it has been able to offer brand name products at prices lower than can be found at other discount outlets. Because of its size, TradeSmart can purchase bulk inventory directly from manufacturers, and the economies of scale it derives from such purchases can be passed on to consumers in the form of lower prices.

In addition to low prices, TradeSmart offers an extremely liberal product return policy. Customers are permitted to return products for virtually any reason, and with little regard to the time period covered by manufacturers' warranties. In fact, just a few days ago, a customer returned a digital pager that was more than two years old. TradeSmart gave the customer a full refund even though the pager appeared to have been run over by a car, which, if true, clearly would have voided the manufacturer's warranty. In another instance, a customer was given a refund when he returned the camcorder he had purchased three days earlier to record his daughter's wedding festivities. The customer could not describe the camcorder's malfunction—he said "it just didn't work right." The customer refused an offer to replace the camcorder; instead, he insisted on a full refund, which he was given. The manager of the customer relations department suspected that the customer had "purchased" the camcorder intending all along to return it after his daughter's wedding. But, TradeSmart's return policy does not dissuade customers from this practice. According to Ed David-son, vice president of customer relations, TradeSmart is willing to stand behind every product it sells, regardless of the problem, because the company believes such a policy is needed to attract and keep loyal customers in such a competitive industry. The company's motto—"Customer Satis-faction Is Our Business"—is displayed prominently throughout TradeSmart stores.

With such a liberal return policy, how does TradeSmart keep its prices so low? Actually, TradeSmart ships the returned products back to the manufacturer as defective products, so the return costs are passed on to the manufacturers. According to manufacturers, only 1 out of every 6 products returned by TradeSmart actually is defective. But, when the manufacturers complain about such returns as used products that have no mechanical problems, TradeSmart reminds them that the company does not have a service department, so its personnel are not knowledgeable concern-ing the technical circuitry of the products—the products are returned to the manufacturers with the customers' complaints attached. TradeSmart's inventory manager would contend that the com-pany does not intentionally deceive or take advantage of the manufacturers' return policies and warranties. Do you agree with TradeSmart's return policy? Is it ethical? What action would you take if you were one of TradeSmart's suppliers?

Summary

This chapter discussed inventory management. The following key concepts are covered.

- **Inventory management** involves determining how much inventory to hold, when to place orders, and how many units to order.
- **Inventory** can be grouped into three categories: (1) raw materials, (2) work-in-process, and (3) finished goods.
- **Inventory costs** can be divided into three types: carrying costs, ordering costs, and stock-out costs. In general, carrying costs increase as the level of inventory rises, but ordering costs and stock-out costs decline with larger inventory holdings.
- **Total carrying cost (TCC)** is equal to the percentage cost of carrying inventory (C) times the purchase price per unit of inventory (PP) times the average number of units held (A): $TCC = (C)(PP)(A)$.

- **Total ordering cost (TOC)** is equal to the fixed cost of placing an order (O) times the number of orders placed per year (N): TOC = (O)(N).
- **Total inventory costs (TIC)** are equal to carrying costs plus ordering costs: TIC = TCC + TOC.
- The **economic ordering quantity (EOQ)** model is a formula for determining the order quantity that will minimize total inventory costs:

$$EOQ = \sqrt{\frac{2(O)(T)}{(C)(PP)}}$$

Here O is the fixed cost per order, T is annual sales in units, C is the percentage cost of carrying inventory, and PP is the purchase price per unit.
- The **reorder point** is the inventory level at which new items must be ordered.
- **Safety stocks** are held to avoid shortages (1) if demand increases or (2) if shipping delays are encountered. The cost of carrying safety stocks is equal to the percentage cost of carrying inventories times the purchase price per unit times the number of units held as the safety stock. These costs are separate from those used in the EOQ model.
- Firms use inventory control systems such as the **red-line method** and the **two-bin method,** as well as **computerized inventory control systems,** to help them keep track of actual inventory levels and to ensure that inventory levels are adjusted as sales change. **Just-in-time (JIT) systems** are also used to hold down inventory costs and, simultaneously, to improve the production process. The **ABC system** categorizes inventory items to ensure that the most important ones are reviewed most often.

Questions

11-1   If a firm calculates its optimal inventory of widgets to be 1,000 units when the general rate of inflation is 2 percent, is it true that the optimal inventory (in units) will almost certainly rise if the general rate of inflation climbs to 10 percent? Explain.

11-2   Indicate by a (+), (−), or (0) whether each of the following events would probably cause average annual inventories (the sum of the inventories held at the end of each month of the year divided by 12) to rise, fall, or be affected in an indeterminant manner:

Our suppliers switch from delivering by train to air freight.   _____
We change from producing just in time to meet seasonal sales to steady,
year-round production. (Sales peak at Christmas.)   _____
Competition in the markets in which we sell increases.   _____
The rate of general inflation increases.   _____
Interest rates rise; other things are constant.   _____

11-3   A firm can reduce its investment in inventory by having its suppliers hold raw materials inventories and its customers hold finished goods inventories. Explain actions a firm can take which would result in larger inventories for its suppliers and customers and smaller inventories for itself. What are the limitations of such actions?

11-4 The toy business is subject to large seasonal demand fluctuations. What effect would such fluctuations have on inventory decisions of toy manufacturers and toy retailers?

11-5 "Every firm should use the EOQ model to determine the optimal level of inventory to maintain." Discuss the accuracy of this statement with respect to the form of the EOQ model presented in this chapter.

Self-Test Problems

(Solutions Appear in Appendix B)
Define each of the following terms:

Key terms   **ST-1** **a.** carrying costs; ordering costs
            b. economic ordering quantity (EOQ); EOQ model
            c. reorder point; stock-out cost; goods in transit; safety stocks
            d. red-line method; two-bin method; computerized inventory control system
            e. just-in-time system; out-sourcing; ABC system

EOQ and total inventory costs   **ST-2** The Homemade Bread Company buys and then sells (as bread) 2.6 million bushels of wheat annually. The wheat must be purchased in multiples of 2,000 bushels. Ordering costs, which include grain elevator removal charges of $3,500, are $5,000 per order. Annual carrying costs are 2 percent of the purchase price of $5 per bushel. The company maintains a safety stock of 200,000 bushels. The delivery time is 6 weeks.

a. What is the EOQ?

b. At what inventory level should an order be placed to prevent having to draw on the safety stock?

c. What are the total inventory costs, including the costs of carrying the safety stock?

d. The wheat processor agrees to pay the elevator removal charges if Homemade Bread will purchase wheat in quantities of 650,000 bushels. Would it be to Homemade Bread's advantage to order this alternative quantity?

Problems

Inventory cost   **11-1** Computer Supplies Inc. must order floppy diskettes from its supplier in lots of one dozen boxes. Given the following information, complete the table below and determine the economic ordering quantity of floppy diskettes for Computer Supplies Inc.

Annual demand: 26,000 dozen

Cost per order placed: $30.00

Carrying cost: 20%

Price per dozen: $7.80

Order Size (dozens)	250	500	1,000	2,000	13,000	26,000
Number of orders	_____	_____	_____	_____	_____	_____
Average inventory	_____	_____	_____	_____	_____	_____
Carrying cost	_____	_____	_____	_____	_____	_____
Order cost	_____	_____	_____	_____	_____	_____
Total cost	_____	_____	_____	_____	_____	_____

EOQ   **11-2**   Krogh Toys, a large manufacturer of toys and dolls, uses large quantities of flesh-colored cloth in its doll production process. Throughout the year, the firm uses 1,250,000 square yards of this cloth. The fixed costs of placing and receiving an order are $2,000, which includes a $1,500 setup charge at the mill. The price of the cloth is $2.50 per square yard, and the annual cost of carrying this inventory item is 20 percent of the price. Krogh maintains a 12,500-square-yard safety stock. The cloth supplier requires a 2-week lead time from order to delivery.

a. What is the EOQ for this cloth?

b. What is the average inventory dollar value, including the safety stock?

c. What is the total cost of ordering and carrying the inventory, including the safety stock? (Assume that the safety stock is on hand at the beginning of the year.)

d. Using a 52-week year, at what inventory unit level should an order be placed? (Again, assume the 12,500-square-yard safety stock is on hand.)

EOQ and inventory costs   **11-3**   The following inventory data have been established for the Thompson Company:

1. Orders must be placed in multiples of 100 units.

2. Annual sales are 338,000 units.

3. The purchase price per unit is $6.

4. Carrying cost is 20 percent of the purchase price of goods.

5. Fixed order cost is $48.

6. Desired safety stock is 12,000 units; this amount is on hand initially.

7. Two weeks are required for delivery.

a. What is the EOQ?

b. How many orders should Thompson place each year?

c. At what inventory level should an order be made? [Hint: Reorder point = Safety stock + (Lead time × Usage rate) − Goods in transit.]

d. Calculate the total cost of ordering and carrying inventories if the order quantity is (1) 4,000 units, (2) 4,800 units, or (3) 6,000 units. (4) What are the total costs if the order quantity is the EOQ?

Changes in EOQ   **11-4**   The following relationships for inventory costs have been established for the Dalrymple Corporation:

1. Annual sales are 585,000 units.

2. The purchase price per unit is $2.00.

3. The carrying cost is 26 percent of the purchase price of goods.

4. The cost per order placed is $169.

5. Desired safety stock is 10,000 units (on hand initially).

6. Two weeks are required for delivery.

a. What is the economic ordering quantity? What is the total cost of ordering and carrying inventories at the EOQ?

b. What is the optimal number of orders to be placed?

c. At what inventory level should Dalrymple order? How would your answer change if the delivery time was six days?

d. If annual unit sales double, what is the percent increase in the EOQ? What is the elasticity of EOQ with respect to sales (percent change in EOQ/percent change in sales)?

e. If the cost per order doubles, what is the elasticity of EOQ with respect to cost per order?

f. If the carrying cost declines by 50 percent, what is the elasticity of EOQ with respect to that change?

g. If the purchase price declines by 50 percent, what is the elasticity of EOQ with respect to that change?

Exam-Type Problem

The problem included in this section is set up in such a way that it could be used as a multiple-choice exam problem.

EOQ **11-5** Green Thumb Garden Centers sells 240,000 bags of lawn fertilizer annually. The optimal safety stock (which is on hand initially) is 1,200 bags. Each bag costs Green Thumb $4, inventory carrying costs are 20 percent, and the cost of placing an order with its supplier is $25.

   a. What is the economic ordering quantity?
   b. What is the maximum inventory of fertilizer?
   c. What will Green Thumb's average inventory be?
   d. How often must the company order?

Integrative Problem

EOQ model **11-6** Dan Edwards, Financial Vice-President of Shield Chemicals Corporation, was requested by the company's president to take a look at the company's inventory position. The president thinks that inventories may be too high as a result of the production manager's tendency to make large production runs. Edwards has decided to examine the situation for one key product, 100-pound drums of general purpose insecticide. Each drum costs $320 to produce, but there is a $10,000 setup cost for each production run. Annual sales of the product are 25,000 drums, and the annual carrying cost is 20 percent of inventory value. The company has been producing 5,000 drums per run and making another production run when the stock on hand falls to 2,000 drums. Sales are uniform throughout the year.

   a. Edwards believes that the EOQ model should be used to help determine the optimal inventory situation for this product. What is the EOQ formula, and what are the key assumptions underlying this model?
   b. What is the formula for total inventory costs?
   c. What is the EOQ for the 100-pound drum of insecticide? What will the total inventory costs be for this product if the EOQ is produced?
   d. What is Shield's added cost if it produces 2,000 drums per run rather than the EOQ quantity? What if it produces 3,500 drums per production run?
   e. Suppose it takes 2 weeks for Shield to set up production, make and test the insecticide, and package it before the product is ready for sale. Assuming certainty in production time and usage, at what inventory level should Shield begin production? (Assume a 52-week year, and assume that Shield produces the EOQ amount.)
   f. Of course, there is uncertainty in Shield's usage rate as well as in the length of the production process, so the company must carry a safety stock to avoid running out of the 100-pound drums of insecticide and having to lose sales. If a 500-drum safety stock is carried, what effect would this have on total inventory costs? At what inventory level will the firm have to make another production run? What protection does the safety stock provide if usage increases or if production is delayed?
   g. Now suppose that if Shield produced quantities of 3,500 or more drums per run, its $320 per drum production cost could be reduced by 1 percent. Should the company do this? Why or why not?
   h. For most of Shield's products, inventory usage is not uniform throughout the year but, rather, follows some seasonal pattern. Could the EOQ model be used in this situation? If so, how?
   i. How would these factors affect the use of the EOQ model?

1. "Just-in-time" (JIT) procedures.
2. The use of air freight for deliveries.
3. Computerized inventory control systems.
4. Flexible plant designs which reduce setup costs and make small production runs more feasible.

Computer-Related Problem

Work the problem in this section only if you are using the computer problem diskette.

EOQ and inventory costs

11-7 Use the model in File C11 to work this problem.

a. Refer to Problem 11-2. Suppose the mill offers to lower the fixed cost to $750 if Krogh will increase its order size from 100,000 (as found in Part a of Problem 11-2) to 183,500 square yards. Would it be to Krogh's advantage to order under this alternative?

b. Now suppose the mill offers to lower the fixed cost to $1,250 if Krogh will order 140,000 square yards at a time. Should Krogh accept this alternative?

CHAPTER 12

Short-Term Financing

Figgie International, Inc., based in Willoughby, Ohio, operates more than twenty businesses in a variety of industries, including insurance, sporting goods, and fire trucks. Recently, Figgie found itself amid a cash shortage. To meet its cash needs, the company sought to increase the line of credit at its bank by almost 50 percent; in addition, Figgie factored, or sold off, some of its accounts receivable. The funds Figgie obtained from these two financing sources helped improve the company's liquidity position, ultimately keeping the company out of bankruptcy.

Similarly, in the summer of 1994, Metro-Goldwyn-Mayer, Inc. (MGM) arranged a $350 million revolving line of credit with a banking group headed by Chemical Bank. This financing source was considered crucial to the survival of MGM, which was taken over by Credit Lyonnais SA, a French bank, in 1992 because of financial difficulties. Even though MGM has produced such legendary movies as *Gone With the Wind, The Wizard of Oz,* and *Thelma and Louise,* it has not generated a profit since 1986, and its financial position is so precarious that it is on the brink of extinction. To recoup its investment of more than $2 billion, Credit Lyonnais had only a couple of years to improve the financial condition of MGM and sell the company; according to current banking laws in the United States, the French bank was required to decrease its ownership to less than 25 percent by 1997. It was hoped the added line of credit would improve MGM's short-term financial position and help the movie studio complete more films, thus increasing its chances of long-run survival.

At about the same time, Woolworth Corporation pulled out of the commercial paper market, because investors were not receptive to lending the firm additional funds, given its declining financial position at the time (April 1994). In fact, Woolworth used some of its approximately $1.5 billion credit lines to reduce the amount of commercial paper it had outstanding in an effort to decrease its reliance on this short-term financing alternative. Woolworth's actions were not unusual, given the capricious nature of the commercial paper market. Recently, such companies as Marriott and

Continued

Westinghouse have had to rely on their banks because they experienced problems raising short-term funds in the commercial paper market.

As you read this chapter, think about the various sources available to companies for financing in the short run. As you will see, the costs and availability of short-term funds can vary widely, both over time and from alternative sources.

In Chapter 8 we discussed the decisions the financial manager must make concerning alternative current asset financing policies. We also showed how debt maturities can affect both risk and expected returns: Although short-term debt generally is riskier than long-term debt, it also generally is less expensive, and it can be obtained faster and under more flexible terms. The primary purpose of this chapter is to examine the different types of short-term credit that are available to the financial manager. We also examine the types of issues the financial manager must consider when selecting among the various types of short-term credit.

Sources of Short-Term Financing

SHORT-TERM CREDIT
Any liability originally scheduled for repayment within one year.

Statements about the flexibility, cost, and riskiness of short-term debt versus long-term debt depend, to a large extent, on the type of short-term credit that actually is used. **Short-term credit** is defined as any liability *originally* scheduled for payment within one year. There are numerous sources of short-term funds, and in the following sections we describe four major types: (1) accruals, (2) accounts payable (trade credit), (3) bank loans, and (4) commercial paper. In addition, we discuss the cost of bank loans and the factors that influence a firm's choice of a bank.

Accruals

Firms generally pay employees on a weekly, biweekly, or monthly basis, so the balance sheet typically will show some accrued wages. Similarly, the firm's own estimated income taxes, the social security and income taxes withheld from employee payrolls, and the sales taxes collected generally are paid on a weekly, monthly, or quarterly basis, so the balance sheet typically will show some accrued taxes along with accrued wages.

ACCRUALS
Continually recurring short-term liabilities; liabilities such as wages and taxes that increase spontaneously with operations.

As we showed in Chapter 8, **accruals** increase automatically, or spontaneously, as a firm's operations expand. Further, this type of debt generally is considered "free" in the sense that no explicit interest is paid on funds raised through accruals. However, a firm ordinarily cannot control its accruals: The timing of wage payments is set by economic forces and industry custom, while tax payment dates are established by law. Thus, firms use all the accruals they can, but they have little control over the levels of these accounts.

Self-Test Questions

What types of short-term credits are classified as accruals?

What is the "explicit" cost of accruals?

How much control do financial managers have over the dollar amount of accruals?

Accounts Payable (Trade Credit)

TRADE CREDIT
The term given to the credit created when one firm buys on credit from another firm.

Firms generally make purchases from other firms on credit, recording the debt as an *account payable.* This type of financing, called **trade credit,** is the largest single category of short-term debt, representing about 40 percent of the current liabilities for the average nonfinancial corporation. The percentage is somewhat larger for smaller firms: Because small companies often do not qualify for financing from other sources, they rely especially heavily on trade credit.[1]

Trade credit is a *spontaneous* source of financing in the sense that it arises from ordinary business transactions. For example, suppose a firm makes average purchases of $2,000 a day on terms of net 30, meaning that it must pay for goods 30 days after the invoice date. As we saw in Chapter 8, on average, the firm will owe 30 times $2,000, or $60,000, to its suppliers. If its sales, and consequently its purchases, were to double, then its accounts payable also would double, to $120,000. So, simply by growing, the firm would have spontaneously generated an additional $60,000 of financing. Similarly, if the terms under which it bought were extended from 30 to 40 days, its accounts payable would expand from $60,000 to $80,000. Thus, lengthening the credit period, as well as expanding sales and purchases, generates additional financing.

The Cost of Trade Credit

As we discussed in Chapter 10, firms that sell on credit have a *credit policy* that includes certain *terms of credit.* For example, Microchip Electronics sells on credit with terms of 2/10, net 30, which means that Microchip gives its customers a 2 percent discount from the invoice price if payment is made within 10 days of the billing date; otherwise, if the discount is not taken, the full invoice amount is due and must be paid within 30 days of the billing date.

Note that the *true* price of the products Microchip offers is the net price, which is 98 percent of the list price, because any customer can purchase an item at a 2 percent "discount" as long as payment is made within 10 days. Consider Personal Computer Company (PCC), which buys its memory chips from Microchip. One commonly used memory chip is listed at $100, so the true cost to PCC is $98. Now if PCC wants an additional 20 days of credit beyond the 10-day

---

[1]In a credit sale, the seller records the transaction as a receivable; the buyer, as a payable. We examined accounts receivable as an asset investment in Chapter 10. Our focus in this chapter is on accounts payable, a liability item. We also should note that if a firm's accounts payable exceed its receivables, it is said to be *receiving net trade credit,* whereas if its receivables exceed its payables, it is *extending net trade credit.* Smaller firms frequently receive net credit; larger firms generally extend it.

discount period, it will incur a finance charge of $2 per chip for that credit. Thus, the $100 list price can be thought of as follows:

$$\text{List price} = \$98 \text{ true price} + \$2 \text{ finance charge.}$$

The question that PCC must ask before it takes the additional 20 days of credit from Microchip is whether the firm could obtain similar credit with better terms from some other lender, say a bank. In other words, could 20 days of credit be obtained for less than $2 per item?

PCC buys an average of 44,100 memory chips from Microchip each year (assume 360 days in the year), which, at the net or true price, amounts to an average annual purchase equal to $4,321,800, or $12,005 per day. For simplicity, assume that Microchip is PCC's only supplier. If PCC pays on the 10th day and takes the discount, its payables will average 10($12,005) = $120,050. Thus, PCC will receive $120,050 of credit from its only supplier, Microchip Electronics.

Now suppose PCC decides to take the additional 20 days credit and thus must pay the finance charge. Because PCC now will pay on the 30th day, its accounts payable will increase to 30($12,005) = $360,150.[2] Under these circumstances, Microchip will be supplying PCC with an additional $240,100 = $360,150 − $120,050 of credit, which it could use to build up its cash account, to pay off debt, to expand inventories, or even to extend more credit to its own customers and hence to increase its own accounts receivable. So, it should be apparent that a firm's policy with regard to taking or not taking cash discounts can have a significant effect on its financial statements. If PPC does not take the cash discount, its accounts payable balance will be $240,100 greater than if it does take the discount ($360,150 compared to $120,050).

The additional credit offered by Microchip has a cost—PCC must pay the finance charge by forgoing the 2 percent discount on its purchases from Microchip. By forgoing the discount, PCC actually will pay $100 rather than $98 per chip, so its annual cost for the chips will be $100 × 44,100 = $4,410,000 instead of $4,321,800. The additional cost should be considered a finance charge for being able to keep the funds an additional 20 days. So, the annual financing cost is $4,410,000 − $4,321,800 = $88,200. Dividing the $88,200 financing cost by the $240,100 *average* annual *additional* credit received if the cash discount is not taken, we find the implicit cost of the additional trade credit to be 36.7 percent:

$$\frac{\text{Approximate}}{\text{percentage cost}} = \frac{\$88,200}{\$240,100} = 36.7\%$$

Should PCC take the discount, or should it wait 20 days and pay the full invoice price? If PCC can borrow from its bank (or from other sources) at an interest rate less than 36.7 percent, it should take the discount by borrowing from its bank to

---

[2]A question arises here: Should accounts payable reflect gross purchases or purchases net of discounts? Although generally accepted accounting principles permit either treatment on the grounds that the difference is not material, most accountants prefer to record payables net of discounts, or at "true" prices, and then to report the higher payments that result from not taking discounts as an additional expense, called "discounts lost." Thus, *we show accounts payable net of discounts even if the company does not expect to take the discount.*

obtain any additional funds it needs—PPC should *not* obtain credit in the form of accounts payable by forgoing discounts if cheaper sources, such as the bank, are available.

The following equation can be used to calculate the *approximate* percentage cost, on an annual basis, of not taking cash discounts—the cost of forgoing discounts:

12-1

$$\text{Approximate cost of forgoing a cash discount (\%)} = \frac{\text{Discount percent}}{100 - \frac{\text{Discount}}{\text{percent}}} \times \frac{360 \text{ days}}{\frac{\text{Total days of}}{\text{credit available}} - \frac{\text{Discount}}{\text{period}}}$$

The numerator of the first term, Discount percent, is the dollar cost per $100 invoice value of not taking the discount, while the denominator in this term, (100 − Discount percent), represents the funds the firm has available by not taking the discount. Thus, the first term in Equation 12-1 is the percent cost of using trade credit as a source of financing for the number of days in the credit period beyond the discount period. The denominator of the second term is the number of days of extra credit obtained by not taking the discount, so the entire second term shows how many times each year the percent cost of the trade credit would be incurred if the firm continues this practice. To illustrate the equation, the approximate cost of not taking a discount when the terms are 2/10, net 30, is calculated as follows:

$$\frac{\text{Approximate}}{\text{percentage cost}} = \frac{2}{100 - 2} \times \frac{360}{30 - 10} = \frac{2}{98} \times \frac{360}{20}$$

$$= 0.02041 \times 18 = 0.367 = 36.7\%$$

The approximation formula does not take into account compounding, so, if we use Equation 12-1 to compute the cost of forgoing a cash discount, the result actually is the *simple* annual percentage rate we discussed in Chapter 6 (Equation 6-11). Therefore, in effective annual interest terms, the cost of trade credit is much higher. The discount amounts to interest, and with terms of 2/10, net 30, the firm gains use of the funds for $30 - 10 = 20$ days, so there are $360/20 = 18$ "interest periods" per year. Remember that the first term in Equation 12-1, (Discount percent)/(100 − Discount percent) = 2/98 = 0.0204, is the periodic interest rate. This rate is paid 18 times each year, so, considering *compounding*, according to Equation 6-8 (look back to Chapter 6), the effective annual cost (rate) of trade credit is

$$\text{Effective annual rate} = (1.0204)^{18} - 1.0 = 1.439 - 1.0 = 43.9\%$$

Thus, the 36.7 percent approximate cost calculated with Equation 12-1 understates the true cost of trade credit.

Notice that, according to Equation 12-1, the cost of trade credit per credit period always is the same as long as the terms of credit do not change—in our example, the cost is 2/98 = 0.0204. Therefore, the cost of using trade credit for financing can be reduced by delaying payment of accounts payable. For example, if PCC could get away with paying in 50 days rather than in the specified 30 days, then the effective credit period would become $50 - 10 = 40$ days, the number of times the discount would be lost would fall from 18 to $360/40 = 9$, and the approximate cost would drop from 36.7 percent to 18.4 percent. Similarly, the effective annual rate would drop from 43.9 percent to 19.9 percent.

STRETCHING ACCOUNTS PAYABLE
The practice of deliberately paying accounts payable late.

The practice of paying trade credit beyond the credit period, or deliberately becoming a delinquent account, is called **stretching accounts payable.** In periods of excess capacity, firms might be able to get away with *stretching* because suppliers need the business. But there are consequences associated with credit delinquency, such as being branded a "slow payer"—the most serious is that credit might be cut off altogether.

The cost of the additional trade credit that is incurred by not taking discounts can be worked out for other credit terms. Some illustrative costs are shown in Table 12-1. As these figures show, the cost of not taking discounts can be substantial. Incidentally, throughout the chapter, we assume that payments are made either on the *last day* for taking discounts or on the *last day* of the credit period, unless otherwise noted. It would be foolish to pay, say, on the fifth day or on the twentieth day if the credit terms were 2/10, net 30. A firm always should pay its creditors at the last possible time under the conditions of the credit agreement, unless the benefits of early payment (lower price) are greater than the costs associated with early payment (opportunity to use the funds). You should follow the same logic—*pay your bills as late as possible without jeopardizing either your status as a good customer or your credit.* If you pay at the last possible time allowed under the payment terms (do not become delinquent), then you will get to use your funds for the maximum time and you will maintain good relationships with the businesses.

Components of Trade Credit: Free versus Costly

"FREE" TRADE CREDIT
Credit received during the discount period.

On the basis of the preceding discussion, trade credit can be divided into two components: (1) **"free" trade credit,** which involves credit received during the discount period and which for PCC amounts to 10 days' net purchases, or $120,050, and (2) **costly trade credit,** which involves credit in excess of the free trade credit and whose cost is an implicit one based on the forgone dis-

TABLE 12-1

Comparison of the Cost of Forgoing a Cash Discount under Various Terms of Credit

Credit Terms	Cost of Additional Credit if the Cash Discount Is Not Taken	
	Approximate Cost	Effective Cost
1/10, net 20	36.36%	43.59%
1/10, net 30	18.18	19.83
2/10, net 20	73.47	106.95
2/10, net 30	36.73	43.86
3/15, net 45	37.11	44.12
3/10, net 100	12.37	12.96

COSTLY TRADE CREDIT
Credit taken in excess of "free" trade credit, whose cost is equal to the discount lost.

counts.[3] PCC could obtain $240,100, or 20 days' net purchases, of nonfree trade credit at a cost of more than 37 percent. *Financial managers always should use the free component, but they should use the costly component only after analyzing the cost of this source of financing to make sure that it is less than the cost of funds that could be obtained from other sources.* Under the terms of trade found in most industries, the costly component will involve a relatively high percentage cost (usually greater than 25 percent), so stronger firms will take the cash discounts offered and avoid using trade credit as a source of additional financing.

As we noted earlier, firms can and sometimes do deviate from the stated credit terms, thus altering the percentage cost figures cited earlier. For example, a California manufacturing firm that buys on terms of 2/10, net 30 makes a practice of paying in 15 days (rather than 10), but it still takes discounts. Its treasurer simply waits until 15 days after receipt of the goods to pay, and then writes a check for the invoiced amount less the 2 percent discount. The company's suppliers want its business, so they tolerate this practice. Similarly, a Wisconsin firm that also buys on terms of 2/10, net 30 does not take discounts, but it pays in 60 rather than in 30 days, thus "stretching" its trade credit. As we saw earlier, both practices reduce the cost of trade credit. Neither of these firms is "loved" by its suppliers, and neither could continue these practices in times when suppliers operate at full capacity and have order backlogs, but these practices can and do reduce the costs of trade credit during times when suppliers have excess capacity.

Self-Test Questions

What is trade credit?

What is the difference between free trade credit and costly trade credit?

What is the formula for finding the approximate cost of trade credit? What is the formula for the effective annual cost rate of trade credit?

How does the cost of costly trade credit generally compare with the cost of other short-term sources of funds?

Short-Term Bank Loans

Commercial banks, whose loans generally appear on firms' balance sheets as notes payable, are second in importance to trade credit as a source of short-term financing.[4] The influence of banks actually is greater than it appears from the dollar amounts they lend because banks provide *nonspontaneous* funds. As a firm's financing needs increase, it specifically requests additional funds from its bank. If

---

[3]There is some question as to whether any credit is really "free," because the supplier will have a cost of carrying receivables which must be passed on to the customer in the form of higher prices. Still, if suppliers sell on standard credit terms such as 2/10, net 30, and if the base price cannot be negotiated downward for early payment, then for all intents and purposes the 10 days of trade credit is indeed "free."

[4]Although commercial banks remain the primary source of short-term loans, other sources are available. For example, in 1995 GE Capital Corporation (GECC) had several billion dollars in commercial loans outstanding. Firms such as GECC, which was initially established to finance consumers' purchases of GE's durable goods, often find business loans to be more profitable than consumer loans.

traditionally has been the lowest rate banks charge. Rates on other loans generally are scaled up from the prime rate.[7]

Bank rates vary widely over time depending on economic conditions and Federal Reserve policy. When the economy is weak, then (1) loan demand usually is slack, (2) inflation is low, and (3) the Fed also makes plenty of money available to the system. As a result, rates on all types of loans are relatively low. Conversely, when the economy is booming, loan demand typically is strong, and the Fed restricts the money supply; the result is high interest rates. As an indication of the kinds of fluctuations that can occur, the prime rate during 1980 rose from 11 percent to 21 percent in just four months. In more recent times, the prime rate remained constant at 6 percent throughout 1993, but the Fed raised interest rates six times in 1994, causing the prime rate to jump to 8½ percent by January 1995. Interest rates on other bank loans also vary, generally moving with the prime rate.

Interest paid on a bank loan generally is calculated in one of three ways: (1) *simple interest,* (2) *discount interest,* and (3) *add-on interest.* These three approaches are explained in the following sections.

Computing the Annual Cost (Rate) of Bank Loans

Before we describe the specifics of each of the three approaches to computing the interest paid on bank loans, it will be useful to briefly discuss how the effective annual rate of return (% cost) and the simple rate are calculated.[8] As an individual, you might enter some of the loan arrangements we discuss below, so it is important that you have an understanding of how the cost of a loan is computed. Remember from Chapter 6 that, in general terms, the effective annual rate is computed using Equation 6-8:

6-8

$$\text{Effective annual rate} = \left[1 + \frac{i_{\text{SIMPLE}}}{m}\right]^m - 1.0$$

$$= (1 + \text{Periodic rate})^m - 1.0$$

where m is the number of compounding (borrowing) periods in one year (i.e., if the loan is for one month, m = 12). For any type of credit, the *actual interest rate per period* can be computed using the following equation:

---

[7]In recent years many banks have been lending to the very strongest companies at rates below the prime rate. As we discuss later in this chapter, larger firms have ready access to the commercial paper market, and if banks want to do business with these larger companies, they must match or at least come close to the commercial paper rate. As competition in financial markets increases, as it has been doing because of the deregulation of banks and other financial institutions, "administered" rates such as the prime rate are giving way to flexible, negotiated rates based on market conditions.

[8]This is a review of material we covered in Chapter 6—we choose to review it here because of the importance of the subject.

$$
\begin{aligned}
\text{Periodic} \atop \text{rate (cost)} &= \frac{\text{Cost of borrowing as a percent of the amount borrowed}}{\text{Usable funds as a percent of the amount borrowed}} \\[2mm]
&= \frac{\left(\dfrac{\text{Dollar cost of borrowing}}{\text{Amount borrowed}}\right)}{\left(\dfrac{\text{Amount of usable funds}}{\text{Amount borrowed}}\right)} \\[4mm]
&= \frac{\text{Dollar cost of borrowing}}{\text{Amount of usable funds}}
\end{aligned}
$$

12-2

In this equation, the numerator represents the amount that must be paid for using the funds borrowed (either in dollar terms or stated as a percent of the amount borrowed), which includes the interest paid, charges for commitment fees, and so on. The denominator represents the amount of the loan that actually can be used (spent) by the borrower (either in dollar terms or stated as a percent of the amount borrowed), which is not necessarily the same as the amount borrowed, because discounts or other costs might be deducted from the loan proceeds. When loan restrictions prevent the borrower from using the entire amount of the loan, as we will see, the effective annual rate paid for the loan increases.

We mentioned in Chapter 6 that banks generally state their loan rates using the *annual percentage rate (APR)*, which is an approximation of the effective annual rate. The APR, or simple interest, which does not account for interest compounding, can be computed using Equation 6-11:

6-11

$$
\text{Annual} \atop \text{percentage rate} = \text{APR} = (\text{Periodic rate}) \times (m) = i_{\text{SIMPLE}}
$$

To see the application of these equations, consider the credit terms of 2/10, net 30. If the firm does not take the cash discount, then it effectively pays 2¢ to borrow 98¢ for a 20-day period, so the cost of using the funds for an additional 20 days is:

$$
\text{Periodic rate} = \frac{2\text{¢}}{98\text{¢}} = 0.020408 \approx 2.041\%
$$

There are m = 18 20-day periods in a 360-day year, so, using Equation 6-11, the simple rate, or approximate cost, associated with the trade credit is:

$$
i_{\text{SIMPLE}} = 0.02041 \times 18 = 0.367 = 36.7\%
$$

Using Equation 6-8, the effective annual cost (rate) of using trade credit with these terms as a source of short-term financing is:

$$\text{Effective annual rate} = (1 + 0.02041)^{18} - 1.0 = 1.439 - 1.0 = 0.439 = 43.9\%$$

These results are identical to those reported earlier both for the *approximate cost of forgoing a cash discount* and for the *effective cost of forgoing a cash discount.*

Regular, or Simple, Interest

SIMPLE INTEREST LOAN
Both the amount borrowed and the interest charged on that amount are paid at the maturity of the loan; there are no payments made before maturity.

FACE VALUE
The amount of the loan, or the amount borrowed; also called the *principal amount* of the loan.

With a **simple interest loan,** the borrower receives the **face value** of the loan (amount borrowed) and repays both the principal and interest at maturity. For example, with a simple interest loan of $10,000 at 12 percent for one year, the borrower receives the $10,000 upon approval of the loan and pays back the $10,000 principal plus $10,000(0.12) = $1,200 in interest at maturity (one year later). The 12 percent is the quoted, or simple, interest rate. On this 1-year loan, the effective annual rate also is 12 percent, because the borrower pays $1,200 interest to use $10,000 for the entire year.

$$\text{Effective annual rate} = \left(1 + \frac{\$1,200}{\$10,000}\right)^{1} - 1 = 0.12 = 12\%$$

The only case in which the effective annual rate is the same as the simple interest rate is if the borrower has use of the entire face value of the loan for one full year, and the only cost associated with the loan is the interest paid on the face value. In such cases, interest compounding occurs annually. However, if the loan is for a term of less than one year, say 90 days, then intrayear compounding should be considered. Consider the simple interest loan with the characteristics described above, except the term of the loan is 90 days. The *effective rate per period* is 0.12/4 = 0.03 = 3 percent, so $300 in interest would be paid for using $10,000 for a 90-day period, and the effective annual rate would be calculated as follows:

$$\text{Effective annual rate} = \left(1 + \frac{\$300}{\$10,000}\right)^{4} - 1 = (1 + 0.03)^{4} - 1 = 0.1255 = 12.55\%$$

The bank gets the interest sooner than under a 1-year loan, hence the effective rate is higher.

The simple rate for this 90-day loan is

$$i_{\text{SIMPLE}} = \frac{\$300}{\$10,000} \times \frac{360}{90} = (0.03) \times 4 = 0.12 = 12\%,$$

which is the same as the simple interest rate because the simple rate computation does not consider intrayear interest compounding.

DISCOUNT INTEREST LOAN
A loan in which the interest, which is calculated on the amount borrowed, is paid at the beginning of the loan period; interest is paid in advance.

Discount Interest

With a **discount interest loan,** the bank deducts the interest "up front" (*discounts* the loan) so the borrower receives less than the face value of the loan. For example, on a 1-year, $10,000 discounted loan with a 12 percent quoted (simple) rate, the interest is $10,000(0.12) = $1,200, so the borrower obtains the use of only $10,000 − $1,200 = $8,800. The rate per period, which is one year in this case, is 13.64 percent:

$$\text{Rate per period} = \frac{0.12(\$10,000)}{\$10,000 - 0.12(\$10,000)} = \frac{0.12(\$10,000)}{\$10,000(1 - 0.12)} = \frac{\$1,200}{\$8,800}$$

$$= \frac{0.12}{1 - 0.12} = \frac{0.12}{0.88}$$

$$= 0.1364 = 13.64\% = \text{Effective annual rate}$$

The effective annual rate and the simple rate also equal 13.64 percent, because the rate per period does not have to be "annualized"—the loan is a 1-year loan. The effective annual rate for this discounted loan is considerably greater than the effective annual rate for the simple interest loan with the same quoted rate and the same maturity because the borrower does not get to "use" the entire face value of the loan. In this case, the borrower can use only 88 percent of the amount borrowed (face value), but the dollar interest payment is computed on 100 percent of the amount borrowed rather than the amount available for use.

If the discount loan is for a period of less than one year, interest compounding must be considered to determine the effective annual rate. For example, if you borrow $10,000 at a simple rate of 12 percent, discount interest, for 3 months, then m = 12/3 = 4, and the dollar interest payment is (0.12/4)($10,000) = $300, so the rate per period and the effective annual rate are computed as follows:

$$\text{Rate per period} = \frac{0.03(\$10,000)}{\$10,000 - 0.03(\$10,000)} = \frac{\$300}{\$10,000 - \$300}$$

$$= \frac{0.03}{1 - 0.03} = \frac{0.03}{0.97}$$

$$= 0.0309 = 3.09\%$$

$$\text{Effective annual rate} = (1.0 + 0.0309)^4 - 1$$

$$= 0.1296 = 12.96\%$$

From this computation, it should be apparent that discount interest imposes less of a penalty on shorter-term loans than on longer-term loans.

The simple rate for this 90-day loan would be

$$i_{\text{SIMPLE}} = \frac{0.03}{0.97} \times \frac{360}{90}$$

$$= 0.0309 \times 4$$

$$= 0.1237 = 12.37\%$$

Notice that a discounted loan represents the same situation as using trade credit as a source of short-term financing. For example, if a firm has a supplier that offers credit terms of 3/10, net 100 (very unusual terms), as Table 12-1 shows, both the effective annual rate and the simple rate, or approximate cost, of the trade credit would be the same as that for the 90-day discounted loan with a simple rate of 12 percent.

Installment Loans: Add-On Interest

ADD-ON INTEREST
Interest that is calculated and then added to the amount borrowed to obtain the total dollar amount to be paid back in equal installments.

Lenders typically charge **add-on interest** on various types of installment loans. The term *add-on* means that the interest is calculated and then added to the amount borrowed to obtain the total dollar amount to be paid back in equal installments. To illustrate, suppose you borrow $10,000 on an add-on basis at a simple rate of 12 percent, with the loan to be repaid in 12 monthly installments. At a 12 percent add-on rate, you will pay a total interest charge of $10,000(0.12) = $1,200, and a total of $11,200 in twelve equal payments throughout the year. The monthly payments would be $11,200/12 = $933.33. Therefore, each month, you would pay $100 interest (1/12 of the total interest) and $833.33 principal repayment (1/12 of the $10,000 borrowed). Because the loan is paid off in monthly installments, you have the use of the full $10,000 only for the first month, and the outstanding balance declines by $833.33 monthly so that only $833.33 in principal is due at the beginning of the last month of the loan. Thus, you are paying $1,200 for the use of only about half the loan's face amount, because the average outstanding balance of the loan is only about $5,000. Therefore, we can *approximate* the rate per period, which is one year in this case, as follows:

$$\frac{\text{Approximate rate}}{\text{per period}} = \frac{\$1,200}{\left(\frac{\$10,000}{2}\right)} = 0.24 = 24\%$$

To determine the precise effective rate of an add-on loan, we have to apply the techniques used to compute the present value of an annuity (discussed in Chapter 6). First, consider the preceding situation. If you want to borrow $10,000 for one year, on a monthly installment basis, beginning in one month, you would have to make twelve payments equal to $933.33. In effect, then, the bank is buying a 12-period annuity for $10,000, so the $10,000 is the present value of the annuity. The cash flow time line for this annuity would be:

```
    0        1        2       11       12
    |--------+--------+-- · · --+--------|
($10,000)  $933.33  $933.33  $933.33  $933.33
```

With a financial calculator, enter PV = −10000, PMT = 933.33, N = 12, and then press I to obtain 1.7880. However, this is a monthly rate, which, when annualized, yields:[9]

$$\text{Effective annual rate} = (1 + 0.01788)^{12} - 1 = 0.2370 = 23.70\%$$

The simple rate for an installment loan is difficult to compute, because the rate per period changes for each installment payment. This occurs because the dollar amount of interest associated with each payment remains constant, but the out-

---

[9]Note that if an installment loan is paid off ahead of schedule, additional complications arise. For a discussion of this point, see Dick Bonker, "The Rule of 78," *Journal of Finance* (June 1976), 877–888.

standing balance of the loan, which is the amount owed, decreases with each payment. For example, in the above situation, you would pay $933.33 each month, of which $100 represents interest. For the first month of the loan, you would have use of the entire $10,000 borrowed, so the interest rate for that month would be $100/$10,000 = 0.01 = 1%. But in the last month you have use of only $833.33 principal which remains due, so the *interest rate for that month* would be $100/$833.33 = 0.12 = 12%. One way to compute the simple rate for an installment loan is to use the average amount of usable funds, or the average principal due, and proceed with the computation given in Equation 6-11. In this case, the result would be

$$i_{SIMPLE} = \frac{\$100}{\left(\frac{\$10,000}{2}\right)} \times 12 = \frac{\$100}{\$5,000} \times 12$$

$$= 0.02 \times 12 = 0.24 = 24\%,$$

which is the same result found by computing the approximate annual rate of the installment loan. This is not a coincidence—neither computation considers the compounding of interest.

Simple Interest with Compensating Balances

Compensating balances can raise the effective rate on a loan. To illustrate, suppose a firm *needs* $10,000 to pay for some equipment that it recently purchased. A bank offers to lend the company money for one year at a 12 percent simple rate, but the company must maintain a *compensating balance (CB)* equal to 20 percent of the loan amount (principal, or face value). What is the effective annual rate on the loan?

First, note that the firm needs to be able to use $10,000 to pay for the equipment. The firm might or might not already have a balance in its checking account that can be used to satisfy all or part of the compensating balance. If the firm's checking account balance is sufficient to cover the compensating balance requirement, then the amount of the loan can be $10,000 because none of this amount would have to be put aside to satisfy the compensating balance requirement. The cost of this loan would be the same as we computed in the section titled *Regular, or Simple, Interest.*

If the firm's checking account balance is not sufficient to cover the compensating balance requirement, it must borrow more than $10,000 because some of the funds borrowed will have to be put aside to satisfy the compensating balance requirement. In this case, the question is: How much must be borrowed so the firm will have $10,000 available for use? To answer this question, first let's compute the compensating balance requirement:

12-3

$$\text{Compensating balance requirement} = CB = \text{Loan amount} \times \text{Compensating balance as a percent}$$

$$= \text{Loan amount} \times \%CB$$

So, *if the firm has a checking account balance equal to zero,* the amount of the borrowed funds that actually can be used is computed as:

12-4

$$\begin{aligned} \text{Usable} \atop \text{funds} &= \left(\text{Loan} \atop \text{amount} \right) - CB \\ &= \left(\text{Loan} \atop \text{amount} \right) - \left[\left(\text{Loan} \atop \text{amount} \right) \times \%CB \right] \\ &= \left(\text{Loan} \atop \text{amount} \right) (1 - \%CB) \end{aligned}$$

If we know how much of the amount borrowed actually is needed as "usable funds," Equation 12-4 can be rearranged to solve for the amount that must be borrowed (loan amount) to provide the needed funds:

12-5

$$\frac{\text{Required}}{\text{loan amount}} = \frac{\text{Amount of usable funds needed}}{1 - \%CB}$$

So, if the firm has nothing in its checking account, it must borrow $12,500 to be able to satisfy the 20 percent compensating balance requirement and have $10,000 available to pay for the equipment:

$$\frac{\text{Required}}{\text{loan amount}} = \frac{\$10,000}{1 - 0.20} = \$12,500$$

If the firms borrows $12,500, the compensating balance requirement would be $2,500 = $12,500(0.20), which means the firm actually could use $12,500 − $2,500 = $10,000 of the face value of the loan—the remaining $2,500 would have to be "set aside" to satisfy the compensating balance requirement. The interest paid on the loan at the end of the year will be $1,500 = $12,500(0.12). But, because the firm will be able to use only $10,000 of the amount borrowed, the rate per period, which is one year, is 15 percent:

$$\frac{\text{Rate per}}{\text{period}} = \frac{(0.12)\$12,500}{\$12,500(1 - 0.20)} = \frac{\$1,500}{\$10,000}$$

$$= \frac{0.12}{(1 - 0.20)} = \frac{0.12}{0.80}$$

$$= 0.15 = 15\% = \frac{\text{Effective}}{\text{annual rate}}$$

If the loan has a term of 90 days rather than one year, the simple rate would be $0.12/4 = 0.03$, and the rate per period and the effective annual rate would be:

$$\frac{\text{Rate}}{\text{per period}} = \frac{0.03(\$12,500)}{\$12,500(1 - 0.20)} = \frac{\$375}{\$10,000}$$

$$= \frac{0.03}{(1 - 0.20)} = \frac{0.03}{0.80}$$

$$= 0.0375 = 3.75\%$$

$$\frac{\text{Effective}}{\text{annual rate}} = (1 + 0.0375)^{\frac{360}{90}} - 1 = (1.0375)^4 - 1$$

$$= 0.1587 = 15.87\%$$

The simple rate for this 90-day loan would be the same as the effective rate for a one-year loan, because compounding is not considered:

$$i_{\text{SIMPLE}} = \frac{\$375}{\$10,000} \times \frac{360}{90} = (0.0375) \times 4 = 0.15 = 15\%$$

If a firm normally keeps a positive checking account balance at the lending bank, then: (1) less needs to be borrowed to have a specific amount of funds available for use, and (2) the effective cost of the loan will be lower. Regardless of the reason the firm maintains a positive checking account balance, we can consider the amount that is in the account is available for use by the firm. For example, if our firm normally maintains a working balance equal to $1,000 in its checking account, then the amount of usable funds that has to be provided by the loan is $1,000 less than if the checking account balance was equal to zero. The numerator in Equation 12-5 can be modified easily to reflect the fact that the amount of usable funds that needs to be provided by the loan is reduced:

12-5a

$$\frac{\text{Required}}{\text{loan amount}} = \frac{\begin{array}{c}\text{Amount of usable} \quad \text{Checking} \\ \text{funds needed} \quad - \quad \text{account balance}\end{array}}{1 - \%CB}$$

So, if the firm has a checking account balance equal to $1,000, the amount of usable funds provided by the loan needs to be $9,000 = $10,000 − $1,000, and the amount that must be borrowed to meet these needs is:

$$\frac{\text{Required}}{\text{loan amount}} = \frac{\$10,000 - \$1,000}{1.0 - 0.20} = \frac{\$9,000}{0.80} = \$11,250$$

If the firm borrows $11,250, the compensating balance requirement will be $2,250. The firm already has $1,000 in its checking account, so the remaining $1,250 needed to satisfy the compensating balance requirement must be taken from the loan proceeds, leaving $10,000 for the firm to use as it pleases.

Because the loan has a term of one year, the effective annual rate is the same as the rate per period, which can be found as follows:

$$\text{Rate per period} = \frac{0.12(\$11,250)}{\$11,250 - [\$11,250(0.20) - \$1,000]}$$

$$= \frac{\$1,350}{\$11,250 - \$1,250} = \frac{\$1,350}{\$10,000}$$

$$= \frac{0.12}{1.0 - \left[0.20 - \frac{\$1,000}{\$11,250}\right]} = \frac{0.12}{0.80 + 0.089} = \frac{0.12}{0.889}$$

$$= 0.1350 = 13.50\% = \text{Effective annual rate}$$

From this computation, you can see the $1,000 that already exists in the firm's checking account effectively increases the percent of the loan's face value that is available for use from 80 percent to almost 89 percent. This results in a decrease in the effective rate, because *the greater the percent available for use, the closer the relative cost of the loan is to the quoted, or simple, rate.*

What would the effective annual rate be if this were a 90-day loan? The 90-day simple rate equals $0.12/4 = 0.03$, and the computations for the rate per period and the effective annual rate are:

$$\text{Rate per period} = \frac{0.03(\$11,250)}{\$11,250 - [0.20(\$11,250) - \$1,000]} = \frac{\$337.50}{\$10,000}$$

$$= \frac{0.03}{1.0 - \left[0.20 - \frac{\$1,000}{\$11,250}\right]} = \frac{0.03}{0.80 + 0.089} = \frac{0.03}{0.889}$$

$$= 0.03375 = 3.375\%$$

$$\text{Effective annual rate} = (1 + 0.03375)^{\frac{360}{90}} - 1 = (1.03375)^4 - 1$$

$$= 0.1420 = 14.20\%$$

The simple rate for this 90-day loan is:

$$i_{\text{SIMPLE}} = \frac{\$337.50}{\$10,000} \times \frac{360}{90} = 0.03375 \times 4 = 0.1350 = 13.50\%$$

Discount Interest with Compensating Balances

The above analysis can be extended to the case where compensating balances are required and the loan is on a discount basis. In this situation, if a firm that has nothing in its checking account needs $10,000 for one year and a 20 percent compensating balance (CB) is required on a 12 percent discount loan, $14,705.88 must be borrowed. *If the entire amount of the compensating balance requirement must be taken out of the amount of the loan,* the required loan amount can be computed by recognizing that the amount of usable funds from a discount loan equals the amount borrowed less the amount of the interest payment *and* the amount of the compensating balance requirement. In this case, the amount of usable funds is:

$$
\begin{aligned}
\text{12-6}\quad
\frac{\text{Usable}}{\text{funds}} &= \left(\frac{\text{Loan}}{\text{amount}}\right) - \text{CB} - \frac{\text{Interest}}{\text{payment}} \\[2mm]
&= \left(\frac{\text{Loan}}{\text{amount}}\right) - \left[\left(\frac{\text{Loan}}{\text{amount}}\right) \times \%\text{CB}\right] - \left[\left(\frac{\text{Loan}}{\text{amount}}\right) \times i_{\text{SIMPLE}}\right] \\[2mm]
&= \left(\frac{\text{Loan}}{\text{amount}}\right)(1 - \%\text{CB} - i_{\text{SIMPLE}})
\end{aligned}
$$

The required loan amount can be calculated by modifying Equation 12-5:

$$
\text{12-7}\qquad
\frac{\text{Required}}{\text{loan amount}} = \frac{\text{Amount of usable funds needed}}{1 - \%\text{CB} - i_{\text{SIMPLE}}}
$$

$$
= \frac{\$10{,}000}{1.0 - 0.20 - 0.12} = \frac{\$10{,}000}{0.68} = \$14{,}705.88
$$

If the face value of the loan is $14,705.88, the compensating balance requirement is $14,705.88 × 0.20 = $2,941.18, and the dollar interest (discount amount) is $14,705.88 × 0.12 = $1,764.71. So, if the firm borrows $14,705.88, and it has no funds in a checking account, only $10,000 ≈ $14,705.88 − $2,941.18 − $1,764.71 (rounding difference of 1¢) of the face value actually can be used by the firm, because $2,941.18 must be put aside to satisfy the compensating balance requirement and the bank takes the $1,764.71 interest payment "off the top" of the loan. For this loan, then, the effective annual rate, which is the same as the rate per period because the term of the loan is one year, equals 17.65%:

$$
\begin{aligned}
\frac{\text{Rate per}}{\text{period}} &= \frac{\$14{,}705.88(0.12)}{\$14{,}705.88 - \$14{,}705.88(0.20) - \$14{,}705.88(0.12)} \\[2mm]
&= \frac{\$1{,}764.71}{\$14{,}705.88 - \$2{,}941.18 - \$1{,}764.71} = \frac{\$1{,}764.71}{\$10{,}000} \\[2mm]
&= \frac{0.12}{1.0 - 0.20 - 0.12} = \frac{0.12}{0.68} \\[2mm]
&= 0.1765 = 17.65\% = \frac{\text{Effective}}{\text{annual rate}}
\end{aligned}
$$

If the loan was for 90 days, the 90-day simple rate would be 0.12/4 = 0.03 = 3%, and the amount that must be borrowed so that $10,000 can be used is $12,987:

$$
\frac{\text{Required}}{\text{loan amount}} = \frac{\$10{,}000}{1.0 - 0.20 - 0.03} = \frac{\$10{,}000}{0.77} = \$12{,}987
$$

The rate per period for this loan would be:

$$\text{Rate per period} = \frac{\$12{,}987(0.03)}{\$12{,}987 - \$12{,}987(0.20) - \$12{,}987(0.03)}$$

$$= \frac{\$389.61}{\$12{,}987 - \$2{,}597.40 - \$389.61} = \frac{\$389.61}{\$10{,}000}$$

$$= \frac{0.03}{1.0 - 0.20 - 0.03} = \frac{0.03}{0.77}$$

$$= 0.039 = 3.90\%$$

So, the effective annual rate and the simple rate equal:

$$\text{Effective annual rate} = (1 + 0.039)^4 - 1 = 0.1652 = 16.52\%$$

$$i_{\text{SIMPLE}} = 0.039 \times \frac{360}{90} = 0.1558 = 15.58\%$$

In our example, compensating balances and discount interest combined to push the effective rate of interest up from 12 percent to 17.65 percent on a loan with a one-year maturity. Note, however, that in this analysis we assumed that the compensating balance requirement forced the firm to increase its bank deposits by the total amount of the compensating balance. If the company normally carries cash balances which could be used to supply all or part of the compensating balances, we would have to adjust the calculations along the lines discussed in the preceding section, and the effective annual rate would be less than 17.65 percent.

Self-Test Questions

What are some different ways that banks can calculate interest on loans?

What effect does a compensating balance requirement have on the effective interest rate on a loan?

Under what circumstances will the simple rate and the effective annual cost of a loan be equal?

Choosing a Bank

Individuals whose only contact with their bank is through the use of its checking services generally choose a bank for the convenience of its location and the competitive cost of its services. However, a business that borrows from banks must look at other criteria, and a potential borrower seeking banking relations should recognize that important differences exist among banks. Some of these differences are considered next.

Willingness to Assume Risks

Banks have different basic policies toward risk. Some banks are inclined to follow relatively conservative lending practices, while others engage in what are properly termed "creative banking practices." These policies reflect partly the personalities of officers of the bank and partly the characteristics of the bank's deposit liabilities. Thus, a bank with fluctuating deposit liabilities in a static community will tend to be a conservative lender, while a bank whose deposits are growing with little interruption might follow more liberal credit policies. Similarly, a large bank with broad diversification over geographic regions or across industries can obtain the benefit of combining and averaging risks. Thus, marginal credit risks that might be unacceptable to a small bank or specialized bank can be pooled by a large branch banking system to reduce the overall risk of a group of marginal accounts.

Advice and Counsel

Some bank loan officers are active in providing counsel and in stimulating development loans to firms in their early and formative years. Certain banks have specialized departments that make loans to firms expected to grow and thus to become more important customers. The personnel of these departments can provide valuable counseling to customers.

Loyalty to Customers

Banks differ in the extent to which they will support the activities of borrowers in bad times. This characteristic is referred to as the degree of *loyalty* of the bank. Some banks might put great pressure on a business to liquidate its loans when the firm's outlook becomes clouded, whereas others will stand by the firm and work diligently to help it get back on its feet. An especially dramatic illustration of this point was Bank of America's bailout of Memorex Corporation. The bank could have forced Memorex into bankruptcy, but instead it loaned the company additional capital and helped it survive a bad period. Memorex's stock price subsequently rose on the New York Stock Exchange from $1.50 to $68, so Bank of America's help was indeed beneficial.

Specialization

Banks differ greatly in their degrees of loan specialization. Larger banks have separate departments that specialize in different kinds of loans—for example, real estate loans, farm loans, and commercial loans. Within these broad categories, there might be a specialization by line of business, such as steel, machinery, cattle, or textiles. The strengths of banks also are likely to reflect the nature of the business and the economic environments in which they operate. For example, some California banks have become specialists in lending to electronics companies, while many Midwest banks are agricultural specialists. A sound firm can obtain more creative cooperation and more active support by going to a bank that has experience and familiarity with its particular type of business. Therefore, a bank that is excellent for one firm might be unsatisfactory for another.

Maximum Loan Size

The size of a bank can be an important factor. Because the maximum loan a bank can make to any one customer is limited to 15 percent of the bank's capital accounts (capital stock plus retained earnings), it generally is not appropriate for large firms to develop borrowing relationships with small banks.

Merchant Banking

The term *merchant bank* originally was applied to banks which not only loaned depositors' money but also provided customers with equity capital and financial advice. Prior to 1933, U.S. commercial banks performed all types of merchant banking functions. However, about one-third of the U.S. banks failed during the Great Depression, in part because of these activities, so in 1933 the Glass-Steagall Act was passed in an effort to reduce banks' exposure to risk. In recent years, commercial banks have tried to get back into merchant banking, in part because their foreign competitors offer such services, and U.S. banks need to be able to compete with their foreign counterparts for multinational corporations' business. Currently, the larger banks, often through holding companies, do offer merchant banking, at least to a limited extent. This trend probably will continue, and, if it does, corporations will need to consider a bank's ability to provide a full range of commercial and merchant banking services when choosing a bank.

Other Services

Some banks also provide cash management services (see Chapter 9), assist with electronic funds transfers, help firms obtain foreign exchange, and the like, and the availability of such services should be taken into account when selecting a bank. Also, if the firm is a small business whose manager owns most of its stock, the bank's willingness and ability to provide trust and estate services also should be considered.

Self-Test Question

What are some factors that should be considered when choosing a bank?

Commercial Paper

COMMERCIAL PAPER
An unsecured, short-term promissory note issued by large, financially sound firms to raise funds.

Commercial paper is a type of unsecured promissory note issued by large, strong firms, and it is sold primarily to other business firms, to insurance companies, to pension funds, to money market mutual funds, and to banks. This form of financing has grown rapidly in recent years—in 1995, the amount of commercial paper outstanding was approximately equal to the amount of regular business loans.

Use of Commercial Paper

The use of commercial paper is restricted to a comparatively small number of firms that are *exceptionally* good credit risks. Dealers prefer to handle the paper of firms whose net worth is $100 million or more and whose annual borrowing exceeds $10 million. One potential problem with commercial paper is that a debtor who is in temporary financial difficulty might receive little help because commercial paper dealings generally are less personal than are bank relationships.

Thus, banks generally are more able and willing to help a good customer weather a temporary storm than is a commercial paper dealer. On the other hand, using commercial paper permits a corporation to tap a wider range of credit sources, including financial institutions outside its own area and industrial corporations across the country, and this can reduce interest costs.

Maturity and Cost

Generally, commercial paper is issued in denominations of $100,000 or more, so few individuals can afford to *directly* invest in the commercial paper market. Maturities of commercial paper vary from one to nine months, with an average of about five months.[10] The rate on commercial paper fluctuates with supply and demand conditions—it is determined in the marketplace, varying daily as conditions change. Generally, the rates on commercial paper are lower than the stated prime rate of interest. In fact, in the first part of 1995, commercial paper rates, which were about the same as the T-bill rates, averaged about 2½ percentage points below the published prime rate.

Commercial paper is called a discount instrument because it is sold at a price below its face, or maturity, value. So, the cost of using commercial paper as a source of financing is computed the same as for a discount interest loan.

Self-Test Questions

What is commercial paper?

What types of companies can use commercial paper to meet their short-term financing needs?

How does the cost of commercial paper compare to the cost of short-term bank loans? To the cost of Treasury bills?

Use of Security in Short-Term Financing

SECURED LOAN
A loan backed by collateral; for short-term loans, the collateral often is either inventory or receivables, or both.

Thus far we have not addressed the question of whether loans should be secured. Commercial paper never is secured, but all other types of loans can be secured if this is deemed necessary or desirable. Given a choice, it ordinarily is better to borrow on an unsecured basis because the bookkeeping costs of **secured loans** often are high. However, weak firms might find that they can borrow only if they put up some type of security, or that by using security they can borrow at a lower rate.

Several different kinds of collateral can be employed, including marketable securities, land or buildings, equipment, inventory, and accounts receivable. Marketable securities make excellent collateral, but few firms that need loans also hold such portfolios. Similarly, real property (land and buildings) and equipment are good forms of collateral, but they generally are used as security for long-term loans

---

[10]The maximum maturity without SEC registration is 270 days. Also, commercial paper can be sold only to "sophisticated" investors; otherwise, SEC registration would be required even for maturities of 270 days or less.

rather than for working capital loans. Therefore, most secured short-term business borrowing involves the use of accounts receivable and inventories as collateral.

To understand the use of security, consider the case of a Chicago hardware dealer who wanted to modernize and expand his store. He requested a $200,000 bank loan. After examining his business's financial statements, the bank indicated that it would lend him a maximum of $100,000 and that the interest rate would be 12 percent, discount interest, for an effective rate of 13.6 percent. The owner had a substantial personal portfolio of stocks, and he offered to put up $300,000 of high-quality stocks to support the $200,000 loan. The bank then granted the full $200,000 loan, and at a rate of only 11 percent, simple interest. The store owner also might have used his inventories or receivables as security for the loan, but processing costs would have been high.[11]

UNIFORM COMMERCIAL CODE
A system of standards that simplifies procedures for establishing loan security.

In the past, state laws have varied greatly with regard to the use of security in financing. Today, however, nearly every secured loan is established under the **Uniform Commercial Code,** which has standardized and simplified the procedures for establishing loan security. The heart of the Uniform Commercial Code is the *Security Agreement,* a standardized document on which the specific pledged assets are listed. The assets can be items of equipment, accounts receivable, or inventories. Procedures under the Uniform Commercial Code for using accounts receivable and inventories as security for short-term credit are described in the following sections.

Accounts Receivable Financing

PLEDGING RECEIVABLES
Using accounts receivables as collateral for a loan.

RECOURSE
The lender can seek payment from the borrowing firm when receivables' accounts used to secure a loan are uncollectible.

FACTORING
The outright sale of receivables.

Accounts receivable financing involves either the pledging of receivables or the selling of receivables (called *factoring*). The **pledging** of accounts receivable is characterized by the fact that the lender not only has a claim against the receivables but also has **recourse** to the borrower: If the person or firm that bought the goods does not pay, the selling firm (borrower) rather than the lender must take the loss. Therefore, the risk of default on the pledged accounts receivable remains with the borrower. The buyer of the goods ordinarily is not notified about the pledging of the receivables, and the financial institution that lends on the security of accounts receivable generally is either a commercial bank or one of the large industrial finance companies.

Factoring, or *selling accounts receivable,* involves the purchase of accounts receivable by the lender (called a *factor*), generally without recourse to the borrower, which means that if the purchaser of the goods does not pay for them, the lender (factor) rather than the seller of the goods (borrower) takes the loss. Under factoring, the customer who purchased the goods typically is notified of the transfer and is asked to make payment directly to the lending institution. Because the factor assumes the risk of default on bad accounts, it generally carries out the credit investigation. Accordingly, factors provide not only money but also a credit department for the borrower. Incidentally, the same financial institutions that make loans against pledged receivables also serve as factors. Thus, depending on

---

[11]The term *asset-based financing* is often used as a synonym for *secured financing.* In recent years accounts receivable have been used as security for long-term bonds, and this permits corporations to borrow from lenders such as pension funds rather than being restricted to banks and other traditional short-term lenders.

the circumstances and the wishes of the borrower, a financial institution will provide either type of receivables financing.

PROCEDURE FOR PLEDGING ACCOUNTS RECEIVABLE   The financing of accounts receivable is initiated by a legally binding agreement between the seller of the goods and the financing institution. The agreement sets forth in detail the procedures to be followed and the legal obligations of both parties. Once the working relationship has been established, the seller periodically takes a batch of invoices to the financing institution. The lender reviews the invoices and makes credit appraisals of the buyers. Invoices of companies that do not meet the lender's credit standards are not accepted for pledging.

The financial institution seeks to protect itself at every phase of the operation. First, selection of sound invoices is one way the lender safeguards itself. Second, if the buyer of the goods does not pay the invoice, the lender still has recourse against the seller (the borrowing firm). Third, additional protection is afforded the lender because the loan generally will be less than 100 percent of the pledged receivables; for example, the lender might advance the selling firm only 75 percent of the amount of the pledged invoices. The percent advanced depends on the quality of the accounts pledged.

PROCEDURE FOR FACTORING ACCOUNTS RECEIVABLE   The procedures used in factoring are somewhat different from those for pledging. Again, an agreement between the seller and the factor specifies legal obligations and procedural arrangements. When the seller receives an order from a buyer, a credit approval slip is written and immediately sent to the factoring company for a credit check. If the factor approves the credit, shipment is made and the invoice is stamped to notify the buyer to make payment directly to the factoring company. If the factor does not approve the sale, the seller generally refuses to fill the order; if the sale is made anyway, the factor will not buy the account.

The factor normally performs three functions: (1) credit checking, (2) lending, and (3) risk bearing. Consider a typical factoring situation: The goods are shipped, and even though payment is not due for 30 days, the factor immediately makes funds available to the borrower (the seller of the goods). Suppose $10,000 worth of goods is shipped. Further, assume that the factoring commission for credit checking and risk bearing is 2½ percent of the invoice price, or $250, and that the interest expense is computed at a 9 percent annual rate on the invoice balance, or $75 = [$10,000(0.09/360)] × 30 days. The selling firm's accounting entry is as follows:

Cash	$9,175	
Interest expense	75	
Factoring commission	250	
Reserve due from factor on collection account	500	
Accounts receivable		$10,000

The $500 due from the factor upon collection of the account is a reserve established by the factor to cover disputes between the seller and buyers over damaged goods, goods returned by the buyers to the seller, and the failure to make an outright sale of goods. The reserve is paid to the selling firm when the factor collects on the account.

Factoring normally is a continuous process instead of the single cycle just described. The firm that sells the goods receives an order; it transmits this order to the factor for approval; upon approval, the firm ships the goods; the factor advances the invoice amount minus withholdings to the seller; the buyer pays the factor when payment is due; and the factor periodically remits any excess in the reserve to the seller of the goods. Once a routine has been established, a continuous circular flow of goods and funds takes place between the seller, the buyers of the goods, and the factor. Thus, once the factoring agreement is in force, funds from this source are *spontaneous* in the sense that an increase in sales will automatically generate additional credit.

Visa and MasterCard represent a prime example of nonrecourse factoring. When you purchase from a retailer such as Wal-Mart using Visa or MasterCard, the retailer is paid only 95 to 97 percent of the invoice by these credit companies. Visa and MasterCard charges the 3 to 5 percent discount because they provide credit-checking services and suffer any losses due to customer nonpayment—the retailer does not incur these costs.

COST OF RECEIVABLES FINANCING   Both accounts receivable pledging and factoring are convenient and advantageous, but they can be costly. The credit-checking and risk-bearing fee is 1 to 3 percent of the amount of invoices accepted by the factor, and it could be even more if the buyers are poor credit risks. The cost of money is reflected in the interest rate (usually 2 to 3 percentage points over the prime rate) charged on the unpaid balance of the funds advanced by the factor.

EVALUATION OF RECEIVABLES FINANCING   It cannot be said categorically that accounts receivable financing is either a good or a bad way to raise funds. Among the advantages is, first, the flexibility of this source of financing: As the firm's sales expand, more financing is needed, but a larger volume of invoices, and hence a larger amount of receivables financing, is generated automatically. Second, receivables can be used as security for loans that otherwise would not be granted. Third, factoring can provide the services of a credit department that otherwise might be available only at a higher cost.

Accounts receivable financing also has disadvantages. First, when invoices are numerous and relatively small in dollar amount, the administrative costs involved might be excessive. Second, because receivables represent the firm's most liquid noncash assets, some trade creditors might refuse to sell on credit to a firm that factors or pledges its receivables on the grounds that this practice weakens the firm's financial strength.

FUTURE USE OF RECEIVABLES FINANCING   It is easy to make a prediction at this point: In the future, accounts receivable financing will increase in relative importance. Computer technology is advancing rapidly toward the point where credit records of individuals and firms can be kept on disks and magnetic tapes. For example, one device used by retailers consists of a box which, when an individual's magnetic credit card is inserted, gives a signal that the credit is "good" and that a bank is willing to "buy" the receivable created as soon as the store completes the sale. The cost of handling invoices will be reduced greatly over present-day costs because the new systems will be so highly automated. This will make it possible to use accounts receivable financing for very small sales, and it will reduce the cost of all receivables financing. The net result will be a marked expansion of accounts receivable financing. In fact, when consumers use credit cards such as MasterCard or Visa, the seller is in effect factoring receivables. The seller receives the amount of the purchase, minus a percentage fee, the next working day. The buyer receives 30 days' (or so) credit, at which time he or she remits payment directly to the credit card company or sponsoring bank.

Inventory Financing

A substantial amount of credit is secured by business inventories. If a firm is a relatively good credit risk, the mere existence of the inventory might be a sufficient basis for receiving an unsecured loan. However, if the firm is a relatively poor risk, the lending institution might insist upon security in the form of a *lien* against the inventory. Methods for using inventories as security are discussed in this section.

BLANKET LIENS The *inventory blanket lien* gives the lending institution a lien against all the borrower's inventories. However, the borrower is free to sell inventories, and thus the value of the collateral can be reduced below the level that existed when the loan was granted. A blanket lien generally is used when the inventory put up as collateral is relatively low priced, fast moving, and difficult to identify individually.

TRUST RECEIPTS Because of the inherent weakness of the blanket lien, another procedure for inventory financing has been developed—the *trust receipt,* which is an instrument acknowledging that the goods are held in trust for the lender. Under this method, the borrowing firm, as a condition for receiving funds from the lender, signs and delivers a trust receipt for the goods. The goods can be stored in a public warehouse or held on the premises of the borrower. The trust receipt states that the goods are held in trust for the lender or are segregated on the borrower's premises on the lender's behalf and that any proceeds from the sale of the goods must be transmitted to the lender at the end of each day. Automobile dealer financing is one of the best examples of trust receipt financing.

One defect of trust receipt financing is the requirement that a trust receipt be issued for specific goods. For example, if the security is autos in a dealer's inventory, the trust receipts must indicate the cars by registration number. In order to validate its trust receipts, the lending institution must send someone to the borrower's premises periodically to see that the auto numbers are listed correctly, because auto dealers who are in financial difficulty have been known to sell cars backing trust receipts and then use the funds obtained for other operations rather than to repay the bank. Problems are compounded if the borrower has a number of different locations, especially if they are separated geographically from the lender. To offset these inconveniences, *warehousing* has come into wide use as a method of securing loans with inventory.

WAREHOUSE RECEIPTS Warehouse receipt financing is another way to use inventory as security. A *public warehouse* is an independent third-party operation engaged in the business of storing goods. Items that must age, such as tobacco and liquor, are often financed and stored in public warehouses. When the inventory products used as collateral are moved to public warehouses, the financing arrangement is termed *terminal warehousing.* Sometimes terminal warehousing is not practical because of the bulkiness of goods and the expense of transporting them to and from the borrower's premises. In such cases, a *field warehouse* might be established on the borrower's grounds. To provide inventory supervision, the lending institution employs a third party in the arrangement, the field warehousing company, which acts as its agent.

Field warehousing can be illustrated by a simple example. Suppose a firm which has iron stacked in an open yard on its premises needs a loan. A field warehousing concern can place a temporary fence around the iron, erecting a sign stating, "This is a field warehouse supervised by the Smith Field Warehousing Corporation," and then assign an employee to supervise and control the fenced-in inventory.

This example illustrates the three essential elements for the establishment of a field warehouse: (1) public notification, (2) physical control of the inventory, and (3) supervision by a custodian of the field warehousing concern. When the field warehousing operation is relatively small, the third condition is sometimes violated by hiring an employee of the borrower to supervise the inventory. This practice is viewed as undesirable by most lenders because there is no control over the collateral by a person independent of the borrowing firm.[12]

ACCEPTABLE PRODUCTS   Canned foods account for about 17 percent of all field warehouse loans. In addition, many other types of products provide a basis for field warehouse financing. Some of these are miscellaneous groceries, which represent about 13 percent; lumber products, about 10 percent; and coal and coke, about 6 percent. These products are relatively nonperishable and are sold in well-developed, organized markets. Nonperishability protects the lender if it should have to take over the security. For this reason, a bank would not make a field warehousing loan on perishables such as fresh fish; but frozen fish, which can be stored for a long time, can be field warehoused.

COST OF FINANCING   The fixed costs of a field warehousing arrangement are relatively high; such financing therefore is not suitable for a very small firm. If a field warehousing company sets up a field warehouse, it typically will set a minimum charge of about $25,000 per year, plus about 1 to 2 percent of the amount of credit extended to the borrower. Furthermore, the financing institution will charge an interest rate of two to three percentage points over the prime rate. An efficient field warehousing operation requires an inventory of at least $1 million.

EVALUATION OF INVENTORY FINANCING   The use of inventory financing, especially field warehouse financing, as a source of funds has many advantages. First, the amount of funds available is flexible because the financing is tied to the growth of inventories, which in turn is related directly to financing needs. Second, the field warehousing arrangement increases the acceptability of inventories as loan

---

[12]This absence of independent control was the main cause of a breakdown that resulted in more than $200 million of losses on loans to the Allied Crude Vegetable Oil Company by Bank of America and other banks. American Express Field Warehousing Company was handling the operation, but it hired men from Allied's own staff as custodians. Their dishonesty was not discovered because of another breakdown—the fact that the American Express touring inspector did not actually take a physical inventory of the warehouses. As a consequence, the swindle was not discovered until losses running into hundreds of millions of dollars had been suffered.

SMALL BUSINESS

Receivables Financing by a Small Firm

To stimulate growth, small firms often find that they must offer customers credit. If rapid sales growth does result, then accounts receivable will grow equally or perhaps even faster. This, in turn, brings with it a need for additional financing. Larger firms, with established earning power, generally have no trouble raising growth capital, but a small firm with no track record might face a real problem.

Accounts receivable are highly liquid, so they are attractive to lenders as collateral. The small firm can either pledge its receivables or factor them to help bring in growth capital.

In the case of pledged receivables, the firm needing capital merely uses its receivables as collateral for the loan. Pledging receivables is especially sensible for the small firm that has customers with better credit histories than the firm itself, because this allows the firm to take advantage of the strength of its customer base. However, the firm ultimately must bear the risk of nonpayment, and it gets only part of the funds due from its customers because receivables cannot be pledged for full face value.

The other alternative is factoring, which involves the sale of receivables to a third party, called the "factor." This arrangement is without recourse, meaning that the factor must bear any credit risks inherent in the receivables. Thus, it is the responsibility of the factor to check the customers' creditworthiness and to collect the receivables. A small firm employing a factor therefore gets more than just credit—the factor generally takes over the credit analysis and collection functions almost entirely. The firm would not need a credit department either for checking credit or for collecting receivables. But factors are in business to make money, so it stands to reason that the company would have to pay for the factor's services. The principal decision, then, is whether the comparatively high cost of the factor is warranted in view of the full set of services that it would receive, including short-term capital, credit analysis, and collection services.

There are good reasons why many small firms find that factors are indeed an economical alternative. The small firm has its own special expertise—perhaps buying and selling building materials—while factors have their own expertise—credit services. Economies of scale exist, so the factor's services might be a bargain when compared to the costs of maintaining a credit department and being exposed to credit risks. In deciding on the use of a factor, the small firm must consider not only the financial cost of other forms of financing, such as that offered by the bank, but also the cost of the credit services provided by the factor. In addition, the small firm needs to consider the availability of other sources of funds—it might be that factoring is the most convenient alternative.

For small firms with limited managerial resources and limited experience in monitoring and collecting credit accounts, factors might be more than worth the cost. The small firm's comparative advantage is its ability to deliver a product; the factor's advantage is its ability to provide financial and credit services. Therefore, it might be best to have the firm do what it does best and to have the factor provide financing and credit services.

---

collateral; some inventories simply would not be accepted by a bank as security without such an arrangement. Third, the necessity for inventory control and safe-keeping as well as the use of specialists in warehousing often results in improved warehouse practices, which in turn save handling costs, insurance charges, theft losses, and so on. Thus, field warehousing companies often save money for firms in spite of the costs of financing that we have discussed. The major disadvantages of field warehousing include the paperwork, physical separation requirements, and, for small firms, the fixed-cost element.

Self-Test Questions

What is a secured loan?

What two types of current assets are pledged as security for short-term loans?

Differentiate between pledging accounts receivable and factoring accounts receivable.

Identify the services a factor normally provides.

List the advantages and disadvantages of accounts receivable financing.

Describe three methods of inventory financing.

What are some advantages and disadvantages of inventory financing?

Summary

This chapter examined (1) the different types of short-term credit available to firms, (2) the decisions financial managers make when selecting among types of short-term credit, and (3) decisions regarding the use of security to obtain credit. The key concepts covered are listed below.

- **Short-term credit** is defined as any liability originally scheduled for payment within one year. The four major sources of short-term credit are (1) accruals, (2) accounts payable, (3) bank loans, and (4) commercial paper.
- **Accruals,** which are continually recurring short-term liabilities, represent free, spontaneous credit.
- **Accounts payable,** or **trade credit,** is the largest category of short-term debt. This credit arises spontaneously as a result of purchases on credit. Firms should use all the **free trade credit** they can obtain, but they should use **costly trade credit** only if it is less expensive than other forms of short-term debt. Suppliers often offer discounts to customers who pay within a stated discount period. The following equation might be used to calculate the approximate percentage cost, on an annual basis, of not taking discounts:

$$\frac{\text{Approximate}}{\text{percentage}} = \frac{\text{Discount percent}}{100 - \frac{\text{Discount}}{\text{percent}}} \times \frac{360}{\frac{\text{Total days of}}{\text{credit available}} - \frac{\text{Discount}}{\text{period}}}$$

- **Bank loans** are an important source of short-term credit. Interest on bank loans might be quoted as **simple interest, discount interest,** or **add-on interest.** The effective rate on a discount or add-on loan always exceeds the quoted simple rate. In general, the effective cost of a bank loan can be computed as follows:

$$\frac{\text{Effective}}{\text{annual rate}} = (1 + \text{Rate per period})^m - 1.0$$

where m is the number of borrowing (compounding) periods in one year (i.e., if the loan is for one month, m = 12). The rate per period can be computed using the following equation:

$$\text{Periodic} \atop \text{rate (cost)} = \frac{\text{Cost of borrowing as a percent of the amount borrowed}}{\text{Usable funds as a percent of the amount borrowed}}$$

$$= \frac{\left(\dfrac{\text{Dollar cost of borrowing}}{\text{Amount borrowed}}\right)}{\left(\dfrac{\text{Amount of usable funds}}{\text{Amount borrowed}}\right)} \qquad (12\text{-}2)$$

$$= \frac{\text{Dollar cost of borrowing}}{\text{Amount of usable funds}}$$

- When a bank loan is approved, a **promissory note** is signed. It specifies: (1) the amount borrowed, (2) the percentage interest rate, (3) the repayment schedule, (4) the collateral, and (5) any other conditions to which the parties have agreed.

- Banks sometimes require borrowers to maintain **compensating balances,** which are deposit requirements set at between 10 percent and 20 percent of the loan amount. Compensating balances generally raise the effective rate of interest on bank loans.

- A **line of credit** is an understanding between the bank and the borrower indicating the maximum amount of credit the bank will extend to the borrower.

- A **revolving credit** agreement is a formal line of credit which involves a **commitment fee.**

- **Commercial paper** is unsecured short-term debt issued by a large, financially strong corporation. Although the cost of commercial paper is lower than the cost of bank loans, commercial paper's maturity is limited to 270 days, and it can be used only by large firms with exceptionally strong credit ratings.

- Sometimes a borrower will find it necessary to borrow on a **secured basis,** in which case the borrower pledges assets such as real estate, securities, equipment, inventories, or accounts receivable as collateral for the loan.

- Accounts receivable financing involves either **pledging** or **factoring** receivables. Under a pledging arrangement the lender not only gets a claim against the receivables but also has recourse to the borrower. Factoring involves the purchase of accounts receivable by the lender, generally without recourse to the borrower.

- There are three primary methods of inventory financing: (1) An **inventory blanket lien** gives the lender a lien against all of the borrower's inventories. (2) A **trust receipt** is an instrument that acknowledges that goods are held in trust for the lender. (3) Under **warehouse receipt** financing, the lender employs a third party to exercise control over the borrower's inventory and to act as the lender's agent.

- **Pledging receivables** is especially sensible for a small firm that has customers with better credit histories than the firm itself, as this allows the firm to take advantage of the strength of its customer base.

- For small firms with limited managerial resources and limited experience in monitoring and collecting credit accounts, **factoring** might be more than worth the cost. The small firm's comparative advantage is its ability to deliver a product; the factor's advantage is its ability to provide financial and credit services.

Questions

12-1 "Firms can control their accruals within fairly wide limits; depending on the cost of accruals, financing from this source will be increased or decreased." Discuss.

12-2 Is it true that both trade credit and accruals represent a spontaneous source of capital for financing growth? Explain.

12-3 Is it true that most firms are able to obtain some free trade credit and that additional trade credit often is available, but at a cost? Explain.

12-4 The availability of bank credit often is more important to a small firm than to a large one. Why?

12-5 What kinds of firms use commercial paper? Could Mama and Papa Gus's Corner Grocery borrow using this form of credit?

12-6 Suppose a firm can obtain funds by borrowing at the prime rate or by selling commercial paper.
   a. If the prime rate is 7½ percent, what is a reasonable estimate for the cost of commercial paper?
   b. If a substantial cost differential exists, why might a firm like this one actually borrow some of its funds in each market?

12-7 Can you think of some firms that might allow you to purchase on credit, but probably would factor your receivables account?

Self-Test Problems

(Solutions Appear in Appendix B)

Key terms   **ST-1** Define each of the following terms:
   a. accruals
   b. trade credit; stretching accounts payable; free trade credit; costly trade credit
   c. promissory note; line of credit; revolving credit agreement
   d. prime rate
   e. simple interest; discount interest; add-on interest
   f. compensating balance (CB); commitment fee
   g. commercial paper
   h. secured loan
   i. Uniform Commercial Code
   j. pledging receivables; factoring
   k. recourse
   l. inventory blanket lien; trust receipt; warehouse receipt financing; field warehouse

Receivables financing   **ST-2** The Naylor Corporation is considering two methods of raising working capital: (1) a commercial bank loan secured by accounts receivable and (2) factoring accounts receivable. Naylor's bank has agreed to lend the firm 75 percent of its average monthly accounts receivable balance of $250,000 at an annual interest rate of 9 percent. The bank loan is in the form of a series of 30-day loans. The loan would be discounted, and a 20 percent compensating balance would also be required.
    A factor has agreed to purchase Naylor's accounts receivable and to advance 85 percent of the balance to the firm. The 15 percent of receivables not loaned to the firm under the factoring arrangement is held in a reserve account. The factor would charge a 3.5 percent factoring commission and annual interest of 9 percent on the invoice price, less both the factoring commission and the reserve account.

The monthly interest payment would be deducted from the advance. If Naylor chooses the factoring arrangement, it can eliminate its credit department and reduce operating expenses by $4,000 per month. In addition, bad debt losses of 2 percent of the monthly receivables will be avoided.

a. What is the annual dollar cost associated with each financing arrangement?

b. Discuss some considerations other than cost that may influence management's decision between factoring and a commercial bank loan.

Problems

Cash discounts **12-1** Suppose a firm makes purchases of $3.6 million per year under terms of 2/10, net 30 and takes discounts.

a. What is the average amount of accounts payable net of discounts? (Assume that the $3.6 million of purchases is net of discounts—that is, gross purchases are $3,673,469, discounts are $73,469, and net purchases are $3.6 million. Also, use 360 days in a year.)

b. Is there a cost of the trade credit the firm uses?

c. If the firm did not take discounts but it did pay on the due date, what would be its average payables and the approximate and effective annual costs of this nonfree trade credit? Assume the firm records accounts payable net of discounts.

d. What would its approximate and effective annual costs of not taking discounts be if it could stretch its payments to 40 days?

Trade credit versus bank credit **12-2** Gallinger Corporation projects an increase in sales from $1.5 million to $2 million, but it needs an additional $300,000 of current assets to support this expansion. The money can be obtained from the bank at an interest rate of 13 percent, discount interest; no compensating balance is required. Alternatively, Gallinger can finance the expansion by no longer taking discounts, thus increasing accounts payable. Gallinger purchases under terms of 2/10, net 30, but it can delay payment for an additional 35 days—paying in 65 days and thus becoming 35 days past due—without a penalty because of its suppliers' current excess capacity problems.

a. Based strictly on effective annual interest rate comparisons, how should Gallinger finance its expansion?

b. What additional qualitative factors should Gallinger consider before reaching a decision?

Cost of bank loans **12-3** The UFSU Corporation intends to borrow $450,000 to support its short-term financing requirements during the next year. The company is evaluating its financing options at the bank where it maintains its checking account. UFSU's checking account balance, which averages $50,000, can be used to help satisfy any compensating balance requirements the bank might impose. The financing alternatives offered by the bank include:

Alternative 1: A discount interest loan with a simple interest of 9.5 percent and no compensating balance requirement.

Alternative 2: A 10 percent simple interest loan that has a 15 percent compensating balance requirement.

Alternative 3: A $1 million revolving line of credit with simple interest of 9¼ percent paid on the amount borrowed and a ¼ percent commitment fee.

a. Compute the effective cost (rate) of each financing alternative assuming UFSU borrows $450,000. Which alternative should UFSU use?

f. Dellvoe is considering using secured short-term financing. What is a secured loan? What two types of current assets can be used to secure loans?

g. What are the differences between pledging receivables and factoring receivables? Is one type generally considered better?

h. What are the differences among the three forms of inventory financing? Is one type generally considered best?

i. Dellvoe had expected a really strong market for office equipment for the year just ended, and in anticipation of strong sales, the firm increased its inventory purchases. However, sales for the last quarter of the year did not meet its expectations, and now Dellvoe finds itself short on cash. The firm expects that its cash shortage will be temporary, lasting only 3 months. (The inventory has been paid for and cannot be returned to suppliers. In the office equipment market, designs change nearly every two years, and Dellvoe's inventory reflects the new design changes, so its inventory is not obsolete.) Dellvoe has decided to use inventory financing to meet its short-term cash needs. It estimates that it will require $800,000 for inventory financing during this 3-month period. Dellvoe has negotiated with the bank for a 3-month, $1,000,000 line of credit with terms of 10 percent annual interest on the used portion, a 1 percent commitment fee on the unused portion, and a $125,000 compensating balance at all times.

Expected inventory levels to be financed are as follows:

Month	Amount
January 1996	$800,000
February	500,000
March	300,000

Calculate the cost of funds from this source, including interest charges and commitment fees. (Hint: Each month's borrowings will be $125,000 greater than the inventory level to be financed because of the compensating balance requirement.)

Computer-Related Problem

Work the problem in this section only if you are using the computer problem diskette.

Factoring receivables   **12-16**   Use the model in File C12 to work this problem. Refer to Problem 12-7.

a. Would it be to Cooley's advantage to offer to pay the factor a commission of 2.5 percent if it would lower the interest rate to 10.5 percent annually?

b. Assume a commission of 2 percent and an interest rate of 12 percent. What would be the total cost of the factoring arrangement if Cooley's funds needed rose to $650,000? Would the factoring arrangement be profitable under these circumstances?

PART V

Capital Budgeting

CHAPTER 13

Capital Budgeting Techniques

A MANAGERIAL PERSPECTIVE

After five years of planning and $3.5 billion in costs for development and for new factories and equipment, General Motors in the summer of 1990 began production of a new compact car—the Saturn. For the project to be viable, GM needed to sell 500,000 Saturns a year. Unfortunately for GM, this has not happened. Even though consumers seem to like the Saturn concept, annual sales (less than 300,000) have been well below the amount needed for GM to begin to call the project a viable investment. Some people believe GM has used the Saturn project as a loss leader to attract first-time new car buyers and as a means to satisfy federal regulations concerning the average fuel economy of the line of cars it offers.

In mid-1994, Chrysler introduced its new compact car—the Neon, which is sold under the Dodge and Plymouth name. The new car has a price tag that is comparable to the Ford Escort and the Saturn, but it has extra features, including dual front air bags and a more advanced, "sportier" engine. Because Chrysler used plant and equipment that it already had, only about $1.3 billion was spent to develop the Neon. For this reason, most analysts believe the Neon will be a money-making project for Chrysler.

In April 1995, Chrysler introduced a new minivan—the first since it introduced the original minivan in 1983. The new minivan is roomier, has many more features, and is more stylish than the older models, the Dodge Caravan and the Chrysler Voyager, which will be phased out. The price to develop the new minivan was $2.3 billion. But, based on the public's reaction to the prototypes shown at auto shows, the minivan project is sure to be a success.

GM's Saturn project and Chrysler's Neon and minivan projects are examples of massive capital budgeting ventures, which required numerous analyses and critical decisions before the billions of dollars necessary for development and implementation were spent. The principles set forth in this chapter as well as the next chapter offer insights into how capital budgeting decisions such as these are made.

SOURCES: "Here Comes GM's Saturn," *Business Week*, April 9, 1990; "Autos: Neon May Be a Bright Light for Chrysler," *The Wall Street Journal*, April 23, 1993; and "How Many Rebates Can Fit in a Minivan?" *Business Week*, February 13, 1995.

In previous chapters we have seen how investors value corporate securities and determine required rates of return, and we also have seen how managers make working capital decisions, including decisions to increase current assets. Now we turn to investment decisions involving the fixed assets of a firm, or *capital budgeting*. Here the term *capital* refers to fixed assets used in production, while a *budget* is a plan that details projected inflows and outflows during some future period. Thus, the capital budget is an outline of planned expenditures on fixed assets, and **capital budgeting** is the process of analyzing projects and deciding which are acceptable investments and which actually should be purchased.

CAPITAL BUDGETING
The process of planning expenditures on assets whose cash flows are expected to extend beyond one year.

Our treatment of capital budgeting is divided into two chapters. First, this chapter gives an overview and explains the basic techniques used in capital budgeting analysis. Then, in Chapter 14, we consider how the cash flows associated with capital budgeting projects are estimated and how risk is considered in capital budgeting decisions.

Importance of Capital Budgeting

A number of factors combine to make capital budgeting decisions perhaps the most important ones financial managers must make. First, the impact of capital budgeting is long-term—thus the firm loses some decision-making flexibility when capital projects are purchased. For example, when a firm invests in an asset with a 10-year economic life, its operations are affected for 10 years—the firm is "locked in" by the capital budgeting decision. Further, because asset expansion is fundamentally related to expected future sales, a decision to buy a fixed asset that is expected to last 10 years involves an implicit 10-year sales forecast.

An error in the forecast of asset requirements can have serious consequences. If the firm invests too much in assets, it will incur unnecessarily heavy expenses. But if it does not spend enough on fixed assets, it might find inefficient production and inadequate capacity lead to lost sales that are difficult, if not impossible, to recover.

Timing also is important in capital budgeting—capital assets must be ready to come "on line" when they are needed; otherwise, opportunities might be lost. For example, consider what happened to Decopot, a decorative tile company with no formal capital budgeting process. Decopot attempted to operate at full capacity as often as possible. This was not a bad idea, because demand for Decopot's product and services was relatively stable. But, about four years ago, Decopot began to experience intermittent spurts of additional demand for its products. Decopot could not satisfy the additional demand because it did not have the capacity to produce any more products—customers had to be turned away. The spurts in demand continued, so senior management decided to add capacity to increase production so the additional orders could be filled. It took nine months to get the additional capacity ready. Finally, Decopot was ready for the increased demand the next time it arrived. Unfortunately, the "next time" never came, because competitors had expanded their operations a year earlier, which allowed them to fill customers' orders when Decopot could not—many of Decopot's customers now are the competitors' customers. If Decopot had properly forecasted demand and planned its capacity requirements, it would have been able to maintain or perhaps even increase its market share; instead, its market share decreased.

Effective capital budgeting can improve both the timing of asset acquisitions and the quality of assets purchased. A firm that forecasts its needs for capital assets in advance will have an opportunity to purchase and install the assets before they are needed. Unfortunately, like Decopot, many firms do not order capital assets until they approach full capacity or are forced to replace worn-out equipment. If many firms order capital assets at the same time, backlogs result, prices increase, and firms are forced to wait for the delivery of machinery; in general, the quality of the capital assets deteriorates. If a firm foresees its needs and purchases capital assets early, it can avoid these problems.

Finally, capital budgeting also is important because the acquisition of fixed assets typically involves substantial expenditures, and before a firm can spend a large amount of money, it must have the funds available—large amounts of money are not available automatically. Therefore, a firm contemplating a major capital expenditure program must arrange its financing well in advance to be sure the funds required are available.

Self-Test Questions

Why are capital budgeting decisions so important to the success of a firm?

Why is the sales forecast a key element in a capital budgeting decision?

Generating Ideas for Capital Projects

The same general concepts that we developed for security analysis are involved in capital budgeting. However, whereas a set of stocks and bonds exists in the securities market, and investors select from this set, capital budgeting projects are created by the firm. For example, a sales representative might report that customers are asking for a particular product that the company does not currently produce. The sales manager then discusses the idea with the marketing research group to determine the size of the market for the proposed product. If it appears likely that a significant market does exist, cost accountants and engineers will be asked to estimate production costs. If it appears that the product can be produced and sold at a sufficient profit, the project will be undertaken.

A firm's growth, and even its ability to remain competitive and to survive, depends upon a constant flow of ideas for new products, ways to make existing products better, and ways to produce output at a lower cost. Accordingly, a well-managed firm will go to great lengths to develop good capital budgeting proposals. Some firms even provide incentives to employees to encourage suggestions that lead to beneficial investment proposals. If a firm has capable and imaginative executives and employees, and if its incentive system is working properly, many ideas for capital investment will be advanced.

Because some capital investment ideas will be good and others will not, procedures must be established for evaluating the worth of such projects to the firm. Our topic in the remainder of this chapter is the evaluation of the acceptability of capital projects.

Self-Test Question

How does a firm generate ideas for capital projects?

Project Classifications

REPLACEMENT DECISIONS
Whether to purchase capital assets to take the place of existing assets to maintain existing operations.

EXPANSION DECISIONS
Whether to purchase capital projects and add them to existing assets to *increase* existing operations.

INDEPENDENT PROJECTS
Projects whose cash flows are not affected by the acceptance or nonacceptance of other projects.

MUTUALLY EXCLUSIVE PROJECTS
A set of projects in which the acceptance of one project means the others cannot be accepted.

Capital budgeting decisions generally are termed either *replacement decisions* or *expansion decisions.* **Replacement decisions** involve determining whether capital projects should be purchased to take the place of (replace) existing assets that might be worn out, damaged, or obsolete. Usually the replacement projects are necessary to maintain or improve profitable operations using the existing production levels. On the other hand, if a firm is considering whether to *increase* operations by adding capital projects to existing assets that will help produce either more of its existing products or entirely new products, **expansion decisions** are made. For example, Ziff-Davis Publishing Company, the largest publisher of computer magazines in the United States, including *PC Magazine* and *PC Week,* formed a 13-member board in January 1995 to help direct the company's effort to *expand* into new businesses, such as CD-ROM products, television ventures, and high-tech services. The decisions concerning which new areas Ziff-Davis should enter are *expansion decisions.*

Some of the capital budgeting decisions Ziff-Davis Publishing will have to make will involve *independent projects,* while others will involve *mutually exclusive projects.* **Independent projects** are projects whose cash flows are not affected by one another, so the acceptance of one project does not affect the acceptance of the other project(s)—*all independent projects can be purchased if they are all acceptable.* For example, if Ziff-Davis decided to purchase the ABC television network, it still could publish a new magazine about personal computers. On the other hand, if a capital budgeting decision involves **mutually exclusive projects,** then when one project is taken on, the other(s) must be rejected—*only one mutually exclusive project can be purchased, even if they all are acceptable.* For example, Alldome Sports, Ltd. has a parcel of land on which it wants to build either a golf course for public use or a domed stadium that would be used by professional sports teams. The land is not large enough for both alternatives, so if Alldome chooses to build the golf course, it could not build the stadium, and vice versa.

In general, relatively simple calculations and only a few supporting documents are required for most replacement decisions, especially maintenance-type investments in profitable plants. More detailed analysis is required for cost-reduction replacements, for expansion of existing product lines, and especially for investments in new products or areas. Also, within each category projects are broken down by their dollar costs: Larger investments require both more detailed analysis and approval at a higher level within the firm. Thus, although a plant manager might be authorized to approve maintenance expenditures up to $10,000 on the basis of a relatively unsophisticated analysis, the full board of directors might have to approve decisions that involve either amounts over $1 million or expansions into new products or markets. Statistical data generally are lacking for new product decisions, so here judgments, as opposed to detailed cost data, are especially important.

Self-Test Question

Identify and briefly explain how capital project classification categories are used.

Similarities between Capital Budgeting and Security Valuation

Conceptually, capital budgeting involves exactly the same six steps that are used in security analysis:

1. The cost of the project must be determined. This is similar to finding the price that must be paid for a stock or bond.
2. Management estimates the cash flows expected from the project, including the salvage value of the asset at the end of its expected life. This is similar to estimating the future dividend or interest payment stream on a stock or bond, along with the stock's expected selling price or the bond's maturity value.
3. The riskiness of the projected cash flows must be estimated. For this assessment, management needs information about the probability distributions of the cash flows.
4. Given the project's riskiness, management determines the appropriate rate of return to use for discounting the cash flows.
5. The present value of the expected cash flows is computed to obtain an estimate of the asset's value to the firm. This is equivalent to finding the present value of a stock's expected future dividends.
6. The present value of the expected cash inflows is compared with the investment, or cost, required to acquire the asset; if the PV of the cash flows exceeds the cost, the project should be accepted. Otherwise, it should be rejected. Alternatively, the expected rate of return on the project can be calculated, and if this rate of return exceeds the rate of return considered appropriate for the project, it should be accepted.

If an individual investor identifies and invests in a stock or bond whose market price is less than its true value, the value of the investor's portfolio will increase. Similarly, if a firm identifies (or creates) an investment opportunity with a present value greater than its cost, the value of the firm will increase. Thus, there is a very direct link between capital budgeting and stock values: The more effective the firm's capital budgeting procedures, the higher the price of its stock.

Self-Test Questions

List the six steps in the capital budgeting process, and compare them with the steps in security valuation.

Explain how capital budgeting is related to the wealth-maximization goal that should be pursued by the financial manager of a firm.

Capital Budgeting Evaluation Techniques

The basic methods used by businesses to evaluate projects and to decide whether they should be accepted for inclusion in the capital budget are: (1) payback, (2) net present value (NPV), and (3) internal rate of return (IRR). As you will see, to determine a project's acceptability using any of these three techniques, its expected cash flows are needed. However, unlike the other two, the payback method does not consider the time value of money—so, we call payback a

---

FIGURE 13-1

Net Cash Flows for Projects S and L

| Year | Expected After-Tax Net Cash Flows, CF_t | |
(t)	Project S	Project L
0^a	$(3,000)	$(3,000)
1	1,500	400
2	1,200	900
3	800	1,300
4	300	1,500

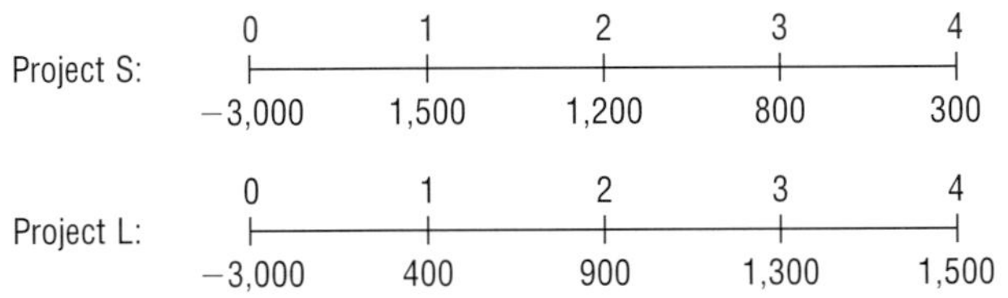

Project S:

0	1	2	3	4
−3,000	1,500	1,200	800	300

Project L:

0	1	2	3	4
−3,000	400	900	1,300	1,500

[a]CF_0 represents the initial investment, or net cost of the project.

---

nondiscounting technique, and NPV and IRR *discounting techniques.* We will explain how each evaluation criterion is calculated, and then we will determine how well each performs in terms of identifying those projects which will maximize the firm's stock price.

We use the tabular and time line cash flow data shown in Figure 13-1 for Projects S and L to illustrate all the methods, and throughout this chapter we assume that the projects are equally risky. Note that the cash flows, CF_t, are expected values and that they have been adjusted to reflect taxes, salvage values, and any other changes in cash flows associated with the capital projects.[1] Also, we assume that all cash flows occur at the end of the designated year. Incidentally, the S stands for *short* and the L for *long:* Project S is a short-term project in the sense that its cash inflows tend to come in sooner than L's.

Payback Period

PAYBACK PERIOD
The length of time before the original cost of an investment is recovered from the expected cash flows.

The **payback period,** defined as the expected number of years required to recover the original investment, is the simplest and, as far as we know, the oldest *formal* method used to evaluate capital budgeting projects. To compute a project's payback period, simply add up the expected cash flows for each year until the amount initially invested in the project is recovered. The total amount of time, including the fraction of a year if appropriate, that it takes to recapture the

---

[1]Perhaps the most difficult part of the capital budgeting process is the estimation of the relevant cash flows. For simplicity, the net cash flows are treated as given in this chapter, which allows us to focus on our main area of concern, the capital budgeting evaluation techniques. However, in Chapter 14 we will discuss cash flow estimation in detail. Also, remember that working capital is defined as the firm's current assets and that net working capital is current assets minus current liabilities.

FIGURE 13-2

Payback Period for Project S and Project L

PROJECT S:

	0	1	2	3	4
Net cash flow	−3,000	1,500	1,200	800	300
Cumulative net cash flow	−3,000	−1,500	−300	500	800

PROJECT L:

	0	1	2	3	4
Net cash flow	−3,000	400	900	1,300	1,500
Cumulative net cash flow	−3,000	−2,600	−1,700	−400	1,100

original amount invested is the payback period. The payback calculation process for both Project S and Project L is diagrammed in Figure 13-2.

The *exact* payback period can be found using the following formula:

13-1

$$\text{Payback} = \begin{array}{c}\text{Year before full}\\ \text{recovery of}\\ \text{original investment}\end{array} + \left(\frac{\text{Unrecovered cost at start of year}}{\text{Total cash flow during year}}\right)$$

The diagram in Figure 13-2 shows that the payback period for Project S is between two years and three years, so, using Equation 13-1, the exact payback period is

$$\text{Payback}_\text{S} = 2 + \frac{300}{800} = 2.4 \text{ years}$$

Applying the same procedure to Project L, we find Payback$_\text{L}$ = 3.3 years.

Using payback to make capital budgeting decisions is based on the concept that it is better to recover the cost of (investment in) a project sooner rather than later. Therefore, Project S is considered better than Project L because it has a lower payback. *As a rule, a project is considered acceptable if its payback is less than the maximum cost recovery time established by the firm.* For example, if the firm requires projects to have a payback of three years or less, Project S would be acceptable but Project L would not.

The payback method is very simple, which explains why payback traditionally has been one of the most popular capital budgeting techniques. But payback ignores the time value of money, so relying solely on this method could lead to incorrect decisions—at least if our goal is to maximize value. If a project has a payback of three years, we know how quickly the initial investment will be covered by the expected cash flows, but this information does not provide any indication of whether the return on the project is sufficient to cover the cost of the funds invested. In addition, when payback is used, the cash flows beyond the payback period are ignored. For example, even if Project L had a fifth year of cash flows equal to $50,000, its payback would remain 3.3 years, which is less desirable than the payback of 2.4 years for Project S. But, with the additional $50,000 cash flow, Project L probably would be preferred.

Even with its deficiencies, payback does provide information on how long funds will be tied up in a project. Thus, the shorter the payback period, other things held constant, the greater is the project's liquidity. Also, because cash flows expected in the distant future generally are regarded as being riskier than near-term cash flows, the payback often is used to get a rough indication of a project's riskiness—a shorter payback *suggests* less risk.

Net Present Value (NPV)

NET PRESENT VALUE (NPV) METHOD
A method of evaluating capital investment proposals by finding the present value of the net cash flows, discounted at the rate of return required by the firm.

DISCOUNTED CASH FLOW (DCF) TECHNIQUES
Methods of evaluating investment proposals that employ time value of money concepts; two of these are the net present value and internal rate of return methods.

To correct for the major defect of any *nondiscounting* technique—ignoring the time value of money—methods were developed to include consideration of the time value of money. One such method is the **net present value (NPV) method,** which relies on **discounted cash flow (DCF) techniques.** To implement this approach, we proceed as follows:

1. Using the rate of return required by the firm, compute the present value of *all* the cash flows, whether inflows or outflows, associated with a project during its life.
2. Sum the cash flows' present values to get the project's NPV.
3. *A project is considered acceptable if its NPV is positive; it is not acceptable if its NPV is negative.* If projects with positive NPVs are purchased, the value of the firm will increase; purchasing negative NPV projects will lower the value of the firm. In general, higher NPV projects are better than lower NPV projects. So, if two projects are mutually exclusive, and *both have positive NPVs,* the one with the higher NPV should be chosen.

NPV is computed using the following equation:

13-2

$$NPV = CF_0 + \frac{CF_1}{(1 + k)^1} + \frac{CF_2}{(1 + k)^2} + \ldots + \frac{CF_n}{(1 + k)^n}$$

$$= \sum_{t=0}^{n} \frac{CF_t}{(1 + k)^t}$$

Here CF_t is the expected net cash flow at Period t, and k is the rate of return required by the firm to invest in this project.[2] Cash outflows (expenditures on the project, such as the cost of buying equipment or building factories) are treated as negative cash flows. For our Projects S and L, only CF_0 is negative, but for many large projects such as the Alaska Pipeline, an electric generating plant, or Chrysler's Neon project, outflows occur for several years before operations begin and cash flows turn positive.

---

[2]The rate of return required by the firm generally is termed the firm's *cost of capital,* because it is the average rate the firm must pay for the funds used to purchase capital projects. The concept of cost of capital will be discussed in Chapter 15.

At a 10 percent required rate of return, Project S's NPV is $161.33:

CASH FLOW TIME LINE FOR PROJECT S:

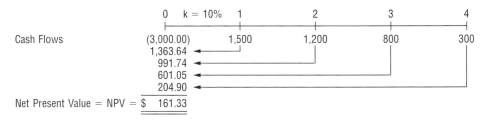

Cash Flows

| | 0 | k = 10% | 1 | 2 | 3 | 4 |

Using the same process, we find $NPV_L = 108.67. On this basis, both projects should be accepted if they are independent, but S should be the one chosen if they are mutually exclusive. Project S is more desirable than Project L even though Project S is expected to provide cash flows totaling $3,800 over its life, which is $300 less than the $4,100 Project L is expected to provide—Project S is more desirable because its cash flows are provided sooner; thus they can be reinvested sooner than those from Project L.

If you look at the cash flow time line for Project S, you can see that it has a positive NPV because the initial investment of $3,000 is recovered on a present value basis prior to the end of the project's life. In fact, if we use the payback concept developed in the previous section, we can compute how long it would take to recapture the initial outlay of $3,000 using the discounted cash flows given in the cash flow time line—the sum of the present values of the cash flows for the first three years is $2,956.43, so all of the $3,000 cost is not recovered until 3 years $+ [($3,000 - $2,956.43) ÷ $204.90] = 3.21$ years. Therefore, on a present value basis, it takes 3.21 years for Project S to recover, or pay back, its

DISCOUNTED PAYBACK
The length of time it takes for a project's *discounted* cash flows to repay the cost of the investment.

original cost. This is called the **discounted payback** of Project S—it is the length of time it takes for a project's *discounted* cash flows to repay the cost of the investment. The discounted payback for Project L is 3.90 years, so Project S is more acceptable. Unlike the traditional payback computation discussed in the previous section, the discounted payback computation *does* consider the time value of money.

It is not hard to calculate the NPV as was done with the time line by using Equation 13-2 and a *regular* calculator, along with the interest rate tables. However, the most efficient way to find the NPV is with a financial calculator. Different calculators are set up somewhat differently, but they all have a section of memory called the "cash flow register," which is used for uneven cash flows such as those in Projects S and L (as opposed to equal annuity cash flows). A solution process for Equation 13-2 is literally programmed into financial calculators, and all you have to do is enter the cash flows (being sure to observe the signs) in the order they occur, along with the value of k = I. At that point you have (in your calculator) this equation:

$$NPV_S = -3,000 + \frac{1,500}{(1.10)^1} + \frac{1,200}{(1.10)^2} + \frac{800}{(1.10)^3} + \frac{300}{(1.10)^4}$$

Notice that the equation has one unknown—NPV. Now all you need to do is ask the calculator to solve the equation for you, which you do by pressing the NPV key (and, on some calculators, the "compute" key). The answer, 161.33, will appear on the screen.[3]

Rationale for the NPV Method

The rationale for the NPV method is straightforward. An NPV of zero signifies that the project's cash flows are just sufficient to repay the invested capital and to provide the required rate of return on that capital. If a project has a positive NPV, then it generates more cash than is needed to service its debt and to provide the required return to shareholders, and this excess cash accrues solely to the firm's stockholders. Therefore, if a firm takes on a project with a positive NPV, the position of the stockholders is improved because the firm's value is greater. In our example, shareholders' wealth would increase by $161.33 if the firm takes on Project S but by only $108.67 if it takes on Project L. Viewed in this manner, it is easy to see why Project S is preferred to Project L, and it also is easy to see the logic of the NPV approach.[4]

Internal Rate of Return (IRR)

In Chapter 7, we presented procedures for finding the yield to maturity, or rate of return, on a bond—if you invest in the bond and hold it to maturity, you can expect to earn the YTM on the money you invested. Exactly the same concepts are employed in capital budgeting when the **internal rate of return (IRR) method** is used. The **IRR** is the rate of return the firm expects to earn if the project is purchased; thus it is defined as the discount rate that equates the

---

INTERNAL RATE OF RETURN (IRR) METHOD
A method of evaluating investment proposals using the rate of return on an asset investment, which is calculated by finding the discount rate that equates the present value of future cash flows to the investment's cost.

IRR
The discount rate that forces the PV of a project's expected cash flows to equal its cost. IRR is similar to the YTM on a bond.

---

[3]Refer to the manual that came with your calculator to determine how the CF function is used. The steps for computing the NPV for Project S using the HP 17B are shown below:

1. Go to the cash flow (CFLO) menu and clear if FLOW(0) = ? does not appear on the screen.
2. Enter CF_0 as follows: 3000 **+/−** **INPUT**.
3. Enter CF_1 as follows: 1500 **INPUT**.
4. Now the calculator will ask you if 1500 is for Period 1 only or if it also is used for several following periods. Because it is used only for Period 1, press **INPUT** to answer "1." Alternatively, you could press **EXIT** and then **#T?** to turn off the prompt for the remainder of the problem. For some problems, you will want to use the repeat feature.
5. Enter the remaining CFs, being sure to turn off the prompt or else to specify "1" for each entry.
6. Once all the CFs have been entered, press **EXIT** and then **CALC**.
7. Now enter k = I = 10% as follows: 10 **I%**.
8. Now press **NPV** to get the answer, NPV = $161.33.

[4]This description of the process is somewhat oversimplified. Both analysts and investors anticipate that firms will identify and accept positive NPV projects, and current stock prices reflect these expectations. Thus, stock prices react to announcements of new capital projects only to the extent that such projects were not already expected. In this sense, we can think of a firm's value as consisting of two parts: (1) the value of its existing assets and (2) the value of its "growth opportunities," or projects with positive NPVs. AT&T is a good example of this: The company has the world's largest long-distance network plus telephone manufacturing facilities, both of which provide current earnings and cash flows, and it has Bell Labs, which has the *potential* for creating new products in the computer/telecommunications area that could be extremely profitable. Security analysts (and investors) thus analyze AT&T as a company with a set of cash-producing assets plus a set of growth opportunities that will materialize if and only if the company can come up with a number of positive NPV projects through its capital budgeting process.

present value of a project's expected cash flows to the investment outlay, or cost. As long as the rate of return *expected* from a project—its IRR—is greater than the rate of return *required* by the firm for such an investment, the project is acceptable.

We can use the following equation to solve for a project's IRR:

13-3

$$CF_0 + \frac{CF_1}{(1 + IRR)^1} + \frac{CF_2}{(1 + IRR)^2} + \cdots + \frac{CF_n}{(1 + IRR)^n} = 0$$

$$\sum_{t=0}^{n} \frac{CF_t}{(1 + IRR)^t} = 0$$

For Project S, the cash flow time line is:

CASH FLOW TIME LINE FOR PROJECT S:

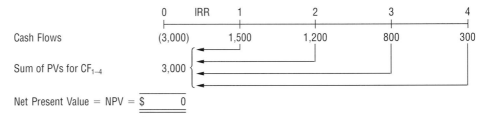

	0	IRR	1	2	3	4
Cash Flows	(3,000)		1,500	1,200	800	300
Sum of PVs for CF$_{1-4}$	3,000					
Net Present Value = NPV =	\$ 0					

Using Equation 13-3, here is the setup for computing IRR$_L$:

$$-3,000 + \frac{1,500}{(1 + IRR)^1} + \frac{1,200}{(1 + IRR)^2} + \frac{800}{(1 + IRR)^3} + \frac{300}{(1 + IRR)^4} = 0$$

Although it is easy to find the NPV without a financial calculator, this is *not* true of the IRR. If the cash flows are constant from year to year, then we have an annuity, and we can use annuity factors discussed in Chapter 6 to find the IRR. However, if the cash flows are not constant, as is generally the case in capital budgeting, then it is difficult to find the IRR without a financial calculator. Without a calculator, you basically have to solve Equation 13-3 by trial and error—try some discount rate (or corresponding PVIF factors) and see if the equation solves to zero, and if it does not, try a different discount rate until you find one that forces the equation to equal zero. The discount rate that causes the equation to equal zero is defined as the IRR. For a realistic project with a fairly long life, the trial and error approach is a tedious, time-consuming task.

Fortunately, it is easy to find IRRs with a financial calculator. You follow almost identical procedures to those used to find the NPV. First, you enter the cash flows as shown on the preceding time line into the calculator's cash flow register. In effect, you have entered the cash flows into the equation shown below the time line. Note that we now have one unknown, IRR, or the discount rate which forces the equation to equal zero. The calculator has been programmed to solve for the IRR, and you activate this program by pressing the key labeled "IRR." Then the calculator solves for IRR and displays it on the screen. Here are the IRRs for Project S and Project L, found using a financial calculator:[5]

$$IRR_S = 13.1\%$$

$$IRR_L = 11.4\%$$

REQUIRED RATE OF RETURN, OR HURDLE RATE
The discount rate (cost of funds) that the IRR must exceed for a project to be considered acceptable.

Projects that have IRRs greater than their **required rates of return,** or **hurdle rates,** *are acceptable investments.* If the hurdle rate required by the firm is 10 percent, then both Project S and Project L are acceptable. If they are mutually exclusive, Project S is more acceptable than Project L because $IRR_S > IRR_L$. If the required rate of return is 14 percent, both projects should be rejected.

Notice that the internal rate of return formula, Equation 13-3, simply is the NPV formula, Equation 13-2, solved for the particular discount rate that forces the NPV to equal zero. Thus, the same basic equation is used for both methods, but in the NPV method the discount rate, k, is specified and the NPV is found, whereas in the IRR method the NPV is set equal to zero, and the interest rate that forces this equality (the IRR) is determined.

Mathematically, the NPV and IRR methods always will lead to the same accept/reject decisions for independent projects: *If a project's NPV is positive, its IRR will exceed k, while if NPV is negative, k will exceed the IRR.* However, NPV and IRR can give conflicting rankings for mutually exclusive projects. This point will be discussed in more detail shortly.

Rationale for the IRR Method

Why is the particular discount rate that equates a project's cost with the present value of its expected cash flows so special? Because the IRR on a project is its expected rate of return, and if this return exceeds the cost of the funds used to finance the project, a surplus remains after paying for the funds, and this surplus accrues to the firm's stockholders. Therefore, *taking on a project whose IRR exceeds its required rate of return, or cost of funds, increases shareholders' wealth.* On the other hand, if the internal rate of return is less than the cost of funds, then taking on the project imposes a cost on current stockholders. Consider what would happen if you borrowed funds at a 15 percent interest rate to invest in the stock market, and the stocks you picked earned only 13 percent. You still have to pay the 15 percent interest, so you end up losing 2 percent on the investment. On the other hand, anything you earn in excess of 15 percent is yours to keep, because only 15 percent in interest has to be paid to the lender. So, 15 percent is your *cost of funds,* which is what you must *require* your investments to earn to break even. It is this "breakeven" characteristic that makes the IRR useful in evaluating capital projects.

---

[5]To find the IRR with an HP 17B, repeat the steps given in footnote 3, then press the IRR% key. You always should get both the NPV and the IRR after entering the input data, before clearing the cash flow register.

INDUSTRY PRACTICE

Practice What We Preach (Teach)

The three capital budgeting techniques presented in this chapter traditionally have been considered the most popular by corporate financial managers. Just how popular are they? Do firms use methods that help to maximize value? A recent study of some of the 1990 *Business Week* 1000 firms provides insight concerning which methods companies use to make capital budgeting decisions.[1] The results indicate that each of the methods discussed in this chapter is relied on to some extent to help to make final decisions about the acceptability of capital budgeting projects. About 60 percent of the companies indicated that they use the traditional payback period either as a primary or as a secondary method for capital budgeting decisions. But, it appears that less than one third of the companies rely on payback as the *primary* capital budgeting technique—this represents a significant decrease from three decades ago when the number was greater than 60 percent. Nearly 90 percent of the companies responded that they use such present value techniques

as net present value (NPV) and internal rate of return (IRR) either as a primary or as a secondary capital budgeting decision methodology. It is interesting to note that about 60 percent of the companies indicated that *both* NPV and IRR are the primary techniques used to make capital budgeting decisions. It seems, for the most part, that financial managers recognize these techniques provide correct decisions with respect to value maximization. The financial managers also were asked whether using IRR presented any problems, especially with regard to multiple internal rates of return and ranking differences when compared to NPV. Most of the financial managers indicated either that they had not heard of these problems or that such problems rarely occurred. In addition, it appears that most of the companies that face such problems chose to use NPV rather than IRR for their capital budgeting decisions.

For the most part, it appears that companies use more sophisticated capital budgeting techniques today than in previous times. Even those firms that prefer payback period seem to have switched to the discounted payback period. Thus, indications are that firms do use the methods we profess in finance courses such as this.

[1]Glenn H. Petry and James Sprow, "The Theory of Finance in the 1990s," *The Quarterly Review of Economics and Finance*, (Winter 1993), pp. 359–381.

Self-Test Questions

What three methods for evaluating capital budgeting proposals were discussed in this section?

Describe each method, and give the rationale for its use.

What two methods always lead to the same accept/reject decision for independent projects?

What two pieces of information does the payback provide that are not provided by the other methods?

Comparison of the NPV and IRR Methods

The NPV for Project S is $161.33. What does this mean? If the project is purchased, the value of the firm will increase by $161.33. The IRR for Project S is 13.1 percent. What does this mean? If a firm purchases Project S, it will earn a 13.1 percent rate of return on its investment. We generally measure wealth in dollars, so the NPV method should be used to accomplish the goal of maximizing shareholders' wealth. In reality, using the IRR method could lead to investment decisions that increase, but do not maximize, wealth. We choose to discuss the IRR method and compare it to the NPV method because many corporate executives are familiar with the meaning of IRR, it is entrenched in the corporate world, and it does have some virtues. Therefore, it is important that finance students understand the IRR method and be prepared to explain why, at times, a project with a lower IRR might be preferable to one with a higher IRR.

NPV Profiles

NET PRESENT VALUE (NPV) PROFILE
A curve showing the relationship between a project's NPV and various discount rates (required rates of return).

A graph that shows a project's NPV at various discount rates (required rates of return) is termed the project's **net present value (NPV) profile;** profiles for Project L and Project S are shown in Figure 13-3. To construct the profiles, we first note that at a zero discount rate, the NPV simply is the total of the undiscounted cash flows of the project; thus, at a zero discount rate NPV_S = $800, and NPV_L = $1,100. These values are plotted as the Y intercepts in Figure 13-3. Next, we calculate the projects' NPVs at various discount rates, say 5 percent, 10 percent, and 15 percent, and plot these values. The points plotted on our graph for each project are shown at the bottom of the figure.[6]

Recall that the IRR is defined as the discount rate at which a project's NPV equals zero. Therefore, the point where its *NPV profile crosses the X axis indicates a project's internal rate of return.* Because we calculated IRR_S and IRR_L in an earlier section, we have two other points which we can use in plotting the projects' NPV profiles. NPV profiles can be very useful in project analysis, and we will use them often in the remainder of the chapter.[7]

NPVs and the Required Rate of Return

CROSSOVER RATE
The discount rate at which the NPV profiles of two projects cross and, thus, at which the projects' NPVs are equal.

Figure 13-3 shows that the NPV profiles of both Project L and Project S decline as the discount rate increases. But notice in the figure that Project L has the higher NPV at low discount rates, while NPV_S exceeds NPV_L if the discount rate is greater than 8.1 percent. We term this point the **crossover rate** because, at a discount rate equal to 8.1 percent, NPV_S = NPV_L = $268—if k < 8.1 percent, NPV_S < NPV_L, and if k > 8.1 percent, NPV_S > NPV_L.[8] Notice also that Project L's NPV is "more sensitive" to changes in the discount rate than is NPV_S; that is, Project L's net present value profile has the steeper slope, indicating that a given change in k has a larger effect on NPV_L than on NPV_S.

To see why Project L has the greater sensitivity, recall first that the cash flows from Project S are received faster than those from Project L—in a payback sense,

---

[6]To calculate the points with a financial calculator, enter the cash flows into the cash flow register, enter k = I = 0, and press the NPV key to find the NPV at a zero cost of capital. Then enter k = I = 5 to override the zero, and press NPV to get the NPV at 5 percent. Repeat these steps for 10, 15, and 20 percent.

[7]Notice that the NPV profiles are curved—they are *not* straight lines. Also, the NPVs approach the t = 0 cash flow (the cost of the project) as the discount rate increases without limit. This occurs because, at an infinitely high discount rate, the PV of the inflows would be zero, so NPV at (k = ∞) is CF_0, which in our example is −$3,000.

[8]The crossover rate is easy to calculate. Simply go back to Figure 13-1, where we first show the two projects' cash flows. Now calculate the difference in the cash flows for Project S and Project L in each year. The differences are CF_S − CF_L = $0, + $1,100, + $300, −$500, and −$1,200, respectively. Enter these values into the cash flow register of a financial calculator, press the IRR key, and the crossover rate, 8.11, appears. Be sure to enter CF_0 = 0.

FIGURE 13-3

NPV Profiles for Project S and Project L

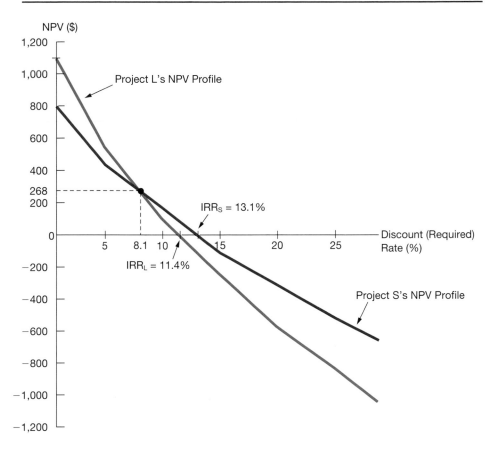

Discount Rate	NPV$_S$	NPV$_L$
0%	$800.00	$1,100.00
5	454.89	554.32
10	161.33	108.67
15	(90.74)	(259.24)
20	(309.03)	(565.97)

S is a short-term project, while L is a long-term project. The impact of an increase in the discount rate is much greater on distant than on near-term cash flows. To illustrate, consider the present value of $100 to be received in one year. If the $100 is discounted at 10 percent its present value is $90.91, but if it is discounted at 15 percent its present value is $86.96; so a 5 percentage point increase in the discount rate results in a $(86.96 - 90.91) \div 90.91 = 4.3$ percent decrease in the present value of the $100 to be received in one year. Now consider the present value of $100 to be received in ten years. If the discount rate is 10 percent, the present value of this $100 is $38.55; but if the discount rate is 15 percent, the present value of the $100 is $24.72; so a 5 percentage point increase in the discount rate results in a $(24.72 - 38.55) \div 38.55 = 35.9$ percent decrease in the present value. Thus, the farther into the future the cash flows are, the greater their sensitivity to discount rate changes. Consequently, if a project has most of its cash flows coming in the early years, its NPV will not be lowered very much if the required rate of return increases, but a project whose cash flows come later will be severely penalized by high capital costs. Accordingly, Project L, which has its largest cash flows in the later years, is hurt badly when the required rate of return is high, while Project S, which has relatively rapid cash flows, is affected less by high discount rates.

Independent Projects

If two projects are *independent,* then the NPV and IRR criteria always lead to the same *accept/reject decision*: If NPV analysis indicates a project is acceptable, it also would be acceptable using IRR analysis. To see why this is so, look back at Figure 13-3, focus on Project L's profile, and notice that (1) the IRR criterion for acceptance is that the required rate of return is less than (or to the left of) the IRR and (2) whenever the required rate of return is less than the IRR, its NPV is positive. Thus, at any required rate of return less than 11.4 percent, Project L will be acceptable by both the NPV and the IRR criteria, while both methods reject the project if the required rate of return is greater than 11.4 percent. Project S— and all other independent projects under consideration—could be analyzed similarly, and *in every case, if a project is acceptable using the IRR method, then the NPV method also will show it is acceptable.*

Mutually Exclusive Projects

Now assume that Project S and Project L are *mutually exclusive* rather than independent. That is, we can choose either Project S or Project L, or we can reject both, but we cannot accept both projects. Notice in Figure 13-3 that as long as the required rate of return is *greater than* the crossover rate of 8.1 percent, NPV_S is larger than NPV_L. IRR_S exceeds IRR_L; therefore, if k is greater than the crossover rate of 8.1 percent, the two methods lead to the selection of the same project. However, if the required rate of return is less than 8.1 percent, the NPV method ranks Project L higher. But, because $IRR_S > IRR_L$, *a conflict exists*—if the required rate of return is less than the crossover rate, NPV says choose Project L over Project S, while IRR says the opposite. Which answer is correct? Logic suggests that the NPV method is better because it selects the project that adds the most to shareholder wealth.

There are two basic conditions that can cause NPV profiles to cross and thus lead to conflicts between NPV and IRR: (1) when *project size (or scale) differences* exist, meaning that the cost of one project is larger than that of the other, or (2) when *timing differences* exist, meaning that the timing of cash flows from the two projects differs such that most of the cash flows from one project come in the early years and most of the cash flows from the other project come in the later years, as occurs with Project S and Project L.[9]

---

[9]Of course, it is possible for mutually exclusive projects to differ with respect to both scale and timing. Also, if mutually exclusive projects have different lives (as opposed to different cash flow patterns over a common life), this introduces further complications, and for meaningful comparisons, some mutually exclusive projects must be evaluated over a common life.

When either size or timing differences occur, the firm will have different amounts of funds to invest in the various years, depending on which of the two mutually exclusive projects it chooses. For example, if one project costs more than the other, then the firm will have more money at t = 0 to invest elsewhere if it selects the smaller project. Similarly, for projects of equal size, the one with the larger early cash inflows provides more funds for reinvestment in the early years. Given this situation, the rate of return at which differential cash flows can be invested is an important consideration.

The critical issue in resolving conflicts between mutually exclusive projects is this: How useful is it to generate cash flows earlier rather than later? The value of early cash flows depends on the rate at which we can reinvest these cash flows. *The NPV method implicitly assumes that the rate at which cash flows can be reinvested is the required rate of return, whereas the IRR method implies that the firm has the opportunity to reinvest at the project's IRR.* These assumptions are inherent in the mathematics of the discounting process. The cash flows actually can be withdrawn as dividends by the stockholders and spent on beer and pizza, but the NPV method still assumes that cash flows can be reinvested at the required rate of return, while the IRR method assumes reinvestment at the project's IRR.

Which is the better assumption—that cash flows can be reinvested at the required rate of return or that they can be reinvested at the project's IRR? The firm's required rate of return actually represents the rate the firm pays for the funds it uses to purchase capital budgeting projects—this rate is called the firm's *cost of capital.* At the very least, a firm could repurchase the bonds and stocks it has issued to raise capital budgeting funds. If a firm did repurchase its *capital* using the cash flows from a project, it would be investing at the cost of capital, or required rate of return. On the other hand, to reinvest at the internal rate of return associated with a capital project, the firm would have to be able to reinvest the project's cash flows in another project with an identical IRR—such projects generally do not exist or it is not feasible to reinvest in such projects. Consequently, we conclude that the *best* **reinvestment rate assumption** *is the required rate of return, which is implicit in the NPV method.* This, in turn, leads us to prefer the NPV method, at least for firms willing and able to obtain capital at a cost reasonably close to their current cost of capital.

We should reiterate that, *when projects are independent, the NPV and IRR methods both give exactly the same accept/reject decision.* However, *when evaluating mutually exclusive projects,* especially those that differ in scale and/or timing, *the NPV method should be used.*

REINVESTMENT RATE ASSUMPTION
The assumption that cash flows from a project can be reinvested (1) at the cost of capital, if using the NPV method, or (2) at the internal rate of return, if using the IRR method.

Multiple IRRs

There is one other situation in which the IRR approach might not be usable—when projects have unconventional cash flow patterns. A project has a *conventional* cash flow pattern if it has cash outflows (costs) in one or more periods at the beginning of its life followed by a series of cash inflows. If, however, a project has a large cash outflow either sometime during or at the end of its life, then it has an *unconventional* cash flow pattern. Projects with unconventional cash flow patterns present unique difficulties when the IRR method is used, including the possibility of **multiple IRRs.**

MULTIPLE IRRs
The situation in which a project has two or more IRRs.

Multiple IRRs result from the manner in which Equation 13-3 must be solved to arrive at a project's IRR. The mathematical rationale and the solution to multiple IRRs will not be discussed here. Instead, we want you to be aware that multiple IRRs can exist, because this possibility complicates capital budgeting evaluation using the IRR method. In addition, many financial calculators cannot compute the IRR for projects that have unconventional cash flows, because there is not a single solution. In such cases, you would have to use NPV profiles, which essentially is a trial-and-error process.

How many IRRs can a project with an unconventional cash flow pattern have? Each time there is an interruption in the direction of the cash flows associated with the implementation of the project, there will be an IRR solution. For example, a conventional cash flow pattern has only one net cash outflow at the beginning of the project's life, so the direction of the cash flows changes (is interrupted) once from negative (outflow) to positive (inflow), and there is only one IRR solution. A project that requires two net cash outflows in nonconsecutive years after the project is in operation will have three IRR solutions because the cash flow pattern has three direction changes, or interruptions—one after the initial cost is paid and two others caused by the net cash outflows required later in the life of the project. Figure 13-4 illustrates the multiple IRR problem with a strip mining project that costs $1.6 million. The mine will produce a cash inflow of $10 million at the end of Year 1, but $10 million must be spent at the end of Year 2 to restore the land to its original condition. Two IRRs exist for this project—25 percent and 400 percent. The NPV profile for the mine shows that the project would have a positive NPV, and thus be acceptable, if the firm's required rate of return is between 25 percent and 400 percent.

FIGURE 13-4

NPV Profile for Project M

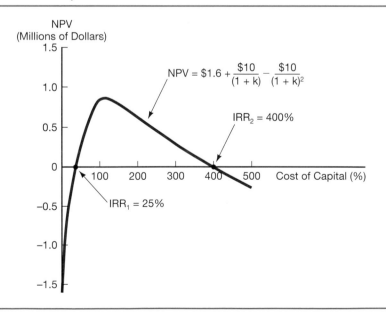

Self-Test Questions

Describe how NPV profiles are constructed.

What is the crossover rate, and how does it affect the choice between mutually exclusive projects?

What are the two basic conditions that can lead to conflicts between the NPV and IRR methods?

What is the underlying cause of conflicts between the NPV and IRR methods?

If a conflict exists, should the capital budgeting decision be made on the basis of the NPV or the IRR ranking? Why?

Explain the difference between conventional and unconventional cash flow patterns.

What is the "multiple IRR problem," and what condition is necessary for its occurrence?

Conclusions on the Capital Budgeting Decision Methods

In this chapter, we have discussed the methods most often used by firms to make capital budgeting decisions. In this discussion, we compared the methods against one another to highlight their relative strengths and weaknesses, and in the process we probably created the impression that "sophisticated" firms should use only one method in the decision process—NPV. However, virtually all capital budgeting decisions are analyzed by computer, so it is easy to calculate and list all the decision measures: payback, discounted payback, NPV, and IRR. In making the accept/reject decision, most large, sophisticated firms such as IBM, GE, and General Motors calculate and consider multiple measures because each provides decision makers with a somewhat different piece of relevant information.

Payback and discounted payback provide an indication of both the risk and the *liquidity* of a project—a long payback means that (1) the investment dollars will be locked up for many years, hence the project is relatively illiquid, and (2) the project's cash flows must be forecast far out into the future, hence the project probably is quite risky. A good analogy for this is the bond valuation process. An investor should never compare the yields to maturity on two bonds without considering their terms to maturity because a bond's riskiness is significantly influenced by its maturity.

NPV is important because it gives a direct measure of the dollar benefit (on a present value basis) to the firm's shareholders, so we regard NPV as the best single measure of *profitability*. IRR also measures profitability, but here it is expressed as a percentage rate of return, which many decision makers, especially nonfinancial managers, seem to prefer. Further, IRR contains information concerning a project's "safety margin," which is not inherent in NPV. To illustrate, consider the following two projects: Project T costs $10,000 at t = 0 and is expected to return $16,500 at the end of 1 year, while Project B costs $100,000 and has an expected payoff of $115,500 after 1 year. At a 10 percent required rate of return, both projects have an NPV of $5,000, so by the NPV rule we should be indifferent between the two. However, Project T actually provides a much larger margin for error. Even if its realized cash inflow were almost 40 percent below the $16,500 forecast, the firm would still recover its $10,000 investment. On the other hand, if Project B's inflows fell by only 14 percent from the forecasted $115,500, the firm would not recover its investment. Further, if no inflows were generated at all, the firm would lose only $10,000 with Project T but $100,000 if it took on Project B.

The NPV contains no information about either the "safety margin" inherent in a project's cash flow forecasts or the amount of capital at risk, but the IRR does provide "safety margin" information—Project T's IRR is a whopping 65.0 percent, while Project B's IRR is only 15.5 percent. As a result, the realized return could fall substantially for Project T, and it would still make money. Note, though, that the IRR method has a reinvestment assumption that probably is unrealistic, and it is possible for projects to have multiple IRRs. Both of these problems can be corrected using the modified IRR calculation that is discussed in Appendix 13A.

In summary, the different methods provide different types of information to decision makers. Because it is easy to calculate them, all should be considered in the decision process. For any specific decision, more weight might be given to one method than another, but it would be foolish to ignore the information provided by any of the methods.

Self-Test Questions

Describe the advantages and disadvantages of the capital budgeting methods discussed in this chapter.

Should capital budgeting decisions be made solely on the basis of a project's NPV?

The Post-audit

POST-AUDIT
A comparison of the actual and expected results for a given capital project.

An important aspect of the capital budgeting process is the **post-audit,** which involves (1) comparing actual results with those predicted by the project's sponsors and (2) explaining why any differences occurred. For example, many firms require that the operating divisions send a monthly report for the first six months after a project goes into operation, and a quarterly report thereafter, until the project's results are up to expectations. From then on, reports on the project are handled like those of other operations.

The post-audit has two main purposes:

1. **Improve forecasts.** When decision makers are forced to compare their projections to actual outcomes, there is a tendency for estimates to improve. Conscious or unconscious biases are observed and eliminated; new forecasting methods are sought as the need for them becomes apparent; and people simply tend to do everything better, including forecasting, if they know that their actions are being monitored.
2. **Improve operations.** Businesses are run by people, and people can perform at higher or lower levels of efficiency. When a divisional team has made a forecast about an investment, its members are, in a sense, putting their reputations on the line. If costs are above predicted levels, sales below expectations, and so on, executives in production, marketing, and other areas will strive to im-

prove operations and to bring results into line with forecasts. In a discussion related to this point, an IBM executive made this statement: "You academicians worry only about making good decisions. In business, we also worry about making decisions good."

The post-audit is not a simple process—a number of factors can cause complications. First, we must recognize that each element of the cash flow forecast is subject to uncertainty, so a percentage of all projects undertaken by any reasonably venturesome firm will necessarily go awry. This fact must be considered when appraising the performances of the operating executives who submit capital expenditure requests. Second, projects sometimes fail to meet expectations for reasons beyond the control of the operating executives and for reasons that no one could realistically be expected to anticipate. For example, the 1990–1992 recession adversely affected many projects. Third, it is often difficult to separate the operating results of one investment from those of a larger system. Although some projects stand alone and permit ready identification of costs and revenues, the actual cost savings that result from a new computer system, for example, might be very hard to measure. Fourth, it is often hard to hand out blame or praise because the executives who were actually responsible for a given decision might have moved on by the time the results of a long-term investment are known.

Because of these difficulties, some firms tend to play down the importance of the post-audit. However, observations of both businesses and governmental units suggest that the best-run and most successful organizations are the ones that put the greatest emphasis on post-audits. Accordingly, we regard the post-audit as being one of the most important elements in a good capital budgeting system.

Self-Test Questions

What is done in the post-audit?

Identify several purposes of the post-audit.

What are some factors that can cause complications in the post-audit?

ETHICAL DILEMMA

This Is a Good Investment—Be Sure the Numbers Show That It Is!

Oliver Greene is the assistant to the financial manager at Cybercomp, Inc., which is a company that develops software to drive network communications for personal computers. Oliver joined Cybercomp three years ago, following his graduation from college. His primary responsibility has been to evaluate capital budgeting projects and make investment recommendations to the board of directors. Oliver enjoys his job very much—he often finds himself challenged with interesting tasks, and he is paid extremely well for what he does.

Last week, Oliver started evaluating the capital projects that have been proposed for investment this year. One of the proposals is to purchase NetWare Products, a company that manufactures circuit boards, called network cards, which are required to achieve communication connectivity between personal computers. Cybercomp packages network cards with the software it sells, but it currently purchases them from another manufacturer. The proposal, which was submitted by Nadine Wilson, Cybercomp's CEO, suggests the company can reduce costs and increase profit margins by producing the network cards in house.

Oliver barely had time to scan the proposal when he was summoned to Mrs. Wilson's office. The meeting was short and to the point. Mrs. Wilson instructed Oliver to "make the numbers for NetWare Products look good, because we *want* to buy that company." She also gave Oliver an evaluation of NetWare completed two years ago by an independent appraiser that suggests NetWare might not be worth the amount Cybercomp is willing to pay. Mrs. Wilson instructed Oliver to find a way to rebut the findings of the report.

Oliver was troubled by the meeting he had with Mrs. Wilson. His "gut feeling" was that something was wrong. But, he hadn't yet had time to carefully examine the proposal—his evaluation was very cursory, and he was far from making a final decision concerning the acceptability of the capital budgeting project proposed by Mrs. Wilson. Oliver felt like he needed much more information before forming a final recommendation.

Oliver has spent the entire day examining the appraisal report provided by Mrs. Wilson and trying to gather additional information about the proposed investment. The report contains some background information concerning NetWare's operations, but crucial financial data are missing. Further investigation into NetWare Products has produced little information. Oliver has discovered that the company's stock is closely held by a small group of investors who owns numerous businesses and who generously contributes to the local university, which happens to be Mrs. Wilson's alma mater. In addition, Oliver's secretary has informed him that the gossip around the "water cooler" at Cybercomp is that Mrs. Wilson and the owners of NetWare are old college buddies, and she might even have a stake in NetWare.

This morning, Mrs. Wilson called Oliver and repeated her feelings concerning the purchase of NetWare. This time she said: "We really want to purchase NetWare. Some people might not believe so, but this is a very good deal. It's your job to make the numbers work—that's why we pay you the big bucks." As a result of the conversation, Oliver has the impression his job might be jeopardized if he doesn't make the "right" decision. This added pressure has made Oliver very tense. What should he do? What would you do if you were Oliver? Would your answer change if you knew Mrs. Wilson had recently sold much of her Cybercomp stock?

Summary

This chapter discussed the capital budgeting process, and the key concepts covered are listed below.

- **Capital budgeting** is the process of analyzing potential fixed asset investments. Capital budgeting decisions are probably the most important ones financial managers must make.
- The **payback period** is defined as the expected number of years required to recover a project's cost. The regular payback method ignores cash flows beyond the payback period, and it does not consider the time value of money. The payback does, however, provide an indication of a project's risk and liquidity because it shows how long the invested capital will be "at risk."
- The **discounted payback method** is similar to the regular payback method except that it discounts cash flows at the project's required rate of return. Like the regular payback, it ignores cash flows beyond the discounted payback period.
- The **net present value (NPV) method** discounts all cash flows at the project's required rate of return and then sums those cash flows. The project is accepted if this sum, called the NPV, is positive.
- The **internal rate of return (IRR)** is defined as the discount rate which forces a project's NPV to equal zero. The project is accepted if the IRR is greater than the project's required rate of return.
- The NPV and IRR methods make the same accept/reject decisions for **independent projects,** but if projects are **mutually exclusive,** then ranking

Capital Budgeting in the Small Firm

The allocation of capital in small firms is as important as it is in large ones. In fact, given their lack of access to the capital markets, it is often more important in the small firm because the funds necessary to correct mistakes might not be available. Also, large firms with capital budgets of $100 million or more allocate capital to numerous projects, so a mistake on one project can be offset by successes with others—large firms benefit from project diversification.

In spite of the importance of capital expenditures to small business, studies of the way capital budgeting decisions are made generally suggest that many small firms use "back-of-the-envelope" analysis, or perhaps no analysis at all. For example, when L. R. Runyon studied 214 firms with net worths of from $500,000 to $1,000,000, he found that almost 70 percent relied upon either payback or some other questionable criteria; only 14 percent used a discounted cash flow analysis; and about 9 percent indicated that they used no formal analysis at all.[1] Studies of larger firms, on the other hand, generally find that most analyze capital budgeting decisions using discounted cash flow techniques.

We are left with a puzzle. Capital budgeting is clearly important to small firms, yet these firms tend not to use the tools that have been developed to improve capital budgeting decisions. Why does this situation exist? One argument is that managers of small firms simply are not well trained; they are unsophisticated. This argument suggests that the managers would make greater use of sophisticated techniques if they understood them better. Another argument relates to the fact that management talent is a scarce resource in small firms, and the demands on their time might be such that they simply cannot afford the time to analyze projects using sophisticated methods, even if they did understand them. A third argument relates to the cost of analyzing capital projects. Some of the analyses' costs are fixed, and it might not be economical to incur them if the project itself is relatively small. This argument suggests that small firms with small projects might actually be making the sensible decision when they rely upon management's "gut feeling."

In his study, Runyon also found that small firms tend to be cash oriented. They are concerned with basic survival, so they tend to look at expenditures from the standpoint of near-term effects on cash. This cash and survival orientation leads to a focus on a relatively short time horizon, and this, in turn, might lead to an emphasis on the payback method. The limitations of payback are well known, but in spite of those limitations, the technique is popular in small business, as it gives the firm a "feel" for when the cash committed to an investment will be recovered and thus be available to repay loans or for new opportunities. Therefore, small firms that are cash oriented and have limited managerial resources might find the payback method an appealing compromise between the need for extensive analysis on the one hand and the high costs of analysis on the other.

Remember from our discussion in the chapter that the single most appealing argument for the use of net present value in capital budgeting decisions is that NPV gives an explicit measure of the effect of the investment on the value of the firm: If NPV is positive, the investment will increase the value of the firm and make its owners wealthier. In small firms, however, the stock often is not traded in public markets, so its value cannot be observed. Also, for reasons of control many small business owners and managers might not want to broaden ownership by going public. It is difficult to argue for value-based techniques when the value of the firm and its required rate of return are unobservable. Furthermore, in a closely held firm the objectives of the individual owner-manager might extend beyond the firm's monetary value.

In general, we know that small firms make less extensive use of DCF techniques than larger firms. This might be a rational decision resulting from a conscious or subconscious conclusion that the costs of sophisticated analyses outweigh their benefits; it might reflect nonmonetary goals of small businesses' owner-managers; or it might reflect difficulties in estimating the values needed for DCF analysis but not payback. However, nonuse of DCF methods also might reflect a weakness in many small business organizations. *We simply do not know.* We do know that small businesses must do all they can to compete effectively with big business, and to the extent that a small business fails to use DCF methods because its manager is unsophisticated or uninformed, it might be putting itself at a serious competitive disadvantage.

[1] L. R. Runyon, "Capital Expenditure Decision Making in Small Firms," *Journal of Business Research,* September 1983, pp. 389–397.

conflicts can arise. If conflicts arise, the NPV method generally should be used. The NPV and IRR methods are both superior to the payback, but NPV is generally the single best measure of a project's profitability.

- The NPV method assumes that cash flows can be reinvested at the firm's required rate of return, while the IRR method assumes reinvestment at the project's IRR. Because **reinvestment at the required rate of return generally is a better (closer to the truth) assumption,** the NPV is superior to the IRR.
- Sophisticated managers consider several of the project evaluation measures because the different measures provide different types of information.
- The **post-audit** is a key element of capital budgeting. By comparing actual results with predicted results, and then determining why differences occurred, decision makers can improve both their operations and their forecasts of projects' outcomes.
- Small firms tend to use the payback method rather than a "sophisticated" method. This might be a rational decision because (1) the *cost* of a DCF analysis *might outweigh the benefits* for the project being considered, (2) the firm's *required rate of return cannot be estimated accurately,* or (3) the small business owner might be considering *nonmonetary goals.*

Although this chapter has presented the basic elements of the capital budgeting process, there are many other aspects of this crucial topic. Some of the more important ones are discussed in the following chapter.

Questions

13-1   How is a project classification scheme (for example, replacement, expansion into new markets, and so forth) used in the capital budgeting process?

13-2   Explain why the NPV of a relatively long-term project, defined as one for which a high percentage of its cash flows is expected in the distant future, is more sensitive to changes in the required rate of return than is the NPV of a short-term project.

13-3   Explain why, if two mutually exclusive projects are being compared, the short-term project might have the higher ranking under the NPV criterion if the required rate of return is high, but the long-term project might be deemed better if the required rate of return is low. Would changes in the required rate of return ever cause a change in the IRR ranking of two such projects?

13-4   In what sense is a reinvestment rate assumption embodied in the NPV and IRR methods? What is the assumed reinvestment rate of each method?

13-5   "If a firm has no mutually exclusive projects, only independent ones, and it also has both a constant required rate of return and projects with conventional cash flow patterns, then the NPV and IRR methods will always lead to identical capital budgeting decisions." Discuss this statement. What does it imply about using the IRR method in lieu of the NPV method? If each of the assumptions made in the question were changed (one by one), how would these changes affect your answer?

13-6   Are there conditions under which a firm might be better off if it were to choose a machine with a rapid payback rather than one with a larger NPV?

13-7   A firm has $100 million available for capital expenditures. It is considering investing in one of two projects; each has a cost of $100 million. Project A has an IRR of 20 percent and an NPV of $9 million. It will be terminated at the end of one year at a profit of $20 million, resulting in an immediate increase in earnings per share (EPS). Project B, which cannot be postponed, has an IRR of 30 percent and an NPV of $50 million. However, the firm's short-run EPS will be reduced if it accepts Project B because no revenues will be generated for several years.

 a. Should the short-run effects on EPS influence the choice between the two projects?

 b. How might situations like the one described here influence a firm's decision to use payback as a part of the capital budgeting process?

Self-Test Problems

(Solutions Appear in Appendix B)

Key terms   **ST-1**   Define each of the following terms:

 a. the capital budget; capital budgeting; strategic business plan

 b. regular payback period; discounted payback period

 c. independent projects; mutually exclusive projects

 d. DCF techniques; net present value (NPV) method

 e. internal rate of return (IRR) method; IRR

 f. NPV profile; crossover rate

 g. unconventional cash flow patterns; multiple IRRs

 h. hurdle rate; required rate of return; cost of capital

 i. reinvestment rate assumption

 j. post-audit

Project analysis   **ST-2**   You are a financial analyst for Damon Electronics Company. The director of capital budgeting has asked you to analyze two proposed capital investments, Projects X and Y. Each project has a cost of $10,000, and the required rate of return for each project is 12 percent. The projects' expected net cash flows are as follows:

	Expected Net Cash Flows	
Year	Project X	Project Y
0	$(10,000)	$(10,000)
1	6,500	3,500
2	3,000	3,500
3	3,000	3,500
4	1,000	3,500

 a. Calculate each project's payback period, net present value (NPV), and internal rate of return (IRR).

 b. Which project or projects should be accepted if they are independent?

 c. Which project should be accepted if they are mutually exclusive?

 d. How might a change in the required rate of return produce a conflict between the NPV and IRR rankings of these two projects? Would this conflict exist if k were 5%? (Hint: Plot the NPV profiles.)

 e. Why does the conflict exist?

Problems

Payback, NPV, and   **13-1**   Project K has a cost of $52,125, and its expected net cash inflows are $12,000 per
IRR calculations   year for 8 years.

 a. What is the project's payback period (to the closest year)?

      b. The required rate of return for the project is 12 percent. What is the project's NPV?

      c. What is the project's IRR? (Hint: Recognize that the project is an annuity.)

      d. What is the project's discounted payback period, assuming a 12 percent required rate of return?

NPV and IRR analysis   **13-2** Derek's Donuts is considering two mutually exclusive investments. The projects' expected net cash flows are as follows:

| | **Expected Net Cash Flows** | |
Year	Project A	Project B
0	$(300)	$(405)
1	(387)	134
2	(193)	134
3	(100)	134
4	500	134
5	500	134
6	850	134
7	100	0

      a. Construct NPV profiles for Projects A and B.

      b. What is each project's IRR?

      c. If you were told that each project's required rate of return was 12 percent, which project should be selected? If the required rate of return was 15 percent, what would the proper choice be?

      d. Looking at the NPV profiles constructed in Part a, what is the approximate crossover rate, and what is its significance?

Timing differences   **13-3** The Southwestern Oil Exploration Company is considering two mutually exclusive plans for extracting oil on property for which it has mineral rights. Both plans call for the expenditure of $12,000,000 to drill development wells. Under Plan A, all the oil will be extracted in one year, producing a cash flow at t = 1 of $14,400,000. Under Plan B, cash flows will be $2,100,000 per year for 20 years.

      a. Construct NPV profiles for Plans A and B, identify each project's IRR, and indicate the approximate crossover rate of return.

      b. Suppose a company has a required rate of return of 12 percent, and it can get unlimited capital at that cost. Is it logical to assume that it would take on all available independent projects (of average risk) with returns greater than 12 percent? Further, if all available projects with returns greater than 12 percent have been taken on, would this mean that cash flows from past investments would have an opportunity cost of only 12 percent, because all the firm could do with these cash flows would be to replace money that has a cost of 12 percent? Finally, does this imply that the required rate of return is the correct rate to assume for the reinvestment of a project's cash flows?

Scale differences   **13-4** The Chaplinsky Publishing Company is considering two mutually exclusive expansion plans. Plan A calls for the expenditure of $40 million on a large-scale, integrated plant which will provide an expected cash flow stream of $6.4 million per year for 20 years. Plan B calls for the expenditure of $12 million to build a somewhat less efficient, more labor-intensive plant which has an expected cash flow stream of $2.72 million per year for 20 years. Chaplinsky's required rate of return is 10 percent.

      a. Calculate each project's NPV and IRR.

      b. Graph the NPV profiles for Plan A and Plan B. From the NPV profiles constructed, approximate the crossover rate.

c. Give a logical explanation, based on reinvestment rates and opportunity costs, for why the NPV method is better than the IRR method when the firm's required rate of return is constant at some value such as 10 percent.

Exam-Type Problems

The problems included in this section are set up in such a way that they could be used as multiple-choice exam problems.

NPVs, IRRs, and payback for independent projects

13-5 Olsen Engineering is considering including two pieces of equipment, a truck and an overhead pulley system, in this year's capital budget. The projects are independent. The cash outlay for the truck is $17,100 and that for the pulley system is $22,430. Each piece of equipment has an estimated life of 5 years. The annual after-tax cash flow expected to be provided by the truck is $5,100, and for the pulley, it is $7,500. The firm's required rate of return is 14 percent. Calculate the IRR, the NPV, and the payback period for each project, and indicate which project(s) should be accepted.

NPVs and IRRs for mutually exclusive projects

13-6 Horrigan Industries must choose between a gas-powered and an electric-powered forklift truck for moving materials in its factory. Since both forklifts perform the same function, the firm will choose only one. (They are mutually exclusive investments.) The electric-powered truck will cost more, but it will be less expensive to operate; it will cost $22,000, whereas the gas-powered truck will cost $17,500. The required rate of return that applies to both investments is 12 percent. The life for both types of truck is estimated to be 6 years, during which time the net cash flows for the electric-powered truck will be $6,290 per year and those for the gas-powered truck will be $5,000 per year. Annual net cash flows include depreciation expenses. Calculate the NPV and IRR for each type of truck, and decide which to recommend.

Capital budgeting decisions

13-7 Project S costs $15,000 and is expected to produce benefits (cash flows) of $4,500 per year for 5 years. Project L costs $37,500 and is expected to produce cash flows of $11,000 per year for 5 years. Calculate the NPV, IRR, and payback period for each project, assuming a required rate of return of 14 percent. If the projects are independent, which project(s) should be selected? If they are mutually exclusive projects, which project actually should be selected?

Present value of costs

13-8 The Cordell Coffee Company is evaluating the within-plant distribution system for its new roasting, grinding, and packing plant. The two alternatives are (1) a conveyor system with a high initial cost but low annual operating costs and (2) several forklift trucks, which cost less but have considerably higher operating costs. The decision to construct the plant has already been made, and the choice here will have no effect on the overall revenues of the project. The required rate of return for the plant is 9 percent, and the projects' expected net costs are listed below:

	Expected Net Cash Flows	
Year	Conveyor	Forklift
0	$(300,000)	$(120,000)
1	(66,000)	(96,000)
2	(66,000)	(96,000)
3	(66,000)	(96,000)
4	(66,000)	(96,000)
5	(66,000)	(96,000)

a. What is the present value of costs of each alternative? Which method should be chosen?

b. What is the IRR of each alternative?

NPV and IRR   **13-9**   Your company is considering two mutually exclusive projects, C and R, whose costs and cash flows are shown below:

Year	Project C	Project R
0	$(14,000)	$(22,840)
1	8,000	8,000
2	6,000	8,000
3	2,000	8,000
4	3,000	8,000

The projects are equally risky, and their required rate of return is 12 percent. You must make a recommendation concerning which project should be purchased. To determine which is more appropriate, compute the NPV and IRR of each project.

NPV and IRR   **13-10**   The after-tax cash flows for two mutually exclusive projects have been estimated, and the following information has been provided:

Year	Machine D	Machine Q
0	$(2,500)	$(2,500)
1	2,000	0
2	900	1,800
3	100	1,000
4	100	900

The company's required rate of return is 14 percent, and it can get an unlimited amount of capital at that cost. What is the IRR of the *better* project? (Hint: Note that the better project might not be the one with the higher IRR.)

NPV and IRR   **13-11**   Diamond Hill Jewelers is considering the following independent projects:

Year	Project Y	Project Z
0	$(25,000)	$(25,000)
1	10,000	0
2	9,000	0
3	7,000	0
4	6,000	36,000

Which project(s) should be accepted if the required rate of return for the projects is 10 percent? Compute the NPVs and the IRRs for both projects.

Integrative Problem

Basics of capital budgeting   **13-12**   Your boss, the chief financial officer (CFO) for Unilate Textiles, has just handed you the estimated cash flows for two proposed projects. Project L involves adding a new item to the firm's fabric line; it would take some time to build up the market for this product, so the cash inflows would increase over time. Project S involves an add-on to an existing line, and its cash flows would decrease over time. Both projects have 3-year lives because Unilate is planning to introduce an entirely new fabric at that time.

Here are the net cash flow estimates (in thousands of dollars):

	Expected Net Cash Flows	
Year	Project L	Project S
0	$(100)	$(100)
1	10	70
2	60	50
3	80	20

Depreciation, salvage values, net working capital requirements, and tax effects are all included in these cash flows.

The CFO also made subjective risk assessments of each project and concluded that the projects both have risk characteristics which are similar to the firm's average project. Unilate's required rate of return is 10 percent. You must now determine whether one or both of the projects should be accepted.

a. What is capital budgeting? Are there any similarities between a firm's capital budgeting decisions and an individual's investment decisions?

b. What is the difference between independent and mutually exclusive projects? Between projects with conventional cash flows and projects with unconventional cash flows?

c. (1) What is the payback period? Find the paybacks for Project L and Project S.

　(2) What is the rationale for the payback? According to the payback criterion, which project or projects should be accepted if the firm's maximum acceptable payback is 2 years, and Project L and Project S are independent? Mutually exclusive?

　(3) What is the difference between the regular payback and the discounted payback?

　(4) What are the main disadvantages of the regular payback? Is the payback method of any real usefulness in capital budgeting decisions?

d. (1) Define the term *net present value (NPV)*. What is each project's NPV?

　(2) What is the rationale behind the NPV method? According to NPV, which project or projects should be accepted if they are independent? Mutually exclusive?

　(3) Would the NPVs change if the required rate of return changed?

e. (1) Define the term *internal rate of return (IRR)*. What is each project's IRR?

　(2) How is the IRR on a project related to the YTM on a bond?

　(3) What is the logic behind the IRR method? According to IRR, which projects should be accepted if they are independent? Mutually exclusive?

　(4) Would the projects' IRRs change if the required rate of return changed?

f. (1) Draw the NPV profiles for Project L and Project S. At what discount rate do the profiles cross?

　(2) Look at the NPV profile graph without referring to the actual NPVs and IRRs. Which project or projects should be accepted if they are independent? Mutually exclusive? Explain. Do your answers apply for any discount rate less than 23.6 percent?

g. (1) What is the underlying cause of ranking conflicts between NPV and IRR?

　(2) What is the "reinvestment rate assumption," and how does it affect the NPV versus IRR conflict?

　(3) Which method is the best? Why?

Computer-Related Problem

Work the problem in this section only if you are using the computer problem diskette.

NPV and IRR analysis **13-13** Use the model in File C13 to solve this problem. West Coast Chemical Company (WCCC) is considering two mutually exclusive investments. The projects' expected net cash flows are as follows:

	Expected Net Cash Flows	
Year	**Project A**	**Project B**
0	$(45,000)	$(50,000)
1	(20,000)	15,000
2	11,000	15,000
3	20,000	15,000
4	30,000	15,000
5	45,000	15,000

a. Construct NPV profiles for Projects A and B.

b. Calculate each project's IRR. Assume the required rate of return is 13 percent.

c. If the required rate of return for each project is 13 percent, which project should West Coast select? If the required rate of return were 9 percent, what would be the proper choice? If the required rate of return were 15 percent, what would be the proper choice?

d. At what rate do the NPV profiles of the two projects cross?

e. Project A has a large cash flow in Year 5 associated with ending the project. WCCC's management is confident of Project A's cash flows in Years 0 to 4 but is uncertain about what its Year 5 cash flow will be. (There is no uncertainty about Project B's cash flows.) Under a worst case scenario, Project A's Year 5 cash flow will be $40,000, whereas under a best case scenario, the cash flow will be $50,000. Redo Parts a, b, and d for each scenario, assuming a 13 percent required rate of return. Press the F10 function key on the computer keyboard to see the new NPV profiles. If the required rate of return for each project is 13 percent, which project should be selected under each scenario?

APPENDIX 13A

Modified Internal Rate of Return (MIRR)

MODIFIED IRR (MIRR)
The discount rate at which the present value of a project's cost is equal to the present value of its terminal value, where the terminal value is found as the sum of the future values of the cash inflows, compounded at the firm's required rate of return (cost of capital).

In spite of a strong academic preference for NPV, surveys indicate that many business executives prefer IRR over NPV. Apparently, these managers find it intuitively more appealing to analyze investments in terms of percentage rates of return than dollars of NPV. But, remember from the discussion in the chapter that the IRR method assumes the cash flows from the project are reinvested at a rate of return equal to the IRR, which we generally view as unrealistic. Given this fact, can we devise a percentage evaluator that is better than the regular IRR? The answer is yes—we can modify the IRR and make it a better indicator of relative profitability, hence better for use in capital budgeting. The new measure is called the **modified IRR,** or **MIRR,** and it is defined as follows:

13A-1

$$PV\ costs = PV\ terminal\ value$$

$$\sum_{t=0}^{n} \frac{COF_t}{(1+k)^t} = \frac{\sum_{t=0}^{n} CIF_t(1+k)^{n-t}}{(1+MIRR)^n}$$

$$PV\ costs = \frac{TV}{(1+MIRR)^n}$$

Here COF refers to cash outflows (negative numbers), or the costs associated with the project, and CIF refers to cash inflows (all positive numbers). The left term is simply the PV of the investment outlays when discounted at the project's required rate of return, and the numerator of the right term is the future value of the inflows, assuming that the cash inflows are reinvested at the project's required rate of return. The future value of the cash inflows is also called the *terminal value,* or *TV.* The discount rate that forces the PV of the TV to equal the PV of the costs is defined as the MIRR.[1]

If the investment costs are all incurred at t = 0, and if the first operating inflow occurs at t = 1, as is true for our illustrative Projects S and L which we first presented in Figure 13-1, then this equation can be used:

13A-1a

$$Cost = \frac{TV}{(1+MIRR)^n} = \frac{\sum_{t=1}^{n} CIF_t(1+k)^{n-t}}{(1+MIRR)^n}$$

We can illustrate the calculation with Project S:

Cash Flow Time Line for Project S:

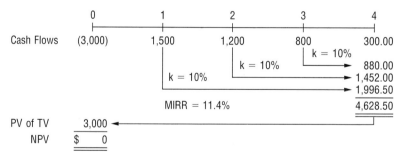

Using the cash flows as set out on the time line, first find the terminal value by compounding each cash inflow at the 10 percent required rate of return. Then, enter into your

---

[1]There are several alternative definitions for the MIRR. The differences relate primarily to whether negative cash flows which occur after positive cash flows begin should be compounded and treated as part of the TV or discounted and treated as a cost. Our definition (which treats all negative cash flows as investments and thus discounts them) generally is the most appropriate procedure. For a complete discussion, see William R. McDaniel, Daniel E. McCarty, and Kenneth A. Jessell, "Discounted Cash Flow with Explicit Reinvestment Rates: Tutorial and Extension." *The Financial Review,* August 1988, pp. 369–385.

calculator PV = −3,000, FV = 4628.5, and N = 4, and press the I key to find MIRR$_S$ = 11.4%. Similarly, we find MIRR$_L$ = 11.0%.

The modified IRR has a significant advantage over the regular IRR. MIRR assumes that cash flows are reinvested at the required rate of return, while the regular IRR assumes that cash flows are reinvested at the project's own IRR. Because reinvestment at the required rate of return (cost of funds) generally is more correct, the modified IRR is a better indicator of a project's true profitability. MIRR also solves the multiple IRR problem. To illustrate, with k = 10%, Project M (the strip mine project) has MIRR = 5.6% versus the 10 percent required rate of return, so it should be rejected. This is consistent with the decision based on the NPV method at k = 10%, NPV = −$0.77 million.

Is MIRR as good as NPV for choosing between mutually exclusive projects? If two projects are of equal size and have the same life, then NPV and MIRR always will lead to the same project selection decision. Thus, for any projects like our Projects S and L, if NPV$_S$ > NPV$_L$, then MIRR$_S$ > MIRR$_L$, and the kinds of conflicts we encountered between NPV and the regular IRR will not occur. Also, if the projects are of equal size but differ in lives, the MIRR always will lead to the same decision as the NPV if the MIRRs are both calculated using as the terminal year the life of the longer project. (Just fill in zeros for the shorter project's missing cash flows.) However, if the projects differ in size, then conflicts can still occur. For example, if we were choosing between a large project and a small mutually exclusive one, then we might find NPV$_L$ > NPV$_S$, but MIRR$_S$ > MIRR$_L$.

Our conclusion is that the modified IRR is superior to the regular IRR as an indicator of a project's "true" rate of return, or "expected long-term rate of return," but the NPV method is still better for choosing among competing projects that differ in size because it provides a better indicator of the extent to which each project will increase the value of the firm.

Problem

MIRR and multiple rates of return

13A-1 The Upton Uranium Company is deciding whether it should open a strip mine, the net cost of which is $2 million. Net cash inflows are expected to be $13 million, all coming at the end of Year 1. The land must be returned to its natural state at a cost of $12 million, payable at the end of Year 2.

  a. Plot the project's NPV profile. (Hint: Calculate NPV at k = 0, 10%, 80%, and 450%, and possibly at other k values.)

  b. Should the project be accepted if k = 10%? If k = 20%? Explain your reasoning.

  c. Can you think of some other capital budgeting situations in which negative cash flows during or at the other end of the project's life might lead to multiple IRRs?

  d. What is the project's MIRR at k = 10%? At k = 20%? Does the MIRR method lead to the same accept/reject decision as the NPV method?

CHAPTER 14

Project Cash Flows and Risk

When RJR Nabisco canceled its smokeless cigarette project, *The Wall Street Journal* called it "one of the most stunning new product disasters in recent history." RJR had spent over $300 million on the product and had test marketed it for five months. The company had even built a new plant and was all set to produce smokeless cigarettes in huge quantities.

The new cigarette had two fatal flaws—it had to be lit with a special lighter and even then it was hard to light, and many, if not most, smokers didn't like the taste. These problems were well known early on, yet RJR still pumped money into the project.

What led RJR's top managers to downplay the flaws and to spend $300 million on a bad product? According to industry observers, many people inside the company were aware of the seriousness of the situation, but they were afraid to voice their concerns because they were afraid they would offend the top managers. The top managers, meantime, were so infatuated with their "new toy" that they assumed consumers would embrace the smokeless cigarette in spite of its obvious flaws. Interestingly, most of the top managers smoked, but none smoked the new smokeless cigarette!

RJR was not a well-run company, even though it was entrenched in highly profitable markets and was generating billions of dollars of cash each year. The smokeless cigarette project didn't kill the company, but it did contribute to the downfall of the management team that backed the project. Had RJR's top managers followed the procedures set forth in this chapter, perhaps they would still be in control of the company.

The basic principles of capital budgeting were covered in Chapter 13. Now we examine some additional issues, including cash flow estimation and incorporating risk into the capital budgeting decision.

Cash Flow Estimation

CASH FLOW
The actual cash, as opposed to accounting net income, that a firm receives or pays during some specified period.

The most important, but also the most difficult, step in the analysis of a capital project is estimating its **cash flows**—the investment outlays and the net cash flows expected after the project is purchased. Many variables are involved in cash flow estimation, and many individuals and departments participate in the process. For example, the forecasts of unit sales and sales prices normally are made by the marketing group based on their knowledge of advertising effects, the state of the economy, competitors' reactions, and trends in consumers' tastes. Similarly, the capital outlays associated with a new product generally are determined by the engineering and product development staffs, while operating costs are estimated by cost accountants, production experts, personnel specialists, purchasing agents, and so forth.

Because it is difficult to make accurate forecasts of the costs and revenues associated with a large, complex project, forecast errors can be quite large. For example, when several major oil companies decided to build the Alaska Pipeline, the original cost estimates were in the neighborhood of $700 million, but the final cost was closer to $7 billion. Similar (or even worse) miscalculations are common in forecasts of product design costs. Further, as difficult as plant and equipment costs are to estimate, sales revenues and operating costs over the life of the project generally are even more uncertain. For example, several years ago Federal Express developed an electronic delivery service system (ZapMail). It used the correct capital budgeting technique, NPV, but it incorrectly estimated the project's cash flows: Projected revenues were too high, and projected costs were too low, and virtually no one was willing to pay the price required to cover the project's costs. As a result, cash flows failed to meet the forecasted levels, and Federal Express ended up losing about $200 million on the venture. This example demonstrates a basic truth—if cash flow estimates are not reasonably accurate, any analytical technique, no matter how sophisticated, can lead to poor decisions and hence to operating losses and lower stock prices. Because of its financial strength, Federal Express was able to absorb the losses on the project without problem, but the ZapMail venture could have forced a weaker firm into bankruptcy.

The financial staff's role in the forecasting process includes (1) coordinating the efforts of the other departments, such as engineering and marketing, (2) ensuring that everyone involved with the forecast uses a consistent set of economic assumptions, and (3) making sure that no biases are inherent in the forecasts. This last point is extremely important, because division managers often become emotionally involved with pet projects or develop empire-building complexes, both of which can lead to cash flow forecasting biases that make bad projects look good—on paper. The RJR smokeless cigarette project discussed earlier is an example of this problem.

It is almost impossible to overstate the difficulties one can encounter with cash flow forecasts. Also, it is difficult to overstate the importance of these forecasts. In this chapter, we will give you a sense of some of the inputs that are involved in forecasting the cash flows associated with a capital project and in minimizing forecasting errors.

Self-Test Questions

What is the most important step in the analysis of a capital project?

What is the financial staff's role in the capital projects forecasting process?

Relevant Cash Flows

RELEVANT CASH FLOWS
The specific cash flows that should be considered in a capital budgeting decision.

One important element in cash flow estimation is the determination of **relevant cash flows,** which are defined as the specific set of cash flows that should be considered in the capital budgeting decision. This process can be rather difficult, but two cardinal rules can help financial analysts avoid mistakes: (1) Capital budgeting decisions must be based on *cash flows after taxes,* not accounting income, and (2) only *incremental cash flows* are relevant to the accept/reject decision. These two rules are discussed in detail in the following sections.

Cash Flow versus Accounting Income

In capital budgeting analysis, *after-tax cash flows, not accounting profits,* are used—it is cash that pays the bills and can be invested in capital projects, not profits. Cash flows and accounting profits can be very different. To illustrate, consider Table 14-1, which shows how accounting profits and cash flows are related to one another. We assume that Unilate Textiles is planning to start a new division at the end of 1996; that sales and all costs, except depreciation, represent actual cash flows and are projected to be constant over time; and that the division will

TABLE 14-1		
Accounting Profits versus Net Cash Flow (thousands of dollars)		
	Accounting Profits	**Cash Flows**
I. 1997 Situation		
Sales	$ 50,000	$ 50,000
Costs except depreciation	(25,000)	(25,000)
Depreciation	(15,000)	—
Net operating income or cash flow	$ 10,000	$ 25,000
Taxes based on operating income (30%)	(3,000)	(3,000)
Net income or net cash flow	$ 7,000	$ 22,000
Net cash flow = Net income plus depreciation = $7,000 + $15,000 = $22,000		
II. 2002 Situation		
Sales	$ 50,000	$ 50,000
Costs except depreciation	(25,000)	(25,000)
Depreciation	(5,000)	—
Net operating income or cash flow	$ 20,000	$ 25,000
Taxes based on operating income (30%)	(6,000)	(6,000)
Net income or net cash flow	$ 14,000	$ 19,000
Net cash flow = Net income plus depreciation = $14,000 + $5,000 = $19,000		

use accelerated depreciation, which will cause its reported depreciation charges to decline over time.[1]

The top section of the table shows the situation in the first year of operations, 1997. Accounting profits are $7 million, but the division's net cash flow—money which is available to Unilate—is $22 million. The $7 million profit is the *return on the funds* originally invested, while the $15 million of depreciation is a *return of part of the funds* originally invested, so the $22 million cash flow consists of both a return *on* and a return *of* part of the invested capital.

The bottom part of the table shows the situation projected for 2002. Here reported profits have doubled because of the decline in depreciation, but net cash flow is down sharply because taxes have doubled. The amount of money received by the firm is represented by the cash flow figure, not the net income figure. And, though accounting profits are important for some purposes, it is cash flows that are relevant for the purposes of setting a value on a project using discounted cash flow (DCF) techniques—cash flows can be reinvested to create value, profits cannot. Therefore, in capital budgeting, we are interested in net cash flows, defined as

$$\text{Net cash flow} = \text{Net income} \quad + \text{Depreciation}$$
$$= \text{Return } on \text{ capital} + \text{Return } of \text{ capital}$$

not in accounting profits per se.[2]

Incremental Cash Flows

In evaluating a capital project, we are concerned only with those cash flows that result directly from the decision to accept the project. These cash flows, called **incremental cash flows,** represent the changes in the firm's total cash flows that occur as a direct result of accepting the project. To determine if a specific cash flow is considered incremental, we need to find out whether it is affected by the purchase of the project. Cash flows that will change because the project is purchased are *incremental cash flows* that need to be included in the capital budgeting evaluation; cash flows that are not affected by the purchase of the project are

INCREMENTAL CASH FLOW
The change in a firm's net cash flow attributable to an investment project.

---

[1]Depreciation procedures are discussed in detail in accounting courses, but we do provide a summary and review in Appendix 14A at the end of this chapter. The tables provided in Appendix 14A are used to calculate depreciation charges used in the chapter examples. In some instances, we simplify the depreciation assumptions in order to reduce the arithmetic. Because Congress changes depreciation procedures fairly frequently, it is always necessary to consult the latest tax regulations before developing actual capital budgeting cash flows.

[2]Actually, net cash flow should be adjusted to reflect all noncash charges, not just depreciation. However, for most projects, depreciation is by far the largest noncash charge. Also, notice that Table 14-1 ignores interest charges, which would be present if the firm used debt. Most firms do use debt and hence finance part of their capital budgets with debt. Therefore, the question has been raised as to whether interest charges should be reflected in capital budgeting cash flow analysis. The consensus is that interest charges should *not* be dealt with explicitly in capital budgeting—rather, the effects of debt financing are reflected in the cost of capital which is used to discount the cash flows. If interest were subtracted, and cash flows were then discounted, we would be double counting the cost of debt.

not relevant to the capital budgeting decision. Unfortunately, identifying the relevant cash flows for a project is not always as simple as it seems. Some special problems in determining incremental cash flows are discussed next.

SUNK COSTS   Sunk costs are not incremental costs, and they should *not* be included in the analysis. A **sunk cost** is an outlay that already has been committed or that already has occurred and hence is not affected by the accept/reject decision under consideration. To illustrate, in 1995 Unilate Textiles considered building a distribution center in New England in an effort to increase sales in that area of the country. To help with its evaluation, in 1994 Unilate hired a consulting firm to perform a site analysis and provide a feasibility study for the project; the cost was $100,000, and this amount was expensed for tax purposes in 1994. Is this 1994 expenditure a relevant cost with respect to the 1995 capital budgeting decision? The answer is no—the $100,000 is a sunk cost, and Unilate cannot recover this money, regardless of whether the new distribution center is built. In some cases, a particular project has a negative NPV when all the associated costs, including sunk costs, are considered. But on an incremental basis the project is acceptable because the incremental cash flows are large enough to produce a positive NPV on the incremental investment.

SUNK COST
A cash outlay that already has been incurred and that cannot be recovered regardless of whether the project is accepted or rejected.

OPPORTUNITY COSTS   The second potential problem relates to **opportunity costs,** defined here as the cash flows that could be generated from assets the firm already owns provided they are not used for the project in question. To illustrate, Unilate already owns a piece of land that is suitable for a distribution center. When evaluating the prospective center in New England, should the cost of the land be disregarded because no additional cash outlay would be required? The answer is no, because there is an opportunity cost inherent in the use of the property. In this case, the land could be sold to yield $150,000 after taxes. Use of the site for the distribution center would require forgoing this inflow, so the $150,000 must be charged as an opportunity cost against the project. Note that the proper land cost in this example is the $150,000 market-determined value, irrespective of whether Unilate originally paid $50,000 or $500,000 for the property. (What Unilate paid would, of course, have an effect on taxes and hence on the after-tax opportunity cost.)

OPPORTUNITY COST
The return on the best alternative use of an asset; the highest return that will not be earned if funds are invested in a particular project.

EXTERNALITIES: EFFECTS ON OTHER PARTS OF THE FIRM   The third potential problem involves the effects of a project on other parts of the firm; economists call these effects **externalities.** For example, Unilate does have some existing customers in New England who would use the new distribution center because its location would be more convenient than the North Carolina distribution center they have been using. The sales, and hence profits, generated by these customers would not be new to Unilate; rather, they would represent a transfer from one distribution center to another. Thus, the net revenues produced by these customers should not be treated as incremental income in the capital budgeting decision. Although they often are difficult to quantify, externalities such as these should be considered.

EXTERNALITIES
The effect accepting a project will have on the cash flows in other parts (areas) of the firm.

SHIPPING AND INSTALLATION COSTS   When a firm acquires fixed assets, it often must incur substantial costs for shipping and installing the equipment. These charges are added to the invoice price of the equipment when the total cost of the project is being determined. Also, for depreciation purposes, the *depreciable basis* of an asset, which is the total amount that can be depreciated, includes the purchase price and any additional expenditures required to make the asset operational, including shipping and installation. Therefore, the full cost of the equipment, including shipping and installation costs, is used as the depreciable basis when depreciation charges are calculated. So, if Unilate Textiles bought a computer with an invoice price of $100,000, and paid another $10,000 for shipping and installation, then the full cost of the computer, and its depreciable basis, would be $110,000.

Keep in mind that depreciation is a noncash expense, so there is not a cash outflow associated with the recognition of depreciation expense each year. But, because depreciation is an expense, it affects the taxable income of a firm, thus the amount of taxes paid by the firm, which is a cash flow.

INFLATION   Inflation is a fact of life, and it should be recognized in capital budgeting decisions. If expected inflation is not built into the determination of expected cash flows, then the calculated net present value and internal rate of return will be incorrect—both will be artificially low. It is easy to avoid inflation bias—simply build inflationary expectations into the cash flows used in the capital budgeting analysis. Expected inflation should be reflected in the revenue and cost figures, thus the annual net cash flow forecasts. The required rate of return does not have to be adjusted by the firm for inflation expectations because investors include such expectations when establishing the rate at which they are willing to permit the firm to use their funds—it is investors who decide at what rates a firm can raise funds in the capital markets.

Self-Test Questions

Briefly explain the difference between accounting income and net cash flow. Which should be used in capital budgeting? Why?

Explain what these terms mean, and assess their relevance in capital budgeting: incremental cash flow, sunk cost, opportunity cost, externality, shipping plus installation costs, and depreciable basis.

Explain why incremental analysis is important in capital budgeting.

How should inflation expectations be included in analysis of capital projects?

Identifying Incremental Cash Flows

Generally, when we identify the incremental cash flows associated with a capital project, we separate them according to when they occur during the life of the project. In most cases, we can classify a project's incremental cash flows as (1) cash flows that occur *only at the start* of the project's life—time period 0, (2) cash flows that *continue throughout* the project's life—time periods 1 through n, and (3) cash flows that occur *only at the end,* or the termination, of the project—time period n. We discuss these three incremental cash flow classifications and identify some of the relevant cash flows in the following sections. But keep in mind, when identifying the incremental cash flows for capital budgeting, the primary question is which cash flows will be affected by the purchase of the project—if a cash flow does not change, it is not relevant for the capital budgeting analysis.

Initial Investment Outlay

INITIAL INVESTMENT OUTLAY
Includes the incremental cash flows associated with a project that will occur only at the start of a project's life, CF_0.

The **initial investment outlay** refers to the incremental cash flows that *occur only at the start of a project's life, CF_0.* The initial investment includes such cash flows as the purchase price of the new project and shipping and installation costs. If the capital budgeting decision is a *replacement decision,* the initial investment also must take into account the cash flows associated with the disposal of the old, or replaced, asset, which include any cash received or paid to scrap the old asset and any tax effects associated with the disposal.

In many cases, the addition or replacement of a capital asset has an impact on the net working capital of the firm. For example, normally, additional inventories are required to support a new operation, and expanded sales also lead to additional accounts receivable. If Unilate builds the new distribution center in New England, the inventories held at that location will be *in addition to* the inventories currently held at its other distribution centers. It is estimated the New England distribution center will require $5 million of inventory to operate normally, so Unilate must purchase an additional $5 million of inventory if the distribution center is built. This cash flow is considered part of the initial investment because the $5 million inventory increase will occur only when the distribution center opens. This inventory increase and any increase in accounts receivable resulting from the *additional* sales expected to be generated by the New England distribution center must be financed. But, as we saw in Chapter 4, Unilate can expect its accounts payable and accruals to increase spontaneously as a result of the expanded operations, and this will reduce the net cash needed to finance inventories and receivables. The difference between the required increase in current assets and the spontaneous increase in current liabilities is the *change in net working capital.* If this change is positive, as it generally is for expansion projects like the new distribution center being considered by Unilate, then additional financing, over and above the cost of the fixed assets, is needed to fund the increase in current assets.

We should note that there are instances where the change in net working capital associated with a capital project actually results in a decrease in the firm's current funding requirements, which frees up cash flows for investment. Usually this occurs if the project being considered is much more efficient than the existing asset(s). In any event, *the change in net working capital that results from the acceptance of a project is an incremental cash flow that must be considered in the capital budgeting analysis.* And, because the changes in net working capital requirements occur at the start of the project's life, this cash flow impact is an incremental cash flow that is included as a part of the initial investment outlay.

Incremental Operating Cash Flow

Most capital projects also affect the day-to-day cash flows generated by the firm. For example, if Unilate purchases a new weaving machine to replace a machine it has been using for ten years, it will be able to reduce its total operating costs by $10 million. The cost reduction would result because the technological advancements of the new machine would allow Unilate to use less electricity and fewer raw materials (wool, cotton, and so on) in its manufacturing process. These cost savings, as well as any changes in depreciation expense, will affect the taxes paid by Unilate each year the new machine is in service. Thus, Unilate's normal *operating cash flows* will change if the project is accepted. We define **incremental operating cash flows** as the changes in day-to-day cash flows that result from the purchase of a capital project. The impact of incremental operating cash flows continues until the firm disposes of the asset.

INCREMENTAL OPERATING CASH FLOWS
The changes in day-to-day cash flows that result from the purchase of a capital project and continue until the firm disposes of the asset.

In most cases, the *incremental operating cash flows* for each year can be computed directly by using the following equation:

14-1

$$
\begin{aligned}
\text{Incremental operating cash flow}_t &= \Delta NI_t + \Delta Depr_t \\[4pt]
&= \Delta EBT_t \times (1 - T) + \Delta Depr_t \\[4pt]
&= (\Delta S_t - \Delta OC_t - \Delta Depr_t) \times (1 - T) + \Delta Depr_t \\[4pt]
&= (\Delta S_t - \Delta OC_t) \times (1 - T) + T(\Delta Depr_t)
\end{aligned}
$$

The symbols in Equation 14-1 are defined as follows:

Δ = the Greek symbol delta, which represents the change in something.

$\Delta NI_t = NI_{t,accept} - NI_{t,reject}$ = the change in net income in period t that results from accepting the capital project; the subscript *accept* is used to indicate the firm's operations that would exist if the project is accepted, and the subscript *reject* indicates the level of operations that would exist if the project is rejected—the existing situation *without* the project.

$\Delta Depr_t = Depr_{t,accept} - Depr_{t,reject}$ = the change in depreciation expense in period t that results from accepting the project.

$\Delta EBT_t = EBT_{t,accept} - EBT_{t,reject}$ = the change in earnings before taxes in period t that results from accepting the project.

$\Delta S_t = S_{t,accept} - S_{t,reject}$ = the change in sales revenues in period t that results from accepting the project.

$\Delta OC_t = OC_{t,accept} - OC_{t,reject}$ = the change in operating costs, excluding depreciation, in period t that results from accepting the project.

T = Marginal tax rate.

We have emphasized that depreciation is a *noncash* expense. So why is the change in depreciation expense included in the computation of incremental operating cash flow shown in Equation 14-1? The change in depreciation expense needs to be computed because, when depreciation changes, taxable income changes, and so does the amount of income taxes paid, and the amount of taxes paid to Uncle Sam is a cash flow.

Terminal Cash Flow

TERMINAL CASH FLOW
The *net* cash flow that occurs at the end of the life of a project, including the cash flows associated with (1) the final disposal of the project and (2) returning the firm's operations to where they were before the project was accepted.

The **terminal cash flow** occurs at the end of the life of the project, and it is associated with (1) the final disposal of the project and (2) returning the firm's operations to where they were before the project was accepted. Consequently, the terminal cash flow includes the salvage value, which could be either positive (selling the asset) or negative (paying for removal), and the tax impact of the disposition of the project. In addition, we generally assume the firm returns to the operating level that existed prior to the acceptance of the project; thus, any working capital accounts changes that occurred at the beginning of the project's life will be reversed at the end of its life. For example, as an expansion project's life approaches termination, inventories will be sold off and not replaced, and receivables also will be converted to cash. As these changes occur, the firm will receive an end-of-project cash flow equal to the net working capital requirement that occurred when the project was begun. Unilate expects the life of the New England distribution center to be 10 years, so the inventories at that location will be reduced to zero in the tenth year. Because inventories will not have to be replenished during the last sales period, cash flows in Year 10 will increase by $5 million.

Self-Test Questions

Identify the three classifications for the incremental cash flows associated with a project, and give examples of the cash flows that would be in each category.

Why are the changes in net working capital recognized as incremental cash flows both at the beginning and the end of a project's life?

Capital Budgeting Project Evaluation

To this point, we have discussed several important aspects of cash flow analysis. Now we illustrate cash flow estimation for expansion projects and for replacement projects.

Expansion Projects

EXPANSION PROJECT
A project that is intended to increase sales.

Remember from Chapter 13 that an **expansion project** is defined as one that calls for the firm to invest in new assets to *increase* sales. We illustrate an expansion project analysis with a project that is being considered by Household Energy Products (HEP), a Dallas-based technology company. HEP's research and development department has created a computerized home appliance control device that will increase a home's energy efficiency by simultaneously controlling all household appliances, large and small, the air-conditioning/heating system, the water heater, the security system, and the filtration and heating systems for pools and spas. At this point, HEP wants to decide whether it should proceed with full-scale production of the appliance control device.

HEP's marketing department plans to target sales of the appliance computer toward the owners of larger homes; the computer is cost effective only in homes with 2,500 or more square feet of living space. The marketing vice-president believes that annual sales would be 15,000 units if the units are priced at $2,000 each, so annual sales are estimated at $30 million. The engineering department has determined the firm would need no additional manufacturing or storage space; it would just need the equipment to manufacture the devices. The necessary equipment would be purchased and installed at the end of 1996, and it would cost $9.5 million, not including the $500,000 that would have to be paid for shipping and installation. The equipment would fall into the MACRS 5-year class for the purposes of depreciation (see Appendix 14A).

The project would require an initial increase in net working capital equal to $4 million, primarily because the raw materials required to produce the devices will significantly increase the amount of inventory HEP currently holds. The investment necessary to increase net working capital will be made on December 31, 1996. The project's estimated economic life is 4 years. At the end of that time, the equipment would have a market value of $2 million and a book value of $1.7 million. The production department has estimated that variable manufacturing costs would total 60 percent of sales and fixed overhead costs, excluding depreciation, would be $5 million a year. Depreciation expenses would vary from year to year in accordance with the MACRS rates.

HEP's marginal tax rate is 40 percent; its cost of funds, or required rate of return, is 15 percent; and, for capital budgeting purposes, the company's policy is to assume that operating cash flows occur at the end of each year. Because the plant would begin operations on January 1, 1997, the first *operating cash flows* would occur on December 31, 1997.

ANALYSIS OF THE CASH FLOWS   The first step in the analysis is to summarize the initial investment outlays required for the project; this is done in the 1996 column of Table 14-2. For HEP's appliance control device project, the initial cash outlays consist of the purchase price of the needed equipment, the cost of shipping and installation, and the required investment in net working capital (NWC). Notice that these cash flows do not carry over in the years 1997–2000—they occur only at the start of the project. Thus, the *initial investment outlay* is $14 million.

Having estimated the investment requirements, we must now estimate the cash flows that will occur once production begins; these are set forth in the 1997 through 2000 columns of Table 14-2. The operating cash flow estimates are based on information provided by HEP's various departments. The depreciation amounts were obtained by multiplying the depreciable basis by the MACRS recovery allowance rates as set forth in the footnote to Table 14-2. Using Equation 14-1 and the information for HEP's appliance control device project provided earlier, the incremental operating cash flows for each year are easy to compute. The numbers used in the following computations are in thousands of dollars, and they correspond to those shown in Table 14-2:

Year	Incremental Operating Cash Flow Computation
1997	$5,000 = ($30,000 − $18,000 − $5,000)(1 − 0.40) + $2,000(0.40)
1998	5,480 = (30,000 − 18,000 − 5,000)(1 − 0.40) + 3,200(0.40)
1999	4,960 = (30,000 − 18,000 − 5,000)(1 − 0.40) + 1,900(0.40)
2000	4,680 = (30,000 − 18,000 − 5,000)(1 − 0.40) + 1,200(0.40)

TABLE 14-2

HEP Expansion Project Net Cash Flows, 1996–2000 (thousands of dollars)

	1996	1997	1998	1999	2000
I. Initial Investment Outlay					
Cost of new asset	$(9,500)				
Shipping and installation	(500)				
Increase in net working capital	(4,000)				
Initial investment	$(14,000)				
II. Incremental Operating Cash Flow					
Sales revenues		$ 30,000	$ 30,000	$ 30,000	$ 30,000
Variable costs (60% of sales)		(18,000)	(18,000)	(18,000)	(18,000)
Fixed costs		(5,000)	(5,000)	(5,000)	(5,000)
Depreciation on new equipment[a]		(2,000)	(3,200)	(1,900)	(1,200)
Earning before taxes (EBT)		$ 5,000	$ 3,800	$ 5,100	$ 5,800
Taxes (40%)		(2,000)	(1,520)	(2,040)	(2,320)
Net income		$ 3,000	$ 2,280	$ 3,060	$ 3,480
Add back depreciation		2,000	3,200	1,900	1,200
Incremental operating cash flows		$ 5,000	$ 5,480	$ 4,960	$ 4,680
III. Terminal Cash Flow					
Return of net working capital					$ 4,000
Net salvage value (see Table 14-3)					1,880
Terminal cash flow					$ 5,880
IV. Annual Net Cash Flow					
Total net cash flow each year	$(14,000)	$ 5,000	$ 5,480	$ 4,960	$ 10,560
Net present value (15%)	$ 3,790				

[a]Depreciation for the new equipment was calculated using MACRS (see Appendix 14A):

	1997	1998	1999	2000
Percent depreciated	20	32	19	12

These percentages were multiplied by the depreciable basis of $10,000 to get the depreciation each year.

As you can see from this analysis, the *incremental operating cash flow* differs each year only because the depreciation expense, and thus the impact depreciation has on taxes, differs each year.

The final cash flow component we need to compute is the terminal cash flow. For this computation, remember the $4 million investment in net working capital will be recovered in 2000. Also, we need an estimate of the net cash flows from the disposal of the equipment in 2000. Table 14-3 shows the calculation of the net salvage value for the equipment. It is expected that the equipment will be sold for more than its book value, which means the company will have to pay taxes on the capital gain because, in essence, the equipment was depreciated too quickly, allowing HEP to reduce its tax liability by too much in the years 1997–2000. The book value is calculated as the depreciable basis (purchase price plus shipping and installation) minus the accumulated depreciation. The net cash flow

TABLE 14-3

HEP Expansion Project Net Salvage Value, 2000 (thousands of dollars)

I.	**Book Value of HEP's Project in 2000**	
	Cost of new asset in 1996	$ 9,500
	Shipping and installation	500
	Depreciable basis of asset	$10,000
	Depreciation from 1997–2000	
	$= (0.20 + 0.32 + 0.19 + 0.12) \times \$10,000$	(8,300)
	Book value in 2000	$ 1,700
II.	**Tax Impact of the Sale of HEP's Project in 2000**	
	Selling price of asset in 2000	$ 2,000
	Book value of asset in 2000	(1,700)
	Gain (loss) on sale of asset	$ 300
	Taxes (40%)	$ 120
III.	**Net Salvage Value, CF, in 2000**	
	Cash flow from sale of project	$ 2,000
	Tax impact of sale	(120)
	Net salvage value cash flow	$ 1,880

from salvage merely is the sum of the salvage value and the tax impact resulting from the sale of the equipment, $1.88 million in this case. Thus, the *terminal cash flow* is $5.88 million.

Notice that the total net cash flow for the year 2000 is the sum of the incremental cash flow for the year and the terminal cash flow. In the final year of a project's economic life, the firm incurs two types of cash flow—the incremental operating cash flow attributed to the project and the terminal cash flow associated with the disposal of the project. For the appliance control device project HEP is considering, the incremental operating cash flow in 2000 is $4.68 million and the terminal cash flow is $5.88 million, so the total expected new cash flow in 2000 is $10.56 million.

MAKING THE DECISION   A summary of the data and the computation of the project's NPV are provided with the following cash flow time line. The amounts are in thousands of dollars, just like in Table 14-2.

CASH FLOW TIME LINE FOR HEP'S APPLIANCE CONTROL DEVICE PROJECT:

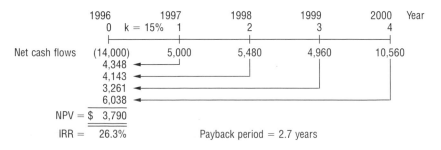

The project appears to be acceptable using the NPV and IRR methods, and it also would be acceptable if HEP required a payback period of three years. Note, however, that the analysis thus far has been based on the assumption that the project has the same degree of risk as the company's average project. If the project was judged to be riskier than an average project, it would be necessary to increase the required rate of return used to compute the NPV. Later in this chapter, we will extend the evaluation of this project to include a risk analysis.

Replacement Analysis

All companies make replacement decisions. The analysis relating to replacements is the same as that for expansion projects—identify the relevant cash flows and then find the net present value of the project. But, to some extent, identifying the *incremental* cash flows associated with a replacement project is more complicated than for an expansion project, because the cash flows from both the new asset *and* the old asset must be considered. **Replacement analysis** is illustrated with another HEP example.

REPLACEMENT ANALYSIS
An analysis involving the decision of whether to replace an existing asset that is still productive with a new asset.

A lathe for trimming molded plastics was purchased 10 years ago at a cost of $7,500. The machine had an expected life of 15 years at the time it was purchased, and management originally estimated, and still believes, that the salvage value will be zero at the end of the 15-year life. The machine is being depreciated on a straight line basis; therefore, its annual depreciation charge is $500, and its present book value is $2,500 = $7,500 − 10($500).

HEP is considering the purchase of a new special-purpose machine to replace the lathe. The new machine, which can be purchased for $12,000 (including freight and installation), will reduce labor and raw materials usage sufficiently to cut operating costs from $7,500 to $4,000. This reduction in costs will cause before-tax profits to rise by $7,500 − $4,000 = $3,500 per year.

It is estimated that the new machine will have a useful life of 5 years, after which it can be sold for $2,000. The old machine's actual current market value is $1,000, which is below its $2,500 book value. If the new machine is acquired, the old lathe will be sold to another company rather than exchanged for the new machine. Net working capital requirements will increase by $1,000 if the lathe is replaced by the new machine; this increase will occur at the time of replacement. By an IRS ruling, the new machine falls into the 3-year MACRS class, and, because the risk associated with the new machine is considered average for HEP, the project's required rate of return is 15 percent. Should the replacement be made?

Table 14-4 shows the worksheet format HEP uses to analyze replacement projects. Determining the relevant cash flows for a *replacement decision* is more involved than for an expansion decision, because we need to consider the fact that the cash flows associated with the replaced asset will not continue after the new asset is purchased—*the cash flows associated with the new asset will take the place of the cash flows associated with the old asset.* So, because we want to evaluate how the acceptance of a capital budgeting project *changes* cash flows, we must compute the increase or decrease in cash flows that results from the replacement of the old asset with the new asset. Let's examine the cash flows computed in Table 14-4.

First, the initial investment outlay of $11,400 includes the cash flows associated with the cost of the new asset and the change in net working capital, which also is included in the initial investment computation for the expansion decision

---

TABLE 14-4

HEP Replacement Project Net Cash Flows, 1996–2000

	1996	1997	1998	1999	2000	2001
I. *Initial Investment Outlay*						
Cost of new asset	$(12,000)					
Change in net working capital	(1,000)					
Net cash flow from sale of old asset[a]	1,600					
Initial investment	$(11,400)					
II. *Incremental Operating Cash Flows*						
Δ Operating costs		$ 3,500	$ 3,500	$ 3,500	$ 3,500	$ 3,500
Δ Depreciation[b]		(3,460)	(4,900)	(1,300)	(340)	500
Δ Earnings before taxes (EBT)		40	(1,400)	2,200	3,160	4,000
Δ Taxes (40%)		(16)	560	(880)	(1,264)	(1,600)
Δ Net income		24	(840)	1,320	1,896	2,400
Add back Δ depreciation		3,460	4,900	1,300	340	(500)
Incremental operating cash flows		$ 3,484	$ 4,060	$ 2,620	$ 2,236	$ 1,900
III. *Terminal Cash Flow*						
Return of net working capital						$ 1,000
Net salvage value of new asset[c]						1,200
Terminal cash flow						$ 2,200
IV. *Annual Net Cash Flows*						
Total net cash flow each year	$(11,400)	$ 3,484	$ 4,060	$ 2,620	$ 2,236	$ 4,100
Net present value (15%)	$(261)					

---

[a]The net cash flow from the sale of the old (replaced) asset is computed as follows:

Selling price (market value)	$ 1,000
Subtract book value	(2,500)
Gain (loss) on sale of asset	(1,500)
Tax impact of sale of asset	600
Net cash flow from the sale of asset = $1,000 + $600 = $1,600	

[b]The change in depreciation expense is computed by comparing the depreciation of the new asset with the depreciation that would have existed if the old asset was *not* replaced. The old asset has been depreciated on a straight line basis, with 5 years of $500 depreciation remaining. The new asset will be depreciated using the rates for the 3-year MACRS class (see Appendix 14A). So the change in annual depreciation would be:

Year	New Asset Depreciation		Old Asset Depreciation		Change in Depreciation
1997	$12,000 × 0.33 = $ 3,960	−	$500	=	$3,460
1998	12,000 × 0.45 = 5,400	−	500	=	4,900
1999	12,000 × 0.15 = 1,800	−	500	=	1,300
2000	12,000 × 0.07 = 840	−	500	=	340
2001	= 0	−	500	=	(500)
	Accumulated depreciation = $12,000				

[c]The book value of the new asset in 2001 will be zero, because the entire $12,000 has been written off. So the net salvage value of the new asset in 2001 is computed as follows:

Selling price (market value)	$ 2,000
Subtract book value	(0)
Gain (loss) on sale of asset	2,000
Tax impact of sale of asset	(800)
Net salvage value of the new asset = $2,000 − $800 = $1,200	

shown in Table 14-2. But when a replacement asset is purchased, the asset being replaced must be removed from operations. If the asset can be sold to another firm or to a scrap dealer, its disposal will generate a positive cash flow; if the firm must pay to have the old asset removed, the cash flow will be negative. If the firm disposes of the old asset at a value different from its book value (its purchase price less accumulated depreciation), there will be a tax effect. In our example, the old asset has a book value equal to $2,500, but it can be sold for only $1,000. So HEP will incur a capital loss equal to $-$1,500 = $1,000 $-$ $2,500 if it replaces the lathe with the new machine. This loss will result in a tax savings equal to (Loss) $\times$ (T) = ($1,500) $\times$ (0.4) = $600 to account for the fact that HEP did not adequately depreciate the old asset to reflect its market value. Consequently, the disposal of the old asset will generate a positive cash flow equal to $1,600—the $1,000 selling price plus the $600 tax savings.

The $1,600 HEP will receive from the disposal of the lathe reduces the amount of cash required to purchase the new machine and to support the increased working capital needs, so the initial investment outlay is $11,400 = $12,000 + $1,000 $-$ $1,600. Any cash flows associated with disposing of the old asset must be included in the computation of the initial investment. If you think about it, the computation of the initial investment outlay for replacement decisions is similar to determining the amount you would need to purchase a new automobile to replace your old one—if the purchase price of the new car is $15,000 and the dealer is willing to give you $5,000 for your old car as a trade-in, then the amount you need is only $10,000; but, if you need to pay someone to take your old car out of the garage because that is where you are going to keep the new car at night, then the total amount you need to purchase the new car actually is greater than $15,000.

Next, we need to compute the incremental operating cash flow each year. Section II of Table 14-4 shows these computations. The procedure is the same as before—determine how operating cash flows will change if the new machine is purchased to replace the lathe. Remember, the new machine is expected to decrease operating costs from $7,500 to $4,000, thus increase operating profits by $3,500—less cash will have to be spent to operate the new machine. Had the replacement resulted in an increase in sales in addition to the reduction in costs (that is, if the new machine had been both larger and more efficient), then this amount would also be reported. Also, note that the $3,500 cost savings is constant over the years 1997–2001; had the annual savings been expected to change over time, this fact would have to be built into the analysis.

The change in depreciation expense must be computed to determine the impact such a change will have on the taxes paid by the firm. If the new machine is purchased, the $500 depreciation expense of the lathe (old asset) no longer will be relevant for tax purposes; instead, the depreciation expense for the new machine will be used. For example, in 1997, the depreciation expense for the new machine will be $3,960 because, according to the 3-year MACRS classification, 33 percent of the cost of the new asset can be depreciated in the year it is purchased. Because HEP will dispose of the lathe if it buys the new machine, in 1997 it will replace the $500 depreciation expense associated with the lathe with the $3,960 depreciation expense associated with the new machine, and the depreciation expense will increase by $3,460 = $3,960 $-$ $500. The computations for the remaining years are the same. Notice in 2001 the change in depreciation is negative. This results because the new machine will be fully depreciated at the end of 2000, so there is nothing left to write off in 2001; thus, if the lathe is replaced, its depreciation of $500 will be replaced by the new machine's depreciation of $0 in 2001, which is a change of −$500.

The terminal cash flow includes $1,000 for the return of net working capital, because a "normal" net working capital level will be restored at the end of the new machine's life—any additional accounts receivable created by the purchase of the new machine will be collected and any additional inventories required by the new machine will be drawn down and not replaced. The net salvage value of the new machine is $1,200. It is expected that the new machine can be sold in 2001 for $2,000, but $800 in taxes will have to be paid on the sale because the new machine will be fully depreciated by the time of the sale.[3] Thus, the terminal cash flow equals $2,200 = $1,000 + $1,200.

MAKING THE DECISION   A summary of the data and the computation of the project's NPV are provided with the following cash flow time line:

CASH FLOW TIME LINE FOR HEP'S REPLACEMENT PROJECT:

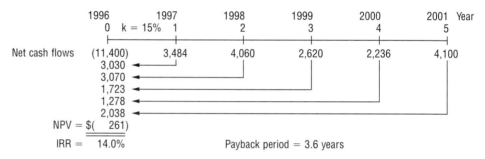

According to the NPV and IRR methods, HEP should not replace the lathe with the new machine.

Before we leave our discussion of replacement decisions, we should note that a replacement decision involves comparing two mutually exclusive projects: retaining the old asset versus buying a new one. To simplify matters, in our replacement example we assumed that the new machine had a life equal to the remaining life of the old machine. If, however, we were choosing between two mutually exclusive alternatives with significantly different lives, an adjustment would be necessary to make the results of the capital budgeting analysis for the two projects comparable. To attain comparability, we can either (1) use a common life for the evaluation of the two projects, or (2) compute the annual annuity that could be produced from the dollar amount of the NPV of each project. Both of these procedures are described in Appendix 14B. We mention the unequal life problem here to make you aware that the evaluation of mutually exclusive projects with significantly different lives requires a slightly different analysis to ensure a correct decision is made.

---

[3]In this analysis, the salvage value of the old machine is zero. However, if the old machine was expected to have a positive salvage value at the end of 5 years, replacing the old machine now would eliminate this cash flow. Thus, the after-tax salvage value of the old machine would represent an opportunity cost to the firm, and it would be included as a Year 5 cash outflow in the terminal cash flow section of the worksheet.

Self-Test Question

Explain and differentiate between the capital budgeting analyses required for expansion and for replacement projects.

Introduction to Project Risk Analysis

STAND-ALONE RISK
The risk an asset would have if it were a firm's only asset; it is measured by the variability of the asset's expected returns.

CORPORATE (WITHIN-FIRM) RISK
Risk not considering the effects of stockholders' diversification; it is measured by a project's effect on the firm's earnings variability.

BETA (MARKET) RISK
That part of a project's risk that cannot be eliminated by diversification; it is measured by the project's beta coefficient.

To this point, we have assumed the projects being evaluated have the same risk as the projects that the firm currently possesses. However, there are three separate and distinct types of project risk that need to be examined to determine if the required rate of return used to evaluate a project should be different than the average required rate of the firm. The three risks are: (1) the project's own **stand-alone risk,** or the risk it exhibits when evaluated alone rather than as part of a combination of assets (a portfolio)—the effect of the project on the other assets of the firm is disregarded; (2) **corporate,** or **within-firm, risk,** which is the effect a project has on the total (overall) riskiness of the company, without considering which risk component, systematic or unsystematic, is affected—the effect the project has on the stockholders' own personal diversification is disregarded; and (3) **beta,** or **market, risk,** which is project risk assessed from the standpoint of a stockholder who holds a well-diversified portfolio. As we shall see, a particular project might have high stand-alone risk, yet taking it on might not have much effect on either the firm's risk or that of its owners because of portfolio, or diversification, effects.

A project's stand-alone risk is measured by the variability of the project's expected returns; its corporate risk is measured by the project's impact on the firm's earnings variability; and its beta risk is measured by the project's effect on the firm's beta coefficient. Taking on a project with a high degree of either stand-alone risk or corporate risk will not necessarily affect the firm's beta to any great extent. However, if the project has highly uncertain returns, and if those returns are highly correlated with returns on the firm's other assets and also with most other assets in the economy, the project will exhibit a high degree of all three types of risk. For example, suppose General Motors decides to undertake a major expansion to build solar-powered autos. GM is not sure how its technology will work on a mass production basis, so there are great risks in the venture—its stand-alone risk is high. Management also estimates that the project will have a higher probability of success if the economy is strong, because people will have more money to spend on the new autos. This means that the project will tend to do well if GM's other divisions also do well and to do badly if other divisions do badly. This being the case, the project will also have high corporate risk. Finally, because GM's profits are highly correlated with those of most other firms, the project's beta coefficient also will be high. Thus, this project will be risky under all three definitions of risk.

Beta risk is important because of its direct effect on a firm's stock price: Beta affects the firm's required rate of return, k, and k affects the stock price. Corporate risk also is important for three primary reasons:

1. Undiversified stockholders, including the owners of small businesses, are more concerned about corporate risk than about beta risk.

2. Empirical studies of the determinants of required rates of return (k) generally find that both beta and corporate risk affect stock prices. This suggests that investors, even those who are well diversified, consider factors other than beta risk when they establish required returns.

3. The firm's stability is important to its managers, workers, customers, suppliers, and creditors, as well as to the community in which it operates. Firms that are in serious danger of bankruptcy, or even of suffering low profits and reduced output, have difficulty attracting and retaining good managers and workers. Also, both suppliers and customers are reluctant to depend on weak firms, and such firms have difficulty borrowing money at reasonable interest rates. These factors tend to reduce risky firms' profitability and hence the prices of their stocks; thus, they also make corporate risk significant.

Therefore, corporate risk is important even if a firm's stockholders are well diversified.

Self-Test Questions

What are the three types of project risk?

How is a project's stand-alone risk measured?

How is corporate risk measured?

How is beta risk measured?

List three reasons why corporate risk is important.

Techniques for Measuring Stand-alone Risk

What about a project's stand-alone risk—is it of any importance to anyone? In theory, stand-alone risk should be of little or no concern, because we know diversification can eliminate some of this type of risk. However, it is of great importance for the following reasons:

1. It is easier to estimate a project's stand-alone risk than its corporate risk, and it is far easier to measure stand-alone risk than beta risk.

2. In the vast majority of cases, all three types of risk are highly correlated—if the general economy does well, so will the firm, and if the firm does well, so will most of its projects. Thus, stand-alone risk generally is a good proxy for hard-to-measure corporate and beta risk.

3. Because of Points 1 and 2, if management wants a reasonably accurate assessment of a project's riskiness, it should spend considerable effort on determining the riskiness of the project's own cash flows—that is, its stand-alone risk.

The starting point for analyzing a project's stand-alone risk involves determining the uncertainty inherent in the project's cash flows. This analysis can be handled in a number of ways, ranging from informal judgments to complex economic and statistical analyses involving large-scale computer models. To illustrate what is involved, we shall refer to Household Energy Products' appliance control computer project that we discussed earlier. Many of the individual cash flows that were shown in Table 14-2 are subject to uncertainty. For example, sales for each year were projected at 15,000 units to be sold at a net price of $2,000 per unit, or $30 million in total. Actual unit sales almost certainly would be somewhat higher or lower than 15,000, however, and also the sales price might turn out to be different from the projected $2,000 per unit. In effect, the sales quantity and the sales price estimates are expected values taken from probability distributions, as are many of the other values that were shown in Table 14-2. The distributions could be relatively "tight," reflecting small standard deviations and low risk, or they could be "flat," denoting a great deal of uncertainty about the final value of the variable in question and hence a high degree of stand-alone risk.

The nature of the individual cash flow distributions, and their correlations with one another, determine the nature of the NPV distribution and, thus, the project's stand-alone risk. We next discuss three techniques for assessing a project's stand-alone risk: (1) sensitivity analysis, (2) scenario analysis, and (3) Monte Carlo simulation.

Sensitivity Analysis

SENSITIVITY ANALYSIS
A risk analysis technique in which key variables are changed and the resulting changes in the NPV and the IRR are observed.

The cash flows used to determine the acceptability of a project result from forecasts of uncertain events, such as economic conditions in the future and expected demand for a product. Intuitively, then, we know the cash flow amounts used to determine the net present value of a project might be significantly different from what actually happens in the future; but those numbers represent our best and most confident prediction concerning the expected cash flows associated with a project. We also know that if a key input variable, such as units sold, changes, the project's NPV also will change. **Sensitivity analysis** is a technique that shows exactly how much the NPV will change in response to a given change in an input variable, other things held constant.

Sensitivity analysis begins with a base case situation, which is developed using the expected values for each input. To illustrate, consider the data given in Table 14-2, in which projected income statements for HEP's computer project were shown. The values used to develop the table, including unit sales, sales price, fixed costs, and variable costs, are the most likely, or base case, values, and the resulting $3.79 million NPV shown in Table 14-2 is called the base case NPV. Now we ask a series of "what if" questions: What if unit sales fall 10 percent below the most likely level? What if the sales price per unit falls? What if variable costs are 66 percent of dollar sales rather than the expected 60 percent? Sensitivity analysis is designed to provide the decision maker with answers to questions such as these.

In a sensitivity analysis, each variable is changed by several specific percentage points above and below the expected value, holding other things constant; then a new NPV is calculated for each of these values; finally, the set of NPVs is plotted against the variable that was changed. Figure 14-1 shows the computer project's sensitivity graphs for three of the key input variables. The table below the graphs gives the NPVs that were used to construct the graphs. The slopes of the lines in the graphs show how sensitive NPV is to changes in each of the inputs: *the steeper the slope, the more sensitive the NPV is to a change in the variable.* In the figure we see that the project's NPV is very sensitive to changes in variable costs, less sensitive to changes in unit sales, and not very sensitive at all to changes in the required rate of return.

If we were comparing two projects, the one with the steeper sensitivity lines would be regarded as riskier because for that project a relatively small error in estimating a variable such as variable cost per unit would produce a large error in

FIGURE 14-1

Sensitivity Analysis (thousands of dollars)

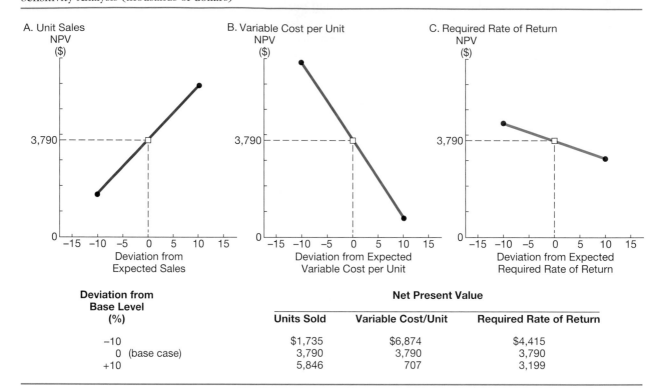

Deviation from Base Level (%)	Net Present Value		
	Units Sold	**Variable Cost/Unit**	**Required Rate of Return**
−10	$1,735	$6,874	$4,415
0 (base case)	3,790	3,790	3,790
+10	5,846	707	3,199

the project's expected NPV. Thus, sensitivity analysis can provide useful insights into the riskiness of a project.

Before we move on, two additional points about sensitivity analysis warrant attention. First, computer spreadsheet models, such as *Lotus 1-2-3,* are ideally suited for performing sensitivity analysis. We used a *Lotus 1-2-3* model to conduct the analyses represented in Figure 14-1; it generated the NPVs and then drew the graphs. Second, we could have plotted all the sensitivity lines on one graph; this would have facilitated direct comparisons of the sensitivities among different input variables.

Scenario Analysis

Although sensitivity analysis probably is the most widely used risk analysis technique, it does have limitations. Consider, for example, a proposed coal mine project whose NPV is highly sensitive to changes in output, in variable costs, and in sales price. However, if a utility company has contracted to buy a fixed amount of coal at an inflation-adjusted price per ton, the mining venture might be quite safe in spite of its steep sensitivity lines. *In general, a project's stand-alone risk depends on both (1) the sensitivity of its NPV to changes in key variables and (2) the range of likely values of these variables as reflected in their probability distributions.* Because sensitivity analysis considers only the first factor, it is incomplete.

Scenario analysis is a risk analysis technique that considers both the sensitivity of NPV to changes in key variables and the likely range of variable values. In a scenario analysis, the financial analyst asks operating managers to pick a "bad" set of circumstances (low unit sales, low sales price, high variable cost per unit, high construction cost, and so on) and a "good" set. The NPVs under the bad and good conditions are then calculated and compared to the expected, or base case, NPV.

As an example, let us return to the appliance control computer project. Assume that HEP's managers are fairly confident of their estimates of all the project's cash flow variables except price and unit sales. Further, they regard a drop in sales below 10,000 units or a rise above 20,000 units as being extremely unlikely. Similarly, they expect the sales price as set in the marketplace to fall within the range of $1,500 to $2,500. Thus, 10,000 units at a price of $1,500 defines the lower bound, or the **worst case scenario,** whereas 20,000 units at a price of $2,500 defines the upper bound, or the **best case scenario.** Remember that the **base case** values are 15,000 units and a price of $2,000.

To carry out the scenario analysis, we use the worst case variable values to obtain the worst case NPV and the best case variable values to obtain the best case NPV.[4] We actually performed the analysis using a *Lotus 1-2-3* model, and Table 14-5 summarizes the results of this analysis. We see that under the base case (or most likely case) forecast a positive NPV results; the worst case produces a negative NPV; and the best case results in a very large positive NPV.

We can use the results of the scenario analysis to determine the expected NPV, the standard deviation of NPV, and the coefficient of variation. To begin, we need an estimate of the probabilities of occurrence of the three scenarios, the Pr_i values. Suppose management estimates that there is a 20 percent probability of the worst case scenario occurring, a 60 percent probability of the base case, and a 20 percent probability of the best case. Of course, it is *very difficult* to estimate scenario probabilities accurately.

The scenario probabilities and NPVs constitute a probability distribution of returns just like those we dealt with in Chapter 5, except that the returns are measured in dollars instead of in percentages (rates of return). The expected NPV (in thousands of dollars) is $4,475:[5]

$$\text{Expected NPV} = \sum_{i=1}^{n} Pr_i(\text{NPV}_i)$$

$$= 0.20(-\$6,487) + 0.60(\$3,790) + 0.20(\$17,494) = \$4,475$$

SCENARIO ANALYSIS	

A risk analysis technique in which "bad" and "good" sets of financial circumstances are compared with a most likely, or base case, situation.

WORST CASE SCENARIO
An analysis in which all the input variables are set at their worst reasonably forecasted values.

BEST CASE SCENARIO
An analysis in which all the input variables are set at their best reasonably forecasted values.

BASE CASE
An analysis in which all the input variables are set at their most likely values.

---

[4]We could have included worst and best case values for fixed and variable costs, income tax rates, salvage values, and so on. For illustrative purposes, we limited the changes to only two variables. Also, note that we are treating sales price and quantity as independent variables; that is, a low sales price could occur when unit sales were low, and a high sales price could be coupled with high unit sales, or vice versa. As we discuss in the next section, it is relatively easy to vary these assumptions if the facts of the situation suggest a different set of conditions.

[5]Note that the expected NPV is *not* the same as the base case NPV, $3,790 (in thousands). This is because the two uncertain variables, sales volume and sales price, are multiplied together to obtain dollar sales, and this process causes the NPV distribution to be skewed to the right. A big number times another big number produces a very big number, which in turn causes the average, or expected value, to be increased.

TABLE 14-5

Scenario Analysis (dollars, except sales price, are in thousands)

Scenario	Sales Volume (Units)	Sales Price	NPV	Probability of Outcome (Pr_i)	NPV × Pr_i
Worst case	10,000	$1,500	$ (6,487)	0.20	$(1,297)
Most likely case	15,000	2,000	3,790	0.60	2,274
Best case	20,000	2,500	17,494	0.20	3,499
				1.00	Expected NPV = $ 4,475[a]
					σ_{NPV} = $ 7,630
					CV_{NPV} = 1.7

[a]There is a $1 rounding effect in the result.

The standard deviation of the NPV is $7,630 (in thousands of dollars):

$$\sigma_{NPV} = \sqrt{\sum_{i=1}^{n} Pr_i(NPV_i - \text{Expected NPV})^2}$$

$$= \sqrt{0.20(-\$6,487 - \$4,475)^2 + 0.60(\$3,790 - \$4,475)^2 + 0.20(\$17,494 - \$4,475)^2}$$

$$= \$7,630$$

Finally, the project's coefficient of variation is 1.7:

$$CV_{NPV} = \frac{\sigma_{NPV}}{\text{Expected NPV}} = \frac{\$7,630}{\$4,475} = 1.7$$

Now the project's coefficient of variation can be compared with the coefficient of variation of HEP's "average" project to get an idea of the relative riskiness of the appliance control computer project. HEP's existing projects, on average, have a coefficient of variation of about 1.0, so, on the basis of this stand-alone risk measure, HEP's managers would conclude that the appliance computer project is riskier than the firm's "average" project.

Scenario analysis provides useful information about a project's stand-alone risk. However, it is limited in that it considers only a few discrete outcomes (NPVs) for the project, even though there really are an infinite number of possibilities. In the next section, we describe a more rigorous method of assessing a project's stand-alone risk.

MONTE CARLO SIMULATION
A risk analysis technique in which probable future events are simulated on a computer, generating estimated rates of return and risk indexes.

Monte Carlo Simulation

Monte Carlo simulation, so named because this type of analysis grew out of work on the mathematics of casino gambling, ties together sensitivities and input variable probability distributions.[6] However, simulation requires a relatively pow-

---

[6]The use of simulation analysis in capital budgeting was first reported by David B. Hertz, "Risk Analysis in Capital Investments," *Harvard Business Review,* January–February 1964, pp. 95–106.

erful computer, coupled with an efficient financial planning software package, whereas scenario analysis can be done using a PC with a spreadsheet program or even using a calculator.

The first step in a computer simulation is to specify the probability distribution of each uncertain cash flow variable. Once this has been done, the simulation proceeds as follows:

1. The computer chooses at random a value for each uncertain variable based on the variable's specified probability distribution. For example, a value for unit sales would be chosen and used in the first model run.

2. The value selected for each uncertain variable, along with values for fixed factors such as the tax rate and depreciation charges, are then used in the model to determine the net cash flows for each year, and these cash flows are then used to determine the project's NPV in the first run.

3. Steps 1 and 2 are repeated many times, say 500, resulting in 500 NPVs, which make up a probability distribution.

The output produced by simulation is a probability distribution that can be used to determine the most likely range of outcomes to be expected from a project. This provides the decision maker with a better idea of the various outcomes that are possible than is available from a point estimate of the NPV. Simulation software packages also can be used to estimate the probability of NPV > 0, of IRR > k, and so on. This additional information can be quite helpful in assessing the riskiness of a project.

Limitations of Scenario and Simulation Analysis

Despite its obvious appeal, Monte Carlo simulation has not been widely used in industry. One major problem is specifying the correlations among the uncertain cash flow variables. The problem is not insurmountable, but it is important not to underestimate the difficulty of obtaining valid estimates of probability distributions and correlations among the variables.[7]

Another problem with both scenario and simulation analyses is that, even when the analyses have been completed, no clear-cut decision rule emerges. We end up with an expected NPV and a distribution about this expected value, and we can use these statistics to judge the project's stand-alone risk. However, the analyses do not provide a means to determine whether a project's profitability as measured by its expected NPV is sufficient to compensate for its risk as measured by its σ_{NPV} or CV_{NPV}.

Finally, scenario and simulation analyses ignore the effects of diversification, both among projects within the firm and by investors in their personal investment portfolios. Thus, an individual project might have highly uncertain returns when evaluated on a stand-alone basis, but if those returns are not correlated with the returns on the firm's other assets, the project might not be very risky in terms of either corporate or market risk.

---

[7]For more insight into the difficulties involved in estimating probability distributions and correlations in practice, see K. Larry Hastie, "One Businessman's View of Capital Budgeting," *Financial Management,* Winter 1974, pp. 36–43. Hastie was treasurer of Bendix Corporation.

Self-Test Questions

List three reasons why, in practice, a project's stand-alone risk is important.

Differentiate between sensitivity and scenario analyses. Why might scenario analysis be preferable to sensitivity analysis?

What is Monte Carlo simulation?

Identify some problems with (1) sensitivity analysis, (2) scenario analysis, and (3) Monte Carlo simulation.

Beta (or Market) Risk

The types of risk analysis discussed thus far in the chapter provide insights into a project's risk and thus help managers make better accept/reject decisions. However, these risk measures do not take account of portfolio risk, and they do not specify whether a project should be accepted or rejected. In this section, we show how the CAPM can be used to help overcome those shortcomings. Of course, the CAPM has shortcomings of its own, but it nevertheless offers useful insights into risk analysis in capital budgeting.

Beta Risk and Required Rate of Return for a Project

To begin, recall from Chapter 5 that the Security Market Line equation expresses the risk/return relationship as follows:

$$k_S = k_{RF} + (k_M - k_{RF})\beta_S$$

As an example, consider the case of Erie Steel Company, an integrated steel producer operating in the Great Lakes region. For simplicity, assume that Erie is all equity financed, so its cost of equity is also its average required rate of return, or cost of capital. Erie's beta $= \beta = 1.1$; $k_{RF} = 8\%$; and $k_M = 12\%$. Thus, Erie's cost of equity is 12.4 percent:

$$k_S = 8\% + (12\% - 8\%)1.1 = 12.4\%$$

This suggests that investors should be willing to give Erie money to invest in average risk projects if the company expects to earn 12.4 percent or more on this money. Here again, by average risk we mean projects having risk similar to the firm's existing assets. Therefore, as a first approximation, Erie should invest in capital projects if and only if these projects have an expected return of 12.4 percent or more.[8] In other words, Erie should use 12.4 percent as its discount rate to determine the NPVs of any average risk project it is considering.

Suppose, however, that taking on a particular project will cause a change in Erie's beta coefficient and hence change the company's required rate of return. For example, suppose Erie is considering the construction of a fleet of barges to

---

[8]To simplify things somewhat, we assume at this point that the firm uses only equity capital. If debt is used, the cost of capital used must be a weighted average of the costs of debt and equity. This point is discussed at length in Chapter 15.

INDUSTRY PRACTICE

Greater Risk? Greater Return, Please.

Indications are that financial managers are quite concerned about risk when making capital budgeting decisions. A recent survey of financial managers suggests that about 75 percent of companies use different required rates of return to account for risk differences when making capital budgeting decisions—only 25 percent use a single rate for all capital projects.[1] Most of the financial managers indicated that they attempt to compute the cost of the funds used by their firms, and that rate is appropriate for determining the acceptability of projects with average risk only. For riskier projects, some of the companies adjust the expected cash flows, but most raise the rates of return required from such investments. In addition, some firms use a reduced minimum payback period to evaluate projects with above-average risk. While this approach is not common, it appears manufacturers and

retailing firms are more likely to use an adjusted payback period to account for project risk than are financial service organizations, service companies, or utilities.

It is interesting to note that firms generally do not attempt to use probability distributions to estimate cash flows for projects, unless the outlay is extremely large. Perhaps the attitude is that it is not worth the effort to assign probabilities unless the project constitutes a major investment. When determining the terminal value of capital projects, most firms use either the expected market value or the book value of the asset at the anticipated liquidation date; in many cases, these values are expected to be the same.

In summary, it appears firms do make adjustments to the various techniques used for making capital budgeting decisions when the risks of the projects differ significantly from the average. And, the most common approach for adjusting for project risk is to raise the discount rate (required rate of return) used to compute the project's net present value.

[1] Glenn H. Petry and James Sprow, "The Theory of Finance in the 1990s," *The Quarterly Review of Economics and Finance* (Winter 1993), pp. 359-381.

---

haul iron ore, and the barge operation has a beta of 1.5 rather than 1.1. Because the firm itself might be regarded as a "portfolio of assets," and because the beta of any portfolio is a weighted average of the betas of its individual assets, taking on the barge project will cause the overall corporate beta to rise to somewhere between the original beta of 1.1 and the barge project's beta of 1.5. The exact value of the new beta will depend on the relative size of the investment in barge operations versus Erie's other assets. If 80 percent of Erie's total funds end up in basic steel operations with a beta of 1.1 and 20 percent in barge operations with a beta of 1.5, the new corporate beta will be 1.18:

$$\text{New beta} = 0.8(1.1) + 0.2(1.5) = 1.18$$

This increase in Erie's beta coefficient will cause its stock price to decline unless the increased beta is offset by a higher expected rate of return. Note that taking on the new project will cause the *overall* corporate required rate of return to rise from the original 12.4 percent to 12.7 percent because the new beta will be 1.18. This higher average rate can be earned only if the new project generates a return *substantially* higher than the existing assets are providing. Because Erie's overall return is based on its portfolio of assets, the return required from the barge project must be sufficiently high so that, in combination with returns of the other assets, the average return is 12.7 percent; only 20 percent of the average return will be provided by the barge project.

FIGURE 14-2

Using the Security Market Line Concept in Capital Budgeting

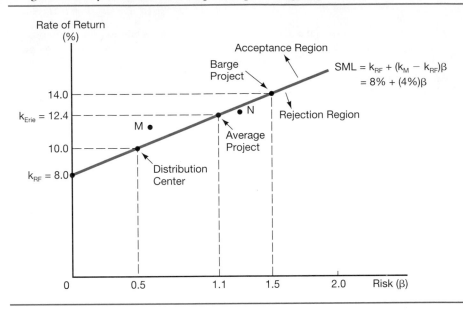

This line of reasoning leads to the conclusion that if the beta coefficient for each project, β_{proj}, could be determined, then a **project required rate of return, k_{proj},** which includes an adjustment for risk, could be found for each individual project using the following equation:

PROJECT REQUIRED RATE OF RETURN, k_{proj}
The risk-adjusted required rate of return for an individual project.

$$k_{proj} = k_{RF} + (k_M - k_{RF})\beta_{proj}$$

Thus, for basic steel projects with $\beta = 1.1$, Erie should use 12.4 percent as the required rate of return. The barge project, with $\beta = 1.5$, should be evaluated at a 14 percent required rate of return:

$$k_{Barge} = 8\% + (4\%)1.5 = 14.0\%$$

On the other hand, a low-risk project such as a new steel distribution center with a beta of only 0.5 would have a required rate of return of 10 percent.

Figure 14-2 gives a graphic summary of these concepts as applied to Erie Steel. Note the following points:

1. The SML is a Security Market Line like the one we developed in Chapter 5. It shows how investors are willing to make trade-offs between risk as measured by beta and expected returns. The higher the beta risk, the higher the rate of return needed to compensate investors for bearing this risk. The SML specifies the nature of this relationship.

2. Erie Steel initially had a beta of 1.1, so its required rate of return on average risk investments was 12.4 percent.

3. High-risk investments such as the barge line require higher rates of return, whereas low-risk investments such as the distribution center require lower rates of return. If Erie concentrates its new investments in either high- or low-risk projects as opposed to average risk ones, its corporate beta will either rise or fall from the current value of 1.1. Consequently, Erie's required rate of return on common stock would change from its current value of 12.4 percent.

4. If the expected rate of return on a given capital project lies *above* the SML, the expected rate of return on the project is more than enough to compensate for its risk, and the project should be accepted. Conversely, if the project's rate of return lies *below* the SML, it should be rejected. Thus, Project M in Figure 14-2 is acceptable, whereas Project N should be rejected. N has a higher expected return than M, but the differential is not enough to offset its much higher risk.

Measuring Beta Risk for a Project

PURE PLAY METHOD
An approach used for estimating the beta of a project in which a firm identifies companies whose only business is the product in question, determines the beta for each firm, and then averages the betas to find an approximation of its own project's beta.

In Chapter 5 (Appendix), we discussed the estimation of betas for stocks, and we indicated that it is difficult to estimate *true* future betas. The estimation of project betas is even more difficult and more fraught with uncertainty. One way a firm can try to measure the beta risk of a project is to find *single-product* companies in the same line of business as the project being evaluated, and then use the betas of those companies to determine the required rate of return for the project being evaluated. This technique is termed the **pure play method,** and the single-product companies that are used for comparisons are called *pure play firms.* For example, if Erie could find three existing single-product firms that operate barges, it could use the average of the betas of those firms as a proxy for the barge project's beta.

The pure play approach can be used only for major assets such as whole divisions, and even then it is frequently difficult to implement because it is often impossible to find pure play proxy firms. However, when IBM was considering going into personal computers, it was able to obtain data on Apple Computer and several other essentially pure play personal computer companies. This is often the case when a firm considers a major investment outside its primary field.

Self-Test Questions

What is meant by the term *average risk project*? How could you find the required rate of return for a project with average risk, low risk, and high risk?

Complete the following sentence: An increase in a company's beta coefficient would cause its stock price to decline unless . . .

Explain why a firm should accept a given capital project if its expected rate of return lies above the SML. What if the expected rate of return lies on or below the SML?

What is the pure play method, and how is it used to estimate a project's beta?

Project Risk Conclusions

We have discussed the three types of risk normally considered in capital budgeting analysis—stand-alone risk, within-firm (or corporate) risk, and beta (or market) risk—and we have discussed ways of assessing each. However, two important questions remain: (1) Should a firm be concerned with stand-alone and corporate risk in its capital budgeting decisions? and (2) what do we do when the stand-alone or within-firm risk assessments and the beta risk assessment lead to different conclusions?

These questions do not have easy answers. From a theoretical standpoint, well-diversified investors should be concerned only with beta risk, managers should be concerned only with stock price maximization, and these two factors should lead to the conclusion that beta risk ought to be given virtually all the weight in capital budgeting decisions. However, if investors are not well diversified, if the CAPM does not operate exactly as theory says it should, or if measurement problems keep managers from having confidence in the CAPM approach in capital budgeting, it might be appropriate to give stand-alone and corporate risk more weight than financial theorists suggest. Note also that the CAPM ignores bankruptcy costs, even though such costs can be substantial, and that the probability of bankruptcy depends on a firm's corporate risk, not on its beta risk. Therefore, one can easily conclude that even well-diversified investors should want a firm's management to give at least some consideration to a project's corporate risk instead of concentrating entirely on beta risk.

Although it would be desirable to reconcile these problems and to measure project risk on some absolute scale, the best we can do in practice is to determine project risk in a somewhat nebulous, relative sense. For example, we can generally say with a fair degree of confidence that a particular project has more or less stand-alone risk than the firm's average project. Then, assuming that stand-alone and corporate risk are highly correlated (which is typical), the project's stand-alone risk will be a good measure of its corporate risk. Finally, assuming that beta risk and corporate risk are highly correlated (as is true for most companies), a project with more corporate risk than average will also have more beta risk, and vice versa for projects with low corporate risk.[9]

Self-Test Questions

In theory, is it correct for a firm to be concerned with stand-alone and corporate risk in its capital budgeting decisions? Should the firm be concerned with these risks in practice?

If a project's stand-alone, corporate, and beta risk are highly correlated, would this make the task of measuring risk easier or harder? Explain.

How Project Risk Is Considered in Capital Budgeting Decisions

Thus far, we have seen that purchasing a capital project can affect a firm's beta risk, its corporate risk, or both. We also have seen that it is extremely difficult to quantify either type of risk. In other words, although it might be possible to reach the general conclusion that one project is riskier than another, it is difficult to develop a really good *measure* of project risk. This lack of precision in measuring project risk makes it difficult to incorporate differential risk into capital budgeting decisions.

---

[9]For example, see M. Chapman Findlay III, Arthur E. Gooding, and Wallace Q. Weaver, Jr., "On the Relevant Risk for Determining Capital Expenditure Hurdle Rates," *Financial Management,* Winter 1976, pp. 9–16.

RISK-ADJUSTED DISCOUNT RATE
The discount rate (required rate of return) that applies to a particular risky stream of income; it is equal to the risk-free rate of interest plus a risk premium appropriate to the level of risk attached to a particular project's income stream.

In reality, most firms incorporate project risk in capital budgeting decisions using the **risk-adjusted discount rate** approach. With this approach, the required rate of return, which is the rate at which the expected cash flows are discounted, is adjusted if the project's risk is substantially different from the average risk associated with the firm's existing assets. Therefore, average risk projects would be discounted at the rate of return required of projects that are considered "average", or normal for the firm; above-average risk projects would be discounted at a higher-than-average rate; and below-average risk projects would be discounted at a rate below the firm's average rate of return. Unfortunately, because risk cannot be measured precisely, there is no accurate way of specifying exactly how much higher or lower these discount rates should be; given the present state of the art, *risk adjustments are necessarily judgmental and somewhat arbitrary.*

Although the process is not exact, many companies use a two-step procedure to develop risk-adjusted discount rates for use in capital budgeting. First, the overall required rate of return is established for the firm's existing assets. This process is completed on a division-by-division basis for very large firms, perhaps using the CAPM. Second, all projects generally are classified into three categories—high risk, average risk, and low risk. Then, the firm or division uses the average required rate of return as the discount rate for average risk projects, reduces the average rate by one or two percentage points when evaluating low-risk projects, and raises the average rate by several percentage points for high-risk projects. For example, if a firm's basic required rate of return is estimated to be 12 percent, an 18 percent discount rate might be used for a high-risk project and a 9 percent rate for a low-risk project. Average risk projects, which constitute about 80 percent of most capital budgets, would be evaluated at the 12 percent rate of return. Table 14-6 contains an example of the application of risk-adjusted discount rates for the evaluation of four projects. Each of the four projects has a 5-year life, and each is expected to generate a constant cash flow stream during its life; therefore, each project's future cash flow pattern represents an annuity. The analysis shows that only Project A and Project C are acceptable when risk is considered. Notice, though, that if the average required rate of return is used to evaluate all the projects, Project C and Project D would be considered acceptable because their IRRs

TABLE 14-6

Capital Budgeting Decisions Using Risk-Adjusted Discount Rates

Project	Project Risk	Required Return (%)	Estimated Life	Initial Investment Outlay—CF_0	Incremental Operating Cash Flows—CF_1–CF_5	NPV	IRR
A	low	9	5	$(10,000)	$2,700	$ 502	10.9%
B	average	12	5	(11,000)	3,000	(186)	11.3
C	average	12	5	(9,000)	2,500	12	12.1
D	high	18	5	(12,000)	3,800	(117)	17.6

Project Risk Classification	Required Rate of Return (%)
Low	9
Average	12
High	18

are greater than 12 percent. Using the average required rate of return would lead to an incorrect decision. Thus, *if project risk is not considered in capital budgeting analysis, incorrect decisions are possible.*

This risk-adjusted discount rate approach is far from precise, but it does at least recognize that different projects have different risks, and projects with different risks should be evaluated using different required rates of return.

Self-Test Questions

How are risk-adjusted discount rates used to incorporate project risk into the capital budget decision process?

Briefly explain the two-step process many companies use to develop risk-adjusted discount rates for use in capital budgeting.

Capital Rationing

CAPITAL RATIONING
A situation in which a constraint is placed on the total size of the firm's capital investment.

Capital budgeting decisions typically are made on the basis of the techniques presented in Chapter 13 and applied as described in this chapter—independent projects are accepted if their NPVs are positive, and choices among mutually exclusive projects are made by selecting the one with the highest NPV. In this analysis, it is assumed that if in a particular year the firm has an especially large number of good projects, management simply will go into the financial markets and raise whatever funds are required to finance all of the acceptable projects. However, some firms do set limits on the amount of funds they are willing to raise, and, if this is done, the capital budget must also be limited. This situation is known as **capital rationing.**

Elaborate and mathematically sophisticated models have been developed to help firms maximize their values when they are subject to capital rationing. However, a firm that subjects itself to capital rationing is deliberately forgoing profitable projects, and hence it is not truly maximizing its value. This point is well known, so few sophisticated firms ration capital today. Therefore, we shall not discuss it further, but you should know what the term *capital rationing* means.

Self-Test Questions

What is meant by the term *capital rationing*?

Why do few sophisticated firms ration capital today?

Summary

This chapter presented two issues in capital budgeting: cash flow estimation and evaluation, and risk analysis in capital budgeting. The key concepts covered are listed below.

- The most important, but also the most difficult, step in analyzing a capital budgeting project is estimating the **incremental after-tax cash flows** the project will produce.
- Incremental cash flows can be classified as (1) the **initial investment outlay,** which includes cash flows that occur only at the start of a project's life, (2) **incremental operating cash flows** that continue throughout the life of

the project, and (3) the **terminal cash flow,** which is the net cash flow at the end, or the termination, of the project.

• In determining incremental cash flows, **opportunity costs** (the cash flow forgone by using an asset) must be included, but **sunk costs** (cash outlays that have been made and that cannot be recouped) should not be included. Any **externalities** (effects of a project on other parts of the firm) should also be reflected in the analysis. In addition, **inflation** effects must be considered in project analysis. The best procedure is to build inflation directly into the cash flow estimates.

• Capital projects often require an additional investment in **net working capital (NWC).** An increase in NWC must be included in the Year 0 initial cash outlay and then shown as a cash inflow in the project's final year.

• **Replacement analysis** is slightly different from that for **expansion projects** because the cash flows from the old asset must be considered in replacement decisions.

• A project's **stand-alone risk** is the risk the project would have if it were the firm's only asset and if the firm's stockholders held only that one stock. Stand-alone risk is measured by the variability of the asset's expected returns, and it is often used as a proxy for both beta and corporate risk because (1) beta and corporate risk are difficult to measure and (2) the three types of risk are usually highly correlated.

• **Within-firm,** or **corporate, risk** reflects the effects of a project on the firm's risk, and it is measured by the project's effect on the firm's earnings variability. Stockholder diversification is not taken into account.

• **Beta risk** reflects the effects of a project on the risks borne by stockholders, assuming stockholders hold diversified portfolios. In theory, beta risk should be the most relevant type of risk.

• **Corporate risk** is important because it influences the firm's ability to use low-cost debt, to maintain smooth operations over time, and to avoid crises that might consume management's energy and disrupt employees, customers, suppliers, and the community.

• **Sensitivity analysis** is a technique which shows how much an output variable such as NPV will change in response to a given change in an input variable such as sales, other things held constant.

• **Scenario analysis** is a risk analysis technique in which the best and worst case NPVs are compared with the project's expected NPV.

• **Monte Carlo simulation** is a risk analysis technique in which a computer is used to simulate probable future events and thus to estimate the profitability distribution and riskiness of a project.

• The **pure play method** can be used to estimate betas for large projects or for divisions.

• The **risk-adjusted discount rate** is the rate used to evaluate a particular project. The discount rate is increased for projects that are riskier than the firm's average project but is decreased for less risky projects.

• **Capital rationing** occurs when management places a constraint on the size of the firm's capital budget during a particular period.

Both the measurement of risk and its incorporation into capital budgeting involve judgment. It is possible to use a quantitative technique such as simulation as an aid to judgment, but in the final analysis the assessment of risk in capital budgeting is a subjective process.

Questions

14-1   Cash flows rather than accounting profits are listed in Table 14-2. What is the basis for this emphasis on cash flows as opposed to net income?

14-2   Look at Table 14-4 and answer these questions:
    a.   Why is the net salvage value shown in Section III reduced for taxes?
    b.   How is the change in depreciation computed?
    c.   What would happen if the new machine permitted a reduction in net working capital?
    d.   Why are the cost savings shown as a positive amount?

14-3   Explain why sunk costs should not be included in a capital budgeting analysis, but opportunity costs and externalities should be included.

14-4   Explain how net working capital is recovered at the end of a project's life, and why it is included in a capital budgeting analysis.

14-5   In general, is an explicit recognition of incremental cash flows more important in new project or replacement analysis? Why?

14-6   Why is it true, in general, that a failure to adjust expected cash flows for expected inflation biases the calculated NPV downward?

14-7   Define (a) simulation analysis, (b) scenario analysis, and (c) sensitivity analysis. If AT&T were considering two investments, one calling for the expenditure of $200 million to develop a satellite communications system and the other involving the expenditure of $12,000 for a new truck, on which one would the company be more likely to use simulation analysis?

14-8   Distinguish between beta (or market) risk, within-firm (or corporate) risk, and stand-alone risk for a project being considered for inclusion in the capital budget. Which type of risk do you believe should be given the greatest weight in capital budgeting decisions? Explain.

14-9   Suppose Reading Engine Company, which has a high beta as well as a great deal of corporate risk, merged with Simplicity Patterns Inc. Simplicity's sales rise during recessions, when people are more likely to make their own clothes, and, consequently, its beta is negative but its corporate risk is relatively high. What would the merger do to the costs of capital in the consolidated company's locomotive engine division and in its patterns division?

14-10   Suppose a firm estimates its required rate of return for the coming year to be 10 percent. What are reasonable required rates of return for evaluating average risk projects, high risk projects, and low risk projects?

Self-Test Problems

(Solutions appear in Appendix B)

Key terms   **ST-1**   Define each of the following terms:
    a.   cash flow; accounting income; relevant cash flow
    b.   incremental cash flow; sunk cost; opportunity cost; externalities; inflation bias
    c.   initial investment outlay; incremental operating cash flow; terminal cash flow
    d.   change in net working capital; expansion project
    e.   salvage value
    f.   replacement analysis
    g.   stand-alone risk; within-firm risk; market risk
    h.   corporate risk

i. sensitivity analysis
j. scenario analysis
k. Monte Carlo simulation analysis
l. coefficient of variation versus standard deviation
m. project beta versus corporate beta
n. pure play method of estimating project betas
o. risk-adjusted discount rate; project required rate of return
p. capital rationing

New project analysis   ST-2   You have been asked by the president of Ellis Construction Company, headquartered in Toledo, to evaluate the proposed acquisition of a new earthmover. The mover's basic price is $50,000, and it will cost another $10,000 to modify it for special use by Ellis Construction. Assume that the mover falls into the MACRS 3-year class. (See Table 14A-2 for MACRS recovery allowance percentages.) It will be sold after 3 years for $20,000, and it will require an increase in net working capital (spare parts inventory) of $2,000. The earthmover purchase will have no effect on revenues, but it is expected to save Ellis $20,000 per year in before-tax operating costs, mainly labor. Ellis's marginal tax rate is 40 percent.

a. What is the company's net initial investment outlay if it acquires the earthmover? (That is, what are the Year 0 cash flows?)
b. What are the incremental operating cash flows in Years 1, 2, and 3?
c. What is the terminal cash flow in Year 3?
d. If the project's required rate of return is 10 percent, should be earthmover be purchased?

Replacement analysis   ST-3   The Dauten Toy Corporation currently uses an injection molding machine that was purchased 2 years ago. This machine is being depreciated on a straight line basis toward a $500 salvage value, and it has 6 years of remaining life. Its current book value is $2,600, and it can be sold for $3,000 at this time. Thus, the annual depreciation expense is ($2,600 − $500)/6 = $350 per year.

Dauten is offered a replacement machine which has a cost of $8,000, an estimated useful life of 6 years, and an estimated salvage value of $800. This machine falls into the MACRS 5-year class. (See Table 14A-2 for MACRS recovery allowance percentages.) The replacement machine would permit an output expansion, so sales would rise by $1,000 per year; even so, the new machine's much greater efficiency would still cause operating expenses to decline by $1,500 per year. The new machine would require that inventories be increased by $2,000, but accounts payable would simultaneously increase by $500.

Dauten's marginal tax rate is 40 percent, and its required rate of return is 15 percent. Should it replace the old machine?

Corporate risk analysis   ST-4   The staff of Heymann Manufacturing has estimated the following net cash flows and probabilities for a new manufacturing process:

| Year | Net Cash Flows | | |
	Pr = 0.2	Pr = 0.6	Pr = 0.2
0	$(100,000)	$(100,000)	$(100,000)
1	20,000	30,000	40,000
2	20,000	30,000	40,000
3	20,000	30,000	40,000
4	20,000	30,000	40,000
5	20,000	30,000	40,000
5*	0	20,000	30,000

Line 0 gives the cost of the process, Lines 1 through 5 give operating cash flows, and Line 5* contains the estimated salvage values. Heymann's required rate of return for an average risk project is 10 percent.

a. Assume that the project has average risk. Find the project's expected NPV. (Hint: Use expected values for the net cash flow in each year.)

b. Find the best case and worst case NPVs. What is the probability of occurrence of the worst case if the cash flows are perfectly dependent (perfectly positively correlated) over time? If they are independent over time?

c. Assume that all the cash flows are perfectly positively correlated: that is, there are only three possible cash flow streams over time: (1) the worst case, (2) the most likely, or base, case, and (3) the best case, with probabilities of 0.2, 0.6, and 0.2, respectively. These cases are represented by each of the columns in the table. Find the expected NPV, its standard deviation, and its coefficient of variation.

d. The coefficient of variation of Heymann's average project is in the range 0.8 to 1.0. If the coefficient of variation of a project being evaluated is greater than 1.0, 2 percentage points are added to the firm's required rate of return. Similarly, if the coefficient of variation is less than 0.8, 1 percentage point is deducted from the required rate of return. What is the project's required rate of return? Should Heymann accept or reject the project?

Problems

New project analysis   **14-1**   You have been asked by the president of your company to evaluate the proposed acquisition of a spectrometer for the firm's R&D department. The equipment's base price is $140,000, and it would cost another $30,000 to modify it for special use by your firm. The spectrometer, which falls into the MACRS 3-year class, would be sold after 3 years for $60,000. (See Table 14A-2 for MACRS recovery allowance percentages.) Use of the equipment would require an increase in net working capital (spare parts inventory) of $8,000. The spectrometer would have no effect on revenues, but it is expected to save the firm $50,000 per year in before-tax operating costs, mainly labor. The firm's marginal tax rate is 40 percent.

a. What is the initial investment outlay associated with this project? (That is, what is the Year 0 net cash flow?)

b. What are the incremental operating cash flows in Years 1, 2, and 3?

c. What is the terminal cash flow in Year 3?

d. If the project's required rate of return is 12 percent, should the spectrometer be purchased?

New project analysis   **14-2**   The Ewert Company is evaluating the proposed acquisition of a new milling machine. The machine's base price is $108,000, and it would cost another $12,500 to modify it for special use by the firm. The machine falls into the MACRS 3-year class, and it would be sold after 3 years for $65,000. (See Table 14A-2 for MACRS recovery allowance percentages.) The machine would require an increase in net working capital (inventory) of $5,500. The milling machine would have no effect on revenues, but it is expected to save the firm $44,000 per year in before-tax operating costs, mainly labor. Ewert's tax rate is 34 percent.

a. What is the initial investment outlay of the machine for capital budgeting purposes? (That is, what is the Year 0 net cash flow?)

b. What are the incremental operating cash flows in years 1, 2, and 3?

c. What is the terminal cash flow in Year 3?

d. If the project's required rate of return is 12 percent, should the machine be purchased?

Replacement analysis   14-3   Atlantic Control Company purchased a machine 2 years ago at a cost of $70,000. At that time, the machine's expected economic life was 6 years and the expected salvage value was $10,000. It is being depreciated using the straight line method so that its book value in 4 more years is $10,000.

A new machine can be purchased for $80,000, including shipping and installation costs. The new machine has an economic life estimated to be 4 years. MACRS depreciation will be used, and the machine will be depreciated over its 3-year class life. (See Table 14A-2 for MACRS recovery allowance percentages.) During its 4-year life, the new machine will reduce cash operating expenses by $20,000 per year. Sales are not expected to change. But the new machine will require net working capital to be increased by $4,000. At the end of its useful life, the machine is estimated to have a market value of $2,500.

The old machine can be sold today for $20,000. If it is not replaced, the company believes the old machine can be used for another 4 years; in 4 years the old machine will be worthless, so its market value will be $0. The firm's tax rate is 40 percent. The appropriate required rate of return is 10 percent.

a. If the new machine is purchased, what is the amount of the initial investment outlay at Year 0?

b. What incremental operating cash flows will occur at the end of Years 1 through 4 as a result of replacing the old machine?

c. What is the terminal cash flow at the end of Year 4 if the new machine is purchased?

d. What is the NPV of this project? Should Atlantic replace the old machine?

Replacement analysis   14-4   The Boyd Bottling Company is contemplating the replacement of one of its bottling machines with a newer and more efficient one. The old machine has a book value of $600,000 and a remaining useful life of 5 years. The firm does not expect to realize any return from scrapping the old machine in 5 years, but it can sell it now to another firm in the industry for $265,000. The old machine is being depreciated toward a zero salvage value, or by $120,000 per year, using the straight line method.

The new machine has a purchase price of $1,175,000, an estimated useful life and MACRS class life of 5 years, and an estimated market value of $145,000 at the end of 5 years. (See Table 14A-2 for MACRS recovery allowance percentages.) It is expected to economize on electric power usage, labor, and repair costs, which will save Boyd $230,000 each year. In addition, it is expected the new machine will reduce the number of defective bottles, which will save an additional $25,000 annually. The company's tax rate is 40 percent and it has a 12 percent required rate of return.

a. What is the initial investment outlay required for the new machine?

b. Calculate the annual depreciation allowances for both machines, and compute the change in the annual depreciation expense if the replacement is made.

c. What are the incremental operating cash flows in Years 1 through 5?

d. What is the terminal cash flow in Year 5?

e. Should the firm purchase the new machine? Support your answer.

f. In general, how would each of the following factors affect the investment decision, and how should each be treated?

(1) The expected life of the existing machine decreases.

(2) The required rate of return is not constant but is increasing as Boyd adds more projects into its capital budget for the year.

Risky cash flows   14-5   The Singleton Company must decide between two mutually exclusive investment projects. Each project costs $6,750 and has an expected life of 3 years. Annual net cash flows from each project begin 1 year after the initial investment is made and have the following probability distributions:

Project A		Project B	
Probability	Net Cash Flows	Probability	Net Cash Flows
0.2	$6,000	0.2	$ 0
0.6	6,750	0.6	6,750
0.2	7,500	0.2	18,000

Singleton has decided to evaluate the riskier project at a 12 percent rate and the less risky project at a 10 percent rate.

a. What is the expected value of the annual net cash flows from each project? What is the coefficient of variation (CV_{NPV})? (Hint: Use Equation 5-3 from Chapter 5 to calculate the standard deviation of Project A. $\sigma_B = \$5,798$ and $CV_B = 0.76$.)

b. What is the risk-adjusted NPV of each project?

c. If it were known that Project B was negatively correlated with other cash flows of the firm whereas Project A was positively correlated, how would this knowledge affect the decision? If Project B's cash flows were negatively correlated with gross national product (GNP), would that influence your assessment of its risk?

CAPM approach to risk adjustment   **14-6**   Goodtread Rubber Company has two divisions: the tire division, which manufactures tires for new autos, and the recap division, which manufactures recapping materials that are sold to independent tire recapping shops throughout the United States. Because auto manufacturing fluctuates with the general economy, the tire division's earnings contribution to Goodtread's stock price is highly correlated with returns on most other stocks. If the tire division were operated as a separate company, its beta coefficient would be about 1.50. The sales and profits of the recap division, on the other hand, tend to be countercyclical because recap sales boom when people cannot afford to buy new tires. The recap division's beta is estimated to be 0.5. Approximately 75 percent of Goodtread's corporate assets are invested in the tire division and 25 percent are invested in the recap division.

Currently, the rate of interest on Treasury securities is 9 percent, and the expected rate of return on an average share of stock is 13 percent. Goodtread uses only common equity capital, so it has no debt outstanding.

a. What is the required rate of return on Goodtread's stock?

b. What discount rate should be used to evaluate capital budgeting projects? Explain your answer fully and, in the process, illustrate your answer with a project that costs $160,000, has a 10-year life, and provides expected after-tax net cash flows of $30,000 per year.

Scenario analysis   **14-7**   Your firm, Agrico Products, is considering the purchase of a tractor which will have a net cost of $36,000, will increase pretax operating cash flows before taking account of depreciation effects by $12,000 per year, and will be depreciated on a straight line basis to zero over 5 years at the rate of $7,200 per year, beginning the first year. (Annual cash flows will be $12,000, before taxes, plus the tax savings that result from $7,200 of depreciation.) The board of directors is having a heated debate about whether the tractor actually will last 5 years. Specifically, Joan Lamm insists that she knows of some tractors that have lasted only 4 years. Alan Grunewald agrees with Lamm, but he argues that most tractors do give 5 years of service. Judy Maese says she has known some to last for as long as 8 years.

Given this discussion, the board asks you to prepare a scenario analysis to ascertain the importance of the uncertainty about the tractor's life. Assume a 40 percent marginal tax rate, a zero salvage value, and a required rate of return of 10 percent. (Hint: Here straight line depreciation is based on the MACRS class life of the tractor and is not affected by the actual life. Also, ignore the half-year convention for this problem.)

Exam-Type Problems

The problems included in this section are set up in such a way that they could be used as multiple-choice exam problems.

Replacement analysis   **14-8**   The Gehr Company is considering the purchase of a new machine tool to replace an obsolete one. The machine being used for the operation has both a tax book value and a market value of zero; it is in good working order, however, and will last physically for at least another 10 years. The proposed replacement machine will perform the operation so much more efficiently that Gehr engineers estimate it will produce after-tax cash flows (labor savings and depreciation) of $9,000 per year. The new machine will cost $40,000 delivered and installed, and its economic life is estimated to be 10 years. It has zero salvage value. The firm's required rate of return is 10 percent, and its tax rate is 34 percent. Should Gehr buy the new machine?

Replacement analysis   **14-9**   Galveston Shipyards is considering the replacement of an 8-year-old riveting machine with a new one that will increase earnings before depreciation from $27,000 to $54,000 per year. The new machine will cost $82,500, and it will have an estimated life of 8 years and no salvage value. The new machine will be depreciated over its 5-year MACRS recovery period. (See Table 14A-2 for MACRS recovery allowance percentages.) The firm's marginal tax rate is 40 percent, and the firm's required rate of return is 12 percent. The old machine has been fully depreciated and has no salvage value. Should the old riveting machine be replaced by the new one?

Risk adjustment   **14-10**   The risk-free rate of return is 9 percent, and the market risk premium is 5 percent. The beta of the project under analysis is 1.4, with expected net cash flows estimated to be $1,500 per year for 5 years. The required investment outlay on the project is $4,500.
a. What is the required risk-adjusted return on the project?
b. Should the project be accepted?

Beta risk   **14-11**   Pappas Computer Corporation, a producer of office equipment, currently has assets of $15 million and a beta of 1.4. The risk-free rate is 8 percent and the market risk premium is 5 percent. Pappas would like to expand into the risky home computer market. If the expansion is undertaken, Pappas would create a new division with $3.75 million in assets. The new division would have a beta of 1.8.
a. What is Pappas's current required rate of return?
b. If the expansion is undertaken, what would be the firm's new beta? What is the new overall required rate of return, and what rate of return must the home computer division produce to leave the new overall required rate of return unchanged?

Integrative Problems

Capital budgeting and cash flow estimation   **14-12**   Unilate Textiles is evaluating a new product, a silk/wool blended fabric. Assume that you were recently hired as assistant to the director of capital budgeting, and you must evaluate the new project.

The fabric would be produced in an unused building adjacent to Unilate's Southern Pines plant; Unilate owns the building, which is fully depreciated. The required equipment would cost $200,000, plus an additional $40,000 for shipping and installation. In addition, inventories would rise by $25,000, while accounts payable would go up by $5,000. All of these costs would be incurred at t = 0. By a special ruling, the machinery could be depreciated under the MACRS system as 3-year property.

The project is expected to operate for 4 years, at which time it will be terminated. The cash inflows are assumed to begin one year after the project is undertaken, or at t = 1, and to continue out to t = 4. At the end of the project's life (t = 4), the equipment is expected to have a salvage value of $25,000.

Unit sales are expected to total 100,000 five-yard rolls per year, and the expected sales price is $2.00 per roll. Cash operating costs for the project (total operating costs less depreciation) are expected to total 60 percent of dollar sales. Unilate's marginal tax rate is 40 percent, and its required rate of return is 10 percent. Tentatively, the silk/wool blend fabric project is assumed to be of equal risk to Unilate's other assets.

You have been asked to evaluate the project and to make a recommendation as to whether it should be accepted or rejected. To guide you in your analysis, your boss gave you the following set of questions.

a. Draw a cash flow time line which shows when the net cash inflows and outflows will occur, and explain how the time line can be used to help structure the analysis.

b. Unilate has a standard form which is used in the capital budgeting process—see Table IP14-1. Part of the table has been completed, but you must replace the blanks with the missing numbers. Complete the table in the following steps:

  (1) Complete the unit sales, sales price, total revenues, and operating costs excluding depreciation lines.

  (2) Complete the depreciation line.

  (3) Now complete the table down to net income and then down to net operating cash flows.

  (4) Now fill in the blanks under Year 0 and Year 4 for the initial investment outlay and the terminal cash flows, and complete the "cash flow time line" (net cash flow). Discuss working capital. What would have happened if the machinery were sold for less than its book value?

c. (1) Unilate uses debt in its capital structure, so some of the money used to finance the project will be debt. Given this fact, should the projected cash flows be revised to show projected interest charges? Explain.

  (2) Suppose you learned that Unilate had spent $50,000 to renovate the building last year, expensing these costs. Should this cost be reflected in the analysis? Explain.

  (3) Now suppose you learned that Unilate could lease its building to another party and earn $25,000 per year. Should that fact be reflected in the analysis? If so, how?

  (4) Now assume that the silk/wool blend fabric project would take away profitable sales from Unilate's cotton/wool blend fabric business. Should that fact be reflected in your analysis? If so, how?

d. Disregard all the assumptions made in Part c, and assume there was no alternative use for the building over the next 4 years. Now calculate the project's NPV, IRR, and regular payback. Do these indicators suggest that the project should be accepted?

e. If this project had been a replacement rather than an expansion project, how would the analysis have changed? Think about the changes that would have to occur in the cash flow table, but no calculations are required.

TABLE IP14-1

Unilate's Silk/Wool Blend Project (thousands of dollars)

End of Year:	0	1	2	3	4
Unit sales (thousands)			100		
Price/unit		$ 2.00	$ 2.00		
Total revenues				$200.0	
Costs excluding depreciation			($120.0)		
Depreciation				(36.0)	(16.8)
Total operating costs		($199.2)	($228.0)		
Earnings before taxes (EBT)				$ 44.0	
Taxes		(0.3)			(25.3)
Net income				$26.4	
Depreciation		79.2		36.0	
Incremental operating CF		$ 79.7			$54.7
Equipment cost					
Installation					
Increase in inventory					
Increase in accounts payable					
Salvage value					
Tax on salvage value					
Return of net working capital					
Cash flow time line (Net CF)	$(260.00)				$89.7
Cumulative CF for payback	(260.0)	(180.3)			63.0

$$NPV =$$
$$IRR =$$
$$Payback =$$

f. Assume that inflation is expected to average 5 percent over the next 4 years; that this expectation is reflected in the required rate of return; and that inflation will increase variable costs and revenues by the same percentage, 5 percent. Does it appear that inflation has been dealt with properly in the analysis? If not, what should be done, and how would the required adjustment affect the decision?

Risk analysis 14-13 Problem 14-12 contained the details of a new-project capital budgeting evaluation being conducted by Unilate Textiles. Although inflation was considered in the initial analysis, the riskiness of the project was not considered. The expected cash flows considering inflation as they were estimated in Problem 14-12 (in thousands of dollars) are given in the following table. Unilate's required rate of return is 10 percent. You have been asked to answer the following questions.

a. (1) What are the three levels, or types, of project risk that are normally considered?
(2) Which type is the most relevant?
(3) Which type is the easiest to measure?
(4) Are the three types of risk generally highly correlated?
b. (1) What is sensitivity analysis?
(2) Discuss how one would perform a sensitivity analysis on the unit sales, salvage value, and required rate of return for the project. Assume that each of these variables deviates from its base case, or expected, value by

TABLE IP14-2

	Year				
	0	1	2	3	4
Investment in:					
Fixed assets	($240)				
Net working capital	(20)				
Unit sales (thousands)		100	100	100	100
Sales price (dollars)		$2.100	$2.205	$2.315	$2.431
Total revenues		$210.0	$220.5	$231.5	$243.1
Cash operating costs (60%)		(126.0)	(132.3)	(138.9)	(145.9)
Depreciation		(79.2)	(108.0)	(36.0)	(16.8)
Earnings before taxes (EBT)		$ 4.8	($ 19.8)	$ 56.6	$ 80.4
Taxes (40%)		(1.9)	7.9	(22.6)	(32.2)
Net income		$ 2.9	($ 11.9)	$ 34.0	$ 48.2
Plus depreciation		79.2	108.0	36.0	16.8
Net operating cash flow		$ 82.1	$ 96.1	$ 70.0	$ 65.0
Salvage value					25.0
Tax on SV (40%)					(10.0)
Recovery of NWC					20.0
Net cash flow	($260)	$ 82.1	$ 96.1	$ 70.0	$100.0
Cumulative cash flow for payback:	(260.0)	(177.9)	(81.8)	(11.8)	88.2

NPV at 10% cost of capital = $15.0
IRR   = 12.6%

plus and minus 10 percent, 20 percent, and 30 percent. Explain how you would calculate the NPV, IRR, and the payback for each case.

(3) What is the primary weakness of sensitivity analysis? What are its primary advantages?

c. Assume that you are confident about the estimates of all the variables that affect the project's cash flows except unit sales. If product acceptance is poor, sales would be only 75,000 units a year, while a strong consumer response would produce sales of 125,000 units. In either case, cash costs would still amount to 60 percent of revenues. You believe that there is a 25 percent chance of poor acceptance, a 25 percent chance of excellent acceptance, and a 50 percent chance of average acceptance (the base case).

(1) What is the worst case NPV? The best case NPV?

(2) Use the worst, most likely (or base), and best case NPVs and probabilities of occurrence to find the project's expected NPV, standard deviation (σ_{NPV}), and coefficient of variation (CV_{NPV}).

d. (1) Assume that Unilate's average project has a coefficient of variation (CV_{NPV}) in the range of 1.25 to 1.75. Would the silk/wool blend fabric project be classified as high-risk, average risk, or low-risk? What type of risk is being measured here?

(2) Based on common sense, how highly correlated do you think the project would be to the firm's other assets? (Give a correlation coefficient, or range of coefficients, based on your judgment.)

(3) How would this correlation coefficient and the previously calculated σ combine to affect the project's contribution to corporate, or within-firm, risk? Explain.

e. (1) Based on your judgment, what do you think the project's correlation co-efficient would be with respect to the general economy and thus with returns on "the market"?

(2) How would correlation with the economy affect the project's market risk?

f. (1) Unilate typically adds or subtracts 3 percentage points to the overall re-quired rate of return to adjust for risk. Should the project be accepted?

(2) What subjective risk factors should be considered before the final deci-sion is made?

g. Define scenario analysis and simulation analysis, and discuss their principal advantages and disadvantages. (Note that you have already done scenario anal-ysis in Part c.)

h. (1) Assume that the risk-free rate is 10 percent, the market risk premium is 6 percent, and the new project's beta is 1.2. What is the project's required rate of return on equity based on the CAPM?

(2) How does the project's market risk compare with the firm's overall mar-ket risk?

(3) How does the project's stand-alone risk compare with that of the firm's average project?

(4) Briefly describe how you could estimate the project's beta. How feasible do you think that procedure actually would be in this case?

(5) What are the advantages and disadvantages of focusing on a project's mar-ket risk?

Computer-Related Problem

Work the problem in this section only if you are using the computer problem diskette.

Expansion project   **14-14**   Use the computerized model in File C14 to work this problem. Golden State Bak-ers Inc. (GSB) has an opportunity to invest in a new dough machine. GSB needs more productive capacity, so the new machine will not replace an existing ma-chine. The new machine costs $260,000 and will require modifications costing $15,000. It has an expected useful life of 10 years, will be depreciated using the MACRS method over its 5-year class life, and has an expected salvage value of $12,500 at the end of Year 10. (See Table 14A-2 for MACRS recovery allowance percentages.) The machine will require a $22,500 investment in net working cap-ital. It is expected to generate additional sales revenues of $125,000 per year, but its use also will increase annual cash operating expenses by $55,000. GSB's re-quired rate of return is 10 percent, and its marginal tax rate is 40 percent. The machine's book value at the end of Year 10 will be zero, so GSB will have to pay taxes on the $12,500 salvage value.

a. What is the NPV of this expansion project? Should GSB purchase the new machine?

b. Should GSB purchase the new machine if it is expected to be used for only 5 years and then sold for $31,250? (Note that the model is set up to handle a 5-year life; you need only enter the new life and salvage value.)

c. Would the machine be profitable if revenues increased by only $105,000 per year? Assume a 10-year project life and a salvage value of $12,500.

Replacement Chain (Common Life) Approach

REPLACEMENT CHAIN (COMMON LIFE) APPROACH
A method of comparing projects of unequal lives which assumes that each project can be replicated as many times as necessary to reach a common life span; the NPVs over this life span are then compared, and the project with the higher common life NPV is chosen.

Although the analysis in Figure 14B-1 suggests that Project C should be selected, this analysis is incomplete, and the decision to choose Project C actually is incorrect. If we choose Project F, we will have the opportunity to make a similar investment in 3 years, and if cost and revenue conditions continue at the Figure 14B-1 levels, this second investment also will be profitable. However, if we choose Project C, we will not have this second investment opportunity. Therefore, to make a proper comparison of Projects C and F, we could apply the **replacement chain (common life) approach;** that is, we could find the NPV of Project F over a 6-year period and then compare this extended NPV with the NPV of Project C over the same 6 years.

The NPV for Project C as calculated in Figure 14B-1 already is over the 6-year common life. For Project F, however, we must expand the analysis to include the replacement of F in Year 3, resulting in the following 6-year time line:[11]

	0 k = 15%	1	2	3	4	5	6
	(20,000)	7,000	13,000	12,000	7,000	13,000	12,000
				(20,000)			
Net CF	(20,000)	7,000	13,000	(8,000)	7,000	13,000	12,000

Extended life NPV$_F$ at 15% = \$6,310

Here we make the assumption that Project F's cost and annual cash inflows will not change if the project is repeated in 3 years, and that HEP's required rate of return will remain at 15 percent. Project F's extended NPV is \$6,310. This is the value that should be compared with Project C's NPV, \$5,374. Because Project F's "true" NPV is greater than that of Project C, Project F should be selected.

Equivalent Annual Annuity Approach

EQUIVALENT ANNUAL ANNUITY (EAA) METHOD
A method that calculates the annual payments a project would provide if it were an annuity. When comparing projects of unequal lives, the one with the higher equivalent annual annuity should be chosen.

Although the preceding example illustrates why an extended analysis is necessary if we are comparing mutually exclusive projects with different lives, the arithmetic is generally more complex in practice. For example, one project might have a 6-year life versus a 10-year life for the other. This would require a replacement chain analysis over 30 years, the lowest common denominator of the two lives. In such a situation, it is often simpler to use a second procedure, the **equivalent annual annuity (EAA) method,** which involves three steps:

1. Find each project's NPV over its initial life. In Figure 14B-1, we found NPV$_C$ = \$5,374 and NPV$_F$ = \$3,807.
2. Find the constant annuity cash flow (the equivalent annual annuity [EAA]) that has the same present value as each project's NPV. For Project F, here is the time line:

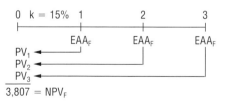

---

[11]We also could set up Project F's extended time line as follows:

1. The Stage 1 NPV is \$3,807.
2. The Stage 2 NPV is also \$3,807, but this value will not accrue until Year 3, so its value today, discounted at 15 percent, is \$2,503.
3. The extended life NPV is thus \$3,807 + \$2,503 = \$6,310.

To find the value of EAA_F, with a financial calculator, enter -3807 as the PV, k = I = 15, and N = 3, and solve for PMT. The answer is \$1,667. This cash flow stream, when discounted back 3 years at 15 percent, has a present value equal to Project F's original NPV, \$3,807. The payment figure we found, \$1,667, is called the project's *equivalent annual annuity (EAA)*. The EAA for Project C was found similarly to be \$1,420. Thus, Project C has an NPV equivalent to an annuity of \$1,420 per year, while Project F's NPV is equivalent to an annuity of \$1,667.

3. Assuming that continuous replacements can and will be made each time a project's life ends, these EAAs will continue on out to infinity; that is, they will constitute perpetuities. Recognizing that the value of a perpetuity is V = PMT/k, w can find the net present values of the infinite EAAs of Projects C and F as follows:

$$\text{Infinite horizon } NPV_C = \$1,420/0.15 = \$\ 9,467.$$
$$\text{Infinite horizon } NPV_F = \$1,667/0.15 = \$11,113.$$

In effect, the EAA method assumes that each project will, if taken on, be replaced each time it wears out and will provide cash flows equivalent to the calculated annuity value. The PV of this infinite annuity is then the infinite horizon NPV for the project. Because the infinite horizon NPV of F exceeds that of C, Project F should be accepted. Therefore, the EAA method leads to the same decision rule as the replacement chain method—accept Project F.

The EAA method often is easier to apply than the replacement chain method, but the replacement chain method is easier to explain to decision makers. Still, the two methods always lead to the same decision if consistent assumptions are used. Also, note that Step 3 of the EAA method is not really necessary—we could have stopped after Step 2 because the project with the higher EAA will always have the higher NPV over any common life *if the same required rate of return* is used for the projects.

When should we worry about unequal life analysis? As a rule, the unequal life issue (1) does not arise for independent projects, but (2) can arise if mutually exclusive projects with significantly different lives are being evaluated. However, even for mutually exclusive projects, it is not always appropriate to extend the analysis to a common life. This should only be done if there is a high probability that the projects will actually be replicated beyond their initial lives.

We should note several potentially serious weaknesses inherent in this type of unequal life analysis: (1) If inflation is expected, then replacement equipment will have a higher price, and both sales prices and operating costs will probably change. Thus, the static conditions built into the analysis would be invalid. (2) Replacements that occur down the road would probably employ new technology, which in turn might change the cash flows. This factor is not built into either replacement chain analysis or the EAA approach. (3) It is difficult enough to estimate the lives of most projects, so estimating the lives of a series of projects is often just a speculation. (4) If reasonably strong competition is present, the profitability of projects will be eroded over time, and that would reduce the need to extend the analysis beyond the projects' initial lives.

In view of these problems, no experienced financial analyst would be too concerned about comparing mutually exclusive projects with lives of, say, 8 years and 10 years. Given all the uncertainties in the estimation process, such projects would, for all practical purposes, be assumed to have the same life. Still, it is important to recognize that a problem does exist if mutually exclusive projects have substantially different lives. When we encounter such problems in practice, we build expected inflation and/or possible efficiency gains directly into the cash flow estimates, and then use the replacement chain approach (but not the equivalent annual annuity method). The cash flow estimation is more complicated, but the concepts involved are exactly the same as in our example.

Problems

Unequal lives   **14B-1**   Keenan Clothes Inc. is considering the replacement of its old, fully depreciated knitting machine. Two new models are available: Machine 190-3, which has a cost of $190,000, a 3-year expected life, and after-tax cash flows (labor savings and depreciation) of $87,000 per year; and Machine 360-6, which has a cost of $360,000, a 6-year life, and after-tax cash flows of $98,300 per year. Knitting machine prices are not expected to rise because inflation will be offset by cheaper components (microprocessors) used in the machines. Assume that the required rate of return appropriate for evaluating the machines is 14 percent.

    a. Should the firm replace its old knitting machine, and, if so, which new machine should it use?

    b. Suppose the firm's basic patents will expire in 9 years, and the company expects to go out of business at that time. Assume further that the firm depreciates its assets using the straight line method, that its marginal tax rate is 40 percent, and that the used machines can be sold at their book values. Under these circumstances, should the company replace the old machine? Explain.

Unequal lives   **14B-2**   Zappe Airlines is considering two alternative planes. Plane A has an expected life of 5 years, will cost $100, and will produce net cash flows of $30 per year. Plane B has a life of 10 years, will cost $132, and will produce net cash flows of $25 per year. Zappe plans to serve the route for 10 years. Inflation in operating costs, airplane costs, and fares is expected to be zero, and the company's required rate of return is 12 percent. By how much would the value of the company increase if it accepted the better project (plane)? Assume all costs and cash flows are in millions of dollars.

PART VI

The Cost of Capital, Leverage, and Dividend Policy

CHAPTER 15

The Cost of Capital

A MANAGERIAL PERSPECTIVE

In January 1995, Boomtown, Inc., a small Nevada gaming company, announced its intention to purchase National Gaming, a New Jersey casino developer. According to Boomtown's management, the purpose of the acquisition was to improve liquidity and strengthen the company's financial position. But, the stockholders balked at the deal, primarily because they believed the transaction would boost Boomtown's cost of capital to more than 20 percent. With such a high cost of capital, Boomtown would have difficulty finding growth opportunities (acceptable capital budgeting projects) in the future, and, quite possibly, the burden of the high financing costs eventually could force the firm into bankruptcy. Thus, Boomtown's stockholders wanted the deal blocked or restructured to reduce the impact on the company's cost of capital—the stockholders realized that a high cost of capital would be detrimental to their wealth position. And, just as home buyers prefer to avoid high mortgage rates, companies should avoid using funds with high costs.

On the other side of the coin, Federated Department Stores was successful in its attempt to acquire R. H. Macy & Company in 1994. Federated, which had emerged from bankruptcy in 1992, was able to purchase Macy, which had been in bankruptcy since 1992, primarily because Citibank and Chemical Bank arranged a $2.8 billion loan package with a moderate interest rate. The arrangement did not increase Federated's debt position much, thus its cost of debt was not affected significantly—in fact, Federated was able to save about $40 million in interest with the bank arrangement compared to similar borrowing alternatives. The fact that the new capital needed for the acquisition was not expected to change Federated's existing cost of capital position was critical to the success of the deal.

Firms raise capital in the financial markets, where interest rates and other yields change continuously. We know that as interest rates change, so do the costs associated with the various types of capital. For instance, in 1994, interest rates increased dramatically while stock prices dropped, which means that companies had to pay higher costs for using investors' funds. As you

Continued

read this chapter, keep in mind that firms need funds provided by investors to take advantage of acceptable capital budgeting projects. The financial marketplace, which consists of investors like you, determines the "price" firms will have to pay for the funds they use. It is essential for us to be able to determine the "price," or the cost, of the capital used by a firm so that we know if the funds are being invested appropriately.

It is vitally important that a firm knows how much it pays for the funds used to purchase assets. The average return required by the firm's investors determines how much must be paid to attract funds—it is the firm's average cost of funds, which more commonly is termed the *cost of capital*. The firm's cost of capital is very important because it represents the minimum rate of return that must be earned from investments, such as capital budgeting projects, to ensure the value of the firm does not decrease—the cost of capital is the firm's *required rate of return*. For example, if investors provide funds to a firm for an average cost of 15 percent, wealth will decrease if the funds are used to generate returns less than 15 percent, wealth will not change if exactly 15 percent is earned, and wealth will increase if returns greater than 15 percent can be generated.

In this chapter, we discuss the concept of cost of capital, how the average cost of capital is determined, and how the cost of capital is used in financial decision making. Most of the models and formulas used in this chapter are the same ones we developed in Chapter 7, where we described how stocks and bonds are valued by investors. How much it costs a firm for its funds is based on the return demanded by investors—if the return offered by the firm is not high enough, then investors will not provide sufficient funds. In other words, the rate of return an investor earns on a corporate security effectively is a cost to the firm of using those funds, so the same models are used by investors and by corporate treasurers to determine required rates of return.

Our first topic in this chapter is the logic of the weighted average cost of capital. Next, we consider the costs of the major types of capital, after which we see how the costs of the individual components of the capital structure are brought together to form a weighted average cost of capital.

The Logic of the Weighted Average Cost of Capital

It is possible to finance a firm entirely with equity funds by issuing only stock. In that case, the cost of capital used to analyze capital budgeting decisions should be the company's required return on equity. However, most firms raise a substantial portion of their funds as long-term debt, and some also use preferred stock. For these firms, their cost of capital must reflect the average cost of the various sources of long-term funds used, not just the firms' costs of equity.

Assume that Unilate Textiles has a 10 percent cost of debt and a 13.7 percent cost of equity. Further, assume that Unilate has made the decision to finance next year's projects by selling debt only. The argument is sometimes made that the cost of capital for these projects is 10 percent because only debt will be used to finance them. However, this position is incorrect. If Unilate finances a particular set of projects with debt, the firm will be using up some of its potential for obtaining new debt in the future. As expansion occurs in subsequent years, Unilate will at some point find it necessary to raise additional equity to prevent the debt ratio from becoming too large.

To illustrate, suppose Unilate borrows heavily at 10 percent during 1996, using up its debt capacity in the process, to finance projects yielding 11.5 percent. In 1997 it has new projects available that yield 13 percent, well above the return on 1996 projects, but it cannot accept them because they would have to be financed with 13.7 percent equity money. To avoid this problem, Unilate should be viewed as an ongoing concern, and *the cost of capital used in capital budgeting should be calculated as a weighted average, or combination, of the various types of funds generally used, regardless of the specific financing used to fund a particular project.*

Self-Test Question

Why should the cost of capital used in capital budgeting be calculated as a weighted average of the various types of funds the firm generally uses, regardless of the specific financing used to fund a particular project?

Basic Definitions

CAPITAL COMPONENT
One of the types of capital used by firms to raise money.

The items on the right-hand side of a firm's balance sheet—various types of debt, preferred stock, and common equity—are its **capital components.** Any increase in total assets must be financed by an increase in one or more of these capital components.

Capital is a necessary factor of production, and, like any other factor, it has a cost. The cost of each component is called the *component cost* of that particular type of capital; for example, if Unilate can borrow money at 10 percent, its component cost of debt is 10 percent.[1] Throughout this chapter we concentrate on debt, preferred stock, retained earnings, and new issues of common stock, which are the four major capital structure components. We will use the following symbols to designate specific component costs of capital:

k_d = interest rate on the firm's debt = before-tax component cost of debt. For Unilate, k_d = 10%.

$k_d(1 - T) = k_{dT}$ = after-tax component cost of debt, where T is the firm's marginal tax rate. k_{dT} is the debt cost used to calculate the weighted average cost of capital. For Unilate, T = 40%, so $k_{dT} = k_d(1 - T) = 10\%(1 - 0.4) = 10\%(0.6) = 6.0\%$.

k_{ps} = component cost of preferred stock. Unilate has no preferred stock at this time, but, as new funds are raised, the company plans to issue preferred stock. The cost of preferred stock, k_{ps}, will be 10.3 percent.

---

[1] We will see shortly that there is both a before-tax and an after-tax cost of debt; for now it is sufficient to know that 10 percent is the before-tax component cost of debt.

k_s = component cost of retained earnings (or internal equity). It is identical to the k_s developed in Chapters 5 and 7 and defined there as the required rate of return on common stock. As we will see shortly, for Unilate, $k_s \approx 13.7\%$.

k_e = component cost of external equity obtained by issuing new common stock as opposed to retaining earnings. As we shall see, it is necessary to distinguish between common equity needs that can be satisfied by retained earnings and the common equity needs that are satisfied by selling new stock. This is why we distinguish between internal and external equity, k_s and k_e. Further, k_e is always greater than k_s. For Unilate, $k_e \approx 14.3\%$.

WACC = the weighted average cost of capital. In the future, when Unilate needs *new* capital to finance asset expansion, it will raise part of the new funds as debt, part as preferred stock, and part as common equity (with common equity coming either from retained earnings or from the issuance of new common stock).[2] We will calculate WACC for Unilate Textiles shortly.

CAPITAL STRUCTURE
The combination, or mix, of different types of capital used by a firm.

These definitions and concepts are explained in detail in the remainder of the chapter, where we develop a marginal cost of capital (MCC) schedule that can be used in capital budgeting. Later, in Chapter 16, we will extend the analysis to determine the mix of types of capital, which is termed the **capital structure,** that will minimize the firm's cost of capital and thereby maximize its value.

Self-Test Question

Identify the firm's four major capital structure components, and give their respective component cost symbols.

Cost of Debt, k_{dT}

AFTER-TAX COST OF DEBT, k_{dT}
The relevant cost of new debt, taking into account the tax deductibility of interest; used to calculate the WACC.

The **after-tax cost of debt, k_{dT},** is the interest rate on debt, k_d, less the tax savings that result because interest is deductible. This is the same as k_d multiplied by $(1 - T)$, where T is the firm's marginal tax rate:

$$
\begin{array}{l}
\text{15-1} \\
\end{array}
$$

$$
\begin{array}{l}
\text{After-tax} \\
\text{component cost of debt}
\end{array} = k_{dT} = \begin{array}{l}
\text{Bondholders' required} \\
\text{rate of return}
\end{array} - \begin{array}{l}
\text{Tax} \\
\text{savings}
\end{array}
$$

$$
= k_d - k_d \times T = k_d(1 - T)
$$

In effect, the government pays part of the cost of debt because interest is tax deductible. Therefore, if Unilate can borrow at an interest rate of 10 percent, and

---

[2]Firms try to keep their debt, preferred stock, and common equity in optimal proportions; we will learn how they establish these proportions in Chapter 16. However, firms do not try to maintain any proportional relationship between the common stock and retained earnings accounts as shown on the balance sheet—for capital structure purposes, common equity is common equity, whether it comes from selling new common stock or from retaining earnings.

if it has a marginal tax rate of 40 percent, then its after-tax cost of debt is 6 percent:

$$k_{dT} = k_d(1 - T) = 10\%(1.0 - 0.4) = 10\%(0.6) = 6.0\%$$

We use the after-tax cost of debt because the value of the firm's stock, which we want to maximize, depends on *after-tax* cash flows. Because interest is a deductible expense, it produces tax savings which reduce the net cost of debt, making the after-tax cost of debt less than the before-tax cost. We are concerned with after-tax cash flows, so after-tax rates of return are appropriate.[3]

Note that the cost of debt is the interest rate on *new* debt, not that on already outstanding debt; in other words, we are interested in the *marginal* cost of debt. Our primary concern with the cost of capital is to use it for capital budgeting decisions—for example, a decision about whether or not to obtain the capital needed to acquire a new machine tool. The rate at which the firm has borrowed in the past is a sunk cost, and it is irrelevant for cost of capital purposes.

In Chapter 7, we solved the following equation to find k_d, the rate of return, or yield to maturity, for a bond:

$$P_0 = \sum_{t=1}^{N} \frac{INT}{(1 + k_d)^t} + \frac{M}{(1 + k_d)^N}$$

where INT is the dollar coupon interest paid per period, M is the face value repaid at maturity, and N is the number of interest payments remaining until maturity.

Assume that Unilate is going to issue a new 9 percent coupon bond in a few days. The bond has face value of $1,000 and a 20-year life, and interest is paid annually. If the market price of similar risk bonds is $915, what is Unilate's k_d? The solution is set up as follows:

$$\$915 = \frac{\$90}{(1 + k_d)^1} + \frac{\$90}{(1 + k_d)^2} + \cdots + \frac{\$1,090}{(1 + k_d)^{20}}$$

Whether you use the trial-and-error method, the time value of money functions on your calculator, or the approximation equation given in Chapter 7, you should find k_d is 10 percent, which is the before-tax cost of debt for this bond.[4] Unilate's

---

[3]The tax rate is *zero* for a firm with losses. Therefore, for a company that does not pay taxes, the cost of debt is not reduced; that is, in Equation 15-1 the tax rate equals zero, so the after-tax cost of debt is equal to the interest rate.

[4]It should also be noted that we have ignored flotation costs (the costs incurred for new issuances) on debt because almost all the debt issued by small and medium sized firm is privately placed and hence has no flotation cost. However, if bonds are publicly placed and do involve flotation costs, the solution value of k_d in this formula is used as the before-tax cost of debt:

$$P_0(1 - F) = \sum_{t=1}^{N} \frac{INT}{(1 + k_d)^t} + \frac{M}{(1 + k_d)^N}$$

Here F is the percentage amount of the bond flotation, or issuing, cost; N is the number of periods to maturity; INT is the dollars of interest per period; M is the maturity value of the bond; and k_d is the cost of debt adjusted to reflect flotation costs. If we assume that the bond in the example calls for annual payments, that it has a 20-year maturity, and that F = 2%, then the flotation-adjusted, before-tax cost of debt is 10.23 percent versus 10 percent before the flotation adjustment.

marginal tax rate is 40 percent, so the after-tax cost of debt, k_{dT}, is 6% = 10%(1 − 0.40).

Self-Test Questions

Why is the after-tax cost of debt rather than the before-tax cost used to calculate the weighted average cost of capital?

Is the relevant cost of debt the interest rate on already outstanding debt or that on new debt? Why?

Cost of Preferred Stock, k_{ps}

COST OF PREFERRED STOCK, k_{ps}
The rate of return investors require on the firm's preferred stock. k_{ps} is calculated as the preferred dividend, D_{ps}, divided by the net issuing price, NP.

In Chapter 7, we found that the dividend associated with preferred stock, D_{ps}, is constant, and that preferred stock has no stated maturity. Thus, D_{ps} represents a perpetuity, and the component **cost of preferred stock, k_{ps},** is the preferred dividend, D_{ps}, divided by the net issuing price, NP, or the price the firm receives after deducting flotation costs, which are the costs of issuing the stock:

15-2

$$\text{Component cost of preferred stock} = k_{ps} = \frac{D_{ps}}{NP} = \frac{D_{ps}}{P_0 - \text{Flotation costs}}$$

For example, Unilate is going to issue preferred stock that pays a $10 dividend per share and sells for $100 per share in the market. It will cost 3 percent, or $3 per share, to issue the new preferred stock, so Unilate will net $97 per share. Therefore, Unilate's cost of preferred stock is 10.3 percent:

$$k_{ps} = \frac{\$10}{\$97} = 0.103 = 10.3\%$$

No tax adjustments are made when calculating k_{ps} because preferred dividends, unlike interest expense on debt, are not tax deductible, so there are no tax savings associated with the use of preferred stock.

Self-Test Questions

Does the component cost of preferred stock include or exclude flotation costs? Explain.

Is a tax adjustment made to the cost of preferred stock? Why or why not?

Cost of Retained Earnings, k_s

The costs of debt and preferred stock are based on the returns investors require on these securities. Similarly, the **cost of retained earnings, k_s,** is the rate of return stockholders require on equity capital the firm obtains by retain-

**COST OF RETAINED
EARNINGS, k_s**
The rate of return required
by stockholders on a firm's
common stock.

ing earnings that otherwise could be distributed to common stockholders as dividends.[5]

The reason we must assign a cost of capital to retained earnings involves the *opportunity cost principle.* The firm's after-tax earnings literally belong to its stockholders. Bondholders are compensated by interest payments, and preferred stockholders by preferred dividends, but the earnings remaining after interest and preferred dividends belong to the common stockholders, and these earnings serve to compensate stockholders for the use of their capital. Management can either pay out the earnings in the form of dividends or retain the earnings and reinvest them in the business. If management decides to retain earnings, there is an opportunity cost involved—stockholders could have received the earnings as dividends and invested this money in other stocks, in bonds, in real estate, or in anything else. Thus, the firm should earn a return on earnings it retains that is at least as great as the stockholders themselves could earn on alternative investments of comparable risk.

What rate of return can stockholders expect to earn on equivalent-risk investments? First, recall from Chapter 7 that stocks normally are in equilibrium, with the expected and required rates of return being equal: $\hat{k}_s = k_s$. Therefore, we can assume that Unilate's stockholders expect to earn a return of k_s on their money. *If the firm cannot invest retained earnings and earn at least k_s, it should pay these funds to its stockholders and let them invest directly in other assets that do provide this return.*[6]

Whereas debt and preferred stocks are contractual obligations that have easily determined costs, it is not as easy to measure k_s. However, we can employ the principles developed in Chapters 5 and 7 to produce reasonably good cost of equity estimates. To begin, we know that if a stock is in equilibrium (which is the typical situation), then its required rate of return, k_s, is also equal to its expected rate of return, $\hat{k}_s$. Further, its required return is equal to a risk-free rate, k_{RF}, plus a risk premium, RP, whereas the expected return on a constant growth stock is equal to the stock's dividend yield, D_1/P_0, plus its expected growth rate, g:

15-3	Required rate of return = Expected rate of return
	$$k_s = k_{RF} + RP \quad = \quad \frac{D_1}{P_0} + g = \hat{k}_s$$

Because the two must be equal, we can estimate k_s either as $k_s = k_{RF} + RP$ or as $k_s = D_1/P_0 + g$. Actually, three methods are commonly used for finding the cost of retained earnings: (1) the CAPM approach, (2) the bond-yield-plus-risk-premium

---

[5]The term *retained earnings* can be interpreted to mean either the balance sheet item "retained earnings," consisting of all the earnings retained in the business throughout its history, or the income statement item "additions to retained earnings." The income statement item is used in this chapter; for our purpose, *retained earnings* refers to that part of current earnings not paid out in dividends and hence available for reinvestment in the business this year.

[6]Dividends and capital gains are taxed differently, with long-term gains being taxed at a lower rate than dividends for many stockholders. That makes it beneficial for companies to retain earnings rather than to pay them out as dividends, and that, in turn, results in a relatively low cost of capital for retained earnings. This point is discussed in Chapter 17.

approach, and (3) the discounted cash flow (DCF) approach. These three approaches are discussed in the following sections.

The CAPM Approach

The Capital Asset Pricing Model (CAPM) we developed in Chapter 5 is:

15-4

$$k_s = k_{RF} + (k_M - k_{RF})\beta_s$$

Equation 15-4 shows that the CAPM estimate of k_s begins with the risk-free rate, k_{RF}, to which is added a risk premium that is based on the stock's relation to the market as measured by its β_s and the magnitude of the market risk premium, which is the difference between the market return, k_M, and the risk-free rate, k_{RF}.

To illustrate the CAPM approach, assume that $k_{RF} = 7\%$, $k_M = 11\%$, and $\beta_s = 1.6$ for Unilate's common stock. Using the CAPM approach, Unilate's cost of retained earnings, k_s, is calculated as follows:

$$k_s = 7\% + (11\% - 7\%)(1.6) = 7\% + 6.4\% = 13.4\%$$

It should be noted that although the CAPM approach appears to yield an accurate, precise estimate of k_s, there actually are several problems with it. First, as we saw in Chapter 5, if a firm's stockholders are not well diversified, they might be concerned with total risk rather than with market risk only (measured by β); in this case the firm's true investment risk will not be measured by its beta, and the CAPM procedure will understate the correct value of k_s. Further, even if the CAPM method is valid, it is difficult to obtain correct estimates of the inputs required to make it operational: (1) There is controversy about whether to use long-term or short-term Treasury yields for k_{RF}; and (2) Both β_s and k_M should be estimated values, which often are difficult to obtain.

Bond-Yield-plus-Risk-Premium Approach

Although it is a subjective procedure, analysts often estimate a firm's cost of common equity by adding a risk premium of three to five percentage points to the interest rate on the firm's own long-term debt. It is logical to think that firms with risky, low-rated, and consequently high-interest-rate debt also will have risky, high-cost equity. Using this logic to estimate the cost of common stock is relatively easy, because all we have to do is add a risk premium to a readily observable debt cost. For example, Unilate's cost of equity might be estimated as follows:

$$k_s = \text{Bond yield} + \text{Risk premium} = 10\% + 4\% = 14\%$$

Because the 4 percent risk premium is a judgmental estimate, the estimated value of k_s also is judgmental. Empirical work in recent years suggests that the risk premium over a firm's own bond yield generally has ranged from 3 to 5 percentage points, so this method is not likely to produce a precise cost of equity—about all it can do is get us "into the right ballpark."

Discounted Cash Flow (DCF) Approach

In Chapter 7 we learned that both the price and the expected rate of return on a share of common stock depend, ultimately, on the dividends expected on the stock, and the value of a share of stock can be written:

15-5

$$P_0 = \frac{D_1}{(1 + k_s)^1} + \frac{D_2}{(1 + k_s)^2} + \cdots + \frac{D_\infty}{(1 + k_s)^\infty}$$

$$= \sum_{t=1}^{\infty} \frac{D_t}{(1 + k_s)^t}$$

Here P_0 is the current price of the stock; D_t is the dividend expected to be paid at the end of Year t; and k_s is the required rate of return. If dividends are expected to grow at a constant rate, then, as we saw in Chapter 7, Equation 15-5 reduces to:

15-5a

$$P_0 = \frac{D_1}{k_s - g}$$

We can solve Equation 15-5a for k_s to estimate the required rate of return on common equity, which for the marginal investor also is equal to the expected rate of return:

15-6

$$k_s = \hat{k}_s = \frac{D_1}{P_0} + g$$

Thus, investors expect to receive a dividend yield, D_1/P_0, plus a capital gain, g, for a total expected return of $\hat{k}_s$, and in equilibrium this expected return also is equal to the required return, k_s. From this point on, we will assume that equilibrium exists, and we will use the terms k_s and $\hat{k}_s$ interchangeably.

It is relatively easy to determine the dividend yield, but it is difficult to establish the proper growth rate. If past growth rates in earnings and dividends have been relatively stable, and if investors appear to be projecting a continuation of past trends, then g can be based on the firm's historical growth rate. However, if the company's past growth has been abnormally high or low, either because of its own unique situation or because of general economic fluctuations, then historical growth probably should not be used. Security analysts regularly make earnings and dividend growth forecasts, looking at such factors as projected sales, profit margins, and competitive factors. For example, *Value Line*, which is available in most libraries, provides growth rate forecasts for 1,700 companies, and Merrill Lynch, Salomon Brothers, and other organizations make similar forecasts.

Therefore, someone making a cost of capital estimate can obtain several analysts' forecasts, average them, and use the average as a proxy for the growth expectations, g.[7]

To illustrate the DCF approach, suppose Unilate's stock sells for $23; it is expected the next dividend (in 1996) will be $1.31; and its expected long-term growth rate is 8 percent. Unilate's expected and required rate of return, and hence its cost of retained earnings, is 13.7 percent:

$$\hat{k}_s = k_s = \frac{\$1.31}{\$23.00} + 0.08 = 0.057 + 0.08 = 0.137 = 13.7\%$$

This 13.7 percent is the minimum rate of return that management must expect to earn to justify retaining earnings and plowing them back into the business rather than paying them out to stockholders as dividends.

We have used three methods to estimate the cost of retained earnings, which actually is a single number. To summarize, we found the cost of common equity to be (1) 13.4 percent using the CAPM method; (2) 14.0 percent with the bond-yield-plus-risk-premium approach; and (3) 13.7 percent using the constant growth model, the DCF approach. It is not unusual to get different estimates, because each of the approaches is based on different assumptions—the CAPM assumes investors are well diversified, the bond-yield-plus-risk-premium approach assumes the cost of equity is closely related to the firm's cost of debt, and the constant growth model assumes the firm's dividends and earnings will grow at a constant rate far into the future. So, which estimate should be used? Probably all of them. Many analysts will use multiple approaches to estimate a single value, then average the results. For Unilate, then, the average of the estimates is 13.7% = (13.4% + 14.0% + 13.7%)/3.

People experienced in estimating equity capital costs recognize that both careful analysis and sound judgment are required. It would be nice to pretend that judgment is unnecessary and to specify an easy, precise way of determining the exact cost of equity capital. Unfortunately, this is not possible—finance is in large part a matter of judgment, and we simply must face that fact.

Self-Test Questions

Why must a cost be assigned to retained earnings?

What are the three approaches for estimating the cost of retained earnings?

Identify some problems with the CAPM approach.

What is the reasoning behind the bond-yield-plus-risk-premium approach?

Which of the components of the constant growth DCF formula is most difficult to estimate? Why?

---

[7]Analysts' growth rate forecasts are usually for five years into the future, and the rates provided represent the average growth rate over that five-year horizon. Studies have shown that analysts' forecasts represent the best source of growth rate data for DCF cost of capital estimates. See Robert Harris, "Using Analysts' Growth Rate Forecasts to Estimate Shareholder Required Rates of Return," *Financial Management*, Spring 1986.

Cost of Newly Issued Common Stock, or External Equity, k_e

COST OF NEW COMMON EQUITY, k_e
The cost of external equity; based on the cost of retained earnings, but increased for flotation costs.

FLOTATION COSTS
The expenses incurred when selling new issues of securities.

The **cost of new common equity, k_e,** or external equity capital, is higher than the cost of retained earnings, k_s, because there is a cost to issuing new stock. Because the firm incurs costs when selling new securities, called **flotation costs,** the full market value of the stock cannot be used for investments—only the amount left after paying flotation costs is available. Thus, the cost of issuing new common stock (external equity), k_e, is greater than the cost of retained earnings (internal equity), k_s, because there are no flotation costs associated with retained earnings.

In general, the cost of issuing new equity, k_e, can be found by modifying the DCF formula used to compute the cost of retained earnings, k_s, to obtain the following equation:

15-7

$$k_e = \frac{D_1}{NP} + g = \frac{D_1}{P_0(1 - F)} + g$$

Here F is the percentage flotation cost incurred in selling the new stock issue, so $P_0(1 - F)$ is the net price per share received by the company.

If Unilate can issue new common stock at a flotation cost of 10 percent, k_e is computed as follows:

$$k_e = \frac{\$1.31}{\$23(1 - 0.10)} + 0.08 = \frac{\$1.31}{\$20.70} + 0.08 = 0.143 = 14.3\%$$

Using the DCF approach to estimate the cost of retained earnings, we found that investors require a return of $k_s = 13.7\%$ on the stock. However, because of flotation costs, the company must earn more than 13.7 percent on funds obtained by selling stock if it is to provide a 13.7 percent return. Specifically, if the firm earns 14.3 percent on funds obtained from new stock, then earnings per share will not fall below previously expected earnings, the firm's expected dividend can be maintained, and, as a result, the price per share will not decline. If the firm earns less than 14.3 percent, then earnings, dividends, and growth will fall below expectations, causing the price of the stock to decline. If it earns more than 14.3 percent, the price of the stock will rise.

The reason for the flotation adjustment can be made clear by a simple example. Suppose Weaver Realty Company has $100,000 of assets and no debt, it earns a 15 percent return (or $15,000) on its assets, and it pays all earnings out as dividends, so its growth rate is zero. The company has 1,000 shares of stock outstanding, so EPS = DPS = $15 = $15,000/1,000, and $P_0 = \$100 = \$100,000/1,000$. Weaver's cost of equity is thus $k_s = \$15/\$100 + 0 = 15\%$. Now suppose Weaver can get a return of 15 percent on new assets. Should it sell new stock to acquire new assets? If it sold 1,000 new shares of stock to the public for $100 per share, but it incurred a 10 percent flotation cost on the issue, it would net $100 − 0.10($100) = $90 per share, or $90,000 in total. It would then invest this $90,000 and earn 15 percent, or $13,500. Its new *total* earnings would be $28,500, which would consist of $15,000 generated from the old assets plus $13,500 from the

---

INDUSTRY PRACTICE

Cost of Equity—Theoretical Versus Ad Hoc Models

In this chapter, we describe three methods to estimate a firm's cost of internal equity—capital asset pricing model (CAPM), bond-plus-risk-premium, and discounted cash flow (DCF). Which, if any of these approaches, actually is used by firms to compute the cost of equity capital?

Before answering, perhaps we should determine whether firms even attempt to compute the cost of equity. The results of a recent survey of large firms in the United States indicate that more than 80 percent of all firms actually calculate the cost of equity capital. This is a stark contrast to the findings from 20 years ago, when about 60 percent of firms did *not* compute the cost of equity.

It is interesting that the most popular method to compute the cost of equity capital also is the method that is considered most theoretical in nature—the CAPM. More than 40 percent of all firms indicated they use the CAPM, and most of these firms consider the CAPM as the principal means for determining the cost of equity. The primary reasons given for not using the CAPM methodology are that (1) it is not understood, and (2) it is not considered appropriate. Both of these "excuses" can be mitigated by better educating financial managers about the usefulness of the CAPM.

The bond-yield-plus-risk-premium method proved to be almost as popular as the CAPM for computing the cost of equity capital. This is an interesting finding, given the fact that the bond-yield-plus-risk-premium method is considered an *ad hoc* approach while the

CAPM is the method that theorists would recommend. In reality, many of the firms use both methods.

Another interesting finding was that, except in the utilities industry, only about 10 percent of the firms indicated they use the DCF method to compute the cost of equity capital. In contrast, about 62 percent of the utilities revealed that they use the DCF model as one of the approaches for determining the cost of equity. Perhaps the reason for this is that the DCF model traditionally has been the method used by utilities and public service commissions for determining the return on (cost of) equity that is considered permissible for such monopolies.

When asked how the weights used to compute the weighted average cost of capital (WACC) are determined, most of the firms indicated that the book values of debt and equity are used. Less than 20 percent indicated that market values are computed. And, about one fourth of the firms said the target, or desired, debt and equity ratios (weights) are used. This is not a surprising finding, because most financial managers believe that these three approaches produce about the same weights for a firm's capital structure.

In summary, indications are that firms actually do compute the cost of equity capital, and the methods most often used include those discussed in this chapter.

SOURCE: Glenn H. Petry and James Sprow, "The Theory and Practice of Finance in the 1990s," *The Quarterly Review of Economics and Finance,* Winter 1993, 359–381.

---

new assets. But the $28,500 would have to be distributed equally to the 2,000 shares of stock that now would be outstanding. Therefore, Weaver's EPS and DPS would decline from $15 to $14.25 = $28,500/2,000$. Because its EPS and DPS would fall, the price of the stock also would fall from $P_0 = \$100$ to $P_1 = \$14.25/0.15 = \$95.00$. This result occurs because investors have put up $100 per share, but the company has received and invested only $90 per share. Thus, we see that the $90 must earn more than 15 percent to provide investors with a 15 percent return on the $100 they put up.

We can use Equation 15-7 to compute the return Weaver must earn on the $90,000 of new assets—that is, the amount raised with the new issue:

$$k_e = \frac{\$15}{\$100(1 - 0.10)} + 0 = 0.1667 = 16.67\%$$

If Weaver invests the funds from the new common stock issue at 16.67%, here is what would happen:

$$\text{New total earnings} = \$15,000 + \$90,000(0.16667) = \$30,000$$

$$\text{New EPS and DPS} = \$30,000/2,000 = \$15$$

$$\text{New price} = \$15/0.15 = \$100 = \text{Original price}$$

Thus, if the return on the new assets is equal to k_e as calculated by Equation 15-7, then EPS, DPS, and the stock price will all remain constant. If the return on the new assets exceeds k_e, then EPS, DPS, and P_0 will rise. This confirms the fact that, because of flotation costs, the cost of external equity exceeds the cost of equity raised internally from retained earnings.

Self-Test Questions

Why is the cost of external equity capital higher than the cost of retained earnings?

How can the DCF model be changed to account for flotation costs?

Weighted Average Cost of Capital, WACC

TARGET (OPTIMAL) CAPITAL STRUCTURE
The percentages of debt, preferred stock, and common equity that will maximize the price of the firm's stock.

WEIGHTED AVERAGE COST OF CAPITAL (WACC)
A weighted average of the component costs of debt, preferred stock, and common equity.

As we will see in the next chapter, each firm has an optimal capital structure, or mix of debt, preferred stock, and common equity, that causes its stock price to be maximized. Therefore, a rational, value-maximizing firm will establish a **target (optimal) capital structure** and then raise new capital in a manner that will keep the actual capital structure on target over time. In this chapter we assume that the firm has identified its optimal capital structure, it uses this optimum as the target, and it raises funds so it remains constantly on target. How the target is established will be examined in Chapter 16.[8]

The target proportions of debt, preferred stock, and common equity, along with the component costs of capital, are used to calculate the firm's **weighted average cost of capital (WACC)**. To illustrate, suppose Unilate Textiles has determined that in the future it will raise new capital according to the following proportions: 45 percent debt, 5 percent preferred stock, and 50 percent common equity (retained earnings plus common stock). In the preceding sections, we found that Unilate's before-tax cost of debt, k_d, is 10 percent, so its after-tax cost of debt, k_{dT}, is $6.0\% = 10\%(1 - 0.40)$; its cost of preferred stock, k_{ps}, is 10.3 percent; and its cost of common equity, k_s, is 13.7 percent if all of its equity financing comes from retained earnings. Now we can calculate Unilate's weighted average cost of capital (WACC) as follows:

---

[8]Note that only long-term debt is included in the capital structure. Unilate uses its cost of capital in the capital budgeting process, which involves long-term assets, and it finances those assets with long-term capital. Thus, current liabilities do not enter the calculation. We will discuss this point in more detail in Chapter 16. Also, see Eugene F. Brigham and Louis C. Gapenski, *Intermediate Financial Management,* 5th ed. (Fort Worth, Tex.: The Dryden Press, 1996), Chapter 6.

$$
\textbf{15-9} \quad WACC = \left[\left(\begin{array}{c} \text{Proportion} \\ \text{of} \\ \text{debt} \end{array} \right) \times \left(\begin{array}{c} \text{After-tax} \\ \text{cost of} \\ \text{debt} \end{array} \right) \right] + \left[\left(\begin{array}{c} \text{Proportion} \\ \text{of preferred} \\ \text{stock} \end{array} \right) \times \left(\begin{array}{c} \text{Cost of} \\ \text{preferred} \\ \text{stock} \end{array} \right) \right] + \left[\left(\begin{array}{c} \text{Proportion} \\ \text{of common} \\ \text{equity} \end{array} \right) \times \left(\begin{array}{c} \text{Cost of} \\ \text{common} \\ \text{equity} \end{array} \right) \right]
$$
$$
= \quad w_d k_{dT} \quad + \quad w_{ps} k_{ps} \quad + \quad w_s (k_s \text{ or } k_e)
$$

$$
= 0.45(6\%) + 0.05(10.3\%) + 0.50(13.7\%) \approx 10.1\%
$$

Here w_d, w_{ps}, and w_s are the weights used for debt, preferred stock, and common equity, respectively.

Every dollar of new capital that Unilate obtains consists of 45¢ of debt with an after-tax cost of 6 percent, 5¢ of preferred stock with a cost of 10.3 percent, and 50¢ of common equity (all from additions to retained earnings) with a cost of 13.7 percent. The average cost of each whole dollar, WACC, is 10.1 percent as long as these conditions continue. If the component costs of capital change when new funds are raised in the future, then WACC changes. We discuss changes in the component costs of capital in the next section.

Self-Test Question

How do you calculate the weighted average cost of capital? Write out the equation.

The Marginal Cost of Capital, MCC

MARGINAL COST OF CAPITAL (MCC)
The cost of obtaining another dollar of new capital; the weighted average cost of the last dollar of new capital raised.

The marginal cost of any item is the cost of another unit of that item; for example, the marginal cost of labor is the cost of adding one additional worker. The marginal cost of labor might be $25 per person if 10 workers are added but $35 per person if the firm tries to hire 100 new workers because it will be harder to find that many people willing and able to do the work. The same concept applies to capital. As the firm tries to attract more new dollars, at some point the cost of each dollar will increase. Thus, the **marginal cost of capital (MCC)** is defined as the *cost of the last dollar of new capital that the firm raises, and the marginal cost rises as more and more capital is raised during a given period.*

In the preceding section, we computed Unilate's WACC to be 10.1 percent. As long as Unilate keeps its capital structure on target, and as long as its debt has an after-tax cost of 6 percent, its preferred stock a cost of 10.3 percent, and its common equity a cost of 13.7 percent, then its weighted average cost of capital will be 10.1%. Each dollar the firm raises will consist of some long-term debt, some preferred stock, and some common equity, and the cost of the whole dollar will be 10.1 percent—its marginal cost of capital (MCC) will be 10.1 percent.

MARGINAL COST OF CAPITAL (MCC) SCHEDULE
A graph that relates the firm's weighted average cost of each dollar of capital to the total amount of new capital raised.

The MCC Schedule

A graph that shows how the WACC changes as more and more new capital is raised by the firm is called the **marginal cost of capital schedule.** Figure 15-1 shows Unilate's MCC schedule if the cost of debt, cost of preferred stock, and cost of common equity *never* change. Here the dots represent dollars raised, and

FIGURE 15-1

Marginal Cost of Capital (MCC) Schedule for Unilate Textiles

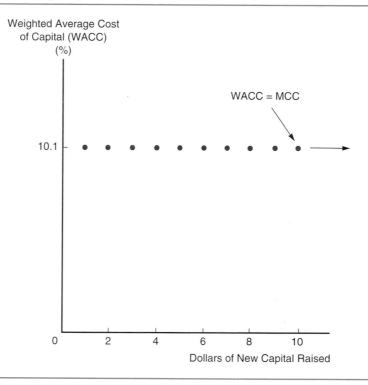

because each dollar of new capital will have an average cost equal to 10.1 percent, the marginal cost of capital (MCC) for Unilate is constant at 10.1 percent under the assumptions we have used to this point.

Do you think Unilate actually could raise an unlimited amount of new capital at the 10.1 percent cost? Probably not, because, as a practical matter, as a company raises larger and larger amounts of funds during a given time period, the costs of those funds begin to rise, and as this occurs, the weighted average cost of each new dollar also rises. Thus, companies cannot raise unlimited amounts of capital at a constant cost—at some point, the cost of each new dollar will increase, no matter what its source (debt, preferred stock, or common equity).

How much can Unilate raise before the cost of its funds increases? As a first step to determining the point at which the MCC begins to rise, recognize that although the company's balance sheet shows total long-term capital of $720 million at the end of 1995, all of this capital was raised in the past, and it has been invested in assets that now are being used in operations. If Unilate wants to raise any new (marginal) capital so that the total amount consists of 45 percent debt, 5 percent preferred stock, and 50 percent common equity, then to raise $1,000,000 in new capital, the company should issue $450,000 of new debt, $50,000 of new preferred stock, and $500,000 of new common equity. The new common equity could come from two sources: (1) retained earnings, defined as that part of this year's profits that management decides to retain in the business rather than pay out as dividends (but not earnings retained in the past, because these amounts already have been invested in existing assets); or (2) proceeds from the sale of new common stock.

We know that Unilate's WACC will be 10.1 percent as long as the after-tax cost of debt is 6 percent, the cost of preferred stock is 10.3 percent, and the funds needed from common equity can be satisfied by retained earnings with a cost of 13.7 percent ($k_s = 13.7\%$). But what happens if Unilate expands so rapidly that the retained earnings for the year are not sufficient to meet the common equity needs, forcing the firm to sell new common stock? Earlier, we determined that the cost of issuing new common stock, k_e, will be 14.3 percent, because the flotation costs associated with the new issue will be 10 percent. Because the cost of common equity increases when common stock has to be issued, the WACC also increases.

How much new capital can Unilate raise before it exhausts its retained earnings and is forced to sell new common stock? In other words, where will an increase in the MCC schedule occur?

In Chapter 4, we forecast that Unilate's 1996 net income would be $70 million and that $34 million would be paid out as dividends, so $36 million would be added to retained earnings (the payout ratio would be about 49 percent). Thus, Unilate can invest in capital projects to the point where the common equity needs equal $36 million before new common stock has to be issued. Remember, though, that when Unilate needs new funds, the target capital structure indicates only 50 percent of the total should be common equity; the remainder of the funds should come from issues of bonds (45 percent) and preferred stock (5 percent). Because common equity makes up 50 percent of the total capital raised, we know:

$$\text{Common equity} = 0.50(\text{Total new capital raised})$$

We can use this relationship to determine how much *total new capital*—debt, preferred stock, and retained earnings—can be raised before the $36 million of retained earnings is exhausted and Unilate is forced to sell new common stock. Just set the common equity needs equal to the retained earnings amount, and solve for the total new capital amount:

$$\frac{\text{Common}}{\text{equity}} = \frac{\text{Retained}}{\text{earnings}} = \$36\text{ million} = 0.50\left(\frac{\text{Total new}}{\text{capital raised}}\right)$$

$$\left(\frac{\text{Total new}}{\text{capital raised}}\right) = \frac{\$36\text{ million}}{0.50} = \$72\text{ million}$$

Thus, Unilate can raise a total of $72 million before it has to sell new common stock to finance its capital projects.

If Unilate needs *exactly* $72 million in new capital, the breakdown of the amount that would come from each source of capital and the computation for the weighted average cost of capital (WACC) would be:

Capital Source	Weight	Amount in Millions	After-Tax Component Cost	WACC
Debt	0.45	$32.4	6.0%	2.7%
Preferred stock	0.05	3.6	10.3	0.5
Common equity	0.50	36.0	13.7	6.9
	1.00	$72.0		WACC$_1$ = 10.1%

Therefore, if Unilate needs exactly $72 million in new capital in 1996, the $36 million increase in retained earnings will be just enough to satisfy the common equity requirement, so the firm will not need to sell new common stock and its weighted average cost of capital (WACC) will be 10.1 percent. But what will happen if Unilate needs more than $72 million in new capital in 1996? If Unilate needs $74 million, for example, retained earnings will not be sufficient to cover the $37 million common equity requirements (50 percent of the total funds), so new common stock will have to be sold. The cost of issuing new common stock, k_c, is greater than the cost of retained earnings, k_s, hence the WACC will be greater. If Unilate raises $74 million in new capital, the breakdown of the amount that would come from each source of capital and the computation for the weighted average cost of capital (WACC) would be:

Capital Source	Weight	Amount in Millions	After-Tax Component Cost	WACC
Debt	0.45	$33.3	6.0%	2.7%
Preferred stock	0.05	3.7	10.3	0.5
Common equity	0.50	37.0	14.3	7.2
	1.00	$74.0	WACC$_2$ =	10.4%

The WACC will be greater because Unilate will have to sell new common stock, which has a higher component cost than retained earnings. Consequently, if Unilate's capital budgeting needs are greater than $72 million, new common stock will need to be sold, and its WACC will increase. The $72 million in total new capital is defined as the *retained earnings break point,* because above this amount of total capital, a break, or jump, in Unilate's MCC schedule occurs. In general, **a break point (BP)** is defined as the dollar of *new total capital* that can be raised before an increase occurs in the firm's weighted average cost of capital.

BREAK POINT (BP)
The dollar value of new capital that can be raised before an increase occurs in the firm's weighted average cost of capital.

Figure 15-2 graphs Unilate's marginal cost of capital schedule with the retained earnings break point. Each dollar has a weighted average cost of 10.1 percent until the company has raised a total of $72 million. This $72 million will consist of $32.4 million of new debt with an after-tax cost of 6 percent, $3.6 million of preferred stock with a cost of 10.3 percent, and $36.0 million of retained earnings with a cost of 13.7 percent. However, if Unilate raises one dollar over $72 million, each new dollar will contain 50¢ of equity *obtained by selling new common equity at a cost of 14.3 percent;* therefore, WACC jumps from 10.1 percent to 10.4 percent, as calculated earlier and shown in Table 15-1.

Note that we really don't think the MCC jumps by precisely 0.3 percent when we raise $1 over $72 million. Thus, Figure 15-2 should be regarded as an approximation rather than as a precise representation of reality. We will return to this point later in the chapter.

Other Breaks in the MCC Schedule

There is a jump, or break, in Unilate's MCC schedule at $72 million of new capital because new common stock needs to be sold. Could there be other breaks in the schedule? Yes, there could. For example, suppose Unilate could obtain only $54 million of debt at a 10 percent interest rate, with any additional debt costing 12 percent. This would result in a second break point in the MCC schedule, at the point where the $54 million of 10 percent debt is exhausted. At what amount of

FIGURE 15-2

Marginal Cost of Capital Schedule for Unilate Textiles Using Both Retained Earnings and New Common Stock

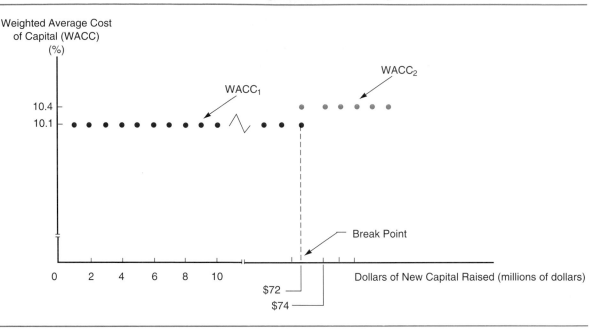

total financing would the 10 percent debt be used up? We know that this total financing will amount to $54 million of debt plus some amount of preferred stock and common equity. If we let BP_{Debt} represent the total financing at this second break point, then we know that 45 percent of BP_{Debt} will be debt, so

$$0.45(BP_{Debt}) = \$54 \text{ million}$$

Solving for BP_{Debt}, we have

$$BP_{Debt} = \frac{\text{Maximum amount of 10\% debt}}{\text{Proportion of debt}} = \frac{\$54 \text{ million}}{0.45} = \$120 \text{ million}$$

Thus, there will be another break in the MCC schedule after Unilate has raised a total of $120 million, and this second break results from an increase in the cost of debt. The higher after-tax cost of debt (7.2 percent versus 6.0 percent) will result in a higher WACC. For example, if Unilate needs $130 million for capital budgeting projects, the WACC would be 10.9 percent:

Capital Source	Weight	Amount in Millions	After-Tax Component Cost	WACC
Debt	0.45	$ 58.5	7.2%	3.2%
Preferred stock	0.05	6.5	10.3	0.5
Common equity	0.50	65.0	14.3	7.2
	1.00	$130.0		WACC$_3$ = 10.9%

TABLE 15-1

TABLE 15-1

WACC and Break Points for Unilate's MCC Schedule

I. Break Points

1. $BP_{\text{Retained earnings}} = \$36,000,000/0.50 = \$72,000,000$

2. $\quad\quad BP_{\text{Debt}} = \$54,000,000/0.45 = \$120,000,000$

II. Weighted Average Cost of Capital (WACC)

1. New Capital Needs: $0–$72,000,000

	Breakdown of Funds at $72,000,000	Weight	×	After-Tax Component Cost	=	WACC
Debt (10%)	$32,400,000	0.45		6.0%		2.7%
Preferred stock	3,600,000	0.05		10.3		0.5
Common equity (Retained earnings)	36,000,000	0.50		13.7		6.9
	$72,000,000	1.00			$WACC_1 =$	10.1%

2. New Capital Needs: $72,000,001–$120,000,000

	Breakdown of Funds at $120,000,000	Weight	×	After-Tax Component Cost	=	WACC
Debt (10%)	$ 54,000,000	0.45		6.0%		2.7%
Preferred stock	6,000,000	0.05		10.3		0.5
Common equity (New stock issue)	60,000,000	0.50		14.3		7.2
	$120,000,000	1.00			$WACC_2 =$	10.4%

3. New Capital Needs: above $120,000,000

	Breakdown of Funds at $130,000,000	Weight	×	After-Tax Component Cost	=	WACC
Debt (12%)	$ 58,500,000	0.45		7.2%		3.2%
Preferred stock	6,500,000	0.05		10.3		0.5
Common equity (New stock issue)	65,000,000	0.50		14.3		7.2
	$130,000,000	1.00			$WACC_3 =$	10.9%

In other words, the next dollar beyond $120 million will consist of 45¢ of 12 percent debt (7.2 percent after taxes), 5¢ of 10.3 percent preferred stock, and 50¢ of new common stock at a cost of 14.3 percent (retained earnings were used up much earlier), and this marginal dollar will have a cost of $WACC_3 = 10.9\%$.

The effect of this second WACC increase is shown in Figure 15-3. Now there are two break points, one caused by using up all the retained earnings and the other by using up all the 10 percent debt. With the two breaks, there are three different WACCs: $WACC_1 = 10.1\%$ for the first $72 million of new capital; $WACC_2 = 10.4\%$ in the interval between $72 million and $120 million; and $WACC_3 = 10.9\%$ for all new capital beyond $120 million.[9]

[9]When we use the term *weighted average cost of capital,* we are referring to the WACC, which is the cost of $1 raised partly as debt, partly as preferred, and partly as equity. We could also calculate the average cost of all the capital the firm raised during a given year. For example, if Unilate raised $150 million, the first $72 million would have a cost of 10.1 percent, the next $48 million a cost of

How is an MCC schedule constructed?

If there are n breaks in the MCC schedule, how many different WACCs are there? Why?

Combining the MCC and Investment Opportunity Schedules

Now that we have calculated the MCC schedule, we can use it to develop a discount rate for use in the capital budgeting process; that is, *we can use the MCC schedule to find the cost of capital for determining projects' net present values (NPVs)* as discussed in Chapter 13.

To understand how the MCC schedule is used in capital budgeting, assume that Unilate Textiles has three financial executives: a financial vice-president (VP), a treasurer, and a director of capital budgeting (DCB). The financial VP asks the treasurer to develop the firm's MCC schedule, and the treasurer produces the schedule shown earlier in Figure 15-3. At the same time, the financial VP asks the DCB to draw up a list of all projects that are potentially acceptable. The list shows each project's cost, projected annual net cash inflows, life, and IRR. These data are presented at the bottom of Figure 15-5. For example, Project A has a cost of $39 million, it is expected to produce inflows of $9 million per year for 6 years, and, therefore, it has an IRR of 10.2 percent. Similarly, Project C has a cost of $36 million, it is expected to produce inflows of $10 million per year for 5 years, and thus it has an IRR of 12.1 percent. (NPVs cannot be shown yet because we do not yet know the marginal cost of capital.) For simplicity, we assume now that all projects are independent as opposed to mutually exclusive, that they are equally risky, and that their risks are all equal to those of the firm's average existing assets.

The DCB then plots the IRR data shown at the bottom of Figure 15-5 as the **investment opportunity schedule (IOS)** shown in the graph. The IOS schedule shows, in rank order, how much money Unilate could invest at different rates of return (IRRs). Figure 15-5 also shows Unilate's MCC schedule as it was developed by the treasurer and plotted in Figure 15-3. Now consider Project C: its IRR is 12.1 percent, and it can be financed with capital that costs only 10.1 percent; consequently, it should be accepted. Recall from Chapter 13 that if a project's IRR exceeds its cost of capital, its NPV also will be positive; therefore, Project C also must be acceptable by the NPV criterion. Projects B, D, and E can be analyzed similarly; they are all acceptable because IRR > MCC = WACC and hence NPV > 0. Project A, on the other hand, should be rejected because its IRR < MCC and therefore its NPV < 0.

People sometimes ask this question: "If we took Project A first, it would be acceptable because its 10.2 percent return would exceed the 10.1 percent cost of money used to finance it. Why couldn't we do this?" The answer is that we are seeking, in effect, to maximize the excess of *returns over costs,* or the area that is above the WACC but below the IOS. We accomplish this by graphing (and accepting) the most profitable projects first.

Another question that sometimes arises is this: "What would happen if the MCC cut through one of the projects? For example, suppose the second break point in the MCC schedule had occurred at $100 million rather than at $120 million, causing the MCC schedule to cut through Project E. Should we then accept Project E?" If Project E could be accepted in part, we would take on only part of

INVESTMENT OPPORTUNITY SCHEDULE (IOS)
A graph of the firm's investment opportunities ranked in order of the projects' internal rates of return.

FIGURE 15-5

Combining the MCC and IOS Schedules to Determine the Optimal Capital Budget

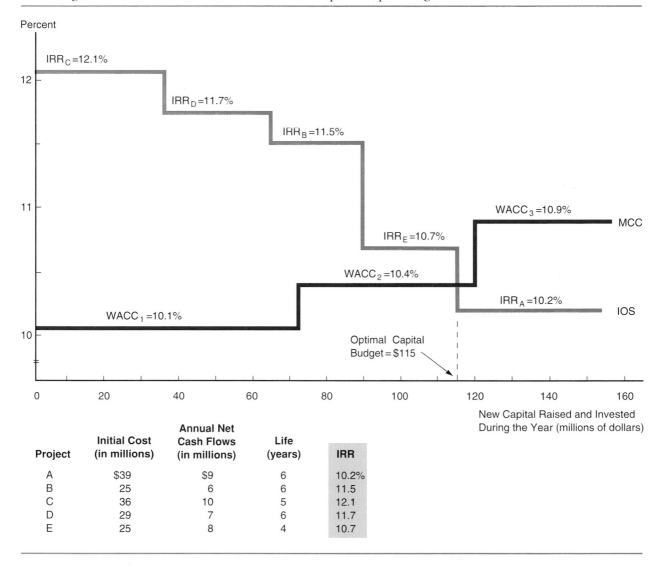

Project	Initial Cost (in millions)	Annual Net Cash Flows (in millions)	Life (years)	IRR
A	$39	$9	6	10.2%
B	25	6	6	11.5
C	36	10	5	12.1
D	29	7	6	11.7
E	25	8	4	10.7

it. Otherwise, the answer would be determined by (1) finding the average cost of the funds needed to finance Project E (some of the money would cost 10.4 percent and some 10.9 percent) and (2) comparing the average cost of this money with the 10.7 percent return on the project. We should accept Project E if its return exceeds the average cost of the $25 million needed to finance it.

The preceding analysis as summarized in Figure 15-5 reveals a very important point: *The cost of capital used in the capital budgeting process as discussed in Chapters 13 and 14 actually is determined at the intersection of the IOS and MCC schedules. If the cost of capital at the intersection (WACC$_2$ = 10.4% in Figure 15-5) is used, then the firm will make correct accept/reject decisions, and* *its level of financing and investment will be optimal. If it uses any other rate, its capital budget will not be optimal.*

The intersection WACC as determined in Figure 15-5 should be used to find the NPVs of new projects that are about as risky as the firm's existing assets, but this corporate cost of capital should be adjusted up or down to find NPVs for projects with higher or lower risk than the average project. This point was discussed in Chapter 14, in connection with the Home Energy Products appliance control computer example.

Self-Test Questions

Differentiate between the MCC and IOS schedules.

How is the corporate cost of capital, which is used to evaluate average risk projects to determine their NPVs, found?

As a rule, should a firm's cost of capital as determined in this chapter be used to evaluate all of its capital budgeting projects? Explain.

Summary

This chapter showed how (1) the weighted average cost of capital (WACC) is computed for a firm, and (2) the MCC schedule is developed for use in the capital budgeting process. The following key concepts were covered.

- The cost of capital to be used in capital budgeting decisions is the **weighted average** of the various types of capital the firm uses, typically debt, preferred stock, and common equity.
- The **component cost of debt** is the after-tax cost of new debt. It is found by multiplying the cost of new debt by $(1 - T)$, where T is the firm's marginal tax rate: $k_{dT} = k_d(1 - T)$.
- The **component cost of preferred stock** is calculated as the preferred dividend divided by the net issuing price, where the net issuing price is the price the firm receives after deducting flotation costs: $k_{ps} = D_{ps}/[P_0(1 - F)] = D_{ps}/NP$.
- The **cost of common equity** is the cost of retained earnings as long as the firm has retained earnings, but the cost of equity becomes the cost of new common stock once the firm has exhausted its retained earnings.
- The **cost of retained earnings** is the rate of return required by stockholders on the firm's common stock, and it can be estimated using one of three methods: (1) the **CAPM approach,** (2) the **bond-yield-plus-risk-premium approach,** and (3) the **dividend-yield-plus-growth-rate,** or DCF, **approach.**
- To use the **CAPM approach,** one (1) estimates the firm's beta, (2) multiplies this beta by the market risk premium to determine the firm's risk premium, and (3) adds the firm's risk premium to the risk-free rate to obtain the firm's cost of retained earnings: $k_s = k_{RF} + (k_M - k_{RF})\beta_s$.
- The **bond-yield-plus-risk-premium approach** calls for adding a risk premium of from 3 to 5 percentage points to the firm's interest rate on long-term debt: $k_s = $ Bond yield $+ $ RP.
- To use the **dividend-yield-plus-growth-rate approach,** which also is called the **DCF approach,** one adds the firm's expected growth rate to its expected dividend yield: $k_s = D_1/P_0 + g$.

SMALL BUSINESS

The Cost of Equity Capital for Small Firms

The three equity cost estimating techniques discussed in this chapter (DCF, bond-yield-plus-risk-premium, and CAPM) have serious limitations when applied to small firms. First, many small, rapidly growing firms do not now and will not in the foreseeable future pay dividends. For firms like this, the constant growth model simply is not applicable. In fact, it is difficult to imagine any dividend model that would be of practical benefit for such firms because of the difficulty of estimating dividends and growth rates. Second, the bond-yield-plus-risk-premium technique cannot be used for firms that do not have bond issues outstanding, and many small firms do not issue bonds. And, third, the CAPM often is not usable because the stocks of many small firms are not traded publicly, so we cannot calculate those firms' betas. For the privately owned firm, we might use the "pure play" CAPM technique, which involves finding a firm in the same line of business with publicly held stock, estimating that firm's beta, and then using this second firm's beta as a replacement for that of the small business in question. But these "large" firms' betas would have to be subjectively modified to reflect their larger sizes and more established positions, as well as to take account of the differences in the nature of their products and their capital structures as compared to the smaller firms.

FLOTATION COSTS FOR SMALL ISSUES We know that when external equity capital is raised, flotation costs increase the cost of equity capital beyond what it would be for internal funds. These external flotation costs are especially significant for smaller firms, and they can substantially affect capital budgeting decisions involving external equity funds. According to the latest Securities and Exchange Commission data, the average flotation costs of small common stock offerings generally are four to five times greater than those of large firms (greater than $50 million). Thus, small firms are at a substantial disadvantage because of the effects of flotation costs.

THE SMALL-FIRM EFFECT A number of researchers have observed that portfolios of small-firm stocks have earned consistently higher average returns than those of large-firm stocks; this is called the "small-firm effect." On the surface, it would seem to be advantageous to the small firm to provide average returns in the stock market that are higher than those of large firms. In reality, this is bad news for the small firm—the small-firm effect means that the capital market demands higher returns on stocks of small firms than on otherwise similar stocks of large firms. Therefore, the basic cost of equity capital is higher for small firms. This compounds the high flotation cost problem noted earlier.

It might be argued that stocks of small firms are riskier than those of large ones and that this accounts for the differences in returns. However, the larger returns for small firms remain larger even after adjusting for the effects of their higher risks. Higher returns reflect higher costs of capital, so we must conclude that small firms do have higher capital costs than otherwise similar large firms. The manager of a small firm should take this factor into account when estimating the firm's cost of equity capital. In general, the cost of equity capital appears to be about four percentage points higher for small firms than for large, New York Stock Exchange firms with similar risk characteristics.

- The **cost of new common equity** is higher than the cost of retained earnings because the firm incurs **flotation expenses** to sell stock. To find the cost of new common equity, the stock price is first reduced by the flotation expense, then the dividend yield is calculated on the basis of the price the firm actually will receive, and finally the expected growth rate is added to this **adjusted dividend yield:** $k_e = D_1/[P_0(1 - F)] + g$.
- Each firm has an **optimal capital structure,** defined as that mix of debt, preferred stock, and common equity which *minimizes* its **weighted average cost of capital (WACC):**

$$WACC = w_d k_{dT} + w_{ps} k_{ps} + w_s(k_s \text{ or } k_e)$$

- The **marginal cost of capital (MCC)** is defined as the cost of the last dollar of new capital that the firm raises. The MCC increases as the firm raises more and more capital during a given period. A graph of the MCC plotted against dollars raised is the **MCC schedule.**
- A **break point** will occur in the MCC schedule each time the cost of one of the capital components increases.
- The **investment opportunity schedule (IOS)** is a graph of the firm's investment opportunities, ranked in order of their internal rates of return (IRR).
- The MCC schedule is combined with the IOS schedule, and the intersection defines the **corporate cost of capital,** which is used to evaluate average-risk capital budgeting projects.
- The three equity cost estimation techniques discussed in this chapter have **serious limitations when applied to small firms,** thus increasing the need for the small-business manager to use judgment.
- The average flotation cost for small firms is much greater than for large firms. As a result, a small firm would have to earn considerably more on the same project than a large firm. Also, the capital market demands higher returns on stocks of small firms than on otherwise similar stocks of large firms—this is called the **small-firm effect.**

The concepts developed in this chapter are extended in Chapter 16, where we consider the effect of the capital structure on the cost of capital.

Questions

15-1   In what sense does the marginal cost of capital schedule represent a series of average costs?

15-2   The financial manager of a large national firm was overheard making the following statement: "We try to use as much retained earnings as possible for capital budgeting purposes because there is no *explicit* cost to these funds, and this allows us to invest in relatively low yielding projects that would not be feasible if we had to issue new common stock. We actually use retained earnings to invest in projects with yields below the coupon rate on our bonds." Comment on the validity of this statement.

15-3   How would each of the following affect a firm's cost of debt, k_{dT}; its cost of equity, k_s; and its weighted average cost of capital, WACC? Indicate by a plus (+), a minus (−), or a zero (0) if the factor would raise, lower, or have an indeterminate effect on the item in question. Assume other things are held constant. Be prepared to justify your answer, but recognize that several of the parts probably have no single correct answer; these questions are designed to stimulate thought and discussion.

	\multicolumn{3}{c}{**Effect on**}	
	k_{dT}	k_s	**WACC**
a. The corporate tax rate is lowered.	_____	_____	_____
b. The Federal Reserve tightens credit.	_____	_____	_____
c. The firm uses more debt; that is, it increases its debt/assets ratio.	_____	_____	_____
d. The dividend payout ratio is increased.	_____	_____	_____
e. The firm doubles its amount of capital it raises during the year.	_____	_____	_____

	Effect on		
	k_{dT}	k_s	**WACC**
f. The firm expands into a risky new area.	_____	_____	_____
g. The firm merges with another firm whose earnings are countercyclical both to those of the first firm and to the stock market.	_____	_____	_____
h. The stock market falls drastically, and the firm's stock falls along with the rest.	_____	_____	_____
i. Investors become more risk averse.	_____	_____	_____
j. The firm is an electric utility with a large investment in nuclear plants. Several states propose a ban on nuclear power generation.	_____	_____	_____

15-4 Suppose a firm estimates its MCC and IOS schedules for the coming year and finds that they intersect at the point 10%, $10 million. What cost of capital should be used to evaluate average projects, high-risk projects, and low-risk projects?

Self-Test Problems

(Solutions Appear in Appendix B)

Key terms **ST-1** Define each of the following terms:

    a. after-tax cost of debt, k_{dT}; capital component cost

    b. cost of preferred stock, k_p

    c. cost of retained earnings, k_s

    d. cost of new common equity, k_e

    e. flotation cost, F

    f. target capital structure; capital structure components

    g. weighted average cost of capital, WACC

    h. marginal cost of capital, MCC

    i. marginal cost of capital schedule; break point, BP

    j. investment opportunity schedule, IOS

Optimal capital budget **ST-2** Lancaster Engineering Inc. (LEI) has the following capital structure, which it considers to be optimal:

Debt	25%
Preferred stock	15
Common equity	60
	100%

LEI's expected net income this year is $34,285.72; its established dividend payout ratio is 30 percent; its marginal tax rate is 40 percent; and investors expect earnings and dividends to grow at a constant rate of 9 percent in the future. LEI paid a dividend of $3.60 per share last year, and its stock currently sells at a price of $60 per share.

    LEI can obtain new capital in the following ways:

Common: New common stock has a flotation cost of 10 percent for up to $12,000 of new stock and 20 percent for all common over $12,000.

Preferred: New preferred stock with a dividend of $11 can be sold to the public at a price of $100 per share. However, flotation costs of $5 per share will be incurred for up to $7,500 of preferred, and flotation costs will rise to $10 per share, or 10 percent, on all preferred over $7,500.

Debt: Up to $5,000 of debt can be sold at an interest rate of 12 percent; debt in the range of $5,001 to $10,000 must carry an interest rate of 14 percent; and all debt over $10,000 will have an interest rate of 16 percent.

LEI has the following independent investment opportunities:

Project	Cost at t = 0	Annual Net Cash Flow	Project Life	IRR
A	$10,000	$2,191.20	7 years	12.0%
B	10,000	3,154.42	5	17.4
C	10,000	2,170.18	8	14.2
D	20,000	3,789.48	10	13.7
E	20,000	5,427.84	6	

   a. Find the break points in the MCC schedule.
   b. Determine the cost of each capital structure component.
   c. Calculate the weighted average cost of capital in the interval between each break in the MCC schedule.
   d. Calculate the IRR for Project E.
   e. Construct a graph showing the MCC and IOS schedules.
   f. Which projects should LEI accept?

Problems

Cost of retained earnings   **15-1**   The earnings, dividends, and stock price of Talukdar Technologies Inc. are expected to grow at 7 percent per year in the future. Talukdar's common stock sells for $23 per share, its last dividend was $2.00, and the company will pay a dividend of $2.14 at the end of the current year.
   a. Using the discounted cash flow approach, what is its cost of retained earnings?
   b. If the firm's beta is 1.6, the risk-free rate is 9 percent, and the average return on the market is 13 percent, what will be the firm's cost of equity using the CAPM approach?
   c. If the firm's bonds earn a return of 12 percent, what will k_s be using the bond-yield-plus-risk-premium approach? (Hint: Use the midpoint of the risk premium range discussed in the text.)
   d. Based on the results of Parts a through c, what would you estimate Talukdar's cost of retained earnings to be?

Cost of retained earnings   **15-2**   The Shrieves Company's EPS was $6.50 in 1995 and $4.42 in 1990. The company pays out 40 percent of its earnings as dividends, and the stock sells for $36.
   a. Calculate the past growth rate in earnings. (Hint: This is a 5-year growth period.)
   b. Calculate the *next* expected dividend per share, D_1. [D_0 = 0.4($6.50) = $2.60.] Assume that the past growth rate will continue.
   c. What is the cost of retained earnings, k_s, for the Shrieves Company?

Break point calculations   **15-3**   The Simmons Company expects earnings of $30 million next year. Its dividend payout ratio is 40 percent, and its debt/assets ratio is 60 percent. Simmons uses no preferred stock.

a. What amount of retained earnings does Simmons expect next year?

b. At what amount of financing will there be a break point in the MCC schedule?

c. If Simmons can borrow $12 million at an interest rate of 11 percent, another $12 million at a rate of 12 percent, and any additional debt at a rate of 13 percent, at what points will rising debt costs cause breaks in the MCC schedule?

Calculation of g and EPS   **15-4**   Rowell Products' stock is currently selling for $60 a share. The firm is expected to earn $5.40 per share this year and to pay a year-end dividend of $3.60.

a. If investors require a 9 percent return, what rate of growth must be expected for Rowell?

b. If Rowell reinvests retained earnings in projects whose average return is equal to the stock's expected rate of return, what will be next year's EPS? [Hint: g = b(ROE), where b = fraction of earnings retained.]

Weighted average   **15-5**   On January 1, 1996, the total assets of the Dexter Company were $270 million. cost of capital   The firm's present capital structure, which follows, is considered to be optimal. Assume that there is no short-term debt.

Long-term debt	$135,000,000
Common equity	135,000,000
Total liabilities and equity	$270,000,000

New bonds will have a 10 percent coupon rate and will be sold at par. Common stock, currently selling at $60 a share, can be sold to net the company $54 a share. Stockholders' required rate of return is estimated to be 12 percent, consisting of a dividend yield of 4 percent and an expected growth rate of 8 percent. (The next expected dividend is $2.40, so $2.40/$60 = 4%.) Retained earnings are estimated to be $13.5 million. The marginal tax rate is 40 percent. Assuming that all asset expansion (gross expenditures for fixed assets plus related working capital) is included in the capital budget, the dollar amount of the capital budget, ignoring depreciation, is $135 million.

a. To maintain the present capital structure, how much of the capital budget must Dexter finance by equity?

b. How much of the new equity funds needed will be generated internally? Externally?

c. Calculate the cost of each of the equity components.

d. At what level of capital expenditure will there be a break in Dexter's MCC schedule?

e. Calculate the WACC (1) below and (2) above the break in the MCC schedule.

f. Plot the MCC schedule. Also, draw in an IOS schedule that is consistent with both the MCC schedule and the projected capital budget. (Any IOS schedule that is consistent will do.)

Weighted average   **15-6**   The following tabulation gives earnings per share figures for the Brueggeman cost of capital   Company during the preceding 10 years. The firm's common stock, 7.8 million shares outstanding, is now (1/1/96) selling for $65 per share, and the expected dividend at the end of the current year (1996) is 55 percent of the 1995 EPS. Because investors expect past trends to continue, g may be based on the earnings growth rate. (Note that nine years of growth are reflected in the data.)

Year	EPS	Year	EPS
1986	$3.90	1991	$5.73
1987	4.21	1992	6.19
1988	4.55	1993	6.68
1989	4.91	1994	7.22
1990	5.31	1995	7.80

The current interest rate on new debt is 9 percent. The firm's marginal tax rate is 40 percent. Its capital structure, considered to be optimal, is as follows:

Debt	$104,000,000
Common equity	156,000,000
Total liabilities and equity	$260,000,000

a. Calculate Brueggeman's after-tax cost of new debt and of common equity, assuming that new equity comes only from retained earnings. Calculate the cost of equity as $k_s = D_1/P_0 + g$.

b. Find Brueggeman's weighted average cost of capital, again assuming that no new common stock is sold and that all debt costs 9 percent.

c. How much can be spent on capital investments before external equity must be sold? (Assume that retained earnings available for 1996 are 45 percent of 1995 earnings. Obtain 1995 earnings by multiplying 1995 EPS by the shares outstanding.)

d. What is Brueggeman's weighted average cost of capital (cost of funds raised in excess of the amount calculated in Part c) if new common stock can be sold to the public at $65 a share to net the firm $58.50 a share? The cost of debt is constant.

Optimal capital budget   **15-7**   Ezzell Enterprises has the following capital structure, which it considers to be optimal under present and forecasted conditions:

Debt (long-term only)	45%
Common equity	55
Total liabilities and equity	100%

For the coming year, management expects after-tax earnings of $2.5 million. Ezzell's past dividend policy of paying out 60 percent of earnings will continue. Present commitments from its banker will allow Ezzell to borrow according to the following schedule:

Loan Amount	Interest Rate
$0 to $500,000	9% on this increment of debt
$500,001 to $900,000	11% on this increment of debt
$900,001 and above	13% on this increment of debt

The company's marginal tax rate is 40 percent; the current market price of its stock is $22 per share; its *last* dividend was $2.20 per share; and the expected growth rate is 5 percent. External equity (new common) can be sold at a flotation cost of 10 percent.

Ezzell has the following investment opportunities for the next year:

Project	Cost	Annual Cash Flows	Project Life	IRR
1	$675,000	$155,401	8 years	
2	900,000	268,484	5	15.0%
3	375,000	161,524	3	
4	562,500	185,194	4	12.0
5	750,000	127,351	10	11.0

Management asks you to help determine which projects (if any) should be undertaken. You proceed with this analysis by answering the following questions (or performing the tasks) as posed in a logical sequence:

a. How many breaks are there in the MCC schedule? At what dollar amounts do the breaks occur, and what causes them?

b. What is the weighted average cost of capital in each of the intervals between the breaks?

c. What are the IRR values for Projects 1 and 3?

d. Graph the IOS and MCC schedules.

e. Which projects should Ezzell's management accept?

f. What assumptions about project risk are implicit in this problem? If you learned that Projects 1, 2, and 3 were of above-average risk, yet Ezzell chose the projects which you indicated in Part e, how would this affect the situation?

g. The problem stated that Ezzell pays out 60 percent of its earnings as dividends. How would the analysis change if the payout ratio were changed to zero, to 100 percent, or somewhere in between? (No calculations are necessary.)

Exam-Type Problems

The problems included in this section are set up in such a way that they could be used as multiple-choice exam problems.

After-tax cost of debt **15-8** Calculate the after-tax cost of debt under each of the following conditions:
a. Interest rate, 13 percent; tax rate, 0 percent.
b. Interest rate, 13 percent; tax rate, 20 percent.
c. Interest rate, 13 percent; tax rate, 34 percent.

After-tax cost of debt **15-9** The McDaniel Company's financing plans for next year include the sale of long-term bonds with a 10 percent coupon. The company believes it can sell the bonds at a price that will provide a yield to maturity of 12 percent. If the marginal tax rate is 34 percent, what is McDaniel's after-tax cost of debt?

Cost of preferred stock **15-10** Maness Industries plans to issue some $100 par preferred stock with an 11 percent dividend. The stock is selling on the market for $97.00, and Maness must pay flotation costs of 5 percent of the market price. What is the cost of the preferred stock for Maness?

Cost of new common stock **15-11** The Choi Company's next expected dividend, D_1, is $3.18; its growth rate is 6 percent; and the stock now sells for $36. New stock can be sold to net the firm $32.40 per share.
a. What is Choi's percentage flotation cost, F?
b. What is Choi's cost of new common stock, k_c?

Weighted average cost of capital **15-12** The Gupta Company's cost of equity is 16 percent. Its before-tax cost of debt is 13 percent, and its marginal tax rate is 40 percent. The stock sells at book value. Using the following balance sheet, calculate Gupta's after-tax weighted average cost of capital:

Assets		Liabilities and Equity	
Cash	$ 120	Long-term debt	$1,152
Accounts receivable	240	Equity	1,728
Inventories	360		
Plant and equipment, net	2,160		
Total assets	$2,880	Total liabilities and equity	$2,880

Optimal capital budget   **15-13**   The Mason Corporation's present capital structure, which is also its target capital structure, calls for 50 percent debt and 50 percent common equity. The firm has only one potential project, an expansion program with a 10.2 percent IRR and a cost of $20 million but which is completely divisible; that is, Mason can invest any amount up to $20 million. The firm expects to retain $3 million of earnings next year. It can raise up to $5 million in new debt at a before-tax cost of 8 percent, and all debt after the first $5 million will have a cost of 10 percent. The cost of retained earnings is 12 percent, and the firm can sell any amount of new common stock desired at a constant cost of new equity of 15 percent. The firm's marginal tax rate is 40 percent. What is the firm's optimal capital budget?

Optimal capital budget   **15-14**   The management of Ferri Phosphate Industries (FPI) is planning next year's capital budget. FPI projects its net income at $7,500, and its payout ratio is 40 percent. The company's earnings and dividends are growing at a constant rate of 5 percent; the last dividend, D_0, was $0.90; and the current stock price is $8.59. FPI's new debt will cost 14 percent. If FPI issues new common stock, flotation costs will be 20 percent. FPI is at its optimal capital structure, which is 40 percent debt and 60 percent equity, and the firm's marginal tax rate is 40 percent. FPI has the following independent, indivisible, and equally risky investment opportunities:

Project	Cost	IRR
A	$15,000	17%
B	20,000	14
C	15,000	16
D	12,000	15

What is FPI's optimal capital budget?

Risk-adjusted optimal capital budget   **15-15**   Refer to Problem 15-14. Management now decides to incorporate project risk differentials into the analysis. The new policy is to add 2 percentage points to the cost of capital of those projects significantly riskier than average and to subtract 2 percentage points from the cost of capital of those which are substantially less risky than average. Management judges Project A to be of high risk, Projects C and D to be of average risk, and Project B to be of low risk. No projects are divisible. What is the optimal capital budget after adjustment for project risk?

Weighted average cost of capital   **15-16**   Florida Electric Company (FEC) uses only debt and equity. It can borrow unlimited amounts at an interest rate of 10% as long as it finances at its target capital structure, which calls for 45 percent debt and 55 percent common equity. Its last dividend was $2; its expected constant growth rate is 4 percent; its stock sells at a price of $25; and new stock would net the company $20 per share after flotation costs. FEC's marginal tax rate is 40 percent, and it expects to have $100 million of retained earnings this year. Two projects are available: Project A has a cost of $200 million and a rate of return of 13 percent, while Project B has a cost of $125 million and a rate of return of 10 percent. All the company's potential projects are equally risky.

a. What is FEC's cost of equity from newly issued stock?

b. What is FEC's marginal cost of capital; i.e., what WACC cost rate should it use to evaluate capital budgeting projects (these two projects plus any others that might arise during the year, provided the cost of capital schedule remains as it is currently)?

After-tax cost of debt **15-17** A company's 6 percent coupon rate, semiannual payment, $1,000 par value bond that matures in 30 years sells at a price of $515.16. The company's marginal tax rate is 40 percent. What is the firm's component cost of debt for purposes of calculating the WACC? (Hint: Base your answer on the simple rate, not the EAR.)

Marginal cost of equity **15-18** Chicago Paints Corporation has a target capital structure of 40 percent debt and 60 percent common equity. The company expects to have $600 of after-tax income during the coming year, and it plans to retain 40 percent of its earnings. The current stock price is $P_0 = 30, the last dividend was $D_0 = 2.00, and the dividend is expected to grow at a constant rate of 7 percent. New stock can be sold at a flotation cost of F = 25 percent. What will Chicago Paints's marginal cost of *equity* capital (not the WACC) be if it raises a total of $500 of new capital?

Integrative Problem

Cost of capital **15-19** Assume that you were recently hired as assistant to Jerry Lehman, financial VP of Coleman Technologies. Your first task is to estimate Coleman's cost of capital. Lehman has provided you with the following data, which he believes may be relevant to your task:

(1) The firm's marginal tax rate is 40 percent.

(2) The current price of Coleman's 12% coupon, semiannual payment, noncallable bonds with 15 years remaining to maturity is $1,153.72. Coleman does not use short-term interest-bearing debt on a permanent basis. New bonds would be privately placed with no flotation cost.

(3) The current price of the firm's 10 percent, $100 par value, quarterly dividend, perpetual preferred stock is $113.10. Coleman would incur flotation costs of $2.00 per share on a new issue.

(4) Coleman's common stock is currently selling at $50 per share. Its last dividend (D_0) was $4.19, and dividends are expected to grow at a constant rate of 5 percent in the foreseeable future. Coleman's beta is 1.2; the yield on T-bonds is 7 percent; and the market risk premium is estimated to be 6 percent. For the bond-yield-plus-risk-premium approach, the firm uses a 4 percentage point risk premium.

(5) Up to $300,000 of new common stock can be sold at a flotation cost of 15 percent. Above $300,000, the flotation cost would rise to 25 percent.

(6) Coleman's target capital structure is 30 percent long-term debt, 10 percent preferred stock, and 60 percent common equity.

(7) The firm is forecasting retained earnings of $300,000 for the coming year.

To structure the task somewhat, Lehman has asked you to answer the following questions.

a. (1) What sources of capital should be included when you estimate Coleman's weighted average cost of capital (WACC)?

(2) Should the component costs be figured on a before-tax or an after-tax basis?

(3) Should the costs be historical (embedded) costs or new (marginal) costs?

b. What is the market interest rate on Coleman's debt and its component cost of debt?

c. (1) What is the firm's cost of preferred stock?

(2) Coleman's preferred stock is riskier to investors than its debt, yet the yield to investors is lower than the yield to maturity on the debt. Does this suggest that you have made a mistake? (Hint: Think about taxes.)

d. **(1)** Why is there a cost associated with the retained earnings?

(2) What is Coleman's estimated cost of retained earnings using the CAPM approach?

(3) Why is the T-bond rate a better estimate of the risk-free rate for cost of capital purposes than the T-bill rate?

e. What is the estimated cost of retained earnings using the discounted cash flow (DCF) approach?

f. What is the bond-yield-plus-risk-premium estimate for Coleman's cost of retained earnings?

g. What is your final estimate for k_s?

h. What is Coleman's cost for up to $300,000 of newly issued common stock, k_{e1}?

i. Explain in words why new common stock has a higher percentage cost than retained earnings.

j. **(1)** What is Coleman's overall, or weighted average, cost of capital (WACC) when retained earnings are used as the equity component?

(2) What is the WACC after retained earnings have been exhausted and Coleman uses up to $300,000 of new common stock with a 15 percent flotation cost?

(3) What is the WACC if more than $300,000 of new common equity is sold?

k. **(1)** At what amount of new investment would Coleman be forced to issue new common stock? To put it another way, what is the largest capital budget the company could support without issuing new common stock? Assume that the 30/10/60 target capital structure will be maintained.

(2) At what amount of new investment would Coleman be forced to issue new common stock with a 25 percent flotation cost?

(3) What is a marginal cost of capital (MCC) schedule? Construct a graph which shows Coleman's MCC schedule.

l. Coleman's Director of Capital Budgeting has identified the following potential projects:

Project	Cost	Life	Cash Flow	IRR
A	$700,000	5 years	$218,795	17.0%
B	500,000	5	152,705	16.0
B′	500,000	20	79,881	15.0
C	800,000	5	219,185	11.5

Projects B and B′ are mutually exclusive, whereas the remainder are independent. All the projects are equally risky. Assume that project B′ is not repeatable.

(1) Plot the IOS schedule on the same graph that contains your MCC schedule. What is the firm's marginal cost of capital for capital budgeting purposes?

(2) What is the dollar size, and the included projects, in Coleman's optimal capital budget? Explain your answer fully.

(3) Would Coleman's MCC schedule remain constant at 12.8 percent beyond $2 million regardless of the amount of capital required?

(4) If $WACC_3$ had been 18.5 percent rather than 12.8 percent, but the second WACC break point had still occurred at $1,000,000, how would that have affected the analysis?

m. Suppose you learned that Coleman could raise only $200,000 of new debt at a 10 percent interest rate and that new debt beyond $200,000 would have a yield to investors of 12 percent. Trace back through your work and explain how this new fact would change the situation.

Computer-Related Problem

Work the problem in this section only if you are using the computer problem diskette.

Marginal cost of capital   **15-20**   Use the model in File C15 to work this problem.

a. Refer to Problem 15-7. Now assume that the debt ratio is increased to 65 percent, causing all interest rates to rise by 1 percentage point, to 10 percent, 12 percent, and 14 percent, and causing g to increase from 5 to 6 percent. What happens to the MCC schedule and the capital budget?

b. Assume the facts as in Part a, but suppose Ezzell's marginal tax rate falls (1) to 20 percent or (2) to 0 percent. How would this affect the MCC schedule and the capital budget?

c. Ezzell's management would now like to know what the optimal capital budget would be if earnings were as high as $3.25 million or as low as $1 million. Assume a 40 percent marginal tax rate.

d. Would it be reasonable to use the model to analyze the effects of a change in payout ratio without changing other variables?

CHAPTER 16

Capital Structure

In 1992, British Petroleum (BP) Company began what was considered a "massive" debt-reduction program to restructure its mix of capital financing. According to David Simon, chairman of the board, BP's debt ratio was well above the desired 35 percent, so drastic measures were needed. Therefore, the company initiated a plan to reduce debt by about $6 billion, or by nearly 39 percent, over a four-year period. In the first 30 months of the plan, debt was reduced by nearly $5 billion. Investors have viewed BP's actions favorably—BP's stock price jumped more than 38 percent from the end of 1993 to mid 1995.

Other companies that recently have changed their mixtures of debt and equity (capital structures) include Curtis Mathes, IBM, and Lockheed. IBM reduced its debt-equity ratio from 61 percent in 1993 to 33 percent in 1994 so that its financing mix was more in line with its target capital structure. Similarly, Lockheed Corporation decreased its debt by more than $2 billion in hopes of reducing its debt ratio from nearly 50 percent to its target of 30 percent to 35 percent. And, in 1995, Curtis Mathes sold Southwest Memory, Inc. to boost its profit position, which had deteriorated due to the high degree of financial leverage Southwest Memory imposed. The sale of Southwest Memory allowed Curtis Mathes to reduce its financial risk by significantly improving its debt ratio.

At a time when many firms were actively reducing debt, other firms were not afraid to take on more debt. For example, American General Corporation, considered one of the best capitalized insurance companies in the United States, recently purchased Franklin Life Insurance Company from American Brands, Inc. for nearly $2 billion. Though the acquisition increased American General's debt, industry analysts believe the company has such a low debt ratio that it can afford to take on more debt via additional acquisitions. Indeed, Harold Hook, chairman and CEO, has informed stockholders the company intends to double its size by the year 2000 by taking advantage of acquisition opportunities that might exist for well-capitalized firms such as American General. In its previous acquisitions, American General has

Continued

been careful not to overburden itself with debt by following the strategy of quickly paying off debt with the profits provided by the acquired operations. As it pursues its growth objectives in the future, American General is expected to follow the same strategy, thus maintaining its stature as a well-capitalized organization.

The decision as to how much debt and equity a firm should have is extremely important. As you read this chapter, consider the factors that should be examined to determine what the appropriate mixture of debt and equity (capital structure) is for a firm. This chapter should help you understand why BP, Curtis Mathes, IBM, and Lockheed took steps to reduce their debt ratios and how American General expects to utilize its capital base to achieve its growth objectives. Throughout the chapter, keep the following question in mind: For a particular firm, is there an optimal capital structure that will maximize its value?

In Chapter 15, when we calculated the weighted average cost of capital for use in capital budgeting, we took the capital structure weights, or the mix of securities the firm uses to finance its assets, as a given. However, if the weights are changed, the calculated cost of capital, and thus the set of acceptable projects, also will change. Further, changing the capital structure will affect the riskiness inherent in the firm's common stock, and this will affect the return demanded by stockholders, k_s, and the stock's price, P_0. Therefore, the choice of a capital structure is an important decision.

The Target Capital Structure

TARGET CAPITAL STRUCTURE
The mix of debt, preferred stock, and common equity with which the firm plans to finance its investments.

As we shall see, the firm first analyzes a number of factors, and then it establishes a **target capital structure.** This target might change over time as conditions vary, but at any given moment the firm's management has a specific capital structure in mind, and individual financing decisions should be consistent with this target. If the actual debt ratio is below the target level, expansion capital probably will be raised by issuing debt, whereas if the debt ratio is above the target, stock probably will be sold to bring the firm back in line with the target ratio.

Capital structure policy involves a trade-off between risk and return:

- Using more debt raises the riskiness of the firm's earnings stream.
- However, a higher debt ratio generally leads to a higher expected rate of return.

The higher risk associated with greater debt tends to lower the stock's price, but the higher expected rate of return makes the stock more attractive to investors, which in turn ultimately increases the stock's price. Therefore, *the optimal capital structure is the one that strikes a balance between risk and return so as to maximize the price of the stock.*

Four primary factors influence capital structure decisions.

1. The first is the firm's *business risk,* or the riskiness that would be inherent in the firm's operations if it used no debt. The greater the firm's business risk, the lower the amount of debt that is optimal.

2. The second key factor is the firm's *tax position.* A major reason for using debt is that interest is tax deductible, which lowers the effective cost of debt. However, if much of a firm's income already is sheltered from taxes by accelerated depreciation or tax loss carry-forwards, its tax rate will be low, and in this case debt will not be as advantageous as it would be to a firm with a higher effective tax rate.

3. The third important consideration is *financial flexibility,* or the ability to raise capital on reasonable terms under adverse conditions. Corporate treasurers know that a steady supply of capital is necessary for stable operations, which in turn are vital for long-run success. They also know that when money is tight in the economy, or when a firm is experiencing operating difficulties, a strong balance sheet is needed to obtain funds from suppliers of capital.

4. The fourth debt-determining factor has to do with *managerial conservatism or aggressiveness* with regard to borrowing. Some managers are more aggressive than others; hence, some firms are more inclined to use debt in an effort to boost profits. This factor does not affect the optimal, or value-maximizing, capital structure, but it does influence the target capital structures that firms actually establish.

These four points largely determine the target capital structure, but, of course, operating conditions can cause the actual capital structure to vary from the target at any given time. For example, Illinois Power has a target debt ratio of about 45 percent, but large losses associated with a nuclear plant forced it to write down its common equity, and that raised the debt ratio above the target level. Subsequently, the company eliminated its dividends and took other steps to get its equity back up to the target level.

Self-Test Questions

What are the four factors that affect the target capital structure?

In what sense does capital structure policy involve a tradeoff between risk and return?

Business and Financial Risk

In Chapter 5, when we examined risk from the viewpoint of the individual investor, we distinguished between market risk, which is measured by the firm's beta coefficient, and total risk, which includes both beta risk and a type of risk that can be eliminated by diversification. Then, in Chapter 14, we examined risk from the viewpoint of the corporation, and we considered how capital budgeting decisions affect the riskiness of the firm. There again we distinguished between beta risk (the effect of a project on the firm's beta) and corporate risk (the effect of the project on the firm's total risk).

Now we introduce two new dimensions of risk:

1. *Business risk,* which is the riskiness of the firm's operations if it uses no debt.
2. *Financial risk,* which is the additional risk placed on the common stockholders as a result of the firm's decision to use debt.

Conceptually, the firm has a certain amount of risk inherent in its production and sales operations; this is its business risk. When it uses debt, it partitions this risk and concentrates most of it on one class of investors—the common stockholders.[1]

Business Risk

Business risk is defined as the uncertainty inherent in projections of future returns on assets (ROA), or of returns on equity (ROE) if the firm uses no debt. Business risk is the single most important determinant of capital structure. Consider Bigbee Electronics Company, a firm that currently uses 100 percent equity. Figure 16-1 gives some clues about Bigbee's business risk. The graph shows the trend in ROE (and ROA) from 1985 through 1995, and it gives both security analysts and Bigbee's management an idea of the degree to which ROE has varied in the past and might vary in the future. Comparing the actual results to the trend line, you can see that Bigbee's ROE has fluctuated significantly since 1985.

Bigbee's past fluctuations in ROE were caused by many factors—booms and recessions in the national economy, successful new products introduced both by Bigbee and by its competitors, labor strikes, a fire in Bigbee's major plant, and so on. Similar events will doubtless occur in the future, and when they do, ROE will rise or fall. Further, there always is the possibility that a long-term disaster might strike, permanently depressing the company's earning power. For example, a competitor could introduce a new product that would permanently lower Bigbee's earnings.[2] This element of uncertainty about Bigbee's future ROE is the company's *basic business risk.*

Business risk varies from one industry to another and also among firms in a given industry. Further, business risk can change over time. For example, the electric utilities were regarded for years as having little business risk, but a combination of events in the 1970s and 1980s altered their situation, producing sharp declines in ROE for some companies, and greatly increasing the industry's business risk. Today, food processors and grocery retailers frequently are cited as examples of industries with low business risk, whereas cyclical manufacturing industries, such as steel, are regarded as having especially high business risk. Smaller companies, especially single-product firms, also have a relatively high degree of business risk.[3]

---

[1]Using preferred stock also adds to financial risk. To simplify matters somewhat, in this chapter we shall consider only debt and common equity.

[2]Two examples of "safe" industries that turned out to be risky are the railroads just before automobiles, airplanes, and trucks took away most of their business and the telegraph business just before telephones came on the scene. Also, numerous individual companies have been hurt, if not destroyed, by antitrust actions, fraud, or just plain bad management.

[3]We have avoided any discussion of market versus company-specific risk in this section. We note now that (1) any action that increases business risk will generally increase a firm's beta coefficient but (2) a part of business risk as we define it generally will be company-specific and hence subject to elimination through diversification by the firm's stockholders.

FIGURE 16-1

Bigbee Electronics Company: Trend in ROE, 1985–1995, and Subjective Probability Distribution of ROE, 1995

a. Trend in Return on Equity (ROE)

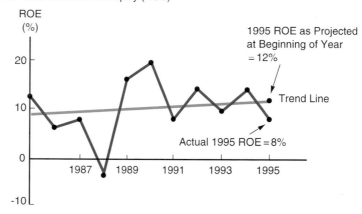

b. Subjective Probability Distribution of ROE

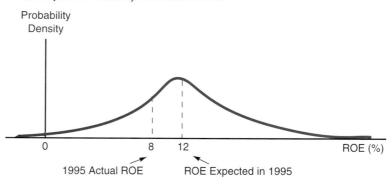

Business risk depends on a number of factors, the more important of which are the following:

1. **Demand (unit sales) variability.** The more stable the unit sales of a firm's products, other things held constant, the lower its business risk.
2. **Sales price variability.** Firms whose products are sold in highly volatile markets are exposed to more business risk than similar firms whose output prices are relatively stable.
3. **Input price variability.** Firms whose input prices (labor, product costs, and so on) are highly uncertain are exposed to a high degree of business risk.
4. **Ability to adjust output prices for changes in input prices.** Some firms have little difficulty in raising the prices of their products when input costs

rise, and the greater the ability to adjust selling prices, the lower the degree of business risk. This factor is especially important during periods of high inflation.

5. **The extent to which costs are fixed: operating leverage.** If a high percentage of a firm's costs are fixed and hence do not decline when demand falls off, this increases the company's business risk. This factor is called *operating leverage,* and it was discussed at length in Chapter 4.

Each of these factors is determined partly by the firm's industry characteristics, but each also is controllable to some extent by management. For example, most firms can, through their marketing policies, take actions to stabilize both unit sales and sales prices; however, this stabilization might require either large expenditures on advertising or price concessions to induce customers to commit to purchasing fixed quantities at fixed prices in the future. Similarly, firms like Bigbee Electronics can reduce the volatility of future input costs by negotiating long-term labor and materials supply contracts, but they might have to agree to pay prices somewhat above the current market price to obtain these contracts.[4]

Financial Risk

FINANCIAL RISK
The portion of stockholders' risk, over and above basic business risk, resulting from the manner in which the firm is financed.

FINANCIAL LEVERAGE
The extent to which fixed-income securities (debt and preferred stock) are used in a firm's capital structure.

Financial risk is the additional risk placed on the common stockholders as a result of using **financial leverage,** which results when a firm uses fixed-income securities (debt and preferred stock) to raise capital. Conceptually, the firm has a certain amount of risk inherent in its operations; this is its business risk, which is defined as the uncertainty inherent in projections of future ROA. In Chapter 4, we saw that a firm intensifies the business risk borne by the common stockholders when financial leverage is created through the use of debt and preferred stock. To illustrate, suppose 10 people decide to form a corporation to manufacture running shoes. There is a certain amount of business risk in the operation. If the firm is capitalized only with common equity, and if each person buys 10 percent of the stock, then each investor will bear an equal share of the business risk. However, suppose the firm is capitalized with 50 percent debt and 50 percent equity, with 5 of the investors putting up their capital as debt and the other 5 putting up their money as equity. In this case, the cash flows received by the debtholders are based on a contractual agreement, so the investors who put up the equity will have to bear essentially all the business risk, and their position will be twice as risky as it would have been had the firm been financed only with equity. Thus, *the use of debt intensifies the firm's business risk borne by the common stockholders.*

In the next section, we will explain how financial leverage affects a firm's expected earnings per share, the riskiness of those earnings, and, consequently, the price of the firm's stock. As you will see, the value of a firm that has no debt first rises as it substitutes debt for equity, then hits a peak, and finally declines as the use of debt becomes excessive. The objective of our analysis is to determine the

---

[4]For example, in 1995 utilities could buy coal in the spot market for about $30 per ton, but under a 5-year contract, the cost was about $50 per ton. Clearly, the price for reducing uncertainty was high!

capital structure at which value is maximized; this point is then used as the *target capital structure*.[5]

Self-Test Questions

What is the difference between business risk and financial risk?

Identify and briefly explain some of the more important factors that affect business risk.

Which of the factors identified in the preceding question can management control?

Why does business risk vary from one industry to another?

What creates financial risk?

Determining the Optimal Capital Structure

We can illustrate the effects of financial leverage using the data shown in Table 16-1 for an illustrative company we will call Firm B. As shown in the top section of the table, the company has no debt. Should it continue the policy of using no debt, or should it start using financial leverage? If it does decide to substitute debt for equity, how far should it go? As in all such decisions, the correct answer is that it should *choose the capital structure that will maximize the price of its stock.*

EBIT/EPS Analysis of the Effects of Financial Leverage

Changes in the use of debt will cause changes in earnings per share (EPS) and, consequently, in the stock price. To understand the relationship between financial leverage and EPS, first consider Table 16-2, which shows how Firm B's cost of debt would vary if it used different percentages of debt in its capital structure. Naturally, the higher the percentage of debt, the riskier the debt, hence the higher the interest rate lenders will charge.

Now consider Table 16-3, which shows how expected EPS varies with changes in financial leverage. Section I of the table begins with a probability distribution of sales; we assume for simplicity that sales can take on only three values, $100,000, $200,000, or $300,000. In the remainder of Section I we calculate EBIT at each of the three sales levels. Note that in Section I we assume that both sales and operating costs are independent of financial leverage. Therefore, the three

---

[5]In this chapter we examine capital structures on a book value (or balance sheet) basis. An alternative approach is to calculate the market values of debt, preferred stock, and common equity and then to reconstruct the balance sheet on a market value basis. Although the market value approach is more consistent with financial theory, bond rating agencies and most financial executives focus their attention on book values. Moreover, the conversion from book to market values is a complicated process, and because market value capital structures change with stock market fluctuations, they are thought by many to be too unstable to serve as operationally useful targets. Finally, exactly the same insights are gained from the book value and market value analyses. For all these reasons, a market value analysis of capital structure is better suited for advanced finance courses.

TABLE 16-1

Data on Firm B

I. Balance Sheet on 12/31/95

Current assets	$100,000	Debt	$ 0
Net fixed assets	100,000	Common equity (10,000 shares)	200,000
Total assets	$200,000	Total liabilities and equity	$200,000

II. Income Statement for 1995

Sales		$200,000
Fixed operating costs	$(40,000)	
Variable operating costs	(120,000)	(160,000)
Earnings before interest and taxes (EBIT)		$ 40,000
Interest		0
Taxable income		$ 40,000
Taxes (40%)		(16,000)
Net income		$ 24,000

III. Other Data

1. Earnings per share = EPS = $24,000/10,000 shares = $2.40.
2. Dividends per share = DPS = $24,000/10,000 shares = $2.40. (Thus, firm B pays out all its earnings as dividends.)
3. Book value per share = $200,000/10,000 shares = $20.
4. Market price per share = P_0 = $20. (Thus, the stock sells at its book value, so M/B = 1.0.)
5. Price/earnings ratio = P/E = $20/$2.40 = 8.33 times.

TABLE 16-2

Interest rates for Firm B with Different Debt/Assets Ratios

Amount Borrowed[a]	Debt/Assets Ratio	Interest Rate, k_d, on All Debt
$ 20,000	10%	8.0%
40,000	20	8.3
60,000	30	9.0
80,000	40	10.0
100,000	50	12.0
120,000	60	15.0

[a]We assume that the firm must borrow in increments of $20,000. We also assume that Firm B is unable to borrow more than $120,000, or 60 percent of assets, because of restrictions in its corporate charter.

TABLE 16-3

Firm B: EPS with Different Amounts of Financial Leverage (thousands of dollars, except Per-Share Figures)

I. Calculation of EBIT

Probability of indicated sales	0.2	0.6	0.2
Sales	$100.0	$200.0	$300.0
Fixed costs	(40.0)	(40.0)	(40.0)
Variable costs (60% of sales)	(60.0)	(120.0)	(180.0)
Total costs (except interest)	($100.0)	($160.0)	($220.0)
Earnings before interest and taxes (EBIT)	$ 0.0	$ 40.0	$ 80.0

II. Situation if Debt/Assets (D/A) = 0%

EBIT (from Section I)	$ 0.0	$ 40.0	$ 80.0
Less interest	(0.0)	(0.0)	(0.0)
Earnings before taxes (EBT)	$ 0.0	$ 40.0	$ 80.0
Taxes (40%)	(0.0)	(16.0)	(32.0)
Net income	$ 0.0	$ 24.0	$ 48.0
Earnings per share (EPS) on 10,000 shares[a]	$ 0.0	$ 2.40	$ 4.80
Expected EPS		$ 2.40	
Standard deviation of EPS		$ 1.52	
Coefficient of variation		0.63	

III. Situation if Debt/Assets (D/A) = 50%

EBIT (from Section I)	$ 0.0	$ 40.0	$ 80.0
Less interest (0.12 × $100,000)	(12.0)	(12.0)	(12.0)
Earnings before taxes (EBT)	($ 12.0)	$ 28.0	$ 68.0
Taxes (40%; tax credit on losses)	4.8	(11.2)	(27.2)
Net income	($ 7.2)	$ 16.8	$ 40.8
Earnings per share (EPS) on 5,000 shares[a]	($ 1.44)	$ 3.36	$ 8.16
Expected EPS		$ 3.36	
Standard deviation of EPS		$ 3.04	
Coefficient of variation		0.90	

[a]The EPS figures can also be obtained using the following formula, in which the numerator amounts to an income statement at a given sales level laid out horizontally:

$$EPS = \frac{(Sales - Fixed\ costs - Variable\ costs - Interest)(1 - Tax\ rate)}{Shares\ outstanding} = \frac{(EBIT - I)(1 - T)}{Shares\ outstanding}$$

For example, with zero debts and Sales = $200,000, EPS is $2.40:

$$EPS_{D/A = 0} = \frac{(\$200,000 - \$40,000 - \$120,000 - 0)(0.6)}{10,000} = \$2.40$$

With 50 percent debt and Sales = $200,000, EPS is $3.36:

$$EPS_{D/A = 0.5} = \frac{(\$200,000 - \$40,000 - \$120,000 - \$12,000)(0.6)}{5,000} = \$3.36$$

The sales level at which EPS will be equal under the two financing policies, or the indifference level of sales, S_I, can be found by setting $EPS_{D/A = 0}$ equal to $EPS_{D/A = 0.5}$ and solving for S_I:

$$EPS_{D/A = 0} = \frac{(S_I - \$40,000 - 0.6S_I - 0)(0.6)}{10,000} = \frac{(S_I - \$40,000 - 0.6S_I - \$12,000)(0.6)}{5,000} = EPS_{D/A = 0.5}$$

$$S_I = \$160,000$$

By substituting this value of sales into either equation, we can find EPS_I, the earnings per share at this indifference point. In our example, $EPS_I = \$1.44$.

EBIT figures ($0, $40,000, and $80,000) will always remain the same, no matter how much debt Firm B uses.[6]

Section II of Table 16-3, the zero-debt case, calculates Firm B's earnings per share at each sales level under the assumption that the company continues to use no debt. Net income is divided by the 10,000 shares outstanding to obtain EPS. If sales are as low as $100,000, EPS will be zero, but it will rise to $4.80 at a sales level of $300,000. The EPS at each sales level then is multiplied by the probability of that sales level and summed to calculate the expected EPS, which is $2.40. We also calculate the standard deviation of EPS and the coefficient of variation as indicators of the firm's risk at a zero debt ratio: $\sigma_{EPS} = \$1.52$, and $CV_{EPS} = 0.63$.[7]

Section III of the table shows the financial results that could be expected if Firm B were financed with a debt/assets ratio of 50 percent. In this situation, $100,000 of the $200,000 total capital would be debt. The interest rate on the debt, 12 percent, is taken from Table 16-2. With $100,000 of 12 percent debt outstanding, the company's interest expense in Table 16-3 would be $12,000 per year. This is a fixed cost—it is the same regardless of the level of sales—and it is deducted from the EBIT values as calculated in the top section. With debt = 0, there would be 10,000 shares outstanding. However, if half of the equity were replaced by debt (debt = $100,000), there would be only 5,000 shares outstanding, and we must use this fact to determine the EPS figures that would result at each of the three possible sales levels.[8] With a debt/assets ratio of 50 percent, the EPS figure would be −$1.44 if sales were as low as $100,000; it would rise to $3.36 if sales were $200,000; and it would soar to $8.16 if sales were as high as $300,000.

The EPS distributions under the two financial structures are graphed in Figure 16-2, where we use continuous distributions rather than the discrete distributions

---

[6]In the real world, capital structure *does* at times affect EBIT. First, if debt levels are excessive, the firm probably will not be able to finance at all if its earnings are low at a time when interest rates are high. This could lead to stop-start construction and research and development programs, as well as to the necessity of passing up good investment opportunities. Second, a weak financial condition (i.e., too much debt) could cause a firm to lose sales. For example, prior to the time that its huge debt forced Eastern Airlines into bankruptcy, many people refused to buy Eastern tickets because they were afraid the company would go bankrupt and leave them holding unusable tickets. Third, financially strong companies are able to bargain hard with unions as well as with their suppliers, whereas weaker ones may have to give in simply because they do not have the financial resources to carry on the fight. Finally, a company with so much debt that bankruptcy is a serious threat will have difficulty attracting and retaining managers and employees, or it will have to pay premium salaries. People value job security, and financially weak companies simply cannot provide such protection. For all these reasons, it is not totally correct to say that a firm's financial policy has no effect on its operating income.

Note also that EBIT is dependent on operating leverage. If we were analyzing a firm with either more or less operating leverage, the top section of Table 16-3 would be quite different: Fixed and variable costs would be different, and the range of EBIT over the various sales levels would be narrower if the company used a lower degree of operating leverage but wider if it used more operating leverage.

[7]See Chapter 5 for a review of procedures for calculating standard deviations and coefficients of variation. Recall that the advantage of the coefficient of variation is that it permits better comparisons when the expected values of EPS vary, as they do here for the two capital structures.

[8]We assume in this example that the firm could change its capital structure by repurchasing common stock at its book value of $100,000/5,000 shares = $20 per share. However, the firm might actually have to pay a higher price to repurchase its stock on the open market. If Firm B had to pay $22 per share, then it could repurchase only $100,000/$22 = 4,545 shares, and in this case, expected EPS would be only $16,800/(10,000 − 4,545) = $16,800/5,455 = $3.08 rather than $3.36.

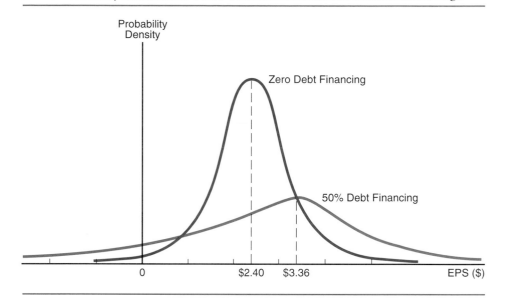

FIGURE 16-2

Firm B: Probability Distributions of EPS with Different Amounts of Financial Leverage

contained in Table 16-3. Although expected EPS would be much higher if financial leverage were employed, the graph makes it clear that the risk of low or even negative EPS would also be higher if debt were used.

Another view of the relationships among expected EPS, risk, and financial leverage is presented in Figure 16-3. The tabular data in the lower section were calculated in the manner set forth in Table 16-3, and the graphs plot these data. Here we see that expected EPS rises until the firm is financed with 50 percent debt. Interest charges rise, but this effect is more than offset by the declining number of shares outstanding as debt is substituted for equity. However, EPS peaks at a debt ratio of 50 percent. Beyond this amount, interest rates rise so rapidly that EPS is depressed despite the falling number of shares outstanding.

The right panel of Figure 16-3 shows that risk, as measured by the coefficient of variation of EPS, rises continuously and at an increasing rate as debt is substituted for equity.

We see, then, that using leverage has both good and bad effects: Higher leverage increases expected earnings per share (in this example, until the D/A ratio equals 50 percent), but it also increases the firm's risk. Clearly, the debt ratio should not exceed 50 percent, but where, in the range of 0 to 50 percent, should it be set? This issue is discussed in the following sections.

EPS Indifference Analysis

EPS INDIFFERENCE POINT
The level of sales at which EPS will be the same whether the firm uses debt or common stock financing.

Another way of considering the data on Firm B's two financing methods is shown in Figure 16-4, which depicts the **EPS indifference point**—that is, the point at which EPS is the same regardless of whether the firm uses debt or common stock. At a low level of sales, EPS is much higher if stock rather than debt is used. However, the debt line has a steeper slope, showing that earnings per share will go up

FIGURE 16-3

Firm B: Relationships among Expected EPS, Risk, and Financial Leverage

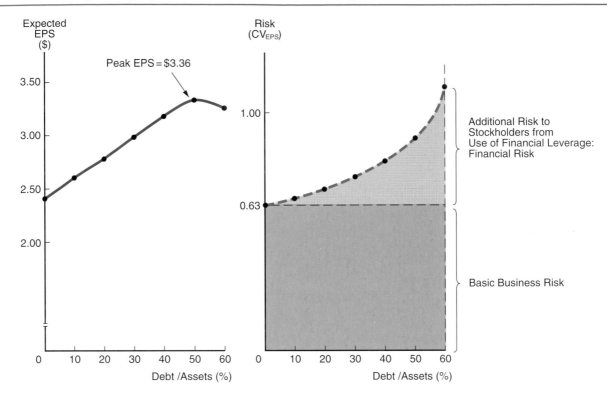

Debt/Assets Ratio	Expected EPS	Standard Deviation of EPS	Coefficient of Variation
0%[a]	$2.40[a]	$1.52[a]	0.63[a]
10	2.56	1.69	0.66
20	2.75	1.90	0.69
30	2.97	2.17	0.73
40	3.20	2.53	0.79
50[a]	3.36[a]	3.04[a]	0.90[a]
60	3.30	3.79	1.15

[a]Values for D/A = 0 and D/A = 50 percent are taken from Table 16-3. Values at other D/A ratios were calculated similarly.

faster with increases in sales if debt is used. The two lines cross at sales of $160,000. Below that level, EPS would be higher if the firm used more common stock; above it, debt financing would produce higher earnings per share.

If we were certain that sales would never again fall below $160,000, bonds would be the preferred method of financing the increase in assets. But we cannot know this for certain. In fact, investors know that in a number of previous years,

FIGURE 16-4

Earnings per Share for Stock and Debt Financing

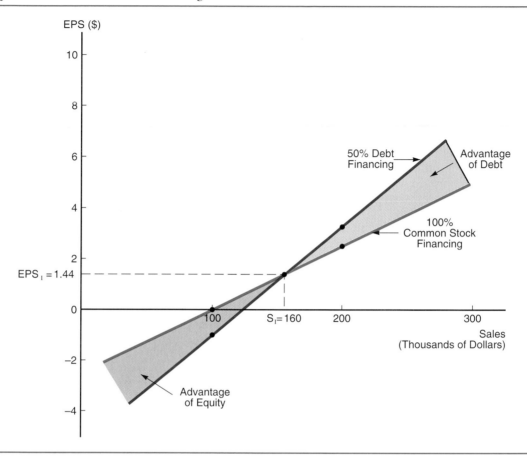

1. These values of the indifference level of sales, S_I and EPS_I, are the same as those obtained algebraically in Table 16-3. These relationships would be somewhat different if we did not assume that stock can be repurchased at book value.

2. We can also develop an equation to find the sales level at which EPS is the same under different degrees of financial leverage:

$$EPS_1 = \frac{S_I - F - VC - I_1}{Shares_1} = \frac{S_I - F - VC - I_2}{Shares_2} = EPS_2$$

Here, EPS_1 and EPS_2 are the EPSs at two debt levels; S_I is the sales indifference level at which $EPS_1 = EPS_2 = EPS_I$; I_1 and I_2 are interest charges at the two debt levels; $Shares_1$ and $Shares_2$ are shares outstanding at the two debt levels; F is the fixed costs; and V = variable costs = Sales × v, where v is the variable cost percentage. Solving for S_I, we obtain this expression:

$$S_I = \left[\frac{(Shares_2)(I_1) - (Shares_1)(I_2)}{Shares_2 - Shares_1} + F \right] \left(\frac{1}{1 - v} \right)$$

In our example,

$$S_I = \left[\frac{(5,000)(0) - (10,000)(\$12,000)}{-5,000} + \$40,000 \right] \left(\frac{1}{0.4} \right)$$

$$= \$160,000$$

sales have fallen below this critical level, and if any of several detrimental events should occur in the future, sales again would fall below $160,000. On the other hand, If sales continue to expand, higher earnings per share would result from the use of bonds, and this is an advantage that no investor would want to forgo.

Internal Equity First, External Equity Last

There has long been a debate concerning the relevance of financing decisions on the value of the firm. The controversy is centered around the question of whether a change in the firm's capital structure has an impact on its value. According to empirical evidence, stock prices do change when firms alter capital structures. But, there still is a question as to the reason stock prices react to capital structure changes. The reactions could result because capital structure changes provide information to investors either about the firm's optimal capital structure, if one exists, or about investment opportunities, which affect the value of the firm.

A survey of Fortune 500 firms provides some insight into the attitudes of financial officers concerning capital structure financing decisions. According to the results, nearly 85 percent of firms reported that retained earnings was their first choice of financing long-term needs, about 15 percent indicated that debt was preferable, and none of the firms listed new equity, either common or preferred, as their first preference. Almost 40 percent of the firms said issuing new common stock would be their last choice of alternatives for raising capital. This is not surprising, considering the fact that the cost of new common equity is greater than the other sources of capital. In addition, more than 60 percent of the firms indicated

that they prefer to use debt and preferred stock to avoid diluting the ownership position of common stockholders. Other important factors that were mentioned include restrictions contained in existing debt contracts, cash flows expected from the asset to be financed, and risk.

More than 85 percent of the firms indicated that financial flexibility and long-term survival are important factors to consider when making financing decisions. About 75 percent stated that firm value, stable cash flows, and financial independence significantly influence the capital structure of a company.

The results of the survey seem to suggest that firms do not have a specific capital structure in mind when deciding how to best finance capital budgeting projects. They prefer to maintain a flexible capital structure than to operate at what might be considered a more rigid optimal position. Therefore, changes in capital structure probably should be perceived as an indication of management's desire to raise funds to acquire projects rather than an indication that management is consciously adjusting the financial make-up of the firm to maximize value.

SOURCE: J. Michael Pinegar and Lisa Wilbricht, "What Managers Think of Capital Structure Theory: A Survey," *Financial Management,* Winter 1989, 82–89.

The Effect of Capital Structure on Stock Prices and the Cost of Capital

As we saw in Figure 16-3, Firm B's expected EPS is maximized at a debt/assets ratio of 50 percent. Does this mean that Firm B's optimal capital structure calls for 50 percent debt? The answer is a resounding no—*the optimal capital structure is the one that maximizes the price of the firm's stock, and this always calls for a debt ratio that is lower than the one that maximizes expected EPS.*

This statement is demonstrated in Table 16-4, which develops Firm B's estimated stock price and weighted average cost of capital at different debt/assets ratios. The debt cost and EPS data in Columns 2 and 3 were taken from Table 16-2 and Figure 16-3. The beta coefficients shown in Column 4 were estimated. Recall from Chapter 5 that a stock's beta measures its relative volatility compared with the volatility of an average stock. It has been demonstrated both theoretically and empirically that a firm's beta increases with its degree of financial leverage. The exact nature of this relationship for a given firm is difficult to estimate, but the values given in Column 4 do show the approximate nature of the relationship for Firm B.

TABLE 16-4

Stock Price and Cost of Capital Estimates for Firm B with Different Debt/Assets Ratios

Debt/ Assets (1)	k_d (2)	Expected EPS (and DPS)[a] (3)	Estimated Beta (4)	$k_s = [k_{RF} + (k_M - k_{RF})\beta_s]$[b] (5)	Estimated Price[c] (6)	Resulting P/E Ratio (7)	Weighted Average Cost of Capital, WACC[d] (8)
0%	—	$2.40	1.50	12.0%	$20.00	8.33	12.00%
10	8.0%	2.56	1.55	12.2	20.98	8.20	11.46
20	8.3	2.75	1.65	12.6	21.83	7.94	11.08
30	9.0	2.97	1.80	13.2	22.50	7.58	10.86
40	10.0	3.20	2.00	14.0	22.86	7.14	10.80
50	12.0	3.36	2.30	15.2	22.11	6.58	11.20
60	15.0	3.30	2.70	16.8	19.64	5.95	12.12

[a]Firm B pays all of its earnings out as dividends, so EPS = DPS.

[b]We assume that $k_{RF} = 6\%$ and $k_M = 10\%$. Therefore, at debt/assets equal to zero, $k_s = 6\% + (10\% - 6\%)1.5 = 6\% + 6\% = 12\%$. Other values of k_s are calculated similarly.

[c]Because all earnings are paid out as dividends, no retained earnings will be plowed back into the business, and growth in EPS and DPS will be zero. Hence, the zero growth stock price model developed in Chapter 7 can be used to estimate the price of Firm B's stock. For example, at debt/assets = 0,

$$P_0 = \frac{DPS}{k_s} = \frac{\$2.40}{0.12} = \$20$$

Other prices were calculated similarly.

[d]Column 8 is found by use of the weighted average cost of capital (WACC) equation developed in Chapter 15:

$$WACC = w_d k_d (1 - T) + w_s k_s$$

$$= (D/A)(k_{dT}) + (1 - D/A)k_s$$

For example, at D/A = 40%,

$$WACC = 0.4(10\%)(0.6) + 0.6(14.0\%) = 10.80\%$$

Assuming that the risk-free rate of return, k_{RF}, is 6 percent and that the required return on an average stock, k_M, is 10 percent, we can use the CAPM equation to develop estimates of the required rates of return, k_s, for Firm B as shown in Column 5. Here we see that k_s is 12 percent if no financial leverage is used, but k_s rises to 16.8 percent if the company finances with 60 percent debt, the maximum permitted by its charter.

Figure 16-5 graphs Firm B's required rate of return on equity at different debt levels. The figure also shows the composition of Firm B's required return: the risk-free rate of 6 percent and the premiums for both business and financial risk, which were discussed earlier in this chapter. As you can see from the graph, the business risk premium does not depend on the debt level—it remains constant at 6 percent at all debt levels. However, the financial risk premium varies depending on the debt level—the higher the debt level, the greater the premium for financial risk.

The zero growth stock valuation model developed in Chapter 7 is used in Table 16-4, along with the Column 3 values of DPS and the Column 5 values of k_s, to

FIGURE 16-5

Firm B's Required Rate of Return on Equity at Different Debt Levels

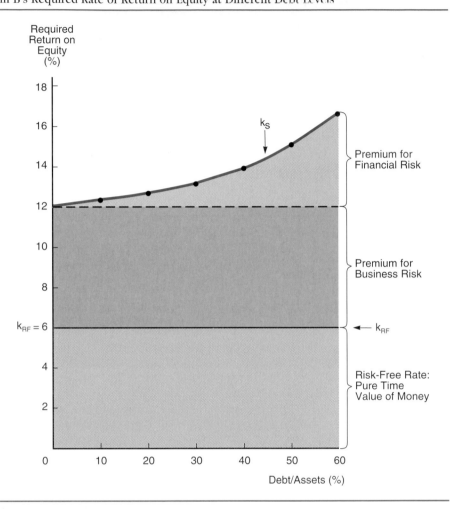

develop the estimated stock prices shown in Column 6. Here we see that the expected stock price first rises with financial leverage, hits a peak of $22.86 at a debt/assets ratio of 40 percent, and then begins to decline. *Thus, Firm B's optimal capital structure calls for 40 percent debt.*

The price/earnings ratios shown in Column 7 were calculated by dividing the price in Column 6 by the expected earnings given in Column 3. We use the pattern of P/E ratios as a check on the "reasonableness" of the other data. Other things held constant, P/E ratios should decline as the riskiness of a firm increases, and that pattern does exist in our illustrative case. Also, at the time Firm B's data were being analyzed, the P/Es shown here were generally consistent with those of zero-growth companies with varying amounts of financial leverage. Thus, the data in Column 7 reinforce our confidence in the reasonableness of the estimated prices shown in Column 6.

Finally, Column 8 shows Firm B's weighted average cost of capital, WACC, calculated as described in Chapter 15, at the different capital structures. If the company uses zero debt, its capital is all equity, so WACC = k_s = 12%. As the firm

FIGURE 16-6

Relationship between Firm B's Capital Structure and Its EPS, Cost of Capital, and Stock Price

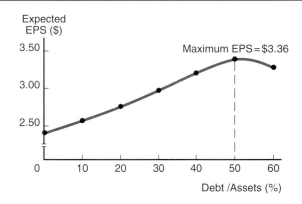

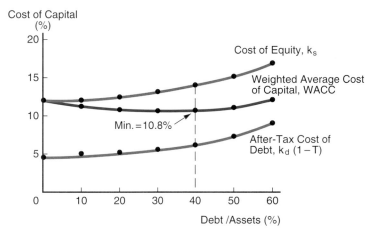

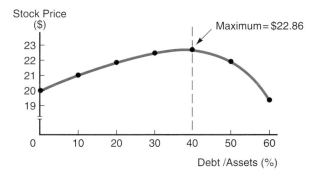

begins to use lower-cost debt, its weighted average cost of capital declines. However, as the debt ratio increases, the costs of both debt and equity rise, and the increasing costs of the two components begin to offset the fact that larger amounts of the lower-cost component are being used. At 40 percent debt, WACC hits a minimum, and it rises after that as the debt ratio is increased.

The EPS, cost of capital, and stock price data shown in Table 16-4 are plotted in Figure 16-6. As the graph shows, the debt/assets ratio that maximizes Firm B's expected EPS is 50 percent. However, the expected stock price is maximized, and the cost of capital is minimized, at a 40 percent debt ratio. Thus, *the optimal capital structure calls for 40 percent debt and 60 percent equity. Management should set its target capital structure at these ratios, and if the existing ratios are off target, it should move toward the target when new security offerings are made.*

Self-Test Questions

Explain the following statement: "Using leverage has both good and bad effects."

What does the EPS indifference point show? What occurs at sales below this point? What occurs at sales above this point?

Is the optimal capital structure the one that maximizes expected EPS? Explain.

Explain the following statement: "At the optimal capital structure, a firm has minimized its cost of capital." Do stockholders want the firm to minimize its cost of capital?

Degree of Leverage[9]

In Chapter 4 we showed that leverage, whether operating or financial, is created when a firm has fixed costs associated either with its sales and production operations or with its financing characteristics. And we found that the two types of leverage, operating and financial, are interrelated. Therefore, if Firm B *reduced* its operating leverage, this probably would lead to an *increase* in its optimal use of financial leverage. On the other hand, if the firm decided to *increase* its operating leverage, its optimal capital structure probably would call for *less* debt.

The theory of finance has not been developed to the point where we can actually specify simultaneously the optimal levels of operating and financial leverage. However, we can see how operating and financial leverage interact through an analysis of the *degree of leverage concept* we introduced in Chapter 4.

Degree of Operating Leverage (DOL)

DEGREE OF OPERATING LEVERAGE (DOL)
The percentage change in operating income (EBIT) associated with a given percentage change in sales.

The **degree of operating leverage (DOL)** is defined as the percentage change in operating income (or EBIT) associated with a given percentage change in sales. Thus, the degree of operating leverage is

16-1

$$DOL = \frac{\text{Percentage change in NOI}}{\text{Percentage change in sales}} = \frac{\frac{\Delta EBIT}{EBIT}}{\frac{\Delta Sales}{Sales}} = \frac{\frac{\Delta EBIT}{EBIT}}{\frac{\Delta Q}{Q}}$$

According to Equation 16-1, the DOL is an index number that measures the effect of a change in sales on operating income, or EBIT.

---

[9]A more detailed discussion of leverage is presented in Chapter 4. The derivations of the equations contained in this section are included in the footnotes in that chapter.

DOL for a particular level of production and sales, Q, can be computed using the following equation:

16-2

$$DOL_Q = \frac{Q(P - V)}{Q(P - V) - F}$$

or, based on dollar sales rather than units,

16-2a

$$DOL_S = \frac{S - VC}{S - VC - F} = \frac{\text{Gross profit}}{\text{EBIT}}$$

Here Q is the initial units of output, P is the average sales price per unit of output, V is the variable cost per unit, F is fixed operating costs, S is initial sales in dollars, and VC is total variable costs. Equation 16-2 normally is used to analyze a single product, such as IBM's PC, whereas Equation 16-2a is used to evaluate an entire firm with many types of products for which "quantity in units" and "sales price" are not meaningful.

Applying Equation 16-2a to data for Firm B at a sales level of $200,000 as shown in Table 16-3, we find its degree of operating leverage to be 2.0:

$$DOL_{\$200,000} = \frac{\$200,000 - \$120,000}{\$200,000 - \$120,000 - \$40,000} = \frac{\$80,000}{\$40,000} = 2.0$$

Thus, an X percent increase in sales will produce a 2X percent increase in EBIT. For example, a 50 percent increase in sales, starting from sales of $200,000, will result in a 50%(2.0) = 100% increase in EBIT. This situation is confirmed by examining Section I of Table 16-3, where we see that a 50 percent increase in sales, from $200,000 to $300,000, causes EBIT to double. Note, however, that if sales decrease by 50 percent, then EBIT will decrease by 100 percent; according to Table 16-3, EBIT decreases to $0 if sales decrease to $100,000.

Note also that the DOL is specific to the initial sales level; thus, if we evaluated it from a sales base of $300,000, there would be a different DOL:

$$DOL_{\$300,000} = \frac{\$300,000 - \$180,000}{\$300,000 - \$180,000 - \$40,000} = \frac{\$120,000}{\$80,000} = 1.5$$

In general, if a firm is operating at close to its breakeven level, the degree of operating leverage will be high, but DOL declines the higher the base level of sales is above breakeven sales.

Degree of Financial Leverage (DFL)

Operating leverage affects earnings before interest and taxes (EBIT), whereas financial leverage affects earnings after interest and taxes, or the earnings available to common stockholders. In terms of Table 16-3, operating leverage affects the

DEGREE OF FINANCIAL LEVERAGE (DFL)
The percentage change in earnings available to common stockholders associated with a given percentage change in earnings before interest and taxes.

top section of the income statement, whereas financial leverage affects the lower section. *Financial leverage takes over where operating leverage leaves off, further magnifying the effects on earnings per share of changes in the level of sales.*

The **degree of financial leverage (DFL)** is defined as the percentage change in earnings per share that results from a given percentage change in earnings before interest and taxes (EBIT), and it is calculated as follows:[10]

> **16-3**
> $$\text{DFL} = \frac{\text{Percent change in EPS}}{\text{Percent change in EBIT}} = \frac{\frac{\Delta \text{EPS}}{\text{EPS}}}{\frac{\Delta \text{EBIT}}{\text{EBIT}}} = \frac{\text{EBIT}}{\text{EBIT} - I}$$

For Firm B at sales of $200,000 and an EBIT of $40,000, the degree of financial leverage with a 50 percent debt ratio is

$$\text{DFL}_{S\,=\,\$200,000,\ D/TA\,=\,50\%} = \frac{\$40,000}{\$40,000 - \$12,000} = 1.43$$

Therefore, a 100 percent increase in EBIT would result in a 100(1.43) = 143 percent increase in earnings per share. This can be confirmed by referring to the lower section of Table 16-3, where we see that a 100 percent increase in EBIT, from $40,000 to $80,000, produces a 143 percent increase in EPS:

$$\%\Delta \text{EPS} = \frac{\Delta \text{EPS}}{\text{EPS}_0} = \frac{\$8.16 - \$3.36}{\$3.36} = \frac{\$4.80}{\$3.36} = 1.43 = 143\%$$

If no debt were used, the degree of financial leverage would by definition be 1.0, so a 100 percent increase in EBIT would produce exactly a 100 percent increase in EPS. This can be confirmed from the data in Section II of Table 16-3.

Degree of Total Leverage (DTL)

DEGREE OF TOTAL LEVERAGE (DTL)
The percentage change in EPS that results from a given percentage change in sales; DTL shows the effects of both operating leverage and financial leverage.

We have seen that (1) the greater the degree of operating leverage (or fixed operating costs), the more sensitive EBIT will be to changes in sales, and (2) the greater the degree of financial leverage (fixed financial costs), the more sensitive EPS will be to changes in EBIT. Therefore, if a firm uses a considerable amount of both operating and financial leverage, then even small changes in sales will lead to wide fluctuations in EPS.

Equation 16-2 for the degree of operating leverage can be combined with Equation 16-3 for the degree of financial leverage to produce the equation for the

---

[10]This equation applies only if the firm has no preferred stock. See Chapter 4 for the equation that is appropriate when preferred stock exists.

degree of total leverage (DTL), which shows how a given change in sales will affect earnings per share. Here are three equivalent equations for DTL:

$$DTL = (DOL) \times (DFL)$$

$$DTL = \frac{Q(P - V)}{Q(P - V) - F - I}$$

$$DTL = \frac{S - VC}{S - VC - F - I} = \frac{Gross\ profit}{EBIT - I}$$

For Firm B at sales of $200,000, we can substitute data from Table 16-3 into Equation 16-4 to find the degree of total leverage if the debt ratio is 50 percent:

$$DTL_{S\ =\ \$200,000,\ D/TA\ =\ 50\%} = \frac{\$200,000 - \$120,000}{\$200,000 - \$120,000 - \$40,000 - \$12,000} = \frac{\$80,000}{\$28,000}$$

$$= (2.00) \times (1.43) = 2.86$$

We can use the degree of total leverage (DTL) to find the new earnings per share (EPS_1) for any given percentage increase in sales, proceeding as follows:

$$EPS_1 = EPS_0 + EPS_0[(DTL) \times (\%\Delta Sales)]$$

$$= EPS_0[1.0 + (DTL) \times (\%\Delta Sales)]$$

For example, a 50 percent (or 0.5) increase in sales, from $200,000 to $300,000, would cause EPS_0 ($3.36 as shown in Section III of Table 16-3) to increase to $8.16:

$$EPS_1 = \$3.36[1.0 + (2.86)(0.5)] = \$3.36(2.43) = \$8.16$$

This figure agrees with the one for EPS shown in Table 16-3.

The degree of leverage concept is useful primarily for the insights it provides regarding the joint effects of operating and financial leverage on earnings per share. The concept can be used to show management the impact of financing the firm with debt versus common stock. For example, management might find that the current capital structure is such that a 10 percent decline in sales would produce a 50 percent decline in earnings, whereas with a different financing package, thus a different degree of total leverage, a 10 percent sales decline would cause earnings to decline by only 20 percent. Having the alternatives stated in this manner gives decision makers a better idea of the ramifications of alternative financing plans, hence different capital structures.[11]

Self-Test Questions

Give the formula for calculating the degree of operating leverage (DOL), and explain what DOL is.

Why is the DOL different at various sales levels?

Give the formula for calculating the degree of financial leverage (DFL), and explain what this calculation means.

Give the formula for calculating the degree of total leverage (DTL), and explain what DTL is.

Why is the degree of leverage concept useful?

Liquidity and Cash Flow Analysis

There are some practical difficulties with the types of analyses described thus far in the chapter, including the following:

1. It is virtually impossible to determine exactly how either P/E ratios or equity capitalization rates (k_s values) are affected by different degrees of financial leverage. The best we can do is make educated guesses about these relationships. Therefore, management rarely, if ever, has sufficient confidence in the type of analysis set forth in Table 16-4 and Figure 16-6 to use it as the sole determinant of the target capital structure.

2. The managers might be more or less conservative than the average stockholder, so management might set a somewhat different target capital structure than the one that would maximize the stock price. The managers of a publicly owned firm never would admit this, because unless they owned voting control, they would be removed from office very quickly. However, in view of the uncertainties about what constitutes the value-maximizing capital structure, management could always say that the target capital structure employed is, in its judgment, the value-maximizing structure, and it would be difficult to prove otherwise. Still, if management is far off target, especially on the low side, then chances are very high that some other firm or management group will take over the company, increase its leverage, and thereby raise its value.

---

[11]The degree of leverage concept also is useful for investors. If firms in an industry are classified as to their degrees of total leverage, an investor who is optimistic about prospects for the industry might favor those firms with high leverage, and vice versa if industry sales are expected to decline. However, it is very difficult to separate fixed from variable costs. Accounting statements generally do not contain this breakdown, so the analyst must make the separation in a judgmental manner. Note that costs really are fixed, variable, and "semivariable," for if times get tough enough, firms will sell off depreciable assets and thus reduce depreciation charges (a fixed cost), lay off "permanent" employees, reduce salaries of the remaining personnel, and so on. For this reason, the degree of leverage concept generally is more useful in explaining the general nature of the relationship than in developing precise numbers, and any numbers developed should be thought of as approximations rather than as exact specifications.

3. Managers of large firms, especially those that provide vital services such as electricity or telephones, have a responsibility to provide continuous service; therefore, they must refrain from using leverage to the point where the firms' long-run viability is endangered. Long-run viability might conflict with short-run stock price maximization and capital cost minimization.[12]

TIMES-INTEREST-EARNED (TIE) RATIO
A ratio that measures the firm's ability to meet its annual interest obligations; calculated by dividing earnings before interest and taxes by interest charges.

For all these reasons, managers are concerned about the effects of financial leverage on the risk of bankruptcy, and an analysis of this factor is therefore an important input in all capital structure decisions. Accordingly, managements give considerable weight to financial strength indicators such as the **times-interest-earned (TIE) ratio.** The lower this ratio, the higher the probability that a firm will default on its debt and be forced into bankruptcy.

The tabular material in the lower section of Figure 16-7 shows Firm B's expected TIE ratio at several different debt/assets ratios. If the debt/assets ratio was only 10 percent, the expected TIE would be a high 25 times, but the interest coverage ratio would decline rapidly if the debt ratio was increased. Note, however, that these coverages are expected values at different debt ratios; the actual TIE for any debt ratio will be higher if sales exceed the expected $200,000 level, but lower if sales fall below $200,000.

The variability of the TIE ratio is highlighted in the graph in Figure 16-7, which shows the probability distributions of the TIEs at debt/assets ratios of 40 percent and 60 percent. The expected TIE is much higher if only 40 percent debt is used. The relationship between actual companies' TIEs and debt ratios will be examined later, in Table 16-5. Even more important is the fact that with less debt, there is a much lower probability of a TIE of less than 1.0, the level at which the firm is not earning enough to meet its required interest payment and thus is seriously exposed to the threat of bankruptcy.[13]

Self-Test Question

Why do managers give considerable weight to the TIE ratio when they make capital structure decisions? Why not just use the capital structure that maximizes the stock price?

---

[12]Recognizing this fact, most public service commissions require utilities to obtain the commission's approval before issuing long-term securities, and Congress has empowered the SEC to supervise the capital structures of public utility holding companies. However, in addition to concern over the firms' safety, which suggests low debt ratios, both managers and regulators recognize a need to keep all costs as low as possible, including the cost of capital. Because a firm's capital structure affects its cost of capital, regulatory commissions and utility managers try to select capital structures that will minimize the cost of capital, subject to the constraint that the firm's financial flexibility not be endangered.

[13]Note that cash flows, which include depreciation, can be sufficient to cover required interest payments even though the TIE is less than 1.0. Thus, at least for a while, a firm might be able to avoid bankruptcy even though its operating income is less than its interest charges. However, most debt contracts stipulate that firms must maintain the TIE ratio above some minimum level, say, 2.0 or 2.5, or else they cannot borrow any additional funds, which can severely constrain operations. Such potential constraints, as much as the threat of actual bankruptcy, limit the use of debt.

FIGURE 16-7

Firm B: Probability Distributions of Times-Interest-Earned Ratios with Different Capital Structures

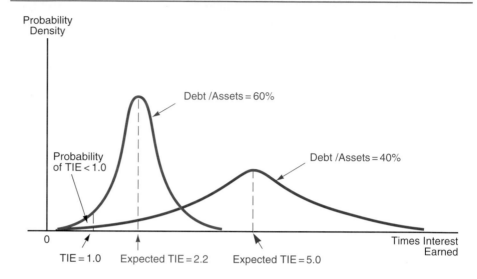

Debt/Assets	Expected TIE[a]
0%	Undefined
10	25.0
20	12.0
30	7.4
40	**5.0**
50	3.3
60	**2.2**

[a]TIE = EBIT/Interest. For example, when debt/assets = 50%, TIE = $40,000/$12,000 = 3.3. Data are from Tables 16-2 and 16-3.

Capital Structure Theory

Capital structure theory has been developed along two main lines: (1) tax benefit/bankruptcy cost trade-off theory and (2) signaling theory. These two theories are discussed in this section.

Trade-off Theory

Modern capital structure theory began in 1958, when Professors Franco Modigliani and Merton Miller (hereafter MM) published what is considered by many to be the most influential finance article ever written.[14] MM proved, under a very

---

[14]Franco Modigliani and Merton H. Miller, "The Cost of Capital, Corporation Finance, and the Theory of Investment," *American Economic Review,* June 1958. Modigliani and Miller both won Nobel prizes for their work.

restrictive set of assumptions, including there exist no personal taxes, no broker-age costs, constant interest rates, and no bankruptcy, that, because of the tax de-ductibility of interest on corporate debt, a firm's value rises continuously as it uses more debt, and hence its value will be maximized by financing almost entirely with debt.

Because several of the assumptions outlined by MM obviously were, and are, unrealistic, MM's position was only the beginning of capital structure research. Subsequent researchers, and MM themselves, extended the basic theory by relax-ing the assumptions. Other researchers attempted to test the various theoretical models with actual data to see exactly how stock prices and capital costs are affected by capital structure. Both the theoretical and the empirical results have added to our understanding of capital structure, but none of these studies has produced results that can be used to precisely identify a firm's optimal capital structure. A summary of the theoretical and empirical research to date is ex-pressed graphically in Figure 16-8. Here are the key points in the figure:

1. The fact that interest is a deductible expense makes debt less expensive than common or preferred stock. In effect, the government pays, or subsidizes, part of the cost of debt capital, or, to put it another way, debt provides *tax shelter benefits.* As a result, using debt causes more of the firm's operating income (EBIT) to flow through to investors, so the more debt a company uses, the higher its value, and the higher the price of its stock. Under the assumptions of the original Modigliani-Miller paper, their analysis led to the conclusion that the firm's stock price will be maximized if it uses virtually 100 percent debt,

---

FIGURE 16-8

Effect of Leverage on the Value of Firm B's Stock

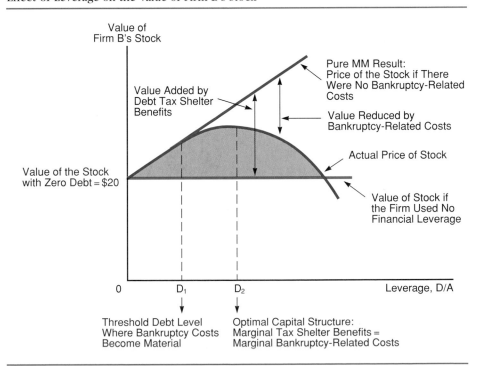

and the line labeled "Pure MM Result" in Figure 16-8 expresses their relationship between stock prices and debt.

2. The MM assumptions do not hold in the real world. First, interest rates rise as the debt ratio increases. Second, expected tax rates fall at high debt levels, and this also reduces the expected value of the debt tax shelter. And, third, the probability of bankruptcy, which brings with it lawyers' fees and other costs, increases as the debt ratio increases.

3. There is some threshold level of debt, labeled D_1 in Figure 16-8, below which the effects noted in Point 2 are immaterial. Beyond D_1, however, the bankruptcy-related costs become increasingly important, and they reduce the tax benefits of debt at an increasing rate. In the range from D_1 to D_2, bankruptcy-related costs reduce but do not completely offset the tax benefits of debt, so the firm's stock price rises (but at a decreasing rate) as the debt ratio increases. However, beyond D_2 bankruptcy-related costs exceed the tax benefits, so from this point on increasing the debt ratio lowers the value of the stock. Therefore, D_2 is the optimal capital structure.

4. Both theory and empirical evidence support the preceding discussion. However, statistical problems prevent researchers from identifying Points D_1 and D_2 precisely, so the graphs shown in Figures 16-6 and 16-8 must be taken as approximations, not as precisely defined functions.

5. Another disturbing aspect of capital structure theory as expressed in Figure 16-8 is the fact that many large, successful firms, such as Apple and Microsoft, use far less debt than the theory suggests. This point led to the development of signaling theory, which is discussed below.

Signaling Theory

SYMMETRIC INFORMATION
The situation in which investors and managers have identical information about the firm's prospects.

ASYMMETRIC INFORMATION
The situation in which managers have different (better) information about their firm's prospects than do outside investors.

MM assumed that investors have the same information about a firm's prospects as its managers—this is called **symmetric information,** because both those who are inside the firm (managers and employees) and those who are outside the firm (investors) have identical information. However, we know that in fact managers often have better information about their firms than do outside investors. This is called **asymmetric information,** and it has an important effect on the optimal capital structure. To see why, consider two situations, one in which the company's managers know that its prospects are extremely favorable (Firm F) and one in which the managers know that the future looks very unfavorable (Firm U).

Suppose, for example, that Firm F's research and development labs have just discovered a cure for the common cold, but the product is not patentable. Firm F's managers want to keep the new product a secret for as long as possible to delay competitors' entry into the market. New plants and distribution facilities must be built to exploit the new product, so capital must be raised. How should Firm F's management raise the needed capital? If the firm sells stock, then, when profits from the new product start flowing in, the price of the stock will rise sharply, and the purchasers of the new stock will have made a bonanza. The current stockholders (including the managers) also will do well, but not as well as they would have if the company had not sold stock before the price increased, because then they would not have had to share the benefits of the new product with the new stockholders. *Therefore, one would expect a firm with very favorable prospects to try to avoid selling stock and, rather, to raise any required new capital by other means, including using debt beyond the normal target capital structure.*[15]

Now let's consider Firm U. Suppose its managers have information that new orders are off sharply because a competitor has installed new technology that has improved its products' quality. Firm U must upgrade its own facilities, at a high cost, just to maintain its recent sales level. As a result, its return on investment will fall (but not by as much as if it took no action, which would lead to a 100 percent loss through bankruptcy). How should Firm U raise the needed capital? Here the situation is just the reverse of that facing Firm F, which did not want to sell stock so as to avoid having to share the benefits of future developments. *A firm with unfavorable prospects would want to sell stock, which would mean bringing in new investors to share the losses!*[16]

The conclusions from all this are that firms with extremely bright prospects prefer not to finance through new stock offerings, whereas firms with poor prospects do like to finance with outside equity. How would you, as an investor, react to this conclusion? You ought to say, "If I see that a company plans to issue new stock, this should worry me, because I know that management would not want to issue stock if future prospects looked good, but it would want to issue stock if things looked bad. Therefore, I should lower my estimate of the firm's value, other things held constant, if I read an announcement of a new stock offering." Of course, the negative reaction would be stronger if the stock sale was by a large, established company such as GM or IBM, which surely has many financing options, than if it was by a small company such as GeneSplicer. For GeneSplicer, a stock sale might mean truly extraordinary investment opportunities that were so large that they just could not be financed without a stock sale.

If you gave the preceding answer, your views are completely consistent with those of sophisticated portfolio managers of such institutions as Morgan Guaranty Trust. *So, in a nutshell, the announcement of a stock offering by a mature firm that seems to have multiple financing alternatives is taken as a* **signal** *that the firm's prospects as seen by its management are not bright.* This, in turn, suggests that when a mature firm announces a new stock offering, the price of its stock should decline. Empirical studies have shown that this situation does indeed exist.[17]

What are the implications of all this for capital structure decisions? The answer is that firms should, in normal times, maintain a **reserve borrowing capacity** that can be used in the event that some especially good investment opportunities come along. *This means that firms should, in normal times, use less debt than would be suggested by the tax benefit/bankruptcy cost trade-off expressed in Figure 16-8.*

Signaling/asymmetric information concepts also have implications for the marginal cost of capital (MCC) curve as discussed in Chapter 15. There we saw that the weighted average cost of capital (WACC) jumped when retained earnings were exhausted and the firm was forced to sell new common stock to raise equity.

SIGNAL
An action taken by a firm's management that provides clues to investors about how management views the firm's prospects.

RESERVE BORROWING CAPACITY
The ability to borrow money at a reasonable cost when good investment opportunities arise; firms often use less debt than specified by the MM optimal capital structure to ensure that they can obtain debt capital later if they need to.

---

[15]It would be illegal for Firm F's managers to purchase more shares on the basis of their inside knowledge of the new product. They could be sent to jail if they did.

[16]Of course, Firm U would have to make certain disclosures when it offered new shares to the public, but it might be able to meet the legal requirements without fully disclosing management's worst fears.

[17]Paul Asquith and David W. Mullins, Jr., "The Impact of Initiating Dividend Payments on Shareholders' Wealth," *Journal of Business,* January 1983, pp. 77–96.

The jump in the WACC, or the break in the MCC schedule, was attributed only to flotation costs. However, if the announcement of a stock sale causes a decline in the price of the stock, then k as measured by $k = D_1/P_0 + g$ will rise because of the decline in P_0. This factor reinforces the effects of flotation costs, and perhaps it is an even more important explanation for the jump in the MCC schedule at the point at which new stock must be issued. For example, assume that $P_0 = \$10$, $D_1 = \$1$, $g = 5\%$, and $F = 10\%$. Therefore, $k_s = 10\% + 5\% = 15\%$, and k_e, the cost of external equity, is 16.1 percent:

$$k_e = \frac{D_1}{P_0(1 - F)} + g = \frac{\$1}{\$10(1.0 - 0.10)} + 0.05 = 0.161 = 16.1\%$$

Suppose, however, that the announcement of a stock sale causes the market price of the stock to fall from $P_0 = \$10$ to $P_0 = \$8$. This will produce an increase in the costs of both retained earnings (k_s) and external equity:

$$k_s = \frac{D_1}{P_0} + g = \frac{\$1}{\$8} + 0.05 = 0.175 = 17.5\%$$

$$k_e = \frac{D_1}{P_0(1 - F)} + g = \frac{\$1}{\$8(1.0 - 0.10)} + 0.05 = 0.189 = 18.9\%$$

This would, of course, have further implications for capital budgeting. Specifically, it would make it even more difficult for a marginal project to show a positive NPV if the project required the firm to sell stock to raise capital.

If you find this discussion of capital structure theory somewhat confusing, or at least imprecise, you are not alone. In truth, no one knows how to identify precisely the optimal capital structure for a firm or how to measure precisely the effect of the firm's capital structure on either its value or its cost of capital. In real life, capital structure decisions must be made more on the basis of judgment than numerical analysis. Still, an understanding of the theoretical issues as presented here is essential to making sound judgments on capital structure issues.

Self-Test Questions

What does it mean when one hears, "The MM capital structure theory involves a trade-off between the tax benefits of debt and costs associated with actual or potential bankruptcy"?

Explain how *asymmetric information* and *signals* affect capital structure decisions.

What is meant by reserve borrowing capacity, and why is it important for firms?

Variations in Capital Structures among Firms

As might be expected, wide variations in the use of financial leverage occur both across industries and among the individual firms in each industry. Table 16-5 illustrates differences for selected industries; the ranking is in descending order of common equity ratios, as shown in Column 1.

TABLE 16-5

Capital Structure Percentages, 1993: Four Industries Ranked by Common Equity Ratios

Industry	Common Equity (1)	Preferred Stock (2)	Total Debt (3)	Long-Term Debt (4)	Short-Term Debt (5)	Times-Interest-Earned Ratio (6)	Return on Equity (7)
Drugs	76.2%	0.0%	23.8%	14.7%	9.1%	24.0×	33.4%
Electronics	65.8	0.4	33.8	18.2	15.6	5.2	14.6
Retailing	62.0	2.6	35.4	33.8	1.6	5.0	14.7
Utilities	39.0	6.2	54.8	51.5	3.3	2.6	10.4
Composite (average of all industries, not just those listed above)	45.2%	1.8%	53.0%	34.6%	18.4%	2.2×	9.4%

NOTE: These ratios are based on accounting (or book) values. Stated on a market-value basis, the equity percentages would rise because most stocks sell at prices that are much higher than their book values.

SOURCE: *Compustat* Industrial Data Tape, 1993.

Drug companies do not use much debt (their common equity ratios are high); the uncertainties inherent in industries that are cyclical, oriented toward research, or subject to huge product liability suits render the heavy use of debt unwise. On the other hand, utilities traditionally have used large amounts of debt, particularly long-term debt—their fixed assets make good security for mortgage bonds, and their relatively stable sales make it safe for them to carry more debt than would be true for firms with more business risk.

Particular attention should be given to the times-interest-earned (TIE) ratio because it gives a measure of how safe the debt is and how vulnerable the company is to financial distress. TIE ratios depend on three factors: (1) the percentage of debt, (2) the interest rate on the debt, and (3) the company's profitability. Generally, the least leveraged industries, such as the drug industry, have the highest coverage ratios, whereas the utility industry, which finances heavily with debt, has a low average coverage ratio.

Wide variations in capital structures also exist among firms within given industries—for example, although the average common equity ratio in 1993 for the electronics industry was 65.8 percent, Lamson and Sessions's equity ratio was about 29 percent, Zenith had 55 percent equity, and Unitrode had no long-term debt, so its equity ratio was nearly 100 percent. Thus, factors unique to individual firms, including managerial attitudes, play an important role in setting target capital structures.

Self-Test Question

Why do wide variations in the use of financial leverage occur both across industries and among the individual firms in each industry?

Summary

In this chapter we discussed the concept of optimal capital structure, and examined the effects of financial leverage on stock prices, earnings per share, and the cost of capital. The key concepts covered are summarized on the following page.

- A firm's **optimal capital structure** is that mix of debt and equity that maximizes the price of the firm's stock. At any point in time, the firm's management has a specific **target capital structure** in mind, presumably the optimal one, although this target might change over time.
- Several factors influence a firm's capital structure decisions. These factors include the firm's (1) **business risk,** (2) **tax position,** (3) need for **financial flexibility,** and (4) **managerial conservatism or aggressiveness.**
- **Business risk** is the uncertainty associated with projections of a firm's future returns on equity. A firm will tend to have low business risk if the demand for its products is stable, if the prices of its inputs and products remain relatively constant, if it can adjust its prices freely if its costs increase, and if a high percentage of its costs are variable and hence decrease as its output and sales decrease. Other things the same, the lower a firm's business risk, the higher its optimal debt ratio.
- **Financial leverage** is the extent to which fixed-income securities (debt and preferred stock) are used in a firm's capital structure. **Financial risk** is the added risk to stockholders that results from financial leverage.
- The **EPS indifference point** is the level of sales at which EPS will be the same whether the firm uses debt or common stock financing. Equity financing will be better if the firm's sales end up below the EPS indifference point, whereas debt financing will be better at higher sales levels.
- The **degree of operating leverage (DOL)** shows how changes in sales affect operating income, whereas the **degree of financial leverage (DFL)** shows how changes in operating income affect earnings per share. The **degree of total leverage (DTL)** shows the percentage change in EPS resulting from a given percentage change in sales: $DTL = DOL \times DFL$.
- Modigliani and Miller developed a **trade-off theory of capital structure,** where debt is useful because interest is **tax deductible,** but debt brings with it costs associated with actual or potential bankruptcy. Under MM's theory the optimal capital structure strikes a balance between the tax benefits of debt and the costs associated with bankruptcy.
- An alternative (or, really, complementary) theory of capital structure relates to the **signals** given to investors by a firm's decision to use debt or stock to raise new capital. The use of stock is a negative signal, while using debt is a positive or at least a neutral signal. Therefore, companies try to maintain a **reserve borrowing capacity,** and this means using less debt in "normal" times than the MM trade-off theory would suggest.

Although it is theoretically possible to determine the optimal capital structure, as a practical matter we cannot estimate this structure with precision. Accordingly, financial executives generally treat the optimal capital structure as a range—for example, 40 percent to 50 percent debt—rather than as a precise point, such as 45 percent. The concepts discussed in this chapter help managers understand the factors they should consider when they set the target capital structure ranges for their firms.

Questions

16-1 "One type of leverage affects both EBIT and EPS. The other type affects only EPS." Explain what this statement means.

16-2 Explain why the following statement is true: "Other things the same, firms with relatively stable sales are able to carry relatively high debt ratios."

16-3 Why is EBIT generally considered to be independent of financial leverage? Why might EBIT actually be influenced by financial leverage at high debt levels?

16-4 If a firm went from zero debt to successively higher levels of debt, why would you expect its stock price to first rise, then hit a peak, and then begin to decline?

16-5 Why is the debt level that maximizes a firm's expected EPS generally higher than the one that maximizes its stock price?

16-6 When the Bell System was broken up, the old AT&T was split into a new AT&T plus seven regional telephone companies. The specific reason for forcing the breakup was to increase the degree of competition in the telephone industry. AT&T had a monopoly on local service, long distance, and the manufacture of all the equipment used by telephone companies, and the breakup was expected to open most of these markets to competition. In the court order that set the terms of the breakup, the capital structures of the surviving companies were specified, and much attention was given to the increased competition telephone companies could expect in the future. Do you think the optimal capital structure after the breakup should be the same as the pre-breakup optimal capital structure? Explain your position.

16-7 Assume that you are advising the management of a firm that is about to double its assets to serve its rapidly growing market. It must choose between a highly automated production process and a less automated one, and it must also choose a capital structure for financing the expansion. Should the asset investment and financing decisions be jointly determined, or should each decision be made separately? How would these decisions affect one another? How could the degree of leverage concept be used to help management analyze the situation?

16-8 Your firm's R&D department has been working on a new process that, if it works, can produce oil from coal at a cost of about $5 per barrel versus a current market price of $20 per barrel. The company needs $10 million of external funds at this time to complete the research. The results of the research will be known in about a year, and there is about a 50-50 chance of success. If the research is successful, your company will need to raise a substantial amount of new money to put the idea into production. Your economists forecast that although the economy will be depressed next year, interest rates will be high because of international monetary problems. You must recommend how the currently needed $10 million should be raised—as debt or as equity. How would the potential impact of your project influence your decision?

Self-Test Problems

(Solutions Appear in Appendix B)

Key terms   **ST-1** Define each of the following terms:
- *a.* target capital structure; optimal capital structure; target range
- *b.* business risk; financial risk; total risk
- *c.* financial leverage
- *d.* EPS indifference point
- *e.* degree of operating leverage (DOL)
- *f.* degree of financial leverage (DFL)
- *g.* degree of total leverage (DTL)
- *h.* times-interest-earned (TIE) ratio
- *i.* symmetric information; asymmetric information

j. trade-off theory; signaling theory

k. reserve borrowing capacity

Financial leverage   **ST-2**   Gentry Motors Inc., a producer of turbine generators, is in this situation: EBIT = $4 million; tax rate = T = 35%; debt outstanding = D = $2 million; k_d = 10%; k_s = 15%; shares of stock outstanding = $Shrs_0$ = 600,000; and book value per share = $10. Since Gentry's product market is stable and the company expects no growth, all earnings are paid out as dividends. The debt consists of perpetual bonds.

a. What are Gentry's earnings per share (EPS) and its price per share (P_0)?

b. What is Gentry's weighted average cost of capital (WACC)?

c. Gentry can increase its debt by $8 million, to a total of $10 million, using the new debt to buy back and retire some of its shares at the current price. Its interest rate on debt will be 12 percent (it will have to call and refund the old debt), and its cost of equity will rise from 15 percent to 17 percent. EBIT will remain constant. Should Gentry change its capital structure?

d. If Gentry did not have to refund the $2 million of old debt, how would this affect things? Assume that the new and still outstanding debt are equally risky, with k_d = 12%, but that the coupon rate on the old debt is 10 percent.

e. What is Gentry's TIE coverage ratio under the original situation and under the conditions of Part c of this question?

Problems

Risk analysis   **16-1**   *a.* Given the following information, calculate the expected value for Firm C's EPS. $E(EPS_A)$ = $5.10, and σ_A = $3.61; $E(EPS_B)$ = $4.20, and σ_B = $2.96; and σ_C = $4.11.

| | Probability | | | | |
	0.1	0.2	0.4	0.2	0.1
Firm A: EPS_A	($1.50)	$1.80	$5.10	$8.40	$11.70
Firm B: EPS_B	(1.20)	1.50	4.20	6.90	9.60
Firm C: EPS_C	(2.40)	1.35	5.10	8.85	12.60

b. Discuss the relative riskiness of the three firms' (A, B, and C) earnings.

Operating leverage effects   **16-2**   Merville Corporation will begin operations next year to produce a single product at a price of $12 per unit. Merville has a choice of two methods of production: Method A, with variable costs of $6.75 per unit and fixed operating costs of $675,000; and Method B, with variable costs of $8.25 per unit and fixed operating costs of $401,250. To support operations under either production method, the firm requires $2,250,000 in assets, and it has established a debt ratio of 40 percent. The cost of debt is k_d = 10 percent. The tax rate is irrelevant for the problem, and fixed *operating* costs do not include interest.

a. The sales forecast for the coming year is 200,000 units. Under which method would EBIT be more adversely affected if sales did not reach the expected levels? (Hint: Compare DOLs under the two production methods.)

b. Given the firm's present debt, which method would produce the greater percentage increase in earnings per share for a given increase in EBIT? (Hint: Compare DFLs under the two methods.)

c. Calculate DTL under each method, and then evaluate the firm's total risk under each method.

d. Is there some debt ratio under Method A that would produce the same DTL_A as the DTL_B that you calculated in Part c? (Hint: Let DTL_A = DTL_B = 2.90 as calculated in Part c, solve for I, and then determine the amount of debt that is consistent with this level of I. Conceivably, debt could be *negative,* which implies holding liquid assets rather than borrowing.)

Degree of leverage **16-3** Wei Communications Corporation (WCC) supplies headphones to airlines for use with movie and stereo programs. The headphones sell for $288 per set, and this year's sales are expected to be 45,000 units. Variable production costs for the expected sales under present production methods are estimated at $10,200,000, and fixed production (operating) costs at present are $1,560,000. WCC has $4,800,000 of debt outstanding at an interest rate of 8 percent. There are 240,000 shares of common stock outstanding, and there is no preferred stock. The dividend payout ratio is 70 percent, and WCC is in the 40 percent marginal tax bracket.

The company is considering investing $7,200,000 in new equipment. Sales would not increase, but variable costs per unit would decline by 20 percent. Also, fixed operating costs would increase from $1,560,000 to $1,800,000. WCC could raise the required capital by borrowing $7,200,000 at 10 percent or by selling 240,000 additional shares at $30 per share.

a. What would be WCC's EPS (1) under the old production process, (2) under the new process if it uses debt, and (3) under the new process if it uses common stock?

b. Calculate DOL, DFL, and DTL under the existing setup and under the new setup with each type of financing. Assume that the expected sales level is 45,000 units, or $12,960,000.

c. At what unit sales level would WCC have the same EPS, assuming it undertakes the investment and finances it with debt or with stock? (Hint: V = variable cost per unit = $8,160,000/45,000, and EPS = [(PQ − VQ − F − I)(1 − T)]/Shrs. Set EPS_{Stock} = EPS_{Debt} and solve for Q.)

d. At what unit sales level would EPS = 0 under the three production/financing setups—that is, under the old plan, the new plan with debt financing, and the new plan with stock financing? (Hint: Note that V_{Old} = $10,200,000/45,000, and use the hints for Part c, setting the EPS equation equal to zero.)

e. On the basis of the analysis in Parts a through d, which plan is the riskiest, which has the highest expected EPS, and which would you recommend? Assume here that there is a fairly high probability of sales falling as low as 25,000 units, and determine EPS_{Debt} and EPS_{Stock} at that sales level to help assess the riskiness of the two financing plans.

Financing alternatives **16-4** The Strasburg Company plans to raise a net amount of $270 million to finance new equipment and working capital in early 1996. Two alternatives are being considered: Common stock may be sold to net $60 per share, or bonds yielding 12 percent may be issued. The balance sheet and income statement of the Strasburg Company prior to financing are as follows:

The Strasburg Company:
Balance Sheet as of December 31, 1995
(millions of dollars)

Current assets	$ 900.00	Accounts payable	$ 172.50
Net fixed assets	450.00	Notes payable to bank	255.00
		Other current liabilities	225.00
		Total current liabilities	$ 652.50
		Long-term debt (10%)	300.00
		Common stock, $3 par	60.00
		Retained earnings	337.50
Total assets	$1,350.00	Total liabilities and equity	$1,350.00

The Strasburg Company:
Income Statement for Year Ended
December 31, 1995
(millions of dollars)

Sales	$2,475.00
Operating costs	2,227.50
Earnings before interest and taxes (10%)	$ 247.50
Interest on short-term debt	15.00
Interest on long-term debt	30.00
Earnings before taxes	$ 202.50
Taxes (40%)	81.00
Net income	$ 121.50

The probability distribution for annual sales is as follows:

Probability	Annual Sales (millions of dollars)
0.30	$2,250
0.40	2,700
0.30	3,150

Assuming that EBIT is equal to 10 percent of sales, calculate earnings per share under both the debt financing and the stock financing alternatives at each possible level of sales. Then calculate expected earnings per share and σ_{EPS} under both debt and stock financing. Also, calculate the debt ratio and the times-interest-earned (TIE) ratio at the expected sales level under each alternative. The old debt will remain outstanding. Which financing method do you recommend?

Exam-Type Problems

The problems included in this section are set up in such a way that they could be used as multiple-choice exam problems.

Financial leverage effects **16-5** The firms HL and LL are identical except for their leverage ratios and interest rates on debt. Each has $20 million in assets, earned $4 million before interest and taxes in 1995, and has a 40 percent marginal tax rate. Firm HL, however, has a leverage ratio (D/TA) of 50 percent and pays 12 percent interest on its debt, whereas LL has a 30 percent leverage ratio and pays only 10 percent interest on debt.
    a. Calculate the rate of return on equity (net income/equity) for each firm.
    b. Observing that HL has a higher return on equity, LL's treasurer decides to raise the leverage ratio from 30 to 60 percent, which will increase LL's interest rate on all debt to 15 percent. Calculate the new rate of return on equity for LL.

Financial leverage effects **16-6** The Damon Company wishes to calculate next year's return on equity under different leverage ratios. Damon's total assets are $14 million, and its marginal tax rate is 40 percent. The company is able to estimate next year's earnings before interest and taxes for three possible states of the world: $4.2 million with a 0.2 probability, $2.8 million with a 0.5 probability, and $700,000 with a 0.3 probability. Calculate Damon's expected return on equity, standard deviation, and coefficient of variation for each of the following leverage ratios, and evaluate the results:

Leverage (Debt/Total Assets)	Interest Rate
0%	—
10	9%
50	11
60	14

Integrative Problem

Optimal capital structure   **16-7**   Assume that you have just been hired as business manager of Campus Deli and Sub Shop (CDSS), which is located adjacent to the campus. Sales were $1,350,000 last year; variable costs were 60 percent of sales; and fixed costs were $40,000. Therefore, EBIT totaled $500,000. Because the University's enrollment is capped, EBIT is expected to be constant over time. Since no expansion capital is required, CDSS pays out all earnings as dividends. The management group owns about 50 percent of the stock, which is traded in the over-the-counter market.

CDSS currently has no debt—it is an all equity firm—and its 100,000 shares outstanding sell at a price of $20 per share. The firm's marginal tax rate is 40 percent. On the basis of statements made in your finance text, you believe that CDSS's shareholders would be better off if some debt financing were used. When you suggested this to your new boss, she encouraged you to pursue the idea, but to provide support for the suggestion.

You then obtained from a local investment banker the following estimates of the costs of debt and equity at different debt levels (in thousands of dollars):

Amount Borrowed	k_d	k_s
$ 0	—	15.0%
250	10.0%	15.5
500	11.0	16.5
750	13.0	18.0
1,000	16.0	20.0

If the firm were recapitalized, debt would be issued, and the borrowed funds would be used to repurchase stock. Stockholders, in turn, would use funds provided by the repurchase to buy equities in other fast food companies similar to CDSS. You plan to complete your report by asking and then answering the following questions.

a. (1) What is business risk? What factors influence a firm's business risk?

(2) What is operating leverage, and how does it affect a firm's business risk?

b. (1) What is meant by the terms *financial leverage* and *financial risk*?

(2) How does financial risk differ from business risk?

c. Now, to develop an example that can be presented to CDSS's management. As an illustration, consider two hypothetical firms—Firm U, with zero debt financing, and Firm L, with $10,000 of 12 percent debt. Both firms have $20,000 in total assets and a 40 percent marginal tax rate, and they face the following EBIT probability distribution for next year:

Probability	EBIT
0.25	$2,000
0.50	3,000
0.25	4,000

(1) Complete the following partial income statements and the set of ratios for Firm L.

	Firm U			Firm L		
Assets	$20,000	$20,000	$20,000	$20,000	$20,000	$20,000
Equity	$20,000	$20,000	$20,000	$10,000	$10,000	$10,000
Probability	0.25	0.50	0.25	0.25	0.50	0.25
Sales	$ 6,000	$ 9,000	$12,000	$ 6,000	$ 9,000	$12,000
Operating costs	4,000	6,000	8,000	4,000	6,000	8,000
Earnings before interest and taxes	$ 2,000	$ 3,000	$ 4,000	$ 2,000	$ 3,000	$ 4,000
Interest (12%)	0	0	0	1,200		1,200
Earnings before taxes	$ 2,000	$ 3,000	$ 4,000	$ 800	$	$ 2,800
Taxes (40%)	800	1,200	1,600	320		1,120
Net income	$ 1,200	$ 1,800	$ 2,400	$480	$	$ 1,680
ROE	6.0%	9.0%	12.0%	4.8%	%	16.8%
TIE	∞	∞	∞	1.7$\times$	$\times$	3.3$\times$
Expected ROE		9.0%			10.8%	
Expected TIE		∞			2.5$\times$	
σ_{ROE}		2.1%			4.2%	
σ_{TIE}		0			0.6$\times$	

(2) What does this example illustrate concerning the impact of financial leverage on expected rate of return and risk?

d. With the preceding points in mind, now consider the optimal capital structure for CDSS.

   (1) To begin, define the term *optimal capital structure.*
   (2) Describe briefly, without using numbers, the sequence of events that would occur if CDSS decided to recapitalize and to increase its use of debt.
   (3) Assume that shares could be repurchased at the current market price of $20 per share. Calculate CDSS's expected EPS and TIE at debt levels of $0, $250,000, $500,000, $750,000, and $1,000,000. How many shares would remain after recapitalization under each scenario?
   (4) What would be the new stock price if CDSS recapitalizes with $250,000 of debt? $500,000? $750,000? $1,000,000? Recall that the payout ratio is 100 percent, so g = 0.
   (5) Considering only the levels of debt discussed, what is CDSS's optimal capital structure?
   (6) Is EPS maximized at the debt level that maximizes share price? Why?
   (7) What is the WACC at the optimal capital structure?

e. Suppose you discovered that CDSS had more business risk than you originally estimated. Describe how this would affect the analysis. What if the firm had less business risk than originally estimated?

f. What is meant by the terms *degree of operating leverage (DOL), degree of financial leverage (DFL),* and *degree of total leverage (DTL)?* If fixed costs total $40,000 and the company uses $500,000 of debt, what are CDSS's degrees of each type of leverage? Of what practical use is the degree of leverage concept?

g. What are some factors a manager should consider when establishing his or her firm's target capital structure?

b. Put labels on the following graph, and then discuss the graph as you might use it to explain to your boss why CDSS might want to use some debt.

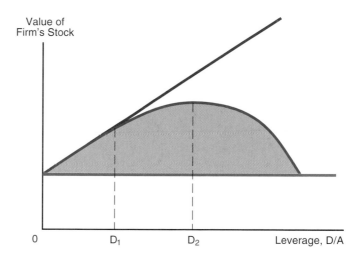

Value of Firm's Stock

0   D₁   D₂   Leverage, D/A

i. How does the existence of asymmetric information and signaling affect capital structure?

Computer-Related Problem

Work the problem in this section only if you are using the computer problem diskette.

Effects of financial leverage   **16-8** Use the model in File C16 to work this problem.

a. Rework Problem 16-4, assuming that the old long-term debt will not remain outstanding but, rather, that it must be refinanced at the new long-term interest rate of 12 percent. What effect does this have on the decision to refinance?

b. What would be the effect on the refinancing decision if the rate on long-term debt fell to 5 percent or rose to 20 percent, assuming that all long-term debt must be refinanced?

c. Which financing method would be recommended if the stock price (1) rose to $105 or (2) fell to $30? (Assume that all debt will have an interest rate of 12 percent.)

d. With $P_0 = \$60$ and $k_d = 12\%$, change the sales probability distribution to the following:

| Alternative 1 | | Alternative 2 | |
Sales	Probability	Sales	Probability
$2,250	0	$ 0	0.3
2,700	1.0	2,700	0.4
3,150	0	7,500	0.3

What are the implications of these changes?

CHAPTER 17

Dividend Policy

Unisys Corporation, currently a manufacturer of computers and related products for commercial and defense companies, had paid a regular dividend to common stockholders for almost 100 years. But, in September 1990, the board of directors decided to suspend the payment of future common stock dividends. According to James Unruh, president and CEO, the dividend suspension was in the "best interests" of shareholders—the board felt Unisys needed to strengthen its financial condition to improve shareholder wealth.

Suspending the common stock dividend saved Unisys more than $162 million a year, and allowed the company to reinvest the funds internally to reduce debt. By eliminating the cash drain associated with the common stock dividend payment, Unisys was able to reduce its amount of debt by more than one half in four years—the debt ratio fell from nearly 70 percent in 1990 to just over 50 percent in 1994. At the same time, Unisys increased its net income from a loss of a little more than $250 million in 1990 to a gain of nearly $250 million in 1994.

The dividend-cutting strategy worked—though more improvement is needed. Today, Unisys has much less debt than it did in 1990, and both its capital structure and profit position have been strengthened greatly. There is no clear indication when Unisys will resume dividend payments to its common stockholders. Many experts believe Unisys is risky, but a good investment for the future.

How has the stock of Unisys been affected by the dividend policy change made by the board in 1990? When Unisys announced the dividend suspension, the price of its common stock dropped more than 25 percent in one day and by about one third of its value within one week—trading at just under $5 per share, the value of Unisys common stock was 76 percent lower than its high during the previous twelve-month period, and 90 percent lower than its high value during the previous five years. Obviously the dividend suspension was not greeted favorably by the stockholders. Four and one half years after the suspension, the value of Unisys stock had increased

Continued

more than 120 percent, to $11, even though dividends still were not being paid. It seems the stockholders realized the dividend suspension in 1990 was beneficial for long-run stability and wealth maximization.

As you can see from the Unisys example, a firm's dividend policy can affect its cash position, capital structure, and value. As you read this chapter, keep in mind the reason Unisys suspended its common stock dividend. Consider the impact a particular dividend policy can have on the cash position of a firm, and how a change in dividend policy can affect the value of a firm.

Optimal Dividend Policy
The dividend policy that strikes a balance between current dividends and future growth and maximizes the firm's stock price.

Dividend policy involves the decision to pay out earnings or to retain them for reinvestment in the firm. Remember that according to the constant dividend growth model given in Chapter 7, the value of common stock can be computed as $P_0 = D_1/(k_s - g)$. This equation shows that if the firm adopts a policy of paying out more cash dividends, D_1 will rise, which will tend to increase the price of the stock. However, if cash dividends are increased, then less money will be available for reinvestment and the expected future growth rate will be lowered, which will depress the price of the stock. Thus, changing the dividend has two opposing effects. *The* **optimal dividend policy** *for a firm strikes that balance between current dividends and future growth that maximizes the price of the stock.*

In this chapter, we examine factors that affect the optimal dividend policy and the types of dividend policies generally used by firms.

Dividend Policy and Stock Value

A number of factors influence dividend policy, including the investment opportunities available to the firm, alternative sources of funds, and stockholders' preferences for current versus future income. The major goal of this chapter is to show how these factors interact to determine a firm's optimal dividend policy. We begin by examining whether dividend policy affects the value of a firm's common stock.

Dividend Irrelevance—Dividend Policy Does Not Affect Stock Value

Dividend Irrelevance Theory
The theory that a firm's dividend policy has no effect on either its value or its cost of capital.

It has been argued that dividend policy has no effect on either the price of a firm's stock or its cost of capital—that is, that dividend policy is *irrelevant*. The principal proponents of the **dividend irrelevance theory** are Merton Miller and Franco Modigliani (MM).[1] They argued that the value of the firm is determined only by its basic earning power and its business risk; in other words, MM argued that the value of the firm depends only on the income produced by its assets, *not* on how this income is split between dividends and retained earnings (and hence growth).

MM based their proposition solely on theoretical grounds; thus, they had to make some assumptions in order to develop a manageable theory. They assumed

---

[1]Merton H. Miller and Franco Modigliani, "Dividend Policy, Growth, and the Valuation of Shares," *Journal of Business,* October 1961, pp. 411–433.

that individuals neither pay taxes nor commissions on investments, firms do not go bankrupt, a firm's dividend policy does not affect its capital budgeting decisions, and investors are indifferent as to whether a firm pays dividends or retains earnings to invest in growth opportunities—thus, the dividend policy does not affect the cost of common equity. Given these assumptions, MM argued (correctly) that investors care *only* about the *total returns* they receive, not whether they receive those returns in the form of dividends or capital gains. Thus, *if the MM theory of dividend irrelevance is correct, there exists no optimal dividend policy, because dividend policy does not affect the value of the firm.*

Dividend Relevance—Dividend Policy Does Affect Stock Value

DIVIDEND RELEVANCE THEORY
The value of a firm is affected by its dividend policy—the optimal dividend policy is the one that maximizes the firm's value.

Obviously the assumptions made by MM are unrealistic. In the real world, investors might prefer one dividend policy over another; if so, a firm's dividend policy is relevant. According to the **dividend relevance theory,** then, dividend policy can affect the value of a firm through investors' preferences.

One of MM's assumptions that has been hotly debated is that dividend policy does not affect investors' required rate of return on equity, k_s. For example, Myron Gordon and John Lintner argued investors prefer to receive dividends "today" because current dividend payments are more certain than the future capital gains that *might* result from investing retained earnings in growth opportunities, so k_s should decrease as the dividend payout is increased.[2] In effect, Gordon and Lintner said that investors value a dollar of expected dividends more highly than a dollar of expected capital gains because the dividend yield component, D_1/P_0, is less risky than the capital gains component, g, in the total expected return equation, $\hat{k}_s = D_1/P_0 + g$.

Another factor that might cause investors to prefer one dividend policy over another, thus affecting the cost of common equity, is the tax effect of dividend receipts. Investors must pay taxes at the time dividends and capital gains are received. Dividends are associated with ownership of the stock; thus, if a firm pays out dividends this year, the owners must pay taxes on those dividends *this year.* On the other hand, capital gains are not taxed until the investment is sold, which can be many years into the future. So, depending on his or her tax situation, an investor might prefer either a payout of current earnings as dividends, or capital gains associated with growth in stock value. Investors who prefer to delay the impact of taxes would be willing to pay more for low payout companies than for otherwise similar high payout companies, and vice versa.

Self-Test Questions

Differentiate between the dividend irrelevance and dividend relevance theories.

What are some assumptions made by Modigliani and Miller concerning the dividend irrelevance theory?

How might taxes affect investors' preferences concerning the receipt of dividends and capital gains?

---

[2]Myron J. Gordon, "Optimal Investment and Financing Policy," *Journal of Finance,* May 1963, pp. 264–272, and John Lintner, "Dividends, Earnings, Leverage, Stock Prices, and the Supply of Capital to Corporations," *Review of Economics and Statistics,* August 1962, pp. 243–269.

Investors and Dividend Policy

Though academic researchers have studied the dividend policy issue extensively, they have yet to reach definitive conclusions about which dividend theory is more correct. As a result, the issue remains unresolved; researchers at this time simply cannot tell corporate decision makers exactly how dividend policy affects stock prices and capital costs. But, from the research, some views have been presented concerning investors' reactions to dividend policy changes and why firms have particular dividend policies. Three of these views are discussed in this section.

Information Content, or Signaling

If investors expect a company's dividend to increase by 5 percent per year, and if, in fact, the dividend is increased by 5 percent, then the stock price generally will not change significantly on the day the dividend increase is announced. In Wall Street parlance, such a dividend increase would be "discounted," or *anticipated*, by the market. However, if investors expect a 5 percent increase, but the company actually increases the dividend by 25 percent—say from $2 to $2.50—this generally would be accompanied by an increase in the price of the stock. Conversely, a less-than-expected dividend increase, or a reduction, generally would result in a price decline.

The fact that large dividend increases generally cause stock price increases suggests to some that investors in the aggregate prefer dividends to capital gains. However, MM argued differently. They noted the well-established facts that corporations are always reluctant to cut dividends and, consequently, that managers do not raise dividends unless they anticipate higher, or at least stable, earnings in the future. Therefore, according to MM, this means that a larger-than-expected dividend increase is taken by investors as a "signal" that the firm's management forecasts improved future earnings, whereas a dividend reduction signals a forecast of poor earnings. Thus, MM claimed that investors' reactions to changes in dividend payments do not show that investors prefer dividends to retained earnings; rather, the stock price changes simply indicate that important information is contained in dividend announcements—in effect, dividend announcements provide investors with information previously known only to management. This theory is referred to as the **information content, or signaling, hypothesis.**

INFORMATION CONTENT (SIGNALING) HYPOTHESIS
The theory that investors regard dividend changes as signals of management's earnings forecasts.

Clientele Effect

CLIENTELE EFFECT
The tendency of a firm to attract the type of investor who likes its dividend policy.

MM also suggested that a **clientele effect** might exist, and, if so, this might help explain why stock prices change after announced changes in dividend policy. Their argument went like this: A firm sets a particular dividend payout policy, which then attracts a "clientele" consisting of those investors who like this particular dividend policy. For example, some stockholders, such as university endowment funds and retired individuals, prefer current income to future capital gains, so they want the firm to pay out a high percentage of its earnings. Other stockholders have no need for current investment income—they would simply reinvest any dividend income received, after first paying income taxes on it, so they favor a low payout ratio.

If the firm retained and reinvested earnings rather than paying dividends, those stockholders who need current income would be disadvantaged. They presumably could realize some capital gains, but they would have to go to the trouble and expense of selling some of their shares to obtain cash. Because brokerage costs are quite high on small transactions, selling a few shares to obtain periodic income would be expensive and inefficient. Also, some institutional investors (or trustees for individuals) are precluded from selling stock and then "spending capital." On the other hand, if the firm paid out most of its income, other stockholders who did not need current cash income would be forced to receive such income, pay taxes on it, and then go to the trouble and expense of reinvesting what is left of their dividends after taxes. MM concluded from all this that those investors who desired current investment income would purchase shares in high-dividend-payout firms, whereas those who did not need current cash income would invest in low-payout firms. This suggests that firms' stockholders are attracted to companies because they have particular dividend policies.

Free Cash Flow Hypothesis

If it is the intent of the financial manager to maximize the value of the firm, then investors should prefer that a firm pay dividends only if acceptable capital budgeting opportunities do not exist. We know that acceptable capital budgeting projects increase the value of the firm. We also know that, because flotation costs are incurred when issuing new stock, it costs a firm more to raise funds using new common equity than it does using retained earnings. So, to maximize value, where possible, a firm should use retained earnings rather than issue new common stock to finance capital budgeting projects. Thus, dividends should be paid only when *free cash flows* in excess of capital budgeting needs exist. If management does otherwise, the firm's value will not be maximized.

FREE CASH FLOW HYPOTHESIS
All else equal, firms that pay dividends from cash flows that cannot be reinvested in positive net present value projects, which are termed *free cash flows,* have higher values than firms that retain such free cash flows.

According to the **free cash flow hypothesis,** the firm should distribute any earnings that cannot be reinvested at a rate at least as great as the investors' required rate of return, k_s. Everything else equal, firms that retain *free cash flows* will have lower values than firms that distribute *free cash flows,* because the firms that retain free cash flows actually decrease investors' wealth by investing in projects with IRR $< k_s$.

The free cash flow hypothesis might help to explain why investors react differently to identical dividend changes made by similar firms. For example, a firm's stock price will not change dramatically if it reduces its dividend for the purpose of investing in capital budgeting projects with positive NPVs. On the other hand, a company that reduces its dividend simply to increase free cash flows will experience a significant decline in the market value of its stock, because the dividend reduction is not in the best interests of the stockholders—in this case, an agency problem exists. Thus, the free cash flow hypothesis suggests the dividend policy can provide information about the firm's behavior with respect to wealth maximization.

Self-Test Question

Define (1) information content, (2) the clientele effect, and (3) the free cash flow hypothesis, and explain how each helps explain stock price reactions to changes in dividend policy.

Dividend Policy in Practice

We have provided some insights concerning the relevance of dividend policy and how investors might view dividend payments from firms. However, no one has been able to develop a formula that can be used to tell management specifically how a given dividend policy will affect a firm's stock price.

Even though no dividend policy formula exists, managements still must establish dividend policies. This section discusses several alternative policies that are used in practice.

Type of Dividend Payments

The dollar amounts of dividends paid by firms follow a variety of patterns. In general, though, firms pay dividends using one of the four payout policies discussed in this section.

RESIDUAL DIVIDEND POLICY   In practice, dividend policy is very much influenced by investment opportunities and by the availability of funds with which to finance new investments. This fact has led to the development of a **residual dividend policy,** which states that a firm should follow these steps when deciding how much earnings should be paid out as dividends: (1) determine the optimal capital budget for the year, (2) determine the amount of capital needed to finance that budget, (3) use retained earnings to supply the equity component to the extent possible, and (4) pay dividends only if more earnings are available than are needed to support the optimal capital budget. The word *residual* means "left over," and the residual policy implies that dividends should be paid only out of "leftover" earnings, or *free cash flows.*

The basis of the residual policy is the fact that *investors prefer to have the firm retain and reinvest earnings rather than pay them out in dividends if the rate of return the firm can earn on reinvested earnings exceeds the rate investors, on average, can themselves obtain on other investments of comparable risk.* For example, if the corporation can reinvest retained earnings at a 14 percent rate of return, whereas the best rate the average stockholder can obtain if the earnings are passed on in the form of dividends is 12 percent, then stockholders will prefer to have the firm retain the profits.

To continue, we saw in Chapter 15 that the cost of retained earnings is an *opportunity cost* that reflects rates of return available to equity investors. If a firm's stockholders can buy other stocks of equal risk and obtain a 12 percent dividend-plus-capital-gains yield, then 12 percent is the firm's cost of retained earnings. The cost of new outside equity raised by selling common stock will be higher than 12 percent because of the costs of floating the issue.

Most firms have a target capital structure that calls for at least some debt, so new financing is done partly with debt and partly with equity. As long as the firm finances with the optimal mix of debt and equity, and as long as it uses only internally generated equity (retained earnings), its marginal cost of each new dollar of capital will be minimized. Internally generated equity is available for financing a certain amount of new investment, but beyond that amount the firm must turn to more expensive new common stock. At the point where new stock must be sold, the cost of equity, and consequently the marginal cost of capital, rises.

RESIDUAL DIVIDEND POLICY
A policy in which the dividend paid is set equal to the actual earnings minus the amount of retained earnings necessary to finance the firm's optimal capital budget.

FIGURE 17-1

Texas and Western Transport Company: Marginal Cost of Capital

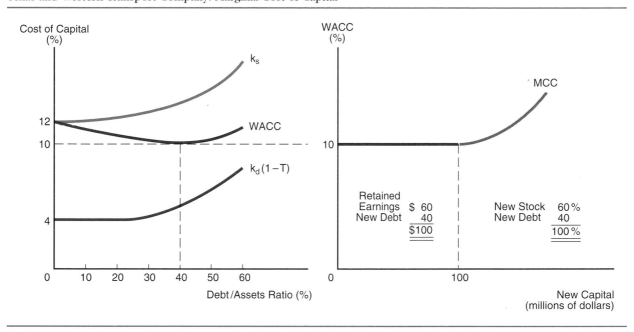

These concepts, which were developed in Chapter 15, are illustrated in Figure 17-1 with data from the Texas and Western (T&W) Transport Company. T&W has a marginal cost of capital of 10 percent. However, this cost rate assumes that all new equity comes from retained earnings. Therefore, MCC = 10% as long as retained earnings are available, but MCC begins to rise at the point where new stock must be sold.

T&W has $60 million of net income and a 40 percent optimal debt ratio. Provided it does not pay cash dividends, T&W can make net investments (investments in addition to asset replacements financed from depreciation) of $100 million, consisting of $60 million from retained earnings plus $40 million of new debt supported by the retained earnings, at a 10 percent marginal cost of capital. Therefore, its MCC is constant at 10 percent up to $100 million of capital, beyond which it rises as the firm begins to use more expensive new common stock.

Suppose T&W's director of capital budgeting has determined that the optimal capital budget requires an investment equal to $70 million. The $70 million will be financed using $28 million debt ($70 million × 0.40) and $42 million in common equity ($70 million × 0.60). So the $60 million retained earnings will be more than sufficient to cover the common equity financing requirement, and the *residual* of $18 million ($60 million − $42 million) can be paid out as dividends to stockholders.

Now suppose T&W's optimal capital budget is $150 million. Should dividends be paid? Not if T&W follows the residual dividend policy. The $150 million capital budgeting needs will be financed with $60 million debt ($150 million × 0.40) and $90 million common equity ($150 million × 0.60). The common equity financing requirement of $90 million exceeds the $60 million retained earnings available, so $30 million of new common equity will have to be issued. The new, or external, common equity will have a higher cost than retained earnings, so the marginal cost of capital for T&W will be higher. Under these conditions, T&W should not pay dividends to its stockholders. If the company pays part of its earnings in dividends, the marginal cost of capital would be even higher because more common stock will have to be issued to account for the amount of retained earnings paid out as dividends. For example, if T&W pays stockholders $20 million in dividends, it still needs $90 million of common equity to satisfy the capital budgeting requirements. In this case, $50 million of external equity will be required, which means T&W's marginal cost of capital will increase sooner—new common equity will have to be issued when $40 million rather than $60 million of retained earnings are used. So, to maximize value, T&W should retain all of its earnings for capital budgeting needs. Consequently, *according to the residual dividend policy, a firm that has to issue new common stock to finance capital budgeting needs does not have residual earnings, and dividends will be zero.*

Because both the earnings level and the capital budgeting needs of a firm vary from year to year, strict adherence to the residual dividend policy would result in dividend variability—one year the firm might declare zero dividends because investment opportunities were good, but the next year it might pay a large dividend because investment opportunities were poor. Similarly, fluctuating earnings would also lead to variable dividends even if investment opportunities were stable over time. Thus, following the residual dividend policy would be optimal only if investors were not bothered by fluctuating dividends. However, if investors prefer stable, dependable dividends, k_s would be higher, and the stock price lower, if the firm followed the residual theory in a strict sense rather than attempting to stabilize its dividends over time.

STABLE, PREDICTABLE DIVIDENDS   In the past, many firms set a specific annual dollar dividend per share and then maintained it, increasing the annual dividend only if it seemed clear that future earnings would be sufficient to allow the new dividend to be maintained. A corollary of that policy was this rule: *Never reduce the annual dividend.*

More recently, inflation plus reinvested earnings have tended to push earnings up, so many firms that would otherwise have followed the stable dollar dividend payment policy have switched over to a "stable growth rate" policy. Here the firm sets a target growth rate for dividends (for example, 6 percent per year) and strives to increase dividends by this amount each year. Obviously, earnings must be growing at a reasonably steady rate for this policy to be feasible, but where it can be followed, such a policy provides investors with a stable real income.

A fairly typical dividend policy, that of Eastman Kodak, is illustrated in Figure 17-2. Kodak's payout ratio ranged from 42 percent to 50 percent from 1978 to 1982, and it averaged about 46 percent during those 5 years. Although the payout ratio fluctuated somewhat, earnings were relatively stable during those years, and dividends clearly tracked earnings. After 1982, Kodak's earnings were much less stable. Global competition intensified, Kodak lost a major suit to Polaroid, and booms and recessions alternated to lead to earnings variability. Management stopped increasing the dividend when earnings fell, but did not cut the dividend, even when earnings failed to cover the dividend. Thus, in 1985 and 1986, the payout ratio was more than 100 percent of earnings. Maintaining the dividend was Kodak's way of signaling to stockholders that management was confident that the earnings decline was only temporary and that earnings would soon resume their

FIGURE 17-2

Eastman Kodak: Earnings per Share and Dividends per Share, 1978–1999

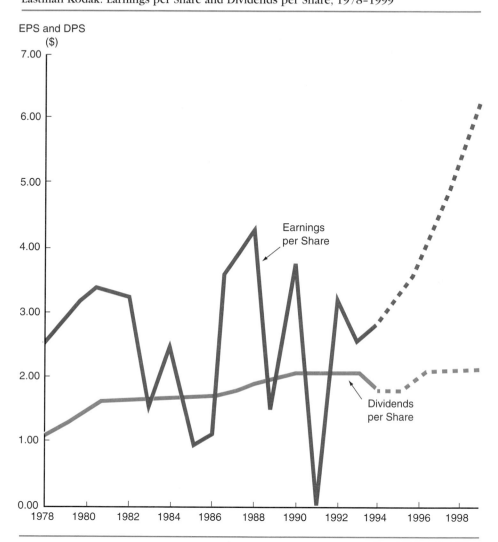

SOURCE: *Value Line*, December 1994. Projected values are shown as dashed lines.

upward trend. This was, indeed, the case. Kodak's earnings increased by more than 300 percent from 1985 to 1990, moving the 1990 dividend payout ratio to about 50 percent, which is in the 45 percent to 50 percent payout range Kodak likes. In 1991, Kodak's earnings dropped due to a sluggish economy and the company's heavy debt burden, but Kodak maintained its dividend at the 1990 level, which caused its payout ratio to be 40 times earnings. Even though earnings improved in 1992 and 1993, Kodak did not increase the dividend. The primary reason dividends were not changed is because Kodak planned to begin a restructuring of the company in 1994 to sell off businesses not related to its core imaging business. The restructuring created uncertainty with respect to near-term cash flows, so Kodak actually decreased dividends in 1994. But, Kodak is expected to return to its stable, and sometimes increasing, dividend by 1996, after the uncertainty of the restructuring is resolved.

The dashed lines beyond 1994 in Figure 17-2 represent the forecasts of a major investment advisory service, *Value Line,* whose analysts believe that Kodak's earnings will grow at a rate of about 15 percent per year and that, over the long term, Kodak will increase dividends as earnings grow. During the forecast period, 1995–1999, *Value Line* projects that Kodak will pay out about 45 percent of earnings.

STABLE, PREDICTABLE DIVIDENDS
Payment of a specific dollar dividend each year, or periodically increasing the dividend at a constant rate—the annual dollar dividend is relatively predictable by investors.

There are two good reasons for paying **stable, predictable dividends** rather than following the residual dividend policy. First, given the existence of the information content, or signaling, idea, a fluctuating payment policy would lead to greater uncertainty, hence to a higher k_s and a lower stock price, than would exist under a stable policy. Second, many stockholders use dividends for current consumption, and they would be put to trouble and expense if they had to sell part of their shares to obtain cash if the company cut the dividend; this is in addition to the anxiety a significant dividend cut would cause them. Further, it is possible for most firms to avoid these problems. Even though the optimal dividend as prescribed by the residual policy might vary somewhat from year to year, actions such as delaying some investment projects, departing from the target capital structure during a particular year, or even issuing new common stock make it possible for a company to avoid the problems associated with unstable dividends. As a rule, stable, predictable dividends imply more certainty than variable dividends, thus a lower k_s and a higher firm value.

CONSTANT PAYOUT RATIO   It would be possible for a firm to pay out a constant *percentage* of earnings, but because earnings surely will fluctuate, this policy would mean that the dollar amount of dividends would vary. For example, if it had paid out a constant percentage of earnings, Eastman Kodak would have had to cut its dividend in several different years, and this probably would have caused its stock price to fall sharply. (Kodak's stock price was relatively stable during the 1980s and the first half of the 1990s, in spite of earnings fluctuations. Had it cut the dividend to keep the payout ratio constant, the stock price would have "fallen out of bed" several times if investors interpreted the dividend reduction as a signal that management thought the earnings declines were permanent.)

If Kodak had followed the policy of paying a constant percentage of earnings per share, say 50 percent, the dividends per share paid since 1978 would have fluctuated exactly the same as earnings per share as shown in Figure 17-2. Thus, with the constant payout ratio dividend policy, investors would have had much greater uncertainty concerning the expected dividends each year, and chances are k_s also would be greater.

EXTRA DIVIDEND
A supplemental dividend paid in years when the firm does well, and excess funds are available for distribution.

LOW REGULAR DIVIDEND PLUS EXTRAS   A policy of paying a low regular dividend plus a year-end extra in good years is a compromise between a stable, predictable dividend and a constant payout rate. Such a policy gives the firm flexibility, yet investors can count on receiving at least a minimum dividend. Therefore, if a firm's earnings and cash flows are quite volatile, this policy might be its best choice. The directors can set a relatively low regular dividend—low enough so that it can be maintained even in low-profit years or in years when a considerable amount of retained earnings is needed—and then supplement it with an **extra dividend** in years when excess funds are available. Ford, General Motors, and other auto companies, whose earnings fluctuate widely from year to year, formerly followed such a policy, but in recent years they have joined the crowd and now follow our first choice, a stable, predictable dividend policy.

Payment Procedures

Dividends normally are paid quarterly, and, if conditions permit, the dividend is increased once each year. For example, Kodak paid $0.40 per quarter in 1994, or at an annual rate of $1.60. In common financial parlance, we say that in 1994 Kodak's regular quarterly dividend was 40¢, and its annual dividend was $1.60. In late 1994, Kodak's board of directors met, reviewed projections for 1995, and decided to keep the 1995 dividend at $1.60. The directors announced their intentions to maintain the $1.60 rate, so stockholders could count on receiving it unless the company experienced unanticipated operating problems.

The actual payment procedure is as follows:

DECLARATION DATE
The date on which a firm's board of directors issues a statement declaring a dividend.

1. **Declaration date.** On the **declaration date**—say, on November 13—the board of directors meets and declares the regular dividend, issuing a statement similar to the following: "On November 13, 1995, the directors of the XYZ Company met and declared the regular quarterly dividend of 50¢ per share, payable to holders of record on December 6, payment to be made on January 4, 1996." For accounting purposes, the declared dividend becomes an actual liability on the declaration date, and if a balance sheet were constructed, the amount ($0.50) × (Number of shares outstanding) would appear as a current liability, and retained earnings would be reduced by a like amount.

HOLDER-OF-RECORD DATE
(DATE OF RECORD)
The date the company opens the ownership books to determine who will receive the dividend—the stockholders of record on this date receive the dividend.

2. **Holder-of-record date.** At the close of business on the **holder-of-record date,** or **date of record,** December 6, the company closes its stock transfer books and produces a list of shareholders as of that date. If XYZ Company is notified of the sale and transfer of some stock before 5 P.M. on December 6, then the new owner receives the dividend. However, if notification is received after December 6, the previous owner of the stock gets the dividend check, because his or her name appears on the company's ownership records.

3. **Ex-dividend date.** Suppose Jean Buyer buys 100 shares of stock from John Seller on December 4. Will the company be notified of the transfer in time to list Buyer as the new owner and thus pay the dividend to her? To avoid conflict, the securities industry has set up a convention of declaring that the right to the dividend remains with the stock until two business days prior to the holder-of-record date; two days before that date, the right to the dividend no longer goes with the shares. The date when the right to the dividend leaves the stock is called the **ex-dividend date.** In this case, the ex-dividend date is two days prior to December 6, or December 4:

EX-DIVIDEND DATE
The date on which the right to the current dividend no longer accompanies a stock; it is usually two working days prior to the holder-of-record date.

	December 3	Buyer receives the dividend
Ex-dividend date:	December 4	Seller receives the dividend
	December 5	
Holder-of-record date:	December 6	

Therefore, if Buyer is to receive the dividend, she must buy the stock on or before December 3. If she buys it on December 4 or later, Seller will receive the dividend because he will be the official holder of record.

The XYZ dividend amounts to $0.50, so the ex-dividend date is important. Barring fluctuations in the stock market, one normally would expect the price of a stock to drop approximately by the amount of the dividend on the ex-dividend date. Thus, if XYZ closed at $30½ on December 3, it probably would open at about $30 on December 4.[3]

4. **Payment date.** The company actually mails the checks to the holders of record on January 4, the **payment date.**

Dividend Reinvestment Plans

In recent years most larger companies have instituted **dividend reinvestment plans (DRPs),** whereby stockholders can automatically reinvest dividends received in the stock of the paying corporation.[4] There are two types of DRPs: (1) plans that involve only "old" stock that already is outstanding and (2) plans that involve newly issued stock. In either case, the stockholder must pay income taxes on the amount of the dividends even though stock rather than cash is received.

Under the "old-stock" type of plan, the stockholder chooses between receiving dividend checks or having the company use the dividends to buy more stock in the corporation. If the stockholder elects reinvestment, a bank, acting as trustee, takes the total funds available for reinvestment, purchases the corporation's stock on the open market, and allocates the shares purchased to the participating stockholders' accounts on a *pro rata* basis. The transactions costs of buying shares (brokerage costs) are low because of volume purchases, so these plans benefit small stockholders who do not need cash dividends for current consumption.

---

[3]Tax effects cause the price decline on average to be less than the full amount of the dividend. Suppose you were an investor in the 40 percent tax bracket. If you bought XYZ's stock on December 3, you would receive the dividend, but you would almost immediately pay 40 percent of it out in taxes. Thus, you would want to wait until December 4 to buy the stock if you thought you could get it for $0.50 less per share. Your reaction, and those of others, would influence stock prices around dividend payment dates. Here is what would happen:

1. Other things held constant, a stock's price should rise during the quarter, with the daily price increase (for XYZ) equal to $0.50/90 = $0.005556. Therefore, if the price started at $30 just after its last ex-dividend date, it would rise to $30.50 on December 3.

2. In the absence of taxes, the stock's price would fall to $30 on December 4 and then start up as the next dividend accrual period began. Thus, over time, if everything else were held constant, the stock's price would follow a sawtooth pattern if it were plotted on a graph.

3. Because of taxes, the stock's price would neither rise by the full amount of the dividend nor fall by the full dividend amount when it goes ex-dividend.

4. The amount of the rise and subsequent fall would depend on the average investor's marginal tax rate.

See Edwin J. Elton and Martin J. Gruber, "Marginal Stockholder Tax Rates and the Clientele Effect," *Review of Economics and Statistics,* February 1970, pp. 68–74, for an interesting discussion of this concept.

[4]See Richard H. Pettway and R. Phil Malone, "Automatic Dividend Reinvestment Plans," *Financial Management,* Winter 1973, pp. 11–18, for an excellent discussion of this topic.

Don't Touch That Dividend—Unless It Is Absolutely Necessary

Which dividend policy—residual dividends, stable, predictable dividends, constant payout ratio, or low regular dividend plus extras—do firms prefer? Many studies have been completed to find the answer to this question, and all concluded that firms prefer to maintain relatively stable dividends and will go to great extremes to ensure dividends are not reduced. More than 90 percent of firms have indicated that dividend stability suggests greater certainty to stockholders, thus higher stock prices than the other dividend policies. Financial managers state that dividends should be decreased only if income is significantly less than normal for extended periods of time. Similarly, dividends should be increased only if profits increase and future profitability is expected to continue.

To illustrate a firm's reluctance to cut dividend payments, consider the actions of two well-known retailers, Kmart and Woolworth. At the beginning of 1995, Kmart cut its quarterly dividend in half, from 24 cents to 12 cents per share. The primary reason given for the dividend cut was the need to reinvest the funds internally for capital improvements, which, according to experts, was necessary to improve the prospects of taking back some market share lost to Wal-Mart. Prior to the decrease, Kmart was not generating profits sufficient to cover the $440 million annual dividend payment, and continued payment of this amount surely would cause increased financial headaches in the future. As expected, the dividend decrease caused the price of Kmart's stock to decrease; but, the price dropped by only 50 cents on the day the cut was announced, primarily because investors "saw it coming."

Also in 1995, Woolworth's poor capital structure caused it to eliminate its quarterly dividend of 15 cents per share, as well as to decrease its capital budget by more than 25 percent, in an effort to improve its financial position. This was the second time in a year Woolworth had decreased its dividend—nine months earlier the dividend was halved to help improve the company's cash position. Previously, many experts believed the primary reason to buy Woolworth's stock was its attractive dividend payment. Since the dividend cut in 1994, the price of Woolworth's stock has dropped more than 25 percent, with much of that decrease coming after the dividend was eliminated in 1995. The stock price would have decreased even more significantly, except investors expected the change in dividend policy—Woolworth has been struggling financially for a few years.

On the other side of the coin, investors react favorably when firms increase dividend payouts. Just the *expectation* by investors that a dividend payment will increase is sufficient to cause the firm's stock price to increase. For example, at the end of 1994, Chrysler had such a large amount of cash that experts were certain its quarterly dividend of 25 cents per share would be increased; the only question was by how much. At about the same time, experts were speculating that IBM was poised to increase its quarterly dividend of 25 cents per share, which would signal shareholders that the ailing computer and business machines manufacturer had begun to see the benefits of its restructuring attempts, and that future prospects were good. This would be the first increase since dividend cuts began in 1992, when the quarterly dividend was slashed from $1.21 to 54 cents per share; it was cut to 25 cents in July 1993. For both Chrysler and IBM, experts believed the firms' futures were promising enough that the increased dividend payments could be absorbed without causing added financial difficulties—the stocks of both companies reacted favorably.

The "new-stock" type of DRP provides for dividends to be invested in newly issued stock; hence, these plans raise new capital for the firm. AT&T, Florida Power & Light, Union Carbide, and many other companies have had such plans in effect in recent years, using them to raise substantial amounts of new equity capital. No fees are charged to stockholders, and many companies offer stock at a discount of 5 percent below the actual market price. The companies absorb these costs as a trade-off against the flotation costs that would have been incurred had they sold stock through investment bankers rather than through the dividend re-investment plans.[5]

Self-Test Questions

Explain the logic of the residual dividend policy, the steps a firm would take to implement it, and why it is more likely to be used to establish a long-run payout target than to set the actual year-by-year payout ratio.

Describe the stable, predictable dividend policy, and give two reasons why a firm might follow such a policy.

Explain what a low-regular-dividend-plus-extras policy is and why a firm might follow such a policy.

Describe the constant payout ratio dividend policy. Why is this policy probably not as popular as a stable, predictable dividend policy?

Why is the ex-dividend date important to investors?

Differentiate between the two types of dividend reinvestment plans.

Factors Influencing Dividend Policy

Thus far in the chapter we have described the major theories that deal with the effects of dividend policy on the value of a firm, and we have discussed alternative payment policies. Firms choose a particular policy based on managements' beliefs concerning which dividend theory is most correct, plus a host of other factors as described below. The factors firms take into account might be grouped into four broad categories: (1) constraints on dividend payments, (2) investment opportunities, (3) availability and cost of alternative sources of capital, and (4) effects of dividend policy on k_s. Each of these categories has several subparts, which we discuss in the following paragraphs.

Constraints

1. **Bond covenants.** Debt contracts often contain *covenants,* or restrictions, that limit dividend payments to earnings generated after the loan was granted. Also, contracts often stipulate that no dividends can be paid unless the current ratio, times-interest-earned ratio, and other safety ratios exceed stated minimums.

2. **Impairment of capital rule.** Dividend payments cannot exceed the balance sheet item "retained earnings." This legal restriction, known as the *impairment*

---

[5]Interestingly, DRPs are forcing corporations to reexamine their basic dividend policies. A high partic-ipation rate in a DRP suggests that stockholders might be better off if the firm simply reduced cash dividends, as this would save stockholders some personal income taxes. Quite a few firms are survey-ing their stockholders to learn more about their preferences and to find out how they would react to a change in dividend policy. A more rational approach to basic dividend policy decisions might emerge from this research.

Also, it should be noted that companies either use or stop using new-stock DRPs depending on their need for equity capital. Florida Power & Light recently stopped offering a new-stock DRP with a 5 percent discount because its need for equity capital declined once it had completed a nuclear-powered generating plant.

of capital rule, is designed to protect creditors. Without the rule, a company that was in trouble might distribute most of its assets to stockholders and leave its debtholders out in the cold. (Liquidating dividends can be paid out of capital, but they must be indicated as such, and they must not reduce capital below the limits stated in debt contracts.)

3. **Availability of cash.** Cash dividends can be paid only with cash. Thus, a shortage of cash in the bank can restrict dividend payments. However, the ability to borrow can offset this factor.

4. **Penalty tax on improperly accumulated earnings.** To prevent wealthy individuals from using corporations to avoid personal taxes, the Tax Code provides for a special surtax on improperly accumulated income. Thus, if the IRS can demonstrate that a firm's dividend payout ratio is being held down deliberately to help its stockholders avoid personal taxes, the firm is subject to heavy penalties. This factor generally is relevant only to privately owned firms.

Investment Opportunities

1. **Capital budgeting opportunities.** If a firm has a large number of acceptable capital budgeting projects, the dividend payout ratio generally will be low, and vice versa if there are few acceptable capital budgeting projects.

2. **Possibility of accelerating or delaying projects.** The ability to accelerate or to postpone projects will permit a firm to adhere more closely to its target dividend policy.

Alternative Sources of Capital

1. **Cost of selling new stock.** If a firm needs to finance a given level of investment, it can obtain equity by retaining earnings or by selling new common stock. If flotation costs (including any negative signaling effects of a stock offering) are high, k_e will be well above k_s, making it better to set a low payout ratio and to finance through retention rather than through sale of new common stock. On the other hand, a high dividend payout ratio is more feasible for a firm whose flotation costs are low. Flotation costs differ among firms—for example, the flotation percentage generally is higher for small firms, so they tend to set low payout ratios.

2. **Ability to substitute debt for equity.** A firm can finance a given level of investment with either debt or equity. As noted earlier, low stock flotation costs permit a more flexible dividend policy because equity can be raised either by retaining earnings or by selling new stock. A similar situation holds for debt policy: If the firm can adjust its debt ratio without raising costs sharply, it can maintain a stable dollar dividend, even if earnings fluctuate, by using a variable debt ratio. The shape of the average cost of capital curve (Figure 17-1 shown earlier) determines the practical extent to which the debt ratio can be varied. If the average cost of capital curve is relatively flat over a wide range, then a higher payout ratio is more feasible than it would be if the curve had a V shape.

3. **Control.** If management is concerned about maintaining control, it might be reluctant to sell new stock, hence the company might retain more earnings than it otherwise would. However, if stockholders want higher dividends and a proxy fight looms, then the dividend will be increased.

Effects of Dividend Policy on k_s

The effects of dividend policy on k_s might be considered in terms of four factors: (1) stockholders' desire for current versus future income, (2) perceived riskiness of dividends versus capital gains, (3) the tax advantage of capital gains over dividends, and (4) the information content of dividends (signaling). Because we discussed each of these factors in detail earlier, we need only note here that the importance of each factor in terms of its effect on k_s varies from firm to firm depending on the makeup of its current and possible future stockholders.

It should be apparent from our discussion thus far that dividend policy decisions truly are exercises in informed judgment, not decisions that can be quantified precisely. Even so, to make rational dividend decisions, financial managers must consider all the points discussed in the preceding sections.

Self-Test Questions

Identify the four broad categories of factors that affect dividend policy.

What constraints affect dividend policy?

How do investment opportunities affect dividend policy?

How does the availability and cost of outside capital affect dividend policy?

Stock Dividends and Stock Splits

Stock dividends and stock splits are related to the firm's cash dividend policy. The rationale for stock dividends and splits can best be explained through an example. We will use Porter Electronic Controls Inc., a $700 million electronic components manufacturer, for this purpose. Since its inception, Porter's markets have been expanding, and the company has enjoyed growth in sales and earnings. Some of its earnings have been paid out in dividends, but some also are retained each year, causing earnings per share and market price per share to grow. The company began its life with only a few thousand shares outstanding, and, after some years of growth, each of Porter's shares had a very high EPS and DPS. When a "normal" P/E ratio was applied, the derived market price was so high that few people could afford to buy a "round lot" of 100 shares. This limited the demand for the stock and thus kept the total market value of the firm below what it would have been if more shares, at a lower price, had been outstanding. To correct this situation, Porter "split its stock," as described in the next section.

Stock Splits

STOCK SPLIT
An action taken by a firm to increase the number of shares outstanding, such as doubling the number of shares outstanding by giving each stockholder two new shares for each one formerly held.

Although there is little empirical evidence to support the contention, there is nevertheless a widespread belief in financial circles that an *optimal, or psychological, price range* exists for stocks. "Optimal" means that if the price is within this range, the price/earnings ratio, hence the value of the firm, will be maximized. Many observers, including Porter's management, believe that the best range for most stocks is from $20 to $80 per share. Accordingly, if the price of Porter's stock rose to $80, management probably would declare a two-for-one **stock split,** thus doubling the number of shares outstanding, halving the earnings and dividends per share, and thereby lowering the price of the stock. Each stockholder would have more shares, but each share would be worth less. If the post-split price were $40, Porter's stockholders would be exactly as well off as they were before the split, because they would have twice as many shares at half the price as before the split. However, if the price of the stock were to stabilize above $40, stockholders would be better off. Stock splits can be of any size—for example, the stock could be split two-for-one, three-for-one, one-and-a-half-for-one, or in any other way.[6]

Stock Dividends

Stock dividends are similar to stock splits in that they "divide the pie into smaller slices" without affecting the fundamental position of the current stockholders. On a 5 percent stock dividend, the holder of 100 shares would receive an additional 5 shares (without cost); on a 20 percent stock dividend, the same holder would receive 20 new shares; and so on. Again, the total number of shares is increased, so earnings, dividends, and price per share all decline. If a firm wants to reduce the price of its stock, should it use a stock split or a stock dividend? Stock splits generally are used after a sharp price run-up to produce a large price reduction. Stock dividends typically are used on a regular annual basis to keep the stock price more or less constrained. For example, if a firm's earnings and dividends were growing at about 10 percent per year, its stock price would tend to go up at about that same rate, and it would soon be outside the desired trading range. A 10 percent annual stock dividend would maintain the stock price within the optimal trading range.

Balance Sheet Effects

Although the economic effects of stock splits and stock dividends are virtually identical, accountants treat them somewhat differently. On a two-for-one split, the shares outstanding are doubled, and the stock's par value is halved. This treatment is shown in the middle section of Table 17-1 for Porter Electronic Controls, using a pro forma 1996 balance sheet.

The bottom section of Table 17-1 shows the effect of a 20 percent stock dividend. With a stock dividend, the par value is not reduced, but an accounting entry is made transferring capital from the retained earnings account to the common stock and paid-in capital accounts. The transfer from retained earnings is calculated as follows:

$$
\underset{\substack{\text{Dollars} \\ \text{transferred from} \\ \text{retained earnings}}}{17\text{-}1} = \begin{pmatrix} \text{Number} \\ \text{of shares} \\ \text{outstanding} \end{pmatrix} \times \begin{pmatrix} \text{Stock} \\ \text{dividend as} \\ \text{a percent} \end{pmatrix} \times \begin{pmatrix} \text{Market} \\ \text{price of} \\ \text{the stock} \end{pmatrix}
$$

---

[6]Reverse splits, which reduce the shares outstanding, can even be used. For example, a company whose stock sells for $5 might employ a one-for-five reverse split, exchanging 1 new share for 5 old ones and raising the value of the shares to about $25, which is within the optimal range. LTV Corporation did this after several years of losses had driven its stock price down below the optimal range.

TABLE 17-1

Porter Electronic Controls Inc.: Stockholders' Equity Accounts, Pro Forma, December 31, 1996

Before a Stock Split or Stock Dividend	
Common stock (5 million shares outstanding, $1 par)	$ 5,000,000
Additional paid-in capital	10,000,000
Retained earnings	285,000,000
Total common stockholders' equity	$300,000,000
Book value per share	$60.00
After a Two-for-One Stock Split	
Common stock (10 million shares outstanding, $0.50 par)	$ 5,000,000
Additional paid-in capital	10,000,000
Retained earnings	285,000,000
Total common stockholders' equity	$300,000,000
Book value per share	$30.00
After a 20 Percent Stock Dividend	
Common stock (6 million shares outstanding, $1 par)[a]	$ 6,000,000
Additional paid-in capital[b]	89,000,000
Retained earnings[b]	205,000,000
Total common stockholders' equity	$300,000,000
Book value per share	$50.00

[a]Shares outstanding are increased by 20 percent, from 5 million to 6 million.

[b]A transfer equal to the market value of the new shares is made from the retained earnings account to the additional paid-in capital *and* common stock accounts:

Transfer = (5,000,000 shares)(0.2)($80) = $80,000,000

Of this $80 million, ($1 par)(1,000,000 shares) = $1,000,000 goes to common stock and $79 million to paid-in capital.

Porter has 5 million shares outstanding, and they sell for $80 each, so a 20 percent stock dividend would require the transfer of $80 million:

$$\text{Dollars transferred} = (5,000,000)(0.2)(\$80) = \$80,000,000$$

As shown in the table, $1 million of this $80 million is added to the common stock account and $79 million to the additional paid-in capital account. The retained earnings account is reduced from $285 million to $205 million.[7]

---

[7]Note that Porter could not pay a stock dividend that exceeded 71.25 percent (3,562,500 shares); a stock dividend of that percentage would exhaust the retained earnings. Thus, a firm's ability to declare stock dividends is constrained by the amount of its retained earnings. Of course, if Porter had wanted to pay a 50 percent stock dividend, it could have just switched to a 1.5-for-one stock split and accomplished the same thing in terms of the number of shares owned by stockholders.

Dividend Policy for Small Businesses

The dividend policy decision involves determining the amount of earnings to distribute to stockholders. Although most large, mature firms pay out a portion of earnings each year, many small, rapidly growing firms pay no dividends at all. As the small firm grows, so does its need for financing, and because small businesses have limited access to the capital markets, they rely on internal financing (retained earnings) to a greater extent than larger firms. Over time, though, as the firm and its products mature, its access to the capital markets improves, its growth will slow, its financing requirements will lessen, and at some point it will begin to pay dividends.

Apple Computer can be used to illustrate this process. Apple was founded in 1977, and its first year sales were $660,000. In 1978, sales increased by 550 percent, to $3.6 million, and the company earned a profit of $660,000. Growth continued at a rapid pace in the following years. Initially, all the stock was owned by the founders and a few venture capitalists. These investors wanted to ensure the company's success, and they also were more interested in capital gains than in taxable dividends, so the firm did not pay any dividends. Indeed, from 1978 through 1986, all earnings were plowed back and used to support growth, which averaged about 50 percent annually. We should also point out that, until 1994, Apple never issued debt; it chose instead to support its early growth by retaining earnings and by occasionally issuing additional shares of common stock. Apple had 119 million shares of stock outstanding in late 1994, up from 33 million in 1978.

By 1988, new competitors had entered the market, and Apple's growth was slowing down. *Value Line*'s analysts estimated that Apple's revenues would grow at an annual rate of 26 percent during the period 1988 to 1993. Although a growth rate of 26 percent per year is well above average, it is far below Apple's earlier growth rate of 50 percent. On the basis of these growth forecasts, Apple's board of directors met early in 1987 and declared an annual dividend of $0.24 per share. The stock price reacted favorably, so the annual dividend was raised in 1988 to $0.32, and on up to $0.48 by 1994.

This story illustrates three points. First, small, rapidly growing firms generally need to retain all their earnings, and also to obtain additional capital from outside sources, to support growth. Growth requires cash, and even highly profitable companies like Apple have difficulty generating enough cash from earnings both to support rapid growth and to pay dividends. Second, as the firm matures, its growth will slow down, and its need for funds will diminish. Thus, when Apple's growth began to slow down, it no longer needed to retain all its earnings, so it began to pay a small dividend. Third, the market recognizes that new, profitable firms often grow so fast that they must raise needed funds through new issues of common stock, and such issues can be considered indications that the firm's managers anticipate extraordinarily good investment opportunities.

Price Effects

Several empirical studies have examined the effects of stock splits and stock dividends on stock prices.[8] These studies suggest that investors see stock splits and stock dividends for what they are—*simply additional pieces of paper.* If stock dividends and splits are accompanied by higher earnings and cash dividends, then

---

[8]See C. A. Barker, "Evaluation of Stock Dividends," *Harvard Business Review,* July–August 1958, pp. 99–114. Barker's study has been replicated several times in recent years, and his results are still valid—they have withstood the test of time. Another excellent study, using an entirely different methodology, reached similar conclusions; see Eugene F. Fama, Lawrence Fisher, Michael C. Jensen, and Richard Roll, "The Adjustment of Stock Prices to New Information," *International Economic Review,* February 1969, pp. 1–21.

investors will bid up the price of the stock. However, if stock dividends are not accompanied by increases in earnings and cash dividends, the dilution of earnings and dividends per share causes the price of the stock to drop by the same percentage as the stock dividend. Thus, the fundamental determinants of price are the underlying earnings and cash dividends per share, and stock splits and stock dividends merely cut the pie into thinner slices.

Self-Test Questions

What is the rationale for a stock split?

Differentiate between the accounting treatments for stock splits and stock dividends.

What is the effect of stock splits and dividends on stock prices?

Summary

Dividend policy involves the decision to pay out earnings versus retaining them for reinvestment in the firm, and dividend policy decisions can have either favorable or unfavorable effects on the price of a firm's stock. The key concepts covered are listed below.

- The **optimal dividend policy** is that policy which strikes the exact balance between current dividends and future growth that maximizes the price of the firm's stock.
- Miller and Modigliani developed the **dividend irrelevance theory,** which holds that a firm's dividend policy has no effect either on the value of its stock or on its cost of capital.
- Those who believe in **dividend relevance** suggest that a particular dividend policy might be preferred because dividends are considered less risky than potential capital gains, taxes must be paid on dividends received in the current period, while taxes on capital gains can be deferred until the stock is sold, and so on.
- Because empirical tests of the theories have been inconclusive, *academicians simply cannot tell corporate managers how a change in dividend policy will affect stock prices and capital costs.* Thus, actually determining the optimal dividend policy is a matter of judgment.
- Dividend policy should reflect the existence of the **information content of dividends (signaling), the clientele effect,** and **the free cash flow effect.** The information content, or signaling, hypothesis states that investors regard dividend changes as a signal of management's forecast of future earnings. According to the clientele effect, a firm will attract investors who like the firm's dividend policy. And the free cash flow effect suggests that firms with few capital budgeting opportunities and great amounts of cash should have higher dividend payout ratios if the value maximization goal is pursued.
- In practice, most firms try to follow a policy of paying a **stable, predictable dividend.** This policy provides investors with a stable, dependable income, and it also gives investors information about management's expectations for earnings growth through signaling effects.
- Other dividend policies used include: (1) the **residual dividend policy,** in which dividends are paid out of earnings left over after the capital budget has

been financed; (2) the **constant payout ratio policy,** in which a constant *percentage* of earnings is targeted to be paid out; and (3) the **low-regular-dividend-plus-extras policy,** in which the firm pays a constant, low dividend that can be maintained even in bad years and then pays an extra dividend in good years.

- A **dividend reinvestment plan (DRP)** allows stockholders to have the company automatically use their dividends to purchase additional shares of the firm's stock. DRPs are popular with investors who do not need current income because the plans allow stockholders to acquire additional shares without incurring normal brokerage fees.

- Other factors, such as **legal constraints, investment opportunities, availability and cost of funds from other sources,** and **taxes,** are considered by managers when they establish dividend policies.

- A **stock split** is an action taken by a firm to increase the number of shares outstanding. Normally, splits reduce the price per share in proportion to the increase in shares because splits merely *divide the pie into smaller slices.* A **stock dividend** is a dividend paid in additional shares of stock rather than in cash. Both stock dividends and splits are used to keep stock prices within an "optimal," or psychological, range.

- Small, rapidly growing firms generally need to **retain all their earnings,** and to obtain additional capital from outside sources, to support growth. As the firm matures, its growth will slow down, and its need for funds will diminish. The market recognizes that new, profitable firms often grow so fast that they simply must issue common stock and that such issues indicate that the firm's managers anticipate extraordinarily good investment opportunities.

Questions

17-1 As an investor, would you rather invest in a firm that has a policy of maintaining (a) a constant payout ratio, (b) a stable, predictable dividend per share with a target dividend growth rate, or (c) a constant regular quarterly dividend plus a year-end extra when earnings are sufficiently high or corporate investment needs sufficiently low? Explain your answer, stating how these policies would affect your required rate of return, k_s. Also, discuss how your answer might change if you were a student, a 50-year-old professional with peak earnings, or a retiree.

17-2 How would each of the following changes tend to affect the average dividend payout ratios for corporations, other things held constant? Explain your answers.
   a. an increase in the personal income tax rate
   b. a liberalization of depreciation for federal income tax purposes—that is, faster tax write-offs
   c. a rise in interest rates
   d. an increase in corporate profits
   e. a decline in corporate investment opportunities
   f. permission for corporations to deduct dividends for tax purposes as they now can do with interest charges
   g. a change in the Tax Code so that both realized and unrealized capital gains in any year were taxed at the same rate as dividends

17-3 Most firms would like to have their stock selling at a high P/E ratio, and they would also like to have a large number of different shareholders. Explain how stock dividends or stock splits might help achieve these goals.

17-4   What is the difference between a stock dividend and a stock split? As a stockholder, would you prefer to see your company declare a 100 percent stock dividend or a two-for-one split? Assume that either action is feasible.

17-5   "The cost of retained earnings is less than the cost of new outside equity capital. Consequently, it is totally irrational for a firm to sell a new issue of stock and to pay dividends during the same year." Discuss this statement.

17-6   Would it ever be rational for a firm to borrow money in order to pay dividends? Explain.

17-7   Give arguments to support both the relevance and the irrelevance of paying dividends.

17-8   One position expressed in the financial literature is that firms set their dividends as a residual after using income to support new investment.

   a.   Explain what a residual dividend policy implies, illustrating your answer with a graph showing how different conditions could lead to different dividend payout ratios.

   b.   Could the residual dividend policy be consistent with (1) a stable, predictable dividend policy, (2) a constant payout ratio policy, and/or (3) a low-regular-dividend-plus-extras policy? Answer in terms of both short-run, year-to-year consistency and longer-run consistency.

   c.   Think back to Chapter 16, where we considered the relationship between capital structure and the cost of capital. If the WACC-versus-debt-ratio plot was shaped like a sharp V, would this have a different implication for the importance of setting dividends according to the residual policy than if the plot was shaped like a shallow bowl (or a flattened U)?

Self-Test Problems

(Solutions appear in Appendix B)

Key terms   **ST-1**   Define each of the following terms:

   a.   optimal dividend policy

   b.   dividend irrelevance theory; dividend relevance theory

   c.   information content, or signaling, hypothesis; clientele effect; free cash flow hypothesis

   d.   residual dividend policy; stable, predictable dividend policy; constant payout ratio policy; low-regular-dividend-plus-extras policy

   e.   declaration date; holder-of-record date; ex-dividend date; payment date

   f.   dividend reinvestment plan (DRP)

   g.   stock split; stock dividend

Alternative dividend policies   **ST-2**   Components Manufacturing Corporation (CMC) has an all-common-equity capital structure. It has 200,000 shares of $2 par value common stock outstanding. When CMC's founder, who was also its research director and most successful inventor, retired unexpectedly to the South Pacific in late 1995, CMC was left suddenly and permanently with materially lower growth expectations and relatively few attractive new investment opportunities. Unfortunately, there was no way to replace the founder's contributions to the firm. Previously, CMC found it necessary to plow back most of its earnings to finance growth, which averaged 12 percent per year. Future growth at a 5 percent rate is considered realistic, but that level would call for an increase in the dividend payout. Further, it now appears that new investment projects with at least the 14 percent rate of return required by CMC's stockholders ($k_s = 14\%$) would amount to only $800,000 for 1996 in comparison to a projected $2,000,000 of net income. If the existing 20 percent dividend payout were continued, retained earnings would be $1.6 million in 1996, but, as noted, investments that yield the 14 percent cost of capital would amount to only $800,000.

The one encouraging thing is that the high earnings from existing assets are expected to continue, and net income of $2 million is still expected for 1996. Given the dramatically changed circumstances, CMC's management is reviewing the firm's dividend policy.

a. Assuming that the acceptable 1996 investment projects would be financed entirely by earnings retained during the year, calculate DPS in 1996, assuming that CMC uses the residual payment policy.

b. What payout ratio does your answer to Part a imply for 1996?

c. If a 60 percent payout ratio is maintained for the foreseeable future, what is your estimate of the present market price of the common stock? How does this compare with the market price that should have prevailed under the assumptions existing just before the news about the founder's retirement? If the two values of P_0 are different, comment on why.

d. What would happen to the price of the stock if the old 20 percent payout were continued? Assume that if this payout is maintained, the average rate of return on the retained earnings will fall to 7.5 percent and the new growth rate will be

$$g = (1.0 - \text{Payout ratio})(\text{ROE})$$

$$= (1.0 - 0.2)(7.5\%) = (0.8)(7.5\%) = 6.0\%$$

Problems

Stock dividend **17-1** The McLaughlin Corporation declared a 6 percent stock dividend. Construct a pro forma balance sheet showing the effect of this action. The stock was selling for $37.50 per share, and a condensed version of McLaughlin's balance sheet as of December 31, 1995, before the dividend, follows (millions of dollars):

Cash	$ 112.5	Debt	$1,500
Other assets	2,887.5	Common stock (75 million	
		shares outstanding, $1 par)	75
		Paid-in capital	300
		Retained earnings	1,125
Total assets	$3,000.0	Total liabilities and equity	$3,000

Alternative dividend policies **17-2** In 1995 the Sirmans Company paid dividends totaling $3,600,000 on net income of $10.8 million. 1995 was a normal year, and for the past 10 years, earnings have grown at a constant rate of 10 percent. However, in 1996, earnings are expected to jump to $14.4 million, and the firm expects to have profitable investment opportunities of $8.4 million. It is predicted that Sirmans will not be able to maintain the 1996 level of earnings growth—the high 1996 earnings level is attributable to an exceptionally profitable new product line introduced that year—and the company will return to its previous 10 percent growth rate. Sirmans's target debt ratio is 40 percent.

a. Calculate Sirmans's total dividends for 1996 if it follows each of the following policies:

(1) Its 1996 dividend payment is set to force dividends to grow at the long-run growth rate in earnings.

(2) It continues the 1995 dividend payout ratio.

(3) It uses a pure residual dividend policy (40 percent of the $8.4 million investment is financed with debt).

(4) It employs a regular-dividend-plus-extras policy, with the regular dividend being based on the long-run growth rate and the extra dividend being set according to the residual policy.

b. Which of the preceding policies would you recommend? Restrict your choices to the ones listed, but justify your answer.

c. Assume that investors expect Sirmans to pay total dividends of $9,000,000 in 1996 and to have the dividend grow at 10 percent after 1996. The total market value of the stock is $180 million. What is the company's cost of equity?

d. What is Sirmans's long-run average return on equity? [Hint: g = (Retention rate) × (ROE) = (1.0 − Payout rate) × (ROE).]

e. Does a 1996 dividend of $9,000,000 seem reasonable in view of your answers to Parts c and d? If not, should the dividend be higher or lower?

Dividend policy and capital structure

17-3 Ybor City Tobacco Company has for many years enjoyed a moderate but stable growth in sales and earnings. However, cigar consumption and consequently Ybor's sales have been falling recently, primarily because of an increasing awareness of the dangers of smoking to health. Anticipating further declines in tobacco sales for the future, Ybor's management hopes eventually to move almost entirely out of the tobacco business and into a newly developed, diversified product line in growth-oriented industries. The company is especially interested in the prospects for pollution-control devices because its research department has already done much work on the problems of filtering smoke. Right now the company estimates that an investment of $15 million is necessary to purchase new facilities and to begin operations on these products, but the investment could be earning a return of about 18 percent within a short time. The only other available investment opportunity totals $6 million and is expected to return about 10.4 percent.

The company is expected to pay a $3.00 dividend on its 3 million outstanding shares, the same as its dividend last year. The directors might, however, change the dividend if there are good reasons for doing so. Total earnings after taxes for the year are expected to be $14.25 million; the common stock is currently selling for $56.25; the firm's target debt ratio (debt/assets ratio) is 45 percent; and its marginal tax rate is 40 percent. The costs of various forms of financing are as follows:

New bonds, $k_d = 11\%$. This is a before-tax rate.

New common stock sold at $56.25 per share will net $51.25.

Required rate of return on retained earnings, $k_s = 14\%$.

a. Calculate Ybor's expected payout ratio, the break point at which the marginal cost of capital (MCC) rises, and its MCC above and below the point of exhaustion of retained earnings at the current payout. (Hint: k_s is given, and D_1/P_0 can be found. Then, knowing k_s and D_1/P_0, g can be determined.)

b. How large should Ybor's capital budget be for the year?

c. What is an appropriate dividend policy for Ybor? How should the capital budget be financed?

d. How might risk factors influence Ybor's cost of capital, capital structure, and dividend policy?

e. What assumptions, if any, do your answers to the preceding parts make about investors' preferences for dividends versus capital gains (in other words, what are investors' preferences regarding the D_1/P_0 and g components of k_s)?

Exam-Type Problems

The problems included in this section are set up in such a way that they could be used as multiple-choice exam problems.

External equity financing   **17-4**   Northern California Heating and Cooling Inc. has a six-month backlog of orders for its patented solar heating system. To meet this demand, management plans to expand production capacity by 40 percent with a $10 million investment in plant and machinery. The firm wants to maintain a 40 percent debt-to-total-assets ratio in its capital structure; it also wants to maintain its past dividend policy of distributing 45 percent of last year's net income. In 1995, net income was $5 million. How much external equity must Northern California seek at the beginning of 1996 to expand capacity as desired?

Dividend payout   **17-5**   The Garlington Corporation expects next year's net income to be $15 million. The firm's debt ratio currently is 40 percent. Garlington has $12 million of profitable investment opportunities, and it wishes to maintain its existing debt ratio. According to the residual dividend policy, how large should Garlington's dividend payout ratio be next year?

Stock split   **17-6**   After a five-for-one stock split, the Swensen Company paid a dividend of $0.75 per new share, which represents a 9 percent increase over last year's pre-split dividend. What was last year's dividend per share?

Dividend payout   **17-7**   The Scanlon Company's optimal capital structure calls for 50 percent debt and 50 percent common equity. The interest rate on its debt is a constant 10 percent; its cost of common equity from retained earnings is 14 percent; the cost of equity from new stock is 16 percent; and its marginal tax rate is 40 percent. Scanlon has the following investment opportunities:

Project A: Cost = $5 million; IRR = 20%.
Project B: Cost = $5 million; IRR = 12%.
Project C: Cost = $5 million; IRR = 9%.

Scanlon expects to have net income of $7,287,500. If Scanlon bases its dividends on the residual policy, what will its payout ratio be?

Integrative Problem

Dividend policy   **17-8**   Information Systems Inc. (ISI), which develops software for the health care industry, was founded 5 years ago by Donald Brown and Margaret Clark, who are still its only stockholders. ISI has now reached the stage where outside equity capital is necessary if the firm is to achieve its growth targets yet still maintain its target capital structure of 60 percent equity and 40 percent debt. Therefore, Brown and Clark have decided to take the company public. Until now, Brown and Clark have paid themselves reasonable salaries but routinely reinvested all after-tax earnings in the firm, so dividend policy has not been an issue. However, before talking with potential outside investors, they must decide on a dividend policy.

Assume that you were recently hired by Arthur Adamson & Company (AA), a national consulting firm, which has been asked to help ISI prepare for its public offering. Martha Millon, the senior AA consultant in your group, has asked you to make a presentation to Brown and Clark in which you review the theory of dividend policy and discuss the following questions.

a. (1) What is meant by the term *dividend policy*?

   (2) The terms *irrelevance* and *relevance* have been used to describe theories regarding the way dividend policy affects a firm's value. Explain what these terms mean, and briefly discuss the relevance of dividend policy.

   (3) Explain the relationships between dividend policy and (1) stock price and (2) the cost of equity under each dividend policy theory.

(4) What results have empirical studies of the dividend theories produced? How does all this affect what we can tell managers about dividend policy?

b. Discuss (1) the information content, or signaling, hypothesis, (2) the clientele effect, (3) the free cash flow hypothesis, and (4) their effects on dividend policy.

c. (1) Assume that ISI has an $800,000 capital budget planned for the coming year. You have determined that its present capital structure (60 percent equity and 40 percent debt) is optimal, and its net income is forecasted at $600,000. Use the residual dividend policy approach to determine ISI's total dollar dividend and payout ratio. In the process, explain what the residual dividend policy is, and use a graph to illustrate your answer. Then, explain what would happen if net income were forecasted at $400,000, or at $800,000.

(2) In general terms, how would a change in investment opportunities affect the payout ratio under the residual payment policy?

(3) What are the advantages and disadvantages of the residual policy? (Hint: Don't neglect signaling and clientele effects.)

d. What are some other commonly used dividend payment policies? What are their advantages and disadvantages? Which policy is most widely used in practice?

e. What is a dividend reinvestment plan (DRP), and how does it work?

f. What are stock dividends and stock splits? What are the advantages and disadvantages of stock dividends and splits? When should a stock dividend as opposed to a stock split be used?

Computer-Related Problem

Work the problem in this section only if you are using the computer problem diskette.

Dividend policy and capital structure

17-9 Use the model in File C17 to work this problem. Refer to Problem 17-3. Assume that Ybor's management is considering a change in the firm's capital structure to include more debt; thus, management would like to analyze the effects of an increase in the debt ratio to 60 percent. The treasurer believes that such a move would cause lenders to increase the required rate of return on new bonds to 12 percent and that k_s would rise to 14.5 percent.

a. How would this change affect the optimal capital budget?

b. If k_s rose to 16 percent, would the low-return project be acceptable?

c. Would the project selection be affected if the dividend was reduced to $1.88 from $3.00, still assuming $k_s = 16$ percent?

PART VII

Strategic Long-Term Financing Decisions

CHAPTER 18
Common Stock and the Investment Banking Process

CHAPTER 19
Long-Term Debt

CHAPTER 20
Alternative Financing Arrangements and Corporate Restructuring

CHAPTER 21
Multinational Managerial Finance

Common Stock and the Investment Banking Process

During the past few years, the initial public offering (IPO) market has been extremely active. In 1993, a record number of companies used the IPO market to "go public"—707 IPOs raised more than $41 billion. The second and third most active years were 1994 and 1992, respectively. More than 600 IPOs worth nearly $29 billion were issued in 1994, while about $24 billion was raised through 517 IPOs in 1992. The IPO market slowed somewhat at the beginning of 1995. During the first quarter of 1995, the number of IPOs was nearly 50 percent less than the first quarter of 1994, and the total dollar value of the IPOs was more than 50 percent lower.

In recent years, the most popular IPOs have been those associated with technologically innovative companies, especially those that develop software and produce peripheral equipment for computers. The demand for such stocks has been so great that, in many cases, their prices have skyrocketed. For example, both Integrated Silicon, a manufacturer of integrated circuits for computers, and Oak Technology, a manufacturer of semiconductors for computers, went public in February 1995—the initial offering price for Integrated Silicon's stock was $13 per share, and it was $14 for Oak Technology. And, in March 1995, the IPOs of Horizon Bancorp, a savings and loan association, and Tivoli Systems, a developer of software, were offered for $7 and $14 per share, respectively. By mid-April, the stock of Oak Technology was up 93 percent at $27 per share. The increase in value for the other companies' stocks was even greater—Horizon Bancorp was up more than 300 percent, Integrated Silicon had increased nearly 190 percent, and the gain on Tivoli Systems' stock was about 170 percent.

In many cases, the demand for IPOs is greatest on the day of issue. For example, on February 10, 1995, General Magic, a PC software developer, went public with an offering of 5.5 million shares at $14 per share. When the offering reached the market, demand was so great that the price of the stock quickly jumped to $32, before settling at $26⅝ at the end of the day,

Continued

673

a 90 percent increase from the initial offering price. Remedy Corporation, a producer of software for computer networks, went public on March 20, 1995 at $23 per share, then it rose to $43.50 before closing at $34, a 48 percent increase from the initial price. Larry Garlick, chairman and CEO, certainly was pleased with the success of Remedy's IPO—not only did the company raise more than $41 million of new capital, but Garlick also saw the value of his 16 percent ownership in the company increase to more than $42 million (not a bad return on the $700,000 investment he made just five years earlier).

Even though IPOs offer the potential to earn significant returns, they are not the panacea many investors think. Obviously, many IPOs do very well at the time they are introduced to the market; but, most of the profits are earned by company insiders and institutional investors like pension funds, not the average investor. Evidence shows that during the first five years, the value of IPOs declines by about 39 percent, and it is the average investor that generally gets hurt. For example, within two weeks of its issue, General Magic's IPO was selling at $18 per share, down nearly one-third from its February 10 closing price; within three months of issue, it was selling for $11.75, $2.25 less than its initial offering price.

As you read this chapter, keep in mind that investment in common stock, whether an IPO or the stock from a "blue chip" company like IBM, is risky. Understanding the concepts presented in this chapter will help you avoid some of the pitfalls commonly made by "naive" investors, especially when investing in IPOs.

When we discussed capital structure decisions in Chapter 16, we did not spend much time on the specific characteristics of common stock or debt, nor did we discuss the process through which such securities are issued. However, these "details" actually are quite important. Therefore, in this and the following two chapters we will examine some of the characteristics of different equities (stock), and of the many different types of debt, and we will discuss how firms actually raise long-term capital. The focus in this chapter is on common stock.

Balance Sheet Accounts and Definitions

COMMON EQUITY
The sum of the firm's common stock, paid-in capital, and retained earnings, which equals the common stockholders' total investment in the firm stated at book value.

An understanding of legal and accounting terminology is vital to both investors and financial managers if they are to avoid misinterpretations and possibly costly mistakes. Therefore, we begin our analysis of common stock with a discussion of accounting and legal issues. Consider first Table 18-1, which shows the **common equity** section of Unilate Textiles' balance sheet. Unilate's owners—its stockholders—have authorized management to issue a total of 40 million shares, and management thus far actually has issued (or sold) 25 million shares. Each share has a

	TABLE 18-1		

Unilate Textiles: Common Equity Accounts as of December 31 (millions of dollars)

	1995	1994
Common stock (40 million shares authorized, 25 million shares outstanding, $1 par)	$ 25	$ 25
Additional paid-in capital	105	105
Retained earnings	293	260
Total common stockholders' equity (net worth)	$423	$390
Book value per share	$16.92	$15.60

PAR VALUE
The nominal or face value of a stock or bond.

RETAINED EARNINGS
The balance sheet account that indicates the total amount of earnings the firm has not paid out as dividends throughout its history; these earnings have been reinvested in the firm.

ADDITIONAL PAID-IN CAPITAL
Funds received in excess of par value when a firm sells stock.

BOOK VALUE PER SHARE
The accounting value of a share of common stock; equal to the common equity (common stock plus additional paid-in capital plus retained earnings) divided by the number of shares outstanding.

par value of $1; this is the minimum amount for which new shares can be issued.[1]

During 1995 Unilate earned $62 million, paid $29 million in dividends, and retained $33 million. The $33 million was added to the $260 million accumulated **retained earnings** shown on the year-end 1994 balance sheet to produce the $293 million retained earnings at year-end 1995. Thus, since its inception, Unilate has retained, or plowed back, a total of $293 million. This is money that belongs to the stockholders and that they could have received in the form of dividends. Instead, the stockholders chose to let management reinvest the $293 million in the business so growth could be achieved.

Now consider the $105 million **additional paid-in capital.** This account shows the difference between the stock's par value and what new stockholders paid when they bought newly issued shares. For example, in 1980, when Unilate was formed, 15 million shares were issued at par value; thus, the first balance sheet showed a zero for paid-in capital and $15 million for the common stock account. However, in 1983, to raise funds for expansion projects, Unilate issued 10 million shares at a market price of $11.50 per share—total value of the issue was $115 million. At that time, the common stock account was increased by $10 million ($1 par value for the 10 million shares issued), and the remainder of the $115 million issue value, $105 million, was added to additional paid-in capital. Unilate has not issued any more stock since 1983, so the only change in the common equity section since that time has been in retained earnings.

The **book value per share** shown in Table 18-1 is computed by dividing the amount of total stockholders' equity, which also is called net worth, by the number of shares outstanding. Unilate's book value per share increased in 1995 to $16.92, from $15.60 in 1994. Whenever stock is sold at a price above book value or the change in retained earnings is positive, book value will increase, and vice versa. Because book value is a historical cost amount, investors prefer that the

---

[1]A stock's par value is an arbitrary figure that originally indicated the minimum amount of money stockholders had put up. Today, firms generally are not required to establish a par value for their stock. Thus, Unilate Textiles could have elected to use "no-par" stock, in which case the common stock and additional paid-in capital accounts would have been consolidated under one account called *common stock,* which would show a 1995 balance of $130 million. For simplicity, in Chapter 3 we did not show the detailed breakdown of Unilate's common equity accounts. For purposes of the present discussion it is necessary to show the detail as given in Table 18-1.

market value of stock be greater than its book value; a stock that is selling below its book value might suggest the company is experiencing financial difficulty.

Self-Test Questions

How is book value per share calculated, and is it generally equal to the par and market values?

What differences would there be in the stockholders' equity accounts of a firm that has par value stock and one that has no-par stock?

How does the amount of earnings retained by a firm affect its common equity accounts?

Legal Rights and Privileges of Common Stockholders

The common stockholders are the owners of a corporation, and as such they have certain rights and privileges. The most important of these rights are discussed in this section.

Control of the Firm

The stockholders have the right to elect the firm's directors, who in turn elect the officers who manage the business. In a small firm, the major stockholder typically assumes the positions of president and chairperson of the board of directors. In a large, publicly owned firm, the managers typically have some stock, but their personal holdings are insufficient to provide voting control. Thus, the managements of most publicly owned firms can be removed by the stockholders if they decide a management team is not effective.

Various state and federal laws stipulate how stockholder control is to be exercised. First, corporations must hold an election of directors periodically, usually once a year, with the vote taken at the annual meeting. Frequently, one-third of the directors are elected each year for a three-year term. Each share of stock normally has one vote; thus, the owner of 1,000 shares has 1,000 votes. Stockholders can appear at the annual meeting and vote in person, but typically they transfer their right to vote to a second party by means of an instrument known as a **proxy.** Management always solicits stockholders' proxies and usually gets them. However, if earnings are poor and stockholders are dissatisfied, an outside group might solicit the proxies in an effort to overthrow management and take control of the business. This is known as a **proxy fight.**

The question of control has become a central issue in finance in recent years. The frequency of proxy fights has increased, as have attempts by one corporation to take over another by purchasing a majority of the outstanding stock. This action is called a **takeover.** Some well-known examples of recent takeover battles include KKR's acquisition of RJR Nabisco, Chevron's acquisition of Gulf Oil, and AT&T's takeover of NCR.

Managers who do not have majority control (more than 50 percent of their firms' stock) are very much concerned about proxy fights and takeovers, and many attempt to get stockholder approval for changes in their corporate charters that would make takeovers more difficult. For example, a number of companies

PROXY
A document giving one person the authority to act for another, typically the power to vote shares of common stock.

PROXY FIGHT
An attempt by a person or group of people to gain control of a firm by getting its stockholders to grant that person or group the authority to vote their shares in order to elect a new management team.

TAKEOVER
An action whereby a person or group succeeds in ousting a firm's management and taking control of the company.

INDUSTRY PRACTICE

Unionized Shareholder Voting—Is It Self-Serving?

In recent years, labor unions have become more active in the proxy fights of corporations in an effort to include union-related proposals on the voting slates at annual meetings. The number of proposals put forth by either union members or the trustees of union pension funds doubled from 1993 to 1994.

Most of the time, the union-initiated proposals were considered legitimate because they relate to the administration of the corporations involved. But, there are many examples of self-serving proposals that are introduced generally for the sole purpose of improving employment conditions, labor relations, and so on. Such proposals are not allowed by the Securities and Exchange Commission (SEC), because they are not concerned with corporate governance and shareholders' interests. For example, in 1994, a union employee of Roadway Services Inc. proposed that the executives of the trucking company be compensated based on the dollar amount invested in the workers. In a similar case, some employees of Dow Jones & Co. proposed that the CEO's compensation be limited to no more than 20 times the pay of the average employee, and that any annual increase in executive compensation be no more than the percentage salary increase received by the average employee. Not coincidentally, the Dow Jones' proposals were filed at the same time the company was negotiating a new contract with one of its employees' unions. In any event, if implemented, proposals like these could create an agency problem for executives—satisfy employees and thus receive greater compensation, or maximize shareholders' wealth. For that reason, unless union-related proposals are concerned with corporate governance, generally the SEC does not allow them on the ballot at corporations' annual meetings. Even if some union-related proposals are disallowed, the fact that the number of proposals presented by unions, union members, or their representatives has risen significantly in recent years clearly indicates that the influence of unions at annual meetings is increasing.

It is obvious that labor unions have become more noticeable with respect to initiations of proposals to be voted on at shareholders' meetings. Many union members believe the union-related proposals should be self-serving. But, should a union work to increase the salaries and the labor conditions of its members, even if such actions depress the value of the stock held in the employees' pension fund? What do you think?

SOURCE: "Labor Unions Increasingly Initiate Proxy Proposals," *The Wall Street Journal*, March 1, 1994.

---

have gotten their stockholders to agree (1) to elect only one-third of the directors each year (rather than electing all directors each year), (2) to require 75 percent of the stockholders (rather than 50 percent) to approve a merger, and (3) to vote in a "poison pill" provision that would allow the stockholders of a firm that is taken over by another firm to buy shares in the second firm at a reduced price. The third provision makes the acquisition unattractive and thus wards off hostile takeover attempts. Managements seeking such changes generally cite a fear that the firm will be picked up at a bargain price, but it often appears that managers' concerns about their own positions might be an even more important consideration.

The Preemptive Right

PREEMPTIVE RIGHT
A provision in the corporate charter or bylaws that gives common stockholders the right to purchase on a *pro rata* basis new issues of common stock (or convertible securities).

Common stockholders often have the right, called the **preemptive right,** to purchase any additional shares sold by the firm. In some states the preemptive right automatically is included in every corporate charter; in others it is necessary to insert it specifically into the charter.

The purpose of the preemptive right is twofold. First, it protects the power of control of current stockholders. If it were not for this safeguard, the management of a corporation under criticism from stockholders could prevent stockholders from removing it from office by issuing a large number of additional shares and purchasing these shares itself. Management could thereby secure control of the corporation and frustrate the will of the current stockholders.

The second, and more important, reason for the preemptive right is that it protects stockholders against a dilution of value. For example, suppose 1,000 shares of common stock, each with a price of $100, were outstanding, making the total market value of the firm $100,000. If an additional 1,000 shares were sold at $50 a share, or for $50,000, this would raise the total market value of the firm to $150,000. When the total market value is divided by the new total shares outstanding, a value of $75 a share is obtained. The old stockholders thus lose $25 per share, and the new stockholders have an instant profit of $25 per share. Thus, selling common stock at a price below the market value would dilute its price and would transfer wealth from the present stockholders to those who were allowed to purchase the new shares. The preemptive right prevents such occurrences.

Self-Test Questions

Identify some actions that companies have taken to make takeovers more difficult.

What are the two primary reasons for the existence of the preemptive right?

Types of Common Stock

CLASSIFIED STOCK
Common stock that is given a special designation, such as Class A, Class B, and so forth, to meet special needs of the company.

Although most firms have only one type of common stock, in some instances **classified stock** is used to meet the special needs of the company. Generally, when special classifications of stock are used, one type is designated Class A, another Class B, and so on. Small, new companies seeking to obtain funds from outside sources frequently use different types of common stock. For example, when Genetic Concepts went public, its Class A stock was sold to the public and paid a dividend, but this stock did not have voting rights until five years after its issue. Its Class B stock, which was retained by the organizers of the company, had full voting rights for five years, but the legal terms stated that dividends could not be paid on the Class B stock until the company had established its earning power by building up retained earnings to a designated level. The use of classified stock thus enabled the public to take a position in a conservatively financed growth company without sacrificing income, while the founders retained absolute control during the crucial early stages of the firm's development. At the same time, outside investors were protected against excessive withdrawals of funds by the original owners. As is often the case in such situations, the Class B stock was called **founders' shares.**

FOUNDERS' SHARES
Stock owned by the firm's founders that has sole voting rights but generally has restricted dividends for a specified number of years.

Note that "Class A," "Class B," and so on, have no standard meanings. Most firms have no classified shares, but a firm that does could designate its Class B shares as founders' shares and its Class A shares as those sold to the public, while another could reverse these designations. Still other firms could use stock classifications for entirely different purposes. For example, when General Motors acquired Hughes Aircraft for $5 billion, it paid in part with a new Class H common, GMH, which had limited voting rights and whose dividends were tied to Hughes's performance as a GM subsidiary. The reasons for the new stock were reported to be (1) that GM wanted to limit voting privileges on the new classified stock because of management's concern about a possible takeover and (2) that Hughes employees wanted to be rewarded more directly on Hughes's own performance than would have been possible through regular GM stock.[2]

 Self-Test Question

What are some reasons why a company might use classified stock?

Evaluation of Common Stock as a Source of Funds

Thus far the chapter has covered the main characteristics of common stock. Now we will appraise stock financing both from the viewpoint of the corporation and from a social perspective.

From the Corporation's Viewpoint

The advantages and disadvantages of using common stock as a financing source are listed in this section.

ADVANTAGES   Common stock offers several advantages to the corporation:

1. Common stock does not legally obligate the firm to make payments to stockholders: Only if the company generates earnings and has no pressing internal needs for them will it pay dividends.
2. Common stock carries no fixed maturity date—it never has to be "repaid" as would a debt issue.
3. Because common stock cushions creditors against losses, the sale of common stock generally increases the creditworthiness of the firm. This, in turn, raises its bond rating, lowers its cost of debt, and increases its future ability to use debt.
4. If a company's prospects look bright, then common stock often can be sold on better terms than debt. Stock appeals to certain groups of investors because (a) it typically carries a higher expected total return (dividends plus capital gains) than does preferred stock or debt, and (b) because stock represents the ownership of the firm, it provides the investor with a better hedge against unanticipated inflation because common dividends tend to rise during inflationary periods.[3]

---

[2]GM's deal posed a problem for the NYSE, which had a rule against listing any company's common stock if the company had any nonvoting common stock outstanding. GM made it clear that it was willing to delist if the NYSE did not change its rules. The NYSE concluded that such arrangements as GM had made were logical and were likely to be made by other companies in the future, so it changed its rules to accommodate GM.

[3]For common stock in general, the rate of increase in dividends has slightly exceeded the rate of inflation since 1970.

DISADVANTAGES   Disadvantages associated with issuing common stock include the following:

1. The sale of common stock gives some voting rights, and perhaps even control, to new stockholders. For this reason, additional equity financing often is avoided by managers who are concerned about maintaining control. The use of founders' shares and other classes of common stock can mitigate this problem.

2. Common stock gives new owners the right to share in the income of the firm; if profits soar, then new stockholders will share in this bonanza, whereas if debt had been used, new investors would have received only a fixed return, no matter how profitable the company had been.[4]

3. As we shall see, the costs of underwriting and distributing common stock usually are higher than those for debt or preferred stock. Flotation costs for common stock characteristically are higher because (a) the costs of investigating an equity security investment are higher than those for a comparable debt security, and (b) stocks are riskier than debt, meaning that investors must diversify their equity holdings, so a given dollar amount of new stock must be sold to a larger number of purchasers than the same amount of debt.

4. As we saw in Chapter 16, if the firm has more equity than is called for in its optimal capital structure, the average cost of capital will be higher than necessary. Therefore, a firm would not want to sell stock if the sale caused its equity ratio (1.0 minus the debt ratio) to exceed the optimal level.

5. Under current tax laws, common stock dividends are not deductible as an expense for tax purposes, but bond interest is deductible. As we saw in Chapter 15, taxes raise the relative cost of equity as compared with debt.

From a Social Viewpoint

From a social viewpoint, common stock is a desirable form of financing because it makes businesses less vulnerable to the consequences of declines in sales and earnings. Common stock financing involves no fixed charge payments that might force a faltering firm into bankruptcy. From the standpoint of the economy as a whole, if too many firms used too much debt, business fluctuations would be amplified, and minor recessions could turn into major ones. Not long ago, when the level of leveraged mergers and buyouts was raising the aggregate debt ratio (the average debt ratio of all firms), the Federal Reserve and other authorities voiced concern over the possible dangers created by the situation, and congressional leaders debated the wisdom of social controls over corporations' use of debt. Like most important issues, this one is debatable, and the debate centers around who can better determine "appropriate" capital structures—corporate managers or government officials.[5]

---

[4]This point has given rise to an important theory: "If a firm sells a large issue of bonds, this is a signal that management expects the company to earn high profits on investments financed by the new capital and that it does not wish to share these profits with new stockholders. On the other hand, if the firm issues stock, this is a signal that its prospects are not so bright." This issue was discussed earlier in Chapters 16 and 17.

[5]When business executives hear someone say, "I'm from Washington and I'm here to help you," they generally cringe, and often with good reason. On the other hand, a stable national economy does require sound businesses, and too much debt can lead to corporate instability.

Self-Test Questions

What are the major advantages and disadvantages of common stock financing?

From a social viewpoint, why is common stock a desirable form of financing?

The Market for Common Stock

CLOSELY HELD CORPORATION
A corporation that is owned by a few individuals who are typically associated with the firm's management.

PUBLICLY OWNED CORPORATION
A corporation that is owned by a relatively large number of individuals who are not actively involved in its management.

OVER-THE-COUNTER (OTC) MARKET
The network of dealers that provides for trading securities not listed on organized exchanges.

ORGANIZED SECURITY EXCHANGE
A formal organization, having a tangible physical location, that facilitates trading in designated ("listed") securities. The two major national security exchanges in the United States are the New York Stock Exchange (NYSE) and the American Stock Exchange (AMEX).

SECONDARY MARKET
The market in which "used" stocks are traded after they have been issued by corporations.

PRIMARY MARKET
The market in which firms issue new securities to raise corporate capital.

Some companies are so small that their common stocks are not actively traded; they are owned by only a few people, usually the companies' managers. Such firms are said to be *privately owned,* or **closely held, corporations,** and their stock is called *closely held stock.* In contrast, the stocks of most larger companies are owned by a large number of investors, most of whom are not active in management. Such companies are said to be **publicly owned corporations,** and their stock is called *publicly held stock.*

As we saw in Chapter 2, the stocks of smaller publicly owned firms are not listed on an exchange; they trade in the **over-the-counter (OTC) market,** and the companies and their stocks are said to be *unlisted.* However, larger publicly owned companies generally apply for listing on an **organized security exchange,** and they and their stocks are said to be *listed.* As a rule, companies are first listed on a regional exchange, such as the Pacific Coast or Midwest Exchange. Then, as they grow, they move up to the American Stock Exchange (AMEX) and the New York Stock Exchange (NYSE). More than 7,000 stocks are traded in the OTC market, but in terms of market value of both outstanding shares and daily transactions, the NYSE generates about 60 percent of the business with its listing of under 2,000 stocks.

Institutional investors such as pension trusts, insurance companies, and mutual funds own about 35 percent of all common stocks. These institutions buy and sell fairly actively, however, so they account for about 75 percent of all transactions. Thus, the institutional investors have a heavy influence on the prices of individual stocks.

Types of Stock Market Transactions

We can classify stock market transactions into three distinct types:

1. **Trading in the outstanding shares of established, publicly owned companies: the secondary market.** Unilate Textiles has 25 million shares of stock outstanding. If the owner of 100 shares sells his or her stock, the trade is said to have occurred in the **secondary market.** Thus, the market for outstanding shares, or used shares, is the secondary market. The company receives no new money when sales occur in this market.

2. **Additional shares sold by established, publicly owned companies: the primary market.** If Unilate decides to sell (or issue) an additional 1 million shares to raise new equity capital, this transaction is said to occur in the **primary market.**[6]

---

[6]Recall that Unilate has 40 million shares authorized but only 25 million outstanding; thus, it has 15 million authorized but unissued shares. If it had no authorized but unissued shares, management could increase the authorized shares by obtaining stockholders' approval, which would generally be granted without any arguments.

3. **New public offerings by privately held firms: the primary market.** When Coors Brewing Company, which was owned by the Coors family at the time, decided to sell some stock to raise capital needed for a major expansion program, it took its stock public—whenever stock in a closely held corporation is offered to the public for the first time, the company is said to be **going public.**[7] The market for stock that has recently gone public normally is called the **initial public offering (IPO) market.**

Firms can go public without raising any additional capital. For example, the Ford Motor Company was once owned exclusively by the Ford family. When Henry Ford died, he left a substantial part of his stock to the Ford Foundation. When the Foundation later sold some of this stock to the general public, the Ford Motor Company went public, even though the company raised no capital in the transaction.

A firm generally *goes public* when growth opportunities no longer can be financed solely by debt and the existing stockholder base, which generally consists of the original owners and current managers of the corporation and a few investors not actively involved in the company's management. The purpose of going public is to increase the ownership base and the funding sources available to the company so that growth opportunities can be better financed and the firm's value can be increased more than otherwise would be possible. Thus, as a firm experiences greater and greater growth and its size expands significantly, there generally is pressure to go public. Unfortunately, when a firm does go public, the "red tape" increases, because financial reporting and disclosure guidelines and security regulations are more restrictive for public firms than for private firms.

Going Public
The act of selling stock to the public at large by a closely held corporation or its principal stockholders.
Initial Public Offering (IPO) Market
The market consisting of stocks of companies that have just gone public.

The Decision to List the Stock

In order to have its stock listed, a company must apply to an exchange, pay a relatively small fee, and meet the exchange's minimum requirements. These requirements relate to the size of the company's net income as well as to the number of shares outstanding and in the hands of outsiders (as opposed to the number held by insiders, who generally do not trade their stock very actively). The company also must agree to disclose certain information to the exchange; this information is designed to help the exchange track trading patterns and thus try to prevent manipulation of the stock's price.[8] The size qualifications increase as one moves from the regional exchanges to the AMEX and on to the NYSE.

---

[7]The stock Coors offered to the public was designated Class B, and it was nonvoting. The Coors family retained the founders' shares, called Class A stock, which carried full voting privileges. The company was large enough to obtain an NYSE listing, but at that time the Exchange had a requirement that listed common stocks must have full voting rights, which precluded Coors from obtaining an NYSE listing. Currently, Coors is traded over the counter.

[8]It is illegal for anyone to attempt to manipulate the price of a stock. Prior to the creation of the SEC in the 1930s, syndicates would buy and sell stock back and forth at rigged prices for the purpose of deceiving the public into thinking that a particular stock was worth more or less than its true value. The exchanges, with the encouragement and support of the SEC, utilize sophisticated computer programs to help spot any irregularities that suggest manipulation. They can identify the exact day and time of each trade, and the broker who executed it, and they can require the broker to disclose the name of the person for whom the trade was made. Such a system can obviously help identify manipulators. This same system also helps to identify illegal insider trading, as discussed in the next section.

Assuming that a company qualifies, many people believe that listing is beneficial both to it and to its stockholders. Listed companies receive a certain amount of free advertising and publicity, and their status as a listed company enhances their prestige and reputation. This might have a beneficial effect on the sales of the firm's products, and it probably is advantageous in terms of lowering the required rate of return on its common stock. Investors respond favorably to increased information, increased liquidity, and confidence that the quoted price is not being manipulated. By providing investors with these benefits in the form of listing their companies' stock, financial managers might lower their firms' costs of capital and increase the value of their stocks.

Regulation of Securities Markets

SECURITIES AND EXCHANGE COMMISSION (SEC)
The U.S. goverment agency that regulates the issuance and trading of stocks and bonds.

Sales of new securities, as well as operations in the secondary markets, are regulated by the **Securities and Exchange Commission (SEC)** and, to a lesser extent, by each of the 50 states. For the most part, the SEC regulations are intended to (1) ensure investors receive fair financial disclosure from publicly traded companies, and (2) discourage fraudulent and misleading behavior by firms' investors, owners, and employees to manipulate stock prices. The primary elements of SEC regulation are:

REGISTRATION STATEMENT
A statement of facts filed with the SEC about a company that plans to issue securities.
PROSPECTUS
A document describing a new security issue and the issuing company.

1. The SEC has jurisdiction over all interstate offerings of new securities to the public in amounts of $1.5 million or more. A company wishing to issue new stock must file a **registration statement** that provides financial, legal, and technical information about the company. A **prospectus** that summarizes the information in the registration statement generally is provided to prospective investors for use in selling the securities. SEC lawyers and accountants analyze both the registration statement and the prospectus; if the information is inadequate or misleading, the SEC will delay or stop the public offering.

2. The SEC also regulates all national securities exchanges, and companies whose securities are listed on an exchange must file annual reports similar to the registration statement with both the SEC and the exchange.

INSIDERS
Officers, directors, major stockholders, or others who might have inside information on a company's operations.

3. The SEC has control over stock trades by corporate **insiders.** Officers, directors, and major stockholders must file monthly reports of changes in their holdings of the corporation's stock. Any *short-term* profits from such transactions must be handed over to the corporation.

4. The SEC has the power to prohibit manipulation by such devices as pools (aggregations of funds used to affect prices artificially) or wash sales (sales between members of the same group to record artificial transaction prices).

5. The SEC has control over the form of the proxy and the way the company uses it to solicit votes.

MARGIN REQUIREMENT
The percentage of a security's purchase price that must be deposited by investors.
MARGIN CALL
Call from a broker asking for more money to support a stock purchase loan.

Control over the flow of credit into securities transactions is exercised by the Board of Governors of the Federal Reserve System. The Fed exercises this control through the **margin requirement,** which represents the percentage of the purchase price that must be deposited (invested) by investors—the percentage that can be borrowed is equal to 100 percent less the margin requirement set by the Fed. If a great deal of margin borrowing has been going on, a decline in stock prices can result in inadequate loan coverages, which would force stockbrokers to issue **margin calls,** which in turn would require investors either to put up more money or to have their margined stock sold to pay off their loans. Such forced sales would further depress the stock market and could set off a downward spiral. The margin requirement currently is 50 percent.

States also have some control over the issuance of new securities within their boundaries. This control usually is exercised by a "corporation commissioner" or someone with a similar title. State laws relating to securities sales are called **blue sky laws,** because they were put into effect to keep unscrupulous promoters from selling securities that offered the "blue sky" but which actually had little or no asset backing.

BLUE SKY LAWS
State laws that prevent the sale of securities having little or no asset backing.

The securities industry itself realizes the importance of stable markets, sound brokerage firms, and no perception of stock manipulation. Therefore, the various exchanges work closely with the SEC to police transactions on the exchanges and to maintain the integrity and credibility of the system. Similarly, the National Association of Securities Dealers (NASD) cooperates with the SEC to police trading in the OTC market. These industry groups also cooperate with regulatory authorities to set net worth and other standards for securities firms, to develop insurance programs to protect the customers of brokerage houses, and the like.

In general, government regulation of securities trading, as well as industry self-regulation, is designed to ensure that investors receive information that is as accurate as possible, that no one artificially manipulates the market price of a given stock, and that corporate insiders do not take advantage of their position to profit in their companies' stocks at the expense of other stockholders. Neither the SEC, the state regulators, nor the industry itself can prevent investors from making foolish decisions or from having bad luck, but regulators can and do help investors obtain the best data possible for making sound investment decisions.

Self-Test Questions

Differentiate between a closely held corporation and a publicly owned corporation.

Differentiate between a listed stock and an unlisted stock.

Differentiate between the primary and secondary markets.

Differentiate between a registration statement and a prospectus.

What is the primary purpose of regulating securities trading, whether it is imposed by law or self-imposed?

The Investment Banking Process

The role of investment bankers was discussed in general terms in Chapter 2, where we learned that (1) investment banking is quite different from commercial banking, (2) the major investment banking houses often are divisions of large financial service corporations engaged in a wide range of activities, and (3) investment bankers help firms issue new securities in the primary markets and also operate as brokers in the secondary markets. For example, Merrill Lynch has a brokerage department that operates thousands of offices as well as an investment banking department that helps companies issue securities, take over other companies, and the like. Of course, Merrill Lynch's brokers also sell securities that have been issued through their investment banking departments. In this section we describe how securities are issued, and we explain the role of investment bankers in this process.

Raising Capital: Stage I Decisions

The firm itself makes some preliminary decisions on its own, including the following:

1. **Dollars to be raised.** How much new capital do we need?
2. **Type of securities used.** Should stock, bonds, or a combination be used? Further, if stock is to be issued, should it be offered to existing stockholders or sold directly to the general public?
3. **Competitive bid versus negotiated deal.** Should the company simply offer a block of its securities for sale to the highest bidder, or should it sit down with an investment banker and negotiate a deal? These two procedures are called *competitive bids* and *negotiated deals.* Only a handful of the largest firms on the NYSE, whose securities already are well-known to the investment banking community, are in a position to use the competitive bid process. The investment banks would have to do a large amount of investigative work in order to bid on an issue unless they already were quite familiar with the firm, and the costs involved would be too high to make it worthwhile unless the investment bank was sure of getting the deal. Therefore, the vast majority of offerings of stock or bonds are made on a negotiated basis.
4. **Selection of an investment banker.** Assuming the issue is to be negotiated, which investment banker should the firm use? Older firms that have "been to market" before already will have established a relationship with an investment banker, although it is easy enough to change bankers if the firm is dissatisfied. However, a firm that is just going public will have to choose an investment bank, and different investment banking houses are better suited for different companies. The older, larger "establishment houses" like Morgan Stanley deal mainly with large companies like AT&T, IBM, and Exxon. Other bankers specialize in more speculative issues like initial public offerings. Table 18-2 lists in ranked order the top ten investment bankers in the U.S. during the first three months of 1995, as measured by the dollar amount of securities underwritten.

Raising Capital: Stage II Decisions

Stage II decisions, which are made jointly by the firm and its selected investment banker, include the following:

1. **Reevaluating the initial decisions.** The firm and its investment banker will reevaluate the initial decisions about the size of the issue and the type of securities to use. For example, the firm initially might have decided to raise $50 million by selling common stock, but the investment banker might convince management that it would be better off, in view of current market conditions, to limit the stock issue to $25 million and to raise the other $25 million as debt.

2. **Best efforts or underwritten issues.** The firm and its investment banker must decide whether the investment banker will work on a best efforts basis or underwrite the issue. In a **best efforts arrangement,** the investment

BEST EFFORTS ARRANGEMENT
Agreement for the sale of securities in which the investment bank handling the transaction gives no guarantee that the securities will be sold.

TABLE 18-2

Top Ten U.S. Investment Bankers, 1995

1. Merrill Lynch	6. J. P. Morgan
2. Goldman Sachs	7. Salomon Brothers
3. Lehman Brothers	8. Bear Stearns
4. Morgan Stanley	9. Donaldson Lufkin
5. CS First Boston	10. First Tennessee

NOTE: Rankings are based on the dollar volume of debt and equity underwritings by U.S. firms managed during the first three months of 1995.

SOURCE: *The Wall Street Journal,* April 3, 1995.

UNDERWRITTEN ARRANGEMENT
Agreement for the sale of securities in which the investment bank guarantees the sale of the securities, thus agreeing to bear any risks involved in the transaction.

UNDERWRITER'S SPREAD
The difference between the price at which the investment banking firm buys an issue from a company and the price at which the securities are sold in the primary market—it represents the investment banker's gross profit on the issue.

FLOTATION COSTS
The costs associated with issuing new stocks or bonds.

OFFERING PRICE
The price at which common stock is sold to the public.

banker does not guarantee that the securities will be sold or that the company will get the cash it needs. In an **underwritten arrangement,** the investment banker generally assures the company the entire issue will be sold, so the investment banker bears significant risks in such an offering. For example, the very day IBM signed an underwritten agreement to sell $1 billion of bonds in 1979, interest rates rose sharply, and bond prices fell. IBM's investment bankers lost somewhere between $10 million and $20 million. Had the offering been on a best efforts basis, IBM would have been the loser.

3. **Issuance costs.** The investment banker's fee must be negotiated, and the firm also must estimate the other expenses it will incur in connection with the issue—lawyers' fees, accountants' costs, printing and engraving, and so on. Usually, the investment banker will buy the issue from the company at a discount below the price at which the securities are to be offered to the public, and this **underwriter's spread** covers the investment banker's costs and provides a profit.

Table 18-3 gives an indication of the **flotation costs** associated with public issues of bonds, preferred stock, and common stock. As the table shows, costs as a percentage of the proceeds are higher for stocks than for bonds, and costs also are higher for small issues than for large issues. The relationship between size of issue and flotation costs is primarily due to the existence of fixed costs: certain costs must be incurred regardless of the size of the issue, so the percentage flotation cost is quite high for small issues.

4. **Setting the offering price.** If the company already is publicly owned, the **offering price** will be based on the existing market price of the stock or the yield on the bonds. For common stock, the most typical arrangement calls for the investment banker to buy the securities at a prescribed number of points below the closing price on the last day of registration. For example, on July 1, 1995, the stock of Unilate Textiles had a current price of $23.00, and it had traded between $20 and $25 a share during the previous three months. Unilate and its underwriter agreed that the investment banker would buy 5 million new shares at $1 below the closing price on the last day of registration, which was expected to be in early October. The stock actually closed at $20.50 on the day the SEC released the issue, so the company received $19.50 a share. The shares then were sold to the public at a price of $20.50. As is typical, Unilate's agreement had an escape clause that provided for the contract to be voided if the price of the stock had fallen below a predetermined figure. In the illustrative case, this "upset" price was set at $18.50 a share. Thus, if the clos-

TABLE 18-3

Costs of Flotation for Underwritten, Nonrights Offerings (Expressed as a Percentage of Gross Proceeds)

Size of Issue (millions of dollars)	Bonds			Preferred Stock			Common Stock		
	Underwriting Commission	Other Expenses	Total Costs	Underwriting Commission	Other Expenses	Total Costs	Underwriting Commission	Other Expenses	Total Costs
Under 1.0	10.0%	4.0%	14.0%	—	—	—	13.0%	9.0%	22.0%
1.0–1.9	8.0	3.0	11.0	—	—	—	11.0	5.9	16.9
2.0–4.9	4.0	2.2	6.2	—	—	—	8.6	3.8	12.4
5.0–9.9	2.4	0.8	3.2	1.9%	0.7%	2.6%	6.3	1.9	8.2
10.0–19.9	1.2	0.7	1.9	1.4	0.4	1.8	5.1	0.9	6.0
20.0–49.9	1.0	0.4	1.4	1.4	0.3	1.7	4.1	0.5	4.6
50.0 and over	0.9	0.2	1.1	1.4	0.2	1.6	3.3	0.2	3.5

NOTES:

1. Small issues of preferred are rare, so no data on preferred issues below $5 million are given.

2. Flotation costs tend to rise somewhat when interest rates are cyclically high, because when money is in relatively tight supply, the investment bankers will have a more difficult time placing issues with permanent investors. Thus, the figures shown in the table represent averages, and actual flotation costs vary somewhat over time.

SOURCES: Securities and Exchange Commission, *Cost of Flotation of Registered Equity Issues* (Washington, D.C.: U.S. Goverment Printing Office, December 1974); Richard H. Pettway, "A Note on the Flotation Costs of New Equity Capital Issues of Electric Companies," *Public Utilities Fortnightly,* March 18, 1982; Robert Hansen, "Evaluating the Costs of a New Equity Issue," *Midland Corporate Finance Journal,* Spring 1986; and informal surveys of common stock, preferred stock, and bond issues conducted by the authors.

ing price of the shares on the last day of registration had been $18, Unilate would have had the option of withdrawing from the agreement.

Investment bankers have an easier job if an issue is priced relatively low, but the issuer of the securities naturally wants as high a price as possible. Therefore, an inherent conflict of interest on price exists between the investment banker and the issuer. However, if the issuer is financially sophisticated and makes comparisons with similar security issues, the investment banker will be forced to price close to the market.

It is important to note that *if pressure from the new shares drives down the price of the stock, all shares outstanding, not just the new shares, will be affected.* Thus, if Unilate's stock fell from $23.00 to $20.50 as a result of the financing, and if the price remained at that new level, the company would incur a loss of $2.50 on each of the 25 million shares previously outstanding, or a total market value loss of $62.5 million. In a sense, that loss would be a *flotation cost* because it would be a cost associated with the new issue. However, if the company's prospects really were poorer than investors had thought, then most of the price decline eventually would have occurred anyway. On the other hand, if the company's prospects are not really all that bad (if the signal was incorrect), then over time Unilate's stock price would increase, and the company would not suffer a permanent loss of $62.5 million.

If the company is going public for the first time, it will have no established price (or demand curve), so the investment bankers will have to estimate the equilibrium price at which the stock will sell after issue. Both the "Small Business" section and Problem 18-2 at the end of this chapter illustrate in some detail the process involved. If the offering price is set below the true equilibrium price, the stock will rise sharply after issue, and the company and its original stockholders will have given away too many shares to raise the required capital. If the offering price is set above the true equilibrium price, either the issue will fail or, if the bankers succeed in selling the stock, their investment clients will be unhappy when the stock subsequently falls to its equilibrium level. Therefore, it is important that the equilibrium price be approximated as closely as possible.

Selling Procedures

Once the company and its investment bankers have decided how much money to raise, the type of securities to issue, and the basis for pricing the issue, they will prepare and file a registration statement and prospectus with the SEC. It generally takes about 20 days for the issue to be approved by the SEC. The final price of the stock (or the interest rate on a bond issue) is set at the close of business the day the issue clears the SEC, and the securities are then offered to the public the following day.

Investment bankers must pay the issuing firm within four days of the time the offering officially begins, so, typically, the investment bankers sell the stock within a day or two after the offering begins. But, on occasion investment bankers miscalculate, set the offering price too high, and are unable to move the issue. Similarly, the market might decline during the offering period, which again would force the investment bankers to reduce the price of the stock. In either instance, on an underwritten offering the firm would still receive the price that was agreed upon, and the investment bankers would have to absorb any losses that were incurred.

Because they are exposed to large potential losses, investment bankers typically do not handle the purchase and distribution of an issue singlehandedly unless it is a very small one. If the amount of money involved is large and the risk of price fluctuations substantial, an investment banker forms an **underwriting syndicate** in an effort to minimize the amount of risk each one carries. The investment banking house which sets up the deal is called the **lead,** or **managing, underwriter.**

In addition to the underwriting syndicate, on larger offerings still more investment bankers are included in a **selling group,** which handles the distribution of securities to individual investors. The selling group includes all members of the underwriting syndicate plus additional dealers who take relatively small participations (or shares of the total issue) from the syndicate members. Thus, the underwriters act as wholesalers, whereas members of the selling group act as retailers. The number of investment banking houses in a selling group depends partly on the size of the issue; for example, the one set up when Communications Satellite Corporation (Comsat) went public consisted of 385 members.

Shelf Registrations

The selling procedures described previously, including the 20-day minimum waiting period between registration with the SEC and sale of the issue, apply to most security sales. However, large, well-known public companies that issue securities frequently might file a master registration statement with the SEC and then update it with a short-form statement just prior to each individual offering. In such a case, a company could decide at 10 a.m. to sell registered securities and have the sale

UNDERWRITING SYNDICATE
A syndicate of investment firms formed to spread the risk associated with the purchase and distribution of a new issue of securities.

LEAD, OR MANAGING, UNDERWRITER
The member of an underwriting syndicate that actually *manages* the distribution and sale of a new security offering.

SELLING GROUP
A group (network) of brokerage firms formed for the purpose of distributing a new issue of securities.

SHELF REGISTRATION
A procedure used by large, well-established firms to issue new securities on very short notice.

completed before noon. This procedure is known as **shelf registration** because in effect the company puts its new securities "on the shelf" and then sells them to investors when it thinks the market is right.

Maintenance of the Secondary Market

In the case of a large, established firm like General Motors, the investment banking firm's job is finished once it has disposed of the stock and turned the net proceeds over to the company. However, in the case of a company going public for the first time, the investment banker is under an obligation to maintain a market for the shares after the issue has been completed. Such stocks typically are traded in the over-the-counter market, and the lead underwriter generally agrees to "make a market" in the stock and to keep it reasonably liquid. The company wants a good market to exist for its stock, as do its stockholders. Therefore, if the investment banking house wants to do business with the company in the future, to keep its own brokerage customers happy, and to have future referral business, it will hold an inventory of the shares and help to maintain an active secondary market in the stock.

Self-Test Questions

What is the sequence of events when a firm decides to issue new securities?

What type of firm would use a shelf registration? Explain.

What is an underwriting syndicate, and why is it important in the investment banking process?

Emerging Trends

The Depository Institutions Deregulation and Monetary Control Act of 1980 had the desirable effect of increasing competition among financial institutions, which benefited both savers and borrowers, and it also slowed the decline of U.S. banks in the world markets. However, the act had several serious shortcomings, and at the time this text is being written (spring 1995), the financial services industry is undergoing some significant changes. In particular, limited branch banking recently has been introduced, and Congress currently is considering repealing the Glass-Steagall Act, which prohibits commercial banks from engaging in investment banking practices.

It is unclear how the final legislation will shape up, but it is likely that U.S. banks will gain new powers to engage in security underwritings and that branching powers will be extended. However, only the strongest banks will be given these expanded powers. The result is likely to be a system of larger, stronger, and more diversified banks, yet more competition probably will exist in our financial markets.

Self-Test Question

What are some important new developments that are taking place in the financial markets?

SMALL BUSINESS

Why Go Public for Less Than You're Worth?

For many entrepreneurs, making an initial public offering (IPO) of their company's equity is a dream come true. After their years of sacrifice and hard work, the company finally is a success. The value of that sacrifice is realized by going public. Many observers are amazed that the successful entrepreneur appears willing to sell equity in his or her firm for too little money—on average, IPOs are *underpriced.*

Stocks are underpriced if they begin trading in the public markets at a price that is higher than the offering price. An example would be a stock that was sold in an IPO for $12.00 which begins trading immediately after the IPO for $15.00 per share.

This underpricing is a puzzle. The company going public, and any current shareholders of the privately owned firm who are selling as part of the public offering, receive, on average, the IPO price minus a commission or "discount" of roughly 8 percent. Even if the existing shareholders do not sell any of their own shares in the IPO, but instead sell only the company's shares, they still are hurt by underpricing because their ownership in the firm is diluted more than it would have been had the shares been fully priced.

The large returns of IPOs in the public market are not caused by the companies' performances after the IPOs. They do not mean that the firms showed high earnings growth after the IPOs—the higher returns generally occur on the *first trading day.* This simply means that the IPO securities were sold at a price below their value.

Why would issuers in IPOs (i.e., selling companies) willingly sell their stocks for less than their true value? There are a number of theories to explain underpricing, but there is no widespread consensus on the reasons for underpricing. Some possible explanations follow.

One explanation for underpricing is that the issuing companies' owners are not as knowledgeable as their underwriters; if owners have the same knowledge as underwriters, issues would be fully priced. This theory might explain some occurrences of underpricing, such as isolated instances in which an unethical underwriter (who presumably would not last long in the business) knowingly misinforms the issuer. However, some underwriters themselves have gone public, acting as their own underwriters, and they also have had substantial first-day returns—underpricing.

A popular theory among academicians is that underpricing occurs to keep *uninformed* investors in the market. According to this theory, there are some well-informed investors who regularly watch the IPO market to identify those that are mispriced. These *informed* investors, therefore, buy only the underpriced issues. However, such informed investors do not have enough capital to buy all the shares of any offering. On the other hand, uninformed investors tend to buy every IPO, believing significant returns will be realized. Thus, uninformed investors tend to buy a lot of stock in the overpriced or correctly priced offerings, but will obtain only a small portion of the offerings in which the informed investors are active. And, unless the set of all offerings is underpriced on average, then uninformed investors would consistently lose money, they would leave the market, and the market would break down. Thus, this theory argues, the IPO market must experience general underpricing to function. Early empirical evidence is consistent with this theory.

The most popular theory with underwriters and venture capitalists is what might be called the "good taste in the mouth" theory. According to this theory, if the company underprices its issue in an IPO, investors will be more receptive to future "seasoned" issues from the same firm. Note, too, that most IPOs involve only 10 percent to 20 percent of the stock, so the original owners still have 80 percent to 90 percent of the shares.

All these theories have a similar implication: An IPO with less uncertainty concerning its value will tend to be more fully priced. This suggests that firms can prepare themselves for public offerings at higher prices by using more prestigious underwriters to issue IPOs, by using reputable, visible accountants for their audits, and by acquiring venture capital investment from more reputable capitalists.

The phenomenon of underpricing IPO shares remains a puzzle to finance academicians. We think we have some of the answers, but the questions are not yet settled. Meanwhile, an issuer should be aware that most IPOs are underpriced by a meaningful amount and that this underpricing is almost certainly related to the risk and uncertainty of the business. This is important information to consider when deciding when the firm should make its initial public offering.

ETHICAL DILEMMA   *It's a "Painful" Decision—By George!*

George Anderson works as an analyst for Roberts, Stephens, and Kilmer (RSK), one of the largest investment banking firms in the United States. His primary job is to analyze initial public offerings (IPOs) planned by firms that want to "go public" to determine the viability of such stock issues. RSK relies on Anderson's evaluations when negotiating with companies that want to enter the markets with IPOs, which can be very risky propositions for investment bankers.

RSK currently is handling the IPO of BioPharm, a pharmaceutical company based in Oregon. Created by a brilliant biochemist named Henry Scott, the company has developed and marketed a number of new drugs since its start in 1985. George Anderson's evaluation of BioPharm indicates that the potential for the company is tremendous, especially if its newest drug, which offers a cure for arthritis, is approved by the Food and Drug Administration (FDA). According to Anderson's report, BioPharm has a very bright future even if the FDA does not approve the arthritis drug. BioPharm's IPO is scheduled to go to the market tomorrow at a price of $20 per share.

This morning, when he got to work and turned on his computer, Anderson discovered he had a number of e-mail messages marked urgent. The messages were sent by Rachel Raymond, a newspaper reporter from Washington, D.C. who specializes in articles about medical issues, including physician care, surgical practices, and pharmaceutical research and development. In essence, the messages indicated an unidentified source told Rachel that, within the next few days, the FDA will announce BioPharm's arthritis treatment has been rejected. George's repeated attempts to contact Rachel about her e-mail messages have been unsuccessful.

Because he could not get in touch with Rachel, George has made inquiries throughout the day to determine the validity of Rachel's messages. The only information he has been able to verify is that William Mezina, CEO of BioPharm, has sold a significant portion of his stock holdings in the company during the past few days. Attempts to corroborate the content of Rachel's messages proved futile—sources at the FDA will not comment, and a flash fire at BioPharm has temporarily interrupted its communications systems.

At this point George is beside himself, because the BioPharm IPO is supposed to be distributed when the markets open tomorrow. RSK has invested considerable funds to get the IPO ready for its introduction tomorrow, and withholding the issue would cost the firm a substantial amount. But, if RSK goes ahead with the issue as planned and, within a few days or weeks, the FDA announces the arthritis drug has been rejected, the per price of BioPharm's IPO probably will plunge significantly. Even worse, if later it can be proven that RSK knew about the FDA's rejection of the arthritis drug, there might be future legal ramifications because withholding such information from stockholders could be considered fraud. What should George do? Should he try to delay the IPO, even though the content of Rachel's messages has not been corroborated at this time?

Summary

This chapter is more descriptive than analytical, but a knowledge of the issues discussed here is essential to an understanding of finance. The key concepts covered are listed below.

- **Stockholders' equity** consists of the firm's common stock, paid-in capital (funds received in excess of the par value), and retained earnings (earnings not paid out as dividends).
- **Book value per share** is equal to stockholders' equity divided by the number of shares of stock outstanding. A stock's book value often is different from its par value and its market value.

- A **proxy** is a document that gives one person the power to act for another person, typically the power to vote shares of common stock. A proxy fight occurs when an outside group solicits stockholders' proxies in order to vote a new management team into office.
- Stockholders often have the right to purchase any additional shares sold by the firm. This right, called the **preemptive right,** protects the control of the present stockholders and prevents dilution of the value of their stock.
- The major **advantages of common stock financing** are as follows: (1) there is no obligation to make fixed payments, (2) common stock never matures, (3) the use of common stock increases the creditworthiness of the firm, and (4) stock often can be sold on better terms than debt.
- The major **disadvantages of common stock financing** are (1) it extends voting privileges to new stockholders, (2) new stockholders share in the firm's profits, (3) the costs of stock financing are high, (4) using stock can raise the firm's cost of capital, and (5) dividends paid on common stock are not tax deductible.
- A **closely held corporation** is one that is owned by a few individuals who typically are associated with the firm's management.
- A **publicly owned corporation** is one that is owned by a relatively large number of individuals who are not actively involved in its management.
- **Going public** facilitates stockholder diversification, increases liquidity of the firm's stock, makes it easier for the firm to raise capital, and establishes a value for the firm. However, reporting costs are high, operating data must be disclosed, and public ownership might make it harder for management to maintain control of the firm.
- Security markets are regulated by the **Securities and Exchange Commission (SEC).**
- An **investment banker** assists in the issuing of securities by helping the firm determine the size of the issue and the type of securities to be used, by establishing the selling price, by selling the issue, and, in some cases, by maintaining an after-market for the stock.
- A *small firm's stock* sold in an **initial public offering (IPO)** often increases in price immediately after issue, with the largest price increases being associated with issues where uncertainties are greatest.

Questions

18-1 Examine Table 18-1. Suppose Unilate Textiles sold 2 million shares, with the company netting $25 per share. Construct a statement of the equity accounts to reflect this sale.

18-2 The SEC attempts to protect investors who are purchasing newly issued securities by requiring issuers to provide relevant financial information to prospective investors. However, the SEC does not provide an opinion about the real value of the securities; hence, an investor might pay too much for some stock and consequently lose heavily. Do you think the SEC should, as a part of every new stock or bond offering, render an opinion to investors on the proper value of the securities being offered? Explain.

18-3 How do you think each of the following items would affect a company's ability to attract new capital and the flotation (issuing) costs involved in doing so?

a. A decision to list a company's stock; the stock now trades in the over-the-counter market.

b. A decision of a privately held company to go public.

c. The increasing importance of institutions in the stock and bond markets.

d. The trend toward financial conglomerates as opposed to stand-alone investment banking houses.

e. Elimination of the preemptive right.

f. The introduction of shelf registrations.

18-4 Before entering a formal agreement, investment bankers carefully investigate the companies whose securities they underwrite; this is especially true of the issues of firms going public for the first time. Because the bankers do not themselves plan to hold the securities but intend to sell them to others as soon as possible, why are they so concerned about making careful investigations?

18-5 It frequently is stated that the primary purpose of the preemptive right is to allow individuals to maintain their proportionate share of the ownership and control of a corporation.

a. How important do you suppose this consideration is for the average stockholder of a firm whose shares are traded on the New York or American Stock Exchanges?

b. Is the preemptive right likely to be of more importance to stockholders of publicly owned or closely held firms? Explain.

18-6 Why would management be interested in getting a wider distribution of its shares?

Self-Test Problem

Key terms **ST-1** Define each of the following terms:

a. common equity; paid-in capital; retained earnings

b. par value; book value per share; market value per share

c. proxy; proxy fight; takeover

d. preemptive right

e. classified stock; founders' shares

f. closely held corporation; publicly owned corporation

g. over-the-counter (OTC) market; organized security exchange

h. primary market; secondary market

i. going public; new issue market; initial public offering (IPO)

j. Securities and Exchange Commission (SEC); registration statement; shelf registration; blue sky laws; margin requirements; margin call; insiders

k. prospectus

l. best efforts arrangement; underwritten arrangement

m. underwriters' spread; flotation costs; offering price

n. underwriting syndicate; lead, or managing, underwriter; selling group

Problems

Profit (loss) on **18-1** Security Brokers Inc. specializes in underwriting new issues by small firms. On a
a new stock issue   recent offering of Barenbaum Inc., the terms were as follows:

Price to public	$7.50 per share
Number of shares	3 million
Proceeds to Barenbaum	$21,000,000

The out-of-pocket expenses incurred by Security Brokers in the design and distribution of the issue were $450,000. What profit or loss would Security Brokers incur if the issue were sold to the public at an average price of

a. $7.50 per share?

b. $9.00 per share?

c. $6.00 per share?

Setting the price of
a new issue of stock

18-2 U-Fix-It, a small home improvement building supplier, has been successful and has enjoyed a good growth trend. Now U-Fix-It is planning to go public with an issue of common stock, and it faces the problem of setting an appropriate price on the stock. The company's management and its investment bankers believe that the proper procedure is to select several similar firms with publicly traded common stock and to make relevant comparisons.

Several home improvement building suppliers are reasonably similar to U-Fix-It with respect to product mix, size, asset composition, and debt/equity proportions. Of these companies, Home Headquarters and Lows are most similar. When analyzing the following data, assume that 1990 and 1995 were reasonably normal years for all three companies; that is, these years were neither especially good nor especially bad in terms of sales, earnings, and dividends. At the time of the analysis, k_{RF} was 10 percent and k_M was 15 percent. Home Headquarters is listed on the AMEX and Lows on the NYSE, while U-Fix-It will be traded in the OTC market.

	Home Headquarters	Lows	U-Fix-It (Totals)
Earnings per share			
1995	$ 3.60	$ 6.00	$ 960,000
1990	2.40	4.40	652,800
Price per share			
1995	$28.80	$52.00	—
Dividends per share			
1995	$ 1.80	$ 3.00	$ 480,000
1990	1.20	2.20	336,000
Book value per share, 1995	$24.00	$44.00	$7,200,000
Market/book ratio, 1995	120%	118%	—
Total assets, 1995	$22.4 million	$ 65.6 million	$16.0 million
Total debt, 1995	$ 9.6 million	$ 24.0 million	$ 8.8 million
Sales, 1995	$32.8 million	$112.0 million	$29.6 million

a. Assume that U-Fix-It has 100 shares of stock outstanding. Use this information to calculate earnings per share (EPS), dividends per share (DPS), and book value per share for U-Fix-It. (Hint: U-Fix-It's 1995 EPS = $9,600.)

b. Calculate earnings and dividend growth rates for the three companies. (Hint: U-Fix-It's EPS g is 8%.)

c. On the basis of your answer to Part a, do you think U-Fix-It's stock would sell at a price in the same "ballpark" as that of Home Headquarters and Lows—that is, in the range of $25 to $100 per share?

d. Assuming that U-Fix-It's management can split the stock so that the 100 shares could be changed to 1,000 shares, 100,000 shares, or any other number, would such an action make sense in this case? Why?

e. Now assume that U-Fix-It did split its stock and has 400,000 shares. Calculate new values for EPS, DPS, and book value per share. (Hint: U-Fix-It's new 1995 EPS is $2.40.)

f. Return on equity (ROE) can be measured as EPS/book value per share or as total earnings/total equity. Calculate ROEs for the three companies for 1995. (Hint: U-Fix-It's 1995 ROE = 13.3%.)

g. Calculate dividend payout ratios for the three companies. (Hint: U-Fix-It's 1995 payout ratio is 50%.)

h. Calculate debt/total assets ratios for the three companies. (Hint: U-Fix-It's 1995 debt ratio is 55%.)

i. Calculate the P/E ratios for Home Headquarters and Lows based on 1995 data. Are these P/E ratios reasonable in view of relative growth, payout, and ROE data? If not, what other factors might explain them? (Hint: Home Headquarters' P/E = 8×.)

j. Now determine a range of values for U-Fix-It's stock price, with 400,000 shares outstanding, by applying Home Headquarters's and Lows's P/E ratios, price/ dividends ratios, and price/book value ratios to your data for U-Fix-It. For example, one possible price for U-Fix-It's stock is (P/E Home Headquarters)(EPS U-Fix-It) = 8($2.40) = $19.20 per share. Similar calculations would produce a range of prices based on both Home Headquarters's and Lows's data. (Hint: Our range was $19.20 to $21.60.)

k. Using the equation $k_s = D_1/P_0 + g$, find approximate k_s values for Home Headquarters and Lows. Then use these values in the constant growth stock price model to find a price for U-Fix-It's stock. (Hint: We averaged the EPS and DPS g's for U-Fix-It.)

l. At what price do you think U-Fix-It's shares should be offered to the public? You will want to select a price that will be low enough to induce investors to buy the stock but not so low that it will rise too sharply immediately after it is issued. Think about relative growth rates, ROEs, dividend yields, and total returns $(k_s = D_1/P_0 + g)$.

Exam-Type Problems

The problems included in this section are set up in such a way that they could be used as multiple-choice exam problems.

Book value per share

18-3 Atlantic Coast Resources Company had the following balance sheet at the end of 1995:

Atlantic Coast Resources Company: Balance Sheet, December 31, 1995

		Accounts payable	$ 64,400
		Notes payable	71,400
		Long-term debt	151,200
		Common stock (30,000 authorized, 20,000 shares outstanding)	364,000
		Retained earnings	336,000
Total assets	$987,000	Total liabilities and equity	$987,000

a. What is the book value per share of Atlantic's common stock?

b. Suppose the firm sold the remaining authorized shares and netted $32.55 per share from the sale. What would be the new book value per share?

Underwriting and flotation expenses

18-4 The Taussig Company, whose stock price now is $30, needs to raise $15 million in common stock. Underwriters have informed Taussig's management that it must price the new issue to the public at $27.53 per share to ensure the shares will be sold. The underwriters' compensation will be 7 percent of the issue price, so Taussig will net $25.60 per share. Taussig also will incur expenses in the amount of

$360,000. How many shares must Taussig sell to net $15 million after underwriting and flotation expenses?

Integrative Problem

Investment banking process

18-5 Gonzales Food Stores, a family-owned grocery store chain headquartered in El Paso, is considering a major expansion. The proposed expansion would require Gonzales to raise $10 million in additional capital. Because Gonzales currently has a debt ratio of 50 percent, and because the family members already have all their funds tied up in the business, the owners cannot supply any additional equity, so the company will have to sell stock to the public. However, the family wants to ensure that they retain control of the company. This would be Gonzales's first stock sale, and the owners are not sure just what would be involved. Therefore, they have asked you to research the process and to help them decide exactly how to raise the needed capital. In doing so, you should answer the following questions.

   a. What are the advantages to Gonzales of financing with stock rather than bonds? What are the disadvantages of using stock?

   b. Is the stock of Gonzales Food Stores currently publicly held or privately owned? Would this situation change if the stock sale were made?

   c. What is classified stock? Would there be any advantage to Gonzales of designating the stock currently outstanding as "founders' shares"? What type of common stock should Gonzales sell to the public to allow the family to retain control of the business?

   d. What does the term *going public* mean? What would be the advantages to the Gonzales family of having the firm go public? What would be the disadvantages?

   e. What does the term *listed stock* mean? Do you think that Gonzales's stock would be listed shortly after the company goes public? If not, where would the stock trade?

   f. Suppose the firm has decided to issue $10 million of Class B nonvoting stock. Now Gonzales must select an investment banker. Do you think it should select a banker on the basis of a competitive bid or do a negotiated deal? Explain.

   g. Without doing any calculations, give a brief description of the procedures by which Gonzales and its investment banker will determine the price at which the stock will be offered to the public.

   h. What is a prospectus? Why does the SEC require all firms to file registration statements and distribute prospectuses to potential stockholders before selling stock?

   i. If Gonzales goes public and sells shares which the public buys at a price of $10 per share, what will be the approximate percentage cost, including both underwriting costs and other costs? Assume the company sells 1.5 million shares. Would the cost be higher or lower if the company already were publicly owned?

   j. Would you recommend that Gonzales have the issue underwritten or sold on a best efforts basis? Why? What would be the difference in costs between the two procedures?

   k. If some of the Gonzales family members wanted to sell some of their own shares in order to diversify at the same time the company was selling new shares to raise expansion capital, would this be feasible?

CHAPTER 19

Long-Term Debt

During the last two decades, the use of debt has increased significantly in all sectors of the economy—households, businesses, and governments. The increase in business debt has been attributed primarily to the merger and acquisition frenzy that occurred in the 1980s, especially prior to 1989. Much of the merger activity was financed with debt, and some firms even "leveraged up" to make themselves less attractive takeover targets. Consequently, the average debt ratio of companies increased significantly during this era. In 1980, the average firm was financed with about 43 percent debt; by 1989, the debt ratio was more than 57 percent. The greatest increases in the issuance of corporate debt occurred from 1984 through 1988, which also was the period when there was an unprecedented number of mergers and acquisitions. Debt financing was attractive during this period because, compared to the period from 1979 to 1983, interest rates had decreased considerably and remained relatively stable.

The result of the leveraging activity that occurred in the 1980s was that more stock was taken out of the capital market than was put back in through new issues—from 1984 to 1990, a net $640 billion of stock was replaced by debt; nearly $200 billion, 7.5 percent of the outstanding equity at the time, was retired in the fourth quarter of 1988.

In the latter part of 1989, economic growth started to slow and firms began to "deleverage." The burden of servicing high amounts of debt motivated many firms to improve their cash flow positions. Stock repurchases slowed, while new stock issues increased—in 1991 and 1992 new stock issues exceeded repurchases by an average of more than $20 billion per year. Unfortunately, at this pace, it would take almost 30 years to recover the amount of equity that was converted into debt in the 1980s.

Debt ratios of companies have decreased somewhat during the 1990s, but the de-leveraging effort has not significantly changed the overall debt position of the business sector. Many firms have found that lower interest rates in the 1990s, especially in 1993, have helped them to reduce interest payments substantially through refinancing, which obviates the need to

Continued

697

replace debt entirely—experts estimate that refinancing with cheaper debt has reduced annual interest on all business debt by as much as $35 billion per year. And, in 1994, stocks performed poorly, making them less attractive for raising funds and more attractive for firms to repurchase. In fact, 1994 stock buybacks were the highest since the record-setting activity of the late 1980s. Companies that repurchased more than $1 billion of their outstanding stock include Philip Morris, whose total buyback of more than $7 billion was almost $6 billion greater than the next largest buyback, Anheuser-Busch, 3M, and Toys "Я" Us. At the same time, 1994 new equity issues were down more than 42 percent and debt issues were up about 17 percent compared to 1993.

From recent events, it appears that businesses in the United States have started to "re-leverage." It is unclear which direction firms will go in the future, but merger and acquisition activity is on the increase once again, and this will help sustain the current "re-leveraging" movement. In any event, it appears that many companies will experience increasing debt ratios and be saddled with servicing large amounts of debt for some time in the future. As you read this chapter, consider the positive and negative effects of debt on both businesses and our economy.

Different groups of investors prefer different types of securities, and investors' tastes change over time. Thus, astute financial managers offer a variety of securities, and they package their new security offerings at each point in time to appeal to the greatest possible number of potential investors. In this chapter, we consider the various types of long-term debt available to financial managers.

FUNDED DEBT
Long-term debt; "funding" means replacing short-term debt with securities of longer maturity.

Long-term debt often is called **funded debt.** When a firm "funds" its short-term debt, this means that it replaces short-term debt with securities of longer maturity. Funding does not imply that the firm places money with a trustee or other repository; it is simply part of the jargon of finance, and it means that the firm replaces short-term debt with permanent capital. Pacific Gas & Electric Company (PG&E) provides a good example of funding. PG&E has a continuous construction program, and it typically uses short-term debt to finance construction expenditures. However, once short-term debt increases to about $100 million, the company sells a stock or bond issue, uses the proceeds to pay off (or fund) its bank loans, and starts the cycle again. There is a fixed cost involved in selling stocks or bonds which makes it quite expensive to issue small amounts of these securities. Therefore, the process used by PG&E and other companies is quite logical.

Traditional Debt Instruments

There are many types of long-term debt instruments: term loans, bonds, secured and unsecured notes, marketable and nonmarketable debt, and so on. In this section, we briefly discuss the traditional long-term debt instruments, after which we examine some important features of debt contracts. Finally, we consider some innovations in long-term debt financing.

Term Loans

A **term loan** is a contract under which a borrower agrees to make a series of interest and principal payments on specific dates to the lender. Term loans usually are negotiated directly between the borrowing firm and a financial institution—generally a bank, an insurance company, or a pension fund. Although term loans' maturities vary from 2 to 30 years, most are for periods in the 3-year to 15-year range.[1]

Term loans have three major advantages over public offerings—*speed, flexibility,* and *low issuance costs.* Because they are negotiated directly between the lender and the borrower, formal documentation is minimized. The key provisions of a term loan can be worked out much more quickly than those for a public issue, and it is not necessary for the loan to go through the Securities and Exchange Commission registration process. A further advantage of term loans has to do with future flexibility. If a bond issue is held by many different bondholders, it is virtually impossible to obtain permission to alter the terms of the agreement, even though new economic conditions might make such changes desirable. With a term loan, the borrower generally can sit down with the lender and work out mutually agreeable modifications to the contract.

The interest rate on a term loan can be either fixed for the life of the loan or variable. If a fixed rate is used, generally it will be set close to the rate on bonds of equivalent maturity and risk. If the rate is variable, it usually will be set at a certain number of percentage points over either the prime rate, the commercial paper rate, the T-bill rate, the T-bond rate, or the London Inter-Bank Offered Rate (LIBOR), which is the rate of interest offered by the largest and strongest London banks on deposits of other large banks of the highest credit standing. Then, when the index rate goes up or down, so does the rate charged on the outstanding balance of the term loan. Rates might be adjusted annually, semiannually, quarterly, monthly, or on some other basis, depending on what the contract specifies. In 1995, over 60 percent of the dollar amount of all term loans made by banks had floating rates, up from virtually zero in 1970. With the increased volatility of interest rates in recent years, banks and other lenders have become increasingly reluctant to make long-term, fixed-rate loans.

Bonds

A **bond** is a long-term contract under which a borrower agrees to make payments of interest and principal on specific dates to the holder of the bond. Although bonds traditionally have been issued with maturities of between 20 and 30 years, in recent years shorter maturities, such as 7 to 10 years, have been used to an increasing extent. Bonds are similar to term loans, but a bond issue generally is advertised, offered to the public, and actually sold to many different investors. Indeed, thousands of individual and institutional investors might purchase bonds when a firm sells a bond issue, whereas there generally is only one lender in the

---

[1]Most term loans are amortized, which means they are paid off in equal installments over the life of the loan. Amortization protects the lender against the possibility that the borrower will not make adequate provisions for the loan's retirement during the life of the loan. See Chapter 6 for a review of amortization. Also, if the interest and principal payments required under a term loan agreement are not met on schedule, the borrowing firm is said to have defaulted, and it can then be forced into bankruptcy.

case of a term loan.[2] With bonds the interest rate generally is fixed, although in recent years there has been an increase in the use of various types of floating rate bonds. There also are a number of different types of bonds, the more important of which are discussed below.

MORTGAGE BOND
A bond backed by fixed assets. First mortgage bonds are senior in priority to claims of second mortgage bonds.

MORTGAGE BONDS   With a **mortgage bond,** the corporation pledges certain assets as security for the bond. To illustrate, in 1995 Scobes Corporation needed $10 million to build a major regional distribution center. Bonds in the amount of $4 million, secured by a mortgage on the property, were issued. (The remaining $6 million was financed with equity capital.) If Scobes defaults on the bonds, the bondholders can foreclose on the property and sell it to satisfy their claims.

If Scobes chooses to, it can issue *second mortgage bonds* secured by the same $10 million plant. In the event of liquidation, the holders of these second mortgage bonds would have a claim against the property, but only after the first mortgage bondholders had been paid off in full. Thus, second mortgages are sometimes called *junior mortgages,* because they are junior in priority to the claims of *senior mortgages,* or *first mortgage bonds.*

INDENTURE
A formal agreement (contract) between the issuer of a bond and the bondholders.

All mortgage bonds are written subject to an **indenture,** which is a legal document that spells out in detail the rights of both the bondholders and the corporation (bond issuer). The indentures of most major corporations were written 20, 30, 40, or more years ago. These indentures generally are "open ended," meaning that new bonds might be issued from time to time under the existing indenture. However, the amount of new bonds that can be issued almost always is limited to a specified percentage of the firm's total "bondable property," which generally includes all plant and equipment. For example, Savannah Electric Company can issue first mortgage bonds totaling up to 60 percent of its fixed assets. If its fixed assets totaled $1 billion, and if it had $500 million of first mortgage bonds outstanding, it could, by the property test, issue another $100 million of bonds (60% of $1 billion = $600 million).

DEBENTURE
A long-term bond that is not secured by a mortgage on specific property.

DEBENTURES   A **debenture** is an unsecured bond, and as such it provides no lien against specific property as security for the obligation. Therefore, debenture holders are general creditors whose claims are protected by property not otherwise pledged. In practice, the use of debentures depends both on the nature of the firm's assets and on its general credit strength. An extremely strong company, such as IBM, will tend to use debentures; it simply does not need to put up property as security for its debt. Debentures also are issued by companies in industries in which it would not be practical to provide security through a mortgage on fixed assets. Examples of such industries are the large mail-order houses and commercial banks, which characteristically hold most of their assets in the form of inventory or loans, neither of which is satisfactory security for a mortgage bond.

SUBORDINATED DEBENTURE
A bond having a claim on assets only after the senior debt has been paid off in the event of liquidation.

SUBORDINATED DEBENTURES   The term *subordinate* means "below," or "inferior to," and, in the event of bankruptcy, subordinated debt has claims on assets only after senior debt has been paid off. **Subordinated debentures** might be subordinated

---

[2]However, for very large term loans, 20 or more financial institutions might form a syndicate to grant the credit. Also, it should be noted that a bond issue can be sold to one lender (or to just a few); in this case, the issue is said to be "privately placed." Companies that place bonds privately do so for the same reasons that they use term loans—speed, flexibility, and low issuance costs.

either to designated notes payable (usually bank loans) or to all other debt. In the event of liquidation or reorganization, holders of subordinated debentures cannot be paid until all senior debt, as named in the debentures' indenture, has been paid.

OTHER TYPES OF BONDS   Several other types of bonds are used sufficiently often to warrant mention. First, **convertible bonds** are securities that are convertible into shares of common stock, at a fixed price, at the option of the bondholder. Convertibles have a lower coupon rate than nonconvertible debt, but they offer investors a chance for capital gains in exchange for the lower coupon rate. Bonds issued with **warrants** are similar to convertibles. Warrants are options which permit the holder to buy stock for a stated price, thereby providing a capital gain if the price of the stock rises. Bonds that are issued with warrants, like convertibles, carry lower coupon rates than straight bonds. **Income bonds** pay interest only when the firm has sufficient income to cover the interest payments. Thus, these securities cannot bankrupt a company, but from an investor's standpoint they are riskier than "regular" bonds. **Putable bonds** are bonds that can be turned in and exchanged for cash at the bondholder's option; generally, the option to turn in the bond can be exercised only if the firm takes some specified action, such as being acquired by a weaker company or increasing its outstanding debt by a large amount. With an **indexed,** or **purchasing power, bond,** which is popular in countries plagued by high rates of inflation, the interest rate payment is based on an inflation index such as the consumer price index; the interest paid rises automatically when the inflation rate rises, thus protecting the bondholders against inflation.

CONVERTIBLE BOND
A bond that is exchangeable, at the option of the holder, for common stock of the issuing firm.

WARRANT
A long-term option to buy a stated number of shares of common stock at a specified price.

INCOME BOND
A bond that pays interest to the holder only if the interest is earned by the firm.

PUTABLE BOND
A bond that can be redeemed at the bondholder's option.

INDEXED (PURCHASING POWER) BOND
A bond that has interest payments based on an inflation index to protect the holder from inflation.

Self-Test Questions

What are the three major advantages that term loans have over public offerings?

Differentiate between term loans and bonds.

Differentiate between mortgage bonds and debentures.

Define convertible bonds, bonds with warrants, income bonds, putable bonds, and indexed bonds.

Why do bonds with warrants and convertible bonds have lower coupon rates than bonds that do not have these features?

Specific Debt Contract Features

A firm's managers are concerned with both the effective cost of debt and any restrictions in debt contracts that might limit the firm's future actions. In this section, we discuss features that could affect either the cost of the firm's debt or the firm's future flexibility.

Bond Indentures

In Chapter 1 we discussed *agency problems,* which relate to conflicts of interest among corporate stakeholders—stockholders, bondholders, and managers. Bondholders have a legitimate fear that once they lend money to a company and are "locked in" for up to 30 years, the company will take some action that is designed to benefit stockholders but that harms bondholders. For example, RJR Nabisco, when it was highly rated, sold 30-year bonds with a low coupon rate, and investors bought those bonds in spite of the low yield because of their low risk. Then, after the bonds had been sold, the company announced plans to issue a great deal more debt, increasing the expected rate of return to stockholders but also increasing the riskiness of the bonds. RJR's bonds fell 20 percent the week the announcement was made. Safeway Stores and a number of other companies have done the same thing, and their bondholders also lost heavily as the market yield on the bonds rose and drove the prices of the bonds down.

TRUSTEE
An official who ensures that the bondholders' interests are protected and that the terms of the indenture are carried out.

Investors attempt to reduce agency problems by use of legal restrictions designed to ensure, insofar as possible, that the company does nothing to cause the quality of its bonds to deteriorate after they have been issued. The indenture is the legal document that spells out the rights of the bondholders and the corporation. A **trustee,** usually a bank, is assigned to represent the bondholders and to make sure that the terms of the indenture are carried out. The indenture might be several hundred pages in length, and it will include **restrictive covenants** that cover such points as the conditions under which the issuer can pay off the bonds prior to maturity, the level at which the issuer's times-interest-earned ratio must be maintained if the company is to sell additional bonds, and restrictions against the payment of dividends when earnings do not meet certain specifications.

RESTRICTIVE COVENANT
A provision in a debt contract that constrains the actions of the borrower.

The trustee is responsible both for making sure the covenants are not violated and for taking appropriate action if they are. What constitutes "appropriate action" varies with the circumstances. It might be that to insist on immediate compliance would result in bankruptcy, which in turn might lead to large losses on the bonds. In such a case, the trustee might decide that the bondholders would be better served by giving the company a chance to work out its problems rather than by forcing it into bankruptcy.

The Securities and Exchange Commission approves indentures for publicly traded bonds and makes sure that all indenture provisions are met before allowing a company to sell new securities to the public. The indentures of many larger corporations were written back in the 1930s or 1940s, and many issues of new bonds, all covered by the same indenture, have been sold through the years. The interest rates on the bonds, and perhaps also the maturities, will change from issue to issue, but bondholders' protection as spelled out in the indenture will be the same for all bonds of a given type.[3]

Call Provisions

CALL PROVISION
A provision in a bond contract that gives the issuer the right to redeem the bonds under specified terms prior to the normal maturity date.

Most bonds contain a **call provision,** which gives the issuing corporation the right to call the bonds for redemption. The call provision generally states that the company must pay the bondholders an amount greater than the par value for the bonds when they are called. The additional sum, which is termed a *call premium,* typically is set equal to one year's interest if the bonds are called during the first year, and the premium declines at a constant rate of INT/N each year thereafter, where INT = annual interest and N = original maturity in years. For example, the call premium on a $1,000 par value, 10-year, 10 percent bond gen-

---

[3]A firm will have different indentures for each major type of bonds it issues, including its first mortgage bonds, its debentures, its convertibles, and so on.

erally would be $100 if it were called during the first year, $90 during the second year (calculated by reducing the $100, or 10 percent, premium by one-tenth), and so on. However, bonds usually are not callable until several years (generally 5 to 10) after they were issued; bonds with these *deferred calls* are said to have *call protection.*

Suppose a company sold bonds or preferred stock when interest rates were relatively high. Provided the issue is callable, the company could sell a new issue of low-yielding securities if and when interest rates drop. It could then use the proceeds to retire the high-rate issue and thus reduce its interest expense. This process is called **refunding.**

REFUNDING
Retiring an existing bond issue with the proceeds of a newly issued bond.

Sinking Funds

SINKING FUND
A required annual payment designed to amortize a bond or preferred stock issue.

A **sinking fund** is a provision that facilitates the orderly retirement of a bond issue (or an issue of preferred stock). Typically, the sinking fund provision requires the firm to retire a portion of the bond issue each year. On rare occasions the firm might be required to deposit money with a trustee, which invests the funds and then uses the accumulated sum to retire the bonds when they mature. Failure to meet the sinking fund requirement causes the bond issue to be thrown into default, which might force the company into bankruptcy. Obviously, a sinking fund can constitute a dangerous cash drain on the firm.

In most cases, the firm is given the right to handle the sinking fund in either of two ways:

1. The company can call in for redemption (at par value) a certain percentage of the bonds each year; for example, it might be able to call 2 percent of the total original amount of the issue at a price of $1,000 per bond. The bonds are numbered serially, and those called for redemption are determined by a lottery administered by the trustee.
2. The company might buy the required amount of bonds in the open market.

The firm will choose the least-cost method. If interest rates have risen, causing bond prices to fall, it will buy bonds in the open market at a discount; if interest rates have fallen, it will call the bonds. Note that a call for sinking fund purposes is quite different from a refunding call as discussed earlier. A sinking fund call requires no call premium, but only a small percentage of the issue normally is callable in any one year.

Self-Test Questions

How do trustees and indentures reduce agency problems for bondholders?

What are the two ways a sinking fund can be handled? Which method will be chosen by the firm if interest rates have risen? What if interest rates have fallen?

What is the difference between a call for sinking fund purposes and a refunding call?

Are securities that provide for a sinking fund regarded as being riskier than those without this type of provision? Explain.

Why is a call provision so advantageous to a bond issuer? When will the issuer initiate a refunding call? Why?

Bond Innovations

Zero (or Very Low) Coupon Bonds

ZERO COUPON BOND

A bond that pays no annual interest but is sold at a discount below par, thus providing compensation to investors in the form of capital appreciation.

Some bonds pay no interest but are offered at a substantial discount below their par values and hence provide capital appreciation rather than interest income. These securities are called **zero coupon bonds** (*"zeros"*), or *original issue discount bonds (OIDs)*. Corporations first used zeros in a major way in 1981. In recent years, many large companies like IBM and J. C. Penney have used them to raise billions of dollars. Municipal governments also sell "zero munis," and investment bankers have in effect created zero coupon Treasury bonds by "stripping" the interest payments and selling only the right to receive principal repayment at maturity.

Not all original issue discount bonds (OIDs) have zero coupons. For example, a company might sell an issue of 5-year bonds with a 3 percent coupon at a time when other bonds with similar ratings and maturities are yielding 9 percent. If an investor purchases these bonds at a price of $762.62, the yield to maturity would be 9 percent. The discount of $1,000 − $762.62 = $237.38 represents the capital appreciation the bondholder would receive for holding the bond for five years. Thus, zero coupon bonds are just one type of original issue discount bond. Any nonconvertible bond whose coupon rate is set below the going market rate at the time of its issue will sell at a discount, and it will be classified as an OID bond.

OID bonds have lost favor with many individual investors in recent years primarily because the interest income that must be reported each year for tax purposes includes the dollar amount of interest actually received, which is $0 for zero coupons, plus the annual *pro rated* capital appreciation. For example, the purchaser of the 3 percent coupon bond mentioned earlier actually would receive $30 interest each year. But the interest income reported for tax purposes would be $30 + ($237.38/5) = $77.48. Thus, taxes would have to be paid on *pro rated* capital gains which would not be received for five years ($47.48 each year). For this reason, most OID bonds currently are held by institutional investors, such as insurance companies and pension funds, rather than individual investors.

Shortly after corporations began to issue zeros, investment bankers figured out a way to create zeros from U.S. Treasury bonds, which are issued only in coupon form. In 1982 Salomon Brothers bought $1 billion of 12 percent, 30-year Treasuries. Each bond had 60 coupons worth $60 each, which represented the interest payments due every 6 months. Salomon then in effect clipped the coupons and placed them in 60 piles; the last pile also contained the now "stripped" bond itself, which represented a promise of $1,000 in the year 2012. These 60 piles of U.S. Treasury promises were then placed with the trust department of a bank and used as collateral for "zero coupon U.S. Treasury Trust Certificates," which are, in essence, zero coupon Treasury bonds. A pension fund that expected to need money in 1997 could have bought 15-year certificates backed by the interest the Treasury will pay in 1997. Treasury zeros are, of course, safer than corporate zeros, so they are very popular with pension fund managers.

Corporate (and municipal) zeros generally are callable at the option of the issuer, just like coupon bonds, after some stated call protection period. The call price is set at a premium over the accrued value at the time of the call. Stripped

U.S. Treasury bonds (Treasury zeros) generally are not callable because the Treasury normally sells noncallable bonds. Thus, Treasury zeros are completely protected against reinvestment risk (the risk of having to invest cash flows from a bond at a lower rate because of a decline in interest rates).

Floating Rate Debt

In the early 1980s, inflation pushed interest rates up to unprecedented levels, causing sharp declines in the prices of long-term bonds. Even some supposedly "risk-free" U.S. Treasury bonds lost fully half their value, and a similar situation occurred with corporate bonds, mortgages, and other fixed-rate, long-term securities. As a result, many lenders became reluctant to lend money at fixed rates on a long-term basis, and they would do so only at extraordinarily high rates.

There normally is a *maturity risk premium* embodied in long-term interest rates; this premium is designed to offset the risk of declining bond prices if interest rates rise. Prior to the 1970s, the maturity risk premium on 30-year bonds was about one percentage point, meaning that under normal conditions, a firm might expect to pay about one percentage point more to borrow on a long-term basis rather than on a short-term basis. However, in the early 1980s, the maturity risk premium is estimated to have jumped to about three percentage points, which made long-term debt very expensive relative to short-term debt. Lenders were able and willing to lend on a short-term basis, but corporations were correctly reluctant to borrow on a short-term basis to finance long-term assets—such action is extremely dangerous. Therefore, there was a situation in which lenders did not want to lend on a long-term basis, but corporations needed long-term money. The problem was solved by the introduction of long-term, floating rate debt.

FLOATING RATE BOND
A bond whose interest rate fluctuates with shifts in the general level of interest rates.

A typical **floating rate bond** works as follows. The coupon rate is set for, say, the initial six-month period, after which it is adjusted every six months based on some market rate. Some corporate issues have been tied to the Treasury bond rate, while other issues have been tied to short-term rates. Many additional provisions can be included in floating rate issues; for example, some are convertible to fixed rate debt, whereas others have upper and lower limits ("caps" and "collars") on how high or low the yield can go.

Floating rate debt is advantageous to investors because the interest rate moves up if market rates rise. This causes the market value of the debt to be stabilized, and it also provides lenders such as banks with income which is better geared to their own obligations. Moreover, floating rate debt is advantageous to corporations because by using it, firms can issue debt with a long maturity without committing themselves to paying a historically high rate of interest for the entire life of the loan. Of course, if interest rates were to move even higher after a floating rate note had been signed, the borrower would have been better off issuing conventional, fixed rate debt.

Junk Bonds

Prior to the 1980s, fixed-income investors such as pension funds and insurance companies generally were unwilling to buy risky bonds, so it was almost impossible for risky companies to raise capital in the public bond markets. These companies, if they could raise debt capital at all, had to do so in the term loan market, where the loan could be tailored to satisfy the lender. Then, in the late 1970s,

JUNK BOND
A high-risk, high-yield bond used to finance mergers, leveraged buyouts, and troubled companies.

Michael Milken of the investment banking firm Drexel Burnham Lambert, relying on historical studies which showed that risky bonds yielded more than enough to compensate for their risk, began to convince certain institutional investors of the merits of purchasing risky debt. Thus was born the **junk bond,** a high-risk, high-yield bond issued to finance a leveraged buyout (LBO), a merger, or a troubled company. For example, when Ted Turner attempted to buy CBS, he planned to finance the acquisition by issuing junk bonds to CBS's stockholders in exchange for their shares. Similarly, Public Service of New Hampshire financed construction of its troubled Seabrook nuclear plant with junk bonds, and junk bonds were used in the RJR Nabisco LBO. In junk bond deals, the debt ratio generally is extremely high, so the bondholders must bear as much risk as stockholders normally would. The bonds' yields reflect this fact—a coupon rate of 25 percent per annum was required to sell the Public Service of New Hampshire bonds.

The emergence of junk bonds as an important type of debt is another example of how the investment banking industry adjusts to and facilitates new developments in capital markets. In the 1980s, mergers and takeovers increased dramatically. People like T. Boone Pickens and Ted Turner thought that certain old-line, established companies were run inefficiently and were financed too conservatively, and they wanted to take these companies over and restructure them. Michael Milken and his staff at Drexel Burnham Lambert began an active campaign to persuade certain institutions (often S&Ls) to purchase high-yield bonds. Milken developed expertise in putting together deals that were attractive to the institutions yet apparently feasible in the sense that projected cash flows were sufficient to meet the required interest payments. The fact that interest on the bonds was tax deductible, combined with the much higher debt ratios of the restructured firms, also increased after-tax cash flows and helped make the deals appear feasible.

The development of junk bond financing has done as much as any single factor to reshape the U.S. financial scene. The existence of these securities led directly to the loss of independence of Gulf Oil and hundreds of other companies, and it led to major shake-ups in such companies as CBS, Union Carbide, and USX (formerly U.S. Steel). It also caused Drexel Burnham Lambert to leap from essentially nowhere in the 1970s to become the most profitable investment banking firm during the 1980s.

The phenomenal growth of the junk bond market was impressive, but controversial. Significant risk, combined with unscrupulous dealings, created significant losses for investors. In early 1989, Drexel Burnham Lambert was forced into bankruptcy, and "junk bond king" Michael Milken eventually was sent to jail for his role in misleading investors in the junk bond market. These events badly tarnished the junk bond market, which also came under severe criticism for fueling takeover fires and adding to the cost of the S&L bailout. Additionally, the realization that high leverage can spell trouble—as when Campeau, with $3 billion in junk financing, filed for bankruptcy in early 1990—has slowed the growth in the junk bond market.

Self-Test Questions

Explain how the cash flows related to an issue of zero coupon bonds are determined.

TABLE 19-1								

Moody's and S&P Bond Ratings

	High Quality		**Investment Grade**		**Junk Bonds**			
					Substandard		**Speculative**	
Moody's	Aaa	Aa	A	Baa	Ba	B	Caa	C
S&P	AAA	AA	A	BBB	BB	B	CCC	D

NOTE: Both Moody's and S&P use "modifiers" for bonds rated below triple A. S&P uses a plus and minus system; thus, A+ designates the strongest A-rated bonds and A− the weakest. Moody's uses a 1, 2, or 3 designation, with 1 denoting the strongest and 3 the weakest; thus, within the double-A category, Aa1 is the best, Aa2 is average, and Aa3 is the weakest.

What problem was solved by the introduction of long-term floating rate debt, and how is the rate on such bonds actually set?

For what purposes have junk bonds typically been used?

Bond Ratings

INVESTMENT GRADE BONDS
Bonds rated A or triple-B; many banks and other institutional investors are permitted by law to hold only investment grade or better bonds.

Since the early 1900s, bonds have been assigned quality ratings that reflect their probability of going into default. The two major rating agencies are Moody's Investors Service (Moody's) and Standard & Poor's Corporation (S&P). These agencies' rating designations are shown in Table 19-1.[4] The triple- and double-A bonds are extremely safe. Single-A and triple-B bonds are strong enough to be called **investment grade bonds,** and they are the lowest-rated bonds that many banks and other institutional investors are permitted by law to hold. Double-B and lower bonds are speculative, or junk bonds; they have a significant probability of going into default, and many financial institutions are prohibited from buying them.

Bond Rating Criteria

Bond ratings are based on both qualitative and quantitative factors. Some of the factors considered by the bond rating agencies include the financial strength of the company as measured by various ratios, collateral provisions, seniority of the debt, restrictive covenants, provisions such as a sinking fund or a deferred call, litigation possibilities, regulation, and so on. Representatives of the rating agencies have consistently stated that no precise formula is used to set a firm's rating; all the factors listed, plus others, are taken into account, but not in a mathematically precise manner. Statistical studies have borne out this contention, for researchers who have tried to predict bond ratings on the basis of quantitative data have had only limited success, indicating that the agencies use subjective judgment when establishing a firm's rating.[5]

[4]In the discussion to follow, reference to the S&P code is intended to imply the Moody's code as well. Thus, triple-B bonds mean both BBB and Baa bonds; double-B bonds mean both BB and Ba bonds; and so on.

[5]See Ahmed Belkaoui, *Industrial Bonds and the Rating Process* (London: Quorum Books, 1983).

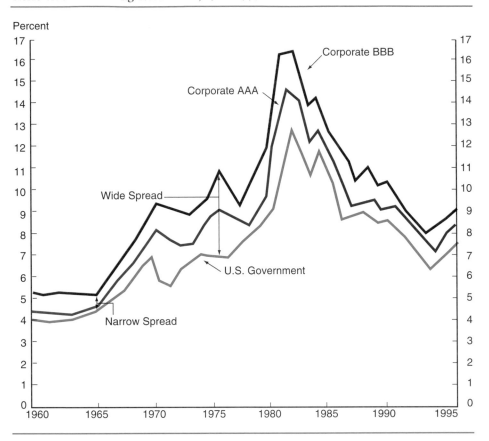

FIGURE 19-1

Yields on Selected Long-Term Bonds, 1960–1995

SOURCE: *Federal Reserve Bulletin,* various issues.

Importance of Bond Ratings

Bond ratings are important both to firms and to investors. First, because a bond's rating is an indicator of its default risk, the rating has a direct, measurable influence on the bond's interest rate and the firm's cost of debt. Second, most bonds are purchased by institutional investors rather than individuals, and many institutions are restricted to investment-grade securities. Thus, if a firm's bonds fall below BBB, it will have a difficult time selling new bonds because many potential purchasers will not be allowed to buy them.

As a result of their higher risk and more restricted market, lower-grade bonds have higher required rates of return, k_d, than high-grade bonds. Figure 19-1 illustrates this point. In each of the years shown on the graph, U.S. government bonds have had the lowest yields, corporate AAA have been next, and corporate BBB bonds have had the highest yields. The figure also shows that the gaps between yields on the three types of bonds vary over time, indicating that the cost differentials, or risk premiums, fluctuate from year to year. This point is highlighted in Figure 19-2, which gives the yields on the three types of bonds and the risk pre-

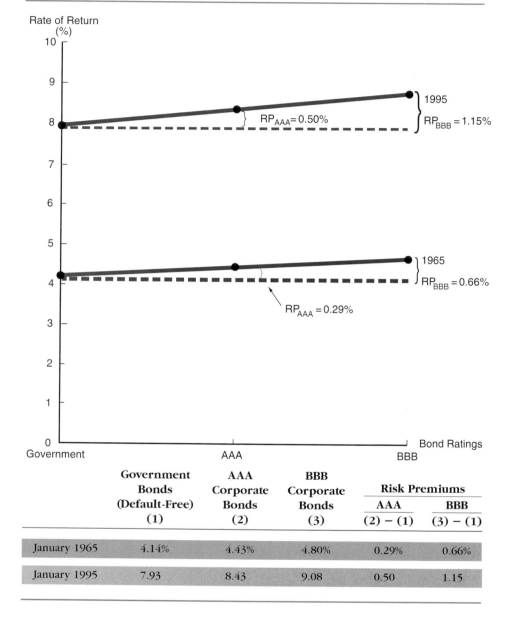

FIGURE 19-2

Relationship between Bond Ratings and Bond Yields, January 1965 and January 1995

	Government Bonds (Default-Free) (1)	AAA Corporate Bonds (2)	BBB Corporate Bonds (3)	Risk Premiums	
				AAA (2) − (1)	BBB (3) − (1)
January 1965	4.14%	4.43%	4.80%	0.29%	0.66%
January 1995	7.93	8.43	9.08	0.50	1.15

miums for AAA bonds and BBB bonds in January 1965 and January 1995.[6] Note first that the risk-free rate, or vertical axis intercept, rose more than 3¾ percentage points from 1965 to 1995, primarily reflecting the increase in realized and anticipated inflation. Second, the slope of the line also has increased since 1965, indicating an increase in investors' risk aversion. Thus, the penalty for having a

---

[6]The term *risk premium* should reflect only the difference in expected (and required) returns between two securities that results from differences in their risk. However, the differences between yields to maturity on different types of bonds consist of (1) a true risk premium; (2) a liquidity

low credit rating varies over time. Occasionally, as in 1965, the penalty is relatively small, but at other times, as in 1995, it is large. These slope differences reflect investors' risk aversion. In January 1995, there was fear of an increase in inflation, and at such times there is a "flight to quality," Treasuries are in great demand, and the premium on low-quality over high-quality bonds increases.

Changes in Ratings

Changes in a firm's bond rating affect both its ability to borrow long-term capital and the cost of that capital. Rating agencies review outstanding bonds on a periodic basis, occasionally upgrading or downgrading a bond as a result of its issuer's changed circumstances. For example, in February 1995, *Standard & Poor's CreditWeek* reported that Melville Corporation's medium-term debt ratings were lowered from AA− to A+, reflecting (1) the outlook that revenues from the company's apparel and footwear products were not expected to improve earnings from historically low levels, and (2) concerns about the tenuous operations of Kay-Bee Toys, a company owned by Melville. In the same month, S&P upgraded Arrow Electronics' subordinated debt from BB+ to BBB, because it was felt that the world's largest distributor of electronic components and computer products had successfully reduced its debt ratio and improved its coverage of interest, despite recent acquisitions of rival firms.

 Self-Test Questions

Name the two major rating agencies and some factors that affect bond ratings.

Why are bond ratings important both to firms and to investors?

Rationale for Using Different Types of Securities

Why are there so many different types of long-term securities? At least a partial answer to this question might be seen in Figure 19-3, which depicts the now familiar risk/return trade-off function drawn to show the risk and the expected after-tax returns for the various securities of Allied Air Products.[7] First, U.S. Treasury bills, which represent the risk-free rate, are shown for reference. The

---

premium, which reflects the fact that U.S. Treasury bonds are more readily marketable than most corporate bonds; (3) a call premium, because most Treasury bonds are not callable whereas corporate bonds are; and (4) an expected loss differential, which reflects the probability of loss on the corporate bonds. As an example of the last point, suppose the yield to maturity on a BBB bond was 10 percent versus 7 percent on government bonds, but there was a 5 percent probability of total default loss on the corporate bond. In this case, the expected return on the BBB bond would be 0.95(10%) + 0.05(0%) = 9.5%, and the risk premium would be 2.5 percent, not the full 3 percentage point difference in "promised" yields to maturity. Because of all these points, the risk premiums given in Figure 19-2 overstate somewhat the true (but unmeasurable) risk premiums.

[7]The yields in Figure 19-3 are shown on an after-tax basis to the recipient. If yields were on a before-tax basis, those on preferred stocks would lie below those on bonds because of the tax treatment of preferreds. In essence, 70 percent of preferred dividends are tax exempt to corporations owning preferred shares, so a preferred stock with a 10 percent pre-tax yield will have a higher after-tax return to a corporation in the 34 percent tax bracket than will a bond with a 12 percent yield.

FIGURE 19-3

Allied Air Products: Risk and Expected Returns on Different Classes of Securities

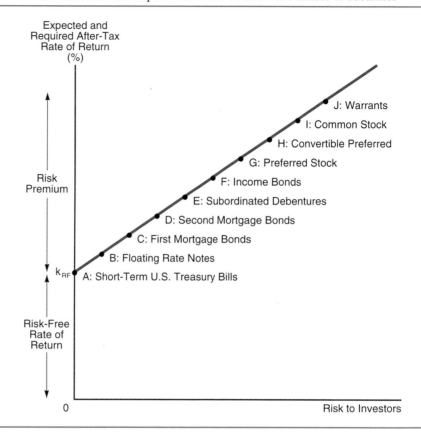

lowest-risk long-term securities offered by Allied are its floating rate notes; these securities are free of interest rate risk, but they are exposed to some risk of default. The first mortgage bonds are somewhat riskier than the notes (because the bonds are exposed to interest rate risk), and they sell at a somewhat higher required and expected after-tax return. The second mortgage bonds are even riskier, so they have a still higher expected return. Subordinated debentures, income bonds, and preferred stocks are all increasingly risky, and their expected returns increase accordingly. The firm's convertible preferred is riskier than its straight preferred, but less risky than its common stock. Allied's warrants, the riskiest security it issues, have the highest required return. (Preferred stock, warrants, and convertibles all will be discussed in Chapter 20.)

Why does Allied issue so many different classes of securities? Why not offer just one type of bond, plus common stock? The answer lies in the fact that different investors have different risk/return trade-off preferences, so to appeal to the broadest possible market, Allied must offer securities that attract as many different types of investors as possible. Also, different securities are more popular at different points in time, and firms tend to issue whatever is popular at the time they need money. Used wisely, a policy of selling differentiated securities to take advantage of market conditions can lower a firm's overall cost of capital below what it would be if the firm used only one class of debt.

Self-Test Questions

List the different types of securities in order of highest to lowest risk.

Why do corporations issue so many different classes of securities?

Factors Influencing Long-Term Financing Decisions

As we show in this section, many factors influence a firm's long-term financing decisions. The factors' relative importance varies among firms at any point in time and for any given firm over time, but any company planning to raise new long-term capital should consider each of these points.

Target Capital Structure

As we discussed in Chapter 16, firms typically establish target capital structures, and one of the most important considerations in any financing decision is how the firm's actual capital structure compares to its target structure. However, few firms finance each year exactly in accordance with their target capital structures, primarily because exact adherence would increase their flotation costs: Because smaller issues of new securities have proportionally larger flotation costs, firms tend to use debt one year and equity the next.

Making fewer but larger security offerings would cause a firm's capital structure to fluctuate above and below its optimal level rather than stay right on target. However, as we discussed in Chapter 16, small fluctuations about the optimal capital structure have little effect either on a firm's cost of debt and equity or on its overall cost of capital. Also, investors would recognize that its actions were prudent and that the firm would save substantial amounts of flotation costs by financing in this manner. Therefore, even though firms do tend to finance over the long haul in accordance with their target capital structures, flotation costs have a definite influence on the specific financing decisions in any given year.

Maturity Matching

Assume that Allied Air Products decides to float a single $13.5 million nonconvertible bond issue with a sinking fund. It must next choose a maturity for the issue, taking into consideration the shape of the yield curve, management's own expectations about future interest rates, and the maturity of the assets being financed. In the case at hand, Allied's capital projects during the next two years consist primarily of new, automated manufacturing equipment. This equipment has an expected economic life of 10 years (even though it falls into the MACRS 5-year class life). Should Allied finance the debt portion of the capital raised for this equipment with 5-year, 10-year, 20-year, or 30-year debt, or with debt of some other maturity? *One approach is to match the maturity of the liabilities with the maturity of the assets being financed.*

Note that some of the new capital for the machinery will come from common stock, which generally is considered to be a perpetual security with an infinite maturity. Of course, common stock always can be repurchased in the open market or by other means, so its effective maturity can be reduced significantly, but generally it has no maturity.

Debt maturities, however, are specified at the time of issue. If Allied financed its capital budgets over the next two years with 10-year sinking fund bonds, it would be matching its asset and liability maturities. The cash flows resulting from the new machinery should be sufficient to make the interest and sinking fund payments on the issue, and the bonds would be retired as the machinery wore out. If Allied used 1-year debt, it would have to pay off the loan with cash flows derived from assets other than the machinery in question. If its operations were stable, the company probably could roll over the 1-year debt, but if interest rates rose, then it would have to pay a higher rate. If Allied subsequently experienced difficulties, its lenders might be hesitant to extend the loan, and the company might be unable to obtain new short-term debt at any reasonable rate. At the other extreme, if it used 20-year or 30-year debt, Allied still would have to service the debt long after the assets purchased with the debt had been scrapped and had ceased providing cash flows, and this would worry potential lenders.

For all these reasons, one commonly used financing strategy is to match debt maturities with asset maturities. In recognition of this fact, firms do consider maturity relationships, and this factor has a major influence on the type of debt securities used.

Interest Rate Levels

Financial managers also consider interest rate levels, both absolute and relative, when making financing decisions. For example, long-term interest rates were high by historic standards in 1981 and 1982, so many managers were reluctant to issue long-term debt and thus lock in those high costs for long periods. We already know that one solution to this problem is to use long-term debt with a call provision. Callability permits the company to refund the issue should interest rates drop, as they did in 1993. But there is a cost, because firms must pay more if they make their debt callable. Alternatively, a firm might finance with short-term debt whenever long-term rates are historically high, and then, assuming that interest rates subsequently fall, sell a long-term issue to replace the short-term debt. Of course, this strategy has its risks. If interest rates climb even higher, the firm will be forced to renew the short-term debt at higher and higher rates, or to replace the short-term debt with a long-term bond which costs more than it would have cost earlier.

Forecasted Interest Rates

At a time when the interest rate on AAA corporate bonds was over 10 percent, which was high by historical standards, Exxon's investment bankers advised the company to tap the Eurodollar bond market for relatively cheap fixed rate financing.[8] At the time, Exxon could have issued its bonds in London at 0.4 percentage points *below* comparable-maturity Treasury bonds. However, one Exxon officer was quoted as cautioning, "I say so what. The absolute level of rates is too high. We would rather wait." The managers of Exxon, as well as those of many other companies, were betting that the next move in interest rates would be down

---

[8]A *Eurodollar bond* is a bond sold outside the United States but denominated in U.S. dollars.

This example illustrates that firms do base their financing decisions on expectations about future interest rates. In Exxon's case, the financial staff turned out to be correct. However, the success of such a strategy requires interest rate forecasts to be right more often than they are wrong, and it is very difficult to find someone with a long-term forecasting record better than 50-50.

The Firm's Current and Forecasted Conditions

If a firm's current financial condition is poor, its managers might be reluctant to issue new long-term debt, because (1) a new bond issue probably would trigger a review by the rating agencies, and (2) long-term debt issued when a firm is in poor financial condition costs more and is subject to more severe restrictive covenants than debt issued from a strong position. Thus, a firm that is in a weakened condition but which is forecasting an improvement would be inclined to delay permanent financing until things improved. Conversely, a firm that is strong now but whose forecasts indicate a potentially bad time just ahead would be motivated to finance long term now rather than to wait. These scenarios imply that the capital markets are inefficient in the sense that investors do not have as much information about the firm's future as does its management. This situation undoubtedly is true at times.

The firm's earnings outlook, and the extent to which forecasted higher earnings per share are reflected in stock prices, also has an effect on the choice of securities. If a successful research and development program has just been concluded, and, consequently, management forecasts higher earnings than do most investors, the firm would not want to issue common stock. It would use debt, and then, after earnings had risen and pushed up the stock price, it would sell common stock to restore the capital structure to its target level.

Restrictions in Existing Debt Contracts

Earlier we discussed the fact that Savannah Electric has at times been restricted from issuing new first mortgage bonds by its indenture coverage requirements. This is just one example of how indenture covenants can influence a firm's financing decisions. Restrictions on the current ratio, the debt ratio, and so on, can also restrict a firm's ability to use different types of financing at a given time.

Availability of Collateral

Generally, secured long-term debt will be less costly than unsecured debt. Thus, firms with large amounts of general-purpose (as opposed to specialized) fixed assets are likely to use a relatively large amount of debt, especially mortgage bonds. Additionally, each year's financing decision will be influenced by the amount of newly acquired assets that are available as security for new bonds.

Self-Test Questions

Do most firms finance each year exactly in accordance with their target capital structures? Why or why not?

Why is the matching of debt maturities with asset maturities a commonly used financing strategy?

If a firm's current financial condition is expected to improve shortly, why might its managers be reluctant to issue new long-term debt?

Which type of firm is more likely to use a relatively large amount of debt, a firm with general-purpose fixed assets or one with specialized fixed assets? Explain.

Bankruptcy and Reorganization

During recessions bankruptcies normally rise, and the recession of 1991–1992 was no exception. The 1991–1992 casualties included Pan Am, Carter Hawley Hale Stores, Continental Airlines, R. H. Macy & Company, Zale Corporation, and McCrory Corporation. Because of its importance, at least a brief discussion of bankruptcy is warranted within the chapter.

When a business becomes *insolvent,* it does not have enough cash to meet scheduled interest and principal payments. A decision must then be made whether to dissolve the firm through *liquidation* or to permit it to *reorganize* and thus stay alive. These issues are addressed in Chapter 7 and Chapter 11 of the federal bankruptcy statutes, and the final decision is made by a federal bankruptcy court judge.

The decision to force a firm to liquidate or to permit it to reorganize depends on whether the value of the reorganized firm is likely to be greater than the value of the firm's assets if they were sold off piecemeal. In a reorganization, a committee of unsecured creditors is appointed by the court to negotiate with management on the terms of a potential reorganization. The reorganization plan might call for a *restructuring* of the firm's debt, in which case the interest rate might be reduced, the term to maturity lengthened, or some of the debt might be exchanged for equity. The point of the restructuring is to reduce the financial charges to a level that the firm's cash flows can support. Of course, the common stockholders also have to give up something—they normally see their position eroded as a result of additional shares being given to debtholders in exchange for accepting a reduced amount of debt principal and interest. A trustee might be appointed by the court to oversee the reorganization, or the existing management might be allowed to retain control.

Liquidation occurs if the company is deemed to be too far gone to be saved— if it is worth more dead than alive. If the bankruptcy court orders a liquidation, assets are distributed as specified in Chapter 7 of the Bankruptcy Act. As a rule, proceeds are distributed to secured creditors first, then wages and taxes are paid; the remaining proceeds are distributed in order to unsecured creditors, to preferred stockholders, and finally to common stockholders, if anything is left. The priority of claims established by federal bankruptcy statutes *must* be followed when distributing the proceeds from a liquidated firm.

Self-Test Questions

When a business becomes insolvent, what two alternatives are available?

Differentiate between a liquidation and a reorganization.

In the case of liquidation who gets paid first and who gets paid last?

Refunding Operations

A great deal of long-term debt was issued at very high interest rates during the late 1970s and early 1980s. Since then, interest rates have fallen, and the call protection periods of many bonds have expired. As a result, corporations and government units are retiring old bonds and replacing them with lower interest rate new bonds—this process is termed *refunding.*

Bond refunding analysis is similar to capital budgeting analysis, as discussed in Chapters 13 and 14. Also, bond refunding can be compared to the process individuals go through to refinance a house—an existing debt (mortgage) with a high interest rate is replaced by a new debt (mortgage) with a lower interest rate.

The refunding decision actually involves two separate questions: (1) Would it be profitable to call an outstanding issue now and to replace it with a new issue? (2) Even if refunding currently is profitable, would it be better to call now or to postpone the refunding to a later date?

As noted above, refunding decisions are similar to capital budgeting decisions, and the net present value method is the primary tool that should be used. In essence, the costs of undertaking the refunding operation (the investment outlay) are compared to the present value of the interest that will be saved if the high interest rate bond is called and replaced with a new, low interest rate bond. If the net present value of refunding is positive, then the refunding should take place. The costs of the refunding operation consist primarily of the call premium on the old bond issue and the flotation costs associated with selling the new issue. The cash flow benefits consist primarily of the interest expenses that will be saved if the company replaces high-cost debt with low-cost debt. The discount rate used to find the present value of the interest savings is the after-tax cost of new debt—the interest saved is the difference between two relatively certain cash flow streams, so the difference essentially is riskless. Therefore, a low discount rate should be used, and that rate is today's after-tax cost of new debt in the market.

To illustrate the refunding decision, consider the Strasburg Communications Corporation, which has a $100 million, 13 percent, semiannual coupon bond outstanding with 10 years remaining to maturity. The bond has a call provision that permits the company to retire the issue by calling in the bonds at an 8 percent call premium. Investment bankers have assured Strasburg that it could issue an additional $100 million of new 10 percent coupon, 10-year bonds that pay interest semiannually. Flotation costs on the new refunding issue will amount to $4,000,000. Predictions are that long-term interest rates are unlikely to fall below 10 percent. Strasburg's marginal tax rate is 40 percent. Should the company refund the $100 million of 13 percent semiannual coupon bonds?

Strasburg's refunding analysis is presented in Table 19-2. Because the marginal tax rate is 40 percent, the company's after-tax cost of new debt is equal to 6 percent, or 3 percent per 6-month period. And, because the bonds have semiannual coupons, there will be 20 semiannual periods in the analysis.

The net present value of refunding is positive, so Strasburg should refund the old bond issue—the firm's value will be increased by $1,389,727 if the old bond is retired.

TABLE 19-2

NPV Refunding Analysis

> **Cost of Refunding at t = 0**
>
> | | |
> |---|---:|
> | Call premium on old bond (0.08 × $100 million) | $ 8,000,000 |
> | Flotation costs on new issue | 4,000,000 |
> | Total initial outlay | $ 12,000,000 |
>
> **Semiannual Interest Savings Due to Refunding: t = 1 to 20**
>   **(10 years of payments twice a year)**
>
> | | |
> |---|---:|
> | Interest on old bond [(0.13/2) × $100 million] | $ 6,500,000 |
> | Interest on new bond [(0.10/2) × $100 million] | 5,000,000 |
> | Interest savings per period | $ 1,500,000 |
> | Increased taxes due to lower interest payment[a] | |
> | (0.40 × $1,500,000) | $(600,000) |
> | Net interest savings | $ 900,000 |
>
> **Refunding Time Line:**
>
> | | | 1 | 10 Year |
> |---|---|---|---|
> | 0 | k = 3%   1 | 2 | 20 Interest period |
>
> | | | | | | |
> |---|---:|---:|---:|---|---:|
> | Initial outlay | (12,000,000) | | | | |
> | Interest savings | 0 | 900,000 | 900,000 | ··· | 900,000 |
> | Net cash flow | (12,000,000) | 900,000 | 900,000 | ··· | 900,000 |
>
> NPV of refunding at $k_{dT}/2$ = [0.10 (1 − 0.40)]/2 = 3% is $1,389,727

---

[a]Strasburg's interest expense will decrease by $1,500,000, thus taxable income will increase by $1,500,000, if the new bond is issued. Strasburg will have to pay 0.40 × $1,500,000 = $600,000 additional taxes on this increased taxable income.

Self-Test Questions

In what respects is bond refunding analysis similar to capital budgeting analysis?

What two questions are involved in the bond refunding decision?

What are the primary costs and the primary benefits in a bond refunding analysis?

Why is the after-tax cost of debt used as the discount rate in a bond refunding analysis?

Summary

This chapter described the characteristics, advantages, and disadvantages of the major types of long-term debt securities. The key concepts covered are listed below.

- **Term loans** and **bonds** are long-term debt contracts under which a borrower agrees to make a series of interest and principal payments on specific dates to the lender. A term loan generally is sold to one lender (or a few), while a bond typically is offered to the public and sold to many different investors.

- There are many different types of bonds. They include **mortgage bonds, debentures, convertibles, bonds with warrants, income bonds, putable bonds,** and **purchasing power (indexed) bonds.** The return required on each type of bond is determined by the bond's riskiness.

- A bond's **indenture** is a legal document that spells out the rights of the bondholders and of the issuing corporation. A **trustee** is assigned to make sure that the terms of the indenture are carried out.

- A **call provision** gives the issuing corporation the right to redeem the bonds prior to maturity under specified terms, usually at a price greater than the maturity value (the difference is a **call premium**). A firm typically will call a bond and refund it if interest rates fall substantially.

- A **sinking fund** is a provision that requires the corporation to retire a portion of the bond issue each year. The purpose of the sinking fund is to provide for the orderly retirement of the issue.

- Some innovations in long-term financing include **zero coupon bonds,** which pay no annual interest but which are issued at a discount; **floating rate debt,** whose interest payments fluctuate with changes in the general level of interest rates; and **junk bonds,** which are high-risk, high-yield instruments issued by firms which use a great deal of financial leverage.

- Bonds are assigned **ratings** that reflect the probability of their going into default. The higher a bond's rating, the less risky it is considered, so the lower its interest rate.

- A firm's long-term financing decisions are influenced by its **target capital structure,** the **maturity of its assets,** current and forecasted **interest rate levels,** the firm's current and forecasted **financial condition, restrictions** in its existing debt contracts, and the suitability of its assets for use as **collateral.**

- **Bankruptcy** is an important consideration both to companies that issue debt and to investors, for it has a profound effect on all parties. **Refunding,** or paying off high interest rate debt with new, lower cost debt, also is an important consideration, because many firms that issued long-term debt in the early 1980s at rates of 12 percent or more now have an opportunity to refund this debt at a cost of about 9 percent or less.

Questions

19-1   What effect would each of the following items have on the interest rate a firm must pay on a new issue of long-term debt? Indicate whether each factor would tend to raise, lower, or have an indeterminate effect on the interest rate, and then explain why.

   a. The firm uses bonds rather than a term loan.
   b. The firm uses nonsubordinated debentures rather than first mortgage bonds.
   c. The firm makes its bonds convertible into common stock.
   d. If the firm makes its debentures subordinate to its bank debt, what will the effect be
      (1) On the cost of the debentures?
      (2) On the cost of the bank debt?
      (3) On the average cost of total debt?
   e. The firm sells income bonds rather than debentures.

    f. The firm must raise $100 million, all of which will be used to construct a new plant, and it is debating the sale of first mortgage bonds or debentures. If it decides to issue $50 million of each type, as opposed to $75 million of first mortgage bonds and $25 million of debentures, how will this affect

        (1) The cost of debentures?

        (2) The cost of mortgage bonds?

        (3) The weighted average cost of the $100 million?

    g. The firm puts a call provision on its new issue of bonds.

    h. The firm includes a sinking fund on its new issue of bonds.

    i. The firm's bonds are downgraded from A to BBB.

19-2 Rank the following securities from lowest (1) to highest (8) in terms of their riskiness for an investor. All securities (except the Treasury bond) are for a given firm. If you think two or more securities are equally risky, indicate so.

    a. income bond   _____

    b. subordinated debentures—noncallable   _____

    c. first mortgage bond—no sinking fund   _____

    d. common stock   _____

    e. U.S. Treasury bond   _____

    f. first mortgage bond—with sinking fund   _____

    g. subordinated debentures—callable   _____

    h. term loan   _____

19-3 A sinking fund can be set up in one of two ways:

    (1) The corporation makes annual payments to the trustee, who invests the proceeds in securities (frequently government bonds) and uses the accumulated total to retire the bond issue at maturity.

    (2) The trustee uses the annual payments to retire a portion of the issue each year, either calling a given percentage of the issue by a lottery and paying a specified price per bond or buying bonds on the open market, whichever is cheaper.

Discuss the advantages and disadvantages of each procedure from the viewpoint of both the firm and its bondholders.

19-4 Draw an SML graph. Put a dot on the graph to show (approximately) where you think a particular company's bonds would lie. Add a dot to represent a riskier company's bonds.

Self-Test Problems

(Solutions Appear in Appendix B)

Key terms   **ST-1** Define each of the following terms:

    a. funded debt

    b. term loan; bond

    c. mortgage bond

    d. debenture; subordinated debenture

    e. convertible bond; warrant; income bond; putable bond; indexed, or purchasing power, bond

    f. indenture; restrictive covenant

    g. trustee

    h. call provision; sinking fund

    i. zero coupon bond; original issue discount bond (OID)

    j. floating rate bond

    k. junk bond

    l. investment grade bonds

    m. maturity matching

Sinking fund   **ST-2**   The Vancouver Development Company has just sold a $100 million, 10-year, 12 percent bond issue. A sinking fund will retire the issue over its life. Sinking fund payments are of equal amounts and will be made *semiannually,* and the proceeds will be used to retire bonds as the payments are made. Bonds can be called at par for sinking fund purposes, or the funds paid into the sinking fund can be used to buy bonds in the open market.

a. How large must each semiannual sinking fund payment be?

b. What will happen, under the conditions of the problem thus far, to the company's debt service requirements per year for this issue over time?

c. Now suppose Vancouver Development set up its sinking fund so that equal annual amounts, payable at the end of each year, are paid into a sinking fund trust held by a bank, with the proceeds being used to buy government bonds that pay 9 percent interest. The payments, plus accumulated interest, must total $100 million at the end of 10 years, and the proceeds will be used to retire the bonds at that time. How large must the annual sinking fund payment be now?

d. What are the annual cash requirements for covering bond service costs under the trusteeship arrangement described in Part c? (Note: Interest must be paid on Vancouver's outstanding bonds but not on bonds that have been retired.)

e. What would have to happen to interest rates to cause the company to buy bonds on the open market rather than call them under the original sinking fund plan?

Problems

Perpetual bond analysis   **19-1**   In 1936 the Canadian government raised $55 million by issuing bonds at a 3 percent annual rate of interest. Unlike most bonds issued today, which have a specific maturity date, these bonds can remain outstanding forever; they are, in fact, perpetuities.

At the time of issue, the Canadian government stated in the bond indenture that cash redemption was possible at face value ($100) on or after September 1966; in other words, the bonds were callable at par after September 1966. Believing that the bonds would in fact be called, many investors purchased these bonds in 1965 with expectations of receiving $100 in 1966 for each perpetual bond they had. In 1965 the bonds sold for $55, but a rush of buyers drove the price to just below the $100 par value by 1966. Prices fell dramatically, however, when the Canadian government announced that these perpetual bonds were indeed perpetual and would not be paid off.

The bonds' market price declined to $42 in December 1966. Because of their severe losses, hundreds of Canadian bondholders formed the Perpetual Bond Association to lobby for face value redemption of the bonds, claiming that the government had reneged on an implied promise to redeem the bonds. Government officials in Ottawa insisted that claims for face value payment were nonsense, for the bonds were and always had been clearly identified as perpetuals. One Ottawa official stated, "Our job is to protect the taxpayer. Why should we pay $55 million for less than $25 million worth of bonds?"

Here are some questions relating to the Canadian issue that will test your understanding of bonds in general:

a. Would it make sense for a business firm to issue bonds like the Canadian government bonds described here? Would it matter whether the firm was a proprietorship or a corporation?

b. Suppose the U.S. government today sold $100 million each of these four types of bonds: 5-year bonds, 50-year bonds, "regular" perpetuities, and Canadian-type perpetuities. Rank the bonds from the one with the lowest to the one with the highest expected interest rate. Explain your answer.

c. (1) Suppose that because of pressure by the Perpetual Bond Association, you believe that the Canadian government will redeem this particular perpetual bond issue in 4 years. Which course of action would be more advantageous to you if you owned the bonds: (a) sell your bonds today at $55.99, or (b) wait 4 years and have them redeemed? Assume that similar-risk bonds earn 9 percent today and that interest rates are expected to remain at this level for the next 4 years.

   (2) If you had the opportunity to invest your money in bonds of similar risk, at what rate of return would you be indifferent to the choice of selling your perpetuals today or having them redeemed in 4 years—that is, what is the expected yield to maturity on the Canadian bonds?

d. Show mathematically the perpetuities' value if they yield 6.1 percent, pay $3 interest annually, and are considered "regular" perpetuities. Show what would happen to the price of the bonds if the going interest rate fell to 2 percent.

e. Are the Canadian bonds more likely to be valued as "regular" perpetuities if the going rate of interest is above or below 3 percent? Why?

f. Do you think the Canadian government would have taken the same action with regard to retiring the bonds if the interest rate had fallen rather than risen after they were issued?

g. Do you think the Canadian government was fair or unfair in its actions? Give the pros and cons, and justify your reason for thinking that one outweighs the other. Would it matter if the bonds had been sold to "sophisticated" as opposed to "naive" purchasers?

Zero coupon bond   **19-2**   Filkins Farm Equipment needs to raise $4.5 million for expansion, and its investment bankers have indicated that 5-year zero coupon bonds could be sold at a price of $567.44 for each $1,000 bond. Filkins's marginal tax rate is 40 percent.

a. How many $1,000 par value zero coupon bonds would Filkins have to sell to raise the needed $4.5 million?

b. What would be the after-tax yield on the zeros (1) to an investor who is tax exempt and (2) to a taxpayer in the 31 percent marginal tax bracket?

c. What would be the after-tax cost of debt to Filkins if it decides to issue the zeros?

Exam-Type Problems

The problems included in this section are set up in such a way that they could be used as multiple-choice exam problems.

Loan payment computation   **19-3**   Suppose a firm is setting up a term loan. What are the annual payments for a $10 million loan under the following terms:

a. 8 percent, 5 years?

b. 8 percent, 10 years?

c. 14 percent, 5 years?

d. 14 percent, 10 years?

Yield to call   **19-4**   Six years ago The Parrish Company sold a 19-year bond issue with a 14 percent annual coupon rate and a 9 percent call premium. Today Parrish called the bonds. The bonds originally were sold at their face value of $1,000. Compute the realized rate of return for investors who purchased the bonds when they were issued and who surrender them today in exchange for the call price.

EAR on zero coupon bonds   **19-5**   Assume that the city of Tampa sold an issue of $1,000 maturity value, tax-exempt (muni), zero coupon bonds 3 years ago. The bonds had a 25-year maturity when they were issued, and the interest rate built into the issue was a simple 10 percent, but with semiannual compounding. The bonds are now callable at a premium of

10 percent over the *accrued value*. What effective annual rate of return would an investor who bought the bonds when they were issued and who still owns them earn if they are called today?

Bond refunding   **19-6**   The city of Gainesville issued $1,000,000 of 14 percent coupon, 30-year, semi-annual payment, tax-exempt muni bonds 10 years ago. The bonds had 10 years of call protection, but now Gainesville can call the bonds if it chooses to do so. The call premium would be 10 percent of the face amount. New 20-year, 12 percent, semiannual payment bonds can be sold at par, but flotation costs on this issue would be 2 percent, or $20,000. What is the net present value of the refunding? (HINT: Approach this problem just like the capital budgeting problems in Chapters 13 and 14.)

Integrative Problem

Long-term debt financing   **19-7**   Hospital Development Corporation (HDC) needs $10 million to build a regional testing laboratory in Birmingham. Once the lab is completed and fully operational, which should take about 5 years, HDC will sell it to a health maintenance organization (HMO). HDC tentatively plans to raise the $10 million by selling 5-year bonds, and its investment bankers have indicated that either regular or zero coupon bonds can be used. Regular coupon bonds would sell at par and would have annual payment coupons of 12 percent, and zero coupon bonds would also be priced to yield 12 percent annually. Either bond would be callable after 3 years, on the anniversary date of the issue, at a premium of 6 months' interest for the regular bonds or 5 percent over the accrued value on the call date for zero coupon bonds. HDC's marginal tax rate is 40 percent. As assistant to HDC's treasurer, you have been assigned the task of making a recommendation as to which type of bonds to issue. As part of your analysis, you have been asked to answer the following questions.

a. What is the difference between a bond and a term loan? What are the advantages of a term loan over a bond?

b. Suppose HDC issues bonds and uses the medical center (land and buildings) as collateral to secure the issue. What type of bond would this be? Suppose that instead of using secured bonds HDC had decided to sell debentures. How would this affect the interest rate that HDC would have to pay on the $10 million of debt?

c. What is a bond indenture? What are some typical provisions the bondholders would require HDC to include in its indenture?

d. HDC's bonds will be callable after 3 years. If the bonds were not callable, would the required interest rate be higher or lower than 12 percent? What would be the effect on the rate if the bonds were callable immediately? What are the advantages to HDC of making the bonds callable?

e. (1) Suppose HDC's indenture included a sinking fund provision which required the company to retire one-fifth of the bonds each year. Would this provision raise or lower the interest rate required on the bonds?

   (2) How would the sinking fund operate?

   (3) Why might HDC's investors require it to use a sinking fund?

   (4) For this particular issue, would it make sense to include a sinking fund?

f. If HDC were to issue zero coupon bonds, what initial price would cause the zeros to have an annual (EAR) return of 12 percent? How many $1,000 par value zeros would HDC have to sell to raise the needed $10 million? How many regular 12 percent coupon bonds would HDC have to sell?

g. Set up a time line which shows the accrued value of the zeros at the end of Years 1 through 5, along with the annual after-tax cash flows from the zeros

(1) to an investor in the 28 percent tax bracket and (2) to HDC. (HINT: The investor has to pay taxes on the annual *accrued value increase* of the bonds.)

h. What would be the after-tax yield to maturity on each type of bond to an investor in the 28 percent tax bracket? What would be the after-tax cost of debt to HDC?

i. If interest rates were to fall, causing HDC to call the bonds (either the zero or the coupon) at the end of Year 3, what would be the after-tax yield to call on each type of bond to an investor in the 28 percent tax bracket?

j. HDC is an A-rated firm. Suppose HDC's bond rating was (1) lowered to triple-B or (2) raised to double-A. Who would make these changes, and what would the changes mean? What would be the effect of these changes on the interest rate required on HDC's new long-term debt and on the market value of HDC's outstanding debt?

k. What are some of the factors a firm like HDC should consider when deciding whether to issue long-term debt, short-term debt, or equity? Why might long-term debt be HDC's best choice for this project?

l. What is meant by the terms *default, insolvent, liquidation, reorganization, bankruptcy, Chapter 11,* and *Chapter 7*?

m. In what sense is a bond refunding decision similar to a capital budgeting decision?

CHAPTER 20

Alternative Financing Arrangements and Corporate Restructuring

The growth of convertible securities, which are financial assets that can be exchanged for such other financial assets as common stock, has been phenomenal during the last decade. In 1994, the market for convertibles was more than $125 billion, an increase of nearly 360 percent from ten years earlier. Convertible bonds and convertible preferred stock are the most popular convertible securities—new issues of these convertibles increased by more than 375 percent from 1990 to 1993.

Many firms use convertibles because they feel that funds can be raised more cheaply than with "straight" debt or preferred stock. For example, in 1989, MCI Corporation issued $1.3 billion of convertible bonds at rates that were significantly lower than non-convertible debt. The price of MCI's stock never reached the point where it was attractive for investors to convert, so the bonds were called by the company in 1993 when market interest rates were extremely low. Home Depot issued more than $800 million of convertible debt in 1992. The coupon interest rate of 4.5 percent was 1.5 percent lower than most top-rated convertibles issued at that time, and more than 3.5 percent lower than the average rate of AAA rated, non-convertible debt. Even at such a low rate, the issue was extremely well received by investors. Home Depot expects its convertible debt to be retired when the price of its common stock increases.

Convertibles are attractive to investors because they offer the opportunity to earn the substantial returns available with stocks, but they also offer the stability associated with debt. From 1991 through 1993, convertibles provided double-digit returns to investors. But, in 1994, the market for convertibles was hit hard from both sides—interest rates increased substantially, which lowered the values of bonds, and, at the same time, the performance of the stock market was poor. Consequently, the market for convertibles also suffered. Selling pressure resulted in an average loss of about 5 percent on convertible investments. For example, in January 1994, Boston Chicken,

Continued

which was trading at a phenomenal price-to-earnings ratio of 100, issued $130 million of convertible bonds with a coupon interest of 4.5 percent. On the first day of trading, the value of the issues decreased 5 percent; by the end of the year, the convertible issue was trading at 70 percent of its face value.

In the spring of 1995, the market for convertibles appeared to be picking up. At that time, investors could benefit from the depressed values carried over from 1994—many convertibles were selling at discounts ranging from 10 to 20 percent. In addition, companies found that much of the money that was taken out of the convertibles' market in 1994 was available to fund new issues in 1995.

As the financial markets strengthen, convertibles gain popularity; but, when the financial markets weaken, selling pressure results and convertibles lose favor with investors. Like other financial assets, convertibles are risky—most experts would caution investors not to put large portions of their investments in convertible securities; diversify instead. Once you have read this chapter and understand the concepts presented, you should be able to make informed decisions regarding convertibles, as well as preferred stock and other "hybrid" securities.

In the two preceding chapters, we examined the use of common stock and various types of debt. In this chapter, we examine some other types of long-term financing arrangements used by financial managers. We give only fundamental descriptions of these alternative sources of financing to enlighten you that a variety of means by which a firm can raise funds does exist. The fact is there are many variations and combinations of financial assets that exist today, and it would take multiple volumes to describe them all. Firms often engage in "creative financing" when seeking different ways to attract investors, so you should not be surprised to see new forms of financing emerge on a continuous basis. In addition, because firms have become extremely "creative" when determining how to finance mergers and acquisitions, we briefly discuss mergers and merger activity at the end of the chapter.

The purpose of this chapter is to provide you with a basic understanding of (1) some financing techniques we have not discussed in previous chapters, and (2) corporate restructuring through mergers and leveraged buyouts. If you want more in-depth discussions, you should look in either an upper-level corporate finance text or an investments text.

Preferred Stock

Preferred stock is a *hybrid* security—it is similar to bonds in some respects and to common stock in others. The hybrid nature of preferred stock becomes apparent when we try to classify it in relation to bonds and common stock. Like bonds, preferred stock has a par value. Preferred dividends also are similar to interest payments in that they are fixed in amount and generally must be paid before common stock dividends can be paid. However, if the preferred dividend is not earned, the directors can omit (or "pass") it without throwing the company into bankruptcy. So, although preferred stock has a fixed payment like bonds, a failure to make this payment will not lead to bankruptcy.

Accountants classify preferred stock as equity and report it in the equity portion of the balance sheet under "preferred stock" or "preferred equity." However, financial analysts sometimes treat preferred stock as debt and sometimes as equity, depending on the type of analysis being made. If the analysis is being made by a common stockholder, the key consideration is the fact that the preferred dividend is a fixed charge which reduces the amount that can be distributed to common shareholders, so from the common stockholder's point of view preferred stock is similar to debt. Suppose, however, that the analysis is being made by a bondholder studying the firm's vulnerability to failure in the event of a decline in sales and income. If the firm's income declines, the debtholders have a prior claim to the available income ahead of preferred stockholders, and if the firm fails, debtholders have a prior claim to assets when the firm is liquidated. Thus, to a bondholder, preferred stock is similar to common equity.

From management's perspective, preferred stock lies between debt and common equity. Because failure to pay dividends on preferred stock will not force the firm into bankruptcy, preferred stock is safer to use than debt. At the same time, if the firm is highly successful, the common stockholders will not have to share that success with the preferred stockholders because preferred dividends are fixed. Remember, however, that the preferred stockholders do have a higher priority claim than the common stockholders. We see, then, that preferred stock has some of the characteristics of debt and some of the characteristics of common stock, and it is used in situations in which conditions are such that neither debt nor common stock is entirely appropriate.

Major Provisions of Preferred Stock Issues

Preferred stock has a number of features, the most important of which are discussed in the following sections.

PRIORITY TO ASSETS AND EARNINGS   Preferred stockholders have priority over common stockholders with regard to earnings and assets. Thus, dividends must be paid on preferred stock before they can be paid on the common stock, and, in the event of bankruptcy, the claims of the preferred shareholders must be satisfied before the common stockholders receive anything. To reinforce these features, most preferred stocks have coverage requirements similar to those on bonds. These restrictions limit the amount of preferred stock a company can use, and they also require a minimum level of retained earnings before common dividends can be paid.

PAR VALUE   Unlike common stock, preferred stock always has a par value (or its equivalent under some other name), and this value is important. First, the par value establishes the amount due the preferred stockholders in the event of liquidation. Second, the preferred dividend frequently is stated as a percentage of the par value. For example, an issue of Duke Power's preferred stock has a par value of $100 and a stated dividend of 7.8 percent of par. The same results would, of course, be produced if this issue of Duke's preferred stock simply called for an annual dividend of $7.80.

CUMULATIVE DIVIDENDS
A protective feature on preferred stock that requires preferred dividends previously not paid to be paid before any common dividends can be paid.

CUMULATIVE DIVIDENDS   Most preferred stock provides for **cumulative dividends;** that is, any preferred dividends not paid in previous periods must be paid before common dividends can be paid. The cumulative feature is a protective device, for if the preferred stock dividends were not cumulative, a firm could avoid paying preferred and common stock dividends for, say, 10 years, plowing back all its earnings, and then pay a huge common stock dividend but pay only the stipulated annual dividend to the preferred stockholders. Obviously, such an action effectively would void the preferred position the preferred stockholders are supposed to have. The cumulative feature helps prevent such abuses.[1]

CONVERTIBILITY   Approximately 40 percent of the preferred stock that has been issued in recent years is convertible into common stock. For example, each share of Enron's $10.50 Class J preferred stock can be converted into 3.413 shares of its common stock at the option of the preferred shareholders.

OTHER PROVISIONS   Some other provisions occasionally found in preferred stocks include the following:

1. **Voting rights.** Although preferred stock is not voting stock, preferred stockholders generally are given the right to vote for directors if the company has not paid the preferred dividend for a specified period, such as ten quarters. This feature motivates management to make every effort to pay preferred dividends.
2. **Participating.** A rare type of preferred stock is one that participates with the common stock in sharing the firm's earnings. Participating preferred stocks generally work as follows: (a) the stated preferred dividend is paid—for example, $5 a share; (b) the common stock is then entitled to a dividend in an amount up to the preferred dividend; (c) if the common dividend is raised, say to $5.50, the preferred dividend must likewise be raised to $5.50.
3. **Sinking fund.** In the past (before the mid-1970s), few preferred issues had sinking funds. Today, however, most newly issued preferred stocks have sinking funds that call for the purchase and retirement of a given percentage of the preferred stock each year. If the amount is 2 percent, which frequently is used, the preferred issue will have an average life of 25 years and a maximum life of 50 years.
4. **Call provision.** A call provision gives the issuing corporation the right to call in the preferred stock for redemption. As in the case of bonds, call provisions generally state that the company must pay an amount greater than the par value of the preferred stock, the additional sum being termed a **call premium.** For example, Trivoli Corporation's 12 percent, $100 par value preferred stock, issued in 1991, is noncallable for 10 years, but it might be called at a price of $112 after 2001.

CALL PREMIUM
The amount in excess of par value that a company must pay when it calls a security.

---

[1]Note, however, that compounding is absent in most cumulative plans—in other words, the unpaid preferred dividends themselves earn no return. Also, many preferred issues have a limited cumulative feature; for example, unpaid preferred dividends might accumulate for only three years.

5. **Maturity.** Before the mid-1970s, most preferred stock was perpetual—it had no maturity and never needed to be paid off. Today, however, most new preferred stock has a sinking fund and thus an effective maturity date.

Pros and Cons of Preferred Stock

As noted below, there are both advantages and disadvantages to financing with preferred stock.

ISSUER'S VIEWPOINT   By using preferred stock, a firm can fix its financial costs and thus keep more of the potential future profits for its existing set of common stockholders, yet still avoid the danger of bankruptcy if earnings are too low to meet these fixed charges. Also, by selling preferred rather than common stock, the firm avoids sharing ownership control with new investors.

However, preferred stock does have a major disadvantage from the issuer's standpoint: It has a higher after-tax cost of capital than debt. The major reason for this higher cost is taxes: Preferred dividends are not deductible as a tax expense, whereas interest expense is deductible.[2] This makes the component cost of preferred stock much greater than that of bonds—the after-tax cost of debt is approximately two-thirds of the stated coupon rate for profitable firms, whereas the cost of preferred stock is the full percentage amount of the preferred dividend. Of course, the deductibility differential is most important for issuers that are in relatively high tax brackets. If a company pays little or no taxes because it is unprofitable or because it has a great deal of accelerated depreciation, the deductibility of interest does not make much difference. Thus, the lower a company's tax bracket, the more likely it is to issue preferred stock.

INVESTOR'S VIEWPOINT   In designing securities, the financial manager must consider the investor's point of view. It is sometimes asserted that preferred stock has so many disadvantages to both the issuer and the investor that it should never be issued. Nevertheless, preferred stock is being issued in substantial amounts. It provides investors with a steadier and more assured income than common stock, and it has a preference over common in the event of liquidation. In addition, 70 percent of the preferred dividends received by corporations are not taxable. For this reason, most preferred stock is owned by corporations.

The principal disadvantage of preferred stock from an investor's standpoint is that, although preferred stockholders bear some of the ownership risks, their returns are limited. Other disadvantages are (1) preferred stockholders have no legally enforceable right to dividends, even if a company earns a profit, and (2) *for individual as opposed to corporate investors,* after-tax bond yields generally are higher than those on preferred stock, even though the preferred is riskier.

---

[2]One would think that a given firm's preferred stock would carry a higher coupon rate than its bonds because of the preferred's greater risk from the holder's viewpoint. However, 70 percent of preferred dividends *received* by corporate owners are exempt from income taxes, and this has made preferred stock very attractive to corporate investors. Therefore, most preferred stock is owned by corporations, and in recent years high-grade preferreds, on average, have sold on a lower-yield basis, before taxes, than high-grade bonds. On an after-tax basis, though, the yield on preferred stock generally is greater than the yield on high-grade corporate bonds.

Self-Test Questions

Explain the following statement: "Preferred stock is a hybrid."

Identify and briefly explain some of the key features of preferred stock.

What are the advantages and disadvantages of preferred stock from an issuer's viewpoint?

What are the advantages and disadvantages of preferred stock from an investor's viewpoint?

Leasing

Firms generally own fixed assets and report them on their balance sheets, but it is the *use* of buildings and equipment that is important, not their ownership per se. One way of obtaining the use of assets is to buy them, but an alternative is to lease them. Prior to the 1950s, leasing generally was associated with real estate—land and buildings. Today, however, it is possible to lease virtually any kind of fixed asset, and in 1995 about 25 percent of all new capital equipment acquired by businesses was leased.

Types of Leases

Leasing takes three different forms: (1) sale-and-leaseback arrangements, (2) operating leases, and (3) straight financial, or capital, leases.

SALE AND LEASEBACK
An operation whereby a firm sells land, buildings, or equipment and simultaneously leases the property back for a specified period under specific terms.

SALE AND LEASEBACK   Under a **sale and leaseback,** a firm that owns land, buildings, or equipment sells the property and simultaneously executes an agreement to lease the property back for a particular period under specific terms. The purchaser could be an insurance company, a commercial bank, a specialized leasing company, or even an individual investor. The sale-and-leaseback plan is an alternative to taking out a mortgage loan.

LESSEE
The party that uses, rather than the one who owns, the leased property.

LESSOR
The owner of the leased property.

The firm that sells the property, or the **lessee,** immediately receives the purchase price from the buyer, or the **lessor.**[3] At the same time, the seller-lessee firm retains the use of the property just as if it had borrowed and mortgaged the property to secure the loan. Note that under a mortgage loan arrangement, the financial institution normally would receive a series of equal payments just sufficient to amortize the loan while providing a specified rate of return to the lender on the outstanding balance. Under a sale-and-leaseback arrangement, the lease payments are set up in exactly the same way; the payments are set so the investor-lessor recoups the purchase price and earns a specified rate of return on the investment.

OPERATING LEASE
A lease under which the lessor maintains and finances the property; also called a *service lease.*

OPERATING LEASES   **Operating leases,** sometimes called *service leases,* provide for both *financing* and *maintenance.* IBM is one of the pioneers of the operating lease contract, and computers and office copying machines, together with automobiles and trucks, are the primary types of equipment involved. Ordinarily, these leases call for the lessor to maintain and service the leased equipment, and the cost of providing maintenance is built into the lease payments.

---

[3]The term *lessee* is pronounced "less-ee," not "lease-ee," and *lessor* is pronounced "less-or."

Another important characteristic of operating leases is the fact that they frequently are *not fully amortized;* in other words, the payments required under the lease contract are not sufficient to recover the full cost of the equipment. However, the lease contract is written for a period considerably shorter than the expected economic life of the leased equipment, and the lessor expects to recover all investment costs through subsequent renewal payments, through subsequent leases to other lessees, or by selling the leased equipment.

A final feature of operating leases is that they frequently contain a *cancellation clause,* which gives the lessee the right to cancel the lease before the expiration of the basic agreement. This is an important consideration for the lessee, for it means that the equipment can be returned if it is rendered obsolete by technological developments or if it no longer is needed because of a decline in the lessee's business.

FINANCIAL LEASE
A lease that does not provide for maintenance services, is not cancelable, and is fully amortized over its life; also called a *capital lease.*

FINANCIAL, OR CAPITAL, LEASES   **Financial leases,** sometimes called *capital leases,* are differentiated from operating leases in three respects: (1) they do *not* provide for maintenance services, (2) they are *not cancelable,* and (3) they are *fully amortized* (that is, the lessor receives rental payments which are equal to the full price of the leased equipment plus a return on the investment). In a typical financial lease arrangement, the firm that will use the equipment (the lessee) selects the specific items it requires and negotiates the price and delivery terms with the manufacturer. The user firm then negotiates terms with a leasing company and, once the lease terms are set, arranges to have the lessor buy the equipment from the manufacturer or the distributor. When the equipment is purchased, the user firm simultaneously executes the lease agreement.

Financial leases are similar to sale-and-leaseback arrangements, except that the leased equipment is new and the lessor buys it from a manufacturer or a distributor instead of from the user-lessee. A sale and leaseback might thus be thought of as a special type of financial lease, and both sale-and-leasebacks and financial leases are analyzed in the same manner.[4]

Financial Statement Effects

OFF-BALANCE-SHEET FINANCING
Financing in which the assets and liabilities involved do not appear on the firm's balance sheet.

Lease payments are shown as operating expenses on a firm's income statement, but under certain conditions, neither the leased assets nor the liabilities under the lease contract appear on the firm's balance sheet. For this reason, leasing often is called **off-balance-sheet financing.** This point is illustrated in Table 20-1 by the balance sheets of two hypothetical firms, B (for Buy) and L (for Lease). Initially, the balance sheets of both firms are identical, and both have debt ratios of 50 percent. Each firm then decides to acquire fixed assets which cost $100. Firm B borrows $100 to make the purchase, so both an asset and a liability are recorded on its balance sheet, and its debt ratio is increased to 75 percent. Firm L leases the equipment, so its balance sheet is unchanged. The lease might call for fixed charges as high as or even higher than those on the loan, and the obligations

---

[4]For a lease transaction to qualify as a lease for *tax purposes,* and thus for the lessee to be able to deduct the lease payments, the life of the lease must not exceed 80 percent of the expected life of the asset, and the lessee cannot be permitted to buy the asset at a nominal value. These conditions are IRS requirements, and they should not be confused with the FASB requirements discussed later in the chapter concerning the capitalization of leases. It is important to consult lawyers and accountants to ascertain whether a prospective lease meets current IRS regulations.

TABLE 20-1

Balance Sheet Effects of Leasing

Before Asset Increase				After Asset Increase							
Firms B and L				Firm B—Purchases Asset				Firm L—Leases Asset			
Current Assets	$ 50	Debt	$ 50	Current Assets	$ 50	Debt	$150	Current Assets	$ 50	Debt	$ 50
Fixed Assets	50	Equity	50	Fixed Assets	150	Equity	50	Fixed Assets	50	Equity	50
Total	$100		$100	Total	$200		$200	Total	$100		$100
	Debt ratio = 50%				Debt ratio = 75%				Debt ratio = 50%		

FASB #13

The statement of the Financial Accounting Standards Board that details the conditions and procedures for capitalizing leases.

assumed under the lease might be equally or more dangerous from the standpoint of financial safety, but the firm's debt ratio remains at 50 percent.

To correct this problem, the Financial Accounting Standards Board issued **FASB #13,** which requires that, for an unqualified audit report, firms that enter into financial (or capital) leases must restate their balance sheets to report leased assets as fixed assets and the present value of future lease payments as a debt. This process is called *capitalizing the lease,* and its net effect is to cause Firms B and L to have similar balance sheets, both of which will resemble the one shown for Firm B after the asset increase.[5]

The logic behind FASB #13 is as follows. If a firm signs a lease contract, its obligation to make lease payments is just as binding as if it had signed a loan agreement. The failure to make lease payments can bankrupt a firm just as surely as can the failure to make principal and interest payments on a loan. Therefore, for all intents and purposes, a financial lease is identical to a loan.[6] This being the case, when a firm signs a lease agreement, it has, in effect, raised its "true" debt ratio and thereby changed its "true" capital structure. Accordingly, if the firm previously had established a target capital structure, and if there is no reason to think that the optimal capital structure has changed, then using lease financing requires additional equity backing in exactly the same manner as does the use of debt financing.

If a disclosure of the lease in the Table 20-1 example were not made, then investors could be deceived into thinking that Firm L's financial position is stronger than it actually is. Even if the lease were disclosed in a footnote, investors might not fully recognize its impact and might not see that Firms B and L essentially are in the same financial position. If this were the case, Firm L would have increased its true amount of debt through a lease arrangement, but its required return on debt, k_d, its required return on equity, k_s, and consequently its weighted average cost of capital would have increased less than those of Firm B, which borrowed directly. Thus, investors would be willing to accept a lower return from

---

[5]FASB #13, "Accounting for Leases," November 1976, spells out in detail the conditions under which leases must be capitalized and the procedures for doing so.

[6]There are, however, certain legal differences between loans and leases. For example, in a bankruptcy liquidation, the lessor is entitled to take possession of the leased asset, and, if the value of the asset is less than the required payments under the lease, the lessor can enter a claim (as a general creditor) for one year's lease payments. In a bankruptcy reorganization, the lessor receives the asset plus three years' lease payments if needed to bring the value of the asset up to the remaining investment in the lease.

Firm L because they would view it as being in a stronger financial position than Firm B. These benefits of leasing would accrue to stockholders at the expense of new investors, who were, in effect, being deceived by the fact that the firm's balance sheet did not fully reflect its true liability situation. This is why FASB #13 was issued.

A lease will be classified as a capital lease, and hence be capitalized and shown directly on the balance sheet, if *any one* of the following conditions exists:

1. Under the terms of the lease, ownership of the property effectively is transferred from the lessor to the lessee.
2. The lessee can purchase the property or renew the lease at less than a fair market price when the lease expires.
3. The lease runs for a period equal to or greater than 75 percent of the asset's life. Thus, if an asset has a 10-year life and if the lease is written for more than 7.5 years, the lease must be capitalized.
4. The present value of the lease payments is equal to or greater than 90 percent of the initial value of the asset.[7]

These rules, together with strong footnote disclosures for operating leases, are sufficient to ensure that no one will be fooled by lease financing. Thus, leases are recognized to be essentially the same as debt, and they have the same effects as debt on the firm's required rate of return. Therefore, leasing generally will not permit a firm to use more financial leverage than could be obtained with conventional debt.

Evaluation by the Lessee

Any prospective lease must be evaluated by both the lessee and the lessor. The lessee must determine whether leasing an asset will be less costly than buying it, and the lessor must decide whether the lease will provide a reasonable rate of return. Because our focus in this text primarily is on managerial finance as opposed to investments, we restrict our analysis to that conducted by the lessee.[8]

In the typical case, the events leading to a lease arrangement follow the sequence described in the following list. We should note that a great deal of theoretical literature exists about the correct way to evaluate lease-versus-purchase decisions, and some very complex decision models have been developed to aid in the analysis. The analysis given here, however, leads to the correct decision in every case we have ever encountered.

1. The firm decides to acquire a particular building or piece of equipment. This decision is based on regular capital budgeting procedures, and it is not an issue

---

[7]The discount rate used to calculate the present value of the lease payments must be the lower of (1) the rate used by the lessor to establish the lease payments or (2) the rate of interest which the lessee would have paid for new debt with a maturity equal to that of the lease.

[8]The lessee typically is offered a set of lease terms by the lessor, which generally is a bank, a finance company such as General Electric Capital (the largest U.S. lessor), or some other institutional lender. The lessee can accept or reject the lease, or shop around for a better deal. In this chapter, we take the lease terms as given for purposes of our analysis. See Chapter 17 of Eugene F. Brigham and Louis C. Gapenski, *Intermediate Financial Management,* 5th ed. (Fort Worth, Tex.: The Dryden Press, 1996), for a discussion of lease analysis from the lessor's standpoint, including a discussion of how a potential lessee can use such an analysis in bargaining for better terms.

in the typical lease analysis. In a lease analysis, we are concerned simply with whether to finance the machine by a lease or by a loan.

2. Once the firm has decided to acquire the asset, the next question is how to finance it. Well-run businesses do not have excess cash lying around, so new assets must be financed in some manner.

3. Funds to purchase the asset could be obtained by borrowing, by retaining earnings, or by issuing new stock. Alternatively, the asset could be leased. Because of the FASB #13 capitalization/disclosure provision for leases, we assume that a lease would have the same capital structure effect as a loan.

As indicated earlier, a lease is comparable to a loan in the sense that the firm is required to make a specified series of payments, and a failure to make these payments can result in bankruptcy. Thus, it is most appropriate to compare the cost of lease financing with that of debt financing.[9] The lease-versus-borrow-and-purchase analysis is illustrated with data on the Richards Electronics Company. The following conditions are assumed:

1. Richards plans to acquire equipment with a 4-year life which has a cost of $10,000 delivered and installed.

2. Richards can either purchase the equipment using a 4-year, 10 percent loan or lease the equipment for 4 years at a rental charge of $3,000 per year, payable at the end of the year. If Richards leases the equipment, the lessor will own it upon the expiration of the lease.[10]

3. The equipment definitely will be used for 4 years, at which time its estimated net salvage value will be $600. Richards plans to continue using the equipment, so (1) if it purchases the equipment, the company will keep it, and (2) if it leases the equipment, the company will exercise an option to buy it at its estimated salvage (residual) value, $600.

4. The lease contract stipulates that the lessor will maintain the equipment. However, if Richards borrows and buys, it will have to bear the cost of maintenance, which will be performed by the equipment manufacturer at a fixed contract rate of $400 per year, payable at the end of the year.

5. The equipment falls in the MACRS 3-year class life, and for this analysis we assume that Richards's effective marginal tax rate is 40 percent.

NPV ANALYSIS   Table 20-2 shows the cash flows that would be incurred each year under the two financing plans. All cash flows occur at the end of the year, and the CF_t values are shown on Lines 5 and 10 of Table 20-2 for buying and leasing respectively.

The top section of the table (Lines 1–6) is devoted to the cost of owning (borrowing and buying). Lines 1–4 show the individual cash flow items. Line 5 summarizes the annual net cash flows that Richards will incur if it finances the

---

[9]The analysis should compare the cost of leasing to the cost of debt financing regardless of how the asset actually is financed. The asset actually might be purchased with available cash if it is not leased, but because leasing is a substitute for debt financing, a comparison between the two still is appropriate.

[10]Lease payments can occur at the beginning of the year or at the end of the year. In this example, we assume end-of-year payments, but we demonstrate beginning-of-year payments in Self-Test Problem ST-2.

TABLE 20-2

Richards Electronics Company: NPV Lease Analysis

	Year				
	0	**1**	**2**	**3**	**4**
I. Cost of Owning					
1. Net purchase price	$(10,000)				
2. Maintenance cost		$ (400)	$ (400)	$ (400)	$ (400)
3. Maintenance cost tax savings		160	160	160	160
4. Depreciation tax savings		1,320	1,800	600	280
5. Net cash flow	$(10,000)	$ 1,080	$ 1,560	$ 360	$ 40
6. Present value of owning (k = 6%)	$(7,258.8)				
II. Cost of Leasing					
7. Lease payment		$(3,000)	$(3,000)	$(3,000)	$(3,000)
8. Lease payment tax savings		1,200	1,200	1,200	1,200
9. Purchase option price					(600)
10. Net cash flow	$ 0	$(1,800)	$(1,800)	$(1,800)	$(2,400)
11. Present value of leasing (k = 6%)	$(6,712.4)				
III. Cost Comparision					
12. Net advantage to leasing	$ 546.4 = $7,258.8 − $6,712.4				

NOTE: A line-by-line explanation of the table follows.

1. If Richards buys the equipment, it will have to spend $10,000 on the purchase. Alternatively, we could show all the financing flows associated with a $10,000 loan, net of taxes, but the result would be the same because the PV of those flows would be exactly $10,000.
2. If the equipment is owned, Richards must pay $400 at the end of each year for maintenance.
3. The $400 maintenance expense is tax deductible, so it will produce a tax savings of $160 = 0.4($400) each year.
4. If Richards buys the equipment, it can depreciate the equipment for tax purposes, and thus lower the taxes paid through lower taxable income. The tax savings in each year is equal to Tax rate × (Depreciation expense) = 0.4(Depreciation expense). As shown in Appendix 14A, the MACRS rate for 3-year property are 0.33, 0.45, 0.15, and 0.07 in Years 1–4, respectively. To illustrate the calculation of the depreciation tax savings, consider Year 2. The depreciation expense is 0.45($10,000) = $4,500, and the tax savings is 0.4($4,500) = $1,800.
5. Sum lines 1–4 to find the net cash flows associated with owning the equipment.
6. The PV of the Line 5 cash flows, discounted at 6 percent, is −$7,258.8.
7. The annual end-of-year lease payment is $3,000.
8. Because the lease payment is tax deductible, a tax savings of $1,200 = 0.4($3,000) results for each year.
9. Because Richards plans to continue to use the equipment after the lease expires, it must purchase the equipment for $600 at the end of Year 4 if it leases.
10. Sum Lines 7–9 to find the net cash flows associated with leasing.
11. The PV of the Line 10 cash flows, discounted at 6 percent, is −$6,712.4.
12. The net advantage to leasing is the difference between the PV cost of owning and the PV cost of leasing = $7,258.8 − $6,712.4 = $546.4. Because the NAL is positive, leasing is favored over borrowing and buying.

equipment with a loan. The present values of these cash flows are summed to find the present value of the cost of owning, which is shown on Line 6 in the Year 0 column. (Note that with a financial calculator, we would input the cash flows as shown on Line 5 into the cash flow register, input the interest rate, I = 6, and then press the NPV key to obtain the PV of owning the equipment.) Section II of the table calculates the present value cost of leasing. The cash flows associated with the lease are shown on Lines 7–9, and Line 10 gives the annual net cash flow. The present value of the cash flows is shown on Line 11. Finally, the net advantage to leasing, which is the difference between the present value of purchasing and the present value of leasing, is shown on Line 12. The result of the analysis shown in Table 20-2 indicates that Richards should lease rather than purchase the equipment.

The rate used to discount the cash flows is a critical issue. In Chapter 5, we saw that the riskier a cash flow, the higher the required return associated with a series of cash flows. This same principle was observed in our discussion of capital budgeting, and it also applies in lease analysis. Just how risky are the cash flows under consideration here? Most of them are relatively certain, at least when compared with the types of cash flow estimates that were developed in capital budgeting. For example, the loan payment schedule is set by contract, as is the lease payment schedule. The depreciation expenses are established by law and generally are not subject to change, and, in many cases, the annual maintenance cost is fixed by contract as well. The tax savings are somewhat uncertain because tax rates can change, although tax rates do not change significantly very often. The residual, or salvage, value is the least certain of the cash flows, but even here Richards's management is fairly confident that it will want to acquire the property and also that the cost of doing so will be close to $600. Because the cash flows under both the lease and the borrow-and-purchase alternatives are reasonably certain, they should be discounted at a relatively low rate. Most analysts recommend that the company's cost of debt be used, and this rate seems reasonable in our example. Further, because all the net cash flows are on an after-tax basis, *the after-tax cost of debt,* which is 6 percent, *should be used.*

Factors That Affect Leasing Decisions

The basic method of analysis set forth in Table 20-2 is sufficient to handle most situations. However, certain factors warrant additional comments.

RESIDUAL VALUE
The value of leased property at the end of the lease term.

ESTIMATED RESIDUAL VALUE   It is important to note that the lessor will own the property upon the expiration of the lease. The estimated end-of-lease value of the property is called the **residual value.** Superficially, it would appear that if residual value is expected to be large, owning would have an advantage over leasing. However, if expected residual value is large—as it might be under inflation for certain types of equipment as well as if real property is involved—then competition among leasing companies will force leasing rates down to the point where potential residual value will be fully recognized in the lease contract rate. Thus, the existence of a large residual value on equipment is not likely to bias the decision against leasing.

INCREASED CREDIT AVAILABILITY   As noted earlier, leasing sometimes is said to have an advantage for firms that are seeking the maximum degree of financial leverage. First, it sometimes is argued that a firm can obtain more money, and for a longer period, under a lease arrangement than under a loan secured by the asset. Second, because some leases do not appear on the balance sheet, lease financing has been said to give the firm a stronger appearance in a superficial credit analysis, thus permitting it to use more leverage than it could if it did not lease. There might be some truth to these claims for smaller firms. However, now that larger firms are required to capitalize major leases and to report them on their balance sheets, this point is of questionable validity.

Self-Test Questions

Define each of these terms: (1) sale-and-leaseback arrangements, (2) operating leases, and (3) financial, or capital, leases.

What is off-balance-sheet financing? What is FASB #13? How are the two related?

List the sequence of events, for the lessee, leading to a lease arrangement.

Why is it appropriate to compare the cost of lease financing with that of debt financing?

Options

OPTION
A contract that gives the option holder the right to buy or sell an asset at some predetermined price within a specified period of time.

An **option** is a contract that gives its holder the right to buy or sell an asset at some predetermined price within a specified period of time. "Pure options" are instruments that are created by outsiders (generally investment banking firms) rather than by the firm itself; they are bought and sold primarily by investors (or speculators). However, financial managers should understand the nature of options because this will help them structure warrant and convertible financings.

Option Types and Markets

There are many types of options and option markets. To understand how options work, suppose you owned 100 shares of IBM stock that, on March 16, 1995, sold for $83.50 per share. You could sell to someone else the right to buy your 100 shares at any time during the next 4 months at a price of, say, $90 per share. The $90 is called the **striking,** or **exercise, price.** Such options exist, and they are traded on a number of option exchanges, with the Chicago Board Options Exchange (CBOE) being the oldest and largest. This type of option is known as a **call option,** because the option holder can "call" in 100 shares of stock for purchase any time during the option period. The seller of a call option is known as an option writer. An investor who writes a call option against stock held in his or her portfolio is said to be selling *covered options;* options sold without the stock to back them up are called *naked options.*

STRIKING (EXERCISE) PRICE
The price that must be paid (buying or selling) for a share of common stock when an option is exercised.

CALL OPTION
An option to buy, or "call," a share of stock at a certain price within a specified period.

On March 16, 1995, IBM's 4-month, $90 call options sold on the CBOE for $1.75 each. Thus, for ($1.75)(100) = $175, you could buy an option contract that would give you the right to purchase 100 shares of IBM at a price of $90 per share at any time during the 4-month period. If the stock stayed below $90 during that period, you would lose your $175, but if the stock's price rose to $100, your $175 investment would be worth ($100 − $90)(100) = $1,000. That translates into a very healthy rate of return on your $175 investment. Incidentally, if the stock price did go up, you probably would not actually exercise your options to buy the stock; rather, you would sell the options to another option buyer, at a price of at least $10 per option—you originally paid only $1.75.

PUT OPTION
The option to sell a specified number of shares of stock at a prespecified price during a particular period.

You also can buy an option that gives you the right to sell a stock at a specified price at some time in the future—this is called a **put option.** For example, suppose you expect IBM's stock price to decline from its current level sometime during the next 4 months. For $187.50 = $1.875 × 100 you could buy a 4-month put option giving you the right to sell 100 shares (which you would not necessarily own) at a price of $80 per share ($80 is the put option striking price). If you bought a 100-share put contract for $187.50 and IBM's stock price actually fell to $70, you would make ($80 − $70)(100) = $1,000 minus the $187.50 you paid for the put option, for a net profit (before taxes and commissions) of $812.50.

Options trading is one of the hottest financial activities in the United States today. The leverage involved makes it possible for speculators with just a few dollars to make a fortune almost overnight. Also, investors with sizable portfolios can sell options against their stocks and earn the value of the options (minus brokerage commissions) even if the stocks' prices remain constant. Still, those who have profited most from the development of options trading are security firms, which earn very healthy commissions on such trades.

The corporations on whose stocks options are written, such as IBM, have nothing to do with the options market. They neither raise money in that market nor have any direct transactions in it, and option holders neither receive dividends nor vote for corporate directors (unless they exercise their options to purchase the stock, which few actually do). There have been studies by the SEC and others as to whether options trading stabilizes or destabilizes the stock market and whether it helps or hinders corporations seeking to raise new capital. The studies have not been conclusive, but options trading is here to stay, and many regard it as the most exciting game in town.

Option Values

The value of an option is closely related to the value of the *underlying* stock, which is the stock on which the option is written, and the striking price. For example, an investor who purchases call options hopes that the value of the underlying stock goes above the striking price during the option period, because then the option could be exercised at a gross profit equal to the market value of the stock less the striking price. In this case, the investor is said to have an **in-the-money option,** because he or she can exercise the call option by purchasing the stock at the striking price and then immediately sell the stock for its market value, which is greater than the striking price. For example, if IBM's stock sells for $100 at the end of June, call options with a striking price of $90 would be in-the-money, because the option holder could exercise the options by paying the option seller $9,000 for 100 shares of IBM stock, and then the stock could be sold on the NYSE for $10,000—the financial benefit of exercising to the option holder would be $1,000 before commissions and taxes. If the market value of IBM's stock is $85, or any other amount below the striking price, the call is said to be an **out-of-the-money option,** because it would not be favorable for the option holder to exercise the call—if the investor were to exercise the call option, there would be a financial loss because the stock would be purchased at a value (the $90 striking price) greater than it could be sold (the $85 market value). The opposite relationship holds for put options, because the striking price represents the price at which an investor can *sell* the stock to the put option writer (seller). To be able to sell to the put option writer, the investor first must *buy* the stock in the market (for example, on the NYSE). Thus, for a put option to be in-the-money, the striking price must be above the market value of the underlying stock.

IN-THE-MONEY OPTION
When it is beneficial financially for the option holder to exercise the option.

OUT-OF-THE-MONEY OPTION
When it is *not* beneficial financially for the option holder to exercise the option—a loss would be incurred if the option is exercised.

As you can see, both the value of the underlying stock and the striking price of the option are very important in determining whether an option is in-the-money or out-of-the-money. If an option is out-of-the-money on its expiration date, it is worthless. Therefore, the stock price and the striking price are important for determining the market value of an option. In fact, options are called *derivative securities* because their values are dependent on, or derived from, the value of the underlying asset and the striking price.

In addition to the stock price and the striking price, the value of an option also depends on (1) the option's time to maturity and (2) the variability of the underlying stock's price, as explained below:

1. The longer an option has to run, the greater its value. If a call option expires at 3 p.m. today, there is not much chance that the stock price will go way up. Therefore, the option will sell at close to the difference between the stock price and the striking price (P_s − striking price), or zero if this difference is negative. On the other hand, if it has a year to go, the stock price could rise sharply, pulling the option's value up with it.

2. An option on an extremely volatile stock will be worth more than one on a very stable stock. We know that an option on a stock whose price rarely moves will not offer much chance for a large gain. On the other hand, an option on a stock that is highly volatile could provide a large gain, so such an option will be valuable. Note also that because losses on options are limited, large declines in a stock's price do not have a corresponding bad effect on call option holders. Therefore, stock price volatility can only enhance the value of an option.[11]

If everything else were held constant, then the longer an option's life, the higher its market price would be, no matter the type of option. Also, the more volatile the price of the underlying stock, the higher the option's market price, regardless of the option type.

Self-Test Questions

Differentiate between a call option and a put option.

---

[11]To illustrate this point, suppose that for $2 you could buy a call option on a stock now selling for $20. The striking price is also $20. Now suppose the stock is highly volatile, and you think it has a 50 percent probability of selling for either $10 or $30 when the option expires in one month. What is the expected value of the option? If the stock sells for $30, the option will be worth $30 − $20 = $10. Because there is a 50-50 chance that the stock will be worth $10 or $30, the expected value of the option is $5:

Expected value of option = 0.5(0) + 0.5($10) = $5.

To be exactly correct, we would have to discount the $5 back for one month.

Now suppose the stock was more volatile, with a 50-50 chance of being worth zero or $40. Here the option would be worth

Expected value of option = 0.5(0) + 0.5($20) = $10.

This demonstrates that the greater the volatility of the stock, the greater the value of the option. This result occurs because the large loss on the stock ($20) had no more of an adverse effect on the option holder than the small loss ($10). Thus, call option holders benefit greatly if a stock goes way up, but they do not lose too badly if it drops all the way to zero. These concepts have been used to develop formulas for pricing options, with the most widely used formula being the Black-Scholes model, which is discussed in most investments texts.

Do the corporations on whose stocks options are written raise money in the options market? Explain.

Explain how these factors affect the value of an option: (1) the time remaining before the option expires and (2) the volatility of the underlying stock.

How is the value of a call option affected by the value of the underlying stock and the striking price? How is the value of a put option affected by these factors?

Warrants

WARRANT
A long-term option issued by a corporation to buy a stated number of shares of common stock at a specified price.

A **warrant** is an option *issued by a company* which gives the holder the right to buy a stated number of shares of the company's stock at a specified price. Generally, warrants are distributed along with debt, and they are used to induce investors to buy a firm's long-term debt at a lower interest rate than otherwise would be required. For example, when Pan-Pacific Airlines (PPA) wanted to sell $50 million of 20-year bonds in 1992, the company's investment bankers informed the financial vice-president that straight bonds would be difficult to sell and that an interest rate of 14 percent would be required. However, the investment bankers suggested as an alternative that investors would be willing to buy bonds with an annual coupon rate as low as 10⅜ percent if the company would offer 30 warrants with each $1,000 bond, each warrant entitling the holder to buy one share of common stock at a price of $22 per share. The stock was selling for $20 per share at the time, and the warrants would expire in 1998 if they had not been exercised previously.

Why would investors be willing to buy Pan-Pacific's bonds at a yield of only 10⅜ percent in a 14 percent market just because warrants were offered as part of the package? The answer is that warrants are long-term options, and they have a value for the reasons set forth in the previous section. In the PPA case, this value offset the low interest rate on the bonds and made the entire package of low interest bonds plus warrants attractive to investors.

Use of Warrants in Financing

Warrants generally are used by small, rapidly growing firms as "sweeteners" to help sell either debt or preferred stock. Such firms frequently are regarded as being very risky, and their bonds can be sold only if the firms are willing to pay extremely high rates of interest and to accept very restrictive indenture provisions. To avoid this, firms such as Pan-Pacific often offer warrants along with their bonds. However, some strong firms also have used warrants. In one of the largest financings of any type ever undertaken by a business firm, AT&T raised $1.57 billion by selling bonds with warrants. This marked the first use ever of warrants by a large, strong corporation.

Getting warrants along with bonds enables investors to share in a company's growth if that firm does in fact grow and prosper; therefore, investors are willing to accept a lower bond interest rate and less restrictive indenture provisions. A bond with warrants has some characteristics of debt and some of equity. It is a hybrid security that provides the financial manager with an opportunity to expand the firm's mix of securities and to appeal to a broader group of investors, thus lowering the firm's cost of capital.

DETACHABLE WARRANT
A warrant that can be detached from a bond and traded independently of it.

Virtually all warrants today are **detachable warrants,** meaning that after a bond with attached warrants has been sold, the warrants can be detached and traded separately from the bond. Further, when these warrants are exercised, the bonds themselves (with their low coupon rate) will remain outstanding. Thus, the warrants will bring in additional equity while leaving low interest rate debt on the books.

The warrants' exercise price generally is set at from 10 percent to 30 percent above the market price of the stock on the date the bond is issued. For example, if the stock sells for $10, the exercise price will probably be set in the $11 to $13 range. If the firm does grow and prosper, and if its stock price rises above the exercise price at which shares can be purchased, warrant holders will turn in their warrants, along with cash equal to the stated exercise price, in exchange for stock. Without some incentive, however, many warrants would never be exercised until just before expiration. Their value in the market would be greater than their exercise value; thus holders would sell warrants rather than exercise them.

There are three conditions which encourage holders to exercise their warrants: (1) Warrant holders surely will exercise warrants and buy stock if the warrants are about to expire with the market price of the stock above the exercise price. This means that if a firm wants its warrants exercised soon in order to raise capital, it should set a relatively short expiration date. (2) Warrant holders will tend to exercise voluntarily and buy stock if the company raises the dividend on the common stock by a sufficient amount. Because no dividend is paid on the warrant, it provides no current income. However, if the common stock pays a high dividend, it provides an attractive dividend yield. Therefore, the higher the stock's dividend, the greater the opportunity cost of holding the warrant rather than exercising it. Thus, if a firm wants its warrants exercised, it can raise the common stock's divi-

STEPPED-UP EXERCISE PRICE
An exercise price that is specified to be higher if a warrant is exercised after a designated date.

dend. (3) Warrants sometimes have **stepped-up exercise prices,** which prod owners into exercising them. For example, the Mills Agricorp has warrants outstanding with an exercise price of $25 until December 31, 1997, at which time the exercise price will rise to $30. If the price of the common stock is over $25 just before December 31, 1997, many warrant holders will exercise their options before the stepped-up price takes effect.

Another useful feature of warrants is that they generally bring in funds only if such funds are needed. If the company grows, it probably will need new equity capital. At the same time, this growth will cause the price of the stock to rise and the warrants to be exercised, thereby allowing the firm to obtain additional cash. If the company is not successful and cannot profitably employ additional money, the price of its stock probably will not rise sufficiently to induce exercise of the options.

Self-Test Questions

What three conditions would encourage holders to exercise their warrants?

Do warrants bring in additional funds to the firm when exercised? Explain.

Explain how a firm can use warrants to issue debt with a lower cost than similar debt without warrants.

Convertibles

CONVERTIBLE SECURITY
A security, usually a bond or preferred stock, that is exchangeable at the option of the holder for the common stock of the issuing firm.

Convertible securities are bonds or preferred stocks that can be exchanged for common stock at the option of the holder. Unlike the exercise of warrants, which provides the firm with additional funds, conversion does not bring in additional capital—debt or preferred stock simply is replaced by common stock. Of course, this reduction of debt or preferred stock will strengthen the firm's balance sheet and make it easier to raise additional capital, but this is a separate action.

Conversion Ratio and Conversion Price

CONVERSION RATIO, CR
The number of shares of common stock that might be obtained by converting a convertible bond or share of convertible preferred stock.

One of the most important provisions of a convertible security is the **conversion ratio, CR,** defined as the number of shares of stock the convertible holder receives upon conversion. Related to the conversion ratio is the conversion price, P_c, which is the effective price paid for the common stock obtained by converting a convertible security. The relationship between the conversion ratio and the conversion price can be illustrated by the convertible debentures issued at par value by Bee TV, Inc. in 1995. At any time prior to maturity on July 1, 2015, a debenture holder can exchange a bond for 20 shares of common stock; therefore, CR = 20. The bond has a par value of $1,000, so the holder would be relinquishing this amount upon conversion. Dividing the $1,000 par value by the 20 shares received gives a conversion price of P_c = $50 a share:

20-1

$$\text{Conversion price} = P_c = \frac{\text{Par value of bond}}{\text{Conversion ratio}}$$

$$= \frac{\$1,000}{20} = \$50$$

Like a warrant's exercise price, the conversion price usually is set at from 10 percent to 30 percent above the prevailing market price of the common stock at the time the convertible issue is sold. Generally, the conversion price and ratio are fixed for the life of the bond, although sometimes a stepped-up conversion price is used.

Another factor that might cause a change in the conversion price and ratio is a standard feature of almost all convertibles—the clause protecting the convertible against dilution from stock splits, stock dividends, and the sale of common stock at prices below the conversion price. The typical provision states that if common stock is sold at a price below the conversion price, the conversion price must be lowered (and the conversion ratio raised) to the price at which the new stock was issued. Also, if the stock is split (or if a stock dividend is declared), the conversion price must be lowered by the percentage of the stock split (or stock dividend). If this protection were not contained in the contract, a company could completely thwart conversion by the use of stock splits. Warrants are similarly protected against such dilution.

Use of Convertibles in Financing

Convertibles offer three important advantages from the *issuer's* standpoint. First, convertibles, like bonds with warrants, permit a company to sell debt with a lower interest rate and with less restrictive covenants than straight bonds. Second, convertibles generally are subordinated to mortgage bonds, bank loans, and other senior debt, so financing with convertibles leaves the company's access to "regular" debt unimpaired. Third, convertibles provide a way of selling common stock at prices higher than those currently prevailing. Many companies actually want to sell common stock and not debt, but they believe that the price of their stock temporarily is depressed. The financial manager might know, for example, that earnings are depressed because of start-up costs associated with a new project, but he or she might expect earnings to rise sharply during the next year or so, pulling the price of the stock along. In this case, if the company sold stock now it would be giving up too many shares to raise a given amount of money. However, if it sets the conversion price at 20 percent to 30 percent above the present market price of the stock, then 20 percent to 30 percent fewer shares will have to be given up when the bonds are converted. Notice, however, that management is counting on the stock's price rising sufficiently above the conversion price to make the bonds attractive in conversion. If earnings do not rise and pull the stock price up, and hence if conversion does not occur, the company could be saddled with debt in the face of low earnings, which could be disastrous.

How can the company be sure that conversion will occur if the price of the stock rises above the conversion price? Typically, convertibles contain a call provision that enables the issuing firm to force bondholders to convert. Suppose the conversion price is $50, the conversion ratio is 20, the market price of the common stock has risen to $60, and the call price on the convertible bond is $1,050. If the company calls the bond, bondholders could either convert into common stock with a market value of $1,200 or allow the company to redeem the bond for $1,050. Naturally, bondholders prefer $1,200 to $1,050, so conversion will occur. The call provision therefore gives the company a means of *forcing* conversion, but only if the market price of the stock is greater than the conversion price.

Convertibles are useful, but they do have three important disadvantages. (1) The use of a convertible security might in effect give the issuer the opportunity to sell common stock at a price higher than it could sell stock otherwise. However, if the common stock increases greatly in price, the company probably would have been better off if it had used straight debt in spite of its higher interest rate and then later sold common stock to refund the debt. (2) If the company truly wants to raise equity capital, and if the price of the stock does not rise sufficiently after the bond is issued, then the firm will be stuck with debt. (3) Convertibles typically have a low coupon interest rate, an advantage that will be lost when conversion occurs. Warrant financings, on the other hand, permit the company to continue to use the low-coupon debt for a longer period.

Self-Test Questions

Does the exchange of convertible securities for common stock bring in additional funds to the firm? Explain.

How do you calculate the conversion price?

What are the key advantages and disadvantages of convertibles?

Reporting Earnings When Warrants or Convertibles Are Outstanding

If warrants or convertibles are outstanding, a firm theoretically can report earnings per share in one of three ways:

1. **Simple EPS.** The earnings available to common stockholders are divided by the average number of shares *actually* outstanding during the period.
2. **Primary EPS.** The earnings available are divided by the average number of shares that would have been outstanding if warrants and convertibles *likely to be converted* in the near future had actually been exercised or converted.
3. **Fully diluted EPS.** This is similar to primary EPS except that all warrants and convertibles are *assumed to be exercised or converted,* regardless of the likelihood of either occurring.

Simple EPS is virtually never reported by firms which have warrants or convertibles likely to be exercised or converted; the SEC prohibits use of this figure, and it requires that primary and fully diluted earnings be shown on the income statement.

Self-Test Question

Differentiate between simple EPS, primary EPS, and fully diluted EPS.

Leveraged Buyouts (LBOs)

LEVERAGED BUYOUT (LBO)
A transaction in which a firm's publicly owned stock is bought up in a mostly debt-financed tender offer, and a privately owned, highly leveraged firm results.

With the extraordinary merger activity that took place in the 1980s, we witnessed a huge increase in the popularity of **leveraged buyouts,** or **LBOs.** The number and size of LBOs jumped significantly during this period. This development occurred for the same reasons that mergers and divestitures occurred—the existence of potential bargains, situations in which companies were using insufficient leverage, and the development of the junk bond market, which facilitated the use of leverage in takeovers.

LBOs can be initiated in one of two ways: (1) The firm's own managers can set up a new company whose equity comes from the managers themselves, plus some equity from pension funds and other institutions. This new company then arranges to borrow a large amount of money by selling junk bonds through an investment banking firm. With the financing arranged, the management group then makes an offer to purchase all the publicly owned shares through a tender offer. (2) A specialized LBO firm, with Kohlberg, Kravis, & Roberts (KKR) being the largest and best known, will identify a potential target company, go to the management, and suggest that an LBO deal be done. KKR and other LBO firms have billions of dollars of equity, most put up by pension funds and other large investors, available for the equity portion of the deals, and they arrange junk bond financing just as would a management-led group. Generally, the newly formed

---

"Deja Vu" All Over Again?

The largest leveraged buyout (LBO) in history was finalized February 1989 when Kohlberg Kravis Roberts & Co. (KKR), a large and powerful LBO firm, acquired RJR Nabisco for just over $25 billion. The deal evolved in October 1988, when a group headed by Ross Johnson, chairman of RJR Nabisco at the time, offered stockholders $75 per share in an attempt to purchase the company and take it private; the total offer was equal to nearly $18 billion. Within days, Henry Kravis and George Roberts, KKR's leaders, started a bidding war by offering $90 per share for RJR Nabisco. Ultimately KKR won the war, and paid $109 per share, which was nearly twice the per share market price at the time the first buyout offer was made by Johnson. Of the $25 billion paid, only $1.35 billion represented equity invested by KKR; the rest was financed by debt, and was raised primarily in the junk bond market. At the time the RJR Nabisco LBO was finalized, there was a great deal of skepticism about whether the deal would be successful. Some experts speculated that the phenomenal price paid for the RJR Nabisco LBO was the result of a battle of egos between two very powerful individuals; others believed the LBO was a good deal. In any event, the degree of financial leverage, thus the risk, associated with the LBO was substantial.

Several years after the RJR Nabisco LBO, experts have dubbed the "deal of the century" the "turkey of the century." The average annual return earned by KKR on its investment in the LBO appears to be only in the single digits range, quite a contrast to the 25 percent to 30 percent returns KKR normally sees, and well below expectations given the risk involved. According to analysts, KKR made two fundamental mistakes with the RJR Nabisco deal: (1) too much was paid for the buyout, and (2) the investment was made in the wrong industry (tobacco).

Not long after KKR put together the LBO, the junk bond market tumbled. To save RJR from insolvency, in July 1990, KKR refinanced some of the debt by infusing another $1.7 billion of equity; this increased KKR's equity position to about $3.1 billion. Then in 1991, KKR took RJR Nabisco public with an initial public offering (IPO) of 100 million shares at a price of $11.25 per share. The stock sold by KKR represented 60 percent equity ownership in RJR Nabisco. KKR believed the funds raised through the IPO could be used to better stabilize the financial position of RJR. Unfortunately, legal and competitive battles in the tobacco industry have resulted in very lackluster operating performances by RJR in the 1990s. In 1993, RJR's primary competitor, Philip Morris, started an aggressive campaign to increase its market share in the tobacco industry by significantly cutting cigarette prices and increasing advertising expenses. These actions surprised RJR, so it "missed the boat" and was left behind by Philip Morris—RJR's profit decreased by 50 percent in 1993. At the same time, increases in both regulation and litigation contributed to a heightened social awareness and a degree of negativism with respect to investing in tobacco companies. Consequently, tobacco stocks have been shunned by many investors in the 1990s. In the middle of 1994, RJR Nabisco stock sold for about $5 per share, less than one half its IPO price two years earlier.

On September 12, 1994, KKR made a bid to acquire Borden Inc., a large food processor, for approximately $14.25 per share. To pay for the $2 billion buyout, KKR exchanged 275 million shares of RJR Nabisco stock for Borden's stock. This move reduced KKR's ownershp of RJR from 40 percent to 17.5 percent. Then, in February and March of 1995, KKR sold its remaining stake in RJR through Borden. Six years after it consummated the "deal of the century," KKR had dumped RJR Nabisco and totally removed itself from the situation.

During the same period KKR was divesting its remaining interest in RJR, RJR Nabisco Holdings Corporation sold to the public nearly 20 percent of Nabisco Brands, the food division of RJR Nabisco. According to experts, the Nabisco Brands IPO was such a hit that there was a good chance RJR would sell the rest of Nabisco Brands by 1997. This would put RJR and Nabisco where they were in 1985 before RJR purchased Nabisco Brands; RJR would be an independent tobacco company and Nabisco would be an independent food company, and both would be independent of KKR. After a little more than a decade, RJR and Nabisco Brands have come "full circle"— starting with a merger, proceeding through the biggest LBO in history, and ultimately splitting up into two companies that are publicly owned once again.

company will have at least 80 percent debt, and sometimes the debt ratio is as high as 98 percent. Thus, the term *leveraged* is most appropriate.

To illustrate an LBO, consider the $25 billion leveraged buyout of RJR Nabisco by KKR. RJR, a leading producer of tobacco and food products with such brands as Winston, Camel, Planters, Ritz, and Oreo, was trading at about $55 a share. Then F. Ross Johnson, the company's president and CEO, announced a $75 per share, or $17.6 billion, offer to take the firm private. The day after the announcement, RJR's stock soared to $77.25, which indicated that investors thought that the final price would be even higher than Johnson's opening bid. A few days later, KKR offered $90 per share, or $20.6 billion, for the firm. The battle between the two bidders continued until late November, when RJR's board accepted a revised KKR bid of cash and securities worth about $106 per share, for a total value of about $25.1 billion.

Was RJR worth $25 billion, or did Henry Kravis and his partners let their egos govern their judgment? At the time the LBO was initiated, analysts believed that the deal was workable, but barely. Six years later, KKR had disposed of all its interest in RJR Nabisco, and many experts were calling the biggest LBO in history the biggest financial flop in history. More information about the history of KKR's ownership of RJR Nabisco is provided in The Industry Practice box in this chapter.

It is not clear if LBOs are, on balance, a good or a bad idea. Some government officials, and others, have stated a belief that the leverage involved might destabilize the economy. On the other hand, LBOs certainly have stimulated some lethargic managements, and that is good. Good or bad, though, LBOs are helping to reshape the face of corporate America.

Self-Test Questions

Identify and briefly explain the two ways in which an LBO can be initiated.

How has the development of the junk bond market affected the use of LBOs?

Mergers

MERGER
The combination of two (or more) firms to form a single firm.

Mergers have taken place at a feverish pace during the past decade. The brief discussion in this section will help you understand the motivations behind all this activity.[12]

---

[12]The purpose of this section is to provide you with a general understanding of mergers, the motivation for mergers, and merger activity in the United States. Merger analysis, which is the evaluation of the attractiveness of a merger, should be conducted in the same manner as capital budgeting analysis—if the present value of the cash flows expected to result from the merger exceeds the price that must be paid for the company being acquired, then the merger has a positive net present value and the acquiring firm should proceed with the acquisition. Because the very nature of the merger process is complex, we choose not to discuss the specifics of merger analysis in this section. For a detailed discussion of merger analysis, see Chapter 24 of Eugene F. Brigham and Louis C. Gapenski, *Intermediate Financial Management*, 5th ed. (Fort Worth, Tex.: The Dryden Press, 1996).

Rationale for Mergers

There are five principal reasons two or more firms are merged to form a single firm.

1. **Synergy.** The primary motivation for most mergers is to increase the value of the combined enterprise—the hope is that **synergy** exists, so that the value of the company formed by the merger is greater than the sum of the values of the individual companies taken separately. Synergistic effects can arise from four sources: (1) *operating economies of scale* occur when cost reductions result from the combination of the companies; (2) *financial economies* might include a higher price/earnings ratio, a lower cost of debt, or a greater debt capacity; (3) *differential management efficiency* generally results when one firm is relatively inefficient, so the merger improves the profitability of the acquired assets; and (4) *increased market power* occurs if reduced competition exists after the merger. Operating and financial economies are socially desirable, as are mergers that increase managerial efficiency; but mergers that reduce competition are both undesirable and often illegal.[13]

2. **Tax Considerations.** Tax considerations have stimulated a number of mergers. For example, a firm that is highly profitable and in the highest corporate tax bracket could acquire a company with large accumulated tax losses, then use those losses to shelter its own income.[14] Similarly, a company with large losses could acquire a profitable firm. Also, tax considerations could cause mergers to be a desirable use for excess cash. For example, if a firm has a shortage of internal investment opportunities compared to its cash flows, it will have excess cash, and its options for disposing of this excess cash are to (1) pay an extra dividend, (2) invest in marketable securities, (3) repurchase its own stock, or (4) purchase another firm. If the firm pays an extra dividend, its stockholders will have to pay taxes on the distribution. Marketable securities such as Treasury bonds provide a good temporary parking place for money, but the rate of return on such securities is less than that required by stockholders. A stock repurchase might result in a capital gain for the remaining stockholders, but it could be disadvantageous if the company has to pay a high price to acquire the stock, and, if the repurchase is designed solely to avoid paying dividends, it might be challenged by the IRS. However, using surplus cash to acquire another firm has no immediate tax consequences for either the acquiring firm or its stockholders, and this fact has motivated a number of mergers.

---

[13]In the 1880s and 1890s, many mergers occurred in the United States, and some of them clearly were directed toward gaining market power at the expense of competition rather than increasing operating efficiency. As a result, Congress passed a series of acts designed to ensure that mergers are not used as a method of reducing competition. Today, the principal acts include the Sherman Act (1890), the Clayton Act (1914), and the Celler Act (1950). These acts make it illegal for firms to combine in any manner if the combination will lessen competition. They are administered by the antitrust division of the Justice Department and by the Federal Trade Commission. For example, in a recent case, the Justice Department filed an antitrust suit against Microsoft, the largest producer of software for personal computers, to block its attempt to take over Intuit, producer of popular financial software. The suit caused Microsoft to drop its takeover attempt in May 1995.

[14]Mergers undertaken only to use accumulated tax losses probably would be challenged by the IRS. However, because many factors are present in any given merger, it is hard to prove that a merger was motivated only, or even primarily, by tax considerations.

3. **Purchase of Assets below their Replacement Cost.** Sometimes a firm will become an acquisition candidate because the replacement value of its assets is considerably higher than its market value. For example, in the 1980s oil companies could acquire reserves more cheaply by buying out other oil companies than by exploratory drilling. This factor was a motive in Chevron's acquisition of Gulf Oil. The acquisition of Republic Steel (the sixth largest steel company) by LTV (the fourth largest) provides another example of a firm's being purchased because its purchase price was less than the replacement value of its assets. LTV found that it was less costly to purchase Republic Steel for $700 million than it would have been to construct a new steel mill. At the time, Republic's stock was selling for less than one-third of its book value. However, the merger did not help LTV's inefficient operations—ultimately, the company filed for bankruptcy.

4. **Diversification.** Managers often claim that diversification helps to stabilize the firm's earnings and thus reduce corporate risk. Therefore, diversification often is given as a reason for mergers. Stabilization of earnings certainly is beneficial to a firm's employees, suppliers, and customers, but its value to stockholders and debtholders is less clear. If an investor is worried about earnings variability, he or she probably could diversify through stock purchases (investment portfolio adjustment) more easily than the firm could through acquisitions.

5. **Maintaining Control.** Some mergers and takeovers are considered *hostile* because the management of the acquired firm opposes the merger. One reason for the hostility is that the managers of the acquired companies generally lose their jobs, or at least their autonomy. Therefore, managers who own less than 51 percent of the stock in their firms look to devices that will lessen the chances of their firms' being taken over. Mergers can serve as such a device. For example, when Enron was under attack, it arranged to buy Houston Natural Gas Company, paying for Houston primarily with debt. That merger made Enron much larger and hence harder for any potential acquirer to "digest." Also, the much higher debt level resulting from the merger made it hard for any acquiring company to use debt to buy Enron. Such **defensive mergers** are difficult to defend on economic grounds. The managers involved invariably argue that synergy, not a desire to protect their own jobs, motivated the acquisition, but there can be no question that many mergers have been designed more for the benefit of managers than for stockholders.

DEFENSIVE MERGER
A merger designed to make a company less vulnerable to a takeover.

Types of Mergers

HORIZONTAL MERGER
A combination of two firms that produce the same type of good or service.
VERTICAL MERGER
A merger between a firm and one of its suppliers or customers.
CONGENERIC MERGER
A merger of firms in the same general industry, but for which no customer or supplier relationship exists.

Economists classify mergers into four groups: (1) horizontal, (2) vertical, (3) congeneric, and (4) conglomerate. A **horizontal merger** occurs when one firm combines with another in its same line of business. For example, the merger of Chevron and Gulf Oil was a horizontal merger because both firms were petroleum producers. An example of a **vertical merger** is a steel producer's acquisition of one of its own suppliers, such as an iron or coal mining firm. The 1993 merger of Merck & Co., a manufacturer of health care products, and Medco Containment, the largest mail-order pharmacy service, is an example of a vertical merger. Congeneric means "allied in nature or action;" hence, a **congeneric merger** involves related enterprises but not producers of the same product (horizontal) or firms in a producer-supplier relationship (vertical). Examples of congeneric mergers include Viacom's acquisitions of Paramount Communications and Blockbuster Entertainment in 1994. Viacom owns several television stations and cable systems and distributes television programming, while Paramount produces movies and other entertainment shown both on television and in theaters and Blockbuster's principal business is the rental of movies, most of which previously have been shown in theaters. A **conglomerate merger** occurs when unrelated enterprises combine, as illustrated by Mobil Oil's acquisition of Montgomery Ward.

CONGLOMERATE MERGER
A merger of companies in totally different industries.

Operating economies (and also anticompetitive effects) are dependent on the type of merger involved. Vertical and horizontal mergers generally provide the greatest synergistic operating benefits, but they also are the ones most likely to be attacked by the U.S. Department of Justice. In any event, it is useful to think of these economic classifications when analyzing the feasibility of a prospective merger.

Merger Activity

Four major "merger waves" have occurred in the United States. The first was in the late 1800s, when consolidations occurred in the oil, steel, tobacco, and other basic industries. The second was in the 1920s, when the stock market boom helped financial promoters consolidate firms in a number of industries, including utilities, communications, and autos. The third was in the 1960s, when conglomerate mergers were the rage, while the fourth began in the early 1980s, and it is still going strong.

The current "merger mania" has been sparked by several factors: (1) the depressed level of the dollar relative to foreign currencies, which has made U.S. companies look cheap to foreign buyers; (2) the unprecedented level of inflation that existed during the 1970s and early 1980s, which increased the replacement value of firms' assets even while a weak stock market reduced their market values; (3) the general belief among the major natural resource companies that it is cheaper to "buy reserves on Wall Street" through mergers than to explore and find them in the field; (4) attempts to ward off raiders by use of defensive mergers; (5) the development of the junk bond market, which has made it possible to use far more debt in acquisitions than had been possible earlier; and (6) the increased globalization of business, which has led to increased economies of scale and to the formation of worldwide corporations.

The statistics that describe the latest merger wave suggest it ranks as the largest in history. Table 20-3 lists the top five mergers of all time in the United States—each has occurred since the mid 1980s. In the past two years, merger and acquisition activity has increased significantly, and there is indication this trend will continue for at least two to three more years. For example, in 1993, the total value of all mergers was approximately $147 billion, the greatest activity since 1988, and this amount increased by 58 percent to more than $232 billion in 1994. Also, as Table 20-4 shows, the size of the individual mergers has grown—in 1994, there were 51 mergers and acquisitions valued at $1 billion or more, up from 23 in 1993. As we write this text in 1995, it appears the pace and size of mergers and acquisitions has not decreased—the volume of merger activity in the first quarter of 1995 was more than $73 billion, which is 36 percent higher than the first quarter of 1994, and the highest since the first quarter of 1989.

TABLE 20-3

The Five Largest Mergers in the United States (billions of dollars)

Companies	Year	Value	Type of Transaction
AT&T–McCaw Cellular	1994	$18.9	Acquisition for stock and assumption of debt
Time–Warner	1989	14.0	Acquisition for cash, stock, and debt
Chevron–Gulf	1984	13.3	Acquisition for cash
Philip Morris–Kraft	1988	12.9	Acquisition for stock
Bristol Myers–Squibb	1989	11.5	Acquisition for stock
Texaco–Getty	1984	10.1	Acquisition for cash and notes

NOTE: KKR's acquisition of RJR Nabisco exceeded $25 billion, but that transaction was an LBO, not a merger.

TABLE 20-4

The Largest Mergers in the United States in 1993 and 1994 (billions of dollars)

1994 Mergers Companies	Value	1993 Mergers Companies	Value
AT&T–McCaw Cellular	$18.9	Merck–Medco Containment	$6.2
Viacom–Paramount	9.6	Columbia Healthcare–	
American Home Products–		Galen Health Care	4.2
American Cyanamid	9.3	Sprint–Centel	4.0
Viacom–Blockbuster Ent.	8.0	Primerica–Travelers	4.0
Columbia Healthcare–		Hanson–Quantum Chemical	3.2
HCA-Hospital Corp.	5.6		

SOURCE: *Institutional Investor,* March issues for 1994 and 1995.

Many of the mergers in 1993 and 1994 resulted either because the acquired firms were considered undervalued or because it was felt economies of scale could produce less costly combined operations. The fear of such governmental reforms as regulation, deregulation, and deficit reduction measures probably was the primary reason most of the merger activity occurred in the health care, telecommunications, and financial services industries. Experts expect these industries and other industries, such as defense, consumer products, and natural resources, to become significantly reshaped as merger activity continues in the future.

Self-Test Questions

What are the four primary motives behind most mergers?

From what sources do synergistic effects arise?

How have tax considerations stimulated mergers?

Is diversification to reduce stockholder risk a valid motive for mergers? Explain.

Explain briefly the four economic classifications of mergers.

What factors have sparked the most recent *merger mania?*

SMALL BUSINESS

Lease Financing for Small Businesses

Earlier in this chapter we saw that, under certain conditions, leasing an asset can be less costly than borrowing to purchase the asset. For the small firm, leasing often offers three additional advantages: it (1) conserves cash, (2) makes better use of managers' time, and (3) provides financing quickly.

CONSERVING CASH   Small firms often have limited cash resources. Because many leasing companies do not require the lessee to make even a small down payment, and because leases often are for longer terms and thus require lower payments than bank loans, leasing can help the small firm conserve its cash. Leasing companies also might be willing to work with a company to design a flexible leasing package that will help the lessee preserve its cash during critical times. For example, when Surgicare of Central Jersey opened its first surgical center, the firm did not have sufficient cash to pay for the necessary equipment. Surgicare's options were to borrow at a high interest rate, to sell stock to the public (which is difficult for a start-up firm), or to lease the equipment. Surgicare's financial vice-president, John Rutzel, decided to lease the needed equipment from Copelco Financial Services, a leasing company which specializes in health-care equipment. Copelco allowed Surgicare to make very low payments for the first 6 months, slightly higher payments during the second 6 months, and level payments thereafter. These unique lease terms "got Surgicare through the start-up phase, when cash flow was the critical consideration."

FREEING MANAGERS FOR OTHER TASKS   Most small-business owners find that they never have enough time to get everything done—being in charge of sales, operations, budgeting, and everything else, they are

simply spread too thin. If an asset is owned, the firm must maintain it in good working condition and also keep records on its use for tax depreciation purposes. However, leasing assets frees the business's owner of these duties. First, paperwork is reduced because maintenance records, depreciation schedules, and other records do not have to be maintained on leased assets. Second, less time might have to be spent "shopping around" for the right equipment because leasing companies, that generally specialize in a particular industry, can often provide the manager with the information necessary to select the needed assets. Third, because the assets can be traded in if they become obsolete, the initial choice of equipment is less critical. And fourth, the burden of servicing and repairing the equipment often can be passed on to the lessor.

OBTAINING ASSETS QUICKLY AND INEXPENSIVELY   Many new, small firms find that banks are unwilling to lend them money at a reasonable cost. However, because leasing companies retain the ownership of the equipment, they might be more willing to take chances with start-up firms. When Ed Lavin started Offset Printing Company, his bank would not lend him the money to purchase the necessary printing presses—the bank wanted to lend only to firms with proven track records. Lavin arranged to lease the needed presses from Eaton Financial, which also advised him on the best type of equipment to meet his needs. As Lavin's company grew, he expanded by leasing additional equipment. Thus, (1) leasing allowed Lavin to go into business when his bank was unwilling to help, (2) his leasing company provided him with help in selecting equipment, and (3) the leasing company also provided additional capital to meet his expansion needs.

Summary

This chapter discussed three hybrid forms of long-term financing: (1) preferred stock, (2) leasing, and (3) option securities. In addition, the concept of LBOs and the reasons for mergers were explained. The key concepts covered are listed below.

* **Preferred stock** is a hybrid security having some characteristics of debt and some of equity. Equity holders view preferred stock as being similar to debt because it has a claim on the firm's earnings ahead of the claim of the common

stockholders. Bondholders, however, view preferred as equity because debt-holders have a prior claim on the firm's income and assets.

- The primary **advantages of preferred stock to the issuer** are (1) preferred dividends are limited and (2) failure to pay them will not bankrupt the firm. The primary disadvantage to the issuer is that the cost of preferred is higher than that of debt because preferred dividend payments are not tax deductible.

- To the **investor,** preferred stock offers the advantage of **more dependable income** than common stock, and, to a corporate investor, **70 percent of such dividends are not taxable.** The principal disadvantages to the investor are that the **returns are limited** and the investor has **no legally enforceable right to a dividend.**

- **Leasing** is a means of obtaining the use of an asset without purchasing that asset. The three most important forms of leasing are (1) **sale-and-leaseback arrangements,** under which a firm sells an asset to another party and leases the asset back for a specified period under specific terms; (2) **operating leases,** under which the lessor both maintains and finances the asset; and (3) **financial leases,** under which the asset is fully amortized over the life of the lease, the lessor does not normally provide maintenance, and the lease is not cancelable.

- The **decision to lease or buy an asset** is made by comparing the financing costs of the two alternatives and choosing the financing method with the lower cost. All cash flows should be discounted at the after-tax cost of debt because lease analysis cash flows are relatively certain and are on an after-tax basis.

- An **option** is a contract that gives its holder the right to buy or sell an asset at some predetermined price within a specified period of time. Options features are used by firms to "sweeten" debt offerings.

- A **warrant** is an option issued by a firm that gives the holder the right to purchase a stated number of shares of stock at a specified price within a given period. A warrant will be exercised if it is about to expire and the stock price is above the exercise price.

- A **convertible security** is a bond or preferred stock that can be exchanged for common stock. When conversion occurs, debt or preferred stock is replaced with common stock, but no money changes hands.

- The **conversion** of bonds or preferred stock by their holders **does not provide additional funds** to the company, but it does result in a lower debt ratio. The **exercise of warrants does provide additional funds,** which strengthens the firm's equity position, but it still leaves the debt or preferred stock on the balance sheet. Thus, low interest rate debt remains outstanding when warrants are exercised, but the firm loses this advantage when convertibles are converted.

- A **leveraged buyout (LBO)** is a transaction in which a firm's publicly owned stock is bought up in a mostly debt-financed tender offer, and a privately owned, highly leveraged firm results. Often, the firm's own management initiates the LBO.

- The reasons **mergers** take place include (1) *synergy,* (2) *tax considerations,* (3) low *asset values,* (4) *diversification,* and (5) ownership *control.* Mergers can be classified as **horizontal, vertical, congeneric,** or **conglomerate.**

- For the small firm, leasing offers three advantages: (1) **cash is conserved,** (2) **managers' time is freed** for other tasks, and (3) **financing often can be obtained quickly** and at a relatively low cost.

Questions

20-1   For purposes of measuring a firm's leverage, should preferred stock be classified as debt or equity? Does it matter if the classification is being made by (a) the firm's management, (b) creditors, or (c) equity investors?

20-2   You are told that one corporation just issued $100 million of preferred stock and another purchased $100 million of preferred stock as an investment. You are also told that one firm has an effective tax rate of 20 percent whereas the other is in the 34 percent bracket. Which firm is more likely to have bought the preferred? Explain.

20-3   One often finds that a company's bonds have a higher before-tax yield than its preferred stock, even though the bonds are considered to be less risky than the preferred to an investor. What causes this yield differential?

20-4   Distinguish between operating leases and financial leases. Would a firm be more likely to finance a fleet of trucks or a manufacturing plant with an operating lease?

20-5   One alleged advantage of leasing voiced in the past was that it kept liabilities off the balance sheet, thus making it possible for a firm to obtain more leverage than it otherwise could have. This raised the question of whether both the lease obligation and the asset involved should be capitalized and shown on the balance sheet. Discuss the pros and cons of capitalizing leases and related assets.

20-6   Suppose there were no IRS restrictions on what constitutes a valid lease. Explain in a manner that a legislator might understand why some restrictions should be imposed.

20-7   Suppose Congress changed the tax laws in a way that (1) permitted equipment to be depreciated over a shorter period, (2) lowered corporate tax rates, and (3) reinstated the investment tax credit. Discuss how each of these changes would affect the relative use of leasing versus conventional debt in the U.S. economy.

20-8   What effect does the expected growth rate of a firm's stock price (subsequent to issue) have on its ability to raise additional funds through (a) convertibles and (b) warrants?

20-9   *a.* How would a firm's decision to pay out a higher percentage of its earnings as dividends affect each of the following?
(1) The value of its long-term warrants.
(2) The likelihood that its convertible bonds will be converted.
(3) The likelihood that its warrants will be exercised.
b. If you owned the warrants or convertibles of a company, would you be pleased or displeased if it raised its payout rate from 20 percent to 80 percent? Why?

20-10   Suppose a company simultaneously issues $50 million of convertible bonds with a coupon rate of 9 percent and $50 million of pure bonds with a coupon rate of 12 percent. Both bonds have the same maturity. Does the fact that the convertible issue has the lower coupon rate suggest that it is less risky than the pure bond? Would you regard its cost of capital as being lower on the convertible than on the pure bond? Explain. (Hint: Although it might appear at first glance that the convertible's cost of capital is lower, this is not necessarily the case because the interest rate on the convertible understates its cost. Think about this.)

20-11   Describe how LBOs are used to finance acquisitions.

Self-Test Problems

(Solutions Appear in Appendix B)

Key terms **ST-1** Define each of the following terms:
a. cumulative dividends
b. lessee; lessor
c. sale and leaseback; operating lease; financial lease
d. off-balance-sheet financing
e. FASB #13
f. residual value
g. option; striking, or exercise, price; call option; put option
h. warrant; detachable warrant; stepped-up exercise price
i. convertible security; conversion ratio, CR
j. simple EPS; primary EPS; fully diluted EPS
k. leveraged buyout (LBO)
l. merger; synergy

Lease analysis **ST-2** The Olsen Company has decided to acquire a new truck. One alternative is to lease the truck on a 4-year contract for a lease payment of $10,000 per year, with payments to be made at the beginning of each year. The lease would include maintenance. Alternatively, Olsen could purchase the truck outright for $40,000, financing with a bank loan for the net purchase price, amortized over a 4-year period at an interest rate of 10 percent per year, payments to be made at the end of each year. Under the borrow-to-purchase arrangement, Olsen would have to maintain the truck at a cost of $1,000 per year, payable at year-end. The truck falls into the MACRS 3-year class. It has a salvage value of $10,000, which is the expected market value after 4 years, at which time Olsen plans to replace the truck irrespective of whether it leases or buys. Olsen has a marginal tax rate of 40 percent.
a. What is Olsen's PV cost of leasing?
b. What is Olsen's PV cost of owning? Should the truck be leased or purchased?
c. The appropriate discount rate for use in Olsen's analysis is the firm's after-tax cost of debt. Why?
d. The salvage value is the least certain cash flow in the analysis. How might Olsen incorporate the higher riskiness of this cash flow into the analysis?

Problems

Balance sheet effects of leasing **20-1** Two textile companies, Meyer Manufacturing and Haugen Mills, began operations with identical balance sheets. A year later, both required additional manufacturing capacity at a cost of $200,000. Meyer obtained a 5-year, $200,000 loan at an 8 percent interest rate from its bank. Haugen, on the other hand, decided to lease the required $200,000 capacity from American Leasing for 5 years; an 8 percent return was built into the lease. The balance sheet for each company, before the asset increases, is as follows:

		Debt	$200,000
		Equity	200,000
Total assets	$400,000	Total liabilities and equity	$400,000

a. Show the balance sheet of each firm after the asset increase, and calculate each firm's new debt ratio. (Assume Haugen's lease is kept off the balance sheet.)

b. Show how Haugen's balance sheet would have looked immediately after the financing if it had capitalized the lease.

c. Would the rate of return (1) on assets and (2) on equity be affected by the choice of financing? How?

Lease analysis   20-2   As part of its overall plant modernization and cost reduction program, the management of Teweles Textile Mills has decided to install a new automated weaving loom. In the capital budgeting analysis of this equipment, the IRR of the project was found to be 20 percent versus a project required return of 12 percent.

The loom has an invoice price of $250,000, including delivery and installation charges. The funds needed could be borrowed from the bank through a 4-year amortized loan at a 10 percent interest rate, with payments to be made at the *end* of each year. In the event that the loom is purchased, the manufacturer will contract to maintain and service it for a fee of $20,000 per year paid at the end of each year. The loom falls in the MACRS 5-year class, and Teweles's marginal tax rate is 40 percent.

Apilado Automation Inc., maker of the loom, has offered to lease the loom to Teweles for $70,000 upon delivery and installation (at t = 0) plus 4 additional annual lease payments of $70,000 to be made at the end of Years 1 through 4. (Note that there are 5 lease payments in total.) The lease agreement includes maintenance and servicing. Actually, the loom has an expected life of 8 years, at which time its expected salvage value is zero; however, after 4 years, its market value is expected to equal its book value of $42,500. Teweles plans to build an entirely new plant in 4 years, so it has no interest in either leasing or owning the proposed loom for more than that period.

a. Should the loom be leased or purchased?

b. The salvage value clearly is the most uncertain cash flow in the analysis. Assume that the appropriate salvage value *pretax* discount rate is 15 percent. What would be the effect of a salvage value risk adjustment on the decision?

c. The original analysis assumed that Teweles would not need the loom after 4 years. Now assume that the firm will continue to use it after the lease expires. Thus, if it leased, Teweles would have to buy the asset after 4 years at the then existing market value, which is assumed to equal the book value. What effect would this requirement have on the basic analysis? (No numerical analysis is required; just verbalize.)

Convertible bond   20-3   The Swift Company was planning to finance an expansion in the summer of 1996. The principal executives of the company agreed that an industrial company like theirs should finance growth by means of common stock rather than by debt. However, they believed that the price of the company's common stock did not reflect its true worth, so they decided to sell a convertible bond.

a. What is the conversion price of the issue? The conversion ratio will be 5.0; that is, each convertible bond can be converted into five shares of common. (The face value of the bond will be $1,000.)

b. Do you think the convertible bond should include a call provision? Why or why not?

Financing alternatives   20-4   The Cox Computer Company has grown rapidly during the past 5 years. Recently its commercial bank urged the company to consider increasing its permanent financing. Its bank loan under a line of credit has risen to $150,000, carrying a 10 percent interest rate, and Cox has been 30 to 60 days late in paying trade creditors.

Discussions with an investment banker have resulted in the decision to raise $250,000 at this time. Investment bankers have assured Cox that the following alternatives are feasible (flotation costs will be ignored):

- *Alternative 1:* Sell common stock at $10 per share.
- *Alternative 2:* Sell convertible bonds at a 10 percent coupon, convertible into 80 shares of common stock for each $1,000 bond (that is, the conversion price is $12.50 per share).
- *Alternative 3:* Sell debentures with a 10 percent coupon; each $1,000 bond will have 80 warrants to buy one share of common stock at $12.50.

Charles Cox, the president, owns 80 percent of Cox's common stock and wishes to maintain control of the company; 50,000 shares are outstanding. The following are summaries of Cox's latest financial statements:

Balance Sheet

		Current liabilities	$200,000
		Common stock, $1 par	50,000
		Retained earnings	25,000
Total assets	$275,000	Total liabilities and equity	$275,000

Income Statement

Sales	$550,000
All costs except interest	(495,000)
EBIT	$ 55,000
Interest	(15,000)
EBT	$ 40,000
Taxes at 40%	(16,000)
Net income	$ 24,000
Shares outstanding	50,000
Earnings per share	$0.48
Price/earnings ratio	18×
Market price of stock	$8.64

a. Show the new balance sheet under each alternative. For Alternatives 2 and 3, show the balance sheet after conversion of the debentures or exercise of the warrants. Assume that $150,000 of the funds raised will be used to pay off the bank loan and the rest to increase total assets.

b. Show Charles Cox's control position under each alternative, assuming that he does not purchase additional shares.

c. What is the effect on earnings per share of each alternative if it is assumed that earnings before interest and taxes will be 20 percent of total assets?

d. What will be the debt ratio under each alternative?

e. Which of the three alternatives would you recommend to Charles Cox, and why?

Exam-Type Problem

The problem included in this section is set up in such a way that it could be used as a multiple-choice exam problem.

Lease versus buy   **20-5**   Maltese Mining Company must install $1.5 million of new machinery in its Nevada mine. It can obtain a bank loan for 100 percent of the required amount. Alternatively, a Nevada investment banking firm which represents a group of investors believes that it can arrange for a lease financing plan. Assume that the following facts apply:

(1) The equipment falls in the MACRS 3-year class.

(2) Estimated maintenance expenses are $75,000 per year.

(3) Maltese's marginal tax rate is 40 percent.

(4) If the money is borrowed, the bank loan will be at a rate of 15 percent, amortized in 4 equal installments to be paid at the end of each year.

(5) The tentative lease terms call for end-of-year payments of $400,000 per year for 4 years.

(6) Under the proposed lease terms, the lessee must pay for insurance, property taxes, and maintenance.

(7) Maltese must use the equipment if it is to continue in business, so it will almost certainly want to acquire the property at the end of the lease. If it does, then under the lease terms it can purchase the machinery at its fair market value at that time. The best estimate of this market value is the $250,000 salvage value, but it could be much higher or lower under certain circumstances.

To assist management in making the proper lease-versus-buy decision, you are asked to answer the following questions.

a. Assuming that the lease can be arranged, should Maltese lease, or should it borrow and buy the equipment? Explain.

b. Consider the $250,000 estimated salvage value. Is it appropriate to discount it at the same rate as the other cash flows? What about the other cash flows—are they all equally risky? (Hint: Riskier cash flows are normally discounted at higher rates, but when the cash flows are *costs* rather than *inflows,* the normal procedure must be reversed.)

Integrative Problem

Lease analysis **20-6** Martha Millon, capital acquisitions manager for Heath Financial Services Inc., has been asked to perform a lease-versus-buy analysis on a new stock price quotation system for Heath's Sarasota branch office. The system would receive current prices, record the information for retrieval by the branch's brokers, and display current prices in the lobby.

The equipment costs $1,200,000, and, if it is purchased, Heath could obtain a term loan for the full amount at a 10 percent cost. The loan would be amortized over the 4-year life of the equipment, with payments made at the end of each year. The equipment is classified as special purpose, and hence it falls into the MACRS 3-year class. If the equipment is purchased, a maintenance contract must be obtained at a cost of $25,000, payable at the beginning of each year.

After 4 years the equipment will be sold, and Millon's best estimate of its residual value at that time is $125,000. Because technology is changing rapidly in real-time display systems, however, the residual value is very uncertain.

As an alternative, National Leasing is willing to write a 4-year lease on the equipment, including maintenance, for payments of $340,000 at the *beginning* of each year. Heath's marginal tax rate is 40 percent. Help Millon conduct her analysis by answering the following questions.

a. (1) Why is leasing sometimes referred to as "off-balance-sheet" financing?

(2) What is the difference between a capital lease and an operating lease?

(3) What effect does leasing have on a firm's capital structure?

b. (1) What is Heath's present value cost of owning the equipment? (Hint: Set up a table whose bottom line is a "time line" which shows the net cash flows over the period t = 0 to t = 4, and then find the PV of these net cash flows, or the PV cost of owning.)

(2) Explain the rationale for the discount rate you used to find the PV.

c. (1) What is Heath's present value cost of leasing the equipment? (Hint: Again, construct a time line.)

(2) What is the net advantage to leasing? Does your analysis indicate that Heath should buy or lease the equipment? Explain.

d. Now assume that Millon believes the equipment's residual value could be as low as $0 or as high as $250,000, but she stands by $125,000 as her expected value. She concludes that the residual value is riskier than the other cash flows in the analysis, and she wants to incorporate this differential risk into her analysis. Describe how this could be accomplished. What effect would it have on Heath's lease decision?

e. Millon knows that her firm has been considering moving to a new downtown location for some time, and she is concerned that these plans may come to fruition prior to the expiration of the lease. If the move occurs, the company would obtain completely new equipment, and hence Millon would like to include a cancellation clause in the lease contract. What effect would a cancellation clause have on the riskiness of the lease?

Computer-Related Problem

Work the problem in this section only if you are using the computer problem diskette.

Lease versus buy   **20-7**   Use the model in File C20 to work this problem.

a. Refer to Problem 20-5. Determine the lease payment at which Maltese would be indifferent to buying or leasing; that is, find the lease payment which equates the NPV of leasing to that of buying. (Hint: Use trial and error.)

b. Using the $400,000 lease payment, what would be the effect if Maltese's tax rate fell to 20 percent? What would be the effect if the tax rate fell to zero percent? What do these results suggest?

Multinational Managerial Finance[1]

In the 1960s and 1970s, the major players in international markets were the U.S. multinational corporations such as IBM, which obtained about 20 percent of its revenues from abroad. These giants treated foreign operations as distant appendages for producing products designed and engineered back home. The chain of command and nationality of the company were clear.

Today, however, the situation has changed dramatically. The United States no longer dominates the world economy, and innovation, new technologies, and capital flow in many different directions. The most sophisticated companies are making breakthroughs in foreign labs, obtaining capital from foreign investors, and putting foreign employees on the fast track to the top. Now, dozens of America's top manufacturers, including Dow Chemical, Colgate-Palmolive, Gillette, Hewlett-Packard, and Xerox sell more of their products outside the United States than at home. Service firms are not far behind, as 40 percent of McDonald's sales are in the foreign market, and about 20 percent of the revenues received by both Citicorp and Disney result from foreign business.

The trend is even more pronounced in profits. In the past several years, Coca-Cola made more money in both the Pacific and Western Europe than it did in the United States. As companies begin to reap half or more of their sales and profits from abroad, they are blending into the foreign landscape to win acceptance and avoid political hassles.

At the same time, foreign-based multinationals are arriving on American shores in greater numbers than ever before. Sweden's ABB, the Netherlands' Philips Electronics, France's state-owned Thomson Electronics, and Japan's Fujitsu all are waging campaigns to be identified as American companies that employ Americans, transfer technology to America, and help the U.S. trade balance and overall economic health. Few Americans know, or likely care, that Thomson owns the RCA name in consumer electronics, Philips owns Magnavox, or Britain's Cadbury Schweppes PLC paid $1.7 billion to

Continued

---

[1]This chapter was coauthored by Professor Roy L. Crum of the University of Florida.

purchase Dr. Pepper/Seven Up Companies in February 1995. In 1994, foreign companies invested $57 billion to acquire, merge with, or form joint ventures with U.S. firms.

These "world companies" raise a host of questions for governments seeking to shape their nations' economic destinies. For example, does it make any difference what a company's nationality is as long as it provides jobs? What nation controls the technology developed by multinational corporations? What obligations do these companies have to adhere to rules imposed by Washington, Paris, or Tokyo on their foreign operations? And if a U.S. firm makes copiers in Japan and exports them to the United States, should they be counted in the trade deficit in the same way as Toyotas imported from Japan?

Managers of multinational companies face a wide range of issues that are not present when a company operates in a single country. In this chapter, we highlight the key differences between multinational and domestic corporations, and we discuss the impact of these differences on managerial finance for U.S. businesses.

Multinational Corporations

MULTINATIONAL CORPORATION
A firm that operates in two or more countries.

The term **multinational corporation** is used to describe a firm that operates in two or more countries. During the period since World War II, a new and fundamentally different form of international commercial activity has developed, and it has increased greatly worldwide economic and political interdependence. Rather than merely buying resources from foreign concerns, multinational firms now make direct investments in fully integrated operations, with worldwide entities controlling all phases of the production process—from extraction of raw materials, through the manufacturing process, to distribution to consumers throughout the world. Today, multinational corporate networks control a large and growing share of the world's technological, marketing, and productive resources.

There are five principal reasons companies, both U.S. and foreign, go "international."

1. **To seek new markets.** After a company has saturated its home market, growth opportunities often are better in foreign markets. Thus, such home-grown firms as Coca-Cola and McDonald's have aggressively expanded into overseas markets, and foreign firms such as Sony and Toshiba now dominate the U.S. consumer electronics market.
2. **To seek raw materials.** It is not surprising that many U.S. oil companies, such as Exxon, have major subsidiaries around the world to ensure access to the basic resources needed to sustain the company's primary business line.
3. **To seek new technology.** No single nation holds a commanding advantage in all technologies, so companies scour the globe for leading scientific and design ideas. For example, Xerox has introduced over 80 different office copiers in the United States that were engineered and built by its Japanese joint venture, Fuji Xerox.

Whirlpool Jumps Into the "WorldPool"

Whirlpool Corporation is the world's largest manufacturer of major home appliances, which include washing machines, clothes dryers, and ovens and ranges, to name a few. But, until it spent approximately $1 billion to purchase the appliance division of Philips Electronics, Europe's largest electronics firm, Whirlpool was simply the largest appliance manufacturer in the United States. The acquisition of the Dutch-based firm's appliance unit was part of Whirlpool's plan to start building a prominent multinational organization; it was accomplished in two stages—Whirlpool purchased 47 percent of Philips' appliance unit in January 1989, and the remaining 53 percent was purchased in July 1991. The acquisition immediately thrust Whirlpool into the global marketplace, but not exactly in the manner the company had hoped. Whirlpool found that the operations it purchased needed an overhaul to make the company a viable competitor in Europe as well as internationally.

The Philips' appliance unit was profitable when Whirlpool acquired it, but just barely, and profits as well as product market share had been declining. The market Philips had built for the appliances was somewhat limited in the European community, and the companies that manufactured the appliances were provincial with respect to their home countries. Whirlpool found that the inter-country systems were not synchronized—for example, appliances made in Germany and Italy contained no common parts. So, to coordinate the operations from each country, Whirlpool created a continental organization called Whirlpool Europe. Under the aegis of Whirlpool Europe, the independent companies that previously existed in individual countries were merged to form a network of regional companies. The network allowed Whirlpool both to consolidate the research and development functions at Whirlpool Europe and to share information and better communicate with Whirlpool operations in the United States. The reorganization of the European companies also included centralized inventory and production management, which allowed Whirlpool to use production "platforms" to achieve more uniformity in

ordering materials and manufacturing and distributing the appliances. More common products were manufactured with more shared parts. Prior to the acquisition, Philips used approximately 1,600 suppliers—Whirlpool cut that number in half. In one case, for example, Philips purchased the power cords used on its refrigerators from 17 suppliers, but Whirlpool cut that number to two.

The coordination and consolidation effort has allowed Whirlpool to cut operating costs, decrease inventories, and increase profit margins. The "platform" manufacturing process provides Whirlpool the opportunity to manufacture two or three brand name products at the same plant; by using a standard design and common parts inside its ovens, for example, Whirlpool now produces its top-of-the-line Bauknecht ovens at the same location it produces its own brand name ovens and cheaper ovens that carry the name Ignis. Such cost-cutting moves have increased the efficiency, along with profits, at Whirlpool Europe—this trend as well as gains in market share, is expected to continue.

As Whirlpool pares its European operations further, many analysts in the United States believe the company will continue its successful expansion overseas. But, some European analysts believe Whirlpool is trying to standardize a continent that consists of many cultures with many different tastes and needs. It is their opinion that the European marketplace cannot be treated as uniform. Whirlpool executives disagree. In fact, in July 1994, the company agreed to purchase Kelvinator of India Ltd., India's largest maker of refrigerators, for $110 million. Whirlpool's plans are to apply the knowledge it has gained through Whirlpool Europe to enter the Asian appliance market. Ultimately, Whirlpool wants to be able to produce its products all over the world, and to have those products used worldwide. To achieve this dream, Whirlpool cannot look back, because such companies as GE and Electrolux are only a step behind.

SOURCE: "Call It Worldpool," *Business Week* (November 28, 1994).

4. **To seek production efficiency.** Companies in high production cost countries are shifting production to low-cost countries. For example, GE has production and assembly plants in Mexico, South Korea, and Singapore, and even Japanese manufacturers have shifted some of their production to lower cost countries

in the Pacific Rim. The ability to shift production from country to country has important implications for labor costs in all countries. For example, when Xerox threatened to move its copier rebuilding work to Mexico, its union in Rochester, New York, agreed to work rule and productivity improvements that kept the operation in the United States. Some multinational companies make almost daily decisions on where to shift production. When Dow Chemical saw European demand for a certain solvent declining, the company scaled back production at a German plant and shifted it to another chemical which previously had been imported from the United States. Relying on complex computer models for making such decisions, Dow runs its plants at higher capacity and thus keeps capital costs down.

5. **To avoid political and regulatory hurdles.** The primary reason for Japanese auto companies to move production to the United States was to get around U.S. import quotas. Now, Honda, Nissan, Toyota, Mazda, and Mitsubishi all assemble automobiles or trucks in the United States. Similarly, one of the factors that prompted U.S. pharmaceutical maker SmithKline and Britain's Beecham to merge was that they wanted to avoid licensing and regulatory delays in their largest markets, Western Europe and the United States. Now, SmithKline Beecham can identify itself as an inside player in both Europe and the United States.

During the 1980s and the 1990s, investments in the United States by foreign corporations have increased significantly. This "reverse" investment, which is of increasing concern to U.S. government officials, actually has been growing at a higher rate in the past few years than has U.S. investment abroad. This trend is important because of its implication for eroding the traditional doctrine of independence and self-reliance that always has been a hallmark of U.S. policy. Just as U.S. corporations with extensive overseas operations are said to use their economic power to exert substantial economic and political influence over host governments around the world, it is feared that foreign corporations might gain similar sway over U.S. policy. However, these developments suggest an increasing degree of mutual influence and interdependence among business enterprises and nations, to which the United States is not immune.

During the past decade, some dramatic international changes have taken place, including the breakup, both politically and economically, of the former Soviet Union, the collapse of communism in many Eastern European countries, the reunification of Germany, and the political revolution in South Africa. Future events will include the continued phasing in of the European Economic Community with one Eurocurrency and the determination of how to help the cash-starved Eastern Bloc nations. Also, there has been a war with Iraq and continuing turbulence in the Middle East. These events, and others which surely will occur, have an impact on the world economy.

Self-Test Questions

What is a multinational corporation?

Why do companies "go international"?

Multinational versus Domestic Managerial Finance

In theory, the concepts and procedures discussed in the previous chapters of the text are valid for both domestic and multinational operations. However, several problems uniquely associated with the international environment increase the complexity of the manager's task in a multinational corporation, and they often force the manager to alter the way alternative courses of action are evaluated and compared. Six major factors distinguish managerial finance as practiced by firms operating entirely within a single country from management by firms that operate in several different countries:

1. **Different currency denominations.** Cash flows in various parts of a multinational corporate system generally are denominated in different currencies. Hence, an analysis of exchange rates, and the effects of fluctuating currency values, must be included in all financial analyses.

2. **Economic and legal ramifications.** Each country in which the firm operates will have its own unique political and economic institutions, and institutional differences among countries can cause significant problems when a firm tries to coordinate and control the worldwide operations of its subsidiaries. For example, differences in tax laws among countries can cause a particular transaction to have strikingly dissimilar after-tax consequences, depending on where the transaction occurred. Similarly, differences in legal systems of host nations complicate many matters, from the simple recording of a business transaction to the role played by the judiciary in resolving conflicts. Such differences can restrict multinational corporations' flexibility to deploy resources as they wish, and can even make procedures illegal in one part of the company that are required in another part. These differences also make it difficult for executives trained in one country to operate effectively in another.

3. **Language differences.** The ability to communicate is critical in all business transactions, and here persons who are American born and raised often are at a disadvantage because they generally are fluent only in English, while European and Japanese businesspeople usually are fluent in several languages, including English. Thus, it is easier for internationals to invade U.S. markets than it is for Americans to penetrate international markets. The importance of this factor cannot be stressed too strongly.

4. **Cultural differences.** Even within geographic regions long considered fairly homogeneous, different countries have unique cultural heritages that shape values and influence the role of business in the society. Multinational corporations find that such matters as defining the appropriate goals of the firm, attitudes toward risk taking, dealings with employees, the ability to curtail unprofitable operations, and so on, can vary dramatically from one country to the next.

5. **Role of governments.** Most traditional models in finance assume the existence of a competitive marketplace in which the terms of trade are determined by the participants. The government, through its power to establish basic ground rules, is involved in this process, but its participation is minimal. Thus, the market provides both the primary barometer of success and the indicator of the actions that must be taken to remain competitive. This view of the process is reasonably correct for the United States and a few other major

industrialized nations, but it does not accurately describe the situation in most of the world. Frequently, the terms under which companies compete, the actions that must be taken or avoided, and the terms of trade on various transactions are determined not in the marketplace, but by direct negotiation between the host government and the multinational corporation. This is essentially a political process, and it must be treated as such. Thus, our traditional financial models have to be recast to include political and other noneconomic facets of the decision.

6. **Political risk.** The distinguishing characteristic of a nation that differentiates it from a multinational corporation is that the nation exercises sovereignty over the people and property in its territory. Hence, a nation is free to place constraints on the transfer of corporate resources and even to expropriate (take for public use) the assets of a firm without compensation. This is political risk, and it tends to be largely a given rather than a variable that can be changed by negotiation. Political risk varies from country to country, and it must be addressed explicitly in any financial analysis. Another aspect of political risk is terrorism against U.S. firms or executives abroad. For example, U.S. executives have been captured and held for ransom in several South American and Middle Eastern countries.

These six factors complicate managerial finance within multinational firms, and they increase the risks faced by the firms involved. However, prospects for high profits often make it worthwhile for firms to accept these risks, and to learn how to minimize or at least live with them.

Self-Test Question

Identify and briefly explain six major factors that complicate managerial finance within multinational firms.

Exchange Rates

EXCHANGE RATE
The number of units of a given currency that can be purchased for one unit of another currency.

An **exchange rate** specifies the number of units of a given currency that can be purchased, or *exchanged,* for one unit of another currency. Exchange rates appear in the financial sections of newspapers each day. Selected rates from the March 24, 1995, issue of *The Wall Street Journal* are given in Table 21-1. The values shown in Column 1 are the number of U.S. dollars required to purchase one unit of foreign currency on March 23, 1995; this is called a *direct quotation.* Thus, the direct U.S. dollar quotation on March 23, 1995, for the German mark is $0.7126 because one German mark could be bought for 71.26 cents. The exchange rates given in Column 2 represent the number of units of foreign currency that can be purchased for one U.S. dollar; these are called *indirect quotations.* The indirect quotation for the German mark is DM1.4033. (The "DM" stands for deutsche mark; it is equivalent to the symbol "$.") The normal practice in the United States is to use indirect quotations (Column 2) for all currencies other than British pounds, for which direct quotations are given. Thus, we speak of the pound as "selling at $1.59" but of the German mark as "being at 1.40."

TABLE 21-1

Illustrative Exchange Rates, March 23, 1995

	Direct Quotation: U.S. Dollars Required to Buy One Unit of Foreign Currency (1)	Indirect Quotation: Number of Units of Foreign Currency per U.S. Dollar (2)
British pound	$1.5944	0.6272
Canadian dollar	0.7109	1.4067
French franc	0.20131	4.9675
German mark	0.7126	1.4033
Greek drachma	0.004336	230.65
Indian rupee	0.03167	31.58
Italian lira	0.0005799	1,724.50
Japanese yen	0.011344	88.15
Mexican peso	0.1449275	6.9000
Netherland (Dutch) guilder	0.6358	1.5727
Norwegian krone	0.1599	6.2545
Saudi Arabian riyal	0.26662	3.7506
Singaporean dollar	0.7067	1.4150
South African rand	0.2777	3.6008
Spanish peseta	0.007725	129.45
Swedish krona	0.1373	7.2825
Swiss franc	0.8599	1.1629

NOTE: Column 2 is the inverse of Column 1; however, rounding differences do occur.
SOURCE: *The Wall Street Journal*, March 24, 1995.

It also is a universal convention on the world's foreign currency exchanges to state all exchange rates except British pounds on a "dollar basis"—that is, as the foreign currency price of one U.S. dollar as reported in Table 21-1, Column 2. Thus, in all currency trading centers, whether in New York, Frankfurt, London, Tokyo, or anywhere else, the exchange rate for the German mark on March 23, 1995, would be displayed as DM1.4033. This convention eliminates confusion when comparing quotations from one trading center with those from another.

We can use the rates in Table 21-1 to show how one computes exchange rates. Suppose a vacationing American tourist flies from New York to London, then to Paris, then on to Munich, and finally back to New York. When she arrives at London's Heathrow Airport on March 23, 1995, she goes to the bank to check the foreign exchange listing. The rate she observes for U.S. dollars is $1.5944; this means that 1 pound will cost her $1.5944. Assume that she exchanges $2,000 for $2,000/$1.5944 = £1,254.39 and enjoys a week's vacation in London, spending £754.39 while there (the symbol £ represents the British pound denomination).

At the end of the week she travels to Dover to catch the Hovercraft to Calais on the coast of France and realizes that she needs to exchange her 500 remaining British pounds for French francs. However, what she sees on the board is the direct quotation between pounds and dollars ($1.5944) and the indirect quotation between francs and dollars (FF4.9675). (For our purposes, we assume that the exchange rates in effect on March 23 remain in effect throughout our example. This is very unrealistic for reasons explained later in this chapter.) The exchange rate between pounds and francs is called a *cross rate,* and it is computed as follows:

$$\text{Cross rate} = \frac{\text{Dollars}}{\text{Pound}} \times \frac{\text{Francs}}{\text{Dollar}} = \frac{\text{Francs}}{\text{Pound}}$$

$$= \$1.5944 \text{ per pound} \times 4.9675 \text{ francs per dollar}$$

$$= 7.9202 \text{ francs per pound}$$

Therefore, for every British pound she would receive 7.9202 French francs, so she would receive $7.9202 \times 500 \approx 3{,}960$ francs.

When she finishes touring in France and arrives in Germany, the American tourist again needs to determine a cross rate, this time between French francs and German marks. The dollar-basis quotes she sees, as shown in Table 21-1, are FF4.9675 per dollar and DM1.4033 per dollar. To find the cross rate, she must divide the two dollar-basis rates:

$$\text{Cross rate} = \frac{\frac{\text{Marks}}{\text{Dollar}}}{\frac{\text{Francs}}{\text{Dollar}}} = \frac{\text{Marks}}{\text{Dollar}} \times \frac{\text{Dollar}}{\text{Franc}} = \frac{\text{Marks}}{\text{Franc}}$$

$$= \frac{\text{DM1.4033 per \$}}{\text{FF4.9675 per \$}} = 0.2825 \text{ marks per franc}$$

Then, if she had FF2,000 remaining, she could exchange them for $0.2825 \times 2{,}000$ = DM565, or 565 marks.

Finally, when her vacation ends and she returns to New York, the quotation she sees is DM1.4033, which tells her that she can buy 1.4033 marks for a dollar. She now holds 50 marks, so she wants to know how many U.S. dollars she will receive for her marks. First, she must find the reciprocal of the quoted indirect rate,

$$\frac{1}{\text{DM1.4033}} = \$0.7126 \text{ per mark}$$

which is the direct quote shown in Table 21-1, Column 1. Then she will end up with

$$\$0.7126 \text{ per mark} \times \text{DM50} = \$35.63$$

In this example, we made two very important and generally incorrect assumptions. First, we assumed that our traveler had to calculate the appropriate cross rates. For retail transactions, it is customary to display the cross rates directly instead of a series of dollar rates. Second, we assumed that exchange rates remain constant over time. Actually, exchange rates vary every day, often dramatically. We will have more to say about exchange rate fluctuations in the next section.

Self-Test Questions

What is an exchange rate?

Explain the difference between direct and indirect quotations.

What is a cross rate?

The International Monetary System

FIXED EXCHANGE RATE SYSTEM
The world monetary system in existence after World War II until 1971, under which the value of the U.S. dollar was tied to gold, and the values of the other currencies were pegged to the U.S. dollar.

From the end of World War II until August 1971, the world was on a **fixed exchange rate system** administered by the International Monetary Fund (IMF). Under this system the U.S. dollar was linked to gold at a *fixed* price of $35 per ounce, and other currencies then were tied to the dollar. Exchange rates between other currencies and the dollar were controlled within narrow limits but then adjusted periodically. For example, in 1964 the British pound was adjusted to $2.80 for 1 pound, with a 1 percent permissible fluctuation around this rate.

Fluctuations in exchange rates occur because of changes in the supply of and demand for dollars, pounds, and other currencies. These supply and demand changes have two primary sources. First, changes in the demand for currencies depend on changes in imports and exports of goods and services. For example, U.S. importers must buy British pounds to pay for British goods, whereas British importers must buy U.S. dollars to pay for U.S. goods. If U.S. imports from Great Britain exceeded U.S. exports to Great Britain, there would be a greater demand for pounds than for dollars; this would drive up the price of the pound relative to that of the dollar. In terms of Table 21-1, the dollar cost of a pound might rise from $1.5944 to $2.0000. The U.S. dollar would be said to be *depreciating,* whereas the pound would be *appreciating.* In this example, the primary cause of the change would be the U.S. **deficit trade balance** with Great Britain. Of course, if U.S. exports to Great Britain were greater than U.S. imports from Great Britain, Great Britain would have a deficit trade balance with the United States.[2]

DEFICIT TRADE BALANCE
The situation where a country imports more than it exports.

Changes in the demand for a currency, and hence exchange rate fluctuations, also depend on capital movements. For example, suppose interest rates in Great Britain were higher than those in the United States. To take advantage of the high British interest rates, U.S. banks, corporations, and even sophisticated individuals could buy pounds with dollars and then use those pounds to purchase high-yielding British securities. These purchases would tend to drive up the price of pounds.[3]

---

[2]If the dollar value of the pound moved up from $1.5944 to $2.00, this increase in the value of the pound would mean that British goods would now be more expensive in the U.S. market. For example, a box of candy costing 1 pound in England would rise in price in the United States from $1.59 to $2.00. Conversely, U.S. goods would become cheaper in England. For example, the British could now buy goods worth $2.00 for 1 pound, whereas before the exchange rate change, 1 pound would buy merchandise worth only $1.59. These price changes would, of course, tend to reduce British exports and increase imports, and this, in turn, would lower the exchange rate, because people in the United States and other nations would be buying fewer pounds to pay for English goods. However, before 1971 the 1 percent limit severely constrained the market's ability to reach an equilibrium between trade balances and exchange rates.

[3]Such capital inflows also would tend to drive down British interest rates. If rates were high in the first place because of efforts by the British monetary authorities to curb inflation, the international

Before August 1971 exchange rate fluctuations were kept within the narrow 1 percent limit by regular intervention of the British government in the market. When the value of the pound was too low, the Bank of England would step in and buy pounds, offering gold or foreign currencies in exchange. These government purchases pushed up the pound rate. Conversely, when the pound rate was too high, the Bank of England would sell pounds. The central banks of other countries operated similarly.

DEVALUATION
The process of officially reducing the value of a country's currency relative to other currencies.

Of course, a central bank's ability to control its exchange rate was limited by its supply of gold and foreign currencies. With the approval of the IMF, a country could **devalue** its currency—which means to officially lower its value relative to other currencies—if it experienced persistent difficulty over a long period in preventing its exchange rate from falling below the lower limit, and if its central bank was running out of the gold and other currencies that could be used to buy its own currency and thus prop up its price. For just these reasons the British pound was devalued from $2.80 per pound to $2.50 per pound in 1967. This lowered the price of British goods in the United States and elsewhere and raised the prices of foreign goods in Britain, thus stopping the British deficit trade balance that had been putting pressure on the pound in the first place. Conversely, a nation with

REVALUATION
The process of officially increasing the value of a country's currency relative to other currencies.

an export surplus and a strong currency might **revalue** its currency upward, as West Germany did twice in the 1960s.

Devaluations and revaluations occurred only rarely before 1971. They usually were accompanied by severe international financial repercussions, partly because nations tended to postpone these needed measures until economic pressures had built up to explosive proportions. For this and other reasons the old international monetary system came to a dramatic end in the early 1970s, when the U.S. dollar, the foundation upon which all other currencies were anchored, was cut loose from the gold standard and, in effect, allowed to "float."

FLOATING EXCHANGE RATES
The system whereby exchange rates are for the most part not fixed by government policy but are allowed to float up or down in accordance with supply and demand.

The United States and the other major nations currently operate under a system of **floating exchange rates,** whereby currency prices are allowed to seek their own levels without much governmental intervention. The central bank of each country still intervenes in the foreign exchange market, buying and selling its currency to smooth out exchange rate fluctuations to some extent, and there have been agreements by groups of countries to keep the relative values of their currencies within a predetermined range. Such an agreement by the "Group of Seven" at the Seoul Economic Summit in October 1985 caused the U.S. dollar to fall substantially against most major currencies. This action was endorsed as appropriate at the Washington Economic Summit in September 1987. The "Group of Seven" also was responsible for helping to stabilize the falling dollar in early 1988.

---

currency flows would tend to thwart that effort. This is one of the reasons domestic and international economics are so closely linked.

A good example of this occurred during the summer of 1981. In an effort to curb inflation, the Federal Reserve Board helped push U.S. interest rates to record levels. This, in turn, caused an outflow of capital from European nations to the United States. The Europeans were suffering from a severe recession and wanted to keep interest rates down in order to stimulate investment, but U.S. policy made this difficult because of international capital flows.

Each central bank also tries to keep its average exchange rate at a level deemed desirable by its government's economic policy. This is important because exchange rates have a profound effect on the levels of imports and exports, which in turn influence the level of domestic employment. For example, if a country is having a problem with unemployment, its central bank might encourage a *decline* in the value of its currency. This would cause its goods to be cheaper in world markets and thus stimulate exports, production, and domestic employment. Conversely, the central bank of a country that is operating at full capacity and experiencing inflation might try to raise the value of its currency to reduce exports and increase imports. Under the current floating rate system, however, such intervention can affect the situation only temporarily, because market forces will prevail in the long run.

Figure 21-1 shows how the values of German marks and Japanese yen moved in comparison with the dollar from 1981 to 1995. The *dollar* strengthened, or appreciated, against the mark from 1981 to 1985 but then weakened, or depreciated, from 1985 to 1995, with slight reversals in 1989, 1991, and 1993. The Japanese *yen* was relatively stable against the dollar in the first five years, but then it appreciated from 1985 to 1988 (fewer yen were required to buy a dollar), depreciated in 1989, and then appreciated again from 1990 to 1995. In fact, at the time this text was written in March 1995, the value of the yen was at a post–World War II high, 88 yen per dollar, meaning the value of the dollar was extremely low relative to the yen—analysts expected the dollar to fall to 75 yen by the end of the year.

Exchange rate fluctuations can have a profound impact on international monetary transactions. For example, in 1985 it cost Honda Motors 2,380,000 yen to build a particular model in Japan and ship it to the United States. The model carried a U.S. sticker price of $12,000. Because the $12,000 sales price was the equivalent of (238 yen per dollar) × ($12,000) = 2,856,000 yen, the automaker had built a 20 percent markup into the U.S. sales price. However, three years later, the dollar had depreciated to 128 yen. Now, if the model still sold for $12,000, the yen return to Honda would be only (128 yen per dollar) × ($12,000) = 1,536,000 yen, and the automaker would be losing about 35 percent on each auto sold. Even though U.S. prices held firm, the 46 percent depreciation of the dollar against the yen turned a healthy profit into a loss. In fact, for Honda to maintain its 20 percent markup, in 1988, the model had to be sold in the United States for (2,856,000 yen) ÷ (128 yen per dollar) = $22,312.50; in March 1995, the same car would have had to be sold for $32,454.55 when $1 was worth 88 yen. No wonder Honda now builds its most popular model, the Accord, in Marysville, Ohio!

You might be thinking that it takes years for major fluctuations in exchange rates to occur. However, major changes can occur in much shorter periods. Suppose, on January 1, 1995, a Japanese investor wanted to take advantage of the comparatively high interest rates on U.S. Treasury securities, so he bought a T-bill for $9,700 that would be worth $10,000 at the end of June. This works out to about a 6 percent annual return. In January, the exchange rate was 100 yen per dollar, so the T-bill cost the investor 100($9,700) = 970,000 yen. If, at maturity, the exchange rate was only 85 yen per dollar, the investor's yen return would be 85($10,000) = 850,000 yen. Thus, exchange rate fluctuations turned the 6 percent expected return into a loss of nearly 25 percent (annualized).

FIGURE 21-1

Yen and Mark Exchange Rates, 1981–1995

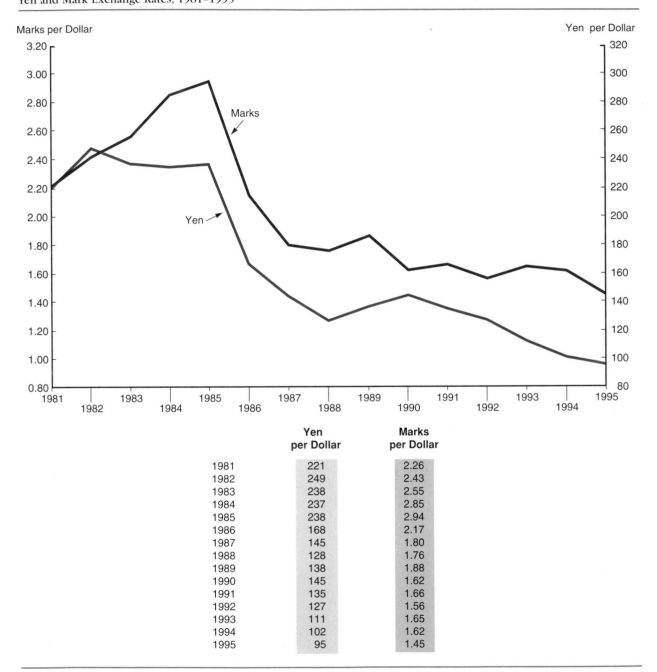

	Yen per Dollar	Marks per Dollar
1981	221	2.26
1982	249	2.43
1983	238	2.55
1984	237	2.85
1985	238	2.94
1986	168	2.17
1987	145	1.80
1988	128	1.76
1989	138	1.88
1990	145	1.62
1991	135	1.66
1992	127	1.56
1993	111	1.65
1994	102	1.62
1995	95	1.45

NOTE: The exchange rates listed above are annual averages—the 1995 averages are based on the exchange rates for the first quarter of the year.

SOURCE: *Federal Reserve Bulletin.*

The inherent volatility of exchange rates under a floating system increases the uncertainty of the cash flows for a multinational corporation. Because these cash flows are generated in many parts of the world, they are denominated in many different currencies. Because exchange rates change, the dollar-equivalent value of the consolidated cash flows can fluctuate. This is known as **exchange rate risk,** and it is a major factor differentiating the multinational corporation from a purely domestic one. However, there exists a variety of ways for a multinational corporation to manage and limit its exchange rate risk, and several of them are discussed in the next section.

EXCHANGE RATE RISK
The risk that exchange rates will change, causing the value of a cash flow to change.

Before closing our discussion of the international monetary system, we should note that not all currencies are convertible. A currency is **convertible** when the issuing nation allows it to be traded in the currency markets and is willing to redeem the currency at market rates. This means that, except for limited central bank influence, the issuing government loses control over the value of its currency. Lack of convertibility creates major problems for international trade. For example, consider the situation faced by Pepsico when it wanted to open a chain of Pizza Hut restaurants in the Soviet Union prior to its breakup. The Russian ruble was not convertible, so Pepsico could not take the profits from its restaurants out of the Soviet Union in the form of rubles. If it took rubles out, no mechanism existed to exchange the rubles for dollars, so the investment in the Soviet Union seemingly was worthless to a U.S. company. But Pepsico arranged to use the ruble profits from the restaurants to buy Russian vodka, which it then shipped to the United States and sold. The profits on the vodka sales, which were in dollars, contained the profits from the Russian restaurants, as well as any added profits made on the vodka import business.

CONVERTIBLE CURRENCY
A currency that can be readily exchanged for other currencies.

Self-Test Questions

What is the difference between a fixed exchange rate system and a floating rate system? Which system is better? Explain.

What does it mean to say that the dollar is depreciating with respect to the British pound? For a U.S. consumer of British goods, would this be good or bad? How could consumption changes arrest the decline of the dollar?

What is a convertible currency?

Trading in Foreign Exchange

Importers, exporters, and tourists, as well as governments, buy and sell currencies in the foreign exchange market. For example, when a U.S. automobile trader imports cars from Germany, payment probably will be made in German marks. The importer buys marks (through its bank) in the foreign exchange market, much as one buys common stocks on the New York Stock Exchange. However, whereas stock exchanges have organized trading floors, the foreign exchange market consists of a network of brokers and banks based in New York, London, Tokyo, and

TABLE 21-2

Selected Spot and Forward Exchange Rates, March 23, 1995
(number of units of foreign currency per U.S. dollar)

	Spot Rate	30 Days	90 Days	180 Days	Forward Rate at a Premium or a Discount
British pound	0.6272	0.6269	0.6273	0.6286	discount
French franc	4.9675	4.9763	4.9930	5.0070	discount
German mark	1.4033	1.4009	1.3980	1.3934	premium
Japanese yen	88.1500	87.8600	87.2500	86.2400	premium
Swiss franc	1.1629	1.1601	1.1550	1.1474	premium

NOTES:

a. These are representative quotes as provided by a sample of New York banks. Forward rates for other currencies and for other lengths of time can often be negotiated.

b. When it takes more units of a foreign currency to buy one dollar in the future, the value of the foreign currency is less in the forward market than in the spot market. Thus, the forward rate is at a discount to the spot rate.

SOURCE: *The Wall Street Journal,* March 24, 1995.

other world financial centers. Most buy-and-sell orders are conducted by computer and telephone.[4]

Spot Rates and Forward Rates

SPOT RATE
The effective exchange rate for a foreign currency for delivery on (approximately) the current day.

FORWARD EXCHANGE RATE
An agreed-upon price at which two currencies will be exchanged at some future date.

DISCOUNT ON FORWARD RATE
The situation when the spot rate is less than the forward rate.

The exchange rates shown earlier in Table 21-1 are known as **spot rates,** which means the rate paid for delivery of the currency "on the spot" or, in reality, two days after the day of the trade. For most of the world's major currencies, it also is possible to buy (or sell) currencies for delivery at some agreed-upon future date, usually 30, 90, or 180 days from the day the transaction is negotiated. This rate is known as the **forward exchange rate.** For example, if a U.S. firm must make payment to a Swiss firm in 90 days, as Table 21-2 shows, the U.S. firm's treasurer can buy Swiss francs today for delivery in 90 days, paying the 90-day forward rate of $0.8658 per Swiss franc (which equals 1.1550 SF per dollar). Forward rates are analogous to futures prices on commodity exchanges, where contracts are drawn up for wheat or corn to be delivered at agreed-upon prices at some future date. The contract is signed today, and the dollar cost of the Swiss francs then is known with certainty. Purchase of a forward contract is one technique for eliminating the volatility of future cash flows caused by fluctuations in exchange rates. This technique, which is called "hedging," will be discussed in more detail shortly.

Forward rates for 30-, 90-, and 180-day delivery, along with the spot rates for March 23, 1995, for the more commonly traded currencies are given in Table 21-2. If one can obtain *more* of the foreign currency for a dollar in the forward than in the spot market, the forward currency is less valuable than the spot currency, and the forward currency is said to be selling at a **discount.** Thus, because

---

[4]For a more detailed explanation of exchange rate determination and operations of the foreign exchange market, see Steven Bell and Bryan Kettell, *Foreign Exchange Handbook* (Westport, Conn.: Quorum Books, 1983).

1 dollar could buy 0.6272 British pounds in the spot market but 0.6286 pounds in the 180-day forward market, forward pounds sell at a discount compared to spot pounds. Conversely, if a dollar would buy *fewer* units of a currency in the forward market than in the spot market, the forward currency is worth more dollars than the spot currency, and the forward currency is said to be selling at a **premium.** For example, in Table 21-2, you can see that the spot rate for the Japanese yen was 88.15 and the 180-day forward rate was 86.24; so a dollar would buy fewer yen in the forward market than in the spot market—thus the forward yen sold for a premium.

PREMIUM ON FORWARD RATE
The situation when the spot rate is greater than the forward rate.

Hedging in the Foreign Exchange Markets

HEDGING EXCHANGE RATE EXPOSURE
The process whereby a firm protects itself from the effects of future exchange rate fluctuations.

Individuals and corporations can buy or sell forward currencies as a means of **hedging exchange rate exposure.** For example, suppose that on March 23, 1995, a U.S. firm buys televisions from a Japanese manufacturer for 100 million Japanese yen. Payment is to be made in Japanese yen 90 days after the goods are shipped, or on June 21, so the Japanese firm extends trade credit for 90 days. The U.S. company is apprehensive that the dollar will depreciate relative to the Japanese yen because of large trade deficits. If the Japanese yen appreciates rapidly, more dollars will be required to buy the 100 million yen, and the profits on the television sets will be lost. Still, the U.S. firm does not want to forgo 90 days of free trade credit by paying cash. It can take the trade credit and protect itself by contracting to purchase 100 million Japanese yen for delivery in 90 days. The 90-day rate is 87.25 yen per dollar, so the contract would require the firm to pay (100,000,000 yen) ÷ (87.25 yen per dollar) = $1,146,132 in 90 days when it takes delivery of the 100 million yen. When payment comes due on June 21, 1995, regardless of the spot rate on that day, the U.S. firm can obtain the needed Japanese yen at the agreed-upon price of $1,146,132. The U.S. firm is said to have covered its trade payables with a *forward market hedge.*

Note that it would cost the firm 100,000,000/88.15 = $1,134,430 to buy the yen on the spot market on March 23, and, because the forward contract is selling at a premium, the firm effectively will pay an extra $1,146,132 − $1,134,430 = $11,702 by buying the forward contract and waiting 90 days to pay the Japanese manufacturer. There are additional costs involved in the hedging transaction— commissions must be paid to purchase the forward contract.

The forward market permits multinational firms to transfer exchange rate risk to professional risk takers, for a price. Forward contracts can be written in any amount, for any length of time, and between any two currencies as long as the two parties to the contract are in agreement. Some forward contracts are entered into directly by individuals or firms without going through an intermediary. Normally, however, forward contracts are negotiated between banks and their clients and are tailored to the specific needs of the client.[5]

---

[5]To supplement forward contracts, which tend to be specialized, the Chicago Mercantile Exchange opened its International Monetary Market (IMM) currency futures market in 1972. A futures contract is similar to a forward contract, except a futures contract is standardized and traded in secondary markets whereas forward contracts generally are not. The IMM currently offers futures contracts on the British pound, Canadian dollar, German mark, Japanese yen, Swiss franc, and Australian dollar. Because an organized market exists for futures contracts, they can be executed more rapidly than

Self-Test Questions

Differentiate between spot and forward exchange rates.

Briefly explain what it means for a forward currency to sell at a discount, or at a premium.

What does "hedging exchange rate exposure" mean? Explain why a firm might wish to do this and how it might be done.

Inflation, Interest Rates, and Exchange Rates

Relative inflation rates, or the rates of inflation in foreign countries compared with that in the home country, have many implications for multinational financial decisions. Obviously, relative inflation rates will influence future production costs at home and abroad. Equally important, inflation affects relative interest rates as well as exchange rates. Both of these factors influence the methods chosen by multinational corporations for financing their foreign investments, and both have a notable effect on the profitability of foreign investments.

The currencies of countries with higher inflation rates than that of the United States tend to depreciate over time against the dollar. Some countries for which this has been the case include France, Italy, Mexico, and all the South American nations. On the other hand, the currencies of Germany, Switzerland, and Japan, which at times have had less inflation than the United States, have appreciated relative to the dollar. In fact, *a foreign currency will, on average, depreciate (or appreciate) at a percentage rate approximately equal to the amount by which its inflation rate exceeds (or is less than) our own.*

Relative inflation rates also are reflected in interest rates. The interest rate in any country is determined largely by its inflation rate; this point was discussed in Chapter 2. Therefore, countries currently experiencing higher rates of inflation than the United States also tend to have higher interest rates, whereas the reverse is true for countries with lower inflation rates.

It is tempting for the treasurer of a multinational corporation to borrow in the countries with the lowest interest rates. However, this is not always the best strategy. Suppose, for example, that interest rates in Germany are lower than those in the United States because Germany has a lower inflation rate. A U.S. multinational firm could save interest by borrowing in Germany. However, the relationship of the two countries' inflation rates will cause the mark to appreciate in the future, so the *dollar cost* of annual interest and principal payments on this debt will rise over time. Thus, the lower interest rate could be more than offset by losses from

---

forward contracts can be negotiated. However, futures contracts are limited to a few currencies, and have such standardized terms as maturity and denomination.

Firms engaged in international trade can hedge with futures or with forward contracts. When used for hedging purposes, both instruments produce the same result, even though each differs with respect to when the profit or loss associated with the contract is recognized. With a futures contract, the profit or loss is recognized daily (called marking to the market), while the profit or loss associated with a forward contract is not recognized until the actual delivery date (the end of the contract). If the purpose is to hedge, both the futures and the forward contracts will have the same profit or loss at the date the required currency is delivered, and that profit or loss will be sufficient to offset the change in exchange rates that might have occurred during the contract period.

currency appreciation. Similarly, one should not expect multinational corporations to avoid borrowing in a country like Brazil, where interest rates are very high, because future depreciation of the Brazilian cruzeiro could make such borrowing relatively inexpensive.

Self-Test Questions

What effects do relative inflation rates have on relative interest rates?

What happens over time to the currencies of countries with higher inflation rates than that of the United States? To those with lower inflation rates?

Why might a multinational corporation decide to borrow in a country like Brazil, where interest rates are high, rather than in a country like Germany, where interest rates are low?

International Capital Markets

Direct foreign investment by U.S. multinational corporations is one way for U.S. citizens to invest in world markets. Another way is to purchase stocks, bonds, or various money market instruments issued in foreign countries. U.S. citizens actually do invest substantial amounts in the stocks and bonds of large corporations headquartered in Europe, and to a lesser extent in firms headquartered in the Far East and South America. They also buy securities issued by foreign governments. Such investments in foreign corporations are known as *portfolio investments,* and they are distinguished from direct investments in physical assets by U.S. corporations.

Eurodollar Market

EURODOLLAR
A U.S. dollar deposited in a bank outside the United States.

A **Eurodollar** is a U.S. dollar deposited in a bank outside the United States.[6] The bank in which the deposit is made might be a host country institution, such as Barclay's Bank in London; the foreign branch of a U.S. bank, such as Citibank's Paris branch; or even a foreign branch of a third-country bank, such as Barclay's Paris branch. Most Eurodollar deposits are for $500,000 or more, and they have maturities ranging from overnight to about 5 years.

The major difference between Eurodollar deposits and regular U.S. time deposits is their geographic locations. The two types of deposits do not involve different currencies—in both cases, dollars are on deposit. However, Eurodollars are outside the direct control of the U.S. monetary authorities, so U.S. banking regulations, such as fractional reserves and FDIC insurance premiums, do not apply. The absence of these costs means that interest rates paid on Eurodollar deposits often tend to be higher than domestic U.S. rates on equivalent instruments.

Although the dollar is the leading international currency, German marks, Swiss francs, Japanese yen, and other currencies also are deposited outside their home countries; these *Eurocurrencies* are handled the same as Eurodollars.

---

[6]Although they are called Eurodollars because they originated in Europe, Eurodollars really are any dollars deposited outside the United States.

Eurodollars are borrowed by U.S. and foreign corporations and governments that need dollars for various purposes, especially to pay for goods exported from the United States and to invest in the U.S. stock market. Also, U.S. dollars are used as an international currency, or international medium of exchange, and many Eurodollars are used for this purpose. It is interesting to note that Eurodollars actually were "invented" by the Soviets in 1946. International merchants did not trust the Soviets or their rubles, so the Soviets bought some dollars (for gold), deposited them in a Paris bank, and then used these dollars to buy goods in the world markets. Others soon found it convenient to use dollars this same way, and soon the Eurodollar market was in full swing.

Eurodollars always are held in interest-bearing accounts. The interest rate paid on these deposits depends (1) on the bank's lending rate, as the interest a bank earns on loans determines its willingness and ability to pay interest on deposits, and (2) on rates of return available on U.S. money market instruments. If rates in the United States were above Eurodollar deposit rates, these funds would be sent back and invested in the United States, whereas if Eurodollar deposit rates were significantly above U.S. rates, which is more often the case, more dollars would be sent out of the United States to become Eurodollars. Given the existence of the Eurodollar market, and the easy flow of dollars to and from the United States, it is easy to see why interest rates in the United States cannot be insulated from those in other parts of the world.

LIBOR
The London InterBank Offer Rate, which represents the interest rate offered by the best London banks on deposits of other large, very creditworthy banks.

Interest rates on Eurodollar deposits (and loans) are tied to a standard rate known by the acronym **LIBOR,** which stands for *London InterBank Offer Rate.* LIBOR is the rate of interest offered by the largest and strongest London banks on deposits of other large banks of the highest credit standing. In March 1995, LIBOR rates were nearly three quarters of a percentage point above domestic U.S. bank rates on time deposits of the same maturity—5.51 percent for 3-month CDs versus 6.25 percent for LIBOR CDs. The Eurodollar market essentially is a short-term market; most loans and deposits are for less than one year.

International Bond Markets

Any bond sold outside the country of the borrower is called an international bond. However, there are two important types of international bonds: foreign bonds and Eurobonds. **Foreign bonds** are bonds sold by a foreign borrower but denominated in the currency of the country in which the issue is sold. For instance, Bell Canada might need U.S. dollars to finance the operations of its subsidiaries in the United States. If it decides to raise the needed capital in the domestic U.S. bond market, the bond will be underwritten by a syndicate of U.S. investment bankers, denominated in U.S. dollars, and sold to U.S. investors in accordance with SEC and applicable state regulations. Except for the foreign origin of the borrower (Canada), this bond will be indistinguishable from those issued by equivalent U.S. corporations. Because Bell Canada is a foreign corporation, however, the bond will be called a *foreign bond.*

FOREIGN BOND
A bond sold by a foreign borrower but denominated in the currency of the country in which it is sold.

EUROBOND
A bond sold in a country other than the one in whose currency the bond is denominated.

The term **Eurobonds** is used to designate any bond sold in some country other than the one in whose currency the bond is denominated. Examples include a British firm's issue of pound bonds sold in France or a Ford Motor Company issue denominated in dollars and sold in Germany. The institutional arrangements by which Eurobonds are marketed are different from those for most other bond issues, with the most important distinction being a far lower level of required disclosure than normally is found for bonds issued in domestic markets, particularly in the United States. Governments tend to be less strict when regulating securities denominated in foreign currencies than they are on home-currency securities because the bonds' purchasers generally are more "sophisticated." The lower disclosure requirements result in lower total transaction costs for Eurobonds.

Eurobonds appeal to investors for several reasons. Generally, they are issued in bearer form rather than as registered bonds, so the names and nationalities of investors are not recorded. Individuals who desire anonymity, whether for privacy reasons or for tax avoidance, find Eurobonds to their liking. Similarly, most governments do not withhold taxes on interest payments associated with Eurobonds.

More than half of all Eurobonds are denominated in dollars; bonds in Japanese yen, German marks, and Dutch guilders account for most of the rest. Although centered in Europe, Eurobonds truly are international. Their underwriting syndicates include investment bankers from all parts of the world, and the bonds are sold to investors not only in Europe but also in such faraway places as Bahrain and Singapore. Until recently, Eurobonds were issued solely by multinational firms, by international financial institutions, or by national governments. Today, however, the Eurobond market also is being tapped by purely domestic U.S. firms such as electric utilities, which find that by borrowing overseas they can lower their debt costs.

 ### Self-Test Questions

Differentiate between foreign portfolio investments and direct foreign investments.

What are Eurodollars?

Do you think the development of the Eurodollar market has made it easier or more difficult for the Federal Reserve to control U.S. interest rates?

Differentiate between foreign bonds and Eurobonds.

Why do Eurobonds appeal to investors?

Multinational Capital Budgeting

In the previous sections, we have discussed the general environment in which multinational firms operate. In the remainder of the chapter we will see how international factors affect key corporate decisions, beginning in this section with capital budgeting.

Although the basic principles of capital budgeting analysis are the same for both foreign and domestic operations, some key differences need to be mentioned. First, cash flow estimation generally is much more complex for overseas investments. Most multinational firms set up a separate subsidiary in each foreign country in which they operate, and the relevant cash flows for these subsidiaries are the dividends and royalties repatriated to the parent company. Second, these cash flows must be converted to the currency of the parent company and thus are subject to future exchange rate changes. For example, General Motors' German subsidiary might make a profit of 150 million marks in 1995, but the value of these profits to GM will depend on the dollar/mark exchange rate. How many dollars is 150 million marks worth? This is the relevant issue for GM's managers and stockholders.

Third, dividends and royalties normally are taxed by both foreign and home-country governments. Furthermore, a foreign government might restrict the amount of cash that can be **repatriated** to the parent company. For example, some governments place a ceiling, stated as a percentage of the company's net worth, on the amount of cash dividends that can be paid by a subsidiary to its parent company. Such restrictions normally are intended to force multinational firms to reinvest earnings in the host country, although restrictions sometimes are imposed to prevent large currency outflows, which might affect the exchange rate.

REPATRIATION OF EARNINGS The process of sending cash flows from a foreign subsidiary back to the parent company.

Whatever the host country's motivation, the result is that the parent corporation cannot use cash flows blocked in the foreign country to pay current dividends to its shareholders, nor does it have the flexibility to reinvest cash flows elsewhere in the world, where expected returns might be higher. Therefore, from the perspective of the parent organization, *the cash flows relevant for the analysis of a foreign investment are the financial cash flows that the subsidiary legally can send back to the parent.* The present value of these cash flows is found by applying an appropriate discount rate, and this present value then is compared to the parent's required investment in the project to determine the project's NPV.

In addition to the complexities of the cash flow analysis, *the cost of capital might be different for a foreign project than for an equivalent domestic project because foreign projects might be more or less risky.* A higher risk could arise from two primary sources—(1) exchange rate risk and (2) political risk—while a lower risk might result from international diversification.

As we discussed earlier, exchange rate risk reflects the inherent uncertainty about the home currency value of cash flows sent back to the parent. In other words, foreign projects have an added risk element that relates to what the basic cash flows will be worth in the parent company's home currency. The foreign currency cash flows to be turned over to the parent must be converted into U.S. dollars by translating them at expected future exchange rates. An analysis should be conducted to ascertain the effects of exchange rate variations, and, on the basis of this analysis, an exchange rate risk premium should be added to the domestic cost of capital to reflect the *exchange rate risk* inherent in the investment. As we have seen, sometimes it is possible to hedge against exchange rate fluctuations, but it might not be possible to hedge completely, especially on long-term projects, and, in addition, the costs of hedging must be subtracted from the project's cash flows.

POLITICAL RISK The risk of expropriation of a foreign subsidiary's assets by the host country, or of unanticipated restrictions on cash flows to the parent company.

Political risk refers to any action (or the probability of such action) by a host government which reduces the value of a company's investment. It includes at one extreme the expropriation without compensation of the subsidiary's assets; but it also includes less drastic actions that reduce the value of the parent firm's investment in the foreign subsidiary, such as higher taxes, tighter repatriation or currency controls, and restrictions on prices charged. The risk of expropriation of U.S. assets abroad is small in traditionally friendly and stable countries such as Great Britain or Switzerland. However, in Latin America, Africa, the Far East, and Eastern Europe, the risk might be substantial. Past expropriations include those of ITT and Anaconda Copper in Chile, Gulf Oil in Bolivia, Occidental Petroleum in

Libya, Enron Corporation in Peru, and the assets of many companies in Iraq, Iran, and Cuba.

Generally, political risk premiums are not added to the cost of capital to adjust for this risk. If a company's management has a serious concern that a given country might expropriate foreign assets, it simply will not make significant investments in that country. Expropriation is viewed as a catastrophic or ruinous event, and managers have been shown to be extraordinarily risk averse when faced with ruinous loss possibilities. However, companies can take steps to reduce the potential loss from expropriation in three major ways: (1) by financing the subsidiary with local capital, (2) by structuring operations so that the subsidiary has value only as a part of the integrated corporate system, and (3) by obtaining insurance against economic losses from expropriation from a source such as the Overseas Private Investment Corporation (OPIC). In the latter case, insurance premiums would have to be added to the project's cost.

Self-Test Questions

List some key differences in capital budgeting as applied to foreign versus domestic operations.

What are the relevant cash flows for an international investment?

Why might the cost of capital for a foreign project differ from that of an equivalent domestic project? Could it be lower?

What adjustments might be made to the domestic cost of capital for a foreign investment due to exchange rate risk and political risk?

International Capital Structures

Significant differences have been observed in the capital structures of U.S. corporations in comparison to their German and Japanese counterparts. For example, the Organization for Economic Cooperation and Development (OECD) recently reported that, on average, Japanese firms use about 85 percent debt to total assets (in book value terms), German firms use nearly 65 percent, and U.S. firms use approximately 50 percent. Of course, different countries use somewhat different accounting conventions with regard to (1) reporting assets on a historical versus a replacement cost basis, (2) the treatment of leased assets, (3) pension plan funding, and (4) capitalizing versus expensing R&D costs, and these differences make comparisons difficult. Still, even after adjusting for accounting differences, researchers find that Japanese and German firms use considerably more financial leverage than U.S. companies.

Why do international differences in financial leverage exist? It seems logical to attribute the differences to dissimilar tax structures. Although the interest on corporate debt is deductible in each country, and individuals must pay taxes on dividends and interest received, capital gains are not taxed in either Germany or Japan. The conclusions from this analysis are: (1) From a tax standpoint, corporations should be equally inclined to use debt in all three countries. (2) Because capital gains are not taxed in Germany or Japan, but are taxed in the United States, and because capital gains are associated more with stocks than with bonds, investors in Germany and Japan should show a preference for stocks compared with U.S. investors. (3) Investor preferences should lead to relatively low equity capital costs in Germany and Japan, and this, in turn, should cause German and Japanese firms to use more equity capital than their U.S. counterparts. Of course, this is exactly the opposite of the actual capital structures, so differential tax laws cannot explain the observed capital structure differences.

If tax rates cannot explain the different capital structures, what else might be an appropriate explanation? Another possibility relates to bankruptcy costs. Actual bankruptcy, and even the threat of potential bankruptcy, imposes a costly burden on firms with large amounts of debt. Note, though, that the threat of bankruptcy is dependent on the probability of bankruptcy. In the United States, equity monitoring costs are comparatively low—corporations produce quarterly reports, pay quarterly dividends, and must comply with relatively stringent audit requirements. These conditions are less prevalent in the other countries. Conversely, debt monitoring costs are probably lower in Germany and Japan than in the United States. In Germany and Japan, the bulk of corporate debt consists of bank loans as opposed to publicly issued bonds; but, more important, the banks are closely linked to the corporations that borrow from them. German and Japanese banks often (1) hold major equity positions in their debtor corporations, (2) vote the shares of individual shareholders for whom banks hold shares in trust, and (3) have bank officers sit on the boards of debtor corporations. Given these close relationships, the banks are much more directly involved with the debtor firms' affairs, and as a result they also are more accommodating than U.S. bondholders in the event of financial distress. This, in turn, suggests that any given amount of debt gives rise to a lower threat of bankruptcy for a German or a Japanese firm than for a U.S. firm with the same amount of business risk. Thus, an analysis of both bankruptcy costs and equity monitoring costs leads to the conclusion that U.S. firms should have more equity and less debt than firms in Japan and Germany.

We cannot state that one financial system is better than another in the sense of making the firms in one country more efficient than those in another. However, as U.S. firms become increasingly involved in worldwide operations, they must become increasingly aware of worldwide conditions, and they must be prepared to adapt to conditions in the various countries in which they do business.

Self-Test Question

Why do international differences in financial leverage exist?

Multinational Working Capital Management

Cash Management

The objectives of cash management in a multinational corporation are similar to those in a purely domestic corporation: (1) to speed up collections and to slow down disbursements as much as is feasible, and hence to maximize net float; (2) to shift cash as rapidly as possible from those parts of the business where it is not needed to those parts where it is needed; and (3) to try to put temporary cash balances to work earning positive returns. Multinational companies use the same general procedures for achieving these goals as domestic firms, but because of longer distances and more serious mail delays, lockbox systems and electronic funds transfers are even more important.

Although multinational and domestic corporations have the same objectives and use similar procedures, the multinational corporation faces a far more complex task. As was mentioned earlier in our discussion of political risk, foreign governments often place restrictions on transfers of funds out of the country, so although IBM can transfer money from its Salt Lake City office to its New York concentration bank just by pressing a few buttons, a similar transfer from its Buenos Aires office is far more complex. Buenos Aires funds are denominated in australs (Argentina's equivalent of the dollar), so the australs must be converted to dollars before the transfer. If there is a shortage of dollars in Argentina, or if the Argentinean government wants to conserve the dollars in the country to use for the purchase of strategic materials, then conversion, and hence the transfer, might be blocked. Even if no dollar shortage exists in Argentina, the government might still restrict funds outflows if those funds represent profits or depreciation rather than payments for purchased materials or equipment because many countries, especially the less developed countries, want profits reinvested in the country in order to stimulate economic growth.

Once it has been determined what funds can be transferred out of the various nations in which a multinational corporation operates, it is important to get those funds to locations where they will earn the highest returns. Whereas domestic corporations tend to think in terms of domestic securities, multinationals are more likely to be aware of investment opportunities all around the world. Most multinational corporations use one or more global concentration banks, located in money centers such as London, New York, Tokyo, Zurich, or Singapore, and their staffs in those cities, working with international bankers, are able to take advantage of the best rates available anywhere in the world.

Credit Management

Like most other aspects of finance, credit management in the multinational corporation is similar to but more complex than that in a purely domestic business. First, granting credit is riskier in an international context because, in addition to the normal risks of default, the multinational corporation also must worry about exchange rate changes between the time a sale is made and the time a receivable is collected. We know, though, that hedging can reduce this type of risk, but at a cost.

Credit policy generally is more important for a multinational corporation than for a purely domestic firm for two reasons. First, much U.S. trade is with poorer, less developed nations, and in such situations granting credit generally is a necessary condition for doing business. Second, and in large part as a result of the first point, developed nations whose economic health depends upon exports often help their manufacturing firms compete internationally by granting credit to foreign countries. In Japan, for example, the major manufacturing firms have direct ownership ties with large "trading companies" engaged in international trade, as well as with giant commercial banks. In addition, a government agency, the Ministry of International Trade and Industry (MITI), helps Japanese firms identify

ETHICAL DILEMMA   *Is It a Licensing Fee, a Commission, or Something Else?*

The government-owned Telecommunications Corporation of India (TCI) wants to upgrade and improve its telephone and communications systems. Teledata Corporation, an American manufacturer of chips and communications electronics for computers, currently is negotiating for a contract to supply TCI with the internal computer components it needs. The negotiations seem to be going very well; in fact, sources from the Indian government have assured Teledata executives that their company's bid for the project is the best TCI has received. Teledata very much wants the TCI contract because the exposure will help the company's plan to expand its presence in foreign markets.

Throughout the negotiations, Teledata has dealt exclusively with a member of India's parliament. Because he is on the government committee that oversees TCI's operations, Teledata executives believed the Indian lawmaker could help guide the company with respect to proper bidding procedures and other traditions of doing business with the government-owned company. And, in fact, his help has been invaluable.

Now that the bidding/negotiating process is nearly complete, the Indian lawmaker has suggested to Teledata executives that they can assure the company wins the TCI contract by paying a $2 million licensing fee to import goods into India. According to the lawmaker, the import license is essential to conduct business in India, and, when awarding contracts, the Indian government favors companies that already have paid the fee—payment of the fee is a sign of commitment. Teledata's executives are skeptical, though, because they believe the fee actually represents a bribe to sway the government officials who ultimately will decide which company gets the TCI contract.

When confronted about the import licensing fee, the Indian lawmaker admitted it was more of a tradition than a requirement of the government, but that it must be paid before a government contract would be awarded to a foreign company. He even suggested that Teledata executives call the fee a sales commission if that made them more comfortable. The lawmaker assured the executives that there is nothing illegal about paying the fee—it is done all the time in India. Teledata's executives don't know what to do. Regardless of what they call it, if the $2 million is not paid, Teledata almost assuredly will not get the TCI contract. But, paying bribes to foreign governments is illegal in the United States. What should Teledata's executives do?

Summary

This chapter presents the differences between multinational and domestic managerial finance. The key concepts covered are listed below.

- **International operations** have become increasingly important to individual firms and to the national economy. A **multinational corporation** is a firm that operates in two or more nations.
- Companies go "international" for five primary reasons: (1) to **seek new markets,** (2) to **seek raw materials,** (3) to **seek new technology,** (4) to **seek production efficiency,** and (5) to **avoid trade barriers.**
- Six major factors distinguish managerial finance as practiced by domestic firms from that of multinational corporations: (1) **different currency denominations,** (2) **economic and legal ramifications,** (3) **languages,** (4) **cultural differences,** (5) **role of governments,** and (6) **political risk.**
- The number of U.S. dollars required to purchase one unit of foreign currency is called a **direct quotation,** while the number of units of foreign currency that can be purchased for one U.S. dollar is an **indirect quotation.**
- Financial forecasting is especially difficult for multinational firms because **exchange rate fluctuations** make it difficult to estimate the dollars that overseas operations will produce.

- Prior to August 1971, the world was on a **fixed exchange rate system** whereby the U.S. dollar was linked to gold, and other currencies were then tied to the dollar. After August 1971, the world monetary system changed to a floating system whereby major world currency rates float with market forces, largely unrestricted by any internationally agreed-upon limits. The central bank of each country does intervene in the foreign exchange market, buying and selling its currency to smooth out exchange rate fluctuations, but only to a limited extent.
- **Spot rates** are the rates paid for delivery of currency "on the spot," while the **forward exchange rate** is the rate paid for delivery of currency at some agreed-upon future date, usually 30, 90, or 180 days from the day the transaction is negotiated. The forward rate can be at either a **premium** or a **discount** to the spot rate.
- Granting credit is riskier in an international context because, in addition to the normal risks of default, the multinational firm must worry about **exchange rate changes** between the time a sale is made and the time a receivable is collected.
- Credit policy is especially important for a multinational firm for two reasons: (1) Much of the U.S. trade is with less developed nations, and in such situations granting credit is a necessary condition for doing business. (2) The governments of nations such as Japan whose economic health depends upon exports often help their manufacturing firms compete internationally by granting credit to foreign customers.
- Foreign investments are similar to domestic investments, but political risk and exchange rate risk must be considered. **Political risk** is the risk the foreign government will take some action that will decrease the value of the investment, while **exchange rate risk** is the risk of losses due to fluctuations in the value of the dollar relative to the values of foreign currencies.
- Investments in **international capital projects** expose the investing firm to exchange rate risk and political risk. The relevant cash flows in international capital budgeting are the dollar cash flows that can be turned over to the parent company.
- **Eurodollars** are U.S. dollars deposited in banks outside the United States. Interest rates on Eurodollars are tied to **LIBOR,** the London InterBank Offer Rate.
- U.S. firms often find that they can raise long-term capital at a lower cost outside the United States by selling bonds in the international capital markets. International bonds might be either **foreign bonds,** which are exactly like regular domestic bonds except that the issuer is a foreign company, or **Eurobonds,** which are bonds sold in a foreign country but denominated in the currency of the issuing company's home country.

Questions

21-1 Exchange rates fluctuate under both the fixed exchange rate and floating exchange rate systems. What, then, is the difference between the two systems?

21-2 If the French franc depreciates against the U.S. dollar, can a dollar buy more or fewer French francs as a result?

21-3 If the United States imports more goods from abroad than it exports, foreigners will tend to have a surplus of U.S. dollars. What will this do to the value of the dollar with respect to foreign currencies? What is the corresponding effect on foreign investments in the United States?

21-4   Why do U.S. corporations build manufacturing plants abroad when they could build them at home?

21-5   Most firms require higher rates of return on foreign projects than on identical projects located at home. Why?

21-6   What is a Eurodollar? If a French citizen deposits $10,000 in Chase Manhattan Bank in New York, have Eurodollars been created? What if the deposit is made in Barclay's Bank in London? Chase Manhattan's Paris branch? Does the existence of the Eurodollar market make the Federal Reserve's job of controlling U.S. interest rates easier or more difficult? Explain.

Self-Test Problem

(Solutions appear in Appendix B.)

Key terms   **ST-1**   Define each of the following terms:
    a. multinational corporation
    b. exchange rate
    c. fixed exchange rate system; floating exchange rates
    d. deficit trade balance
    e. devaluation; revaluation
    f. exchange rate risk; convertible currency
    g. spot rate; forward exchange rate
    h. discount on forward rate; premium on forward rate
    i. hedging exchange rate exposure
    j. repatriation of earnings; political risk
    k. Eurodollar; Eurobond; foreign bond

Problems

Exchange rates   **21-1**   Table 21-1 lists foreign exchange rates for March 23, 1995. On that day how many dollars would be required to purchase 1,000 units of each of the following: Indian rupees, Italian lira, Japanese yen, Mexican pesos, and Saudi Arabian riyals?

Exchange rates   **21-2**   Look up the 5 currencies in Problem 21-1 in the foreign exchange section of a current issue of *The Wall Street Journal.*
    a. What is the current exchange rate for changing dollars into 1,000 units of rupees, lira, yen, pesos, and riyals?
    b. What is the percentage gain or loss between the March 23, 1995, exchange rate and the current exchange rate for each of the currencies in Part a?
    c. Describe whether the value of each currency appreciated or depreciated from March 23, 1995, to the current period.

Exchange rate changes   **21-3**   Early in September 1983, it took 245 Japanese yen to equal $1. Eleven years and six months later, in March 1995, that exchange rate had fallen to 88 yen to $1. Assume the price of a Japanese-manufactured automobile was $8,000 in September 1983 and that its price changes were in direct relation to exchange rates (the price *in yen* has not changed).
    a. Has the price, in dollars, of the automobile increased or decreased during the 11½-year period because of changes in the exchange rate?
    b. What would be the dollar price of the automobile on March 23, 1995, again assuming that the car's price changes only with exchange rates?

Hedging   **21-4**   Chavalier French Imports has agreed to purchase 15,000 cases of French wine for 16 million francs at today's spot rate. The firm's financial manager, George Racette, has noted the following current spot and forward rates:

	U.S. Dollar/Franc	Franc/U.S. Dollar
Spot	0.20131	4.9675
30-day forward	0.20095	4.9763
90-day forward	0.20028	4.9930
180-day forward	0.19972	5.0070

On the same day Mr. Racette agrees to purchase 15,000 more cases of wine in 3 months at the same price of 16 million francs.

a. What is the price of the wine, in U.S. dollars, if it is purchased at today's spot rate?

b. What is the cost, in dollars, of the second 15,000 cases if payment is made in 90 days and the spot rate at that time equals today's 90-day forward rate?

c. If Mr. Racette is concerned about the dollar losing value relative to the franc in the next 90 days, what can he do to reduce his exposure to exchange rate risk?

d. If he does not hedge his exposure to exchange rate risk, and the exchange rate for the French franc is 4.75 to $1 in 90 days, how much will he have to pay for the wine (in dollars)?

Exam-Type Problems

The problems included in this section are set up in such a way that they could be used as multiple-choice exam problems.

Exchange rate **21-5** If British pounds sell for $1.60 (U.S.) per pound, what should dollars sell for in pounds per dollar?

Currency appreciation **21-6** Suppose that 1 French franc could be purchased in the foreign exchange market for 20 U.S. cents today. If the franc appreciated 10 percent tomorrow against the dollar, how many francs would a dollar buy tomorrow?

Cross exchange rates **21-7** Recently the exchange rate between U.S. dollars and the French franc was FF4.97 = $1, and the exchange rate between the dollar and the British pound was £1 = $1.60. What was the exchange rate between francs and pounds?

Cross exchange rates **21-8** Look up the 3 currencies in Problem 21-7 in the foreign exchange section of a current issue of *The Wall Street Journal*. What is the current exchange rate between francs and pounds?

Foreign investment analysis **21-9** After all foreign and U.S. taxes, a U.S. corporation expects to receive 3 pounds of dividends per share from a British subsidiary this year. The exchange rate at the end of the year is expected to be $1.67 per pound, and the pound is expected to depreciate 5 percent against the dollar each year for an indefinite period. The dividend (in pounds) is expected to grow at 10 percent a year indefinitely. The parent U.S. corporation owns 10 million shares of the subsidiary. What is the present value in dollars of its equity ownership of the subsidiary? Assume a cost of equity capital of 14 percent for the subsidiary.

Exchange rate gains/losses **21-10** You are the vice-president of International InfoXchange, headquartered in Chicago, Illinois. All shareholders of the firm live in the United States. Earlier this month you obtained a loan of 5 million Canadian dollars from a bank in Toronto to finance the construction of a new plant in Montreal. At the time the loan was received, the exchange rate was 71 U.S. cents to the Canadian dollar. By the end of the month it has unexpectedly dropped to 65 cents. Has your company made a gain or loss as a result, and by how much?

Integrative Problem

Multinational
managerial finance

21-11   Citrus Products Inc. is a medium-sized producer of citrus juice drinks with groves in Indian River County, Florida. Until now, the company has confined its operations and sales to the United States, but its CEO, George Gaynor, wants to expand into Europe. The first step would be to set up sales subsidiaries in Spain and Portugal, then set up a production plant in Spain, and, finally, distribute the product throughout the European common market. The firm's financial manager, Ruth Schmidt, is enthusiastic about the plan, but she is worried about the implications of the foreign expansion on the firm's managerial finance process. She has asked you, the firm's most recently hired financial analyst, to develop a 1-hour tutorial package that explains the basics of multinational managerial finance. The tutorial will be presented at the next board of director's meeting. To get you started, Ms. Schmidt has supplied you with the following list of questions.

a. What is a multinational corporation? Why do firms expand into other countries?

b. What are the six major factors that distinguish multinational managerial finance from managerial finance as practiced by a purely domestic firm?

c. Consider the following illustrative exchange rates.

	U.S. Dollars Required to Buy One Unit of Foreign Currency
Spanish peseta	0.0076
Portuguese escudo	0.0055

   (1) Are these currency prices direct quotations or indirect quotations?
   (2) Calculate the indirect quotations for pesetas and escudos.
   (3) What is a cross rate? Calculate the two cross rates between pesetas and escudos.
   (4) Assume Citrus Products can produce a liter of orange juice and ship it to Spain for $1.75. If the firm wants a 50 percent markup on the product, what should the orange juice sell for in Spain?
   (5) Now assume Citrus Products begins producing the same liter of orange juice in Spain. The product costs 200 pesetas to produce and ship to Portugal, where it can be sold for 400 escudos. What is the dollar profit on the sale?
   (6) What is exchange rate risk?

d. Briefly describe the current international monetary system. How does the current system differ from the system that was in place prior to August 1971?

e. What is a convertible currency? What problems arise when a multinational company operates in a country whose currency is not convertible?

f. What is the difference between spot rates and forward rates? When is the forward rate at a premium to the spot rate? At a discount? How can a firm use the forward markets to hedge a future currency transaction?

g. What impact does relative inflation have on interest rates and exchange rates?

h. Briefly discuss the international capital markets.

i. What is the impact of multinational operations on each of the following managerial finance topics?
   (1) cash management
   (2) capital budgeting decisions
   (3) credit management
   (4) inventory management

APPENDIX A

Mathematical Tables

TABLE A-1

Present Value of $1 Due at the End of n Periods:

EQUATION:

$$PVIF_{i,n} = \frac{1}{(1 + i)^n}$$

FINANCIAL CALCULATOR KEYS:

n	i	0	1.0
N	**I**	**PV**	**PMT** **FV**

Table Value

Period	1%	2%	3%	4%	5%	6%	7%	8%	9%	10%
1	.9901	.9804	.9709	.9615	.9524	.9434	.9346	.9259	.9174	.9091
2	.9803	.9612	.9426	.9246	.9070	.8900	.8734	.8573	.8417	.8264
3	.9706	.9423	.9151	.8890	.8638	.8396	.8163	.7938	.7722	.7513
4	.9610	.9238	.8885	.8548	.8227	.7921	.7629	.7350	.7084	.6830
5	.9515	.9057	.8626	.8219	.7835	.7473	.7130	.6806	.6499	.6209
6	.9420	.8880	.8375	.7903	.7462	.7050	.6663	.6302	.5963	.5645
7	.9327	.8706	.8131	.7599	.7107	.6651	.6227	.5835	.5470	.5132
8	.9235	.8535	.7894	.7307	.6768	.6274	.5820	.5403	.5019	.4665
9	.9143	.8368	.7664	.7026	.6446	.5919	.5439	.5002	.4604	.4241
10	.9053	.8203	.7441	.6756	.6139	.5584	.5083	.4632	.4224	.3855
11	.8963	.8043	.7224	.6496	.5847	.5268	.4751	.4289	.3875	.3505
12	.8874	.7885	.7014	.6246	.5568	.4970	.4440	.3971	.3555	.3186
13	.8787	.7730	.6810	.6006	.5303	.4688	.4150	.3677	.3262	.2897
14	.8700	.7579	.6611	.5775	.5051	.4423	.3878	.3405	.2992	.2633
15	.8613	.7430	.6419	.5553	.4810	.4173	.3624	.3152	.2745	.2394
16	.8528	.7284	.6232	.5339	.4581	.3936	.3387	.2919	.2519	.2176
17	.8444	.7142	.6050	.5134	.4363	.3714	.3166	.2703	.2311	.1978
18	.8360	.7002	.5874	.4936	.4155	.3503	.2959	.2502	.2120	.1799
19	.8277	.6864	.5703	.4746	.3957	.3305	.2765	.2317	.1945	.1635
20	.8195	.6730	.5537	.4564	.3769	.3118	.2584	.2145	.1784	.1486
21	.8114	.6598	.5375	.4388	.3589	.2942	.2415	.1987	.1637	.1351
22	.8034	.6468	.5219	.4220	.3418	.2775	.2257	.1839	.1502	.1228
23	.7954	.6342	.5067	.4057	.3256	.2618	.2109	.1703	.1378	.1117
24	.7876	.6217	.4919	.3901	.3101	.2470	.1971	.1577	.1264	.1015
25	.7798	.6095	.4776	.3751	.2953	.2330	.1842	.1460	.1160	.0923
26	.7720	.5976	.4637	.3607	.2812	.2198	.1722	.1352	.1064	.0839
27	.7644	.5859	.4502	.3468	.2678	.2074	.1609	.1252	.0976	.0763
28	.7568	.5744	.4371	.3335	.2551	.1956	.1504	.1159	.0895	.0693
29	.7493	.5631	.4243	.3207	.2429	.1846	.1406	.1073	.0822	.0630
30	.7419	.5521	.4120	.3083	.2314	.1741	.1314	.0994	.0754	.0573
35	.7059	.5000	.3554	.2534	.1813	.1301	.0937	.0676	.0490	.0356
40	.6717	.4529	.3066	.2083	.1420	.0972	.0668	.0460	.0318	.0221
45	.6391	.4102	.2644	.1712	.1113	.0727	.0476	.0313	.0207	.0137
50	.6080	.3715	.2281	.1407	.0872	.0543	.0339	.0213	.0134	.0085
55	.5785	.3365	.1968	.1157	.0683	.0406	.0242	.0145	.0087	.0053

TABLE A-1

continued

Period	12%	14%	15%	16%	18%	20%	24%	28%	32%	36%
1	.8929	.8772	.8696	.8621	.8475	.8333	.8065	.7813	.7576	.7353
2	.7972	.7695	.7561	.7432	.7182	.6944	.6504	.6104	.5739	.5407
3	.7118	.6750	.6575	.6407	.6086	.5787	.5245	.4768	.4348	.3975
4	.6355	.5921	.5718	.5523	.5158	.4823	.4230	.3725	.3294	.2923
5	.5674	.5194	.4972	.4761	.4371	.4019	.3411	.2910	.2495	.2149
6	.5066	.4556	.4323	.4104	.3704	.3349	.2751	.2274	.1890	.1580
7	.4523	.3996	.3759	.3538	.3139	.2791	.2218	.1776	.1432	.1162
8	.4039	.3506	.3269	.3050	.2660	.2326	.1789	.1388	.1085	.0854
9	.3606	.3075	.2843	.2630	.2255	.1938	.1443	.1084	.0822	.0628
10	.3220	.2697	.2472	.2267	.1911	.1615	.1164	.0847	.0623	.0462
11	.2875	.2366	.2149	.1954	.1619	.1346	.0938	.0662	.0472	.0340
12	.2567	.2076	.1869	.1685	.1372	.1122	.0757	.0517	.0357	.0250
13	.2292	.1821	.1625	.1452	.1163	.0935	.0610	.0404	.0271	.0184
14	.2046	.1597	.1413	.1252	.0985	.0779	.0492	.0316	.0205	.0135
15	.1827	.1401	.1229	.1079	.0835	.0649	.0397	.0247	.0155	.0099
16	.1631	.1229	.1069	.0930	.0708	.0541	.0320	.0193	.0118	.0073
17	.1456	.1078	.0929	.0802	.0600	.0451	.0258	.0150	.0089	.0054
18	.1300	.0946	.0808	.0691	.0508	.0376	.0208	.0118	.0068	.0039
19	.1161	.0829	.0703	.0596	.0431	.0313	.0168	.0092	.0051	.0029
20	.1037	.0728	.0611	.0514	.0365	.0261	.0135	.0072	.0039	.0021
21	.0926	.0638	.0531	.0443	.0309	.0217	.0109	.0056	.0029	.0016
22	.0826	.0560	.0462	.0382	.0262	.0181	.0088	.0044	.0022	.0012
23	.0738	.0491	.0402	.0329	.0222	.0151	.0071	.0034	.0017	.0008
24	.0659	.0431	.0349	.0284	.0188	.0126	.0057	.0027	.0013	.0006
25	.0588	.0378	.0304	.0245	.0160	.0105	.0046	.0021	.0010	.0005
26	.0525	.0331	.0264	.0211	.0135	.0087	.0037	.0016	.0007	.0003
27	.0469	.0291	.0230	.0182	.0115	.0073	.0030	.0013	.0006	.0002
28	.0419	.0255	.0200	.0157	.0097	.0061	.0024	.0010	.0004	.0002
29	.0374	.0224	.0174	.0135	.0082	.0051	.0020	.0008	.0003	.0001
30	.0334	.0196	.0151	.0116	.0070	.0042	.0016	.0006	.0002	.0001
35	.0189	.0102	.0075	.0055	.0030	.0017	.0005	.0002	.0001	*
40	.0107	.0053	.0037	.0026	.0013	.0007	.0002	.0001	*	*
45	.0061	.0027	.0019	.0013	.0006	.0003	.0001	*	*	*
50	.0035	.0014	.0009	.0006	.0003	.0001	*	*	*	*
55	.0020	.0007	.0005	.0003	.0001	*	*	*	*	*

*The factor is zero to four decimal places.

TABLE A-2

Present Value of an Annuity of $1 per Period for n Periods:

EQUATION:

$$PVIFA_{i,n} = \sum_{t=1}^{n} \frac{1}{(1+i)^t} = \frac{1 - \dfrac{1}{(1+i)^n}}{i} = \frac{1}{i} - \frac{1}{i(1+i)^n}$$

FINANCIAL CALCULATOR KEYS:

| n | i | 1.0 | 0 |

N   I   PV   PMT   FV

Table Value

Number of Periods	1%	2%	3%	4%	5%	6%	7%	8%	9%
1	0.9901	0.9804	0.9709	0.9615	0.9524	0.9434	0.9346	0.9259	0.9174
2	1.9704	1.9416	1.9135	1.8861	1.8594	1.8334	1.8080	1.7833	1.7591
3	2.9410	2.8839	2.8286	2.7751	2.7232	2.6730	2.6243	2.5771	2.5313
4	3.9020	3.8077	3.7171	3.6299	3.5460	3.4651	3.3872	3.3121	3.2397
5	4.8534	4.7135	4.5797	4.4518	4.3295	4.2124	4.1002	3.9927	3.8897
6	5.7955	5.6014	5.4172	5.2421	5.0757	4.9173	4.7665	4.6229	4.4859
7	6.7282	6.4720	6.2303	6.0021	5.7864	5.5824	5.3893	5.2064	5.0330
8	7.6517	7.3255	7.0197	6.7327	6.4632	6.2098	5.9713	5.7466	5.5348
9	8.5660	8.1622	7.7861	7.4353	7.1078	6.8017	6.5152	6.2469	5.9952
10	9.4713	8.9826	8.5302	8.1109	7.7217	7.3601	7.0236	6.7101	6.4177
11	10.3676	9.7868	9.2526	8.7605	8.3064	7.8869	7.4987	7.1390	6.8052
12	11.2551	10.5753	9.9540	9.3851	8.8633	8.3838	7.9427	7.5361	7.1607
13	12.1337	11.3484	10.6350	9.9856	9.3936	8.8527	8.3577	7.9038	7.4869
14	13.0037	12.1062	11.2961	10.5631	9.8986	9.2950	8.7455	8.2442	7.7862
15	13.8651	12.8493	11.9379	11.1184	10.3797	9.7122	9.1079	8.5595	8.0607
16	14.7179	13.5777	12.5611	11.6523	10.8378	10.1059	9.4466	8.8514	8.3126
17	15.5623	14.2919	13.1661	12.1657	11.2741	10.4773	9.7632	9.1216	8.5436
18	16.3983	14.9920	13.7535	12.6593	11.6896	10.8276	10.0591	9.3719	8.7556
19	17.2260	15.6785	14.3238	13.1339	12.0853	11.1581	10.3356	9.6036	8.9501
20	18.0456	16.3514	14.8775	13.5903	12.4622	11.4699	10.5940	9.8181	9.1285
21	18.8570	17.0112	15.4150	14.0292	12.8212	11.7641	10.8355	10.0168	9.2922
22	19.6604	17.6580	15.9369	14.4511	13.1630	12.0416	11.0612	10.2007	9.4424
23	20.4558	18.2922	16.4436	14.8568	13.4886	12.3034	11.2722	10.3711	9.5802
24	21.2434	18.9139	16.9355	15.2470	13.7986	12.5504	11.4693	10.5288	9.7066
25	22.0232	19.5235	17.4131	15.6221	14.0939	12.7834	11.6536	10.6748	9.8226
26	22.7952	20.1210	17.8768	15.9828	14.3752	13.0032	11.8258	10.8100	9.9290
27	23.5596	20.7069	18.3270	16.3296	14.6430	13.2105	11.9867	10.9352	10.0266
28	24.3164	21.2813	18.7641	16.6631	14.8981	13.4062	12.1371	11.0511	10.1161
29	25.0658	21.8444	19.1885	16.9837	15.1411	13.5907	12.2777	11.1584	10.1983
30	25.8077	22.3965	19.6004	17.2920	15.3725	13.7648	12.4090	11.2578	10.2737
35	29.4086	24.9986	21.4872	18.6646	16.3742	14.4982	12.9477	11.6546	10.5668
40	32.8347	27.3555	23.1148	19.7928	17.1591	15.0463	13.3317	11.9246	10.7574
45	36.0945	29.4902	24.5187	20.7200	17.7741	15.4558	13.6055	12.1084	10.8812
50	39.1961	31.4236	25.7298	21.4822	18.2559	15.7619	13.8007	12.2335	10.9617
55	42.1472	33.1748	26.7744	22.1086	18.6335	15.9905	13.9399	12.3186	11.0140

TABLE A-2

continued

Number of Periods	10%	12%	14%	15%	16%	18%	20%	24%	28%	32%
1	0.9091	0.8929	0.8772	0.8696	0.8621	0.8475	0.8333	0.8065	0.7813	0.7576
2	1.7355	1.6901	1.6467	1.6257	1.6052	1.5656	1.5278	1.4568	1.3916	1.3315
3	2.4869	2.4018	2.3216	2.2832	2.2459	2.1743	2.1065	1.9813	1.8684	1.7663
4	3.1699	3.0373	2.9137	2.8550	2.7982	2.6901	2.5887	2.4043	2.2410	2.0957
5	3.7908	3.6048	3.4331	3.3522	3.2743	3.1272	2.9906	2.7454	2.5320	2.3452
6	4.3553	4.1114	3.8887	3.7845	3.6847	3.4976	3.3255	3.0205	2.7594	2.5342
7	4.8684	4.5638	4.2883	4.1604	4.0386	3.8115	3.6046	3.2423	2.9370	2.6775
8	5.3349	4.9676	4.6389	4.4873	4.3436	4.0776	3.8372	3.4212	3.0758	2.7860
9	5.7590	5.3282	4.9464	4.7716	4.6065	4.3030	4.0310	3.5655	3.1842	2.8681
10	6.1446	5.6502	5.2161	5.0188	4.8332	4.4941	4.1925	3.6819	3.2689	2.9304
11	6.4951	5.9377	5.4527	5.2337	5.0286	4.6560	4.3271	3.7757	3.3351	2.9776
12	6.8137	6.1944	5.6603	5.4206	5.1971	4.7932	4.4392	3.8514	3.3868	3.0133
13	7.1034	6.4235	5.8424	5.5831	5.3423	4.9095	4.5327	3.9124	3.4272	3.0404
14	7.3667	6.6282	6.0021	5.7245	5.4675	5.0081	4.6106	3.9616	3.4587	3.0609
15	7.6061	6.8109	6.1422	5.8474	5.5755	5.0916	4.6755	4.0013	3.4834	3.0764
16	7.8237	6.9740	6.2651	5.9542	5.6685	5.1624	4.7296	4.0333	3.5026	3.0882
17	8.0216	7.1196	6.3729	6.0472	5.7487	5.2223	4.7746	4.0591	3.5177	3.0971
18	8.2014	7.2497	6.4674	6.1280	5.8178	5.2732	4.8122	4.0799	3.5294	3.1039
19	8.3649	7.3658	6.5504	6.1982	5.8775	5.3162	4.8435	4.0967	3.5386	3.1090
20	8.5136	7.4694	6.6231	6.2593	5.9288	5.3527	4.8696	4.1103	3.5458	3.1129
21	8.6487	7.5620	6.6870	6.3125	5.9731	5.3837	4.8913	4.1212	3.5514	3.1158
22	8.7715	7.6446	6.7429	6.3587	6.0113	5.4099	4.9094	4.1300	3.5558	3.1180
23	8.8832	7.7184	6.7921	6.3988	6.0442	5.4321	4.9245	4.1371	3.5592	3.1197
24	8.9847	7.7843	6.8351	6.4338	6.0726	5.4509	4.9371	4.1428	3.5619	3.1210
25	9.0770	7.8431	6.8729	6.4641	6.0971	5.4669	4.9476	4.1474	3.5640	3.1220
26	9.1609	7.8957	6.9061	6.4906	6.1182	5.4804	4.9563	4.1511	3.5656	3.1227
27	9.2372	7.9426	6.9352	6.5135	6.1364	5.4919	4.9636	4.1542	3.5669	3.1233
28	9.3066	7.9844	6.9607	6.5335	6.1520	5.5016	4.9697	4.1566	3.5679	3.1237
29	9.3696	8.0218	6.9830	6.5509	6.1656	5.5098	4.9747	4.1585	3.5687	3.1240
30	9.4269	8.0552	7.0027	6.5660	6.1772	5.5168	4.9789	4.1601	3.5693	3.1242
35	9.6442	8.1755	7.0700	6.6166	6.2153	5.5386	4.9915	4.1644	3.5708	3.1248
40	9.7791	8.2438	7.1050	6.6418	6.2335	5.5482	4.9966	4.1659	3.5712	3.1250
45	9.8628	8.2825	7.1232	6.6543	6.2421	5.5523	4.9986	4.1664	3.5714	3.1250
50	9.9148	8.3045	7.1327	6.6605	6.2463	5.5541	4.9995	4.1666	3.5714	3.1250
55	9.9471	8.3170	7.1376	6.6636	6.2482	5.5549	4.9998	4.1666	3.5714	3.1250

TABLE A-3

Future Value of $1 at the End of n Periods:

EQUATION:

$FVIF_{i,n} = (1 + i)^n$

FINANCIAL CALCULATOR KEYS:

n   i   1.0   0

| N | I | PV | PMT | FV |

Table
Value

Period	1%	2%	3%	4%	5%	6%	7%	8%	9%	10%
1	1.0100	1.0200	1.0300	1.0400	1.0500	1.0600	1.0700	1.0800	1.0900	1.1000
2	1.0201	1.0404	1.0609	1.0816	1.1025	1.1236	1.1449	1.1664	1.1881	1.2100
3	1.0303	1.0612	1.0927	1.1249	1.1576	1.1910	1.2250	1.2597	1.2950	1.3310
4	1.0406	1.0824	1.1255	1.1699	1.2155	1.2625	1.3108	1.3605	1.4116	1.4641
5	1.0510	1.1041	1.1593	1.2167	1.2763	1.3382	1.4026	1.4693	1.5386	1.6105
6	1.0615	1.1262	1.1941	1.2653	1.3401	1.4185	1.5007	1.5869	1.6771	1.7716
7	1.0721	1.1487	1.2299	1.3159	1.4071	1.5036	1.6058	1.7138	1.8280	1.9487
8	1.0829	1.1717	1.2668	1.3686	1.4775	1.5938	1.7182	1.8509	1.9926	2.1436
9	1.0937	1.1951	1.3048	1.4233	1.5513	1.6895	1.8385	1.9990	2.1719	2.3579
10	1.1046	1.2190	1.3439	1.4802	1.6289	1.7908	1.9672	2.1589	2.3674	2.5937
11	1.1157	1.2434	1.3842	1.5395	1.7103	1.8983	2.1049	2.3316	2.5804	2.8531
12	1.1268	1.2682	1.4258	1.6010	1.7959	2.0122	2.2522	2.5182	2.8127	3.1384
13	1.1381	1.2936	1.4685	1.6651	1.8856	2.1329	2.4098	2.7196	3.0658	3.4523
14	1.1495	1.3195	1.5126	1.7317	1.9799	2.2609	2.5785	2.9372	3.3417	3.7975
15	1.1610	1.3459	1.5580	1.8009	2.0789	2.3966	2.7590	3.1722	3.6425	4.1772
16	1.1726	1.3728	1.6047	1.8730	2.1829	2.5404	2.9522	3.4259	3.9703	4.5950
17	1.1843	1.4002	1.6528	1.9479	2.2920	2.6928	3.1588	3.7000	4.3276	5.0545
18	1.1961	1.4282	1.7024	2.0258	2.4066	2.8543	3.3799	3.9960	4.7171	5.5599
19	1.2081	1.4568	1.7535	2.1068	2.5270	3.0256	3.6165	4.3157	5.1417	6.1159
20	1.2202	1.4859	1.8061	2.1911	2.6533	3.2071	3.8697	4.6610	5.6044	6.7275
21	1.2324	1.5157	1.8603	2.2788	2.7860	3.3996	4.1406	5.0338	6.1088	7.4002
22	1.2447	1.5460	1.9161	2.3699	2.9253	3.6035	4.4304	5.4365	6.6586	8.1403
23	1.2572	1.5769	1.9736	2.4647	3.0715	3.8197	4.7405	5.8715	7.2579	8.9543
24	1.2697	1.6084	2.0328	2.5633	3.2251	4.0489	5.0724	6.3412	7.9111	9.8497
25	1.2824	1.6406	2.0938	2.6658	3.3864	4.2919	5.4274	6.8485	8.6231	10.835
26	1.2953	1.6734	2.1566	2.7725	3.5557	4.5494	5.8074	7.3964	9.3992	11.918
27	1.3082	1.7069	2.2213	2.8834	3.7335	4.8223	6.2139	7.9881	10.245	13.110
28	1.3213	1.7410	2.2879	2.9987	3.9201	5.1117	6.6488	8.6271	11.167	14.421
29	1.3345	1.7758	2.3566	3.1187	4.1161	5.4184	7.1143	9.3173	12.172	15.863
30	1.3478	1.8114	2.4273	3.2434	4.3219	5.7435	7.6123	10.063	13.268	17.449
40	1.4889	2.2080	3.2620	4.8010	7.0400	10.286	14.974	21.725	31.409	45.259
50	1.6446	2.6916	4.3839	7.1067	11.467	18.420	29.457	46.902	74.358	117.39
60	1.8167	3.2810	5.8916	10.520	18.679	32.988	57.946	101.26	176.03	304.48

TABLE A-3

continued

Period	12%	14%	15%	16%	18%	20%	24%	28%	32%	36%
1	1.1200	1.1400	1.1500	1.1600	1.1800	1.2000	1.2400	1.2800	1.3200	1.3600
2	1.2544	1.2996	1.3225	1.3456	1.3924	1.4400	1.5376	1.6384	1.7424	1.8496
3	1.4049	1.4815	1.5209	1.5609	1.6430	1.7280	1.9066	2.0972	2.3000	2.5155
4	1.5735	1.6890	1.7490	1.8106	1.9388	2.0736	2.3642	2.6844	3.0360	3.4210
5	1.7623	1.9254	2.0114	2.1003	2.2878	2.4883	2.9316	3.4360	4.0075	4.6526
6	1.9738	2.1950	2.3131	2.4364	2.6996	2.9860	3.6352	4.3980	5.2899	6.3275
7	2.2107	2.5023	2.6600	2.8262	3.1855	3.5832	4.5077	5.6295	6.9826	8.6054
8	2.4760	2.8526	3.0590	3.2784	3.7589	4.2998	5.5895	7.2058	9.2170	11.703
9	2.7731	3.2519	3.5179	3.8030	4.4355	5.1598	6.9310	9.2234	12.166	15.917
10	3.1058	3.7072	4.0456	4.4114	5.2338	6.1917	8.5944	11.806	16.060	21.647
11	3.4785	4.2262	4.6524	5.1173	6.1759	7.4301	10.657	15.112	21.199	29.439
12	3.8960	4.8179	5.3503	5.9360	7.2876	8.9161	13.215	19.343	27.983	40.037
13	4.3635	5.4924	6.1528	6.8858	8.5994	10.699	16.386	24.759	36.937	54.451
14	4.8871	6.2613	7.0757	7.9875	10.147	12.839	20.319	31.691	48.757	74.053
15	5.4736	7.1379	8.1371	9.2655	11.974	15.407	25.196	40.565	64.359	100.71
16	6.1304	8.1372	9.3576	10.748	14.129	18.488	31.243	51.923	84.954	136.97
17	6.8660	9.2765	10.761	12.468	16.672	22.186	38.741	66.461	112.14	186.28
18	7.6900	10.575	12.375	14.463	19.673	26.623	48.039	85.071	148.02	253.34
19	8.6128	12.056	14.232	16.777	23.214	31.948	59.568	108.89	195.39	344.54
20	9.6463	13.743	16.367	19.461	27.393	38.338	73.864	139.38	257.92	468.57
21	10.804	15.668	18.822	22.574	32.324	46.005	91.592	178.41	340.45	637.26
22	12.100	17.861	21.645	26.186	38.142	55.206	113.57	228.36	449.39	866.67
23	13.552	20.362	24.891	30.376	45.008	66.247	140.83	292.30	593.20	1178.7
24	15.179	23.212	28.625	35.236	53.109	79.497	174.63	374.14	783.02	1603.0
25	17.000	26.462	32.919	40.874	62.669	95.396	216.54	478.90	1033.6	2180.1
26	19.040	30.167	37.857	47.414	73.949	114.48	268.51	613.00	1364.3	2964.9
27	21.325	34.390	43.535	55.000	87.260	137.37	332.95	784.64	1800.9	4032.3
28	23.884	39.204	50.066	63.800	102.97	164.84	412.86	1004.3	2377.2	5483.9
29	26.750	44.693	57.575	74.009	121.50	197.81	511.95	1285.6	3137.9	7458.1
30	29.960	50.950	66.212	85.850	143.37	237.38	634.82	1645.5	4142.1	10143.
40	93.051	188.88	267.86	378.72	750.38	1469.8	5455.9	19427.	66521.	*
50	289.00	700.23	1083.7	1670.7	3927.4	9100.4	46890.	*	*	*
60	897.60	2595.9	4384.0	7370.2	20555.	56348.	*	*	*	*

*FVIF > 99,999.

TABLE A-4

Future Value of an Annuity of $1 per Period for n Periods:

EQUATION:

$$FVIFA_{i,n} = \sum_{t=1}^{n} (1 + i)^{n-t} = \frac{(1 + i)^n - 1}{i}$$

FINANCIAL CALCULATOR KEYS:

n   i   0   1.0

[N] [I] [PV] [PMT] [FV]

Table
Value

Number of Periods	1%	2%	3%	4%	5%	6%	7%	8%	9%	10%
1	1.0000	1.0000	1.0000	1.0000	1.0000	1.0000	1.0000	1.0000	1.0000	1.0000
2	2.0100	2.0200	2.0300	2.0400	2.0500	2.0600	2.0700	2.0800	2.0900	2.1000
3	3.0301	3.0604	3.0909	3.1216	3.1525	3.1836	3.2149	3.2464	3.2781	3.3100
4	4.0604	4.1216	4.1836	4.2465	4.3101	4.3746	4.4399	4.5061	4.5731	4.6410
5	5.1010	5.2040	5.3091	5.4163	5.5256	5.6371	5.7507	5.8666	5.9847	6.1051
6	6.1520	6.3081	6.4684	6.6330	6.8019	6.9753	7.1533	7.3359	7.5233	7.7156
7	7.2135	7.4343	7.6625	7.8983	8.1420	8.3938	8.6540	8.9228	9.2004	9.4872
8	8.2857	8.5830	8.8923	9.2142	9.5491	9.8975	10.260	10.637	11.028	11.436
9	9.3685	9.7546	10.159	10.583	11.027	11.491	11.978	12.488	13.021	13.579
10	10.462	10.950	11.464	12.006	12.578	13.181	13.816	14.487	15.193	15.937
11	11.567	12.169	12.808	13.486	14.207	14.972	15.784	16.645	17.560	18.531
12	12.683	13.412	14.192	15.026	15.917	16.870	17.888	18.977	20.141	21.384
13	13.809	14.680	15.618	16.627	17.713	18.882	20.141	21.495	22.953	24.523
14	14.947	15.974	17.086	18.292	19.599	21.015	22.550	24.215	26.019	27.975
15	16.097	17.293	18.599	20.024	21.579	23.276	25.129	27.152	29.361	31.772
16	17.258	18.639	20.157	21.825	23.657	25.673	27.888	30.324	33.003	35.950
17	18.430	20.012	21.762	23.698	25.840	28.213	30.840	33.750	36.974	40.545
18	19.615	21.412	23.414	25.645	28.132	30.906	33.999	37.450	41.301	45.599
19	20.811	22.841	25.117	27.671	30.539	33.760	37.379	41.446	46.018	51.159
20	22.019	24.297	26.870	29.778	33.066	36.786	40.995	45.762	51.160	57.275
21	23.239	25.783	28.676	31.969	35.719	39.993	44.865	50.423	56.765	64.002
22	24.472	27.299	30.537	34.248	38.505	43.392	49.006	55.457	62.873	71.403
23	25.716	28.845	32.453	36.618	41.430	46.996	53.436	60.893	69.532	79.543
24	26.973	30.422	34.426	39.083	44.502	50.816	58.177	66.765	76.790	88.497
25	28.243	32.030	36.459	41.646	47.727	54.865	63.249	73.106	84.701	98.347
26	29.526	33.671	38.553	44.312	51.113	59.156	68.676	79.954	93.324	109.18
27	30.821	35.344	40.710	47.084	54.669	63.706	74.484	87.351	102.72	121.10
28	32.129	37.051	42.931	49.968	58.403	68.528	80.698	95.339	112.97	134.21
29	33.450	38.792	45.219	52.966	62.323	73.640	87.347	103.97	124.14	148.63
30	34.785	40.568	47.575	56.085	66.439	79.058	94.461	113.28	136.31	164.49
40	48.886	60.402	75.401	95.026	120.80	154.76	199.64	259.06	337.88	442.59
50	64.463	84.579	112.80	152.67	209.35	290.34	406.53	573.77	815.08	1163.9
60	81.670	114.05	163.05	237.99	353.58	533.13	813.52	1253.2	1944.8	3034.8

TABLE A-4

continued

Number of Periods	12%	14%	15%	16%	18%	20%	24%	28%	32%	36%
1	1.0000	1.0000	1.0000	1.0000	1.0000	1.0000	1.0000	1.0000	1.0000	1.0000
2	2.1200	2.1400	2.1500	2.1600	2.1800	2.2000	2.2400	2.2800	2.3200	2.3600
3	3.3744	3.4396	3.4725	3.5056	3.5724	3.6400	3.7776	3.9184	4.0624	4.2096
4	4.7793	4.9211	4.9934	5.0665	5.2154	5.3680	5.6842	6.0156	6.3624	6.7251
5	6.3528	6.6101	6.7424	6.8771	7.1542	7.4416	8.0484	8.6999	9.3983	10.146
6	8.1152	8.5355	8.7537	8.9775	9.4420	9.9299	10.980	12.136	13.406	14.799
7	10.089	10.730	11.067	11.414	12.142	12.916	14.615	16.534	18.696	21.126
8	12.300	13.233	13.727	14.240	15.327	16.499	19.123	22.163	25.678	29.732
9	14.776	16.085	16.786	17.519	19.086	20.799	24.712	29.369	34.895	41.435
10	17.549	19.337	20.304	21.321	23.521	25.959	31.643	38.593	47.062	57.352
11	20.655	23.045	24.349	25.733	28.755	32.150	40.238	50.398	63.122	78.998
12	24.133	27.271	29.002	30.850	34.931	39.581	50.895	65.510	84.320	108.44
13	28.029	32.089	34.352	36.786	42.219	48.497	64.110	84.853	112.30	148.47
14	32.393	37.581	40.505	43.672	50.818	59.196	80.496	109.61	149.24	202.93
15	37.280	43.842	47.580	51.660	60.965	72.035	100.82	141.30	198.00	276.98
16	42.753	50.980	55.717	60.925	72.939	87.442	126.01	181.87	262.36	377.69
17	48.884	59.118	65.075	71.673	87.068	105.93	157.25	233.79	347.31	514.66
18	55.750	68.394	75.836	84.141	103.74	128.12	195.99	300.25	459.45	700.94
19	63.440	78.969	88.212	98.603	123.41	154.74	244.03	385.32	607.47	954.28
20	72.052	91.025	102.44	115.38	146.63	186.69	303.60	494.21	802.86	1298.8
21	81.699	104.77	118.81	134.84	174.02	225.03	377.46	633.59	1060.8	1767.4
22	92.503	120.44	137.63	157.41	206.34	271.03	469.06	812.00	1401.2	2404.7
23	104.60	138.30	159.28	183.60	244.49	326.24	582.63	1040.4	1850.6	3271.3
24	118.16	158.66	184.17	213.98	289.49	392.48	723.46	1332.7	2443.8	4450.0
25	133.33	181.87	212.79	249.21	342.60	471.98	898.09	1706.8	3226.8	6053.0
26	150.33	208.33	245.71	290.09	405.27	567.38	1114.6	2185.7	4260.4	8233.1
27	169.37	238.50	283.57	337.50	479.22	681.85	1383.1	2798.7	5624.8	11198.0
28	190.70	272.89	327.10	392.50	566.48	819.22	1716.1	3583.3	7425.7	15230.3
29	214.58	312.09	377.17	456.30	669.45	984.07	2129.0	4587.7	9802.9	20714.2
30	241.33	356.79	434.75	530.31	790.95	1181.9	2640.9	5873.2	12941.	28172.3
40	767.09	1342.0	1779.1	2360.8	4163.2	7343.9	22729.	69377.	*	*
50	2400.0	4994.5	7217.7	10436.	21813.	45497.	*	*	*	*
60	7471.6	18535.	29220.	46058.	*	*	*	*	*	*

*FVIFA > 99,999.

Solutions to Self-Test Problems

Note: Except for Chapter 1, we do not show an answer for ST-1 problems because they are verbal rather than quantitative in nature.

Chapter 1

ST-1 Refer to the marginal glossary definitions or relevant chapter sections to check your responses.

Chapter 2

ST-2 *a.* Average = (6% + 7% + 8% + 9%)/4 = 30%/4 = 7.5%.

   b. $k_{\text{T-bond}} = k^* + IP = 3.0\% + 7.5\% = 10.5\%$.

   c. If the 5-year T-bond rate is 11 percent, the inflation rate is expected to average approximately $11\% - 3\% = 8\%$ during the next 5 years. Thus, the implied Year 5 inflation rate is 10 percent:

$$8\% = (6\% + 7\% + 8\% + 9\% + I_5)/5$$

$$40\% = 30\% + \text{Infl}_5$$

$$\text{Infl}_5 = 10\%.$$

ST-3

	1996	1997	1998
Thompson's Taxes as a Corporation			
Income before salary and taxes	$60,000	$ 90,000	$110,000
Less: salary	(40,000)	(40,000)	(40,000)
Taxable income, corporate	$20,000	$ 50,000	$ 70,000
Total corporate tax	(3,000)[a]	(7,500)	(12,500)

Salary	$40,000	$ 40,000	$ 40,000
Less exemptions and deductions	(16,350)	(16,350)	(16,350)
Taxable personal income	$23,650	$ 23,650	$ 23,650
Total personal tax	(3,548)[b]	(3,548)	(3,548)
Combined corporate and personal tax:	$ 6,548	$ 11,048	$ 16,048

Thompson's Taxes as a Proprietorship

Total income	$60,000	$ 90,000	$110,000
Less: exemptions and deductions	(16,350)	(16,350)	(16,350)
Taxable personal income	$43,650	$ 73,650	$ 93,650
Tax liability of proprietorship	$(7,282)[c]	$(15,682)	$ (21,336)
Advantage to being a corporation:	$ 734	$ 4,634	$ 5,288

[a]Corporate tax in 1996 = (0.15)($20,000) = $3,000.

[b]Personal tax (if Thompson incorporates) in 1996 = (0.15)($23,650) = $3,548.

[c]Proprietorship tax in 1996 = $5,700 + (0.28)($43,650 − $38,000)

$$= \$5,700 + \$1,582$$
$$= \$7,282$$

The corporate form of organization allows Thompson to pay the lowest taxes in each year; therefore, on the basis of taxes over the 3-year period, Thompson should incorporate his business. However, note that to get money out of the corporation so he can spend it, Thompson will have to have the corporation pay dividends, which will be taxed to Thompson, and thus he will, sometime in the future, have to pay additional taxes.

Chapter 3

ST-2 Billingsworth paid $2 in dividends and retained $2 per share. Since total retained earnings rose by $12 million, there must be 6 million shares outstanding. With a book value of $40 per share, total common equity must be $40(6 million) = $240 million. Since Billingsworth has $120 million of debt, its debt ratio must be 33.3 percent:

$$\frac{\text{Debt}}{\text{Assets}} = \frac{\text{Debt}}{\text{Debt} + \text{Equity}} = \frac{\$120 \text{ million}}{\$120 \text{ million} + \$240 \text{ million}}$$
$$= 0.333 = 33.3\%.$$

ST-3 *a.* In answering questions such as this, always begin by writing down the relevant definitional equations, then start filling in numbers. Note that the extra zeros indicating millions have been deleted in the calculations below.

(1)
$$\text{DSO} = \frac{\text{Accounts receivable}}{\text{Sales}/360}$$

$$40 = \frac{\text{A/R}}{\$1,000/360}$$

A/R = 40($2.778) = $111.1 million.

(2)
$$\text{Quick ratio} = \frac{\text{Current assets} - \text{Inventories}}{\text{Current liabilities}} = 2.0$$

$$= \frac{\text{Cash and marketable securities} + \text{A/R}}{\text{Current liabilities}} = 2.0$$

$$2.0 = \frac{\$100 + \$111.1}{\text{Current liabilities}}$$

Current liabilities = ($100 + $111.1)/2 = $105.6 million.

(3)
$$\text{Current ratio} = \frac{\text{Current assets}}{\text{Current liabilities}} = 3.0$$

$$= \frac{\text{Current assets}}{\$105.6} = 3.0$$

Current assets = 3.0($105.6) = $316.7 million.

(4)
$$\text{Total assets} = \text{Current assets} + \text{Fixed assets}$$
$$= \$316.7 + \$283.5 = \$600.1 \text{ million.}$$

(5)
$$\text{ROA} = \text{Profit margin} \times \text{Total assets turnover}$$

$$= \frac{\text{Net income}}{\text{Sales}} \times \frac{\text{Sales}}{\text{Total assets}}$$

$$= \frac{\$50}{\$1,000} \times \frac{\$1,000}{\$600.1}$$

$$= 0.05 \times 1.667 = 0.0833 = 8.33\%.$$

(6)
$$\text{ROE} = \frac{\text{NI}}{\text{Equity}}$$

$$12.0\% = \frac{\$50}{\text{Equity}}$$

$$\text{Equity} = \frac{\$50}{0.12}$$

$$= \$416.7 \text{ million.}$$

(7)
$$\text{Total assets} = \text{Total claims} = \$600.1 \text{ million}$$

$$\text{Current liabilities} + \text{Long-term debt} + \text{Equity} = \$600.1 \text{ million}$$

$$\$105.6 + \text{Long-term debt} + \$416.7 = \$600.1 \text{ million}$$

$$\text{Long-term debt} = \$600.1 - \$105.6 - \$416.7 = \$77.8 \text{ million.}$$

b. Kaiser's average sales per day were $1,000/360 = $2.8 million. Its DSO was 40, so A/R = 40($2.8) = $111.1 million. Its new DSO of 30 would cause A/R = 30($2.8) = $83.3 million. The reduction in receivables would be $111.1 − $83.3 = $27.8 million, which would equal the amount of cash generated.

(1)
$$\text{New equity} = \text{Old equity} - \text{Stock bought back}$$

$$- \$416.7 - \$27.8$$

$$= \$388.9 \text{ million.}$$

Thus,

$$\text{New ROE} = \frac{\text{Net income}}{\text{New equity}}$$

$$= \frac{\$50}{\$388.9}$$

$$= 12.86\% \text{ (versus old ROE of 12.0\%).}$$

(2)

$$\text{New ROA} = \frac{\text{Net income}}{\text{Total assets} - \text{Reduction in A/R}}$$

$$= \frac{\$50}{\$600.1 - \$27.8}$$

$$= 8.74\% \text{ (versus old ROA of 8.33\%).}$$

(3) The old debt is the same as the new debt:

$$\text{Debt} = \text{Total claims} - \text{Equity}$$

$$= \$600.1 - \$416.7 = \$183.4 \text{ million.}$$

$$\text{Old total assets} = \$600.1 \text{ million.}$$

$$\text{New total assets} = \text{Old total assets} - \text{Reduction in A/R}$$

$$= \$600.1 - \$27.8$$

$$= \$572.3 \text{ million.}$$

Therefore,

$$\frac{\text{Debt}}{\text{Old total assets}} = \frac{\$183.4}{\$600.1} = 30.6\%,$$

while

$$\frac{\text{New debt}}{\text{New total assets}} = \frac{\$183.4}{\$572.3} = 32.0\%.$$

Chapter 4

ST-2 *a.* (1) Determine the variable cost per unit at present, using the following definitions and equations:

$$Q = \text{units of output (sales)} = 5,000.$$

$$P = \text{average sales price per unit of output} = \$100.$$

$$F = \text{fixed operating costs} = \$200,000.$$

$$V = \text{variable costs per unit.}$$

$$\text{EBIT} = P(Q) - F - V(Q)$$

$$\$50,000 = \$100(5,000) - \$200,000 - V(5,000)$$

$$5,000V = \$250,000$$

$$V = \$50.$$

(2) Determine the new EBIT level if the change is made:

$$\text{New EBIT} = P_2(Q_2) - F_2 - V_2(Q_2)$$

$$= \$95(7{,}000) - \$250{,}000 - \$40(7{,}000)$$

$$= \$135{,}000.$$

(3) Determine the incremental EBIT:

$$\Delta\text{EBIT} = \$135{,}000 - \$50{,}000 = \$85{,}000.$$

(4) Estimate the approximate rate of return on the new investment:

$$\Delta\text{ROA} = \frac{\Delta\text{EBIT}}{\text{Investment}} = \frac{\$85{,}000}{\$400{,}000} = 21.25\%.$$

Since the ROA exceeds Olinde's average cost of capital, this analysis suggests that Olinde should go ahead and make the investment.

b.

$$\text{DOL} = \frac{Q(P - V)}{Q(P - V) - F}$$

$$\text{DOL}_{\text{Old}} = \frac{5{,}000(\$100 - \$50)}{5{,}000(\$100 - \$50) - \$200{,}000} = 5.00.$$

$$\text{DOL}_{\text{New}} = \frac{7{,}000(\$95 - \$40)}{7{,}000(\$95 - \$40) - \$250{,}000} = 2.85.$$

This indicates that operating income will be less sensitive to changes in sales if the production process is changed; thus the change would reduce risks. However, the change would increase the breakeven point. Still, with a lower sales price, it might be easier to achieve the higher new breakeven volume.

$$\textit{Old:}\ Q_{\text{BE}} = \frac{F}{P - V} = \frac{\$200{,}000}{\$100 - \$50} = 4{,}000\ \text{units.}$$

$$\textit{New:}\ Q_{\text{BE}} = \frac{F}{P_2 - V_2} = \frac{\$250{,}000}{\$95 - \$40} = 4{,}545\ \text{units.}$$

c. The incremental ROA is:

$$\Delta\text{ROA} = \frac{\Delta\text{Profit}}{\Delta\text{Sales}} \times \frac{\Delta\text{Sales}}{\Delta\text{Assets}}.$$

Using debt financing, the incremental profit associated with the investment is equal to the incremental profit found in Part a minus the interest expense incurred as a result of the investment:

$$\Delta\text{Profit} = \text{New profit} - \text{Old profit} - \text{Interest}$$

$$= \$135{,}000 - \$50{,}000 - 0.08(\$400{,}000)$$

$$= \$53{,}000.$$

The incremental sales is calculated as:

$$\Delta Sales = P_2Q_2 - P_1Q_1$$

$$= \$95(7,000) - \$100(5,000)$$

$$= \$665,000 - \$500,000$$

$$= \$165,000.$$

$$ROA = \frac{\$53,000}{\$165,000} \times \frac{\$165,000}{\$400,000} = 13.25\%.$$

The return on the new equity investment still exceeds the average cost of funds (10%), so Olinde should make the investment.

d.

$$DFL = \frac{EBIT}{EBIT - I}$$

$$DFL_{New} = \frac{\$135,000}{\$135,000 - \$32,000}$$

$$= 1.31.$$

$$EBIT_{financial\ BEP} = \$32,000$$

Chapter 5

ST-2 a. The average rate of return for each stock is calculated by simply averaging the returns over the five-year period. The average return for each stock is 18.90 percent, calculated for Stock A as follows:

$$k_{Avg} = (-10.00\% + 18.50\% + 38.67\% + 14.33\% + 33.00\%)/5$$

$$= 18.90\%.$$

The realized rate of return on a portfolio made up of Stock A and Stock B would be calculated by finding the average return in each year as k_A(% of Stock A) + k_B(% of Stock B) and then averaging these yearly returns:

Year	Portfolio AB's Return, k_{AB}
1991	(6.50%)
1992	19.90
1993	41.46
1994	9.00
1995	30.65
	$k_{Avg} = 18.90\%$

b. The standard deviation of returns is estimated, using Equation 5-3a, as follows (see Footnote 4):

$$\text{Estimated } \sigma = S = \sqrt{\frac{\sum_{t=1}^{n} (\bar{k}_t - \bar{k}_{Avg})^2}{n - 1}}. \qquad \textbf{(5-3a)}$$

For Stock A, the estimated σ is 19.0 percent:

$$\sigma_A = \sqrt{\frac{(-10.00 - 18.9)^2 + (18.50 - 18.9)^2 + \ldots + (33.00 - 18.9)^2}{5 - 1}}$$

$$= \sqrt{\frac{1,445.92}{4}} = 19.0\%.$$

The standard deviation of returns for Stock B and for the portfolio are similarly determined, and they are as follows:

	Stock A	Stock B	Portfolio AB
Standard deviation	19.0	19.0	18.6

c. Since the risk reduction from diversification is small (σ_{AB} falls only from 19.0 to 18.6 percent), the most likely value of the correlation coefficient is 0.9. If the correlation coefficient were -0.9, the risk reduction would be much larger. In fact, the correlation coefficient between Stocks A and B is 0.92.

d. If more randomly selected stocks were added to the portfolio, σ_p would decline to somewhere in the vicinity of 15 percent; see Figure 5-7, σ_p would remain constant only if the correlation coefficient were $+ 1.0$, which is most unlikely. σ_p would decline to zero only if the correlation coefficient, r, were equal to zero and a large number of stocks were added to the portfolio, or if the proper proportions were held in a two-stock portfolio with r $= -1.0$.

Chapter 6

ST-2 **a.**

1/1/96   8%   1/1/97   1/1/98   1/1/99   1/1/2000
├──────────────┼───────────────┼───────────────┤
       $-1,000$ FV = ?

$1,000 is being compounded for 3 years, so your balance on January 1, 2000, is $1,259.71:

$$FV_n = PV(1 + i)^n = \$1,000(1 + 0.08)^3 = \$1,259.71.$$

Alternatively, using a financial calculator, input N = 3, I = 8, PV = -1000, PMT = 0, and FV = ? FV = $1,259.71.

b.

1/1/96   1/1/97   1/1/98   1/1/99   1/1/2000
  2%
├─┼─┼─┼─┼─┼─┼─┼─┼─┼─┼─┼─┤
       $-1,000$ FV = ?

The effective annual rate for 8 percent, compounded quarterly, is

$$\text{Effective annual rate} = \left(1 + \frac{0.08}{4}\right)^4 - 1.0$$

$$= (1.02)^4 - 1.0 = 0.0824 = 8.24\%.$$

Therefore, FV = $1,000(1.0824)^3 = \$1,000(1,2681) = \$1,268.10$. Alternatively, use FVIF for 2%, 3 $\times$ 4 = 12 periods:

$$FV_{12} = \$1,000(FVIF_{2\%,12}) = \$1,000(1.2682) = \$1,268.20.$$

Alternatively, using a financial calculator, input N = 12, I = 2, PV = −1000, PMT = 0, and FV = ? FV = $1,268.24.

Note that since the interest factors are carried to only four decimal places, rounding errors occur. Rounding errors also occur between calculator and tabular solutions.

c.

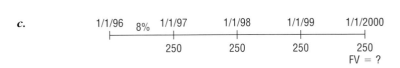

1/1/96   8%   1/1/97   1/1/98   1/1/99   1/1/2000

                250   250   250   250

                                             FV = ?

As you work this problem, keep in mind that the tables assume that payments are made at the end of each period. Therefore, you may solve this problem by finding the future value of an annuity of $250 for 4 years at 8 percent:

$$FVA_4 = PMT(FVIFA_{i,n}) = \$250(4.5061) = \$1,126.53.$$

Alternatively, using a financial calculator, input N = 4, I = 8, PV = 0, PMT = −250, and FV = ? FV = $1,126.53.

d.

1/1/96   8%   1/1/97   1/1/98   1/1/99   1/1/2000

                ?   ?   ?   ?

                                          FV = 1,259.71

N = 4; I = 8%; PV = 0; FV = $1,259.71; PMT = ?; PMT = $279.56.

$$PMT(FVIFA_{8\%,4}) = FVA_4$$

$$PMT(4.5061) = \$1,259.71$$

$$PMT = \$1,259.71/4.5061 = \$279.56.$$

Therefore, you would have to make 4 payments of $279.56 each to have a balance of $1,259.71 on January 1, 2000.

ST-3   **a.** Set up a time line like the one in the preceding problem:

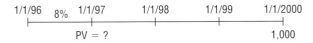

1/1/96   8%   1/1/97   1/1/98   1/1/99   1/1/2000

            PV = ?   1,000

Note that your deposit will grow for 3 years at 8 percent. The fact that it is now January 1, 1996, is irrelevant. The deposit on January 1, 1997, is the PV, and the FV is $1,000. Here is the solution:

N = 3; I = 8%; PMT = 0; FV = $1,000; PV = ?; PV = $793.83.

$$FV_3(PVIF_{8\%,3}) = PV$$

$$PV = \$1,000(0.7938) = \$793.80 = \text{Initial deposit to accumulate } \$1,000.$$

(Difference due to rounding error.)

b.

```
1/1/96   8%   1/1/97        1/1/98        1/1/99        1/1/2000
 ├───────────┼─────────────┼─────────────┼─────────────┤
            PMT           PMT           PMT           PMT
                                                    FV = 1,000
```

Here we are dealing with a 4-year annuity whose first payment occurs one year from today, on 1/1/97, and whose future value must equal $1,000. You should modify the time line to help visualize the situation. Here is the solution:

$$N = 4; I = 8\%; PV = 0; FV = \$1,000; PMT = ?; PMT = \$221.92.$$

$$PMT(FVIFA_{8\%,4}) = FVA_4$$

$$PMT = \frac{FVA_4}{(FVIFA_{8\%,4})}$$

$$= \frac{\$1,000}{4.5061} = \$221.92 = \begin{array}{l}\text{Payment necessary} \\ \text{to accumulate } \$1,000.\end{array}$$

c. This problem can be approached in several ways. Perhaps the simplest is to ask this question: "If I received $750 on 1/1/97 and deposited it to earn 8 percent, would I have acquired $1,000 on 1/1/2000?" The answer is no:

```
1/1/96   8%   1/1/97        1/1/98        1/1/99        1/1/2000
 ├───────────┼─────────────┼─────────────┼─────────────┤
            -750                                      FV = ?
```

$$FV_3 = \$750(1.08)^3 = \$944.78.$$

This indicates that you should let your father make the payments rather than accept the lump sum of $750.

You could also compare the $750 with the PV of the payments:

```
1/1/96   8%   1/1/97        1/1/98        1/1/99        1/1/2000
 ├───────────┼─────────────┼─────────────┼─────────────┤
           221.92         221.92         221.92         221.92
           PV = ?
```

$$N = 4; I = 8\%; PMT = -\$221.92; FV = 0; PV = ?; PV = \$735.03.$$

$$PMT(PVIFA_{8\%,4}) = PVA_4$$

$$\$221.92(3.3121) = \$735.02 = \begin{array}{l}\text{Present value at } 1/1/96 \\ \text{of the required payments.}\end{array}$$

(Difference due to rounding error.)

This is less than the $750 lump sum offer, so your initial reaction might be to accept the lump sum of $750. However, this would be a mistake. The problem is that when you found the $735.02 PV of the annuity, you were finding the value of the annuity *today,* on January 1, 1996. You were comparing $735.02 today with the lump sum of $750 one year from now. This is, of course, invalid. What you should have done was take the $735.02, recognize that this is the PV of an annuity as of January 1, 1996, multiply $735.02 by 1.08 to get $793.82, and compare $793.82 with the lump sum of $750. You would then take your father's offer to make the payments rather than take the lump sum on January 1, 1997. If you solved the PV for an annuity due, you would find the same answer.

d.

1/1/96	$i = ?$	1/1/97	1/1/98	1/1/99	1/1/2000

-750 $1,000$

$N = 3$; $PV = -\$750$; $PMT = 0$; $FV = \$1,000$; $I = ?$; $I = 10.0642\%$.

$$PV(FVIF_{i,3}) = FV$$

$$FVIF_{i,3} = \frac{FV}{PV}$$

$$= \frac{\$1,000}{\$750} = 1.3333.$$

Use the Future Value of $1 table (Table A-3 in Appendix A) for 3 periods to find the interest rate corresponding to an FVIF of 1.3333. Look across the Period 3 row of the table until you come to 1.3333. The closest value is 1.3310, in the 10 percent column. Therefore, you would require an interest rate of approximately 10 percent to achieve your $1,000 goal. The exact rate required, found with a financial calculator, is 10.0642 percent. Solving directly, $i = (1.3333)^{\frac{1}{3}} - 1 = 10.0642\%$.

e.

1/1/96	$i = ?$	1/1/97	1/1/98	1/1/99	1/1/2000

186.29 186.29 186.29 186.29
$FV = 1,000$

$N = 4$; $PV = 0$; $PMT = -\$186.29$; $FV = \$1,000$; $I = ?$; $I = 19.9997\%$.

$$PMT(FVIFA_{i,4}) = FVA_4$$

$$\$186,29(FVIFA_{i,4}) = \$1,000$$

$$FVIFA_{i,4} = \frac{\$1,000}{\$186.29} = 5.3680.$$

Using Table A-4 at the end of the book, we find that 5.3680 corresponds to a 20 percent interest rate. You might be able to find a borrower willing to offer you a 20 percent interest rate, but there would be some risk involved—he or she might not actually pay you your $1,000 on January 1, 2000.

f.

1/1/96	4%	1/1/97	1/1/98	1/1/99	1/1/2000

400 PMT   PMT   PMT   PMT   PMT   PMT
$FV = 1,000$

Find the future value of the original $400 deposit:

$$FV_6 = PV(FVIF_{4\%,6}) = \$400(1.2653) = \$506.12.$$

This means that on January 1, 2000, you need an additional sum of $493.88:

$$\$1,000.00 - \$506.12 = \$493.88.$$

This will be accumulated by making 6 equal payments which earn 8 percent compounded semiannually, or 4 percent each 6 months:

$$N = 6; I = 4\%; PV = 0; FV = \$493.88; PMT = ?; PMT = 74.46.$$

$$PMT(FVIFA_{4\%,6}) = FVA_6$$

$$PMT = \frac{FVA_6}{(FVIFA_{4\%,6})}$$

$$= \frac{\$493.88}{6.6330} = \$74.46.$$

Alternatively, using a financial calculator, input N = 6, I = 4, PV = −400, FV = 1000, and PMT = ? PMT = $74.46.

g.
$$\text{Effective annual rate} = \left(1 + \frac{i_{SIMPLE}}{m}\right)^m - 1.0$$

$$= \left(1 + \frac{0.08}{2}\right)^2 - 1 = (1.04)^2 - 1$$

$$= 1.0816 - 1 = 0.0816 = 8.16\%.$$

h. There is a reinvestment rate risk here because we assumed that funds will earn an 8 percent return in the bank. In fact, if interest rates in the economy fall, the bank will lower its deposit rate because it will be earning less when it lends out the funds you deposited with it. If you buy certificates of deposit (CDs) that mature on the date you need the money (1/1/2000), you will avoid the re-investment risk, but that would work only if you were making the deposit today. Other ways of reducing reinvestment rate risk will be discussed later in the text.

ST-4   Bank A's effective annual rate is 8.24 percent:

$$\text{Effective annual rate} = \left(1 + \frac{0.08}{4}\right)^4 - 1.0$$

$$= (1.02)^4 - 1 = 1.0824 - 1$$

$$= 0.0824 = 8.24\%.$$

Now Bank B must have the same effective annual rate:

$$\left(1 + \frac{i}{12}\right)^{12} - 1.0 = 0.0824$$

$$\left(1 + \frac{i}{12}\right)^{12} = 1.0824$$

$$1 + \frac{i}{12} = (1.0824)^{1/12}$$

$$1 + \frac{i}{12} = 1.00662$$

$$\frac{i}{12} = 0.00662$$

$$i = 0.07944 = 7.94\%.$$

Thus, the two banks have different quoted rates—Bank A's quoted rate is 8 percent, while Bank B's quoted rate is 7.94 percent; however, both banks have the same effective annual rate of 8.24 percent. The difference in their quoted rates is due to the difference in compounding frequency.

Chapter 7

ST-2   a. This is not necessarily true. Because G plows back two-thirds of its earnings, its growth rate should exceed that of D, but D pays higher dividends ($6 versus $2). We cannot say which stock should have the higher price.

    b. Again, we just do not know which price would be higher.

    c. This is false. The changes in k_d and k_s would have a greater effect on G—its price would decline more.

    d. The total expected return for D is $\hat{k}_D = D_1/P_0 + g = 15\% + 0\% = 15\%$. The total expected return for G will have D_1/P_0 less than 15 percent and g greater than 0 percent, but $\hat{k}_G$ should be neither greater nor smaller than D's total expected return, 15 percent, because the two stocks are stated to be equally risky.

    e. We have eliminated a, b, c, and d, so e should be correct. On the basis of the available information, D and G should sell at about the same price, $40; thus, $\hat{k}_s$ = 15% for both D and G. G's current dividend yield is $2/$40 = 5%. Therefore, g = 15% − 5% = 10%.

ST-3   a. Pennington's bonds were sold at par; therefore, the original YTM equaled the coupon rate of 12%.

    b.

$$V_d = \sum_{t=1}^{50} \frac{\$120/2}{\left(1 + \dfrac{0.10}{2}\right)^t} + \frac{\$1,000}{\left(1 + \dfrac{0.10}{2}\right)^{50}}$$

$$= \$60(\text{PVIFA}_{5\%,50}) + \$1,000(\text{PVIF}_{5\%,50})$$

$$= \$60(18.2559) + \$1,000(0.0872)$$

$$= \$1,095.35 + \$87.20 = \$1,182.55.$$

Alternatively, with a financial calculator, input the following: N = 50, I = 5, PMT = 60, FV = 1000, and PV = ? PV = $1,182.56.

    c.

$$\text{Current yield} = \text{Annual coupon payment/Price}$$

$$= \$120/\$1,182.55$$

$$= 0.1015 = 10.15\%.$$

$$\text{Capital gains yield} = \text{Total yield} - \text{Current yield}$$

$$= 10\% - 10.15\% = -0.15\%.$$

    d.

$$\$916.42 = \sum_{t=1}^{13} \frac{\$60}{(1 + k_d/2)^t} + \frac{\$1,000}{(1 + k_d/2)^{13}}.$$

Using Equation 7-3, the approximate YTM is:

$$\text{YTM} \approx \frac{\$60 + \left(\dfrac{\$1,000 - \$916.42}{13}\right)}{\left[\dfrac{2(\$916.42) + \$1,000}{3}\right]}$$

$$= 7\%$$

At k_d = 7%:

$$V_d = \text{INT}(\text{PVIFA}_{7\%,13}) + M(\text{PVIF}_{7\%,13})$$

$$\$916.42 = \$60(8.3577) + \$1,000(0.4150)$$

$$= \$501.46 + \$415.00 = \$916.46.$$

Therefore, the YTM on July 1, 1996, was 14 percent. Alternatively, with a financial calculator, input the following: N = 13, PV = −916.42, PMT = 60, FV = 1000, and $k_{d/2}$ = I = ? Calculator solution = $k_{d/2}$ = 7.00%; therefore, k_d = 14.00%.

e.

$$\text{Current yield} = \$120/\$916.42 = 13.09\%.$$

$$\text{Capital gains yield} = 14\% - 13.09\% = 0.91\%.$$

ST-4   The first step is to solve for g, the unknown variable, in the constant growth equation. Since D_1 is unknown but D_0 is known, substitute $D_0(1 + g)$ as follows:

$$\hat{P}_0 = P_0 = \frac{D_1}{k_s - g} = \frac{D_0(1 + g)}{k_s - g}$$

$$\$36 = \frac{\$2.40(1 + g)}{0.12 - g}.$$

Solving for g, we find the growth rate to be 5 percent:

$$\$4.32 - \$36g = \$2.40 + \$2.40g$$

$$\$38.4g = \$1.92$$

$$g = 0.05 = 5\%.$$

The next step is to use the growth rate to project the stock price 5 years hence:

$$\hat{P}_5 = \frac{D_0(1 + g)^6}{k_s - g}$$

$$= \frac{\$2.40(1.05)^6}{0.12 - 0.05}$$

$$= \$45.95.$$

$$[\text{Alternatively, } \hat{P}_5 = \$36(1.05)^5 = \$45.95.]$$

Therefore, Ewald Company's expected stock price 5 years from now, $\hat{P}_5$, is $45.95.

ST-5   *a.* (1) Calculate the PV of the dividends paid during the supernormal growth period:

$$D_1 = \$1.1500(1.15) = \$1.3225.$$

$$D_2 = \$1.3225(1.15) = \$1.5209.$$

$$D_3 = \$1.5209(1.13) = \$1.7186.$$

$$PV\, D = \$1.3225(0.8929) + \$1.5209(0.7972) + \$1.7186(0.7118)$$

$$= \$1.1809 + \$1.2125 + \$1.2233$$

$$= \$3.6167 \approx \$3.62.$$

(2) Find the PV of Snyder's stock price at the end of Year 3:

$$\hat{P}_3 = \frac{D_4}{k_s - g} = \frac{D_3(1 + g)}{k_s - g}$$

$$= \frac{\$1.7186(1.06)}{0.12 - 0.06}$$

$$= \$30.36.$$

$$PV\ \hat{P}_3 = \$30.36(0.7118) = \$21.61.$$

(3) Sum the two components to find the value of the stock today:

$$\hat{P}_0 = \$3.62 + \$21.61 = \$25.23.$$

Alternatively, the cash flows can be placed on a time line as follows:

Enter the cash flows into the cash flow register, I = 12, and press the NPV key to obtain P_0 = $25.23.

b.

$$\hat{P}_1 = \$1.5209(0.8929) + \$1.7186(0.7972) + \$30.36(0.7972)$$

$$= \$1.3580 + \$1.3701 + \$24.2030$$

$$= \$26.9311 \approx \$26.93.$$

(Calculator solution: $26.93.)

$$\hat{P}_2 = \$1.7186(0.8929) + \$30.36(0.8929)$$

$$= \$1.5345 + \$27.1084$$

$$= \$28.6429 \approx \$28.64.$$

(Calculator solution: $28.64.)

c.

Year	Dividend Yield	+	Capital Gains Yield	=	Total Return
1	$\dfrac{\$1.3225}{\$25.23} \approx 5.24\%$		$\dfrac{\$26.93 - \$25.23}{\$25.23} \approx 6.74\%$		$\approx 12\%$
2	$\dfrac{\$1.5209}{\$26.93} \approx 5.65\%$		$\dfrac{\$28.64 - \$26.93}{\$26.93} \approx 6.35\%$		$\approx 12\%$
3	$\dfrac{\$1.7186}{\$28.64} \approx 6.00\%$		$\dfrac{\$30.36 - \$28.64}{\$28.64} \approx 6.00\%$		$\approx 12\%$

Chapter 8

ST-2 *a.* and *b.*

**Income Statements for Year Ended December 31, 1995
(Thousands of Dollars)**

	Vanderheiden Press		Herrenhouse Publishing	
	a	b	a	b
EBIT	$ 30,000	$ 30,000	$ 30,000	$ 30,000
Interest	(12,400)	(14,400)	(10,600)	(18,600)
Taxable income	$ 17,600	$ 15,600	$ 19,400	$ 11,400
Taxes (40%)	(7,040)	(6,240)	(7,760)	(4,560)
Net income	$ 10,560	$ 9,360	$ 11,640	$ 6,840
Equity	$100,000	$100,000	$100,000	$100,000
Return on equity	10.56%	9.36%	11.64%	6.84%

The Vanderheiden Press has a higher ROE when short-term interest rates are high, whereas Herrenhouse Publishing does better when rates are lower.

c. Herrenhouse's position is riskier. First, its profits and return on equity are much more volatile than Vanderheiden's. Second, Herrenhouse must renew its large short-term loan every year, and if the renewal comes up at a time when money is very tight, when its business is depressed, or both, then Herrenhouse could be denied credit, which could put it out of business.

ST-3 **The Calgary Company: Alternative Balance Sheets**

	Restricted (40%)	Moderate (50%)	Relaxed (60%)
Current assets	$1,200,000	$1,500,000	$1,800,000
Fixed assets	600,000	600,000	600,000
Total assets	$1,800,000	$2,100,000	$2,400,000
Debt	$ 900,000	$1,050,000	$1,200,000
Equity	900,000	1,050,000	1,200,000
Total liabilities and equity	$1,800,000	$2,100,000	$2,400,000

The Calgary Company: Alternative Income Statements

	Restricted	Moderate	Relaxed
Sales	$3,000,000	$3,000,000	$3,000,000
EBIT	450,000	450,000	450,000
Interest (10%)	(90,000)	(105,000)	(120,000)
Earnings before taxes (EBT)	$ 360,000	$ 345,000	$ 330,000
Taxes (40%)	(144,000)	(138,000)	(132,000)
Net income	$ 216,000	$ 207,000	$ 198,000
ROE	24.0%	19.7%	16.5%

Chapter 9

ST-2 a. First determine the balance on the firm's checkbook and the bank's records as follows:

	Firm's Checkbook	Bank's Records
Day 1: Deposit $500,000; write check for $1,000,000	($500,000)	$500,000
Day 2: Write check for $1,000,000	($1,500,000)	$500,000
Day 3: Write check for $1,000,000	($2,500,000)	$500,000
Day 4: Write check for $1,000,000; deposit $1,000,000	($2,500,000)	$500,000

After Upton has reached a steady state, it must deposit $1,000,000 each day to cover the checks written three days earlier.

b. The firm has 3 days of float; not until Day 4 does the firm have to make any additional deposits.

c. As shown above, Upton should try to maintain a balance on the bank's records of $500,000. On its own books it will have a balance of *minus* $2,500,000.

ST-3 First, determine the annual benefit to Kroncke from the reduction in cash balances under each plan:

$$\text{Average daily collections} = (30)(\$30,000) = \$900,000.$$

DTC:

Current collection float: $900,000 per day $\times$ 5 days = $4,500,000
New collection float: $900,000 per day $\times$ 3 days   =   2,700,000
Float reduction: $1,800,000

Kroncke can reduce its average cash balances by $1,800,000 by using DTCs, and it can earn 11 percent, which will provide $198,000 of additional income:

$$\text{Additional income} = (\$1,800,000)(0.11) = \$198,000.$$

Wire transfer:

Current collection float: $900,000 per day $\times$ 5 days = $4,500,000
New collection float: $900,000 per day $\times$ 1 day   =   900,000
Float reduction: $3,600,000

Kroncke can reduce its cash balances by $3,600,000 by using wire transfers, which will increase income by $396,000:

$$\text{Additional income} = (\$3,600,000)(0.11) = \$396,000.$$

Next, compute the annual cost of each transfer method:

Number of transfers = 30 × 260 = 7,800 per year.

Fixed lockbox cost = $14,000 × 12 = $168,000 per year.

DTC:

Total costs = (7,800)($0.75) + $168,000 = $173,850.

Wire transfer:

Total costs = (7,800)($11) + $168,000 = $253,800.

Finally, calculate the net additional income resulting from each transfer method:

DTC:

$198,000 − $173,850 = $24,150.

Wire transfer:

$396,000 − $253,800 = $142,200.

Therefore, Kroncke should adopt the lockbox system and transfer funds from the lockbox operators to the regional concentration banks using wire transfers.

Chapter 10

ST-2 Under the current credit policy, the Boca Grande Company has no discounts, has collection expenses of $50,000, has bad debt losses of (0.02)($10,000,000) = $200,000, and has average accounts receivable of (DSO)(Average sales per day) = (30)($10,000,000/360) = $833,333. The firm's cost of carrying these receivables is (Variable cost ratio)(A/R)(Cost of capital) = (0.80)($833,333)(0.16) = $106,667. It is necessary to multiply by the variable cost ratio because the actual *investment* in receivables is less than the dollar amount of the receivables.

Proposal 1: Lengthen the credit period to net 30 so that

1. Sales increase by $1 million.
2. Discounts = $0.
3. Bad debt losses = (0.02)($10,000,000) + (0.04)($1,000,000)
    = $200,000 + $40,000
    = $240,000.
4. DSO = 45 days on all sales.
5. New average receivables = (45)($11,000,000/360) = $1,375,000.
6. Cost of carrying receivables = (v)(k)(Average accounts receivable)
    = (0.80)(0.16)($1,375,000)
    = $176,000.
7. Collection expenses = $50,000.

Analysis of proposed change:

	Income Statement under Current Policy	Effect of Change	Income Statement under New Policy
Gross sales	$10,000,000	+$1,000,000	$11,000,000
Less discounts	(0)	+ (0)	(0)
Net sales	$10,000,000	+$1,000,000	$11,000,000
Production costs (80%)	(8,000,000)	+ (800,000)	(8,800,000)
Profit before credit costs and taxes	$ 2,000,000	+$ 200,000	$ 2,200,000
Credit-related costs			
Cost of carrying receivables	(106,667)	+ (69,333)	(176,000)
Collection expenses	(50,000)	+ (0)	(50,000)
Bad debt losses	(200,000)	+ (40,000)	(240,000)
Profit before taxes	$ 1,643,333	+$ 90,667	$ 1,734,000
Federal-plus-state taxes (40%)	(657,333)	+ (36,267)	(693,600)
Net income	$ 986,000	+$ 54,400	$ 1,040,400

The proposed change appears to be a good one, assuming the assumptions are correct.

Proposal 2: Shorten the credit period to net 20 so that

1. Sales decrease by $1 million.

2. Discount = $0.

3. Bad debt losses = (0.01)($9,000,000) = $90,000.

4. DSO = 22 days.

5. New average receivables = (22)($9,000,000/360) = $550,000.

6. Cost of carrying receivables = (v)(k)(Average accounts receivable)
   = (0.80)(0.16)($550,000)
   = $70,400.

7. Collection expenses = $50,000.

Analysis of proposed change:

	Income Statement under Current Policy	Effect of Change	Income Statement under New Policy
Gross sales	$10,000,000	($1,000,000)	$9,000,000
Less discounts	(0)	(0)	(0)
Net sales	$10,000,000	($1,000,000)	$9,000,000
Production costs (80%)	(8,000,000)	800,000	(7,200,000)

Profit before credit costs and taxes	$ 2,000,000	($ 200,000)	$1,800,000
Credit-related costs			
Cost of carrying receivables	(106,667)	36,267	(70,400)
Collection expenses	(50,000)	(0)	(50,000)
Bad debt losses	(200,000)	110,000	(90,000)
Profit before taxes	$ 1,643,333	($ 53,733)	$1,589,600
Federal-plus-state taxes (40%)	(657,333)	21,493	(635,840)
Net income	$ 986,000	($ 32,240)	$ 953,760

This change reduces net income, so it should be rejected. Boca Grande will increase profits by accepting Proposal 1 to lengthen the credit period from 25 days to 30 days, assuming all assumptions are correct. This may or may not be the *optimal,* or profit-maximizing, credit policy, but it does appear to be a movement in the right direction.

Chapter 11

ST-2 *a.*

$$EOQ = \sqrt{\frac{2(O)(T)}{(C)(PP)}}$$

$$= \sqrt{\frac{(2)(\$5,000)(2,600,000)}{(0.02)(\$5.00)}}$$

$$= 509,902 \text{ bushels.}$$

Because the firm must order in multiples of 2,000 bushels, it should order in quantities of 510,000 bushels.

b.

$$\text{Average weekly sales} = 2,600,000/52$$

$$= 50,000 \text{ bushels.}$$

$$\text{Reorder point} = 6 \text{ weeks' sales} + \text{Safety stock}$$

$$= 6(50,000) + 200,000$$

$$= 300,000 + 200,000$$

$$= 500,000 \text{ bushels.}$$

c. Total inventory costs:

$$TIC = (C)PP\left(\frac{Q}{2}\right) + O\left(\frac{T}{Q}\right) + (C)(PP)(\text{Safety stock})$$

$$= (0.02)(\$5)\left(\frac{510,000}{2}\right) + (\$5,000)\left(\frac{2,600,000}{510,000}\right) + (0.02)(\$5)(200,000)$$

$$= \$25,500 + \$25,490.20 + \$20,000$$

$$= \$70,990.20.$$

d. Ordering costs would be reduced by $3,500 to $1,500. By ordering 650,000 bushels at a time, the firm can bring its total inventory cost to $58,500:

$$TIC = (0.02)(\$5)\left(\frac{650,000}{2}\right) + (\$1,500)\left(\frac{2,600,000}{650,000}\right) + (0.02)(\$5)(200,000)$$

$$= \$32,500 + \$6,000 + \$20,000$$

$$= \$58,500.$$

Because the firm can reduce its total inventory costs by ordering 650,000 bushels at a time, it should accept the offer and place larger orders. (Incidentally, this same type of analysis is used to consider any quantity discount offer.)

Chapter 12

ST-2   a.

Commercial bank loan

Amount loaned	= (0.75)($250,000)	= $187,500
Discount	= (0.09/12)($187,500) =	(1,406)
Compensating balance	= (0.20)($187,500)	= (37,500)
Amount received		= $148,594
Interest expense	= (0.09)($187,500)	= $ 16,875
Credit department*	= ($4,000)(12)	= 48,000
Bad debts*	= (0.02)($250,000)(12) =	60,000
Total annual costs		= $124,875

*The costs of the credit department and bad debts are expenses that will be incurred if a bank loan is used, but these costs will be avoided if the firm accepts the factoring arrangement.

Factoring

Amount loaned	= (0.85)($250,000)	= $212,500
Commission for period	= (0.035)($250,000)	= (8,750)
Prepaid interest	= (0.09/12)($203,750) =	(1,528)
Amount received		= $202,222
Annual commission	= ($8,750)(12)	= $105,000
Annual interest	= (0.09)($203,750)	= 18,338
Total annual costs		= $123,338

b. The factoring costs are slightly lower than the cost of the bank loan, and the factor is willing to advance a significantly greater amount. On the other hand, the elimination of the credit department could reduce the firm's options in the future.

Chapter 13

ST-2   a. *Payback:*

To determine the payback, construct the cumulative cash flows for each project:

	Cumulative Cash Flows	
Year	Project X	Project Y
0	($10,000)	($10,000)
1	(3,500)	(6,500)
2	(500)	(3,000)
3	2,500	500
4	3,500	4,000

$$\text{Payback}_X = 2 + \frac{\$500}{\$3,000} = 2.17 \text{ years.}$$

$$\text{Payback}_Y = 2 + \frac{\$3,000}{\$3,500} = 2.86 \text{ years.}$$

Net present value (NPV):

$$\text{NPV}_X = -\$10,000 + \frac{\$6,500}{(1.12)^1} + \frac{\$3,000}{(1.12)^2} + \frac{\$3,000}{(1.12)^3} + \frac{\$1,000}{(1.12)^4}$$

$$= \$966.01.$$

$$\text{NPV}_Y = -\$10,000 + \frac{\$3,500}{(1.12)^1} + \frac{\$3,500}{(1.12)^2} + \frac{\$3,500}{(1.12)^3} + \frac{\$3,500}{(1.12)^4}$$

$$= \$630.72.$$

Alternatively, using a financial calculator, input the cash flows into the cash flow register, enter I = 12, and then press the NPV key to obtain $\text{NPV}_X = \$966.01$ and $\text{NPV}_Y = \$630.72$.

Internal rate of return (IRR):
To solve for each project's IRR, find the discount rates which equate each NPV to zero:

$$\text{IRR}_X = 18.0\%.$$

$$\text{IRR}_Y = 15.0\%.$$

b. The following table summarizes the project rankings by each method:

	Project Which Ranks Higher
Payback	X
NPV	X
IRR	X

Note that all methods rank Project X over Project Y. In addition, both projects are acceptable under the NPV and IRR criteria. Thus, both projects should be accepted if they are independent.

c. In this case, we would choose the project with the higher NPV at k = 12%, or Project X.

d. To determine the effects of changing the cost of capital, plot the NPV profiles of each project. The crossover rate occurs at about 6 to 7 percent (6.2%).

NPV Profiles for Projects X and Y

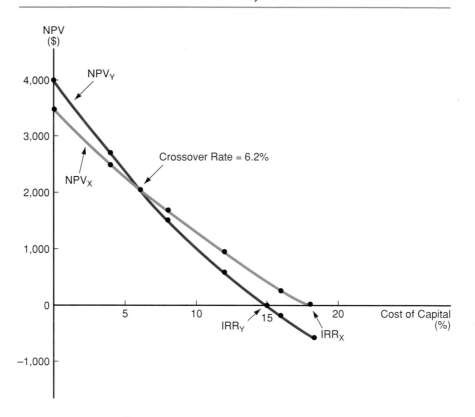

Required Rate of Return	NPV$_X$	NPV$_Y$
0%	$3,500	$4,000
4	2,545	2,705
8	1,707	1,592
12	966	631
16	307	(206)
18	5	(585)

If the firm's required rate of return is less than 6 percent, a conflict exists because NPV$_Y$ > NPV$_X$, but IRR$_X$ > IRR$_Y$. Therefore, if k were 5 percent, a conflict would exist.

e. The basic cause of the conflict is differing reinvestment rate assumptions between NPV and IRR. NPV assumes that cash flows can be reinvested at the cost of capital, while IRR assumes reinvestment at the (generally) higher IRR. The high reinvestment rate assumption under IRR makes early cash flows especially valuable, and hence short-term projects look better under IRR.

Chapter 14

ST-2   a. *Estimated investment outlay:*

Price	($50,000)
Modification	(10,000)
Change in net working capital	(2,000)
Total investment outlay	($62,000)

b. *Incremental operating cash flows:*

	Year 1	Year 2	Year 3
1. After-tax cost savings[a]	$12,000	$12,000	$12,000
2. Depreciation[b]	19,800	27,000	9,000
3. Depreciation tax savings[c]	7,920	10,800	3,600
Net cash flow (1 + 3)	$19,920	$22,800	$15,600

[a]$20,000 (1 − T).

[b]Depreciable basis = $60,000; the MACRS percentage allowances are 0.33, 0.45, and 0.15 in Years 1, 2, and 3, respectively; hence, depreciation in Year 1 = 0.33($60,000) = $19,800, and so on. There will remain $4,200, or 7 percent, undepreciated after Year 3; it would normally be taken in Year 4.

[c]Depreciation tax savings = T(Depreciation) = 0.4($19,800) = $7,920 in Year 1, and so on.

c. *Terminal cash flow:*

Salvage value	$20,000
Tax on salvage value[a]	(6,320)
Net working capital recovery	2,000
	$15,680

[a]Sales price	$20,000
Less book value	(4,200)
Taxable income	$15,800
Tax at 40%	$ 6,320

Book value = Depreciable basis − Accumulated depreciation
= $60,000 − $55,800 = $4,200.

d. *Project NPV:*

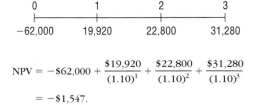

$$NPV = -\$62,000 + \frac{\$19,920}{(1.10)^1} + \frac{\$22,800}{(1.10)^2} + \frac{\$31,280}{(1.10)^3}$$

$$= -\$1,547.$$

Alternatively, using a financial calculator, input the cash flows into the cash flow register, enter I = 10, and then press the NPV key to obtain NPV = −$1,547. Because the earthmover has a negative NPV, it should not be purchased.

ST-3   *First determine the initial investment outlay:*

Purchase price	($8,000)
Sale of old machine	3,000
Tax on sale of old machine	(160)[a]
Change in net working capital	(1,500)[b]
Total investment	($6,660)

[a]The market value is $3,000 − $2,600 = $400 above the book value. Thus, there is a $400 recapture of depreciation, and Dauten would have to pay 0.40($400) = $160 in taxes.

[b]The change in net working capital is a $2,000 increase in current assets minus a $500 increase in current liabilities, which totals to $1,500.

Now, examine the operating cash inflows:

Sales increase	$1,000
Cost decrease	1,500
Increase in pretax operating revenues	$2,500

After-tax operating revenue increase:

$$\$2,500(1 - T) = \$2,500(0.60) = \$1,500.$$

Depreciation:

Year	1	2	3	4	5	6
New[a]	$1,600	$2,560	$1,520	$ 960	$ 880	$ 480
Old	350	350	350	350	350	350
Change	$1,250	$2,210	$1,170	$ 610	$ 530	$ 130
Depreciation Tax savings[b]	$ 500	$ 884	$ 468	$ 244	$ 212	$ 52

[a]Depreciable basis = $8,000. Depreciation expense in each year equals depreciable basis times the MACRS percentage allowances of 0.20, 0.32, 0.19, 0.12, 0.11, and 0.06 in Years 1–6, respectively.

[b]Depreciation tax savings = T(Δ Depreciation) = 0.4(Δ Depreciation).

Now recognize that at the end of Year 6 Dauten would recover its net working capital investment of $1,500, and it would also receive $800 from the sale of the replacement machine. However, since the machine would be fully depreciated, the firm must pay 0.40($800) = $320 in taxes on the sale. Also, by undertaking the replacement now, the firm forgoes the right to sell the old machine for $500 in Year 6; thus, this $500 in Year 6 must be considered an opportunity cost in that year. No tax would be due because the $500 salvage value would equal the old machine's Year 6 book value.

Finally, place all the cash flows on a time line:

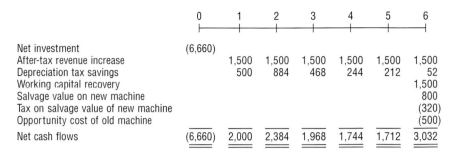

	0	1	2	3	4	5	6
Net investment	(6,660)						
After-tax revenue increase		1,500	1,500	1,500	1,500	1,500	1,500
Depreciation tax savings		500	884	468	244	212	52
Working capital recovery							1,500
Salvage value on new machine							800
Tax on salvage value of new machine							(320)
Opportunity cost of old machine							(500)
Net cash flows	(6,660)	2,000	2,384	1,968	1,744	1,712	3,032

The net present value of this incremental cash flow stream, when discounted at 15 percent, is $1,335. Thus, the replacement should be made.

ST-4 a. First, find the expected cash flows:

Year	Expected Cash Flows
0	$0.2(-\$100,000) + 0.6(-\$100,000) + 0.2(\ \$100,000) = (\$100,000)$
1	$0.2(\$20,000)\quad + 0.6(\$30,000)\quad + 0.2(\$40,000)\quad = \$30,000$
2	$\$30,000$
3	$\$30,000$
4	$\$30,000$
5	$\$30,000$
5*	$0.2(\$0)\quad\quad + 0.6(\$20,000)\quad + 0.2(\$30,000)\quad = \$18,000$

	0	1	2	3	4	5
	−100,000	30,000	30,000	30,000	30,000	48,000

Next, determine the NPV based on the expected cash flows:

$$NPV = -\$100,000 + \frac{\$30,000}{(1.10)^1} + \frac{\$30,000}{(1.10)^2} + \frac{\$30,000}{(1.10)^3}$$
$$+ \frac{\$30,000}{(1.10)^4} + \frac{\$48,000}{(1.10)^5} = \$24,900.$$

Alternatively, using a financial calculator, input the cash flows in the cash flow register, enter I = 10, and then press the NPV key to obtain NPV = $24,900.

b. For the worst case, the cash flow values from the cash flow column farthest on the left are used to calculate NPV:

	0	1	2	3	4	5
	−100,000	20,000	20,000	20,000	20,000	20,000

$$NPV = -\$100,000 + \frac{\$20,000}{(1.10)^1} + \frac{\$20,000}{(1.10)^2} + \frac{\$20,000}{(1.10)^3}$$
$$+ \frac{\$20,000}{(1.10)^4} + \frac{\$20,000}{(1.10)^5} = \$24,184.$$

Similarly, for the best case, use the values from the column farthest on the right. Here the NPV is $70,259.

If the cash flows are perfectly dependent, then the low cash flow in the first year will mean a low cash flow in every year. Thus, the probability of the worst case occurring is the probability of getting the $20,000 net cash flow in Year 1, or 20 percent. If the cash flows are independent, the cash flow in each year can be low, high, or average, and the probability of getting all low cash flows will be

$$0.2(0.2)(0.2)(0.2)(0.2) = 0.2^5 = 0.00032 = 0.032\%.$$

c. The base case NPV is found using the most likely cash flows and is equal to $26,142. This value differs from the expected NPV of $24,900 because the Year 5 cash flows are not symmetric. Under these conditions, the NPV distribution is as follows:

P_r	NPV
0.2	($24,184)
0.6	26,142
0.2	70,259

Thus, the expected NPV is $0.2(-\$24,184) + 0.6(\$26,142) + 0.2(\$70,259) = \$24,900$. As is generally the case, the expected NPV is the same as the NPV of the expected cash flows found in Part a. The standard deviation is $29,904:

$$\sigma^2_{NPV} = 0.2(-\$24,184 - \$24,900)^2 + 0.6(\$26,142 - \$24,900)^2$$
$$+ 0.2(\$70,259 - \$24,900)^2$$
$$= \$894,261,126.$$
$$\sigma_{NPV} = \sqrt{\$894,261,126} = \$29,904.$$

The coefficient of variation, CV, is $29,904/$24,900 = 1.20.

d. Since the project's coefficient of variation is 1.20, the project is riskier than average, and hence the project's risk-adjusted cost of capital is 10% + 2% = 12%. The project now should be evaluated by finding the NPV of the expected cash flows, as in Part a, but using a 12 percent discount rate. The risk-adjusted NPV is $18,357, and therefore the project should be accepted.

Chapter 15

ST-2 a. A break point will occur each time a low-cost type of capital is used up. We establish the break points as follows, after first noting that LEI has $24,000 of retained earnings:

$$\text{Retained earnings} = (\text{Total earnings})(1.0 - \text{Payout})$$
$$= \$34,285.72(0.7)$$
$$= \$24,000.$$

$$\text{Break point} = \frac{\text{Total amount of low-cost capital of a given type}}{\text{Proportion of this type of capital in the capital structure}}.$$

Capital Used Up	Break Point Calculation			Break Number
Retained earnings	BP_{RE}	$= \dfrac{\$24,000}{0.60}$	$= \$40,000$	2
10% flotation common	$BP_{10\%E}$	$= \dfrac{\$24,000 + \$12,000}{0.60}$	$= \$60,000$	4
5% flotation preferred	$BP_{5\%P}$	$= \dfrac{\$7,500}{0.15}$	$= \$50,000$	3
12% debt	$BP_{12\%D}$	$= \dfrac{\$5,000}{0.25}$	$= \$20,000$	1
14% debt	$BP_{14\%D}$	$= \dfrac{\$10,000}{0.25}$	$= \$40,000$	2

Summary of break points

(1) There are three common equity costs and hence two changes and, therefore, two equity-induced breaks in the MCC. There are two preferred costs and hence one preferred break. There are three debt costs and hence two debt breaks.

(2) The numbers in the third column of the table designate the sequential order of the breaks, determined after all the break points were calculated. Note that the second debt break and the break for retained earnings both occur at $40,000.

(3) The first break point occurs at $20,000, when the 12 percent debt is used up. The second break point, $40,000, results from using up both retained earnings and the 14 percent debt. The MCC curve also rises at $50,000 and $60,000, as preferred stock with a 5 percent flotation cost and common stock with a 10 percent flotation cost, respectively, are used up.

b. Component costs within indicated total capital intervals are as follows: Retained earnings (used in interval $0 to $40,000):

$$k_s = \frac{D_1}{P_0} + g = \frac{D_0(1 + g)}{P_0} + g$$

$$= \frac{\$3.60(1.09)}{\$60} + 0.09$$

$$= 0.0654 + 0.09 \qquad\qquad = 15.54\%.$$

Common with F = 10% ($40,001 to $60,000):

$$k_e = \frac{D_1}{P_0(1.0 - F)} + g = \frac{\$3.924}{\$60(0.9)} + 9\% \qquad\qquad = 16.27\%.$$

Common with F = 20% (over $60,000):

$$k_e = \frac{\$3.924}{\$60(0.8)} + 9\% \qquad\qquad = 17.18\%.$$

Preferred with F = 5% ($0 to $50,000):

$$k_p = \frac{D_p}{P_0 - \text{Flotation costs}} = \frac{\$11}{\$100(0.95)} \qquad\qquad = 11.58\%.$$

Preferred with F = 10% (over $50,000):

$$k_p = \frac{\$11}{\$100(0.9)} \qquad = 12.22\%.$$

Debt at k_d = 12% ($0 to $20,000):

$$k_{dT} = k_d(1 - T) = 12\%(0.6) \qquad = 7.20\%.$$

Debt at k_d = 14% ($20,001 to $40,000):

$$k_{dT} = 14\%(0.6) \qquad = 8.40\%.$$

Debt at k_d = 16% (over $40,000):

$$k_{dT} = 16\%(0.6) \qquad = 9.60\%.$$

c. WACC calculations within indicated total capital intervals:
   (1) $0 to $20,000 (debt = 7.2%, preferred = 11.58%, and retained earnings [RE] = 15.54%):

$$WACC_1 = w_d k_{dT} + w_p k_p + w_s k_s$$
$$= 0.25(7.2\%) + 0.15(11.58\%) + 0.60(15.54\%) = 12.86\%.$$

   (2) $20,001 to $40,000 (debt = 8.4%, preferred = 11.58%, and RE = 15.54%):

$$WACC_2 = 0.25(8.4\%) + 0.15(11.58\%) + 0.60(15.54\%) = 13.16\%.$$

   (3) $40,001 to $50,000 (debt = 9.6%, preferred = 11.58%, and equity = 16.27%):

$$WACC_3 = 0.25(9.6\%) + 0.15(11.58\%) + 0.60(16.27\%) = 13.90\%.$$

   (4) $50,001 to $60,000 (debt = 9.6%, preferred = 12.22%, and equity = 16.27%):

$$WACC_4 = 0.25(9.6\%) + 0.15(12.22\%) + 0.60(16.27\%) = 14.00\%.$$

   (5) Over $60,000 (debt = 9.6%, preferred = 12.22%, and equity = 17.18%):

$$WACC_5 = 0.25(9.6\%) + 0.15(12.22\%) + 0.60(17.18\%) = 14.54\%.$$

d. IRR calculation for Project E:

$$PVIFA_{k,6} = \frac{\$20,000}{\$5,427.84} = 3.6847.$$

This is the factor for 16 percent, so IRR_E = 16%.
Alternatively, N = 6, PV = −20000, PMT = 5427.84, and I = ? I = 16.00%.

e. See the graph of the MCC and IOS schedules for LEI at the top of the next page.

LEI: MCC and IOS Schedules

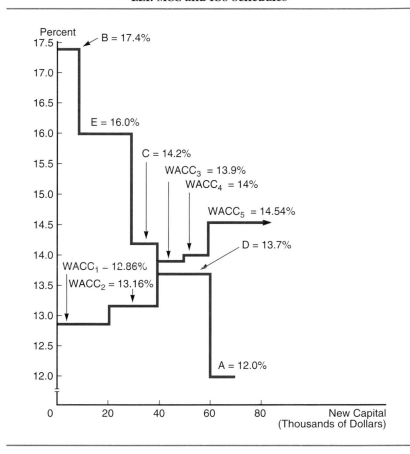

f. LEI should accept Projects B, E, and C. It should reject Projects A and D because their IRRs do not exceed the marginal costs of funds needed to finance them. The firm's capital budget would total $40,000.

Chapter 16

ST-2   *a.*

EBIT	$4,000,000
Interest ($2,000,000 × 0.10)	(200,000)
Earnings before taxes (EBT)	$3,800,000
Taxes (35%)	(1,330,000)
Net income	$2,470,000

$$EPS = \$2,470,000/600,000 = \$4.12.$$

$$P_0 = \$4.12/0.15 = \$27.47.$$

b.

$$Equity = 600,000 \times (\$10) = \$6,000,000.$$

$$Debt = \$2,000,000.$$

$$Total\ capital = \$8,000,000.$$

$$WACC = w_d[k_d(1 - T)] + w_sk_s$$

$$= (2/8)[(10\%)(1 - 0.35)] + (6/8)(15\%)$$

$$= 1.63\% + 11.25\%$$

$$= 12.88\%.$$

c.

EBIT	$4,000,000
Interest ($10,000,000 $\times$ 0.12)	(1,200,000)
Earnings before taxes (EBT)	$2,800,000
Taxes (35%)	(980,000)
Net income	$1,820,000

Shares bought and retired:

$$\Delta Shrs = \Delta Debt/P_0 = \$8,000,000/\$27.47 = 291,227.$$

New outstanding shares:

$$Shrs_1 = Shrs_0 - \Delta Shrs = 600,000 - 291,227 = 308,773.$$

New EPS:

$$EPS = \$1,820,000/308,773 = \$5.89.$$

New price per share:

$$P_0 = \$5.89/0.17 = \$34.65 \text{ versus } \$27.47.$$

Therefore, Gentry should change its capital structure.

d. In this case, the company's net income would be higher by $(0.12 - 0.10)$ $(\$2,000,000)(1 - 0.35) = \$26,000$ because its interest charges would be lower. The new price would be

$$P_0 = \frac{(\$1,820,000 + \$26,000)/308,773}{0.17} = \$35.18.$$

In the first case, in which debt had to be refunded, the bondholders were compensated for the increased risk of the higher debt position. In the second case, the old bondholders were not compensated; their 10 percent coupon perpetual bonds would now be worth

$$\$100/0.12 = \$833.33,$$

or $1,666,667 in total, down from the old $2 million, or a loss of $333,333. The stockholders would have a gain of

$$(\$35.18 - \$34.65)(308,773) = \$163,650.$$

This gain would, of course, be at the expense of the old bondholders. (There is no reason to think that bondholders' losses would exactly offset stockholders' gains.)

e.
$$\text{TIE} = \frac{\text{EBIT}}{\text{I}}.$$

$$\text{Original TIE} = \frac{\$4,000,000}{\$200,000} = 20 \text{ times.}$$

$$\text{New TIE} = \frac{\$4,000,000}{\$1,200,000} = 3.33 \text{ times.}$$

Chapter 17

ST-2 a.

Projected net income	$2,000,000
Less projected capital investments	(800,000)
Available residual	$1,200,000
Shares outstanding	200,000

$$\text{DPS} = \$1,200,000/200,000 \text{ shares} = \$6 = D_1.$$

b.

$$\text{EPS} = \$2,000,000/200,000 \text{ shares} = \$10.$$

$$\text{Payout ratio} = \text{DPS/EPS} = \$6/\$10 = 60\%, \text{ or}$$

$$\text{Total dividends/NI} = \$1,200,000/\$2,000,000 = 60\%.$$

c.

$$\text{Currently, } P_0 = \frac{D_1}{k_s - g} = \frac{\$6}{0.14 - 0.05} = \frac{\$6}{0.09} = \$66.67.$$

Under the former circumstances, D_1 would be based on a 20 percent payout on $10 EPS, or $2. With $k_s = 14\%$ and $g = 12\%$, we solve for P_0:

$$P_0 = \frac{D_1}{k_s - g} = \frac{\$2}{0.14 - 0.12} = \frac{\$2}{0.02} = \$100.$$

Although CMC has suffered a severe setback, its existing assets will continue to provide a good income stream. More of these earnings should now be passed on to the shareholders, as the slowed internal growth has reduced the need for funds. However, the net result is a 33 percent decrease in the value of the shares.

d. If the payout ratio were continued at 20 percent, even after internal investment opportunities had declined, the price of the stock would drop to $2/(0.14 − 0.06) = $25 rather than to $66.67. Thus, an increase in the dividend payout is consistent with maximizing shareholder wealth.

Because of the downward-sloping IOS curve, the greater the firm's level of investment, the lower the average ROE. Thus, the more money CMC retains and invests, the lower its average ROE will be. We can determine the average ROE under different conditions as follows:

Old situation (with founder active and 20 percent payout):

$$g = (1.0 - \text{Payout ratio})(\text{Average ROE})$$

$$12\% = (1.0 - 0.2)(\text{Average ROE})$$

$$\text{Average ROE} = 12\%/0.8 = 15\% > k_s = 14\%.$$

Note that the *average* ROE is 15 percent, whereas the *marginal* ROE is presumably equal to 14 percent.

New situation (with founder retired and a 60 percent payout):

$$g = 6\% = (1.0 - 0.6)(\text{ROE})$$

$$\text{ROE} = 6\%/0.4 = 15\% > k_s = 14\%.$$

This suggests that the new payout is appropriate and that the firm is taking on investments down to the point at which marginal returns are equal to the cost of capital.

Chapter 19

ST-2 a. $100,000,000/10 = $10,000,000 per year, or $5 million each 6 months. Since the $5 million will be used to retire bonds immediately, no interest will be earned on it.

b. The debt service requirements will decline. As the amount of bonds outstanding declines, so will the interest requirements (amounts given in millions of dollars):

Semiannual Payment Period (1)	Sinking Fund Payment (2)	Outstanding Bonds on Which Interest Is Paid (3)	Interest Payment[a] (4)	Total Bond Service (2) + (4) = (5)
1	$5	$100	$6.0	$11.0
2	5	95	5.7	10.7
3	5	90	5.4	10.4
.	.	.	.	.
.	.	.	.	.
.	.	.	.	.
20	5	5	0.3	5.3

[a]Interest is calculated as $[(0.12)/2](\text{Column 3})$; for example: interest in Period 2 = $(0.06)(\$95) = \$5.7$.

The company's total cash bond service requirement will be $21.7 million for the first year. The requirement will decline by 0.12($10,000,000) = $1,200,000 per year for the remaining years.

c. Here we have a 10-year, 9 percent annuity whose compound value is $100 million, and we are seeking the annual payment, PMT. The solution can be obtained with a financial calculator. Input N = 10, I = 9, PV = 0, and FV = 100000000, and press the PMT key to obtain $6,582,009.

We could also find the solution using this equation:

$$\$100,000,000 = \sum_{t=1}^{10} \text{PMT}(1+k)^t$$

$$= \text{PMT}(\text{FVIFA}_{9\%,10})$$

$$= \text{PMT}(15.193)$$

$$\text{PMT} = \$6,581,979 = \text{sinking fund payment.}$$

The difference is due to rounding the FVIFA to 3 decimal places.

d. Annual debt service costs will be $100,000,000(0.12) + $6,582,009 = $18,582,009.

e. If interest rates rose, causing the bond's price to fall, the company would use open market purchases. This would reduce its debt service requirements.

Chapter 20

ST-2   a. *Cost of leasing:*

	Beginning of Year			
	0	**1**	**2**	**3**
Lease payment (AT)[a]	($ 6,000)	($6,000)	($6,000)	($6,000)
PVIFs (6%)[b]	1.000	0.9434	0.8900	0.8396
PV of leasing	($ 6,000)	($5,660)	($5,340)	($5,038)
Total PV cost of leasing =	($22,038)			

[a]After-tax payment = $10,000(1 − T) = $10,000(0.60) = $6,000.

[b]This is the after-tax cost of debt: 10%(1 − T) = 10%(0.60) = 6.0%.

Alternatively, using a financial calculator, input the following data after switching your calculator to "BEG" mode: N = 4, I = 6, PMT = −6000, and FV = 0. Then press the PV key to arrive at the answer of ($22,038). Now switch your calculator back to "END" mode.

b. *Cost of owning:*

Depreciable basis = $40,000.

Here are the cash flows under the borrow-and-buy alternative:

	End of Year				
	0	**1**	**2**	**3**	**4**
1. Depreciation schedule					
(a) Depreciable basis		$40,000	$40,000	$40,000	$40,000
(b) Allowance		0.33	0.45	0.15	0.07
(c) Depreciation		13,200	18,000	6,000	2,800
2. Cash outflows					
(d) Net purchase price	($40,000)				
(e) Depreciation tax savings		5,280[a]	7,200	2,400	1,120
(f) Maintenance (AT)		(600)	(600)	(600)	(600)
(g) Salvage value (AT)					6,000
(h) Total cash outflows	($40,000)	$ 4,680	$ 6,600	$ 1,800	$ 6,520
PVIFs	1.000	0.9434	0.8900	0.8396	0.7921
PV of owning	($40,000)	$ 4,415	$ 5,874	$ 1,511	$ 5,164
Total PV cost of owning =	($23,036)				

[a]Depreciation(T) = $13,200(0.40) = $5,280.

Alternatively, input the cash flows for the individual years in the cash flow register and input I = 6, then press the NPV button to arrive at the answer of ($23,036). Because the present value of the cost of leasing is less than that of owning, the truck should be leased: $23,036 − $22,038 = $998, net advantage to leasing.

c. The discount rate is based on the cost of debt because most cash flows are fixed by contract and, consequently, are relatively certain. Thus, the lease cash flows have about the same risk as the firm's debt. Also, leasing is considered to be a substitute for debt. We use an after-tax cost rate because the cash flows are stated net of taxes.

d. Olsen could increase the discount rate on the salvage value cash flow. This would increase the PV cost of owning and make leasing even more advantageous.

Answers to End-of-Chapter Problems

We present here some intermediate steps and final answers to selected end-of-chapter problems. Please note that your answer may differ slightly from ours due to rounding errors. Also, although we hope not, some of the problems may have more than one correct solution, depending upon what assumptions are made in working the problem. Finally, many of the problems involve some verbal discussion as well as numerical calculations; this verbal material is not presented here.

2-1 *a.* $k_1 = 9.20\%$; $k_5 = 7.20\%$.

2-3 *a.* 5.4%.
    b. 7.4%.
    c. 5-yr bond = 7.9%.

2-5 $Tax_{1996} = \$0$; Initial $tax_{1998} = \$4,500$; Initial $tax_{1999} = \$15,450$; Final $tax_{1999} = \$0$.

2-6 *a.* 1996 advantage as a corporation = $1,456; 1997 advantage = $4,056; 1998 advantage = $5,356.

2-7 *a.* Personal tax = $20,280.
    c. IBM yield = 7.59; choose FLA bonds.
    d. 18.18%.

2-8 *a.* k_1 in Year 2 = 13%.

2-9 k_1 in Year 2 = 15%; Year 2 inflation = 11%.

2-10 Tax = $107,855; NI = $222,145; Marginal tax rate = 39%; Average tax rate = 33.8%.

2-11 *a.* Tax = $61,250.
    b. Tax = $15,600.
    c. Tax = $4,680.

2-12 1.5%.

2-13 AT&T bonds = 8.8%.

2-14 6.0%.

3-2 *a.* Current ratio = 1.98×; DSO = 75 days; Total assets turnover = 1.7×; Debt ratio = 61.9%.

3-3 A/P = $90,000; Inv = $67,500; FA = $160,500.

3-5 *a.* Quick ratio = 0.85×; DSO = 37 days; ROE = 13.1%; Debt ratio = 54.8%.

3-6 $\dfrac{NI}{S} = 2\%$; $\dfrac{D}{A} = 40\%$.

3-7 $262,500; 1.19×.

3-8 Sales = $2,511,628; DSO = 37 days.

3-9 TIE = 3.5×.

3-10 ROE = 24.5%; ROA = 9.8%.

3-11 *a.* +5.54%.
    b. (2) +3.21%.

3-12 Total sources = $102; Net increase in cash and marketable securities = $19.

3-13 **a.** NI = \$900,000; CF = \$2,400,000.
  b. CF = \$3,000,000.

4-1 **a.** Notes payable = \$31.44 million.
  b. Current ratio = 2.00×; ROE = 14.2%.
  c. (1) −\$14.28 million.
     (2) Total assets = \$147 million; Notes payable
        = \$3.72 million.
     (3) Current ratio = 4.25×; ROE = 10.84%.

4-2 **a.** Total assets = \$33,534; AFN = \$2,128.
  b. Notes payable = \$4,228; AFN = \$70;
     ΔInterest = \$213.

4-3 **a.** DOL = 2.5; DFL = 3.0.

4-4 **a.** First pass AFN = \$667.
  b. Increase in notes payable = \$51; Increase in
     C/S = \$368.

4-5 **a.** (1) − \$60,000.
  b. Q_{BE} = 14,000.
  c. (1) −1.33.

4-6 **a.** (2) \$125,000.
  b. Q_{BE} = 7,000.
  c. Q_{CBE} = 2,600.

4-7 **a.** \$2,000.
  b. DFL = 1.8.
  c. \$3,000.

4-8 **a.** (1) −\$75,000.
     (2) \$175,000.
  b. Q_{BE} = 140,000.
  c. (1) −8.3.
     (2) 15.0.
     (3) 5.0.

4-9 **a.** \$480,000.
  b. \$18,750.

4-10 **a.** FC_A = \$80,000; VC_A = \$4.80/unit;
     P_A = \$8.00/unit.

4-11 AFN = \$360.

4-12 **a.** 40,000.
  b. (\$0.30).
  c. 48,000.
  d. DOL = 3.0; DFL = 1.7.

5-1 **a.** \$0.5 million.

5-2 **a.** 13.5%.
  b. 1.8.
  c. k_F = 8% + 5.5%β_F.
  d. 17.9%.

5-3 **a.** $\bar{k}_A$ = 11.30%.
  c. σ_A = 20.8%; σ_P = 20.1%.

5-4 **a.** $\hat{k}_M$ = 13.5%; $\hat{k}_J$ = 11.6%.
  b. σ_M = 3.85%; σ_J = 6.22%.
  c. CV_M = 0.29; CV_J = 0.54.

5-5 **a.** $\hat{k}_Y$ = 14%.
  b. σ_X = 12.20%.

5-6 **a.** β_B = 2.
  b. k_B = 12.5%.

5-7 **a.** k_j = 15.5%.
  b. (1) k_j = 16.5%.
  c. (1) k_j = 18.1%.

5-8 β_{New} = 1.16.

5-9 β_p = 0.7625; k_p = 12.1%.

5-10 4.5%.

5A-1 **a.** β = 0.62.

5A-2 **a.** β_A = 1.0; β_B = 0.5.
  c. k_A = 14%; k_B = 11.5%.

6-1 **a.** \$530.
  d. \$445.

6-2 **a.** \$895.40.
  b. \$1,552.90.
  c. \$279.20.
  d. \$500.03; \$867.14.

6-3 **a.** ≈ 10 years.
  c. ≈ 4 years.

6-4 **a.** \$6,374.96.
  d. (1) \$7,012.46.

6-5 **a.** \$2,457.84.
  c. \$2,000.
  d. (1) \$2,703.62.

6-6 **a.** Stream A: \$1,251.21.

6-7 **b.** 7%.
  c. 9%.
  d. 15%.

6-8 **a.** \$881.15.
  b. \$895.40.
  c. \$903.05.
  d. \$908.35.

6-9 **b.** \$279.20.
  c. \$276.85.
  d. \$443.70.

6-10 **a.** \$5,272.40.
  b. \$5,374.00.

6-11 **a.** 1st City = 7%; 2nd City = 6.66%.

6-12 **a.** PMT = \$6,594.94.
  b. \$13,189.87.

6-13 **a.** Z = 9%; B = 8%.
    b. Z = $558.39; $135.98; 32.2%; B = $548.33; $48.33; 9.7%.

6-14 **a.** $61,203.
    b. $11,020.
    c. $6,841.

6-15 **a.** $176,792.
    b. $150,257.

6-16 $1,000 today is worth more.

6-17 **a.** 15% (or 14.87%).

6-18 APR = 8.0%; EAR = 8.24%.

6-19 12%.

6-20 9%.

6-21 **a.** $33,872.
    b. $26,243.04 and $0.

6-22 $1,205.55.

6-23 $\approx$ 15 years.

6-24 5 years; $1,885.09.

6-25 $PV_{7\%}$ = $1,428.57; $PV_{14\%}$ = $714.29.

6-26 $984.88 $\approx$ $985.

6-27 $1,901.

6-28 **a.** $260.73.
    b. $263.34.

6-29 k_{SIMPLE} = 15.19%.

6-30 $4,971.

7-1 **a.** $1,251.26.
    b. $898.90.

7-2 **a.** $1,250.
    b. $833.33.
    d. At 8%, V_d = $1,196.31.

7-3 **b.** PV = $5.29.
    d. $30.01.

7-4 **a.** 7%.
    b. 5%.
    c. 12%.

7-5 **a.** (1) $9.50.
       (2) $13.33.
    b. (1) Undefined.

7-6 **a.** $7.20.
    b. $41.60.
    c. $35.28.

7-7 **a.** $1,000.
    b. IBM = $812.59; GM = $711.89.
    d. 5.0%.

7-8 **a.** Dividend 1998 = $2.66.
    b. P_0 = $39.42.
    c. Dividend yield 1996 = 5.10%; 2000 = 7.00%.

7-9 **a.** P_0 = $54.11.

7-10 **b.** P_0 = $21.43.
    c. P_0 = $26.47.
    e. P_0 = $40.54.

7-11 **a.** New price = $31.34.
    b. beta = 0.49865.

7-12 **a.** V_L at 5 percent = $1,518.97; V_L at 8 percent = $1,171.15; V_L at 12 percent = $863.79.

7-13 **a.** 8.02%.

7-14 **a.** YTM at $829 $\approx$ 15%.

7-15 **a.** 13.3%.
    b. 10%.
    c. 8%.
    d. 5.7%.

7-16 $23.75.

7-17 **a.** k_C = 10.6%; k_D = 7%.

7-18 $25.03.

7-19 IBM bond = 9.33%.

7-20 10.2%.

7-21 P_0 = $19.89.

8-1 **b.** 20 days.

8-2 **a.** (1) 110 days.
       (2) 80 days.
    d. (1) 141 days.
       (2) 114 days.

8-3 **a.** 32.
    b. $288,000.
    c. $45,000.
    d. (1) 30.
       (2) $378,000.

8-4 **a.** ROE_T = 11.75%; ROE_M = 10.80%; ROE_R = 9.16%.

8-5 **a.** 72.
    b. $396,000.
    d. Decrease to 57.

8-6 **a.** 51.
    b. (1) 2.33.
       (2) 11.67%.
    c. (1) 42.
       (2) 2.46.
       (3) 12.3%.

9-1 **a.** $1,600,000.
    c. Bank = $1,200,000; Books = −$5,200,000.

9-2 *b.* $164,400.

9-3 *b.* Oct. loan = $22,800.

9-4 *b.* $420,000.
    c. $35,000.

9-5 *a.* Wire transfer.
    b. $7,250.

9-6 *a.* Net float = $30,000.
    b. $16,000.

9-7 *a.* $103,350.
    b. $97,500.

9A-1 *a.* $45,000.

10-1 *a.* DSO_O = 27 days; DSO_N = 22.5 days.
    b. D_O = $15,680; D_N = $38,220.
    c. C_O = $10,125; C_N = $10,969.
    e. NI_Δ = +$68,770.

10-2 NI_3 = $59,700; NI_4 = $22,344; NI_5 = $15,708.

10-3 NI_Δ = +$13,350.

10-4 *a.* DSO = 28 days.
    b. $70,000.

10-5 NI_Δ = ($60,578).

10-6 $70.

11-1 EOQ = 1000.

11-2 *a.* EOQ = 100,000.
    b. $156,250.
    c. TIC = $56,250.
    d. 60,577.

11-3 *a.* EOQ = 5,200.
    b. 65.
    c. 14,600.
    d. (3) TIC = $20,704.

11-4 *a.* EOQ = 19,500.
    b. 30.
    c. 32,500.
    d. 41%.

11-5 *a.* EOQ = 3,873.
    b. 5,073 bags.
    c. 3,137 bags.
    d. Every 6 days.

12-1 *a.* $100,000.
    c. (1) $300,000.
        (2) Approximate cost = 36.73%;
            Effective cost = 43.86%.

12-2 *a.* $EAR_{DISC.}$ = 14.9%.

12-3 *a.* Alternative 3 EAR = 9.56%.
    b. Alternative 2 $470,588.

12-4 *a.* 11.73%.
    b. 12.09%.
    c. 18%.

12-5 *b.* $384,615.
    c. Cash = $126.90; NP = $434.60.

12-6 *a.* (1) $27,500.
       (3) $25,833.

12-7 *a.* $515,464.

12-8 *a.* $46,167.
    b. $40,667.

12-9 *b.* 14.69%.
    d. 20.99%.

12-10 *a.* 44.54%.

12-11 *a.* 12% *b.* 11.25% *c.* 11.48%
    d. 16%; Alternative b.

12-12 Approximate cost = 14.69%; Effective cost = 15.65%.

12-13 N/P = 13.64%.

12-14 *d.* 8.3723%.

13-1 *b.* NPV = $7,486.20.
    d. DPP = 6.51 yrs.

13-2 *b.* IRR_A = 17.8%; IRR_B = 24.0%.

13-3 *a.* IRR_A = 20%; IRR_B = 16.7%;
       Crossover rate ≈ 16%.

13-4 *a.* NPV_A = $14,486,808; NPV_B = $11,156,893;
       IRR_A = 15.03%; IRR_B = 22.26%.

13-5 NPV_T = $409; IRR_T = 15%; Accept;
    NPV_P = $3,318; IRR_P = 20%; Accept.

13-6 NPV_E = $3,861; IRR_E = 18%; NPV_G = $3,057;
    IRR_G = 18%; Purchase electric-powered forklift; it has a higher NPV.

13-7 NPV_S = $448.86; NPV_L = $263.89; IRR_S = 15.24%; IRR_L = 14.29%.

13-8 *a.* PV_C = −$556,717; PV_F = −$493,407; Forklift should be chosen.

13-9 NPV_C = $1,256; IRR_C = 17.3%; NPV_R = $1,459.

13-10 IRR_Q = 15.6%.

13-11 Accept Project Y.

14-1 *a.* ($178,000).
    b. $52,440; $60,600; $40,200.
    c. $48,760.
    d. NPV = −$19,549; Do not purchase.

14-2 *a.* ($126,000).
    b. $42,560; $47,477; $35,186.
    c. $51,268.
    d. NPV = $11,385; Purchase.

14-3 *a.* ($52,000).
    b. $18,560; $22,400; $12,800; $10,240.
    c. $1,500.

d. NPV = $1,021; Replace the old machine.

14-4 ***a.*** ($776,000).
  c. $199,000; $255,400; $194,300; $161,400; $156,700.
  d. $115,200.
  e. NPV = $436.77; Purchase the new machine.

14-5 ***a.*** Expected CF_A = $6,750; Expected CF_B = $7,650; CV_A = 0.0703.
  b. NPV_A = $10,037; NPV_B = $11,624.

14-6 ***a.*** 14%.

14-7 NPV_5 = $2,211; NPV_4 = −$2,080; NPV_8 = $13,329.

14-8 NPV = 15,301; Buy the new machine.

14-9 NPV = $22,329; Replace the old machine.

14-10 ***a.*** 16%.
  b. NPV = $411; Accept.

14-11 ***a.*** 15%.
  b. 1.48; 15.4%; 17%.

14A-1 PV = $1,273,389.

14B-1 ***a.*** NPV_{190-3} = $20,070; NPV_{360-6} = $22,256.

14B-2 NPV_A = $12.76 million

15-1 ***a.*** 16.3%.
  b. 15.4%.
  c. 16%.

15-2 ***a.*** 8%.
  b. $2.81.
  c. 15.8%.

15-3 ***a.*** $18 million.
  b. BP = $45 million.
  c. BP_1 = $20 million; BP_2 = $40 million.

15-4 ***a.*** g = 3%.
  b. EPS = $5.562.

15-5 ***a.*** $67,500,000.
  c. k_s = 12%; k_e = 12.4%.
  d. $27,000,000.
  e. $WACC_1$ = 9%; $WACC_2$ = 9.2%.

15-6 ***a.*** k_{dT} = 5.4%; k_s = 14.6%.
  b. WACC = 10.92%.
  d. WACC = 11.36%.

15-7 ***a.*** 3 breaks; BP_{D_1} = $1,111,111; BP_{RE} = $1,818,182; BP_{D_2} = $2,000,000.
  b. $WACC_1$ = 10.96%; $WACC_2$ = 11.50%; $WACC_3$ = 12.14%; $WACC_4$ = 12.68%.
  c. IRR_1 = 16%; IRR_3 = 14%.

15-8 ***a.*** 13%.
  b. 10.4%.
  c. 8.58%.

15-9 7.92%.

15-10 11.94%.

15-11 ***a.*** F = 10%.
  b. k_e = 15.8%.

15-12 WACC = 12.72%.

15-13 $10 million.

15-14 $42,000.

15-15 $62,000.

15-16 ***a.*** 14.40%.
  b. 10.62%.

15-17 7.2%.

15-18 k_e = 16.5%.

16-1 ***a.*** $5.10.

16-2 ***a.*** DOL_A = 2.80; DOL_B = 2.15; Method A.
  b. DFL_A = 1.32; DFL_B = 1.35; Method B.
  d. Debt = $129,310; D/A = 5.75%.

16-3 ***a.*** EPS_{Old} = $2.04; New: EPS_D = $4.74; EPS_S = $3.27.
  b. DOL_{Old} = 2.30; DOL_{New} = 1.60; DFL_{Old} = 1.47; $DFL_{New, Stock}$ = 1.15; $DTL_{New, Debt}$ = 2.53.
  c. 33,975 units.
  d. $Q_{New, Debt}$ = 27,225 units.

16-4 Debt used: E(EPS) = $5.78; σ_{EPS} = $1.05; E(TIE) = 3.49×.
  Stock used: E(EPS) = $5.51; σ_{EPS} = $0.85; E(TIE) = 6.00×.

16-5 ***a.*** ROE_{LL} = 14.6%; ROE_{HL} = 16.8%.
  b. ROE_{LL} = 16.5%.

16-6 No leverage: $\widehat{ROE}$ = 10.5%; σ = 5.4%; CV = 0.51; 60% leverage: $\widehat{ROE}$ = 13.7%; σ = 13.5%; CV = 0.99.

17-1 CS = $79.50; PIC = $464.25; RE = $956.25.

17-2 ***a.*** (1) $3,960,000.
    (2) $4,800,000.
    (3) $9,360,000.
    (4) Regular = $3,960,000; Extra = $5,400,000.
  c. 15%.
  d. 15%.

17-3 ***a.*** PO = 63.16%; BP = $9.55 million; $WACC_1$ = 10.67%; $WACC_2$ = 10.96%.
  b. $15 million.

17-4 $3,250,000.

17-5 Payout = 52%.

17-6 D_0 = $3.44.

17-7 Payout = 31.39%.

18-1 *a.* $1,050,000.
    b. $5,550,000.
    c. ($3,450,000).

18-2 *a.* EPS_{1995} = $9,600; DPS_{1995} = $4,800;
       BV_{1995} = $72,000/share.
    b. g_{EPS}: HH = 8.4%; L = 6.4%; U = 8%;
       g_{DPS}: HH = 8.4%; L = 6.4%; U = 7.4%.
    e. EPS_{1995} = $2.40; DPS_{1995} = $1.20;
       BV_{1995} = $18/share.
    f. ROE_{HH} = 15.00%; ROE_L = 13.64%;
       ROE_U = 13.33%.
    i. P/E_{HH} = 8×; P/E_L = 8.65×.
    k. k_{HH} = 15.2%; k_L = 12.5%; U-Fix-It's price:
       $P_0(HH)$ = $17.23; $P_0(L)$ = $26.93.

18-3 *a.* $35.00.
    b. $34.18.

18-4 600,000 shares.

19-1 *d.* at k_d = 6.1%, V = $49.18;
      at k_d = 2%, V = $150.

19-2 *a.* 7,930 bonds.
    b. (1) 12%.
       (2) 8.28%.
    c. 7.2%.

19-3 *a.* $2,504,571 or $2,504,565.
    b. $1,490,291 or $1,490,295.
    c. $2,912,819 or $2,912,835.
    d. $1,917,141 or $1,917,135.

19-4 15.03%.

19-5 12.37%.

19-6 $30,463.

20-1 *a.* D/A_H = 50%; D/A_M = 67%.

20-2 *a.* PV cost of owning = −$185,112; PV cost of
      leasing = −$187,534; Purchase loom.

20-3 *a.* $20.

20-4 *b.* Percent ownership: Original = 80%;
      Plan 1 = 53%; Plans 2 and 3 = 57%.
    c. EPS_0 = $0.48; EPS_1 = $0.60; EPS_2 = $0.64;
      EPS_3 = $0.86.
    d. D/A_1 = 13%; D/A_2 = 13%; D/A_3 = 48%.

20-5 *a.* PV cost of leasing = ($954,639); Lease
      equipment.

21-1

Dollars per 1,000 Units of:				
Rupees	Lira	Yen	Pesos	Riyals
$31.67	$0.58	$11.34	$144.93	$266.62

21-3 *b.* $22,273.

21-4 *a.* $3,220,996.
    b. $3,204,480.
    d. $3,368,421.

21-5 0.625 pounds per dollar.

21-6 4.5455 francs per dollar.

21-7 7.95 francs per pound.

21-9 $55.67/share or Total value = $556,666,667.

21-10 $300,000 gain.

Selected Equations and Data

Chapter 2

$$k = k^* + IP + DRP + LP + MRP = k_{RF} + DRP + LP + MRP.$$

$$k_{RF} = k^* + IP.$$

$$IP_n = \frac{I_1 + I_2 + \ldots I_n}{n}.$$

$$\text{Equivalent } \textbf{pretax} \text{ yield on taxable investment} = \frac{\text{Yield on tax-free investment}}{1 - T}.$$

Chapter 3

$$\text{Current ratio} = \frac{\text{Current assets}}{\text{Current liabilities}}.$$

$$\text{Quick, or acid test, ratio} = \frac{\text{Current assets} - \text{Inventories}}{\text{Current liabilities}}.$$

$$\text{Inventory turnover ratio} = \frac{\text{Cost of goods sold}}{\text{Inventories}}.$$

$$DSO = \frac{\text{Days sales outstanding}}{} = \frac{\text{Receivables}}{\text{Average sales per day}} = \frac{\text{Receivables}}{\text{Annual sales}/360}.$$

$$\text{Fixed assets turnover ratio} = \frac{\text{Sales}}{\text{Net fixed assets}}.$$

$$\text{Total assets turnover ratio} = \frac{\text{Sales}}{\text{Total assets}}.$$

$$\text{Debt ratio} = \frac{\text{Total debt}}{\text{Total assets}}.$$

$$\text{Times-interest-earned (TIE) ratio} = \frac{\text{EBIT}}{\text{Interest charges}}.$$

$$\text{Fixed charge coverage ratio} = \frac{\text{EBIT} + \text{Lease payments}}{\text{Interest charges} + \text{Lease payments} + \left[\dfrac{\text{Sinking fund payments}}{(1 - \text{Tax rate})}\right]}.$$

$$\text{Profit margin on sales} = \frac{\text{Net income}}{\text{Sales}}.$$

$$\text{Return on total assets (ROA)} = \frac{\text{Net income}}{\text{Total assets}}.$$

$$\text{ROA} = \left(\begin{array}{c}\text{Profit}\\\text{margin}\end{array}\right)\left(\begin{array}{c}\text{Total assets}\\\text{turnover}\end{array}\right) = \left(\frac{\text{Net income}}{\text{Sales}}\right)\left(\frac{\text{Sales}}{\text{Total assets}}\right).$$

$$\text{Return on common equity (ROE)} = \frac{\begin{array}{c}\text{Net income available to}\\\text{common stockholders}\end{array}}{\text{Common equity}}.$$

$$\text{Price/earnings (P/E) ratio} = \frac{\text{Market price per share}}{\text{Earnings per share}}.$$

$$\text{Earnings per share} = \frac{\text{Net income available to common stockholders}}{\text{Number of common shares outstanding}}.$$

$$\text{Book value per share} = \frac{\text{Common equity}}{\text{Shares outstanding}}.$$

$$\text{Market/book (M/B) ratio} = \frac{\text{Market price per share}}{\text{Book value per share}}.$$

Chapter 4

$$\text{Full capacity sales} = \frac{\text{Sales level}}{\begin{array}{c}\text{Percentage of capacity used}\\\text{to generate sales level}\end{array}}.$$

$$\text{TC} = \text{F} + \text{VQ}.$$

$$Q_{BE} = \frac{F}{P - V} = \frac{F}{\text{Contribution margin}}.$$

$$S_{BE} = P \times Q_{BE} = \frac{F}{1 - \dfrac{V}{P}} = \frac{F}{\text{Gross profit margin}}.$$

$$Q_{CBE} = \frac{F - \text{noncash outlays}}{P - V}.$$

$$DOL = \frac{\frac{\Delta EBIT}{EBIT}}{\frac{\Delta Q}{Q}}.$$

$$DOL_Q = \frac{Q(P - V)}{Q(P - V) - F}.$$

$$DOL_S = \frac{S - VC}{S - VC - F} = \frac{\text{Gross profit}}{EBIT}.$$

$$EBIT = PQ - VQ - F.$$

$$EBIT_{\text{financial BEP}} = I + \frac{D_{ps}}{(1 - T)}.$$

$$DFL = \frac{\frac{\Delta EPS}{EPS}}{\frac{\Delta EBIT}{EDIT}}.$$

$$DFL = \frac{EBIT}{EBIT - I}; \text{ if preferred stock} = 0.$$

$$DFL = \frac{EBIT}{EBIT - [\text{Financial BEP}]}.$$

$$DTL = DOL \times DFL = \frac{S - VC}{EBIT - I}; \text{ if preferred stock} = 0.$$

$$DTL = \frac{\text{Gross profit}}{EBIT - [\text{Financial BEP}]}.$$

Chapter 5

$$\text{Expected rate of return} = \hat{k} = \sum_{i=1}^{n} Pr_i k_i.$$

$$\text{Variance} = \sigma^2 = \sum_{i=1}^{n} (k_i - \hat{k})^2 Pr_i.$$

$$\text{Standard deviation} = \sigma = \sqrt{\sum_{i=1}^{n} (k_i - \hat{k})^2 Pr_i}.$$

$$CV = \frac{\sigma}{\hat{k}}.$$

$$\hat{k}_p = \sum_{j=1}^{n} w_j \hat{k}_j.$$

$$\beta_p = \sum_{j=1}^{n} w_j \beta_j.$$

$$SML = k_j = k_{RF} + (k_M - k_{RF})\beta_j = k_{RF} + (RP_M)\beta_j.$$

$$\beta = \frac{Y_2 - Y_1}{X_2 - X_1} = \text{slope coefficient in } \bar{k}_{jt} = a + \beta \bar{k}_{Mt} + e_t.$$

Chapter 6

$$FV_n = PV(1 + i)^n = PV(FVIF_{i,n}).$$

$$PV = FV_n\left(\frac{1}{1 + i}\right)^n = FV_n(1 + i)^{-n} = FV_n(PVIF_{i,n}).$$

$$PVIF_{i,n} = \frac{1}{FVIF_{i,n}}.$$

$$FVIFA_{i,n} = \frac{(1 + i)^n - 1}{i}.$$

$$PVIFA_{i,n} = \frac{1 - \frac{1}{(1 + i)^n}}{i}.$$

$$FVA_n = PMT(FVIFA_{i,n}).$$

$$FVA_{n,DUE} = PMT[FVIFA_{i,n}(DUE)] = PMT[(FVIFA_{i,n})(1 + i)].$$

$$PVA_n = PMT(PVIFA_{i,n}).$$

$$PVA_{n,DUE} = PMT[PVIFA_{i,n}(DUE)] = PMT[(PVIFA_{i,n})(1 + i)].$$

$$PV_{PERPETUITY} = \frac{Payment}{Interest\ rate} = \frac{PMT}{i}.$$

$$PV_{Uneven\ stream} = \sum_{t=1}^{n} CF_t\left(\frac{1}{1 + i}\right)^t = \sum_{t=1}^{n} CF_t(PVIF_{i,t}).$$

$$FV_{Uneven\ stream} = \sum_{t=1}^{n} CF_t(1 + i)^{n - t} = \sum_{t=1}^{n} CF_t(FVIF_{i,n - t}).$$

$$FV_n = PV\left(1 + \frac{i_{SIMPLE}}{m}\right)^{mn}.$$

$$Effective\ annual\ rate = \left(1 + \frac{i_{SIMPLE}}{m}\right)^m - 1.0.$$

$$Periodic\ rate = i_{PER} = \frac{i_{SIMPLE}}{m}.$$

$$i_{SIMPLE} = APR = (Periodic\ rate)(m).$$

$$FV_n = PV(e^{in}).$$

$$PV = FV_n(e^{-in}).$$

Chapter 7

$$\text{Asset value} = V = \sum_{t=1}^{N} \frac{\hat{CF_t}}{(1 + k)^t}.$$

$$V_d = \sum_{t=1}^{N} \frac{INT}{(1 + k_d)^t} + \frac{M}{(1 + k_d)^N}$$

$$= INT(PVIFA_{k_d,N}) + M(PVIF_{k_d,N}).$$

$$V_d = \sum_{t=1}^{2N} \frac{INT/2}{(1 + k_d/2)^t} + \frac{M}{(1 + k_d/2)^{2N}} = \frac{INT}{2}(PVIFA_{k_d/2,2N}) + M(PVIF_{k_d/2,2N}).$$

$$\text{Approx. yield} \atop \text{to maturity} = \frac{INT + \left(\dfrac{M - V_d}{N}\right)}{\left[\dfrac{2(V_d) + M}{3}\right]}.$$

$$\text{Price of callable bond} = \sum_{t=1}^{N} \frac{INT}{(1 + k_d)^t} + \frac{\text{Call price}}{(1 + k_d)^{Nc}}.$$

$$V_{ps} = \frac{D_{ps}}{k_{ps}}.$$

$$k_{ps} = \frac{D_{ps}}{V_{ps}}.$$

$$\hat{P}_0 = \text{PV of expected future dividends} = \sum_{t=1}^{\infty} \frac{D_t}{(1 + k_s)^t}.$$

$$\hat{P}_0 = \frac{D_0(1 + g)}{k_s - g} = \frac{D_1}{k_s - g} \text{ if growth, g, is constant.}$$

$$\hat{k}_s = \frac{D_1}{P_0} + g.$$

Chapter 8

$$\text{Account} \atop \text{balance} = \left(\text{Amount of} \atop \text{daily activity}\right) \times \left(\text{Average life} \atop \text{of the account}\right).$$

$$\text{Inventory conversion} \atop \text{period} = \frac{\text{Inventory}}{\text{CGS}/360}.$$

$$\text{Receivables collection} \atop \text{period} = DSO = \frac{\text{Receivables}}{\text{Sales}/360}.$$

$$\text{Payables} \atop \text{deferral period} = DPO = \frac{\text{Accounts payable}}{\text{CGS}/360}.$$

$$\text{Cash} \atop \text{conversion} \atop \text{cycle} = \text{Inventory} \atop \text{conversion} \atop \text{period} + \text{Receivables} \atop \text{collection} \atop \text{period} - \text{Payables} \atop \text{deferral} \atop \text{period}.$$

Chapter 9

$$\text{Annual} \atop \text{savings} = \text{Credit sales} \atop \text{per day} \times \text{Decrease in} \atop \text{collection delays} \times \text{Opportunity} \atop \text{cost}.$$

$$\text{Total costs of cash balances} = \text{Holding costs} + \text{Transactions costs}$$
$$= \frac{\text{Cash}}{2}(k) + \frac{T}{\text{Cash}}(O).$$

$$\text{Cash*} = \sqrt{\frac{2(O)(T)}{k}}.$$

Chapter 10

$$\text{Average} \atop \text{daily sales} = ADS = \frac{\text{Annual sales}}{360} = \frac{(\text{Units sold})(\text{Sales price})}{360}.$$

$$\text{Days sales} \atop \text{outstanding} = DSO = \frac{\text{Receivables}}{ADS}.$$

$$\text{Cost of carrying receivables} = [(DSO)(\text{Sales}/360)(v)](k_{AR}).$$

Chapter 11

$$\text{Average inventory} = A = \frac{\text{Units per order}}{2} = \frac{T/N}{2} = \frac{Q}{2}.$$

$$\text{Total carrying cost} = TCC = (C)(PP)(A) = (C)(PP)\left(\frac{Q}{2}\right).$$

$$\text{Total ordering cost} = TOC = (O)(N) = O\left(\frac{T}{Q}\right).$$

$$\text{Total inventory cost} = TIC = TCC + TOC$$

$$= (C)(PP)(A) + (O)(N)$$

$$= (C)(PP)\left(\frac{Q}{2}\right) + O\left(\frac{T}{Q}\right).$$

$$\text{Economic ordering quantity} = EOQ = \sqrt{\frac{2(O)(T)}{(C)(PP)}}.$$

$$\text{Reorder point} = (\text{Lead time in weeks} \times \text{Weekly usage}) - \text{Goods in transit}.$$

Chapter 12

$$\text{Approximate cost of foregoing a cash discount (\%)} = \frac{\text{Discount percent}}{100 - \substack{\text{Discount} \\ \text{percent}}} \times \frac{360 \text{ days}}{\substack{\text{Total days of} \\ \text{credit available}} - \substack{\text{Discount} \\ \text{period}}}.$$

$$\text{Periodic rate (cost)} = \frac{\text{Dollar cost of borrowing}}{\text{Amount of usable funds}}.$$

$$\text{Effective annual rate} = \left[1 + \frac{i_{\text{SIMPLE}}}{m}\right]^m - 1.0 = [1 + \text{Periodic rate}]^m - 1.0.$$

$$\text{Annual percentage rate} = APR = (\text{Periodic rate}) \times (m) = i_{\text{SIMPLE}}.$$

$$\text{Periodic rate}_{\text{(Discount)}} = \frac{\text{Interest}}{\substack{\text{Amount of} \\ \text{usable funds}}} = \frac{(\text{Loan amount})\left(\frac{i_{\text{SIMPLE}}}{m}\right)}{(\text{Loan amount})\left(1 - \frac{i_{\text{SIMPLE}}}{m}\right)}.$$

$$\text{Periodic rate}_{\left(\substack{\text{Compensating} \\ \text{balance}}\right)} = \frac{\text{Interest}}{\substack{\text{Amount of} \\ \text{usable funds}}} = \frac{(\text{Loan amount})\left(\frac{i_{\text{SIMPLE}}}{m}\right)}{\left(\substack{\text{Loan} \\ \text{amount}}\right)(1 - \%CB)}.$$

$$\text{Compensating balance requirement} = CB = \frac{\text{Loan}}{\text{amount}} \times \substack{\text{Compensating balance} \\ \text{as a percent}}.$$

$$\substack{\text{Usable funds if} \\ \text{checking is \$0}}_{\left(\substack{\text{Compensating} \\ \text{balance}}\right)} = \left(\substack{\text{Loan} \\ \text{amount}}\right) - CB = \left(\substack{\text{Loan} \\ \text{amount}}\right)(1 - \%CB).$$

$$\substack{\text{Required loan amount} \\ \text{if checking is \$0}}_{\left(\substack{\text{Compensating} \\ \text{balance}}\right)} = \frac{\substack{\text{Amount of usable} \\ \text{funds needed}}}{1 - \%CB}.$$

$$\text{Periodic rate}_{\left(\substack{\text{Discount \&} \\ \text{compensating balance}}\right)} = \frac{\text{Interest}}{\substack{\text{Amount of} \\ \text{usable funds}}} = \frac{(\text{Loan amount})\left(\frac{i_{\text{SIMPLE}}}{m}\right)}{\left(\substack{\text{Loan} \\ \text{amount}}\right)\left(1 - \%CB - \frac{i_{\text{SIMPLE}}}{m}\right)}.$$

$$\substack{\text{Usable funds if} \\ \text{checking is \$0}} = \left(\substack{\text{Loan} \\ \text{amount}}\right) - CB - \frac{\text{Interest}}{\text{payment}} = \left(\substack{\text{Loan} \\ \text{amount}}\right)\left[1 - \%CB - \left(\frac{i_{\text{SIMPLE}}}{m}\right)\right].$$

$$\substack{\text{Required loan amount} \\ \text{if checking is \$0}} {}_{\left(\substack{\text{Discount \&} \\ \text{compensating balance}}\right)} = \frac{\substack{\text{Amount of usable} \\ \text{funds needed}}}{1 - \%CB - \left(\frac{i_{\text{SIMPLE}}}{m}\right)}.$$

$$\substack{\text{Required loan amount for} \\ \text{a loan with a compensating} \\ \text{balance requirement} \\ \text{if checking balance is} > \$0} = \frac{\substack{\text{Amount of usable} \\ \text{funds needed}} - \substack{\text{Checking} \\ \text{account balance}}}{1 - \%CB}.$$

$$\substack{\text{Approximate} \\ \text{periodic rate}_{(\text{Add-on})}} = \frac{\text{Interest}}{\left(\frac{\text{Amount received}}{2}\right)}.$$

Chapter 13

$$\text{Payback} = \substack{\text{Year before full} \\ \text{recovery of} \\ \text{original investment}} + \left(\frac{\substack{\text{Unrecovered cost} \\ \text{at start of year}}}{\substack{\text{Total cash flow} \\ \text{during year}}}\right).$$

$$\text{NPV} = CF_0 + \frac{CF_1}{(1 + k)^1} + \frac{CF_2}{(1 + k)^2} + \ldots + \frac{CF_n}{(1 + k)^n}$$

$$= \sum_{t=0}^{n} \frac{CF_t}{(1 + k)^t}.$$

$$\text{IRR: } CF_0 + \frac{CF_1}{(1 + \text{IRR})^1} + \frac{CF_2}{(1 + \text{IRR})^2} + \ldots + \frac{CF_n}{(1 + \text{IRR})^n} = 0$$

$$\sum_{t=0}^{n} \frac{CF_t}{(1 + \text{IRR})^t} = 0.$$

$$\text{MIRR: PV costs} = \sum_{t=0}^{n} \frac{COF_t}{(1 + k)^t} = \frac{\sum_{t=0}^{n} CIF_t(1 + k)^{n-t}}{(1 + \text{MIRR})^n} = \frac{TV}{(1 + \text{MIRR})^n}.$$

Chapter 14

Net cash flow = Net income + Depreciation.

$$\substack{\text{Incremental} \\ \text{operating CF}_t} = \Delta NI_t + \Delta Depr_t = (\Delta S_t - \Delta OC_t)(1 - T) + T(\Delta Depr_t).$$

$$E(\text{NPV}) = \sum_{i=1}^{n} Pr_i(\text{NPV}_i).$$

$$\sigma_{\text{NPV}} = \sqrt{\sum_{i=1}^{n} Pr_i[\text{NPV}_i - E(\text{NPV})]^2}.$$

$$CV_{NPV} = \frac{\sigma_{NPV}}{E(NPV)}.$$

$$k_p = k_{RF} + (k_M - k_{RF})\beta_p.$$

Chapter 15

After-tax component cost of debt $= k_{dT} = k_d(1 - T)$.

$$\begin{matrix} \text{Component cost} \\ \text{of preferred stock} \end{matrix} = k_{ps} = \frac{D_{ps}}{NP} = \frac{D_{ps}}{P_0 - \text{Flotation costs}}.$$

$$k_s = k_{RF} + RP = \frac{D_1}{P_0} + g = \hat{k}_s.$$

$$k_s = k_{RF} + (k_M - k_{RF})\beta_s.$$

$$k_s = \text{Bond yield} + \text{Risk premium}.$$

$$k_e = \frac{D_1}{P_0(1 - F)} + g = \frac{D_1}{NP} + g.$$

$$WACC = w_d k_{dT} + w_p k_p + w_s(k_s \text{ or } k_e).$$

$$BP = \frac{\text{Total amount of lower-cost capital of a given type}}{\text{Proportion of this type of capital in the capital structure}}.$$

Chapter 16

$$EPS = \frac{(S - F - VC - I)(1 - T)}{\text{Shares outstanding}} = \frac{(EBIT - I)(1 - T)}{\text{Shares outstanding}}.$$

$$DOL_Q = \frac{Q(P - V)}{Q(P - V) - F}.$$

$$DOL_S = \frac{S - VC}{S - VC - F} = \frac{\text{Gross profit}}{EBIT}.$$

$$DFL = \frac{EBIT}{EBIT - I}.$$

$$DTL = \frac{Q(P - V)}{Q(P - V) - F - I} = \frac{S - VC}{S - VC - F - I} = \frac{\text{Gross profit}}{EBIT - I} = (DOL)(DFL).$$

$$EPS_1 = EPS_0[1 + (DTL)(\%\Delta Sales)].$$

Chapter 17

$$\begin{matrix} \text{Dollars transferred} \\ \text{from retained} \\ \text{earnings due to} \\ \text{stock dividend} \end{matrix} = \begin{pmatrix} \text{Number of} \\ \text{shares} \\ \text{outstanding} \end{pmatrix} \begin{pmatrix} \text{Stock} \\ \text{dividend as} \\ \text{a percent} \end{pmatrix} \begin{pmatrix} \text{Market} \\ \text{price of} \\ \text{the stock} \end{pmatrix}.$$

Chapter 20

$$\text{Conversion price} = P_c = \frac{\text{Par value of bond}}{\text{Conversion ratio}}.$$

Chapter 21

$$\frac{\text{Cross}}{\text{rate}} = \frac{\text{Dollars}}{\text{Currency 1}} \times \frac{\text{Currency 2}}{\text{Dollars}} = \frac{\text{Currency 2}}{\text{Currency 1}}.$$

Index

C